# HANDBOOK OF
# Exchange Rates

Wiley Handbooks in
**FINANCIAL ENGINEERING AND ECONOMETRICS**

Advisory Editor
**Ruey S. Tsay**
*The University of Chicago Booth School of Business, USA*

A complete list of the titles in this series appears at the end of this volume.

# HANDBOOK OF Exchange Rates

Edited by

JESSICA JAMES

IAN W. MARSH

LUCIO SARNO

WILEY

A John Wiley & Sons, Inc., Publication

Published by John Wiley & Sons, Inc., Hoboken, New Jersey
Published simultaneously in Canada



For general information on our other products and services or for technical support, please contact our Customer Care Department within the United States at (800) 762-2974, outside the United States at (317) 572-3993 or fax (317) 572-4002.

Wiley also publishes its books in a variety of electronic formats. Some content that appears in print may not be available in electronic formats. For more information about Wiley products, visit our web site at www.wiley.com.

***Library of Congress Cataloging-in-Publication Data:***

Handbook of exchange rates / [edited by] Jessica James, Ian W. Marsh, Lucio Sarno.
pages cm. – (Wiley handbooks in financial engineering and econometrics ; 2)
Includes bibliographical references and index.
ISBN 978-0-470-76883-9
1. Foreign exchange rates. 2. Foreign exchange. I. James, Jessica, 1968– II. Marsh, Ian W., 1966– III. Sarno, Lucio.
HG3810.H35 2012
332.4′56–dc23

2011052323

Printed in the United States of America

10 9 8 7 6 5 4 3 2 1

For my children Zach and Miriam, my constant sources of inspiration!

*Jessica James*

To my wonderful wife Michela

*Ian W. Marsh*

To my fantastic wife Julia

*Lucio Sarno*

# Contents

PREFACE XXIII

CONTRIBUTORS XXVII

PART ONE
Overview

1 FOREIGN EXCHANGE MARKET STRUCTURE, PLAYERS, AND EVOLUTION 3

1.1 Introduction, 3
1.2 Geography and Composition of Currency Trading, 4
1.2.1 Which Currencies are Traded? 6
1.2.2 What Instruments are Traded? 9
1.2.3 How is Trading Regulated? 9
1.3 Players and Information in FX Markets, 11
1.3.1 Who Needs Liquidity? 12
1.3.2 Who Provides Liquidity? 15
1.3.3 Asymmetric Information and Exchange Rate Determination, 19
1.4 Electronic Trading Revolution in FX Markets, 21
1.4.1 The Telephone Era, 22
1.4.2 The Rise of the Computer, 22
1.4.3 Recent Developments in Electronic Trading, 30
1.5 Survey of Multibank FX Platforms, 35
1.6 Summary, 38
Glossary, 39
Acknowledgments, 41
References, 42

2 MACRO APPROACHES TO FOREIGN EXCHANGE DETERMINATION 45

2.1 Introduction, 45
2.2 Models of the Nominal Exchange Rate, 46
2.2.1 The Monetary Model, 46
2.2.2 Portfolio Balance Models, 49
2.2.3 Empirical Evidence, 51
2.3 Real Models of the Real Exchange Rate, 54
2.3.1 Purchasing Power Parity, 55
2.3.2 Balassa–Samuelson and Productivity-Based Models, 56
2.3.3 Two-Good Models, 59
2.4 New Directions in Exchange-Rate Modeling, 60
2.4.1 Taking Reaction Functions Seriously, 60
2.4.2 The Impact of Financial Globalization, 63
2.4.3 The Risk Premium and Order Flow, 64
2.5 Conclusions, 65
Acknowledgments, 65
References, 66

3 MICRO APPROACHES TO FOREIGN EXCHANGE DETERMINATION 73

3.1 Introduction, 73
3.2 Perspectives on Spot-Rate Dynamics, 74
3.2.1 Decomposition of Depreciation Rates, 74
3.2.2 Macro- and Microperspectives, 77
3.3 Currency Trading Models and their Implications, 80
3.3.1 The Portfolio Shifts Model, 81
3.3.2 Empirical Implications, 88
3.4 Exchange Rates, Order Flows, and the Macro Economy, 95
3.4.1 A Micro-Based Macro model, 96
3.4.2 Empirical Implications, 100
3.5 Conclusion, 105
Appendix, 105
3.6 Acknowledgment, 108
References, 108

4 THE EXCHANGE RATE IN A BEHAVIORAL FINANCE FRAMEWORK 111

4.1 Introduction, 111
4.1.1 Mainstream Exchange Rate Models, 111
4.1.2 Away from the Mainstream, 113

4.2 Exchange Rate Puzzles, 114
4.2.1 Disconnect Puzzle and Excess Volatility Puzzle, 114
4.2.2 Unit Root Property, 115
4.2.3 Volatility Clustering, 118
4.2.4 Fat-Tailed Distributed Exchange Rate Returns, 119
4.3 A Prototype Behavioral Model of the Foreign Exchange Market, 122
4.4 Conclusion, 127
References, 129

5 THE EVOLUTION OF EXCHANGE RATE REGIMES AND SOME FUTURE PERSPECTIVES 133

5.1 Introduction, 133
5.2 A Brief History of Currency Regimes, 135
5.3 Performance of the *Laisser-Faire* Exchange Rate System, 1973–2010, 138
5.3.1 Market Discipline, 139
5.3.2 Economic Policy Coordination, 140
5.3.3 Integration of Emerging Market Countries into the Global Economy, 140
5.4 Trends in Currency Use, 141
5.4.1 Global Imbalances and the Financial Crisis of 2007–2009, 143
5.5 Prospects for the Future, 144
5.5.1 The Current System, 144
5.5.2 Toward a more Managed International Monetary System? 146
5.5.3 How and When Will Reform Occur? 150
5.5.4 A Global Nominal Anchor? 151
5.6 Concluding Comments, 153
Appendix A: A Formal Test of Hollowing Out, 154
References, 156

PART TWO
Exchange Rate Models and Methods

6 PURCHASING POWER PARITY IN ECONOMIC HISTORY 161

6.1 Introduction, 161

6.2 Categorization of Purchasing-Power-Parity Theories, 162
6.3 Historical Application of PPP: Premodern Periods, 163
6.3.1 Ancient Period, 163
6.3.2 Medieval Period, 164
6.3.3 Sixteenth-Century Spain, 165
6.4 Techniques of Testing PPP Theory in Economic-History Literature, 165
6.4.1 Comparative-Static Computation, 165
6.4.2 Regression Analysis, 165
6.4.3 Testing for Causality, 165
6.4.4 Nonstationarity and Spurious Regression, 166
6.4.5 Testing for Stationarity, 167
6.4.6 Cointegration Analysis, 167
6.5 Price Variable in PPP Computations, 168
6.6 Modern Period: Testing of PPP, 169
6.6.1 Early North America, 169
6.6.2 Bullionist Periods, 170
6.6.3 Floating Rates—Second-Half of Nineteenth Century, 171
6.6.4 Classic Metallic Standards, 172
6.6.5 World War I, 172
6.6.6 Floating Rates—1920s, 173
6.6.7 1930s, 175
6.6.8 Interwar Period, 175
6.6.9 Spain—Long Term, 176
6.6.10 Guatemala—Long Term, 176
6.7 Analysis of U.S. Return to Gold Standard in 1879, 177
6.8 Establishment and Assessment of a Fixed Exchange Rate in Interwar Period, 177
6.8.1 United Kingdom, 177
6.8.2 France, 179
6.9 Conclusions, 180
References, 181

7 Purchasing Power Parity in Tradable Goods 189

7.1 Introduction, 189
7.2 The LOP and Price Indices, 190
7.3 Empirical Evidence on the LOP, 194
7.3.1 Early Tests of the LOP, 194
7.3.2 The Border Effect, 194
7.3.3 Barriers to Arbitrage and Nonlinearities, 195

7.3.4 The Tradable Versus Nontradable Goods Dichotomy, 198
7.3.5 The Aggregation Bias and Micro Price Studies, 199
7.4 Purchasing Power Parity, 200
7.4.1 Transitory and Structural Disparities from Parity, 203
7.5 Aggregating from the LOP to PPP: What Can We Infer? 205
7.5.1 An Eyeball Analysis of PPP, 207
7.6 Conclusion and Implications, 213
Appendix: TAR Modeling, 214
Acknowledgments, 215
References, 215

8 STATISTICAL AND ECONOMIC METHODS FOR EVALUATING EXCHANGE RATE PREDICTABILITY 221

8.1 Introduction, 221
8.2 Models for Exchange Rate Predictability, 224
8.2.1 A Present Value Model for Exchange Rates, 224
8.2.2 Predictive Regressions, 226
8.3 Statistical Evaluation of Exchange Rate Predictability, 228
8.4 Economic Evaluation of Exchange Rate Predictability, 231
8.4.1 The Dynamic FX Strategy, 231
8.4.2 Mean-Variance Dynamic Asset Allocation, 231
8.4.3 Performance Measures, 232
8.4.4 Transaction Costs, 234
8.5 Combined Forecasts, 235
8.6 Empirical Results, 237
8.6.1 Data on Exchange Rates and Economic Fundamentals, 237
8.6.2 Predictive Regressions, 242
8.6.3 Statistical Evaluation, 244
8.6.4 Economic Evaluation, 249
8.7 Conclusion, 256
Appendix A: The Bootstrap Algorithm, 259
Acknowledgments, 260
References, 260

**9 When Are Pooled Panel-Data Regression Forecasts of Exchange Rates More Accurate than the Time-Series Regression Forecasts? 265**

9.1 Introduction, 265
9.2 Panel Data Exchange Rate Determination Studies, 267
9.3 Asymptotic Consequences of Pooling, 268
9.3.1 Predictive Regression Estimated on Full Sample, 268
9.3.2 Out-of-Sample Prediction, 271
9.4 Monte Carlo Study, 272
9.5 An Illustration with Data, 275
9.6 Conclusions, 278
References, 279

**10 Carry Trades and Risk 283**

10.1 Introduction, 283
10.2 The Carry Trade: Basic Facts, 285
10.2.1 What is a Carry Trade? 285
10.2.2 Measuring the Returns to the Carry Trade, 286
10.3 Pricing the Returns to the Carry Trade, 290
10.4 Empirical Findings, 293
10.4.1 Traditional Risk Factors, 293
10.4.2 Factors Derived from Currency Returns, 299
10.5 Time-Varying Risk and Rare Events, 308
10.6 Conclusion, 311
Acknowledgments, 311
References, 311

**11 Currency Fair Value Models 313**

11.1 Introduction, 313
11.2 Models/Taxonomy, 315
11.2.1 "Adjusted PPP": Harrod-Balassa-Samuelson and Penn Effects, 315
11.2.2 The Behavioral Equilibrium Exchange Rate Family of Models, 316
11.2.3 The Underlying Balance (UB) Approach, 320
11.2.4 External Sustainability (ES) Approach, 324
11.2.5 The Natural Real Exchange Rate (NATREX), 325
11.2.6 The Indirect Fair Value (IFV), 325
11.3 Implementation Choices and Model Characteristics, 328
11.3.1 Horizon/Frequency, 329

11.3.2 Direct Econometric Estimation Versus "Methods of Calculation", 331
11.3.3 Treatment of External Imbalances , 332
11.3.4 Real Versus Nominal Exchange Rates, 333
11.3.5 Bilateral Versus Effective Exchange Rate, 333
11.3.6 Time Series Versus Cross Section or Panel, 336
11.3.7 Model Maintenance, 336
11.4 Conclusion, 337
Acknowledgments, 338
References, 339

12 TECHNICAL ANALYSIS IN THE FOREIGN EXCHANGE MARKET 343

12.1 Introduction, 343
12.2 The Practice of Technical Analysis, 345
12.2.1 The Philosophy of Technical Analysis, 345
12.2.2 Types of Technical Analysis, 346
12.3 Studies of Technical Analysis in the Foreign Exchange Market, 350
12.3.1 Why Study Technical Analysis? 350
12.3.2 Survey Evidence on the Practice of Technical Analysis, 350
12.3.3 Computing Signals and Returns, 351
12.3.4 Early Studies: Skepticism before the Tide Turns, 353
12.3.5 Pattern Recognition, Intraday Data, and Other Exchange Rates, 353
12.4 Explaining The Success of Technical Analysis, 355
12.4.1 Data Snooping, Publication Bias, and Data Mining, 355
12.4.2 Temporal Variation in Trading Rule Returns, 357
12.4.3 Do Technical Trading Returns Compensate Investors for Bearing Risk? 359
12.4.4 Does Foreign Exchange Intervention Create Trading Rule Profits? 361
12.4.5 Do Cognitive Biases Create Trading Rule Profits? 363
12.4.6 Do Markets Adapt to Arbitrage Away Trading Rule Profits? 365
12.5 The Future of Research on Technical Analysis, 366
12.6 Conclusion, 367
Acknowledgments, 368
References, 368

**13** MODELING EXCHANGE RATES WITH INCOMPLETE INFORMATION 375

13.1 Introduction, 375
13.2 Basic Monetary Model, 376
13.3 Information Heterogeneity, 379
13.4 Model Uncertainty, 381
13.5 Infrequent Decision Making, 385
13.6 Conclusion, 388
Acknowledgments, 388
References, 389

**14** EXCHANGE RATES IN A STOCHASTIC DISCOUNT FACTOR FRAMEWORK 391

14.1 Introduction, 391
14.2 Exchange Rates and Stochastic Discount Factors, 392
14.2.1 Stochastic Discount Factors, 392
14.2.2 Real Exchange Rates and Currency Risk Premia, 395
14.3 Empirical Evidence, 398
14.3.1 From UIP Regressions to Currency Portfolios, 398
14.3.2 Annual Currency Excess Returns and Aggregate Risk, 399
14.3.3 Monthly Currency Excess Returns, 403
14.3.4 Implications for Stochastic Discount Factors, 403
14.3.5 Predictability of Currency Excess Returns, 405
14.4 Models, 407
14.4.1 Habits, 407
14.4.2 Long-Run Risk, 411
14.4.3 Disaster Risk, 414
14.5 Conclusion, 417
References, 417

**15** VOLATILITY AND CORRELATION TIMING IN ACTIVE CURRENCY MANAGEMENT 421

15.1 Introduction, 421
15.2 Dynamic Models for Volatility and Correlation, 424
15.2.1 The Set of Multivariate Models, 425
15.2.2 The Set of Univariate Models for Volatility Timing, 427
15.2.3 Pairwise Model Comparisons, 427
15.2.4 Estimation and Forecasting, 427

15.3 The Economic Value of Volatility and Correlation Timing, 428
15.3.1 The Dynamic Strategy, 428
15.3.2 Dynamic Asset Allocation with CRRA Utility, 428
15.3.3 Performance Measures, 429
15.3.4 Transaction Costs, 430
15.4 Parameter Uncertainty in Bayesian Asset Allocation, 430
15.5 Model Uncertainty, 431
15.5.1 The BMA Strategy, 432
15.5.2 The BMW Strategy, 432
15.6 Empirical Results, 432
15.6.1 Data and Descriptive Statistics, 432
15.6.2 Bayesian Estimation, 433
15.6.3 Evaluating Volatility and Correlation Timing, 434
15.7 Conclusion, 440
Appendix A: Univariate Models for Volatility Timing, 442
Appendix B: Parameter Uncertainty and the Predictive Density, 443
Acknowledgments, 444
References, 444

PART THREE

# FX Markets and Products

16 ACTIVE CURRENCY MANAGEMENT PART I: IS THERE A PREMIUM FOR CURRENCY INVESTING (BETA) 451
16.1 Introduction, 451
16.2 Beta in the Foreign Exchange Markets, 453
16.2.1 Understanding the FX Carry Trade, 453
16.2.2 FX Carry as a Broader Strategy, 454
16.2.3 FX Trend-Based Strategies, 456
16.2.4 Value-Based Strategies Within FX, 458
16.2.5 USD Directional Trade, 459
16.2.6 Correlation between these FX Strategies and Other Forms of Beta, 460
16.2.7 Weighted Portfolio of FX Strategies, 461
16.3 Multiple Forms of FX Beta, 463
16.4 Carry FX Indices from Banks, 463
16.5 Trend-Following FX Indices from Banks, 465

16.6 Conclusion, 466
References, 467

17 Active Currency Management Part II: Is There Skill or Alpha in Currency Investing? 469

17.1 Introduction, 469
17.2 Alternative Currency Management Mandates, 471
17.2.1 Features of a Currency Mandate, 471
17.2.2 Structural and Operational Choices, 474
17.2.3 The Alpha Continuum and Implications of Active Currency Mandates, 475
17.3 Benchmarks for Currency Fund Management, 475
17.3.1 A Basic Factor Model for Currency Returns, 477
17.4 Empirical Evidence with the Barclay Currency Traders Index and Individual Fund Managers, 479
17.4.1 Empirical Evidence with the Barclay Currency Traders Index, 479
17.4.2 Individual Currency Manager Returns, 483
17.4.3 Alternative Information Ratio, 491
17.5 Empirical Evidence: Fund Managers on the DB FX Select Platform, 494
17.5.1 Grouping Managers into a Fund of Funds, 494
17.6 Conclusions and Investment Implications, 496
References, 497

18 Currency Hedging for International Bond and Equity Investors 501

18.1 Introduction, 501
18.2 Overview of Empirical Hedging Studies, 502
18.3 Return and Volatility Impact of Currency Hedging, 504
18.3.1 Theoretical Background, 504
18.3.2 Methodology, 506
18.3.3 Summary of Findings on the Return and Volatility Impact of Currency Hedging, 523
18.4 Hedge Instruments—Currency Forwards versus Options, 524
18.4.1 Why Do Hedge Cash Flows Matter? 524
18.4.2 Historical Performance of Hedging with Options, 525
18.4.3 Summary of Findings on Hedging with Options Versus Forwards, 530

18.5 Managing Tracking Error in Forward Hedges, 531
18.5.1 How Often to Rebalance? 531
18.5.2 Trigger-Based Versus Regular Rebalancing, 537
18.5.3 Summary of Findings on Hedge Rebalancing, 537
18.6 Conclusions, 539
References, 541

19 FX RESERVE MANAGEMENT 543

19.1 FX Reserve Management, 543
19.2 FX Reserve Uses, 543
19.3 FX Reserve Sources, 544
19.4 Objectives of Reserves Management, 545
19.5 Techniques of Reserve Management, 545
19.6 Historical Perspective, 546
19.7 What Assets Do Central Banks Hold? 547
19.8 Constraints, 548
19.9 External Managers, 549
19.10 Costs of Accumulation and Holding of Reserves, 549
19.11 Diversification, 550
19.12 Challenges to Diversification and Size of Reserves, 550
19.13 Changing Role of the Dollar as the International Reserve Currency, 552
19.14 Reserve Management if the Dollar is Replaced as the Reserve Currency, 555
19.15 Conclusion, 557
Acknowledgments, 557
References, 557

20 HIGH FREQUENCY FINANCE: USING SCALING LAWS TO BUILD TRADING MODELS 561

20.1 Introduction, 561
20.2 The Intrinsic Time Framework, 563
20.3 Scaling Laws, 565
20.3.1 The New Scaling Laws, 566
20.3.2 The Coastline, 571
20.4 The Scale of Market Quakes, 572
20.5 Trading Models, 575
20.5.1 Overview, 575
20.5.2 Coastline Trader, 576
20.5.3 Monthly Statistics, 578
20.6 Conclusion, 580

Acknowledgments, 580
References, 580

**21** ALGORITHMIC EXECUTION IN FOREIGN EXCHANGE 583

21.1 Introduction, 583
21.1.1 Drawing from the Equity Market, 584
21.1.2 What is Going to Work for Foreign Exchange? 585
21.2 Key Components of an Algorithmic Execution Framework, 587
21.2.1 Smart Order Routing (SOR), 587
21.2.2 Intelligence, 588
21.2.3 Speed, 589
21.3 Types of Algorithms, 590
21.3.1 Time Slicers, 590
21.3.2 Sweeper, 590
21.3.3 Iceberg, 590
21.3.4 Opportunistic, 590
21.3.5 Participators, 592
21.3.6 Internalization Strategies, 592
21.3.7 Dynamic Algorithms, 593
21.4 What Execution Strategies are Most Effective? 593
21.4.1 Measuring Performance, 594
21.5 Looking Forward, 594
Appendix A, 594
References, 595

**22** FOREIGN EXCHANGE STRATEGY BASED PRODUCTS 597

22.1 Introduction, 597
22.2 Evolution of the Foreign Exchange Market, 598
22.2.1 Disappointing Early Years, 598
22.2.2 Emergence of "Puzzles" in FX, 599
22.2.3 Growth of FX Market Turnover and Currency Managers, 600
22.3 Foreign Exchange Investable Indices and Strategy-Based Products, 604
22.3.1 Why Profit Opportunities Exist? 604
22.3.2 Beta and Alpha in Foreign Exchange, 605
22.3.3 Why is FX Attractive? 611
22.3.4 Why use Strategy-Based FX Products? 617

22.4 Conclusion, 618
References, 618

**23 FOREIGN EXCHANGE FUTURES, FORWARDS, AND SWAPS 621**

23.1 Introduction, 621
23.2 Market Basics and Size, 623
23.2.1 FX Outright Forwards and Futures, 623
23.2.2 FX Swaps and Cross-Currency Swaps, 626
23.2.3 Market Size, 633
23.3 Dislocations of the FX and Cross-Currency Swap Markets under Financial Crises, 635
23.3.1 Japan Premium Case in the Late 1990s, 635
23.3.2 The Global Financial Crisis from 2007, 637
23.4 Conclusion, 641
Acknowledgments, 641
References, 641

**24 FX OPTIONS AND VOLATILITY DERIVATIVES: AN OVERVIEW FROM THE BUY-SIDE PERSPECTIVE 645**

24.1 Introduction, 645
24.2 Why Would One Bother with an Option? 646
24.2.1 History, 646
24.2.2 FX Options, 647
24.3 Market for FX Options, 653
24.3.1 Overview, 653
24.3.2 Players, 654
24.3.3 Setting the Price, 656
24.4 Volatility, 658
24.4.1 Overview of Models, 658
24.4.2 Some Stylized Facts and Implied Moments, 662
24.4.3 Is Volatility an Asset Class? 664
24.4.4 Anti-Black Swan Strategies, 672
24.4.5 Black Swan Strategies, 674
24.5 FX Options from the Buy-Side Perspective, 681
24.5.1 Strike versus Leverage, 681
24.5.2 Implied Distribution, 683
24.5.3 Long-Dated Options versus Short-Dated Option, 687
24.5.4 Black Swan Fund, 690
24.5.5 Currency Hedging of Illiquid Assets, 691

Acknowledgment, 693
References, 693

# PART FOUR
# FX Markets and Policy


## 25 A Common Framework for Thinking about Currency Crises 697

25.1 Introduction, 697
25.2 The KFG Model, 699
25.3 Extensions, 704
25.3.1 Attack-Conditional Monetary Policy, 704
25.3.2 Devaluation, 705
25.3.3 Sterilization and Interest Rate Defense, 707
25.3.4 Lender of Last Resort and Currency Crises, 709
25.4 Empirical Work, 711
25.5 Conclusion, 712
References, 713

## 26 Official Intervention in the Foreign Exchange Market 715

26.1 Introduction, 715
26.2 Official FX Interventions and Reserve Accumulation: Stylized Facts, Motives, and Effects, 719
26.3 Empirical Evidence on the Effectiveness of Official FX Interventions, 723
26.3.1 A Simple Conceptual Framework, 724
26.3.2 Time-Series Approach: Evidence on Effectiveness and Channels, 726
26.3.3 Event-Study Approach: Evidence on Longer-Term Effectiveness, 737
26.4 Conclusions, 744
26.5 Acknowledgements, 744
References, 745

## 27 Exchange Rate Misalignment—The Case of the Chinese Renminbi 749

27.1 Introduction, 749
27.2 Background, 750
27.3 Undervalued or Overvalued, 752
27.3.1 The FEER Misalignment Estimate, 752
27.3.2 The Penn Effect Regression, 755

27.3.3 Data Revision, 757
27.4 Concluding Remarks, 760
Acknowledgments, 761
References, 761

28 CHOOSING AN EXCHANGE RATE REGIME 765
28.1 Five Advantages of Fixed Exchange Rates, 766
28.2 Econometric Evidence on the Bilateral Trade Effects of Currency Regimes, 768
28.2.1 Time-Series Dimension, 769
28.2.2 Omitted Variables, 770
28.2.3 Endogeneity of the Currency Decision, 771
28.2.4 Implausible Magnitude of the Estimate, 772
28.2.5 Country Size, 773
28.3 Five Advantages of Floating Exchange Rates, 773
28.4 How to Weigh Up the Advantages of Fixing Versus Floating, 775
28.5 Country Characteristics That Should Help Determine the Choice of Regime, 776
28.6 Alternative Nominal Anchors, 778
References, 779

INDEX 783

# Preface

The Foreign Exchange market, as we know, was born in the 1970s. To us in the second decade of the third millennium, mainly accustomed to freely floating and convertible currencies, the events that led to its birth would seem almost incredible. It is huge news when a government, via its central bank, intervenes to shift its currency or keep it stable. But from the end of World War II to the mid-1970s, pegs and interventions were the norm for almost all currencies.

The post war era gave us the Bretton Woods agreement that set the United States as the world's reserve currency and pegged most others to it. The United States was backed by gold, and the stability that this system brought enabled trade flows to enormously grow worldwide. This was deliberate; in the preceding decades, the architects of the system had seen how economic stresses could lead countries to war and were driven by a desire to promote trade and allow the world economy to grow.

However, the Vietnam war brought a growing US trade deficit and a drift of the alignment of the United States and the US dollar with the rest of the world. Pressure grew on the exchange rates and one by one, led by the Japanese yen, the currency became freely convertible and floating. By 1976, the gold standard was no more present and the majority of the world's currencies had the form we know today.

From that not-so-auspicious beginning grew the world's largest market. Today, according to the 2010 BIS report, currencies to the value of over US$4 trillion are traded each working day in global markets. The total value of global equity is a fraction of this amount. In most countries, the traded volume of the currency vastly exceeds the total amount of government debt. Foreign exchange has indeed come of age.

But what is it like, compared to other rates? It is not an interest rate. An interest rate is highly predictable and stable between close to zero, and perhaps exceptionally 15%. Outside these ranges, interest rates historically do not last long; high rates are often followed by spiralling hyperinflations, and negative rates do not occur without anomalous market stresses. It is not an equity, which has a floor at zero and is at least expected to appreciate with inflation.

There is a symmetry to foreign exchange, which is lacking in other market rates. One is "long" or "short" of an equity; in foreign exchange to be long of one currency is to be short of another. It is a rate of exchange and not an ownership of an asset. It has no floor or ceiling, no particular "stable region." As befits the largest global market, it is also the easiest and cheapest to trade in, with transactions often costing just a single basis point—1% of 1%—in bid-offer spread.

How and why has it grown to such a size? Partly, it is the nature of the beast and the way it is traded. Most foreign exchange transactions are done on a margined basis, with the principal amounts being notional only. Thus, for a simple forward trade of 1 month's duration, where a rate of exchange is locked in for 1 month ahead, no capital is exchanged at the start. At the end, the difference between the agreed rate and the market rate is paid out, scaled by the notional amount of the deal. This is usually at most a few percent of this notional amount. So one can see that it is unnecessary to actually own a sum of money equal to the notional amount—it is more of a scaling factor to the deal. Hence, the notional flows in the market can be very large relative to a smaller capital base.

Another reason for the size of the foreign exchange flows is that speculative trades, which have grown vastly in size and number over the last few years, are usually leveraged. The foreign exchange market is somewhat less volatile than the equity or commodity market, and so to generate comparable profits, profit seeking traders usually apply a multiplier to the notional amount. The last decade has seen the development of foreign exchange as an asset class, where structures suitable for investors are created around foreign exchange transactions. These often utilize large notional amounts to generate returns.

These additions increase an already considerable bulk of foreign exchange trades in the market. One critical activity made possible by the advent of floating exchange rates is hedging. Overseas investments can have their value drastically altered by fluctuations in the foreign exchange rates; hedges allow investors and corporates to immunize their portfolios and cashflows against these variations. Thus the growth of overseas investment has itself driven the volume of foreign exchange transactions higher; the investments, particularly less volatile fixed income instruments, will be significantly affected by foreign exchange movements unless they are hedged.

What are the instruments that make up this flow? The vast majority are spot and forward transactions, but the option market is also deep and liquid. This market came into its own in 1983 when Garman and Kolhagen published the formula for an option on a foreign exchange rate. Additionally, a vast variety of structures may be constructed, which allow investors or corporates to eliminate or transform risks, or gain exposure to specific areas and events.

Why do we need a Handbook of Exchange Rates? In part because it is so important, and in part because it is evolving so rapidly. In the last 5 years, we have seen the growth of foreign exchange as an asset class, which 10 years ago was the exclusive property of large trading floors and a few fund managers. Most large investors will now have a portion of their risk allocated to active strategies, which deliver fundlike returns derived from positioning themselves in the foreign exchange market. Another significant change is the growth of correlation and volatility derivatives. The correlation of rates has become a traded quantity, allowing a remarkably subtle set of risks and rewards to be accessed. The fascinating dynamics of high frequency data are now largely understood via scaling laws, to the extent that co-location—the siting of trading hubs close to exchanges—is becoming an issue; the speed of light has become a limiting factor in foreign exchange trading.

Another fascinating development is strongly connected with the correlation properties of foreign exchange rates. In floating emerging markets, the majority of foreign exchange rates are closely connected with their equity markets for obvious reasons. So high is this correlation that one can replicate emerging market equity indices to good accuracy using only foreign exchange rates—with their greater liquidity and low trading costs. Other interesting correlations are those between the Japanese yen or Australian dollar to the world's equity markets. So strong is the negative (in the case of the Yen) or positive (the Australian dollar) correlation that currency positions are often used to hedge equity drawdowns. So the foreign exchange market is being used to proxy for other rates. Its liquidity and depth make this attractive, though market stresses could bring an end to some of these useful correlations.

The Handbook is designed to span this extensive subject, with experts in the different areas contributing to each section. In planning the book, we drew up a list of the key subjects deserving of a chapter and against each we wrote the name of the key people in that topic. In almost every case, to our delight, those people accepted our invitation to contribute. As a result, the chapters have been written by leading specialists in their fields, often with extensive experience in academia and/or professional practice. Each chapter then benefitted from the feedback of at least one anonymous referee and at least one coeditor, and most authors kindly also acted as referees.

The initial section "Overview" covers structure, regimes, and general underlying behaviors. Part 2 covers models and methods, focussing on the predictability—or lack of it—of foreign exchange rates. In Part 3, we go to the practitioner side of the subject to cover hedging, active management, high frequency trading, and products. Part 4 wraps up with a look at policy and a framework for analyzing currency crises. The chapters are mainly in the form of self-contained surveys, and trace the key developments in a well-defined topic with specific reference to the relevant research frontier. Some contributions also present new empirical findings, especially where competing paradigms are evaluated. So rapid has the evolution of this market been, that it would not be surprising if in a few years there are many new chapters to add! Alternatively, market stresses and political crises can influence foreign exchange rates to an enormous extent. It is easy to forget that our current regime of floating market determined rates is recent, and by no means the norm in a historical context. The foreign exchange market is a fascinating subject, which never stops evolving.

We owe a debt of gratitude to many people for helping us bring this project to a successful conclusion: the contributing authors, for the high quality of their chapters; the many anonymous referees who provided, without exception, valuable feedback to the authors; and Chiara Banti who collated the chapters and worked very hard to copy edit the first draft of the Handbook. Needless to say, without their help, we would never have completed this project.

Jessica James
Ian W. Marsh
Lucio Sarno

# Contributors

SAEED AMEN, Nomura, London, UK

NAOHIKO BABA, Goldman Sachs Japan Co. Ltd., Tokyo, Japan

PHILIPPE BACCHETTA, Department of Economics, University of Lausanne, Lausanne, Switzerland; CEPR

CRAIG BURNSIDE, Department of Economics, Duke University, Durham, NC, USA; CEPR; NBER

GINO CENEDESE, Bank of England, London, UK

YIN-WONG CHEUNG, Department of Economics and Finance, City University of Hong Kong, Hong Kong

MENZIE CHINN, Robert M. La Follette School of Public Affairs; Department of Economics, University of Wisconsin-Madison, Madison, WI, USA; NBER

JAMES E. DALTON, CitiFX Intelligent Orders, Citigroup, London, UK

PAUL DE GRAUWE, Department of Economics, University of Leuven, Leuven, Belgium

PASQUALE DELLA CORTE, Imperial College, London, UK

ALEXANDRE DUPUIS, Olsen Ltd., Zurich, Switzerland; Centre for Computational Finance and Economic Agents (CCFEA), University of Essex, UK

MARTIN D. D. EVANS, Department of Economics, Georgetown University, Washington DC, USA; NBER

ROBERT FLOOD, University of Notre Dame, Notre Dame, IN, USA

JEFFREY A. FRANKEL, Kennedy School of Government, Harvard University, Cambridge, MA, USA; NBER

MARCEL FRATZSCHER, European Central Bank, Frankfurt/Main, Germany

KRISTJAN KASIKOV, CitiFX Quantitative Investor Solutions, Citigroup, London, UK

GEOFFREY KENDRICK, Nomura, London, UK

MICHAEL R. KING, Richard Ivey School of Business, University of Western Ontario, Canada

RICHARD M. LEVICH, Finance Department, Stern School of Business, New York University, New York, NY, USA

Hanno Lustig, UCLA Anderson School of Management, Los Angeles, CA, USA; NBER

Nancy Marion, Dartmouth College, Hanover, NH, USA

Nelson Mark, Department of Economics, University of Notre Dame, Notre Dame, IN, USA; NBER

Ian W. Marsh, Cass Business School, London, UK

Paul R. Masson, Rotman School of Management, University of Toronto, Toronto, Canada

Christopher J. Neely, Research Department, Federal Reserve Bank of St. Louis, St. Louis, MI, USA

Lawrence H. Officer, University of Illinois at Chicago, Chicago, IL, USA

Richard B. Olsen, Olsen Ltd., Zurich, Switzerland; Centre for Computational Finance and Economic Agents (CCFEA), University of Essex, UK

Carol Osler, Brandeis International Business School, Brandeis University, Waltham, MA, USA

Frank Packer, Bank for International Settlements, Basel, Switzerland

Evgenia Passari, Cass Business School, London, UK

Michael J. Paulus, Hongkong and Shanghai Banking Corporation (HSBC), Hong Kong

Momtchil Pojarliev, Hathersage Capital Management LLC, South Norwalk, CT, USA

Dagfinn Rime, Research Department, Norges Bank, Oslo, Norway; Norwegian University of Science and Technology

Pablo Rovira Kaltwasser, University of Leuven, Leuven, Belgium

Yuji Sakurai, UCLA Anderson School of Management, Los Angeles, CA, USA

Lucio Sarno, Cass Business School, London, UK; CEPR

Aysu Secmen, CitiFX Quantitative Investor Solutions, Citigroup, New York, USA

Thomas Stopler, Goldman Sachs, London, UK

Donggyu Sul, University of Texas, Dallas, TX, USA

Oleg Svirschi, Record Currency Management, London, UK

Ilias Tsiakas, Department of Economics and Finance, University of Guelph, Guelph, Ontario, Canada

Eric van Wincoop, Department of Economics, University of Virginia, VA, USA; NBER

Adrien Verdelhan, Department of Finance, MIT Sloan School of Management, Cambridge, MA, USA; NBER

Paul A. Weller, Tippie College of Business, University of Iowa, Iowa City, IA, USA

Juan Yepez Albornoz, Department of Economics, University of Notre Dame, Notre Dame, IN, USA

# PART ONE

# Overview

CHAPTER ONE

# Foreign Exchange Market Structure, Players, and Evolution

**MICHAEL R. KING**
Richard Ivey School of Business, University of Western Ontario

**CAROL OSLER**
Brandeis International Business School, Brandeis University

**DAGFINN RIME**
Norges Bank, Norwegian University of Science and Technology

## 1.1 Introduction

It would be hard to overstate the importance of exchange rates for the world economy. They affect output and employment through real exchange rates. They affect inflation through the cost of imports and commodity prices. They affect international capital flows through the risks and returns of different assets. Exchange rates are justifiably a major focus for policymakers, the public, and, of course, the media.

To understand exchange rates, it is essential to know how these prices are determined. This chapter describes the FX market and presents new evidence on recent trends, thereby setting the stage for the rest of the handbook. It presents stylized facts on the market's size and composition. It then describes more closely the motives, incentives, and constraints of the major players. Trading is a search problem, and the constraints and costs related to this search are affected by the structure of the market. Our starting point is that the exchange rates are

*Handbook of Exchange Rates*, First Edition. Edited by Jessica James, Ian W. Marsh, and Lucio Sarno.

primarily driven by new information about economic fundamentals. In this light, we review which agents bring information to the market and exactly how their information becomes embedded in the market price.

The chapter describes the momentous changes in trading practices and market structure which have taken place over the recent decades. It concludes by presenting new evidence on some of the most recent technological advances. Twenty-five years ago, most FX trading involved the telephone and all trading involved institutions: individuals were essentially shut out. Trading was opaque, there was a sharp division between interdealer trading and dealer–customer trading, and market concentration among dealers was low.

Today, only the least liquid corners of the FX market can still be described this way. In the liquid markets, telephones are obsolete. New electronic trading platforms have streamlined trade processing and settlement, reduced operational risks, and lowered trading costs. Lower trading costs have enabled the participation of retail traders and the adoption of new strategies such as high frequency trading—a form of computer-automated trading that relies on high execution speeds to make profits from small price movements. Since streaming real-time prices are now available to virtually all participants, these markets are now regarded as transparent. On some of the new platforms, any trader can provide liquidity, so the division between dealers and their most sophisticated customers is, at times, ambiguous. To remain competitive, the major dealing banks have made heavy investments in software and hardware, which has led to sharply higher concentration among market makers.

## 1.2 Geography and Composition of Currency Trading

Given the pervasive influence of exchange rates, it is no surprise that the dollar value of trading activity in spot and forward FX market dwarfs most other economic measures (BIS, 2010). With daily average turnover estimated at $2.0 trillion, the market is 36 times larger than the combined exports and imports for the world's 35 largest economies, 16 times their combined GDP, and roughly 10 times exchange-traded equity turnover.

FX trading volume has exploded reflecting an electronic revolution that has lowered trading costs, attracted new groups of market participants, and enabled aggressive new trading strategies. Between 1998 and 2010, turnover in the FX market grew by over 250% (BIS, 2010). The associated 8.4% average annual growth rate far exceeds the contemporary 5.5% annual expansion of global real GDP (Table 1.1).

Many aspects of the FX market remain constant despite the electronic revolution. As has been true for decades, the markets remain decentralized with high liquidity and continuous trading (Lyons, 2001; Rime, 2003; Osler, 2009). As ever, the trading day begins when dealers arrive for work in Australia and Asia. Activity then moves to Europe when markets open in Frankfurt, London, and Paris, and finishes late in the afternoon in New York. As always, there is no

**TABLE 1.1 FX Turnover and Growth: Comparison with Trade, GDP, and Equity Trading Volume**

| | 1992 | 1995 | 1998 | 2001 | 2004 | 2007 | 2010 |
|---|---|---|---|---|---|---|---|
| | | | | (a) Volumes | | | |
| All instruments | 857 | 1135 | 1713 | 1480 | 2013 | 3296 | 3981 |
| Spot total | 434 | 475 | 637 | 461 | 657 | 996 | 1490 |
| Forwards total | 65 | 93 | 143 | 156 | 217 | 359 | 475 |
| Growth, spot, and forwards | — | 44% | 54% | 9% | 40% | 65% | 32% |
| | | | | (b) Ratios | | | |
| Spot/Trade | 31 | 29 | 30 | 18 | 21 | 23 | 36 |
| Spot/GDP | 10 | 10 | 11 | 7 | 10 | 12 | 16 |
| Spot/Equity volume | 35 | 25 | 14 | 4 | 9 | 7 | 9 |

Note: Panel (a): Constant 2010 values, in billions USD, for volumes based on BIS Triennial FX surveys corrected for interdealer and cross-border double-counting (i.e., "net–net" basis according to terminology of the BIS Triennial survey). Constant values are created by using SDR rates. "All instruments" includes spot, forwards, swaps, currency swaps, options, and other derivatives as defined in the survey. Panel (b): Ratio of spot volumes to trade volumes (import and exports), GDP, and equity volumes of 35 countries. The aggregate spot volumes are created using the currencies of the same 35 countries (EUR for the EU countries after 1999). All volumes in panel b are monthly nominal values, where daily FX volume is multiplied by 20 (trading days), and yearly numbers for trade, GDP, and equity volumes are divided by 12. For 2010, we use IMF forecasts. The countries are AR, AT, AU, BE, BR, CA, CH, CL, CN, CO, DE, ES, FI, FR, GB, GR, HK, ID, IE, IN, IT, JP, KR, MX, MY, NZ, PE, PH, PT, SE, SG, TH, TR, US, and ZA.

*Sources:* Trade and GDP data are from IMF WEO, equity volumes are from World Federation of Exchanges (WFE), and FX volumes are from BIS Triennial FX Survey.

time during the day when the market formally closes, although there is a brief lull in activity between about 19:00 and 22:00 GMT, when most New York traders have gone home and most Sydney traders are still on their way to work (Figure 1.1). As ever, overall market liquidity is deepest when both London and New York are open, though liquidity for most individual currencies tends to be deepest during their local trading hours.

FX trading remains heavily concentrated in London, which captures over one-third of global trading, and New York, which captures almost one-fifth of trading (Table 1.2). London's traditional dominance in FX grew out of the United Kingdom's worldwide economic dominance in the nineteenth century. It remains secure at the beginning of the twenty-first century because of its geographic location: London's morning session overlaps with Asian trading and its afternoon session overlaps with New York's trading. Trading in the Asia-Pacific region, which in aggregate accounts for about one-quarter of global trading, is dispersed among Tokyo, Hong Kong, Singapore, and Sydney. Latin America, Africa, and the Middle East each account for less than 1% of global turnover.

Despite the continued dominance of London and New York, there have been some subtle shifts in the global distribution of currency trading. The advent of the euro (EUR) brought a decline in the share of European trading

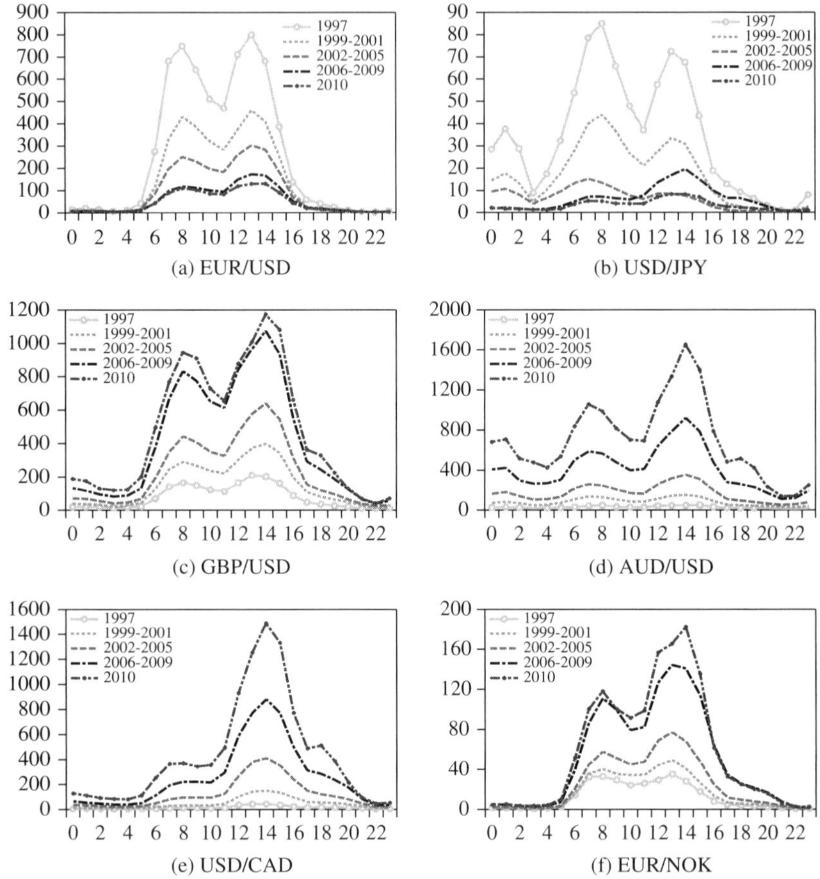


**FIGURE 1.1** Average daily interdealer trading activity by the hour across different currencies. Note: The horizontal axis shows hour of the day (GMT) and the vertical axis shows the average number of trades. The five lines are for 1997, 4-year averages for 1998–2001, 2002–2005, and 2006–2009, respectively, and 2010. From example GBP/USD (c), we see the growth in number of trades since 1997. The exchange rates EUR/USD and USD/JPY are now primarily traded on the competing platform EBS, hence the decrease in number of trades from 1997 to 2010 for these two exchange rates. *Source*: Thomson Reuters Matching.

outside of London. Meanwhile, rapid economic growth in Asia has supported a surge in trading in the Asian regional centers. Hong Kong and Singapore now vie in importance with traditional European centers such as Switzerland and France.

## 1.2.1 WHICH CURRENCIES ARE TRADED?

Another unchanging aspect of the FX market is the dominance of the US dollar (USD), which is still involved on one side of roughly three-quarters of all spot

**TABLE 1.2 Geographical Distribution of Global Foreign Exchange Market Turnover (%)**

| Country | 1995 | 1998 | 2001 | 2004 | 2007 | 2010 |
|---|---|---|---|---|---|---|
| United Kingdom | 29.3 | 32.6 | 32.0 | 32.0 | 34.6 | 36.7 |
| United States | 16.3 | 18.3 | 16.1 | 19.1 | 17.4 | 17.9 |
| Japan | 10.3 | 7.0 | 9.0 | 8.0 | 5.8 | 6.2 |
| Singapore | 6.6 | 6.9 | 6.1 | 5.1 | 5.6 | 5.3 |
| Switzerland | 5.4 | 4.4 | 4.5 | 3.3 | 5.9 | 5.2 |
| Hong Kong SAR | 5.6 | 3.8 | 4.0 | 4.1 | 4.2 | 4.7 |
| Australia | 2.5 | 2.3 | 3.2 | 4.1 | 4.1 | 3.8 |
| France | 3.8 | 3.7 | 2.9 | 2.6 | 3.0 | 3.0 |
| Denmark | 1.9 | 1.3 | 1.4 | 1.6 | 2.1 | 2.4 |
| Germany | 4.8 | 4.7 | 5.4 | 4.6 | 2.4 | 2.1 |
| Canada | 1.9 | 1.8 | 2.6 | 2.3 | 1.5 | 1.2 |
| Sweden | 1.2 | 0.8 | 1.5 | 1.2 | 1.0 | 0.9 |
| Korea | — | 0.2 | 0.6 | 0.8 | 0.8 | 0.9 |
| Russia | — | 0.3 | 0.6 | 1.1 | 1.2 | 0.8 |
| Luxembourg | 1.2 | 1.1 | 0.8 | 0.6 | 1.0 | 0.7 |
| Belgium | 1.7 | 1.3 | 0.6 | 0.8 | 1.2 | 0.6 |
| Finland | 0.3 | 0.2 | 0.1 | 0.1 | 0.2 | 0.6 |
| Spain | 1.1 | 1.0 | 0.5 | 0.5 | 0.4 | 0.6 |
| Italy | 1.5 | 1.4 | 1.0 | 0.9 | 0.9 | 0.6 |
| India | — | 0.1 | 0.2 | 0.3 | 0.9 | 0.5 |

Note: Country percentage shares of daily average global total in April. Country volumes are adjusted for local interdealer double-counting but not cross border (i.e., "net–gross" basis according to terminology of the BIS Triennial survey). Countries are sorted based on 2010 market share.
*Source:* BIS Triennial FX Survey.

transactions (Table 1.3).[1] The dollar's dominance reflects the market's practice of trading minor currencies via a major currency (called the *vehicle currency*). A trade from Mexican pesos (MXP) to Australian dollars (AUD), for example, would typically involve two trades, one from MXP to USD and the second from USD to AUD. This "vehicle" trading through the major crosses concentrates liquidity in a narrower range of currency pairs, reducing overall transaction costs.

[1]Every currency has a three-letter currency code, such as CAD for the Canadian dollar. These codes have been developed by the International Organization for Standardization (www.iso.org). In labeling currency pairs, market practice is to express the base currency first, as in "dollar–yen" or USD/JPY, which should be read as Japanese yen (JPY) per USD. Major exchange rates have nicknames: USD/CHF is "swissie" and NZD/USD is "kiwi." GBP/USD is "cable" in reference to the first trans-Atlantic telegraph cable that connected FX traders in London and New York.

**TABLE 1.3 Currency Distribution of Spot Turnover (%)**

| | 1992 | 1995 | 1998 | 2001 | 2004 | 2007 | 2010 |
|---|---|---|---|---|---|---|---|
| USD | 72 | 71 | 78 | 84 | 85 | 79 | 80 |
| EUR | 69 | 75 | 58 | 43 | 44 | 42 | 46 |
| JPY | 20 | 22 | 24 | 26 | 21 | 20 | 20 |
| GBP | 14 | 9 | 12 | 11 | 13 | 15 | 14 |
| CHF | 9 | 8 | 7 | 7 | 7 | 9 | 6 |
| AUD/CAD/NOK/NZD | 4 | 5 | 5 | 9 | 10 | 12 | 15 |
| BRL/RUB/INR/CNY | — | — | 1 | 2 | 3 | 4 | 3 |
| All others | 12 | 10 | 15 | 18 | 17 | 19 | 15 |
| Total | 200 | 200 | 200 | 200 | 200 | 200 | 200 |

*Note*: Total spot volume in a currency as percentage share of total global spot volume. First four rows show the G4-currencies. EUR includes legacy currencies. The total equals 200 since two currencies are involved in each transaction. "BRL/RUB/INR/CNY" represent the Brazilian real, Russian ruble, Indian rupee, and Chinese renminbi, respectively (the "BRIC" currencies).
*Source:* BIS Triennial FX Survey.

The EUR is involved in 46% of trades, in part because it serves as the vehicle currency within the eurozone.[2] The next most actively traded currencies are the JPY (20%) and the UK pound (GBP, 14%). Together, these four currencies are known as "the majors" (or G4).[3]

The next tier below the majors comprises the AUD (7.5%), the Swiss franc (CHF, 6.2%), and the Canadian dollar (CAD, 5.2%). A notable recent shift is the rising share of the so-called commodity currencies, specifically the AUD, CAD, NOK, and the New Zealand dollar (NZD). These currencies' combined share rose from 7% in 1998 to 16% in 2010.

The share of emerging-market currencies rose sharply in the 1990s but has been fairly stable around 18% since then. Nonetheless, currencies from the most advanced emerging markets, such as the South Korean won (KRW) and Hong Kong dollar (HKD), have more than doubled their market share since 1998 and now rival the Swedish krona (SEK). Turnover in more recently emerging countries, such as Turkey, Thailand, Brazil, and India, has grown even faster.

The conventions governing the quotation of different currency pairs have also been fairly stable over time. Most exchange rates are expressed as units of a given currency required to purchase 1 USD. The exceptions are the EUR, the GBP, the AUD, and the NZD, which are quoted as the base currency (i.e., EUR/USD = USD per EUR). Most exchange rates are quoted to five significant digits, with the final (or smallest) digit known as a "pip."[4]

[2]As an example, in interdealer spot trading, the volumes traded in EUR/ NOK (Norwegian krone) are 10 times larger than the sum of those in USD/NOK, GBP/NOK, and NOK/JPY.

[3]The most actively traded currency pairs have USD or EUR on one side.

[4]A pip is short form for Price Increment Point. In EUR/USD, a one-pip change is, for example, from 1.234<u>5</u> to 1.234<u>6</u>. In most major currency pairs, one pip is roughly one basis point.

### 1.2.2 WHAT INSTRUMENTS ARE TRADED?

The dominance of spot FX trading is another area of relative stability.[5] Daily spot turnover in 2010 was $1.5 trillion while turnover in outright forwards was far lower, at $0.5 trillion (BIS, 2010). A number of other currency-related instruments—FX futures, currency options, FX swaps, and currency swaps—swell total daily turnover in FX market beyond $4.0 trillion (Table 1.4).[6] These assets are traded entirely separately from spot and forward contracts and for entirely different purposes, so they generally have little influence on exchange rates and are not discussed in this chapter.

FX swaps deserve some discussion, however, because of their immense average daily turnover of $1.8 trillion. Like repos in the fixed income markets, FX swaps are primarily used for overnight position management by banks. Collapsing swap volumes following the Lehman Brothers bankruptcy in late 2008 triggered a rapid expansion of central bank swap activity, as authorities tried to stabilize the world banking system (Baba and Packer, 2009; Melvin and Taylor, 2009). In 2010, FX swap trading activity remained below its previous peak.

### 1.2.3 HOW IS TRADING REGULATED?

The vast majority of FX trading is essentially unregulated, in striking contrast to the extensive regulations in most equity and bond markets.[7] Governments have learned through experience that dealers will simply move elsewhere if they are regulated. In the 1960s, for example, bond dealers moved offshore when the US government attempted to regulate the foreign issuance of USD denominated bonds in the domestic market.

Some well-known regulations in other asset markets are missing in FX market. Their absence is not a problem because of unique features of the FX market. Short sales restrictions, for example, though severe in most developed equity and bond markets, cannot even be defined in this asset class because the sale of one currency is simply the purchase of another. Other practices

[5]With a spot contract, the exchange rate and the quantity to exchange are agreed initially, and the funds actually change hands ("settle") 2 business days later (1 day later for USD/CAD). A forward contract is similar in structure, but settlement generally happens more than 2 business days later. For "inside forwards," settlement is less than 2 days later.

[6]Currency futures, like forwards, involve an agreement today to exchange two currencies in the future. Future contracts are exchange traded so their characteristics, such as contract size and maturity, are standardized. In contrast, a FX (or currency) option gives the owner the right but not the obligation to buy or sell a currency at an agreed exchange rate during a specified period. Standardized FX option contracts are traded on organized exchanges, while tailor-made contracts are available through individual FX dealers. Currency swaps are the currency equivalent of interest-rate swaps; they essentially allow someone to swap a loan (or bond) in one currency for a loan in another without incurring currency risk if the swap is held until maturity.

[7]Exchange-traded FX instruments fall under the relevant securities regulation in their respective countries. The Chicago Mercantile Exchange, for example, is regulated by the National Futures Association and Commodity Futures Trading Commission.

**TABLE 1.4 Instruments Traded in Global FX Market**

| | 1992 | 1995 | 1998 | 2001 | 2004 | 2007 | 2010 |
|---|---|---|---|---|---|---|---|
| Total | 857 | 1135 | 1713 | 1480 | 2013 | 3296 | 3981 |
| | | | | (a) Shares (%) | | | |
| Spot | 51 | 42 | 37 | 31 | 33 | 30 | 37 |
| FX swaps | 42 | 46 | 48 | 53 | 49 | 52 | 44 |
| Forwards | 8 | 8 | 8 | 11 | 11 | 11 | 12 |
| Currency swaps | — | 0 | 1 | 1 | 1 | 1 | 1 |
| Options and others | 4 | 3 | 6 | 5 | 6 | 6 | 5 |
| | | | | (b) Growth (%) | | | |
| Total | — | 33 | 51 | −14 | 36 | 64 | 21 |
| Spot | — | 9 | 34 | −28 | 42 | 52 | 50 |
| FX swaps | — | 47 | 57 | −5 | 27 | 71 | 4 |
| Forwards | — | 44 | 54 | 9 | 40 | 65 | 32 |
| Currency swaps | — | — | 207 | −23 | 156 | 42 | 37 |
| Options and others | — | 16 | 148 | −27 | 74 | 69 | −1 |
| | | | | (c) Growth contribution (%) | | | |
| Spot | — | 14 | 28 | 75 | 37 | 26 | 72 |
| FX swaps | — | 60 | 52 | 17 | 39 | 55 | 10 |
| Forwards | — | 10 | 9 | −5 | 12 | 11 | 17 |
| Currency swaps | — | — | 1 | 1 | 3 | 1 | 2 |
| Options and others | — | 2 | 10 | 12 | 10 | 7 | 0 |

Note: Total is measured in USD billions, calculated at constant rates. Shares are percentage share out of total, $\frac{x}{\text{Tot}}100$. Growth rates are calculated as $\left(x_t - x_{t-1}\right)/x_{t-1}$. Contribution to total growth is calculated as $\left(x_1 - x_0\right)/\left(\text{Tot}_1 - \text{Tot}_0\right)$.
*Source:* BIS Triennial FX Survey.

that are illegal on most organized exchanges are discouraged in FX by market conventions and best practices. For example, front running of customer orders is widely considered bad practice even though it is not illegal.[8] Fortunately, the FX market is sufficiently liquid that significant manipulation by any single actor is all but impossible during active trading hours for the major currencies.

Since FX market are subject to minimal regulation, they are also subject to minimal reporting requirements, which explains the scarcity of aggregate data on FX trading. Although equity trading volume is a staple on the evening news on any given day, no one knows how much was traded in FX market—not the regulators, not the monetary authorities, and not even the major FX dealers. The only comprehensive information source is the Triennial Central Bank Survey of FX Market Activity, a joint effort of central banks around the world, coordinated

[8] A front-running dealer would buy in the interdealer market for his own account, driving up the price, before filling a customer buy order. Such activity, if suspected, would lead customers to boycott or punish this FX dealer.

every third year in April by the Bank for International Settlements (BIS).[9] In the absence of official sources of high frequency data, most research on currency trading relies on proprietary data from banks and brokers.

## 1.3 Players and Information in FX Market

A key goal of exchange rate economics is to understand currency returns. Exchange rates, like asset prices, more generally, move in response to new information about their fundamental value. Over the past decade, microstructure research has revealed that this "price discovery" process involves different categories of market participants. Each participant's distinct role is determined by (i) whether the agent is a liquidity maker or taker and (ii) the extent to which the agent is informed.

The original FX market participants were traders in goods and services. Currencies came into existence because they solved the problem of the coincidence of wants with respect to goods. Most countries have their own currencies, so international trade in goods requires trade in currencies. The motives for currency exchange have expanded over the centuries to include speculation, hedging, and arbitrage, with the list of key players expanding accordingly. Beyond importers and exporters, the major categories of market participants now include asset managers, dealers, central banks, small individual (retail) traders, and, most recently, high frequency traders.

"Dealers" or "market makers" emerged naturally to fulfill the search function among trading counterparties. Dealers stand ready to trade with anyone needing FX at a moment's notice. To initiate an FX trade, an agent calls a dealer indicating the currency and quantity she/he wishes to trade and asking for the price. The dealer states a price at which she/he is willing to buy (the "bid") and a price at which she/he is willing to sell (the "ask"). Finally, the customer decides whether to buy, sell, or pass. The dealer is compensated for the burdens of liquidity provision, such as bearing inventory risk and screening agents for credit quality, by a favorable gap between the quoted buy and sell prices, the "bid–ask spread." Markets of this structure, known as "over-the-counter" (or OTC) markets, have arisen naturally in contexts including municipal and corporate bonds, derivatives, and equities. Although OTC dealers are under no formal obligation to provide liquidity, they tend to be reliable because otherwise their reputation—and potentially their market share—will suffer.

Existing theory indicates that information is brought to the market by liquidity takers rather than market makers. Among liquidity takers in FX, the evidence indicates that information relevant to short horizons comes from financial customers, especially leveraged investors. Information does not come from firms involved in international trade, small individual traders, or governments/central banks (Bjønnes et al., 2005, 2011; Evans and Lyons, 2006; Nolte and Nolte,

[9] King and Mallo (2010) provide a user's guide to the Triennial survey. Since the mid-1990s, the Triennial Survey has been complemented by more frequent regional surveys conducted in Australia, Canada, Hong Kong, London, New York, Singapore, and Tokyo.

2009; Osler and Vandrovych, 2009; King et al., 2010). To identify whether some category of participant is typically informed, it is standard to examine whether their trades anticipate FX returns. If an agent consistently tends to buy (sell) before prices rise (fall) and the subsequent price change tends to be at least partially permanent, researchers infer that the agent was trading based on information about the asset's fundamental value. Academic studies have long indicated that FX dealers are informed. But, until recently, both theory and practice assumed that this information originated entirely with end-customers (Evans and Lyons, 2002). It is now recognized that dealers bring their own independent information to the market (Bjønnes et al., 2011; Moore and Payne, 2011).

## 1.3.1 WHO NEEDS LIQUIDITY?

Traditionally, the end-customers routinely needing FX liquidity were non-dealer financial institutions on one hand, and corporations and governments on the other. Over the last decade, the set of active FX end-users has been augmented by retail investors and by computer-automated traders known as *algorithmic traders*.

Until the mid-1980s, non-dealer financial institutions, corporations, and governments each traded roughly equal amounts with their FX dealers. Since then trading by corporate customers and governments has maintained an overall market share of 17% on an average, though this share naturally rises and falls with economic activity. During the recessions of 2001 and 2010, for example, their share of activity fell to 15%. The share of financial trading in total trading, by contrast, rose steadily from 20% in 1998 to over 50% in 2010 (Figure 1.2). This trend partly reflects the rapid growth of trading on retail trading platforms,[10] which reached an estimated $125 to 150 billion per day in 2010, equivalent to 8–10% of global spot turnover (King and Rime, 2010). It also reflects rapid growth in algorithmic trading, especially, high frequency trading. Although data on the extent of algorithmic trading are limited, the survey reported in Section 4 suggest that it now accounts for between one-third and one-half of trading in the most liquid currencies.

**1.3.1.1 Financial Institutions.** Financial institutions are a diverse category that includes hedge funds and other asset managers, regional and local banks, broker–dealers, and central banks. Relative to corporate customers, financial institutions trade larger amounts and hold FX positions for far longer. Financial institutions tend to be better informed than other end-users, because they have strong incentives to invest in information acquisition. Since financial institutions use currencies primarily as a store of value, they gain or lose according to changes in the currency's value.

Among financial institutions, leveraged institutional investors—meaning mostly hedge funds and their close cousins the commodity trading advisors (CTAs)—appear to be best informed. This finding seems logical since leveraged institutional investors face particularly intense incentives to acquire information.

[10] Retail trading platforms, so-called "retail aggregators" (RAs), are reported as financial institutions in the BIS Triennial Survey. See more on retail aggregators below.

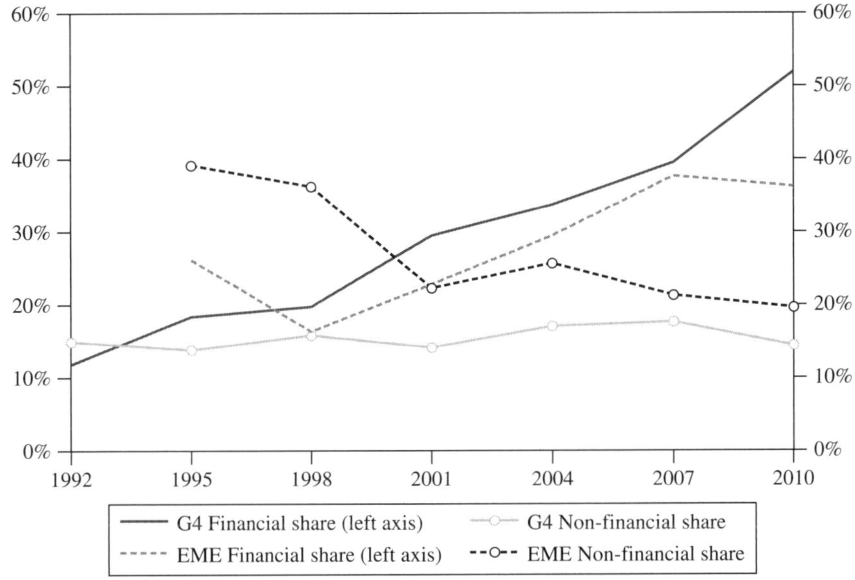


**FIGURE 1.2** **Rising share of financial turnover. Note: Figure shows the share of financial customers (left axis) and non-financial customers (right axis, dot symbols) out of total spot trading. Third group not shown in graph is dealers. G4-currencies (solid lines) are USD, EUR (DEM before 1999), JPY, and GBP; emerging-market currencies (dashed lines) are MXN, KRW, RUB, PLN, TRL, TWD, INR, HUF, ZAR, and BRL.**

Hedge-fund managers are often paid 2% of underlying assets as a flat annual fee and 20% of investment returns. Leveraged currency funds, which grew dramatically during the late 1990s, are known to favor well-defined speculative strategies focused on four factors: fundamentals, interest differentials (i.e., the carry trade), momentum, and volatility.

Unleveraged asset managers ("real-money investors") include mutual funds, pension funds, endowments, and insurance firms. Perhaps surprisingly, such funds often pay little attention to the exchange rate component of returns when choosing asset allocations (Taylor and Farstrup, 2006). Instead, they concentrate on maximizing expected returns to foreign assets measured in the asset's home currency. This approach may be rational given ample evidence that major exchange rates are well approximated by a random walk. Some real-money investors outsource the management of FX exposures to currency overlay managers, who focus on risk reduction, return maximization, or some combination of the two.

FX hedging has become more important among portfolio managers since the financial crisis (Melvin and Prins, 2010). Market participants report that it is common to adopt a 50% hedge ratio, with the hedge reset periodically (e.g., once a month). A 50% ratio minimizes "embarrassment risk," meaning the risk that a firm incurs either an absolute loss (when the rate moves adversely on an unhedged position) or an opportunity loss (when the rate moves favorably on a fully hedged position).

Private financial institutions dominate financial trading on a day-to-day basis, but central banks are noteworthy participants nonetheless. When these public sector institutions intervene to influence exchange rates, their trades are considered informed. Major dealing banks ensure that they know of such trades by cultivating their relationships with central banks. For example, dealers may share market intelligence on a daily basis with these valued clients. Central banks also trade FX as part of the regular procurement process for military and other government functions. Such trades are not considered informative, and central banks often ensure that such trades are not confused with intervention by announcing them in advance.[11]

**1.3.1.2 Corporate Customers.** Corporate customers use FX market to support treasury operations associated with their core business activities such as mining, shipping, and manufacturing. As such, corporations primarily use foreign currencies as a medium of exchange, trade relatively small amounts, and hold these positions only briefly. Most corporate customers choose not to engage in speculative FX trading; indeed some firms explicitly prohibit it. Given their institutional goals, this restriction seems logical. FX forecasting is not among a corporation's "core competencies," so cultivating in-house speculative expertise can be ill-advised (Goodhart, 1988). Further, creating a trading operation is expensive. Not only it is costly to hire currency analysts and traders but also it is expensive to hire the extra staff required to protect against "rogue trader risk," meaning the risk that a single trader brings down the firm (Osler, 2009).[12] Even corporate firms that hedge their foreign cash flows pay little attention to future exchange rate movements. A survey by Bodnar et al. (1998) finds that among corporations that hedge their exposures—as most do—they typically choose hedge ratios between 40% and 50% and favor maturities below 6 months. They also review their currency hedge ratios at most a few times each year. Since corporate customers generally choose not to engage in speculative trading, it is not surprising that their trades do not anticipate short-term returns and are, therefore, not considered informative.

Corporations typically only use the FX market for one side of each exposure. A US multinational needing EUR to pay taxes in Germany, for example, sells its USD to buy the EUR in the FX market but then delivers the currency directly to the German government, bypassing the FX market entirely. Similarly, a Japanese exporter of manufactured goods to the United States receives USD from the American importer and then sells those USD in the FX market.

**1.3.1.3 Retail Investors.** Historically, few private individuals have had sufficient net worth to qualify for a credit line at a FX dealing bank. This barrier to entry effectively made the FX market an entirely wholesale market. Trading

[11]As an example, the Norges Bank trades on behalf of the Norges Bank Investment Management (NBIM), which is Norway's sovereign wealth fund. These trades are announced in advance online (see http://www.norges-bank.no/en/price-stability/foreign-exchange-purchases-for-gpfg/).

[12]A few multinational corporations had FX trading desks as part of their treasury functions before the 2008–2009 financial crisis. Many of these has been closed afterwards.

by small investors was also discouraged by the relatively high bid–ask spreads on small trades, meaning those below $1 million. Retail investors gained access to FX market around the year 2000 with the arrival of internet-based trading platforms tailored to their unique needs, so-called "retail aggregators" (RAs, described below).

Retail investors primarily trade FX spot in the major currency pairs, although the number of emerging-market currencies offered is growing. These individuals or small institutions tend to focus on just one or two currencies and to hold positions for very short time horizons, typically under a day. According to a recent survey (CitiFX Pro, 2010), these traders find the FX market attractive in part because of its low correlation with other markets, its high liquidity, and its 24-h market.

Retail traders should have strong incentives to be informed, since they trade for speculative purposes and employ substantial leverage. The evidence indicates, however, that retail trades are not informed. Their trades do not generally anticipate exchange rate returns (Nolte and Nolte, 2009) and the retail traders themselves are generally unprofitable (Heimer and Simon, 2011). In 2011, Oanda.com claimed that 48% of their retail customers were profitable. A systematic lack of trading acumen also appears to characterize retail traders in equities (Barber and Odean, 2000, 2002; Linnainmaa, 2010). Well-documented forces that might drive traders to stay active even when losing money include wishful thinking and overconfidence (Oberlechner and Osler, 2012).

**1.3.1.4 Algorithmic and High Frequency Traders.** Algorithmic trading is a form of electronic trading where a computer algorithm (or program) determines an order-submission strategy and executes trades without human intervention (Chaboud et al., 2009). Human involvement is limited to designing the algorithm (or algo), monitoring it, and occasionally adjusting the trading parameters. Some algorithms simply automate existing strategies—for example, they break up large trades to minimize transaction costs—while others take advantage of superior execution speeds such as high frequency trading.

High frequency trading relies on a technological advantage to exploit small price discrepancies across different online trading platforms. The time to execute a high frequency trade is measured in milliseconds (where it takes 100 ms to blink). Speed is so essential that high frequency traders co-locate their computer servers as geographically close to the pricing engines of leading electronic trading platforms as possible. Popular high frequency strategies include triangular arbitrage and covered interest rate arbitrage. More commonly, high frequency traders simply pick off dealers' posted quotes that are briefly out of line with the market due to slight time delays between trade instructions and execution (known as *price-latency arbitrage*).

### 1.3.2 WHO PROVIDES LIQUIDITY?

Historically, liquidity in currency markets was provided exclusively by the bigger commercial and investment banks. Over the past decade the spectrum of formal liquidity providers has expanded to include global custodial banks, retail aggregators, and high frequency traders. The rest of this section discusses each agent type in detail.

**1.3.2.1 FX Dealers.** As they have for decades, FX dealers earn income by taking speculative positions and by providing liquidity to customers. Speculation is typically the responsibility of interbank traders, whose positions are only held open a few minutes or hours, and proprietary traders, whose positions are held open for longer periods (Bjønnes and Rime, 2005). Salespeople, who are responsible for maintaining good relationships with customers, are the third major group on a trading floor. To align the interests of FX dealers with those of bank shareholders, dealers receive bonuses tied to their individual profits and the profits of the entire trading floor while their individual risk-taking is constrained by position and loss limits.

Historically, the largest dealing banks earned substantial revenue from both speculative trading and liquidity provision for customers; the smaller dealing banks, by contrast, primarily earned income from customer service (Mende and Menkhoff, 2006). Since the 2007–2009 global financial crisis, proprietary FX trading activity has shrunk dramatically, discouraged by intensified regulatory scrutiny and a smaller appetite for risk. A few top dealers now report that liquidity provision for customers is their biggest source of FX revenue.

When not servicing customers, dealers have historically preferred to trade on the fast and inexpensive interdealer market. In the 1980s and early 1990s, interdealer trading represented over 60% of spot FX trades. In recent years, this fraction (the residual of the two shares presented in Figure 1.2) has declined steadily, and it was most recently estimated at only 35% (BIS, 2010). Reasons for this decline are discussed at length in Section 3 and include greater market transparency and heightened efficiency in matching trades electronically.

Interdealer trading can be carried out either directly in the OTC market or indirectly via FX limit-order markets run by FX brokers (Lyons, 1995). In OTC markets, all trades take place through designated market makers. In limit-order markets, no agents are specifically tasked with providing liquidity. Every agent can either supply ("make") liquidity by placing a limit order or demand ("take") liquidity by entering a market order. Limit orders indicate the prices at which an agent is willing to buy (bid) or sell (offer/ask) a specific quantity. The set of outstanding limit orders, which represents the existing liquidity supply, is known as the *limit-order book*. Orders remain in the limit-order book until executed or cancelled. The best bid or ask prices are known as *the quotes*, and the quantity available at the quotes is the market's "depth." Trades occur when another dealer indicates that she/he wishes to trade immediately by placing a "market order." Market orders are executed against limit orders in the book, beginning with the best-priced limit order and, for large quantities, moving to limit orders with successively less attractive prices.

Interdealer bid–ask spreads in the major currencies are typically 0.5–2.0 pips; those on less liquid currencies, particularly those with exchange controls, can reach 40 pip (Osler et al., 2011). These spreads, like spreads in equity and bond markets, are influenced by inventory risk, as indicated by the positive cross-sectional relation between average spreads and average market volatility (Bollerslev and Melvin, 1994). Nonetheless, the forces that drive FX interdealer spreads vary in striking ways from those that drive equity and bond spreads. FX interdealer spreads are highest during the short overnight period when trading is light and volatility is low. By contrast, spreads in equity and bond markets are typically highest at the market open, when trading and volatility are highest. This difference has been traced to the absence of regulation—and specifically the absence of formal opening and closing hours—in FX (Osler and Yusim, 2009).

Historically, dealers preferred to have zero inventories, so after trading with a customer, the dealer typically passed any accumulated inventory quickly onto other dealers (Lyons, 1995; Bjønnes and Rime, 2005). On the basis of pre-2000 data, estimated inventory half-lives range from a minute for dealers at large banks (Bjønnes and Rime, 2005) to 12 minutes for dealers at small banks (Osler et al., 2011). In recent years, these speeds have come down sharply because of the advancement in electronic trading technologies. If a dealer passed inventory to another dealer, that second dealer typically laid the position off on yet another dealer in a process known as *hot-potato trading* (Lyons, 1997). In other words, the position continued to move until some dealer laid the risk off onto its own customers. In this respect, the FX market differed from some other OTC markets, such as the US municipal bond market or the European government bond market, where dealers "warehouse the risk" and eliminate the inventory via later customer trades, shading their quoted prices to attract trades in their preferred direction (Dunne et al., 2008).

Dealers are perhaps the best-informed agents in FX market. Not only does their order flow anticipate returns (Rime et al., 2010) but it does so better than the trades of any individual group, including leveraged investors (Osler and Vandrovych, 2009). This advantage is thought to reflect, at least in part, the dealers' extensive networks of financial customers. If so, then larger dealers should be better informed than smaller dealers, a prediction that is supported by evidence (Bjønnes et al., 2011).

To increase the amount of customer information coming their way, dealers have historically quoted narrower spreads for larger trades and for financial-customer trades (Ding, 2009; Osler et al., 2011). This pattern is the opposite of that observed in prominent equity markets such as the NYSE. As discussed in Osler et al. (2011), these dealer choices could also be influenced by fixed operating costs and the dealers' stronger bargaining power relative to their least informed customers.

Recent evidence suggests that dealers generate some market-relevant information independently of their customers (Bjønnes et al., 2011). Consistent with this, Moore and Payne (2011) find that dealers specializing in liquid dollar rates can forecast both order flow, which is known to drive returns, and the component of returns that is uncorrelated with flow.

**1.3.2.2 Global Custodian Banks.** Large asset managers typically hire administrators or "custodians" who track their assets, calculate portfolio values, process dividend and interest payments, buy and sell assets, and settle trades. When they need to trade foreign currencies, real-money investors typically do not contact the major banks. Instead, they trade with their custodian, motivated largely by administrative efficiency (DuCharme, 2007).

Consistent with standard practice in the broader FX market, custodial FX trades are handled on a principal basis. Global custodians thus provide a second layer of FX market-making services. The custodian provides liquidity to its clients and, in turn, counts on receiving liquidity from its regular dealing banks. The custodian charges its clients a mark-up over the prices it pays in the interbank market.

Bid–ask spreads on custodial FX trades average a striking 30–40 basis points more than interbank spreads (Osler et al., 2011). This has been traced to the relative opacity of these trades. Typically, when a fund manager instructs its "fund accountant" at the custodian to buy or sell a foreign asset, the order includes instructions to carry out any required FX transactions. As a consequence, the custodian's client gets very little information about the trade; it learns the price actually paid with a delay of days or even weeks and it learns no information at all about the time of the trade or the effective bid–ask spread. This opacity makes it difficult for the fund to monitor execution quality.

In recent years, institutional investors have focused much more on the costs of their FX trades. Transaction cost analysis (TCA) is a growing business and increasingly a requirement for pension funds and other fiduciaries.

Research has not yet examined whether the interbank trades of global custodians are informed, but this could well vary across custodians. Small and mid-sized custodians typically focus exclusively on customer service and their customer trades may not be highly informative since they serve few leveraged investors (Osler et al., 2011). The custodial business has become increasingly concentrated, however, and some large custodians intentionally gather market-relevant information from customers to support speculative position-taking (Ramadorai, 2008).

**1.3.2.3 Retail Aggregators.** In recent years, the emergence of retail FX trading was enabled by the development of a new type of financial intermediary, the retail aggregator (RA). Retail aggregators exclusively operate over internet-trading platforms, bundling small retail trades into larger trades that can be conveniently handled by dealing banks. Some retail aggregators act purely as FX brokers, matching retail trades with quotes from banks. Other retail aggregators combine a broker model with a dealer model; they match some trades but strategically act as the counterparty for others. Retail aggregators typically provide their customers with leverage, which can range up to 200%. They protect themselves against default by insisting that each retail customer posts an initial cash deposit ("margin"). When a trade is executed, the retail aggregator settles it against the margin in the customer's account. When the margin in the retail customer's account is exhausted, the retail aggregator liquidates the retail customer's positions and closes the account immediately. This behavior allows retail aggregators to avoid taking on credit risk from their customers, who must therefore monitor their own trading activity closely.

### 1.3.3 ASYMMETRIC INFORMATION AND EXCHANGE RATE DETERMINATION

For exchange rate modeling, it is important to know not only just which agents bring information to the market but also how their information becomes embedded in the market price. In FX market, this process appears to have at least three steps. First, end-customers reveal their information to market makers indirectly by trading with them. Second, the information becomes embedded in interdealer prices. Third, the information is disseminated widely as quotes in the customer segment of the FX market are adjusted to reflect the new interdealer prices.

The process through which dealers learn information from their customers has already been described. To examine the next step in this process, consider how a dealer adjusts her position after providing liquidity to a customer. As discussed earlier, a dealer who has bought currency from a customer then sells that currency in the interdealer market. The dealer will be especially anxious to trade quickly and aggressively after trading with informed customers (Bjønnes et al., 2011; Osler et al., 2011). An informed customer's purchase implies that the price is likely to rise. If the dealer is short the appreciating currency as a result of the trade, the inventory position represents a bad risk. If the customer is uninformed, however, the dealer has no strong reason for trading aggressively, as there is a 50–50 chance that the associated inventory position will be a winner.

Consistent with this hypothetical dealer behavior, Osler et al. (2011) provide evidence that, after customer trades, dealers are more likely to trade aggressively and in the same direction as the customer if the customer is informed. Similarly, Bjønnes et al. (2011) provide evidence that dealers with larger networks of financial customers tend to trade more aggressively, on average. By contrast, the average aggressiveness of dealer trades is not influenced by the extent of their trading with corporations or governments.

To connect this dealer behavior to price discovery, note that when a dealer sells aggressively, she trades at the lower, less attractive bid price. The downward movement of the interdealer price is consistent with the information implied by the initial informed-customer sale that the price is likely to decline. The interdealer price thus naturally moves to embed the information brought to the market by end-customers. The price shift can be sustained, because other dealers move their own quotes in parallel when they observe the interdealer trade (Goodhart et al., 1996). The interdealer price shift will immediately influence the prices quoted to customers, because these are typically set as a mark-up relative to the interdealer price.

The contemporaneous relationship between daily FX returns and order flow provides evidence consistent with this view of price discovery. (Order flow is defined as the net of aggressive buy trades and aggressive sell trades.) This relationship is positive for financial customers, as one would expect since their individual buy (sell) trades are typically followed by price rises (declines). Dealer order flow also has a positive contemporaneous relationship with daily FX returns.

Since corporate customers are generally uninformed, the price discovery process just described should imply that FX returns are unrelated to corporate order flow. But the contemporaneous relationship between FX returns and corporate order flow is actually negative. That is, on days when corporate customers are net buyers (sellers) of a currency, FX returns are negative (positive) (Bjønnes et al., 2005; Evans and Lyons, 2006; Lyons, 2001; Marsh and O'Rourke, 2005).

The intraday response of corporate customers to changing currency values explains the negative contemporaneous relationship with daily FX returns. Corporate customers are motivated to buy imports inexpensively or to sell exports lucratively. Once a currency has declined in value, imports are less expensive; after a currency gains in value, the effective mark-up on exports is higher. Thus, changes in exchange rates elicit trading responses from corporate customers. Corporate customers can respond nimbly, even though they do not normally monitor the market closely, by using "take-profit" orders, effectively hiring the dealer to monitor the market for them (Osler, 2003, 2005).[13]

Because of their different trading motivations, financial and corporate customers appear to play different roles in exchange rate determination. Sager and Taylor (2006) use a "push-pull" metaphor. When push agents sell a currency to FX dealers, the currency typically depreciates. The depreciation serves to "pull" other agents into the market as buyers. This process has a similar flavor to the model suggested by Evans and Lyons (2002), though their "push" agents are uninformed financial customers and their "pull" agents are risk-averse investors. The evidence suggests, instead, that the push agents tend to be informed financial customers and the pull agents tend to be non-speculative traders.

Corporate customers can also be viewed as unintentional providers of "overnight liquidity" to the market. Dealers provide "immediate liquidity," trading with customers on the assumption that the associated inventory can be off-loaded within the day. But since FX dealers typically end the day with zero inventory, if some end-customers are net buyers on a given day, other end-customers must be net sellers, and vice versa. This second group of customers effectively provides overnight liquidity. The evidence reported above suggests that financial customers tend to demand overnight liquidity and corporate customers tend to supply it.

This analysis of liquidity provision has two key implications for the design of exchange rate models. First, models must include non-financial agents and speculative agents ("investors"). Second, models cannot focus on stock holdings of currencies. It has long been thought that models based on stock positions are equivalent to models based on flows, since flows are simply the first difference of stocks. However, not all flows matter for exchange rate determination. Exchange rates are only influenced by the flows that pass through the currency markets. As noted earlier, currency-market flows include only half of the currency flows generated by corporate customers: when such agents open and then close a FX position, only one leg of the round trip involves the FX market. In short, the first difference of currency holdings are not equivalent to the flows that drive exchange rates, so stock equilibrium models do not conform to critical aspects of the exchange-rate determination process.

[13]A take-profit order instructs a dealer to buy (sell) a specified amount if the price falls (rises) to a certain level.

# 1.4 Electronic Trading Revolution in FX Market

The electronic trading revolution in FX has transformed the market's structure while improving market quality in terms of transparency and transaction costs. This section describes this transformation, which proceeded in two stages. In the first, electronic trading platforms essentially replaced the telephone. In the the second stage, market participants developed previously unanticipated ways to exploit the new technology.

To help clarify the structures, Figure 1.3 provides a stylized depiction of the FX market structure at different points in time. In each frame, the interdealer

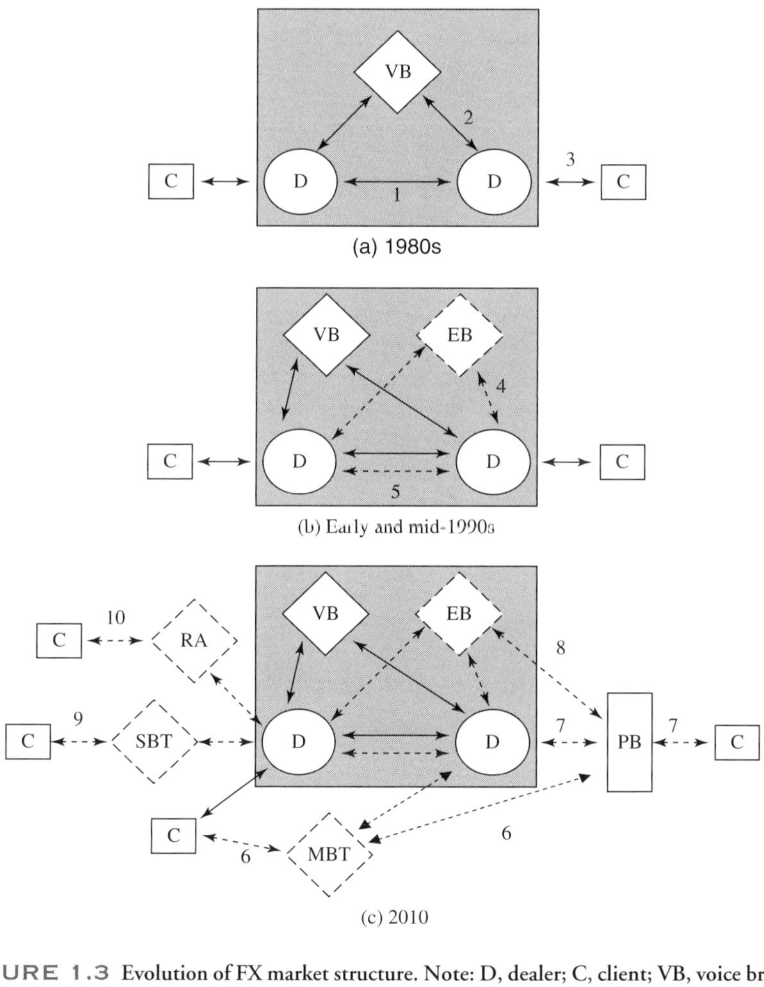


FIGURE 1.3 Evolution of FX market structure. Note: D, dealer; C, client; VB, voice broker; EB, electronic broker; PB, prime broker; MBT, multibank trading system; SBT, single-bank trading system; RA, retail aggregator. Solid lines represent voice execution methods. Dashed lines represent electronic execution methods.

market is represented by the shaded box and the customer market is the area outside the shaded box. Channels for transacting FX are numbered arrows. Solid lines represent voice channels for trading over the telephone; dotted lines represent electronic execution methods.

### 1.4.1 THE TELEPHONE ERA

Currency trading was a sleepy business before exchange rates began floating in the early 1970s. As the business took off, FX trading in the OTC market was handled via telephone lines. Figure 1.3(a) provides a stylized depiction of the market during this period. A customer (C) wishing to trade would call an FX dealer (D) and ask for his current bid and ask quotes. On the basis of the quotes the customer would decide whether to buy the base currency, sell it, or "pass" without trading. Confirmation involved the physical exchange of paperwork between the two back offices. This back-office processing was cumbersome and prone to human error.

In the interdealer market, dealers could call each other directly (line 1) or they could remain anonymous by placing an order with a voice broker (VB) (line 2). The VBs shouted the best available bid and ask prices into open multi-party phone lines that ended in small speakers known as *squawk boxes* on the desks of each dealer. Some emerging-market currencies that are relatively illiquid are still traded this way.

The FX market were fairly opaque during this period, since information about FX trades was proprietary to the two counterparties. The only market-wide source of information was the ongoing announcement of quotes by the voice brokers. Major banks had small networks with implicit agreements to quote tight bid–ask spreads, while smaller banks paid wider spreads. To gather information, dealers often called each other asking for quotes, a practice that required them sometimes to trade. Dealers would also do *hot-potato trading* as described earlier. For these and other reasons, interdealer trading exceeded half of all trading.

### 1.4.2 THE RISE OF THE COMPUTER

Electronic trading platforms first transformed the interdealer market during the late 1980s and then reached the customer market in the 1990s. Most of these early computer systems merely replaced the telephone, leaving the dealer–customer relationship largely intact.

**1.4.2.1 Electronic Trading in the Interdealer Market.** In 1987, Reuters launched a system for bilateral trades between dealers now known as *Thomson Reuters Dealing* (line 5). Although, in principle, it merely replaced telephone conversations with typed messages, it was speedier and more efficient for the dealers and it enhanced operating efficiency by creating electronic trading records. It quickly became the dominant tool for interdealer trading (Rime, 2003).

Transparency in the interdealer market was enhanced by a roughly contemporary Reuters product, the "FXFX" page. This computer page was essentially a screen that provided dealers' indicative quotes for liquid currencies in real time. It thus served as a one-stop-shop for up-to-date price information from many dealers. For roughly a decade, FXFX was the dealers' main source of FX price information for the most liquid currencies.

In 1992, Reuters introduced the first electronic limit-order market to FX, now known as *Thomson Reuters Matching*. Other banks, worried that Reuters might monopolize interdealer trading, formed a consortium and introduced another such platform a year later, the Electronic Broking Service (EBS). With the launch of these competing electronic brokers (EBs), dealers could now trade anonymously and electronically, as shown by line 4 in Figure 1.3(b). Dealers preferred the anonymity of these platforms to direct interdealer trading because it allowed them to work off positions without tipping off their competitors. A trader at, say, Deutsche Bank, would see the EBS screen but would not know the identity of the banks placing the limit orders (say, Citibank and RBS).[14] Dealers also preferred these trading platforms to the voice brokers because they were faster and more operationally efficient.

By the end of the 1990s, the electronic brokers dominated interdealer trading in the liquid currencies. Owing to network externalities, liquidity naturally gravitated to just one platform for each currency. EBS has long dominated interbank trading for the EUR, JPY, and CHF, while Reuters dominates the GBP, AUD, CAD, and the Scandinavian currencies. Voice brokers remain important for less liquid currencies—which are not traded over electronic brokers—so in 2010, they still accounted for 10% of global spot FX trading.

The introduction of interdealer limit-order markets reduced trading costs for small banks, since the anonymous trading environment did not permit price discrimination. The electronic brokers also enhanced market transparency because limit-order prices are "firm," so the brokers' best bid and ask quotes provided a more reliable signal of "the market" than the indicative quotes of the FXFX page. Post trade transparency was enhanced because the electronic brokers also reported trades more efficiently than voice brokers. However, the effect of electronic brokers on trading volume has been ambiguous. Electronic brokers match counterparties more efficiently and may have reduced passing of unwanted inventories among dealers (so-called hot-potato trading). On the other hand, by lowering execution costs, the electronic brokers may have encouraged more speculative trading.

The electronic revolution in FX encompasses trade processing and trading itself. In the late 1990s, the market came to recognize the dangerously high level of settlement risk, the most important operational risk in FX. For the largest FX dealing banks, exposure to even a single counterparty can exceed bank capital. Given the interconnected nature of the financial system, a failure to settle a large FX trade could trigger a string of defaults. Settlement risk arises because traditionally the transfer of the currency across borders occurs during the normal

[14]To ensure that dealers only trade with creditworthy counterparties, FX brokers screen every quote, comparing the existing exposure of a quoting bank (Citi) to its existing credit line with the potentially observing bank (Deutsche).

working hours of its home central bank. If one leg of a FX transaction settles before the other, the party still waiting for settlement faces the risk of counterparty default (Lindley, 2008). This risk was realized in 1974 when Germany's Herstatt Bank failed after markets closed in Europe but before their USD funds had been transferred to other banks. FX settlement risk is, therefore, commonly known as *Herstatt risk*.

Around 1997, a consortium of 74 banks began designing a new electronic settlement system that would address settlement risk. In 2002, "Continuous Linked Settlement" (CLS) Bank began operation (Galati, 2002). CLS Bank reduces Herstatt risk by settling both legs of every trade simultaneously. It also nets payments across member banks before transferring funds, a process known as *multilateral netting*. As a result, only 4% of the aggregate value traded must actually be transferred to complete settlement. CLS Bank has become an integral part of today's FX market. In 2010, it settled roughly 43% of spot FX transactions and it continues to expand the number of currencies it settles and its institutional membership.[15] The success of CLS Bank in minimizing settlement risk was demonstrated by the smooth handling of FX trades following the bankruptcy of Lehman Brothers—a leading FX dealing bank—in September 2008.[16]

**1.4.2.2 Electronic Trading for End-Customers.** By the middle of the 1990s, bid–ask spreads on FX trades had narrowed in the interbank market but they remained unchanged for end-customers, enabling dealers to reap enhanced profits. This profitability spurred intensified competition for customer business and an explosion of new electronic trading platforms targeting customers. With the launch of these electronic trading platforms, the telephone became largely irrelevant to anyone trading liquid currencies. At the same time, the FX market's structure became complex and multilayered, defying easy classification.

As depicted in Figure 1.3(c), trading is now fragmented across many venues. The strict separation between the two tiers of the FX market—interdealer and customer—has broken down with the advent of multibank trading (MBT) systems (line 6) and FX prime brokerage (PB) (line 7). Prime brokerage is a dealer–customer arrangement that allows end-customers such as hedge funds to transact in the interdealer market, either directly (line 7) or via electronic brokers (line 8). Customers increasingly trade with dealers on proprietary trading systems, known as *single-bank trading systems* (SBT) (line 9). Meanwhile, retail aggregators are a new class of agents that allow retail customers to trade FX economically (line 10).

Electronic trading for end-customers began around 1996 when the global custodian State Street launched its proprietary electronic platform, FX Connect. This system simply replaced the telephone with an electronic connection and thus had no effect on either transparency or bid–ask spreads in the FX market. Nonetheless, it allowed State Street and its customers to handle trades more efficiently and with lower operational risk.

---

[15]This figure emerges from comparing CLS Bank data with the 2010 Triennial Survey.

[16]On September 17, 2008, CLS Bank handled more than 1.5 million payment instructions with a gross value of $8.6 trillion—a new record–with no market disruption.

Around 1999, as the US dot-com boom was reaching its peak, a number of independent (non-bank) firms began a more momentous shift in FX market by launching electronic trading platforms for FX that targeted end-customers. These multibank trading systems allowed customers to directly trade with a range of dealers over proprietary computer networks (line 6). The first such platform, Currenex launched in 1999, extended the existing FX market in a natural direction. Instead of calling individual banks in sequence to find the best quote, customers could send a "request-for-quote" (RFQ) to many FX dealers simultaneously. Dealers were required to respond within a few seconds, and end-customers would then trade with the dealer of their choice. In 2000, State Street made FX Connect available to end-users beyond its own customer base, effectively turning it into a multibank trading system. Table 1.5 provides an overview of the leading multibank trading systems for FX.

Other new entrants, such as Hotspot FX (launched in 2000) and Lava (launched in 2001), introduced electronic limit-order platforms directed at the customer markets, allowing end-customers to trade anonymously. These platforms permit end-customers to make liquidity—by placing limit orders—as well as to take it. Since the supply of liquidity from customers could potentially dry up at times, these platforms contract with dealers to stream continuous quotes.

The major banks responded to competition from these new entrants in a number of ways. First, dealers banded together to create their own competitive entrants. A consortium of banks created FXall, a major multibank request for quote system, in 2001. Second, existing platforms have acquired some of the independent platforms. Currenex, for example, was acquired by State Street in 2007 while Lava was acquired by FXall.

**TABLE 1.5 Overview of Largest Multibank Trading Systems for Customers**

| | Instruments that can be traded | | | | | |
|---|---|---|---|---|---|---|
| | Launched | Spot | Forwards | NDFs | Options | Swaps |
| (a) Request-for-quote service | | | | | | |
| State Street's FXConnect | 1996 | y | — | — | — | y |
| FXall | 2001 | y | y | y | — | y |
| 360 Trading Networks | 2002 | y | y | y | y | y |
| Reuters Trading for FX | 2005 | y | — | — | — | y |
| (b) Pretrade anonymous limit-order book | | | | | | |
| Thomson Reuters Matching | 1992 | y | y | y | y | y |
| EBS | 1993 | y | — | y | — | — |
| Currenex | 1999 | y | — | — | — | y |
| Hotspot FX | 2000 | y | — | — | — | — |
| Lava | 2001 | y | y | y | — | y |

Note: Thomson Reuters Matching and EBS started as interdealer electronic brokers and was opened for customers via prime brokerage in 2005 and 2004, respectively. Currenex was acquired by State Street in 2007. NDFs are non-deliverable forward contracts.

Most importantly, the major banks invested heavily in developing proprietary electronic trading platforms for their customers, known as single bank trading systems (SBT). UBS launched FX Trader in 2000, followed by Barclays' BARX in 2001. Deutsche Bank's Autobahn, developed in 1996 to allow real-time trading of US treasury securities, added FX trading in 2002. Goldman Sachs launched its offering in 2003. Citigroup was a relatively late arrival, launching Velocity in 2006. Some single bank trading systems allow customers to enter orders at the daily fixing price or for delayed dealing. On other systems, dealers provide "streaming prices" based on interbank quotes and their proprietary customer trades. Customers can tailor trades to their specific needs with just a few key strokes and buy spot FX at the click of a mouse. Figure 1.4 shows a screen print of Barclay's BARX, illustrating what customers typically see on such platforms.

The advent of customer-focused electronic trading has brought a significant dispersal of trading across platforms, as shown in Table 1.6. In the 1980s, only three out of the five listed platform types were available; in the 1990s, electronic brokers became available for the interbank market, while today both dealers and customers trade side-by-side on several platforms.

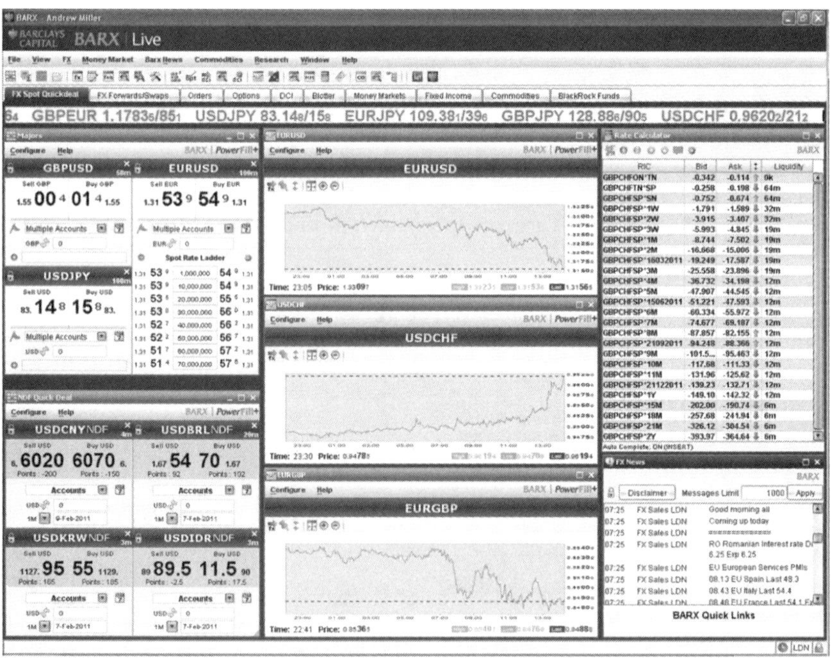


FIGURE 1.4 Screenshot of the BarX platform of Barclays Capital. Note: From the "Sheet-bar" at top, we see all the instruments configured for trading in this particular screen. The upper left panel shows a window for spot trading, where we notice that the GBP/USD and the EUR/USD is quoted with five decimals, while USD/JPY is quoted with three decimals. Earlier, it was customary to quote with four and two decimals, respectively.

**TABLE 1.6 Execution Methods for FX Trading (% Shares)**

| | Inter dealer Direct | Voice Broker | Electronic Broker | Customer Direct | Multibank Trading System | Total |
|---|---|---|---|---|---|---|
| All FX instruments | | | | | | |
| UK, US, and Japan | 15 | 16 | 19 | 39 | 12 | 100 |
| Next 7 countries | 24 | 19 | 17 | 31 | 10 | 100 |
| Remaining 43 countries | 29 | 11 | 24 | 25 | 10 | 100 |
| Spot only | | | | | | |
| UK, US, and Japan | 12 | 8 | 27 | 36 | 16 | 100 |
| - Dealers | 29 | 10 | 34 | 16 | 11 | 100 |
| Next 7 countries | 20 | 11 | 20 | 39 | 11 | 100 |
| - Dealers | 37 | 7 | 28 | 15 | 13 | 100 |
| Remaining 43 countries | 27 | 8 | 27 | 28 | 10 | 100 |
| FX swaps only | | | | | | |
| UK, US, and Japan | 18 | 28 | 15 | 32 | 7 | 100 |
| Next 7 countries | 26 | 23 | 17 | 25 | 9 | 100 |
| Remaining 43 countries | 33 | 15 | 22 | 18 | 12 | 100 |

Note: When comparing national results, FX turnover is on a "net–gross" basis (i.e., only adjusting for local interdealer double counting). "Next 7 countries" are, in descending order of global FX activity, Singapore; Switzerland; Hong Kong SAR; Australia; France; Denmark; and Germany. "Interdealer direct" are trades directly between reporting dealers executed either electronically or by telephone, and "Customer direct" are all direct trades between a customer and a dealer executed either by telephone or on a single-bank trading system.
*Source:* BIS Triennial FX Survey.

The advent of electronic trading for end-customers has had welcome effects on most measures of market quality while simultaneously bringing a perhaps worrying increase in market concentration among dealers. We conclude this section by reviewing these consequences.

*Enhanced transparency.* Pre-trade transparency is greater now that single bank trading and multibank trading systems stream prices continuously. Customers can now monitor developments in FX market directly rather than relying on their dealers. Pre-trade transparency has also been enhanced by the extensive real-time information about limit-order books available on some of the anonymous platforms. Hotspot FX, for example, presents prices and depth at every available level.

Most electronic systems permit customers to record market prices at the time of trade execution and the price impact of their trades. As a result, they can begin to carry out transaction cost analysis, a practice in which agents statistically examine their transaction costs to identify potential sources of efficiency. Transaction cost analysis is already common in equity markets, where it is generally considered essential to responsible asset management. In FX, this practice has not yet been widely embraced because it was infeasible until recently.

*Improved operating efficiency.* Electronic trading enables "straight-through processing" (STP), whereby trades entered electronically can likewise be cleared and settled electronically. Because straight-through processing involves no paperwork and little human intervention, it is almost error free and thus dramatically lowers operational costs and risk.

*Narrower bid–ask spreads.* The introduction of electronic trading for end-customers quickly brought narrower spreads for them. In the 1980s and 1990s, when the FX market was opaque, the spreads paid by corporate customers on small trades were reportedly as large as 20 times interdealer spreads (Bjønnes and Rime, 2005; Goodhart et al., 2002). Even in 2001, corporate spreads on small trades were still three times interdealer spreads or more (Osler et al., 2011). By now, this difference in bid–ask spreads between the two FX market segments has almost disappeared.

Customer electronic trading platforms have pushed down bid–ask spreads in the interdealer market, as well, by lowering dealers' operating costs. Lower operating costs, in turn, have meant that certain cross rates can now be traded directly at tight bid–ask spreads (e.g., EUR/AUD and AUD/JPY). As shown in Figure 1.5, interdealer spreads were on the order of 4-10 basis points in the mid-1990s, but within a decade, they had narrowed to roughly 2 pips (or \$200 for a round trip transaction of EUR \$1 million, which remains as the minimum trade size on electronic brokers). In some of the most liquid markets, such as EUR/USD,

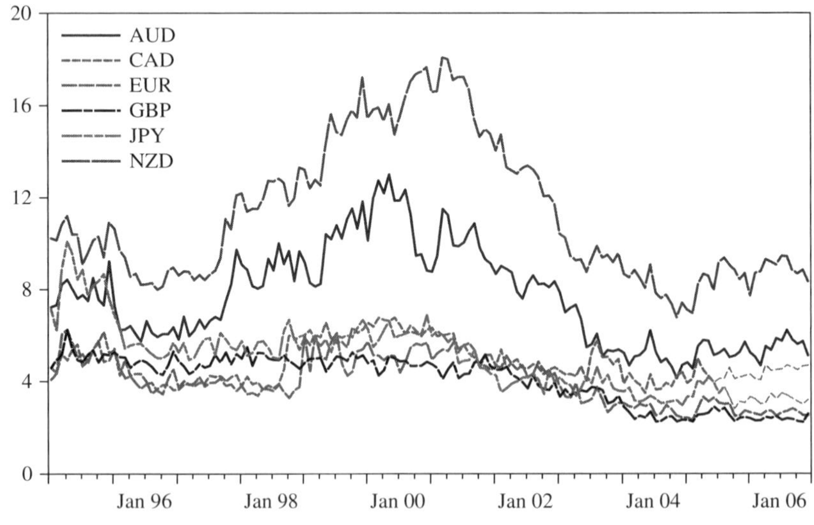


**FIGURE 1.5** **Relative bid–ask spread by currency: January 1995–December 2006. Note: Bid–ask spread in basis points of midquote for several currencies against the USD. All relative spreads shown exhibit negative correlation with a time trend.** ***Source:*** **Olsen and Associates.**

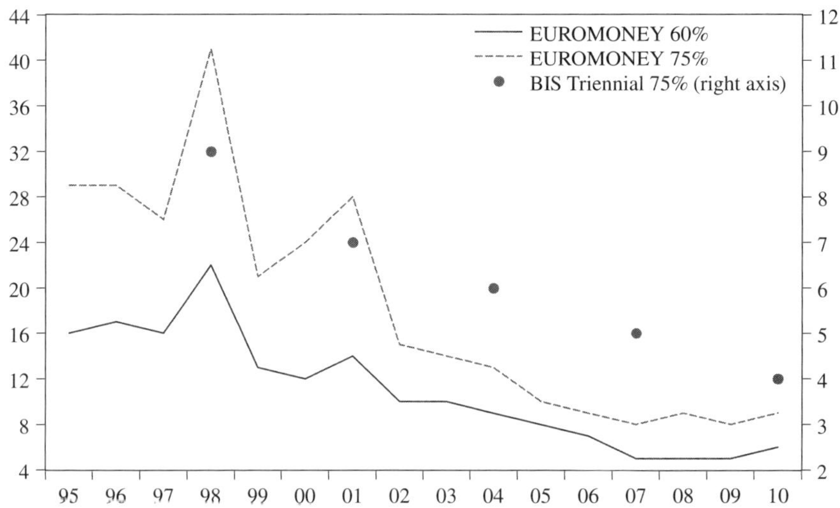


**FIGURE 1.6 Market concentration. Number of banks covering *x*% market share. Note: Dots, measured on right axis, represents number of banks covering 75% of the market according to the BIS Triennial Survey. The dots are weighted average of a selection of 14 countries, where share of the total volume of these 14 countries is used as weight. Lines, on left axis, measure the number of banks covering 60% and 75% of the market using the annual survey by the Euromoney.**

bid–ask spreads during active trading are often narrower than 1 pip. In 2011, one of the major interdealer brokers, EBS, moved to fractional-pip pricing but its competitor Thomson Reuters did not. While EBS is appealing to algorithmic traders, Thomson Reuters is responding to objections from its manual-trading customers, who prefer to see a greater depth of book on their screens.

Bid–ask spreads in the custodial segment have, until recently, resisted the tendency to decline. Beginning in October 2009, a number of lawsuits were filed claiming that global custodian banks had overcharged clients on FX trades. The costs of non-negotiated FX trades by global custodians reportedly dropped by 63% in 2010 relative to earlier years (Diamond, 2011).

*Rising market concentration among dealers.* Customer electronic trading has prompted a striking increase in concentration among FX dealers (Figure 1.6). Because banks have been forced to invest heavily in trading technology even while quoting tighter bid–ask spreads, small banks now find it unprofitable to make markets in the major currencies. Between 1998 and 2010, the top three banks' share of FX trading rose from 19% to 40% as reported in the annual Euromoney survey. Despite this increasing concentration, small and regional banks continue to make markets in their local currencies, profiting from their local expertise and comparative advantage in the provision of credit to customers.

### 1.4.3 RECENT DEVELOPMENTS IN ELECTRONIC TRADING

Once the telephone had been replaced by electronic connections, traders began to identify creative new ways to exploit the potential of electronic trading. Large banks have aggressively moved to internalize trades and to profile their customers. They also provide hedge fund customers with prime brokerage services and regional-bank customers with white labeling of their proprietary trading platforms. Meanwhile, independent proprietary trading firms have developed innovative ways of trading on electronic platforms, such as algorithmic trading.

#### 1.4.3.1 Innovations by the Major Dealing Banks

*White labeling.* Although many small banks have withdrawn from market making in the most liquid currencies, they ensure their customers have access to liquidity by providing the single bank trading platforms of major banks under their own name. This practice, called *white labeling*, has numerous advantages for the major banks. First, it lets them view the small banks' trading flows—and to extract any relevant information—without the expense of evaluating each counterparty's creditworthiness. It also provides major banks with a new revenue stream, supporting the investments required to develop their single bank trading systems. The extent of white labeling is indicated in Table 1.7, which shows that the combined market share of the three largest single bank trading platforms, at roughly 70%, is double the overall market share of the three largest banks, at roughly 35%.

*Internalization of customer trades.* Given the rising market share of the largest dealers, they now have sufficient flow to systematically internalize customer trades. If customer A calls to sell a quantity of JPY, the bank will hold those JPY

**TABLE 1.7 Average Market Share and Years with Top-10 Ranking for Single-Bank Platforms**

| | Share (%) | # Top 10 |
|---|---|---|
| Deutsche Bank (Autobahn) | 36 | 7 |
| UBS (FX Trader) | 22 | 7 |
| Barclays Capital (BARX) | 12 | 7 |
| Citi (Velocity) | 6 | 7 |
| JPMorgan (MorganDirect) | 3 | 3 |
| Goldman Sachs (REDI) | 3 | 5 |
| RBS (SmartPrime) | 3 | 6 |
| HSBC (HSBCnet FXHub) | 2 | 7 |
| Credit Suisse (PrimeTrade FX) | 2 | 3 |
| Morgan Stanley (Passport) | 2 | 2 |

Note: The table shows the average market share (in percentage points) since 2004 up to 2010. The column "#Top 10" states how many years, out of the 7 possible years, that a bank's single-bank platform has ranked top 10.
*Source:* Euromoney FX Survey.

in inventory until customers B and C call to buy JPY, rather than unloading the position in the interdealer market. Electronic trades can be especially profitable to internalize because algorithms allow banks to capture the bid–ask spread with less market risk. Any trades that cannot be matched internally are passed to the dealer's trading desk, where the inventory risk can be managed as before in interdealer markets. In 2007, fewer than 25% of trades were internalized in this way. Today, the top FX dealers are reportedly matching 80% or more of customer trades on their own books. Internalization is another factor contributing to the declining share of interdealer trading in overall trading.

*Customer profiling.* Banks have begun to exploit their new digital trading records to profile the trades of each customer. Dealers examine these data statistically to distinguish three types of trades: (i) directional flows, (ii) non-directional flows, and (iii) predatory high frequency trades. Directional flows are customer trades that are typically associated with subsequent movements in exchange rates and are therefore considered informed. Dealers can use the information embedded in these informed trades either to reduce inventory risk or to guide their speculative position-taking. Non-directional (or uninformed) flows refer to client transactions that are not associated with any predictable price movements. Dealers can safely hold trades with uninformed customers in their inventory and then cross them against other end-customer trades, allowing the dealers to earn the full bid–ask spread. Predatory flows are discussed in greater detail below.

*Prime brokerage.* Leveraged investors have begun trading directly in the interbank markets via prime brokerage arrangements with the biggest dealers. Prime brokerage clients trade with other dealers in the prime broker's name using the prime broker's existing credit lines (Figure 1.3(c), line 7), a privilege for which they pay a fee based on trading volume. Any trades executed with FX dealers other than the prime broker are "given up" to the prime broker, who becomes the counterparty to both legs of the trade. Hedge-fund Z, for example, might pay Bank of America to be its prime broker, thereby gaining access to the EBS and Thomson Reuters trading platforms. After Z buys AUD from, say, HSBC, Bank of America becomes the seller of AUD to Z and the buyer of AUD from HSBC.

For the large banks, prime brokerage arrangements generate new, fee-based revenue that leverages their technology and operating infrastructure. The benefits to end-customers are more varied. End-customers gain leverage, consolidated settlement, clearing, and reporting services.[17] Since many hedge funds have a limited credit history, prime brokerage arrangements provide access to new counterparties and new trading platforms. Prime brokerage also permits a more efficient use of their collateral for margin relationships, since positions can be netted, replacing operational and settlement risk. Finally, prime brokerage provides customers with anonymity, as their counterparties often do not know

[17]For more details on FX prime brokerage, see www.ny.frb.org/fxc/2005/fxc051219a.pdf.

the identity behind a prime brokerage trade. By contrast, hedge funds do not enjoy anonymity when they trade directly with their banks. Historically, some major hedge funds have been concerned that banks would either front run their trades or share information about their activity with others in the market.[18]

Prime brokerage, like many innovations in FX, initially took root in equity and bond markets, which may help explain why the growth of FX prime brokerage has been startlingly rapid. Close to 30% of spot transactions in London were executed via a prime brokerage relationship in April 2010, up from just 15% in 2008.[19]

### 1.4.3.2 Innovations by End-Customers

*Algorithmic trading.* Algorithmic (or algo) trading, described in Section 2, emerged naturally once end-customers had access to sophisticated electronic trading systems. A key turning point came in 2003 when the electronic broker EBS provided an automated interface (AI) to banks, allowing banks to receive streaming price quotes electronically. This innovation opened the door to algorithmic trading in interdealer markets. A few years later, in response to competition from multibank trading systems, EBS and Reuters extended this service to banks' major customers. This development gave hedge funds and other proprietary traders access to interdealer markets for the first time. As shown in Figure 1.7, the share of algorithmic trading on the interdealer brokers has grown rapidly and now exceeds 50%.

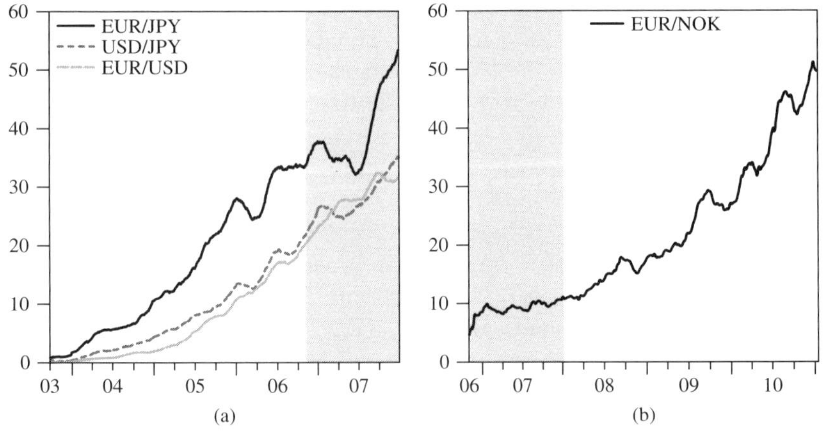


**FIGURE 1.7 Share of algorithmic trading on EBS and Thomson Reuters Dealing. Note: Moving average of share of trades involving at least one machine using gross volumes. (a) Fifty-day moving average of machine-share on EBS for EUR/USD, USD/JPY, and EUR/JPY. (b) Seven-week moving average of machine-share on Reuters D3000 for EUR/NOK. The shaded area marks where the two graphs have overlapping observations. *Source:* Chaboud et al. (2009).**

[18] Soros's Quantum Funds has required banks with which it trades to sign special confidentiality agreements.

[19] See the survey of the London FXJSC at http://www.bankofengland.co.uk/markets/forex/fxjsc/index.htm.

*High frequency trading.* As discussed in Section 2, algorithmic trading has spawned a new form of trading called *high frequency trading*. High frequency trading involves capturing frequent but tiny profits associated with slight transitory price differences across platforms. King and Rime (2010) estimate that high frequency trading now accounts for roughly one-quarter of spot FX turnover. The rise of high frequency trading explains the concentration of trading growth in spot markets, the concentration of that growth in USD and EUR, and the concentration of reported activity in London and the United States. It can also explain why spot trade sizes have been falling while trade numbers have been rising as well as the doubling of exchange-traded contracts on the Chicago Mercantile Exchange (CME) since 2007. By 2010, high frequency traders were active on some single bank trading systems and algorithmic trading was even a dominating feature of smaller currencies such as the NOK (Figure 1.7).

Dealers have mixed reactions toward high frequency trading on their proprietary systems. The high frequency traders' profit is a dealer's loss. As a result, some banks screen out such "predatory" trading using computer algorithms that profile customers based on trading activity. Other banks, however, encourage high frequency trading on in-house systems; they see indirect gains, since the additional liquidity allows them to populate internal pricing engines.

Dealers are generally happy to sponsor high frequency trading firms on multibank platforms through prime brokerage relationships and charge them for using the bank's credit. Nonetheless, FX dealers recognize that they themselves can be "scalped" by price-latency arbitrage, so some post quotes on these platforms only when they proactively want to trade. In addition, most banks have invested heavily in their own high frequency trading capacity. Unsurprisingly, the expansion of high frequency trading has diminished the profitability of this strategy. With high frequency trading less profitable and fewer banks making markets, a number of top high frequency trading firms have begun providing liquidity—and in effect making markets—on anonymous multibank trading platforms as a profitable trading strategy.

A key question that FX market face is whether liquidity provided by high frequency traders is a "mirage" that will dry up in a crisis when it is needed most. High frequency traders engage in market making because it is profitable, but are under no *obligation* to offer liquidity. Most banks, by contrast, will make markets for their customers even during times of stress, in order to maintain their reputation and to win other more lucrative business. The evidence from the 2007–2009 global financial crisis is inconclusive. Following the collapse of Lehman Brothers, the spot markets—where high frequency traders are most active—remained liquid, though spreads widened considerably (Baba and Packer, 2009; Melvin and Taylor, 2009).

*Retail aggregators.* With electronic trading, small trades can automatically be aggregated into larger trades and laid off in the liquid interdealer market. With the advent of such retail aggregators, described in Section 2, individuals with modest wealth—an entirely new class of agents—began trading FX. Retail trading has been one of the fastest growing segments of the market. Such trading, which was negligible in 2001, had reached an estimated $125–150 billion per day, or 8–10% of global spot turnover, by 2010 (King and Rime, 2010).[20] Japanese retail investors are believed to be the most active, representing perhaps 30% or more of spot JPY trading (or more than $20 billion per day). Most of this Japanese trading takes place through margin accounts on the Tokyo Financial Exchange (Terada et al., 2008).

Dealers are happy to provide liquidity to retail aggregators at attractive prices because retail trades are not on average informed, as noted earlier, so there is no adverse-selection risk. Dealers can safely hold retail flows in inventory to cross against future transactions. Table 1.8 shows that retail customers trading over the internet for amounts of $50,000 or less may pay bid–ask spreads as low as 1 pip for the most liquid currency pairs, similar to spreads available to dealers a decade ago.

The rapid growth of retail FX trading has led to increased regulation. Online FX dealers must now be registered and capital requirements have been raised. Further, the United States and Japan have lowered the cap on retail leverage from 100 : 1 to 50 : 1 for major currencies, and in Japan the cap fell further, to 25 : 1, in January 2012. Since there are currently no limits on leverage and limited regulation in the United Kingdom and continental Europe, there is potential for regulatory arbitrage.

Greater regulation has brought industry consolidation. The number of US retail platforms shrank from 47 in 2007 to 11 in 2011; the number of Japanese platforms fell from over 500 in 2005 to around 70 in 2011.

**TABLE 1.8 Bid–Ask Spreads Available From A Retail FX Platform (in Pips)**

| Pair | Spread | Pair | Spread | Pair | Spread |
|---|---|---|---|---|---|
| EUR/USD | 2.3 (1.0) | NZD/USD | 4.0 (1.1) | USD/DKK | 6.8 (1.0) |
| USD/JPY | 2.4 (1.0) | NZD/JPY | 4.4 (1.1) | EUR/CAD | 7.1 (1.3) |
| GBP/USD | 3.0 (1.0) | AUD/JPY | 4.8 (1.4) | USD/SGD | 7.1 (4.7) |
| USD/CHF | 3.0 (1.0) | AUD/CHF | 4.9 (2.6) | GBP/AUD | 8.0 (2.4) |
| AUD/USD | 3.1 (1.1) | AUD/NZD | 5.0 (1.6) | GBP/CAD | 8.3 (3.0) |
| EUR/JPY | 3.1 (1.1) | GBP/JPY | 5.4 (1.1) | EUR/NZD | 9.2 (3.2) |
| EUR/GBP | 3.2 (1.1) | CAD/JPY | 5.7 (1.6) | USD/TRY | 9.2 (4.2) |
| USD/CAD | 3.7 (1.0) | AUD/CAD | 6.0 (2.5) | EUR/TRY | 15.2 (7.2) |
| EUR/CHF | 3.9 (1.4) | EUR/AUD | 6.5 (1.5) | GBP/NZD | 17.4 (7.0) |
| CHF/JPY | 4.0 (1.0) | GBP/CHF | 6.6 (2.0) | USD/HKD | 18.2 (17.2) |

Note: Table shows typical spreads for several exchange rates, together with lowest spread in parenthesis, from the FXCM retail internet platform. The relative spread as a measure of transaction cost varies of course with the level of the exchange rate, but the table shows that for many pairs, there is not much room for decreasing the spread.
*Source:* FXCM (http://www.fxcm.com/forex-spreads.jsp).

[20]Activity via retail aggregators is reported as "Other financial institutions" in the Triennial Central Bank Survey.

*Liquidity aggregators.* With trading dispersed across competing electronic platforms, liquidity could have become fragmented and the markets inefficient. Natural market forces, however, have provided a solution with the development of "liquidity aggregators". Liquidity aggregators are electronic tools that collect streaming price quotes from different sources such as FX dealers, electronic brokers, and multibank trading systems. By aggregating quotes into one executable stream, dealers and end-customers can access the best prices from many platforms simultaneously. Hedge funds have been using these algorithms for several years, and they are now being adopted by large banks.

*Central counterparties.* One more operational innovation may yet take hold in FX market, specifically the introduction of central counterparties (CCPs), which are designed to mitigate counterparty credit risk (i.e., default risk). Although most FX instruments generate little counterparty credit risk, exposures generated by longer-dated FX forwards and options can be substantial. This risk is typically managed in FX using counterparty risk limits set bilaterally and master netting agreements that specify the conditions and procedures associated with default (FXC, NY, 2010).

During the 2008 financial crisis, standard counterparty protections in OTC markets proved inadequate or were questioned for many asset classes. To address this weakness, regulators in the United States and Europe began considering whether to mandate centralized clearing via a central counterparty. The central counterparty reduces counterparty credit risk by stepping into the middle of every trade, becoming the buyer to every seller and the seller to every buyer. The central counterparty requires both parties to post collateral, with a safety margin maintained while any position remains open (Cecchetti et al., 2009). If one party defaults, the central counterparty uses that party's margin to close out the transaction with the other counterparty.

In FX market, central counterparties have been operating for exchange-traded products for some time but have been absent in OTC markets. While the US Treasury has exempted spot and forward FX market from the requirement under the Dodd–Frank Act to use a central counterparty, other FX instruments will be required to adopt this new structure. European authorities are expected to follow the US' lead on this issue.

A 2006 joint attempt by CME and Reuters to launch a central counterparty with the OTC sector, called *FX MarketSpace*, failed in 2008. As of 2010, the CME—which operates the largest central counterparty for exchange-traded FX products—is again planning to launch a central counterparty for OTC derivatives including FX. Unlike the 2006 venture, the planned offering will be operated as a stand-alone, open entity that may prove more popular with market participants.

## 1.5 Survey of Multibank FX Platforms

To better understand FX activity on multibank trading systems and electronic brokers, the authors conducted a survey of 15 institutional and retail platforms. Table 1.9 shows the results from the authors' survey. The 10 institutional

**TABLE 1.9 Survey of 15 Multibank Platforms for FX**

| | Institutional | Retail | Total |
|---|---|---|---|
| Platforms participating | 10 | 5 | 15 |
| *1. What was average daily turnover (in US dollar millions):* | | | |
| In April 2010? | 830,417 | 71,861 | 902,278 |
| In April 2007? | 687,856 | 16,705 | 704,561 |
| Growth from 2007 to 2010 | 21% | 330% | 28% |
| *2. In April 2010, what was the ...* | | | |
| Average daily number of transactions | 396,727 | 1,177,440 | 1,574,167 |
| Average trade size | 2,093,169 | 61,032 | 573,178 |
| *3. What was average daily turnover (in US dollar millions) through your system by FX instrument?* | | | |
| Spot | 436,835 | 70,822 | 507,657 |
| Outright forwards | 11,657 | 444 | 12,101 |
| Non-deliverable forwards (NDFs) | 449 | 0 | 449 |
| FX swaps | 381,387 | 0 | 381,387 |
| Currency options | 89 | 595 | 684 |
| Total | 830,417 | 71,861 | 902,278 |
| *4. Rank customer types by importance for activity (1 = most important)* | | | |
| Banks and other financial institutions | 1 | 2 | — |
| Real money | 2 | 4 | — |
| Hedge-fund / leveraged strategies | 3 | 3 | — |
| Corporates or governments | 4 | — | — |
| Central banks, monetary authorities | 5 | — | — |
| Retail (small individual) trading | 6 | 1 | — |
| *5. What was the share of turnover by value traded in 2010 (2007)?* | | | |
| Algorithmic trading | 35% (38%) | 37% (19%) | — |
| High frequency trading | 18% (15%) | 8% (10%) | — |
| Executed via a prime brokerage account | 19% (7%) | 9% (24%) | — |

Note: The table shows the results from a survey of multibank platforms and retail platforms conducted during fall 2010. The names are (in alphabetical order): Multibank platforms: Currenex, EBS, FXall, FXConnect, Hotstpot FX, Lava Trading, Reuters Trading for Foreign Exchange, Thomson Reuters Dealing, Thomson Reuters Matching, and 360 Trading Networks. Retail platforms: FXCM, FX Direct Dealer, Gain Capital, OANDA, and Saxo Bank.

*Source:* Author's survey.

platforms that participated represent as much as 30% of spot FX trading globally and 22% of FX swaps.[21] The five retail platforms surveyed captured another 5% of global spot FX turnover. Activity on multibank platforms has grown strongly over the past three years, with weighted-average daily turnover rising by 20% for the institutional platforms and by over 300% for the retail platforms. The average trade size is $2 million on institutional platforms and around $60,000 on retail platforms, with the latter handling many more transactions on a typical day.

The most active participants on institutional platforms (in order of importance) are banks, real-money investors, and leveraged investors. Trading on institutional platforms is even more concentrated in spot (53%) and FX swaps (46%) than it is in the rest of the market.

The client base and nature of trading varies considerably across platforms. EBS and Thomson Reuters serve the interbank market, with significant activity by algorithmic and high frequency traders who gain access via prime brokerage relationships. In the case of EBS, there is now almost a 50/50 split between algorithmic traders and manual traders with a keypad. To satisfy both customer types, EBS slowed down execution on its platform by introducing a minimum quote life of 250 ms to prevent flash orders and to level the playing field between computers and humans.

Algorithmic and high frequency trading are also important on other anonymous platforms such as Currenex, Hotspot FX, and Lava. On Hotspot FX, for example, reportedly over 75% of the platform's turnover in 2011 is algorithmic. Across all institutional platforms, the share of algorithmic trading has been stable over the past 3 years at around 35% of activity. High frequency trading represented 18% of turnover in 2010, with all of this activity transacted through prime brokerage relationships.

Real-money investors and corporate customers are most active on request for quote platforms such as FXall, FXConnext, 360Trading Networks, and Reuters Trading for FX. Algo trading on request for quote platforms is a negligible share of activity.

On retail-oriented platforms, activity is concentrated in spot trades in the major bilateral pairs (i.e., EUR/USD, GBP/USD, USD/JPY) or in popular carry trade combinations (AUD/USD, GBP/JPY, EUR/JPY). Carry trade activity has declined over the past 2 years, however, as interest rates have fallen and a number of leveraged investors suffered large losses on their trades.

Four out of the five retail platforms surveyed are US based, but they attract customers globally. Asia represents the fastest growing market, with particular growth in Japan, Taiwan, and Korea. More than a third of retail investors use computer algorithms. This statistic reflects the wide availability of popular software trading packages such as MetaTrader that offer charting and other technical tools and allow users to program their own trading strategies.

While much of retail trading is reportedly intraday, a significant portion involves buy-and-hold investors who trade on fundamentals. A recent survey

[21]The data collected from multibank platforms are not adjusted for interdealer double-counting, so these estimates of their coverage are biased upwards.

by CitiFX Pro found that more than half of traders employ a combination of fundamental and technical analysis, with 36% saying they only use technical analysis. Leverage is important, with the most common range between 50 and 100 times capital. As the regulatory limits on leverage described earlier take hold, these fractions will likely decline.

## 1.6 Summary

This chapter examines the state of play in the global FX market, which reflects both stability and rapid technological change. As ever, currency trading still takes place on a decentralized market in which most customers rely on professional dealers to provide liquidity. Currencies are still traded to facilitate international trade, hedge risk, earn speculative returns, and to profit from market making. The USD, JPY, and EUR remain the dominant currencies and trading is still concentrated in London and New York. The best-informed agents in the market continue to be financial institutions, especially hedge funds. Corporate customers continue to eschew speculative trading in spot markets and provide liquidity.

In the early 1980s, all FX trading was done by phone, transparency was low, and customer transaction costs were high. The lack of transparency resulted in high levels of interdealer trading relative to end-customer trading. In the early 1990s, the introduction of electronic brokers to the interdealer market brought a huge increase in transparency, and the share of interbank trading began to fall even while trading volumes rose.

The electronic revolution finally reached end-customers around 2000, when single-bank platforms and multibank platforms allowed institutional customers to trade electronically with their dealers and with each other. Market transparency rose further, trade processing costs fell due to straight-through processing, and customer bid–ask spreads fell rapidly. Electronic trading has also created access to the market from previously excluded groups, specifically retail trading by individuals and small institutions. Retail trading was made possible by the development of a new type of internet-based trading platform, the retail aggregator. Ongoing attempts to regulate retail trading may bring further market changes in the future.

Innovative trading strategies employed in FX market include white labeling, prime brokerage, algorithmic trading, and high frequency trading. These innovations have complicated the strategic calculus of market making and could potentially undermine liquidity provision in a crisis.

The increasing sophistication of FX trading software and the associated growth of algorithmic and high frequency trading have brought a number of important structural changes to global FX market.

1. Banks are matching a growing share of customer flows on their single-bank trading systems, reducing activity in interdealer markets.
2. Electronic trading has enabled the development of algorithmic strategies, including high frequency trading. In just a few years, high frequency trading has come to dominate trading volume in the major liquid currencies.

3. High frequency traders have gained access to interdealer markets through their prime brokerage relationships, and have engaged in price-latency arbitrage. This activity has led to the breakdown of the traditional gentlemen's agreement among FX dealers to provide continuous, two-way quotes to other market makers.
4. As the top tier FX dealers back away from market making and the traditional profit-making opportunities in high frequency trading are competed away, some high frequency firms are turning to market making as a profitable trading activity. Critics worry that they—and the liquidity they provide—will disappear during times of market stress as these firms are under no obligation to make markets.
5. The top tier banks are investing heavily in computer systems that allow them to profile their customers. This heavy investment has created an effective barrier to entry, and has driven many small banks away from making markets in the most liquid currencies, raising market concentration among the top tier dealers.
6. Smaller and regional banks are now pursuing a hybrid model, acting as customers of the top dealers for the most liquid currencies while still making markets in their local currencies. This division allows banks below the top tier to profit from their local expertise and comparative advantage in the provision of credit to their customers.
7. The increasing tendency for banks to internalize their trading flow and to turn their own platforms into separate liquidity pools may have unexpected consequences on market liquidity. Each bank relies implicitly on the liquidity of the interbank market when quoting to customers. But by intensifying the ongoing fragmentation of FX trading, the dealers' own strategic efforts may compromise this critical liquidity. Only time will tell how this plays out.

## GLOSSARY

**Algorithmic trading:** Automated transactions where a computer algorithm decides the order-submission strategy. See also "High frequency trading."

**Bid–ask spread:** Difference between the price for buying (the dealer's ask) and for selling (the dealer's bid), which measures the transaction costs for executing a trade; often used as an indicator of market liquidity.

**Broker:** A financial intermediary who matches counterparties to a transaction without being a party to the trade. The broker can operate electronically (electronic broker) or by telephone (voice broker).

**Carry trade:** A trading strategy where low yielding currencies are sold to finance the purchase of higher-yielding currencies.

**Central counterparty (CCP):** An independent legal entity that interposes itself between the buyer and the seller of a security, and requires a margin deposit from both sides.

**Counterparty credit risk:** The risk that a counterparty will not settle an obligation in full value, either when due or at any time thereafter.

**Counterparty risk limit:** An institution's maximum aggregate market exposure to an individual counterparty across all uncollateralized trading positions. Established by a dealer's risk managers before agreeing to trade with a given counterparty.

**Credit support annex (CSA):** Document specifying the rules governing the mutual posting of collateral between two counterparties.

**Currency (or FX) futures:** Similar to outright forward, a transaction involving the exchange of two currencies at a rate agreed on the date of the contract for value or delivery (cash settlement) at some time in the future (more than 2 business days or later). Unlike outright forward, currency futures are exchange-traded instruments with standardized characteristics such as contract size and maturity. Four contracts are available with settlement in March, June, September, and December. The biggest currency futures exchange is the CME, followed by the London Futures Exchange. Futures are mainly available for the most liquid currency pairs.

**Currency (or FX) options:** A derivative security giving the holder the right (but not the obligation) to buy or sell a currency at an agreed exchange rate during a specified period. This category includes exotic currency options such as average rate options and barrier options. Currency options are sold in both OTC markets and on exchanges.

**Currency swaps:** A contract committing two counterparties to exchange streams of interest payments denominated in different currencies for an agreed period of time. They typically require an exchange of principal amounts denominated in different currencies at a preagreed exchange rate at inception and at maturity of the contract. Interest payments are then on a fixed, floating, or zero coupon basis. In effect, a currency swap allows a borrower or lender to swap a loan (or bond) in one currency for a loan in another without incurring currency risk if the swap is held until maturity. Currency swaps are directly analogous to interest-rate swaps and do not influence exchange rate dynamics.

**Dealer (or market-maker):** A financial institution whose primary business is entering into transactions on both sides of markets and seeking profits by taking risks in these markets.

**FX swap:** The currency equivalent of a repurchase transaction (or repo): a single transaction with a single counterparty that involves two currency transactions—one purchase and one sale—for two different value dates. The exchange rate for both transactions is agreed at the outset. The typical FX swap combines a spot FX transaction that is offset with an outright forward at a later date, but it is also possible to have two outright forwards.

**High frequency trading (HFT):** An algorithmic trading strategy that profits from incremental price movements with frequent, small trades executed in milliseconds for investment horizons of typically less than 1 day. See also "Algorithmic trading."

**Interdealer market:** The market where FX dealers trade with each other, either bilaterally or through brokers. Also called the *interbank market*, due to the dominance of banks as FX dealers.

**Liquidity aggregators:** Electronic tools that receive streaming price quotes from different sources, such as FX dealers, electronic brokers, and multibank trading systems, and consolidate them into one stream, allowing traders to access the best prices from many platforms simultaneously.

**Margin account:** An account that allows customers to buy securities with money borrowed from a financial intermediary. The customer's cash deposit in the account is called the *margin*.

**Market liquidity:** A characteristic of the market where transactions have a limited impact on prices ("price impact") and can be completed quickly ("immediacy").

**Master netting agreement:** Document specifying various events of default between counterparties and a methodology for closing out positions in such events. It forms part of a master agreement that sets out the responsibilities of trading parties toward each other.

**Multibank trading system (MBT):** An electronic trading system that aggregates and distributes quotes from multiple FX dealers.

**Outright forward:** An agreement between two counterparties to exchange two currencies at a rate agreed on the date of the contract for cash settlement on an agreed future date, which is more or less than two business days later. Non-deliverable forwards do not require physical delivery of a non-convertible currency; instead, the counterparty that loses on the contract simply pays the losses directly to the other counterparty.

**Prime brokerage (PB):** A service offered by banks that allows a client to source funding and market liquidity from a variety of executing dealers while maintaining a credit relationship, placing collateral, and settling with a single entity.

**Reporting dealer:** A bank that is active in FX market, both for its own account and to meet customer demand, and participates in the Triennial Survey.

**Settlement risk:** The risk that a counterparty to a transaction does not deliver payment.

**Single-bank trading system (SBT):** A proprietary electronic trading system operated by an FX dealer for the exclusive use of its customers.

**Spot FX:** A single outright transaction involving the exchange of two currencies at a rate agreed on the date of the contract for cash settlement, which is typically in two business days.

## Acknowledgments

The authors would like to thank the editors, an anonymous referee, Geir Bjønnes, Alain Chaboud, Alex Heath, Colin Lambert, Michael Melvin, Michael Moore, Richard Olsen, and James Whitelaw for their helpful comments and suggestions on the final text. We also thank many anonymous market participants for their discussions and insights. Any remaining errors are our own. The views expressed in this chapter are those of the authors and do not necessarily represent those of the Norges Bank.

## REFERENCES

Baba N, Packer F. From turmoil to crisis: dislocations in the FX swap market before and after the failure of Lehman Brothers. BIS Working Papers 285, Bank for International Settlements; 2009.

Barber BM, Odean T. Trading is hazardous to your wealth: the common stock investment performance of individual investors. J Finance 2000; 55(2): 773–806.

Barber BM, Odean T. Online investors: do the slow die first? Rev Financ Stud 2002; 15(2): 455–488.

BIS. Triennial Central Bank Survey of Foreign Exchange and Derivatives Market Activity in 2010. Bank for International Settlements; Basel, Switzerland, 2010.

Bjønnes GH, Osler CL, Rime D. Sources of information advantage in the foreign exchange market. typescript, Norges Bank; 2011.

Bjønnes GH, Rime D. Dealer behavior and trading systems in foreign exchange markets. J Financ Econ 2005; 75(3): 571–605.

Bjønnes GH, Rime D, Solheim HAa. Liquidity provision in the overnight foreign exchange market. J Int Money Finance 2005; 24(2): 177–198.

Bodnar G, Hayt G, Marston R. 1998 Wharton survey of financial risk management by US non-financial firms. Financ Manage 1998; 27(4): 70–91.

Bollerslev T, Melvin M. Bid-ask spreads and volatility in the foreign exchange market: an empirical analysis. J Int Econ 1994; 36: 355–372.

Cecchetti SG, Gyntelberg J, Hollanders M. Central counterparties for over-the-counter derivatives. BIS Q Rev 2009;(3): 45–58.

Chaboud A, Chiquoine B, Hjalmarsson E, Vega C. Rise of the Machines: Algorithmic Trading in the Foreign Exchange Market. International Finance Discussion Papers 980, Federal Reserve Board; 2009.

CitiFX Pro. Forex Traders' Survey 2010 Results. Web-document, Citi Research Team; 2010.

Diamond R. Banks' profits could take hit in fight over forex fees. Pensions and Investments; 2011 Apr 4.

Ding L. Bid-ask spread and order size in the foreign exchange market: an empirical investigation. Int J Finance Econ 2009; 14(1): 98–105.

DuCharme M. First steps in foreign exchange transaction cost analysis. J Perform Meas 2007; 19–27.

Dunne P, Hau H, Moore M. A Tale of Two Platforms: Dealer Intermediation in the European Sovereign Bond Market. Discussion Paper 6969, CEPR; 2008.

Evans MDD, Lyons RK. Order flow and exchange rate dynamics. J Pol Econ 2002; 110(1): 170–180.

Evans MDD, Lyons RK. Understanding order flow. Int J Finance Econ 2006; 11(1): 3–23.

FXC, NY. Tools for Mitigating Credit Risk in Foreign Exchange Transactions. Web-document Nov., New York Foreign Exchange Committee. Available at http://www.newyorkfed.org/fxc/2010/creditrisktools.pdf. 2010.

Galati G. Settlement risk in foreign exchange markets and CLS Bank. BIS Q Rev 2002;(4): 55–65.

Goodhart CAE. The foreign exchange market: a random walk with a dragging anchor. Economica 1988; 55(220): 437–460.

Goodhart CAE, Ito T, Payne R. One Day in June 1993: a study of the working of the reuters 2000-2 electronic foreign exchange trading system. In: Frankel JA, Galli G, Giovannini A, editors. The microstructure of foreign exchange markets. Chicago: University of Chicago Press; 1996. pp. 107–79.

Goodhart CAE, Love R, Payne R, Rime D. Analysis of spreads in the Dollar/Euro and Deutschemark/Dollar foreign exchange markets. Econ Policy 2002; 17(35): 537–552.

Heimer RZ, Simon D. The Dedicated and the Dabblers: A Social Network for Forex Traders. typescript, Brandeis University; 2011.

King MR, Mallo C. A user's guide to the Triennial Central Bank Survey of foreign exchange market activity. BIS Q Rev 2010;(4): 71–83.

King MR, Rime D. The $4 trillion question: what explains foreign exchange growth since the 2007 survey? BIS Q Rev 2010;(4): 27–42.

King M, Sarno L, Sojli E. Timing exchange rates using order flow: the case of the Loonie. J Bank Finan 2010; 34(12): 2917–2928.

Lindley R. Reducing foreign exchange settlement risk. BIS Q Rev 2008;(3): 53–65.

Linnainmaa JT. Do limit orders alter inferences about investor performance and behavior? J Finance 2010; 65(4): 1473–1506.

Lyons RK. Tests of microstructural hypothesis in the foreign exchange market. J Financ Econ 1995; 39 321–351.

Lyons RK. A simultaneous trade model of the foreign exchange hot potato. J Int Econ 1997; 42 275–298.

Lyons RK. The microstructure approach to exchange rates. Cambridge (MA): MIT Press; 2001.

Marsh IW, O'Rourke C. Customer Order Flow and Exchange Rate Movements: Is There Really Information Content? Working paper, Cass Business School; 2005.

Melvin M, Prins J. The equity hedging channel of exchange rate adjustment. typescript, Blackrock; 2010.

Melvin M, Taylor MP. The crisis in the foreign exchange market. J Int Money Finance 2009; 28(8): 1317–1330.

Mende A, Menkhoff L. Profits and speculation in intra-day foreign exchange trading. J Financ Mark 2006; 9(3): 223–245.

Moore MJ, Payne R. On the sources of private information in FX markets. J Bank Finance 2011; 35(5): 1250–1262.

Nolte I, Nolte S. Customer Trading in the Foreign Exchange Market. Empirical Evidence from an Internet Trading Platform. Working Paper 09-01, FERC; 2009.

Oberlechner T, Osler CL. Survival of overconfidence in currency markets. J Financ Quant Anal 2012. Forthcoming.

Osler CL. Currency orders and exchange-rate dynamics: explaining the success of technical analysis. J Finance 2003; 58(5): 1791–1819.

Osler CL. Stop-loss orders and price cascades in currency markets. J Int Money Finance 2005; 24(2): 219–241.

Osler CL. Market microstructure, foreign exchange. In: Meyers RA, editor. Encyclopedia of Complexity and System Science. New York (NY): Springer; 2009. pp. 5404–5438.

Osler CL, Mende A, Menkhoff L. Price discovery in currency markets. J Int Money Finance 2011; 30(8): 1696–1718.

Osler CL, Vandrovych V. Hedge funds and the origins of private information in currency markets. typescript, Brandeis University; 2009.

Osler CL, Yusim R. Intraday dynamics of foreign-exchange spreads. typescript, Brandeis University; 2009.

Ramadorai T. What determines transaction costs in foreign exchange markets? Int J Finance Econ 2008; 13(1): 14–25.

Rime D. New electronic trading systems in the foreign exchange markets. In: Jones DC, editor. Volume 21, New economy handbook. San Diego (CA): Academic Press; 2003. pp. 471–504.

Rime D, Sarno L, Sojli E. Exchange rate forecasting, order flow and macroeconomic information. J Int Econ 2010; 80(1): 72–88.

Sager MJ, Taylor MP. Under the microscope: the structure of the foreign exchange market. Int J Finance Econ 2006; 11(1): 81–95.

Taylor A, Farstrup A. Active currency management: arguments, considerations, and performance for institutional investors. Darien (CT): CRA RogersCasey International Equity Research; 2006.

Terada T, Higashio N, Iwasaki J. Recent trends in Japanese foreign exchange margin trading. Bank Japan Rev 2008; (3).

CHAPTER TWO

# Macro Approaches to Foreign Exchange Determination

MENZIE D. CHINN
Department of Economics, University of Wisconsin; NBER

## 2.1 Introduction

In this chapter, I review a number of models of exchange rate developed during the post-Bretton Woods era. The approaches are broken down into categories of nominal and real exchange-rate models, with particular reference to the empirical evidence. I then discuss recent approaches that do not neatly fall into either categorization.

The defining feature of the bulk of the models that have been empirically assessed is that they rely upon stock equilibrium conditions, and hence are often categorized as being within the "asset market" approach, to distinguish them from the earlier flow market approach. Although the underpinnings of these models are quite unsatisfying from the perspective of recent theoretical developments, they remain the workhorses of empirical exchange-rate modeling. This is true largely because the empirical implications of, for instance, the New International Macroeconomics (Obstfeld and Rogoff, 1996) have not been proven easy to test in the econometric framework.

For this same reason, most of the empirical evidence discussed in the chapter comes from reduced form or quasi-reduced form specifications, rather from structural (i.e., calibrated) models of economies. While structural approaches, most prominently in the form of dynamic stochastic general equilibrium (DSGE)

*Handbook of Exchange Rates*, First Edition. Edited by Jessica James, Ian W. Marsh, and Lucio Sarno.

models, have become increasing important in the new research, evaluation of goodness of fit remains difficult, for a variety of reasons.[1]

## 2.2 Models of the Nominal Exchange Rate

The early empirical literature pertaining to monetary and portfolio balance models has been surveyed extensively (Frankel and Rose, 1995; Sarno and Taylor, 2002; Taylor, 1995).

In the wake of the collapse of the Bretton Woods system two major strands of models dominated the literature: the monetary and portfolio balance approaches. Both approaches focused on *stocks* of outside assets—money in the former and both money and bonds in the latter. While this perspective is completely natural from today's vantage point, it is easy to forget how much this approach differed from the older flow perspective of the Mundell-Fleming model. This approach stressed current account and capital account flows as the determinants of exchange rates, and was largely superseded in the 1970s. Consequently, I do not discuss this approach in detail.

Although the monetary and portfolio approaches share a focus upon stocks, they differ in their views of the substitutability of capital. In practice, the difference amounts to whether uncovered interest rate parity holds, or whether the forward rate differs from the expected future spot rate by an exchange risk premium. Of the two approaches, by far the most common approach in the nominal exchange-rate literature has been the monetary model.

### 2.2.1 THE MONETARY MODEL

The monetary approach views the exchange rate as the relative price of currencies, when that relative price depends on the relative demands and supplies of the stocks of money. Within that strand, two variants can be discerned: the flexible price (Bilson, 1981; Frenkel, 1976) and sticky price versions (Dornbusch, 1976; Frankel, 1979); in the former, purchasing power parity (PPP) holds continuously, while in the latter, it only holds in the long run. To fix the notation and motivate the empirical modeling, these two models are derived. Assume PPP in log levels,

$$s_t = p_t - p_t^* \tag{2.1}$$

where log $s$ is the nominal exchange rate, expressed in units of home currency per foreign currency, and $p$ is the log price level. Asterisks denote foreign variables. Money-demand functions in the two countries are expressed as

$$m_t^d - p_t = \varphi y_t - \lambda i_t \tag{2.2}$$

[1] Most papers rely upon an informal assessment of how impulse response functions from a calibrated or estimated model conform to priors. In addition, the empirical results are often couched in terms of deviations from steady state, which in practice have to be estimated. See Morley (2010) for discussion.

where $m$ is the log nominal money stock, $y$ is log income, $i$ is the short-term interest rate, and the $d$ superscripts indicate "demand". I assume for simplicity that the money-demand parameters are the same across the two economies. Rearranging, assuming money supply equals money demand, and imposing PPP one obtains

$$s_t = \left(m_t - m_t^*\right) - \varphi\left(y_t - y_t^*\right) + \lambda\left(i_t - i_t^*\right) \tag{2.3}$$

The monetary model yields two key implications. The first is the intuitive result that higher relative income induces a *stronger* currency. The second is that a higher relative interest rate induces a *weaker* currency. Both of these predictions are opposite of those obtained by the static version of the Mundell-Fleming model.

The reasons for these differences are obvious. In the Mundell-Fleming model, higher income induces higher imports, *ceteris paribus*, and hence a weaker currency. In the monetary model, a higher income induces a higher money demand relative to supply, and hence a stronger currency. Also, in the Mundell-Fleming model, a higher interest rate causes a capital inflow, by the *ad hoc* financial account function. In the monetary approach, a higher interest rate causes a lower money demand, relative to money supply, and hence a weaker currency.

In empirical work on the flexible price model, it will prove convenient to work with Equation 2.3. However, additional insight into the intuition of the monetarist approach can be obtained by noting that uncovered interest rate parity (UIP) implies that a higher domestic interest rate implies a weaker currency in the future. To see this, note UIP is denoted by

$$E_t s_{t+1} - s_t \equiv \Delta s_{t+1}^e = i_t - i_t^* \tag{2.4}$$

The object in the middle of the equation is "expected depreciation" based on the time $t$ information set. Substitution of this expression into the Equation 2.3 and rearranging indicate that the current exchange rate is a function of the future expected exchange rate.

$$s_t = \left(\frac{1}{1+\lambda}\right) F_t + \left(\frac{\lambda}{1+\lambda}\right) s_{t+1}^e \tag{2.5}$$

where

$$F_t \equiv \left(m_t - m_t^*\right) - \varphi\left(y_t - y_t^*\right)$$

Repeated substitution for the expected future spot rate will lead to an expression that relates the current spot rate to the current and future discounted expected fundamentals. Clearly, such expressions are not very tractable for empirical work; however, they do yield insights into how changes in expectations about future variables can affect the current exchange rate, even when the current values of macroeconomic variables remain unchanged.

The flexible price monetary approach (sometimes termed the *monetarist* model) yields some very strong predictions. One of the most implausible is that increasing interest differential will be associated with weakening currencies. In the context of a model with PPP holding in both the long run and short run, this result makes sense; positive interest differentials arise from positive inflation differentials (via the Fisher relation). The more rapid a currency loses value against a basket of real goods, the more rapid a currency loses value against another currency, given that PPP links prices of home and foreign real goods.

The positive relationship between the interest differential and the exchange rate runs counter to casual empiricism, at least as far as the developed economies are concerned (economies experiencing high inflation such as Argentina and Brazil during the 1980s are another matter). Hence, consider a sticky price version of the monetary model that allows the PPP condition to hold only in the long run. Then the flexible price monetary model equation for the exchange rate pertains to the long run, Equation 2.3 is rewritten as

$$s_t = \left(\overline{m_t} - \overline{m_t^*}\right) - \varphi\left(\overline{y_t} - \overline{y_t^*}\right) + \lambda\left(\overline{\pi_t} - \overline{\pi_t^*}\right) \tag{2.6}$$

where the overbars denote long-run values, and the secular inflation rates stand in for long-run interest rates, given the Fisher relation holds in the long run.

Overshooting means that exchange rates tend to revert back toward the long-run value at some rate $\theta$. That is, if the exchange rate is too high (the domestic currency too weak), relative to some long-run value, they will then tend to fall toward the long-run value. Assuming rational expectations this suggests the following mechanism:

$$s_{t+1}^e - s_t = -\theta\left(s_t - \overline{s_t}\right) + \left(\pi_t^e - \pi_t^{e^*}\right) \tag{2.7}$$

The $\theta$ parameter is the rate of reversion to the long-run nominal exchange rate, and is an inverse function of the degree of price stickiness. Since higher trend inflation implies a weaker expected future spot exchange rate, the secular inflation differential enters into this expression.

However, by UIP, the left-hand side of Equation 2.7 is also equal to the interest differential. Solving for $s$, and substituting in the expression for the long run $s$, one obtains

$$s_t = \left(m_t - m_t^*\right) - \varphi\left(y_t - y_t^*\right) - (1/\theta)\left(i_t - i_t^*\right) + (\lambda + 1/\theta)\left(\pi_t^e - \pi_t^{e^*}\right) \tag{2.8}$$

This expression can be rewritten as

$$s_t = \left(m_t - m_t^*\right) - \varphi\left(y_t - y_t^*\right) - (1/\theta)\left(r_t - r_t^*\right) + \lambda\left(\pi_t^e - \pi_t^{e^*}\right) \tag{2.9}$$

where $r_t \equiv i_t - \pi_t^e$.

Since the real interest rate shows up in this expression, this model is sometimes called the *real interest differential* model.[2]

The current exchange rate depends positively on current money stocks and inflation rates, and negatively on income levels and interest rates. This result regarding interest rates differs from the flex-price monetary model, because in the short-run inflation rate differentials can differ from interest rate differentials.

The previous models have imposed PPP in the long run. However, there are persuasive reasons for allowing *long-run* deviations from PPP (as discussed in Chapters 6 and 7 of this handbook, on PPP), in which case some real factors enter into nominal exchange-rate determination. One rationale ascribes such deviations to the presence of nontradable goods. Assuming that PPP holds only for tradable goods, one obtains the expression in Equation 2.10 is

$$s_t = \left(m_t - m_t^*\right) - \varphi\left(y_t - y_t^*\right) - (1/\theta)\left(i_t - i_t^*\right) \\ + (\lambda + 1/\theta)\left(\pi_t^e - \pi_t^{e^*}\right) - \alpha\omega_t \tag{2.10}$$

where $\omega \equiv [(p_t^N - p_t^T) - (p_t^{N*} - p_t^{T*})]$, and for simplicity, aggregate and tradable sector inflation rates are assumed to be approximately the same (otherwise, one has to include separate inflation terms).

Equation 2.10 indicates that in addition to the usual monetary factors real factors can also affect the nominal exchange rate; in this case, anything that shifts the intercountry differential in the relative price of tradables to nontradables. This expression is a sticky price version of that used by Clements and Frenkel (1980) and is similar to that used by Wolff (1987).

What determines this relative price? In principle, this variable can be affected by supply factors (changes in endowments and productivity growth) or demand side factors (government spending and changing preferences). This seems to be an important factor for some currencies, but is not usually incorporated in the work on developed country currencies. Furthermore, the exact mechanisms underlying movements in $\omega$ are not usually outlined in such work. Since the determinants of these movements are usually thought of as real factors, I reserve extensive discussion of this approach in Section 2.3.

### 2.2.2 PORTFOLIO BALANCE MODELS

The portfolio balance model differs from the monetary model in that it assumes that assets denominated in different currencies are not perfectly substitutable; this means that returns on bonds, when expressed in a common currency, might differ because of a risk premium.[3] This is shown in a model drawn from

[2]Certain papers focus on the role of the real interest differential in determining the real exchange rate. See Baxter (1994); Edison and Pauls (1993); Meese and Rogoff (1988), and MacDonald and Nagayasu (2000).

[3]Risk premia can arise in models without this particular structure. In more microfounded approaches, the risk premia arise from the correlation of relative returns with consumption growth. The implications of this type of approach are discussed in Section 2.4.

Frankel (1984). Assume perfect capital mobility, so that covered interest parity (CIP) holds while perfect capital substitutability does not. That is, investors view domestic and foreign bonds as imperfect substitutes. Then investor $j$ will allocate her/his holdings in response to expected returns (expressed in a common currency). Aggregating over homogeneous investors yields:

$$\frac{B_t}{S_t B_t^*} = \gamma \left( i_t - i_t^* - E_t \Delta s_{t+1} \right) \tag{2.11}$$

where $B$ and $B^*$ are net supplies of domestic and foreign bonds, and it is assumed for simplicity that governments issue debt denominated only in their own currencies. The term in the parentheses on the right hand side of Equation 2.11 is the deviation from UIP, or equivalently, the exchange risk premium on domestic currency.

This expression indicates that holdings of domestic bonds, relative to foreign currency denominated bonds, are a positive function $\gamma$ of the exchange risk premium. Assuming the functional form for relative bond demand is linear exponential in $\gamma$, then after rearrangement, Equation 2.11 becomes

$$s_t = \gamma_0 + \gamma_1 \left( i_t - i_t^* - E_t \Delta s_{t+1} \right) + b_t - b_t^* \tag{2.12}$$

The difficulty in implementing Equation 2.12 is that the term in the parentheses is unobservable.[4] To obtain an empirically implementable specification, one could assume expected depreciation is zero—an assumption that is consistent with the near random walk exchange rates. Then Equation 2.12 becomes

$$s_t = \gamma_0 + \gamma_1 \left( i_t - i_t^* \right) + b_t - b_t^* \tag{2.13}$$

Notice the equation indicates that as $b^*$ increases $s$ falls (appreciates) : as the stock of foreign assets held by home rises, the exchange rate appreciates.

In the specification represented by Equation 2.13, it is assumed that all investors have the same portfolio preferences, presumably because they consume the same basket of goods.

If on the other hand the home country is a small country, such that only home residents wish to hold domestically denominated assets, then one can equate capital inflows with increases in the supply of foreign assets in the home market. If the home country is large relative to the foreign, then one might want to make the converse assumption. Clearly, neither of these versions fit the typical large country. Then what one needs to specify is a separate asset-demand function for each of the two countries. As long as the responsiveness of home

[4]As in the case of Equation 2.5, one could recursively substitute out for the expected future exchange rate. This would lead to an expression stating that the current exchange rate is determined as a negative function of current and discounted future expected interest rates, and a positive function of current and discounted future expected stocks of domestic currency bonds, relative to foreign denominated bonds. This expression, likes its monetary counterpart, is not tractable from an empirical standpoint.

residents to the expected return on domestic bonds exceeds the responsiveness of foreign residents, then the exchange rate will appreciate in response to cumulated trade balances that reallocate world wealth.[5] In line with this approach, Hooper and Morton (1982) use a real exchange-rate-target current account model to motivate inclusion of cumulated current account balances.[6]

### 2.2.3 EMPIRICAL EVIDENCE

The models described appear to constitute a quite disparate set of approaches; however, in terms of the empirics, the appearance is misleading. The above models can be subsumed into the following general expression:

$$s = f\left(\hat{m}, \hat{y}, \hat{i}, \hat{\pi}, \omega, b, b^{*}, ctb\right) \tag{2.14}$$

where the time subscripts have been suppressed, *ctb* denotes the cumulated trade balance, and the circumflexes denote intercountry differences. Different models imply the inclusion of different regressors within this set.

Most of the earlier studies cited include an empirical component. In most instances, some supportive evidence is found, particularly for the monetary model. Frankel (1979) provides evidence that the sticky price monetary model fit the dollar/deutschemark rate well, using a quasi-reduced form expression. Papell (1984, 1988) estimates the monetary model in a system and finds that the degree of overshooting and undershooting is dependent on the monetary policy being conducted.

However, it is fair to say that the empirical results of the 1980s are not very robust to the addition of new data. The identified relationships often break down with the addition of new data, suggesting model over-fitting. Frankel (1983) provides an early overview of the empirical inadequacies of the monetary (flexible and sticky price), portfolio balance and hybrid models. Particularly in the latter two cases, the key portfolio balance variables—domestic and foreign bond stocks—failed to show up with the correct coefficient signs.

Portfolio balance models of exchange rates are merely transformations of portfolio balance models of the exchange risk premium. The failure of these types of models reflects the failure of attempts to explain the exchange risk premium using measures of government bonds, in the context of an international capital asset pricing model.[7]

The fragile nature of these empirical results motivates a reliance on out-of-sample simulations to guard against in-sample over-fitting. Among the first

[5] So far, we have discussed matters as if the only way in which $B$ and $B^*$ can change is through current account imbalances. In fact, foreign exchange intervention can affect the stock of bonds, and hence the exchange rate. See Dooley and Isard (1982) for one study where the stocks of bonds take into account foreign exchange intervention.

[6] Frankel (1982) uses a portfolio demand for money so that wealth (measured as the sum of current account balances and domestic bonds and money) enters into the regression equation.

[7] See early studies by Frankel and Engel (1984) and more recent surveys by Hodrick (1987) and Engel (1996).

studies to adopt this approach was Meese and Rogoff (1983a,b). These authors tested the out-of-sample forecasting properties of these various exchange-rate models plus the forward rate, a univariate ARIMA, and a vector autoregression (VAR). The procedure involves estimating the models over a certain period, forecast out *k* periods *using the actually realized values of the exogenous variables*, then "roll" the regression sample up a period, to account for parameter variation. This procedure is repeated until all of the remaining data points are exhausted. They then compare the forecasts statistics, mean error (ME), mean absolute error (MAE) and root mean absolute error (RMSE).[8]

Meese and Rogoff (1983a) obtain the surprising result that none of the structural models (nor time series models) consistently outperforms the random walk using any of the metrics, and over any of the forecast horizons. This finding was robust to relaxing coefficient restrictions (like the income elasticity being the same across countries), or replacing one proxy for inflationary expectations with another.

The analysis of exchange-rate forecasts changes dramatically with the development of the literature relating to integrated variables. The study of variables that co-trend, namely the cointegration literature, suggests that one could respecify equations in terms of error correction models. A key issue here is what the nature of the cointegrating vector, that is, the error correction term, would be. In most cases, the cointegration results are based on monetary fundamentals, either imposed or estimated.[9]

One of the implications of long-run relationships holding, and possible short-run nonlinearities, is that long-horizon prediction might be more successful than short horizon. In the earliest implementation of this approach, Nelson Mark (1995) used a calibrated flexible price monetary model to perform out-of-sample predictions of the dollar-deutschemark rate, and finds substantial improvement for the monetary model's performance vis-a-vis the random walk. Chinn and Meese (1995) examine a broader number of models including the flexible price, the Hooper-Morton, and augmented monetary and, imposing the cointegrating vector in an error correction framework, find that a random walk can be outperformed in a statistically significant sense, at longer horizons of 2–3 years.

This set of results is intuitive. The amount of "news" that moves exchange rates month to month that are not captured in typical macroeconomic variables such as money stocks, interest and inflation rates is very large. Most likely, this

[8]Notice that because in these exercises, actually realized values of the exogenous variables are used, the usual argument that asset prices should not be predictable *ex ante* becomes moot. In these forecast comparisons knowledge about contemporaneous information is available. That is, by using the *ex post* values of the exogenous values in the forecasts, one "purges" the forecasts of uncertainty about the future paths of the exogenous variables. Hence, failure can be isolated to the misspecification of the equations.

[9]Error correction terms (ECTs) may be empirically motivated or based on theory. For the former, see for instance MacDonald and Taylor (1994). For the latter, see Edison (1991) who replicates the Meese-Rogoff (1983a) study, but imposes a PPP error correction term. She finds some improvement, especially over longer horizons. See also MacDonald (1995, 1999), MacDonald and Marsh (1997, 1999).

type of news dominates at high frequencies, but is less likely to play a large role at longer horizons. Moreover, the random walk "model" is a very naive model as it yields a "no change" forecast, so as the horizon lengthens, the random walk forecast is more and more likely to be proved wrong.

Nonetheless, these results did not prove to be conclusive. First, Faust et al. (2003) have shown that these long-horizon results are specific to the particular time period examined, particularly in the case of Mark's study.[10] Second, by examining a slightly different set of models and taking into account the possibility of no cointegration, Cheung et al. (2005) find only very limited evidence of improved forecasting ability at long horizons, relative to shorter horizons. Specifically, they examine a more recent set of models developed over the last two decades—interest rate parity,[11] productivity-based models, and "behavioral equilibrium exchange-rate (BEER)" models.[12] The performance of these models is compared against a benchmark model—the Dornbusch-Frankel sticky price monetary model in Equation 2.8. The models are estimated in error correction and first-difference specifications.

Rather than estimating the cointegrating vector over the entire sample and treating it as part of the *ex ante* information set as is commonly done in the literature, they recursively update the cointegrating vector, thereby generating true *ex ante* forecasts. Model performance at various forecast horizons (1 quarter, 4 quarters, 20 quarters) is examined using differing metrics (mean squared error, direction of change), as well as the "consistency" test of Cheung and Chinn (1998).

They find that no model consistently outperforms a random walk, by a mean squared error measure; however, along a direction-of-change dimension certain structural models do outperform a random walk with statistical significance. Moreover, although they find that these forecasts are cointegrated with the actual values of exchange rates, in a large number of cases, the elasticity of the forecasts with respect to the actual values is different from unity. Overall, model/specification/currency combinations that work well in one period will not necessarily work well in another period.

A natural approach to improving the empirical performance of models is to use information across currencies.[13] One example of this approach includes Mark and Sul (2001). They use a panel of 17 exchange rates for industrialized

[10]In addition, Kilian (1999) has argued that the apparent outperformance of the random walk at long horizons is largely spurious. He uses bootstrapping to demonstrate that the performance relative to a random walk is approximately the same at short and long horizons. Kilian argues that only if the underlying vector error correction model is nonlinear might a long-horizon regression outperform a random walk. Kilian and Taylor (2003) argue that even if a specific form of nonlinearity is used, the outperformance may be difficult to detect.

[11]The use of interest rate parity is analogous with the forward rate examined by Meese and Rogoff (1983a,b). One should expect better performance at the long horizon because Chinn and Meredith (2004) and Alexius (2001) find that UIP holds better at long horizons than short.

[12]The productivity-based model and BEER models can be considered variants of the productivity-based model described in Section 2.3.2. See Section 2.3.4.

[13]Another approach is to extend the sample over time. Rapach and Wohar (2002) undertake an analysis of 14 industrialized country exchange rates over a period of 115 years. They assert that they

countries to implement a panel version of Mark's (1995) paper. Specifically, they first test to see whether the exchange rate and the monetary fundamentals are cointegrated in the panel, using a panel version of dynamic ordinary least squares (DOLS). After rejecting the null hypothesis of no cointegration they use the estimated cointegrating vector to conduct long-horizon regressions as in the study of Mark (1995). Monetary fundamentals outpredict a random walk at short and long horizons, over the 1983q2–1997q1 period, when the U.S. dollar is the numeraire currency. The results are slightly different if the numeraire currency is the yen; then the outperformance is not usually statistically significant, although the predictions from the monetary model typically have smaller root mean squared errors than those generated from a random walk forecast (and smaller, as well, than those from a PPP fundamentals model).

Two other examples of using panel cointegration methods include Husted and MacDonald (1998) and Groen (2005). Husted and MacDonald (1998) use panel cointegration techniques derived from Pedroni (1999). They conclude that there is substantial evidence in favor of monetary models of the exchange rate, based on cointegration evidence. Groen (2005) uses a much smaller panel of three currencies and finds both evidence of cointegration of the exchange rate with the monetary fundamentals and model outperformance of a random walk at both short and long horizons. Most recently, Cerra and Saxena (2010) have used a large panel of currencies to find that the monetary model works well at longer horizons.[14]

These results suggest that the empirical versions of the monetary model may enjoy renewed life, as researchers exploit cross-currency variation in order to pin down the coefficient estimates that have proven elusive in the pure time series context.[15]

## 2.3 Real Models of the Real Exchange Rate

Most real models of the exchange rate focus on real—as opposed to nominal—determinants of the price-level-adjusted exchange rate. PPP is a particularly simple version, where the real exchange rate is assumed to be constant. The second portion of the section describes two other approaches to modeling the real exchange rate; the first of these two approaches is associated with the Balassa–Samuelson framework, but more generally allows for the presence of nontradable goods. The second of these approaches encompasses the general equilibrium models of the exchange rate arose in response to the *ad hoc* nature of the extant models of the 1970s. In this sense, they represent the open economy analog to the rejection of *ad hoc* macroeconomic models dominant in the domestic context.

---

find substantial evidence in favor of the monetary approach, despite the fact that the samples span radically different exchange-rate regimes.

[14]See Chapter 9 on panel methods.

[15]For the sake of brevity, I omit the discussion of functional nonlinearities (Chinn, 1991; Diebold and Nason, 1990; Meese and Rose, 1991), threshold autoregression (Taylor and Peel, 2000; Taylor et al., 2001), and regime switching (Engel, 1994; Engel and Hamilton, 1990).

### 2.3.1 PURCHASING POWER PARITY

PPP is one of the most important concepts in international finance. Several excellent surveys exist on the subject, including Breuer (1994); Rogoff (1996), and Taylor and Taylor (2004). While a thoroughgoing discussion of PPP is beyond the scope of this chapter, some discussion of PPP is necessary to set the stage for a discussion of real exchange-rate determination.[16] The simplest statement of PPP is that the common currency price of an identical bundle of goods is equalized:

$$s_t + p_t^* = p_t \tag{2.15}$$

where $p$ corresponds to the price of a bundle of goods.

Notice that there is, in this context, a direct relationship between the deviation from PPP, and the real exchange rate. Suppressing the constant and rearranging (Eq. 2.15), one obtains

$$q_t \equiv s_t - p_t + p_t^* \tag{2.16}$$

where $q$ is measured in domestic units of the domestic basket of goods required to purchase a single basket of foreign goods. If absolute PPP holds, then the (log) real exchange rate should be a zero (and a constant if relative PPP holds). In practice, the distinction is of limited relevance, since one typically has access to only price indexes rather than prices of bundles of goods.

One can decompose the general price index along several dimensions. One is the tradable/nontradable distinction; furthermore, the tradable category can be further divided into importables and exportables. Consider the first dimension; then, writing the general price index as

$$p_t = \alpha p_t^N + (1 - \alpha) p_t^T \tag{2.17}$$

where an $N$ superscript denotes nontradables and $T$ tradables, one obtains the resulting expression for the real exchange rate (assuming the weights are identical):

$$q_t = q_t^T + \alpha \left(\hat{p}_t^N - \hat{p}_t^T\right) \tag{2.18}$$

where $q_t^T \equiv s_t - p_t^T + p_t^{T*}$.

The real exchange rate thus deviates from zero if either tradables prices differ, or the relative price of nontradables versus tradables differs across countries. This decomposition underpins Engel's (1999) analysis of the sources of U.S. real exchange-rate movements.

[16]As I alluded to earlier, there are a myriad of definitions for PPP. I define PPP as pertaining to relationships between relatively broad price indices such as the consumer price index (CPI), the producer price index (PPI), or gross domestic product (GDP) deflator, on the one hand, and the exchange rate on the other. In other words, I will not consider PPP to be a relationship between the exchange rate versus price levels *and other variables*. Some authors have termed such relationships as *generalized PPP*.

The relative price variable may be determined by any number of factors. In the Balassa (1964) and Samuelson (1964) model, relative prices are driven by relative differentials in productivity in the tradable and nontradable sectors.[17] With respect to the East Asian countries there is a widespread belief that such factors are of central importance (Cheung and Lai, 1998; Chinn, 2000).

Relative prices may also be affected by demand side factors. In the long run, the rising preference for services, which are largely nontradable, may induce a trend rise in the relative price of nontradables. Over shorter horizons, government spending on public services may also induce changes in relative prices (DeGregorio and Wolf, 1994; Chinn, 1999).[18]

Early work on PPP relied upon classical regression techniques and addressed the question of whether PPP held on a period-by-period basis. The early literature concluded that absolute PPP did not hold for broad price indices, on a period-by-period basis. One important exception was that identified by Frenkel (1976) who found that during the German hyperinflation of the 1920s, PPP did hold. Hence, the conclusion that PPP held only when nominal (monetary) shocks were large relative to real shocks.

The advent of the unit root and cointegration brought a resurgence in the PPP literature. At the same time, it produced a large amount of confusion between the economically interesting hypothesis of PPP in levels and the statistical hypotheses. To see this, recall from Equation 2.16 that PPP implies that the real exchange rate is equal to a constant. Findings of cointegration, but without unitary coefficients, was sometimes interpreted as "weak" PPP, when it was consistent with a trending real exchange rate. Even when cointegration with unitary coefficients was found, allowance for a deterministic trend meant that the real rate was not constant over time. The issue of PPP at the short and long horizon is examined at further length in Chapter 7 in this *Handbook*.

## 2.3.2 BALASSA–SAMUELSON AND PRODUCTIVITY-BASED MODELS

The basic motivation for most empirical exercises addressing the exchange-rate productivity nexus rely upon the tradable–nontradable distinction highlighted by Balassa (1964) and Samuelson (1964). Recall that in the presence of nontradables one can write the real exchange rate as

$$q_t = q_t^T + \alpha\left(\hat{p}_t^N - \hat{p}_t^T\right)$$

where $q_t^T \equiv s_t - p_t^T + p_t^{T*}$.

[17]This view is adopted in Canzoneri et al. (1996); Chinn (1997a, b); DeGregorio and Wolf (1994) among others. The first two studies examine annual total factor productivity (TFP) data for 14 Organisation for Economic Co-operation and Development (OECD) countries in a panel context, while Chinn (1997a) undertakes a higher frequency analysis. He uses quarterly time series regressions where labor productivity in manufacturing is used as a proxy for relative sectoral productivity, for the United States, Canada, Germany, Japan, and the UK.

[18]See also Chen and Rogoff (2003) for a commodities price channel.

Assuming perfect capital mobility, free intersectoral factor mobility, the internal relative price of traded and nontraded goods is given by

$$p_t^N - p_t^T = a_t^T - a_t^N \tag{2.19}$$

where for expository simplicity the production functions are assumed to be identical; $a^T$ and $a^N$ are the TFP levels in the traded and nontraded sectors, respectively. In words, Equation 2.19 implies that the relative price of traded goods moves one-for-one with the productivity differential. As tradable sector productivity rises relative to nontradable, the price of tradable goods relative to nontradable falls.

Combining Equation 2.19 with Equation 2.18 yields a standard expression for the real exchange rate:

$$q_t = q_t^T + a\left(\hat{a}_t^N - \hat{a}_t^T\right) \tag{2.20}$$

where $q_t^T \equiv s_t - p_t^T + p_t^{T*}$.

In this framework, the real exchange rate is a function of the intercountry relative productivity differential. And if PPP holds for tradable goods, then $q^T$ is 0, and the real exchange rate depends solely on the productivity differential.

A number of papers have examined the relationship expressed in Equation 2.20 for developed economies, including Chinn (1997a, b), DeGregorio and Wolf (1994), Hsieh (1982), Marston (1990), Strauss (1996), and Chinn (1999).

The first three papers, like many others, estimate the real exchange rate and productivity differential relationship in growth rates. Usually, a link is detected. However, the specification allows for permanent shocks to the relationship in levels, which might not be desirable.

The relationship in levels has been more elusive. While Chinn (1997a, b) finds evidence for individual currencies, and Strauss (1996) finds evidence of cointegration using the conventional asymptotic critical values in 8 out of 14 cases, he also finds the parameter restrictions implied by the model are generally rejected.

More evidence of a long-run relationship between the level of the real exchange rate and the productivity differential is found in a panel context. Canzoneri et al. (1999, hereafter CCD) test the proposition in Equation 2.20 using labor productivity differentials and find that it holds fairly well in a panel cointegration context for the OECD countries. They also test the hypothesis that PPP holds for traded goods (i.e., that the second line of Equation 2.20 equals zero), and while they do find evidence of cointegration the estimated coefficients are not of the expected sign. Hence, CCD do not *directly* confirm the proposition embodied in the top line of Equation 2.20.[19]

It is of interest to note that the expressions in Equation 2.18 and the top line of Equation 2.19 *with* $q^T = 0$ require fairly strong assumptions. In particular, if the form of the production functions differs in the two sectors, then the coefficients on tradable and nontradable productivity need not be of equal

[19] Strauss (1999) found slightly more evidence in favor of a role for productivity and government spending for exchange rates.

and opposite sign. Moreover, in some dynamic models incorporating a fixed factor assumption (Rogoff, 1992), the coefficient on nontraded productivity differs from that of traded, because consumption smoothing can only take place through traded goods production.

Finally, if exact PPP does not hold for traded goods, it may be the case that traded sector productivity affects the real exchange rate through the relative price of traded goods. Engel (1999) has argued that this is an important factor for developed country exchange-rate behavior. If this turns out to be the case, then the symmetry restrictions on tradable and nontradable productivity in Equation 2.20 may be invalidated.

Chinn and Johnston (1999) find some evidence that the productivity does not enter in the expected manner, particularly when TFP (which is implied by the theory) is substituted for labor productivity. The analysis is conducted on annual data over 1970–1994 period, using panel DOLS.[20] They find that relative productivity does not have a significant impact on the real exchange rate, but tradable sector productivity does, with a coefficient of −0.420. If one believed that the coefficient-relating relative prices to relative productivities should instead be one, then the implied value is −0.5; the actual point estimate is insignificantly different from this value.

Lee and Tang (2007) provide one of the most recent test of the Balassa–Samuelson hypothesis. Using data for 10 OECD countries over the 1970–1995 period they show (using panel regression techniques) that the findings regarding the link between productivity and the real exchange rate—or the relative price of tradables (bottom line of Equation 2.18—is highly sensitive to the productivity measure that is used. Increases in TFP, which is suggested by theory, tend to *depreciate* the $q^T$, so that the net effect on the real exchange rate is muted.

Ricci, Milessi-Ferretti, and Lee (forthcoming) extend this analysis to a sample encompassing 48 industrial and emerging market economies. They find that while productivity measures have a statistically significant impact on real exchange rates, in the posited direction, the size of the effect is fairly small. Other effects, including those associated with government consumption and net foreign asset accumulation, are also statistically significant.

To sum up, the evidence in favor of the standard Balassa–Samuelson hypothesis is weak, when focusing on the developed economies, and using total factor, rather than labor, productivity. The most recent research suggests that this is the case because PPP rarely holds for traded goods, perhaps because these goods are highly differentiated (see Cheung et al., 1998). In fact, productivity growth in the tradable sector might have a bigger impact on the intercountry price of traded goods than on the relative price of traded to nontraded goods. If this is the case—at least for developed economies—then the difficulty in identifying the productivity/real exchange rate link might be more explicable.

---

[20] Bilateral exchange rates are deflated by general price, while the tradable and nontradable sector TFP data were constructed from the International Sectoral Data Base (ISDB) database which contains TFP disaggregated by sector. The tradable and nontradable categorization is the same as that used by DeGregorio and Wolf (1994). Tradable sectors include agriculture, mining, manufacturing, and transportation, while the nontradable sectors include all other services.

### 2.3.3 TWO-GOOD MODELS

Now depart from the case where there are nontradable goods, and suppose all goods are tradable, these traded goods are not perfect substitutes. One can then define the real exchange rate as the ratio of the two traded goods prices. The nominal exchange rate is then the real exchange rate, adjusted for the stocks of monies. This can be seen most clearly in the Lucas (1982) model.

Assume there are infinitely lived agents in two countries are subject to a stochastic endowment and monetary shocks. The model uses a Clower, or cash-in-advance, constraint to motivate the holding of money. Each agent maximizes discounted utility. In a complete markets framework, with perfect pooling of risk, each trader consumes his/her share of both endowments. Hence, the equilibrium spot price of $Y^*$ in terms of $Y$ (call this $P_{Y*}$ the "real exchange rate") is given by the ratio of the marginal utilities of consumption of the two goods.

The nominal exchange rate is given by the ratio of nominal monies, the amounts of endowments of each good, and the relative price of $Y^*$. This result is interesting, since this implies that as endowments change and the ratio of marginal utilities change, then the real and hence nominal exchange rates also change. Under the typical convention that an increase in endowment of the home good only decreases the relative price slightly, then the exchange rate appreciates.[21] Otherwise, the currency will depreciate.

In terms of observables, the Lucas model is observationally equivalent to the flexible price monetary model. Consider the specification that allows for endowments to be proxied by output. Then the resulting estimating equation is

$$s_t = (m_t - m_t^*) - (y_t - y_t^*) + p_y^* \tag{2.21}$$

where a complicating factor is that $p_{y*}$ depends on the endowments $y$ and $y^*$. This equation is therefore functionally similar to the flexible price monetary model, with the exception of the absence of interest rate terms arises from the binding cash-in-advance constraint. One difference is that, in the monetary approach, the response of the exchange rate to a rise in income is unambiguously negative—that is an increase in home income raises money demand and hence the value of the home currency. Here, notice that as $y$ rises, $p_{y*}$ also rises as before, since more of the home good, holding constant foreign should induce a price change. The more inelastic demand for the home good (the poorer a substitute the home good is for the foreign) the bigger the price drop. Stockman terms this the "relative price effect". On the other hand, as $y$ in Equation 2.21 rises the "money-demand effect" on the exchange rate is negative. Hence there are two offsetting effects.

[21] Lucas (1982) notes the conditions under which the home currency appreciates. Suppose U is homothetic, such that the marginal rate of substitution is a positive, negatively sloped function of the endowment ratio, $r = \eta/\xi$, call it $g(r)$. Then if the derivative of $rg(r)$ with respect to $r$ is greater than zero, then the currency will appreciate. Else, it will depreciate as the terms of trade turn against the home country's goods.

What is the net effect? Given the binding Clower constraint, one knows that the income elasticity of money demand is unity; however, $\partial \ln(p_{y^*})/\partial \ln(y)$ is unknown. If this object is greater than unity because of low substitutability between $y$ and $y^*$, then the overall effect of higher GDP is a *weaker* currency. When $\partial \ln(p_{y^*})/\partial \ln(y) < 1$ (y and $y^*$ are good substitutes) the standard effect of higher income leading to a stronger currency, familiar from the flex-price monetary model, holds. However, only when $\partial \ln(p_{y^*})/\partial \ln(y) = 0$ (perfect substitutability) will the exact *quantitative* result from the flex-price monetary model hold.[22]

Apte et al. (2004) have provided a recent general equilibrium endowment model of the exchange rate that nests the Lucas model, PPP and the Balassa–Samuelson formulation. Using the no-arbitrage condition, homothetic utility functions characterized by constant relative risk aversion, they find that the nominal exchange rate can be expressed as a function of price levels and nominal consumption (really expenditure), where the elasticities of nominal consumption and the price level sum to unity.

$$s_t = p_t - p_t^* - \kappa y_t + \kappa^* y_t^* \tag{2.22}$$

Instead of estimating this equation, they rearrange Equation 2.26 to yield the real exchange rate on the right side. They proxy $y$ using real consumption data and find that there is a long-run cointegrating relationship between the real exchange rate and consumption levels. The authors take this as evidence in favor of the standard power utility model.

Equation 2.22 highlights the fact that microfounded models often yield specifications that are difficult to differentiate empirically from *ad hoc* models.[23]

# 2.4 New Directions in Exchange-Rate Modeling

## 2.4.1 TAKING REACTION FUNCTIONS SERIOUSLY

One strand of development in macroeconomic-based models has involved the incorporation of central bank reaction functions into exchange-rate models. Recent research reports that out-of-sample exchange-rate forecasting can be improved by incorporating monetary policy reaction functions (Taylor rules)

[22]The key distinction in this model vis-a-vis a sticky price monetary model is that the key driving variable in determining real exchange rates is the $p_y$ variable. To see this consider the Dornbusch model. In that framework, a nominal exchange-rate movement gets translated into a deviation from PPP because prices are sticky. In the Stockman model, prices are perfectly flexible, so that movements in the real exchange rates get translated into movements in the nominal exchange rate. Movements in the nominal magnitudes (such as $M$) have an impact on the nominal exchange rate, but not the real. Hence, this model possesses the classical dichotomy between nominal and real variables.

[23]Discussion of "generalized PPP" models and BEER models is covered in Chapter 11 on "fair value models."

into standard models. Essentially, output gaps and inflation gaps are then brought into the determination of exchange rates.

Engel and West (2005) were the first to incorporate Taylor rule fundamentals in a formal derivation of a model of exchange rates. By analyzing the dollar exchange rate, they posited a standard Taylor rule for the United States, and an interest rate targeting rule for the foreign country that incorporated an exchange-rate gap, where the foreign country targets a PPP value of the nominal exchange rate. Combined with interest rate parity (allowing for an exchange risk premium), they solve out for the present value expression for the exchange rate. One of the implications of this present value relationship is, with a discount factor close to unity, the exchange rate *should* be essentially unpredictable. In this context, there is no "exchange rate disconnect," that is, there is no puzzle why the exchange rate does not seem to be predictable on the basis of currently observed fundamentals.

Another implication of the model with highly persistent fundamentals is that the exchange rate should Granger cause the fundamentals. Of course, in their approach, only interest rates and price levels are observable (since target output and inflation are not). For the G-7 bilateral exchange rates, the null hypothesis of no Granger causality is rejected in most cases. By contrast, the null hypothesis that the fundamentals do not cause Granger cause the exchange rate is almost never rejected.

Engel and West also evaluate the model by assessing the correlation between the change in the exchange rates and the change in constructed fundamentals. They construct the fundamentals using either univariate regressions or bivariate VARs (with imposed discount factors), and find that the correlations are positive, thereby supportive of the model.

Engel and West (2006) examine the dollar-deutschemark rate more closely and bring into the analysis estimates of the output and inflation gaps. Depending on the imposed parameters and detrending technique, the correlation between the actual and fitted real exchange-rate changes is as high as 0.49.

Following the insights of Engel and West (2005, 2006), Chinn (2008) takes a more direct route, regressing exchange-rate changes on output and inflation gaps. He finds substantial in-sample predictive power for Taylor rule fundamentals. The analysis proceeds in the following manner. assume that policymakers follow Taylor rules, allowing for smoothing of interest rates as follows:

$$\begin{aligned} i_t = \pi_t + \beta_y \tilde{y}_t + \beta_\pi \tilde{\pi}_t + \beta_q \tilde{q}_t + \bar{r}_t + \rho i_{t-1} \\ \beta_y > 0, \beta_\pi > 0, \beta_q > 0, \rho > 0 \end{aligned} \tag{2.23}$$

where $\tilde{q}$ is the deviation of the real exchange rate from a target exchange rate, and the tildes denote "gaps." The monetary authorities move the policy rate in response to the deviations of output from potential GDP, deviations of inflation from target inflation, after accounting for a natural level of interest rates (i.e., the sum of the natural real interest rate and the inflation rate), as well as a deviation of the real exchange rate from the target rate.

A lagged interest rate is included in order to account for the tendency of central banks to smooth interest rates. The inclusion of the real exchange rate is not uncontroversial; it presupposes that the monetary authority attempts to stabilize the exchange rate. However, it is not an uncommon approach, and has been employed by Clarida et al. (1998), as well as Chinn and Dooley (1998).

To introduce the exchange rate, Chinn drops the uncovered interest parity assumption and rely upon an *ad hoc* characterization of the exchange rate/interest differential relationship.

$$s_{t+k} - s_t = \kappa \left(i_t - i_t^*\right) \qquad \kappa < 0 \tag{2.24}$$

In words, a larger interest differential is associated with an appreciation of the currency over a four quarter horizon.

Combining Equations 2.23 and 2.24 and assuming the foreign country is characterized by a similar Taylor rule, one obtains the following expression:

$$s_{t+k} - s_t = \kappa\beta_y\hat{\tilde{y}}_t + \kappa\left(\beta_y + 1\right)\hat{\pi}_t + \kappa\beta_q\hat{\tilde{q}}_t + \kappa\rho\hat{i}_{t-1} + c \tag{2.25}$$

where the circumflexes indicate intercountry differentials.[24]

This specification accords well with practitioner intuition for how interest rates (and hence exchange rates) move in response to inflation and output gaps. Consider what happens if the inflation gap rises in the United States relative to the foreign economy. Then the Fed will raise the policy rate, thereby appreciating the currency.

What about inflation? This framework implies that when inflation rises above the target level, then the currency will appreciate. Hence, the answer to Clarida and Waldmann's (2008) question "Is bad news about inflation good news for the dollar?" is yes.

Finally, if the real exchange rate rises (currency depreciates), then the central bank will "lean against the wind" and raise interest rates, thereby inducing a strengthening of the currency over the next four quarters.

Chinn (2008) finds that the resulting specification fits well, in sample. In particular, the output and inflation gaps enter in with expected sign, and typically with statistical significance, for the dollar/euro (1999–2007). For a longer period using synthetic dollar/euro exchange rates and variables, the evidence is a little less supportive, particularly with respect to the output gap.[25]

The coefficient on the exchange-rate gap is not often statistically significant. This might be because the importance of this variable depends on the two respective central bank reaction functions ascribing different weights on the

[24]Note that I am imposing the same coefficients for inflation and output gaps for both economies. Hence, this specification is a homogenous, asymmetric specification with smoothing, in Molodtsova and Papell's (2008) lexicon.

[25]There is a substantial complication in terms of implementation, since the output gap is directly observable. It can be measured by either using detrending methods (Hodrick-Prescott (HP) or band-pass filters) or production-function-based approaches. See Chinn (2008) for discussion.

exchange rate. If they ascribe the same weight, then the exchange-rate gap term drops out.

Molodtsova et al. (2008, 2011) and Molodtsova and Papell (2009) investigate the out-of-sample forecasting properties of Taylor-rule-based fundamentals. They find that incorporating Taylor rule variables helps with out-of-sample forecasting at short horizons, improving upon conventional interest rate, PPP or monetary models. For the exchange rates for the legacy currencies of the euro, as well as other key bilateral rates (pound, yen, Swiss franc, Australian and New Zealand dollars), Molodtsova and Papell (2009) find that a specification that allows the coefficients on the gap terms to vary across countries, and the exchange-rate gap to enter, typically does well in out-of-sample forecasting exercises, at the one quarter horizon. This outperformance is statistically significant using tests.

Molodtsova et al. (2011) examine the dollar/euro exchange rate. In this case, they find that the specification imposing common coefficients and omitting the exchange rate and interest rate smoothing does best in out-of-sample forecasting. This is true at the 1-month horizon, as well as longer horizons up to one year.[26] Molodtsova and Papell (2010) show that these results largely survive the arrival of zero interest rate policy to the United States and the euro area.[27]

Benigno (2004), Mark (2009); Corsetti et al. (2011), and Engel et al. (2010) show that monetary policy rules that can, among other things, generate some of the observed persistence in real exchange rates.

Combining monetary fundamentals and policy, with yield curve factors—which reflect expectations and risk premiums—further helps to explain exchange-rate movements and excess currency returns 1 month to 2 years ahead, outperforming the random walk (Chen and Tsang, 2011). Conversely, as Engel and West (2005) show that exchange rates are useful in forecasting future monetary policy, consistent with the idea that the exchange rate reflects the market's expectations of monetary policy. These findings suggest that excess currency returns reflect both real (business cycle) as well as financial factors.

### 2.4.2 THE IMPACT OF FINANCIAL GLOBALIZATION

Another strand of research focuses on the implications of financial globalization, particularly on valuation effects and the impact on exchange rates. With the substantial increase in gross cross-border holdings and assets and liabilities, the debate has shifted from the traditional role of current account imbalances on reallocating net assets, to the roles played by financial variables in explaining exchange rates. Balance sheet and valuation effects, for example, appear to be important in driving exchange rates and in turn real variables.

Confirmation of the quantitative importance of this channel for the United States has been provided by Gourinchas and Rey (2007). They use a log-linearized budget constraint to show how adjustment can be accomplished by a traditional trade channel (changes in net exports) and a financial channel

[26]Less promising results are obtained by Binici and Cheung (2011).

[27]One concern is that Equation 2.24 is *ad hoc* in nature, and represents an empirical relationship.

involving asset and liability returns. One important component of these returns is the exchange-rate change.

Gourinchas and Rey find that exchange-rate effects have contributed to about 30% of U.S. external adjustment since the 1950s. This is not to deny that exchange rates affect net exports, thereby aiding adjustment; rather, this financial adjustment channel results in a high degree of predictability at the 2- to 4-year horizon. Other recent tests also find evidence for the importance of balance sheets variables. Alquist and Chinn (2008), for example, compare the relative predictive power of the sticky price monetary model, uncovered interest rate parity and the Gourinchas and Rey (2007) models, even when assessing bilateral exchange rates. They find some support for the Gourinchas-Rey model at short horizons, even though the G-R model does not make specific predictions about *bilateral* exchange rates. Note that they find no model outperforms the random walk model.

Despite the empirical importance of this financial adjustment channel, it is unclear where this effect is coming from. Gourinchas and Rey argue that the effect is consistent with home bias in asset holdings in the context of a portfolio balance model, but do not provide a formal model.

Evans and Fuertes (2011) also examine the predictive power of the U.S. external position for the U.S. dollar. The innovation they incorporate is to use a VAR to model the trend and cyclical components, and not just the cyclical components as in the study of Gourinchas and Rey.[28]

Finally, some research has sought to more seriously deal with the financial sector, and in particular address the issue of segmented markets. Alvarez et al. (2009) build a two-country model in which the fraction of agents in each country that participate in financial markets varies over time, because of costs in transacting across assets. The exchange rate is much more volatile than the consumption—something difficult to achieve in models with complete markets, but is consistent with real-world observations.

### 2.4.3 THE RISK PREMIUM AND ORDER FLOW

One of the enduring puzzles in international finance is the presence of deviations from uncovered interest parity, when rational expectations is assumed. Alternatively, interest rate parity does not predict either well or the direction of subsequent exchange-rate changes. Chinn (2006) highlights these well-known facts. One way to explain the failure of uncovered interest parity combined with rational expectations (sometimes called the *unbiasedness hypothesis*) is by positing an exchange risk premium. The portfolio balance models discussed in Section 2.2.2 provide one (but not the only) rationale for the existence of an exchange risk premium. The lack of success in relating *ex post* risk premia to government bond stocks (Engel, 1996; Frankel and

[28]The authors log-linearize around zero net exports and net foreign assets, rather than around the balanced growth path as in Gourinchas and Rey.

Engel, 1984) has suggested alternative routes to modeling the exchange risk premia.

Engel (2010) has pointed out that any successful model of the exchange rate must explain why, simultaneously, high interest rate currencies tend to earn excess returns (the forward premium puzzle), and at the same time high real interest rate currencies tend to be stronger than the discounted rationally expected future real interest differentials. This in turn means that if there is an exchange risk premium, it is one that tends to shrink as real interest rates rise.

Deviations from *ex post* uncovered interest parity might arise from other sources. In the very short run, order flow affects exchange-rate behavior over periods varying from minutes to a couple of months (see Chapter 3 on market microstructure effects). It also seems related to the information in order flow about underlying macroeconomic factors. Evans (2010), for example, provides evidence that order-flow information reaching dealers provides information concerning the slowly evolving state of the macroeconomy, information which then in turn affects exchange rate behavior. Chinn and Moore (2011) also show that combining a monetary fundamental model with order-flow information can improve in out-of-sample exchange-rate forecasting.

## 2.5 Conclusions

The literature on macroeconomic determinants has split into several directions over the past few decades, with greater reliance on certain types of models in certain areas. In the theoretical aspects, greater and greater emphasis has been placed on modeling exchange rates in the context of general equilibrium models, using either calibration methods or estimated dynamic stochastic general equilibrium models. In academic empirical work, most of the recent advances have been derived from either the application of new panel econometric methods to existing asset-based approaches (such as the monetary approach) or the time series modeling as applied to newer models incorporating either reaction functions like the Taylor rule or balance sheet variables. Among the theoretical innovations the Taylor fundamentals approach has had a greater impact. This is probably because the data are easier to obtain, and the familiarity and intuitive appeal of the Taylor rules.

Finally, in the practitioner and policy areas pragmatism rules. Differing models gain greater adherence mostly on the basis of goodness of fit; the prevalence of BEER models in assessing currency fair values is one manifestation of that phenomenon.

## Acknowledgments

I thank the editors, Ron Alquist, Yin-Wong Cheung, Jaewoo Lee, David Papell, and the coeditor Ian Marsh for their comments.

## REFERENCES

Alexius A. Uncovered interest parity revisited. Rev Int Econ 2001; 9(3): 505–517.

Alquist R, Chinn M. Conventional and unconventional approaches to exchange rate modeling and assessment. Int J Finance Econ 2008; 13: 2–13.

Alvarez F, Atkeson A, Kehoe PJ. Time-varying risk, interest rates, and exchange rates in general equilibrium. Rev Econ Stud 2009; 76: 851–878.

Apte P, Sercu P, Uppal R. The exchange rate and purchasing power parity: extending the theory and tests. J Int Money Finance 2004; 23: 553–571.

Balassa B. The purchasing power parity doctrine: a reappraisal. J Pol Econ 1964; 72: 584–596.

Baxter M. Real exchange rates and real interest differentials: have we missed the business-cycle relationship? J Monet Econ 1994; 33: 5–37.

Benigno G. Real exchange rate persistence and monetary policy rules. J Monet Econ 2004; 51: 473–502.

Bilson, John F.O. The 'Speculative Efficiency' Hypothesis. J Business 1981; 54(3) (June): 435–451.

Binici M, Cheung Y-W. Exchange rate equations based on interest rate rules: in-sample and out-of-sample performance. mimeo Central Bank of Turkey and UC Santa Cruz; 2011 Feb.

Breuer JB. An assessment of the evidence on purchasing power parity. In: Williamson J, editor. Estimating equilibrium exchange rates. Washington (DC): IIE; 1994. pp. 245–278.

Canzoneri M, Cumby R, Diba B. Relative labor productivity and the real exchange rate in the long run: evidence for a panel of OECD countries. J Int Econ 1999; 47(2): 245–266.

Cerra V, Saxena SC. The monetary model strikes back: evidence from the world. J Int Econ 2010; 81: 184–196.

Chen Y-C, Rogoff K. Commodity currencies. J Int Econ 2003; 60(1): 133–160.

Chen Y-C, Tsang BKP. What does the yield curve tell us about exchange rate predictability? mimeo; 2011.

Cheung Y-W, Chinn M. Integration, cointegration, and the forecast consistency of structural exchange rate models. J Int Money Finance 1998; 17(5) (Oct.): 813–830.

Cheung Y-W, Chinn M, Pascual AG. Empirical exchange rate models of the 1990's: are any fit to survive? J Int Money Finance 2005; 24(7): 1150–1175.

Cheung Y-W, Lai KS. Economic growth and stationarity of real exchange rates: evidence from some fast growing Asian countries. Pac Basin Finance J 1998; 6: 61–76.

Cheung Y-W, Chinn M, Fujii E. Market structure and the persistence of sectoral deviations from purchasing power parity. Int J Finance Econ 2001; 6(2): 95–114.

Chinn M. Some linear and nonlinear thoughts on exchange rates. J Int Money Finance 1991; 10(2): 214–230.

Chinn M. Productivity, Government spending and the real exchange rate: evidence for OECD countries. In: MacDonald R, Stein J, editors. Equilibrium Exchange Rates. Boston: Kluwer Academic Publishers; 1999, 163–190.

Chinn MD. Paper pushers or paper money? Empirical assessment of fiscal and monetary models of exchange rate determination. J Policy Model 1997a; 19(1): 51–78.

Chinn MD. Whither the yen? Implications of an intertemporal model of the Yen/Dollar rate. J Jpn Int Econ 1997b; 11(2): 228–246.

Chinn M. The usual suspects? Productivity and demand shocks and Asia-Pacific real exchange rates. Rev Int Econ 2000; 8: 20–43.

Chinn M. The (Partial) rehabilitation of interest rate parity: longer horizons, alternative expectations and emerging markets. J Int Money Finance 2006; 25(1): 7–21.

Chinn M. Nonlinearities, business cycles and exchange rates. Econ Notes 2008; 37(3): 219–239.

Chinn M, Dooley M. Monetary policy in Japan, Germany and the United States: Does one size fit all? In: Freedman C, editor. Japanese Economic Policy Reconsidered. London: Edward Elgar; 1998. p. 179–217.

Chinn M, Johnston L. The impact of productivity differentials on real exchange rates: beyond the Balassa-Samuelson framework, Working Paper, 442. Santa Cruz (CA): Department of Economics, University of California; 1999 June.

Chinn M, Meese R. Banking on currency forecasts: how predictable is change in money? J Int Econ 1995; 38(1–2): 161–178.

Chinn M, Moore MJ. Order flow and the monetary model of exchange rates: evidence from a novel data set. J Money Credit Bank 2011; 43(8): 1594–1624.

Clarida R, Galí J, Gertler M. Monetary policy rules in practise: some international evidence. Eur Econ Rev 1998; 42: 1033–1-67.

Clarida RH, Waldman D. Is bad news about inflation good news for the exchange rate? And, if so, can that tell us anything about the conduct of monetary policy? In: Campbell J, editor. Asset prices and monetary policy. Chicago: Chicago University Press for NBER; 2008. p. 371–396.

Clements K, Frenkel J. Exchange rates, money, and relative prices: the Dollar-Pound in the 1920s. J Int Econ 1980; 10: 249–262.

Corsetti G, Dedola L, Leduc S. Optimal monetary policy in open economies. In: Friedman B, Woodford M, editors. Volume III, Handbook of monetary economics. Amsterdam: North-Holland; 2011. p. 861–934.

DeGregorio J, Wolf H. Terms of trade, productivity, and the real exchange rate, NBER Working Paper 4807 1994 July.

Diebold FX, Nason J. Nonparametric exchange rate prediction? J Int Econ 1990; 28: 315–332.

Dooley M, Isard P. A portfolio-balance rational-expectations model of the Dollar-Mark exchange rate. J Int Econ 1982; 12(3/4): 257–276.

Dornbusch R. Expectations and exchange rate dynamics. J Pol Econ 1976; 84: 1161–1176.

Edison H. Forecast performance of exchange rate models revisited. Appl Econ 1991; 23: 187–196.

Edison H, Pauls BD. A Re-assessment of the relationship between real exchange rates and real interest rates. J Monet Econ 1993; 31: 165–187.

Engel C. Can the markov switching model forecast exchange rates? J Int Econ 1994; 36(1–2): 151–165.

Engel C. The forward discount anomaly and the risk premium: a survey of recent evidence. J Empir Finance 1996; 3: 123–192.

Engel C. Accounting for US real exchange rate changes. J Pol Econ 1999; 107: 507–538.

Engel C, Hamilton J. Long swings in the exchange rate: are they in the data and do markets know it? Am Econ Rev 1990; 80(4): 689–713.

Engel C, West KD. Exchange rates and fundamentals. J Pol Econ 2005; 113(3): 485–517.

Engel C, West KD. Taylor rules and the Deutschmark–Dollar real exchange rate. J Money Credit Bank 2006; 38(5): 1175–1194.

Engel C, West KD, Zhu M. Global interest rates, monetary policy, and currency returns, Working Paper, draft (University of Wisconsin); 2010.

Evans M. Order flows and the exchange rate disconnect puzzle'. J Int Econ 2010; 80: 58–71.

Evans MDD, Fuertes A. Understanding the Dynamics of the US External Position mimeo. Washington (DC): Georgetown University; 2011.

Faust J, Rogers J, Wright J. Exchange rate forecasting: the Errors We've really made. J Int Econ 2003; 60: 35–60.

Frankel J. On the mark: a theory of floating exchange rates based on real interest differentials. Am Econ Rev 1979; 69: 610–622.

Frankel J. The mystery of the multiplying marks: a modification of the monetary model. Rev Econ Stat 1982; 64: 515–519.

Frankel J. Monetary and portfolio-balance models of exchange rate determination. Econ Interdepend Flexible Exchange Rates. In: Bhandari J, Putnam B, editors. Cambridge, MA: MIT Press; 1983. p. 84–115.

Frankel J. Tests of monetary and portfolio balance models of exchange rate determination. In: Bilson J, Marston R, editors. Exchange rate theory and practice. Chicago: University of Chicago Press for NBER; 1984: 239–260.

Frankel J, Engel C. Do asset-demand functions optimize over the mean and variance of real returns? J Int Econ 1984; 17: 309–323.

Frankel J, Rose A. A survey of empirical research on nominal exchange rates. In: Grossman G, Rogoff K, editors. Volume 3, Handbook of international economics. Amsterdam: North-Holland; 1995.

Frenkel JA. A monetary approach to the exchange rate: doctrinal aspects and empirical evidence. Scand J Econ 1976; 78: 200–224.

Gourinchas P-O, Rey H. International financial adjustment. J Pol Econ 2007; 115(4): 665–773.

Groen JJJ. Exchange rate predictability and monetary fundamentals in a small multi-country panel. J Money Credit Bank 2005; 37(3): 495–516.

Hodrick R. The empirical evidence on the efficiency of forward and futures foreign exchange markets. Chur, Switz.: Harwood Academic Publishers; 1987.

Hooper P, Morton J. Fluctuations in the dollar: a model of nominal and real exchange rate determination. J Int Money Finance 1982; 1: 39–56.

Hsieh D. The determination of the real exchange rate: the productivity approach. J Int Econ 1982; 12(2): 355–362.

Husted S, MacDonald R. Monetary-based models of the exchange rate: a panel perspective. J Int Financ Mark Inst Money 1998; 8: 1–19.

Isard P, Faruqee H, editors. Exchange rate assessment: extensions of the macroeconomic balance approach. Washington (DC): IMF; 1998.

Kilian L. Exchange rates and monetary fundamentals: what do we learn from long-horizon regressions? J Appl Economet 1999; 14: 491–510.

Kilian L, Taylor MP. Why is it so difficult to beat the random walk forecast of exchange rates? J Int Econ 2003; 60: 85–107.

Lee J, Tang M-K. Does productivity growth appreciate the real exchange rate? Rev Int Econ 2007; 15(1): 164–187.

Lucas R. Interest rates and currency prices in a two-country world. J Monet Econ 1982; 10(3): 335–359.

MacDonald R. Floating exchange rates: theories and evidence. London: Unwin Hyman; 1988.

MacDonald R. Long-run exchange rate modeling - a survey of the recent evidence. Int Monet Fund Staff Pap 1995; 42(3): 437–489.

MacDonald R. Exchange rate behaviour: are fundamentals important? Econ J 1999; 109: 673–691.

MacDonald R, Marsh I. On fundamentals and exchange rates: a Casselian perspective. Rev Econ Stat 1997; 79(4): 655–664.

MacDonald R, Marsh I. Exchange rate modelling. Boston (MA): Kluwer Academic Publishers; 1999.

MacDonald R, Nagayasu J. The long-run relationship between real exchange rates and real interest rate differentials. IMF Staff Pap 2000; 47(1): 116–128.

MacDonald R, Taylor M. The monetary model of the exchange rate: long-run relationships, short-run dynamics and how to beat a random walk. J Int Money Finance 1994; 13(3): 276–290.

Mark N. Exchange rates and fundamentals: evidence on long horizon predictability. Am Econ Rev 1995; 85: 201–218.

Mark N. Changing monetary policy rules, learning, and real exchange rate dynamics. J Money Credit Bank 2009; 41: 1047–1070.

Mark N, Sul D. Nominal exchange rates and monetary fundamentals: evidence from a small post-bretton woods panel. J Int Econ 2001; 53(1): 29–52.

Marston R. Systematic movements in real exchange rates in the G-5: evidence on the integration of internal and external markets. J Bank Finance 1990; 14(5): 1023–1044.

Meese R, Rogoff K. Empirical exchange rate models of the seventies: do they fit out of sample? J Int Econ 1983a; 14: 3–24.

Meese R, Rogoff K. The out-of-sample failure of empirical exchange rate models: sampling error or misspecification. In: Frenkel J, editor. Exchange rates and international macroeconomics. Chicago: University of Chicago Press; 1983b. pp. 67–105.

Meese R, Rogoff K. Was it real? The exchange rate-interest differential relation over the modern floating-rate period. J Finance 1988; 43(4): 933–947.

Meese R, Rose A. An empirical assessment of non-linearities in models of exchange rate determination. Rev Econ Stud 1991; 58: 603–619.

Molodtsova T, Papell D. Exchange rate predictability with taylor rule fundamentals. J Int Econ 2009; 77: 167–180.

Molodtsova T, Papell D. Phoenix taylor rule exchange rate forecasting during the financial crisis mimeo, 2010.

Molodtsova T, Nikolsko-Rzhevskyy A, Papell D. Taylor rules with real-time data: a tale of two countries and one exchange rate. J Monet Econ 2008; 55: S64–S79.

Molodtsova T, Nikolsko-Rzhevskyy A, Papell D. Taylor rules and the Euro. J Money Credit Bank 2011; 43: 536–552.

Morley J. The emperor has no clothes. Macroecon Advisers' Macro Focus 2010; 5(2): 1–14.

Obstfeld M, Rogoff K. Foundations of international macroeconomics. Cambridge (MA): MIT Press; 1996.

Papell D. Activist monetary policy and exchange rate overshooting: The DM/Dollar rate. J Int Money Finance 1984; 3: 293–310.

Papell D. Expectations and exchange rate dynamics after a decade of floating. J Int Econ 1988; 25: 303–317.

Pedroni P. Critical values for cointegration tests in heterogeneous panels with multiple regressors. Oxford Bull Econ Stat 1999; 61 (S1) (Nov.): 653–670.

Rapach DE, Wohar ME. Testing the monetary model of exchange rate determination: new evidence from a century of data. J Int Econ 2002; 58: 359–385.

Ricci LA, Milesi-Ferretti GM, Lee J. Real exchange rates and fundamentals: a cross-country perspective. J Money Credit Bank. Forthcoming.

Rogoff K. Traded goods consumption smoothing and the random walk behavior of the real exchange rate. Bank Japan Monet Econ Studies 1992; 10(2): 1–29.

Rogoff K. The purchasing power parity puzzle. J Econ Lit 1996; 34(2): 647–668.

Samuelson P. Theoretical notes on trade problems. Rev Econ Stat 1964; 46: 145–154.

Sarno L, Taylor MP. The economics of exchange rates. Cambridge: MIT Press; 2002.

Strauss J. The cointegrating relationship between productivity, real exchange rates and purchasing power parity. J Macroecon 1996; 18(2): 299–313.

Strauss J. Productivity differentials, the relative price of non-tradables and real exchange rates. J Int Money Finance 1999; 18: 383–409.

Taylor MP. The economics of exchange rates. J Econ Lit 1995; 33(1): 13–47.

Taylor MP, Peel DA. Nonlinear adjustment, long-run equilibrium and exchange rate fundamentals. J Int Money Finance 2000; 19(1): 33–53.

Taylor MP, Peel DA, Sarno L. Nonlinear mean-reversion in real exchange rates: towards a solution to the purchasing power parity puzzles. Int Econ Rev 2001; 42(4): 1015–1042.

Taylor AM, Taylor MP. The purchasing power parity debate. J Econ Persp 2004; 18(4) (Fall): 135–158.

Wolff CCP. Time-varying parameters and the out-of-sample forecasting performance of structural exchange rate models. J Business Econ Stat 1987; 5(1): 87–97.

CHAPTER THREE

# Micro Approaches to Foreign Exchange Determination

**MARTIN D. D. EVANS**
Department of Economics, Georgetown University, NBER

**DAGFINN RIME**
Norges Bank, Norwegian University of Science and Technology

## 3.1 Introduction

Micro-based exchange-rate research examines the determination and behavior of spot exchange rates in an environment that replicates the key features of trading in the foreign exchange (FX) market. Traditional macro exchange-rate models pay little attention to how trading in the FX market actually takes place. The implicit assumption is that the details of trading are unimportant for the behavior of exchange rates over months, quarters, or longer. Micro-based models, by contrast, examine how information relevant to the pricing of FX becomes reflected in the spot exchange rate via the trading process. According to this view, trading is not an ancillary market activity that can be ignored when considering exchange-rate behavior. Rather, trading is an integral part of the process through which spot rates are determined and evolved.

The past decade of micro-based research has uncovered a robust and strong empirical relation between exchange rates and measures of FX trading activity. One measure in particular, order flow (i.e., the net of buyer- and seller-initiated FX trades) appears as the proximate driver of exchange-rate changes over horizons ranging from a few minutes to a few months. This finding supports the view

*Handbook of Exchange Rates*, First Edition. Edited by Jessica James, Ian W. Marsh, and Lucio Sarno.

that trading is an integral part of exchange-rate determination. It also stands in stark contrast to the well-known deficiencies of macro models in accounting for exchange-rate variations over horizons shorter than a couple of years.

In this chapter, we provide an overview of micro-based research on exchange-rate determination. Originally, the research was focused on partial equilibrium models—the traditional domain of microstructure research. These models provide an explanation for why order flow is a proximate driver of exchange-rate changes over short horizons. Recent micro-based research focuses on the link between currency trading and macroeconomic conditions in the general equilibrium setting of modern macroeconomic models. This research aims to provide the microfoundations for the exchange-rate dynamics that are missing in traditional macro models. The models provide new perspectives on the behavior of exchange rates over horizons which are relevant to researchers and policy makers concerned with international macroeconomic issues. They also produce theoretical predictions concerning the links between exchange rates, order flow, and macro economic factors which are supported by the data. Thus, we may finally be making some progress toward understanding the links between macro economic conditions and the behavior of exchange rates over macro- and policy-relevant horizons.

We structure our discussion as follows: In Section 3.2, we provide a broad overview of the key differences between the traditional macro view of exchange-rate determination and the micro-based approach. This discussion also provides some perspective on why the empirical performance of macro- and micro-based exchange-rate models is so different. Section 3.3 first lays out the key features of the FX market and describes how they are incorporated into a canonical partial equilibrium model of currency trading. We then discuss the empirical implications of the model and the relevant micro-based empirical literature. Section 3.4 examines the research that links spot-rate dynamics to macro economic conditions via currency trading. Section 3.5 concludes with some thoughts on the directions of future micro-based exchange-rate research.

## 3.2 Perspectives on Spot-Rate Dynamics

We begin by providing a broad perspective on the possible factors that drive spot exchange rates. For this purpose, we first derive a simple decomposition for the period-by-period depreciation rate that must hold in any exchange-rate model; that is, traditional macro models and micro-based models. We then use this decomposition to identify the key differences between micro-based models and their traditional macro counterparts.

### 3.2.1 DECOMPOSITION OF DEPRECIATION RATES

We begin with some definitions. Let $s_t$ denote the log spot exchange rate defined as the domestic price of foreign currency. The log excess return on foreign currency between periods $t$ and $t+1$ is $er_{t+1} = s_{t+1} - s_t + r_t^* - r_t$, where $r_t$ and $r_t^*$

denote the home and foreign one-period nominal interest rates, respectively. We define the FX risk premium, $\delta_t$, as the expected log excess return, $\mathbb{E}_t er_{t+1} = \delta_t$, where $\mathbb{E}_t$ denotes expectations conditioned on period-$t$ information, $\Omega_t$. For the present, all we shall assume is that $\Omega_t$ contains the period-$t$ spot rate and interest rates: $s_t$, $r_t$, and $r^*_t$.

Our aim is to provide a decomposition for the period-by-period depreciation rate, $\Delta s_{t+1} = s_{t+1} - s_t$. For this purpose, we first combine the definitions of $er_{t+1}$ and $\delta_t$ to write

$$\Delta s_{t+1} = r_t - r^*_t + \delta_t + (s_{t+1} - \mathbb{E}_t s_{t+1}). \tag{3.1}$$

In words, the depreciation rate must be equal to the sum of the interest differential, $r_t - r^*_t$; the risk premium, $\delta_t$; and the error in forecasting the period-$t+1$ spot rate, $s_{t+1} - \mathbb{E}_t s_{t+1}$.

To identify the forecast error, we introduce our first economic assumption. In modern macro models short-term interest rates are viewed as the policy instruments of central banks who react to changing macro economic conditions in pursuit of their monetary policy goals. With this in mind, we assume that expectations about the future path of domestic and foreign interest rates follow

$$\begin{aligned}\mathbb{E}_t(r^*_{t+i} - r_{t+i}) = (1 + \gamma_\pi)\mathbb{E}_t\left(\Delta p^*_{t+1+i} - \Delta p_{t+1+i}\right) \\ + \gamma_y \mathbb{E}_t\left(y^*_{t+i} - y_{t+i}\right) - \gamma_q \mathbb{E}_t q_{t+i},\end{aligned} \tag{3.2}$$

for $i > 0$, where $\gamma_\pi$, $\gamma_y$, and $\gamma_q$ are positive coefficients.

Equation (3.2) says that the expected future differential between foreign and domestic rates is higher when: (i) the future difference between foreign and home inflation, $\Delta p^*_{t+1} - \Delta p_{t+1}$, is higher; (ii) the difference between the foreign and home output gaps, $y^*_t - y_t$, widens; or (iii) when the log real exchange rate, $q_t = s_t + p^*_t - p_t$, depreciates. The first two terms are consistent with the widely accepted view that central banks react to higher domestic inflation and output by raising short-term interest rates. The third term captures the idea that some central banks can be expected to react to deviations in the spot rate from its purchasing power parity level—a notion that finds empirical support in Clarida et al. 1998).

We now identify the implications of these interest rate expectations for the behavior of the spot-rate forecast error, $s_{t+1} - \mathbb{E}_t s_{t+1}$. By definition, $s_{t+1} = r^*_{t+1} - r_{t+1} - \delta_{t+1} + \mathbb{E}_{t+1} s_{t+2}$, so taking conditional expectations gives

$$\mathbb{E}_t s_{t+1} = \mathbb{E}_t(r^*_{t+1} - r_{t+1} - \delta_{t+1}) + \mathbb{E}_t s_{t+2}. \tag{3.3}$$

Substituting for interest rate expectations with Equation (3.2), and iterating forward, we find that

$$\mathbb{E}_t s_{t+1} = \mathbb{E}_t \sum_{i=1}^{\infty} \rho^i (f_{t+i} - \delta_{t+i}) + \mathbb{E}_t \lim_{i\to\infty} \rho^i s_{t+i}, \tag{3.4}$$

with $\rho = 1/(1+\gamma_q) < 1$, where macro fundamentals are

$$f_t = (1+\gamma_\pi)\left(\Delta p^*_{t+1} - \Delta p_{t+1}\right) + \gamma_y\left(y^*_t - y_t\right) + \gamma_q(p_t - p^*_t).$$

To rule out the effects of asset-pricing bubbles, we assume that $\mathbb{E}_t \lim_{i\to\infty} \rho^i s_{t+i} = 0$, so that Equation (3.4) becomes

$$\mathbb{E}_t s_{t+1} = \frac{\rho}{1-\rho}\mathbb{E}_t f_t + \frac{1}{1-\rho}\mathbb{E}_t \sum_{i=1}^{\infty} \rho^i \Delta f_{t+i} - \mathbb{E}_t \sum_{i=1}^{\infty} \rho^i \delta_{t+i}. \tag{3.5}$$

Equation (3.5) identifies the expected spot rate next period in terms of the estimate of current macro fundamentals, $\mathbb{E}_t f_t$; forecasts of future changes in fundamentals, $\mathbb{E}_t \Delta f_{t+i}$; and expectations about the future risk premia, $\mathbb{E}_t \delta_{t+i}$.

Finally, we combine Equation (3.3) with the identity, $s_{t+1} = r^*_{t+1} - r_{t+1} - \delta_{t+1} + \mathbb{E}_{t+1} s_{t+2}$, to give

$$s_{t+1} - \mathbb{E}_t s_{t+1} = r^*_{t+1} - r_{t+1} - \delta_{t+1} - \mathbb{E}_t(r^*_{t+1} - r_{t+1} - \delta_{t+1}) + (\mathbb{E}_{t+1} - \mathbb{E}_t) s_{t+2}.$$

Notice that the last term on the right is equal to $(\mathbb{E}_{t+1} - \mathbb{E}_t)\mathbb{E}_{t+1} s_{t+2}$ by the law of iterated expectations. So, substituting for $\mathbb{E}_{t+1} s_{t+2}$ from Equation (3.5) gives

$$\begin{aligned} s_{t+1} - \mathbb{E}_t s_{t+1} &= (1 - \mathbb{E}_t)\left(r^*_{t+1} - r_{t+1}\right) + \frac{\rho}{1-\rho}(\mathbb{E}_{t+1} - \mathbb{E}_t) f_{t+1} \\ &\quad + \frac{1}{1-\rho}(\mathbb{E}_{t+1} - \mathbb{E}_t)\sum_{i=2}^{\infty} \rho^{i-1}\Delta f_{t+i} \\ &\quad - (\mathbb{E}_{t+1} - \mathbb{E}_t)\sum_{i=1}^{\infty} \rho^{i-1}\delta_{t+i}. \end{aligned}$$

Since $\{r_t, r^*_t\} \in \Omega_t$, $(1-\mathbb{E}_t)\left(r^*_{t+1} - r_{t+1}\right) = (1-\mathbb{E}_t)\Delta\left(r^*_{t+1} - r_{t+1}\right)$. We can therefore combine this expression with Equation (3.1) to produce

$$\begin{aligned} \Delta s_{t+1} &= r_t - r^*_t - (1-\mathbb{E}_t)\Delta\left(r_{t+1} - r^*_{t+1}\right) \\ &\quad + \frac{\rho}{1-\rho}(\mathbb{E}_{t+1} - \mathbb{E}_t) f_{t+1} + \frac{1}{1-\rho}(\mathbb{E}_{t+1} - \mathbb{E}_t)\sum_{i=2}^{\infty} \rho^{i-1}\Delta f_{t+i} \\ &\quad + \delta_t - (\mathbb{E}_{t+1} - \mathbb{E}_t)\sum_{i=1}^{\infty} \rho^{i-1}\delta_{t+i}. \end{aligned} \tag{3.6}$$

Equation (3.6) decomposes variations in the depreciation rate into three sets of factors: policy-determined interest rates, revisions in expectations about current and future fundamentals, and the anticipated path for the risk premium. Monetary policy affects the depreciation rate via the period-$t$ differential and via unexpected changes in the interest differential, as identified by the terms in the first line on the right-hand side. The terms in the second line identify the influence of macro fundamentals. These terms only appear because expectations concerning future interest rates are correlated with forecasts of future macro fundamentals. The terms in the last row identify the role of the risk premia. The period-$t$ risk premia, $\delta_t$, affects the depreciation rate via its impact on $\mathbb{E}_t \Delta s_{t+1}$, while the present value term contributes to $s_{t+1} - \mathbb{E}_t s_{t+1}$. Again, we stress that this decomposition follows from just two assumptions: the assumption on interest rate forecasts in Equation (3.2); and the "no bubble" assumption, $\mathbb{E}_t \lim_{i\to\infty} \rho^i s_{t+i} = 0$.

### 3.2.2 MACRO- AND MICROPERSPECTIVES

The decomposition of the depreciation rate in Equation (3.6) allows us to clearly identify the key differences between micro-based exchange-rate models and their traditional macro counterparts. Broadly speaking, these differences appear in two areas: (i) the specification of the conditioning information set used to compute expectations and (ii) the specification of the risk premium, $\delta_t$.

Macro models of exchange-rate determination typically assume that agents (i.e., households, firms, and central banks) have the same information about the structure of the economy and observe its current state. In the context of Equation (3.6), this means that current prices, inflation, and output gaps are also part of the period-$t$ common information set, $\Omega_t$. Assumptions about the risk premium vary. Many traditional models assume some version of uncovered interest parity, so the risk premium is zero or a constant. In contrast, modern macro models identify the risk premium from the covariance between currency returns and the macro risk factors driving the stochastic discount factor (SDF) that prices all financial assets in an economy without arbitrage opportunities. The risk premium can vary in these models, but estimates in the literature are typically close to zero.[1]

With these assumptions, the macro perspective on the factors driving depreciation rates focuses on the terms in the first two lines of Equation (3.6). The first line identifies the effect of current and unanticipated changes in short-term interest rates. In practice, current interest differentials (i.e., $r_t - r_t^*$) typically account for very little of the variation in depreciation rates. Furthermore, central banks change interest rates relatively rarely; and when they do, they often communicate their intentions beforehand so as not to put undue stress on the financial system. As a result, unanticipated changes in short-term interest are not

[1]At their heart, macro models for the risk premium require that (i) any expected excess currency return that differs from zero should covary with the SDF and (ii) differences between expected returns are proportional to the difference in the covariance between returns and the SDF. Unfortunately, researchers have yet to find evidence satisfying the first condition for specifications of the SDF based on macro variables. For example, a comprehensive recent study by Burnside et al. (2007) finds that the excess returns from carry-trade strategies have no significant covariance with a wide array of risk factors.

an important source of spot-rate changes over weeks, months, and quarters.[2] This leaves the terms involving macro fundamentals, $f_t$.

By definition, $(\mathbb{E}_{t+1} - \mathbb{E}_t)f_{t+1} = (\mathbb{E}_{t+1} - \mathbb{E}_t)\left(f_{t+1} - f_{t-1}\right) + (\mathbb{E}_{t+1} - \mathbb{E}_t)f_{t-1}$. So if the current state of the macro economy is common knowledge as macro models assume, $(\mathbb{E}_{t+1} - \mathbb{E}_t)f_{t-1} = 0$, and Equation (3.6) becomes[3]

$$\Delta s_{t+1} \cong \frac{\rho}{1-\rho}(\mathbb{E}_{t+1} - \mathbb{E}_t)\left(f_{t+1} - f_{t-1}\right) + \frac{1}{1-\rho}(\mathbb{E}_{t+1} - \mathbb{E}_t)\sum_{i=2}^{\infty}\rho^{i-1}\Delta f_{t+i}. \tag{3.7}$$

Suppose one-period spans a month or quarter. Under normal circumstances, the first term on the right should be close to zero because macro fundamentals are unlikely to change significantly over this time span. Thus, from a macro perspective, the lion's share of the link between macro fundamentals and monthly/quarterly variations in spot rates must be attributable to the second term on the right-hand side of Equation (3.7): that is, the revisions in forecasts about future changes in fundamentals, $\Delta f_{t+i}$ for $i > 1$. However, the time-series properties of the macro variables used to construct fundamentals, $\hat{f}_t$, in the macro exchange-rate literature imply very little variation in the estimates of the present value of future changes in $\hat{f}_t$. As a result, estimates of the second term in Equation (3.7) using $\hat{f}_t$ account for at most 5% of the variance of the depreciation rates at the monthly and quarterly horizons.[4] This lack of empirical success has given credence to the view that exchange rates are largely disconnected from macro fundamentals; a view Obstfeld and Rogoff (2001) call the exchange-rate disconnect puzzle.

Micro-based models bring a different perspective on spot-rate dynamics for two reasons. First, they consider much richer informational environments where agents have different and incomplete information about market and macro conditions. As a result, the information conditioning expectations in Equation (3.6) no longer represents common public information. Second, micro-based models produce significant variations in the risk premium that are unrelated to the risk factors found in macro models. Consequently, micro-based models can account for variations in spot rates in the absence of changes in interest rates and/or fundamentals.

A key feature of micro-based models is that they treat the spot exchange rate as the price of FX that dealers quote to each other and agents outside the market during trading. Thus, the dynamics of spot exchange rates literally reflects the changes in dealers' FX quotes. This dealer-centered perspective has two critical implications for exchange-rate determination. First, at any point in time, the

[2]This is not to say that unexpected changes in monetary policy have no exchange-rate effects. For example, Faust et al. (2007) found that unexpected changes in the Fed Funds rate accounted for 20% of the variance in the USD/DEM(EUR) depreciation rate in 20 min following the change. The point is simply that such events account for very small fraction of the total variation in spot rates over weeks, months, and longer.

[3]Notice that we focus here only on the terms involving macro fundamentals, or equivalently on circumstances where $r_t = r_t^*$ and $\delta_t = 0$.

[4]See Engel and West (2006) and Mark (2009). Chapter 3 in Evans (2011) contains a detailed discussion of this point.

spot exchange rate can only reflect information known to the dealers making quotes. In terms of Equation (3.6), expectations are conditioned on the period$-t$ common information available to all dealers. Second, information known to dealers will only be embedded in the spot exchange rate if they find it optimal from a trading perspective to base their quotes on that information; i.e., the information is price-relevant. These implications are straightforward but open up new conceptual space for thinking about exchange-rate dynamics.

To illustrate this point, consider the terms involving fundamentals from Equation (3.6), where we replace $\mathbb{E}_t$ by $\mathbb{E}_t^{\mathrm{D}}$ to emphasize that the expectations are conditioned on dealers' information:

$$\frac{\rho}{1-\rho}(\mathbb{E}_{t+1}^{\mathrm{D}} - \mathbb{E}_t^{\mathrm{D}})f_{t+1} + \frac{1}{1-\rho}(\mathbb{E}_{t+1}^{\mathrm{D}} - \mathbb{E}_t^{\mathrm{D}})\sum_{i=2}^{\infty}\rho^{i-1}\Delta f_{t+i}. \tag{3.8}$$

Micro-based models do not assume that dealers have contemporaneous information on all the macro variables that comprise fundamentals. In accordance with reality, information on macro economic conditions only becomes available via the release of macro data with reporting lags of up to several months. Thus, the first term in Equation (3.8) can contribute to short-term variations in spot rates, as dealers learn about the current macro economic conditions that comprise fundamentals. As we shall see, this turns out to be empirically important: Some of the high frequency behavior of spot rates reflects the flow of new information reaching dealers concerning the slowly evolving state of the macro economy.

Variations in the risk premium also play an important role in micro-based models. When dealers determine their FX quotes, they include a risk premium, $\delta_t$, that compensates them for the risks of being a market maker. These risks arise because the dealer stands ready to fill the currency orders of other market participants, and can vary significantly as market conditions change. They are also quite different from the risks faced by other market participants, such as investors, identified in macro models. As a consequence, the terms involving the risk premia from Equation (3.6):

$$\delta_t - (\mathbb{E}_{t+1}^{\mathrm{D}} - \mathbb{E}_t^{\mathrm{D}})\sum_{i=1}^{\infty}\rho^{i-1}\delta_{t+i}, \tag{3.9}$$

play a significant role in the determination of depreciation rates in micro-based models. We discuss this role of the risk premium in Sections 3.3 and 3.4.

Micro-based models also differ from their traditional counterparts in terms of the information sources driving dealers' expectations. As in macro models, dealers can change their expectations in response to public data releases that contain information on past economic conditions. They can also revise their expectations in response to contemporaneously observed macro economic shocks, such as natural disasters, or other public news. More uniquely to micro-models, dealers also receive information from their observations on the patterns of currency trading. This source of information is ignored by macro models, but it turns out to be very important empirically. In particular, one measure of trading activity, order flow, accounts for as much as 60–70% of the variations in spot rates at a daily frequency.

Foreign currency order flow is defined as the difference between the value of purchase and sale orders for FX initiated by traders against dealers spot-rate quotes during a specified trading period. A key element in this definition is the initiator of trade. In every trade, there is a buyer and seller of FX, but only one party to the trade initiates the transaction. The initiator is the one paying transaction costs, and presumably so for a reason. Hence, by tracking who initiates each trade, order flow provides a measure of the information exchanged between counterparties in a series of FX transactions. In micro-based models this information may concern fundamentals and/or the determinants of the risk premium. In the former case, order flow is a proximate driver of the depreciation rate via the terms in Equation (3.8). When order flow conveys information about the risk premium, it is a proximate driver of depreciation rates via the terms in Equation (3.9). We discuss why order flow plays this role below.

In summary, micro-based models bring a new perspective to understanding the sources of spot-rate variations, because they focus on the flow of information reaching dealers and the compensation they require to act as market makers in currency markets. In the sections that follow, we examine the theoretical foundations of these features and discuss the supporting empirical evidence.

## 3.3 Currency Trading Models and their Implications

One goal of micro-based research is to build exchange-rate models from microeconomic foundations that reasonably represent the key features of the FX market. In particular, the aim is to incorporate the institutional implications of how information is transmitted from one agent to another as trading takes place and to study how this information flow is ultimately reflected in the spot exchange rate.

No model can incorporate all the institutional features of trading in the FX market—it is far too complex. Instead, micro-based models focus on a small number of features that are viewed as essential for understanding the main economic mechanisms at work. The structure of the FX market is discussed in more detail in the chapter by King et al. We summarize the key features below.

FX dealers working in banks are the key intermediaries in the FX market. The FX market is a two-tier market in the sense that the end-users of currency trade with dealers in the retail market, and dealers trade with other dealers in the interbank market. Neither the interbank nor the retail market has a physical location. Trades are made by phone or electronically between participants located all around the world, and trading can take place continuously 24 hours a day. However, a majority of the trading in the interbank market involve banks in a few financial centers (Tokyo, Singapore, Frankfurt, New York, and particularly London), and activity is heavily concentrated during the daytime hours of these main financial centers.

In the interbank market, FX dealers trade both directly and indirectly with each other. Direct interdealer trading, typically bilateral "conversations" between two dealers over a computer network called *Reuters D2000-1*, was the dominant form of interbank trading before the mid-1990s. Since then, more and more interbank trades are matched indirectly via the market and limit orders to buy and sell currencies that dealers submit to two electronic brokers, Reuters D2000-2 and EBS.

The lack of a physical location and the structure and number of trading systems implies that no FX dealer has complete information about the state of the interbank market. Direct interdealer trading takes place simultaneously across the interbank market, and dealers only have information on the direct trades they participate in. Electronic brokerages provide market-wide information on transaction prices, and thereby give dealers signals on the market-wide order flow, but the dealers do not observe the structure of limit orders that determine market liquidity. And since there are no regulatory bodies requiring disclosure of trades, the dealers do not know who is behind the trades observed on the electronic brokers.

The FX orders from end-users (often called *customer orders*) received by banks represent the most important source of private information to FX dealers. Dealers working at banks with a large customer base and a world-wide reporting system have a potentially important informational advantage over other market participants (Cheung and Wong, 2000; Cheung et al., 2004). Customer orders come from many different end-user types and may be generated by allocative, speculative, and risk-management factors. Customer orders that are purely a function of current and past currency prices are termed *feedback orders*. FX dealers face constraints on both the duration and size of their FX positions. Their overnight positions are typically small or zero.

### 3.3.1 THE PORTFOLIO SHIFTS MODEL

The Portfolio Shifts (PS) model developed by Lyons (1997) and Evans and Lyons (2002) incorporates many of these features into a model that examines how trading in the interbank and retail tiers of the FX market relates to the evolution of the spot exchange rate. This model describes trading in a single currency pair among a large number of dealers, a broker and between dealers and investors over a stylized trading day. Here, we extend the model to allow for the effects of data releases (see Evans (2011) for a detailed analysis).

**3.3.1.1 Overview.** There is one risky asset representing FX and one risk-free asset with a daily return of $1 + r$. The economy is populated by a continuum of risk-averse investors indexed by $n \in [0, 1]$ and D risk-averse dealers indexed by $d$. Each day, $t$, is split into three trading rounds: I, II, and III. The sequence of events throughout day $t$ is shown in Figure 3.1.

At the start of round I on day $t$, all investors, dealers, and the broker observe the dividend paid to the current holders of FX. The value of the dividend, $D_t$, is assumed to follow a random walk

$$D_t = D_{t-1} + V_t, \tag{3.10}$$

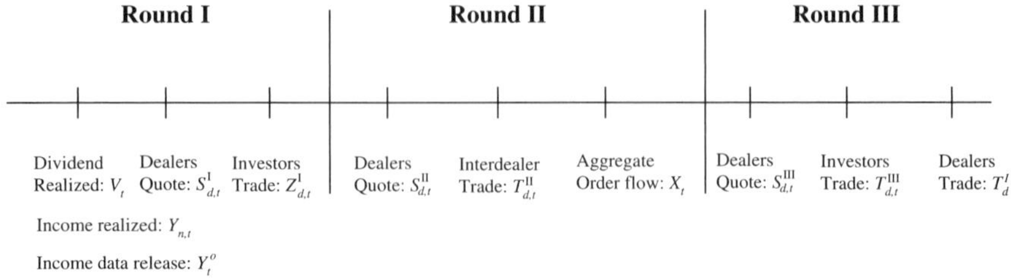


**FIGURE 3.1 Daily timing in the portfolio shifts model.**

where $V_t \sim$ i.i.d.$N(0, \sigma_v^2)$. Realizations of $V_t$ represent the arrival of public macro information over time (e.g., changes in interest rates). At the start of the day, each investor $n$ also receives FX income,

$$Y_{n,t} = Y_t + \xi_{n,t}, \tag{3.11}$$

where $Y_t$ and $\xi_{n,t}$ are i.i.d. mean-zero normal random variables that represent the aggregate and idiosyncratic components of income. $Y_{n,t}$ is private information to each investor and generates a hedging motive for the customer orders in round-I trading. Investors do not initially observe either component; but in equilibrium they learn the value of $Y_t$ by the end of day $t$.

Data releases take place on a prespecified schedule. At the start of round I on a release day, everyone also observes an estimate of aggregate foreign income, $Y_t^o$. This estimate is related to actual foreign income by

$$Y_t^o = Y_t + U_t, \tag{3.12}$$

where $U_t \sim$ i.i.d.$N(0, \sigma_{\mathrm{U}}^2)$.

The retail tier of the market opens in round I. Each dealer simultaneously and independently quotes a scalar price at which they will fill customer orders to buy or sell FX. The round-I price quoted by dealer $d$ is denoted by $S^{\mathrm{I}}_{d,t}$. Prices are publicly observed by all dealers and investors and are good for orders of any size. Investors then place their orders for FX. Orders may be placed with more than one dealer. If two or more dealers quote the same price, the customer order is randomly assigned among them. The customer orders received by dealer $d$ are denoted by $Z^{\mathrm{I}}_{d,t}$. Positive (negative) values of $Z^{\mathrm{I}}_{d,t}$ denote net customer purchases (sales) of FX. As in the actual retail market, customer orders, $Z^{\mathrm{I}}_{d,t}$, are only observed by dealer $d$.

Trading in the interbank tier of the market takes place in round II. The broker and each dealer simultaneously and independently quotes a scalar price for FX, $S^{\mathrm{II}}_{\mathrm{B},t}$ and $\{S^{\mathrm{II}}_{d,t}\}^{\mathrm{D}}_{d=1}$. The quoted prices are observed by all dealers and are good for interdealer trades of any size. Each dealer then simultaneously and independently trades on other dealers' and the broker's quotes. We denote the FX orders made by dealer $d$ as $T^{\mathrm{II}}_{d,t}$ and orders received by dealer $d$ as $Z^{\mathrm{II}}_{d,t}$. Orders received by the broker are denoted by $Z^{\mathrm{II}}_{\mathrm{B},t}$. When dealer $d$ initiates a purchase (sale) of FX, $T^{\text{II}}_{d,t}$ is positive (negative). Positive values of $Z^{\text{II}}_{d,t}$ or $Z^{\text{II}}_{\text{B},t}$ denote purchases of FX initiated by another dealer. Once again, trading with multiple dealers and the broker is feasible. If multiple agents quote the same price, trades are allocated equally between them.[5] At the close of round II trading, all dealers and the broker observe aggregate interdealer order flow:

$$X_t = \sum_{d=1}^{\text{D}} T^{\text{II}}_{d,t}. \tag{3.13}$$

Interdealer order flow, $X_t$, simply aggregates the purchases of FX made by dealers initiating trades against other dealers' quotes and the broker's quote.

The retail tier of the market reopens in round III. The broker and dealers again simultaneously and independently quote prices, $S^{\text{III}}_{\text{B},t}$ and $\{S^{\text{III}}_{d,t}\}^{\text{D}}_{d=1}$, at which they will fill dealer and customer orders, respectively. Investors observe all the prices and then place their orders with dealers. As above, orders may be placed with more than one dealer and are randomly assigned to dealers quoting the same prices. The round III customer orders received by dealer $d$ are denoted by $Z^{\text{III}}_{d,t}$. Once each dealer has filled his customer orders, he can trade with the broker.[6]

Clearly, this sequence of events represents a simplified view of trading in the actual FX market. It does, however, allow us to analyze how information pertinent to the spot exchange rate is learnt by dealers via trading. In particular, the focus of the model is on how information about the aggregate demand for FX contained in the customer orders at the start of the day becomes learnt by dealers and reflected in the FX prices they quote at the end of day. As we shall see, this information aggregation process produces an important empirical prediction linking trading activity to exchange-rate dynamics.

#### 3.3.1.2 Equilibrium.

The model's equilibrium comprises: (i) a set of optimal FX orders by investors in rounds I and III; (ii) a set of optimal FX price quotes by dealers in rounds I–III, and the broker in rounds II and III; and (iii) a set of optimal dealer trading decisions in rounds II and III, such that markets clear (i.e., there is a counterparty for every trade in each round) and the expected utility of investors and dealers are maximized at every decision point.

[5] Unlike round I, there is no random assignment of trades between dealers quoting the same price in round II. This assumption makes the single round of interdealer trading more transparent than customer–dealer trading in round I. Alternatively, we could generate greater transparency in interdealer trading by including multiple rounds of interdealer trading with random assignment, but such a formulation of the model would be much less tractable.

[6] It is tempting to think that the broker plays no real role in the model because he simply quotes the same price as dealers in rounds II and III, but this is not the case. In round III, the presence of the broker allows each dealer to hold no FX inventory overnight, consistent with the efficient risk-sharing allocation, even though each dealer is left with different holdings after filling customer orders. In round II, the broker absorbs the imbalance of trades among dealers so that in aggregate they can achieve their desired FX holdings. For a further discussion of the broker's role, see Chapter 6 in Evans (2011).

*Days without macro data releases.* When all market participants act to maximize expected utility defined over future wealth, the equilibrium of the model is summarized as follows:

1. All dealers quote the same price for FX in each round of trading, that is, $S^i_{d,t} = S^i_t$ for $i = \{\text{I, II, III}\}$. The broker quotes the same price as dealers in rounds II and III. Common quotes are given by

$$S^{\text{I}}_t = S^{\text{III}}_{t-1} - \lambda_{\text{A}} A_{t-1} + \frac{1}{r} V_t, \tag{3.14}$$

$$S^{\text{II}}_t = S^{\text{I}}_t, \qquad \text{and} \tag{3.15}$$

$$S^{\text{III}}_t = S^{\text{II}}_t + \lambda_{\text{A}} A_{t-1} + \lambda_{\text{X}}(X_t - \mathbb{E}[X_t|\Omega^{\text{II}}_t]), \qquad \lambda_{\text{X}} > 0 \tag{3.16}$$

where $A_{t-1}$ denotes investors' aggregate holding of FX at the end of day $t-1$, and $\Omega^{\text{II}}_t$ denotes common information of dealers and the broker at the start of round II.

2. The trades initiated by dealer $d$ in round II are

$$T^{\text{II}}_{d,t} = \alpha_{\text{Z}} Z^{\text{I}}_{d,t} + \alpha_{\text{A}} A_{t-1}, \tag{3.17}$$

and the customer orders received by dealer $d$ in round I are

$$Z^{\text{I}}_{d,t} = (\beta/\text{D}) Y_t + \varepsilon_{d,t}, \qquad \beta < 0 \tag{3.18}$$

where $\sum_{d=1}^{\text{D}} \varepsilon_{d,t} = 0$.

There are several noteworthy features of this equilibrium. First, consider its implications for the behavior of the spot exchange rate at the daily frequency:

$$S^{\text{III}}_t - S^{\text{III}}_{t-1} = \frac{1}{r} V_t + \lambda_{\text{X}}(X_t - \mathbb{E}[X_t|\Omega^{\text{II}}_t]). \tag{3.19}$$

Daily changes in the spot exchange rate are driven by shocks to dividends and unexpected interdealer order flow. The former reflect the effects of public news while the latter conveys information that was initially dispersed across investors and was then aggregated via trading in the FX market.

Dividend shocks play a familiar role in the determination of the spot rate. Realizations of $V_t$ are public information and affect the forecasts of future dividends by all dealers and investors in exactly the same way. Consequently, it should come as no surprise that $V_t$ shocks are immediately reflected in the equilibrium spot rate.[7] That said, it is important to remember that quotes are chosen optimally in this model, so $V_t$ shocks only affect the spot rate because dealers have an incentive to adjust their quotes once the value of $V_t$ is known (Eq. 3.14).

[7]When viewed from the perspective of our decomposition in Equation (3.6), $V_t$ drives the spot rate via the second and third terms on the right-hand side.

The role played by aggregate interdealer order flow in Equation (3.19) is more complex. Notice that it is unexpected interdealer order flow that affects the exchange rate in Equation (3.19). The reason is that dealers adjust their quotes between rounds II and III to account for the new information contained in aggregate interdealer order flow (Eq. (3.16)). The customer orders received by each dealer reflect the difference between the desired and actual FX positions of individual investors. As such, they convey information to dealers about both the current income and the overnight positions of a subset of investors. This information is effectively shared between dealers via interdealer trading in round II. As a result, $X_t$ conveys information about aggregate income and the prior overnight FX position of all investors. Since the latter is already known to dealers, $X_t - \mathbb{E}[X_t|\Omega_t^{\text{II}}]$ is proportional to the new information concerning income that is incorporated into the round III quote, $S_t^{\text{III}}$.

Of course, the mere fact that unexpected interdealer order flow conveys new information about aggregate income to dealers does not explain why $X_t - \mathbb{E}[X_t|\Omega_t^{\text{II}}]$ appears in Equation (3.19). For that, we need to understand why dealers find it optimal to incorporate the new income information they learn into their common round III quote. In short, why is information on aggregate income, $Y_t$, relevant for the pricing of FX? The answer is quite simple. As in the actual market, dealers do not want to hold FX overnight—the risk of holding FX can be shared more efficiently by investors than by individual dealers. Consequently, each dealer's aim in round III is to quote a price that will induce investors to purchase all the FX currently held by dealers. In other words, the round III quote is chosen so that the excess overnight return expected by investors is such that they want to hold the entire existing stock of FX. Obviously, this would not be possible unless all dealers can calculate what the existing stock of FX is. However, since investors' income is the only source of FX, the existing stock can be computed from the history of aggregate income. Thus, information on $Y_t$ is price-relevant, because it reveals to dealers what aggregate overnight FX position investors must be induced to hold.[8] In sum, interdealer order flow conveys information about the shift in the FX portfolios of investors needed to achieve efficient risk sharing. This is the origin of the term, *Portfolio Shifts*.

Another important feature of the model concerns timing. As we noted above, public news concerning current and future dividends is immediately and fully incorporated into the spot exchange rate. By contrast, it takes time for the information concerning income to be reflected in the dealer quotes. The reason for the delay is important. Information about income is originally transmitted to dealers via the customer orders they receive in round I (Eq. 3.18). Thus, each dealer has some information about $Y_t$ at the start of round II, but the information is imprecise. At this point, each dealer could choose to use their private information on $Y_t$ in setting their quote, but this is not optimal in the model's trading environment. Instead, their best strategy is to quote the same price as in round I (which is the same across all dealers and only a function

[8] In terms of the decomposition in Equation (3.6), unexpected order flow induces a change in the risk premium embedded in dealers' round III quotes, and so drives the spot rate via the last term on the right-hand side.

of common round I information), because to do otherwise would expose the dealer to arbitrage trading losses.[9] As a result, the equilibrium spot rate remains unchanged between rounds I and II even though dealers have information about aggregate income. The spot rate only incorporates this information when it becomes common knowledge among dealers. This process of information aggregation takes place via interdealer trading in round II. The best strategy of each dealer is to use their private information concerning income in determining the trade they wish to initiate with other dealers (Eq. 3.17). It is for this reason that interdealer order flow provides information on aggregate income that becomes common knowledge to dealers by the start of round III.

*Days with macro data releases.* On days with data releases (i.e., on days when everyone observes an estimate of aggregate foreign income, $Y_t^o$), the equilibrium of the model is summarized by the following:

1. All dealers quote the same price for FX in each round of trading, and the broker quotes the same price as dealers in rounds II and III. Common quotes are given by

$$S_t^{\text{I}} = S_{t-1}^{\text{III}} - \lambda_{\text{A}} A_{t-1} + \frac{1}{r} V_t - \lambda_{\text{I}} Y_t^o, \qquad \lambda_{\text{I}} > 0, \tag{3.20}$$

$$S_t^{\text{II}} = S_t^{\text{I}}, \qquad \text{and} \tag{3.21}$$

$$S_t^{\text{III}} = S_t^{\text{II}} + \lambda_{\text{A}} A_{t-1} + \lambda_{\text{III}} Y_t^o + \lambda_{\text{X}}^o (X_t - \mathbb{E}[X_t | \Omega_t^{\text{II}}]), \qquad \lambda_{\text{III}} > 0, \lambda_{\text{X}}^o > 0. \tag{3.22}$$

2. The trades initiated by dealer $d$ in round II are

$$T_{d,t}^{\text{II}} = \alpha_{\text{Z}} Z_{d,t}^{\text{I}} + \alpha_{\text{A}} A_{t-1} + \alpha_{\text{Y}} Y_t^o, \qquad \alpha_{\text{Y}} > 0, \tag{3.23}$$

   and the customer orders received by dealer $d$ are in round I are

$$Z_{d,t}^{\text{I}} = (\beta/\text{D})(Y_t - \kappa_{\text{D}} Y_t^o) + \varepsilon_{d,t}, \qquad \beta < 0, \tag{3.24}$$

   where $\mathbb{E}[Y_t | \Omega_t^{\text{I}}] = \kappa_{\text{D}} Y_t^o$ and $\Omega_t^{\text{I}}$ denotes common information of dealers and the broker at the start of round I.

The trade and exchange-rate dynamics described above differ in several important respects from those on non-release days. First, Equations (3.20) and (3.22) show that data releases directly affect the spot-rate quotes dealers make in rounds I and III. Second, data releases affect the pattern of trading in rounds I and II. In round I, the effects show up in the FX orders received by each dealer. In round II, they affect the size of the trade dealers initiate with each other. Data releases also affect the price-impact of interdealer order flow at the start of round III, as measured by the size of the $\lambda_{\text{X}}^o$ coefficient in Equation (3.22).

[9] Equation (3.14) shows that this quote embeds a risk premium of $\lambda_{\text{A}} A_{t-1}$, which also affects dealers' round II trades identified in Equation (3.17).

The intuition behind these results is straightforward. Recall that dealers choose $S_t^{\text{III}}$ using information on foreign income, $Y_t$, to achieve an efficient risk-sharing FX allocation at the end of each trading day. Dealers adjust $S_t^{\text{I}}$ in response to the release of $Y_t^{o}$, because it provides them with incremental information that is useful in forecasting $S_t^{\text{III}}$. They also adjust $S_t^{\text{I}}$ to manage risk. In particular, dealers recognize that the FX orders they receive in round I depend on the difference between investors' desired FX holdings and their existing holdings. They therefore adjust their quotes so as to offset the expected hedging effect of foreign income on investors FX orders. These actions have several important consequences. First, as Equation (3.18) shows, the spot rate immediately appreciates in response to a positive income release. Second, the change in quotes between rounds I and III contains a risk premium based on the data release:

$$S_t^{\text{III}} - S_t^{\text{I}} = \lambda_{\text{A}} A_{t-1} + \lambda_{\text{III}} Y_t^{o} + \lambda_{\text{X}}^{o}(X_t - \mathbb{E}[X_t | \Omega_t^{\text{II}}]). \tag{3.25}$$

The first term on the right-hand side is the risk premium dealers embed in their round I quotes on non-release days, the second shows the incremental premium induced by the release. When dealers observe a positive value for $Y_t^{o}$, they anticipate that investors' aggregate hedging demand for FX will be lower, so they embed a larger risk premium into their round I quotes to make holding FX more attractive to investors. Thus, in contrast with standard macro models, some of the exchange-rate effects of the data release are delayed beyond the release time because dealers have a risk-sharing incentive to adjust the risk premium embedded in their spot-rate quotes. Of course, this only happens here because the information contained in the data release is price-relevant but imprecise. If everyone knew that $Y_t^{o} = Y_t$, dealers would have all the information they needed to quote the efficient risk-sharing spot rate in round I, so that $S_t^{\text{I}} = S_t^{\text{III}}$.

Risk sharing also affects the behavior of order flows. Equation (3.24) implies that customer flows should not be correlated with data releases. The reason is that dealers have a strong risk-sharing incentive to adjust their spot-rate quotes immediately after the release to a level that makes customer order flows unforecastable. The idea that a data release containing bad news for the dollar should trigger positive customer order flow (i.e., customer orders to purchase FX) is simply inconsistent with dealers adjusting their quotes immediately following a data release in an efficient risk-sharing manner. Data releases have a different impact on interdealer flows. As Equation (3.23) shows, the round II trades initiated by each dealer depend on $Y_t^{o}$, and so could be forecast from public information available at the end of round I. This arises because dealers try to take advantage of the predictable change in spot rates between rounds II and III, $S_t^{\text{III}} - S_t^{\text{II}}$ (which equals $S_t^{\text{III}} - S_t^{\text{I}}$ because $S_t^{\text{II}} = S_t^{\text{I}}$). In short, interdealer order flows are forecastable because dealers have an risk-sharing incentive to make customer order flows unforecastable.

Data releases also affect the price-impact of order flow as measured by the $\lambda_{\text{X}}^{o}$ coefficient in Equation (3.22). Intuitively, on non-release days, unexpected order flow represents the first source of information on income all dealers receive, but on release days it is the second source. An unexpected order flow of a given size therefore conveys more new information to dealers on release than non-release days, so they adjust their round III quotes by a larger amount. Notice, also, that order flows on release days provide dealers with more precise information on foreign income than was present in the data release. Investors have an incentive to trade after they observe the data release, because their own foreign income provides them with more precise forecasts of future FX returns than dealers. So, it is through their trades that dealers finally learn the full price-relevance of the data release.

In sum, the discussion above makes clear that the predictions of a micro-based model concerning the exchange-rate effects of data releases differs from the traditional macro view. When a data release contains imprecise but price-relevant information, dealers adjust their spot-rate quotes to accommodate the new information on payoffs and the risk of providing liquidity to the market. This can produce predictable components in both order flows and spot-rate returns following data releases. Data releases also affect the transmission of information to dealers via order flow because they alter trading patterns across the market.

## 3.3.2 EMPIRICAL IMPLICATIONS

**3.3.2.1 Order Flows and FX Returns.** The empirical implications of the PS model were first investigated by Evans and Lyons (2002a). They considered regressions of the daily depreciation rate on interdealer order flow and the change in the nominal interest differential:

$$\Delta s_t = \beta_1 X_t + \beta_2 \Delta(r_t - r_t^*) + \zeta_t. \tag{3.26}$$

These regressions are motivated by Equation (3.19) with $\Delta s_t = s_t - s_{t-1}$, replacing $S_t^{\text{III}} - S_{t-1}^{\text{III}}$, and actual interdealer order flow, $X_t$, replacing $X_t - \mathbb{E}[X_t|\Omega_t^{\text{II}}]$. The first of these substitutions makes the empirical specification comparable to standard macro models but has no significant effect on the estimation results; the second is motivated by the assumption that expected interdealer order flow is zero.[10] The nominal interest differential is included to account for the arrival of public news.[11]

Table 3.1 reproduces regression results from Evans and Lyons (2002) for the DM/USD and JPY/USD spot rates between May 1 and August 31, 1996. Their data on interdealer order flow comes from the Reuters Dealing 2000-1 system. This was the dominant platform for interdealer trading at the time, accounting for approximately 90% of all direct dealer-to-dealer trades. Table 3.1 reports the coefficient estimates and standard errors in parenthesis for five versions of Equation (3.26).

[10]Evans and Lyons do not have information on the size of each transaction and so cannot measure true interdealer order flow (i.e., the difference in *value* between buyer-initiated and seller-initiated trades). However, since there is much less variation in the size of trades than in their direction, their measure for $X_t$ closely approximates true order flow across the market.

[11]Recall that the arrival of public news affects the spot rate via the second, third, and forth terms on the right-hand side of Equation (3.6).

TABLE 3.1 **Estimates of the Portfolio Shifts Model**

| | | Regressors | | | |
|---|---|---|---|---|---|
| | | $X_t$ | $\Delta(r_t - r_t^*)$ | $r_{t-1} - r_{t-1}^*$ | $R^2$ |
| DM/USD | I | $2.14^a$ (0.29) | 0.51 (0.26) | | 0.64 |
| | II | $2.15^a$ (0.29) | | | 0.63 |
| | III | | 0.62 (0.77) | | 0.01 |
| | IV | $2.15^a$ (0.29) | | $0.02^b$ (0.01) | 0.64 |
| | V | | | 0.02 (0.02) | 0.00 |
| JPY/USD | I | $2.86^b$ (0.36) | $2.47^b$ (0.92) | | 0.46 |
| | II | $2.61^b$ (0.36) | | | 0.40 |
| | III | | 0.57 (1.20) | | 0.00 |
| | IV | $2.78^a$ (0.38) | | $0.02^b$ (0.01) | 0.42 |
| | V | | | 0.01 (0.01) | 0.00 |

Notes: The table reports slope coefficients and standard errors.
[a]Statistical significance at the 1% level.
[b]Statistical significance at the 5% level.
*Source:* Evans and Lyons (2002b).

Three features of the estimation results are particularly noteworthy:

1. The coefficient on order flow, $X_t$, is correctly signed and significant, with $t$-statistics above 5 for both the DM/USD and JPY/USD. The positive sign indicates that net dollar purchases—a positive $X_t$–lead to a higher FX price for the dollar. For perspective, the estimated value of 2.1 for the order flow coefficient in the DM/USD equation translates to $1 billion of net purchases increasing the deutschemark price of a dollar by 0.8 pfennigs.
2. Almost all the explanatory power in the regressions is due to order flow. In specifications III and V, where order flow is omitted, the $R^2$ statistics are less than 1% in both the DM/USD and JPY/USD equations. Moreover, the explanatory power of order flow is extraordinarily high. The $R^2$ statistics of 64% and 45% for the DM/USD and JPY/USD equations that include order flow are an order of magnitude higher than those found in other exchange-rate models.
3. The coefficient on the change in the interest differential is correctly signed, but is only significant in the JPY/USD equation. The positive sign arises in the sticky-price monetary model, for example, because an increase in the US interest rate requires an immediate dollar appreciation (i.e., an increase in JPY/USD) to make room for UIP-induced expected dollar depreciation.

Figure 3.2 provides further perspective on the results in Table 3.1. Here the solid plots shows the path of the spot exchange rate over the 4-month sample. The dashed plot shows cumulative order flow over the same period measured

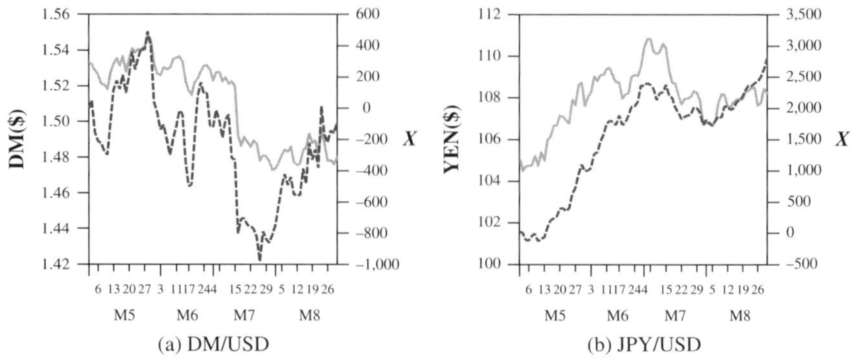


**FIGURE 3.2** Exchange rates (solid) and cumulative order flow (dashed). *Source:* Evans and Lyons (2002).

against the right-hand axis. Cumulative order flow is simply the sum of daily order flow, that is, $X_t^\infty = \sum_{i=1}^{t} X_i$. If all variations in spot rates reflected quote revisions driven only by order flow, the daily change in the spot rate should be proportional to daily order flow; that is, $S_t - S_{t-1} = \lambda_X X_t$. Under these circumstances, $S_t = \lambda_X X_t^\infty$ so the plots should coincide. Figure 3.2 shows that this in not quite the case. Nevertheless, it is hard not to be impressed by the close correspondence between exchange rates and order flow over this sample period.

Figure 3.2 highlights two further features of the relation between order flow and currency returns. First, although the expression in Equation (3.26) is estimated at the daily frequency, the estimation results have implications for the behavior of spot rates over much longer periods. In particular, since there is almost no serial correlation in daily depreciation rates, the $k$-day change in the log spot rate is well approximated by

$$s_t - s_{t-k} \cong \beta_1 X_t^k + \beta_2 \Delta^k (r_t - r_t^*) + \zeta_{t,k},$$

where $X_t^k = \sum_{i=0}^{k-1} X_{t-i}$ denotes order flow during the past $k$ days and $\beta_2 \Delta^k (r_t - r_t^*) + \zeta_{t,k}$ identifies the impact of public news arriving during the same period. Thus, the rate of depreciation over $k$ days will be well approximated by the cumulative effects of order flow, $X_{t,k}$, and the arrival of public news. Figure 3.2 shows that there are many instances where $s_t - s_{t-k} \cong \beta_1 X_t^k$ for significant horizons $k$. This evidence should help dispel the notion that micro-based models have little to say about exchange-rate behavior over macro-relevant time horizons.

The second feature concerns the dynamics of order flow. The plots of cumulative order flow in Figure 3.2 display no significant mean reversion because there is no detectable serial correlation in daily order flows. This feature of the data is important because the empirical specification in Equation (3.26) assumes that realizations of daily order flow represent news to dealers. Thus, daily order flow must be serially uncorrelated if the results in Table 3.1 are to be consistent with the predictions of the PS model.

The estimates in Table 3.1 are based on daily data from the Reuters D2000-1 trading platform—the dominant trading platform in 1996. Evans (2002) reported similar results studying intradaily data from the same source. Since 1996, the electronic brokers EBS and Reuters D2000-2 have taken over as the preferred medium for interdealer trading. However, the basic mechanism in the PS model still applies: interdealer trade is driven by dealers wishing to use the information they obtain from filling the currency orders of their customers. Research using data from the electronic brokers show that the results in Table 3.1 are robust to both frequency and sample period. Danielson and Love (2006); Payne (2003), and Berger et al. (2008) find similar results in intraday analysis, while Breedon and Vitale (2010), Chinn and Moore (2011), Killeen et al. (2006), and Berger et al. (2008) confirm the results for daily to quarterly frequencies.

The strong empirical link between interdealer order flows and daily changes in the spot exchange rate extends to different currencies with lower levels of liquidity than the deutschemark, euro, and yen. Evans and Lyons (2002b) study several smaller European currencies, Smyth (2009) examines the Australian and New Zealand dollar markets, while Scalia (2008) and Menkhoff and Schmeling (2008) study emerging markets such as Czech koruna and Russian ruble.

In the PS model, interbank order flow conveys price-relevant information to dealers that initially entered the market in dispersed form via the customer orders received by individual dealers. Consequently, if interdealer order flow is a proximate driver of exchange rates, as the studies cited above suggest, we should expect to find that customer order flows also have explanatory power in accounting for exchange-rate changes. This is indeed the case. Marsh and O'Rourke (2005) find such a result for major currencies, Bjønnes et al. (2005), King et al. (2010), and Rime (2001) for small open economies, and Gyntelberg et al. (2009), Onur (2008), and Wu (2007) for emerging markets.

The majority of the studies cited above use regressions similar to the Evans and Lyons regression in Equation (3.26). Some, like Payne (2003) and Menkhoff and Schmeling (2008), use the SVAR-approach of Hasbrouck (1991); and some, like Chinn and Moore (2011), Killeen et al. (2006), and Bjønnes et al. (2005), use the framework of cointegration. Despite these differences, all the studies conclude that positive order flow significantly leads to an appreciation of the foreign currency, and that variations in order flow are a major contributor to the variance of exchange-rate changes. To repeat, this is true both for major currencies and emerging market currencies, for interbank and for customer order flows, for recent data samples and data from mid-1990s, and for exchange-rate variations at intraday to quarterly frequencies.

**3.3.2.2 Order Flows and Macro Data Releases.** Empirical micro-based research on the effects of macro data release has taken several different forms. Love and Payne (2008) study transaction prices and order flows from the Reuters electronic brokerage system to study the impact of data releases on trading in the EUR/USD, EUR/GBP, and GBP/USD over 10 months in 1999 and 2000. When they use estimates of a VAR to compare the total effects of data releases on spot-rate changes with the indirect effects induced by order flows, they find that the indirect effects contribute between 30% and 60% of the variance. In other words, a significant fraction of the price-relevant information contained in data release becomes impounded into spot rates via order flow.

Evans and Lyons (2008) develop an alternative econometric model to study the intraday response of spot rates and order flows to data releases. In particular, consistent with the PS model discussed above, they allow the arrival of a data release to affect the process through which the information carried by order flow is impounded to FX quotes. Their results indicate that order flow contributes more to spot-rate adjustment following macro data releases than at other times. This is not what one would expect. If macro releases primarily contain precise information that is directly impounded into dealers' quotes, order flow should contribute less to spot-rate dynamics in the period following the release than at other times. In contrast, the results in Evans and Lyons (2008) strongly suggest that a macro data release triggers trading that reveals new information that affects spot rates indirectly.[12]

Evans and Lyons (2008) also use the PS model to examine the effects of data releases in daily data. As above, data releases affect dealers' quotes directly and indirectly via their impact on order flows. Evans and Lyons (2008) estimate that more than one-third of the total variance in daily spot-rate changes can be related to the direct and indirect effects of macro data releases and other news sources, with indirect effects contributing roughly 60% more than the indirect effects. These estimates clearly indicate that the indirect effects of news operating via order flow are an important component of spot-rate dynamics.

The results from conventional event studies suggest that all the detectable exchange-rate effects of data releases occur within a few minutes. However, this perspective changes when we account for the indirect effects of data releases on exchange rates operating via order flows. Using daily disaggregated customer order flow from Citibank, Evans and Lyons (2005) show that the indirect effects from news may take up to a week. The use of customer data in this study is important for at least two reasons: (i) Since order flow from customers is proprietary information, one would expect that it takes longer for customer trades to become common knowledge than for interdealer trades. (ii) Customers have more first-hand information than dealers about the real-time state of the economy, and hence their trading may be especially informative about the impact of macro releases. Evans and Lyons (2005) find that much of the protracted response of exchange rates to news comes via the order flows of leveraged investors—an end-user class that conducts extensive analysis of news and the macro economy (Bjønnes et al., 2010).

**3.3.2.3 Further Implications.** A number of studies have found that past changes in FX prices have forecasting power for order flows. For example, Danielsson and Love (2006) find highly significant coefficient estimates on lagged price changes in the order flow equation of their simultaneous equation

[12]These findings relate to earlier results in Evans (2002), Evans and Lyons (2002c), and Payne (2003), showing how the price-impact of order flow varies with the level of trading intensity.

model. There is also evidence of forecastability of customer flows at the daily frequency. Sager and Taylor (2008) find that daily customer order flow data from JPMorgan Chase can be predicted with prior FX returns. Do these results establish that order flows largely reflect the actions of dealers and customer following feedback trading strategies, and as such convey rather little new price-relevant information?

The answer to this question is clearly no. From a theoretical perspective, changes in FX prices can be solely driven by the information conveyed by order flow, which is itself forecastable using past changes in FX prices. Indeed, the PS model has precisely this combination of features. Interdealer order flows are the proximate driver of all the intraday changes in FX prices, but the interdealer order flow depends in part on the public pre-existing FX holdings that are correlated with lagged FX price changes. The key point here is that it is the unexpected portion of order flow that conveys the price-relevant information to dealers, so the fact that order flow is to some extent forecastable does not negate its role as a conveyor of price-relevant information.

That said, predictability in order flow can complicate inferences in regressions like Equation (3.26) because the use of actual order flow rather than its unpredictable component introduces "measurement error". Danielsson and Love (2006) show that when one takes account of this "measurement error" the impact from order flow is even higher. Intuitively, only the unexpected component of order flow conveys price-relevant information, so the estimated coefficient on total order flow is biased downwards. Bjønnes et al. (2005) and Killeen et al. (2006) provide some related evidence. They use error correction models to study whether order flows and exchange-rate changes are forecastable using the gap between the current rate and the rate implied by cumulated past order flows: $S_t - \lambda_{\mathrm{X}} X_t^{\infty}$. They find that the gap has forecasting power for future exchange-rate changes but not order flows. These results are consistent with the notion that order flows are a proximate determinant of exchange-rate changes because they convey information.

The PS shifts model also sheds light on the relationship between order flows and portfolio holdings. Recall that the risks of holding FX overnight are more efficiently shared by investors than by dealers, so the price of FX quoted by dealers at the end of each day reflects their desire to close out their existing FX positions. Now, dealers have sufficient information to precisely infer the price at which investors can be induced to hold the existing stock of FX. This means that the aggregate FX holdings of investors at the end of day $t$, $A_t$, follow $A_t = A_{t-1} + Y_t$, where $Y_t$ is aggregate foreign income the investors receive on day $t$. So, an estimate of the day $t$ order flow computed from the change in the foreign currency holdings of investors would be $A_t - A_{t-1} = Y_t$. This estimate differs from the actual order flow that drives spot-rate changes on day $t$. For example, on non-release days, Equation (3.16) implies that aggregate customer order flow from round I trading is $\sum_d Z^{\mathrm{I}}_{d,t} = \beta Y_t$, where $\beta < 0$. Thus, the position-based estimate of order flow is perfectly *negatively* correlated with true order flow. This problem is not specific to the PS model. It occurs whenever there is a frequency miss-match between transactions and the portfolio positions recorded in the data. Unfortunately, it is often overlooked when researchers use portfolio positions to estimate order flows (see, e.g., Froot and Ramadorai, 2005).

Accurate estimates of order flow also require information on the initiator of trade. Often, this information is unavailable, but it can be inferred from institutional knowledge. For example, for typical dealer–customer transactions (e.g., a mutual fund or corporation), the initiative will come from the end-user contacting the bank to ask for some FX quotes. Such inferences about the initiator of trade are impossible in the wholesale interbank market because trade can be initiated by any bank (either directly or indirectly via a market order on an electronic brokerage system). If trading takes place via a limit order market, Evans (2011) shows that it is impossible to accurately identify order flow from data on portfolio holdings without further information on how traders choose between limit and market orders.[13]

Although transactions in the retail FX market are typically initiated by end-users, two features of the market complicate the identification of customer order flow. First, in the past few years, some banks have given their largest customers direct access to the electronic brokerage systems that now dominate trading in the interbank market (e.g., EBS and Reuters 3000). These end-users now can submit both market and limit orders on the same terms as any bank, so it is no longer safe to assume that they are the initiators of every trade. The second complication arises from the use of stop-loss and take-profit orders by end-users. These price-contingent orders provide end-users with a close substitute to the limit orders available on the interbank brokerage systems, but make the identification of order flow from changes in portfolio holdings just as difficult as when end-users can submit limit orders.[14]

The PS model also clarifies how spot rates and order flows should be linked in the long run. Following the work of Hasbrouck (1991), it is common to equate permanent changes in asset prices with the embedding of information. For example, Payne (2003) estimates that more than 40% to the variance of permanent changes in log spot rates is attributable to order flow shocks. Consistent with this finding, Killeen et al. (2006) and Chinn and Moore (2011) show that cumulative interdealer order flow is cointegrated with log spot rates. Using customer data, Bjønnes et al. (2005) find evidence of cointegration while Froot and Ramadorai (2005) and Boyer and van Norden (2006) are using interdealer flows, not customer flows.

The PS model helps make sense of these results. In particular, the model implies that spot rates should be cointegrated with cumulated interdealer order

[13]Evidence from interbank dealers indicate that dealers use market orders when they regard themselves as informed (Bjønnes and Rime, 2005).

[14]The presence of the price-contingent orders need not lead to inaccurate estimates of order flow if purchases and sales of foreign currency implied by take-profit and stop-loss orders are well balanced over the range for spot rates in the data sample. Unfortunately, this does not appear to always be the case. Osler (2003) found that stop-loss buy orders are more strongly clustered above than below trigger points with round numbers, and the opposite is true for stop-loss sell orders. This means that estimates of order flow derived from portfolio holdings may be less accurate when the spot rate is the neighborhood a trigger point with round numbers.

flow because unexpected order flow permanently changes dealers quotes. At the same time, the PS model shows that there is no cointegrating relationship between spot rate and *aggregate* cumulated customer order flow. In equilibrium, investors hold the existing shock of FX at the end of each day, so cumulated customer order flows aggregated over rounds I and III are zero. This feature will be present in any micro-based model where dealers seek to allocate risk efficiently between themselves and other market participants. Consequently, a failure to find cointegration between cumulated customer order flows and spot rates is actually consistent with efficient risk sharing but uninformative about the role that order flow plays in the determination of spot rates. This implication need not apply to *disaggregated* customer flows. For example, suppose one group of end-users is overrepresented in round-I trading and underrepresented in round II. In that case, spot rates could be cointegrated with cumulated order flows of different end-users, as indicated by the results in Bjønnes et al. (2005).

Many papers interpret the empirical relation between exchange rates and order flows in terms of liquidity or information concerning fundamentals. For example, Bjønnes et al. (2011) and Marsh and O'Rourke (2005) argue that differential price-impact of order flow across counterparties is an indication that order flow carries fundamental information, while Froot and Ramadorai (2005) and Berger et al. (2008) suggest that the explanatory power of order flow primarily stems from liquidity disruptions. Assessing the validity of these interpretations is very difficult without a theoretical model that allows for both possibilities. In particular, the PS model shows how order flow conveys information about the hedging demands of investors (i.e., nonfundamental information) that has both short- (intraday) and long-term exchange-rate effects. Thus, classifying the type of information conveyed by order flow according to the persistence of its effects on FX prices is unlikely to be accurate. More generally, risk-averse dealers need to be compensated for the risk of providing liquidity to investors when their trades (in aggregate) convey information on fundamentals such as future interest rates. Consequently, it is hard to conceive of an empirically relevant trading model where a clear dichotomy exists between liquidity and information effects.

## 3.4 Exchange Rates, Order Flows, and the Macro Economy

Microstructure exchange-rate models, such as the PS model, are silent on the potential links between the macro economy and order flows, because they focus on the details of currency trading between different market participants rather than the macro economic factors that ultimately drive the individual trades. More specifically, all the information conveyed by order flow in the PS model concerns the risk premium dealers embed in their spot-rate quotes. Thus, from the perspective of the PS model, the correlation between depreciation rates and order flows observed in the data is attributable to the role that order flow plays in driving the last term on the right-hand side of Equation (3.6):

$$\begin{aligned}\Delta s_{t+1} &= r_t - r_t^* - (1-\mathbb{E}_t)\Delta(r_{t+1} - r_{t+1}^*) \\ &\quad + \frac{\rho}{1-\rho}(\mathbb{E}_{t+1} - \mathbb{E}_t)f_{t+1} + \frac{1}{1-\rho}(\mathbb{E}_{t+1} - \mathbb{E}_t)\sum_{i=2}^{\infty}\rho^{i-1}\Delta f_{t+i} \\ &\quad + \delta_t - (\mathbb{E}_{t+1} - \mathbb{E}_t)\sum_{i=1}^{\infty}\rho^{i-1}\delta_{t+i}.\end{aligned}$$

Clearly, this is a rather narrow perspective. The observed correlation between depreciation rates and order flows could also reflect the fact that order flow conveys information about current and future fundamentals (i.e., via the terms in the second row in the above equation). To address this possibility, recent micro-based research focuses on the role that order flow plays in conveying macro information. This research builds on two central ideas: (i) Only some of the macro information relevant for the current spot rate is publicly known at any point in time. Other information is present in the economy, but it exists in a dispersed microeconomic form. (ii) Since the spot rate literally is the price of FX quoted by dealers, it will only reflect dispersed information once it has been assimilated by dealers—a process that takes place via trading. Below, we provide an overview of a micro-based model developed by Evans and Lyons (2009), which incorporates these ideas and discusses its empirical implications.

### 3.4.1 A MICRO-BASED MACRO MODEL

The economy comprises two countries populated by a continuum of risk-averse agents, indexed by $n \in [0, 1]$; and D risk-averse dealers who act as market makers in the spot FX market.[15] We will refer to the home and foreign countries as the United States and Europe, so the log spot exchange rate, $s_t$, denotes the dollar price of euros. The only other actors in the model are the central banks (i.e., The Federal Reserve (FED) and the European Central Bank (ECB)), who conduct monetary policy by setting short-term nominal interest rates, $r_t$ and $r_t^*$.

**3.4.1.1 An Overview.** The model focuses on the currency trades between agents and dealers at a weekly frequency. At the start of week $t$, all dealers and agents observe a data release that provides information on the state of the economy several weeks earlier. Let $z_t$ denote a vector of variables that completely describe the state of the macro economy in week $t$. This vector contains variables that are directly observable, such as short-term interest rates, and others that only become publicly known with a lag. Each agent $n$ also receives private information concerning his/her current microeconomic environment: $z_t^n = z_t + v_t^n$, where $v_t^n = [v_{i,t}^n]$ is a vector of agent-specific shocks with the property that $\int_0^1 v_{i,t}^n dn = 0$

[15]We use the term *agents* rather than *investors* to emphasize the fact that the demand for foreign currency in this model can depend on more than just the speculative and hedging motives of investors.

for all $i$. Notice that the $z_t^n$ vector represents dispersed private information about macro conditions across the world economy.

Next, all dealers quote a log USD/EUR spot price equal to

$$s_t = \mathbb{E}_t^{\mathrm{D}} s_{t+1} + r_t^* - r_t - \delta_t, \tag{3.27}$$

where $\mathbb{E}_t^{\mathrm{D}}$ denotes expectations conditioned on the common information available to all dealers at the start of week $t$. This information set includes the histories of interest rates and data releases, and the order flows from earlier currency trading. Macro economic conditions affect dealers quotes in Equation (3.27) via their effects on current monetary policy (i.e., $r_t^* - r_t$), and via $\mathbb{E}_t^{\mathrm{D}} s_{t+1}$ insofar, as these expectations are affected by dealers' forecasts for the future interest differential. These forecasts are assumed to incorporate a view on how central banks react to changes in the macro economy, as shown in Equation (3.2) (with $\mathbb{E}_t^{\mathrm{D}}$ replacing $\mathbb{E}_t$):

$$\begin{aligned}\mathbb{E}_t^{\mathrm{D}}(\hat{r}_{t+i} - r_{t+i}) = (1+\gamma_\pi)\mathbb{E}_t^{\mathrm{D}}\left(\Delta p_{t+1+i}^* - \Delta p_{t+1+i}\right) \\ + \gamma_y \mathbb{E}_t^{\mathrm{D}}\left(y_{t+i}^* - y_{t+i}\right) - \gamma_q \mathbb{E}_t^{\mathrm{D}} q_{t+i}.\end{aligned} \tag{3.28}$$

As in the PS model, the risk premium in Equation (3.27) is determined by the requirements of efficient risk sharing. More specifically, in an economy where there is a finite number of risk-averse dealers and a continuum of risk-averse agents, dealers will choose $\delta_t$ such that their expected holdings of risky currencies at the end of week $t$ are zero. We assume that all dealers are located in the United States. They therefore choose the risk premium, $\delta_t$, such that their expected holdings of euros at the end of week $t$ equal zero. These holdings are determined by the history of order flow from all agents. In particular, let $X_{t+1}$ denote the aggregate of all orders from agents for euros received by dealers during week $t$ (i.e., customer order flow), so $I_{t+1} = -\sum_{i=0}^{\infty} X_{t+1-i}$ denotes the euro holdings of all dealers at the end of week-$t$ trading.[16] Efficient risk sharing requires that dealers chose a value for $\delta_t$ such that

$$\mathbb{E}_t^{\mathrm{D}} I_{t+1} = 0. \tag{3.29}$$

Dealers stand ready to fill the foreign currency orders of agents at their quoted price of $s_t$. Once agent $n \in [0, 1]$ observes $s_t$, they place their currency order with a dealer to fill their demand for euros. The order flow for euros from agent $n$ is therefore $\alpha_t^n - \alpha_{t-1}^n$ where $\alpha_t^n$ denotes the week-$t$ euro demand by agent $n$. This demand is given by

$$\alpha_t^n = \alpha_s\left(\mathbb{E}_t^n \Delta s_{t+1} + r_t^* - r_t\right) + h_t^n, \tag{3.30}$$

[16]We identify the order flow from week-$t$ trading with a subscript of $t+1$ to emphasize the fact that dealers cannot use the information it conveys until the start of week $t+1$.

where $\alpha_s > 0$ and $\mathbb{E}_t^n$ denotes expectations conditioned on the information available to agent $n$ after the spot rate is quoted at the start of week $t$. The demand for euros depends on the log excess return expected by the agent and a hedging term, $h_t^n$, that represents the influence of all other factors. Without loss of generality, we may assume that $h_t^n = \alpha_z z_t^n$, for some vector $\alpha_z$, where the vector $z_t^n$ describes the microeconomic environment of agent $n$. The aggregate demand for euros by agents is thus given by

$$\alpha_t = \int_0^1 \alpha_t^n \mathrm{d}n = \alpha_s(\overline{\mathbb{E}}_t^n s_{t+1} - s_t + r_t^* - r_t) + h_t, \tag{3.31}$$

where $\overline{\mathbb{E}}_t^n$ denotes the average of agents' expectations, $\overline{\mathbb{E}}_t^n s_{t+1} = \int_0^1 \mathbb{E}_t^n s_{t+1} \mathrm{d}n$, and $h_t = \alpha_z \int_0^1 z_t^n \mathrm{d}n = \alpha_z z_t$. Notice that the aggregate hedging demand, $h_t$, depends on the state of the macro economy, $z_t$.

For the remainder of the week, dealers trade among themselves. The model abstracts from the details of interdealer trade. Instead, consistent with the PS model, it assumes that all dealers learn the aggregate order flow that resulted from the earlier week-$t$ trades between agents and dealers. This order flow is determined by

$$X_{t+1} = \alpha_t - \alpha_{t-1}. \tag{3.32}$$

Equations (3.31) and (3.32) imply that order flow is driven by changes in the average of agents' expectations concerning future excess returns and the change in the aggregate hedging demand.

Several features distinguish this model from macro exchange-rate models. First, it incorporates the fact that dealers and agents have incomplete and different information about the current state of the macro economy. In contrast, traditional macro models assume that the full current state is common knowledge. Second, the spot rate includes a risk premium that dealers choose to manage risk efficiently. The factors that drive this risk premium in equilibrium are very different from those determining the risk premium in macro models. Third, the model identifies the determinants of order flows and the role they play as a driver of exchange rates. In contrast, currency-trading patterns play no role in exchange-rate determination in macro models.

**3.4.1.2 Equilibrium.** An equilibrium in this model comprises a sequence of spot rates and market-clearing order flows that support and are supported by the endogenous evolution of dealers' common information and agents' private information. Recall that dealers and agents observe current interest rates and the data releases containing information on past macro conditions. Dealers also obtain information from their observations on order flow that is endogenously determined by the trading decisions of agents. Similarly, each agent observes the endogenously determined spot rate together with their microeconomic environment.

Solving for equilibrium spot rates and order flows is complex. But, so long as public information about the current state of macro economy is incomplete, equilibrium order flows provide dealers with information about the macro economy that they will embed in the spot-rate quotes; information that was initially dispersed across agents as their observations on $z_t^n$.

In equilibrium, the weekly depreciation rate takes the same form as Equation (3.6):

$$\Delta s_{t+1} = r_t - r_t^* - (1 - \mathbb{E}_t^{\mathrm{D}})\Delta(r_{t+1} - r_{t+1}^*) + \frac{\rho}{1-\rho}(\mathbb{E}_{t+1}^{\mathrm{D}} - \mathbb{E}_t^{\mathrm{D}})f_{t+1} + \frac{1}{1-\rho}(\mathbb{E}_{t+1}^{\mathrm{D}} - \mathbb{E}_t^{\mathrm{D}})\sum_{i=2}^{\infty}\rho^{i-1}\Delta f_{t+i} + \delta_t - (\mathbb{E}_{t+1}^{\mathrm{D}} - \mathbb{E}_t^{\mathrm{D}})\sum_{i=1}^{\infty}\rho^{i-1}\delta_{t+i}. \tag{3.33}$$

Thus, order flow has the potential to drive the depreciation rate by revising dealers' expectations about fundamentals and the risk premia, $\delta_t$.

Recall that dealers choose $\delta_t$ so that $\mathbb{E}_t^{\mathrm{D}} I_{t+1} = 0$ where $I_{t+1} = I_t - X_{t+1}$, and market clearing requires that the aggregate order flow received by dealers during week-$t$ trading must equal the aggregate change in the demand for euros across all agents: $X_{t+1} = \alpha_t - \alpha_{t-1}$. These two conditions jointly imply that $I_{t+1} + \alpha_t = I_t + \alpha_{t-1} = I_1 + \alpha_0$. For clarity, we normalize $I_1 + \alpha_0$ to equal zero, so efficient risk sharing requires that $0 = \mathbb{E}_t^{\mathrm{D}}\alpha_t$. Combining this restriction with Equation (3.31) gives

$$0 = \alpha_s \mathbb{E}_t^{\mathrm{D}}(\overline{\mathbb{E}}_t^n s_{t+1} - s_t + r_t^* - r_t) + \mathbb{E}_t^{\mathrm{D}} h_t. \tag{3.34}$$

Since $\mathbb{E}_t^{\mathrm{D}}\Delta s_{t+1} + r_t^* - r_t = \delta_t$ from Equation (3.27), and $\mathbb{E}_t^{\mathrm{D}}\overline{\mathbb{E}}_t^n s_{t+1} = \mathbb{E}_t^{\mathrm{D}} s_{t+1} + \mathbb{E}_t^{\mathrm{D}}(\overline{\mathbb{E}}_t^n s_{t+1} - s_{t+1})$ by definition, the first term on the right of Equation (3.34) is equal to $\alpha_s\delta_t + \alpha_s\mathbb{E}_t^{\mathrm{D}}(\overline{\mathbb{E}}_t^n s_{t+1} - s_{t+1})$. We may therefore rewrite Equation (3.34) as

$$\delta_t = \mathbb{E}_t^{\mathrm{D}}[s_{t+1}^e - \frac{1}{\alpha_s}h_t], \tag{3.35}$$

where $s_{t+1}^e = s_{t+1} - \overline{\mathbb{E}}_t^n s_{t+1}$.

Equation (10.9) shows that dealers' choice for the risk premium depend on their estimates of: (i) the aggregate hedging demand for euros, $\mathbb{E}_t^{\mathrm{D}} h_t$; and (ii) the average error agents make when forecasting next week's spot rate, $s_{t+1}^e$. Intuitively, dealers lower the risk premium when they anticipate a rise in the aggregate hedging demand for euros, because the implied fall in the excess return agents' expect will offset their desire to accumulate larger euro holdings. Dealers also reduce the risk premium to offset agents' desire to accumulate larger euro holdings when they are viewed as being too optimistic (on average) about the future spot rate; that is, when $\mathbb{E}_t^{\mathrm{D}} s_{t+1} < \mathbb{E}_t^{\mathrm{D}}\overline{\mathbb{E}}_t^n s_{t+1}$.

In equilibrium, the aggregate order flow the dealers observe at the end of week-$t$ trading reflects the change in aggregate demand for foreign currency by agents between weeks $t-1$ and $t$: $X_{t+1} = \alpha_t - \alpha_{t-1}$. Since dealers know the history of order flow and $\alpha_{t-1} = \sum_{i=0}^{\infty} X_{t-i}$ by market clearing, $\alpha_{t-1} \in \Omega_t^{\mathrm{D}}$. Consequently, unexpected order flow from week-$t$ trading can be written as

$$X_{t+1} - \mathbb{E}_t^{\mathrm{D}} X_{t+1} = \alpha_z(z_t - \mathbb{E}_t^{\mathrm{D}} z_t) + \alpha_s(\overline{\mathbb{E}}_t^n s_{t+1} - \mathbb{E}_t^{\mathrm{D}}[\overline{\mathbb{E}}_t^n s_{t+1}]). \tag{3.36}$$

Thus, order flow contributes new information about the current macro economic conditions, $z_t$, via the aggregate hedging demand, $h_t - \mathbb{E}_t^{\mathrm{D}} h_t = \alpha_z(z_t - \mathbb{E}_t^{\mathrm{D}} z_t)$, and about the average of agents' spot-rate forecasts, $\overline{\mathbb{E}}_t^n s_{t+1}$. These forecasts will embed agents' private expectations concerning future interest rates and the macro economic conditions that affect monetary policy.

Equations (10.9) and (3.36) shed light on the role that heterogeneous information plays in the behavior of the risk premium and order flow. In particular, if agents and dealers have the same spot-rate forecasts (i.e., $\mathbb{E}_t^{\mathrm{D}} s_{t+1} = \mathbb{E}_t^n s_{t+1}$ for all $n \in [0, 1]$), $\mathbb{E}_t^{\mathrm{D}} s_{t+1}^e = 0$ and $\overline{\mathbb{E}}_t^n s_{t+1} = \mathbb{E}_t^{\mathrm{D}}[\overline{\mathbb{E}}_t^n s_{t+1}]$ so Equations (10.9) and (3.36) imply that $\delta_t = -\frac{1}{\alpha_s}\mathbb{E}_t^{\mathrm{D}} h_t$ and $X_{t+1} - \mathbb{E}_t^{\mathrm{D}} X_{t+1} = h_t - \mathbb{E}_t^{\mathrm{D}} h_t$. Here, the risk premium only varies with dealers' estimate of the aggregate hedging demand and order flow simply reflects their estimation error. Under other circumstances, heterogeneity among dealers' and agents' spot-rate forecasts contribute to the variations in the risk premium via $\mathbb{E}_t^{\mathrm{D}} s_{t+1}^e$ and unexpected order flow via $\alpha_s(\overline{\mathbb{E}}_t^n s_{t+1} - \mathbb{E}_t^{\mathrm{D}}[\overline{\mathbb{E}}_t^n s_{t+1}])$.

## 3.4.2 EMPIRICAL IMPLICATIONS

**3.4.2.1 Order Flows and Current Macro Conditions.** Consider the behavior of excess returns, $er_{t+1} = \Delta s_{t+1} + r_t^* - r_t$. Combining this definition with Equations (3.33) and (3.35) gives

$$\begin{aligned} er_{t+1} &= \delta_t + (1 - \mathbb{E}_t^{\mathrm{D}})(r_{t+1}^* - r_{t+1}) \\ &\quad + (\mathbb{E}_{t+1}^{\mathrm{D}} - \mathbb{E}_t^{\mathrm{D}}) \sum_{i=2}^{\infty} \rho^{i-1}\left(f_{t+i} - \frac{1}{\rho} s_{t+i}^e - \frac{1}{\rho\alpha_s} h_{t+i-1}\right). \end{aligned} \tag{3.37}$$

Notice that the second and third terms on the right-hand side depend on the flow of information reaching all dealers between the start of weeks $t$ and $t + 1$. This information flow comprises observations on current interest rates; data releases on past macro variables; and order flow from week-$t$ trading, $X_{t+1}$. Equation (3.37) implies that any of these information sources will affect the excess returns insofar as they convey new information on current monetary policy, future fundamentals, and the risk premia. Thus, the model attributes the strong correlation between foreign currency returns and order flows observed in the data to the important role that order flow plays in this information transmission process.

Following Evans (2010), we can examine this implication of the model with a two-step regression procedure. In the first step, we regress a macro variable $\varkappa_t$ on the cumulation of current and past order flows, $X_{t+1}^{\infty} = \sum_{i=0}^{\infty} X_{t+1-i}$. Under efficient risk sharing $X_{t+1}^{\infty} = X_{t+1} - \mathbb{E}_t^{\mathrm{D}} X_{t+1}$, so the regression coefficient on $X_{t+1}^{\infty}$ should be statistically significant if unexpected order flow from week-$t$ trading contains information about macro variable $\varkappa_t$. In the second step, we regress excess returns on the predicted values from the first stage. The estimated slope coefficient in this regression should be statistically significant when the information concerning $\varkappa_t$ conveyed by order flow is price-relevant.

Table 3.2 reproduces the results from estimating the second-stage regression as reported in Evans (2010). The dependent variable is the excess return on the USD/EUR rate over a 4-week horizon. The independent variables in Panel A are the predicted values from regressions of GDP growth, CPI inflation, and M1 growth in the United States and Germany on cumulated customer order flows for euros received by Citibank. In panel B, the independent variables are the differences between the predicted values for the German and US macro variables. The regressions are estimated at the weekly frequency in data from January 1993 to June 1999.[17]

**TABLE 3.2 Excess Returns and Macro Information**

| | GDP | | CPI | | M1 | | |
|---|---|---|---|---|---|---|---|
| | German | US | German | US | German | US | $R^2$ |
| A: | | | | | | | |
| | 0.14 | −0.68** | | | | | 0.10 |
| | (0.11) | (0.10) | | | | | |
| | | | 0.50** | 0.51** | | | 0.11 |
| | | | (0.20) | (0.11) | | | |
| | | | | | 0.12 | −0.70** | 0.19 |
| | | | | | (0.07) | (0.14) | |
| | 0.14 | −0.11 | −1.14 | 0.48 | 1.65 | 0.69 | 0.29 |
| | (1.90) | (0.80) | (1.45) | (0.83) | (2.28) | (1.15) | |
| B: | | | | | | | |
| | 0.43** | | | | | | 0.15 |
| | (0.08) | | | | | | |
| | | | −0.17** | | | | 0.04 |
| | | | (0.04) | | | | |
| | | | | | 0.26** | | 0.11 |
| | | | | | (0.04) | | |
| | 0.90** | | 0.52** | | 0.19 | | 0.23 |
| | (0.43) | | (0.25) | | (0.30) | | |

Notes: The table reports slope coefficients and standard errors from the second-stage regression using the predicted values for the variables listed at the head of each column. Estimates are calculated at the weekly frequency. The standard errors correct for heteroskedasticity and an MA (3) error process. Statistical significance at the 5% and 1% level is denoted by * and **, respectively.
*Source:* Evans (2010)

[17] Obviously, the macro time series examined are not available at a weekly frequency, so the weekly series for $\varkappa_t$ must first be constructed from a time-series model. The procedure is described in Evans (2010).

The results in Table 3.2 provide strong support for the idea that order flows convey price-relevant information about GDP, prices, and the money stock. The slope coefficients for German inflation, US GDP growth, inflation, and monetary growth are all significant at the 1% level. Insofar, as spot rates reflect the difference between US and EU monetary policy, order flows should carry more price-relevant information about the difference in macro economic conditions between countries. This seems to be the case. As Panel B shows, the slope coefficients on the predicted values for GDP growth and inflation are highly significant. These findings are supported by results in Rime et al. (2010). They show that interdealer order flow has forecasting power for specific macro data releases scheduled in the next week. For example, positive euro order flow forecasts a higher than previously anticipated data release in cases where positive releases are associated with an appreciation of the euro.

**3.4.2.2 Order Flows and Future Macro Conditions.** The model also holds implications for the links between the dynamics of spot rates, order flows, and the future evolution of the macro economy. In particular, dealers' equilibrium quotes can be written as

$$s_t = \bar{s}_t + \frac{1}{1-\rho}\mathbb{E}_t^{\mathrm{D}} \sum_{i=1}^{\infty} \rho^i (\Delta f_{t+i} - \Delta \delta_{t+i}) \tag{3.38}$$

where

$$\bar{s}_t = (r_t^* - r_t) + \frac{\rho}{1-\rho}\mathbb{E}_t^{\mathrm{D}} f_t - \frac{1}{1-\rho}\delta_t.$$

This equation splits the factors affecting dealers' spot-rate quotes into two terms. Current conditions such as interest rats and dealer's estimates of week-$t$ fundamentals affect dealers' quotes via $\bar{s}_t$. Expected changes in future conditions (i.e., inflation, the output gaps, and the risk premium) affect the spot rate via the second term. It is this term that provides the link between spot rates, order flows, and the future path of macro variables.

Equation (3.38) implies that $s_t - \bar{s}_t$ will have forecasting power for any future macro variable, $\varkappa_{t+\tau}$, if dealers expectations, $\mathbb{E}_t^{\mathrm{D}} \varkappa_{t+\tau}$, are correlated with $\mathbb{E}_t^{\mathrm{D}}(\Delta f_{t+i} - \Delta \delta_{t+i})$. Intuitively, dealers will raise their spot-rate quotes relative to $\bar{s}_t$ when their forecasts of future changes in fundamentals increase, so if these forecast are correlated with $\mathbb{E}_t^{\mathrm{D}} \varkappa_{t+\tau}$, variations in $s_t - \bar{s}_t$ will have forecast power for $\varkappa_{t+\tau}$. Equation (3.38) also implies that order flow should generally have incremental forecasting power for future macro variables beyond that contained in $s_t - \bar{s}_t$. To understand why, consider the following identity:

$$\varkappa_{t+\tau} = \mathbb{E}_t^{\mathrm{D}} \varkappa_{t+\tau} + (\mathbb{E}_{t+1}^{\mathrm{D}} - \mathbb{E}_t^{\mathrm{D}}) \varkappa_{t+\tau} + (1 - \mathbb{E}_{t+1}^{\mathrm{D}}) \varkappa_{t+\tau}. \tag{3.39}$$

The first term on the right-hand side identifies dealers' expectations concerning $\varkappa_{t+\tau}$ based on the information they use to quote spot rates at the start of week $t$. The second term identifies the revision in dealers' forecasts between the start of weeks $t$ and $t+1$. The incremental forecasting power of order flow comes from this term, which, by construction, is uncorrelated with $\mathbb{E}_t^{\mathrm{D}} \varkappa_{t+\tau}$. In particular, any information conveyed by $X_{t+1} - \mathbb{E}_t^{\mathrm{D}} X_{t+1}$ concerning $\varkappa_{t+\tau}$ will lead dealers to revise their forecasts of $\varkappa_{t+\tau}$.

This implication of the model can be examined with a regression of $\varkappa_{t+\tau}$ on $s_t$ and other variables known to dealers at the start of week $t$ (as proxies for $\bar{s}_t$), and unexpected order flow from trades between dealers and agents during week $t$. The coefficients on the order flows should be statistically significant if they have incremental forecasting power for the macro variable in question. Furthermore, the portion of the predicted value for $\varkappa_{t+\tau}$ attributable to the order flows should make a significant contribution to the variance of $\varkappa_{t+\tau}$ if the information conveyed by the order flows is economically significant.

Figure 3.3 reproduces the plots from Evans and Lyons (2009) that show the variance contributions of Citibank's customer order flows together with 95% confidence bands for the six macro variables considered in Table 3.2 for horizons $\tau = 1, \ldots, 26$ weeks. In five of the six cases, the contributions rise steadily with the horizon and are quite sizable beyond one quarter. The exception is US GDP growth, where the contribution remains around 15% from the quarterly horizon onward. These plots clearly show that order flows have considerable forecasting power for the future flows of information concerning GDP growth, inflation, and M1 growth at all but the shortest horizons. Clearly, then, these order flows are carrying significant information on future macro economic conditions.

**3.4.2.3 Macro Drivers of the Risk Premium.** Micro-based models have novel implications concerning the behavior of excess currency returns that are related to the way dealers adjust the risk premium embedded in their FX quotes. To illustrate these implications, we combine the definition of excess returns with the identity, $s_{t+1} = \mathbb{E}_t^{\mathrm{D}} s_{t+1} + (s_{t+1} - \mathbb{E}_t^{\mathrm{D}} s_{t+1})$, and Equation (3.27) to give

$$\begin{aligned} er_{t+2} &= \delta_{t+1} + s_{t+2} - \mathbb{E}_{t+1}^{\mathrm{D}} s_{t+2} \\ &= \mathbb{E}_t^{\mathrm{D}} \delta_{t+1} + (\delta_{t+1} - \mathbb{E}_t^{\mathrm{D}} \delta_{t+1}) + (s_{t+2} - \mathbb{E}_{t+1}^{\mathrm{D}} s_{t+2}). \end{aligned} \tag{3.40}$$

This decomposition of returns holds true in any micro-based model irrespective of what determines interests rates and the aggregate hedging demand for foreign currency. We can therefore use it to think about the possible sources of forecastability for future excess returns.

The right-hand side of Equation (3.40) identifies two channels through which forecastability can occur. The first operates via dealers' expectations of next week's risk premium, $\mathbb{E}_t^{\mathrm{D}} \delta_{t+1}$. Any variable known to the dealers at the start of week $t$ could potentially be correlated with $\mathbb{E}_t^{\mathrm{D}} \delta_{t+1}$, and hence have forecasting power for $er_{t+2}$. Notice that this channel rules out any forecasting power for unanticipated order flow from week-$t$ trading because $X_{t+1} - \mathbb{E}_t^{\mathrm{D}} X_{t+1}$ cannot be correlated with $\mathbb{E}_t^{\mathrm{D}} \delta_{t+1}$.The second channel operates via the revision in dealer's estimate of the risk premium, $\delta_{t+1} - \mathbb{E}_t^{\mathrm{D}} \delta_{t+1}$. These revisions occur because dealers change their estimates of the aggregate hedging demand and/or the average error of agents forecasting the future spot rate. They may be triggered either by the arrival of public information at the start of week $t+1$ (e.g., an unanticipated change in interest rates or a macro announcement) or by the

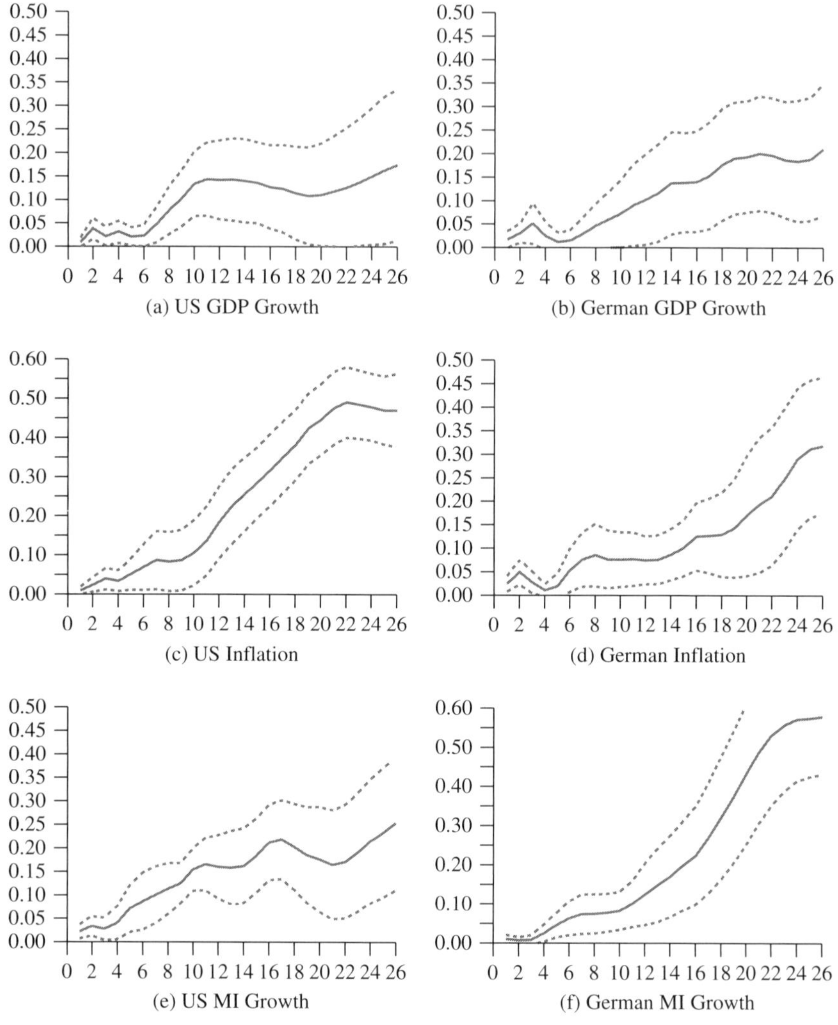


**FIGURE 3.3 Estimated contribution of order flows to the variance of future GDP growth, inflation, and M1 growth by forecasting horizon, $\tau$, measured in weeks. Dashed lines denote 95% confidence bands computed as $\pm 1.96\hat{\sigma}$, where $\hat{\sigma}$ is the standard error of the estimated contribution. *Source:* Evans and Lyons (2009).**

information conveyed by order flow from week $t$ trading, $X_{t+1} - \mathbb{E}_t^{\mathrm{D}} X_{t+1}$. In the latter case, order flow will have forecasting power for future excess returns.

Empirical evidence on the forecasting power of order flow for excess returns was first reported in Evans and Lyons (2007) and Evans and Lyons (2005). These papers examine the in-sample and out-of-sample forecasting power of six customer order flows in the USD/EUR market received by Citibank between January 1993 and June 1999. Evans and Lyons (2007) find that the within-sample forecasting power of these order flows rises with the forecasting horizon, accounting for 16% of returns at 4 weeks. By comparison, the forecasting power of interest differential is in the 2–4% range. There is, of course, a long tradition in the exchange-rate literature of considering out-of-sample forecasting performance. Evans and Lyons (2005) find that out-of-sample forecast using the Citibank order flows account for almost 16% of the sample variance in monthly spot-rate changes. Thus, the forecasting power of order flows appears truly significant from an economic perspective.

How do these empirical findings relate to the micro-based model? To address this question, Evans and Lyons (2009) employ a two-step regression procedure. In the first step, they regress future macro variables on the order flows. The predicted values from this regression are then used to forecast future excess returns. If the order flows contain information about the future macro variables used in the first stage, and that information is used by dealers to revise the risk premium embedded in their FX quotes, the coefficients on second-stage regression should be significant. This turns out to be the case. Evans and Lyons (2009) find that the order flows convey information about the future growth in M1 and in the M1/GDP ratio for the United States and Germany, which has forecasting power for the excess return on the USD/EUR. These findings provide a micro-based explanation for the forecasting results discussed above. They indicate that this forecasting power stems from the fact that order flows convey significant information about future macro economic conditions, specifically M1 and GDP growth, that dealers use to revise the risk premia they embed in their FX quotes.

## 3.5 Conclusion

Micro-based research over the past has made some significant progress toward providing exchange-rate models with empirically relevant microfoundations but much remains to be done. Although empirical research examines the role of order flow in exchange-rate determination spans many currencies, trading mechanisms, and time periods, to date most theoretical research has focused on understanding the behavior of major currency markets with lots of trading activity, such as the USD/EUR and USD/JPY markets. Existing models are less well suited for studying the behavior of exchange rates between other currencies that trade with much less liquidity. Since the currencies of most countries fall into this category, adapting micro-based models to these markets is an important priority for future research. The models also need to expand their focus beyond the spot markets. Trade in forward contracts, currency swaps, and other exchange-rate derivatives account for a large share of FX trading activity, but this portion of the FX market has yet to be studied from a micro-based perspective. This will surely change as data from electronic trading systems becomes more accessible to researchers. Finally, micro-based models hold significant potential for studying the onset and effects of the 2008 world financial crisis on exchange rates and international financial markets.

## APPENDIX

TABLE A **Overview of a Selection of Empirical Papers**

| | Orderflow | Source | Currencies | Period | Frequency |
|---|---|---|---|---|---|
| Berger et al. (2008) | Interbank indirect | EBS | USDEUR; JPYUSD | Jan 1999–Dec 2004 | 1 min to 3 months |
| Bjønnes et al. (2010) | Interbank | Reuters D2000-2 and EBS | USDEUR; DEMUSD | 2–6 Mar 1998; 2–20 Aug 1999 | Trans. time |
| Bjønnes et al. (2005) | End-user, disaggregated | Sveriges Riksbank | SEKEUR | 2 Jan 1994–28 Jun 2002 | Daily |
| Breedon and Vitale (2010) | Interbank indirect | Reuters D2000-2 and EBS | USDEUR | Aug 2000–mid-Jan 2001 | Daily |
| Chinn and Moore (2011) | Interbank indirect | EBS | USDEUR; JPYUSD | Jan 1999–Jan 2007 | Monthly |
| Daníelsson and Love (2006) | Interbank indirect (LSE II) | Reuters D2000-2 | USDEUR | 6 Oct 1999–24 July 2000 | 1 min, 5 min |
| Evans (2002) | Interbank direct | Reuters D2000-1 | DEMUSD | 1 May–31 Aug 1996 | 5 min |
| Evans (2010) | End-user, disaggregated | Citibank | USDEUR | Jan 1993–Jun 1999 | Weekly |
| Boyer and van Norden (2006), Evans and Lyons (2002a,b) | Interbank direct | Reuters D2000-1 | DEMUSD; USDGBP; JPYUSD; CHFUSD; FRFUSD; BEFUSD; ITLUSD and NLGUSD | 1 May–31 Aug 1996 | Daily |
| Evans and Lyons (2005a) | End-user, disaggregated | Citibank | USDEUR | 11 Apr 1993–30 Jun 1999 | Daily |
| Froot and Ramadorai (2005) | End-user | State Street | 18 currencies against USD | 20 Jun 1994–9 Feb 2001 | Daily |
| Gyntelberg et al. (2009) | End-user, disaggregated | Bank of Thailand | THBUSD | 1 Jan 2005–15 Dec 2006 | Daily |
| Killeen et al. (2006) | Interbank indirect | EBS | FFRDEM | Jan 1998–Dec 1998 | Daily |

| | | | | | |
|---|---|---|---|---|---|
| King et al. (2010) | End-user, disaggregated, and interbank | Bank of Canada | CADUSD | 1994–2005 | Daily |
| Love and Payne (2008) | Interbank indirect (LSE II) | Reuters D2000-2 | USDEUR; USDGBP; GBPEUR | 28 Sep 1999–24 Jul 2000 | 1 min |
| Marsh and O'Rourke (2005) | End-user, disaggregated | Royal Bank of Scotland | USD, EUR, JPY, and GBP (6 crosses) | 1 Aug 2002–29 Jun 2004 | Daily |
| Menkhoff and Schmeling (2008) | Interbank indirect | MICEX | RURUSD | 11 Mar–21 Mar 2002 | Full orderbook |
| Onur (2008) | End-user and interbank | Bank of Israel | Israeli Sheqel/Dollar (NISUSD) | Jun 2000–Jun 2006 | Daily |
| Osler (2003) | End-user price-contingent orders | Royal Bank of Scotland | USDEUR; USDGBP; JPYUSD | Aug 1999–11 Apr 2000 | Trans. time |
| Payne (2003) | Interbank indirect (LSE I) | Reuters D2000-2 | DEMUSD | 6–10 Oct 1997 | Trans. time |
| Rime et al. (2010) | Interbank indirect | Reuters D2000-2 | USDEUR; USDGBP; JPYUSD | 13 Feb 2004–14 Feb 2005. | Daily |
| Sager and Taylor (2008) | Interbank direct and end-user | (1) Reuters D2000-1 (Evans-Lyons JPE); (2) JP Morgan; (3) RBS | DEMUSD; JPYUSD; USDEUR; USDGBP; CHFUSD | 1) 1 May–29 Aug, 1996. (2) 1 Jan 1999–9 Jun 2003. (3) 1 Oct 2001–15 May 2003 | Daily |
| Scalia (2008) | Interbank indirect | Reuters D2000-2 | CZKEUR | 1 Jul–31 Dec 2002 | Hourly |
| Smyth (2009) | Interbank indirect | Reuters D2000-2 | NZDUSD; AUDUSD | Jan 2001–Mar 2006 | 1 s, daily, weekly |
| Wu (2007) | End-user and interbank | Bank of Brazil and PTAX | BRLUSD | 1 Jul 1999–30 Jun 2003 | Daily |

## 3.6 Acknowledgment

The views expressed here do not necessarily reflect those of Norges Bank.

## REFERENCES

Berger D, Chaboud A, Chernenko S, Howorka E, Wright J. Order flow and exchange rate dynamics in electronic brokerage system data. J Int Econ 2008; 75: 93–109.

Bjønnes GH, Osler CL, Rime D. Sources of information advantage in the foreign exchange market. typescript, Norges Bank; 2010.

Bjønnes GH, Rime D. Dealer behavior and trading systems in foreign exchange markets. J Financ Econ 2005; 75: 571–605.

Bjønnes GH, Rime D, Solheim HOA. Liquidity provision in the overnight foreign exchange market. J Int Money Finance 2005; 24: 177–198.

Boyer MM, van Norden S. Exchange rates and order flow in the long run. Finance Res Lett 2006; 3: 235–243.

Breedon F, Vitale P. An empirical study of portfolio-balance and information effects of order flow on exchange rates. J Int Money Finance 2010; 29: 504–524.

Burnside C, Eichenbaum M, Kleshchelski I, Rebelo S. The returns to currency speculation. Am Econ Rev 2007; 97: 333–338.

Cheung YW, Chinn MD, Marsh IW. How do U.K.-based foreign exchange dealers think their market operates? Int J Finance Econ 2004; 9: 289–306.

Cheung YW, Wong CYP. A survey of market practioners' views on exchange rate dynamics. J Int Econ 2000; 51: 401–419.

Chinn M, Moore M. Order flow and the monetary model of exchange rates: Evidence from a novel data set. J Money Credit Banking 2011. 43: 1599–1624.

Clarida R, Gali J, Gertler M. Monetary policy rules in practice some international evidence. Eur Econ Rev 1998; 42: 1033–1067.

Daníelsson J, Love R. Feedback trading. Int J Finance Econ 2006; 11: 35–53.

Engel C, West K. Taylor rules and the deutschmark–dollar real exchange rate. J Money Credit Bank 2006; 38: 1175–1194.

Evans MDD. FX trading and exchange rate dynamics. J Finance 2002; 57: 2405–2447.

Evans MDD. Order flows and the exchange rate disconnect puzzle. J Int Econ 2010; 80: 58–71.

Evans MDD. Exchange rate dynamics, Princeton Series in International Finance. Princeton NJ, USA: Princeton University Press; 2011.

Evans MDD, Lyons RK. Order flow and exchange rate dynamics. J Pol Econ 2002a; 110: 170–180.

Evans MDD, Lyons RK. Informational integration and FX trading. J Int Money Finance 2002b; 21: 807–831.

Evans MDD, Lyons RK. Time-varying liquidity in foreign exchange. J Monet Econ 2002c; 49: 1025–1051.

Evans MDD, Lyons RK. Do currency markets absorb news quickly? J Int Money Finance 2005a; 24: 197–217.

Evans MDD, Lyons RK. Meese-ogoff redux: micro-based exchange-rate forecasting. Am Econ Rev Pap Proc 2005b; 95: 405–414.

Evans MDD, Lyons RK. Exchange rate fundamentals and order flow. Working Paper 13151. National Bureau of Economic Research; 2007.

Evans MDD, Lyons RK. How is macro news transmitted to exchange rates? J Financ Econ 2008; 88: 26–50.

Evans MDD, Lyons RK. Forecasting exchange rate fundamentals with order flow. Working paper, Georgetown University; 2009.

Faust J, Rogers J, Wang S, Wright J. The high-frequency response of exchange rates and interest rates to macro economic announcements. J Monet Econ 2007; 54: 1051–1068.

Froot KA, Ramadorai T. Currency returns, intrinsic value, and institutional-investor flows. J Finance 2005; 60: 1535–1566.

Gyntelberg J, Loretan M, Subhanij T, Chan E. International portfolio rebalancing and exchange rate fluctuations in Thailand. Working Paper 287; BIS; 2009.

Hasbrouck J. Measuring the information content of stock trades. J Finance 1991; 46: 179–207.

Killeen WP, Lyons RK, Moore MJ. Fixed versus flexible: lessons from EMS order flow. J Int Money Finance 2006; 25: 551–579.

King M, Sarno L, Sojli E. Timing exchange rates using order flow: the case of the loonie. J Bank Finance 2010; 34: 2917–2928.

Love R, Payne R. Macro economic news, order flows and exchange rates. J Financ Quant Anal 2008; 43: 467–488.

Lyons RK. A simultaneous trade model of the foreign exchange hot potato. J Int Econ 1997; 42: 275–298.

Mark N. Changing monetary policy rules, learning, and real exchange rate dynamics. J Money Credit Bank 2009; 41: 1047–1070.

Marsh IW, O'Rourke C. Customer order flow and exchange rate movements: Is there really information content? Working paper, Cass Business School; 2005.

Menkhoff L, Schmeling M. Local information in foreign exchange markets. J Int Money Finance 2008; 27: 1383–1406.

Obstfeld M, Rogoff K. The six major puzzles in international macro economics: I there a common cause? NBER Macro economics Annual 2000; 2001.

Onur E. The role of asymmetric information among investors in the foreign exchange market. Int J Finance Econ 2008; 13: 368–385.

Osler CL. Currency orders and exchange-rate dynamics: explaining the success of technical analysis. J Finance 2003; 58: 1791–1821.

Payne R. Informed trade in spot foreign exchange markets: an empirical investigation. J Int Econ 2003; 61: 307–329.

Rime D. Trading in foreign exchange markets. [PhD dissertation]. Norway: Norwegian School of Management; 2001.

Rime D, Sarno L, Sojli E. Exchange rate forecasting, order flow and macro economic information. J Int Econ 2010; 80: 72–88.

Sager M, Taylor MP. Commercially available order flow data and exchange rate movements: caveat emptor. J Money Credit Bank 2008; 40: 583–625.

Scalia A. Is foreign exchange intervention effective? Some microanalytical evidence from the Czech Republic. J Int Money Finance 2008; 27: 529–546.

Smyth N. Order flow and the exchange rate changes: A look at the NZD/USD and AUD/USD. Discussion Paper 2009/03, Reserve Bank of New Zealand; 2009.

Wu T. Order flow in the south: anatomy of the Brazilian FX market. typescript, UC Santa Cruz; 2007.

CHAPTER FOUR

# The Exchange Rate in a Behavioral Finance Framework

**PAUL DE GRAUWE**
University of Leuven

**PABLO ROVIRA KALTWASER**
University of Leuven

## 4.1 Introduction

### 4.1.1 MAINSTREAM EXCHANGE RATE MODELS

Ever since the breakdown of the Bretton Woods system in the early 1970s, exchange rate economics became a popular field in economic research. The start of the era of floating exchange rates opened a niche not only for economists but also for policy makers to experiment with new rules, and for financial market practitioners to deal, and ideally make some profits, in the foreign exchange market.

The beginning of the 1970s also coincides with the rapid propagation of the new paradigm of rational expectations (RE) in macroeconomic and finance modeling. Not surprisingly, exchange rate models have been strongly influenced by this intellectual framework, such that as of today the majority of the exchange rate models are based on RE. RE models offer several appealing advantages compared to previous economic theories. Most importantly, they allow the introduction of micro foundations in economic modeling, which means that

*Handbook of Exchange Rates*, First Edition. Edited by Jessica James, Ian W. Marsh, and Lucio Sarno.

decisions made at the individual level are based on optimal forecasts using all available information. As a consequence, in these models, individuals never make systematic mistakes (Sargent and Wallace, 1973; Sargent, 1979; Galí, 2008).

Despite the elegance and popularity of RE models, the validity of this framework has not been free of criticism. The FOREX market provides large amounts of data, and this has opened the possibility to test the validity of theoretical models using many different techniques. Far from giving a conclusive support to the RE paradigm, many puzzling contradictions between the theory and the empirical data have emerged. RE models have, to a large extent, not been able to provide fully satisfactory answers to these puzzles.

To understand why RE models fail to explain several empirical regularities, the framework has been put under the microscope to see where exactly the problems reside. One line of criticism has come surprisingly not from economics but from psychological sciences. Psychologists, and more recently so-called behavioral economists and neurologists alike, have systematically found inconsistencies between the assumptions typically made by economists and the way in which humans actually do behave. Put differently, the homo economicus hypothesis has been challenged Della Vigna and Malmendier (2006), Kahneman and Thaler (2006, 1979), Kahneman et al. (1997, 2003).

A second line of criticism leveled against the RE models concerns the underlying assumption that individual agents are capable of understanding the complexity of the underlying model. Indeed, in RE models, these agents are assumed to use all available information, including the information embedded in the model and the statistical distribution of the shocks hitting the economy. This assumption implies that agents posses incredible cognitive capacities. In reality, individual agents only know and understand a tiny part of the whole "Truth".

A logical implication of RE models is that since there is only one Truth, every agent endowed with RE will make the same optimal plans, and therefore, they will make the same forecasts.[1] Thus it suffices to model only one agent, the representative agent. The use of the representative agent approach robs macroeconomics of much of its specificity. Macroeconomics is about the dynamics that arises when there is heterogeneity, for example, when agents make different forecasts driven by different beliefs. Clearly the representative agent assumption neglects all interactions between agents. The interactions between agents are important in economic modeling, for there are situations that make it possible to think that the dynamics at the aggregate level do not necessarily have to coincide with an optimal behavior at the level of every individual. This is of course nothing else than the definition of the fallacy of composition (Caballero, 1992).

[1] Strictly speaking, it is possible to define several representative agents by assuming that they have access to different information sets and they are rational and form their expectations within the information set available to them (see the literature on rational inattention pioneered by Sims (2010)). Still, however, in this literature, it is normally not allowed for agents to switch information sets. See also Bacchetta and van Wincoop (2003, 2010).

### 4.1.2 AWAY FROM THE MAINSTREAM

Are there alternatives to mainstream exchange rate models? We believe yes. In this chapter, we discuss other approaches to modeling the foreign exchange market. Our basic assumption will be that agents have cognitive limitations, that is, they understand only a small part of the complex world they live in. As a result, they use simple rules to form expectations (heuristics). This does not mean that they are irrational. We introduce rationality into the analysis by assuming that agents are willing to learn, that is, they select the rules based on some fitness (utilitaristic) criterion. This selection mechanism is the discipline that is imposed on the behavior of agents so as to avoid "that everything becomes possible."

Our modeling approach belongs to the literature of agent-based models. In the past 10 years or so, agent-based models have notoriously gained visibility in economics. Several reasons explain this development. While in its beginning, behavioral economics represented only a minor niche outside mainstream economic thinking, today, it represents one of the most active fields of research within economics. This has led to a rebalancing among researchers from a fully rational view of the world to a more boundedly rational form. At the same time, research fields, located mostly in the microeconomic part of the spectrum, have carried out a major reorientation to include the views and findings of behavioral economics. To conclude, the fact that traditional models have not been able to offer fully convincing explanations to several puzzles has led researchers to consider alternative modeling approaches. All this has opened the possibility for agent-based models to enter economics and establish itself as a research field that can provide several contributions in many areas of the economic profession.

The literature on agent-based models has increased over the years. The first paper to develop an agent-based model of the exchange rate was by Frankel and Froot (1986, 1990a, 1990b). Several of the elements of the model that we present here can be traced back to their work. Since then, many alternative models have been proposed and they have become more involved, as they study different phenomena. Kirman (1991), for instance, develops a model of opinion formation as a source of speculative bubbles in the foreign exchange market, Westerhoff (2003a) and Wieland and Westerhoff (2005) analyze the role of central bank interventions in the FOREX market, De Grauwe and Grimaldi (2005) investigate the role of transaction costs on the exchange rate dynamics, Westerhoff and Manzan (2004) study the link between liquidity in the FOREX market and volatility, and Manzan and Westerhoff (2005) study the role of news on the exchange rate dynamics.[2]

A common feature among several papers of the agent-based literature, not only applied to exchange rate models but also to financial markets in general, is the emergence of complex dynamics. Beja and Goldman (1980) and Chiarella (1992) were probably the first to present a model where limit cycles emerged out the interactions of agents. Brock and Hommes (1997), Chiarella et al. (2006), Day and Huang (1990), De Grauwe et al. (1993), Gaunersdorfer (2000), and

[2]Chiarella et al. (2009), Hommes (2006), Lux (2009), and Westerhoff (2009) provide an excellent overview of the agent-based literature.

others have made important contributions showing how deterministic chaos can be an important source of endogenous asset price fluctuations.

In all these papers, the source for endogenous dynamics is the nonlinear nature of interactions between agents. Several approaches have been proposed in the literature. While Frankel and Froot (1986, 1990a, 1990b) introduce a market maker that uses a Bayesian mechanism to dynamically update the weights of chartists' and fundamentalists' forecasts in her own decision rule, Lawrenz and Westerhoff (2003) and Lux and Schornstein (2005) use a genetic algorithm to allow the weights of the different decision rules to vary over time. Using a different approach, Brock and Hommes (1997) introduce the discrete choice model in order to introduce time variability without the need to have a market maker. Alternatively, interactions of agents can be assumed to be governed by a stochastic process as, for instance, Föllmer (1974), Kirman (1991, 1993), Lux (1995, 1998), and Lux and Marchesi (1999, 2000).

The remainder of this chapter is organized as follows: We first discuss a number of well-known empirical puzzles in Section 4.2. We then present a prototype behavioral exchange rate model whose purpose is to mimic these empirical puzzles in Section 4.3. In Section 4.4, we briefly summarize the results of the incumbent literature of complex systems in economics. We conclude in Section 4.4.

## 4.2 Exchange Rate Puzzles

### 4.2.1 DISCONNECT PUZZLE AND EXCESS VOLATILITY PUZZLE

The first stylized fact of the foreign exchange market is composed of two phenomena related to one another. They are the so-called disconnect and excess volatility puzzles. Empirical evidence shows that the market exchange rate is systematically disconnected from its fundamental, and furthermore, that it is considerably more volatile than its fundamental as well.

Figure 4.1 shows this feature for the US Dollar–Euro/Deutsche Mark exchange rate. The upper panel displays the exchange rate level (continuous line) versus its fundamental (dashed line) for the period January, 1993 until February, 2003. The figure shows that the market exchange rate was systematically disconnected from its fundamental over the whole sample period. This fundamental is obtained by Ehrmann and Fratzscher (2005) using a SVAR model, linking the exchange rate to observable macroeconomic variables.

The lower panel of the same figure displays the (log) first differences of the two series shown in the upper panel, that is, the difference (in logs) of the exchange rate and the difference (in logs) of its fundamental between consecutive periods. The figure illustrates the excess volatility puzzle, which is closely related to the previous one. This second puzzle refers to the excess of volatility of the market exchange rate with respect to measures of its fundamental. Again, the

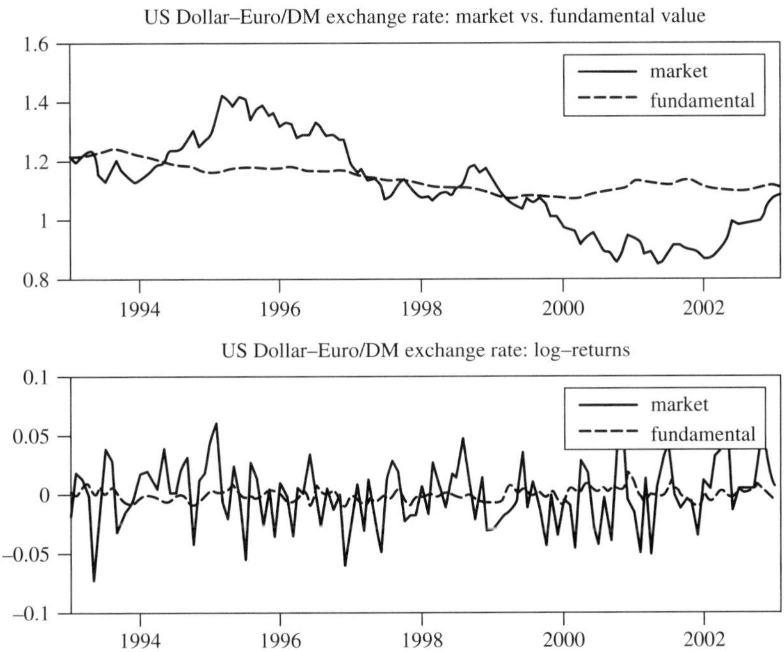


**FIGURE 4.1** Disconnect and excess volatility puzzles. *Source:* Ehrmann and Fratzscher (2005).

figure shown here does not represent a unique case, but rather the general picture that is found in the literature (Baxter and Stockman, 1989; Flood and Rose, 1995; Mussa, 1986).

One could object to the preceding evidence by arguing that since the fundamental exchange rate is not an observable variable, and therefore, has to be estimated, any measure of the fundamental will contain potentially large errors. As a result, if we observe that the market exchange rate is disconnected from the fundamental, this could be due to the fact that we have measured the fundamental incorrectly (e.g., because we used the wrong model of the fundamental). This objection looses much of its power, however, when one considers that the disconnect feature has been observed with many other measures of fundamentals, (Obstfeld and Rogoff, 2000; Taylor and Taylor, 2004). After decades of searching for the fundamentals driving the exchange, and finding that these have very little influence on the market exchange rate, it is fair to conclude that the disconnect puzzle is a robust phenomenon, in need of an explanation, rather than of a denial.

### 4.2.2 UNIT ROOT PROPERTY

The second empirical regularity is the unit root property of spot exchange rates. Assume that we have a series of past values of the market exchange rate, and we would like to forecast its future value. To obtain a forecast, we need to estimate the parameters of a statistical model that describes the relationship between past and future values of the exchange rate. To be more precise, let us define $e_t$ as the (log) exchange rate observed at time $t$. The simplest possible equation describing the dynamics of the exchange rate would be $e_t = \rho e_{t-1} + \varepsilon_t$, where $\varepsilon_t$ are random (stationary) innovations. Empirical estimates of the autoregressive parameter $\rho$ lie systematically around 1 (Cheung et al., 2005; Meese and Rogoff, 1983a,b; Mussa, 1979). Put differently, using standard econometric methods, such as the Dicky–Fuller test and variations of it, one is not able to reject the null hypothesis that the exchange rate level has a unit root. A value of the parameter $\rho = 1$ implies that $e_t = e_{t-1} + \varepsilon_t$, that is, that the exchange rate follows a random walk. Meese and Rogoff (1983a,b) provide strong evidence showing that no structural model of the exchange rate can reliably outperform the forecasting (in) capacity of a naive random walk at short- and medium-run horizons. Since their study, the random walk became the standard benchmark against which the forecasting performance of every exchange rate model is compared to.[3]

At this point, it is perhaps important to distinguish between the unit root property of exchange rates and the their predictability in the short versus the long run. The fact that empirical studies cannot reject the null hypothesis of a unit root on exchange rate data does not proof that the exchange rate level is not forecastable per se. Mark (1995) and Taylor and Taylor (2004), for instance, show evidence of long-run exchange rate predictability but no predictability in the short run. This should not be surprising perhaps, for according to the law of one price, the price of internationally traded goods should be the same everywhere once expressed in a common currency. As a consequence, one should expect that arbitrage in internationally traded goods eliminate, at least partially, deviations from the law of one price. This in turn should allow predicting the movement of the exchange rate in the long run. Additionally, it is possible that a cointegrating relationship governs the long-run dynamics between the exchange rate and its fundamental allowing for long-run predictability. Mark and Choi (1997) and Mark and Sul (2001) find evidence of a long run exchange rate predictability based on a cointegration relationship between the exchange rate and a set of fundamental variables. Empirical studies, however, show that convergence toward the fundamental exchange rate is very slow. Potential explanations for the slow speed of adjustment include nominal price rigidities, the share of nontraded goods in the economy, and also the different weight that goods might have in the consumption basket across different countries.

At the same time, however, the unit root property has been widely seen as strong support of the efficient market view of the foreign exchange market. In a nutshell, the efficient market hypothesis says that if prices fully reflect all available information, then it should not be possible to earn excess returns based

[3]Since the original Meese and Rogoff article, a huge literature has developed that aims at testing the out-of-sample forecasting capacity of structural models of the exchange rate. Although once in a while researchers have claimed victory for their model, this victory was usually short-lived. The consensus today is that the Meese and Rogoff conclusion holds, that is, structural models typically do not outperform random walk forecasts at short horizons.

on information that is already available. That is, market participants will exploit any new piece of information accordingly incorporating it in the price, so as to eliminate all risk-free profit opportunities. The nonpredictability of the exchange rate has led to label the foreign exchange market a *fair game*. According to this view, any change observed in the market exchange rate can only be attributed to the arrival of news. Given that news events are in general not predictable, it should not be surprising that exchange rate models systematically fail to outperform the simple random walk model.

The news model that logically follows from the efficient market hypothesis has often be used to argue that the disconnect puzzle that we discussed earlier is not really a puzzle. The story goes as follows. When there are unforeseen shocks in a fundamental, the market exchange rate overreacts (see the overshooting model of Dornbusch (1976)). A sequence of unforeseen shocks in one or more fundamentals (news) can then lead the exchange rate into one direction for a considerable period of time, leading to the appearance of a disconnect. This explanation is not really convincing when considering the history of exchange rate movements since 1973.[4] Figure 4.2 shows the DM–US dollar exchange rate during 1980–1987. We observe that during the first half of the 1980s, the dollar experienced a strong upward movement, so that in 1985 it had doubled in value against the German mark. In 1985 the crash came, and in 2 years time, the dollar halved in value again against the mark. Something similar occurred during the period 1996–2004. Figure 4.3 shows the Euro–US dollar rate during that period. From 1996 to 2001, the dollar increased by more than 70% against the euro (DM). In 2001, it started a spectacular decline such that at the end of 2004, it was at approximately the same level as it was at the start of the bubble. Thus, it appears that since the start of flexible exchange rates in 1973 the dollar has been involved in two major bubbles and crashes, each of which have lasted 8–9 years.

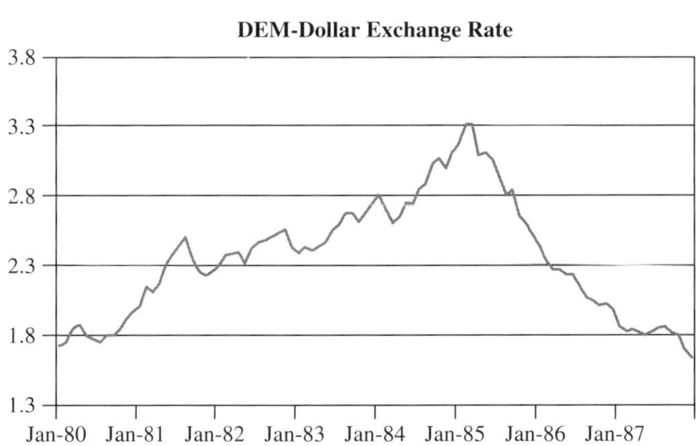


**FIGURE 4.2** **Deutsche Mark–US dollar exchange rate.**

[4]The discussion of this and the next paragraph draws heavily on De Grauwe and Grimaldi (2006).

FIGURE 4.3 Euro–US dollar exchange rate. *Source:* De Grauwe and Grimaldi (2006).

Put differently, since 1973 the dollar was caught by a bubble and crash dynamics about half of the time.

Defenders of the news model will have difficulties in accepting this bubble-and-crashes interpretation of the dollar exchange rate movements. They will typically argue that these movements can be explained by a series of fundamental shocks. For example, it can be argued that the upward movement of the dollar during 1980–1985 was due to a series of positive shocks in US fundamentals, to be followed after 1985 by a series of negative news about US fundamentals during 3 years. A similar interpretation of the dollar movements could be given during 1996–2004. The trouble with this interpretation is that there was simply not enough positive news to account for the long upward movements. Similarly, there was not enough negative news to explain the crashes afterward (Frankel and Froot, 1986).

### 4.2.3 VOLATILITY CLUSTERING

Another well-known empirical regularity of the foreign exchange market is that nonlinear functions of the exchange rate returns, such as the squared and absolute returns, display significant positive autocorrelation, slowly decaying with the length of the lags (Bollersev et al., 1992; Cont et al., 1997; Ding et al., 1993; Ding and Granger, 1996; Engle, 1995). This phenomenon received the name of volatility clustering or volatility persistency.

To put it in simple terms, periods of high and low volatility have a strong tendency to persist over time, alternating each other in an unpredictable way. That is, when there is a large change in the market exchange rate, it is very likely that this "jump" will trigger other big changes in the exchange rate. How slow does volatility decay once a burst in it has unraveled? There is strong empirical evidence showing that the speed of decay is hyperbolic. Let us define the autocorrelation function of absolute returns as $C(\tau) = E\left[|r_\tau||r_{t+\tau}|\right]$. Empirical studies systematically confirm that $C(\tau) \sim \tau^{-y}$. That is, it follows a power law. More remarkable still is that estimates of the parameter $y$ systematically fluctuate in the interval [0.2, 0.3] (Cont et al., 1997; Ding et al., 1993; Liu et al., 1997; Lobato and Savin, 1998; Vandewalle and Ausloos, 1997, 1998). All the previously mentioned studies focus on a uniscaling dimension of the intertemporal dependency of exchange rate volatility. There is, however, an increasing body of studies that finds strong evidence of multiscaling or multifractals in the structure of financial asset returns (Calvet and Fisher, 2002, 2008; Lux, 2008; Mandelbrot, 1999).

The reason why this is an anomaly in standard exchange rate models is that these models are typically linear so that if we observe volatility clustering in the market exchange rate data, we should be able to trace this phenomenon back to the fundamentals. The problem with this view, however, is that there is very little empirical evidence showing that the fundamentals display clusters of volatility that are clearly related to the clustering observed in the exchange rate data.

### 4.2.4 FAT-TAILED DISTRIBUTED EXCHANGE RATE RETURNS

A further anomaly about the exchange rate is the relatively high probability of witnessing an extreme change in it. This phenomenon is shown in Figure 4.4. The upper panel of the figure displays the daily changes of the US$/UK£ exchange rate for the period April, 1971–March, 2010. The lower panel shows 10,000 draws from a normal distribution with standard deviation $\sigma = 0.0061$.[5] The dashed lines correspond to the 0.00001% confidence bounds, that is, the number that is obtained from a normal distribution $N(0, 0.0061)$ with a probability of 0.00001%. The figure shows that while the normally distributed random draws never cross the 0.00001% confidence bounds, the US$/UK £ does so several times. This means that the fluctuations of the empirical series are a lot "wilder", that is, they exhibit fatter tails, than that of the normally distributed random draws. This also means that the exchange rate returns are certainly not normally distributed and therefore belong to another type distribution.

Strictly speaking, the exchange rate returns belong to the Fréchet-type distribution family, for exchange rate returns can be well described by a Pareto law, at least in the tails, and the Pareto law belongs to the Fréchet-type family. Let $| r_t |$ be the absolute value of the changes in the exchange rate between $t$ and $t-1$. According to the Pareto law, the probability of observing a change in the exchange rate, which is larger than a threshold value $x$ is given by $Pr\left(| r_t | > x\right) \sim x^{-\alpha}$. The parameter $\alpha$ determines the speed with which the probability of observing a value of $| r_t | > x$ declines. Empirical studies typically find a value for the parameter $\alpha$ around 3, and therefore exchange rate returns are

[5]The conditional standard deviation of the US$/UK £ series is 0.0061, hence our choice to generate random numbers from a normal distribution with the same standard deviation.

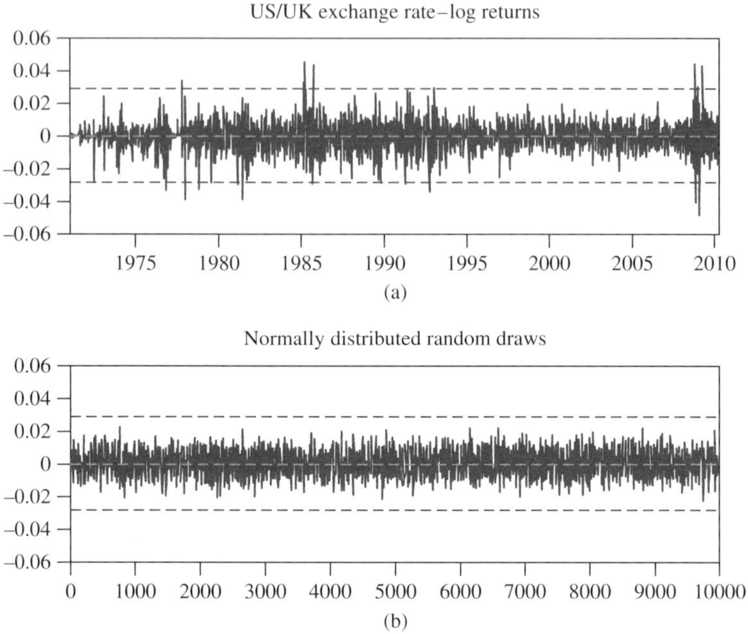


**FIGURE 4.4** **(a) Log returns of the US dollar–UK pound exchange rate and (b) random draws from a normal distribution.**

said to follow an *inverse cubic power law* (Cont et al., 1997; Jansen and de Vries, 1991). It can be shown that the normal distribution belongs to another family of distributions, the Gumbel-type family. Figure 4.5 displays both the Gumbel and the Fréchet distributions. Clearly, the Fréchet distribution has "fatter" tails than the Gumbel family.

Another way of looking at the same phenomenon is to analyze the log–log plot of the inverse empirical cumulative distribution function of the exchange rate. Figure 4.6 displays the inverse cumulative distribution of three different exchange rate series and simultaneously of normally distributed random draws. The figure gives a clear picture; for a given probability level the size of changes in the exchange rate are lot higher than the normally distributed random draws. In other words, the exchange rate changes are "too wild" to be explained by a normal distribution. Additionally, the figure shows another related phenomenon; the distribution of the exchange rate returns has a lower mass at the center of the distribution than the normally distributed random draws, that is, exchange rate returns are leptokurtic.

The distributions belonging to the Pareto-type family (Fréchet case) are characterized by slower tail decay than the distributions of the Gumbel type. That means that the tail decay of the normal distribution (Gumbel type) is faster than the tail decay of the Pareto distribution. This is shown in Figure 4.4, and it helps us to understand why in Figure 4.4a the US$/UK£ series crosses the confidence bounds in several occasions, while in Figure 4.4b, the normally

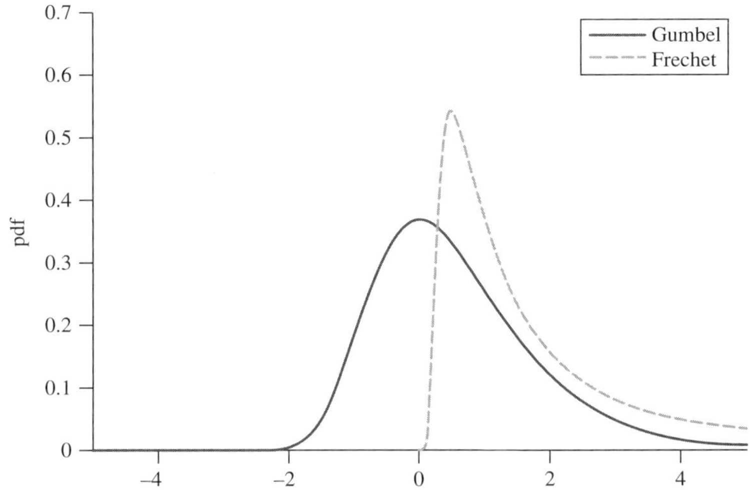


FIGURE 4.5 Gumbel- versus Fréchet-type distributions.

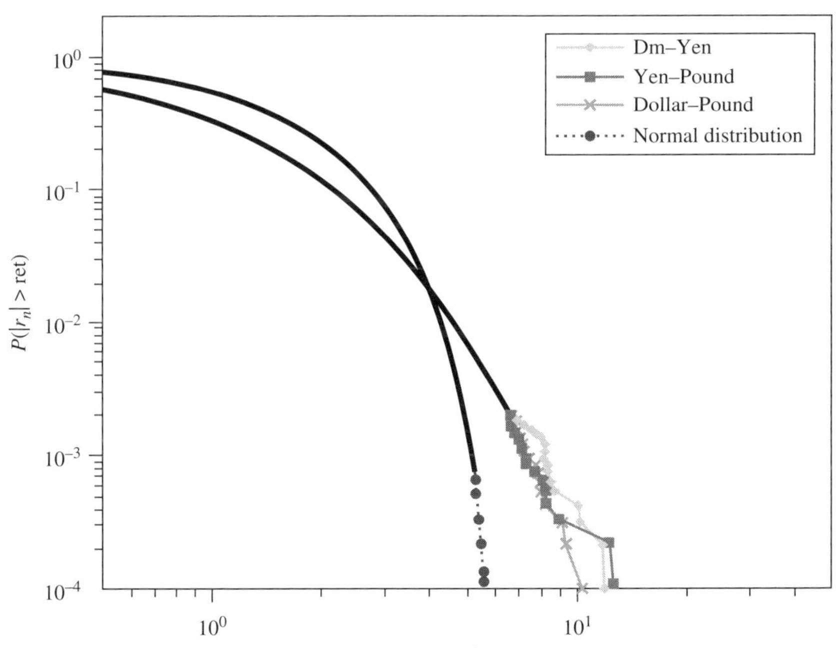


FIGURE 4.6 Log–log plot of empirical exchange rate data versus random draws of the normal distribution. The empirical time series are (parentheses indicate the sample size): Dollar–Pound (9,651), Deutsche Mark–Yen (9,488), and Yen–Pound (9,364).

distributed random draws never do. For this reason also, it is said that the distribution of the exchange rate returns have fat tails. Fat-tailed distributed returns with an $\alpha$ exponent of magnitude 3 is not unique to the US$/UK£ exchange rate. This property has sometimes been called a *universal law*, for it is typically observed at frequencies ranging from tick up to monthly observations in the foreign exchange market, stock exchanges, and commodities markets (Plerou and Stanley, 2008; Stanley et al., 2008).

## 4.3 A Prototype Behavioral Model of the Foreign Exchange Market

In this section, we present a prototype behavioral model of the foreign exchange market. The basic assumptions used in this model are the following. First, individual agents have cognitive limitations in processing and evaluating information. They are not capable of understanding the complexity of the underlying model. Secondly, as they know their cognitive limitations, they do not try to understand the full complexity of the world. Instead, they use simple rules (heuristics) to take positions in the market. Agents in our model are not rational in the traditional sense. That does not mean, however, that they are dumb. On the contrary, they are willing to change and adjust their behavior when the incentive to do so is strong enough. Quite often, a departure from RE is interpreted to imply moving into a world of irrationality. This is not the case in our model. The world in which individual agents cannot hope to understand the underlying complexity of that world, it is reasonable to use simple rules and to subject these rules to regular evaluation.[6] This trial and error mechanism is probably the most fundamental learning mechanism of human beings.

We will assume that there are two types of heuristic rules. One rule is an extrapolative one (a chartist or trend following rule) and the other is a mean-reverting one (a fundamentalist rule). Traders use one of the two rules. The use of the fundamentalist rule leads to the following specification of the excess demand of foreign exchange:

$$d_{f,t} = \alpha\left(S^f - S_t\right) \tag{4.1}$$

where $\alpha > 0$, that is, when the current market exchange rate $S_t$ is below the fundamental exchange rate $S^f$, traders expect the market rate to increase in the future, and therefore they buy foreign exchange at the rate $\alpha$. The reverse happens when $S_t$ exceeds $S^f$. In that case, they expect the exchange rate to decline and

[6]Kahneman and Thaler (2006) make this point clear. They distinguish between expected utility and experienced utility, and they show how expected utility is strongly influenced by the experiences of the recent past. Furthermore, when faced with situations that involve uncertain outcomes in the future, humans use previous experiences as a reference point. This is an intelligent way of solving a particular problem quickly, at expense of opening the possibility for systematic mistakes to take place.

they sell foreign exchange. Here, we assume that the fundamental is exogenously determined by a random walk.

The excess demand function of the traders using a chartist rule is specified as follows:

$$d_{c,t} = \beta(S_t - S_{t-1}) \tag{4.2}$$

where $\beta > 0$. When the exchange rate has increased (declined), traders expect it to continue to increase (decline). As a result, they buy (sell) foreign exchange accordingly.

We assume that a market maker collects the information about the individual orders from the traders and adjust the price in each period $t$.[7] The market value of the exchange rate is given by

$$S_{t+1} = S_t + \mu \sum_i \omega_{i,t} d_{i,t} + \varepsilon_t \tag{4.3}$$

where $\mu > 0$ measures the speed with which the market maker adjusts the exchange rate, $\omega_{i,t}$ is the fraction of traders using the forecasting rule $i$ (where $i = f, c$), and $\varepsilon_t$ is a small normally distributed noise process with variance $\sigma_t^{mm}$. The fraction $\omega_{i,t}$ varies over time. Its value will depend on how successful the use of the rule $i$ is.

Since $\omega_{f,t} + \omega_{c,t} = 1$, we define $x_t = \omega_{f,t} - \omega_{c,t}$, with $x_t \in (-1, 1)$. This allows expressing the fractions of traders as

$$\omega_{f,t} = \frac{1}{2}(1 + x_t) \text{ and } \omega_{c,t} = \frac{1}{2}(1 - x_t) \tag{4.4}$$

As a result, Equation 4.3 can be rewritten as

$$S_{t+1} = S_t + \frac{1}{2}\mu(\alpha(S^f - S_t)(1 + x_t) + \beta(S_t - S_{t-1})(1 - x_t)) + \varepsilon_t \tag{4.5}$$

Because we have not formally defined the law of motion of $\omega_{i,t}$ though, it is not possible to solve equation (4.5) explicitly. Still however, from the definition of $x_t$ above we can say a few things about its dynamic behavior. Let us begin with the simplest case and assume that the population of traders is composed almost exclusively by fundamentalist traders in the market, i.e. when $x_t \to 1$. In this case, abstracting from the noise term, equation (4.5) becomes

$$S_{t+1} = S_t + \alpha\mu(S^f - S_t) \tag{4.6}$$

It is not difficult to show that the exchange rate can only settle down and reach its fundamental in the long if the parameter $\alpha\mu < 1$. Only then will any difference $(S^f - S_{t-1}) \neq 0$ vanish in the long run. Because this would be the only possible solution of the model if we had used the homogeneous agent

[7] This specification goes back to Beja and Goldman (1980).

rational expectation scheme, we will call this steady state the *rational expectations* solution to the model.

Perhaps the most interesting case is when $x_t \to -1$, i.e. when there are almost only trend followers in the market. In this case equation (4.5) becomes

$$S_{t+1} = S_t(1 + \beta\mu) - \beta\mu S_{t-1} \tag{4.7}$$

The stability of the equation depends critically on the condition $\beta\mu < 1$. This time, however, when the exchange rate settles down, i.e. when $S_{t+1} = S_t = S_{t-1} = S_{LR}$, the value $S_{LR}$ does not have to coincide with the rational expectations solution of the model. In other words, equation (4.7) has a continuum of equilibria. This feature is common in the literature on complex systems and allows for the emergence of rich and complex dynamics. It will become clear that the market exchange rate does not necessarily have to settle down in any of these particular steady states. The reason for this is our definition of the state variables $\omega_{i,t}$, which is key for the emergence of complex dynamics.

We now define the dynamics of the population of traders. We will assume that traders adapt their behavior using an evolutionary fitness criterion. This allows introducing discipline into the model in such a way that traders chose their trading strategies not just randomly but based on a utilitarian evolutionary principle. Traders will try a rule and if it turns out to be profitable, they will stick to it. If a particular agent uses a certain trading strategy and there happens to be another more profitable one, she/he will adopt it, departing from the previous one, with a certain probability. The evolutionary dynamics is governed by the profits that traders have made in the recent past when taking positions in the market.

We therefore define the realized profits as

$$\pi_{f,t} = d_{f,t-1}\left(S_t - S_{t-1}\right) \text{ and } \pi_{c,t} = d_{c,t-1}\left(S_t - S_{t-1}\right) \tag{4.8}$$

Following Brock and Hommes (1997), we let the fractions $\omega_{i,t}$ of traders using rule $i$ to be given by the discrete choice probability model.

$$\omega_{f,t} = \frac{\exp(\gamma\pi_{f,t})}{Z_t} \text{ and } \omega_{c,t} = \frac{\exp(\gamma\pi_{c,t})}{Z_t} \tag{4.9}$$

where $Z_t = \sum_i \exp\left(\gamma\pi_{i,t}\right)$.

The discrete choice theory takes the view that individuals make choices based on both a deterministic (rational) and a random component. If $\gamma = 0$ then $\omega_{\text{opt},t} = \omega_{\text{pes},t} = \frac{1}{2}$ and the decision making is purely stochastic. Traders decide to adopt a chartist or a fundamentalist trading rule just by tossing a coin, and the expected value of being 1 or the other type of trader is equal to $\frac{1}{2}$. At the other extreme, if $\beta = \infty$, all randomness disappears and switches are fully governed by the rational component. Combining Equations 4.9 and 4.10, we obtain

$$x_t = \tanh\left(\frac{1}{2}\gamma U_t\right) \tag{4.10}$$

where $U_t = \pi_{f,t} - \pi_{c,t}$ and $x_t \in (-1, +1)$.

The intuition of this result is that an increase in the profitability of the fundamentalist rule relative to the chartist rule, increases the fraction of agents using the fundamentalist rule, and vice versa.

Up to here, we have a two-dimensional system composed by Equations 4.5 and 4.10. Several models of this type have been proposed in the literature within the context of the FOREX market, financial markets in general, and also the macroeconomy (Chiarella et al., 2006; Gaunersdorfer, 2000; Westerhoff, 2003b). One common feature of this literature is the emergence of endogenous fluctuations of the state variables in question, the exchange rate and diffusion index $x_t$ in our case. This is a remarkable difference with the mainstream literature. We will come back to this point later.

Finally, we introduce the notion that the use of the fundamentalist rule is only triggered when the exchange rate is sufficiently far from the fundamental variable (see De Grauwe and Grimaldi (2005)). The reason is that underlying the fundamentalist rule is arbitrage in the goods market. Assume that the fundamental exchange rate is given by the PPP value. Arbitrage in the goods market is triggered only when the deviation between the market exchange rate and the PPP-exchange rate exceeds transactions costs in the goods market. If this deviation is smaller than the transaction costs, arbitrage is not profitable and is switched off. We assume that fundamentalist traders know this. As a result, they will only start buying (selling) foreign exchange when the distance between the market and fundamental rate exceeds transaction costs in the goods market.[8] This means that we write $\alpha$ in Equation 4.1 as

$$\alpha > 0 \text{ if } |S^f - S_t| > C \tag{4.11}$$

and

$$\alpha = 0 \text{ if } |S^f - S_t| \le C \tag{4.12}$$

where $C$ is transaction costs.

The model has a number of nonlinearities making it difficult to derive analytical solutions. We therefore rely on numerical simulations to analyze the types of

[8]This assumption is rooted by the concept of difference limen in psychology. Psychologists define the "difference limen" or "just noticeable difference" as the intensity of a stimulus that when applied to people leads to no reaction or change in behavior. This concept has been used in economic modeling in different contexts, for example, for the quantification of qualitative diffusion indices (Carlson and Parkin, 1975; Carrol, 2003; Seitz, 1988).

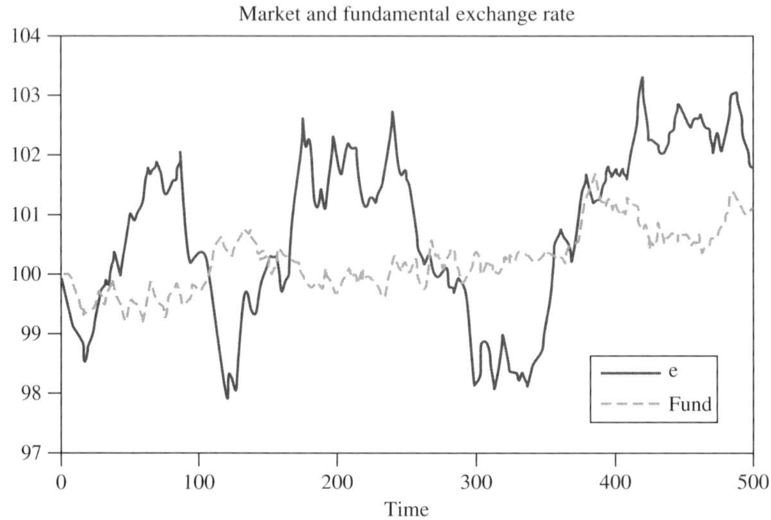


FIGURE 4.7 Simulated exchange rate and its fundamental.

dynamics that emerge from the model.[9] We first show the evolution of the simulated market and fundamental exchange rates, obtained in a representative numerical run. This is shown in Figure 4.7. Two things stand out. First, there appears to be excessive volatility of the simulated market exchange rate (relative to the fundamental). Second, the model produces a strong "disconnect" phenomenon, that is, the market exchange rate is often disconnected from the movements of the fundamental exchange rate. Both phenomena are persistently found in the real world and were discussed in Section 4.2. Thus, our prototype behavioral model mimics the empirical regularities of excess volatility and disconnection. This result has been obtained with other similar behavioral models (see De Grauwe and Grimaldi (2006)). The intuition behind this result is a self-fulfilling mechanism. A series of stochastic shocks can lead the trend followers (chartists) to make better forecasts than the fundamentalist traders. This attracts more traders in using the trend following rule, which in a self-fulfilling way improves the fit of these rules. Bubbles ensue that lead to divergences from the fundamental. At some point, however, as the distance from the fundamental becomes large enough, the exchange rate crashes. Thus, the foreign exchange market is continuously driven by waves of optimism and pessimism, which lead to positive and negative departures from the underlying fundamental. Additionally, using standard econometric methods such as the augmented Dickey Fuller test, it is not possible to reject the null hypothesis that the market exchange rate is governed by a unit root at the 1% level.

Figure 4.8 shows the returns of the simulated exchange rate. We immediately observe the occurrence of large spikes in these returns, suggesting that the

[9]The model is simulated using the following parameter values: $\alpha = 0.2$, $\beta = 0.6$, $\gamma = 1$, $\mu = 2$, $\sigma^{mm} = \sigma^{fund} = 0.1$, $c = 2.5$.

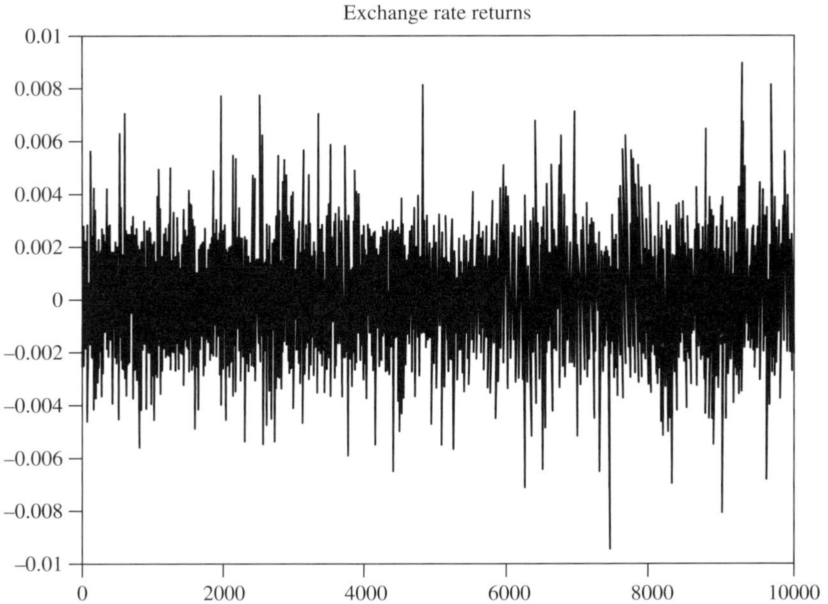


FIGURE 4.8 **Simulated exchange rate returns.**

distribution of the returns is not normal and may exhibit fat tails. To check for this, we show the log–log plot of the inverse cumulative distribution of the simulated returns in Figure 4.9. The figure also displays the cumulative distribution function of a draw of random numbers with normal distribution. We find that the cumulative distribution deviates from the normal, exhibiting both excess kurtosis and fat tails. The latter is also confirmed by the Hill estimator for the existence of fat tails (Hill = 3.8; 4.3; 4.8). Again, our behavioral model mimics an important empirical regularity of the foreign exchange markets relatively well.

## 4.4 Conclusion

In this chapter, we have presented a modeling strategy of the foreign exchange market that departs from the prevailing REs paradigm. Mainstream models have not been able to give a fully convincing explanation of several empirical regularities observed in the foreign exchange market. In this chapter, we have presented a prototype model as an example of an agent-based model. The model assumes that agents have cognitive limitations, that is, they are unable to comprehend the complexities of the underlying model. As a result, they use simple forecasting rules (heuristics). They are rational, however, in that they wish to learn from their mistakes. Thus, they switch to alternative rules if it turns out that these alternative rules perform better than the one in use. This switching

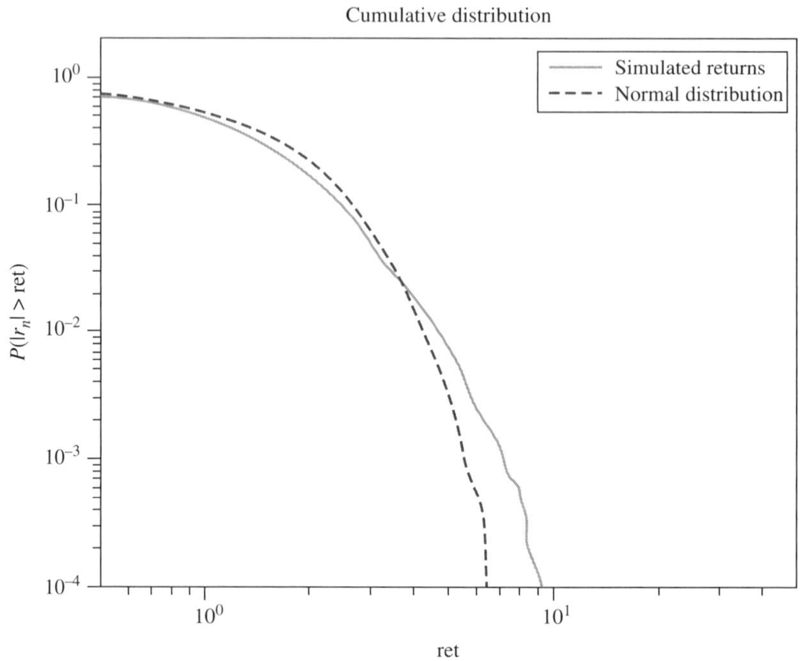


**FIGURE 4.9** Log–log plot of the simulate exchange rate returns (continues line) and random draws from a normal distribution (dotted line).

mechanism provides the basis for the dynamics of the foreign exchange market. In particular, it offers a simple explanation for several phenomena typically observed in the foreign exchange market.

The simulated exchange rate in our model is systematically disconnected from its fundamentals, and it is characterized by excess volatility. At the same time, the model produces fat-tailed distributed exchange rate returns, and moreover the null of a unit root in the exchange rate level cannot be rejected. These results are driven by the switches in the trading strategies of traders. Traders try a trading strategy and when they find out that there is a more profitable alternative, they switch to it, leading to large jumps in the exchange rate level. The exchange rate that is systematically disconnected from its fundamental has to do with the fact that trend following traders never look at the fundamental in order to take positions in the market. Not surprisingly, they act as a destabilizing force.

The model that we have presented here can be expanded in several ways. First, our model assumes only two trading rules that have been chosen in a rather ad hoc way. This is a simplifying assumption that is in fact not rooted in empirical observations. Several studies report that traders actively use many more, and also more involved, trading rules than the ones that we have chosen here. An interesting extension would be to include more trading rules in such a way that they evolve inside the model along the lines of Evstigneev et al. (2009). In our model, we have assumed that the trading costs that apply to fundamentalists are constant. There is in fact no reason why this cost cannot be time varying. A potential extension therefore would be to allow it to vary over time. Our model also assumes no feedback from the market exchange rate to the value of the fundamental, which is assumed to be a random walk. An attractive alternative would be to expand the model, allowing for bidirectional causality between these two variables, as in De Grauwe and Grimaldi (2006).

Agent-based models provide an interesting alternative to mainstream economic models. The recent developments, in the field of behavioral economics have paved the way for models that deviate from full rationality and that favor an evolutionary view of the world. This is an exciting and fast moving field, which we believe is full of promise for the study of the foreign exchange market.

## REFERENCES


Bacchetta P, van Wincoop E. Can information heterogeneity explain the exchange rate determination puzzle? Working Paper 9498, NBER; 2003.

____, ____. Infrequent portfolio decisions: a solution to the forward discount puzzle. Am Econ Rev2010;100(3):870–904.

Baxter M, Stockman AC. Business cycles and the exchange rate system: some international evidence. J Monet Econ 1989;23:377–400.

Beja A, Goldman MB. On the dynamic behavior of prices in disequilibrium. J Finance 1980;35(2):235–247.

Bollersev T, Chou RC, Kroner KF. ARCH modelling in finance. J Economet 1992;52:5–59.

Brock WA, Hommes CH. A rational route to randomness. Econometrica 1997;65(5):1059–1095.

Caballero R. A fallacy of composition. Am Econ Rev 1992;82(5):1279–1292.

Calvet LE, Fisher AJ. Multifractality in asset returns: theory and evidence. Rev Econ Stat 2002;84(3):381–406.

____, ____. Multifractal volatility: theory, forecasting and pricing, Advanced finance series. Academic Press; 2008.

Carlson JA, Parkin M. Inflation expectations. Economica 1975;42:123–138.

Carrol CD. Macroeconomic expectations of households and professional forecasters. Q J Econ 2003;118(1):269–298.

Cheung Y-W, Chinn M, Pascual AG. Empirical exchange rate models of the nineties: are any fit to survive? J Int Money Finance 2005;24:1150–1175.

Chiarella C. The dynamics of speculative behavior. Ann Oper Res 1992;37:101–123.

____, Dieci R, He X-Z. Heterogeneity, market mechanisms, and asset price dynamics. In: Hens T, Schenk-Hoppe KR, editors. Handbook of financial markets: dynamics and evolution. 2009. pp. 277–344.

____, He X-ZH, Hommes C. A dynamic analysis of moving average rules. J Econ Dyn Control 2006;30:1729–1753.

Cont R, Potters M, Bouchaud J-P. Scaling in stock market data: stable laws and beyond. In: Dubrulle B, Graner F, Sornette D, editors. Scale invariance and beyond,

Proceedings of the Les Houches workshop. Les Houches, France: Springer-Verlag; 1997. pp. 1997.

Day RH, Huang W. Bulls, bears and market sheep. J Econ Behav Organ 1990;14:299–329.

De Grauwe P, Dewachter H, Embrechts M. Exchange rate theory: chaotic models of foreign exchange markets. Oxford: Blackwell; 1993.

——, Grimaldi M. Heterogeneity of agents, transaction costs and the exchange rate. J Econ Dyn Control 2005;29:691–719.

——, ——. The exchange rate in a behavioral finance framework. Princeton University Press; 2006.

Della Vigna S, Malmendier U. Paying not to go to the Gym. Am Econ Rev 2006;96(3):694–719.

Ding Z, Granger CWJ. Modelling volatility persistence of speculative returns: a new approach. J Economet 1996;73:185–216.

Ding Z, Granger CWJ, Engle RF. A long memory property of stock market returns and a new model. J Empir Finance 1993;1:1–83.

Ehrmann M, Fratzscher M. Exchange rate and fundamentals: new evidence from real-time data. J Int Money Finance 2005;24:317–341.

Engle RF. ARCH: selected readings. Oxford University Press; 1995.

Evstigneev IV, Hens T, Schenk-Hoppè KR. Evolutionary finance, in handbook the financial markets: dynamics and evolution. North-Holland; 2009.

Föllmer H. Random economies with many interacting agents. J Math Econ 1974;1:51–62.

Flood RP, Rose AK. Fixing exchange rates: a virtual quest for fundamentals. Technical Report 4335. NBER; 1995.

Frankel JA, Froot KA. Understanding the US dollar in the eighties: the expectations of chartists and fundamentalists. Econ Rec 1986;1(2):24–38.

Frankel JA, Froot KA. Chartists, fundamentalists and the demand for dollars. In: Courakis AS, Taylor MP, editors. Private behaviour and government policy in interdependent economies. Oxford University Press; 1990a. pp. 73–126.

Frankel JA, Froot KA. The rationality of the foreign exchange rate: chartists, fundamentalists and trading in the foreign exchange market. Am Econ Rev AEA Pap Proc 1990b;80(2):181–185.

Gaunersdorfer A. Endogenous fluctuations in a simple asset pricing model with heterogeneous beliefs. J Econ Dyn Control 2000;24:799–831.

Haken H. Synergetics: introduction and advanced topics. Berlin: Springer-Verlag; 2004.

Hommes C. Heterogeneous agent models in economics and finance. In: Tesfatsion L, Judd K, editors.Volume 2, Handbook of computational economics, Agent-based computational economics. 2006. pp. 1107–1186.

Jansen DW, de Vries CG. On the frequency of large stock returns: putting booms and busts into perspective. Rev Econ Stat 1991;73(1):18–24.

Kahneman D, Thaler R. Utility maximization and experienced utility. J Econ Persect 2006;20(1):221–234.

——, Tversky A. Prospect theory: an analysis of decisions under risk. Econometrica 1997;47(2):263–291.

———, Wakker PP, Sarin R. Back to bentham? Explorations of experienced utility. Q J Econ 1997;112(2):375–405.

———, Wakker PP, Sarin R. Maps of bounded rationality: psychology for behavioral economics. Am Econ Rev 2003;93(5):1449–1475.

Kirman A. Epidemics of opinion and financial bubbles in financial markets. In: Taylor M, editor. Money and financial markets. Cambridge: Blackwell; 1991. pp. 354–368.

———. Ants, rationality and recruitment. Q J Econ 1993;108:137–156.

———. Correlations in economic time series. Physica A 1997;245:437–440.

Lawrenz C, Westerhoff F. Modeling exchange rate behavior with a genetic algorithm. Comput Econ 2003;21:209–229.

Liu Y, Cizeau P, Meyer M, Peng C-K, Stanley HE. Correlations in economic time series. Physica A 1997;245:437–440.

Lobato IN, Savin NE. Real and spurious long memory properties of stock market data. J Bus Econ Stat 1998;16:261–283.

Lux T. Herd behavior, bubbles and crashes. Econ J 1995;105:881–896.

Lux T. The socioeconomic dynamics of speculative markets: interacting agents, chaos and the fat tails of return distribution. J Econ Behav Organ 1998;245:437–440.

———. The markov-switching multifractal model of asset returns: GMM estimation and linear forecasting of volatility. J Bus Econ Stat 2008;26:194–210.

———. Stochastic behavioural asset-pricing models and the stylized facts. In: Hens T, Schenk-Hoppe KR, editors. Handbook of financial markets: dynamics and evolution. 2009. pp. 161–216.

———, Marchesi M. Scaling and criticality in a stochastic multi-agent model of a financial market. Lett Nat 1999;397:498–500.

———, Marchesi M. Volatility clustering in financial markets: a micro-simulation of interacting agents. Int J Theor Appl Finance 2000;3:675–702.

———, Schornstein S. Genetic learning as an explanation of stylized facts of foreign exchange markets. J Math Econ 2005;41:169–196.

Mandelbrot B. The variation of certain speculative prices. J Bus 1963;35:394–419.

Manzan S, Westerhoff F. Representativeness of news and the exchange rate dynamics. J Econ Dyn Control 2005;29:677–689.

Mark N. Exchange rates and fundamentals: evidence on long-horizon predictability. Am Econ Rev 1995;85:201–218.

———, Choi D-Y. Real exchange rate prediction over long horizons. J Int Econ 1997;43:29–60.

———, Sul D. Nominal exchange rates and monetary fundamentals evidence from a small post-bretton woods panel. J Int Econ 2001;53:29–52.

Meese RA, Rogoff K. Empirical exchange rate models of the seventies. J Int Econ 1983a;14:3–24.

———, ———. The Out-of-sample failure of empirical exchange rate models: sampling error or misspecification? In: Frenkel JA, editor. Exchange rates and international macroeconomics. University of Chicago Press; 1983b. pp. 67–112.

Mussa M. Empirical regularities in the behavior of exchange rates and theories of the foreign exchange market. Carniege-Rochester Conference Series on Public Policy 11; 1979. pp. 9–57.

Obstfeld M, Rogoff K. The six major puzzles in international macroeconomic: is there a Common Cause?, Working Paper 7777, NBER; 2000.

Plerou V, Stanley HE. Stock return distributions: tests of scaling and universality from three distinct stock markets. Phys Rev 2008;77.

Sargent TJ. Macroeconomic theory. New York: Academic Press; 1987.

Sargent TJ, Wallace N. The stability of models of money and growth with perfect foresight. Econometrica 1973;41(6):1043–1048.

Seitz H. The estimation of inflation forecasts from business survey data. Appl Econ 1988;20:427–438.

Sims C. Rational inattention and monetary economics. In: Fried-man BM, Woodford M, editors. Handbook of monetary economics. Elsevier; 2010.

Stanley HE, Plerou V, Gabaix X. A statistical physics view of financial fluctuations: evidence for scaling and Universality. Physica A 2008;387:3967–3981.

Taylor AM, Taylor MP. The purchasing power parity debate. J Econ Prespect 2004;18(4):135–158.

Vandewalle N, Ausloos M. Coherent and random sequences in financial fluctuations. Physica A 1997;246:454–459.

——, ——. Sparseness and roughness of foreign exchange rates. Int J Mod Phys C 1998;9(5):711–719.

Weidlich W, Haag G. Concepts and models of a quantitative sociology: the dynamics of interacting populations. New York: Springer-Verlag; 1983.

Westerhoff F. Central bank interventions and feedback traders. J Int Financ Mark Inst Money 2003a;13(5):419–427.

——. Expectations driven distortions in the foreign exchange market. J Econ Behav Organ 2003b;51:389–412.

——. Exchange rate dynamics: a nonlinear survey. In: Rosser JB Jr, editor. Handbook of research on complexity. Cheltenham: Edward Elgar; 2009. pp. 287–325.

——, Manzan S. Does liquidity in the FX market depend on volatility? Econ Bull 2004;6(10):1–8.

Wieland C, Westerhoff F. Exchange rate dynamics, central bank interventions and chaos control methods. J Economic Behav Organ 2005;58:117–132.

CHAPTER FIVE

# The Evolution of Exchange Rate Regimes and Some Future Perspectives

**PAUL R. MASSON**
Rotman School of Management, University of Toronto

## 5.1 Introduction

For the first time in about three decades, the international monetary system, and, in particular, the constellation of exchange rate regimes, seems to be under reconsideration. Since the breakdown of the Bretton Woods system of pegged but adjustable exchange rates in the early 1970s, global monetary relations have been subject to little official guidance or systematic control—apart from a few episodes of concerted intervention by the major powers. Countries are able to choose among the full range of monetary regimes from fixed to floating and are able to organize their monetary and intervention policies as they see fit. While the International Monetary Fund (IMF) continues to exercise surveillance over exchange rate policies and "exchange rate manipulation" is in principle ruled out by IMF guidelines, in practice, the major countries that do not need to borrow from the IMF can safely ignore its advice.

Indeed, *laisser-faire* in international finance has been the norm, leading some to term this an *international monetary 'nonsystem'*. Unlike the gold standard period, or the Bretton Woods system before the United States closed the 'gold window' that assured convertibility for the US dollar into gold at a fixed price, there is no commodity anchor for fiat currencies. In the decades since the breakdown of Bretton Woods, the US dollar has lost more than 90% of its value

*Handbook of Exchange Rates*, First Edition. Edited by Jessica James, Ian W. Marsh, and Lucio Sarno.

against gold; over that period, a broader index of commodity prices has risen more than fivefold in terms of the dollar. At the same time, exchange rates for the major currencies fluctuate relatively freely and there have been large movements that reflect different monetary policies and economic conditions. The US dollar has experienced a trend depreciation against most other major currencies except the pound sterling. Global liquidity, constituted by international money in circulation in the form of currency issue and bank deposits, expands at a rate that depends on the uncoordinated actions of central banks and the demand for money by private individuals and firms.

In this nonsystem the US dollar continues to be the major international currency, that is, the currency used in international payments and official foreign exchange reserves, to denominate assets and liabilities, for pricing commodities, as anchor for pegged exchange rates, and as vehicle for trading other currencies. Its principal rival is the euro, whose introduction in 1999 marked a milestone in international monetary relations—the first creation by mutual agreement of a true multilateral currency. Nonetheless, the euro's current importance is considerably less than that of the dollar. Other currencies—principally the yen, the pound sterling, and the Swiss franc—have much more minor roles.

The challenge to the current *laisser-faire* system comes from the BRIC countries (Brazil, Russia, India, and China) and more generally, from the rise of other emerging market economies, whose newfound power is manifested in the virtual eclipse of the G8 by the G20. China, in particular, has advocated the replacement of the current system of uncoordinated expansion of international liquidity with one in which international agreement would control the supply of an international currency at the center of the system. In many respects, this proposal is similar to the role initially envisaged for the Special Drawing Right, namely, to become the "principal reserve asset for the international monetary system."

In what follows, the history of currency regimes is briefly reviewed, including the years leading up to the breakdown of Bretton Woods, and then the experience post-1973 is examined. Numerous observers have noted that the current system has at times led both to high exchange rate volatility that seems unrelated to economic fundamentals and to exchange rate misalignments. At the same time, there has been a trend toward more freely floating exchange rates and toward monetary policies based on domestic objectives, typically, inflation targeting, which has successfully kept inflation in check in most countries. The possible role of exchange rate policies in contributing to international imbalances and the global financial crisis of 2008–2009 is the subject of active debate, and there is an emerging consensus that central banks need to include macrofinancial stability, as well as inflation, among their objectives. Nonetheless, the system has proved relatively robust and has allowed considerable discretion in the exercise of monetary policy autonomy.

This robustness needs to be kept in mind when evaluating the chances of a more managed international system taking its place. Much of the discussion of reform in the early 1970s, under the auspices of the Committee of Twenty and by academic economists, is still relevant at present. Those proposals for reform were not adopted precisely because countries were unwilling to abandon the monetary autonomy that a *laisser-faire* system afforded them. The last section considers whether the opportunity of strengthening the rules of the game of the international monetary system is greater now that the financial crisis has exposed fault lines in the current system. In the absence of fundamental reform, enhanced coordination among the major blocs is nevertheless possible, arguably necessary, to lessen exchange rate volatility and improve financial stability. It is argued that policy coordination should be organized around global public goods rather than conflict variables such as bilateral exchange rates or balances of payments.

## 5.2 A Brief History of Currency Regimes

Currency regimes, until recently, have relied on a link to a valuable commodity, usually gold or silver, to establish the value of a currency. While the monetary use of precious metals can be traced back to 2900 BC, this took the form of ingots whose value was based on weight (Eagleton and Williams, 2007, p. 16). Coinage seems to have emerged around 700–800 BC, when Lydian coins made of electrum (a naturally occurring mixture of gold and silver) were struck (Eagleton and Williams, 2007, p. 24). International exchange of currencies was normally based on their bullion value, whatever their value in tale (that is, their nominal value as officially declared). Exchange rates between currencies were thus relatively straightforward and stable—as long as countries linked their currency to the same precious metal and the currency was not "debased." However, the classical gold standard period—when all the major powers linked their domestic currency's value to gold—lasted only from 1896 to 1914.

England was effectively on the gold standard starting in 1817, with silver coins becoming subsidiary currency whose value was established by fiat, not by their (lesser) bullion value (Chown, Chapter 7). However, during much of the nineteenth century, other European countries, the United States, Japan, and India variously had a silver standard or a bimetallic standard whereby both gold and silver coins were supposed to reflect their metallic content. However, the relative market price of the bullion content of gold and silver coins in any given country on a bimetallic standard could differ from the exchange rates implied by their nominal values. If the divergence was too great, this led to the operation of Gresham's law, in which the "bad" money, whose official value was greater than its bullion value, drove out the "good" money. As a result, countries on a bimetallic standard faced the prospect of either the gold or the silver coins disappearing from circulation, if the price of gold relative to silver differed significantly from the exchange rate implicit in the coinage.

From 1815 until 1872, the relative price stayed remarkably constant, fluctuating between 15 and 16 ounces of silver for one ounce of gold (Chown, 1994, Table 8.1). In most cases, these fluctuations were not large enough to provoke melting down coins for industrial or jewelry use. However, another channel for arbitrage was the shipment of currency to a country where it could be minted at a higher value. This made it important for the survival of bimetallism for countries to agree on the ratio and embody a common ratio in their coinage. This was the basis for the Latin Monetary Union; however, the attempt to reach agreement with other countries, including Britain, Germany, and the United States, at the Paris Conference of 1867 was a failure (Chown, 1994, Chapter 9).

Silver discoveries and the increased demand for gold because of the adoption of the gold standard by Germany in 1873 led to the breakdown of the Latin Monetary Union. Its members (France, Italy, Switzerland, and Belgium) subsequently went onto the gold standard, as did the United States in 1896 with its rejection of a silver standard (despite William Jennings Bryan's plea not to "crucify mankind upon a cross of gold"). Thus, until 1914, the world's exchange rate regime was simple and transparent since exchange rates between the major currencies, which were convertible into gold, were defined by their gold content. Nevertheless, currency values could fluctuate within a narrow range, defined by the "gold points," which were the thresholds for profitable arbitrage between currencies. The operation of the gold standard is often considered to have removed discretion over monetary policy, but in fact, its operation was not really so automatic, as central banks used interest rate policy to attract gold and they issued bonds to prevent the money supply from increasing in response to gold inflows (de Cecco, 1974).

The classical gold standard came to an end with the outbreak of war in 1914; countries established limits on the convertibility of their paper currencies into gold as well as restrictions on gold movements abroad. Although most of the major countries resumed a link to gold during the 1920s,[1] the system collapsed a few years later as a result of the economic downturn and banking crises of the Great Depression. Although the classical gold standard was widely thought to have contributed to the free movement of goods and persons and furthered global integration and prosperity (Keynes, 1920, quoted in Yeager, 1996), the system was clearly incompatible with the world economy of the interwar period, given the large accumulation of war debts and the desire to use monetary and fiscal policies to cushion the effects of the global downturn that began in 1929 (Cassell, 1936; Eichengreen, 1992).

The interwar gold standard was characterized by rivalry among key currencies, in particular, the pound sterling and US dollar, in their roles as vehicles for international trade and finance. Many smaller countries pegged to these currencies, rather than to gold directly. This regime is better characterized as a gold exchange standard since these currencies, which could be exchanged into gold, nevertheless carried out most of the functions of international money and other countries often held their reserves not in gold, but in the key currencies. Yeager argues that this attempt to economize on gold contributed to the precariousness of the system (Yeager, 1996, p. 80). When it broke down, exchange rates fluctuated in ways that were viewed as inhibiting adjustment, at times reflecting deliberate attempts to gain competitive advantage by overdepreciating

[1]Starting with Sweden in 1924 and Britain in 1925. France, Belgium and Germany went back on the gold standard later, at currency values that were depreciated relative to the prewar gold content.

one's currency. This period gave flexible exchange rates a bad name, and Nurkse, in an influential study done for the League of Nations, concluded that a return to fixed exchange rates was called for (Nurkse, 1944).

The 1944 conference in Bretton Woods, New Hampshire, created the so-called Bretton Woods regime of pegged but adjustable exchange rates with the dollar at its center. Countries were expected to keep their exchange rates against the dollar within narrow margins, plus or minus 1%, and the United States assured convertibility of the dollar into gold at a fixed rate of $35 per ounce. Exchange rates could be changed in cases of "fundamental disequilibrium," to be monitored by the IMF, which could also provide financing to prevent adjustment from being costly in terms of output losses. Exchange rates of the major currencies did adjust, most notably, the pound sterling, which was devalued in 1949 and 1967, and the French franc, which was devalued in 1957, 1958, and 1969, while the deutsche mark was revalued in 1969. However, arguably, exchange rates adjusted too infrequently since devaluations were resisted due to the loss of face they caused and surplus countries were not constrained to adjust since there was no upper limit to reserves (Yeager, 1996).

Another problem with the system was the role of the center country, the United States, whose currency was the main component of international liquidity and other countries' reserves. Robert Triffin identified the dilemma facing the global economy: in order to supply international liquidity, the United States had to run balance of payments deficits, but these deficits undermined the credibility of the dollar, in particular, the commitment of convertibility into gold (Triffin, 1960). Balance of payments deficits led the United States to put restrictions on capital outflows and to close the gold window (i.e., abandon convertibility) to private holders in 1968, while putting pressure on foreign central banks to not redeem dollars for gold and finally, also closing the gold window to the latter in August, 1971 (as well as imposing an import tariff to put pressure for a readjustment of currency values). The Smithsonian Agreement of December 1971, which appreciated other major currencies against the dollar and increased the price of gold, only succeeded in extending the life of the Bretton Woods regime until March 1973, when all other major currencies floated against the dollar (see Solomon, 1982, for a detailed history of this period).

In the meantime, considerable thought had been given to alternative international monetary systems in which the US dollar would be supplemented as reserve currency by multilateral liquidity creation and in which there would be greater symmetry in the adjustment of surplus and deficit countries. The creation of the special drawing right (SDR) was the main outcome of this process. The SDR gives the automatic right to have access to usable currencies, and was intended to address the Triffin problem mentioned above. However, by the time of the first SDR allocation in 1969, the problem was not a reserve shortage but a glut of US dollars. Thus, the SDR never came close to becoming the "primary reserve asset" of the international monetary system as intended by its creators.

Fundamental reform of the Bretton Woods system was further considered by the Committee of Twenty (representatives of the 20 countries with executive directors at the IMF), but proposals did not command sufficient agreement.

Instead, this reform effort was abandoned and the system (or "nonsystem"[2]) that was created by the floating of currencies against the dollar was made official by the 1976 Jamaica Agreement. This allowed countries to choose any exchange rate regime ranging from a free float to a currency peg (but did not include a peg to gold, which was demonetized).

## 5.3 Performance of the *Laisser-Faire* Exchange Rate System, 1973–2010

The "nonsystem" inherited some of the perceived defects of the Bretton Woods system—no control over international liquidity and asymmetry in the need for adjustment of deficit and surplus countries—supplemented with much greater volatility of exchange rates and at times, large misalignments. At the same time, it allowed much more freedom in the use of monetary policies and no longer obliged countries to defend parities. The flexibility of exchange rates, which facilitated balance of payments adjustment, and the relative absence of rules of the game made the regime relatively robust. In principle, the IMF's Guidelines to Floating ruled out manipulation of exchange rates (for instance, to achieve competitive advantage), and the IMF's surveillance over exchange rate policies existed to rule out negative spillovers. In practice, however, no country was sanctioned for manipulation, and the IMF's advice mostly went unheeded by the major countries, which did not need to access IMF financing.

Assessment of whether the current regime is better or worse than the Bretton Woods system requires addressing two basic issues. First, has the greater flexibility (and consequent volatility) of exchange rates contributed to better balance of payments adjustment (and macroeconomic performance generally)? Second, would the alternative of maintaining fixity of exchange rates be feasible in a context of increasing global financial integration?

Regarding the first issue, since Mussa (1986), it has been recognized that flexible exchange rates have been associated with greater volatility in both *nominal* and *real* exchange rates. This might of course be due to larger shocks during the flexible rate period. However, work by Flood and Rose (1999) concludes that macroeconomic performance seems to be independent of the exchange rate regime—calling into question whether the greater exchange rate volatility since 1973 helped damp the volatility of real variables. Clearly, exchange rate movements not only just serve to achieve macroeconomic adjustment but also induce unneeded fluctuations in international competitiveness.

As for the second issue, the feasibility of a pegged rate system in the present day world, its very breakdown in 1973 is prima facie evidence for a negative answer. But Bayoumi and Eichengreen (1994), who analyze the changes in international monetary regimes starting with the pre-World-War-I gold standard, conclude that it is difficult to identify the causes for the breakdown of Bretton Woods system, as neither increased shocks nor reduced macroeconomic

[2]Williamson, (1976).

flexibility were present. Subsequent exchange rate crises affecting pegged or quasi-fixed exchange rates (the European Monetary System (EMS), Mexico, and Asian emerging markets) confirm the fragility of pegs in a context of high capital mobility and provide strong evidence that reestablishing Bretton Woods system would be impossible. But this leaves open the possibility that a regime of managed floating—intermediate between pegged rates and free floats—might not be both feasible and superior to the current one, producing both balance of payments adjustment and lower exchange rate volatility.

The costs of currency volatility have been hotly debated. Despite a presumption that volatility should have a negative effect on trade, a careful look at economic theory gives an ambiguous answer, and early empirical work suggested that effects in any case were small (Côté, 1994). More recently, interest in this issue has been revived by striking results found by Andrew Rose and others (Frankel and Rose, 2000; Rose, 2000) that trade within currency unions is much greater than the standard gravity model would suggest. Some of this effect seems to come from lower exchange rate volatility, although some is specific to currency unions themselves (Carrère, 2006).

The post-1973 period has, in fact, been characterized by an intensification of economic globalization—despite the fears that exchange rate variability would limit trade and foreign direct investment. As a result, there has been an increase in trade relative to GDP and an even larger increase in cross-border capital flows. Increased economic integration has had a number of causes: (i) technological innovations that have lowered communication and transportation costs; (ii) successive rounds of trade liberalization; and (iii) the inclusion of former communist countries into the world trading and financial system. Increasing capital market integration has also benefited from the introduction of new financial instruments (derivatives, swaps, and forwards) and a reduction in the official barriers to capital flows.

This increased economic integration has had at least three, sometimes conflicting, influences on the global economy. First, it has increased market discipline over government policies, making policymakers more conscious of the need to put their houses in order. Second, it has at times stimulated the perceived need for policy coordination across countries to mitigate unfavorable spillovers. Third, it has helped bring the richer developing countries ("emerging market economies") into world financial affairs, while making them more vulnerable to currency crises.

### 5.3.1 MARKET DISCIPLINE

Financial integration has made the discipline of the market much more stringent. With increased cross-border capital movements, the government cannot rely on a captive market to sell its debt. Flexible exchange rates move quickly to reflect concerns about monetary policy credibility, as was especially evident during the EMS crisis of 1992–1993 and the subsequent emerging market crises. The 2010–2011 euro zone sovereign debt crisis shows that cross-border market discipline can also be exerted strongly in a common currency area. The response of the major industrial countries has been to try to make their monetary and fiscal policies more transparent and sustainable. Inflation targeting has been one manifestation of this, and improved budgetary procedures another. The same forces have been exerted on those emerging market countries that have liberalized their capital accounts, with similar results.

The one notable exception is the United States. Continued demand by other countries for US dollar assets for liquidity purposes and as official foreign exchange reserves has allowed that country to run persistent current account deficits financed at low rates of interest. As a result, the United States is the world's largest net debtor, with a negative net international investment position in excess of $2.7 trillion, about 20% of US GNP.

## 5.3.2 ECONOMIC POLICY COORDINATION

At the same time, the negative spillovers of unsustainable policies and a recognition that the market does not always get it right led to the formation of the G5/G7 in the 1970s and to episodes of policy coordination involving exchange rate intervention and jointly agreed packages of macroeconomic and structural policy measures (Funabashi, 1988). The high points of intervention policy were the Plaza Agreement and Louvre Accord of 1985–1987 to correct the overvaluation of the US dollar and to bring about its subsequent stabilization. The 1978 Bonn Summit also involved a major attempt to coordinate fiscal policies.

Greater coordination of monetary policies has also taken the form of regional agreements. The EMS, created in 1979, aimed to create monetary stability in Europe in the face of global exchange rate instability. It was dealt a major setback in the 1992–1993 EMS crisis, leading to a widening of the bands of fluctuation to ±15% around central parities. It did, nevertheless, help prepare for monetary union. The successful launch of the euro in 1999 has not created the preconditions for macroeconomic policy coordination in Europe that many had hoped, due in part to the failure of the Stability and Growth Pact to exert budget discipline. The sovereign debt crisis affecting Greece, Ireland, Portugal, and Spain that broke out in 2010 led to a recognition that euro zone institutions would have to be strengthened.

In Asia, the Chiang-Mai Initiative aims to achieve monetary integration among ASEAN countries, plus China, Japan, and Korea. At present, this takes the form of swap agreements among the region's central banks, but it may proceed to greater exchange market intervention, target zones, and even a common currency. Africa, the Middle East, and Latin America also have various projects to strengthen regional monetary integration.

## 5.3.3 INTEGRATION OF EMERGING MARKET COUNTRIES INTO THE GLOBAL ECONOMY

Financial integration of developing countries has gone through three phases since 1973. The first phase involved the recycling of petrodollars to developing countries by banks, but with inadequate safeguards to ensure that the recipient countries were investing the funds wisely and would be able to repay their debts. This led to the "lost decade" of the 1980s, when developing countries defaulted and were denied further access to nonofficial lending. The second phase, following the replacement of most of the remaining bank debt by Brady bonds, ushered in a period of major expansion of market-based sovereign bond issues by emerging market countries. This phase was also accompanied by a series of crises, starting with Mexico in 1994, followed by Asia in 1997–98, Brazil in 1999, and so forth. The strength of discipline (for good or bad reasons) that financial markets could exert was brought home to these countries. The third phase was in part a response to the currency crises and was accompanied by major reforms to reduce emerging market countries' vulnerability. These reforms helped align their policies with those of the advanced countries and involved accumulation of foreign exchange reserves, strengthened financial regulation, and improved macroeconomic policies. For instance, a number of countries ranging from Mexico, Brazil, and Indonesia were led to adopt exchange rate flexibility and inflation targeting. At the end of 2010, developing countries held two-thirds of the world's foreign exchange reserves, reversing their share relative to advanced countries of a decade before.

## 5.4 Trends in Currency Use

The currency crises of the EMS, Latin America, and Asia highlighted the fragility of adjustable peg regimes in the context of liberalized capital accounts. This led some to argue that, in fact, only two polar exchange rate regimes were sustainable—namely, a pure float and a hard fix, such as a currency board or a monetary union (Eichengreen, 1994; Obstfeld and Rogoff, 1995). All the intermediate cases of exchange rate regimes, including adjustable pegs and managed floats, were viewed as ultimately condemned to disappear. To quote Eichengreen (1994, pp. 4–5), "... contingent policy rules to hit explicit exchange rate targets will no longer be viable in the twenty-first century ... [C]ountries will be forced to choose between floating exchange rates on the one hand and monetary unification on the other." This theory was called the "two poles" or "hollowing out" hypothesis. It was supported by the well-accepted proposition that countries had to choose at most two among the following three policy objectives, which taken together, were inconsistent: (i) monetary independence; (ii) a pegged exchange rate; and (iii) capital mobility.

Others objected that countries could still choose to trade off one of the policy objectives for the other two and that, moreover, the choice was not all or nothing (Frankel, 1999). For instance, some limits on capital mobility might afford a country some monetary independence even with a pegged exchange rate. Moreover, countries could manage their exchange rates to some extent, without attempting to defend a pegged rate. And countries willing to give up all monetary independence could credibly maintain a pegged rate, despite high capital mobility.[3]

[3]Such as Austria and the Netherlands within the context of the EMS, up until EMU and the replacement of their currencies by the euro.

The classification of exchange rate regimes is subject to much controversy; but the different classifications will not be discussed here. The IMF's revamped classification, reported in the table below, suggests some increase in hard pegs (countries with no separate legal tender and those with currency boards) and floating arrangements and decline in soft pegs over 1996–2007. However, the floats include both managed and independent floats. If we include the former with soft pegs in intermediate exchange rate regimes, as is appropriate, then the trend toward hollowing out of intermediate regimes is modest, at best. In 2007, intermediate regimes still constituted the largest category, prevailing in 130 of 188 countries (Table 5.1).

A formal test of hollowing out using Markov-switching regimes (Appendix A) does not support the disappearance of intermediate regimes. It is true that pegged rate regimes seem to have a limited life span, but this does not preclude countries adopting them for temporary stabilization purposes. History suggests that it is better to think of countries occasionally altering their regime in response to changing circumstances, rather than choosing once and for all the regime that is right for them and keeping that regime for eternity. For instance, adjustable pegs have been chosen by countries facing strong inflationary pressures in a context in which the central bank did not have a great deal of credibility; this policy has been called "exchange-rate-based stabilization." A peg to a stable international currency helps to shore up credibility and to provide a transparent and easily monitored policy rule. While the adjustable peg may not be sustainable forever, it may nevertheless serve as a useful temporary regime for reducing inflation quickly, and it is unrealistic to expect that the circumstances that made such a policy useful in the past will not recur.

This is confirmed when the matrix $P$ of transition probabilities between exchange rate regimes is endogenized using explanatory variables suggested by theories of voluntary and involuntary exits from regimes (Masson and Ruge-Murcia, 2005). Voluntary exits can be explained by optimal currency area criteria, while involuntary exits are those that are consistent with the currency crisis literature. The transition probabilities $p_{ij}$ (the probability of transition from regime $i$ to regime $j$) are allowed to vary over time and made functions of a vector

TABLE 5.1 **Evolution of Exchange Rate Regimes**

| | 1996 | 2001 | 2002 | 2003 | 2004 | 2005 | 2006 | 2007[a] |
|---|---|---|---|---|---|---|---|---|
| Hard pegs | 17 | 21 | 22 | 22 | 22 | 22 | 22 | 23 |
| Soft pegs | 107 | 72 | 73 | 72 | 72 | 76 | 83 | 82 |
| Floating arrangements | 60 | 93 | 92 | 93 | 93 | 89 | 82 | 83 |
| Managed floating | 37 | 43 | 45 | 46 | 49 | 51 | 45 | 48 |
| Independ. floating | 23 | 50 | 47 | 47 | 44 | 38 | 37 | 35 |

[a]April 2007.
*Source*: IMF (2007).

of explanatory variables $X$:

$$P(X_t) = \{p_{ij}(X_t)\} \tag{5.1}$$

The variables in $X$ include inflation, trade openness, GDP growth, and the level of reserves divided by GDP.

Estimation results are different for developed and emerging market economies. The stock of reserves helps explain (inversely) the transition between fixed and intermediate regimes for emerging market countries, but not for developed economies, which do not seem to be constrained by their reserve levels. Low growth helps to explain the transitions from intermediate to floating rate regimes for developed countries, while for emerging economies, high inflation explains transitions both from fixed to intermediate and from intermediate to either fixed or float. This is evidence both of the use of exchange-rate-based stabilization and the ultimate need to exit the peg once cumulated inflation makes a peg untenable.

Thus, poor macroeconomic performance—both low growth and high inflation—leads to changes in policy regime. In response to severe shocks, countries tend to abandon their current policy frameworks and search for alternatives. This was true even of regimes as "iron clad" as the gold standard in the 1930s or Argentina's currency board and convertibility plan, which it exited in 2002. By analogy, one might expect that countries would explore a move back to greater exchange rate fixity if financial turmoil under floating exchange rates became too severe.

### 5.4.1 GLOBAL IMBALANCES AND THE FINANCIAL CRISIS OF 2007–2009

While the evolution of the *laisser-faire* monetary system over its first three decades was accompanied by frequent financial crises affecting developing countries, the advanced countries were largely spared after the EMS crises of 1992–1993. This scenario changed in 2007 when problems in the US subprime mortgage market threatened the banking systems in all the major countries through their holdings of complicated and opaque structured products. While the crisis had many causes, the financial excesses were at least in part fueled by excessive global liquidity and the large current account deficits of the United States that were financed by the buildup of holdings of US assets by foreigners—especially China, whose pegged exchange rate and large current account surpluses forced it to accumulate foreign exchange reserves. By 2010, these amounted to more than two and a half trillion dollars and were still rising.

The crisis highlighted the fundamental absence of control over global liquidity and the lack of pressure on the United States to adjust its macroeconomic policies in order to "live within its means"—that is, to limit its current account deficit and prevent further increases in its indebtedness to foreigners. These deficiencies inspired renewed interest in reform of the international monetary system, with proposals by the BRIC countries to move toward a more managed system with a multilateral reserve asset (Dailami and Masson, 2010). In the following section, the author discusses the prospects for reform and speculates on the evolution of exchange rate arrangements.

## 5.5 Prospects for the Future

The future of exchange rate regimes may be influenced by two distinct types of events. In the context of the current system, or rather "nonsystem" where exchange rate regimes are virtually at the discretion of individual governments, any regime from a pure float to a hard fix is possible—as are regional currencies and dollarization. In light of the experience of the past 40 years, competition among currencies is likely to dictate the choice of international money. However, it is also possible that there might be a concerted move to a different global system—a more managed international monetary system in which the choices of individual countries were constrained and in which the "rules of the game" were made more stringent. Past examples of the latter include, of course, the gold standard and the Bretton Woods system of fixed but adjustable parities, but neither seems likely to be reinstated. Instead, any new system is likely to allow countries to retain considerable flexibility to hit domestic objectives. This is discussed further below, and modifications to the current system are suggested.

### 5.5.1 THE CURRENT SYSTEM

For reasons that have already been discussed, short of a concerted reform, it does not seem likely that the world will converge to a single system, in which all countries let their currencies float freely, despite the arguments of the proponents of such a regime accompanied by inflation targeting (Rose, 2006). The advantages of such a regime have been overstated by its proponents: neither is it true that policy coordination is redundant if all countries adhere to this regime nor does its single-minded focus on inflation to the neglect of financial stability and the risk of asset bubbles seem desirable, especially in the light of the recent global financial crisis. Indeed, a world of exchange rate flexibility and inflation targeting faces two severe problems. First, there is no control over global liquidity, which is the result of the uncoordinated decisions of the central banks issuing key currencies, and this may lead to global asset bubbles or global deflation. Second, exchange rate volatility and misalignments may, at times, be excessive and require a credible commitment to resist them by modifying the policies of systemically important countries. Both these problems require reinforced policy coordination to make the current system work better, and the formation of the G20 and the statements of its leaders indicate agreement, in principle, on the need for greater coordination, if not a road map of how to achieve it.

Another aspect of the current system that can exacerbate the two problems mentioned above is competition for the role of key currency. At present, it is the US dollar that plays this role in most of the uses of an international currency such as in other countries' foreign exchange reserves (where its share is currently about 64%), as a vehicle currency for forex trading (where the dollar is one of the two currencies used in 85% of all global trades), in trade invoicing, in denominating international debt (although the euro is a serious rival here), etc. There has been much speculation, however, that the decline of the dollar, fueled by high US indebtedness to foreigners and continuing large budget deficits, will lead to a much more multipolar international monetary system, with other currencies rivaling the dollar. Chinn and Frankel (2008), for instance, argue that in the coming decade, the euro is likely to take over the top spot, while Persaud (2007) suggests that in the not too distant future, China's renminbi will reflect the importance of China in the global economy—and China's GDP is slated to become the world's largest within a decade or two. Others are sceptical that the economic and political factors that have led to the dollar's dominance will go away, including the dynamism of the US economy in technological innovation, the importance of the US for global security, and the existence of deep and broad US financial markets supported by an independent central bank and a liquid market in Treasury securities (Cooper, 1973; Helleiner, 2009; Posen, 2008). In fact, the euro has disappointed some of its proponents and has so far mainly served as a *regional* currency, not an international one (ECB, 2010). As for the renminbi, it has virtually no international role at present, and China requires further major liberalization of its capital account, exchange rate flexibility, and domestic financial reforms before the renminbi assumes one (Dobson and Masson, 2009).

The creation of a more symmetric, multipolar world monetary system with several key currencies may lead to greater instability, as countries attempt to exert their power and rivalry for the advantages that a global currency brings. In the years leading up to the creation of the euro, there was already concern that a Europe that was more unified and less open to the outside would make policy coordination more difficult (Alogoskoufis and Portes, 1997). Consistent with the theory of hegemonic stability (Kindleberger, 1973), the lack of a global hegemon in the future may threaten stability of the international monetary system (Cohen, 1998, 2000). In fact, trade within regional blocs has continued to grow faster than trade between blocs, suggesting that the forces toward regionalism are outpacing those for globalization. Blocs that are relatively closed to the outside world can more easily use trade protection as a policy weapon to achieve their goals because they are less vulnerable to retaliation. On the monetary front, the example of the euro has led to other projects for regional currencies. They include proposals for common currencies among the countries of the Gulf Cooperation Council, several regional groupings in Africa, MERCOSUR, and the countries of East Asia grouped together in the Chiang Mai Initiative. While these other potential regional currencies have considerably less institutional backing at present than does the euro zone, a world with fewer currencies than the present seems a likely outcome a decade or two later. Strengthening of regional blocs may exacerbate the problems facing the current *laisser-faire* international monetary system and lead to calls for change.

## 5.5.2 TOWARD A MORE MANAGED INTERNATIONAL MONETARY SYSTEM?

The challenge to the role of the dollar may come not from other national currencies, but from the move to a new monetary system in which countries agree to vest responsibility for the control of international liquidity to a global body and take it away from national central banks (Dailami and Masson, 2010). Such a system—which revives Keynes' notion of a world reserve bank—would seem to be the ultimate objective of the proposal by the BRIC countries to increase the attractiveness of the SDR in international financial markets. The SDR, when it was created in the late 1960s, was intended to become the primary reserve asset of the international monetary system—a role that it has never played. Even after the agreement in 2009 for a general allocation to augment the stock of SDRs by $250 billion, they still represent only 4% of global foreign exchange reserves. After a brief flurry of issuance of SDR-linked private securities three decades ago, the private SDR market has become virtually moribund and pegs to the SDR currency basket have also almost disappeared. Thus, the BRIC initiative to revive the importance of the SDR seems a long shot indeed.

More seriously, for the chances that the SDR would replace the dollar and other national currencies in international use, the SDR neither has proved a very attractive reserve asset nor is it a currency on its own—just the right to draw other usable currencies. So issuing more SDRs would not change the amount of national currencies in circulation. While the SDR in its current form could be made into a world currency if governments decided at some stage that they were willing to do so (as EU countries were willing to do for the ECU, which was a basket of currencies that became the euro), the leap required would be enormous. It would presuppose agreement to create in effect a world central bank, which in order to gain legitimacy would itself require strengthening of other global institutions. The prospect of any such agreement seems many decades away, if at all conceivable.

In what other ways could the rules of the game be modified in order to constrain national governments more strictly with the aim of ruling out some of the excesses that were discussed above? It seems clear that ad hoc coordination of policies, whether to intervene in exchange markets (such as those embodied in the 1985 Plaza Agreement) or occasional bargains to modify macroeconomic or structural policies (such as the 1978 Bonn Summit) are not sufficient; they are too dependent on the vagaries of domestic politics and the personalities of those who happen to be in power at the time. There are at least three types of policy rules with automatic triggers that could be envisaged instead: (i) rules on allowable *exchange rate behavior*; (ii) limits on *balance of payments positions*; and (iii) criteria for proscribing beggar-thy-neighbor *macroeconomic policies*.

**5.5.2.1 Exchange Rate Rules.** The Bretton Woods system prevented countries from gaining competitive advantage by engineering depreciations of their currencies, unless a "fundamental disequilibrium" of their balance of payments was present. In contrast, in a world of generalized floating, the opposite problem arises: a country should not be able to achieve a position of competitive advantage by preventing the operation of market forces on its currency's value. This was the objective of the Guidelines to Floating, adopted by the IMF in 1977; it proscribed "currency manipulation," which could be identified (in principle) by evidence of prolonged one-way intervention in exchange markets. In practice, the Guidelines have not been applied—even in the most obvious case of China, which has intervened massively throughout the past decade in the face of enormous current and capital account surpluses, leading it to accumulate the largest foreign exchange reserves ever. The system could be reformed to make the Guidelines effective, for instance, by prescribing penalties that could take effect automatically. As an example, currency manipulation could lead to countervailing duties being authorized by the WTO.

In effect, the current "anything goes" system where all exchange rate regimes are permitted would be considerably narrowed if currency manipulation were ruled out. It is important to understand that all fixed rate systems face periods of sustained one-way intervention; this is true because shocks are serially correlated and their effects are also persistent. This helps explain why the Europeans have never been keen on applying the Guidelines to Floating, because the EMS faced extended periods of speculative attacks against its central parities, and politicians and central bankers used a variety of policies, including intervention, to resist them. A stringent prohibition of one-way intervention would effectively achieve the "hollowing out" of intermediate regimes that its proponents have claimed market forces will eventually do. It would virtually rule out adjustable pegs and impose severe limits on "managed floats." Presumably, currency boards could still be allowed to operate on the presumption that the self-equilibrating changes in the domestic money supply would rule out prolonged one-way accumulation or decumulation of reserves (although the experience, e.g., of Argentina, makes that presumption questionable). So, in effect, it would produce a world in which all currencies floated more or less freely.

As argued above, countries use exchange-rate-based stabilizations because, as a result of large external shocks or policy errors, they want to achieve rapid disinflation and shore up the credibility of the domestic monetary authorities. Ruling out currency manipulation would eliminate this option. While a case might be made that it was desirable to do so, some countries nevertheless would object to any reform of the system along these lines. In any case, a problem arises for the system not so much from exchange-rate-based stabilizations, but rather when countries maintain an undervalued exchange rate to stimulate exports and growth. Obviously, the size of a country matters, and it may be thought that the problem of China should be treated as a one-off since the Chinese authorities have indicated their willingness to embrace greater exchange rate flexibility.

Another type of exchange rate rule would put in place a form of managed floating subject to specific rules designed to combine exchange rate flexibility with measures to prevent excessive volatility and misalignments of currency values. This could take the form of a system of "target zones" for exchange rates—a proposal most closely associated with John Williamson (Williamson, 1993). There are two key elements for its successful operation: agreement on a consistent set of exchange rate targets and effective tools for hitting those targets. On the one hand, countries (and experts) have often disagreed on the "fundamental equilibrium" exchange rates. On the other hand, intervention to defend depreciating currencies alone in the presence of freely mobile capital is likely to be ineffective. A successful system also needs to impose policy adjustments on the appreciating currencies, but it is much more difficult to get their agreement to do so.

Given these difficulties, one could envision relaxing the requirement to maintain exchange rates within narrow margins. However, widening the bands, as was done in the EMS, or making the ranges "soft bands" rather than fixed limits, detracts from the stabilizing benefits of operating a target zone system. Therefore, short of reducing the mobility of capital, it is unlikely that a formal target zone system would be put in place as part of a fundamental reform of the international monetary system (although a de facto grid of what are judged to be equilibrium exchange rates may at times embody a consensus of official views and guide ad hoc currency intervention).

**5.5.2.2 Balance of Payments Rules.** The economic spillovers between countries operate mainly through their balances of payments. Moreover, exchange rate misalignments and inappropriate domestic policies (such as a tax system that discourages saving) can be expected to show up in imbalances in the current account. Hence the interest in using some measure of external payments disequilibrium as a trigger for policy action by the country concerned. This was widely discussed by the G5/G7 and international organizations in the 1970s and 1980s (Frenkel et al., 1990) and was recently revived in a proposal to the G20 by the US Treasury Secretary, Timothy Geithner[4] A country's current account surplus of deficit would be limited to some proportion of its GDP, say 4%. If it exceeded that threshold, the country would have to take policy measures to bring it back within the allowable range.

The earlier consideration of such rules, inspired in part by US current account deficits and Japanese surpluses in the early 1980s highlighted the importance of understanding the source of the current account deficits or surpluses. Deficits can be the result of inadequate saving (including fiscal dissaving) or, instead, a result of unusually attractive investment opportunities. Imbalances are the outcome of the complex interaction of government policies and private sector behavior; a closer analysis is needed to come to a judgment concerning the causes and whether there is reason for concern. Hence the difficulty in coming up with a rule that would link an indicator variable with policy action. So it is hard to imagine a rules-based international regime along these lines, although current account indicators could well be a trigger for international discussion and further analysis.

Another type of balance of payments rule might be to impose a system of constraints on capital movements or on the stocks of foreign assets and liabilities. One could, for instance, prevent countries from acquiring foreign currency debt in excess of their foreign exchange reserves. This proposal was made by Morris

[4]http://graphics8.nytimes.com/packages/pdf/10222010geithnerletter.pdf.

Goldstein (Goldstein, 2002), as a way of reducing the likelihood of emerging market crises. Another possibility would be to prevent accumulation of reserves beyond a certain amount (based on underlying characteristics of the economy, such as GDP, imports, etc.). This would address a concern that the current system (and Bretton Woods system before it) apply asymmetric pressures to adjust on surplus and deficit countries: the latter are forced to adjust since there is a floor to reserves, while the former can, in principle, accumulate unlimited reserves and postpone adjustment indefinitely. Rather than forcing exchange rate flexibility on China, a ceiling on reserves would allow it to choose from the array of policy changes those that it felt would be preferable to avoid the "prolonged one-way intervention" that led to the further accumulation of reserves.

Finally, one could imagine a change in the rules of the game that led to a world in which certain types of capital movements (such as short-term flows) were systematically constrained using capital controls or Tobin taxes—whatever the balance of payments position. While possible in principle, a systemic reform to turn back the clock in this area seems politically unlikely, given the trend toward liberalization, and hard to enforce, given advances in communications technology and the explosion of derivative financial instruments.

**5.5.2.3 Macroeconomic Policy Rules.** International policy coordination in the post-1973 world has ultimately been about the underlying macroeconomic policies, rather than about their symptoms—values taken by exchange rates or balances of payments. However, countries have rarely been able to reach agreement on coordinated policy packages. Could one formalize a set of rules for macroeconomic policies in a way that would limit payments imbalances and excessive exchange rate movements? For instance, countries that operate inflation targeting regimes can be evaluated on whether their inflation target is appropriate (most developed countries aim for a range around 2%, but developing countries have higher targets), and how successful they are at meeting their targets. Fiscal policies are more complicated since they have many dimensions: the level of tax rates, their progressivity, the size and composition of government spending, etc.). An overall measure of the stance of fiscal policy, however, is the fiscal deficit or surplus (perhaps corrected for the cycle). One could formulate an acceptable range for the fiscal position. Countries going outside that range should make policy adjustments to bring the fiscal position back inside the range.

However, the experience of international economic policy coordination since 1973 has shown how complex it is to analyze monetary and fiscal policies. While monetary policy is simpler to evaluate than fiscal policy, there is considerable uncertainty about future inflation. Moreover, monetary policy is not unidimensional: the inclusion of financial stability as an objective makes an assessment of the appropriate level of interest rates much more difficult. As for fiscal policy, the euro zone's attempt to use the fiscal deficit as the sole indicator of the appropriateness of policies has been an abject failure. While this failure has had a number of causes, it underscores the fact that fiscal policy has many objectives and is typically driven by a political process that is hard to constrain.

During the 1990s, the IMF's policy conditionality moved more and more toward detailed conditions on fiscal and structural policies for the countries that borrowed from it. In contrast, those that did not, including the major developed countries as well as the surplus countries such as oil exporters and China, could ignore the IMF's advice proffered in the context of annual Article IV examinations and the semiannual *World Economic Outlook*. A backlash against detailed macroeconomic policy conditions led the IMF in 2007 to refocus its surveillance on exchange rates. However, this had little effect, since surveillance over exchange rate policies has no more teeth than it had before.

Time will tell if the G20's attempt to exert peer pressure on its members' policies (the mutual assessment process (MAP)) will have more effect, but the current dispute over exchange rate levels and current account imbalances illustrates the problem with trying to get agreement on targets for variables that are inherently zero-sum—that is, have a beggar-thy-neighbor aspect. When there is a global shock (inflationary or deflationary), countries would all like to move their exchange rates and/or current accounts in the same direction, either to stimulate demand or to dampen inflationary pressures. The rules of the game of the gold standard or Bretton Woods proscribed this, but nothing similar exists at present. Unless the international rules of the games are reformed, or national policy regimes focus on variables that are international public goods, the G20 will only provide a forum for ad hoc coordination when the situation facing countries is sufficiently different that they can agree to policies that do not simply shift a problem from one country to another.

### 5.5.3 HOW AND WHEN WILL REFORM OCCUR?

It seems certain that the international monetary system will evolve—in some direction or other. We have sketched out some of the possibilities for new rules of the game that could be agreed to in principle by all countries, or at least by a sufficiently large number of countries to enable imposing these rules on other countries. Past experience suggests, however, that the rules of the game are rarely negotiated, but are rather more often adopted unilaterally by countries as a response to the occurrence of a crisis or even more dramatically, to the breakdown of the existing system. They may then be codified by formal agreements that make them into the accepted "rules of the game."

For instance, the Paris Conference of 1867 aimed to extend bimetallism to the international monetary system, but it failed, and in another decade, the Latin Monetary Union had in effect disappeared as all the remaining major countries switched to the gold standard. The Genoa International Monetary Conference of 1922 passed resolutions to establish an institutional framework for cooperation to make the gold exchange standard work, but these resolutions were not adopted by the governments themselves. By the early 1930s, the system had broken down, and flexible exchange rates prevailed through the World War II.

The partial exception, of course, was the Bretton Woods agreement of 1944, which created a universal system[5] with clear rules of the game. However, this was

[5]Although the communist countries did not subscribe to it.

achieved in very special circumstances. Only two countries—the United States and the United Kingdom—were in a position to call the shots, and in the end, it was only one that did so. Moreover, the Bretton Woods system, although it lasted almost three decades, eventually succumbed to market forces. It was patched up by the Smithsonian Agreement of December 1971, hailed by President Nixon as the "greatest monetary agreement in the history of the world," but this lasted barely 2 years. In 1973, there was generalized floating of the major currencies, which emerged when the countries concerned refused to acquire further dollar reserves and to maintain their currencies within margins of agreed parities.

Only a severe crisis is likely to lead to a negotiated reform of the international monetary system of major proportions, and even then, as the Smithsonian Agreement has shown, it may have a very short shelf life. Thus, if one had to speculate on the circumstances likely to trigger reform in the future, it seems more likely to be the result of a series of minor changes—some of them perhaps agreed incremental changes to the rules of the game, others taken unilaterally by a sufficient number of countries—leading to a new regime whose evolution was not completely planned nor foreseen.

### 5.5.4 A GLOBAL NOMINAL ANCHOR?

Given the difficulties in reaching agreement on broad-based international monetary reform, it is worth exploring how market forces could encourage de facto coordination of policies. As suggested above, countries should try to coordinate around "international public goods" rather than "conflict variables," examples of the latter being the exchange rate and the current account. Problems with the latter variables occur at the time of major crisis, when a global shock makes all countries want to see these variables move in the same direction, but by their very nature, a gain for one country is a loss for others. Rules of the game could be devised to rule out using these variables at the expense of others, such as a pegged rate system, but as discussed above, a return to a Bretton-Woods-like system is unlikely.

One common objective of countries is control over inflation, and this helps explain the popularity of inflation targeting monetary policy regimes. But experience has shown that success in meeting inflation objectives (even when countries aim at the same target level of 2%) neither ensures exchange rate stability nor rules out beggar-thy-neighbor behavior. It may be worth considering moving away from national inflation targeting to a regime in which countries target the same basket of goods (and possibly services). If each of the issuers of key currencies committed to stabilizing the value of a basket of international goods and services in terms of its own currency, this would also stabilize their bilateral exchange rates. Most practical would probably be an index of prices of commodities that were actively traded, but it could also be a broader measure of inflation. Note that such a regime would *not* be equivalent to targeting domestic inflation (or the price level) since the basket would not be limited to a country's own goods and services but rather key off international prices. The fact that several key currency countries could target the same basket would allow coordination of policies to emerge naturally, without detailed agreement except on the composition of the basket (each country would target the same average price, but expressed in its *own* currency).

Note that this proposal concerns the key world economies, not the commodity exporters. Frankel (2011) proposes that each of the latter should target its export price. But since that price (in dollars, say) would be largely exogenous, targeting the domestic currency value of the export commodity would transmit the exogenous fluctuations in its dollar price to the country's dollar exchange rate, inducing an appreciation when the commodity's dollar price was high, and the converse when it was low. It would do nothing to stabilize the bilateral exchange rates of the key currencies themselves or the value of a basket of commodities.

By targeting an international price basket, the United States could enhance the attractiveness of the dollar as a key currency and assert its role as a global leader. It might induce other countries to do the same thing and thus promote global exchange rate stability through currency competition. Rather than achieving a managed international monetary system by a negotiated "big bang," this would occur through the voluntary and unilateral policy moves of the major countries. In these circumstances, smaller countries would also find it in their interest to target such a basket. If all countries successfully maintained their currency values in terms of the same price index, their exchange rates would effectively be stabilized within narrow ranges.

Such a system would have the advantage of moving away from a national focus of monetary policies. And because countries could then target the same thing, exchange rate stability would naturally emerge. The issue of what basket to use would of course have to be faced, and this might be the most difficult challenge.

A global inflation target (using an aggregate CPI, GDP deflator, or personal consumption deflator) would be the most attractive on theoretical grounds but would face the greatest data problems. Instead of global inflation, G20 inflation would probably be a sufficiently good approximation, and this index could then provide a centerpiece for G20 coordination. Nevertheless, price indices would have to be harmonized (as in the European Union) for a G20 price index to be a reliable guide to inflation. A narrower index based on a basket of commodities traded on organized exchanges would provide a more straightforward and transparent anchor for policy. Moreover, targeting a basket of widely traded commodities could be implemented by buying and selling those commodities directly or by trading derivative instruments. Thus, a monetary policy commitment could, in principle, be achieved with a fair degree of accuracy in this case. However, the exclusion of manufactures and services might well cause problems if their prices relative to commodities changed in a major way (as has been the case in the past). Targeting a basket of commodities would be a vast improvement over a single-commodity anchor, such as gold, but nevertheless, the aggregate supply of commodities would come into play.

This is actually an old idea[6], which was advanced by Keynes in his *Treatise on Money* and repeated by Richard Cooper at a Bologna-Claremont Monetary

[6]I discovered this by chance, after having reinvented the wheel.

Conference (Mundell et al., 2005, pp. 138–39). Keynes proposed to have countries target a wholesale price index, which as Cooper points out, would have the advantage of including mainly tradable goods whose prices were readily available. Such an index could be stabilized while allowing other prices (in particular, nontraded goods and services) to rise, lessening the risk of overall deflation. Thus, targeting a stable level of wholesale prices could turn out to give an overall rate of inflation roughly equal to 2%. If so, the transition from current inflation targeting regimes to targeting wholesale prices would be eased. An objection to such a regime, however, is that it would target the most flexible prices, not the most sticky, and the latter is the basis for targeting "core inflation" by those countries that have an explicit inflation target. To work well, then, this regime would have to bring about greater flexibility of other prices and wages. This might be the price to be paid for enhanced exchange rate stability—or perhaps a collateral benefit of it.

## 5.6 Concluding Comments

For the first time in decades, the world's international monetary relations are subject to serious scrutiny. The relative decline of the United States and associated concerns about the dollar's value, the creation of the euro, and the rise of emerging market economies all suggest a move away from a system that is centered on the dollar. However, what form an alternative system might take is highly uncertain. One possibility is that a new monetary system with more constraining rules of the game could be put in place after international negotiation and agreement. Such a system would be unlikely to involve fixed exchange rates but could involve greater constraints on exchange rate policies, balance of payments positions, or macroeconomic policies. But past history suggests that reaching agreement on far-reaching international monetary reform is very hard to achieve and difficult to sustain. Moreover, there is considerable inertia in monetary relations. Instead, regime changes, if at all they occur, are often taken unilaterally, under the pressure of market forces.

These considerations lead some to conclude that the dollar's role at the center of the international monetary system is not really threatened and that the current "nonsystem" will continue in place: countries choose their macroeconomic policies and exchange rate regimes in a way that they believe is most conducive to achieving their domestic objectives. Policy coordination, if it occurs at all, is episodic and is a response to situations of generalized crisis.

However, there may be a middle ground in which policy coordination is institutionalized and strengthened through the operation of market forces, provided agreement can be reached on a common target for monetary policies. As discussed above, none of the traditional variables—whether exchange rates, balance of payments positions, or the overall stance of macroeconomic policies—seems to hold out much hope as a basis for rules-based coordination. It is suggested above that targeting a common price index instead might provide incentives for coordination and de facto exchange rate stability. If this were so, exchange rate regimes could evolve in a direction that provided some of the benefits of the Bretton Woods system without the associated currency and balance of payments crises.

## APPENDIX A: A FORMAL TEST OF HOLLOWING OUT

The hypothesis of hollowing out needs to be supported by more than assertion or casual empiricism. In Masson (2001), the hypothesis is formally tested in the context of a Markov-chain model of the transitions between exchange rate regimes. In this model, the probability of moving between the three regimes—fixed, intermediate, and flexible—is assumed to be constant (including the probability of remaining in the current regime). Then, the hollowing out hypothesis can be equated with a test for whether the two polar regimes constitute a *closed set*—there can be transitions toward them from intermediate regimes and transitions between fixed and flexible, but none toward the intermediate regimes. This hypothesis can be tested on the estimated transition matrix. If true, the hypothesis implies that the long-run distribution of exchange rate regimes, obtained by iterating the Markov chain to infinity, would involve fixed and flexible regimes and zero occurrence of intermediate regimes.

Writing this formally, let the transition probabilities be a matrix $P = \{p_{ij}\}$, with the sum across each row equal to unity. Thus, in the general case, the matrix has the following form:

| | Probability of regime in period $t$ | | |
|---|---|---|---|
| Regime in $t$-$1$ | Fix | Intermediate | Float |
| Fix | $p_{11}$ | $p_{12}$ | $p_{13}$ |
| Intermediate | $p_{21}$ | $p_{22}$ | $p_{23}$ |
| Float | $p_{31}$ | $p_{32}$ | $p_{33}$ |

Hollowing out will occur if and only if one or both of the fixed and floating regimes constitute an absorbing state, or if they together constitute a closed set. In either case, there will be transitions away from the intermediate regimes, but no transitions toward them, so the distribution of regimes will in the long run not include any intermediate regimes.

If the fixed rate regime is an absorbing state, then the transition matrix takes the following form (and similarly if float is an absorbing state):

| | Probability of regime in period $t$ | | |
|---|---|---|---|
| Regime in $t$-$1$ | Fix | Intermediate | Float |
| Fix | 1 | 0 | 0 |
| Intermediate | $p_{21}$ | $p_{22}$ | $p_{23}$ |
| Float | $p_{31}$ | $p_{32}$ | $p_{33}$ |

If the two polar regimes constitute a closed set, then

| | Probability of regime in period $t$ | | |
|---|---|---|---|
| Regime in *t-1* | Fix | Intermediate | Float |
| Fix | $p_{11}$ | 0 | $1 - p_{11}$ |
| Intermediate | $p_{21}$ | $p_{22}$ | $p_{23}$ |
| Float | $1 - p_{33}$ | 0 | $p_{33}$ |

The long-run distribution of regimes can be found by iterating the transition matrix. If the initial distribution of regimes is given by $\pi_0$, then the long run (or *invariant*) distribution will be given by $\overline{\pi} = \lim_{n \to \infty} \pi_0 P^n$. It can be verified that in the two cases above, the invariant distribution contains no regimes in the intermediate category.

Testing the hypothesis of hollowing out involves estimating an unrestricted transition matrix and a transition matrix corresponding to an absorbing state or closed set, and doing a likelihood ratio test for equality between them. A difficult issue is the classification of exchange rate regimes into the three categories. The first difficulty is that countries officially report to the IMF regimes that do not correspond to actual behavior. Thus there have been several attempts to identify the actual regime. Second is the issue of dividing lines between fixed, intermediate, and floating. In defining regimes, Masson (2001) reports two classifications and defines fixes and floats relatively narrowly, in order to guard against biasing the test of hollowing out toward rejection (since a somewhat broader definition would produce more transitions away from the poles). Transition matrices are estimated over several time periods, but only estimates for the most recent time period, with the Ghosh et al. (1997) classification, are reported here. These estimates provide the most support for the hollowing out hypothesis.

| Estimated transition matrix, 1990–1997 | | |
|---|---|---|
| 0.9909 | 0.0000 | 0.0091 |
| 0.0055 | 0.9234 | 0.0711 |
| 0.0066 | 0.1093 | 0.8841 |

Test for a closed set of fixes and floats: reject at $p < 0.0001$.
Test of fix as absorbing state: reject at $p = 0.137$.
Test of flex as absorbing state: reject at $p < 0.0001$.

There were no transitions from fix (limited to currency boards and announced pegs with no changes in parities) to intermediate regimes in the sample, explaining why fix as an absorbing state can only be rejected at the 13.7% level[7]. Despite this, the implied invariant distribution gives a significant weight to intermediate regimes, one that is greater than the proportion either of fixes or floats in 1997:

[7]The next decade was to see a notable transition away from a currency board in Argentina.

| | Fix | Intermediate | Float |
|---|---|---|---|
| Distribution in 1997 | 0.1677 | 0.5749 | 0.2575 |
| Invariant distribution | 0.3954 | 0.3554 | 0.2492 |

## REFERENCES

Alogoskoufis G, Portes R. The euro, the dollar, and the international monetary system. In: Masson PR, Krueger TH, Turtelboom BG, editors. EMU and the international monetary system. Washington (DC): International Monetary Fund; 1997.

Bayoumi T, Eichengreen B. Economic performance under alternative exchange rate regimes: some historical evidence. In: Kenen PB, Papadia F, Saccomanni F, editors. The international monetary system. Cambridge, New York: Cambridge University Press; 1994.

Carrère C. Revisiting the effects of regional trading agreements on trade flows with proper specification of the gravity model. Eur Econ Rev 2006;50(2):223–247.

Cassell G. The downfall of the gold standard. London: Oxford at the Clarendon Press; 1936.

Chinn M, Frankel J. Why the euro will rival the dollar. Int Finance 2008;11(1):49–73.

Chown JF. A history of money from AD 800. London, New York: Routledge; 1994.

Cohen BJ. The geography of money. Ithaca (NY): Cornell University Press; 1998.

——. Life at the top: international currencies in the twenty-first century, Essays in International Finance 221. Princeton (NJ): Princeton University; 2000.

Cooper RN. The future of the dollar. Foreign Policy 1973;11:4.

Côté A. Exchange rate volatility and trade, Working Paper No. 94-5; Bank of Canada, Ottawa; 1994.

Dailami M, Masson PR. Toward a more managed international monetary system? Int J 2010;65(2):393–409.

de Cecco M. Money and empire: the international gold standard, 1890–1914. Oxford: Basil Blackwell; 1974.

Dobson W, Masson PR. Will the renminbi become a world currency? China Econ Rev 2009;20(1):124–135.

Eagleton C, Williams J. Money: a history. 2nd ed. London: British Museum Press; 2007.

ECB. The international role of the Euro. Frankfurt: European Central Bank; 2010.

Eichengreen B. Golden fetters: the gold standard and the great depression, 1919–1939. New York, London: Oxford University Press; 1992.

Eichengreen B. International monetary arrangements for the 21st Century. Washington (DC): Brookings; 1994.

Flood RD, Rose AK. Understanding exchange rate volatility without the contrivance of macroeconomics. Econ J 1999;109:660–672.

Frankel JA. No single currency regime is right for all countries or at all times Essays in International Finance 213. Princeton (NJ): Princeton University; 1999.

Frankel JA. How can commodity exporters make fiscal and monetary policy less procyclical? HKS Faculty Research Working Paper Series RWP11-015. Cambridge (MA): Harvard Kennedy School; 2011.

Frankel JA, Rose AK. Estimating the effect of currency unions on trade and output, NBER Working Paper 7857. Cambridge (MA): National Bureau of Economic Research; 2000.

Frenkel JA, Goldstein M, Masson PR. The Rationale for, and effects of, international economic policy coordination. In: Branson WH, Frenkel JA, Goldstein M, editors. International policy coordination and exchange rate fluctuations. Chicago: University of Chicago Press for the National Bureau of Economic Research; 1990.

Funabashi Y. Managing the dollar: from the plaza to the louvre. Washington (DC): Institute for International Economics; 1988.

Ghosh A, Gulde A-M, Ostry J, Wolf H. Does the nominal exchange rate matter? NBER Working Paper 5874. Cambridge (MA): National Bureau of Economic Research; 1997.

Goldstein M. Managed floating plus. Policy analyses in international economics 66. Washington (DC): Peterson Institute for International Economics; 2002.

Helleiner E. Enduring top currency, fragile negotiated currency: politics and the dollar's international role. In: Helleiner E, Kirshner J, editors. The future of the dollar. Ithaca (NY): Cornell University Press; 2009.

IMF. Review of exchange arrangements, restrictions, and controls. Washington (DC): International Monetary Fund; 2007.

Keynes JM. The Economic Consequences of the Peace. New York: Harcourt, Brace & World, 1920.

Kindleberger C. The world in depression, 1929–1939. Berkeley (CA): University of California Press; 1973.

Masson PR. Exchange rate regime transitions. J Dev Econ 2001;64:571–586.

Masson PR, Ruge-Murcia F. Explaining the transitions between exchange rate regimes. Scand J Econ 2005;107(2):261–278.

Mundell R, Zak P, Shaeffer D, editors. International monetarypolicy after the Euro. Cheltenham, UK: Edward Elgar; 2005.

Mussa MM. Nominal exchange rate regimes and the behaviour of the real exchange rate, Carnegie-Rochester Series on Public Policy; Amsterdam: North-Holland 1986. pp. 117–213.

Nurkse R. International currency experience. Princeton (NJ): League of Nations; 1944.

Obstfeld M, Rogoff K. The mirage of fixed exchange rates. J Econ Perspect 1995;9(4):73–96.

Persaud A. Is the Chinese growth miracle built to last? Manuscript; 2007 July.

Posen A. Why the euro will not rival the dollar. Int Finance 2008;11(1):75–100.

Rose AK. One money, one market: the effect of common currencies on trade. Econ Policy 2000;15(30):9–45.

Rose AK. A stable international monetary system emerges: Inflation targeting is Bretton Woods, reversed, NBER Working Paper 12711. Cambridge (MA): National Bureau of Economic Research; 2006.

Solomon R. The international monetary system, 1945–1981. New York: Harper and Row; 1982.

Triffin R. Gold and the Dollar Crisis: The Future of Convertibility. New Haven: Yale University Press, 1960.

Williamson J. The benefits and costs of an international monetary nonsystem. In: Bernstein EM, et al. editors. Reflections on Jamaica, Essays in International Finance 115. Princeton (NJ): Princeton University; 1976. pp. 54–59.

Williamson J. Exchange rate management. Econ J 1993;103:188–197.

Yeager LB. From gold to the ecu: the international monetary system in retrospect. Independent Rev 1996;1:75–99.

# PART TWO

# Exchange Rate Models and Methods

CHAPTER SIX

# Purchasing Power Parity in Economic History

LAWRENCE H. OFFICER
Department of Economics, University of Illinois at Chicago

## 6.1 Introduction

This essay, which draws on Officer (2006), surveys the application of purchasing power parity (PPP) to historical experiences. To be considered in the historical domain and therefore included in this essay, a study's time period must fully antedate the year 1940. This arbitrary bar means that World War II and the Bretton Woods system are "post-history." The many fixed and floating-exchange-rate episodes before Bretton Woods enable a logical ordering of the essay. The literature is surveyed according to historical periods, with each period delineated according to exchange-rate regime or regimes.

Section 6.2 categorizes PPP theories, while Section 6.3 presents applications of PPP to the premodern period. Section 6.4 outlines the various methods of testing the theory, and Section 6.5 discusses the all-important price concept in PPP. Tests of the theory for the modern period (eighteenth century to 1940) are covered in Section 6.6. PPP analysis of the United States return to the gold standard is discussed in Section 6.7. Section 6.8 looks at actual situations (in the interwar period) in which PPP was applied to determine a new exchange rate. Concluding comments are in Section 6.9.

*Handbook of Exchange Rates*, First Edition. Edited by Jessica James, Ian W. Marsh, and Lucio Sarno.

## 6.2 Categorization of Purchasing-Power-Parity Theories

This essay interprets PPP theory broadly.[1] Consider the variables $P$ (domestic price index), $P^*$ (foreign price index), $E$ (nominal exchange rate), $R$ (PPP), and $Q$ (real exchange rate), where $R = P^*/P$ and $Q = ER$. $E$ is defined as the number of units of domestic currency per unit of foreign currency, but may alternatively be expressed as an index number; $R$ may be reexpressed as an index number; and $Q$ is always dimensionless.

Any PPP theory can be represented by the implicit function $G(E, P, P^*, X)$, where $X$ is a vector of variables that can include (i) $E$, $P$, $P^*$ in earliest periods and (ii) additional variables in the current period and in earlier periods. For a specific $G$ function to be considered a PPP theory, it is necessary that certain minimum requirements be satisfied. First, the $G$ equation must be solvable in terms of $E$: $E = g(P, P^*, X)$. The $E$ that results from solving the $G$ function may be the actual exchange rate in the current period, the equilibrium exchange rate in the current period, or the long-run equilibrium exchange rate. Second, partial derivatives must have sign consistent with PPP theory: $\partial E/\partial P > 0$, $\partial E/\partial P^* < 0$.

Inclusion of (ii) variables other than $E$, $P$, and $P^*$ in $G$ results in an "augmented PPP theory" (the term suggested in Officer, 1982, p. 188). Is an augmented PPP theory legitimately classified within the domain of PPP? Reasonable scholars may differ on this point, but a sensible statement is as follows: The greater the importance of $R$ (or $P$ and $P^*$ individually) relative to the other determinants of $E$, the more clearly the augmented theory is in the PPP rubric.

The variables $E$, $P$, and $P^*$ may enter in several ways. The general $G$ function involves a trivariable theory: $E$, $P$, and $P^*$ entering as separate variables. A bivariable theory combines two of these variables; generally, $R$ replaces $P$ and $P^*$ in $G$. The theory is univariable if $Q$ then replaces $R$ and $E$. A theory has the property of "symmetry" if there are identical magnitude effects of the domestic and foreign price levels on the exchange rate ($\partial E/\partial P/\partial E/\partial P^* = -1$) and "proportionality" if that identical magnitude is unity. The theory in terms of the real exchange rate is proportional if $\partial Q/\partial R$ is a constant. Linear or log-linear $G$ functions can yield these properties.

Univariable, bivariable, and trivariable theories may or may not have the property of "exclusiveness" (the term coined by Edison, 1987, p. 378). The $G$ function involves exclusivity (perhaps a better term) if the $X$ vector does not include any variables other than lagged $E$ or lagged $R$ (or lagged $P$ and $P^*$). Define "super-exclusivity" as the absence even of the latter variables; under symmetry, the $G$ function reduces to $G(E, R) = 0$. If PPP theory is univariable and super-exclusive, the $G$ function becomes $G(Q) = 0$. If the $G$ function is linear, it reduces to $Q = c$, where $c$ is a constant.

[1] However, the essay discusses only relative PPP, a reflection of the PPP literature with a historical bent, itself a result of a paucity of data on absolute price levels in the pre-1940 period.

The modern literature considers the *R-E* direction of causation irrelevant and PPP theory simply describes an equilibrium relationship among the nominal exchange rate and price levels. However, traditionally and in the historical literature, PPP theory had a causal component, implicit or explicit: prices determine the exchange rate (say, *R* determines *E*). In terms of the real exchange rate: if *Q* is shocked out of equilibrium, *R* (rather than *E*) changes to restore equilibrium.

What modern economists cannot legitimately deny is that PPP is a monetarist theory and, as such, asserts that, at least in the long run, the nominal exchange rate (*E*—a monetary variable) can be affected only by monetary variables, such as PPP (*R*). In contrast, the real exchange rate (*Q*) is a real variable; correspondingly, in the long run only real variables can affect it.

## 6.3 Historical Application of PPP: Premodern Periods

The "premodern" period denotes human history before the eighteenth century. For the premodern period, the only use of PPP is to assess the extent of the integration of the domestic economy with foreign economies. The closer PPP is to fulfillment, the greater the integration. The best way of using PPP to determine the amount of integration of economies is to test PPP theory statistically; but this method is not possible for premodern economies, because of the lack of data. Alternatively, one could observe either individual-commodity price differences, in domestic currency, at home and abroad, or exchange rates and domestic prices. This technique is usable, even in the absence of recorded price series; for (i) contemporary authors may have written of the price differences or (ii) inferences on price differences may be made by modern scholars on the basis of other information.

Premodern economies are characterized by monetary systems in the realm of a coin standard. Except in China, paper standards were unknown until the eighteenth century. In fact, again except in China, paper money did not even exist until toward the end of the premodern period. Exchange rates were "fixed" at mint parities. According to Einzig (1970, p. 71), foreign-exchange transactions were almost entirely coin-for-coin until the thirteenth century, when bills of exchange became dominant. The "fixity" of exchange rates was not absolute, in two respects. First, mint parities were responsive to depreciation and debasement of coins. Second, specie-point spreads were much wider than in modern times.

### 6.3.1 ANCIENT PERIOD

The few scholars who have examined the issue are unanimous that there was not even a tendency for PPP theory to be fulfilled in ancient times.[2] In particular, there are four reasons why PPP theory did not apply to the Roman Empire. First,

[2] See Burns (1927, p. 417), Einzig (1970, p. 44), and Officer (1982, p. 27).

Roman imports were luxuries, such as valuable furs, amber, carpets, silk, precious stones, and aromatics, which were purchased only by the rich. They were income, rather than price, determined. The own-price elasticity of demand for imports was effectively zero. Second, imports were not produced in the Empire, and had no close domestic substitutes. The cross-price elasticity of demand for imports with respect to domestic commodities was also zero, or close to it.

Third, there were tremendous price differences between Rome and its trading partners.[3] Such price differences are suggestive of arbitrage imperfections, which took two forms: high transportation and commission charges, inherent in the state of transportation and communication technology; high profit margins and risk premiums. Fourth, trade in nonmonetary commodities between the Roman Empire and Asia was largely one-sided. Rome imported luxury goods; but exported nonmonetary commodities to the Far East only in small amounts, because Far Eastern countries had little demand for wine, oils, wool manufactures, and leather manufactures—which were the Empire's principal exportables. Rome did have an abundant exportable that was in demand in the East: silver. To the extent that silver exports were in the form of coin, Rome thereby financed its "balance-of-payments deficit on commodity account." To the extent that the silver was bullion, it can be considered a normal commodity export, reducing the one-sided character of Roman-Eastern trade.

In sum, the economy of the Roman Empire may have been well integrated within itself, but certainly not with the outside world.

## 6.3.2 MEDIEVAL PERIOD

Einzig (1970, p. 99) states that "in the Middle Ages ... exports and imports were largely inelastic and unresponsive to changes in prices or exchanges." Officer (1982, p. 28) suggests reasons for this inelasticity. First, the feudal economy, with its self-sufficiency nature and structured society, had purely luxury imports, as in Roman times. Second, general contraction of trade occurred, both within Europe (the former Roman Empire) and between Europe and Asia. The result was again inapplicability of PPP and the lack of integration between economies, even within Europe.

Over time, trade expanded and parts of Europe coalesced into sovereign regions. Trade among these entities took place, and foreign-exchange markets developed. What used to be intra-Empire trade became foreign trade, with distances and risks less than they had been for Empire-Asian trade. It is reasonable to presume that commodity arbitrage gradually became less imperfect over time, and that there was an increasing tendency toward PPP, as economies became more integrated.

---

[3]Citing the Roman historian Pliny, Einzig (1970, p. 45) reports that "merchants importing Indian goods sold them in Rome at a hundred-fold of what they had paid for them ... the margin between the price of luxuries in their countries of origin and in their countries of destination was [some]thing like 10,000 per cent."

### 6.3.3 SIXTEENTH-CENTURY SPAIN

Spanish scholars of the Salamanca School originated the PPP theory. In their environment, PPP was an indicator not only of integration of the Spanish and outside economies but also of the importance of monetary influences on the exchange rate. The Salamancans made the following empirical observations: (i) Spain had received large inflows of gold and silver from the New World; (ii) the Spanish money stock increased; (iii) the Spanish price level also increased; and (iv) exchange rates had become unfavorable to Spain. Spain (along with England and the rest of Europe) was on a metallic standard. Therefore, what an unfavorable movement in exchange rates meant was a movement in current exchange rates away from mint parities in the direction of specie-export points. This was a lower exchange value for Spanish coin. Thus PPP as an equilibrium theory was fulfilled, at least in an approximate sense. The causal PPP theory was also satisfied, with the obvious causal chain (i)→(ii)→(iii)→(iv).

## 6.4 Techniques of Testing PPP Theory in Economic-History Literature

### 6.4.1 COMPARATIVE-STATIC COMPUTATION

Let $E_0$ denote $E$ in period 0. An obvious test of PPP theory is to measure $P$ and $P^*$ as index numbers with value unity in base period 0 and compute $V = (P/P^*)E_0$ for either one period, a few discontinuous periods or a continuous sequence of periods. The computed $V$ are then compared with the corresponding values of $E$, in a table or graph. Alternatively, $(E/E_0)/(P/P^*)$ is compared with unity. In either case, the closer the computed value to the norm, PPP-predicted, value, the closer is PPP theory to fulfillment. Any noticeable divergences are then explained in terms of non-PPP influences on the exchange rate (augmented PPP theory). One can allow for a lagged effect of $R$ on $E$. Further, investigations of lead-lag relationships are used to test the PPP-postulated direction of causality, from prices to the exchange rate. This entire approach has the advantage of lying outside formal statistical analysis.

### 6.4.2 REGRESSION ANALYSIS

The use of regression analysis was a natural development in testing PPP theory. For example (using lower-case letters to denote logarithms), $e$ is regressed on $P$ and $p^*$ or on $r^{-1}$; $q$ is regressed on a constant. Properties such as symmetry and proportionality can be readily tested in terms of elasticities.

### 6.4.3 TESTING FOR CAUSALITY

The PPP relationship tested can either be an equilibrium relationship or a causal relationship, each being tested directly. A hybrid test involves an equilibrium relationship tested via an imposed causal relationship. The causal direction is indicated by the direction of minimization of the sum of squared errors in regression. Generally, minimization is in the direction of the exchange rate. Some scholars believe that this direction of minimization is applicable only to a floating exchange rate. Under a fixed exchange rate, the "dependent variable" is $p$ and the "independent variable" $ep^*$: the domestic price index is determined by the foreign price index expressed in domestic currency, the "world" price index governing the domestic price. However, Gustav Cassel and other traditionalists considered PPP as the principal determinant of the exchange rate under both a floating exchange rate and the gold standard.[4]

In modern work, testing for causality involves a peculiar definition of causality: Granger causality, a forecasting concept. If $r^{-1}$ aids in the forecasting of $e$ beyond lagged values of $e$, then $r^{-1}$ is said to Granger-cause $e$. Only preceding values of $r^{-1}$ can assist in the forecast; and they can only assist: lagged values of $e$ are also in the forecast equation.

### 6.4.4 NONSTATIONARITY AND SPURIOUS REGRESSION

It came to be realized that regression analysis ignored crucial time-series properties of variables, so that the results and conclusions could be meaningless or spurious. The comparative-static and regression studies of PPP implicitly assume stationarity of the PPP, nominal-exchange-rate, and real-exchange-rate series that are utilized. A stationary series has a constant and finite mean, a constant and finite variance, and convariances that are constant for a given time interval between the observations.

A stationary series has several desirable properties. (i) Computation of the parameters (mean, variance, autocorrelations) of the series is readily accomplished from sample data. (ii) The series exhibits "mean reversion": at least in the long run, the series returns to its mean, the equilibrium value of the series. Deviations of the series from its mean are only temporary. Shocks to the series have only temporary effect. (iii) There is the possibility (although not the necessity) of "short memory," implying a relatively fast reversion to the mean, after any disturbance. (iv) There is no statistical reason why regressions or correlations involving only stationary series would be spurious. The legitimacy of standardized tests for significance stands.

If $d$ is an integer (the usual assumption), the "order of integration" ( $d$) of a series is the minimum number of times that the series must be differenced to achieve stationarity. Traditionally, economists have an either-or-viewpoint of stationarity: a series is stationary as it stands ($d = 0$) or needs to be differenced once to achieve stationarity ($d = 1$). And the conventional wisdom has been that most economic series are in the latter category. Nonstationary series ($d \geq 1$) have disadvantages. (i) They lack a constant mean; or, if they have such a mean, have a nonconstant or even infinite variance. Estimation of parameters of the series cannot be readily effected. (ii) Mean reversion is not present. There is no mean to which to revert; or deviations from a mean persist. (iii) Memory is infinitely long;

[4]See the references in Officer, 1982, p. 194, n. 22.

the "stochastic trend" emanating from disturbances adds new terms without reducing the impact of existing terms. (iv) Regressions and correlations can be spurious with even one of the variables nonstationary, and standard tests of significance give misleading results.

It is now realized that a series can be "fractionally integrated" ($0<d<1$). Such series are mean reverting, but have long memory. It takes a long time for the effects of disturbances to die out. The critical value for $d$ is 1/2. For $d < 1/2$, the series is stationary; for $1/2 \leq d < 1$, the series is nonstationary, because the variance of the series is infinite. In the latter case, stationarity is obtained by first differencing the series. For correlations or regressions involving two fractionally integrated variables, say of orders $d_1$ and $d_2$, spurious results occur for $d_1 + d_2 \geq 1/2$. Of course, if the variables are fractionally cointegrated, then the results would not be spurious.

### 6.4.5 TESTING FOR STATIONARITY

Modern univariate testing of PPP involves testing for the stationarity (order of integration) of the real exchange rate ($q$) as distinct from testing for a constant mean of $q$ (as was formerly done). Only if the series is stationary is there an equilibrium value of the real exchange rate to which the actual value reverts in the long run. Deviations of the actual from the equilibrium (mean) real rate do occur, but they eventually disappear. "Eventually" is not necessarily good enough. For the stationary series, a PPP-shock half-life (the length of time needed for the original deviation of actual $q$ from equilibrium $q$ to be halved) is a crucial statistic. The longer this half-life, the less is PPP theory supported. These tests of PPP are pleasing, because they treat the theory as applicable only to the long run; but the tests are also displeasing, because (i) a PPP-determined mean value is not imposed and (ii) symmetry and proportionality are ignored. In other words, an extremely weak interpretation of PPP is tested.

While a series can be made stationary by first differencing, it is also possible that a transformation short of first differencing might work, for example, taking logarithms of the variables. Also, including the lagged-dependent variable as an explanatory variable might be sufficient. While early studies of PPP paid no attention to stationarity (and, as seen in Section 6.6, these are the bulk of the studies in the economic-history vein), some did make an adjustment—perhaps inadvertently or for some other reason (usually hypothesis specification).

### 6.4.6 COINTEGRATION ANALYSIS

Even if variables are tested and nonstationarity is found, one should not proceed with correcting for spurious correction; for the variables might be cointegrated, that is, a linear combination of the variables is stationary. Cointegration analysis is admirably suited for PPP bivariate or trivariate testing. The cointegration model involves the PPP relationship with zero error, as holding in the long run: it is the long-run equilibrium. Deviations from that relationship occur in the short run, and an error-correction process returns the variables to the long-run relationship: there is mean reversion. Differing speed of adjustment for the exchange rate and for price (or price ratio) is embedded in the error-correction process. Symmetry and proportionality are not imposed, and can be tested. General-to-specific modeling, in which restrictive models are nested within more-general models, can be used here, as with conventional regression analysis. The causal aspect of PPP can also be tested, via the speed-of-adjustment coefficients. Fractional cointegration, involving fractionally integrated variables, is also possible, although rarely performed in the PPP literature.

## 6.5 Price Variable in PPP Computations

Crucial to empirical use and testing of PPP is the price concept, and many price concepts have been used in PPP computations. Ranging from most justifiable to least justifiable (with symbols), they are as follows: GDP deflator (PGDP), GNP deflator (PGNP), consumption deflator (PCONS), retail price index [incorporating consumer price index and cost-of-living index] (RPI), wholesale price index (WPI), export price index (XPI), wage-rate index (WI), component indexes or subindexes of WPI or RPI, and prices of individual commodities.

The bar separating PPP-legitimate price measures is drawn between WPI and XPI. So only results based on PGDP, PGNP, PCONS, RPI, and WPI are included in the survey. PGDP and PGNP have three justifications. First, as stated by Cassel (1928, p. 33), PPP relates to the internal value of currencies, and therefore should be "measured only by general index figures representing as far as possible the whole mass of commodities marketed in the country." PGDP and PGNP fit this criterion better than any other price index. Second, PPP is a macroeconomic theory, and therefore necessitates the usual macro-price concept, PGDP or PGNP, with the former marginally preferred, because it measures the price of production within the country. Third, to the extent that PPP is justified by arbitrage and substitutability of commodities in production and consumption (broadly construed), the price concept underlying PPP should be as broad as possible, again leading to PGDP or PGNP.

Other things being equal, one would like to place WPI below the separation bar while leaving RPI above the bar for two reasons. First, a PPP computed from traded-goods prices alone is close to a truism.[5] Because (i) in any given country, the WPI is heavily weighted with tradables and, in particular, excludes all services and (ii) across countries, arbitrage directly equates prices of tradables (up to transactions costs, including tariffs and transportation charges), a PPP computed from WPIs comes close to making PPP theory a truism. Therefore, WPI biases result in favor of the hypothesis that PPP theory holds, and therefore that the domestic economy is well integrated with the foreign economy. In contrast, the RPI consists of nontradables (services) as well as tradables. Also, the weighting pattern of the WPI need not bear a close relationship with the production

[5]This was pointed out originally by Keynes (1930, pp. 72–74; 1931 [originally published in 1925], pp. 249–250).

weighted (i.e., GDP weighting pattern) of the economy. The WPI incorporates considerable, but unknown, double-counting and even multiple-counting. In contrast, the RPI has a logical weighting pattern. Yet, unfortunately the most widely used price measure in PPP studies is the WPI. For many historical periods, the WPI is the only, or at least the most comprehensive, price index available. Even when alternative indexes exist, researchers often select the WPI. So, on grounds of expediency the WPI just makes the bar.

The XPI is totally composed of tradables. After the joyless decision to include the WPI above the bar, it gives one a certain pleasure to place the XPI below the bar. Also, price measures of individual commodities are excluded, because of their lack of comprehensiveness. WIs are excluded, primarily because PPP theory (and its justifications) pertains to prices of commodities rather than of factors of production. A second reason to exclude WI is the opposite justification for excluding XPI (and only reluctantly including WPI). In contrast to measures heavily weighted with tradables, that can move almost automatically in correspondence with the exchange rate, WI is typically the price of an entity heavily nontradable, and can move *too slowly* relative to the exchange rate.

## 6.6 Modern Period: Testing of PPP

The principal use of PPP in historical research of the modern period (eighteenth century onward) is testing the validity of the theory. Although almost all investigators test the theory for its own sake, in effect, the degree of integration of the domestic with the foreign economy is assessed. Most, but not all, studies pertain to periods of a floating as distinct from fixed exchange rate.

### 6.6.1 EARLY NORTH AMERICA

The earliest date of any PPP testing in this survey is the U.S. colonial period, and all authors paid attention to the stationarity issue. Bordo and Marcotte (1987) found that PPP holds under the South Carolina adjustably fixed exchange rate and proportionality could not be rejected. Choudhry and Luintel (2001) examined Pennsylvania under a floating exchange rate, and PPP results are mixed. Bernholz (2003) examined the period of the 13 colonies in rebellion, during which Congress issued Continental currency. During this paper standard and floating exchange rate, the price of specie (silver coin—representing the exchange rate) did not increase as much as the price index. Bernholz's explanation is the war-inflicted damage on production (supply) of goods and the British blockade, which reduced the value of specie (the currency used in payment for imports).

Grubb (2003, 2005, 2010) compared properties of the real exchange rate for six American colonies (later U.S. states) and Lower Canada in 1748–1775 (colonial period) versus 1796–1811 (Constitution period), with Lower Canada serving as a control. In the colonial period, only Massachusetts and Lower Canada were clearly on specie standards and fixed exchange rates. In the Constitution period, all U.S. states were on a fixed exchange rate—that of the U.S. dollar—by default. Lower Canada was now on a floating exchange rate, by virtue of Britain abandoning the gold standard in 1797. In general, PPP held; but half-lives to shocks were lower in the colonial than Constitution period. As Grubb (2010, p. 141) stated: "Market integration as measured by PPP during 1796–1811 was not superior to market integration during the 1748–1755 colonial period."

### 6.6.2 BULLIONIST PERIODS

A "bullionist period" in economic history has both an empirical and an intellectual characteristics. Empirically, a bullionist period involved a paper standard and floating exchange rate that temporarily interrupted a specie standard and fixed exchange rate. Intellectually, a bullionist period carried with it a "bullionist controversy" regarding the ruling macroeconomic model of the economy. In modern terminology, the competing models are monetarist and nonmonetarist. In particular, "bullionists" were monetarists, and generally exposited a PPP theory of the exchange rate.

Two bullionist experiences that have been subject to PPP testing are the Swedish bullionist period (1745–1776) and the Engish bullionist period (1797–1821). The latter is customarily called the Bank Restriction Period, because the Bank of England's obligation to pay cash (gold) for its note issues was restricted. It may be noted that, while paper money originated in China, banknotes were first issued in Sweden. The Swedish bullionist period began with the paper daler made inconvertible into copper bullion.

Three authors investigated PPP for both episodes. Eagly (1968, 1971) noted increases in the price level and exchange rate in terms of banknotes. Myhrman used growth rates and found positive evidence for PPP. Bernholz, Gärtner, and Heri (hereafter Bernholz et al., 1985) applied a univariate technique to various floating-rate episodes and found that PPP was violated in the short run but held in the long run; however, they paid no attention to stationarity. Bernholz's (1982, 2003) results for Sweden are consistent with those of Bernholz et al.

Turning to authors who examined the Bank Restriction Period exclusively, Angell (1926, p. 484) found no relationship between the British price index and exchange rate. Nachane and Hatekar (1995) rejected cointegration of the British price index and exchange rate. Also, they could not reject that price does not Granger-cause the exchange rate. Their use of the exchange rate on Paris is contrary to other researchers; economic historians generally view the Hamburg exchange as more representative than Paris during the French Revolutionary and Napoleonic Wars. The Nachane and Hatekar observation period extends to 1838, which, with annual data, increases the sample size. However, the effect is a mixture of a "paper standard, floating exchange rate" with a "gold standard, fixed exchange rate."

In contrast, Officer (2000) used quarterly data and limited the sample to the Bank Restriction Period. Another difference is that Officer engaged in multivariate testing, with Bank of England notes, the price of wheat, and external military expenditure as variables in addition to the general price index and exchange rate. While Nachane and Hatekar also employed multiple variables, their testing was entirely bivariate. However, Officer's results regarding PPP were negative, and essentially the same as those of Nachane and Hatekar.

### 6.6.3 FLOATING RATES—SECOND-HALF OF NINETEENTH CENTURY

The greenback-period episode of a paper standard and floating exchange rate encompasses the full years 1862–1878, and has received considerable attention in the literature. Graham (1922) did not mention PPP, and in fact made no formal judgment on the validity of the theory. He stated that the principal determinants of the exchange rate were (i) expectations regarding a Northern victory, during the Civil War, and (ii) net capital inflow, in the postbellum period. However, it is clear from his computations and the context that these influences were secondary, and came into play given the effect of commodity prices on the exchange rate. This was the position also of later authors who offered an augmented PPP theory for the greenback period: Kindahl (1961) and Friedman and Schwartz (1963). None of these authors paid attention to nonstationarity; nor did Farag and Ott (1964) and Thompson (1972). Therefore, the generally positive results of all these early writers were questionable; and the regression analyses of Farag and Ott (1964) and Thompson (1972) could be particularly misleading, as the estimation technique is ordinary least-squares.

Officer (1981) provided some innovations to PPP investigation of the greenback period. Instead of representing the dollar-sterling exchange rate by the price of gold, he constructed a "true" exchange-rate series (the inverse of the dollar-sterling rate) as the ratio of the gold-dollar price of the greenback to the gold-dollar price of the pound; and his price concept is the GNP deflator rather than the WPI. Also, Officer, in effect, corrected for nonstationarity in his regressions. So his positive results for PPP lend credibility to the results of the earlier studies.

Bernholz et al. (1985) obtained their usual qualitative result of short-run PPP violated, long-run return to PPP. Enders (1989) is the only author other than Officer to have addressed nonstationarity, and he trumped Officer because his attention is deliberate rather than inadvertent. However, Enders' results were mixed. Nonstationarity ($d = 1$) could not be rejected for the real exchange rate, while the U.S. and British price indexes (the latter expressed in dollars) were found to be cointegrated. The former result is unfavorable to PPP, the latter is supportivc.

Austria was on a paper standard and floating exchange rate from the mid-nineteenth century, when it left the silver standard, until 1892, when Austria–Hungary joined the gold standard. Especially interesting is the subperiod 1979–1892, during which the paper gulden was worth more than its legal metallic content. The PPP aspect of the Austrian experience was investigated by Yeager (1969) and Myhrman (1976), who reprinted Yeager's graph of the exchange rate and PPP. Yeager (1969) computed correlation coefficients of the exchange rate and PPP, for the variables in percentage-change form, which could produce stationarity, and the results can reasonably be construed as positive evidence for

PPP. Myhrman (1976, p. 190) commented that "both prices and the exchange rate were rather stable but with a rising trend." This remark is suggestive of a possible trend-stationarity characteristic of the variables.

### 6.6.4 CLASSIC METALLIC STANDARDS

With the United States back on the gold standard in 1879 and Britain on gold since the end of the Bank Restriction Period in 1821, it is natural to examine PPP for these two countries in the context of the fixed exchange rate of the gold standard. Enders (1989) offered an identical analysis as for the greenback period. For this period, not only was there cointegration in a bivariate model, but also now nonstationarity of the real exchange rate was rejected—supportive of PPP. In contrast, Grilli and Kaminsky (1991) could not reject nonstationarity in the real exchange rate, destructive of PPP.

Catão and Solomou (2005) investigated real-effective exchange rates for three groups of countries: the gold-standard core group, countries on a silver standard for at least part of their time period (1871–1913), and countries on an inconvertible paper standard for a substantial part of the period. They did not formally test for nonstationarity of the real exchange rate of the countries; rather they accepted stationarity, based on estimated autoregressive coefficients uniformly below unity. Nevertheless, their results are unfavorable to PPP; for they found "large and protracted real exchange rate fluctuations" (Catão and Solomou, 2005, p. 1265).

Considering both the gold standard (1880–1914) and interwar period (1921–1940) for the United Kingdom and Canada versus the United States, McCloskey and Zecher (1984) found that PPP regression forecast errors were not related to U.S. money-market disequilibria—supportive of PPP. Their use of the GNP deflator is to be commended. Hasan (2004) examined PPP for silver-standard India. Among other techniques, he applied fractional-integration modeling. The hypothesis of nonstationarity of the real exchange rate was rejected.

Hegwood and Papell (2002) studied Belgium, France, Germany, and the United States over 1793–1913, which encompassed episodes of the gold standard, silver standard, and paper standard. Impressive is their concept of "quasi-PPP": reversion to mean $q$ that exhibits structural shifts rather than to a constant mean $q$; and half-lives of PPP deviations were short. Structural breaks were associated with economic and political events: the U.S. Civil War, dissolution of the German Confederation, coup d'etat in France, and the 1840s decade of political unrest in Europe.

### 6.6.5 WORLD WAR I

Investigations of PPP for World War I were undertaken by Cassel (1916, 1918, 1919), Heckscher (1930), Keynes (1919), and Bresciani-Turroni (1937). Gustav Cassel, the greatest expositor and propagator of PPP, naturally tested the theory first for his own country. All these studies were comparative-static in nature.

Findings were mixed, and, because there was no attention to nonstationarity, must be viewed with caution.

### 6.6.6 FLOATING RATES—1920s

A tremendous number of PPP studies pertain to the 1920s, especially the first part of that decade. There are several reasons for this concentration. First, all countries on the classical gold standard left gold during World War, resulting in floating exchange rates. During the war, there was exchange-market intervention on the part of some countries, in particular, France and the United Kingdom. However, shortly after the end of the war, almost all exchange rates became freely floating, and remained so for a substantial part of the decade. PPP theory is typically of greater interest to researchers when exchange rates are floating rather than fixed. Second, the United States, which had effectively adopted a paper standard extralegally in April 1917, returned to gold in March 1922. The dollar thus provided an anchor to other countries for a return to a fixed-rate system and for assessing the level and volatility of the exchange rate while their currencies were floating. In particular, the United States was a natural base country for PPP computations. Third, even though World War I marked the end of the nominal international economic supremacy of the United Kingdom and even though that country did not readopt the gold standard until April 1925, its traditional importance as the center country of the classical gold standard made it a natural alternative base country for floating exchange rates of other countries. Fourth, the very fact that the once central country of a metallic standard and fixed-rate system (the gold standard) was now floating made the United Kingdom a most interesting subject of PPP analysis, with the United States (the upstart other center country) as base country. Fifth, for researchers in the final quarter of the twentieth century and beyond, it was natural to compare the floating rates of the post-Bretton Woods period with the floating rates of the 1920s, in particular, from the standpoint of PPP analysis.

The U.K. floating rate of 1919–1925 has been studied by many authors.[6] While there is no consensus, the preponderance of the evidence suggests that the pound sterling in the 1920s floated in the dollar–pound exchange market in a manner consistent with the PPP theory. France had a floating exchange rate in 1919–1926, and this experience has been investigated by various authors.[7] PPP aspects of the German floating rate of 1914–1923 were considered by Bresciani-Turroni (1937), Frenkel (1976), Haberler (1936), Rogers (1929), and Bernholz et al. (1985). For each episode, results have quite different implications regarding the validity of PPP, and no general assessment of the validity of PPP can be made. Other individual-country PPP studies of the 1920s concerned the floating and fixed exchange rate of Sweden, and the floating rates of Switzerland

[6] Ahking (1990), Angell (1926), Cassel (1925a), Crump (1925), Farag and Ott (1964), Grilli and Kaminsky (1991), Hodgson (1972), MacDonald (1985a), Myhrman (1976), Stolper (1948), Taylor (1992), and Michael et al. (1996).

[7] Aliber (1970), Angell (1926), Dulles (1929), Farag and Ott (1964), Myhrman (1976), Pippenger (1973), Rogers (1929), Wasserman (1936), and Sicsic (1992).

and Greece.[8] Generally, results were negative for Sweden, mixed for Switzerland, and positive for Greece.

An impressive, two-volume, assemblage of studies of the post-World-War I monetary and exchange-rate experience of European countries is that of Young (1925a). Papers were contributed by a large number of government officials and academic economists, and many of the writers in effect test the PPP approach to the exchange rate.[9] Almost all the authors adopted a common comparative-static methodology, plotting and tabulating the exchange rate versus the PPP, with the United States as the base country. The following general findings can be discerned: (i) the exchange rate and PPP moved more or less in correspondence; (ii) there was persistent directional deviation of one of these variables from the other; (iii) the usual pattern was that the domestic currency depreciated more than indicated by PPP, that is, the currency was undervalued in the foreign-exchange market; (iv) there was closer correspondence of the exchange rate and PPP in recent years than previously, especially if exchange-rate stabilization had occurred.

Bernholz et al. (1985) applied their model to three countries in the 1920s. The usual results (PPP violated in short run, validated in long run) pertained to Hungary and Poland. Austria was an outlying case, with PPP not holding in the long run.

Many studies tested PPP in the 1920s for multiple domestic countries with the United States as the base country. They fit into two groups: those that ignored stationarity and those that addressed the issue (even if via another route).[10] Distinctive in the first group is the conclusion of Keynes (1923, pp. 101, 106), who later became a critic of PPP, that "even under such abnormal conditions as have existed since the Armistice . . . the Purchasing Power Parity Theory, even in its crude form, has worked passably well"; and Flux's (1924) early use of logarithms in PPP computation. In the studies that addressed stationarity, overall results are more positive than negative for PPP. There are also 1920s studies with the United Kingdom as the base country.[11] No author addressed stationarity, and yet the only positive results are those of Thomas (1972).

Finally, there are 1920s studies which do not have a base country as such. A set of "equal status" countries was selected, and the PPP between pairs of these countries was investigated. One country group consists of the United States, United Kingdom, and France; another group adds Germany to these

[8] For Sweden, Anonymous (1921), Flux (1924), and Cassel (1925a,b); for Switzerland, Junge (1984) and Bleaney (1998); for Greece, Phylaktis (1990, 1992) and Georgoutsos and Kouretas (1992).

[9] The relevant papers are those of Bachi (1925), Jacobson (), Jacobson and Jaeger (1925), Wight (1925a,b,c), Wood (1925a,b,c,d), Young (1925b,c,d,e,f,g), Jacobson et al. ().

[10] The first group consists of Flux (1924), Furniss (1922), Graham (1930), Gregory (1925), Keynes (1923), Lester (1939), Robertson (1922), Tsiang (1959), U.S. Tariff Commission (1922), and Aliber (1962); the second, Hodgson and Phelps (1975), Hakkio (1984), Krugman (1978), Rogalski and Vinso (1977), Thomas (1973a,b), and De Grauwe et al. (1985).

[11] Bachi (1925), Copland (1930), Flux (1924), Gregory (1925), Katzenellenbaum (1925), Thomas (1972).

countries.[12]. All studies were conducted using modern time-series analysis, with explicit attention paid to stationarity. For the first group results were largely mixed; for the second group they were mostly positive. Very impressive is Michael et al. (1997), who specified a nonlinear adjustment process. They concluded that, for country pairs excluding Germany: "Despite the high degree of persistence in PPP deviations, our framework provides strong evidence of mean-reverting behavior for the real exchange rate" (Michael et al., 1997, pp. 876, 877).

### 6.6.7 1930s

In September 1931 the United Kingdom abandoned the gold standard for a managed float, while the United States did not leave gold until March 1933. Broadberry (1987), Whitaker and Hudgins (1977), and Grilli and Kaminsky (1991) performed PPP testing for the United Kingdom during the 1930s, with the United States as the base country. Overall, the results were negative. Graham (1935) White (1935), and Broadberry and Taylor (1992) dealt with the 1930s PPP experience of multiple countries. Overall, again results were not generally positive. The Broadberry-Taylor study is instructive. They examined all pairs in the country group United States, United Kingdom, France, Germany, and could not reject that the real exchange rate is nonstationary ($d = 1$), a failure of PPP. Cointegration results, which pertain to equilibrium PPP, were mixed. Granger causality tests, which address causal PPP, were also mixed. For full samples, prices never Granger-caused exchange rates, but the reverse was sometimes found. Only for subperiods of freely floating rates was there some evidence of prices Granger-causing the exchange rate.

McCloskey and Zecher (1984) found a close weekly relationship between the dollar–pound exchange rate and the U.S. WPI or RPI in 1933, with foreign prices relatively constant. The finding is associated with the depreciation of the dollar, the United States leaving the gold standard. McCloskey and Zecher (1984, p. 143) concluded: "Purchasing power parity is not a failure. On the contrary, by the standards we have examined, it is a great success."

### 6.6.8 INTERWAR PERIOD

Some studies treated the interwar period as a broad expanse, incorporating fixed and floating exchange rates in the same sample. Young (1938) found that there were subperiods defined by PPP and the exchange rate alternately moving together (during one subperiod) and diverging (during the next subperiod). This is not good evidence for PPP. Bunting (1939) graphed the exchange rate against PPP, with the latter alternatively lagged zero, one, two, and three periods. This is a logical way of assessing causal PPP, even though it is defective for the lack of attention to nonstationarity. Even with the lags, there were substantial deviations

[12]Studies of the first group are of Edison (1985); Frenkel (1978); Georgoutsos and Kouretas (2000); MacDonald (1985b); studies of the second group are of Ardeni and Lubian (1989); Frenkel (1980); Michael et al. (1997); Taylor and McMahon (1988)

between the PPP and the exchange rate, and in opposite directions for France and the United Kingdom. Bunting (1939, p. 299) judged: "This is damaging statistical evidence against the purchasing power parity theory." Katano (1956, 1957) computed a number of correlation coefficients; but these are largely devoid of meaning, because of the small number of observations and the danger of spurious correlation. His most interesting result is that deviation from PPP was related to divergence from pure inflation in the countries. Bernholz et al. (1985) exhibited the usual result of PPP validated in the long run while violated in the short run.

## 6.6.9 SPAIN—LONG TERM

Spain was on a floating exchange rate for most of the 1870–1935 period, moving from a free to a managed float in 1931. For 1914–1920, Delaplane (1934, p. 41) used comparative-static computation to note "the wide divergence of purchasing power parity from the [exchange] rate." For the entire 1914–1933 period, his assessment of PPP was, at best, mixed: "In the light of Spanish monetary experience since 1913, one could not attribute more than a rough correspondence between purchasing power parity and exchange" (Delaplane, 1934, p. 211). Using Delaplane's data for the subperiod 1920–1929, Yeager (1976, p. 220) took a more-sanguine view of PPP: "The actual rate kept within the range of 12.5% below to 12.5% above purchasing-power parity in 82.5% of the months."

Sort et al. (2005), following Sabaté et al. (2003), examined the Spanish experience over the full 1870–1935 period. They considered $q$ for the peseta against the British pound, French franc, and U.S. dollar. In the Hedgwood-Papell tradition, allowing for structural breaks in $q$ enables rejection of nonstationarity. These breaks were explained via rumors of restoration of gold convertibility of the peseta in 1927, the pound abandoning the gold standard in 1931, stabilization of the peseta in 1931, and the financial instability of France after World War I. The authors concluded: "one can accept the PPP hypothesis as *a good approximation* of the behaviour of the peseta exchange rate against its main traders and investors between 1870 and 1935."

## 6.6.10 GUATEMALA—LONG TERM

Schweigert (2002) investigated PPP for Guatemala for 1897–1922, during which time the country was on a floating exchange rate. The United States was the base country. The money stock was used to proxy the Guatemalan price index, for which a direct series does not exist. This representation had been adopted by Cassel and Keynes for their World War I studies, absent price data. Results were excellent for PPP. The exchange rate, U.S. price, and Guatemalan money stock were found to be cointegrated. With the coefficient of the exchange rate normalized to unity, one could not reject the hypotheses of symmetry and proportionality (coefficients of U.S. price and Guatemalan money one and minus one, respectively).

## 6.7 Analysis of U.S. Return to Gold Standard in 1879

The successful PPP testing for the greenback period, on the part of Kindahl (1961) and Officer (1981), was based (wholly, for Kindahl; in part, for Officer) on real-exchange-rate computations. These authors put their computations to work to determine (i) the range of real appreciation of the greenback for successful return to the gold standard and (ii) the first year in which a successful return could occur. For (i), the technique was simply to observe the range of the real exchange rate in the postbellum period but excluding 1877–1879, which were years of unusual capital outflow. The resulting range for Kindahl was 9–27% or 8–18%; for Officer, −3 to 18%—all assuming no capital movements. If resumption was to occur at the prewar parity (as in fact did happen), then the U.S. price index could exceed the U.K. price index by a value within the specified range (with both indexes relative to base year 1860). With capital inflow, the real exchange rate (or PPP, with no change in the nominal exchange rate) could exceed the upper limit. With capital outflow, it might have to fall below the lower limit.

To answer (ii), one approach is to find the earliest year in which the real exchange rate falls within the estimated range; but the range might be considered too broad for a confident return and maintenance of the gold standard. Consider, rather, a stronger criterion: the earliest year at which the real exchange rate reached (or almost reaches) 100—the same value as in 1860. For Kindahl, that year was 1879, when his real exchange rate was 101 and the return to gold in fact occurred. For Officer, the year was 1875, when his real exchange rate was 100 and the Resumption Act was passed. That Act specified a return to the gold standard on January 1, 1879—which in fact happened. To some historians of the period, Officer's answer would be too optimistic. For example, Friedman and Schwartz (1963, p. 48) wrote that "the act was little more than the expression of a pious hope." However, they went on to state: "Resumption might well have been successful a year or more earlier than the date set and certainly could have occurred later"—Friedman and Schwartz (1963, p. 85).

## 6.8 Establishment and Assessment of a Fixed Exchange Rate in Interwar Period

This section discusses the use of PPP by government in connection with the setting of a new exchange rate. In the interwar period, there were two interesting cases of PPP computations by the government in order to establish a new, or return to a former, exchange rate: the United Kingdom (1925) and France (1926).

### 6.8.1 UNITED KINGDOM

The U.K. return to gold on April 28, 1925 was the (sole) case of a government predetermining the exchange rate—in this case the prewar gold parity—and using PPP to measure the amount of price-level adjustment at home or abroad required to maintain the rate. France, Czechoslovakia, and Belgium applied PPP to compute the new exchange rate, although less so in France than in the other two countries.

No doubt the U.K. experience is the most famous of all governmental applications of PPP. The floating pound had appreciated from 10% to less than 2% below parity—caused by anticipation of a return to parity, whereupon the prewar exchange value of the pound ($4.86656 per pound) was restored. There was never a question that return to the gold standard would take place, and at the prewar rate. As Sayers (1960, p. 314) commented: "The restoration of the gold standard, at a tacitly assumed rate of 4.86, was government policy throughout . . .". Moggridge (1969, p. 14) agreed: "The Authorities had as their primary aim a return to gold . . . a return to the pre-war parity." There was never any choice as to the fact of return and the rate. According to Sayers (1960, p. 317), one of the advisers of Winston Churchill, Chancellor of the Exchequer, told him: "There's no escape; you have to go back [to gold at the prewar parity]; but it will be hell."

For the authorities, the only question was timing: when the gold standard would be reestablished. Churchill's advisers used the WPI in their PPP computation, which Keynes criticized for virtually validating the existing exchange rate. "This led them to think that the gap to be bridged was perhaps 2 or 3 per cent . . . ."—Keynes (1931 [originally published in 1925], p. 250). So the return to gold occurred on April 28, 1925.

Both contemporary and later economists used PPP to determine the overvaluation of the pound upon re-adoption of the gold standard.[13] The earliest such computation was apparently made by Keynes himself. He contrasted the government WPI-based estimated overvaluation of 2–3%, with his own RPI-based figure of 10–12%. The former estimate was considered biased downward, the latter (in conjunction with PPP based on wages and prices of manufactures) "a much better rough-and-ready guide for this purpose . . . than are the index numbers of wholesale prices" (Keynes, 1931 [originally published in 1925], p. 250). However, as first pointed out by Gregory (1926), Keynes used RPI figures from the state of Massachusetts rather than the national U.S. data of the Bureau of Labor. The presumed reason, according to Gregory, was that only the former series at the time was published on a regular basis. Using the national figures, Gregory obtained results in accord with those of Churchill's advisors. Cassel (1925b, 1926) offered a WPI-based estimate slightly above that ascribed by Keynes to Churchill's advisors.

The computations of later writers used a broader array of indexes and base countries. Moggridge (1972) was the first author to employ the GNP deflator—a superior price index than the WPI and RPI—and found overvaluation to be 11%, consistent with Keynes. Moggridge (1972, p. 105) wrote: "An exchange rate at least 10 per cent lower than $4.86 would probably have been somewhat more

[13] Excluded from the discussion are computations based on wages or export price indexes, as well as estimates emanating from more-general models of exchange-rate determination.

appropriate for sterling." Dimsdale's (1981) estimates were between 1% and 14%, depending on the price index. In addition, he computed a real-effective exchange rate for sterling versus 11 currencies, but only from 1920 and on a 1929 rather than prewar base. The work of Redmond (1984) is impressive for a wide array of alternative base countries as well as for effective-exchange-rate computations; however, as might be expected, estimates are all over the place. Matthews (1986) offered estimates based on the work of Redmond and Moggridge. Taylor's (1992) estimate of 5% overvaluation was based on an error-correction model, and is mentioned because the model is within the PPP rubric.

Certainly, the estimates of overvaluation of the authors have considerable variation. Perhaps most trustworthy are Redmond's figures based on RPI and the effective-exchange-rate concept. These estimates suggest substantial overvaluation, which is consistent with the U.K. post-return experience of balance-of-payments deficits, deflation, and unemployment. Keynes predicted this in 1925, and he was right![14]

### 6.8.2 FRANCE

France re-adopted the gold standard on June 25, 1928, with a par value of 124.21 francs per pound sterling. This emanated from a gold par of exchange only slightly greater than one-fifth the prewar value, when mint parity was 25.225 francs per pound. The genesis of the new par value occurred in 1926, when several French officials made PPP computations yielding ranges of a stabilized rate. The best source of this history is Mouré (1996). In August, Pierre Quesnay's calculations, using WPI and Germany as the base country, yielded appropriate stabilization of 160–170 francs per pound. In November, Jacques Rueff's PPP computations employed both WPI and RPI price indexes, again with Germany as base country. He found the desired stabilization rate to be 120–145. In the same month, Charles Rist recommended the range 140–160.

In fact, the franc was appreciating in the foreign-exchange market. To stem this appreciation, at least temporarily, on December 20, 1926, Prime Minister Raymond Poincaré authorized the Bank of France to stabilize the rate via exchange-market intervention. This was a decision based on fear that appreciation would result in recession and unemployment and reduce Poincaré's political support within a coalition government. "PPP calculations did not decide the stabilization in December 1926" (Mouré, 1996, p. 144). However, as Mouré

[14]In February 1934, Czechoslovakia devalued the crown by 16 2/3%, with the devaluation rate based on a WPI PPP computation. Haberler (1961, p. 49, n. 37) comments that "exactly the same mistake was made [as in the United Kingdom in 1925]." The interpretation of Nurkse (1944, p. 128) was that the rate left no margin for economic expansion, putting downward pressure on the exchange value of the domestic currency. In any event, Czechoslovakia had to devalue a second time, in October 1936. In contrast, Belgium successfully devalued its franc in 1935. The devaluation rate of 28% was decided on the basis of PPP computations, with RPI as the decisive price concept. Further discussion of the Czech experience is in League of Nations (1936, pp. 49–52). The Belgian experience is discussed in League of Nations (1936, pp. 49–50), Nurkse (1944, p. 128), Garnsey (1945), Triffin (1937), and Officer (1982, pp. 143–144).

(1996, p. 144) comments, "the economists' arguments were not without effect." Stabilization was at about 122 francs per pound and the return to the gold standard in 1928 at 124.21. These figures are close to the lower bound of Rueff's PPP computations. Mouré (1996, p. 148) writes: "With regard to choosing a rate of stabilization, PPP calculations offered evidence that was of interest but not decisive . . . "

Keynes (1930 [originally published in 1928]), Cassel (1936), Walter (1951), and Sicsic (1992) provided estimates of undervaluation of the franc with respect to the British pound. The extent, not the direction, of deviation from PPP was the only issue. There is no doubt that undervaluation of the franc worsened the situation of the British, who overvalued the pound. At first, Keynes (1930, p. 114) judged that "the franc . . . fixed . . . at about one-fifth of its pre-war gold value . . . The figure finally chosen seems about right." Yet Keynes (1930, pp. 114–115) went on to state that a PPP computation would involve "a gold value of the franc nearer to one quarter (100 francs to the £) than to one-fifth of the pre-war value." This suggests about a 20% undervaluation (although Keynes did not state which price index he was applying). However, Keynes provided reasons—crudeness of French price indexes, room for domestic prices to rise, effect on export industry, budgetary implications, and avoidance of capital loss on foreign-exchange reserves of the Bank of France—why the French authorities were wise not to follow his computed PPP.

Using the WPI, Cassel, Walter, and Sicsic provided estimates of the undervaluation of the franc in the 6–12% range, the figure depending on the currency of comparison and the price index. These estimates are substantially below Keynes' figure of 20%.[15] Only Sicsic's RPI estimate, 28%, based on a nine-country effective exchange rate, exceeded that of Keynes.

It is not clear whether the French authorities *deliberately* undervalued the franc. According to Mouré, the concern was domestic macroeconomic stability, which explains why (i) the de facto stabilization rate in 1926 was undertaken to keep the franc from appreciating further and (ii) the de jure stabilization rate in 1928 was close to the de facto rate established in 1926.

## 6.9 Conclusions

Why has PPP endured through the centuries and under the rubric of various and varying exchange-rate experiences and monetary standards? This survey of the application of PPP to historical experiences illustrates the controversial nature of PPP—and that nature is one reason for the durability and endurance of PPP. The second reason is that PPP is fundamentally a simple and intuitively appealing theory. The third reason is that it has an inherent concreteness that other exchange-rate theories lack.

Clearly, this survey shows that there is mixed empirical evidence for the applicability of PPP, whether in explaining exchange-rate behavior or in establishing new exchange-rate levels. Yet that result gives rise to a fourth reason for

[15]The estimates for Walter were computed by the this author from data in Walter.

the robustness of PPP: *Whether or not PPP is deemed to hold empirically*, it is useful to know the extent to which the theory is valid. Measurement of *deviations* from PPP is important both for macroeconomic historians and for economic policy makers. As Houthakker (1962, pp. 296–297) wrote: "All in all, it would be most unwise to ignore the unique insight which PPP calculations can afford."

## REFERENCES


Ahking FW. Further results on long-run purchasing power parity in the 1920s. Eur Econ Rev 1990;34:913–919.

Aliber RZ. Speculation in the foreign exchanges: the European experience, 1919–1926. Yale Econ Essays 1962;2:171–245.

____. Speculation in the flexible exchange revisited. Kyklos 1970;23:303–313.

Angell JW. The theory of international prices: history, criticism and restatement. Cambridge (MA): Harvard University Press; 1926.

Anonymous. Is the Swedish exchange overvalued abroad? Skandinaviska Kreditaktiebolaget Quarterly Report; 1921. pp. 36–37.

Ardeni PG, Lubian D. Purchasing power parity during the 1920s. Econ Lett 1989;30:357–362.

Bachi R. Position of the currency and currency reform in Italy. Translated by Jacobson ML. In Young (1925a), Volume 1; 1925. pp. 161–196.

Bernholz P. Flexible exchange rates in historical perspective. Princeton (NJ): International Finance Section, Princeton University; 1982.

____. Monetary regimes and inflation: history, economic and political relationships. Cheltenham: Edward Elgar; 2003.

____, Manfred G, Heri EW. Historical experiences with flexible exchange rates: a simulation of common qualitative characteristics. J Int Econ 1985;19:21–45.

Bleaney M. Purchasing power parity in the 1920s: evidence for the Swiss franc. Appl Econ Lett 1998;5:239–241.

Bordo MD, Marcotte IA. Purchasing power parity in colonial America: some evidence for South Carolina 1732–1774: a comment on the Michener paper. Empirical Studies of Velocity, Real Exchange Rates, Unemployment and Productivity: Carnegie-Rochester Conf. Ser. Public Pol. 1987;27:311–324.

Bresciani-Turroni C. The economics of inflation: a study of currency depreciation in post-war Germany. London: George Allen and Unwin; 1937.

Broadberry SN. Purchasing power parity and the pound-dollar rate in the 1930s. Economica 1987;54:69–78.

____, Taylor MP. In: Broadberry SN, editor. Britain in the international economy. Cambridge: Cambridge University Press; 1992. pp. 369–395.

Bunting FH. The purchasing power parity theory reexamined. South Econ J 1939;5: 282–301.

Burns AR. Money and monetary policy in early times. London: K. Paul, Trench, Trubner; 1927.

Cassel G. The present situation of the foreign exchanges. Econ J 1916;26:62–65.

——. Abnormal deviations in international exchanges. Econ J 1918;28:413–415.

——. The depreciation of the German mark. Econ J 1919;29:492–496.

——. Rates of exchange and purchasing-power parity, Skandinaviska Kreditaktiebolaget Quarterly Report; 1925a April. pp. 17–21.

——. Some recent experiences of monetary policy, Skandinaviska Kreditaktiebolaget *Quarterly Report*; 1925b Oct. pp. 55–58.

——. Exchanges, foreign. Supplementary Volume 1, Encyclopaedia Britannica. 13th ed. London: Encyclopaedia Britannica Company; 1926. pp. 1086–1089.

——. Post-war monetary stabilization. New York: Columbia University Press; 1928.

——. The downfall of the gold standard. Oxford: Clarendon Press; 1936.

Catão LAV, Solomou SN. Effective exchange rates and the classical gold standard adjustment. Am Econ Rev 2005;95:1259–1275.

Choudhry T, Luintel KB. The long-run behaviour of the real exchange rate: evidence from colonial Pennsylvania. Econ Lett 2001;74:25–30.

Copland DB. Credit and currency control. Melbourne: Melbourne University Press; 1930.

Crump N. The New York exchange: a reply to Professor Cassel. J R Stat Soc 1925;88:428–432.

De Grauwe P, Janssens M, Leliaert H. Real-exchange-rate variability from 1920 to 1926 and 1973 to 1982. Princeton (NJ): International Finance Section, Princeton University; 1985.

Delaplane WH. The Spanish Peseta Since 1913. [PhD dissertation]. Duke University; 1934.

Dimsdale NH. British monetary policy and the exchange rate 1920–1938. Oxf Econ Pap 1981;33:306–349.

Dulles EL. The French Franc, 1914–1928. New York: Macmillan; 1929.

Eagly RV. The Swedish and English bullionist controversies: a comparative study of the impact of events on ideas. In: Eagly RV, editor. Events, ideology and economic theory. Detroit: Wayne State University Press; 1968. pp. 13–31.

——. The Swedish bullionist controversy. Philadelphia (PA): American Philosophical Society; 1971.

Edison HJ. Purchasing power parity: a quantitative reassessment of the 1920s experience. J Int Money Finance 1985;4:361–372.

——. Purchasing power parity in the long run: a test of the Dollar/Pound exchange rate (1890–1978). J Money Credit Bank 1987;19:376–387.

Einzig P. The history of foreign exchange. 2nd ed. London: Macmillan; 1970.

Enders W. Unit roots and the real exchange rate before World War I: the case of Britain and the USA. J Int Money Finance 1989;8:59–73.

Farag AA, Ott DJ. Exchange rate determination under fluctuating exchange rates: some empirical evidence. In: Murphy JC, editor. Money in the international order. Dallas (TX): Southern Methodist University Press; 1964. pp. 84–105.

Flux AW. The foreign exchanges. London: P. S. King; 1924.

Frenkel JA. A monetary approach to the exchange rate: doctrinal aspects and empirical evidence. Scand J Econ 1976;78:200–224.

——. Purchasing power parity: doctrinal perspective and evidence from the 1920s. J Int Econ 1978;8:169–191.

——. Exchange rates, prices, and money: lessons from the 1920s. Am Econ Rev 1980;70:235–242.

Friedman M, Schwartz AJ. A monetary history of the United States, 1867–1960. Princeton (NJ): Princeton University Press; 1963.

Furniss ES. Foreign exchange: the financing mechanism of international commerce. Boston (MA): Houghton Mifflin; 1922.

Garnsey ME. Postwar exchange-rate parities. Q J Econ 1945;60:113–135.

Georgoutsos DA, Kouretas GP. Long-run purchasing power parity in the 1920s: the Greek experience. Appl Econ 1992;1301–1306.

——, Kouretas GP. The pound sterling and the Franc Poincaré in the 1920s: long-run relationships, speculation and temporal stability. Appl Financ Econ 2000;10:471–482.

Graham FD. International trade under depreciated paper: the United States, 1862—79. Q J Econ 1922;36:220–273.

——. Exchange, prices, and production in hyper-inflation Germany, 1920–1923. Princeton (NJ): Princeton University Press; 1930.

——. Recent movements in international price levels and the doctrine of purchasing power parity. J Am Stat Assoc 1935;30:159–166.

Gregory TE. Foreign exchange before, during, and after the War. London: Oxford University Press; 1925.

——. The first year of the gold standard. London: Ernest Benn; 1926.

Grilli V, Kaminsky G. Nominal exchange rate regimes and the real exchange rate: evidence from the United States and Great Britain, 1885–1986. J Monet Econ 1991;27:191–212.

Grubb FW. Creating the U.S. Dollar currency union, 1748–1811: a quest for monetary stability or a usurpation of state sovereignty for personal gain. Am Econ Rev 2003;93:1778–1798.

——. State 'Currencies' and the transition to the U.S. Dollar: reply—including a new view from Canada. Am Econ Rev 2005;95:1341–1348.

——. Testing for the economic impact of the U.S. constitution: purchasing power parity across the colonies versus across the states, 1748–1811. J Econ Hist 2010;70:118–145.

Haberler G. The theory of international trade. London: William Hodge; 1936.

Haberler G. A survey of international trade theory. Princeton (NJ): International Finance Section, Princeton University; 1961.

Hakkio CS. A re-examination of purchasing power parity: a multi-country and multi-period study. J Int Econ 1984;17:265–277.

Hasan MS. Univariate time series behaviour of the real exchange rate: evidence from colonial India. Econ Lett 2004;84:75–80.

Heckscher EF. Sweden. In: Heckscher EF, editor. Sweden, Norway, Denmark and Iceland in the World War. New Haven (CT): Yale University Press; 1930. pp. 125–217.

Hegwood ND, Papell DH. Purchasing power parity under the gold standard. South Econ J 2002;69:72–91.

Hodgson JS. An analysis of floating exchange rates: the dollar-sterling rate, 1919–1925. South Econ J 1972;39:249–257.

——. Phelps P. The distributed impact of price-level variation on floating exchange rates. Rev Econ Stat 1975;57:58–64.

Houthakker HS. Exchange rate adjustment. In: Factors Affecting the United States Balance of Payments, Compilation of studies prepared for the Subcommittee on International Exchange and Payments, Joint Economic Committee, 87th Congress. 2nd session. Washington (DC): U.S. Government Printing Office; 1962. pp. 287–304.

Jacobson ML. Russia, In Young (1925a), Volume 2; pp. 185–203.

——, Jaeger R. Germany, In Young (1925a), Volume 1; 1925. pp. 387–3430.

——, Jaeger R, Young JP. Italy, In Young (1925a), Volume 1; 1925. pp. 347–386.

Junge G. Purchasing power parity in the 1920s and the 1970s. Eur Econ Rev 1984;26:73–82.

Katano H. Econometric determination of foreign exchange rate of Japan for 1926–1935. Kobe Econ Bus Rev 1956;3:9–25.

——. Reconstruction of the theory of purchasing power parity. Kobe Econ Bus Rev 1957;4:125–148.

Katzenellenbaum SS. Russian currency and banking, 1914–1924. London: P.S. King; 1925.

Keynes JM. Official figures relating to inflation. Econ J 1919;29:504–506.

——. A tract on monetary reform. London: Macmillan; 1923.

——. Volume 1, A treatise on money. London: Macmillan; 1930.

——. Essays in persuasion. London: Macmillan; 1931.

Kindahl JK. Economic factors in specie resumption: the United States, 1865–79. J Pol Econ 1961;69:30–48.

Krugman PR. Purchasing power parity and exchange rates: another look at the evidence. J Int Econ 1978;8:397–407.

League of Nations. Monetary Review, Money and Banking, 1935/36, Volume 1, Geneva; 1936.

Lester RA. Monetary experiments: early American and recent Scandinavian. Princeton (NJ): Princeton University Press; 1939.

MacDonald R. The Norman Conquest of $4.86 and the asset approach to the exchange rate. J Int Money Finance 1985a;4:373–387.

——. Are deviations from purchasing power parity efficient? Some further answers. Weltwirtsch Arch 1985b;121:638–645.

Matthews KGP. Was sterling overvalued in 1925? Econ Hist Rev 1986;39:572–587.

McCloskey DN, Zecher JR. The success of purchasing power parity: historical evidence and its implications for macroeconomics. In: Bordo MD, Schwartz AJ, editors. A retrospective on the classical gold standard, 1821–1931. Chicago: University of Chicago Press; 1984. pp. 121–150.

Michael P, Nobay AR, Peel DA. Exchange rate dynamics and monetary reforms: theory and evidence from Britain's return to gold. In: Bayoumi T, Eichengreen B, Taylor MP, editors. Modern perspectives on the gold standard. Cambridge: Cambridge University Press; 1996. pp. 341–362.

———, Nobay AR, Peel DA. Transactions costs and nonlinear adjustment in real exchange rates: an empirical investigation. J Polit Econ 1997;105:862–879.

Moggridge DE. The return to gold, 1925. Cambridge: Cambridge University Press; 1969.

———. British monetary policy 1924–1931: the Norman conquest of $4.86. Cambridge: Cambridge University Press; 1972.

Mouré K. Undervaluing the Franc Poincaré. Econ Hist Rev 1996;49:137–153.

Myhrman J. Experiences of flexible exchange rates in earlier periods: theories, evidence and a new view. Scand J Econ 1976;78:169–196.

Nachane DM, Hatekar NR. The bullionist controversy: an empirical reappraisal. Manch Sch 1995;43:412–425.

Nurkse R. International currency experience, League of Nations. Princeton (NJ): Princeton University Press; 1944.

Officer LH. The floating dollar in the greenback period: a test of theories of exchange-rate determination. J Econ Hist 1981;629–650.

———. Purchasing power parity and exchange rates: theory, evidence and relevance. Greenwich (CT): JAI; 1982.

———. The bullionist controversy: a time-series analysis. Int J Finance Econ 2000;5: 197–209.

———. Purchasing power parity: from ancient times to World War II. in EH.Net Encyclopedia, Economic History Services, EH.Net, 2006. 79 pages. http://eh.net/files/graphics/encyclopedia/officer.pdf.

Phylaktis K. Purchasing power parity: the Greek evidence from the 1920s. Greek Econ Rev 1990;12:148–156.

———. Purchasing power parity and cointegration: the Greek evidence from the 1920s. J Int Money Finance 1992;11:502–5513.

Pippenger JE. Speculation in the flexible exchange re-revisited. Kyklos 1973;26:613–618.

Redmond J. The sterling overvaluation in 1925: a multilateral approach. Econ Hist Rev 1984;37:520–532.

Robertson DH. Money. New York: Harcourt, Brace; 1922.

Rogalski RJ, Vinso JD. Price level variations as predictors of flexible exchange rates. J Int Bus Stud 1977;8:71–81.

Rogers JH. The process of inflation in France, 1914–1927. New York: Columbia University Press; 1929.

Sabaté M, Gadea MD, Serrano JM. PPP and structural breaks: the peseta-sterling rate, 50 years of a floating regime. J Int Money Finance 2003;22:613–627.

Sayers RS. The return to gold, 1925. In: Pressnell LS, editor. Studies in the industrial revolution. London: Athlone Press; 1960. pp. 313–327.

Schweigert TE. Nominal and real exchange rates and purchasing power parity during the Guatemalan float, 1897–1922. J Econ Dev 2002;27:127–142.

Sicsic P. Was the franc Poincaré deliberately undervalued? Explor Econ Hist 1992;29:69–92.

Sort MS, Gadea MD, Serrano JM. The Spanish peseta versus the pound sterling, the French franc and the US dollar (1870–1935): a long floating experience. Appl Financ Econ Lett 2005;1:95–99.

Stolper WF. Purchasing power parity and the pound sterling from 1919–1925. Kyklos 1948;2:240–269.

Taylor MP. Dollar-sterling exchange rate in the 1920s: purchasing power parity and the Norman conquest of $4.86. Appl Econ 1992;24:803–811.

——, McMahon PC. Long-run purchasing power parity in the 1920s. Eur Econ Rev 1988;32:179–197.

Thomas LB. Some evidence on international currency experience, 1919–1925. Nebr J Econ Bus 1972;11:145–155.

——. Speculation in the flexible exchange revisited—another view. Kyklos 1973a;26:143–150.

——. Behavior of flexible exchange rates: additional tests from the post-World War I episode. South Econ J 1973b;40:167–182.

Thompson GR. Expectations and the greenback rate, 1862–1878. [PhD dissertation]; University of South Florida; 1972.

Triffin R. La thèorie de la surévaluation monétaire et la devaluation belge. Bull d'Institut de Rech Econ Soc 1937;9:19–52.

Tsiang S-C. Fluctuating exchange rates in countries with relatively stable economies: some European experiences after World War I. Int Monet Fund Staff Pap 1959;7:244–273.

United States Tariff Commission. Depreciated exchange and international trade. Washington (DC): Government Printing Office; 1922.

Walter JT. Foreign exchange equilibrium. Pittsburgh (PA): University of Pittsburgh Press; 1951.

Wasserman MJ. The compression of French wholesale prices during inflation, 1919–1926. Am Econ Rev 1936;26:62–73.

White HG. Foreign exchange rates and internal prices under inconvertible paper currencies. Am Econ Rev 1935;25:259–2272.

Whitaker JK, Hudgins MW Jr. The floating pound sterling of the nineteen-thirties: an econometric study. South Econ J 1977;43:1478–1485.

Wight EVD. Austria, In Young (1925a), Volume 2; 1925a. pp. 9–23.

——. Belgium, In Young (1925a), Volume 2; 1925b. pp. 27–49.

——. Netherlands, In Young (1925a), Volume 2; 1925c. pp. 125–139.

Wood E. Denmark, In Young (1925a), Volume 2; 1925a. pp. 79–97.

——. Norway, In Young (1925a), Volume 2; 1925b. pp. 143–159.

——. Sweden, In Young (1925a); Volume 2; 1925c. pp. 245–266.

——. Switzerland, In Young (1925a), Volume 2; 1925d. pp. 267–289.

Yeager LB. Fluctuating exchange rates in the nineteenth century: the experiences of Austria and Russia. In: Mundell RA, Swoboda AK, editors. Monetary problems of the international economy. Chicago: University of Chicago Press; 1969. pp. 61–89.

——. International monetary relations: theory, history, and policy. 2nd ed. New York: Harper & Row; 1976.

Young JP. European currency and finance. Two volumes. Washington (DC): Government Printing Office; 1925a.

Young JP. Czechoslovakia, In Young (1925a), Volume 2; 1925b. pp. 55–69.

——. France, In Young (1925a), Volume 1; 1925c. pp. 307–346.

_____. Hungary, In Young (1925a), Volume 2; 1925d. pp. 103–124.
_____. Poland, In Young (1925a), Volume 2; 1925e. pp. 163–184.
_____. Spain, In Young (1925a), Volume 2; 1925f. pp. 223–239.
_____. Great Britain, In Young (1925a), Volume 1; 1925g. pp. 273–306.
_____. International trade and finance. New York: Ronald; 1938.

CHAPTER SEVEN

# Purchasing Power Parity in Tradable Goods

IAN W. MARSH
Cass Business School

EVGENIA PASSARI
Cass Business School

LUCIO SARNO
Cass Business School, CEPR

## 7.1 Introduction

In this chapter, we provide a discussion of the law of one price (LOP), the basic building block of purchasing power parity (PPP). The LOP relates to the common-currency prices of similar goods at a disaggregated level, postulating that similar tradable goods, once their national prices are expressed in a common currency, should sell for the same price across different international locations. Aggregating across different tradable goods and services in a sector and then across different sectors, one obtains that the resulting baskets of tradable goods should trade at the same price: this is the notion of PPP in tradable goods. Further aggregating across other goods and services, including nontradables, leads to the conventional PPP hypothesis, which states that national price levels should be equal when expressed in a common currency.

While several surveys exist on PPP, this chapter mainly focuses on internationally tradable goods and services, rather than broad baskets of goods and services, which also include a substantial nontradable component. Specifically, the objective is to understand the properties of deviations from the LOP applied

*Handbook of Exchange Rates*, First Edition. Edited by Jessica James, Ian W. Marsh, and Lucio Sarno.

to internationally tradable goods or sectors, on the basis of the existing empirical evidence published in the leading academic literature. To anticipate our conclusions, we will show that a careful reading of the literature suggests that the LOP holds over long periods of time for the relevant tradable goods and services, and that adjustment occurs in a nonlinear manner such that the larger the current deviation from parity the faster the adjustment toward parity in the future.

The core of the chapter focuses on the specific subset of the relevant literature that analyzes deviations from the LOP applied to individual goods and services and specific sectors. The emphasis will therefore be on tradable items. This literature, while less voluminous than the literature on PPP, is nevertheless substantial, and it has not been summarized in a survey article to date. This is exactly the gap that this study fills, with the ultimate goal to describe the current state of knowledge on the properties of deviations from the LOP, including the persistence of deviations from the LOP across currencies (the speed of reversion to the LOP), and the nature of the shocks. The discussion follows similar steps to the leading surveys on PPP, but with a more specific focus on internationally tradable goods and a specific description of some of the key studies that have best addressed this topic.

The remainder of this chapter is set out as follows: Section 7.2 briefly outlines the LOP and PPP. Section 7.3 provides an overview of the relevant empirical literature on the LOP, followed by a discussion of commodity-arbitrage-based modeling approaches to PPP in Section 7.4. In Section 7.5, we summarize our views on what can be inferred as we aggregate from LOP to PPP, and present a graphical analysis of the behavior of real exchange rates using a range of alternative aggregate price measures. The final section briefly concludes.

## 7.2 The LOP and Price Indices

The LOP states that identical goods, once their national prices are expressed in a common currency, should sell for the same price across different international locations. The LOP is viewed as a long-run proposition about arbitrage in international goods market that suggests that once arbitrage opportunities arise they do not persist forever; adjustment can take place either via prices or via the exchange rate, which moves in such a way as to restore the LOP over time. While in its purest form, the LOP compares *identical* products or services sold in two different geographical locations, the most relevant case in practice is the comparison of *similar* goods, with different origin of production and different pricing currency, for which prices should be very close, after accounting for transaction costs, due to competition in international goods market.

Ignoring transaction costs for the moment, the LOP stated above in its *absolute* version may be written formally as

$$P_{i,t} = P^*_{i,t} S_t \qquad i = 1, 2, \ldots, N \tag{7.1}$$

where $P_{i,t}$ denotes the price of good $i$ in terms of the domestic currency at time $t$, $P^*_{i,t}$ is the price of good $i$ in terms of the foreign currency at time $t$, and $S_t$ is the nominal exchange rate expressed as the domestic price of the foreign currency at time $t$. In its *relative* version, the LOP postulates the relatively weaker condition:

$$\frac{P^*_{i,t+1}S_{t+1}}{P_{i,t+1}} = \frac{P^*_{i,t}S_t}{P_{i,t}} \qquad i = 1, 2, \ldots, N \tag{7.2}$$

Obviously, the absolute LOP implies the relative LOP but not *vice versa*.

By summing up all the traded goods in each country, one obtains the *absolute* version of PPP for tradable goods:

$$\sum_{i=1}^{N}\alpha_i P_{i,t} = S_t\sum_{i=1}^{N}\alpha_i P^*_{i,t}, \tag{7.3}$$

where the weights in the summation satisfy $\sum_{i=1}^{N}\alpha_i = 1$. Alternatively, if the price indices are constructed using a geometric index, then we must form the weighted sum after taking logarithms:

$$\sum_{i=1}^{N}\gamma_i p_{i,t} = s_t + \sum_{i=1}^{N}\gamma_i p^*_{i,t}, \tag{7.4}$$

where the geometric weights in the summation satisfy $\sum_{i=1}^{N}\gamma_i = 1$ and lower case letters denote logarithms. If the aggregate price levels are $P_t$ and $P^*_t$ or, in logarithms, $p_t$ and $p^*_t$, then (according to whether the arithmetic or geometric index is used), we can use Equation 7.3 or 7.4 to derive the (absolute) PPP condition:

$$s_t = p_t - p^*_t \tag{7.5}$$

From Eequation 7.5, it is easily seen that the real exchange rate, defined here in logarithmic form:

$$q_t \equiv s_t - p_t + p^*_t \tag{7.6}$$

may be viewed as a measure of the deviation from PPP.

The PPP hypothesis, as expressed in Equation 7.5, states that national price levels should be equal when expressed in a common currency. Although very few economists would believe that this simple proposition holds at each point in time, a large literature in international finance has examined empirically the validity of PPP over the long run, either by testing whether nominal exchange rates and relative prices move together or by testing whether the real exchange rate has a tendency to revert to a stable equilibrium level over time (see the surveys of Rogoff (1996), Sarno and Taylor (2002), Taylor and Taylor (2004), and Sarno (2008)).

Whether long-run PPP holds or, equivalently, whether the real exchange rate is stationary has important economic implications on a number of fronts. In particular, the degree of persistence in the real exchange rate can be used to infer the principal impulses driving exchange rate movements.[1] Further,

[1] For example, if the real exchange rate is highly persistent then the shocks are likely to be real-side, for example, technology shocks, whereas if it is not very persistent then the shocks must be mainly to aggregate demand, such as monetary policy shocks (Rogoff, 1996).

from a theoretical perspective, if PPP is not a valid long-run international parity condition, this casts doubts on the predictions of much open-economy macroeconomics that is based on the assumption of long-run PPP. Finally, estimates of PPP exchange rates are often used for practical purposes such as determining the degree of misalignment of the nominal exchange rate and the appropriate policy response, the setting of exchange rate parities, the international comparison of national income levels, and the need for exchange rate hedging for a long-run investor. These practical uses of the PPP concept, and in particular the calculation of PPP exchange rates, would obviously be of very limited use if PPP deviations do not settle down to a constant equilibrium level over time.[2]

Clearly, deriving PPP for tradable goods from the LOP introduces a range of index number problems. For example, Equations 7.3 and 7.4 implicitly assume that the same weights are relevant in each country, whereas price index weights will typically differ across countries (perhaps even being zero in one country and nonzero in another for some goods and services) and will also tend to shift through time. In practice, researchers often assume that PPP should hold approximately using the price indices of each country. In the geometric index case, for example, we can rearrange Equation 7.4 to yield

$$\sum_{i=1}^{N} \gamma_i p_{i,t} = s_t + \sum_{i=1}^{N} \gamma_i^* p_{i,t}^* + \sum_{i=1}^{N} (\gamma_i - \gamma_i^*) p_{i,t}^* \tag{7.7}$$

or

$$\sum_{i=1}^{N} \gamma_i p_{i,t} = s_t + \sum_{i=1}^{N} \gamma_i^* p_{i,t}^* + u_t \tag{7.8}$$

where the $\gamma_i^*$ denote the weights in the foreign price index. Clearly, the greater the disparity between national weighting patterns, the greater the apparent disparity—represented by the term $u_t$—from aggregate PPP even when the LOP holds for individual goods. Note that, however, if the geometric price indices are homogeneous of degree 1 (i.e., an equiproportionate increase in all prices will raise the overall price level by the same proportion) then differences in weights across countries will matter less where price impulses affect all goods and services more or less homogeneously. This assumption, while unrealistic in its exact formulation, appears quite plausible since shocks to goods prices tend to have a strong common component that relates to costs of production and inputs, which tend to comove across both countries and goods.[3] Considerable differences may arise, however, where price impulses impinge heterogeneously across the various goods and services in an economy and, in particular, where price inflation

[2]It is also worth noting that the literature refers to the difficulty sometimes encountered in establishing very strong evidence in favor of PPP as the "PPP puzzle" (Rogoff, 1996). This terminology suggests that, should PPP not hold, it would be regarded as an anomaly, a surprising empirical fact, given that international economists tend to believe that some sort of PPP must guide the long-run comovement between exchange rates and relative prices.

[3]In practice, it is more common for national statistical bureaus to use arithmetic rather than geometric price indices, although deviations from PPP arising from this source are not likely to be large.

differs between the tradable and nontradable goods sectors. A particular example of this is the Harrod-Balassa-Samuelson effect, which is discussed later.

One of the key reasons why PPP exchange rate calculations are still somewhat controversial is exactly because of the difficulties of finding comparable baskets of goods to measure purchasing power across countries. If two countries trade different baskets of goods, it is no longer logical to use the LOP to build PPP, since there is no strong reason why one should arrive exactly at the same price level by aggregating baskets of different goods. Moreover, people in different countries typically consume different baskets of goods, and the comparison of the cost of baskets of goods and services using a price index is further complicated because purchasing patterns and even the goods available for purchase differ across countries. For example, it would be desirable to make adjustments for differences in the quality of goods and services, which are hard to measure. All of these issues reflect in PPP disparities.

Despite these issues, there are several arguments to support the notion that the LOP and PPP continue to be useful as approximations to long-run exchange rate behavior. For example, while it is clear that the theoretical construct of identical goods is not realistic when thinking about the LOP in practice, it is quite reasonable to think about similar goods. The notion of similar goods can be thought of as follows: goods are similar when they serve to satisfy the same consumption need; for example, any car will satisfy the need to commute between two different locations. That specific need has an "intrinsic price" that is embedded in the wholesale and consumer price of the car in international markets. It is the intrinsic price that theoretically one would want to use when testing the LOP or PPP, but it is of course not observable. The total price will instead include a number of other factors, such as quality and size, that differ across cars. Moreover, in different export markets, the very same car will also have different prices because of transactions and transport costs, tariffs and taxes, and other adaptations that affect demand and supply (e.g., the need to make cars with right-hand side drive in Britain). The resulting price differentials are not necessarily violations of the LOP, and they are justifiable on grounds related to quality, brand, transaction costs, etc. These price differentials will be bounded by the fact that similar goods are competing in international goods markets very much in the same way as identical goods do, with the main difference being that while competition for identical goods can only occur through prices, competition for similar goods occurs through prices and other attributes such as quality.

Ultimately, however, the soundness of the above arguments is an empirical matter. In this sense, what matters is the empirical evidence from the literature on testing the LOP and PPP for different levels of aggregation in prices and different countries. This literature, as it will be clear at the end of this chapter, indicates that the LOP and PPP tend to work reasonably well across a range of different goods and countries, which is indicative that the above arguments make empirical sense. In general, however, the difficulty in finding evidence strongly supportive of PPP and the difficulties encountered in moving from the LOP to PPP have provided a strong motivation for researchers to investigate the LOP empirically using a variety of disaggregated data.

## 7.3 Empirical Evidence on the LOP

### 7.3.1 EARLY TESTS OF THE LOP

In general, the early econometric studies suggest rejection of the LOP for a broad range of goods and provide empirical evidence both that deviations from the LOP are highly volatile and that the volatility of relative prices is considerably lower than the volatility of nominal exchange rates. This is suggested, for example, by two influential studies carried out in the 1970s. Isard (1977) uses disaggregated data for a number of traded goods and for a number of countries, providing empirical evidence that the deviations from the LOP are large and persistent, and they appear to be highly correlated with exchange rate movements. Richardson (1978) finds very similar results to Isard, by using data for four- and seven-digit standard industrial classification (SIC) categories.[4]

Implicit in the LOP is the assumption that exporters maintain their local currency price in the face of exchange rate movements such that exchange rate pass-through to importers is complete. In this case, we observe the so-called producer-currency pricing. Alternatively, if exporters lower their export prices to fully offset exchange rate changes, prices in the importer's currency will be unchanged, and we observe local-currency pricing and an exchange rate pass-through of zero.

In an early study, Kreinin (1977) documents exchange rate pass-through rates of between 50% (to US import prices) and 100% (for Italian imports). Knetter (1989, 1993) uses high quality disaggregated data (seven digits) and provides evidence that large and persistent price differentials exist for traded goods exported to multiple destinations (e.g., for German beer exported to the United Kingdom as compared to the United States). Herguera (1994) investigates the implications of product differentiation for the price adjustment mechanism in international trade using an imperfect competition model. The model shows that market structure, product differentiation, and strategic behavior can explain the persistent price differential of perfectly substitutable goods across countries (see also Chen and Knez (1995) and Dumas et al. 1995). This is consistent with the "pricing-to-market" (PTM) theory of Krugman (1987) and Dornbusch (1987), whose main feature is that the same good can be given a different price in different countries when oligopolistic firms are supplying it. Goldberg and Knetter (1997) survey the extensive literature on PTM in much more detail.

### 7.3.2 THE BORDER EFFECT

Parsley and Wei (1996) look for convergence toward the LOP in the absence of trade barriers or nominal exchange rate fluctuations by analyzing a panel of 51 prices from 48 cities in the United States. They find that convergence rates substantially higher than those typically found in cross-country data, that

[4]Similarly, Giovannini (1988) uses data on domestic and dollar export prices of Japanese goods and provides evidence that deviations from the LOP—found to be large not only for sophisticated manufacturing goods but also for commodities such as screws, nuts, and bolts—are mainly due to exchange rate movements.

convergence occurs faster for larger price differences, and that rates of convergence are slower for cities further apart. Extending this line of research, Engel and Rogers (1996) use data for both US and Canadian cities and for 14 categories of consumer prices in order to analyze the properties of deviations from the LOP. The authors provide evidence that the distance between cities can explain a considerable amount of the price differential of similar goods in different cities of the same country. Nevertheless, the price differentials are considerably larger for two cities across different countries relative to two equidistant cities in the same country. The estimates of Engel and Rogers suggest that crossing the national border—the so-called "border effect" —increases the volatility of price differentials by the same order of magnitude, which would be generated by the addition of 2500–23,000 extra miles between the cities considered. Rogers and Jenkins (1995) find similar results to Engel and Rogers, providing evidence that the "border effect" is effective in increasing not only the volatility of price differentials but also their persistence.

Crucini et al. (2005a) also show that the volatility of LOP deviations across goods is greater the farther apart are locations; see also Crucini and Shintani (2008) and Crucini et al. (2010). The latter build a single-country, two-city model with nominal rigidities and transportation costs, which predicts that the volatility of LOP deviations is lower for goods with infrequent price adjustment after controlling for distance. They adapt the Engel and Rogers (1996) analysis to examine Japanese retail prices at the city level and find that the distance equivalent of nominal rigidities can be as large as the "width" of the border documented in the literature on international LOP, casting doubt over interpretations of distance as a metric for market segmentation.

### 7.3.3 BARRIERS TO ARBITRAGE AND NONLINEARITIES

Among the possible explanations of the violation of the LOP suggested by the literature, transport costs, tariffs, and nontariff barriers play a dominant role. An estimate of the wedge driven by the costs of transportation is given, for example, by the International Monetary Fund: the difference between the value of world exports computed as "free on board" (FOB) and the value of world imports charged in full, or cost, insurance, and freight (CIF) is estimated at about 10% and is found to be highly variable across countries. Also, even if tariffs have been considerably reduced over time across major industrialized countries, nontariff barriers are still very significant. Governments of many countries often intervene in trade across borders using nontariff barriers in a way that they do not use within their borders (e.g., in the form of strict inspection requirements; see Knetter (1994), Feenstra (1995), Rogoff (1996), and Feenstra and Kendall (1997)).

Frictions in international arbitrage have important implications and, in particular, imply potential nonlinearities in the deviations from the LOP. The idea that there may be nonlinearities in goods arbitrage dates at least from Heckscher (1916), who suggested that there may be significant deviations from the LOP due to international transaction costs between spatially separated markets. A similar viewpoint can be discerned in the writings of Cassel (Cassel, 1922) and, to a greater or lesser extent, in other earlier writers (Officer, 1982). More recently, a number of authors have developed theoretical models of nonlinear real exchange rate adjustment arising from transaction costs in international arbitrage (Benninga and Protopapadakis, 1988; Dumas, 1992; Sercu et al., 1995; O'Connell and Wei, 2002). In most of these models, proportional or "iceberg" transport costs ("iceberg" because a fraction of goods are presumed to "melt" when shipped) create a band for the real exchange rate within which the marginal cost of arbitrage exceeds the marginal benefit. Assuming instantaneous goods arbitrage at the edges of the band typically implies that the thresholds become reflecting barriers.

Some of these studies show that the thresholds should be interpreted more broadly than as simply reflecting shipping costs and trade barriers *per se*, but also as resulting from the sunk costs of international arbitrage and the resulting tendency for traders to wait for sufficiently large arbitrage opportunities to open up before entering the market (see, in particular, Dumas, 1992). O'Connell and Wei (2002) extend the iceberg model to allow for fixed and proportional costs of arbitrage. This results in a two-threshold model where the real exchange rate is reset by arbitrage to an upper or lower inner threshold whenever it hits the corresponding outer threshold. Intuitively, arbitrage will be heavy once it is profitable enough to outweigh the initial fixed cost but will stop short of returning the real rate to the LOP level because of the proportional arbitrage costs.[5]

Some empirical evidence on the effect of transaction costs in this context is provided by Davutyan and Pippenger (1990). Subsequent recent studies modeling nonlinearities in the deviations from the LOP include Michael et al. (1994), Obstfeld and Taylor (1997), O'Connell (1998), Taylor (2001), and O'Connell and Wei (2002). In all these studies, the nonlinear nature of the adjustment process is investigated in terms of a TAR (transition autoregressive) model (Tong, 1990). The TAR model allows for a transaction costs band within which no adjustment in deviations from the LOP takes place, while outside of the band, as goods arbitrage becomes profitable the process switches abruptly to induce convergence toward the LOP. Further, the TAR model can incorporate a delay parameter that reflects the possibility that market participants react to deviations of the LOP from equilibrium with a lag, possibly due to menu costs. Michael et al. (1994) investigate the relative US dollar price of six wheat varieties and provide evidence for nonlinear mean reversion in deviations from the LOP. Obstfeld and Taylor (1997) employ disaggregated data (clothing, food, and fuel) for 32 locations at a monthly frequency from 1980 to 1995, the United States being the reference country. Their estimated thresholds are found to be between

[5]Coleman (1995) suggests that the assumption of instantaneous trade should be replaced with the presumption that it takes time to ship goods. In his approach, transport costs still create a band of no arbitrage for the real exchange rate, beyond which the exchange rate can stray. Once beyond the thresholds, the real rate becomes increasingly mean reverting with the distance from the threshold. Within the transaction costs band, when no trade takes place, the process is divergent so that the exchange rate spends most of the time away from parity.

7% and 10% on an average across different types of goods. They also note that transaction costs to be lower between the US and Asia (about 2–8%) than between the US and Europe (about 9–19%). Using two different sets of relative price panels over the period 1975–1992, O'Connell and Wei (2002) also find strong evidence of nonlinear mean reversion in deviations from the LOP.

Importantly, Taylor (2001) shows that there can also be substantial upward bias in the estimated half-life of adjustment from assuming linear adjustment when, in fact, the true adjustment process is nonlinear. This essentially invalidates studies that employ linear models to examine the persistence properties of deviations from the LOP.[6]

Studies are now cumulating evidence in favor of threshold-type nonlinearity in deviations from the LOP, but they are often based on few commodities or currencies.[7] However, Sarno et al. (2004) provide a broad-based study on the presence of threshold-type nonlinearities in deviations from the LOP and on the ability of the TAR model to characterize them. They investigate the mean-reverting properties for real sectoral dollar exchange rates (deviations from the LOP) *vis-a-vis* five major currencies, for nine sectors since 1974. The results provide evidence suggesting that, in general, the TAR model characterizes well the deviations from the LOP across this broad range of currencies and sectors, yielding plausible estimates of transaction costs and convergence speeds.

We update these results using price data for four major sectors and for three major currency pairs vis-a-vis the US dollar. We obtain monthly price series for clothing and footwear (CL), energy (EN), food (FOD), and services (SRV) sectors from Datastream for the United Kingdom, Japan, Germany, and the United States as the reference country. We collect matching spot exchange rates from the IMF's International Financial Statistics database. The time series of interest are the monthly sectoral real exchange rates (deviations from the LOP) $q_{t(i)}$, constructed in logarithmic terms. The sectoral real exchange rates were normalized to unity at the beginning of the sample period, which runs from January 1991 to March 2011. Details are given in the Appendix of this chapter.

The key findings of Sarno et al. (2004) are confirmed by our results, reported in Table 7.1. First, transactions costs estimates differ widely across sectors. In the United Kingdom, for example, transactions costs for the energy sector are estimated to be of the order of 1%, whereas those for the services sector are some 20%. Second, costs of arbitrage widely fluctuate across countries for a given sector. Transactions costs for clothing range from 3% for Germany up to 19% for the United Kingdom. Conversely, transactions costs for the food sector in the

[6]Taylor (2001) also investigates the impact of temporal aggregation in the data. Using a model in which deviations from the LOP or PPP follow an AR(1) process at a higher frequency than that at which the data is sampled, Taylor shows analytically that the degree of upward bias in the estimated half-life rises as the degree of temporal aggregation increases, that is, as the length of time between observed data points increases. This time aggregation problem is a difficult issue for researchers to deal with, since high frequency data do not exist for prices.

[7]Also, most studies employing TAR models in this context were written before the publication of Hansen's (1996, 1997) work, which provides important econometric contributions for testing linearity against threshold-type nonlinearity and for estimating TAR models.

TABLE 7.1 **TAR Estimation Results: United Kingdom, Japan, and Germany**

| | United Kingdom | | | | Japan | | | | Germany | | | |
|---|---|---|---|---|---|---|---|---|---|---|---|---|
| Sector | CL | EN | FOD | SRV | CL | EN | FOD | SRV | CL | EN | FOD | SRV |
| $\theta$ | 0.19 | 0.01 | 0.05 | 0.20 | 0.03 | 0.15 | 0.10 | 0.09 | 0.06 | 0.03 | 0.16 | 0.02 |
| d | 24 | 24 | 24 | 24 | 21 | 23 | 23 | 23 | 23 | 24 | 24 | 24 |
| $\beta_1$ | 0.914 | 0.924 | 0.941 | 0.902 | 0.988 | 0.953 | 0.964 | 0.969 | 0.985 | 0.929 | 0.959 | 0.969 |
| DW | 2.09 | 1.89 | 2.05 | 2.15 | 1.95 | 1.67 | 1.89 | 1.95 | 1.82 | 1.74 | 1.85 | 1.85 |
| $p$-Value | 0.00 | 0.00 | 0.00 | 0.00 | 0.00 | 0.00 | 0.00 | 0.00 | 0.00 | 0.00 | 0.00 | 0.00 |

Notes: For the following four sectors: clothing and footwear (CL), energy (EN), food (FOD), and services (SRV), the time series of interest are the monthly sectoral real exchange rates (deviations from the LOP) of United Kingdom, Japan, and Germany *vis-a-vis* the USD, constructed in logarithmic terms. The sectoral real exchange rates were normalized to unity at the beginning of the sample period, which spans from January 1991 to March 2011. Sectoral real exchange rates are estimated using a TAR$(p, k, d)$ model, where in all cases the autoregressive order $p = 1$, the number of thresholds $k = 2$ (the thresholds being equal to $-\theta$ and $\theta$, respectively) and $d$ denotes the delay parameter. Coefficient $\beta_1$ is the estimated outer autoregressive parameter that measures the degree of nonlinear mean reversion. Estimation is conducted by sequential least squares. The $p$-value refers to the marginal significance level from executing the Hansen (1997) linearity test.

United Kingdom are relatively low at 5% while in Germany they are estimated to be 16%. Third, the estimated speed of adjustment parameters suggest that adjustment toward LOP is fairly fast with average half-lives of approximately 9 months for the United Kingdom, 24 months for Germany, and 28 months for Japan. However, the delay parameter, which measures the timing of the reaction of market participants to deviations from the LOP, is perhaps longer than one might expect at around 2 years, on an average. This means that deviations for the LOP may be somewhat sticky given the large delay parameter, but that they are not particularly persistent since reversion is quite rapid.

Overall, these results suggest that deviations from the LOP become mean reverting only when they are large enough to generate profitable arbitrage opportunities net of transaction costs. These models, therefore, provide a rationale for threshold-type models of deviations from the LOP that allow for a jump from non-mean-reverting behavior within the transaction costs band to mean-reverting behavior outside the transaction costs band.

### 7.3.4 THE TRADABLE VERSUS NONTRADABLE GOODS DICHOTOMY

Engel (1999) measures the proportion of US real exchange rate movements that can be accounted for by movements in the relative prices of nontradable goods, at all possible horizons from 1 month up to 30 years. The study is performed with five different measures of nontradable goods prices and real exchange rates. The author reports that the relative prices of nontradable goods appear to account for almost none of the movement of US real exchange rates and considers the possibility of mismeasurement of traded goods prices.

Consistent with Engel (1999), Obstfeld and Rogoff (2000) find evidence of very slow mean reversion in shocks to the relative prices of tradables. It is suggested that it does not make much difference whether one uses tradables or nontradables to compute real exchange rates and hence that the properties of PPP deviations are largely the same regardless of the specific price index used. These results hold across a broad set of currencies. However, the traded/nontradable goods distinction is a bit ambiguous at the retail level since many traded goods embody large nontradable components, which makes the dichotomy arbitrary. Nevertheless, the results are somewhat surprising and cannot be attributed solely to price aggregation problems, as many researchers report similar findings even for highly disaggregated data on goods that are perceived as highly tradable (Engel and Rogers, 1996).

There appears to be substantially stronger adjustment of prices to exchange rate changes at the importer level than at the consumer level. Goldberg and Knetter (1997) find that the pass-through of exchange rates to relative international prices is about 50% after 1 year, much faster than what we see in consumer price data. Thus, relatively large elasticities in international trade between exporters and importers can be consistent with exceedingly sluggish adjustment in the relative consumer price of tradables.

The relevance of the dichotomy between tradables and nontradables is, however, supported by other studies. For example, Imbs et al. (2003) find a relationship between the speed of mean reversion of sector-specific real exchange rates and economic determinants such as tradability and exchange rate volatility. Along these lines, Crucini et al. (2005b) study the good-by-good dispersion in the absolute LOP deviations and report that much of this dispersion can be ascribed to how tradable the goods are, as well as to how tradable the inputs required to produce them are. Crucini and Shintani (2008) further stress that the classical tradable/nontradable dichotomy is relevant. They partition items into two categories and find that nontradable goods have more persistence than traded goods across different locations. An important conclusion emerging from this strand of the literature is, therefore, the positive relationship between the goods' tradability and the speed of adjustment toward the equilibrium price (the LOP).

### 7.3.5 THE AGGREGATION BIAS AND MICRO PRICE STUDIES

Imbs et al. (2005) suggest that since sectoral real exchange rates might revert to the mean with different speeds, this heterogeneity could give rise to highly persistent aggregate series while relative price persistence is low on average at a disaggregated level. The authors maintain that the aggregate real exchange rate is persistent because its components have heterogeneous dynamics that standard time series and panel methods fail to control for. They argue that when this heterogeneity is taken into account, the estimated persistence of real exchange rates falls dramatically (its half-life, for instance, falls to around 1 year).

Chen and Engel (2005) question Imbs et al. (2005), citing Engel's (2000) paper that concludes that "for most categories of goods, there is not even evidence that deviations from the LOP tend to be eliminated." Along similar lines, Rogers and Jenkins (1995) and Crucini and Shintani (2008) explicitly find no aggregation bias. This point is given more formal support by Gadea and Mayoral (2009), who discard the notion that there is an aggregation bias in estimates of the persistence of PPP deviations, both theoretically and empirically.

Carvalho and Nechio (2010) build a theoretical model with sticky prices allowing for heterogeneity in the frequency of price changes across sectors. They show that a multisector model calibrated to match microeconomic evidence on the frequency of price changes produces deviations form PPP with a half-life of 45 months. A counterfactual one-sector model with the same average frequency of price adjustment fails to produce persistent deviations from PPP. They argue that this difference is mainly due to the misspecification of the one-sector model and that the aggregation bias is small.

Mayoral and Gadea (2011), using highly disaggregated data for a group of EU countries, report a high degree of heterogeneity along with high and positive skewness in the speed of reversion of the sectoral RERs. Using quantile panel regression analysis, they find that variables related to the market structure of the intermediate inputs and to the price stickiness of the final goods are important for sectoral persistence with the effect of these variables being greater, the higher the quantile.

A separate literature, including contributions by Crucini and Telmer (2007) and Nakamura (2008), however, shows substantially more volatility in LOP deviations than PPP deviations, implying that shocks to individual goods mostly average out in the aggregation to PPP. In other words, aggregation increases persistence and reduces variability.[8]

## 7.4 Purchasing Power Parity

The literature on PPP is voluminous, and we will not survey it comprehensively here (see instead Rogoff (1996), Taylor and Taylor (2004), Officer (2011)). Rather, we concentrate our discussion on research that can be seen as considering PPP as a generalization of LOP based on the commodity-arbitrage view.

A simple consideration of the enormously high volatility of exchange rates compared to the volatility of relative price levels implies that PPP does not hold continuously. Most of the research on PPP has concentrated on whether PPP holds as a long-run proposition. Much of this has been performed through analysis of the unit root properties of real exchange rates. Early evidence was not encouraging, as studies were unable to reject the null hypothesis that real exchange rates contained a unit root, which implies that the level of the real exchange rate does not return to some stable average level (Mark, 1990).[9]

[8]A final issue that is worth noting is the possibility that the failure of the LOP may be explained by institutional factors typical of this century, which have increased the persistence of deviations from the LOP. Nevertheless, Froot, Kim, and Rogoff (1995), using data on prices for grains and other dairy goods in England and Holland for a span of data, which goes from the fourteenth to the twentieth century, provide empirical evidence suggesting that the volatility of the LOP is quite stable during the whole period, regardless of the many regime shifts during the sample.

[9]Officer (2011) contains a survey of the application of such modern econometric tests of PPP using data from historical episodes and notes the mixed empirical evidence.

However, the low power of statistical tests when applied to a relatively short sample span such as the length of the recent float makes rejecting the null difficult. In an illustrative Monte Carlo exercise, Sarno and Taylor (2002) show how, given the observed persistence properties of the real exchange rate, standard unit root tests may be unable to detect stationarity of the real exchange rate (i.e., the validity of long-run PPP), having less than a 50/50 chance to do so for samples spanning up to 100 years. The same problem applies to the LOP (Taylor, 2001). Researchers have sought to overcome the power problem in testing for mean reversion in the real exchange rate either using long-span studies (Lothian and Taylor, 1996; Taylor, 2002) or more powerful panel econometric methods (Abuaf and Jorion, 1990; Frankel and Rose, 1996; O'Connell, 1998; Papell, 1998; Sarno and Taylor, 1998; Taylor and Sarno, 1998). A major issue with long-span studies is that, as noted by Frankel and Rose (1996), the long samples required to generate a reasonable level of statistical power with standard univariate unit root tests may be unavailable for many currencies (perhaps thereby generating a "survivorship bias" in tests on the available data) and, in any case, may potentially be inappropriate because of differences in real exchange rate behavior both across different historical periods and across different nominal exchange rate regimes (Baxter and Stockman, 1989; Taylor, 2002). As for panel-data studies, these provide mixed evidence. While, for example, Frankel and Rose (1996) and Taylor and Sarno (1998) find results favorable to long-run PPP, O'Connell (1998) rejects it on the basis of his empirical evidence.

From the perspective of PPP derived from goods arbitrage, a further weakness of many tests for long-run PPP is that the null hypothesis is of a linear process generating the real exchange rate series, meaning that adjustment is both continuous and of constant speed, regardless of the size of the deviation from PPP. The presence of transaction-costs-based impediments to arbitrage demonstrated above instead implies a nonlinear process for LOP. A number of authors have developed theoretical models of nonlinear real exchange rate adjustment arising from transaction costs in international arbitrage. The arguments made here to rationalize mean reversion in real exchange rates toward PPP are based on ideas that relate to the LOP in the sense that they refer to tradable goods only.[10]

While the abrupt regime change of a threshold model is appropriate when we consider the effects of arbitrage on individual goods prices, it is unrealistic when we model the real exchange rate. At this more aggregated level, the transition to mean-reverting behavior is more likely to be smooth. This behavior can be reproduced by the smooth transition autoregressive (STAR) model of Granger and Teräsvirta (1993), where adjustment is continuous but the speed of adjustment depends on the magnitude of the deviation from equilibrium. Michael et al. (1997) apply an exponential version of this nonlinear model to monthly

[10]However, we argue that this is reasonable given that Engel (1999), in a study that measures the proportion of dollar real exchange rate movements that can be accounted for by movements in the relative prices of nontradable goods, finds that relative prices of nontradable goods appear to account for essentially none of the movement of dollar real exchange rates. Hence, much of the explanation for the time series properties of PPP deviations is likely to reside in the behavior of deviations from the LOP, that is, movements in the relative prices of tradable goods.

interwar data for the French franc–US dollar, French franc–UK sterling and UK sterling–US dollar, as well as for the Lothian and Taylor (1996) long-span data set for 200 years ending in 1992. The systematic pattern in the estimates provides strong evidence of mean-reverting behavior for PPP deviations. Using data for the recent float, moreover, Taylor et al. (2001) provide confirmation that four major real bilateral dollar exchange rates are well characterized by nonlinear mean reverting processes. The estimated model implies an equilibrium level of the real exchange rate in the neighborhood of which the real exchange rate is close to a random walk, becoming increasingly mean reverting with the absolute size of the deviation from equilibrium, consistent with the theoretical arguments on the nature of real exchange rate dynamics in the presence of international arbitrage costs.

Taylor et al. also estimate the impulse response functions corresponding to their estimated nonlinear real exchange rate models. By taking account of nonlinearities, Taylor et al. find the speed of real exchange rate adjustment to be typically much faster than the very slow speeds of real exchange rate adjustment hitherto recorded in the literature. For example, the estimated half-lives (in months) for dollar–sterling and dollar–yen are the following:

| Shock (%): | 40 | 30 | 20 | 10 | 5 | 1 |
|---|---|---|---|---|---|---|
| Dollar–sterling | 10 | 20 | 22 | 26 | 29 | 32 |
| Dollar–yen | 14 | 18 | 24 | 32 | 38 | 42 |

where in the first row we report the size of the shock (in percentage terms) to the log-level of the real exchange rate. The estimated half-lives of these major real dollar exchange rates illustrate the nonlinear nature of the response to shocks, with larger shocks mean reverting much faster than smaller shocks. The dollar–sterling rate displays quite fast mean reversion, ranging from a half-life of under 1 year for the largest shocks of 40% to just under 3 years for small shocks of 1%; for shocks of 5–10%, the half-lives are just over 2 years. The dollar–yen displays higher persistence, with half-lives ranging from 14 to 42 months.

These results therefore suggest that PPP holds among major economies, and nonlinear models yield half-lives in the range of 3–5 years—which Rogoff (1996) terms "glacial"—only for small shocks occurring when the real exchange rate is near its equilibrium. For larger shocks, the speed of mean reversion is much faster, and for dollar–sterling even small shocks of 1–5% have a half-life under 3 years. Sarno and Chowdhury (2003) apply the same methods as Taylor et al. (2001) to real exchange rates constructed using only tradable goods and report even faster adjustment to PPP. These results provide important support for PPP as a long-run equilibrium relationship.[11]

[11]An interesting experiment in terms of gauging the extent to which market integration and the reduction of trade costs impacts on the degree of mean reversion in real exchange rates is provided by the advent of the euro in 1999. Koedijk et al. (2004) provide empirical evidence that the introduction of the euro and, more generally, the process of economic integration in Europe has

A further generalization of this class of models is provided by Sarno and Valente (2006), who use long-span data and apply a general modeling methodology in which regime changes and nonlinearities in the dynamic relationship between exchange rates and prices are explicitly allowed for. They examine the G5 countries across different exchange rate regimes, including the gold standard, the Bretton Woods period, and the floating regime, since the 1970s. Over the sample period examined, the economic history of the countries involved has seen a number of fundamental changes in monetary and exchange rate regimes, institutional structure, and policy targets which, in addition to the continuous evolution of the financial system and various nominal and real shocks, represent serious potential pitfalls to researchers attempting to find an empirical model of the deviations from PPP that is stable over the full sample. Sarno and Valente's results are supportive of long-run PPP for each of the major exchange rates examined and of a simple basic conjecture: under fixed exchange rate regimes relative prices adjust to restore deviations from long-run equilibrium, while nominal exchange rates bear most of the burden of adjustment under flexible exchange rate regimes.[12] Importantly, therefore, the validity of long-run PPP does not appear to depend on the regime in operation, although the adjustment dynamics are regime dependent.

Overall, our reading of the literature suggests that PPP is a good first approximation to the long-run behavior of exchange rates, and that adjustment to PPP displays significant nonlinearities.[13]

### 7.4.1 TRANSITORY AND STRUCTURAL DISPARITIES FROM PARITY

Crucini et al. (2005b) note that a substantial part of empirical and theoretical work in international economics focuses on two questions: what determines whether a deviation from the LOP will be small or large and what determines whether a deviation from the LOP will be long- or short lived. The empirical literature on the first question is very limited due to the lack of price data on comparable goods across locations. The theoretical literature, however, provides some answers, including the models of Dumas (1992) and Sercu et al. (1995), which emphasize the magnitude of shipping costs in consumption goods and physical capital. Furthermore, the models of Krugman (1987) emphasize imperfect competition, while the models of Balassa (1964) and Samuelson (1964) emphasize productivity

---

accelerated convergence to PPP, consistent with a transactions-costs goods-market arbitrage view of PPP. Future research on these data is warranted to refine the estimates of Koedijk et al. (2004) and test for nonlinearities.

[12]Goldfajin and Valdes (1999) and Cheung et al. (2004).

[13]Note that, while the initial results in this literature were established using data for major currencies, their robustness has been extended to a number of emerging currencies. See, among others, Bahmani-Oskooee (1998) and Sarno (2000) on Middle Eastern countries, Liew et al. (2003) and Liew (2004) for Asia, and Anoruo et al. (2006) on Africa. Cerrato and Sarantis (2006, 2007) provide evidence on nonlinear mean reversion in the real exchange rates of many emerging market economies using black market exchange rate data.

differences across tradable and nontradable goods. Finally, the models of Ethier (1979) and Jones and Sanyal (1982) emphasize that much of international trade takes place not in final goods and services but in intermediate inputs.

Overall, it seems rather implausible that the high volatility and strong persistence of PPP deviations could be completely attributed to real factors. As volatilities are found to systematically differ across monetary regimes, it is likely that some combination of nominal shocks and price stickiness might be affecting the short-run volatility of exchange rates. As Obstfeld (2001); Obstfeld and Rogoff (2001), and Burstein et al. (2003) note, it could be that economies are more closed than originally thought, since large sectors are nontradable. In this way, in an economy with price stickiness and a nontradable sector, small monetary shocks can generate high levels of exchange rate volatility (Burstein et al., 2005). As soon as the nontradable share of the economy increases, the economy becomes less "open" and the LOP applies to a smaller fraction of goods, allowing a larger role for exchange rate overshooting and other sources of exchange rate volatility (Hau, 2000, 2002; Obstfeld and Rogoff, 2000).

Furthermore, the PPP hypothesis is based on the concept that the real exchange rate equilibrium remains fixed forever, which is not necessarily true. Several theories that have tried to rationalize the changes in the level of the real exchange rate focus on the net international asset position. Lane and Milesi-Ferretti (2002) find some empirical evidence supporting this argument. They report that countries with larger positive net asset positions tend to have more negative trade balances and appreciated real exchange rates, controlling for other factors and allowing for real return differentials across countries. This finding suggests that if the equilibrium PPP exchange rate changes, the following net wealth changes, and if these shifts are not controlled for in a model, then the exchange rate will seem to deviate from what is falsely assumed to be a fixed PPP rate for too much or for too long.

The other key theory for changing real exchange rate equilibria is built around the notion of nontradable goods. The Harrod-Balassa-Samuelson (HBS) model of equilibrium real exchange rates has recently experienced a revival. In this model, countries are thought to generate wealth by fostering productivity in traded sectors. Meanwhile, all nontradable sectors, in rich and poor countries, remain in technological lethargy. Suppose the LOP holds among traded goods and labor is mobile among sectors but not internationally. As productivity in the traded sector rises, wage levels rise, so prices of nontradable goods will have to rise too. Should one measure the overall price index as a weighted average of tradable and nontradable goods prices, relatively rich countries will tend to have stronger currencies.

Although early studies of the HBS effect found little support in the data from the 1950s to the early 1970s (Officer, 1982), recent research studying later periods has often found support for this hypothesis (De Gregorio et al., 1994; Chinn, 2000; Micossi and Milesi-Ferretti, 1994). This potentially reveals developments in the PPP literature in a broader sense: longer spans of data and wider country samples, along with more powerful econometric techniques, have helped to make the relationship tighter. Furthermore, up to date findings hint that the magnitude of the HBS effect has been variable over time—definitely during the postwar period and possibly going back several centuries (Bergin et al., 2004). A reason could be that the nontradable share has risen over time; however, this effect matches neither the changes that have occurred in terms of magnitude nor the timing of the changes. Another possible explanation is that the productivity advances of tradable and nontradable goods have been different across time. Bergin et al. (2004) develop the hypothesis that trade costs determine tradability patterns, an assumption that allows various productivity shocks to give rise eventually to an endogenous HBS effect. Overall, if the equilibrium exchange rate is moving gradually over time, and our statistical analysis presupposes that the PPP exchange rate is fixed over time, then estimates of the speed of reversion to PPP will be biased. Indeed, allowing for long-run trends in the real exchange rate could be of great importance in understanding PPP deviations. Along these lines, Taylor (2002), reports relatively short half-lives in a 20-country panel when allowance is made for long-run trends in the equilibrium exchange rate. Allowing for nonlinear time trends, Lothian and Taylor (2000) suggest that the half-life of deviations from PPP for the dollar–pound exchange rate may be as low as 2 years. Lothian and Taylor (2008) show that the HBS effect may account for about a third of the variation in this real exchange rate.

Summing up, the equilibrium real exchange rate might trend over the long run due to these wealth effects, productivity effects, and other forces as potential triggers. However, there is substantial uncertainty on the economic importance of HBS effects, which appear to change over time in ways that economists do not fully understand. Hence, our reading suggests that, as a first approximation to the long-run behavior of the real exchange rate, PPP is empirically validated, regardless of the precise basket of goods and services examined and of the proportion of nontradables included in price indices.[14]

## 7.5 Aggregating from the LOP to PPP: What Can We Infer?

We are now in position to discuss what happens empirically to the properties of the LOP as we aggregate from individual tradable goods and services to sectors, and then to all tradables, and finally to all goods (tradables and nontradables).

[14]A more ad hoc formulation that incorporates changing real exchange rate equilibria is the fundamental equilibrium exchange rate (FEER), which comes in a number of different variants. However, in essence, this is a framework that is based on the idea that, especially for emerging countries undergoing major structural change, the real exchange rate equilibrium shifts over time due to HBS effects, terms of trade shocks, and the process of opening up to international trade that typically accompanies the transition of emerging markets to developed markets. Even in these models, typically the uncertainty in parameter estimation is such that it is difficult to make accurate inference on whether a currency is misaligned unless the misalignment is very large, in which case the disparity would be apparent even using PPP rather than a larger model of real exchange rate determination.

The reading of the literature on the LOP applied to individual goods and individual sectors indicates that the LOP holds in the long run. To the extent that the LOP holds for individual goods, it ought to hold for sectors of similar tradable goods. Then, if the LOP holds for each sector of tradable goods, it ought to hold for all tradable goods, that is, the PPP hypothesis for tradable goods *must* hold, given that the LOP holds for individual goods.

Moving one further level up in the aggregation process, and therefore assessing PPP applied to national (e.g., consumer) price indices as opposed to baskets of tradable goods only, is less straightforward from a theoretical standpoint. The inability to extend the arguments about arbitrage in goods markets to nontradable goods and the potential presence of HBS effects does not allow us to infer that PPP must also hold for national price indices. However, we also know from the extensive literature on PPP and on HBS effects that (i) PPP holds in the long run across a number of currencies even when using price indices that include nontradables and, consistent with this, (ii) HBS effects are generally small, albeit varying over time. It is not entirely clear why PPP holds for consumer price indices, given that they include nontradables. Clearly, because of the lack of arbitrage opportunities among nontradables, the mechanism that keeps price levels close to each other across countries cannot be due to the arbitrage forces that underlie the commodity-arbitrage view of the LOP. Cassell's (1922) influential thinking on PPP was that this hypothesis relates to broad price indices and a currency's value. The empirical fact that PPP provides a good first approximation to the long-run behavior of real exchange rates constructed with national price indices lends some support to Cassell's view at this high level of aggregation. At the same time, the argument that catching up in terms of technological innovation and growth across countries mitigates HBS effects is also a likely part of the explanation for this result. While it is not possible to exactly identify the reasons why PPP should hold when applied to both tradables and nontradables, there is plenty of evidence that it does.

The choice of the appropriate price index to be used in computing absolute PPP has been the object of a long debate in the literature, going back at least as far as Keynes (1932). In testing PPP, most studies in the literature have employed official price indices, all of which include some proportion of nontradable goods, for which arbitrage does not occur. Some work on PPP looks at the cost of production of a basket of goods-producer choices (rather than the cost of a basket of goods in terms of consumer choices). For example, Lafrance et al. (1998) and Sarno and Chowdhury (2003) provide evidence that PPP works much better if it is based on costs of production—essentially unit labor costs—or on indices made only of tradable goods, rather than, say, the consumer price index (CPI) from official sources.

Given these problems with using official price indices attempts have been made to construct appropriate price measures for testing PPP. The work of Summers and Heston (1991), has been influential in this context. They developed the "International Comparison Programme" (ICP) data set, which reports estimates of absolute PPP for a long sample period and a number of countries, using a common basket of goods across countries. The ICP is not, however, of great practical help in empirical work since it is constructed at infrequent and long time intervals and, for certain time periods, data are only available for a few countries. Moreover, extensive use of extrapolation has been made in order to solve this problem. Another important development is the PPP spot rate calculated by the OECD, which is not based on indices but on actual prices, allowing the calculation of a direct measure of absolute PPP at annual frequency.

Overall, the above logic and the empirical evidence available to us further indicates that the LOP and PPP provide useful guidance to the long-run behavior of exchange rates. However, it seems plausible that the persistence of deviations from parity will be higher when one moves from the LOP and PPP for tradable goods to variants of PPP that include nontradables. How relevant is this issue empirically?

### 7.5.1 AN EYEBALL ANALYSIS OF PPP

It is instructive to illustrate the above discussions by eyeballing some data on deviations from PPP for a variety of cases. Let us start from Figure 7.1, which plots the time series for the dollar–sterling real exchange rate over the sample period from 1791 to 2010. The data are an updated version of the annual data set used by Lothian and Taylor (1996), using the wholesale price index; we plot the log-real exchange rate in deviation from its mean, so that PPP is obtained when the rate is equal to zero. First, it is interesting how this real exchange rate appears to have a tendency to return to its long-run mean, that is, the PPP equilibrium, although the mean is crossed only 22 times in 210 years of data, indicating a remarkable degree of persistence. Second, the time series suggests that the misalignments have been as large as 40% (both above and below PPP), suggesting that deviations from PPP have been very large indeed at some points in time. Third, the real exchange rate appears to be more persistent when it is in the proximity of the long-run mean, whereas reversion toward the mean happens

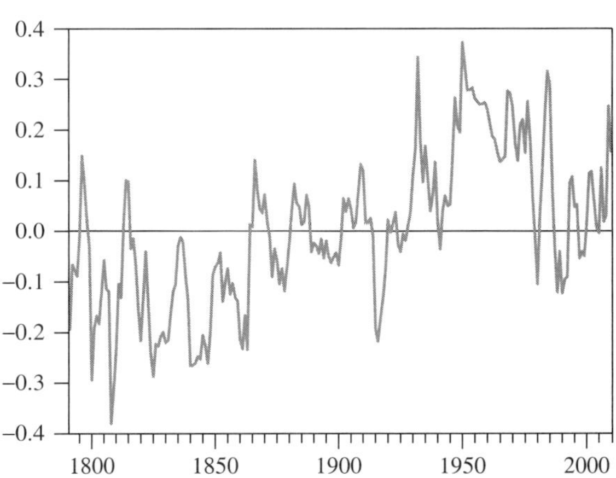


**FIGURE 7.1** Logarithm of GBP/USD real exchange rate, 1791–2010.

more rapidly when the absolute size of the PPP deviation is large, providing visual support for the evidence of nonlinear adjustment discussed earlier. Overall, this eyeball analysis of 210 years of real dollar–sterling illustrates some of the key basic points arising from our reading of the PPP literature: deviations from PPP are stationary, albeit persistent, and are very persistent in the neighborhood of PPP, while being mean-reverting at a faster speed when the deviation from PPP gets larger. Again, this is consistent with the existence of nonlinear dynamics in the real exchange rate, implying that the speed of mean reversion is state dependent.

Now, consider the behavior of the real exchange rate for monthly data over the dollar floating era. Figures 7.2–7.4 show the real exchange rates (again in log-deviations from the mean) for the US dollar against the UK pound and Japanese yen since 1973, and the Deutsche mark-euro since the German unification in 1991, when PPI data for Germany become available. In each graph, we plot three real exchange rates, obtained using three different price indices: CPI (black line), GDP deflator (gray line), and PPI (dotted black line). The graphs confirm the earlier eyeball analysis, but they also illustrate further points. First, the estimate of the PPP equilibrium is made cumbersome in shorter samples because both of the difficulty to estimate the mean accurately and because of the stronger effect of the choice of a base year. This is especially apparent if one compares Figures 7.1 and 7.2, since in the former the pound sterling looks likely to be undervalued in the last couple of years, whereas the latter suggests the pound looks likely to be overvalued. Second, the tendency to revert to PPP appears less strong when looking at shorter samples, consistent with the well-known difficulties of the empirical literature to detect PPP during the post-Bretton Woods period. Third, real exchange rates constructed using different price data are highly correlated and display very similar properties, because the volatility of the deviations from

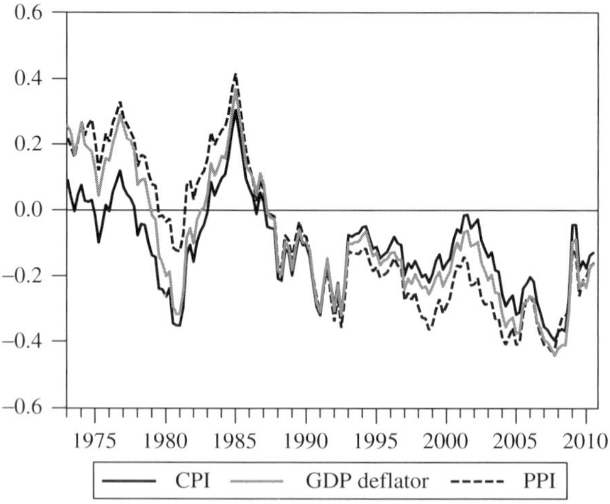


FIGURE 7.2 GBP/USD: real exchange rates calculated using different price indices (1973–2010).

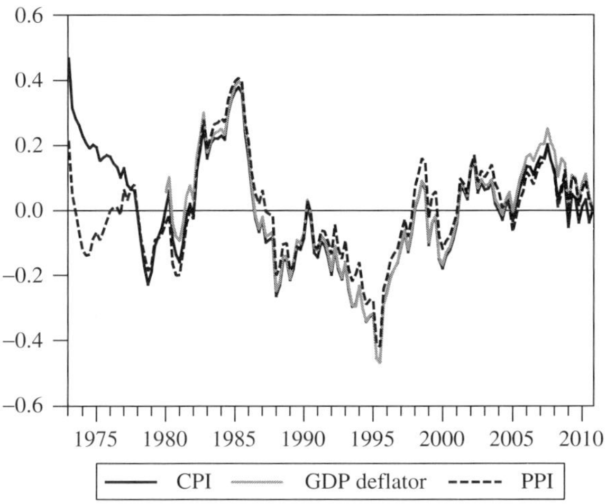


FIGURE 7.3 JPY/USD: real exchange rates calculated using different price indices (1973–2010).

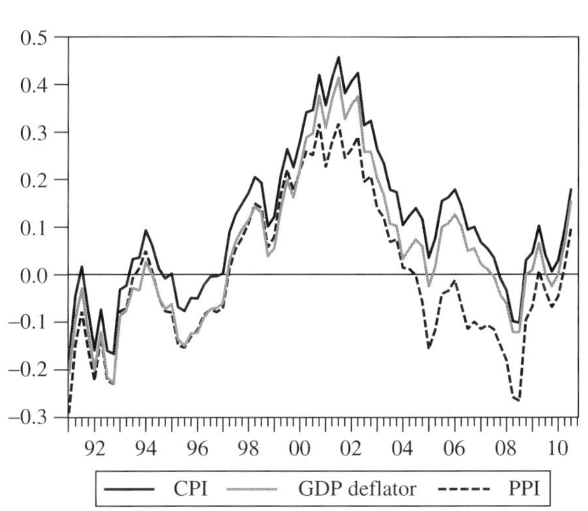


FIGURE 7.4 DEM-EUR/USD: real exchange rates calculated using different price indices (1991–2010).

PPP (for both tradables and nontradables) is largely driven by the volatility of the nominal exchange rate rather than relative prices. This is consistent with the claims by Engel (1999) and Obstfeld and Rogoff (2000). Nevertheless, earlier we argued that PPI-based real exchange rates are more appropriate than CPI- and GDP-based real exchange rates, because of the lower proportion of tradables included in the PPI. While this is not clear from Figure 7.2 a simple calculation illustrates this point. Specifically, if PPI-based real exchange rates are indeed closer to PPP, the cumulative real exchange rate $\Sigma q_t$ must be closer to zero than the other measures.[15] The table below makes it clear that this is indeed the case for the pound and the euro; for the yen the PPI-based real exchange rate only has the second smallest cumulative real exchange rate but all of the three values are actually very small:

| | GDP | PPI | CPI |
|---|---|---|---|
| Japan | 0.00 | 1.14 | −2.76 |
| UK | −14.32 | −13.24 | −17.21 |
| DM-Euro | 3.87 | 0.00 | 8.10 |

As noted above, one problem with the data used generally in LOP and PPP analyses is that they are based on imperfect price indices. A direct approach would use the actual price levels of some combination of goods and services and compare these across countries to arrive at an actual level of PPP (such as the Big Mac Index). This is in principle preferable to price indices, such as the CPI or PPI, because PPP levels would not need to be derived by assuming some earlier base period that represents the PPP equilibrium. In some sense, while the use of price indices allows one to pick a price index that contains more or less tradable goods, there is scope for data mining by choosing the base period that results in PPP working best. For this reason, it is very useful to consider the direct approach and use the OECD's PPP values (OECD, 2006). The OECD calculates direct PPP values in order to make international GDP comparisons, rather than as a tool to forecast currencies. Therefore, it may be seen as more robust and comprehensive than other direct PPP measures.[16]

We retrieve from the OECD the spot exchange PPP value, which is the nominal exchange rate that is needed for PPP to hold, using their direct measures of prices at the annual frequency. The PPPs calculated by the OECD are still price relatives whether they refer to a product group or to an aggregate. It is just that in moving up the levels of aggregation the price relatives refer to increasingly complex assortments of goods and services. Thus, for example, if the PPP for GDP between Germany and the United States is 0.97 euros to the dollar, it means that 0.97 euros has to be spent in Germany to obtain the same volume of final goods and services that 1 dollar purchases in the United States. Note that this does not imply that the baskets of goods and services purchased in both countries will be identical. The composition of the baskets will vary between countries reflecting their economic, social, and cultural differences, but both baskets will, in principle, provide equivalent satisfaction or utility.

[15]Adjustment toward PPP should also be faster, and indeed we find that this is the case, but for the purpose of this discussion, we shall focus on the cumulative deviation from PPP rather than the adjustment to equilibrium.

[16]It is worth noting that some currency managers prefer to use the OECD PPP data exactly for the reasons outlined above. A notable example is Deutsche Bank (2007), whose *FX Value Index* is traded exactly using these OECD PPP data. The index calculates deviations from PPP in the same way as discussed in this section and, in order to take into account the importance of nonlinearities, it trades only in the most misaligned currencies.

We calculate the difference between the observed nominal exchange rate and the spot PPP value, which is essentially a direct measure of the deviation from absolute PPP. Figure 7.5 plots this measure of the deviation from PPP (i.e., the real exchange rate), again for the US dollar against the UK pound, Japanese yen and the Deutsche mark-euro since the collapse of the Bretton Woods system in 1973. Under this measure, PPP is obtained when the real exchange rate equals unity. These graphs illustrate several important points. First, when using a direct measure of absolute PPP, the pound sterling appears to be grossly undervalued at the beginning of the post-Bretton Woods period, the yen slightly undervalued, and the Deutsche mark roughly at PPP. At the end of the sample in 2010, however, the pound sterling and the euro appear very close to PPP, while the yen appears somewhat overvalued. Second, the real exchange rates constructed with OECD direct price measures appear to have the same properties as the real exchange rates obtained using conventional price indices, in the sense that they are persistent and quite volatile, although volatility is difficult to compare given that the OECD data are at annual frequency. However, the persistence does not appear as extreme as in standard aggregate measures of the real exchange rate, and over the 37-year period of this sample, there seems to be a clear tendency toward PPP (unity). Formal unit root tests indicate that these real exchange rates are indeed clearly stationary—that is, they converge to their PPP value in the long run—with high statistical confidence.[17] Also, estimation of regressions designed

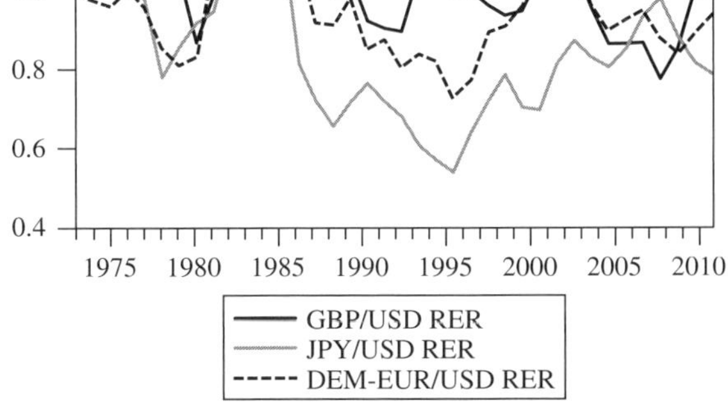


**FIGURE 7.5** Real exchange rates against the USD (1973–2010).

[17] For example, we carried out the panel unit root test of Im et al. (2003) for the null hypothesis of a unit root (PPP not valid) against the alternative hypothesis that each of the real exchange rate series is stationary (PPP valid for all currencies). We also applied a multivariate Augmented Dickey-Fuller test for the same null hypothesis. The null hypothesis was rejected with 99% confidence under both test statistics, lending strong support to long-run PPP for these exchange rates.

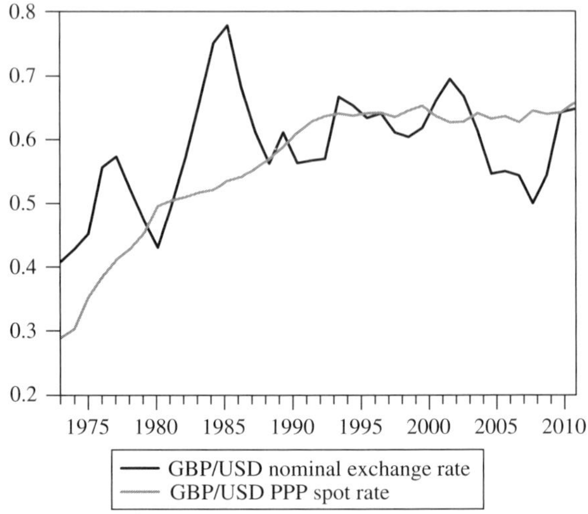


**FIGURE 7.6** GBP/USD nominal exchange rate versus GBP/USD PPP spot rate (OECD Data), 1973–2010.

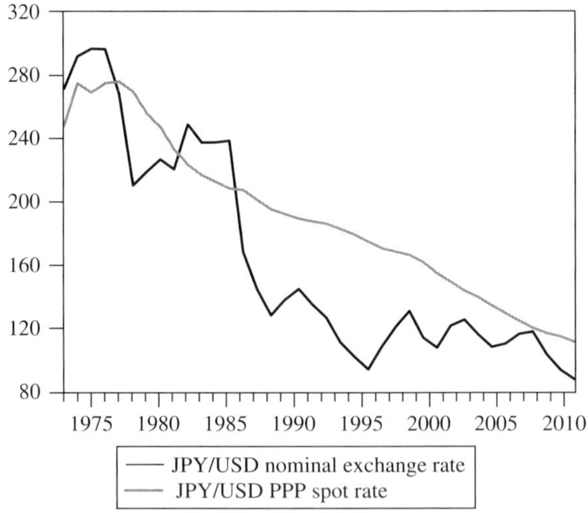


**FIGURE 7.7** JPY/USD nominal exchange rate versus JPY/USD PPP spot rate (OECD Data), 1973–2010.

to understand whether the adjustment to PPP occurs through relative prices or exchange rates indicates that virtually all of the adjustment to PPP occurs via exchange rates, which respond very strongly to past PPP misalignments.

These properties indicate that there is indeed a long-run comovement between nominal exchange rates and relative prices, which we can observe quite clearly in the data. Figures 7.6–7.8 show, for each of the three exchange rates,

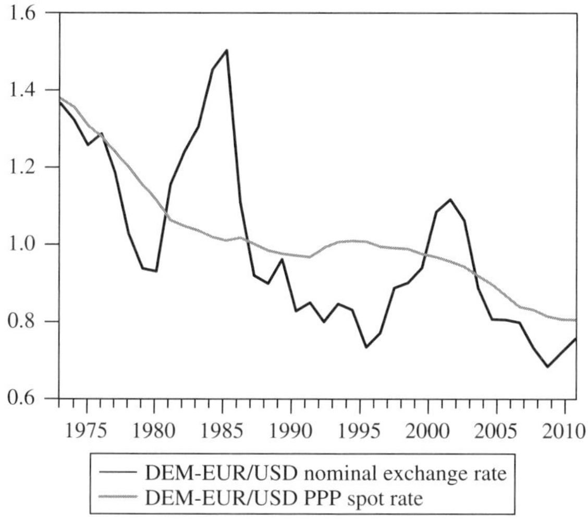


**FIGURE 7.8** **DEM-EUR/USD nominal exchange rate versus DEM-EUR/USD PPP spot rate (OECD Data), 1973–2010.**

the graph of the nominal exchange rate and the relative price provided by the OECD. The graphs make apparent how, while the nominal exchange rate is a lot more volatile than relative prices, exchange rates and prices appear to share the same long-run trend throughout the post-Bretton Woods period. This is exactly what one would expect: the nominal exchange rate moves in the short run in response to a large number of factors, some of which possibly unrelated to economic fundamentals, but over long periods of time there appears to be a remarkable degree of convergence toward PPP. Put another way, while it may be difficult to produce a long-horizon forecast of the nominal exchange rate or relative prices in isolation, this evidence suggests that PPP is a reasonable assumption for long-horizon forecasting of the real exchange rate.

## 7.6 Conclusion and Implications

This chapter has surveyed the empirical evidence on the properties of deviations from the LOP and PPP for tradable goods. While it is fair to say that a universal consensus may not exist yet, the emerging consensus at the present time is converging toward the view that deviations from the LOP are transitory and therefore the LOP holds in the long run among a broad range of tradable goods and currencies.

In our view, a promising strand of research that goes some way toward understanding the behavior of LOP deviations is the literature that has investigated the role of nonlinearities in the adjustment toward the long-run equilibrium implied by the LOP (Obstfeld and Taylor, 1997; Sarno et al., 2004; Blavy and Juvenal, 2009). For example, Sarno et al. (2004) provide evidence of nonlinear reversion toward the LOP in a number of major sectoral exchange rates during the post-Bretton Woods period. However, they also provide evidence of price stickiness and heterogeneity across goods and currencies, as one would expect.

While it would be overly simplistic to believe that all that drives exchange rates is goods prices, the empirical evidence surveyed here suggests that the LOP is at least a good first approximation to the link between exchange rates and goods prices across countries. Put another way, if price differentials of individual goods do not converge to the same number over time (once expressed in the same currency), the drift must be small enough to be statistically and economically insignificant. We also examine some direct measures of absolute PPP using data from the OECD and illustrate that such direct measures lend clear support to PPP as a valid international parity condition.

## APPENDIX: TAR MODELING

Let the deviations from the LOP for a sector $i$ (i.e., the sectoral real exchange rate for sector $i$) be $q_t(i)$. An econometric model that captures the predictions of a discrete switch in $q_t(i)$ is the following symmetric three-regime TAR model:[18]

$$\Delta q_t(i) = \begin{cases} \left[(\beta_1 - 1)(q_{t-1}(i) - \theta_i) + \sum_{j=2}^{p} \beta_j (q_{t-j}(i) - \theta_i)\right] l(q_{t-d}(i) > \theta_i) \\ + \left[\sum_{j=1}^{p-1} \alpha_j \Delta q_{t-j}(i)\right] l(|q_{t-d}(i)| \leq \theta_i) \\ + \left[(\beta_1 - 1)(q_{t-1}(i) + \theta_i) + \sum_{j=2}^{p} \beta_j (q_{t-j}(i) + \theta_i)\right] l(q_{t-d}(i) < -\theta_i) + \varepsilon_{it} \end{cases} \tag{7.9}$$

where $\Delta$ denotes the first difference operator; $\theta_i$ is the threshold parameter for sector $i$; and $q_{t-d}(i)$ represents the threshold variable for sector $i$, with $d$ denoting an integer chosen from the set $\Psi \in [1, \bar{d}]$. The indicator function, given by $l(\cdot)$, takes a value of unity when the bracketed expression is true, and is zero otherwise. The error term $\varepsilon_{it}$ is assumed independently and identically distributed (*iid*) Gaussian. The autoregressive order of $q_t$ is $p \geq 1$. Note that essentially the TAR specified has two regimes given that the behavior of the outer regimes is identical because of the symmetry assumption.

The integer $d$ represents the delay parameter and reflects the possibility that market participants react to deviations of the LOP from equilibrium with a lag.

[18]The TAR model was initially introduced by Tong (1983), although a number of econometric issues concerning TAR specification and estimation have only recently been resolved, primarily by Hansen (1996, 1997).

As long as $|q_{t-d}| \leq \theta$, the time series $q_t$ follows a unit root process. Thus, in this regime (or region), there is no tendency for the series $q_t$ to move back toward equilibrium. Once $|q_{t-d}| > \theta$, however, $q_t$ becomes a stationary process and has a tendency to revert back as long as $\sum_{j=1}^{p} \beta_j < 1$, regardless of whether $q_{t-d}$ is positive or negative. As arbitrage is not profitable in the region defined within the bands, the series will only revert back toward an equilibrium band, here $[-\theta, \theta]$.[19] Also, note that the specified TAR model is deliberately constructed as a symmetric process. This is the case since it is difficult to think of plausible economic arguments why arbitrage forces should vary depending on whether deviations from the LOP are above or below the arbitrage bands.[20]

## Acknowledgments

This research was funded by the Norwegian Ministry of Finance, Asset Management Department. The authors are grateful to Øystein Børsum, Jerry Coakley, Tom Fearnley, and Lawrence Officer for useful discussions. The authors alone are responsible for any errors that may remain.

## REFERENCES

Abuaf N, Jorion P. Purchasing power parity in the long run. J Finance 1990; 45: 157–174.

Anoruo E, Liew VK-S, Elike U. Nonlinear real exchange rate behavior: are the african currencies exceptional? Int Res J Finance Econ 2006; 1: 98–111.

Bahmani-Oskooee M. Do exchange rates follow a random walk process in Middle Eastern Countries? Econ Lett 1998; 58: 339–344.

Balassa B. The purchasing power parity doctrine: a reappraisal. J Pol Econ 1964; 72: 584–596.

Balke NS, Fomby TB. Threshold cointegration. Int Econ Rev 1997; 38: 627–647.

Baxter M, Stockman AC. Business cycles and the exchange rate system. J Monet Econ 1989; 23: 377–400.

Benninga S, Protopapadakis AA. The equilibrium pricing of exchange rates and assets when trade takes time. J Int Econ 1988; 7: 129–149.

[19] A sufficient condition for global stability (stationarity) is that the roots of the autoregression in the outer regime are less than unity in absolute value (Granger and Teräsvirta, 1993; Tjostheim, 1986; Tong, 1990).

[20] Balke and Fomby (1997) define the specified TAR model as the Band-TAR model. An alternative TAR model is the so-called equilibrium-transition autoregressive (EQTAR) model. In the EQTAR model, the time series is allowed to tend toward a precise equilibrium value when the process is outside the region $[-\theta, \theta]$. However, as deviations from the LOP do not *fully* die out in the presence of arbitrage costs, a Band-TAR model is more appealing than an EQTAR model in the present context.

Bergin P, Glick R, Taylor AM. Productivity, tradability, and the long-run price puzzle. FRBSF Working Paper, 2004-08; 2004.

Blavy R, Juvenal L. Mexico's integration into NAFTA markets: a view from sectoral real exchange rates. Fed Reserve Bank St. Louis Rev 2009; 91: 441–464.

Burstein AC, Eichenbaum M, Rebelo S. Large devaluations and the real exchange rate. J Pol Econ 2005; 113: 742–784.

Burstein AT, Neves JC, Rebelo S. Distribution costs and real exchange rate dynamics during exchange-rate-based stabilizations. J Monet Econ 2003; 50: 1189–1214.

Carvalho C, Nechio F. Aggregation and the PPP puzzle in a sticky-price model. *Am Econ Rev* 2010; 101: 2391–2424.

Cassel G. Money and foreign exchange after 1914. London: Constable; 1922.

Cerrato M, Sarantis N. Nonlinear mean reversion in black market real exchange rates. Econ Bull 2006; 6: 1–14.

Cerrato M, Sarantis N. Does purchasing power parity hold in emerging markets? Evidence from a panel of black market exchange rates. Int J Finance Econ 2007; 12: 427–444.

Chen S-S, Engel C. Does 'Aggregation Bias' explain the PPP puzzle? Pac Econ Rev 2005; 10: 49–72.

Chen Z, Knez PJ. Measurement of market integration and arbitrage. Rev Financ Stud 1995; 8: 287–325.

Cheung Y-W, Lai KS, Bergman M. Dissecting the PPP puzzle: the unconventional roles of nominal exchange rate and price adjustments. J Int Econ 2004; 64: 135–150.

Chinn MD. The usual suspects? Productivity and demand shocks and Asia-Pacific real exchange rates. Rev Int Econ 2000; 8: 20–43.

Coleman AMG. Arbitrage, storage and the law of one price: new theory for the time series analysis of an old problem, Princeton University discussion paper; 1995.

Crucini MJ, Shintani M. Persistence in law-of-one-price deviations: evidence from micro-data. J Monet Econ 2008; 55: 629–644.

Crucini MJ, Shintani M, Tsuruga T. The law of one price without the border: the role of distance versus sticky prices. Econ J 2010; 120: 462–480.

Crucini MJ, Telmer CI, Zachariadis M. Price dispersion: the role of borders, distance and location. Vanderbilt University, mimeo; 2005a.

Crucini MJ, Telmer CI, Zachariadis M. Understanding European real exchange rates. Am Econ Rev 2005b; 95: 724–738.

Crucini MJ, Telmer CI. Microeconomic sources of real exchange rate variability. Vanderbilt University, mimeo; 2007.

Davutyan N, Pippenger J. Testing purchasing power parity: some evidence of the effects of transaction costs. Economet Rev 1990; 9: 211–240.

De Gregorio J, Giovannini A, Wolf HC. International evidence on tradable and nontradables inflation. Eur Econ Rev 1994; 38: 1225–1244.

Deutsche Bank. Currencies: value investing. FX Strategy, *%Deutsche Bank Global Markets Research* (Publication of the 29 March 2007); 2007.

Dornbusch R. Purchasing power parity. In: Eatwell J, Milgate M, Newman P, editors. The new palgrave: a dictionary of economics. London, New York: Macmillan, Stockton Press; 1987. pp. 1075–1085.

Dumas B. Dynamic equilibrium and the real exchange rate in spatially separated world. Rev Financ Stud 1992; 5: 153–180.

Dumas B, Jennergren LP, Naslund B. Siegel's paradox and the pricing of currency options. J Int Money Finance 1995; 14: 213–223.

Engel C. Accounting for U.S. real exchange rate changes. J Pol Econ 1999; 107: 507–538.

Engel C. Long-run PPP may not hold after all. J Int Econ 2000; 51: 243–273.

Engel C, Rogers JH. How wide is the border? Am Econ Rev 1996; 86: 1112–1125.

Ethier WJ. Internationally decreasing costs and world trade. J Int Econ 1979; 9: 1–24.

Feenstra RC. Exact hedonic price indexes. Rev Econ Stat 1995; 77: 634–653.

Feenstra RC, Kendall JD. Pass-through of exchange rates and purchasing power parity. J Int Econ 1997; 43: 237–261.

Frankel JA, Rose AK. A panel project on purchasing power parity: mean reversion within and between countries. J Int Econ 1996; 40: 209–224.

Froot KA, Kim M, Rogoff K. The law of one price over 700 years. NBER working paper 5132; 1995.

Gadea MD, Mayoral L. Aggregation is not the solution: the PPP puzzle strikes back. J Appl Economet 2009; 24: 875–894.

Giovannini A. Exchange rates and traded goods prices. J Int Econ 1988; 24: 45–68.

Goldberg PK, Knetter MM. Goods prices and exchange rates: what have we learned? J Econ Lit 1997; 35: 1243–1272.

Granger CWJ, Teräsvirta T. Modeling nonlinear economic relationships. New York: Oxford University Press; 1993.

Goldfajin I, Valdes RO. Liquidity crises and international financial architecture, Unpublished manuscript, Central Bank of Chile, Santiago; 1999.

Hansen BE. Inference when a nuisance parameter is not identified under the null hypothesis. Econometrica 1996; 64: 413–430.

Hansen BE. Inference in TAR models. Stud Nonlin Dyn Economet 1997; 2: 1–14.

Hau H. Exchange rate determination: the role of factor price rigidities and nontradeables. J Int Econ 2000; 50: 421–447.

Hau H. Real exchange rate volatility and economic openness: theory and evidence. J Money Credit Bank 2002; 34: 611–30.

Heckscher EF. Växelkursens grundval vid pappersmyntfot. Ekono Tidskr 1916; 18: 309–312.

Herguera I. Exchange rate uncertainty, market structure and the pass-through relationship. Econ Notes 1994; 23: 292–307.

Im KS, Pesaran MH, Shin Y. Testing for unit roots in heterogeneous panels. J Economet 2003; 115: 53–74.

Imbs J, Mumtaz H, Ravn M, Rey H. Non-linearities and real exchange rates dynamics. J Eur Econ Assoc 2003; 1: 639–649.

Imbs J, Mumtaz H, Ravn M, Rey H. PPP strikes back: aggregation and the real exchange rate. Q J Econ 2005; 120: 1–43.

Isard P. How far can we push the "law of one price "? Am Econ Rev 1977; 67: 942–948.

Jones RW, Sanyal KK. The theory of trade in middle products. Am Econ Rev 1982; 72: 16–31.

Keynes JM. Essays in persuasion. New York: Harcout Brace; 1932.

Knetter MM. Price discrimination by U.S. and German exporters. Am Econ Rev 1989; 79: 198–210.

Knetter MM. International comparisons of price-to-market behavior. Am Econ Rev 1993; 83: 473–486.

Knetter MM. Did the strong dollar increase competition in U.S. product markets? Rev Econ Stat 1994; 76: 192–195.

Koedijk KG, Tims B, van Dijk MA. Purchasing power parity and the Euro Area. J Int Money Finance 2004; 23: 1081–1107.

Kreinin ME. The effect of exchange rate changes on the prices and volume of foreign trade. Int Monet Fund Staff Pap 1977; 24: 297–329.

Krugman PR. Pricing to market when the exchange rate changes. In: Arndt SW, Richardson JD, editors. Real-financial linkages among open economies. Cambridge (MA): MIT Press; 1987. pp. 49–70.

Lafrance R, Osakwe P, Normandin M. Evaluating alternative measures of the real effective exchange rate. Bank of Canada, Working Paper 98-20; 1998.

Lane PR, Milesi-Ferretti GM. External wealth, the trade balance, and the real exchange rate. Eur Econ Rev 2002; 46: 1049–1071.

Liew VK-S. Nonlinear adjustment of ASEAN-5 real exchange rates: symmetrical or asymmetrical? Econ Bull 2004; 6: 1–19.

Liew VK-S, Chong TT-L, Lim K-P. The inadequacy of linear autoregressive model for real exchange rates: empirical evidence from asian economies. Appl Econ 2003; 35: 1387–1392.

Lothian JR, Taylor MP. Real exchange rate behavior: the recent float from the perspective of the past two centuries. J Pol Econ 1996; 104: 488–510.

Lothian JR, Taylor MP. Purchasing power parity over two centuries: strengthening the case for real exchange rate stability. J Int Money Finance 2000; 19: 759–764.

Lothian JR, Taylor MP. Real exchange rates over the past two centuries: how important is the harrod-balassa-samuelson effect? Econ J 2008; 118: 1742–1763.

Mark NC. Real and nominal exchange rates in the long run: an empirical investigation. J Int Econ 1990; 28: 115–136.

Mayoral L, Gadea MD. Aggregate real exchange rate persistence through the lens of sectoral data. J Monet Econ 2011; 58: 290–304.

Michael P, Nobay AR, Peel DA. Purchasing power parity yet again: evidence from spatially separated markets. J Int Money Finance 1994; 13: 637–657.

Michael P, Nobay AR, Peel DA. Transaction costs and nonlinear adjustment in real exchange rates: an empirical investigation. J Pol Econ 1997; 105: 862–879.

Micossi S, Milesi-Ferretti GM. Real exchange rates and the prices of nontradeable goods. IMF Working Paper No. 19; 1994.

Nakamura E. Pass-through in retail and wholesale. Am Econ Rev 2008; 98: 430–437.

Obstfeld M. International macroeconomics: beyond the mundell-fleming model. Int Monet Fund Staff Pap 2001; 47: 1–39.

Obstfeld M, Rogoff K. The six major puzzles in international macroeconomics: is there a common cause? In: Bernanke B, Rogoff K, editors. National bureau of economic research macroeconomics annual 2000. Cambridge (MA); NBER and MIT Press; 2000.

Obstfeld M, Rogoff K. Do we really need a new global monetary compact? In: Alesina A, Barro R, editors. Currency Unions. Stanford University (CA): Hoover Institution Press; 2001.

Obstfeld M, Taylor AM. Nonlinear aspects of goods-market arbitrage and adjustment: Heckscher's commodity points revisited. J Jpn Int Econ 1997; 11: 441–479.

O'Connell PGJ. Market frictions and real exchange rates. J Int Money Finance 1998; 17: 71–95.

O'Connell PGJ, Wei S-J. The bigger they are, the harder they fall: retail price differences across U.S. cities. J Int Econ 2002; 56: 21–53.

Officer LH. Purchasing power parity and exchange rates: theory, evidence and relevance. Greenwich (CT): JAI Press; 1982.

Officer LH. Purchasing power parity in economic history, this volume; 2011.

Papell DH. Searching for stationarity: purchasing power parity under the current float. J Int Econ 1998; 43: 313–332.

Parsley DC, Wei S-J. Convergence to the law of one price without trade barriers or currency fluctuations. Q J Econ 1996; 111: 1211–1236.

Richardson JD. Some empirical evidence on commodity arbitrage and the law of one price. J Int Econ 1978; 8: 341–351.

Rogers JH, Jenkins M. Haircuts or hysteresis? Sources of movements in real exchange rates. J Int Econ 1995; 38: 339–360.

Rogoff R. The purchasing power parity puzzle. J Econ Lit 1996; 34: 647–668.

Samuelson PA. Theoretical notes on trade problems. Rev Econ Stat 1964; 46: 145–154.

Sarno L. Real exchange rate behavior in the middle east: a re-examination. Econ Lett 2000; 66: 127–136.

Sarno L. Purchasing power parity. In: Durlauf SN, Blume LE, editors. The new palgrave dictionary of economics. 2nd revised ed. (online). London: Palgrave MacMillan; 2008.

Sarno L, Chowdhury I. The behaviour of the real exchange rate: evidence from an alternative price index. Econ Notes 2003; 32: 295–333.

Sarno L, Taylor MP. Real exchange rates under the recent float: unequivocal evidence of mean reversion. Econ Lett 1998; 60: 131–137.

Sarno L, Taylor MP. Purchasing power parity and the real exchange rate. Int Monet Fund Staff Pap 2002; 49: 65–105.

Sarno L, Taylor MP, Chowdhury I. Nonlinear dynamics in deviations from the law of one price: a broad-based empirical study. J Int Money Finance 2004; 23: 1–25.

Sarno L, Valente G. Deviations from purchasing power parity under different exchange rate regimes: do they revert and, if so, how? J Bank Finance 2006; 30: 3147–3169.

Sercu P, Uppal R, Van Hulle C. The exchange rate in the presence of transaction costs: implications for tests of purchasing power parity. J Finance 1995; 50: 1309–1319.

Summers R, Heston A. The penn world table (Mark 5): an expanded set of international comparisons, 1950–1988. Q J Econ 1991; 106: 327–368.

Taylor AM. Potential pitfalls for the purchasing power parity puzzle? Sampling and specification biases in mean reversion tests of the law of one price. Econometrica 2001; 69: 473–498.

Taylor AM. A century of purchasing power parity. Rev Econ Stat 2002; 84: 139–50.

Taylor MP, Peel DA, Sarno L. Nonlinear mean-reversion in real exchange rates: towards a solution to the purchasing power parity puzzles. Int Econ Rev 2001; 42: 1015–1042.

Taylor MP, Sarno L. The behaviour of real exchange rates during the post-bretton woods period. J Int Econ 1998; 46: 281–312.

Taylor MP, Taylor AM. The purchasing power parity debate. J Econ Perspect 2004; 8: 135–158.

Tjostheim D. Estimation in nonlinear time series models. Stochastic Processes and Their Applications 1986; 21: 251–73.

Tong H. Threshold models in nonlinear time series analysis. Springer-Verlag New York, NY. 1983.

Tong H. Nonlinear time series: a dynamical system approach. Oxford: Clarendon Press; 1990.

CHAPTER EIGHT

# Statistical and Economic Methods for Evaluating Exchange Rate Predictability

**PASQUALE DELLA CORTE**
Imperial College London

**ILIAS TSIAKAS**
University of Guelph

## 8.1 Introduction

Exchange rate fluctuations are regularly monitored with great interest by policy makers, practitioners, and academics. It is not surprising, therefore, that exchange rate predictability has long been at the top of the research agenda in international finance. Starting with the seminal contribution of Meese and Rogoff (1983), a large body of empirical research finds that models that depend on economically meaningful variables do not provide reliable exchange rate forecasts. This has led to the prevailing view that exchange rates follow a random walk (RW) and hence are not predictable, especially at short horizons.

Several well-known puzzles in foreign exchange (FX) are responsible for this view. First, the "exchange rate disconnect puzzle" concerns the empirical disconnect between exchange rate movements and economic fundamentals such as money supply and real output (Cheung et al., 2005; Mark, 1995; Rogoff and Stavrakeva, 2008). Second, the "forward premium puzzle" implies that on average the interest differential is not offset by a commensurate depreciation of

*Handbook of Exchange Rates*, First Edition. Edited by Jessica James, Ian W. Marsh, and Lucio Sarno.

the investment currency, which is an empirical violation of uncovered interest rate parity. As a result, borrowing in low interest rate currencies and investing in high interest rate currencies forms the basis of the widely used carry trade strategy in active currency management (Brunnermeier et al., 2009; Burnside et al., 2011; Fama, 1984; and Della Corte et al., 2009). Third, there is extensive evidence that purchasing power parity (PPP) holds in the long run (Lothian and Taylor, 1996).

A recent contribution by Engel and West (2005) provides a possible resolution to the difficulty of tying exchange rates to economic fundamentals. Specifically, Engel and West (2005) show analytically that exchange rates can be consistent with present value asset pricing models and still manifest near-RW behavior if two conditions are met: (i) fundamentals integrated are of order 1 and (ii) the discount factor for future fundamentals is near 1.[1]

A model that is nested by the Engel and West (2005) present value relation is a variant of the Taylor (1993) rule used for exchange rate determination. The Taylor rule postulates that the central bank adjusts the short-run nominal interest rate in response to changes in inflation, the output gap, and the exchange rate. Using alternative specifications of Taylor rule fundamentals, Molodtsova and Papell (2009) provide strong evidence of short-horizon exchange rate predictability and hence offer renewed hope for empirical success in this literature. In short, one way to summarize the state of the literature is that it has come full circle: from the Meese and Rogoff (1983) "no predictability at short horizons," to the Mark (1995) "predictability at long but not at short horizons," to the Cheung et al. (2005) "no predictability at any horizon," to finally, the Molodtsova and Papell (2009) "predictability at short horizons with Taylor rule fundamentals."

This chapter aims at connecting these related literatures by providing a comprehensive review of the statistical and economic methods used for evaluating exchange rate predictability, especially out of sample. We assess the short-horizon forecasting performance of a set of widely used empirical exchange rate models that include the RW model, uncovered interest parity, PPP, monetary fundamentals (MF), and $TR_s$ and $TR_a$. Our analysis employs monthly FX data ranging from January 1976 to June 2010 for the 10 most liquid (G10) currencies in the world: the Australian dollar (AUD), Canadian dollar (CAD), Swiss franc (CHF), Deutsche mark \ euro (EUR), British pound (GBP), Japanese yen (JPY), Norwegian kroner (NOK), New Zealand dollar (NZD), Swedish kronor (SEK), and US dollar (USD).[2]

The vast majority of the FX literature uses a well-established statistical methodology for evaluating exchange rate predictability. This methodology typically involves statistical tests of the null hypothesis of equal predictive ability

[1]The assumption of integrated fundamentals of order 1 is widely accepted in the literature. The assumption that the discount factor is close to 1 has been empirically validated by Sarno and Sojli (2009).

[2]Note that we will not be discussing two recent approaches to predicting movements in exchange rates: (i) the microstructure approach that depends on order flow as a measure of net buying pressure for a currency (Evans and Lyons, 2002; Rime et al., 2010) and (ii) the global imbalances approach (Gourinchas and Rey, 2007, and Della Corte et al., 2012).

between the RW benchmark and an alternative empirical exchange rate model. The tests are based on the out-of-sample (OOS) mean squared error (MSE) of the forecasts generated by the models. In this chapter, we discuss the main recent contributions to this methodology.

The most popular method for testing whether the alternative model has a lower MSE than the benchmark is using the Diebold and Mariano (1995) and West (1996) statistic. By design, however, all the models we estimate are nested, and this statistic has a nonstandard distribution when comparing forecasts from nested models. Therefore, we focus on the recent inference procedure by Clark and West (2006, 2007), which accounts for the fact that under the null, the MSE from the alternative model is expected to be greater than that from the RW benchmark because the alternative model introduces noise into the forecasting process by estimating a parameter vector that is not helpful in prediction. For a comprehensive statistical evaluation, we also implement the encompassing test of Clark and McCracken (2001) and the $F$-statistic of McCracken (2007) using bootstrapped critical values. Finally, following Campbell and Thompson (2008) and Welch and Goyal (2008), we also report the OOS $R^2_{\mathrm{oos}}$ measure and a root MSE difference statistic.

In addition to the extensive literature on statistical evaluation, there is also an emerging line of research proposing a methodology for assessing the economic value of exchange rate predictability. A purely statistical analysis of predictability is not particularly informative to an investor, as it falls short of measuring whether there are tangible economic gains from using dynamic forecasts in active portfolio management. We review this approach on the basis of the dynamic asset allocation that is used, among others, by Abhyankar et al. (2005), Bandi and Russell (2006), Bandi et al. (2008), Della Corte et al. (2008), Fleming et al. (2001), Han (2006), Marquering and Verbeek (2004), West et al. (1993) and Della Corte et al. (2009, 2011).

We first design an international asset allocation strategy that exposes a US investor purely to FX risk. The investor builds a portfolio by allocating her wealth between a domestic and a set of foreign bonds and then uses the exchange rate forecasts from each model to predict the USD return of the foreign bonds. We evaluate the performance of the dynamically rebalanced portfolios using mean-variance analysis, which allows us to measure how much a risk-averse investor is willing to pay for switching from a portfolio strategy based on the RW benchmark to an empirical exchange rate model that conditions on economic fundamentals. In contrast to statistical measures of forecast accuracy that are computed separately for each exchange rate, the economic value is assessed for the portfolio generated by a model's forecasts on all exchange rate returns. This contributes to our finding that even modest statistical significance in OOS predictive regressions can lead to large economic benefits for investors.

Our review also includes an assessment of the economic value of combined forecasts. We use a variety of model averaging methods, some of which generate forecast combinations in a naive ad hoc manner, some that exploit statistical measures of past OOS forecasting performance, and some that use economic measures of past predictability. All forecast combinations that we explore are formed ex-ante using the full universe of individual forecasts of each model for each exchange rate. It is important to note that the combined forecasts do not require a view of which model is best at any given period and therefore provide a way for resolving model uncertainty.

To preview our key results, we find strong statistical and economic evidence against the RW benchmark. In particular, empirical exchange rate models based on uncovered interest parity (UIP), PPP, and the $TR_a$ perform better than the RW in OOS prediction using both statistical and economic criteria. We also confirm that conditioning on MF does not generate OOS economic gains. Consistently, the worst performing model is the symmetric Taylor rule ($TR_s$). Finally, combined forecasts formed using a variety of model averaging methods perform even better than individual empirical models. These results are robust to reasonably high transaction costs, the choice of numeraire, and the exclusion of any one currency from the investment opportunity set.

The remainder of the chapter is organized as follows. In the next section, we briefly review the empirical exchange rate models that we estimate and their foundations in asset pricing. Section 8.3 describes the statistical methods we use for evaluating exchange rate predictability. In Section 8.4 we present a general framework for assessing the economic value of forecasting exchange rates for a risk-averse investor with a dynamic mean-variance portfolio allocation strategy. Section 8.5 explains the construction of combined forecasts using a variety of model averaging methods. Section 8.6 reports our empirical results and, finally, Section 8.7 provides the concluding remarks.

## 8.2 Models for Exchange Rate Predictability

In this section, we review the empirical models that we use for evaluating exchange rate predictability. We begin by describing the Engel and West (2005) present value model that nests and motivates many of the predictive regressions we estimate.

### 8.2.1 A PRESENT VALUE MODEL FOR EXCHANGE RATES

The Engel and West (2005) model relates the exchange rate to economic fundamentals and the expected future exchange rate as follows:

$$s_t = (1 - b)(f_{1,t} + z_{1,t}) + b(f_{2,t} + z_{2,t}) + bE_t s_{t+1} \tag{8.1}$$

where $s_t$ is the log of the nominal exchange rate defined as the domestic price of foreign currency, $f_{i,t}$ $(i = 1, 2)$ are the observed economic fundamentals, and $z_{i,t}$ are the unobserved fundamentals that drive the exchange rate. Note that an increase in $s_t$ implies a depreciation of the domestic currency. This is a general asset pricing model that builds on earlier work on pricing stock returns by Campbell and Shiller (1987, 1988) and West (1988).

Iterating forward and imposing the no-bubbles condition leads to the following present value relation:

$$s_t = (1-b)\sum_{j=0}^{\infty} b^j E_t(f_{1,t+j} + z_{1,t+j}) + b\sum_{j=0}^{\infty} b^j E_t(f_{2,t+j} + z_{2,t+j}) \quad (8.2)$$

Engel and West (2005) show that the exchange rate will follow a RW if the discount factor $b$ is close to 1 and either (i) $f_{1,t} + z_{1,t} \sim I(1)$ and $f_{2,t} + z_{2,t} = 0$ or (ii) $f_{2,t} + z_{2,t} \sim I(1)$. Some other well-known exchange rate models take the general form of Equation (1), and in what follows, we discuss two examples.

**8.2.1.1 Monetary Fundamentals.** Consider first the monetary exchange rate models of the 1970s and 1980s, which assume that the money market relation is described by

$$m_t = p_t + \gamma y_t - \alpha i_t + v_{m,t} \quad (8.3)$$

where $m_t$ is the log of the domestic money supply, $p_t$ is the log of the domestic price level, $\gamma > 0$ is the income elasticity of money demand, $y_t$ is the log of the domestic national income, $\alpha > 0$ is the interest rate semielasticity of money demand, $i_t$ is the domestic nominal interest rate, and $v_{m,t}$ is a shock to domestic money demand. A similar equation holds for the foreign economy, where the corresponding variables are denoted by $m_t^*$, $p_t^*$, $y_t^*$, $i_t^*$, and $v_{m,t}^*$. We assume that the parameters $\{\gamma, \alpha\}$ of the foreign money demand are identical to the domestic parameters.

The nominal exchange rate is equal to its PPP value plus the real exchange rate $q_t$

$$s_t = p_t - p_t^* + q_t \quad (8.4)$$

Finally, the interest parity condition is given by

$$E_t s_{t+1} - s_t = i_t - i_t^* + \rho_t \quad (8.5)$$

where $\rho_t$ is the deviation from the UIP condition that is based on rational expectations and risk neutrality. Hence $\rho_t$ can be interpreted either as an expectational error or a risk premium.

Using Equations (8.3)–(8.5) for the domestic and foreign economies and rearranging, we get

$$s_t = \frac{1}{1+\alpha}[m_t - m_t^* - \gamma(y_t - y_t^*) + q_t - (v_{m,t} - v_{m,t}^*) - \alpha\rho_t] + \frac{\alpha}{1+\alpha}E_t s_{t+1} \quad (8.6)$$

This equation takes the form of the original model in Equation (8.1), where the discount factor is given by $b = \alpha/1+\alpha$, the observable fundamentals are $f_{1,t} = m_t - m_t^* - \gamma\left(y_t - y_t^*\right)$, and the unobservable fundamentals are $z_{1,t} = q_t - \left(v_{m,t} - v_{m,t}^*\right)$ and $z_{2,t} = -\rho_t$.

**8.2.1.2 Taylor Rule.** The second model to be nested by the Engel and West (2005) present value relation is the Taylor (1993) rule, where the home country is assumed to set the short-term nominal interest rate according to

$$i_t = \bar{i} + \beta_1 y_t^g + \beta_2(\pi_t - \bar{\pi}) + v_t \tag{8.7}$$

where $\bar{i}$ is the target short-term interest rate, $y_t^g$ is the output gap measured as the percentage deviation of actual real GDP from an estimate of its potential level, $\pi_t$ is the inflation rate, $\bar{\pi}$ is the target inflation rate, and $v_t$ is a shock. The Taylor rule postulates that the central bank raises the short-term nominal interest rate when output is above potential output and/or inflation rises above its desired level.

The foreign country is assumed to follow a Taylor rule that explicitly targets exchange rates (Clarida et al., 1998):

$$i_t^* = -\beta_0(s_t - \bar{s}_t) + \bar{i} + \beta_1 y_t^{*g} + \beta_2(\pi_t^* - \bar{\pi}) + v_t^* \tag{8.8}$$

where $0 < \beta_0 < 1$ and $\bar{s}_t$ is the target exchange rate. For simplicity, we assume that the home and foreign countries target the same interest rate, $\bar{i}$, and the same inflation rate, $\bar{\pi}$. The rule indicates that the foreign country raises interest rates when its currency depreciates relative to the target.[3]

We assume that the foreign central bank targets the PPP level of the exchange rate

$$\bar{s}_t = p_t - p_t^* \tag{8.9}$$

Taking the difference between the home and foreign Taylor rules, using interest parity (Eq. 8.5), substituting the target exchange rate, and solving for $s_t$ gives

$$\begin{aligned} s_t = {} & \frac{\beta_0}{1+\beta_0}(p_t - p_t^*) - \frac{1}{1+\beta_0}[\beta_1(y_t^g - y_t^{*g}) + \beta_2(\pi_t - \pi_t^*) \\ & + v_t - v_t^* + \rho_t] + \frac{1}{1+\beta_0}E_t s_{t+1} \end{aligned} \tag{8.10}$$

This equation also has the general form of the present value model in Equation (Eq. 8.1), where the discount factor is $b = 1/1 + \beta_0$, $f_{1,t} = p_t - p_t^*$ and $z_{2,t} = -\left[\beta_1\left(y_t^g - y_t^{*g}\right) + \beta_2\left(\pi_t - \pi_t^*\right) + v_t - v_t^* + \rho_t\right]$.

## 8.2.2 PREDICTIVE REGRESSIONS

Our empirical analysis is based on six predictive regressions for exchange rate returns, many of which are nested and motivated by the Engel and West (2005) present value model. All predictive regressions have the following same linear structure:

$$\Delta s_{t+1} = \alpha + \beta x_t + \varepsilon_{t+1} \tag{8.11}$$

[3]The argument still follows if the home country also targets exchange rates. It is standard to omit the exchange rate target from Equation (8.3) on the interpretation that US monetary policy has essentially ignored exchange rates (Engel and West, 2005).

where $\Delta s_{t+1} = s_{t+1} - s_t$, $\alpha$ and $\beta$ are constants to be estimated, and $\varepsilon_{t+1}$ is a normal error term. The empirical models differ in the way they specify the economic fundamentals $x_t$ that are used to forecast exchange rate returns.

**8.2.2.1 Random Walk.** The first regression is the RW with drift model that sets $\beta = 0$. Since the seminal work of Meese and Rogoff (1983), this model has become the benchmark in assessing exchange rate predictability. The RW model captures the prevailing view in international finance research that exchange rates are not predictable when conditioning on economic fundamentals, especially at short horizons.

**8.2.2.2 Uncovered Interest Parity.** The second regression is based on the UIP condition:[4]

$$x_t = i_t - i_t^* \tag{8.12}$$

UIP is the cornerstone condition for FX market efficiency. Assuming risk neutrality and rational expectations, it implies that $\alpha = 0$, $\beta = 1$, and the error term is serially uncorrelated. However, numerous empirical studies consistently reject the UIP condition (Engel, 1996; Hodrick, 1987; Sarno, 2005). As a result, it is a stylized fact that estimates of $\beta$ tend to be closer to minus unity than plus unity. This is commonly referred to as the "forward premium puzzle," which implies that high interest currencies tend to appreciate rather than depreciate and forms the basis of the widely used carry trade strategy in active currency management.[5]

**8.2.2.3 Purchasing Power Parity.** The third regression is based on the PPP hypothesis

$$x_t = p_t - p_t^* - s_t \tag{8.13}$$

The PPP hypothesis states that national price levels should be equal when expressed in a common currency and is typically thought of as a long-run condition rather than holding at each point in time (Rogoff, 1996; Taylor and Taylor, 2004).

**8.2.2.4 Monetary Fundamentals.** The fourth regression conditions on MF:

$$x_t = (m_t - m_t^*) - (y_t - y_t^*) - s_t \tag{8.14}$$

The relation between exchange rates and fundamentals defined in Equation (8.14) suggests that a deviation of the nominal exchange rate $s_{t+1}$ from its

---

[4]An alternative way of testing UIP is to estimate the "Fama regression" (Fama, 1984), which conditions on the forward premium. Note that if covered interest parity (CIP) holds, the interest rate differential is equal to the forward premium and testing UIP is equivalent to testing for forward unbiasedness in exchange rates (Bilson, 1981). For recent evidence on CIP see Akram et al. (2008).

[5]Clarida et al. (2003, 2006) and Boudoukh et al. (2006) also show that the term structure of forward exchange (and interest) rates contains valuable information for forecasting spot exchange rates.

long-run equilibrium level determined by the fundamentals $x_t$, requires the exchange rate to move in the future so as to converge toward its long-run equilibrium. The empirical evidence on the relation between exchange rates and fundamentals is mixed. On the one hand, short-run exchange rate variability appears to be disconnected from the underlying fundamentals (Mark, 1995) in what is commonly referred to as the "exchange rate disconnect puzzle." On the other hand, some recent empirical research finds that fundamentals and nominal exchange rates move together in the long run (Groen, 2000; Mark and Sul, 2001).

**8.2.2.5 Taylor Rule.** The final two regressions are based on simple versions of the Taylor (1993) rule. We estimate a $TR_s$

$$x_t = 1.5(\pi_t - \pi_t^*) + 0.1(y_t^g - y_t^{*g}) \tag{8.15}$$

as well as an $TR_a$ that assumes that the foreign central bank also targets the real exchange rate

$$x_t = 1.5(\pi_t - \pi_t^*) + 0.1(y_t^g - y_t^{*g}) + 0.1(s_t + p_t^* - p_t) \tag{8.16}$$

The domestic and foreign output gaps are computed with a Hodrick and Prescott (1997) (HP) filter.[6] The parameters on the inflation difference (1.5), output gap difference (0.1), and the real exchange rate (0.1) are fairly standard in the literature (Engel et al., 2007; Mark, 2009). Alternative versions of the Taylor rule that we do not consider in this chapter may also account for smoothing, where interest rate adjustments are not immediate but gradual, and heterogeneous coefficients for (i) the US versus foreign inflation and (ii) the US versus foreign output gap (Molodtsova and Papell, 2009).

## 8.3 Statistical Evaluation of Exchange Rate Predictability

The success or failure of empirical exchange rate models is typically determined by statistical tests of OOS predictive ability. Our statistical analysis tests for equal predictive ability between one of the empirical exchange rate models we estimate (UIP, PPP, MF, $TR_s$, or $TR_a$) and the benchmark RW model. In effect, we are comparing the performance of a parsimonious restricted null model (the RW, where $\beta = 0$) to a set of larger alternative unrestricted models that nest the parsimonious model (where $\beta \neq 0$).[7]

[6]Note that in estimating the HP trend in sample or out of sample, at any given period $t$, we only use data up to period $t-1$. We then update the HP trend every time, a new observation is added to the sample. This captures as closely as possible the information available to central banks at the time decisions are made.

[7]For a review of forecast evaluation, see West (2006) and Clark and McCracken (2011).

We estimate all empirical exchange rate models using ordinary least squares (OLS) and then run a pseudo-OOS forecasting exercise as follows (Stock and Watson, 2003). Given today's known observables $\{\Delta s_{t+1}, x_t\}_{t=1}^{T-1}$, we define an in-sample (IS) period using observations $\{\Delta s_{t+1}, x_t\}_{t=1}^{M}$, and an OOS period using $\{\Delta s_{t+1}, x_t\}_{t=M+1}^{T-1}$. This exercise produces $P = (T-1) - M$ OOS forecasts. Our empirical analysis uses $T - 1 = 413$ monthly observations, $M = 120$, and $P = 293$.[8]

In what follows, we describe a comprehensive set of statistical criteria for evaluating the OOS predictive ability of empirical exchange rate models. First, we compute the Campbell and Thompson (2008) OOS $R^2$ statistic, $R^2_{\text{oos}}$, that compares the unconditional forecasts of the benchmark RW model to the conditional forecasts of an alternative model. Let $\Delta\bar{s}_{t+1|t}$ denote the one-step-ahead unconditional forecast from the RW and $\Delta\widehat{s}_{t+1|t}$ be the one-step-ahead conditional forecast from the alternative model represented by one of Equations (8.12)–(8.16). Then, the $R^2_{\text{oos}}$ statistic is given by

$$R^2_{\text{oos}} = 1 - \frac{\sum_{t=M+1}^{T-1}(\Delta s_{t+1} - \Delta\widehat{s}_{t+1|t})^2}{\sum_{t=M+1}^{T-1}(\Delta s_{t+1} - \Delta\bar{s}_{t+1|t})^2}.$$

A positive $R^2_{\text{oos}}$ statistic implies that the alternative model outperforms the benchmark RW by having a lower MSE.

Second, we compute the OOS root MSE difference statistic, $\Delta RMSE$, as in Welch and Goyal (2008).

$$\Delta\text{RMSE} = \sqrt{\frac{\sum_{t=M+1}^{T-1}\left(\Delta s_{t+1} - \Delta\bar{s}_{t+1|t}\right)^2}{P}} - \sqrt{\frac{\sum_{t=M+1}^{T-1}\left(\Delta s_{t+1} - \Delta\widehat{s}_{t+1|t}\right)^2}{P}}$$

A positive ΔRMSE denotes that the alternative model outperforms the benchmark RW by having a lower RMSE.

The most popular method for testing whether the alternative model has a lower MSE than the benchmark is using the Diebold and Mariano (1995) and West (1996) statistic, which has an asymptotic standard normal distribution when comparing forecasts from nonnested models. However, as shown by Clark and McCracken (2001) and McCracken (2007), this statistic has a nonstandard distribution when comparing forecasts from nested models and is severely undersized when using standard normal critical values. Clark and McCracken (2001) and McCracken (2007) account for this size distortion by deriving the nonstandard asymptotic distributions for a number of statistical tests as applied to nested models. We report the two tests with the best overall power and

[8]The IS period for $x_t$ ranges from January 1976 to December 1985. The first OOS forecast is for the February 1986 value of $\Delta s_{t+1}$ that depends on the January 1986 value of $x_t$. The last forecast is for June 2010.

size properties: the ENC-F encompassing test statistic proposed by Clark and McCracken (2001) defined as follows:

$$\text{ENC-F} = \frac{\sum_{t=M+1}^{T-1}(\Delta s_{t+1} - \Delta \bar{s}_{t+1|t})^2 - (\Delta s_{t+1} - \Delta \bar{s}_{t+1|t})(\Delta s_{t+1} - \Delta \widehat{s}_{t+1|t})}{P^{-1}\sum_{t=M+1}^{T-1}(\Delta s_{t+1} - \Delta \bar{s}_{t+1|t})^2}$$

and the MSE-F test of McCracken (2007):

$$\text{MSE-F} = \frac{\sum_{t=M+1}^{T-1}(\Delta s_{t+1} - \Delta \bar{s}_{t+1|t})^2 - (\Delta s_{t+1} - \Delta \widehat{s}_{t+1|t})^2}{P^{-1}\sum_{t=M+1}^{T-1}(\Delta s_{t+1} - \Delta \widehat{s}_{t+1|t})^2}$$

When the models are correctly specified, the forecast errors are serially uncorrelated and exhibit conditional homoskedasticity. In this case, Clark and McCracken (2001) and McCracken (2007) numerically generated the asymptotic critical values for the ENC-F and MSE-F tests. When the above conditions are not satisfied, a bootstrap procedure must be used to compute valid critical values, which we discuss later.

Finally, we also apply the recently developed inference procedure by Clark and West (2006, 2007) for testing the null of equal predictive ability of two nested models. This procedure acknowledges the fact that under the null the MSE from the alternative model is expected to be greater than that of the RW benchmark because the alternative model introduces noise into the forecasting process by estimating a parameter vector that is not helpful in prediction. Therefore, finding that the RW has smaller MSE is not clear evidence against the alternative model. Clark and West (2006, 2007) suggest that the MSE should be adjusted as follows:

$$\text{MSE}_{\text{adj}} = \frac{1}{P}\sum_{t=M+1}^{T-1}(\Delta s_{t+1} - \Delta \widehat{s}_{t+1|t})^2 - \frac{1}{P}\sum_{t=M+1}^{T-1}(\Delta \bar{s}_{t+1|t} - \Delta \widehat{s}_{t+1|t})^2 \tag{8.17}$$

Then, a computationally convenient way of testing for equal MSE is to define

$$\widehat{f}_{t+1|t} = (\Delta s_{t+1} - \Delta \bar{s}_{t+1|t})^2 - [(\Delta s_{t+1} - \Delta \widehat{s}_{t+1|t})^2 - (\Delta \bar{s}_{t+1|t} - \Delta \widehat{s}_{t+1|t})^2] \tag{8.18}$$

and to regress $\widehat{f}_{t+1|t}$ on a constant, using the $t$-statistic for a zero coefficient, which we denote by MSE-$t$. Even though the asymptotic distribution of this test is nonstandard (Clark and West (2006, 2007); McCracken, 2007) show that standard normal critical values provide a good approximation and therefore recommend to reject the null if the statistic is greater than +1.282 (for a one-sided 0.10 test) or +1.645 (for a one-sided 0.05 test).[9]

[9]This approximation tends to perform better when forecasts are obtained from rolling regressions than recursive regressions.

The above statistical tests compare the null hypothesis of equal forecast accuracy with the one-sided alternative that forecasts from the unrestricted model are more accurate than those from the restricted benchmark model. Asymptotic critical values for these test statistics, whenever available, tend to be severely biased in small samples. In addition to the size distortion, there may be spurious evidence of return predictability in small samples when the forecasting variable is sufficiently persistent (Nelson and Kim, 1993; Stambaugh, 1999). In order to address these concerns, we obtain bootstrapped critical values for a one-sided test by estimating the model and generating $10,000$ bootstrapped time series under the null. The procedure preserves the autocorrelation structure of the predictive variable and maintains the cross-correlation structure of the residual. The bootstrap algorithm is summarized in Appendix A.

## 8.4 Economic Evaluation of Exchange Rate Predictability

This section describes the framework for evaluating the performance of an asset allocation strategy that exploits predictability in exchange rate returns.

### 8.4.1 THE DYNAMIC FX STRATEGY

We design an international asset allocation strategy that involves trading the USD and nine other currencies: the AUD, CAD, CHF, Deutsche mark \ euro (EUR), GBP, JPY, NOK, NZD, and SEK. Consider a US investor who builds a portfolio by allocating her wealth between 10 bonds: one domestic (US), and nine foreign bonds (Australia, Canada, Switzerland, Germany, UK, Japan, Norway, New Zealand, and Sweden). The yield of the bonds is proxied by euro deposit rates. At each period $t+1$, the foreign bonds yield a riskless return in local currency but a risky return $r_{t+1}$ in USD, whose expectation at time $t$ is equal to $E_t[r_{t+1}] = i_t + \Delta s_{t+1|t}$. Hence the only risk the US investor is exposed to is the FX risk.

In each period the investor takes two steps. First, she uses each predictive regression to forecast the one-period-ahead exchange rate returns. Second, depending on the forecasts of each model, she dynamically rebalances her portfolio by computing the new optimal weights. This setup is designed to assess the economic value of exchange rate predictability by informing us which empirical exchange rate model leads to a better performing allocation strategy.

### 8.4.2 MEAN-VARIANCE DYNAMIC ASSET ALLOCATION

Mean-variance analysis is a natural framework for assessing the economic value of strategies that exploit predictability in the mean and variance. Consider an investor who has a one-period horizon and constructs a dynamically rebalanced portfolio. Computing the time-varying weights of this portfolio requires one-step-ahead forecasts of the conditional mean and the conditional variance–covariance matrix. Let $r_{t+1}$ denote the $K \times 1$ vector of risky asset returns; $\mu_{t+1|t} = E_t[r_{t+1}]$ is the conditional expectation of $r_{t+1}$ and $\Sigma_{t+1|t} = E_t[(r_{t+1} - \mu_{t+1|t})(r_{t+1} - \mu_{t+1|t})']$ is the $K \times K$ conditional variance–covariance matrix of $r_{t+1}$.

Mean-variance analysis may involve three rules for optimal asset allocation: maximum expected utility, maximum expected return, and minimum volatility. Following Della Corte et al. (2009, 2011), our empirical analysis focuses on the maximum expected return strategy, as this is the strategy most often used in active currency management. For details on the maximum expected utility rule and the minimum volatility rule see Han (2006).

The maximum expected return rule leads to a portfolio allocation on the efficient frontier for a given target conditional volatility. At each period $t$, the investor solves the following problem:

$$\max_{w_t} \left\{ \mu_{p,t+1} = w_t'\mu_{t+1|t} + \left(1 - w_t'\iota\right) r_f \right\} \tag{8.19}$$

$$\text{s.t.} \left(\sigma_p^*\right)^2 = w_t' \sum_{t+1|t} w_t \tag{8.20}$$

where $\sum_p^*$ is the target conditional volatility of the portfolio returns. The solution to the maximum expected return rule gives the following risky asset weights:

$$w_t = \frac{\sigma_p^*}{\sqrt{C_t}} \sum_{t+1|t}^{-1} (\mu_{t+1|t} - \iota r_f) \tag{8.21}$$

where $C_t = (\mu_{t+1|t} - \iota r_f)' \sum_{t+1|t}^{-1} (\mu_{t+1|t} - \iota r_f)$

Then, the gross return on the investor's portfolio is

$$R_{p,t+1} = 1 + r_{p,t+1} = 1 + (1 - w_t'\iota) r_f + w_t' r_{t+1} \tag{8.22}$$

Note that we assume that $\sum_{t+1|t} = \overline{\sum}$, where $\overline{\sum}$ is the unconditional covariance matrix of exchange rates returns using available information at time $t$. In other words, we do not model the dynamics of FX return volatility and correlation. Therefore, the optimal weights will vary across the empirical exchange rate models only to the extent that the predictive regressions produce better forecasts of the exchange rate returns.[10]

### 8.4.3 PERFORMANCE MEASURES

We assess the economic value of exchange rate predictability with a set of standard mean-variance performance measures. We begin our discussion with the Fleming et al. (2001) performance fee, which is based on the principle that

[10]See Della Corte et al. (2012) for an economic evaluation of volatility and correlation timing in FX.

at any point in time, one set of forecasts is better than another if investment decisions based on the first set lead to higher average realized utility. The performance fee is computed by equating the average utility of the RW optimal portfolio with the average utility of the alternative (e.g., UIP) optimal portfolio, where the latter is subject to expenses $\mathcal{F}$. Since the investor is indifferent to these two strategies, we interpret $\mathcal{F}$ as the maximum performance fee she will pay to switch from the RW to the alternative (e.g., UIP) strategy. In other words, this utility-based criterion measures how much a mean-variance investor is willing to pay for conditioning on better exchange rate forecasts. The performance fee will depend on $\delta$, which is the investor's degree of relative risk aversion (RRA). To estimate the fee, we find the value of $\mathcal{F}$ that satisfies

$$\sum_{t=0}^{T-1}\left\{\left(R^*_{p,t+1}-\mathcal{F}\right)-\frac{\delta}{2(1+\delta)}\left(R^*_{p,t+1}-\mathcal{F}\right)^2\right\}$$
$$=\sum_{t=0}^{T-1}\left\{R_{p,t+1}-\frac{\delta}{2(1+\delta)}R^2_{p,t+1}\right\} \tag{8.23}$$

where $R^*_{p,t+1}$ is the gross portfolio return constructed using the forecasts from the alternative (e.g., UIP) model and $R_{p,t+1}$ is the gross portfolio return implied by the benchmark RW model.

We also evaluate performance using the premium return, which builds on the Goetzmann et al. (2007) manipulation-proof performance measure and is defined as

$$\mathcal{P}=\frac{1}{(1-\delta)}\ln\left[\frac{1}{T}\sum_{t=0}^{T-1}\left(\frac{R^*_{p,t+1}}{R_f}\right)^{1-\delta}\right]-\frac{1}{(1-\delta)}\ln\left[\frac{1}{T}\sum_{t=0}^{T-1}\left(\frac{R_{p,t+1}}{R_f}\right)^{1-\delta}\right] \tag{8.24}$$

where $R_f = 1 + r_f$. $\mathcal{P}$ is robust to the distribution of portfolio returns and does not require the assumption of a particular utility function to rank portfolios. In contrast, the Fleming et al. (2001) performance fee assumes a quadratic utility function. $\mathcal{P}$ can be interpreted as the certainty equivalent of the excess portfolio returns and hence can also be viewed as the maximum performance fee an investor will pay to switch from the benchmark to another strategy. In other words, this criterion measures the risk-adjusted excess return an investor enjoys for using onc particular exchange rate model rather than assuming a RW. We report both $\mathcal{F}$ and $\mathcal{P}$ in annualized basis points (bps).

In the context of mean-variance analysis, perhaps the most commonly used measure of economic value is the Sharpe ratio ($\mathcal{SR}$). The realized $\mathcal{SR}$ is equal to the average excess return of a portfolio divided by the standard deviation of the portfolio returns. It is well known that because the $\mathcal{SR}$ uses the sample standard deviation of the realized portfolio returns, it overestimates the conditional risk an investor faces at each point in time and hence underestimates the performance of dynamic strategies (Han, 2006; Marquering and Verbeek, 2004).

Finally, we also compute the Sortino ratio ($\mathcal{SO}$), which measures the excess return to "bad" volatility. Unlike the $\mathcal{SR}$, the $\mathcal{SO}$ differentiates between volatility due to "up" and "down" movements in portfolio returns. It is equal to the average excess return divided by the standard deviation of only the negative returns. In other words, the $\mathcal{SO}$ does not take into account positive returns in computing volatility because these are desirable. A large $\mathcal{SO}$ indicates a low risk of large losses.

### 8.4.4 TRANSACTION COSTS

The effect of transaction costs is an essential consideration in assessing the profitability of dynamic trading strategies. We account for this effect in three ways. First, we calculate the performance measures for the case when the bid-ask spread for spot exchange rates is equal to 8 bps. In foreign exchange trading, this is a realistic range for the recent level of transaction costs.[11] We follow the simple approximation of Marquering and Verbeek (2004) by deducting the proportional transaction cost from the portfolio return ex-post. This ignores the fact that dynamic portfolios are no longer optimal in the presence of transaction costs but maintain simplicity and tractability in our analysis.[12]

The second way of accounting for transaction costs acknowledges the fact that for long data samples the transaction costs will likely change over time. Neely et al. (2009) find that the transaction cost for switching from a long to a short position in FX has on an average declined from about 10 bps in the 1970s to about 2 bps in recent years. If we were to keep transaction costs constant over our sample period, we would spuriously introduce a decline in performance by penalizing more recent returns too heavily relative to those early in the sample period. Therefore, we follow Neely et al. (2009) in estimating a simple time trend that assumes that the bid-ask spread was 20 bps at the beginning of our data sample and declined linearly to 4 bps by the end of the sample. The actual one-way transaction cost is half of the bid-ask spread and hence declines from 10 bps to 2 bps. Specifically, the net return from buying a currency at the spot exchange rate at time $t$ and selling at time $t+1$ is equal to $s_{t+1}^{\text{bid}} - s_t^{\text{ask}} = s_{t+1}^{\text{mid}} - s_t^{\text{mid}} - \tau_{t+1}$, where $\tau_{t+1} = \ln \frac{(1-c_{t+1})}{(1+c_t)}$ and $c_{t+1} = 0.5\left(S_{t+1}^{\text{ask}} - S_{t+1}^{\text{bid}}\right)/S_{t+1}^{\text{mid}}$ is the one-way transaction cost (Neely et al. 2009). $S_t$ is the spot exchange rate and $s_t$ is

[11] In recent years, the typical transaction cost a large investor pays in the FX market is 1 pip, which is equal to 0.01 cent. For example, if the USD/GBP exchange rate is equal to 1.5000, 1 pip would raise it to 1.5001 and this would roughly correspond to 1/2 basis point proportional cost.

[12] Our empirical analysis uses the full bid-ask spread. Note, however, that the effective spread is generally lower than the quoted spread, since trading takes place at the best price quoted at any point in time, suggesting that the worse quotes will not attract trades. For example, Goyal and Saretto (2009) and Della Corte et al. (2011) consider effective transaction costs in the range of 50%–100% of the quoted spread. Assuming that the effective spread is less than the quoted spread would make our economic evidence stronger.

$s_t = \ln S_t$. In the first case, we assume a fixed bid-ask spread and hence $\tau_t = \tau$, whereas in the second case, $\tau_t$ is time-varying.[13]

Third, we also calculate the break-even proportional transaction cost, $\tau^{\text{be}}$, that renders investors indifferent to two strategies (Han, 2006). We assume that $\tau$ is a fixed fraction of the value traded in all assets in the portfolio. Then, the cost of the dynamic strategy is $\tau|w_t - \frac{w_{t-1}(1+r_{j,t})}{1 + r_{p,t}}|$ for each asset $j \leq K$. In comparing a dynamic strategy with the benchmark $RW$ strategy, an investor who pays transaction costs lower than $\tau^{\text{be}}$ will prefer the dynamic strategy. Since $\tau^{\text{be}}$ is the proportional cost paid every time the portfolio is rebalanced, we report $\tau^{\text{be}}$ in monthly basis points.[14]

## 8.5 Combined Forecasts

Our analysis has so far focused on evaluating the performance of individual empirical exchange rate models relative to the RW benchmark. Considering a large set of alternative models that capture different aspects of exchange rate behavior without knowing which model is "true" (or best) inevitably generates model uncertainty. In this section, we resolve this uncertainty by exploring whether portfolio performance improves when combining the forecasts arising from the full set of predictive regressions. Even though the potentially superior performance of combined forecasts is known since the seminal work of Bates and Granger (1969), applications in finance are only recently becoming increasingly popular (Timmermann, 2006). Rapach et al. (2010) argue that forecast combinations can deliver statistically and economically significant OOS gains for two reasons: (i) they reduce forecast volatility relative to individual forecasts and (ii) they are linked to the real economy.[15]

Recall that we estimate $N = 6$ predictive regressions, each of which provides an individual forecast $\widehat{\Delta s}_{i,t+1}$ for the one-step-ahead exchange rate return, where $i \leq N$. We define the combined forecast $\widehat{\Delta s}_{c,t+1}$ as the weighted average of the $N$ individual forecasts $\widehat{\Delta s}_{i,t+1}$:

$$\widehat{\Delta s}_{c,t+1} = \sum_{i=1}^{N} \omega_{i,t} \widehat{\Delta s}_{i,t+1} \tag{8.25}$$

where $\{\omega_{i,t}\}_{i=1}^{N}$ are the ex-ante combining weights determined at time $t$.

---

[13]The derivation is as follows $\frac{S_{t+1}^{\text{bid}}}{S_t^{\text{ask}}} = \frac{S_{t+1}^{\text{mid}} - 0.5\left(S_{t+1}^{\text{ask}} - S_{t+1}^{\text{bid}}\right)}{S_t^{\text{mid}} + 0.5\left(S_t^{\text{ask}} - S_t^{\text{bid}}\right)} = \frac{S_{t+1}^{\text{mid}}\left(1 - \frac{0.5\left(S_{t+1}^{\text{ask}} - S_{t+1}^{\text{bid}}\right)}{S_{t+1}^{\text{mid}}}\right)}{S_t^{\text{mid}}\left(1 + \frac{0.5\left(S_t^{\text{ask}} - S_t^{\text{bid}}\right)}{S_t^{\text{mid}}}\right)} = \frac{S_{t+1}^{\text{mid}}(1 - c_{t+1})}{S_t^{\text{mid}}(1 + c_t)}$.

Then, $\ln s_{t+1}^{\text{bid}} - \ln s_{t+1}^{\text{ask}} = \ln s_{t+1}^{\text{mid}} - \ln s_{t+1}^{\text{mid}} - \ln \frac{(1 - c_{t+1})}{(1 + c_t)}$.

[14]For a slightly different calculation, see Jondeau and Rockinger (2008).

[15]For a Bayesian approach to forecast combinations, see Avramov (2002), Cremers (2002), Wright (2008), and Della Corte et al. (2009, 2012).

We form three types of combined forecasts. The first one uses simple model averaging that, in turn, implements three rules: (i) the mean of the panel of forecasts so that $\omega_{i,t} = 1/N$; (ii) the median of the $\{\Delta\widehat{s}_{i,t+1}\}_{i=1}^{N}$ individual forecasts; and (iii) the trimmed mean that sets $\omega_{i,t} = 0$ for the individual forecasts with the smallest and largest values and $\omega_{i,t} = 1/(N-2)$ for the remaining individual forecasts. These combined forecasts disregard the historical performance of the individual forecasts.

The second type of combined forecasts is based on Stock and Watson (2004) and uses statistical information on the past OOS performance of each individual model. In particular, we compute the discounted MSE (DMSE) forecast combination by setting the following weights:

$$\omega_{i,t} = \frac{\text{DMSE}_{i,t}^{-1}}{\sum_{j=1}^{N} \text{DMSE}_{j,t}^{-1}}, \quad \text{DMSE}_{i,t} = \sum_{t=M+1}^{T-1} \theta^{T-1-t} \left(\Delta s_{t+1} - \Delta\widehat{s}_{i,t+1}\right)^2 \tag{8.26}$$

where $\theta$ is a discount factor and $M$ are the first IS observations on which we depend to form the first OOS forecast. For $\theta < 1$, greater weight is attached to the most recent forecast accuracy of the individual models. The DMSE forecasts are computed for three values of $\theta = \{0.90, 0.95, 1.0\}$. The case of no discounting ($\theta = 1$) corresponds to the Bates and Granger (1969) optimal forecast combination when the individual forecasts are uncorrelated. We also compute simpler "most recently best" $MSE(\kappa)$ forecast combinations that use no discounting ($\theta = 1$) and weigh individual forecasts by the inverse of the OOS MSE computed over the last $\kappa$ months, where $\kappa = \{12, 36, 60\}$.

The third type of combined forecasts does not use statistical information on the historical performance of individual forecasts. Instead it exploits the economic information contained in the Sharpe ratio ($\mathcal{SR}$) of the portfolio returns generated by an individual forecasting model over a prespecified recent period. We compute the discounted $\mathcal{SR}$ (DSR) combined forecast by setting the following weights:

$$\omega_{i,t} = \frac{\text{DSR}_{i,t}}{\sum_{j=1}^{N} \text{DSR}_{j,t}}, \quad \text{DSR}_{i,t} = \sum_{t=M+1}^{T-1} \theta^{T-1-t} SR_{t+1} \tag{8.27}$$

Finally, we also compute simpler "most recently best" $SR(\kappa)$ forecast combinations that use no discounting ($\theta = 1$) and weigh individual forecasts by the OOS $\mathcal{SR}$ computed over the last $\kappa$ months, where $\kappa = \{12, 36, 60\}$.

We assess the economic value of combined forecasts by treating them in the same way as any of the individual empirical models. For instance, we compute the performance fee, $\mathcal{F}$, for the DMSE one-month-ahead forecasts and compare it to the RW benchmark. Finally, note that where possible, we use these forecast combination methods not only for the OOS mean prediction but also for the OOS variance covariance matrix that enters the weights in mean-variance asset allocation.

## 8.6 Empirical Results

### 8.6.1 DATA ON EXCHANGE RATES AND ECONOMIC FUNDAMENTALS

The data sample consists of 414 monthly observations ranging from January 1976 to June 2010 and focuses on nine spot exchange rates relative to the USD: the AUD, CAD, CHF, Deutsche mark \ euro (EUR), GBP, JPY, NOK, NZD, and SEK. The exchange rate is defined as the USD price of a unit of foreign currency so that an increase in the exchange rate implies a depreciation of the USD. These data are obtained through the download data program (DDP) of the Board of Governors of the Federal Reserve System.[16]

Table 8.1 provides a detailed description of all data sources we use. For interest rates, we use the one-month euro deposit rate taken from *Datastream* with the following exceptions. For Japan, the euro deposit rate is only available from January 1979, and hence before this date, we use CIP relative to the USD to construct the no-arbitrage riskless rate. The one-month forward exchange rate required to implement CIP is taken from Hai et al. (1997). For Australia, Norway, New Zealand, and Sweden, euro deposit rates are only available from April 1997. For Australia and New Zealand, we combine the money market rate from January 1976 to November 1984 taken from the IMF's *International Financial Statistics* (IFS) and CIP relative to the USD from December 1984 to March 1997 using one-month forward exchange rates taken from *Datastream.* For Norway and Sweden, we use CIP relative to GBP from January 1976 to March 1997, using spot and one-month forward exchange rates from *Datastream.*

Turning to macroeconomic data, we use nonseasonally adjusted M1 data to measure money supply. For the UK, we use M0 because of the unavailability of M1 data. To construct these times series, we combine IFS and national central bank data from *Ecowin.*[17] We deseasonalize the money supply data by implementing the procedure of Gomez and Maravall (2000).

The price level is measured by the monthly consumer price index (CPI) obtained from the OECD's *Main Economic Indicators* (MEI). For Australia and New Zealand, CPI data are published at quarterly frequency, and hence monthly observations are constructed by linear interpolation. For the inflation rate, we use an annual measure computed as the 12-month log-difference of the CPI. We define the output gap as deviations from the HP filter.

Since GDP data are generally available quarterly, we proxy real output by the seasonally adjusted monthly industrial production index (IPI) taken from IFS. For Australia, New Zealand, and Switzerland, however, IPI data are only released at quarterly frequency, and hence we obtain monthly observations via

---

[16]Before the introduction of the euro in January 1999, we used the USD-Deutsche mark exchange rate combined with the official conversion rate between the Deutsche mark and the euro.

[17]For Germany, for the period January 1976 to December 1979, we construct the money supply using data on currency outside banks and demand deposits from *IFS*.

**TABLE 8.1 Data Sources**

| Country | Description | Source | Range | Frequency | Series |
|---|---|---|---|---|---|
| | | *Nominal Exchange Rate* | | | |
| Australia | Spot USD/AUD | Federal Reserve Board | 76:01-10:06 | Monthly | DDP [RXI$US_N.B.AL] |
| Canada | Spot CAD/USD | Federal Reserve Board | 76:01-10:06 | Monthly | DDP [RXI_N.B.CA] |
| Switzerland | Spot CHF/USD | Federal Reserve Board | 76:01-10:06 | Monthly | DDP [RXI_N.B.SZ] |
| Germany | Spot DEM/USD | Federal Reserve Board | 76:01-98:12 | Monthly | H.10 Historical Rates |
| | Spot USD/EUR | Federal Reserve Board | 99:01-10:06 | Monthly | DDP [RXI$US_N.B.EU] |
| UK | Spot USD/GBP | Federal Reserve Board | 76:01-10:06 | Monthly | DDP [RXI$US_N.B.UK] |
| Japan | Spot JPY/USD | Federal Reserve Board | 76:01-10:06 | Monthly | DDP [RXI_N.B.JA] |
| Norway | Spot NOK/USD | Federal Reserve Board | 76:01-10:06 | Monthly | DDP [RXI_N.B.NO] |
| New Zealand | Spot USD/NZD | Federal Reserve Board | 76:01-10:06 | Monthly | DDP [RXI$US_N.B.NZ] |
| Sweden | Spot SEK/USD | Federal Reserve Board | 76:01-10:06 | Monthly | DDP [RXI_N.B.SD] |
| | | *Riskless Rate* | | | |
| Australia | Money Market Rate | IMF IFS | 76:01-84:11 | Monthly | Ecowin [ifs:s19360b00zfm] |
| | Spot AUD/USD | Barclays Bank | 84:12-97:03 | Monthly | Datastream [BBAUDSP] |
| | 1M Fwd AUD/USD | Barclays Bank | 84:12-97:03 | Monthly | Datastream [BBAUD1F] |
| | 1M Euro Deposit Rate | Thomson Reuters | 97:04-10:05 | Monthly | Datastream [ECCAD1M] |
| Canada | 1M Euro Deposit Rate | Thomson Reuters | 76:01-10:05 | Monthly | Datastream [ECAUD1M] |
| Switzerland | 1M Euro Deposit Rate | Thomson Reuters | 76:01-10:05 | Monthly | Datastream [ECSWF1M] |
| Germany | 1M Euro Deposit Rate | Thomson Reuters | 76:01-10:05 | Monthly | Datastream [ECWGM1M] |
| UK | 1M Euro Deposit Rate | Thomson Reuters | 76:01-10:05 | Monthly | Datastream [ECUKP1M] |

| | | | | | |
|---|---|---|---|---|---|
| Japan | Spot JPY/USD | Hai et al. (1997) | 76:01-78:12 | Monthly | Nelson Mark's website |
| | 1M Fwd JPY/USD | Hai et al. (1997) | 76:01-78:12 | Monthly | Nelson Mark's website |
| | 1M Euro Deposit Rate | Thomson Reuters | 79:01-10:05 | Monthly | Datastream [ECJAP1M] |
| Norway | Spot NOK/GBP | Not Specified | 76:01-97:03 | Monthly | Datastream [NORKRON] |
| | 1M Fwd NOK/GBP | Not Specified | 76:01-97:03 | Monthly | Datastream [NORKN1F] |
| | 1M Euro Deposit Rate | Thomson Reuters | 97:04-10:05 | Monthly | Datastream [ECNOR1M] |
| New Zealand | Money Market Rate | IMF IFS | 76:01-84:11 | Monthly | Ecowin [ifs:s19660000zfm] |
| | Spot NZD/USD | Barclays Bank | 84:12-97:03 | Monthly | Datastream [BBNZDSP] |
| | 1M Fwd NZD/USD | Barclays Bank | 84:12-97:03 | Monthly | Datastream [BBNZD1F] |
| | 1M Euro deposit rate | Thomson Reuters | 97:04-10:05 | Monthly | Datastream [ECNZD1M] |
| Sweden | Spot SEK/GBP | Not Specified | 76:01-97:03 | Monthly | Datastream [SWEKRON] |
| | 1M Fwd SEK/GBP | Not Specified | 76:01-97:03 | Monthly | Datastream [SWEDK1F] |
| | 1M Euro deposit rate | Thomson Reuters | 97:04-10:05 | Monthly | Datastream [ECSWE1M] |
| US | 1M Euro deposit rate | Thomson Reuters | 76:01-10:05 | Monthly | Datastream [ECUSD1M] |
| | | *Money Supply* | | | |
| Australia | M1 | Reserve Bank of Australia | 76:01-10:05 | Monthly | EcoWin [ew:aus12045] |
| Canada | M1 | Bank of Canada | 76:01-10:05 | Monthly | EcoWin [ew:can12042] |
| Switzerland | M1 | IMF IFS | 76:01-84:11 | Monthly | EcoWin [ifs:s14634000zfm] |
| | M1 | Swiss National Bank | 84:12-10:05 | Monthly | EcoWin [ew:che12045] |
| Germany | Currency in Circulation | IMF IFS | 76:01-79:12 | Monthly | EcoWin [ifs:s13434a0nzfm] |

(*continued*)

**TABLE 8.1** *(Continued)*

| Country | Description | Source | Range | Frequency | Series |
|---|---|---|---|---|---|
| | Demand Deposits | IMF IFS | 76:01-79:12 | Monthly | EcoWin [ifs:s13434b0nzfm] |
| | M1 | Deutsche Bundesbank | 80:01-10:05 | Monthly | EcoWin [ew:deu12990] |
| UK | M0 | Bank of England | 76:01-10:05 | Monthly | EcoWin [boe:lpmavaa] |
| Japan | M1 | Bank of Japan | 76:01-10:05 | Monthly | EcoWin [ew:jpn12066] |
| Norway | M1 | IMF IFS | 76:01-86:12 | Monthly | EcoWin [ifs:s14234000zfm] |
| | | Norges Bank | 87:01-10:05 | Monthly | EcoWin [ew:nor12045] |
| New Zealand | M1 | IMF IFS | 76:01-77:02 | Monthly | EcoWin [ifs:s19634000zfm] |
| | | Reserve Bank of New Zealand | 77:03-10:05 | Monthly | EcoWin [ew:nzl12045] |
| Sweden | M1 | IMF IFS | 76:01-98:02 | Monthly | EcoWin [ifs:s14435l00zfm] |
| | | Sveriges Riksbank | 98:03-10:05 | Monthly | EcoWin [ew:swe12010] |
| US | M1 | Federal Reserve United States | 76:01-10:05 | Monthly | EcoWin [ew:usa12010] |
| | | *Real Output* | | | |
| Australia | Industrial Production Index | IMF IFS | 69:12-10:06 | Quarterly | EcoWin [ifs:s1936600czfq] |
| Canada | Industrial Production Index | IMF IFS | 70:01-10:05 | Monthly | EcoWin [ifs:s1566600czfm] |
| Switzerland | Industrial Production Index | IMF IFS | 69:04-10:06 | Quarterly | EcoWin [ifs:s1466600bzfq] |
| Germany | Industrial Production Index | IMF IFS | 70:01-10:05 | Monthly | EcoWin [ifs:s1346600czfm] |
| UK | Industrial Production Index | IMF IFS | 70:01-10:05 | Monthly | EcoWin [ifs:s1126600czfm] |
| Japan | Industrial Production Index | IMF IFS | 70:01-10:05 | Monthly | EcoWin [ifs:s1586600czfm] |
| Norway | Industrial Production Index | IMF IFS | 70:01-10:05 | Monthly | EcoWin [ifs:s1426600czfm] |

| | | | | | |
|---|---|---|---|---|---|
| New Zealand | Gross Domestic Product | IMF IFS | 69:12-77:05 | Quarterly | EcoWin [ifs:s19699b0czfy] |
| | Industrial Production Index | IMF IFS | 77:06-10:06 | Quarterly | EcoWin [ifs:s19666eyczfq] |
| Sweden | Industrial Production Index | IMF IFS | 70:01-10:05 | Monthly | EcoWin [ifs:s1446600czfm] |
| United States | Industrial Production Index | IMF IFS | 70:01-10:05 | Monthly | EcoWin [ifs:s1116600czfm] |
| | | | *Price Level* | | |
| Australia | Consumer Price Index | OECD MEI | 74:12-10:06 | Quarterly | EcoWin [oecd:aus_cpalcy01_ixobq] |
| Canada | Consumer Price Index | OECD MEI | 75:01-10:05 | Monthly | EcoWin [oecd:can_cpaltt01_ixobm] |
| Switzerland | Consumer Price Index | OECD MEI | 75:01-10:05 | Monthly | EcoWin [oecd:che_cpaltt01_ixobm] |
| Germany | Consumer Price Index | OECD MEI | 75:01-10:05 | Monthly | EcoWin [oecd:deu_cpaltt01_ixobm] |
| UK | Consumer Price Index | OECD MEI | 75:01-10:05 | Monthly | EcoWin [oecd:gbr_cpaltt01_ixobm] |
| Japan | Consumer Price Index | OECD MEI | 75:01-10:05 | Monthly | EcoWin [oecd:jpn_cpaltt01_ixobm] |
| Norway | Consumer Price Index | OECD MEI | 75:01-10:05 | Monthly | EcoWin [oecd:nor_cpaltt01_ixobm] |
| New Zealand | Consumer Price Index | OECD MEI | 74:12-10:06 | Quarterly | EcoWin [oecd:nzl_cpalcy01_ixobq] |
| Sweden | Consumer Price Index | OECD MEI | 75:01-10:05 | Monthly | EcoWin [oecd:swe_cpaltt01_ixobm] |
| United States | Consumer Price Index | OECD MEI | 75:01-10:05 | Monthly | EcoWin [oecd:usa_cpaltt01_ixobm] |

The table presents a detailed description of the sources of the raw data. The exchange rate data range from January 1976 to June 2010. The riskless rate and the money supply data range from January 1976 to May 2005. Data on real output range from January 1970 to May 2010 and are used to construct the output gap. Data on the price level range from January 1975 to May 2010 and are used to construct the inflation rate. The data are monthly, but quarterly data are used to retrieve monthly observations via linear interpolation when monthly data are not available. The raw money supply is not seasonally adjusted but the raw real output is.

linear interpolation.[18] Orphanides (2001) has recently stressed the importance of using real-time data to estimate Taylor rules for the United States, which are data available to central banks when the policy decisions are made. Since real-time data are not available for most of the countries included in this study, we mimic as closely as possible the information set available to the central banks using quasi-real-time data: although data incorporate revisions, we update the HP trend each period so that ex-post data is not used to construct the output gap. In other words, at time $t$, we only use data up to $t - 1$ to construct the output gap. Using a number of detrending methods, Orphanides and van Norden (2002) showed that most of the difference between fully revised and real-time data comes from using ex-post data to construct potential output and not from the data revisions themselves.[19]

We convert all data but interest rates by taking logs and multiplying by 100. Throughout the rest of the chapter, the symbols $s_t$, $i_t$, $m_t$, $p_t$, $\pi_t$, $y_t$, and $y_t^g$ refer to transformed spot exchange rate, interest rate, money supply, price level, inflation rate, real output, and output gap, respectively. We use an asterisk to denote the transformed data ($i_t^*$, $m_t^*$, $p_t^*$, $\pi_t^*$, $y_t^*$, and $y_t^{g*}$) for the foreign country.

Table 8.2 reports the descriptive statistics for the monthly percentage FX returns, $\Delta s_t$; the difference between domestic and foreign interest rates, $i_t - i_t^*$; the difference in percentage change in price levels, $\Delta\left(p_t - p_t^*\right)$; the difference in percentage change in money supply, $\Delta\left(m_t - m_t^*\right)$; and the difference in percentage change in real output, $\Delta\left(y_t - y_t^*\right)$. For our sample period, the monthly sample means of the FX returns range from $-0.138\%$ for SEK to 0.296% for JPY. The return standard deviations are similar across all exchange rates at about 3% per month. Most FX returns exhibit negative skewness and higher-than-normal kurtosis. Finally, the exchange rate return sample autocorrelations are no higher than 0.10 and decay rapidly. For the economic fundamentals, the notable trends are as follows: (i) $i_t - i_t^*$ are highly persistent with long memory, (ii) $\Delta\left(p_t - p_t^*\right)$ are always negatively skewed, and (iii) $\Delta\left(m_t - m_t^*\right)$ and $\Delta\left(y_t - y_t^*\right)$ have occasionally high kurtosis.

## 8.6.2 PREDICTIVE REGRESSIONS

We test the empirical performance of the models by first estimating the six predictive regressions for nine monthly exchange rates. The regressions include the RW model, UIP, PPP, MF, $TR_s$, and $TR_a$. Table 8.3 presents the OLS estimates with Newey and West (1987) standard errors. We focus primarily on the significance of the slope estimate $\beta$ of the predictive regressions since this would be an indication that the RW benchmark is misspecified.

[18]For New Zealand, IPI data are only available from June 1977. We fill the gap using quarterly GDP data.

[19]The output gap for the first period is computed using real output data from January 1970 to January 1976. In the HP filter, we use a smoothing parameter equal to 14,400 as in Molodtsova and Papell (2009).

**TABLE 8.2 Descriptive Statistics**

| | | Mean | Std | Skew | Kurt | $\rho_1$ | $\rho_3$ | $\rho_6$ | $\rho_{12}$ |
|---|---|---|---|---|---|---|---|---|---|
| AUD | $\Delta s$ | −0.089 | 3.237 | −1.396 | 9.440 | 0.056 | 0.046 | −0.002 | −0.100 |
| | $i - i^*$ | −0.175 | 0.290 | 0.092 | 4.547 | 0.956 | 0.873 | 0.795 | 0.643 |
| | $\Delta(p - p^*)$ | −0.088 | 0.405 | −0.803 | 4.304 | 0.560 | 0.138 | 0.103 | 0.259 |
| | $\Delta(m - m^*)$ | −0.350 | 1.528 | 2.880 | 35.059 | 0.009 | 0.167 | 0.078 | 0.040 |
| | $\Delta(y - y^*)$ | 0.026 | 0.785 | −0.218 | 4.438 | 0.278 | 0.035 | 0.038 | −0.068 |
| CAD | $\Delta s$ | −0.009 | 1.907 | −0.672 | 10.792 | −0.033 | 0.017 | −0.121 | −0.002 |
| | $i - i^*$ | −0.063 | 0.140 | −0.223 | 3.646 | 0.885 | 0.732 | 0.648 | 0.440 |
| | $\Delta(p - p^*)$ | 0.005 | 0.365 | −0.739 | 6.657 | 0.008 | 0.079 | 0.080 | 0.240 |
| | $\Delta(m - m^*)$ | −0.256 | 1.004 | 0.354 | 4.124 | 0.076 | 0.230 | 0.128 | 0.102 |
| | $\Delta(y - y^*)$ | −0.016 | 1.089 | −0.890 | 11.287 | −0.216 | 0.062 | −0.035 | −0.067 |
| CHF | $\Delta s$ | 0.210 | 3.528 | 0.038 | 3.921 | 0.013 | 0.023 | −0.092 | −0.029 |
| | $i - i^*$ | 0.256 | 0.279 | 0.443 | 3.768 | 0.970 | 0.890 | 0.834 | 0.747 |
| | $\Delta(p - p^*)$ | 0.157 | 0.419 | −0.123 | 3.724 | 0.231 | −0.054 | 0.330 | 0.509 |
| | $\Delta(m - m^*)$ | −0.037 | 1.531 | −0.443 | 10.496 | 0.173 | 0.072 | 0.205 | −0.003 |
| | $\Delta(y - y^*)$ | 0.015 | 0.949 | 0.105 | 4.278 | 0.355 | −0.036 | −0.020 | −0.033 |
| EUR | $\Delta s$ | 0.119 | 3.218 | −0.147 | 3.730 | 0.024 | 0.036 | −0.057 | −0.022 |
| | $i - i^*$ | 0.116 | 0.239 | −0.249 | 3.615 | 0.961 | 0.875 | 0.827 | 0.723 |
| | $\Delta(p - p^*)$ | 0.132 | 0.411 | −0.770 | 5.174 | 0.171 | 0.031 | 0.078 | 0.504 |
| | $\Delta(m - m^*)$ | −0.183 | 1.442 | 0.929 | 30.164 | 0.080 | −0.009 | 0.167 | 0.060 |
| | $\Delta(y - y^*)$ | 0.071 | 1.807 | 0.011 | 9.269 | −0.286 | 0.079 | 0.007 | −0.003 |
| GBP | $\Delta s$ | −0.073 | 3.065 | −0.205 | 4.793 | 0.092 | 0.018 | −0.078 | −0.002 |
| | $i - i^*$ | −0.176 | 0.220 | −0.674 | 5.378 | 0.921 | 0.763 | 0.573 | 0.296 |
| | $\Delta(p - p^*)$ | −0.063 | 0.559 | −1.325 | 8.335 | 0.087 | −0.012 | 0.235 | 0.551 |
| | $\Delta(m - m^*)$ | −0.091 | 0.942 | 0.475 | 6.410 | 0.033 | 0.195 | 0.220 | 0.108 |
| | $\Delta(y - y^*)$ | 0.121 | 1.340 | 0.281 | 6.516 | −0.266 | 0.068 | −0.063 | −0.063 |
| JPY | $\Delta s$ | 0.296 | 3.361 | 0.365 | 4.325 | 0.039 | 0.042 | −0.105 | 0.035 |
| | $i - i^*$ | 0.247 | 0.221 | 0.327 | 3.446 | 0.952 | 0.829 | 0.671 | 0.445 |
| | $\Delta(p - p^*)$ | 0.202 | 0.529 | −0.399 | 5.214 | 0.065 | −0.104 | 0.110 | 0.468 |
| | $\Delta(m - m^*)$ | −0.132 | 1.795 | −4.414 | 52.393 | 0.036 | 0.018 | 0.050 | 0.086 |
| | $\Delta(y - y^*)$ | 0.026 | 1.604 | 0.568 | 5.895 | −0.081 | 0.105 | 0.028 | −0.024 |
| NOK | $\Delta s$ | −0.037 | 2.965 | −0.489 | 4.695 | 0.067 | −0.022 | −0.038 | −0.082 |
| | $i - i^*$ | −0.181 | 0.277 | 0.013 | 3.043 | 0.934 | 0.831 | 0.744 | 0.499 |
| | $\Delta(p - p^*)$ | −0.038 | 0.534 | −0.884 | 5.370 | 0.192 | 0.112 | 0.162 | 0.427 |
| | $\Delta(m - m^*)$ | −0.475 | 3.099 | −1.950 | 17.999 | −0.184 | −0.097 | 0.114 | −0.025 |
| | $\Delta(y - y^*)$ | −0.033 | 4.358 | 0.696 | 28.252 | −0.425 | −0.034 | −0.006 | −0.095 |
| NZD | $\Delta s$ | −0.093 | 3.366 | −1.232 | 11.815 | 0.036 | 0.185 | 0.035 | −0.098 |
| | $i - i^*$ | −0.296 | 0.350 | −1.666 | 7.590 | 0.957 | 0.859 | 0.736 | 0.546 |
| | $\Delta(p - p^*)$ | −0.169 | 0.495 | −1.414 | 7.351 | 0.690 | 0.361 | 0.326 | 0.330 |
| | $\Delta(m - m^*)$ | −0.225 | 1.925 | 0.213 | 4.944 | −0.207 | 0.212 | 0.124 | −0.168 |
| | $\Delta(y - y^*)$ | 0.073 | 1.071 | −1.232 | 9.601 | 0.477 | 0.113 | 0.062 | 0.001 |

*(continued)*

TABLE 8.2 (*Continued*)

| | | Mean | Std | Skew | Kurt | $\rho_1$ | $\rho_3$ | $\rho_6$ | $\rho_{12}$ |
|---|---|---|---|---|---|---|---|---|---|
| SEK | $\Delta s$ | −0.138 | 3.192 | −0.876 | 6.427 | 0.104 | 0.062 | −0.104 | −0.034 |
| | $i-i^*$ | −0.148 | 0.277 | −0.826 | 4.141 | 0.937 | 0.837 | 0.749 | 0.543 |
| | $\Delta(p-p^*)$ | −0.045 | 0.546 | −1.103 | 6.226 | 0.199 | 0.048 | 0.102 | 0.342 |
| | $\Delta(m-m^*)$ | −0.184 | 1.443 | 1.650 | 21.307 | 0.010 | 0.050 | 0.124 | −0.023 |
| | $\Delta(y-y^*)$ | 0.107 | 2.803 | 0.086 | 38.324 | −0.297 | 0.047 | 0.030 | −0.026 |

The table presents descriptive statistics for nine major exchange rates and a set of economic fundamentals. $\Delta s$ is the percentage change in the US dollar exchange rate vis-à-vis the Australian dollar (AUD), Canadian dollar (CAD), Swiss franc (CHF), Deutsche mark \ euro (EUR), British pound (GBP), Japanese yen (JPY), Norwegian kroner (NOK), New Zealand dollar (NZD), and Swedish kronor (SEK); $i$ is the one-month interest rate; $\Delta p$ is the percentage change in the price level; $\Delta m$ is the percentage change in the money supply; $\Delta y$ is the percentage change in real output; and the asterisk denotes a non-US value. The exchange rate is defined as US dollars per unit of foreign currency. $\rho_l$ is the autocorrelation coefficient with $l$ lags. The data range from January 1976 to June 2010 for a sample size of 414 monthly observations.

Consistent with the large literature on the forward premium puzzle, the UIP $\beta$ is predominantly negative. The PPP $\beta$ is always positive, and for $TR_a$, it is always negative. For these three cases (UIP, PPP and $TR_a$), the $\beta$ estimates are significant for half of the exchange rates. The least significant slopes are for MF revolving around zero and for $TR_s$ for which they are always negative. Finally, the $R^2_{oos}$ of the predictive regressions is as high as 2.4%, but in most cases, it is below 1%. In conclusion, the predictive regression results demonstrate that the empirical exchange rates models with the most significant slopes are the UIP, PPP, and $TR_a$.

### 8.6.3 STATISTICAL EVALUATION

We assess the statistical performance of the empirical exchange rate models (UIP, PPP, MF, $TR_s$, and $TR_a$) by reporting OOS tests of predictability against the null of the RW. We focus on the following statistics:

**(i)** The $R^2_{oos}$ statistic of Campbell and Thompson (2008). Recall that a positive $R^2_{oos}$ value implies that the alternative model has lower MSE than the benchmark RW. However, even a slightly negative $R^2_{oos}$ may be consistent with a better performing alternative because the calculation of the $R^2_{oos}$ does take into account the adjustment in the MSE proposed by Clark and West (2006, 2007) to account for the noise introduced in forecasting by estimating a parameter that is not helpful in prediction.

**(ii)** The $\Delta RMSE$ statistic, a positive value for which denotes superior OOS performance for the competing model but is subject to the same criticism as the $R^2_{oos}$.

**(iii)** The Clark and McCracken (2001) ENC-F statistic.

**(iv)** The McCracken (2007) MSE-F statistic.

**TABLE 8.3 Predictive Regressions**

| | | RW | UIP | PPP | MF | $TR_s$ | $TR_a$ |
|---|---|---|---|---|---|---|---|
| AUD | $\alpha$ | − 0.089<br>(0.170) | − 0.154<br>(0.160) | − 0.047<br>(0.174) | 0.251<br>(1.380) | − 0.120<br>(0.154) | − 0.076<br>(0.174) |
| | $\beta$ | – | − 0.368<br>(0.433) | 0.019[a]<br>(0.010) | − 0.001<br>(0.005) | − 0.208<br>(0.486) | − 0.178[a]<br>(0.092) |
| | $R^2_{oos}$(%) | – | 0.108 | 0.821 | 0.033 | 0.049 | 0.816 |
| CAD | $\alpha$ | − 0.009<br>(0.097) | − 0.070<br>(0.116) | − 0.288<br>(0.185) | 0.640<br>(0.929) | − 0.008<br>(0.097) | − 0.273<br>(0.172) |
| | $\beta$ | – | − 0.974[a]<br>(0.586) | 0.015[a]<br>(0.008) | − 0.003<br>(0.004) | − 0.025<br>(0.440) | − 0.139[a]<br>(0.074) |
| | $R^2_{oos}$(%) | – | 0.512 | 0.828 | 0.328 | 0.001 | 0.790 |
| CHF | $\alpha$ | 0.210<br>(0.182) | 0.498[b]<br>(0.250) | − 1.735<br>(1.149) | − 1.632<br>(1.075) | 0.322<br>(0.236) | − 1.673<br>(1.067) |
| | $\beta$ | – | − 1.126<br>(0.720) | 0.023[a]<br>(0.014) | 0.009[a]<br>(0.005) | − 0.483<br>(0.686) | − 0.226[a]<br>(0.129) |
| | $R^2_{oos}$(%) | – | 0.793 | 1.028 | 0.690 | 0.173 | 1.104 |
| EUR | $\alpha$ | 0.119<br>(0.171) | 0.192<br>(0.190) | − 0.386<br>(0.374) | − 0.225<br>(0.304) | 0.214<br>(0.194) | − 0.338<br>(0.335) |
| | $\beta$ | – | − 0.630<br>(0.789) | 0.016<br>(0.011) | 0.004<br>(0.004) | − 0.458<br>(0.606) | − 0.157<br>(0.103) |
| | $R^2_{oos}$(%) | – | 0.218 | 0.691 | 0.531 | 0.182 | 0.732 |
| GBP | $\alpha$ | − 0.073<br>(0.168) | − 0.342[a]<br>(0.199) | 2.079<br>(1.387) | − 1.620<br>(1.504) | − 0.106<br>(0.165) | 1.896<br>(1.218) |
| | $\beta$ | – | − 1.529[a]<br>(0.887) | 0.028<br>(0.018) | 0.005<br>(0.005) | − 0.302<br>(0.511) | − 0.257[a]<br>(0.155) |
| | $R^2_{oos}$(%) | – | 1.204 | 1.196 | 0.366 | 0.135 | 1.224 |
| JPY | $\alpha$ | 0.296[a]<br>(0.178) | 0.881[c]<br>(0.211) | − 9.156[a]<br>(5.379) | 0.349[a]<br>(0.193) | 0.487[b]<br>(0.194) | − 9.685[a]<br>(5.145) |
| | $\beta$ | – | − 2.369[c]<br>(0.655) | 0.018[a]<br>(0.010) | 0.003<br>(0.002) | − 0.654[a]<br>(0.399) | − 0.186[a]<br>(0.096) |
| | $R^2_{oos}$(%) | – | 2.431 | 0.977 | 0.332 | 0.396 | 1.150 |
| NOK | $\alpha$ | − 0.037<br>(0.161) | − 0.128<br>(0.173) | − 3.466<br>(2.295) | 0.065<br>(1.240) | − 0.046<br>(0.162) | − 3.076<br>(2.022) |
| | $\beta$ | – | − 0.507<br>(0.551) | 0.020<br>(0.013) | 0.001<br>(0.003) | − 0.253<br>(0.503) | − 0.174<br>(0.115) |
| | $R^2_{oos}$(%) | – | 0.225 | 0.779 | 0.001 | 0.161 | 0.800 |
| NZD | $\alpha$ | − 0.093<br>(0.184) | − 0.387[a]<br>(0.218) | 0.041<br>(0.274) | 0.590<br>(2.797) | − 0.165<br>(0.191) | 0.018<br>(0.239) |
| | $\beta$ | – | − 0.995[a]<br>(0.516) | 0.009<br>(0.011) | − 0.001<br>(0.006) | − 0.284<br>(0.318) | − 0.095<br>(0.097) |
| | $R^2_{oos}$(%) | – | 1.073 | 0.222 | 0.029 | 0.212 | 0.295 |

*(continued)*

TABLE 8.3 (*Continued*)

| | | RW | UIP | PPP | MF | $TR_s$ | $TR_a$ |
|---|---|---|---|---|---|---|---|
| SEK | $\alpha$ | − 0.138 | − 0.130 | − 2.619[a] | − 1.862 | − 0.145 | − 2.668 |
| | | (0.182) | (0.183) | (1.579) | (1.636) | (0.189) | (1.642) |
| | $\beta$ | – | 0.051 | 0.015 | 0.008 | − 0.125 | − 0.150 |
| | | | (0.863) | (0.009) | (0.007) | (0.465) | (0.096) |
| | $R^2_{\text{oos}}$ (%) | – | 0.002 | 0.807 | 0.493 | 0.024 | 0.849 |

The table reports the least squares estimates of the predictive regression $\Delta s_{t+1} = \alpha + \beta x_t + \varepsilon_{t+1}$ for nine major exchange rates defined as USD per unit of foreign currency. $\Delta s_t$ is the monthly percentage exchange rate return. The random walk (RW) model sets $\beta = 0$; the UIP model sets $x_t = i_t - i_t^*$, which is the interest rate differential between the home and foreign country; the PPP model sets $x_t = p_t - p_t^* - s_t$, where $p_t - p_t^*$ is the log-price differential; the monetary fundamentals (MF) model sets $x_t = (m_t - m_t^*) - (y_t - y_t^*) - s_t$, where $m_t - m_t^*$ is the the log-money supply differential and $y_t - y_t^*$ the log-real output differential; the symmetric Taylor rule ($TR_s$) sets $x_t = 1.5\left(\pi_t - \pi_t^*\right) + 0.1(y_t^g - y_t^{g*})$, where $\pi_t - \pi_t^*$ is the inflation differential and $y_t^g - y_t^{g*}$ the real output gap differential; and the asymmetric Taylor rule ($TR_a$) sets $x_t = 1.5(\pi_t - \pi_t^*) + 0.1(y_t^g - y_t^{g*}) + 0.1(s_t + p_t^* - p_t)$, where $s_t + p_t^* - p_t$ is the log-real exchange rate. Newey and West (1987) standard errors are reported in parentheses. The sample period comprises monthly observations from January 1976 to June 2010.
[a]Statistical significance at 10%.
[b]Statistical significance at 5%.
[c]Statistical significance at 1%.

**(v)** The Clark and West (2006, 2007) MSE-t statistic. The null hypothesis for the ENC-F, MSE-F, and MSE-t statistics is that the MSEs for the RW and the competing model are equal against the alternative that the competing model has lower MSE.

One-sided critical values are obtained by generating 10,000 bootstrapped time series as in Mark (1995) and Kilian (1999). The OOS monthly forecasts are obtained in two ways: (i) with rolling regressions that use a 10-year window that generates forecasts for the period of January 1986 to June 2010 and (ii) with recursive regressions for the same forecasting period that successively reestimate the model parameters every time a new observation is added to the sample.

Table 8.4 shows that most of the statistics tend to be negative and hence provide evidence against the alternative model. In many cases, however, the results are not statistically significant. If instead we focus on the Clark and West (2006, 2007) MSE-t statistic, which makes the adjustment to the MSE and is hence more reliable, a different picture emerges. For rolling regressions, the UIP and PPP models have a positive MSE-t statistic for seven of the nine exchange rates, whereas the MF and $TR_a$ models have for for six. The model that is most often significantly different from the RW is the $TR_a$. The worse performing model is the $TR_s$. The results are very similar for recursive regressions. In short, therefore, a careful examination of the empirical evidence reveals that many of the models perform well against the RW with the clear exception of the $TR_s$.

It is important to note that in OOS predictive regressions, lack of statistical significance does not imply lack of economic significance. Campbell and Thompson (2008) show that a small $R^2$ can generate large economic benefits for

**TABLE 8.4 Statistical Evaluation of Exchange Rate Predictability**

| | UIP | PPP | MF | $TR_s$ | $TR_a$ | UIP | PPP | MF | $TR_s$ | $TR_a$ | UIP | PPP | MF | $TR_s$ | $TR_a$ |
|---|---|---|---|---|---|---|---|---|---|---|---|---|---|---|---|
| | | | | | | | | *Rolling Regressions* | | | | | | | |
| | | | AUD | | | | | CAD | | | | | CHF | | |
| $R^2_{oos}$ (%) | −0.98 | −1.88 | −1.92 | −2.14 | −1.52 | 0.53[b] | −1.35 | −1.69 | −2.63 | −1.11 | −1.80 | −1.03 | −0.60 | −1.82 | −3.75 |
| ΔRMSE (%) | −0.02 | −0.03 | −0.03 | −0.04 | −0.03 | 0.01[b] | −0.01 | −0.02 | −0.03 | −0.01 | −0.03 | −0.02 | −0.01 | −0.03 | −0.06 |
| ENC-F | 1.87 | −1.86 | −0.37 | −1.17 | 1.76 | 2.89[a] | −1.04 | −0.40 | −2.92 | −0.07 | 4.35[b] | 2.14 | 5.33[b] | −1.23 | 0.10 |
| MSE-F | −2.85 | −5.41 | −5.51 | −6.14 | −4.39 | 1.56[b] | −3.91 | −4.87 | −7.51 | −3.21 | −5.18 | −2.98 | −1.74 | −5.24 | −10.6 |
| MSE-t | 0.60 | −1.43 | −0.19 | −0.44 | 0.70 | 1.73[b] | −0.79 | −0.24 | −1.30 | −0.04 | 1.00 | 0.92 | 1.62[b] | −0.57 | 0.03 |
| | | | EUR | | | | | GBP | | | | | JPY | | |
| $R^2_{oos}$ (%) | −3.34 | −1.38 | −2.74 | −1.45 | −3.19 | −3.36 | 0.57[b] | −0.87 | −2.05 | 1.29[c] | −0.39 | −0.17[a] | −1.48 | −1.26 | −3.78 |
| ΔRMSE (%) | −0.05 | −0.02 | −0.04 | −0.02 | −0.05 | −0.05 | 0.01[b] | −0.01 | −0.03 | 0.02[c] | −0.01 | 0.01[a] | −0.02 | −0.02 | −0.06 |
| ENC-F | 0.44 | 1.38 | 2.53 | −0.98 | −0.90 | 2.54 | 3.75[b] | 2.62 | −1.78 | 4.98[c] | 3.87[b20] | 3.06[a] | 3.96[a] | 0.77 | −0.69 |
| MSE-F | −9.46 | −3.99 | −7.82 | −4.20 | −9.07 | −9.51 | 1.67[b] | −2.52 | −5.89 | 3.84[c] | −1.14 | −0.50[a] | −4.26 | −3.64 | −10.7 |
| MSE-t | 0.11 | 0.60 | 0.76 | −0.62 | −0.37 | 0.47 | 1.74[b] | 1.42[b] | −1.05 | 2.25[c] | 1.35[a] | 0.95 | 0.85 | 0.44 | −0.20 |
| | | | NOK | | | | | NZD | | | | | SEK | | |
| $R^2_{oos}$ (%) | −2.74 | −1.33 | −2.63 | −3.09 | 0.02[a] | −0.81 | −1.62 | −1.80 | −0.84 | −2.06 | −6.38 | −0.44 | −0.51 | −1.56 | 0.39[b] |
| ΔRMSE (%) | −0.04 | −0.02 | −0.04 | −0.05 | 0.01[b] | −0.01 | −0.03 | −0.03 | −0.01 | −0.03 | −0.10 | −0.01 | −0.01 | −0.03 | 0.01[b] |
| ENC-F | −2.31 | 0.07 | −1.21 | 0.29 | 3.28[a] | 2.04 | −1.42 | 0.22 | 1.30 | 1.25 | −4.10 | 0.92 | 2.00 | −0.63 | 2.60[a] |
| MSE-F | −7.80 | −3.85 | −7.51 | −8.78 | 0.07[a] | −2.35 | −4.68 | −5.18 | −2.43 | −5.93 | −17.6 | −1.28 | −1.49 | −4.51 | 1.13[b] |
| MSE-t | −1.39 | 0.05 | −0.73 | 0.09 | 1.14[a] | 0.70 | −1.26 | 0.09 | 0.69 | 0.68 | −1.31 | 0.64 | 0.87 | −0.30 | 1.25[b] |

*(continued)*

**TABLE 8.4** (*Continued*)

| | UIP | PPP | MF | $TR_s$ | $TR_a$ | UIP | PPP | MF | $TR_s$ | $TR_a$ | UIP | PPP | MF | $TR_s$ | $TR_a$ |
|---|---|---|---|---|---|---|---|---|---|---|---|---|---|---|---|
| | | | | | | | | *Recursive Regressions* | | | | | | | |
| | | | AUD | | | | | CAD | | | | | CHF | | |
| $R^2_{oos}$ (%) | −0.26 | 0.34[a] | −1.21 | −0.34 | 0.91[b] | 0.06 | 0.30[a] | −1.32 | −0.41 | 0.09[a] | −1.68 | 1.11[c] | −0.35 | −0.81 | −2.37 |
| ΔRMSE (%) | 0.00 | 0.01[a] | −0.02 | −0.01 | 0.02[b] | 0.00 | 0.01[a] | −0.01 | 0.00 | 0.01[a] | −0.03 | 0.02[c] | −0.01 | −0.01 | −0.04 |
| ENC-F | −0.25 | 1.36[a] | −0.71 | −0.39 | 2.29[a] | 1.40[a] | 1.26[a] | −0.50 | −0.56 | 0.96 | 2.43 | 2.41[a] | 5.73[c] | −0.30 | 1.12 |
| MSE-F | −0.75 | 1.00 | −3.50 | −0.98 | 2.70[b] | 0.18 | 0.89[a] | −3.81 | −1.20 | 0.27[a] | −4.85[a] | 3.29[c] | −1.02 | −2.36 | −6.79 |
| MSE-t | −0.49 | 0.96 | −0.53 | −1.04 | 1.76[b] | 1.21[a] | 1.16[a] | −0.22 | −1.13 | 0.68 | 0.64 | 1.88[b] | 1.78[b] | −0.17 | 0.36 |
| | | | EUR | | | | | GBP | | | | | JPY | | |
| $R^2_{oos}$ (%) | −1.55 | 0.74[b] | −0.73 | −1.06 | −1.71 | −1.22 | 1.22[c] | −0.33 | −0.69 | 1.64[c] | 0.71[b] | 0.30[a] | −1.67 | −0.85 | −1.64 |
| ΔRMSE (%) | −0.02 | 0.01[b] | −0.01 | −0.02 | −0.03 | −0.02 | 0.02[c] | 0.00 | −0.01 | 0.02[c] | 0.01[b] | 0.01[a] | −0.03 | −0.01 | −0.03 |
| ENC-F | 0.30 | 1.44 | 3.24[b] | −0.74 | −0.13 | 0.91 | 2.65[a] | 1.60 | −0.79 | 3.86[b] | 4.27[b] | 0.98 | 4.10[b] | −0.71 | −0.74 |
| MSE-F | −4.47 | 2.19[b] | −2.12 | −3.06 | −4.93 | −3.54 | 3.62[c] | −0.97 | −2.00 | 4.89[c] | 2.09[b] | 0.87[a] | −4.82 | −2.46 | −4.73 |
| MSE-t | 0.10 | 1.66[b] | 1.10[a] | −0.56 | −0.05 | 0.29 | 1.93[b] | 0.88 | −1.14 | 2.87[c] | 1.78[b] | 0.91 | 1.07[a] | −0.88 | −0.39 |
| | | | NOK | | | | | NZD | | | | | SEK | | |
| $R^2_{oos}$ (%) | −0.50 | 0.68[b] | −1.42 | −1.53 | 1.01[b] | 0.11 | −0.37 | −0.65 | −0.06 | 1.15[c] | −1.00 | 0.72[b] | −0.28 | −0.60 | 0.77[b] |
| ΔRMSE (%) | −0.01 | 0.01[b] | −0.02 | −0.02 | 0.02[b] | 0.00 | −0.01 | −0.01 | 0.00 | 0.02[c] | −0.02 | 0.01[b] | 0.00 | −0.01 | 0.01[b] |
| ENC-F | −0.05 | 1.34 | −1.43 | −1.48 | 2.20[a] | 1.67 | −0.39 | −0.54 | 0.58 | 2.52[a] | −1.22 | 1.40 | 1.50 | −0.78 | 1.68[a] |
| MSE-F | −1.46 | 2.02[b] | −4.11 | −4.42 | 3.00[b] | 0.33 | −1.07 | −1.90 | −0.18 | 3.41[c] | −2.91 | 2.13[b] | −0.82 | −1.74 | 2.27[b] |
| MSE-t | −0.04 | 1.46[b] | −1.29 | −0.88 | 2.00[c] | 0.85 | −0.61 | −0.62 | 0.61 | 2.10[c] | −0.85 | 1.59[b] | 0.71 | −1.31 | 1.69[b] |

The table displays out-of-sample tests of the predictive ability of a set of empirical exchange rate models against the null of a random walk (RW). In addition to RW, we form exchange rate forecasts using five alternative models: uncovered interest parity (UIP), purchasing power parity (PPP), monetary fundamentals (MF), symmetric Taylor rule ($TR_s$) and asymmetric Taylor rule ($TR_a$). The out-of-sample monthly forecasts are obtained in two ways: (i) with rolling regressions that use a 10-year window generating forecasts for the period of January 1986 to June 2010 and (ii) with recursive regressions for the same forecasting period that successively reestimate the model parameters every time a new observation is added to the sample. $R^2_{oos}$ is the Campbell and Thompson (2008) statistic. Δ RMSE is the root mean squared error difference between the RW and the competing model. *ENC-F* is the Clark and McCracken (2001) *F*-statistic, MSE-F is the McCracken (2007) *F*-statistic and MSE-t is the Clark and West (2006, 2007) *t*-statistic, all of which test the null hypothesis of equal mean squared error (MSE) between the RW and the competing model; the alternative hypothesis is that the competing model has lower MSE. One-sided critical values are obtained by generating 10,000 bootstrap samples as in Mark (1995) and Kilian (1999).

[a] Significance level at 90%.

[b] Significance level at 95%.

[c] Significance level at 99%.

investors. They use a mean-variance framework to demonstrate that a good way to judge the magnitude of $R^2$ is to compare it to the square of the Sharpe ratio ($SR^2$). Even a modest $R^2$ can lead to a substantial proportional increase in the expected return by conditioning on the predictive variable $x_t$. Indeed, regressions with large $R^2$ statistics would be too profitable to believe, which is equivalent to the saying "if you are so smart, why aren't you rich?" In the limit, an $R^2$ close to 1 should lead to perfect predictions and hence infinite profits for investors. Furthermore, dynamic asset allocation is, by design, multivariate thus exploiting predictability in all exchange rate series. In the following section, we discuss in detail whether the predictive regressions can generate economic value.

### 8.6.4 ECONOMIC EVALUATION

We assess the economic value of exchange rate predictability by analyzing the performance of dynamically rebalanced portfolios based on one-month-ahead forecasts from the six empirical exchange rate models we estimate. The economic evaluation is conducted both IS and OOS, but again, the main focus of our analysis is OOS. The OOS results we present in this section are based on forecasts constructed according to a recursive procedure that only depends on information up to the month in which the forecast is made. The predictive regressions are then successively reestimated every month.

Our empirical analysis focuses on the Sharpe ratio ($\mathcal{SR}$), the Sortino ratio ($\mathcal{SO}$), the Fleming et al. (2001) performance fee ($\mathcal{F}$), the Goetzmann et al. (2007) premium return measure ($\mathcal{P}$), and the break-even transaction cost $\tau^{\text{be}}$. The $\mathcal{F}$ and $\mathcal{P}$ performance measures are computed for three cases: (i) zero transaction costs; (ii) a bid-ask spread of 8 bps; and (iii) a bid-ask spread of 20 bps at the beginning of the sample that linearly decays to 4 bps at the end of the sample as suggested by Neely et al. (2009). Following Della Corte et al. (2009, 2011), our empirical analysis focuses on the maximum expected return strategy, as this is the strategy most often used in active currency management. We set a volatility target of $\sigma_p^* = 10\%$ and a degree of RRA $\delta = 6$. We have experimented with different $\sigma_p^*$ and $\delta$ values and found that qualitatively, they have little effect on the asset allocation results discussed below.

Table 8.5 reports the IS and OOS portfolio performance and shows that there is high economic value associated with some of the empirical exchange rate models. We first discuss the IS results, which demonstrate that all models outperform the RW, except for the $\text{TR}_\text{s}$). For example, $\mathcal{SR} = 1.30$ for PPP, 1.28 for $\text{TR}_\text{a}$, 1.18 for MF, 1.14 for UIP, 1.08 for RW, and 0.96 for $\text{TR}_\text{s}$. The $\mathcal{SO}$ have higher values ranging from 1.26 for $\text{TR}_\text{s}$ to 2.00 for PPP. Switching from the benchmark RW to another model generates $\mathcal{F} = 285$ annual bps for PPP, 202 bps for $\text{TR}_\text{a}$, 138 for MF, and 83 bps for UIP. The $\mathcal{P}$ performance measure has similar value to $\mathcal{F}$. Furthermore, both measures are largely unaffected by transaction costs. This can be exemplified by the very large value of the monthly $\tau^{\text{be}}$, which are 586 bps for UIP, 328 bps for MF, and 138 bps for PPP.

The literature on exchange rate forecasting is primarily concerned with OOS predictability, and hence we turn our attention to the OOS results. The first

**TABLE 8.5 The Economic Value of Exchange Rate Predictability**

| Strategy | $\mu_p$ | $\sigma_p$ | $\mathcal{SR}$ | $\mathcal{SO}$ | $\mathcal{F}$ | $\mathcal{P}$ | $\tau^{be}$ | $\mathcal{F}_\tau$ | $\mathcal{P}_\tau$ | $\mathcal{F}_8$ | $\mathcal{P}_8$ |
|---|---|---|---|---|---|---|---|---|---|---|---|
| | | | | | *In-Sample* | | | | | | |
| RW | 18.0 | 10.8 | 1.08 | 1.46 | | | | | | | |
| UIP | 19.1 | 11.1 | 1.14 | 1.68 | 83 | 92 | 586 | 83 | 91 | 83 | 91 |
| PPP | 21.5 | 11.6 | 1.30 | 2.00 | 285 | 297 | 138 | 285 | 297 | 285 | 297 |
| MF | 19.9 | 11.5 | 1.18 | 1.64 | 138 | 139 | 328 | 138 | 139 | 138 | 139 |
| $TR_s$ | 16.9 | 11.1 | 0.96 | 1.26 | −127 | −128 | — | −127 | −128 | −127 | −128 |
| $TR_a$ | 19.8 | 10.5 | 1.28 | 1.86 | 202 | 202 | — | 202 | 202 | 202 | 202 |
| | | | | | *Out-of-Sample* | | | | | | |
| RW | 10.8 | 11.4 | 0.54 | 0.73 | | | | | | | |
| UIP | 11.9 | 11.1 | 0.65 | 0.99 | 131 | 143 | 173 | 138 | 153 | 141 | 163 |
| PPP | 13.3 | 11.3 | 0.76 | 0.97 | 252 | 247 | 70 | 230 | 227 | 231 | 208 |
| MF | 11.1 | 11.7 | 0.55 | 0.73 | 10 | 4 | — | 3 | −3 | 11 | 5 |
| $TR_s$ | 7.1 | 11.6 | 0.21 | 0.23 | −384 | −433 | — | −395 | −445 | −392 | −451 |
| $TR_a$ | 12.1 | 11.4 | 0.65 | 0.83 | 130 | 121 | 161 | 162 | 154 | 156 | 174 |

The table shows the in-sample and out-of-sample economic value of a set of empirical exchange rate models for nine nominal spot exchange rates relative to the US dollar. We form exchange rate forecasts using six models: the random walk (RW), uncovered interest parity (UIP), purchasing power parity (PPP), monetary fundamentals (MF), symmetric Taylor rule ($TR_s$), and asymmetric Taylor rule ($TR_a$ ). Using the exchange rate forecasts from each model, we build a maximum expected return strategy subject to a target volatility $\sigma_p^* = 10\%$ for a US investor who every month dynamically rebalances her portfolio investing in a domestic US bond and nine foreign bonds. For each portfolio, we report the annualized percentage mean ($\mu_p$), percentage volatility ($\sigma_p$), Sharpe ratio ($\mathcal{SR}$), and Sortino ratio ($\mathcal{SO}$). $\mathcal{F}$ denotes the performance fee a risk-averse investor is willing to pay for switching from the benchmark RW strategy to a competing strategy. $\mathcal{P}$ is the premium return performance measure. $\mathcal{F}$ and $\mathcal{P}$ are computed for a degree of relative risk aversion equal to 6 and are expressed in annual basis points. $\tau^{be}$ is the break-even proportional transaction cost that cancels out the utility advantage of a given strategy relative to the RW. $\tau^{be}$ is only reported for positive performance measures and is expressed in monthly basis points. $\mathcal{F}_\tau$ ($\mathcal{P}_\tau$) denote the performance fee (premium return) reported net of the bid-ask spread, which is assumed to linearly decay from *20* bps in 1976 to 4 bps in 2010. $\mathcal{F}_8$ and $\mathcal{P}_8$ are computed for a fixed bid-ask spread of 8 bps. The in-sample analysis covers monthly data from January 1976 to June 2010. The out-of-sample analysis runs from January 1986 to June 2010.

thing to notice is that the value of the OOS $\mathcal{SR}$ is smaller than IS. The RW has an OOS $\mathcal{SR} = 0.54$ and is outperformed only by the PPP ($\mathcal{SR} = 0.76$), UIP ($\mathcal{SR} = 0.65$), and $TR_a$ ($\mathcal{SR} = 0.65$). Consistent with a very large literature in FX, neither do the MF models outperform the RW nor do the $TR_s$. The $\mathcal{F}$ values are 252 annual bps for PPP, 131 bps for UIP, 130 bps for $TR_a$, 10 bps for MF, and −384 bps for $TR_s$. The $\mathcal{P}$ measure has slightly higher value than $\mathcal{F}$. Transaction costs seem to be a bit more important OOS than IS. For example, the $\tau^{be}$ are 173 bps for UIP, 161 bps for $TR_a$, and 70 bps for PPP. However, it seems that whether we assume fixed transaction costs or linearly decaying costs makes little difference in the performance of the empirical exchange rate models. In short, our findings demonstrate that it is worth using the UIP, PPP, and $TR_a$

empirical exchange rate models, as their forecasts generate significant economic value.

By design, the dynamic FX strategy invests in nine foreign bonds and thus exploits predictability in nine exchange rates. Since we economically evaluate the performance of portfolios rather than individual exchange rates, it would be interesting to assess whether the superior portfolio performance of one versus another empirical model is driven by one particular currency. Table 8.6 reports the economic value of exchange rate predictability when we remove one of the currencies (and hence one of the bonds) from the investment opportunity set. For example, AUD in Table 8.6 denotes the dynamic allocation strategy that invests in all currencies, except for AUD. The results for excluding one currency at a time show that the best performing models are still the same as before. In sample, all models but the $TR_s$ outperform the RW, whereas out of sample the UIP, PPP, and $TR_a$ are still the best models. Therefore, the empirical evidence suggests that our results are not driven by any one particular currency.

A unique feature of the FX market is that investors trade currencies but all prices are quoted relative to a numeraire. Consistent with the vast majority of the FX literature, we use data on exchange rates relative to the USD. It is of interest, however, to check whether using a different currency as numeraire meaningfully affects the economic value of the empirical exchange rate models. This is a crucially important robustness check since it is straightforward to show analytically that the portfolio returns and their covariance matrix are not invariant to the numeraire. For example, consider taking the point of view of a European investor and hence changing the numeraire currency from the USD to the euro. Then, all previously bilateral exchange rates become cross rates and nine of the previously cross rates become bilateral. Furthermore, converting dollar FX returns into euro FX returns replaces the US bond as the domestic asset by the European bond. It also replaces all US economic fundamentals and MF by Europe's fundamentals. The main question, however, can only be answered empirically: if changing the numeraire also changes the portfolio returns, does the economic value of the empirical exchange rate models also change?

Table 8.7 shows the IS and OOS economic value of exchange rate predictability from the perspective of each of nine countries other than the US. For example, using the AUD as numeraire means that all exchange rates are quoted relative to AUD, all predictive regressions are estimated using the new exchange rates, and the mean-variance economic evaluation is done from the perspective of an Australian investor. The same holds when the numeraire changes to CAD, CHF, EUR, GBP, JPY, NOK, NZD, and SEK. We find that our main results remain robust across all numeraires: the best IS and OOS models are consistently the UIP, the PPP, and the $TR_a$. In terms of Sharpe ratios and performance fees, in sample, the PPP and $TR_a$ outperform the RW for all nine numeraires and UIP does so six of nine times; OOS the PPP outperforms the RW seven of nine times, whereas the UIP and $TR_a$ five of nine times. To conclude, the economic value of exchange rate predictability of the best individual empirical exchange rate models remains robust regardless of the numeraire choice.

**TABLE 8.6 The Economic Value of Exchange Rate Predictability when Removing one Currency**

| | $\mathcal{SR}$ | $\mathcal{SO}$ | $\mathcal{F}$ | $\mathcal{P}$ | $\tau^{be}$ | $\mathcal{SR}$ | $\mathcal{SO}$ | $\mathcal{F}$ | $\mathcal{P}$ | $\tau^{be}$ | $\mathcal{SR}$ | $\mathcal{SO}$ | $\mathcal{F}$ | $\mathcal{P}$ | $\tau^{be}$ |
|---|---|---|---|---|---|---|---|---|---|---|---|---|---|---|---|
| | | | | | | | | *In-Sample* | | | | | | | |
| | | | AUD | | | | | CAD | | | | | CHF | | |
| RW | 1.11 | 1.53 | — | — | — | 0.94 | 1.25 | — | — | — | 0.94 | 1.28 | — | — | — |
| UIP | 1.15 | 1.74 | 56 | 64 | 163 | 0.99 | 1.40 | 60 | 69 | 443 | 1.02 | 1.49 | 91 | 100 | 127 |
| PPP | 1.25 | 1.94 | 219 | 234 | 99 | 1.20 | 1.93 | 304 | 319 | 169 | 1.18 | 1.88 | 281 | 296 | 146 |
| MF | 1.19 | 1.71 | 128 | 130 | 410 | 1.06 | 1.52 | 150 | 153 | 271 | 1.02 | 1.25 | 97 | 83 | 175 |
| $TR_s$ | 0.96 | 1.30 | −148 | −147 | — | 0.81 | 1.05 | −150 | −151 | — | 0.89 | 1.18 | −58 | −62 | — |
| $TR_a$ | 1.21 | 1.78 | 119 | 120 | 454 | 1.20 | 1.61 | 258 | 253 | 176 | 1.19 | 1.75 | 245 | 244 | 99 |
| | | | EUR | | | | | GBP | | | | | JPY | | |
| RW | 1.01 | 1.41 | — | — | — | 1.02 | 1.33 | — | — | — | 0.96 | 1.30 | — | — | — |
| UIP | 1.07 | 1.62 | 67 | 76 | 146 | 1.11 | 1.54 | 107 | 113 | 526 | 0.98 | 1.46 | 32 | 41 | 41 |
| PPP | 1.19 | 1.85 | 235 | 249 | 109 | 1.22 | 1.74 | 256 | 265 | 157 | 1.18 | 1.84 | 271 | 284 | 103 |
| MF | 1.10 | 1.52 | 121 | 118 | 153 | 1.10 | 1.45 | 117 | 117 | 216 | 1.07 | 1.48 | 137 | 136 | 259 |
| $TR_s$ | 0.97 | 1.31 | −43 | −46 | — | 0.89 | 1.15 | −134 | −134 | — | 0.84 | 1.12 | −129 | −129 | — |
| $TR_a$ | 1.27 | 1.83 | 240 | 238 | 62 | 1.18 | 1.59 | 155 | 155 | 103 | 1.16 | 1.72 | 207 | 208 | 162 |
| | | | NOK | | | | | NZD | | | | | SEK | | |
| RW | 0.98 | 1.24 | — | — | — | 1.10 | 1.52 | — | — | — | 1.04 | 1.45 | — | — | — |
| UIP | 1.05 | 1.50 | 89 | 104 | 218 | 1.17 | 1.83 | 85 | 95 | 4 | 1.06 | 1.54 | 35 | 41 | 37 |
| PPP | 1.15 | 1.76 | 215 | 231 | 130 | 1.30 | 2.08 | 278 | 291 | 149 | 1.24 | 1.87 | 249 | 259 | 200 |
| MF | 1.12 | 1.53 | 181 | 187 | 171 | 1.19 | 1.74 | 141 | 143 | 393 | 1.18 | 1.76 | 161 | 168 | 404 |
| $TR_s$ | 0.87 | 1.08 | −123 | −120 | — | 0.96 | 1.34 | −133 | −131 | — | 0.93 | 1.27 | −119 | −118 | — |
| $TR_a$ | 1.15 | 1.71 | 182 | 190 | 314 | 1.23 | 1.92 | 141 | 146 | 88 | 1.28 | 1.92 | 213 | 214 | 206 |

*Out-of-Sample*

| | | | AUD | | | | | CAD | | | | | CHF | | |
|---|---|---|---|---|---|---|---|---|---|---|---|---|---|---|---|
| RW | 0.56 | 0.78 | — | — | — | 0.46 | 0.60 | — | — | — | 0.46 | 0.65 | — | — | — |
| UIP | 0.67 | 1.02 | 118 | 129 | 158 | 0.52 | 0.69 | 71 | 79 | 169 | 0.57 | 0.87 | 131 | 144 | 390 |
| PPP | 0.78 | 1.00 | 249 | 242 | 70 | 0.68 | 0.88 | 251 | 253 | 89 | 0.71 | 0.93 | 287 | 275 | 64 |
| MF | 0.58 | 0.75 | 10 | −1 | — | 0.56 | 0.77 | 110 | 117 | 357 | 0.47 | 0.59 | −1 | −21 | — |
| $TR_s$ | 0.20 | 0.23 | −416 | −465 | — | 0.11 | 0.12 | −397 | −439 | — | 0.23 | 0.26 | −262 | −312 | — |
| $TR_a$ | 0.66 | 0.83 | 102 | 89 | 104 | 0.64 | 0.70 | 206 | 176 | 136 | 0.68 | 0.85 | 252 | 230 | 120 |
| | | | EUR | | | | | GBP | | | | | JPY | | |
| RW | 0.48 | 0.67 | — | — | — | 0.50 | 0.67 | — | — | — | 0.52 | 0.68 | — | — | — |
| UIP | 0.58 | 0.91 | 114 | 123 | 260 | 0.61 | 0.92 | 127 | 139 | 178 | 0.56 | 0.79 | 52 | 64 | 57 |
| *PPP* | 0.70 | 0.91 | 238 | 228 | 55 | 0.66 | 0.86 | 176 | 173 | 59 | 0.70 | 0.92 | 212 | 213 | 63 |
| MF | 0.54 | 0.68 | 50 | 37 | 149 | 0.48 | 0.65 | −39 | −41 | — | 0.54 | 0.76 | 33 | 37 | 19 |
| $TR_s$ | 0.26 | 0.30 | −271 | −306 | — | 0.17 | 0.19 | −376 | −420 | — | 0.17 | 0.19 | −392 | −434 | — |
| $TR_a$ | 0.64 | 0.81 | 172 | 161 | 132 | 0.57 | 0.72 | 75 | 68 | 82 | 0.65 | 0.84 | 151 | 147 | 185 |
| | | | NOK | | | | | NZD | | | | | SEK | | |
| RW | 0.42 | 0.61 | — | — | — | 0.52 | 0.69 | — | — | — | 0.49 | 0.70 | — | — | — |
| UIP | 0.58 | 0.91 | 178 | 188 | 135 | 0.65 | 0.92 | 139 | 150 | 162 | 0.63 | 1.00 | 179 | 186 | 269 |
| PPP | 0.58 | 0.72 | 176 | 166 | 50 | 0.77 | 0.95 | 277 | 270 | 78 | 0.76 | 1.10 | 314 | 312 | 114 |
| MF | 0.45 | 0.56 | 10 | −14 | 2 | 0.52 | 0.69 | −12 | −13 | — | 0.51 | 0.66 | 27 | 8 | 32 |
| $TR_s$ | 0.21 | 0.24 | −225 | −261 | — | 0.16 | 0.17 | −412 | −471 | — | 0.20 | 0.26 | −328 | −335 | — |
| $TR_a$ | 0.53 | 0.64 | 108 | 86 | 112 | 0.60 | 0.76 | 83 | 77 | 164 | 0.65 | 0.92 | 196 | 190 | 157 |

The table shows the in-sample and out-of-sample economic value of a set of empirical exchange rate models when one of the nine foreign currencies is removed from the investment opportunity set. The nine exchange rates include the Australian dollar (AUD), Canadian dollar (CAD), Swiss franc (CHF), Deutsche mark \ euro (EUR), British pound (GBP), Japanese yen (JPY), Norwegian kroner (NOK), New Zealand dollar (NZD), and Swedish kronor (SEK) relative to the US dollar (USD). For example, AUD denotes an investment strategy that invests in all currencies except for AUD. We form exchange rate forecasts using six models: the random walk (RW), uncovered interest parity (UIP), purchasing power parity (PPP, monetary fundamentals (MF), symmetric Taylor rule ($TR_s$) and asymmetric Taylor rule ($TR_a$). Using the exchange rate forecasts from each model, we build a maximum expected return strategy subject to a target volatility $\sigma_p^* = 10\%$ for a US investor who every month dynamically rebalances her portfolio investing in a domestic US bond and nine foreign bonds. For each portfolio, we report the Sharpe ratio ($\mathcal{SR}$) and Sortino ratio ($\mathcal{SO}$). $\mathcal{F}$ denotes the performance fee a risk-averse investor is willing to pay for switching from the benchmark RW strategy to a competing strategy. $\mathcal{P}$ is the premium return performance measure. $\mathcal{F}$ and $\mathcal{P}$ are computed for a degree of relative risk aversion equal to 6 and are expressed in annual basis points. $\tau^{be}$ is the break-even proportional transaction cost that cancels out the utility advantage of a given strategy relative to the RW. $\tau^{be}$ is only reported for positive performance measures and is expressed in monthly basis points. The in-sample analysis covers monthly data from January 1976 to June 2010. The out-of-sample analysis runs from January 1986 to June 2010.

**TABLE 8.7 The Economic Value of Exchange Rate Predictability for Alternative Numeraires**

| | $\mathcal{SR}$ | $\mathcal{SO}$ | $\mathcal{F}$ | $\mathcal{P}$ | $\tau^{be}$ | $\mathcal{SR}$ | $\mathcal{SO}$ | $\mathcal{F}$ | $\mathcal{P}$ | $\tau^{be}$ | $\mathcal{SR}$ | $\mathcal{SO}$ | $\mathcal{F}$ | $\mathcal{P}$ | $\tau^{be}$ |
|---|---|---|---|---|---|---|---|---|---|---|---|---|---|---|---|
| | | | | | | | | *In-Sample* | | | | | | | |
| | | | AUD | | | | | CAD | | | CHF | | | | |
| RW | 1.08 | 1.49 | — | — | — | 1.08 | 1.47 | — | — | — | 1.09 | 1.44 | — | — | — |
| UIP | 0.95 | 1.44 | −141 | −127 | — | 1.10 | 1.46 | 55 | 55 | 114 | 1.28 | 1.82 | 200 | 207 | 137 |
| PPP | 1.24 | 1.94 | 242 | 268 | 54 | 1.32 | 2.03 | 306 | 317 | 116 | 1.41 | 2.27 | 394 | 412 | 378 |
| MF | 0.82 | 1.29 | −285 | −269 | — | 1.07 | 1.86 | −11 | 6 | — | 1.04 | 1.53 | −38 | −26 | — |
| $TR_s$ | 1.06 | 1.39 | −13 | −14 | — | 0.93 | 1.37 | −163 | −155 | — | 1.02 | 1.26 | −72 | −78 | — |
| $TR_a$ | 1.49 | 2.40 | 370 | 373 | 212 | 1.17 | 1.64 | 100 | 103 | 316 | 1.26 | 1.82 | 190 | 194 | 186 |
| | | | EUR | | | | | GBP | | | JPY | | | | |
| RW | 1.09 | 1.44 | — | — | — | 1.07 | 1.47 | — | — | — | 1.09 | 1.47 | — | — | — |
| UIP | 1.25 | 1.74 | 159 | 162 | 170 | 1.18 | 1.73 | 133 | 145 | 61 | 1.16 | 2.01 | 115 | 140 | 92 |
| PPP | 1.35 | 1.98 | 329 | 342 | 245 | 1.23 | 1.85 | 222 | 236 | 124 | 1.38 | 2.01 | 367 | 375 | 251 |
| MF | 1.10 | 1.67 | 13 | 24 | 8 | 1.04 | 1.58 | −37 | −23 | — | 1.08 | 1.51 | 11 | 17 | 23 |
| $TR_s$ | 1.07 | 1.30 | 5 | 1 | 1 | 1.03 | 1.47 | −50 | −49 | — | 1.02 | 1.42 | −86 | −80 | — |
| $TR_a$ | 1.28 | 1.82 | 204 | 208 | 290 | 1.22 | 1.81 | 157 | 157 | 147 | 1.24 | 1.68 | 180 | 183 | 277 |
| | | | NOK | | | | | NZD | | | SEK | | | | |
| RW | 1.08 | 1.50 | — | — | — | 1.07 | 1.53 | — | — | — | 1.08 | 1.50 | — | — | — |
| UIP | 1.26 | 2.19 | 146 | 150 | 827 | 1.05 | 1.46 | −19 | −14 | — | 1.00 | 1.51 | −100 | −98 | — |
| PPP | 1.24 | 1.84 | 235 | 248 | 127 | 1.15 | 1.85 | 129 | 152 | 28 | 1.33 | 1.79 | 340 | 344 | 128 |
| MF | 1.31 | 1.67 | 243 | 239 | 139 | 0.98 | 1.62 | −114 | −107 | — | 1.01 | 1.58 | −62 | −46 | — |
| TRs | 1.14 | 1.57 | 73 | 74 | 8 | 1.06 | 1.47 | −11 | −7 | — | 1.11 | 1.36 | 45 | 37 | 5 |
| TRa | 1.33 | 2.08 | 258 | 265 | 166 | 1.55 | 2.61 | 452 | 452 | 401 | 1.39 | 2.06 | 292 | 294 | 21 |

| | Out-of-Sample | | | | | | | | | | | | | | |
|---|---|---|---|---|---|---|---|---|---|---|---|---|---|---|---|
| | | | AUD | | | | | CAD | | | | | CHF | | |
| RW | 0.54 | 0.75 | — | — | — | 0.54 | 0.74 | — | — | — | 0.54 | 0.73 | — | — | — |
| UIP | 0.25 | 0.36 | −333 | −326 | — | 0.66 | 0.88 | 143 | 141 | 169 | 0.66 | 0.91 | 134 | 136 | 92 |
| PPP | 0.54 | 0.83 | −15 | −2 | — | 0.66 | 0.88 | 130 | 131 | 36 | 0.81 | 1.18 | 318 | 323 | 103 |
| MF | 0.29 | 0.38 | −278 | −280 | — | 0.54 | 0.70 | 20 | 5 | 8 | 0.28 | 0.40 | −320 | −310 | — |
| $TR_s$ | 0.42 | 0.58 | −111 | −113 | — | 0.24 | 0.29 | −313 | −329 | — | 0.33 | 0.45 | −227 | −220 | — |
| $TR_a$ | 0.46 | 0.63 | −81 | −71 | — | 0.60 | 0.77 | 76 | 57 | 121 | 0.26 | 0.33 | −333 | −349 | — |
| | | | EUR | | | | | GBP | | | | | JPY | | |
| RW | 0.54 | 0.73 | — | — | — | 0.53 | 0.74 | — | — | — | 0.54 | 0.73 | — | — | — |
| UIP | 0.64 | 0.94 | 113 | 121 | 89 | 0.64 | 0.99 | 122 | 137 | 47 | 0.59 | 0.94 | 49 | 72 | 23 |
| PPP | 0.68 | 0.97 | 155 | 157 | 56 | 0.51 | 0.71 | −52 | −47 | — | 0.86 | 1.20 | 379 | 381 | 104 |
| MF | 0.42 | 0.51 | −145 | −183 | — | 0.31 | 0.43 | −250 | −244 | — | 0.36 | 0.53 | −191 | −184 | — |
| $TR_s$ | 0.36 | 0.43 | −235 | −259 | — | 0.49 | 0.72 | −38 | −34 | — | 0.33 | 0.41 | −222 | −225 | — |
| $TR_a$ | 0.33 | 0.39 | −254 | −284 | — | 0.74 | 1.02 | 239 | 238 | 102 | 0.34 | 0.42 | −237 | −252 | — |
| | | | NOK | | | | | NZD | | | | | SEK | | |
| RW | 0.53 | 0.74 | — | — | — | 0.53 | 0.75 | — | — | — | 0.54 | 0.74 | — | — | — |
| UIP | 0.50 | 0.80 | −28 | −20 | — | 0.45 | 0.67 | −123 | −111 | — | 0.52 | 0.77 | −21 | −14 | — |
| PPP | 0.65 | 0.92 | 121 | 126 | 37 | 0.77 | 1.03 | 270 | 268 | 45 | 0.61 | 0.85 | 70 | 73 | 22 |
| MF | 0.60 | 0.70 | 73 | 49 | 39 | 0.36 | 0.42 | −173 | −207 | — | 0.17 | 0.23 | −471 | −476 | — |
| TRs | 0.52 | 0.77 | −3 | 2 | — | 0.29 | 0.41 | −223 | −225 | — | 0.47 | 0.54 | −110 | −150 | — |
| TRa | 0.67 | 0.94 | 164 | 163 | 278 | 0.71 | 0.93 | 205 | 197 | 109 | 0.73 | 0.89 | 217 | 198 | 903 |

The table presents the in-sample and out-of-sample economic value of a set of empirical exchange rate models for alternative numeraires other than the US dollar. The set of currencies includes the Australian dollar (AUD), Canadian dollar (CAD), Swiss franc (CHF), Deutsche mark \ euro (EUR), British pound (GBP), Japanese yen (JPY), Norwegian kroner (NOK), New Zealand dollar (NZD), Swedish kronor (SEK), and the US dollar (USD). For example, AUD denotes an investment strategy using AUD as the domestic currency and expressing all exchange rates relative to AUD. We form exchange rate forecasts using six models: the random walk (RW), uncovered interest parity (UIP), purchasing power parity (PPP), monetary fundamentals (MF), symmetric Taylor rule ($TR_s$) and asymmetric Taylor rule ($TR_a$). Using the exchange rate forecasts from each model, we build a maximum expected return strategy subject to a target volatility $\sigma_p^* = 10\%$ for a US investor who every month dynamically rebalances her portfolio investing in a domestic US bond and nine foreign bonds. For each portfolio, we report the Sharpe ratio ($\mathcal{SR}$) and Sortino ratio ($\mathcal{SO}$). $\mathcal{F}$ denotes the performance fee a risk-averse investor is willing to pay for switching from the benchmark RW strategy to a competing strategy. $\mathcal{P}$ is the premium return performance measure. $\mathcal{F}$ and $\mathcal{P}$ are computed for a degree of relative risk aversion equal to 6 and are expressed in annual basis points. $\tau^{be}$ is the break-even proportional transaction cost that cancels out the utility advantage of a given strategy relative to the RW. $\tau^{be}$ is only reported for positive performance measures and is expressed in monthly basis points. The in-sample analysis covers monthly data from January 1976 to June 2010. The out-of-sample analysis runs from January 1986 to June 2010.

In addition to the results associated with individual models, even stronger economic evidence is found for the combined forecasts reported in Table 9.8. Inall cases, forecast combinations significantly outperform the RW model. In fact, the best performing model averaging strategies are those based on the $\mathcal{SR}$. For example, the $SR(\kappa = 12)$ strategy generates (i) $\mathcal{SR} = 0.76$ compared to the RW where $\mathcal{SR} = 0.54$ and (ii) $\mathcal{F} = 254$ annual bps with $\tau^{be} = 128$ monthly bps. It is noteworthy that the simple model average strategy using the mean forecast also generates a high $\mathcal{SR} = 0.74$ and $\mathcal{F} = 234$ bps. Another trend worth mentioning is that the degree of discounting ($\theta$) or the length of the most recently best period ($\kappa$) have little or no effect on the performance of combined forecasts. In short, therefore, there is clear OOS economic evidence on the superiority of combined forecasts relative to the RW benchmark that tends to be robust to the way combined forecasts are formed. Finally, Figure 8.1 compares the OOS Sharpe ratios for the three best performing individual models (UIP, PPP, and $TR_a$) and the $SR(\kappa = 60)$ forecast combination with that of the RW.

## 8.7 Conclusion

Thirty years of empirical research in international finance has attempted to resolve whether exchange rates are predictable. Most of this literature uses statistical criteria for OOS tests of the null of the RW representing no predictability against the alternative of linear models that depend on economic fundamentals. The results of these studies are specific to, among other things, the empirical model and the exchange rate series. The emerging literature has moved in a different direction by providing an economic evaluation of predictability. This second line of research takes the view of an investor who builds a dynamic asset allocation strategy that depends on the forecasts from a set of empirical exchange rate models. The results of these studies are also specific to the empirical model, but instead of providing results for one exchange rate at a time, they evaluate predictability by looking at the performance of dynamically rebalanced portfolios. Finally, there is a third strand of empirical work that forms ex-ante combined forecasts from a set of individual empirical models. The results of these studies are not particular to an empirical model but rather relate to forecast combinations that account for model uncertainty.

This chapter reviews and connects these three loosely related literatures. We illustrate the statistical and economic methodologies by estimating a set of widely used empirical exchange rate models using monthly returns from nine major USD exchange rates. In line with Campbell and Thompson (2008), we show that modest statistical significance can generate large economic benefits for investors with a dynamic FX portfolio strategy. We find three main results (i) empirical models based on UIP, PPP, and the $TR_a$ perform better than the random walk in OOS forecasting using both statistical and economic criteria; (ii) depending on MF or using a symmetric Taylor rule does not generate economic value OOS; and (iii) combined forecasts formed using a variety of model averaging methods perform better than individual empirical models. These results are robust to reasonably high transaction costs, the choice of numeraire, and the exclusion of any one currency from the investment opportunity set.

TABLE 8.8 **The Economic Value of Combined Forecasts**

| | $\mu$ | $\sigma$ | $\mathcal{SR}$ | $\mathcal{SO}$ | $\mathcal{F}$ | $\mathcal{P}$ | $\tau^{be}$ |
|---|---|---|---|---|---|---|---|
| RW | 10.8 | 11.4 | 0.54 | 0.73 | | | |
| | | *Simple Model Averaging* | | | | | |
| Mean | 13.3 | 11.6 | 0.74 | 0.89 | 234 | 206 | 81 |
| Median | 12.0 | 12.0 | 0.61 | 0.74 | 76 | 52 | 21 |
| Trimmed Mean | 12.0 | 12.1 | 0.60 | 0.72 | 65 | 37 | 23 |
| | | *Statistical Model Averaging* | | | | | |
| DMSE($\theta = 0.90$) | 13.2 | 11.7 | 0.72 | 0.87 | 213 | 186 | 71 |
| DMSE ($\theta = 0.95$) | 13.2 | 11.7 | 0.73 | 0.88 | 218 | 191 | 74 |
| DMSE($\theta = 1.00$) | 13.3 | 11.6 | 0.74 | 0.89 | 232 | 204 | 81 |
| MSE($\kappa = 60$) | 13.2 | 11.7 | 0.73 | 0.88 | 222 | 195 | 76 |
| MSE($\kappa = 36$) | 13.2 | 11.7 | 0.73 | 0.88 | 218 | 191 | 74 |
| MSE($\kappa = 12$) | 13.1 | 11.7 | 0.72 | 0.87 | 207 | 179 | 70 |
| | | *Economic Model Averaging* | | | | | |
| DSR($\theta = 0.90$) | 13.4 | 11.5 | 0.76 | 0.96 | 254 | 235 | 128 |
| DSR($\theta = 0.95$) | 13.4 | 11.5 | 0.76 | 0.95 | 255 | 236 | 127 |
| DSR($\theta = 1.00$) | 12.9 | 11.4 | 0.72 | 0.89 | 207 | 187 | 103 |
| SR($\kappa = 60$) | 13.5 | 11.5 | 0.76 | 0.96 | 261 | 241 | 129 |
| SR($\kappa = 36$) | 13.4 | 11.5 | 0.76 | 0.95 | 254 | 234 | 126 |
| SR($\kappa = 12$) | 13.4 | 11.5 | 0.76 | 0.96 | 254 | 235 | 128 |

The table presents the out-of-sample economic value of combined forecasts across a set of empirical exchange rate models. We form forecasts for the nine exchange rates using combinations of six models: the random walk (RW, uncovered interest parity (UIP), purchasing power parity (PPP), monetary fundamentals (MF), symmetric Taylor rule ($TR_s$), and asymmetric Taylor rule ($TR_a$). *Simple Model Averaging* denotes ex-ante combining methods that disregard the past out-of-sample performance of the individual models and use the mean, median, and trimmed mean of the individual forecasts. *Statistical Model Averaging* denotes ex-ante combining methods based on the past out-of-sample mean squared error (MSE) of the individual models. *DMSE*($\theta$) use the inverse of the discounted MSE with $\theta$ as a discount factor. *MSE*($\kappa$) use the inverse of the MSE over the most recent $\kappa$ months. *Economic Model Averaging* denote ex-ante combining methods that use the past out-of-sample Sharpe ratio ($\mathcal{SR}$) of the individual models. *DSR*($\theta$) use the discounted $\mathcal{SR}$ with $\theta$ as a discount factor. *SR*($\kappa$) uses the average $\mathcal{SR}$ over the most recent $\kappa$ months. Using the forecast combinations, we build a maximum expected return strategy subject to a target volatility $\sigma_p^* = 10\%$ for a US investor who every month dynamically rebalances her portfolio investing in a domestic US bond and nine foreign bonds. For each portfolio, we report the Sharpe ratio ($\mathcal{SR}$) and Sortino ratio ($\mathcal{SO}$). $\mathcal{F}$ denotes the performance fee a risk-averse investor is willing to pay for switching from the benchmark *RW* strategy to a competing strategy. $\mathcal{P}$ is the premium return performance measure. $\mathcal{F}$ and $\mathcal{P}$ are computed for a degree of relative risk aversion equal to 6 and are expressed in annual basis points. $\tau^{be}$ is the break-even proportional transaction cost that cancels out the utility advantage of a given strategy relative to the *RW*. $\tau^{be}$ is only reported for positive performance measures and is expressed in monthly basis points. The in-sample analysis covers monthly data from January 1976 to June 2010. The out-of-sample analysis runs from January 1986 to June 2010.

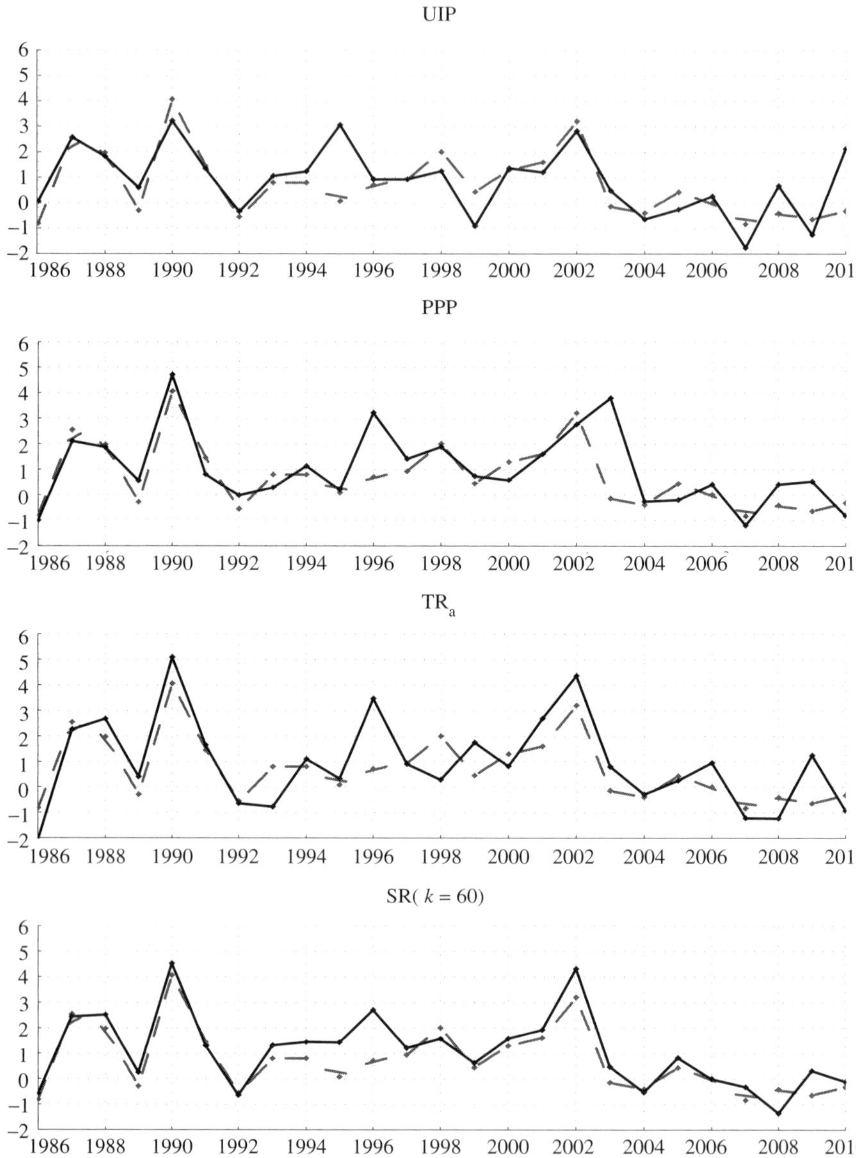


**FIGURE 8.1** Out-of-sample Sharpe ratios. The figure displays the out-of-sample annualized Sharpe ratio ($\mathcal{SR}$) for selected empirical exchange rate models. We show the results from forming exchange rate forecasts using uncovered interest parity (UIP), purchasing power parity (PPP), asymmetric Taylor rule ($TR_a$), and the ex-ante forecast combination method that uses the out-of-sample $\mathcal{SR}$ over the past 60 months ($SR(\kappa = 60)$). All models (solid line) are displayed versus the random walk (RW) benchmark (dashed line). Using the exchange rate forecasts from each model, we build a maximum expected return strategy subject to a target volatility $\sigma_p^* = 10\%$ for a US investor who every month dynamically rebalances her portfolio investing in a domestic US bond and nine foreign bonds. The $\mathcal{SR}$ is computed using the out-of-sample portfolio returns for one year. The out-of-sample period runs from January 1986 to June 2010.

## APPENDIX A: THE BOOTSTRAP ALGORITHM

This appendix summarizes the bootstrap algorithm we use for generating critical values for the OOS test statistics under the null of no exchange rate predictability against a one-sided alternative of linear predictability. Following Mark (1995) and Kilian (1999), the algorithm consists of the following steps:

1. Define the IS period for $\{\Delta s_{t+1}, x_t\}_{t=1}^{M}$ and the OOS period for $\{\Delta s_{t+1}, x_t\}_{t=M+1}^{T-1}$. We generate $P = (T-1) - M$ OOS forecasts $\{\Delta \bar{s}_{t+1|t}, \Delta \widehat{s}_{t+1|t}\}_{t=M+1}^{T-1}$ by estimating the predictive regression

$$\Delta s_{t+1} = \alpha + \beta x_t + \varepsilon_{t+1}$$

   and then computing the test statistic of interest, $\widehat{\tau}$.
2. Define the data generating process (DGP) as

$$\begin{aligned} \Delta s_{t+1} &= \alpha + \beta x_t + u_{1,t+1} \\ x_t &= \mu + \rho_1 x_{t-1} + \ldots + \rho_p x_{t-p} + u_{2,t}, \end{aligned}$$

   and estimate this model subject to the constraint that $\beta$ in the first equation is zero, using the full sample of observations $\{\Delta s_{t+1}, x_t\}_{t=1}^{T-1}$. The lag order $p$ in the second equation is determined by a suitable lag order selection criterion such as the Bayesian information criterion (BIC).
3. Generate a sequence of pseudo-observations $\{\Delta s_t^*, x_{t-1}^*\}_{t=1}^{T-1}$ as follows:

$$\begin{aligned} \Delta s_{t+1}^* &= \widehat{\alpha} + u_{1,t+1}^* \\ x_t^* &= \widehat{\mu} + \widehat{\rho}_1 x_{t-1}^* + \ldots + \widehat{\rho}_p x_{t-p}^* + u_{2,t}^*. \end{aligned}$$

   The pseudo-innovation term $u_t^* = (u_{1,t}^*, u_{2,t}^*)'$ is randomly drawn with replacement from the set of observed residuals $\widehat{u}_t = (\widehat{u}_{1,t}, \widehat{u}_{2,t})'$. The initial observations $\left(x_{t-1}^*, \ldots, x_{t-p}^*\right)'$ are randomly drawn from the actual data. Repeat this step $B = 10{,}000$ times.
4. For each of the $B$ bootstrap replications, define an IS period for $\{\Delta s_{t+1}^*, x_t^*\}_{t=1}^{M}$, and an OOS period for $\{\Delta s_{t+1}^*, x_t^*\}_{t=M+1}^{T-1}$. Then, generate $P$ OOS forecasts $\{\Delta \bar{s}_{t+1|t}^*, \Delta \widehat{s}_{t+1|t}^*\}_{t=M+1}^{T-1}$ by estimating the predictive regression

$$\Delta s_{t+1}^* = \alpha^* + \beta^* x_t^* + u_{1,t+1}^*$$

   both under the null and the alternative for $t = M+1, \ldots, T-1$, and construct the test statistic of interest, $\widehat{\tau}^*$.

**5.** Compute the one-sided $p$-value of $\widehat{\tau}$ as

$$p\text{-value} = \frac{1}{B}\sum_{j=1}^{B} I(\widehat{\tau}^{*} > \widehat{\tau}),$$

where $I(\cdot)$ denotes an indicator function, which is equal to 1 when its argument is true and 0 otherwise.

# Acknowledgments

The authors are grateful to Lucio Sarno and an anonymous referee for useful comments.

## REFERENCES

Abhyankar A, Sarno L, Valente G. Exchange rates and fundamentals: evidence on the economic value of predictability. J Int Econ 2005; 66: 325–348.

Akram F, Rime D, Sarno L. Arbitrage in the foreign exchange market: turning on the microscope. J Int Econ 2008; 76: 237–253.

Avramov D. Stock return predictability and model uncertainty. J Financ Econ 2002; 64: 423–458.

Bandi FM, Russell JR. Separating microstructure noise from volatility. J Financ Econ 2006; 79: 655–692.

Bandi FM, Russell JR, Zhu Y. Using high-frequency data in dynamic portfolio choice. Economet Rev 2008; 27: 163–198.

Bates JM, Granger CWJ. The combination of forecasts. Oper Res Q 1969; 20: 451–468.

Bilson JFO. The 'Speculative Efficiency' hypothesis. J Bus 1981; 54: 435–451.

Boudoukh J, Richardson M, Whitelaw RF. The information in long-maturity forward rates: implications for exchange rates and the forward premium anomaly. working paper, New York University; 2006.

Brunnermeier MK, Nagel S, Pedersen LH. Carry trades and currency crashes, NBER Macroeconomics Annual 2008; 2009. pp. 313–347.

Burnside C, Eichenbaum M, Kleshchelski I, Rebelo S. Do peso problems explain the returns to the carry trade? Rev Financ Stud 2011; 24: 853–891.

Campbell JY, Shiller RJ. Cointegration and tests of present value models. J Pol Econ 1987; 95: 1062–1088.

Campbell JY, Shiller RJ. Stock prices, earnings, and expected dividends. J Finance 1988; 43: 661–676.

Campbell JY, Thompson SB. Predicting excess stock returns out of sample: can anything beat the historical average? Rev Financ Stud 2008; 21: 1509–1531.

Cheung Y-W, Chinn MD, Pascual AG. Empirical exchange rate models of the nineties: are any fit to survive? J Int Money Finance 2005; 24: 1150–1175.

Clarida R, Gali J, Gertler M. Monetary policy rules in practice: some international evidence. Eur Econ Rev 1998; 42: 1033–1067.

Clarida RH, Sarno L, Taylor MP, Valente G. The out-of-sample success of term structure models as exchange rate predictors: a step beyond. J Int Econ 2003; 60: 61–83.

Clarida RH, Sarno L, Taylor MP, Valente G. The role of asymmetries and regime shifts in the term structure of interest rates. J Bus 2006; 79: 1193–1225.

Clark TE, McCracken MW. Tests of equal forecast accuracy and encompassing for nested models. J Economet 2001; 105: 85–110.

Clark TE, McCracken MW. Testing for unconditional predictive ability. In: Hendry D, Clements M, editors. Oxford handbook on economic forecasting. Oxford University Press; 2011. Forthcoming.

Clark TE, West KD. Using out-of-sample mean squared prediction errors to test the martingale difference hypothesis. J Economet 2006; 135: 155–186.

Clark TE, West KD. Approximately normal tests for equal predictive accuracy. J Economet 2007; 138: 291–311.

Cremers M. Stock return predictability: a bayesian model selection perspective. Rev Financ Stud 2002; 15: 1223–1249.

Della Corte P, Sarno L, Sestieri G. The predictive information content of external imbalances for exchange rate returns: how much is it worth? Rev Econ Stat 2012; 94: 100–115.

Della Corte P, Sarno L, Thornton DL. The expectation hypothesis of the term structure of very short-term rates: statistical tests and economic value. J Financ Econ 2008; 89: 158–174.

Della Corte P, Sarno L, Tsiakas I. An economic evaluation of empirical exchange rate models. Rev Financ Stud 2009; 22: 3491–3530.

Della Corte P, Sarno L, Tsiakas I. Spot and forward volatility in foreign exchange. J Financ Econ 2011; 100: 496–513.

Della Corte P, Sarno L, Tsiakas I. Volatility and correlation timing in active currency management. In: James J, Sarno L, Marsh IW, editors. Handbook of exchange rates. London: Wiley; 2012. Forthcoming.

Diebold FX, Mariano RS. Comparing predictive accuracy. J Bus Econ Stat 1995; 13: 253–263.

Engel C. The forward discount anomaly and the risk premium: a survey of recent evidence. J Empir Finance 1996; 3: 123–192.

Engel C, Mark NC, West KD. Exchange rate models are not as bad as you think. NBER Macroeconomics Annual 2007; 2007. pp. 381–441.

Engel C, West KD. Exchange rates and fundamentals. J Pol Econ 2005; 113: 485–517.

Evans MDD, Lyons RK. Order flow and exchange rate dynamics. J Pol Econ 2002; 110: 170–180.

Fama EF. Forward and spot exchange rates. J Monet Econ 1984; 14: 319–338.

Fleming J, Kirby C, Ostdiek B. The economic value of volatility timing. J Finance 2001; 56: 329–352.

Goetzmann W, Ingersoll J, Spiegel M, Welch I. Portfolio performance manipulation and manipulation-proof performance measures. Rev Financ Stud 2007; 20: 1503–1546.

Gomez V, Maravall A. Seasonal adjustment and signal extraction in economic time series. In: Pena D, Tiao GC, Tsay TR, editors. A course in time series analysis. New York: Wiley; 2000.

Gourinchas P-O, Rey H. International financial adjustment. J Pol Econ 2007; 115: 665–703.

Goyal A, Saretto A. Cross-section of option returns and volatility. J Financ Econ 2009; 94: 310–326.

Groen JJJ. The monetary exchange rate model as a long-run phenomenon. J Int Econ 2000; 52: 299–319.

Hai W, Mark NC, Wu Y. Understanding spot and forward exchange rate regressions. J Appl Economet 1997; 12: 715–734.

Han Y. Asset allocation with a high dimensional latent factor stochastic volatility model. Rev Financ Stud 2006; 19: 237–271.

Hodrick RJ. The empirical evidence on the efficiency of forward and futures foreign exchange markets. London: Harwood; 1987.

Hodrick RJ, Prescott EC. Postwar U.S. business cycles: an empirical investigation. J Money Credit Bank 1997; 29: 1–16.

Jondeau E, Rockinger M. Time-variability in higher moments is important for asset allocation. Unpublished Working paper, University of Lausanne; 2008.

Kilian L. Exchange rates and monetary fundamentals: what do we learn from long-horizon regressions? J Appl Economet 1999; 14: 491–510.

Lothian JR, Taylor MP. Real exchange rate behavior: the recent float from the perspective of the past two centuries. J Pol Econ 1996; 104: 488–509.

Mark NC. Exchange rates and fundamentals: evidence on long-horizon predictability. Am Econ Rev 1995; 85: 201–218.

Mark NC. Changing monetary policy rules, learning, and real exchange rate dynamics. J Money Credit Bank 2009; 41: 1047–1070.

Mark NC, Sul D. Nominal exchange rates and monetary fundamentals: evidence from a small post-bretton woods panel. J Int Econ 2001; 53: 29–52.

Marquering W, Verbeek M. The economic value of predicting stock index returns and volatility. J Financ Quant Anal 2004; 39: 407–429.

McCracken MW. Asymptotics for out of sample tests of granger causality. J Economet 2007; 140: 719–752.

Meese RA, Rogoff K. Empirical exchange rate models of the seventies: do they fit out of sample? J Int Econ 1983; 14: 3–24.

Molodtsova T, Papell DH. Out-of-sample exchange rate predictability with taylor rule fundamentals? J Int Econ 2009; 77: 167–180.

Neely CJ, Weller PA, Ulrich JM. The adaptive markets hypothesis: evidence from the foreign exchange market. J Financ Quant Anal 2009; 44: 467–488.

Nelson CR, Kim MJ. Predictable stock returns: the role of small sample bias. J Finance 1993; 48: 641–661.

Newey WK, West KD. A simple, positive semi-definite, heteroskedasticity and autocorrelation consistent covariance matrix. Econometrica 1987; 55: 703–708.

Orphanides A. Monetary policy rules based on real-time data. Am Econ Rev 2001; 91: 964–985.

Orphanides A, van Norden S. The unreliability of output gap estimates in real time. Rev Econ Stat 2002; 84: 569–583.

Rapach DE, Strauss JK, Zhou G. Out-of-sample equity premium prediction: combination forecasts and links to the real economy. Rev Financ Stud 2010; 23: 821–862.

Rime D, Sarno L, Sojli E. Exchange rate forecasting, order flow and macroeconomic information. J Int Econ 2010; 80: 72–88.

Rogoff KS. The purchasing power parity puzzle. J Econ Lit 1996; 34: 647–668.

Rogoff KS, Stavrakeva V. The continuing puzzle of short horizon exchange rate forecasting. NBER Working Paper No. 14071; 2008.

Sarno L. Towards a solution to the puzzles in exchange rate economics: where do we stand? Can J Econ 2005; 38: 673–708.

Sarno L, Sojli E. The feeble link between exchange rates and fundamentals: can we blame the discount factor? J Money Credit Bank 2009; 41: 437–442.

Stambaugh RF. Predictive regressions. J Financ Econ 1999; 54: 375–421.

Stock JH, Watson MW. Forecasting output and inflation: the role of asset prices. J Econ Lit 2003; 41: 788–829.

Stock JH, Watson MW. Combination forecasts of output growth in a seven-country data set. J Forecast 2004; 23: 405–430.

Taylor JB. Discretion versus policy rules in practice. Carnegie-Rochester Conf Ser Publ Policy 1993; 39: 195–214.

Taylor AM, Taylor MP. The purchasing power parity debate. J Econ Perspect 2004; 18: 135–158.

Timmermann A. Forecast combinations. In: Elliott G, Granger CWJ, Timmermann A, editors. Handbook of economic forecasting. Amsterdam: Elsevier; 2006.

Welch I, Goyal A. A comprehensive look at the empirical performance of equity premium prediction. Rev Financ Stud 2008; 21: 1455–1508.

West KD. Dividend innovations and stock price volatility. Econometrica 1988; 56: 37–61.

West KD. Asymptotic inference about predictive ability. Econometrica 1996; 64: 1067–1084.

West KD. Forecast evaluation. In: Elliott G, Granger CW, Timmermann A, editors. Volume 1, Handbook of economic forecasting. 2006. pp. 99–134. Chapter 3.

West KD, Edison HJ, Cho D. A utility-based comparison of some models of exchange rate volatility. J Int Econ 1993; 35: 23–45.

Wright JH. Bayesian model averaging and exchange rate forecasting. J Economet 2008; 146: 329–341.

CHAPTER NINE

# When Are Pooled Panel-Data Regression Forecasts of Exchange Rates More Accurate than the Time-Series Regression Forecasts?

**NELSON C. MARK**
Department of Economics, University of Notre Dame; NBER

**DONGGYU SUL**
University of Texas at Dallas

## 9.1 Introduction

Out-of-sample forecasts of exchange rates in the late 1990s and 2000s generated by time-series regression models have fared poorly. These forecasts are typically dominated (in mean-square error) by the driftless random walk. On the other hand, pooled regression models estimated on panel data (allowing for fixed effects) have, in many instances, performed much better than forecasts generated by time-series regression models. The superior predictive performance of the pooled panel data models is a puzzle because the evidence also reports of significant underlying model heterogeneity, in which case econometric theory tells us that pooling is inappropriate. Groen (2005), Rapach and Wohar (2004),

*Handbook of Exchange Rates*, First Edition. Edited by Jessica James, Ian W. Marsh, and Lucio Sarno.

Basher and Westerlund (2009) address the question about whether or not it is appropriate to pool. In this chapter, we ask when is it (under what conditions) that pooled regression forecasts generate more accurate exchange rate predictions than time-series regressions when the available econometric theory says that you should not pool.

The empirical literature on which we focus traces its origin to, and is motivated toward overturning the findings of Meese and Rogoff (1983), who in studying floating exchange rates in the post Bretton Woods era, demonstrated that the driftless random walk model dominated economic theory-based econometric models (e.g., purchasing-power parity models or simple monetary models) in out-of-sample forecast accuracy. Using time-series regression models, Mark (1995) and Chinn and Meese (1995) were able to overturn Meese and Rogoff (1983) by examination of long-horizon forecasts with error-correction models. The success of these papers was only temporary, however, because it was found that as time passed and more recent data from the 1990s and the 2000s were added to the time-series, the earlier findings of predictability became insignificant (Cheung et al., 2005; Faust et al., 2003; Groen, 1999). At the same time, other research (Lothian and Taylor, 1996; Rapach and Wohar, 2002) added observations to the front-end of the sample by constructing long historical time-series spanning over a 100 years or more. These studies found that simple monetary models and purchasing power-parity-based models have significant predictive ability. These papers are notable because their findings suggest that the inability to predict exchange rates with time-series regression models is a small-sample issue. The long time-span studies can be criticized, however, because they employed data that spanned across both fixed and flexible exchange rate regimes, but they did not control for regime changes. The interpretation of the ability to predict out-of-sample based on a forecasting model estimated across different regimes is not entirely obvious.

One reaction to this state of affairs was to restrict attention to the post Bretton Woods float and to increase sample size in the cross-sectional dimension and exploiting panel data, as in Cerra and Saxena (2010), Groen (2005), Mark and Sul (2001), and Ince (2010). These studies found that forecasts built from pooled regression models estimated on panel data dominate those of time-series regression forecasts and random walk forecasts in mean square.[1] However, the data also tell us that there is significant heterogeneity across countries in the coefficients of the forecasting equation. Econometric theory instructs us in this case that one should not pool. But allowing for heterogeneous constants and slopes would generate little advantage over time-series regression, except to the extent that you could exploit correlated errors and do seemingly unrelated regression. Pooling when there is slope coefficient heterogeneity appears to

[1] Groen (2000) and Husted and MacDonald (1998) exploit panel data to test restrictions implied by the monetary model and find the evidence for the monetary model to be much stronger using panel data, but these papers do not engage in out-of-sample prediction. Rogoff and Stavrakeva (2008) find that panel data models with time dummies do not produce robust forecasting results.

commit, in the cross-sectional dimension, the same sort of error that failure to account for regime changes does in the time-series context.

The next section describes the methodology employed in the panel data exchange rate forecasting literature. In Section 9.3, we discuss the econometric theory that gives us some guidance in seeing the consequences from pooling when there is underlying heterogeneity. Section 9.4 contains a small Monte Carlo study that illustrates some of the ideas and predictions from the econometric theory. Section 9.5 is an application to data and Section 9.6 concludes.

## 9.2 Panel Data Exchange Rate Determination Studies

In a data set of $N$ countries indexed by $i \in [1, N]$ and $T$ time-series observations indexed by $t \in [1, T]$, let $x_{it}$ be a (scalar) prediction variable for $s_{i,t+k}$, the log-exchange rate for country $i$. Mark and Sul (2001) and Cerra and Saxena (2010) investigate the empirical link between the monetary model fundamentals and the exchange rate. They set $x_{i,t}$ to be the deviation of today's exchange rate $s_{i,t}$ from the long-run equilibrium value predicted by economic theory. In the case of the monetary model, $x_{i,t} = f_{i,t} - s_{i,t}$, where $f_{i,t} = (m_{i,t} - m_{0,t}) - \lambda(y_{i,t} - y_{0,t})$, country "0" is the base country, $m$ is the log-money stock, and $y$ is log-real income. They used the panel exchange rate predictive regression

$$s_{i,t+k} - s_{it} = \beta x_{it} + \eta_{i,t+k}$$

where $\eta_{i,t+k} = \gamma_i + \theta_{t+k} + \varepsilon_{i,t+k}$ has an error-component representation with individual (fixed) effect $\gamma_i$, common time effect $\theta_t$, and idiosyncratic effect $\varepsilon_{i,t+k}$. Rapach and Wohar (2004) reject the null hypothesis of slope coefficient homogeneity at the one-percent level using Mark and Sul's data set.

Groen (2005) uses a four-country panel and pools a vector error-correction model (VECM). Letting $X_{i,t} = (s_{i,t}, (m_{i,t} - m_{0,t}), (y_{i,t} - y_{0,t}))'$ and $Z_{i,t-1} = (X'_{i,t-1}, 1)'$, the model he works with is

$$\Delta X_{i,t} = \alpha \left(1, -1, \phi, c_i\right) Z_{i,t-1} + \sum_{j=1}^{p} \Gamma_{i,j} \Delta X_{i,t-j} + \varepsilon_{i,t}$$

where $(1, -1, \phi)$ is the common cointegrating vector and $c_i$ is the regression constant. He finds that out-of-sample forecasts with the pooled VECM, beat the random walk and the unpooled (individual country) VECM forecasts.

In addition to forecasting studies, panel data has been used extensively in exchange rate research. Beginning with Frankel and Rose (1996), many studies have employed panel data to study long-run purchasing power parity (Choi et al., 2006; Papell, 2006; Papell and Theodoridis, 1998, 2001), and cointegrating restrictions imposed by monetary models (Groen, 2000; Husted and MacDonald, 1998; Rogoff and Stavrakeva 2008). To the extent to which these papers pooled in the presence of cross-sectional heterogeneity, our comments may also have applicability.

Engel et al. (2009) and Mark and West (2010) employ factor models to predict the exchange rate. This is another use of panel data, but this sort of work is the topic of a separate paper.

## 9.3 Asymptotic Consequences of Pooling

Let $y_{i,t+k} = s_{i,t+k} - s_{i,t}$, where $s_{i,t}$ is the exchange rate between country $i$ and the base country, in logarithms. Suppose that economic theory suggests to us that $x_{it}$ contains predictive information for future $s_{i,t}$. For example, we might think that the real exchange rate is mean reverting. In this case, we might let $x_{it}$ be the deviation from purchasing-power parity if we thought that the nominal exchange rate chases the relative price differential after a shock. Alternatively, we might let $x_{it}$ be the deviation of $s_{it}$ from a long-run specification of the equilibrium exchange rate. Simple monetary models suggest using some linear combination of the logarithm of country $i$'s money stocks, interest rates, and real GDP relative to those of the base country. Macroeconomic panel data sets typically have $T > N$. The existence of predictive ability has been investigated in 2 ways. The preferred method in the finance literature is to estimate a predictive regression for asset returns—that is, a regression of future returns on currently observed data—and drawing inference on the slope coefficients using the full data set (Daniel, 2001; Fama and French, 1988; Stambaugh, 1999). The preferred method in research on exchange rates has been to employ out-of-sample prediction procedures and to examine the properties of the prediction errors.

### 9.3.1 PREDICTIVE REGRESSION ESTIMATED ON FULL SAMPLE

Suppose that the truth is

$$y_{i,t+1} = \beta x_{it} + \varepsilon_{i,t+1} \tag{9.1}$$

where $\varepsilon_t = (\varepsilon_{1,t}, \ldots, \varepsilon_{N,t}) \overset{\text{iid}}{\sim} (0, \sigma_\varepsilon^2)$. This is the case where the slope is identical across countries. In practice, one always includes a (possibly heterogeneous) constant in the regression, but we will ignore it in the exposition. This is a predictive regression in the sense that future changes in the exchange rate are projected onto current values of $x_{it}$. We will assume that this is a well-behaved regression. This will be true if $x_{it}$ is econometrically exogenous. If this assumption seems too strong, one may assume that an appropriate bias correction method is applied. The asymptotic results that we discuss will not be affected if this is the case. The existence of predictive ability can be tested by estimating the predictive Equation 1 in the full sample ($i = 1, \ldots, N, t = 1, \ldots, T$) and doing a $t$-test of the null hypothesis $H_0 : \beta = 0$ against the alternative $H_A : \beta \neq 0$.

Asymptotic distribution theory tells us that there are advantages to pooling if the truth is given by Equation 1. An easy way to see this is by looking at the convergence rate of the pooled least-squares estimator,

$$\sqrt{NT}(\hat{\beta} - \beta) \xrightarrow{d} N(0, \sigma_{\varepsilon}^2 Q^{-1}) \tag{9.2}$$

where $Q = \text{plim}\left((NT)^{-1}\sum_i \sum_t x_{it}^2\right)$. Thus, the pooled estimator converges in distribution at the rate $\sqrt{NT}$, whereas the least-squares estimator for the time-series regression (not pooled) converges at rate $\sqrt{T}$. This suggests that asymptotically, there is an informational advantage to be gained by expanding the available observations in the cross-sectional dimension when the slopes are identical across $i$.

Now, to compare to the case where there is underlying heterogeneity in the regression slopes, let the truth be

$$y_{i,t+1} = \beta_i x_{i,t} + \varepsilon_{i,t+1} \tag{9.3}$$

$$\beta_i \overset{\text{iid}}{\sim} \left(\beta, \sigma_{\beta}^2\right) \tag{9.4}$$

Equation (13.2.4) characterizes the underlying heterogeneity of the slopes. Evidence of underlying heterogeneity in the slope coefficients across individuals has been reported by Groen (2005); Rapach and Wohar (2004), and Basher and Westerlund (2010). Pooling in the presence of heterogeneous slopes distorts the error term $u_{i,t+1}$ in

$$y_{i,t+1} = \beta x_{it} + u_{i,t+1}$$

$$u_{i,t+1} = \left(\beta_i - \beta\right) x_{it} + \varepsilon_{i,t+1}$$

As a result of this distortion, the asymptotic distribution of the pooled estimator is

$$\sqrt{NT}\left(\hat{\beta} - \beta\right) \xrightarrow{d} N\left(0, \left(\omega^2 Q^{-1} + \sigma_{\varepsilon}^2 Q^{-1}\right)\right) \tag{9.5}$$

where $\omega^2$ and $\sigma_{\varepsilon}^2$ are the asymptotic variances of $\left(\frac{1}{\sqrt{NT}}\sum_{i=1}^{N}\sum_{t=1}^{T}\left(\beta_i - \beta\right) x_{it}^2\right)$ and $\left(\frac{1}{\sqrt{NT}}\sum_{i=1}^{N}\sum_{t=1}^{T}\varepsilon_{i,t+1}\right)$, respectively.

To discuss the pros and cons of pooling, we compare the asymptotic distribution of the time-series regression (OLS) estimator with the pooled regression estimator. Under the null hypothesis of no predictability, $(\beta_i = \beta = 0)$, let us rewrite the asymptotic distribution of the pooled estimator (Eq. 5)) as

$$\sqrt{T}\left(\hat{\beta} - 0\right) \xrightarrow{d} N\left(0, \frac{\omega^2 Q^{-1} + \sigma_{\varepsilon}^2 Q^{-1}}{N}\right) \tag{9.6}$$

The asymptotic distribution of the OLS estimator in the time-series case is, of course,

$$\sqrt{T}\left(\hat{\beta}_i - 0\right) \xrightarrow{d} N\left(0, \sigma_\varepsilon^2 Q^{-1}\right) \tag{9.7}$$

Now, comparing Equations 6 and 7, we see that the asymptotic variance of the pooled regression can easily be smaller than that of the time-series regression estimator because of the $N$ in the denominator. This suggests that under the null hypothesis, the test of the null may be better sized than the pooled regression. This is only a suggestion, however, because in practice there may be many nuisance parameter issues such as cross-sectional and serial dependencies that need to be dealt with and these complications can substantially distort the size of the test. These complications are assumed away here.

An alternative way to see potential advantages from pooling in the presence of slope heterogeneity is through an analysis of local alternative power. Let the sequence of local alternatives be given by

$$\beta_i = \frac{c_i}{\sqrt{T}}, \quad \beta_N = \frac{b}{\sqrt{T}}$$

where $b = \frac{1}{N}\sum_{i=1}^{N} c_i = O(1)$. Here, we consider only the time $T$ dimension under the local alternative in order to compare the power of the test between by pooling and not pooling. Under these circumstances, the estimators in the time-series regression and the pooled regression have the (respective) asymptotic distributions,

$$\frac{\sqrt{T}\left(\hat{\beta}_i - 0\right)}{\sqrt{\sigma_\varepsilon^2 Q^{-1}}} \xrightarrow{d} N\left(\frac{c_i}{\sqrt{\sigma_\varepsilon^2 Q^{-1}}}, 1\right) \tag{9.8}$$

$$\frac{\sqrt{NT}\left(\hat{\beta} - 0\right)}{\sqrt{\Omega}} \xrightarrow{d} N\left(\frac{b}{\sqrt{\Omega}}N, 1\right) \tag{9.9}$$

where $\Omega = \omega^2 Q^{-1} + \sigma_\varepsilon^2 Q^{-1}$. Hence the pooled test is potentially more powerful with even a moderately large $N$ because the local alternative parameter is $bN/\sqrt{\Omega}$. This means as $N$ increases, the alternative moves farther away from the null, which increases the power of the test.

To summarize, if the goal is to test for predictive power, it might make sense to pool whether or not one believes that there is underlying heterogeneity in the slope coefficients. However, this is not to say that one can obtain more accurate forecasts using the pooled prediction equation. We are saying only that the test of the null hypothesis of no predictability can be easier to reject. There are a different set of issues involved in whether or not the pooled forecasts are actually more accurate. We now turn to an analysis of this topic.

### 9.3.2 OUT-OF-SAMPLE PREDICTION

In the exchange rate literature, it is common to assess predictive ability with an analysis of out-of-sample forecasts. We let the full sample size in the time dimension be $T = S + P$. The model is estimated on the sample $t \in [1, S]$ and the observations $t \in [S + 1, S + P]$ are reserved for assessing forecast accuracy. The asymptotic results discussed below assume that $S, P \to \infty$ so that the full sample size $S + P$ increases faster than the portion of the sample used for estimation. The standard practice is to generate the $P$ forecasts with recursively updated model estimates or with models estimated on a rolling sample. To simplify the exposition in this section, we assume that the model is estimated once on the first $S$ observations. However, the empirical work that follows below is done with rolling regressions. While doing so is a bit sloppy, it is innocuous in terms of the asymptotic theory because as $S \to \infty$, the recursive and rolling estimators have the same asymptotic distribution.

Again, let us assume that the truth is given by Equation 1 in which there is no underlying heterogeneity in the slopes and one uses the sample $t \in [1, S]$ to estimate the predictive equation by pooled regression. Let $\hat{\beta}_{NS}$ and $\hat{\beta}_S$ be the pooled and time-series estimators of the slope and $\hat{y}_{i,j}^{\text{pool}} = \hat{\beta}_{NS} x_{i,j}$, $\hat{y}_{i,j}^{\text{time}} = \hat{\beta}_S x_{i,j}$, $j \in [S + 1, S + P]$ be the predictors. Then as $N, S \to \infty$, the forecast errors have the representation

$$\hat{y}_{i,j+1}^{\text{pool}} - y_{i,j+1} = \left(\hat{\beta}_{NS} - \beta\right) x_{i,j} + \varepsilon_{i,j+1} = \varepsilon_{i,j+1} + O_p\left(\frac{1}{\sqrt{NS}}\right)$$

$$\hat{y}_{i,j+1}^{\text{time}} - y_{i,j+1} = \left(\hat{\beta}_{S} - \beta\right) x_{i,j} + \varepsilon_{i,j+1} = \varepsilon_{i,j+1} + O_p\left(\frac{1}{\sqrt{S}}\right)$$

Hence, we have that the pooled forecast should always be more accurate than the time-series forecast in the finite sample. Asymptotically, however, makes no difference whether one pools or not, because there is no difference in forecast accuracy between pooled and unpooled.[2]

Next, let us assume that the slope coefficients vary across countries and the truth is given by Equations 3 and 4. The prediction errors from the pooled regression forecast are now

$$\hat{y}_{i,j+1}^{\text{pool}} - y_{i,j+1} = \left(\hat{\beta}_{NS} - \beta_i\right) x_{i,j} + \varepsilon_{i,j+1}$$

whereas the time-series forecast errors are

$$\hat{y}_{i,j+1}^{\text{time}} - y_{i,j+1} = \left(\hat{\beta}_{iS} - \beta_i\right) x_{i,j} + \varepsilon_{i,j+1}$$

[2]As $S \to \infty$ regardless size of $N$,

$$\text{plim}_{S,P\to\infty} \frac{1}{P} \sum_{t=S+1}^{S+P} \left(\hat{y}_{i,j+1}^{\text{pool}} - y_{i,j+1}\right)^2 = \text{plim}_{S,P\to\infty} \frac{1}{P} \sum_{t=S+1}^{S+P} \left(\hat{y}_{i,j+1}^{\text{time}} - y_{i,j+1}\right)^2 = \sigma_\varepsilon^2.$$

Asymptotically,

$$\text{plim}_{N,S,P\to\infty}\frac{1}{P}\sum_{t=S+1}^{S+P}\left(\hat{y}_{i,j+1}^{\text{pool}}-y_{i,j+1}\right)^2=\sigma_\varepsilon^2+\sigma_x^2\sigma_\beta^2>$$

$$\sigma_\varepsilon^2=\text{plim}_{S,P\to\infty}\frac{1}{P}\sum_{t=S+1}^{S+P}\left(\hat{y}_{i,j+1}^{\text{time}}-y_{i,j+1}\right)^2$$

Asymptotically, therefore, pooling in the presence of underlying slope heterogeneity must lead to less accurate predictions.

The question here is why do researchers often obtain lower mean-square prediction errors (MSPE) from pooled regression forecasts even when slope heterogeneity is present? At a general level, the reason is that guidance on whether to pool or not is based on asymptotic theory that may be inaccurate in any finite sample. To see why this may be the case, we get a clue by examining the difference in the squared prediction errors from the pooled and time-series regressions when there is underlying heterogeneity in the slopes. For any finite $S$ and $P$, as $N\to\infty$, this difference is

$$\begin{aligned}&\left(\hat{y}_{i,j+1}^{\text{pool}}-y_{i,j+1}\right)^2-\left(\hat{y}_{i,j+1}^{\text{time}}-y_{i,j+1}\right)^2\\&=\left[\left(\hat{\beta}_{NS}-\beta_i\right)^2-\left(\hat{\beta}_{iS}-\beta_i\right)^2\right]x_{i,j}^2+o_p(1).\end{aligned}\tag{9.10}$$

Thus, in any finite sample, it is possible for $\left(\hat{\beta}_{NS}-\beta_i\right)^2<\left(\hat{\beta}_{iS}-\beta_i\right)^2$, in which case the pooled predictor will perform better. This is most likely the case when the underlying dispersion in the slope coefficients is not too large.

Probing deeper, however, we can see that for each $i$, the relative forecasting performance depends on two parts: the distance of the pooled estimates $\hat{\beta}_{NS}$ from the unknown true value of $\beta_i$ and the distance between the time-series estimates $\hat{\beta}_{iS}$ and the true value. In practice, with a large $N$ but relatively small $S$, the pooled estimates are robust and do not move around much as the time-series estimates, as the length of the sample changes since its variance of $\hat{\beta}_{NS}$ is $O_p\left(N^{-1}S^{-1}\right)$. Meanwhile, the time-series estimates do tend to move around as $S$ increases because the variance of $\hat{\beta}_{iS}$ is $O_p\left(S^{-1}\right)$. Now, if the pooled estimate is sufficiently stable so that we can treat it as if it is constant, then the relative forecasting performance will primarily depend on the variability of the time-series estimator. In the next section, we explore these ideas further with a small Monte Carlo study.

## 9.4 Monte Carlo Study

In our data-generating process (DGP), the cross-sectional dimension is $N=10$, and the time-series dimension varies from $S+P=100$ to 400. For each time-series length, estimation is performed over half of the sample and prediction over the second half so that $S = P$.

For example, the smallest sample size that we consider is of length 100. The first 50 observations are used to estimate the prediction model and the second 50 are reserved for forecast evaluation.

The DGP for our Monte Carlo work is as follows:

$$y_{i,t+1} = \beta_i x_{it} + \varepsilon_{i,t+1}$$
$$x_{it} \overset{\text{iid}}{\sim} N(0,1)$$
$$\varepsilon_{it} \overset{\text{iid}}{\sim} N(0,1)$$

In terms of the slope heterogeneity, we consider the following three cases for assignment of the slope coefficients:

| $\beta_i$ Assignment | | | |
|---|---|---|---|
| Cross-Sectional Unit | Case 1 | Case 2 | Case 3 |
| 1 | 0.05 | 0.05 | 0.05 |
| 2 | 0.06 | 0.10 | 0.15 |
| 3 | 0.07 | 0.15 | 0.25 |
| 4 | 0.08 | 0.20 | 0.35 |
| 5 | 0.09 | 0.25 | 0.45 |
| 6 | 0.10 | 0.30 | 0.55 |
| 7 | 0.11 | 0.35 | 0.65 |
| 8 | 0.12 | 0.40 | 0.75 |
| 9 | 0.13 | 0.45 | 0.85 |
| 10 | 0.14 | 0.50 | 0.95 |

For each experiment, 2000 replications are performed. We compute the MSPE from the pooled regression forecasts, the time-series regression forecast, and the driftless random walk forecast. Our discussion is limited to these point estimates. Inference issues, while very important, are addressed in a separate chapter of this book (Della Corte and Tsiakas, 2010).[3]

Table 9.1 shows the MSPE comparison between the pooled and time-series forecasts. Bold entries indicate instances in which the MSPE of the pooled forecasts dominate those of the time-series forecasts. We observe two very striking features that corroborate the implications of the asymptotic analysis

[3]The iid assumption for $x_{it}$ is innocuous because the relative forecasting performance expressed in ratios does not depend on $x_{i,j}^2$. With a highly serially correlated regressor, the asymptotic results do not change, but in finite samples, the relative dispersion of $\hat{\beta}_{iT}$ to $\hat{\beta}_{NT}$ may increase with the degrees of serial correlation. If this is the case, the Monte Carlo results may show overly favorable results for the pooled forecasts.

**TABLE 9.1** $\mathbf{MSPE_{pool}/\ MSPE_{time}}$

| $P = S$ | $i = 1$ | $i = 2$ | $i = 3$ | $i = 4$ | $i = 5$ | $i = 6$ | $i = 7$ | $i = 8$ | $i = 0$ | $i = 10$ |
|---|---|---|---|---|---|---|---|---|---|---|
| | | | | | Case 1: $\beta = (0.05, 0.06, \ldots, 0.14)$ | | | | | |
| 50 | **0.990** | **0.989** | **0.989** | **0.987** | **0.987** | **0.988** | **0.989** | **0.988** | **0.990** | **0.989** |
| 60 | **0.992** | **0.990** | **0.991** | **0.990** | **0.989** | **0.990** | **0.990** | **0.990** | **0.991** | **0.992** |
| 70 | **0.993** | **0.993** | **0.993** | **0.991** | **0.991** | **0.992** | **0.991** | **0.992** | **0.993** | **0.993** |
| 100 | **0.996** | **0.995** | **0.994** | **0.994** | **0.994** | **0.994** | **0.994** | **0.994** | **0.995** | **0.995** |
| 200 | **0.999** | **0.998** | **0.997** | **0.997** | **0.997** | **0.997** | **0.997** | **0.997** | **0.998** | **0.999** |
| | | | | | Case 2: $\beta = (0.05, 0.10, \ldots, 0.50)$ | | | | | |
| 50 | 1.041 | 1.018 | 1.003 | **0.994** | **0.988** | **0.989** | **0.993** | 1.003 | 1.020 | 1.040 |
| 60 | 1.044 | 1.021 | 1.005 | **0.994** | **0.991** | **0.990** | **0.996** | 1.006 | 1.022 | 1.043 |
| 70 | 1.041 | 1.024 | 1.006 | **0.998** | **0.992** | **0.992** | **0.997** | 1.008 | 1.022 | 1.044 |
| 100 | 1.046 | 1.025 | 1.010 | 1.000 | **0.994** | **0.995** | 1.000 | 1.010 | 1.026 | 1.045 |
| 200 | 1.047 | 1.028 | 1.012 | 1.002 | **0.998** | **0.998** | 1.003 | 1.012 | 1.028 | 1.049 |
| | | | | | Case 3: $\beta = (0.05, 0.15, \ldots, 0.95)$ | | | | | |
| 50 | 1.199 | 1.115 | 1.053 | 1.009 | **0.991** | **0.990** | 1.009 | 1.050 | 1.114 | 1.193 |
| 60 | 1.192 | 1.116 | 1.053 | 1.014 | **0.993** | **0.993** | 1.011 | 1.056 | 1.116 | 1.195 |
| 70 | 1.195 | 1.112 | 1.055 | 1.014 | **0.994** | **0.994** | 1.013 | 1.056 | 1.116 | 1.198 |
| 100 | 1.201 | 1.117 | 1.057 | 1.017 | **0.996** | **0.997** | 1.017 | 1.056 | 1.116 | 1.200 |
| 200 | 1.201 | 1.119 | 1.060 | 1.020 | **0.999** | 1.000 | 1.021 | 1.061 | 1.120 | 1.200 |

in the previous section. The pooled forecasts tend to dominate the time-series forecasts when (i) the sample size is small in the time dimension and (ii) when the slope heterogeneity across individuals is not too large (i.e., Case 1 as opposed to Case 3).

Table 9.2 reports the MSPE of the time-series regression forecasts relative to the driftless random walk. Beginning with the work of Meese and Rogoff (1983), the random walk has been the standard benchmark against which econometric forecasts are judged in the empirical exchange rate literature. The message from Table 9.2 is that the alternative has to be fairly far away from the null ($\beta_i$ has to be fairly sizable) before predictions from the time-series regression model can beat the random walk, even in sample sizes as large as 200. Typically, in exchange rate research, we have access to short-time series and slope coefficient estimates tend to be small in magnitude.

In Table 9.3, the MSPE of the pooled forecasts are compared to those of the random walk. Again, the pooled forecast will generally perform well relative to the random walk when the underlying model heterogeneity is small and when the time series is short. Notice Case 3. When there is substantial heterogeneity in the slope coefficients, the pooled forecasts dominate the random walk in cases far from the null (large $\beta_i$) and are beaten badly when the $\beta_i$ are small.

TABLE 9.2 $\mathbf{MSPE_{time}/MSPE_{r.w}}$

| $P=S$ | $i=1$ | $i=2$ | $i=3$ | $i=4$ | $i=5$ | $i=6$ | $i=7$ | $i=8$ | $i=9$ | $i=10$ |
|---|---|---|---|---|---|---|---|---|---|---|
| | | | | | Case 1: $\beta=(0.05, 0.06, \ldots, 0.14)$ | | | | | |
| 50 | 1.012 | 1.011 | 1.010 | 1.009 | 1.007 | 1.005 | 1.001 | 1.001 | **0.999** | **0.997** |
| 60 | 1.010 | 1.010 | 1.009 | 1.004 | 1.005 | 1.002 | 1.000 | **0.999** | **0.996** | **0.992** |
| 70 | 1.008 | 1.008 | 1.005 | 1.004 | 1.004 | 1.000 | **0.998** | **0.996** | **0.993** | **0.992** |
| 100 | 1.005 | 1.004 | 1.002 | 1.000 | 1.000 | **0.998** | **0.995** | **0.993** | **0.992** | **0.989** |
| 200 | 1.001 | 1.000 | **0.999** | **0.997** | **0.996** | **0.994** | **0.992** | **0.989** | **0.988** | **0.984** |
| | | | | | Case 2: $\beta=(0.05, 0.10, \ldots, 0.50)$ | | | | | |
| 50 | 1.012 | 1.006 | **0.994** | **0.977** | **0.958** | **0.932** | **0.908** | **0.879** | **0.848** | **0.817** |
| 60 | 1.009 | 1.003 | **0.991** | **0.972** | **0.957** | **0.931** | **0.903** | **0.877** | **0.844** | **0.814** |
| 70 | 1.008 | 1.001 | **0.987** | **0.973** | **0.954** | **0.930** | **0.903** | **0.873** | **0.845** | **0.812** |
| 100 | 1.005 | **0.998** | **0.985** | **0.970** | **0.949** | **0.925** | **0.897** | **0.870** | **0.838** | **0.808** |
| 200 | 1.001 | **0.994** | **0.981** | **0.965** | **0.948** | **0.920** | **0.893** | **0.867** | **0.835** | **0.802** |
| | | | | | Case 3: $\beta=(0.05, 0.15, \ldots, 0.95)$ | | | | | |
| 50 | 1.012 | **0.992** | **0.957** | **0.906** | **0.852** | **0.787** | **0.726** | **0.660** | **0.597** | **0.545** |
| 60 | 1.009 | **0.991** | **0.953** | **0.906** | **0.850** | **0.784** | **0.724** | **0.652** | **0.595** | **0.543** |
| 70 | 1.007 | **0.988** | **0.951** | **0.901** | **0.845** | **0.781** | **0.719** | **0.651** | **0.594** | **0.538** |
| 100 | 1.004 | **0.986** | **0.948** | **0.898** | **0.841** | **0.775** | **0.711** | **0.651** | **0.589** | **0.534** |
| 200 | 1.001 | **0.982** | **0.945** | **0.895** | **0.835** | **0.771** | **0.706** | **0.643** | **0.586** | **0.530** |

## 9.5 An Illustration with Data

In this section, we illustrate these ideas using data for US dollar exchange rates against the currencies of Australia, Canada, Chile, Colombia, the Czech Republic, Denmark, Hungary, Israel, South Korea, Norway, New Zealand, the Philippines, the Russian Federation, Singapore, South Africa, Sweden, Taiwan, the United Kingdom, Japan, Switzerland, and the Euro Area. The dimensions of the data set are $N = 21$, $S + P = 132$. We are using monthly observations that extend from January 1999 through January 2010 obtained from Global Insights.[4] Initially, we use observations from January 1999 through December 2003 to estimate the prediction model and to form forecasts at horizons of 1–24 months ahead. We then recursively update the sample and repeat the estimation and forecast generation. Relative forecast accuracy is measured by Theil's U-Statistic, which is the ratio of the RMPSE (root mean prediction square error) of a particular model to that of the driftless random walk.

[4]For New Zealand and Australia, quarterly CPI is interpolated into monthly. The fundamentals for the euro are an aggregation of variables in the euro zone.

TABLE 9.3 $\mathbf{MSPE_{pool}/MSPE_{r.w}}$

| $P=S$ | $i=1$ | $i=2$ | $i=3$ | $i=4$ | $i=5$ | $i=6$ | $i=7$ | $i=8$ | $i=9$ | $i=10$ |
|---|---|---|---|---|---|---|---|---|---|---|
| | | | | Case 1: $\beta=(0.05,0.06,\ldots,0.14)$ | | | | | | |
| 50 | 1.001 | **0.999** | **0.997** | **0.996** | **0.993** | **0.992** | **0.988** | **0.988** | **0.987** | **0.985** |
| 60 | 1.001 | **0.999** | 1.000 | **0.994** | **0.993** | **0.991** | **0.990** | **0.988** | **0.986** | **0.984** |
| 70 | 1.001 | 1.000 | **0.997** | **0.995** | **0.994** | **0.991** | **0.989** | **0.987** | **0.986** | **0.984** |
| 100 | 1.001 | **0.999** | **0.996** | **0.995** | **0.993** | **0.991** | **0.989** | **0.987** | **0.986** | **0.984** |
| 200 | 1.000 | **0.998** | **0.996** | **0.994** | **0.992** | **0.991** | **0.989** | **0.987** | **0.985** | **0.983** |
| | | | | Case 2: $\beta=(0.05,0.10,\ldots,0.50)$ | | | | | | |
| 50 | 1.053 | 1.024 | **0.998** | **0.971** | **0.946** | **0.920** | **0.900** | **0.878** | **0.860** | **0.843** |
| 60 | 1.054 | 1.025 | **0.996** | **0.966** | **0.948** | **0.921** | **0.897** | **0.879** | **0.859** | **0.844** |
| 70 | 1.050 | 1.025 | **0.994** | **0.972** | **0.947** | **0.922** | **0.899** | **0.877** | **0.860** | **0.843** |
| 100 | 1.051 | 1.023 | **0.996** | **0.970** | **0.944** | **0.919** | **0.896** | **0.877** | **0.857** | **0.842** |
| 200 | 1.048 | 1.022 | **0.994** | **0.968** | **0.946** | **0.918** | **0.895** | **0.877** | **0.858** | **0.840** |
| | | | | Case 3: $\beta=(0.05,0.15,\ldots,0.95)$ | | | | | | |
| 50 | 1.215 | 1.109 | 1.012 | **0.917** | **0.844** | **0.778** | **0.728** | **0.686** | **0.655** | **0.637** |
| 60 | 1.204 | 1.108 | 1.007 | **0.921** | **0.845** | **0.777** | **0.728** | **0.683** | **0.656** | **0.637** |
| 70 | 1.204 | 1.100 | 1.006 | **0.915** | **0.840** | **0.775** | **0.726** | **0.682** | **0.655** | **0.635** |
| 100 | 1.207 | 1.103 | 1.004 | **0.914** | **0.838** | **0.771** | **0.721** | **0.684** | **0.653** | **0.634** |
| 200 | 1.203 | 1.100 | 1.003 | **0.914** | **0.835** | **0.770** | **0.719** | **0.681** | **0.654** | **0.633** |

The predictive variable is based on purchasing-power parity. For country $i$, we set

$$x_{i,t}=\left(p_{it}-p_{0,t}\right)-s_{i,t}$$

where $p$ is the log-price level and the "0" subscript refers to the United States. For the time-series regression, the $k-$month ahead predictive equation is

$$s_{i,t+k}-s_{i,t}=\alpha_i+\beta_i x_{i,t}+\varepsilon_{i,t+k}$$

For the pooled regression case with fixed effects, the predictive equation is

$$s_{i,t+k}-s_{i,t}=\alpha_i+\beta x_{i,t}+\varepsilon_{i,t+k}$$

This is the model of Mark and Sul (2001) but without controls (time-specific dummy variables) for a common time effect. The regression errors are in fact correlated across $i$, and if we were concerned with drawing inference then it would be necessary to model the cross-sectional dependence in the regression error. However, since we are reporting only the point estimates, we can safely ignore this complication.

The relative prediction results are shown in Table 9.4. The table shows the ratio of Theil's U-statistic for the pooled forecast to that of the time-series

TABLE 9.4 **Theil's U-Statistics: Pooled/Time Series**

| Horizon | 1 | 2 | 3 | 4 | 5 | 6 | Avg over 24 |
|---|---|---|---|---|---|---|---|
| Australia | **0.994** | **0.989** | **0.996** | 1.007 | 1.020 | 1.041 | **0.841** |
| Canada | **0.958** | **0.975** | 1.009 | 1.010 | 1.014 | 1.042 | **0.899** |
| Chile | **0.955** | **0.991** | 1.014 | 1.022 | 1.043 | 1.082 | 1.083 |
| Colombia | **0.927** | **0.893** | **0.844** | **0.809** | **0.797** | **0.792** | **0.740** |
| Czech | **0.987** | **0.983** | **0.992** | 1.009 | 1.022 | 1.015 | 1.325 |
| Denmark | **0.974** | **0.979** | **0.960** | **0.973** | **0.982** | **0.991** | **0.779** |
| Hungary | **0.982** | **0.981** | **0.980** | **0.972** | **0.972** | **0.967** | 1.084 |
| Israel | 1.020 | 1.012 | 1.027 | 1.069 | 1.121 | 1.176 | 1.317 |
| Korea | 1.001 | 1.012 | 1.024 | 1.047 | 1.083 | 1.113 | 1.234 |
| Norway | 1.011 | 1.011 | 1.024 | 1.050 | 1.069 | 1.074 | **0.967** |
| NZ | **0.990** | 1.010 | 1.031 | 1.050 | 1.058 | 1.069 | **0.964** |
| Philippines | **0.960** | **0.926** | **0.883** | **0.837** | **0.809** | **0.745** | **0.637** |
| Russia | **0.951** | **0.954** | **0.937** | **0.930** | **0.923** | **0.915** | **0.880** |
| Singapore | **0.956** | **0.951** | **0.964** | **0.975** | **0.993** | **0.991** | **0.886** |
| South Africa | **0.995** | 1.033 | 1.079 | 1.106 | 1.139 | 1.170 | **0.967** |
| Sweden | 1.029 | 1.045 | 1.056 | 1.071 | 1.112 | 1.156 | 1.015 |
| Taiwan | 1.020 | **0.941** | **0.901** | **0.882** | **0.887** | **0.859** | **0.697** |
| UK | 1.010 | 1.057 | 1.102 | 1.133 | 1.174 | 1.219 | 1.388 |
| Japan | 1.002 | 1.018 | 1.043 | 1.089 | 1.114 | 1.151 | 1.617 |
| Swiss | **0.995** | **0.988** | **0.986** | **0.971** | **0.993** | 1.039 | **0.810** |
| Euro | **0.978** | **0.979** | **0.972** | **0.960** | **0.968** | **0.955** | **0.827** |

forecast. We generate forecasts at horizons 1 through 24, but we report only detailed results for horizons 1 through 6. The last column shows the average U-statistic ratio over forecast horizons 1 through 24. Values less than 1 indicate that the pooled forecast is more accurate in the mean-square sense. The pooled forecast is more accurate than the time-series forecast in about half of the cases. As can be seen from the last column, the dominance of the pooled forecasts becomes stronger at the longer horizons.

To help identify when it is that the pooled forecast will dominate the time-series forecast, we work with Equation 11. First, we note that the relative ranking of the mean-square error for currency $i$ depends on the distance between the particular estimator (pooled or unpooled) and the true slope value $\beta_i$,

$$\operatorname{sign}\left\{\frac{1}{P}\sum_{t=S+1}^{S+P}\left(\hat{y}_{i,j+1}^{\text{pool}}-y_{i,j+1}\right)^2-\frac{1}{P}\sum_{t=S+1}^{S+P}\left(\hat{y}_{i,j+1}^{\text{time}}-y_{i,j+1}\right)^2\right\}$$

$$=\operatorname{sign}\left\{\frac{1}{P}\sum_{p=1}^{P}\left\{\left(\hat{\beta}_{NS+p}-\beta_i\right)^2-\left(\hat{\beta}_{iS+p}-\beta_i\right)^2\right\}\right\}$$

Let us call the last expression,

$$\gamma_{P,i} \equiv \frac{1}{P}\sum_{p=1}^{P}\left\{\left(\hat{\beta}_{NS+p}-\beta_i\right)^2-\left(\hat{\beta}_{iS+p}-\beta_i\right)^2\right\}.$$

Then the pooled forecast will dominate the time-series forecast when $\gamma_{P,i} < 0$. To verify this prediction, we compute the average $\gamma_{P,i}$ for one-to-six period ahead forecasts and plot them against the (average of ) the relative Theil's U-statistic in Figure 9.1.[5]

The results conform to the predictions of the theory in that the $\gamma_{P,i}$ are positively correlated with the relative Theil's U-statistics, and the pooled forecasts tend to dominate the time-series forecasts for those $i$ in which $\gamma_{P,i} < 0$. The figure predicts that the pooled forecasts will dominate the time-series forecasts for Columbia, the Philippines, Taiwan, Russia, Singapore, Hungary, Denmark, and the Euro zone, and referring back to Table 9.4 confirms this prediction. Predictions of these exchange rates should be generated by the pooled panel data model. However, currencies of Sweden, the UK, Japan, and Israel should employ time-series regression.

## 9.6 Conclusions

The empirical literature finds that out-of-sample exchange rate forecasts over the 1990s and 2000s from (pooled) panel data models often perform better than

[5] In calculating $\gamma_{P,i}$, we note that the difference in the mean-square errors can be approximated as

$$\begin{aligned}\gamma_{P,i} &= \frac{1}{P}\sum_{p=1}^{P}\left\{\left(\hat{\beta}_{NS+p}-\hat{\beta}_{S+P,i}\right)^2-\left(\hat{\beta}_{iS+p}-\hat{\beta}_{S+P,i}\right)^2\right\}\\ &= \frac{1}{P}\sum_{p=1}^{P}\left(\hat{\beta}_{NS+p}-\beta_i\right)^2-\frac{1}{P}\sum_{p=1}^{P}\left(\hat{\beta}_{iS+p}-\beta_i\right)^2\\ &\quad -2\frac{1}{P}\sum_{p=1}^{P}\left(\hat{\beta}_{NS+p}-\hat{\beta}_{iS+p}\right)\left(\beta_i-\hat{\beta}_{S+P,i}\right)\\ &= \frac{1}{P}\sum_{p=1}^{P}\left(\hat{\beta}_{NS+p}-\beta_i\right)^2-\frac{1}{P}\sum_{p=1}^{P}\left(\hat{\beta}_{iS+p}-\beta_i\right)^2+O_p\left(\frac{1}{\sqrt{S+P}}\right)\end{aligned}$$

as $P \to \infty$. The last step follows since $\left(\beta_i-\hat{\beta}_{S+P,i}\right)=O_p\left(\frac{1}{\sqrt{S+P}}\right)$, but $\left(\hat{\beta}_{NS+p}-\hat{\beta}_{iS+p}\right)=O_p(1)$. Hence, we approximate the unobserved true value $\beta_i$ with the point estimate using the full sample, $\hat{\beta}_{S+P,i}$.

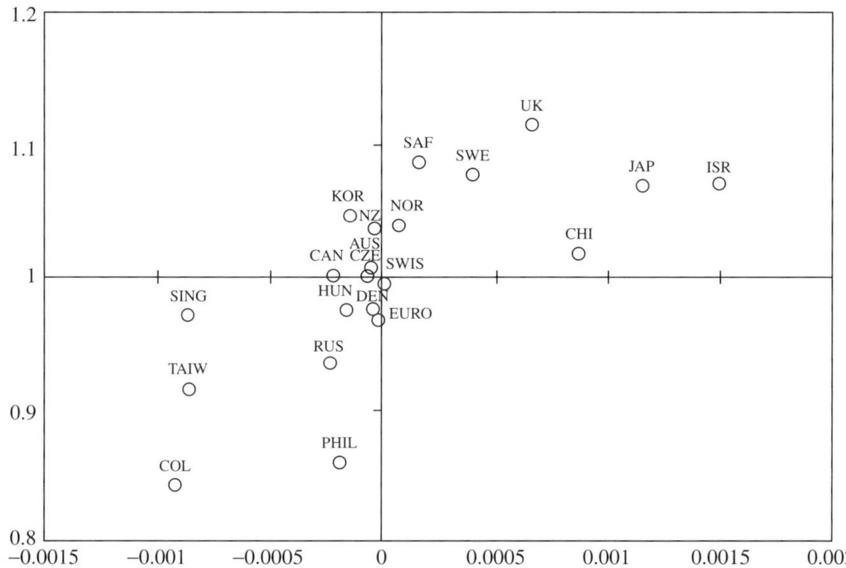


**FIGURE 9.1** **Average of Theil's U-statistic of pooled forecast relative to time-series forecast over horizons 1 through 6 plotted against average $\gamma_{P,i}$.**

those generated from time-series regression models. Researchers have reported these findings, even though there is substantial model heterogeneity across countries (or currencies) and asymptotic analysis tells us that pooling should be inappropriate in this case.

What we have shown is that if one is interested in evaluating out-of-sample forecast ability, pooling does not always generate more accurate forecasts than time-series regression. Pooling dominates when there is not much heterogeneity in the model parameters. When the heterogeneity is great, time-series forecasts should be used. However, if one is interested in testing for predictive ability using the full sample, pooling will result in more powerful tests as long as the model parameters and regressors are uncorrelated with the regression errors. Under these conditions, it makes sense to pool whether or not one believes that there is underlying slope heterogeneity.

## REFERENCES

Basher S, Westerlund J. "Panel cointegration and the monetary exchange rate model," Econ Model, 2009;26:506–513.

Cerra V, Saxena SC. The monetary model strikes back: evidence from the world. J Int Econ 2010;81:184–196.

Cheung Y-W, Chinn MD, Pascual AG. Empirical exchange rate models of the nineties: are any fit to survive? J Int Money Finance 2005;24:1150–1175.

Chinn MD, Meese RA. Banking on currency forecasts: how predictable is change in money? J Int Econ 1995;38:161–178.

Choi C-Y, Mark NC, Sul D. Unbiased estimation of the half-life to PPP convergence in panel data. J Money Credit Bank 2006;38:921\pgsemdash–938.

Daniel K. The power and size of mean reversion tests. J Empir Finance 2001;8:493–535.

Della Corte P, Tsiakas I. Statistical and economic methods for evaluating exchange rate predictability. *mimeo*, University of Warwick; 2010.

Engel C, Mark NC, West KD. Factor model forecasts of exchange rates. *mimeo*, University of Wisconsin; 2009.

Fama EF, French KR. Dividend yields and expected stock returns. J Financ Econ 1988;22:3–25.

Faust J, Rogers JH, Wright J. Exchange rate forecasting: the errors we've really made. J Int Econ 2003;60:35–59.

Frankel JA, Rose AK. A panel project on purchasing power parity: mean reversion within and between countries. J Int Econ 1996;40:209–224.

Groen JJJ. Long horizon predictability of exchange rates: is it for real? Empir Econ 1999;24:451–469.

Groen JJJ. The monetary exchange rate model as a long-run phenomenon. J Int Econ 2000;52:299–319.

Groen JJJ. Exchange rate predictability and monetary fundamentals in a small multi-country panel. J Money Credit Bank 2005;37(3): 495–516.

Husted S, MacDonald R. Monetary-based models of the exchange rate: a panel perspective. J Int Financ Mark Inst Money 1998;8:1–19.

Ince O. Forecasting exchange rates out-of-sample with panel methods and real-time data, *mimeo*, University of Houston; 2010.

Lothian JR, Taylor MP. Real exchange rate behavior: the recent float from the perspective of the past two centuries. J Polit Econ 1996;104:488–510.

Mark NC. Exchange rates and fundamentals: evidence on long-horizon predictability. Am Econ Rev 1995;85:201–218.

Mark NC, Sul D. Nominal exchange rates and monetary fundamentals: evidence from a small post-bretton woods panel. J Int Econ 2001;53:29–52.

Meese R, Rogoff K. Empirical exchange rate models of the 1980's: do they fit out of sample? J Int Econ 1983;14:3–24.

Papell DH. The panel purchasing power parity puzzle. J Money Credit Bank 2006;38:447–467.

Papell DH, Theodoridis H. Increasing evidence of purchasing power parity over the current float. J Int Money Finance 1998;17:41–50.

Papell DH, Theodoridis H. The choice of numeraire currency in panel tests of purchasing power parity. J Money Credit Bank 2001;33:790–803.

Rapach DE, Wohar ME. Testing the monetary model of exchange rate determination: new evidence from a century of data. J Int Econ 2002;58:359–385.

Rapach DE, Wohar ME. Testing the monetary model of exchange rate determination: a closer look at panels. J Int Money Finance 2004;23:867–895.

Rogoff K, Stavrakeva V. The continuing puzzle of short horizon exchange rate forecasting. *mimeo*, Harvard University; 2008.

Stambaugh RF. Predictive regressions. J Financ Econ 1999;54:375–421.

CHAPTER TEN

# Carry Trades and Risk

**CRAIG BURNSIDE**
Department of Economics, Duke University; NBER

## 10.1 Introduction

In a foreign exchange carry trade, an investor borrows funds in a low interest rate currency and lends those funds in a high interest rate currency. The uncovered interest parity (UIP) condition states that the interest rate differential between riskless assets denominated in foreign and domestic currency is equal to the rate at which the foreign currency is expected to depreciate against the domestic currency. If the UIP condition held, an investor engaged in the carry trade would, therefore, expect a zero net payoff. One motivation for investors to engage in the carry trade is, however, that UIP does not appear to hold in the data.[1] If anything, high interest rate currencies are more likely to appreciate than depreciate against low interest rate currencies. Consequently, in historical data, carry trades have earned positive average returns in excess of the interest differentials between the relevant currencies.

If investors expect to earn the interest differential, why do they limit their trading in foreign exchange? The most obvious explanation is that carry trades are risky, and that the average returns to carry trades reflect a risk premium. In this chapter, I review the evidence for and against a variety of risk-premium-based explanations. I first explore traditional factor models, ones that have been used to explain the returns to stock market portfolios. Examples include the CAPM, the Fama–French three-factor model, and the consumption CAPM. I find that these

[1] See Hodrick (1987) and Engel (1996) for reviews of the large literature documenting the failure of UIP.

*Handbook of Exchange Rates*, First Edition. Edited by Jessica James, Ian W. Marsh, and Lucio Sarno.

traditional models fail to explain the returns to the carry trade, defined either as an equally weighted (EW) portfolio of carry trades (as in Burnside et al., 2006, 2011a) or as high-minus-low portfolio of carry trades (as in Lustig et al., 2011). Risk-based explanations of the returns to the carry trade rely on identifying risk factors that covary with the returns. Traditional factors are either uncorrelated with carry-trade returns, that is, they have zero betas, or the betas are much too small to rationalize the magnitude of the returns to the carry trade.

I also examine less traditional factor models. These models adopt risk factors constructed specifically to price currency returns. I begin by studying the returns to portfolios of currencies that have been sorted according to the size of their forward discount. This sorting approach to portfolio construction has a long tradition in the finance literature (see Fama and French, 1993), and was brought to the literature on currency returns by Lustig and Verdelhan (2007). In studying a similar set of currency portfolios I find that three-factor models are quite successful in pricing the cross section of returns. These models are based on Lustig et al. (2011) model, which uses a high-minus-low carry-trade factor, Menkhoff et al.'s (2012) model, which uses a global currency volatility factor, and Rafferty's (2011) model, which uses a global currency skewness or "currency crash" factor. Although these models have some success in explaining currency returns, I find that they do not explain stock returns. Given, as I argued above, that models that do reasonably well in explaining stock returns do not explain currency returns, it appears that there is no unifying risk-based explanation of returns in these two markets.

One plausible explanation for the fact that one set of factors works for currency returns, while another is more successful in explaining stock returns, is that there is some degree of market segmentation. I find this explanation unattractive for the following reason. Although segmentation between currency and stock markets is plausible, factors that price carry trade portfolios ought to have some success in pricing other currency portfolios, such as those based on momentum or value. Burnside et al. (2011b) and Menkhoff et al. (2012) present evidence, however, that the same nontraditional factors that price carry-trade portfolios are unable to price momentum portfolios defined using short-term historical returns. Menkhoff et al. (2012) report more mixed evidence for momentum defined using longer term historical performance. Menkhoff et al. (2011) find that individual-currency characteristics appear to be important in explaining the returns to currency momentum. Alternatively, it could be argued that empirical exercises involving currency returns reveal one component of the global investor's Stochastic discount factor, while those involving stock returns reveal a different component of it. I find this explanation unsatisfying because it effectively renders untestable SDF-based explanations of asset return anomalies.

Finally, I provide evidence that time-varying market risk is unlikely to explain the returns to the carry trade. During the recent financial crisis, carry-trade returns and stock market returns became more highly correlated. This might suggest that covariance at times of market distress explains the returns to the carry trade (see, for example, Lustig et al., 2011). While this is an interesting conjecture, as I show here the degree of covariance seen in the data is insufficient. An alternative explanation is the one pursued by Burnside et al. (2011a), who argue that periods of extreme risk aversion that have not been observed in sample (peso events) can explain the returns to the carry trade and the stock market. I argue, below, that important challenges for future research on peso-event-based models is that they need to explain the empirical success of the nontraditional factor models described above, the time variation in "risk premia" needed to explain the UIP puzzle, and the cross section of stock returns. Julliard and Ghosh (2010) suggest that explaining the cross section of returns is difficult in a model with rare consumption disasters and constant relative risk aversion preferences because rare disasters tend to reduce the cross-sectional dispersion of the model-implied consumption betas.

In Section 10.2, I define the carry trade and measure the returns to two carry trade portfolios in historical data. In Section 10.3, I derive theoretical pricing equations for risk-based explanations and outline the empirical methods used for assessing them. In Section 10.4, I present empirical results. In Section 10.5, I discuss time-varying risk, rare events, and peso problems. In Section 10.6, I conclude.

## 10.2 The Carry Trade: Basic Facts

### 10.2.1 WHAT IS A CARRY TRADE?

In the carry trade, an investor borrows funds in a low interest rate currency and lends in a high interest rate currency. Here, I let the domestic currency be the US dollar (USD) and denote the rate of interest on riskless USD denominated securities as $i_t$. I denote the interest rate on riskless foreign denominated securities as $i_t^*$. Abstracting from transactions costs, the payoff to borrowing one USD in order to lend the foreign currency is

$$\left(1 + i_t^*\right) \frac{S_{t+1}}{S_t} - \left(1 + i_t\right) \tag{10.1}$$

where $S_t$ denotes the spot exchange rate expressed as USD per foreign currency unit (FCU). The payoff to the carry-trade strategy is, therefore:

$$z_{t+1} = \text{sign}(i_t^* - i_t) \left[ \left(1 + i_t^*\right) \frac{S_{t+1}}{S_t} - \left(1 + i_t\right) \right] \tag{10.2}$$

The carry-trade strategy can also be implemented by selling the foreign currency forward when it is at a forward premium ($F_t \geq S_t$) and buying the foreign currency forward when it is at a forward discount ($F_t < S_t$). If the number of FCUs transacted forward is normalized to be $(1 + i_t)/F_t$, then the payoff to this version of the strategy, denoted $z_{t+1}$, is

$$z_{t+1} = \text{sign}(F_t - S_t) \frac{1 + i_t}{F_t} \left(F_t - S_{t+1}\right) \tag{10.3}$$

Covered interest rate parity (CIP) implies that

$$\frac{1+i_t}{1+i_t^*} = \frac{F_t}{S_t} \tag{10.4}$$

When CIP holds, the expressions for $z_{t+1}$in Equations (10.3) and (10.2) are equal to each other. So the strategies are equivalent.

I measure payoffs to the carry trade using Equation (10.3). My empirical analysis focuses on the carry trade implemented at a 1-month horizon, so I mainly work with monthly payoffs. In order to assess the importance of real risk factors that are measured at the quarterly frequency, I also compute quarterly real excess returns to the carry trade. Letting $s$ be the time index for quarterly data, and $t$ be the time index for monthly data, so that $s = t/3$, the quarterly excess return in quarter $s$ is defined as

$$z_s^q = R_t R_{t-1} R_{t-2} - R_t^f R_{t-1}^f R_{t-2}^f \tag{10.5}$$

where

$$R_t = 1 + i_{t-1} + z_t \tag{10.6}$$

is the gross monthly rate of return to investing in the carry trade, and

$$R_t^f = 1 + i_{t-1} \tag{10.7}$$

is the gross monthly risk free return. The quarterly real excess return in quarter $s$ is simply

$$z_s^{qr} = z_s^q/(1+\pi_s) \tag{10.8}$$

where $\pi_s$ is the growth rate of the deflator for the consumption of nondurables and services from the US National Income and Product Accounts.

### 10.2.2 MEASURING THE RETURNS TO THE CARRY TRADE

To measure the returns to the carry trade, I consider trades conducted on a currency by currency basis against the USD. I also consider portfolio-based carry-trade strategies. I implement the trades with historical data using the forward market strategy described above. My data set consists of spot and forward exchange rates from Reuters/WMR and Barclays, available on Datastream, for the euro and the currencies of 20 countries: Australia, Austria, Belgium, Canada, Denmark, France, Germany, Ireland, Italy, Japan, the Netherlands, New Zealand, Norway, Portugal, South Africa, Spain, Sweden, Switzerland, the United Kingdom, and the United States. I use the risk free rate from Kenneth French's database as a measure of the US interest rate.

The raw data are daily observations of spot and 1-month forward exchange rates. I use end of month values of these data to create monthly observations. The data span the period January 1976 to October 2010, with the sample varying by currency. Reuters/WMR exchange rate quotes against the British pound (GBP) are available beginning in 1976. Reuters/WMR exchange rate quotes against the USD are available from January 1997 to October 2010. I construct USD quotes over the longer sample by multiplying GBP/FCU quotes by USD/GBP quotes. I augment the data set with USD quotes from Barclays for the Australian, New Zealand, and South African currencies from 1983 through 1996. Details of the data set are provided in an online appendix available at http://web.duke.edu/~acb8/ctapp.pdf.

Table 10.1 provides summary information about the profitability of carry trades between the USD and the other 20 currencies. On average the annual excess return to the individual-currency strategies is 4.6% with a typical standard deviation of 11.3% (on an annual basis) and an annualized Sharpe ratio of 0.42. This compares favorably with the performance of the US stock market over the same period, which had an average excess return of 6.3%, a standard deviation of 15.7% and a Sharpe ratio of 0.40. While the average carry trade was profitable, the performance of the individual carry trade varies across currencies, with trades against the Swiss franc earning a low 0.6% annual excess return, and trade against the Danish krone earning a high 9.3% annual excess return.

When carry trades are combined in portfolios, their performance is more impressive still. One strategy I consider is to combine all the individual-currency

**TABLE 10.1 Annualized Excess Returns of Investment Strategies**

| | Mean | Standard Deviation | Sharpe Ratio | Skewness | Excess Kurtosis |
|---|---|---|---|---|---|
| Average of individual currency carry trades | 0.0460 | 0.113 | 0.418 | −0.233 | 1.61 |
| Equally weighted carry trade | 0.0458 | 0.051 | 0.903 | −0.531 | 4.23 |
| | (0.0095) | (0.004) | (0.212) | (0.402) | (1.52) |
| HML carry trade | 0.0597 | 0.095 | 0.626 | −0.516 | 1.63 |
| | (0.0164) | (0.006) | (0.192) | (0.206) | (0.77) |
| US stock market | 0.0634 | 0.157 | 0.403 | −0.782 | 2.35 |
| | (0.0277) | (0.010) | (0.189) | (0.278) | (1.14) |

February 1976 to October 2010. Statistics are reported for annualized excess returns. The US stock market return is the value-weighted excess return on all US stocks reported in Kenneth French's database. The equally weighted carry-trade portfolio is formed as the average of up to 20 individual-currency carry trades against the US dollar. The individual currencies are indicated in the text. The HML carry trade strategy is a portfolio that takes an equally weighted long position in the quintile of currencies with the largest forward discounts and an equally weighted short position in the quintile of currencies with the smallest forward discounts against the US dollar. Heteroskedasticity consistent generalized method of moments (GMM) standard errors are in parentheses. The mean excess return of the equally weighted carry trade is not equal to the average mean excess return of the individual-currency carry trades because the sample periods for which the currencies are available varies.

positions in an EW portfolio with the total value of the bet normalized to 1 USD at the time it is initiated. I refer to this strategy as the EW carry trade, and it is the same strategy studied by Burnside et al. (2011a). As Table 10.1 indicates, over the historical sample, the EW strategy had an average annual payoff of 4.6% , with a standard deviation of 5.1% and a Sharpe ratio of 0.90. This shows that there are large diversification gains to combining carry trades in a portfolio.

A second strategy is constructed as follows. In each period, the available currencies in my sample, including the USD, are sorted into five bins according to their forward discount against the USD (of course the USD's forward discount is 0). The first bin includes those currencies with the smallest forward discounts (the lowest interest rates), the second bin the next smallest, etc., with the fifth bin consisting of those currencies with the largest forward discounts (and, therefore, the highest interest rates). I then compute the payoff associated with borrowing $1 in order to invest equally in the riskless securities of the constituent currencies of each bin.[2] This is equivalent to calculating the average value of $(1 + i_t)(S_{t+1} - F_t)/F_t$ for the currencies with the bin. The USD is treated the same as other currencies, with the payoff being zero. This procedure produces five currency portfolios that I refer to as S1, S2, S3, S4, and S5. The second carry-trade portfolio that I study involves investing 1 USD in S5 and −1 USD in S1. This is, effectively, equivalent to executing a carry trade in which the investor borrows the low interest rate currencies in S1 in order to lend funds in the high interest rate currencies in S5. Like Lustig et al. (2011), I refer to this portfolio as the HML carry-trade portfolio.[3] As Table 10.1 indicates, over the historical sample, the HML carry-trade strategy had an average annual excess return of 6.0% , with a standard deviation of 9.5% and a Sharpe ratio of 0.63. Although the HML portfolio had larger average returns than the EW portfolio over the historical sample, it is important to note that it is more highly leveraged than the EW portfolio since it involves a bet size of $2 instead of $1.

Figure 10.1 shows 12-month moving averages of the carry-trade portfolio and the US stock market excess returns. Two features of the returns are worth noting. First, the EW and HML carry-trade returns are positively correlated with each other (the correlation of the raw monthly returns is 0.51) but not perfectly so. Second, neither carry-trade portfolio is strongly correlated with the US stock market, despite their common poor performance in the 2008–2009 financial crisis.

Currency movements are often characterized as being highly skewed. For example, Brunnermeier et al. (2009) note the saying among traders that "exchange

[2]This is the same procedure used by Lustig et al. (2011) and Menkhoff et al. (2012).

[3]The HML portfolio is a close cousin of a market index, the Deutsche Bank G10 Currency Future Harvest (DBCFH). The DBCFH index takes positions in up to six currencies from a list of 10. The index is formed by taking equally weighted long positions vis-à-vis the USD in the three currencies with the highest interest rates, and symmetric short positions vis-à-vis the USD in the three currencies with the lowest interest rates. The currency composition of the DBCFH portfolio is rebalanced quarterly, while the composition of my HML portfolio is rebalanced monthly.

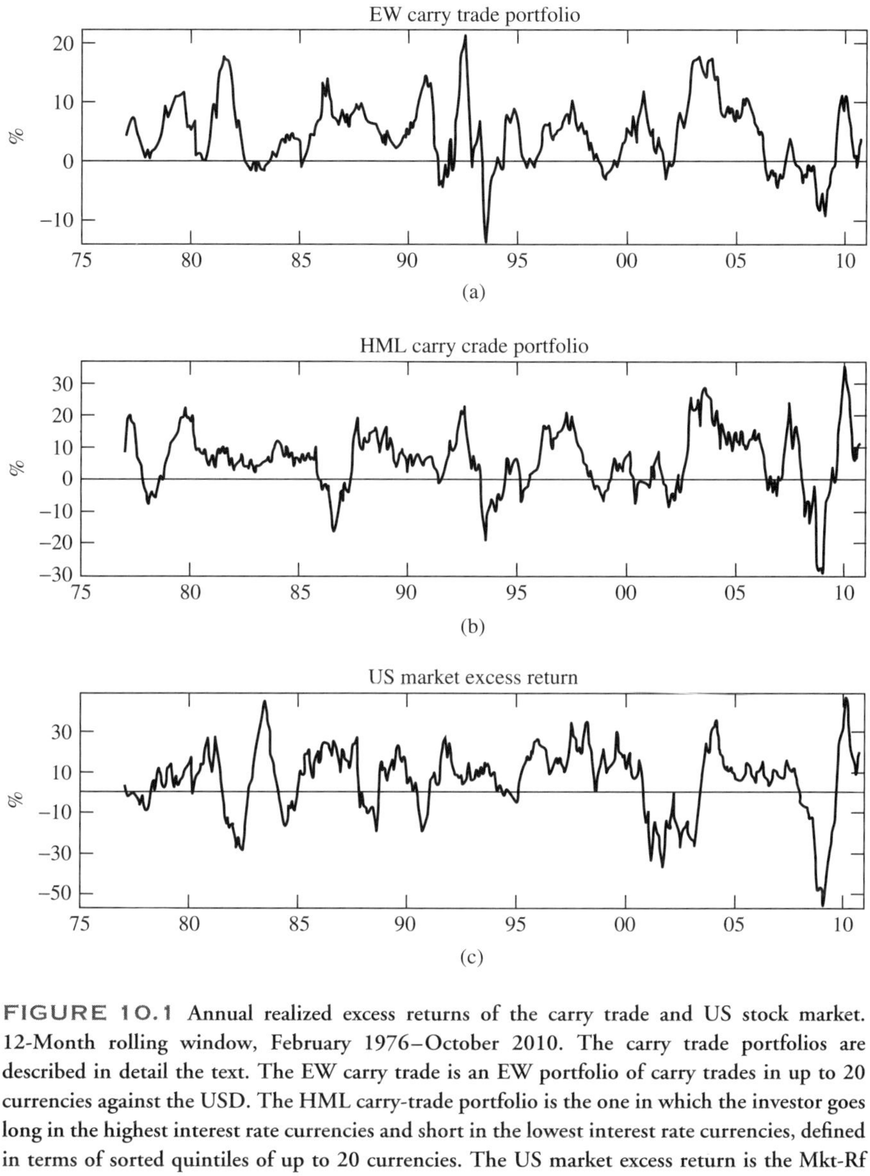


**FIGURE 10.1** **Annual realized excess returns of the carry trade and US stock market. 12-Month rolling window, February 1976–October 2010. The carry trade portfolios are described in detail the text. The EW carry trade is an EW portfolio of carry trades in up to 20 currencies against the USD. The HML carry-trade portfolio is the one in which the investor goes long in the highest interest rate currencies and short in the lowest interest rate currencies, defined in terms of sorted quintiles of up to 20 currencies. The US market excess return is the Mkt-Rf factor from Kenneth French's database.**

rates go up by the stairs and down by the elevator." While there is evidence that large forward discounts are associated with realized negative skewness of carry-trade returns (and large premia with positive skewness), the amount of skewness exhibited by the EW and HML carry-trade portfolios is less than that exhibited by the US stock market, and for the EW portfolio it is not statistically significant (Table 10.1). Currency payoffs display excess kurtosis, with noticeable central peakedness, especially in the case of the EW portfolio.

## 10.3 Pricing the Returns to the Carry Trade

Risk-based explanations of the returns to the carry trade begin from the premise that there is an SDF that prices these returns. In particular, since the carry trade is a zero net-investment strategy, the payoff, $z_t$, must satisfy

$$E_t\left(M_{t+1}z_{t+1}\right) = 0 \tag{10.9}$$

Here $M_{t+1}$ denotes the SDF that prices payoffs denominated in dollars, while $E_t$ is the mathematical expectations operator given information available at time $t$. Equation (10.9) implies that

$$p_t \equiv E_t\left(z_{t+1}\right) = -\frac{\mathrm{cov}_t\left(M_{t+1}, z_{t+1}\right)}{E_t\left(M_{t+1}\right)} \tag{10.10}$$

The variable $p_t$ is referred to as the conditional risk premium and corresponds to the conditional expectation of the payoff. As Equation (10.10) suggests, one approach to learning about risk premia is to build a forecasting model for the payoffs to the carry trade. An approximation to the mathematical expectation in Equation (10.10) is implicit in any forecasting model. Therefore, model forecasts correspond to estimates of the risk premium (Fama, 1984).

Consider an example of an individual-currency carry trade in which the domestic interest rate exceeds the foreign interest rate, that is, $i_t > i_t^*$, or, equivalently that the foreign currency is at a forward premium: $F_t > S_t$. Assume that the carry trader sells $S_t^{-1}$ units, rather than $(1 + i_t)/F_t$ units, of the foreign currency forward. In this case his/her payoff is

$$z_{t+1} = \frac{F_t - S_{t+1}}{S_t} \tag{10.11}$$

so that Equation (10.10) becomes

$$p_t = fp_t - E_t\delta_{t+1} \equiv \frac{\mathrm{cov}_t\left(M_{t+1}, \delta_{t+1}\right)}{E_t\left(M_{t+1}\right)} \tag{10.12}$$

where $\delta_{t+1} = (S_{t+1} - S_t)/S_t$ is the rate of appreciation of the foreign currency, and $fp_t = (F_t - S_t)/S_t$ is the forward premium.

Several features of Equation (10.12) are worthy of note. First, to the extent that the exchange rate is well approximated by a martingale, the risk premium to a carry trade is simply equal to the forward premium, that is, if $E_tS_{t+1} = S_t$ then $p_t = fp_t$. Second, for many currency pairs $\delta_{t+1}$ and $fp_t$ covary negatively in sample.[4] This implies, given Equation (10.12), that for these currency pairs

$$\mathrm{var}(p_t) \geq \mathrm{var}(fp_t) + \mathrm{var}(E_t\delta_{t+1}) \tag{10.13}$$

[4]For early surveys see Hodrick (1987) and Engel (1996). For recent evidence, see Burnside et al. (2006). Bekaert and Hodrick (1992) provide a broad set of evidence on the predictability of currency returns.

and

$$\operatorname{cov}(p_t, E_t\delta_{t+1}) \leq -\operatorname{var}(E_t\delta_{t+1}) \tag{10.14}$$

These inequalities, derived by Fama (1984) and discussed by Engel (1996), put restrictions on the time-series properties of the risk premium that could clearly be tested for a particular model. Any good forecast based model, however, will satisfy Equations (10.13) and (10.14) by construction. To see this, let $\hat{\delta}_{t+1}$ be the time series of one step ahead forecasts of $\delta_{t+1}$ produced by a forecasting model, and let the estimated risk premium be $\hat{p}_t = fp_t - \hat{\delta}_{t+1}$. As long as the forecasts have the property that $\operatorname{cov}(\hat{\delta}_{t+1}, fp_t) \leq 0$ it follows that $\operatorname{var}(\hat{p}_t) \geq \operatorname{var}(fp_t) + \operatorname{var}(\hat{\delta}_{t+1})$ and $\operatorname{cov}(\hat{p}_t, \hat{\delta}_{t+1}) \leq -\operatorname{var}(\hat{\delta}_{t+1})$. Finally, the challenge posed to economic researchers using Equation (10.12) is that the risk premium is equal to the covariance term on the right hand side of the equation. A risk-based explanation of the returns to the carry trade, therefore, relies on identifying an SDF that covaries with the rate of appreciation of the foreign currency. If in-sample risk explains the returns to the carry trade, then this SDF should correspond to some observable time series. As I argue below, finding such an SDF remains an elusive goal of economic research.

My exploration of candidate SDFs focuses on the unconditional moment condition restriction corresponding to Equation (10.9) is

$$E(Mz) = 0 \tag{10.15}$$

I consider SDFs that are linear in vectors of risk factors:

$$M_t = \xi\left[1 - (f_t - \mu)'b\right] \tag{10.16}$$

Here $\xi$ is a scalar, $f_t$ is a $k \times 1$ vector of risk factors, $\mu = E(f_t)$, and $b$ is a $k \times 1$ vector of parameters.

Since the parameter $\xi$ is not identified by Equation (10.15) I set it equal to 1, so that $E(M) = 1$. Given this assumption, Equation (10.15) implies that

$$E(z) = -\operatorname{cov}(M, z) \tag{10.17}$$

Given the model for $M$ given in Equation (10.16), Equation (10.17) can be rewritten as

$$E(z) = \operatorname{cov}(z, f)b \tag{10.18}$$

or as

$$E(z) = \underbrace{\operatorname{cov}(z, f)\,\Sigma_f^{-1}}_{\beta}\,\underbrace{\Sigma_f b}_{\lambda} \tag{10.19}$$

where $\Sigma_f$ is the covariance matrix of $f_t$. Equation (10.19) is the beta representation of the model. The betas, which are population coefficients in a regression of $z_t$ on $f_t$, measure the risk exposure of the payoff, while $\lambda$ is a $k \times 1$ vector of risk premia that is not specific to the payoff.

I assess risk-based explanations of the returns to the carry trade in two ways. First, I ask whether there are risk factors for which the payoffs to the carry trade have statistically and economically significant betas. To answer this question, I run a simple time-series regression of each portfolio's excess return on a vector of candidate risk factors:

$$z_{it} = a_i + f_t' \beta_i + \varepsilon_{it}, \quad t = 1, \ldots, T, \text{ for each } i = 1, \ldots, n \tag{10.20}$$

where $T$ is the sample size and $n$ the number of portfolios being studied.

Second, I ask whether these betas, combined with estimates of $\lambda$, can explain the returns to the carry trade according to Equation (10.19). One way to answer this question is to run a cross-sectional regression of average portfolio excess returns on the estimated betas:

$$\bar{z}_i = \hat{\beta}_i' \lambda + \alpha_i, \qquad i = 1, \ldots, n \tag{10.21}$$

where $\bar{z}_i = \frac{1}{T} \sum_{t=1}^{T} z_{it}$, $\hat{\beta}_i$ is the ordinary least squares (OLS) estimate of $\beta_i$ obtained above, and $\alpha_i$ is a pricing error. Let the OLS estimator of $\lambda$ be $\hat{\lambda} = (\hat{\beta}'\hat{\beta})^{-1}\hat{\beta}'\bar{z}$, where $\bar{z}$ is an $n \times 1$ vector formed from the individual mean returns. Rather than actually running the cross-sectional regression I estimate the parameters of the SDF using the GMM (Hansen, 1982) and the moment restriction (Eq. (10.15)) along with $E(f) = \mu$. Equation (10.15) can be rewritten as

$$E\left(z\left[1 - (f - \mu)' b\right]\right) = 0 \tag{10.22}$$

where $z$ is an $n \times 1$ vector of excess returns, and is equivalent to Equation (10.18). The GMM estimators of $\mu$ and $b$ at each step are $\hat{\mu} = \bar{f}$ and

$$\hat{b} = \left(d_T' W_T d_T\right)^{-1} d_T' W_T \bar{z} \tag{10.23}$$

where $d_T$ is the sample covariance matrix of $z$ with $f$ and $W_T$ a weighting matrix. Estimates of $\lambda$ are obtained from $\hat{b}$ as $\hat{\lambda} = \hat{\Sigma}_f \hat{b}$, where $\hat{\Sigma}_f$ is the sample covariance matrix of $f$. The model's *predicted mean returns* are $d_T\hat{b}$, and are estimates of the right-hand side of Equation (10.18). The *pricing errors* are the residuals, $\hat{\alpha} = \bar{z} - d_T\hat{b}$. In the first GMM step the weighting matrix is $W_T = I_n$, and the estimate of $\lambda$ and the pricing errors are the same as the ones obtained from the cross-sectional regression described above. In subsequent GMM steps the weighting matrix is chosen optimally. A test of the pricing errors is obtained as $J = T\hat{\alpha}' V_T^{-1} \hat{\alpha}$, where $V_T$ is a consistent estimate of the asymptotic covariance matrix of $\sqrt{T}\hat{\alpha}$ and the inverse is generalized. The test statistic is asymptotically distributed as a $\chi^2$ with $n - k$ degrees of freedom. I mainly focus on results obtained by iterating on the GMM estimator to convergence. Burnside (2010a) shows that the first-stage, second-stage, and iterated GMM estimators have similar size properties when calibrated linear factor models are used as the data generating process. However, the iterated estimator has much greater power to reject misspecified models. Burnside (2011) provides further details of the GMM procedure.

## 10.4 Empirical Findings

In this section, I use the empirical methods outlined in the previous section to determine whether there is a candidate SDF that can price the returns to the carry trade. I begin by studying risk factors that have traditionally been used to explain stock returns. These include the CAPM, the Fama–French three factor model, models in which industrial production growth and stock market volatility are used as risk factors, and consumption-based models. I show that none of the SDFs specified in terms of these traditional risk factors explains the returns to the carry trade. I then turn to less traditional models in which the risk factors are, themselves, derived from currency returns. These models have varying degrees of success in pricing carry-trade returns.

### 10.4.1 TRADITIONAL RISK FACTORS

**10.4.1.1 Models for Monthly Returns.** Table 10.2 summarizes the results of running time-series regressions

described by Equation (10.20) for monthly models. Consider, first the CAPM model, which uses the market excess return as a single factor. For the EW carry-trade portfolio the beta is statistically insignificant. It is also economically small. To see this, consider that in order for the CAPM model to explain the return to holding the value weighted US stock market, the annualized value of $\lambda$ must be approximately equal to the average excess return of the stock market, since the beta of the market return is 1. Given that the beta of the EW carry-trade portfolio is 0.028, the CAPM model therefore predicts that the average excess return of the EW carry trade should be 0.028 times the average return on the market, or 0.2% , as opposed to the 4.6% return indicated in Table 10.1. For the HML carry-trade portfolio the beta is larger (0.163) and statistically significant, but it is still economically small. The CAPM model predicts that the average excess return of the HML carry trade should be 0.163 times the average return on the market or 1.0% , as opposed to the 6.0% return indicated in Table 10.1.

The second model is the three-factor model proposed by Fama and French (1993), which uses the excess return to the value-weighted US stock market (Mkt-Rf), the size premium (SMB), and the value premium (HML) as risk factors. Here, the beta associated with the Mkt-Rf factor is statistically significant for both carry-trade portfolios but it remains economically small. The beta associated with the SMB factor is small and statistically insignificant for both carry trade

**TABLE 10.2 Monthly Factor Betas of the Carry-Trade Portfolios**

| | EW Carry Trade | | | | | HML Carry Trade | | | | |
|---|---|---|---|---|---|---|---|---|---|---|
| Factors | Intercept | Beta(s) | | | $R^2$ | Intercept | Beta(s) | | | $R^2$ |
| CAPM | 0.004 | 0.028 | | | 0.008 | 0.004 | 0.163* | | | 0.072 |
| | (0.001) | (0.017) | | | | (0.001) | (0.038) | | | |
| Fama–French factors | 0.004 | 0.042* | −0.034 | 0.037 | 0.020 | 0.003 | 0.185* | 0.080 | 0.156* | 0.100 |
| (Mkt-Rf, SMB, HML) | (0.001) | (0.018) | (0.029) | (0.029) | | (0.001) | (0.042) | (0.047) | (0.055) | |
| Industrial production (IP) | 0.004 | 0.118 | | | 0.003 | 0.005 | 0.171 | | | 0.002 |
| | (0.001) | (0.146) | | | | (0.001) | (0.231) | | | |
| CAPM-IP | 0.003 | 0.029 | 0.129 | | 0.011 | 0.004 | 0.165* | 0.232 | | 0.075 |
| (Mkt-Rf, IP growth) | (0.001) | (0.017) | (0.141) | | | (0.001) | (0.038) | (0.198) | | |
| Realized stock volatility | 0.005 | −0.002 | | | 0.005 | 0.014 | −0.010* | | | 0.038 |
| | (0.002) | (0.002) | | | | (0.003) | (0.004) | | | |
| CAPM stock volatility | 0.005 | 0.023 | −0.001 | | 0.009 | 0.009 | 0.138* | −0.006 | | 0.084 |
| (Mkt-Rf, Stock vol) | (0.002) | (0.020) | (0.002) | | | (0.003) | (0.036) | (0.004) | | |

February 1976 to October 2010. The table reports estimates of the equation $z_t = a + f_t'\beta + \varepsilon_{t+1}$, where $z_t$ is the monthly excess return of a carry-trade portfolio and $f_t$ is a scalar or vector of risk factors. The CAPM factor is the excess return on the value-weighted US stock market (Mkt-Rf), and the Fama–French factors are the Mkt-Rf, SMB, and HML factors (available from Kenneth French's database). The industrial production factor is monthly industrial production growth. The stock volatility factor is realized daily volatility measured monthly. Heteroskedasticity-consistent standard errors are in parentheses. Slope coefficients that are statistically significant at the 5% level are indicated by an asterisk (*).

portfolios. The beta associated with the HML factor is small and statistically insignificant for the EW carry-trade portfolio, but is statistically significant and small for the HML carry-trade portfolio.

The third model uses industrial production growth as a risk factor, while the fourth model uses industrial production growth in conjunction with the Mkt-Rf factor. The betas associated with industrial production growth are not statistically significant for either carry-trade portfolio.

The fifth model uses realized stock return volatility (measured monthly using daily observations of Mkt-Rf) as a risk factor, while the sixth model uses stock volatility in conjunction with the Mkt-Rf factor. For the EW carry trade portfolio, the beta associated with stock market volatility is not statistically significant in either model. For the HML carry-trade portfolio, the beta associated with stock market volatility is statistically significant, but not when Mkt-Rf is included in the regression.

Table 10.3 presents results from estimating each of these models using the iterated GMM estimator. The models are estimated using the EW and HML carry trade portfolios, as well as Fama and French's 25 portfolios sorted on the basis of book to market value and size. First, it is worth noting that in every case the pricing errors of the carry-trade portfolios are statistically significant. None of the models explains the returns earned by these strategies. Second, all of the models are rejected, at the 5% level, by the test of the pricing errors. The only model with reasonably good fit is the Fama and French's (1993) three-factor model. For this model two of the slope coefficients (on Mkt-Rf and HML) are statistically significant, while the third coefficient (on SMB) is close to being significant. The $R^2$ measure of fit for the model is 0.38. But the model does a very poor job of explaining the returns to the carry-trade portfolios.

**10.4.1.2 Models for Quarterly Returns.** Here I consider three risk factors: the growth rate of real consumption of nondurables and services, the growth rate of the service flow from the real stock of durables, and the market return. I consider each of these factors individually, but also use them together in a three-factor model following Yogo (2006), who used the three-factor model to study stock market returns. For the consumption variables I use both conventional timing (where consumption growth and the returns are measured in the same quarter) and Campbell's (2003) timing where consumption growth is measured in the quarter after the returns are realized.

Table 10.4 summarizes the results of running time-series regressions of quarterly real excess returns on the risk factors described above. Consider, first the C-CAPM model, which uses real consumption growth (nondurables plus services) as a single factor. This model can be considered a linear approximation to a simple representative agent model in which households have constant relative risk aversion preferences with risk aversion parameter $b$. For both carry-trade portfolios the beta is small and statistically insignificant. The betas are larger, but remain statistically insignificant, when Campbell's timing is used, and the beta for the HML carry trade has counterintuitive sign.

**TABLE 10.3 GMM Estimates of Monthly Linear Factor Models**

| | $b$ | $\lambda$ (%) | $R^2$ | $J$ | Pricing Errors ($\alpha$) EW Carry | HML Carry |
|---|---|---|---|---|---|---|
| CAPM | 2.18 | 0.45* | −1.86 | 104 | 0.044* | 0.051* |
| | (1.17) | (0.22) | | (0.00) | (0.009) | (0.016) |
| Fama–French factors | | | | | | |
| Mkt-Rf | 3.36* | 0.49* | 0.38 | 91.0 | 0.043* | 0.040* |
| | (1.41) | (0.23) | | (0.00) | (0.009) | (0.017) |
| SMB | 3.15 | 0.24 | | | | |
| | (1.74) | (0.15) | | | | |
| HML | 6.52* | 0.36* | | | | |
| | (1.91) | (0.17) | | | | |
| Industrial prod. (IP) | −5.40 | −0.03 | −9.59 | 108 | 0.046* | 0.060* |
| | (28.1) | (0.14) | | (0.00) | (0.009) | (0.016) |
| CAPM-IP | | | | | | |
| Mkt-Rf | 2.28 | 0.46* | −1.76 | 103 | 0.044* | 0.050* |
| | (1.21) | (0.22) | | (0.00) | (0.009) | (0.016) |
| I.P. growth | 4.64 | 0.02 | | | | |
| | (29.6) | (0.14) | | | | |
| Stock volatility | −0.30 | −9.18 | −3.49 | 85.77 | 0.044* | 0.049* |
| | (0.25) | (6.40) | | (0.00) | (0.009) | (0.017) |
| CAPM stock volatility | | | | | | |
| Mkt-Rf | −1.36 | 0.08 | −6.70 | 80.5 | 0.044* | 0.051* |
| | (1.70) | (0.23) | | (0.00) | (0.010) | (0.018) |
| Stock volatility | −0.41 | −11.1 | | | | |
| | (0.33) | (7.99) | | | | |

February 1976 to October 2010. Test assets are the Fama–French 25 portfolios, and the EW and HML carry-trade portfolios. The CAPM factor is the excess return on the value-weighted US stock market (Mkt-Rf), and the Fama–French factors are the Mkt-Rf, SMB, and HML factors (available from Kenneth French's database). The industrial production factor is monthly industrial production growth. The stock volatility factor is realized daily volatility measured monthly. The table reports iterated GMM estimates of the SDF parameter, $b$, and the factor risk premia, $\lambda$, reported in monthly percent. The $R^2$ is a measure of fit between the mean excess returns and the predicted mean returns. Test statistics, $J$, for the overidentifying restrictions are also reported. The annualized pricing errors of the carry-trade portfolios ($\alpha$) are reported. Heteroskedasticity-consistent standard errors are in parentheses, except for the $J$ statistics, for which the $p$-value is in parentheses. An asterisk (*) indicates statistical significance at the 5% level.

Another model that has received broad attention in the literature is a three-factor model, which I refer to as the extended C-CAPM model, which includes consumption growth, durables growth, and the market return as risk factors. This model is a linear approximation to a representative agent model in which households have recursive preferences over the two types of consumption good. Yogo (2006) uses this model to explain stock returns, while Lustig and Verdelhan

**TABLE 10.4 Quarterly Factor Betas of the Carry-Trade Portfolios**

| | EW Carry Trade | | | | | HML Carry Trade | | | | |
|---|---|---|---|---|---|---|---|---|---|---|
| Factors | Intercept | Beta(s) | | | $R^2$ | Intercept | Beta(s) | | | $R^2$ |
| C-CAPM ($\Delta c$) | 0.012 | −0.021 | | | 0.000 | 0.016 | 0.018 | | | 0.000 |
| | (0.005) | (0.744) | | | | (0.008) | (1.234) | | | |
| Durables ($\Delta d$) | 0.007 | 0.524 | | | 0.009 | 0.018 | −0.196 | | | 0.000 |
| | (0.007) | (0.554) | | | | (0.010) | (0.878) | | | |
| Market return (Mkt) | 0.012 | 0.009 | | | 0.001 | 0.013 | 0.145* | | | 0.061 |
| | (0.002) | (0.031) | | | | (0.011) | (0.068) | | | |
| Extended C-CAPM | 0.007 | −0.325 | 0.641 | 0.014 | 0.012 | 0.013 | −0.437 | 0.130 | 0.148* | 0.062 |
| ($\Delta c$, $\Delta c$, Mkt) | (0.007) | (0.828) | (0.580) | (0.032) | | (0.001) | (1.184) | (0.852) | (0.069) | |
| C-CAPM ($\Delta c$) | 0.011 | 0.119 | | | 0.000 | 0.017 | −0.384 | | | 0.001 |
| (Campbell timing) | (0.004) | (0.605) | | | | (0.007) | (1.170) | | | |
| Durables ($\Delta d$) | 0.007 | 0.495 | | | 0.008 | 0.016 | −0.044 | | | 0.000 |
| (Campbell timing) | (0.007) | (0.576) | | | | (0.011) | (1.010) | | | |
| Extended C-CAPM | 0.007 | −0.203 | 0.568 | 0.014 | 0.010 | 0.013 | −1.646 | 0.604 | 0.172* | 0.077 |
| (Campbell timing) | (0.007) | (0.672) | (0.618) | (0.030) | | (0.011) | (1.064) | (1.021) | (0.072) | |

1976Q2–2009Q4. The table reports estimates of the equation $z_t^{qr} = a + f_t'\beta + \varepsilon_{t+1}$, where $z_t^{qr}$ is the quarterly real excess return of a carry-trade portfolio and $f_t$ is a scalar or vector of risk factors. The C-CAPM factor is the log growth rate of real consumption of nondurables and services, the durables factor is the log growth rate of the service flow of durables assumed to be proportional to the real stock of consumer durables, the market return factor (Mkt) is from Kenneth French's database. "Campbell timing" is explained in the main text. Heteroskedasticity-consistent standard errors are in parentheses. Slope coefficients that are statistically significant at the 5% level are indicated by an asterisk (*).

(2007) use it to explain currency returns. Before turning to the full three-factor model, I study models that use durables growth and the market return as single factors.

Consider, first, the model with the real growth rate of the stock of consumer durables (interpreted as the growth rate of the service flow from durables) as a single factor. For both carry-trade portfolios the beta is statistically insignificant, and it has counterintuitive sign for the HML carry trade. The same is true for Campbell's timing, largely because the growth rate of the stock of durables is highly serially correlated.

Consider, next, the model that uses the market return, as opposed to the market excess return used in the CAPM model, as a single factor. As we saw for the CAPM using monthly data, the beta is small and statistically insignificant for the EW carry-trade portfolio. For the HML carry-trade portfolio the beta is statistically significant, but economically small.

Finally, I enter all three factors together in a single model. None of the factors is statistically significant for the EW carry-trade portfolio, and neither consumption factor displays any significance for the HML carry-trade portfolio. The market return has significance for the HML carry-trade portfolio, but the coefficient is quantitatively small. This evidence, against a consumption-based explanation of the returns to the carry trade, is overwhelming.

Table 10.5 presents results from estimating the C-CAPM and extended C-CAPM models using iterated GMM. The models are estimated using the real excess returns of the EW and HML carry-trade portfolios, as well as Fama and French's 25 portfolios sorted on the basis of book to market value and size. First, it is worth noting that none of the estimated $b$ parameters are statistically significant at the 5% level, although the $\lambda$ associated with the market return is statistically significant for the extended C-CAPM model. Second, for all cases, the pricing errors of the carry-trade portfolios are statistically significant, the models are rejected at the 5% level on the basis of the $J$-statistic, and the $R^2$ measures of fit are negative.

**10.4.1.3 Discussion.** The results in this section suggest that traditional risk factors cannot explain the returns to carry-trade portfolios. At best, the models considered here explain very little of the average returns to the EW and HML carry-trade portfolios, leaving unexplained economically large and statistically significant pricing errors. In every case the models can also be rejected on the basis of statistical tests of the pricing errors.

The reader may be puzzled by the poor performance of the extended C-CAPM model given its prior apparent success in explaining stock returns (Yogo, 2006). The bottom line is that the factors in the model simply do not produce the amount of spread in the betas required for the model to be a success. It is not easy to illustrate the problem for a three-factor model, because there are betas in three dimensions and the partial explanatory power of each factor is what is relevant. To deal with this issue, I construct a calibrated SDF, $\hat{m}_t^Y = 1 - (f_t - \bar{f})'\hat{b}^Y$, where $\hat{b}^Y$ is Yogo's (2006) estimate of the $b$ vector for the extended C-CAPM model, $f_t$ is the vector of relevant risk factors and $\bar{f}$ is their sample mean. I then compute betas for the two carry-trade portfolios and the 25 Fama–French portfolios with

TABLE 10.5 **GMM Estimates of Quarterly Linear Factor Models**

| | $b$ | $\lambda$ (%) | $R^2$ | $J$ | Pricing Errors ($\alpha$) EW Carry | HML Carry |
|---|---|---|---|---|---|---|
| C-CAPM | 68.9 | 0.12 | −7.25 | 66.2 | 0.047* | 0.063* |
| | (50.2) | (0.09) | | (0.00) | (0.012) | (0.021) |
| Extended C-CAPM | | | | | | |
| $\Delta c$ | 3.30 | 0.00 | −1.25 | 65.6 | 0.046* | 0.054* |
| | (53.3) | (0.09) | | (0.00) | (0.010) | (0.018) |
| $\Delta d$ | 5.41 | 0.01 | | | | |
| | (39.0) | (0.09) | | | | |
| Mkt | 2.26 | 1.57* | | | | |
| | (1.21) | (0.73) | | | | |
| Models with Campbell's timing for consumption | | | | | | |
| C-CAPM | 31.1 | 0.06 | −7.27 | 68.5 | 0.047* | 0.064* |
| | (41.4) | (0.07) | | (0.00) | (0.011) | (0.019) |
| Extended C-CAPM | | | | | | |
| $\Delta c$ | −17.1 | 0.01 | −4.20 | 43.4 | 0.045* | 0.057* |
| | (51.9) | (0.08) | | (0.01) | (0.011) | (0.018) |
| $\Delta d$ | 38.0 | 0.08 | | | | |
| | (42.9) | (0.11) | | | | |
| Mkt | 1.44 | 0.74 | | | | |
| | (1.33) | (0.74) | | | | |

1976Q2 to 2009Q4. Test assets are the Fama–French 25 portfolios, and the EW and HML carry-trade portfolios. The C-CAPM factor is the log growth rate of real consumption of nondurables and services, the durables factor is the log growth rate of the service flow of durables assumed to be proportional to the real stock of consumer durables, the market return factor (Mkt) is from Kenneth French's database. The table reports iterated GMM estimates of the SDF parameter, $b$, and the factor risk premia, $\lambda$, reported in quarterly percent. The $R^2$ is a measure of fit between the mean excess returns and the predicted mean returns. Test statistics, $J$, for the overidentifying restrictions are also reported. The annualized pricing errors of the carry-trade portfolios ($\alpha$) are reported. Heteroskedasticity-consistent standard errors are in parentheses, except for the $J$statistics, for which the $p$-value is in parentheses. An asterisk (*) indicates statistical significance at the 5% level.

respect to $\hat{m}_t^Y$. If the model explains the average returns on the 27 portfolios, then 27 estimated betas and the 27 average returns should line up (with negative slope) in a scatter plot. Instead, they are approximately uncorrelated in the cross section (the correlation coefficient is −0.02). Also, only 4 out of the 27 betas are statistically significant at the 5% level. The model simply does not do a good job of explaining currency returns or stock returns over the period 1976–2010.

### 10.4.2 FACTORS DERIVED FROM CURRENCY RETURNS

I turn, now, to less traditional factor models. Here the factors are, themselves, derived from currency returns. In creating factors in this way, the literature, beginning with Lustig et al. (2011), takes inspiration from the literature on stock returns, where it is common to choose risk factors that are, themselves, the returns to particular investment strategies. For example, having identified the size and value premia, Fama and French (1993) construct new risk factors which are the return differentials between, respectively, small and large firms (SMB) and high and low value firms (HML). Similarly, many researchers have used a momentum risk factor to explain stock returns, since Jegadeesh and Titman (1993) identified the momentum anomaly.

**10.4.2.1 Currencies Sorted by Forward Discount.** The Fama and French factors and the momentum factors are created by sorting firms on the basis of characteristics. Take, for example, Fama and French's SMB factor. To construct this factor, Fama and French (1993) sort firms by their market value. This sorting is done once per year at the end of June. Firms in the bottom third in terms of size are used to form a portfolio of small firms. Firms in the top third in terms of size are used to form a portfolio of large firms. The SMB factor is the return differential between the small firm portfolio and the large firm portfolio in each period.

In a similar way, Lustig and Verdelhan (2007) and Lustig et al. (2011) sort currencies into, respectively, eight and six portfolios according to their forward discount against the USD. The sorting is done period by period. Each portfolio is EW and represents the excess return to going long in the constituent currencies while going short in the USD. In Section 10.2.2. I constructed the S1–S5 portfolios in an analogous way, and Menkhoff et al. (2012) follow a similar procedure. These five portfolios are the focus of my empirical work in this section.

Table 10.6 shows the average returns of the five portfolios. Notice that they are monotonically increasing going from S1 to S5. This establishes that sorting currencies on the basis of the forward discount " works," in that it produces a set of portfolios with different expected returns, where the ordering of the expected returns aligns with an observed characteristic of the underlying assets. This result should not come as a surprise. Meese and Rogoff (1983) established that it is hard to produce a currency forecasting model that beats a random walk. If the change in the spot rate for each currency was exactly a random walk then the expected excess returns of S1–S5 would be exactly equal to the forward discount period by period. In that circumstance, sorting done on the basis of the forward discount could not fail to provide portfolios with ordered average returns.

**10.4.2.2 Factors Created from Sorted Portfolios.** Lustig et al. (2011) take the sorting approach one step further by constructing two risk factors that they then use to price the cross section of their six portfolios. The first risk factor, which they call the dollar risk factor and denote RX, is simply the average excess return of the six portfolios. The second risk factor, which they denote $HML_{FX}$, is the return differential between the sixth portfolio (the largest forward discount) and the first portfolio (the smallest forward discount). In an analogous way, I construct two risk factors, one denoted DOL, which is simply the average excess return of the S1–S5 portfolios described above, the other being the excess return

**TABLE 10.6 Factor Betas of the Sorted Currency Portfolios and the Carry-Trade Portfolios**

| | | LRV (2011) | | | Menkhoff et al. (2012) | | | Rafferty (2011) | | |
|---|---|---|---|---|---|---|---|---|---|---|
| Portfolio | Mean Return | DOL | HML Carry | $R^2$ | DOL | VOL | $R^2$ | DOL | SKW | $R^2$ |
| S1 | −0.80% | 0.959* | −0.478* | 0.923 | 0.942* | 0.0216* | 0.736 | 0.948* | −0.0129* | 0.723 |
| | (1.86) | (0.020) | (0.020) | | (0.039) | (0.0056) | | (0.043) | (0.0030) | |
| S2 | −0.28% | 0.901* | −0.116* | 0.857 | 0.893* | −0.0000 | 0.841 | 0.904* | −0.0066* | 0.846 |
| | (1.69) | (0.028) | (0.021) | | (0.030) | (0.0046) | | (0.028) | (0.0021) | |
| S3 | 2.80% | 0.917* | −0.001 | 0.825 | 0.915* | −0.0030 | 0.826 | 0.910* | 0.0044 | 0.827 |
| | (1.80) | (0.027) | (0.026) | | (0.027) | (0.0033) | | (0.027) | (0.0024) | |
| S4 | 3.72% | 0.959* | 0.068* | 0.868 | 0.961* | −0.0044 | 0.864 | 0.957* | 0.0041* | 0.865 |
| | (1.76) | (0.024) | (0.022) | | (0.025) | (0.0027) | (0.025) | (0.0021) | | |
| S5 | 5.17% | 0.959* | 0.522* | 0.933 | 0.986* | −0.0120* | 0.717 | 0.973* | 0.0126* | 0.722 |
| | (2.13) | (0.020) | (0.020) | | (0.034) | (0.0052) | | (0.036) | (0.0031) | |
| EW Carry | 4.58% | 0.184* | 0.264* | 0.371 | 0.196* | −0.0080* | 0.140 | 0.179* | 0.0140* | 0.187 |
| | (0.95) | (0.040) | (0.029) | | (0.045) | (0.0039) | | (0.043) | (0.0029) | |
| HML Carry | 5.97% | 0 | 1* | 1 | 0.044 | −0.0336* | 0.071 | 0.026 | 0.0255* | 0.061 |
| | (1.64) | | | | (0.062) | (0.0094) | | (0.069) | (0.0052) | |

February 1976 to October 2010. The table reports estimates of the equation $z_t = a + f_t'\beta + \varepsilon_{t+1}$, where $z_t$ is the monthly excess return of each of the portfolios indicated and $f_t$ is a $2 \times 1$ vector of the indicated risk factors. The DOL factor is the average excess return to portfolios S1–S5. The HML carry portfolio is the excess return to being long portfolio P5 and short portfolio P1. The VOL factor is a measure of realized global currency volatility. The SKW factor is a measure of realized global currency skewness. Heteroskedasticity-consistent standard errors are in parentheses. Slope coefficients that are statistically significant at the 5% level are indicated by an asterisk (*).

to the HML carry-trade portfolio. Like Lustig, Roussanov and Verdelhan I use these two risk factors to study the cross section of returns of the S1–S5 portfolios.

**10.4.2.3 A Currency Volatility Factor.** Menkhoff et al. (2012) use a factor analogous to DOL, and a factor that measures global currency volatility, to study portfolios similar to S1–S5. Their volatility factor is constructed on a monthly basis and is the average Intra-month realized volatility of the daily log changes in the value of each currency (available in their sample) against the USD. In studying the importance of volatility as a pricing factor, they take inspiration from an earlier literature that suggests exposure to volatility helps explain stock returns (Ang et al. (2006); Da and Schaumburg (2009)). To reexamine their evidence, I construct a volatility factor, VOL, which is measured monthly, and is the average sample standard deviation of the daily log changes in the values of the currencies in my sample against the USD.

**10.4.2.4 A Currency Skewness Factor.** Rafferty (2011) uses a factor analogous to DOL, and a factor that measures global currency skewness, to study portfolios similar to S1–S5. He takes inspiration from the literature on currency crashes and liquidity, for example, Brunnermeier et al. (2009). They tell a story in which carry trades drive currency dynamics until liquidity dries up, traders draw back their positions in tandem, and the currencies which are the targets of their trades crash. Accordingly, one might expect that carry trades are risky because high interest rate currencies are exposed, in tandem, to these crashes. To measure coordinated "crashing" of target currencies, Rafferty constructs a global currency skewness factor. This factor sorts currencies into two groups, one with positive forward discounts (equivalently, positive interest differentials) and the other with negative forward discounts. On a monthly basis he measures the realized skewness of the currencies in the first group, and the *negative* of the skewness of the currencies in the second group. The average, across available currencies, of these skewness statistics is his global currency skewness factor. I construct a similar factor using my data set and refer to it as SKW.

**10.4.2.5 Betas of Currency Factors.** Table 10.6 summarizes the results of running time-series regressions of the monthly excess returns to S1–S5, the EW carry-trade portfolio and the HML carry-trade portfolio on three pairs of risk factors: DOL and the HML carry-trade factor, DOL and VOL, and DOL and SKW. Consistent with the literature, the factors are entered in pairs in the time-series regressions.

The DOL and HML carry factors are highly correlated with the S1–S5 portfolio returns. The betas on the DOL factor are all close to 1 in value and statistically significant. The betas of the HML carry factor run from −0.48 for S1 and increase across the portfolios to a high of 0.52 for S5, although the betas for S2, S3, and S4 are all close to zero. The $R^2$ for the five regressions are all large as well. DOL and HML carry also have positive and significant betas for the EW carry-trade portfolio. Of course, the HML carry portfolio has a beta of 1 with respect to itself.

Should we be surprised by these findings? Not really. Recall, from Table 10.6, that sorting the portfolios on the basis of the forward discount produced a monotonic ordering of the expected returns. In this circumstance, the DOL and HML carry factors will, by construction, create a pattern in the betas similar to what we see in Table 10.6.[5] The reason is simple: DOL is the simple average of the returns to S1–S5. And HML is the difference between the returns to S5 and S1. If the returns to S1–S5 were mutually uncorrelated and had common variance the construction of the factors would then imply a beta of 1 for the DOL factor, and betas of −0.5, 0, 0, 0, and 0.5 for the HML factor. The observed pattern in the betas is very similar to this, with the difference being that the returns to S1–S5 are not mutually uncorrelated and do not have exactly the same variance. In fact, S1–S5 have an interesting factor structure. As Lustig et al. (2011) point out, the covariance structure of S1–S5 implies that two important factors drive most of the time-series variation in the five portfolio returns. Let the covariance matrix of the returns to S1–S5 be $\Sigma_z$, and diagonalize $\Sigma_z$ as $\Sigma_z = P\Lambda P^{-1}$, where $P$ is the matrix whose columns are the orthonormal eigenvectors of $\Sigma_z$ and $\Lambda$ has the corresponding eigenvalues of $\Sigma_z$ on the diagonal and zeros elsewhere. Lustig, Roussanov, and Verdelhan's point is that there are two large eigenvalues, with the others being much smaller. The eigenvectors corresponding to the two largest eigenvalues are close to being proportional to (1, 1, 1, 1, 1) and (−0.5, 0, 0, 0, 0.5). Therefore, if linear combinations of the returns are formed using these vectors, the two resulting "factors" are highly correlated with, respectively, DOL and HML.

Turning now to the DOL and VOL factors, we see that using VOL as a factor, rather than HML Carry, has very little impact on the betas with respect to DOL. The betas with respect to VOL decrease monotonically as we go from S1 to S5 and are statistically significant for the extreme portfolios, being positive for S1 and negative for S5. The betas with respect to VOL are also negative and statistically significant for the EW carry and HML carry portfolios. These findings indicate that when global currency volatility increases, the returns to holding low interest rate currencies increase and the returns to holding high interest rate currencies decrease. That is, low interest rate currencies provide a hedge against increased volatility. The average value of the volatility factor in the sample is 0.6% , indicating that on an annualized basis volatility averages about $0.6 \times \sqrt{365} = 11.5\%$ . The standard deviation of the volatility factor in the sample is 0.2% . The magnitude of the betas for S1 and S5 implies that if volatility went up by one standard deviation, the annualized return to S1 would be 5.5% higher than normal, while the annualized return to S5 would be 3.1% lower than normal.

Similarly, when we consider the DOL and SKW factors, we see that using SKW as a factor has very little impact on the betas with respect to DOL. The betas with respect to SKW increase (almost) monotonically as we go from S1 to S5 and are statistically significant for all portfolios, except S3. The betas are negative for S1 and S2 and positive for S3–S5, as well as for the EW carry and

[5] Burnside (2010b) goes through the details of this "by construction" result.

HML carry portfolios. These findings indicate that during episodes in which intra-month global currency skewness becomes more negative, the returns to holding low interest rate currencies increase and the returns to holding high interest rate currencies decrease. That is, low interest rate currencies provide a hedge against currency crashes, and high interest rate currencies are the most exposed to them. The average value of the skewness factor in the sample is −0.07, with a standard deviation of 0.26. The magnitude of the betas for S1 and S5 implies that if skewness became more negative by one standard deviation, the annualized return to S1 would be 4.1% higher than normal, while the annualized return to S5 would be 4.0% lower than normal.

**10.4.2.6 Cross-Sectional Analysis of Currency Factors.** Table 10.7 presents estimates of the SDF for the three currency factor models, obtained using the first-stage GMM estimator. This estimator is equivalent to running the cross-sectional regression (10.3.13). The results in Table 10.7 use only portfolios S1−S5 in the cross-sectional analysis. Not surprisingly, given our discussion of the betas, each of the models appears to do quite well in explaining the cross section of returns. To see why, recall that in each case the betas with respect to the DOL factor were similar across portfolios and close to 1. This means that the betas of the DOL factor act like a constant in the cross-sectional regression. The $b$ and $\lambda$ estimates associated with the DOL factor end up being statistically insignificant, in each case, because the betas associated with the other factor are centered near zero, and the cross-sectional average of the mean returns of S1−S5 is also, statistically, near zero. The $b$ parameters and risk premia ($\lambda$) associated with the HML carry, VOL and SKW factors are statistically significant at the 5% level (except the $b$ associated with VOL, which is significant at the 10% level). Again, this is not too surprising, because we saw, in Table 10.6, that the betas with respect to these factors tend to increase or decrease monotonically across the five portfolios. Finally, for all models the cross-sectional $R^2$ statistic is large. The model that uses DOL and HML carry ends up being rejected on the basis of the pricing errors at the 5% level. This is because the model does a relatively poor job of explaining the returns on the nonextreme and noncentral portfolios. This is a typical, by-construction, result for factor models based on one-dimensional sorts, where the first factor is the average of the portfolio returns, and the second factor is the difference between the extremes (Burnside, 2010b).

Table 10.8 presents estimates of the SDF for the three currency factor models, obtained using the iterated GMM estimator. Qualitatively and quantitatively, most of the results in Table 10.7 are robust to using the iterated estimator. Rafferty's (2011) skewness-based model has the best fit, and has no individually significant pricing errors, as before. The $R^2$ associated with Menkhoff et al.'s (2012) model falls considerably but the model is still not rejected on the basis of the $J$-statistic despite there being three individually significant pricing errors. The poorer fit in terms of $R^2$ can be understood by the fact that the iterated GMM estimator attempts to shrink the pricing error associated with S2 but at the cost of increasing the pricing errors associated with S1 and S4. The GMM estimator tries to do this because these pricing errors are correlated with each other. Lustig,

**TABLE 10.7 First-Stage GMM Estimates of Linear Factor Models for Sorted Currency Portfolios**

| | $b$ | $\lambda$ (%) | $R^2$ | $J$ | Pricing Errors ($\alpha$) S1 | S2 | S3 | S4 | S5 |
|---|---|---|---|---|---|---|---|---|---|
| Lustig et al. (2011) factors | | | | | | | | | |
| DOL | 2.39 | 0.190 | 0.84 | 9.23 | 0.0010 | −0.0158* | 0.0071 | 0.0109 | −0.0040 |
| | (2.05) | (0.127) | | (0.026) | (0.0060) | (0.0060) | (0.0068) | (0.0064) | (0.0046) |
| HML Carry | 6.97* | 0.539* | | | | | | | |
| | (2.08) | (0.133) | | | | | | | |
| Menkhoff et al. (2012) factors | | | | | | | | | |
| DOL | 0.96 | 0.198 | 0.73 | 4.31 | 0.0060 | −0.0240* | 0.0012 | 0.0070 | 0.0081 |
| | (3.16) | (0.122) | | (0.23) | (0.0043) | (0.0121) | (0.0092) | (0.0081) | (0.0098) |
| VOL | −3.07 | −14.0* | | | | | | | |
| | (1.69) | (5.67) | | | | | | | |
| Rafferty (2011) factors | | | | | | | | | |
| DOL | −2.11 | 0.182 | 0.96 | 1.51 | 0.0033 | −0.0061 | −0.0029 | 0.0061 | −0.0008 |
| | (2.76) | (0.131) | | (0.68) | (0.0054) | (0.0066) | (0.0091) | (0.0074) | (0.0071) |
| SKW | 3.05* | 20.7* | | | | | | | |
| | (0.95) | (6.19) | | | | | | | |

February 1976 to October 2010. Test assets are the sorted currency portfolios S1–S5. The DOL factor is the average excess return to portfolios S1–S5. The HML carry portfolio is the excess return to being long portfolio P5 and short portfolio P1. The VOL factor is a measure of realized global currency volatility. The SKW factor is a measure of realized global currency skewness. The table reports first-stage GMM estimates of the SDF parameter, $b$, and the factor risk premia, $\lambda$, reported in monthly percent. The $R^2$ is a measure of fit between the mean excess returns and the predicted mean returns. Test statistics, $J$, for the overidentifying restrictions are also reported. The annualized pricing errors of the S1–S5 portfolios ($\alpha$) are reported. Heteroskedasticity-consistent standard errors are in parentheses, except for the $J$statistics, for which the $p$-value is in parentheses. An asterisk (*) indicates statistical significance at the 5% level.

**TABLE 10.8 Iterated GMM Estimates of Linear Factor Models for Sorted Currency Portfolios**

| | | $\lambda$ | | | Pricing Errors ($\alpha$) | | | | |
|---|---|---|---|---|---|---|---|---|---|
| | $b$ | (%) | $R^2$ | $J$ | S1 | S2 | S3 | S4 | S5 |
| Lustig et al. (2011) factors | | | | | | | | | |
| DOL | 2.35 | 0.184 | 0.83 | 9.37 | −0.0012 | −0.0159* | 0.0077 | 0.0120* | −0.0001 |
| | (2.03) | (0.127) | | (0.025) | (0.0051) | (0.0060) | (0.0079) | (0.0059) | (0.0043) |
| HML Carry | 6.30* | 0.488* | | | | | | | |
| | (2.03) | (0.133) | | | | | | | |
| Menkhoff et al. (2012) factors | | | | | | | | | |
| DOL | −0.68 | 0.053 | 0.184 | 5.78 | 0.0127* | −0.0085* | 0.0185 | 0.0257* | 0.0306 |
| | (2.64) | (0.135) | | (0.12) | (0.0062) | (0.0038) | (0.0139) | (0.0110) | (0.0176) |
| VOL | −2.26 | −10.3* | | | | | | | |
| | (1.34) | (4.84) | | | | | | | |
| Rafferty (2011) factors | | | | | | | | | |
| DOL | −1.66 | 0.221 | 0.93 | 1.47 | −0.0001 | −0.0098 | −0.0075 | 0.0012 | −0.0064 |
| | (2.72) | (0.136) | | (0.69) | (0.0052) | (0.0091) | (0.0114) | (0.0069) | (0.0087) |
| SKW | 3.14* | 21.4* | | | | | | | |
| | (0.94) | (6.11) | | | | | | | |

February 1976 to October 2010. Test assets are the sorted currency portfolios S1–S5. The DOL factor is the average excess return to portfolios S1–S5. The HML carry portfolio is the excess return to being long portfolio P5 and short portfolio P1. The VOL factor is a measure of realized global currency volatility. The SKW factor is a measure of realized global currency skewness. The table reports iterated GMM estimates of the SDF parameter, $b$, and the factor risk premia, $\lambda$, reported in monthly percent. The $R^2$ is a measure of fit between the mean excess returns and the predicted mean returns. Test statistics, $J$, for the overidentifying restrictions are also reported. The annualized pricing errors of the S1–S5 portfolios ($\alpha$) are reported. Heteroskedasticity-consistent standard errors are in parentheses, except for the $J$ statistics, for which the $p$-value is in parentheses. An asterisk (*) indicates statistical significance at the 5% level.

Roussanov, and Verdelhan's HML carry-based model, despite having a high $R^2$, is statistically rejected, as before. With the iterated GMM estimator the poor fit of the noncentral and nonextreme portfolios, S2 and S4 is highlighted by their statistical significance.

**10.4.2.7 Discussion.** Models with factors based on currency returns seem to do quite well at explaining the returns to sorted portfolios of currencies. In the case of the DOL–HML carry model we have seen that this is not surprising, given that the sorting works (in that it produces an ordering of average returns), and given that both factors are constructed from the portfolios being priced. Indeed, it is somewhat dissatisfying to explain currency returns with the HML carry portfolio when, previously, we were trying to explain the returns of the HML carry portfolio. For the other currency-based models there is no similar issue, but, at the same time, the factors used in these cases are only indirectly linked to theoretical models. In a sense, therefore, we are left with the unsettling question: Why do these models seem to work in pricing the cross section of S1–S5?

If the estimated currency-based models are really informative about the SDFs of investors, then these models should also price stock returns. To see whether they do I reestimate the models of the previous section using the five sorted portfolios, as well as Fama and French's 25 portfolios sorted on the basis of size and value. When the stock market portfolios are added to the cross section, the models fare quite poorly. As Table 10.9 shows, the estimated parameters of the models do not change dramatically. However, the fit of the models and the results of the tests of the overidentifying restrictions suggest that the models simply cannot explain the cross section of stock returns.

This finding suggests that the cross-sectional analysis does not identify investors' SDF, or, to put it differently, a simple risk-based story based on the moment condition (10.9) has not yet been identified. However, the currency-based models are informative. They tell us that carry-trade strategies (like EW carry and HML carry) do better when currencies are less volatile and daily returns are less skewed. They do worse when volatility increases, and skewness becomes more negative. This finding is informative about the forces that drive currency fluctuations even if a satisfactory SDF has yet to be identified.

There are two less pessimistic interpretations of my findings. The first, is that there is some degree of market segmentation, which would make one SDF applicable to stock returns, and another relevant to currency returns. Although this is a logical possibility, there is empirical evidence against it. The nontraditional risk factors, described above, that do reasonably well at explaining currency portfolios sorted on the basis of forward discount, ought to explain other currency portfolios, such as those based on momentum, if they are reflective of currency investors' SDF. Burnside et al. (2011b) and Menkhoff et al. (2012) present evidence, however, that the same nontraditional factors that price carry-trade portfolios are unable to price momentum portfolios defined using short-term historical returns (i.e., when momentum is defined in terms of the previous month's return). Menkhoff et al. (2012) report more mixed evidence for

**TABLE 10.9 GMM Estimates of Linear Factor Models for Sorted Currency and Stock Market Portfolios**

| | $b$ | $\lambda$(%) | $R^2$ | $J$ |
|---|---|---|---|---|
| Lustig et al. (2011) factors | | | | |
| DOL | 1.82 | 0.145 | −1.92 | 97.0 |
| | (1.97) | (0.128) | | (0.000) |
| HML carry | 5.26* | 0.407* | | |
| | (1.94) | (0.134) | | |
| Menkhoff et al. (2012) factors | | | | |
| DOL | 0.30 | 0.053 | −2.70 | 89.3 |
| | (2.14) | (0.135) | | (0.000) |
| VOL | −0.84 | −3.86 | | |
| | (0.73) | (2.96) | | |
| Rafferty (2011) factors | | | | |
| DOL | −2.46 | 0.154 | −2.42 | 56.8 |
| | (2.44) | (0.138) | | (0.001) |
| SKW | 3.02* | 20.4* | | |
| | (0.86) | (4.26) | | |

February 1976 to October 2010. Test assets are the sorted currency portfolios S1–S5 and the Fama–French 25 portfolios sorted on the basis of size and value. The DOL factor is the average excess return to portfolios S1–S5. The HML carry portfolio is the excess return to being long portfolio P5 and short portfolio P1. The VOL factor is a measure of realized global currency volatility. The SKW factor is a measure of realized global currency skewness. The table reports iterated GMM estimates of the SDF parameter, $b$, and the factor risk premia, $\lambda$, reported in monthly percent. The $R^2$ is a measure of fit between the mean excess returns and the predicted mean returns. Test statistics, $J$, for the overidentifying restrictions are also reported. Heteroskedasticity-consistent standard errors are in parentheses, except for the $J$statistics, for which the $p$-value is in parentheses. An asterisk (*) indicates statistical significance at the 5% level.

momentum defined using longer term historical performance. Menkhoff et al. (2011) find that individual-currency characteristics appear to be important in explaining the returns to currency momentum.

The second interpretation of my findings is that empirical exercises involving currency returns identify one component of the global investor's SDF, while those involving stock returns identify another. According to this interpretation, in effect, the fully successful SDF is the sum of the individual SDFs identified by sorting stocks, currencies, and other assets, on the basis of each asset return anomaly. Again, this is a logically coherent explanation, but one I find rather unsatisfying in that it makes SDF-based explanations untestable.

## 10.5 Time-Varying Risk and Rare Events

I concluded, in Section 10.4.1, that standard risk models do not explain the returns to the carry trade. There we saw that the beta of the HML carry-trade portfolio with respect to the CAPM factor is statistically significant, but is much too small (0.163) to explain the risk premium of the carry trade. To explain the roughly 6% risk premium of the HML carry portfolio, the beta would need to be about six times as large. Lustig et al. (2011) agree on this assessment, arguing that "the average beta of $HML_{FX}$ with the US stock market return is too small to explain carry trade risk premia." However, they argue that the beta of the carry trade with respect to the stock market increases during times of financial market distress. Certainly, during the recent mortgage crisis my HML carry-trade factor displayed more correlation than usual with the stock market. However, it seems unlikely that a simple conditional beta story can explain the returns to the carry trade. There are two reasons favoring this conclusion. First, as Figure 10.1 reveals, in historical data, there is no systematic relationship between distress in the stock market (measured by periods of sharp decline) and currency crashes (measured by the period of big losses to the carry trade). Second, time variation in the carry trade's stock market beta, while significant, is quantitatively not large enough. To see this, consider Figure 10.2, which plots betas of the *daily* returns of the HML carry-trade portfolio with respect to the market premium. The betas are computed with a 130 working day (6-month) backward-looking rolling window, but similar results emerge with different windows. Overall, the betas, even at the extremes, are not that large. The figure also shows all dates at which the monthly return to the stock market was −10% or less. If these months initiated periods

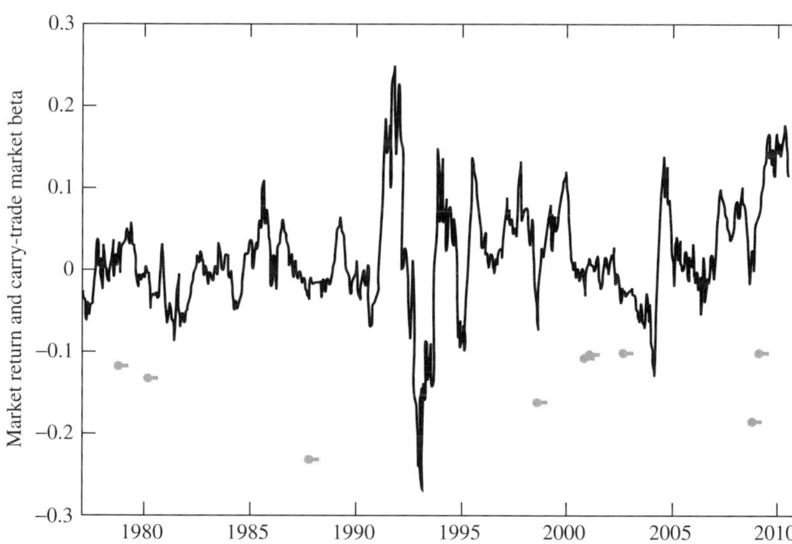


FIGURE 10.2 The time-varying market beta of the HML carry trade portfolio. 6-Month rolling window, January 1977–June 2010. The beta is computed by regressing daily returns to the HML carry-trade portfolio on daily returns to the US stock market, defined as the Mkt-Rf factor from Kenneth French's database. The gray dots mark single months in which the market excess return was less than −10%. The gray lines delineate a 6-month window after but inclusive of each of these dates.

of stock market distress we might expect to see the rolling window betas increase in the 6-month windows inclusive of these events. In some cases, as in the recent crisis, this is what we observe. In other cases, such as the stock market crash at the end of the dot-com boom in 2000–2001, there is no such increase in the beta.

Lustig et al. (2011) briefly explore a potentially related explanation of currency returns. They consider a two-factor model in which one of the factors is DOL and the other factor is a measure of the change in global stock market volatility (the cross-country average of daily intra-month stock market volatility, measured using local currency MSCI indices). They find that the betas of their sorted currency portfolios with respect to stock market volatility decrease with the size of the interest differential. While the second factor is driven out by their HML carry factor in cross-sectional regressions, the relationship between stock market volatility and currency returns may shed light on a common economic explanation of the returns to the carry trade, especially because stock market volatility has been shown to have some power to explain the cross section of stock returns (Ang et al., 2006).

An alternative explanation of the returns to the carry trade is that they reflect out of sample (or peso event) risk.[6] This explanation relies on the notion that Equation (10.9) still holds, but that the observed historical data are not fully representative of the underlying population distribution of the payoffs and the SDF. Burnside et al. (2011a) use currency options data to construct hedged and unhedged versions of the EW carry-trade portfolio. By doing so, and by imposing that Equation (10.9) holds after allowing for peso event risk, they are able to characterize the nature of the hidden peso events. They argue that peso events appear to be the ones in which carry trades incur relatively modest losses. The defining characteristic of a peso event, instead, is the fact that the SDF increases sharply, indicating that investors fear disastrous outcomes.

What remains to be seen is whether the peso-event-based explanation of the returns to the carry trade can be connected to the results discussed above. Can peso risk induce a time-varying risk premium that explains the UIP puzzle? Can peso risk explain the correlation between volatility and skewness factors and carry-trade payoffs? These are open questions for future research. A theme of this chapter is that explanations of asset pricing puzzles that work across markets are not easily identifiable. So, a peso risk story that works for currencies should also work for stock returns. Burnside et al. (2011a) suggest that the same peso event that can rationalize carry-trade returns can also rationalize the return on the overall stock market. Burnside et al. (2011b) suggest that the same peso event that can rationalize carry-trade returns can also rationalize currency momentum returns. Julliard and Ghosh (2010), however, suggest that rare consumption disasters make the cross section of stock returns harder to rationalize, because they reduce the spread of consumption betas in the cross section. Also, if we observe sufficiently many extreme events in markets (e.g., the 2008 financial

[6]Krasker (1980); Lewis (1989), and Kaminsky (1993) explored the role of peso problems in explaining the behavior of foreign exchange markets. More recently Burnside et al. (2011a) ask whether out-of-sample events can explain the returns to the carry trade. Farhi and Gabaix (2008) and Farhi et al. (2009) explore both in-sample and out-of-sample rare events.

crisis, the 2011 European debt crises, and the 2011 downgrade of US Treasury debt by Standard and Poor's) the distinction between theories based on observed risk factors, especially those related to measures of volatility and skewness and unobserved peso events may become less clear. In other words, the in-sample frequency of extreme events may end up being similar to their true frequency.

## 10.6 Conclusion

Carry trades are, on average, profitable. As we have seen, conventional, stock-Market-based models of risk do not explain the returns to the carry trade. Less traditional factors, that are defined in terms of the currency fluctuations, are more successful in explaining currency returns, but do not, conversely, explain the returns to the stock market. This means that, at least for the moment, a unifying explanation of stock market and carry-trade returns based on observed fluctuations in measures of risk remains elusive. An alternative explanation is that carry-trade returns reflect investors' concerns about out-of-sample events. While this story has some appeal, it must, of course, grapple with the evidence that volatility and skewness (or crash risk) factors have explanatory power in sample.

## Acknowledgments

I thank Martin Eichenbaum, Barry Rafferty, Sergio Rebelo, Nikolai Roussanov, Lucio Sarno, and an anonymous referee for their helpful comments.

## REFERENCES

Ang A, Hodrick RJ, Xing Y, Zhang X. The cross-section of volatility and expected returns. J Finance 2006; 61: 259–299.

Bekaert G, Hodrick RJ. Characterizing predictable components in excess returns on equity and foreign exchange markets. J Finance 1992; 47:467–509.

Brunnermeier MK, Nagel S, Pedersen LH. Carry trades and currency crashes. NBER Macroeconomics Annual 2008, 2009; 23:313–347.

Burnside C. Identification and inference in linear stochastic discount factor models. NBER Working paper 16634; 2010a.

Burnside C. Sorts and cross-sectional regressions, mimeo. Duke University; 2010b.

Burnside C. The cross-section of foreign currency risk premia and consumption growth risk: Comment. American Economic Review 2011; 101:3456–76.

Burnside C, Eichenbaum M, Kleshchelski I, Rebelo S. The returns to currency speculation. NBER Working paper 12489; 2006.

Burnside C, Eichenbaum M, Kleshchelski I, Rebelo S. Do peso problems explain the returns to the carry trade? Rev Financ Stud 2011a; 24:853–891.

Burnside C, Eichenbaum M, Rebelo S. Carry trade and momentum in currency markets. Annu Rev Financ Econ 2011b; 3:511–35.

Campbell JY. Consumption-based asset pricing. In: Constantinides GM, Harris M, Stulz R, editors. Volume 1B, Handbook of the economics of finance. Amsterdam: Elsevier; 2003.

Da Z, Schaumburg E. The pricing of volatility risk across asset classes and the Fama-French factors, mimeo, University of Notre Dame; 2009.

Engel C. The forward discount anomaly and the risk premium: a survey of recent evidence. J Empir Finance 1996; 3:123–192.

Fama EF. Forward and spot exchange rates. J Monet Econ 1984; 14:319–338.

Fama E, French KR. Common risk factors in the returns on stocks and bonds. J Financ Econ 1993; 33:3–56.

Farhi E, Fraiberger SP, Gabaix X, Ranciere R, Verdelhan A. Crash risk in currency markets. NBER Working paper 15062; 2009.

Farhi E, Gabaix X. Rare disasters and exchange rates. NBER Working paper 13805; 2008.

Hansen LP. Large sample properties of generalized method of moments estimators. Econometrica 1982; 50:1029–1054.

Hodrick RJ. The empirical evidence on the efficiency of forward and futures foreign exchange markets. Chur, Switzerland: Harwood Academic Publishers; 1987.

Jegadeesh N, Titman S. Returns to buying winners and selling losers: implications for stock market efficiency. J Finance 1993; 48:65–91.

Julliard C, Ghosh A. Can rare events explain the equity premium puzzle? mimeo, Carnegie Mellon University; 2010.

Kaminsky G. Is there a peso problem? Evidence from the dollar/pound exchange rate, 1976–1987. Am Econ Rev 1993; 83:450–472.

Krasker WS. The 'peso problem' in testing the efficiency of forward exchange markets. J Monet Econ 1980; 6:269–276.

Lewis KK. Changing beliefs and systematic rational forecast errors with evidence from foreign exchange. Am Econ Rev 1989; 79:621–636.

Lustig H, Roussanov N, Verdelhan A. Common risk factors in currency markets. Rev Financ Stud 2011; 24:3731–3777.

Lustig H, Verdelhan A. The cross-section of foreign currency risk premia and consumption growth risk. Am Econ Rev 2007; 97:89–117.

Meese RA, Rogoff K. Empirical exchange rate models of the seventies: do they fit out of sample? J Int Econ 1983; 14: 3–24.

Menkhoff L, Sarno L, Schmeling M, Schrimpf A. Currency momentum strategies. Working Paper, Cass Business School, City University, London; 2011.

Menkhoff L, Sarno L, Schmeling M, Schrimpf A. Carry trades and global foreign exchange volatility. J Finance 2012; 67.

Rafferty B. Currency returns, skewness and crash risk, manuscript. Duke University; 2011.

Yogo M. A consumption-based explanation of expected stock returns. J Finance 2006; 61:539–580.

CHAPTER ELEVEN

# Currency Fair Value Models


GINO CENEDESE
Bank of England

THOMAS STOLPER
Goldman Sachs International


## 11.1 Introduction

What is the fair value of a currency? Policymakers and international investors have always been asking this question, and economists have been trying to find answers, proposing many different methodologies to estimate fair value. Simple measures have ranged from relative national price indices (Cassel, 1918) to relative hamburger prices (The Economist, 1986). More elaborate models take into consideration the economic factors, ranging from productivity differentials (Balassa, 1964; Harrod, 1933; Samuelson, 1964) to sex ratios (Du and Wei, 2011). In this chapter, we provide a comprehensive review of models that are used by policymakers and international investors in order to assess exchange rate misalignments from their fair value.

Early references to misaligned currencies go back to the antiquity. Vaughan (1675) uses the example of the Roman coin *as* to illustrate how the "intrinsical value" of a money declined after the reduction of weight of a coin. The author also introduces a notion of fairness linked to exchange rates when calling currency devaluation "an unjust device."

Policymakers need to assess the possible misalignment of currencies for a number of reasons. Exchange rates play a crucial role in a country's external adjustment process, particularly as economies become more and more integrated. At the time of writing, advanced economies have faced some degree of exchange rate realignment since the onset of the recent global financial crisis, whereas this


*Handbook of Exchange Rates*, First Edition. Edited by Jessica James, Ian W. Marsh, and Lucio Sarno.

realignment has been limited for emerging market (EM) economies, creating tensions and constituting a threat to the global recovery [Chapter 1] (IMF, 2011). More generally, substantial misalignments can have severe consequences, as exchange rates may abruptly adjust when the misalignment becomes unsustainable, leading to currency crises generally associated with large output contractions, especially in EMs (Dornbusch et al, 1995; Gourinchas and Obstfeld, 2012; Gupta et al, 2007). In a theory paper, Engel (2011) shows that currency misalignments are inefficient, lower world welfare, and should be targeted by monetary policymakers in a model in which firms price to market and prices are sticky.

Another major use of fair value models is investment advice. Major financial institutions have introduced fully investable and tradable indices that track the performance of fair-valued-based strategies, such as Goldman Sachs FX Valuation Current (Goldman Sachs, 2009) and Deutsche Bank Valuation Index (Deutsche Bank, 2007). Beyond financial investments, variable real exchange rates may influence the location of production facilities chosen by multinationals (Goldberg and Kolstad, 1995) and a fair value estimate may be useful as a long-term forecast.

Given the diverse use of currency fair value models highlighted above, it is important to understand which models are more suitable for a given context. In this chapter, we analyze this issue in detail by surveying and critically assessing a number of fair value models proposed in the literature.[1] We intentionally avoid an extensive discussion of purchasing-power parity (PPP), as this literature is covered in detail in many surveys: see Sarno and Taylor (2003, Chapter 3) and Taylor and Taylor (2004).

Section 11.2 provides an exposition of a number of fair value and equilibrium exchange rate models that are widely used in practice. After briefly discussing theories of long-term deviations from PPP and their practical application to fair value modeling, we focus on the two main families of models, namely, the behavioral equilibrium exchange rate (BEER) and the underlying balance (UB) models. As applied examples, we discuss in more detail the IMF framework and the Goldman Sachs Dynamic Equilibrium Exchange Rate (GSDEER) model. In both cases, we highlight how the estimates of fair value are affected by some typical implementation choices. We also illustrate a fair value concept frequently used by financial market practitioners but not previously formalized in the academic literature. This model, which we dub indirect fair value (IFV), relies on indirect estimation of fair value of the currency by "removing" the speculative components that drive exchange rates in the short run.

In Section 11.3, we discuss the basic characteristics of fair value models with a particular focus on how implicit or explicit design choices typically affect the results, the robustness and the general usability of these models. We argue that there is no explicit answer regarding which model delivers the correct fair value of a currency, because each model has its own individual strengths and weaknesses. We illustrate this point by means of examples, focusing on the practical implementation of the models. For instance, we discuss the sensitivity of

[1]As highlighted below, we focus on the practical implementation of these models. For their theoretical foundations, see Chapter 2 by Menzie Chinn in this Handbook.

UB models with regard to variations in import and export elasticities. Moreover, we discuss how the treatment of the external balance in different models appears responsible for discrepancies between estimation results. Researchers are therefore left with a wide range of choices, and many use a set of models or a combination of these in order to assess exchange rate misalignments.

## 11.2 Models/Taxonomy

Over the years, a number of models of fair value have been developed. Although some approaches are more theoretical, all of these models have been used in applied work, some only occasionally for ad hoc studies, while others are being updated and modified continuously. The latter is particularly true for those models used in the private sector or by international institutions for policy advice. In this category, we include the three fair value models used by the IMF Consultative Group on Exchange Rate Issues (CGER), as well as the Goldman Sachs fair value model.

### 11.2.1 "ADJUSTED PPP": HARROD-BALASSA-SAMUELSON AND PENN EFFECTS

Many studies have tried to measure exchange rate misalignment by exploiting the positive relation between real per capita income and relative prices across countries, that is, the fact that rich countries tend to have higher price levels than poor countries. This empirical relation is also known as the *Penn effect* after the Penn World Table of Summers and Heston (1991), and has been explained usually by appealing to productivity differentials between the tradeable and nontradeable sectors—the Harrod-Balassa-Samuelson effect (Rogoff, 1996). This effect provides a structural interpretation of long-run deviations from PPP (hence the "adjusted PPP" terminology used in many studies) based on real factors that can be exploited for measuring exchange rate misalignments.

The exchange rate misalignment can therefore be measured as the residual of a cross-sectional regression such as

$$q_i = a + b\ln(\mathrm{GDP}_i) + \nu_i \tag{11.1}$$

where $q$ is the log real exchange rate, $a$ and $b$ are coefficients, $\nu$ is the residual term, and GDP is measured in per capita terms, usually relative to the United States and converted using PPP-based exchange rates. Frankel (2006) uses this kind of regression in order to evaluate the renminbi misalignment at two different time points, the years 1990 and 2000. De Broeck and Slok (2006) adopt a similar methodology for measuring the misalignment of the real exchange rates for a number of transition economies at the onset of the transition period. Cheung et al. (2007, 2009) extend the cross-sectional approach of Frankel (2006) by using panel data techniques for a number of specifications, for example, allowing for country fixed effects, random effects, and adding different control variables.

Rodrik (2008) builds an index of currency undervaluation by taking the residuals of an estimated panel regression of real exchange rates on real per capita income allowing for time fixed effects.

### 11.2.2 THE BEHAVIORAL EQUILIBRIUM EXCHANGE RATE FAMILY OF MODELS

Clark and MacDonald (1998) propose the estimation of a reduced-form equation in order to explain the behavior of the real effective exchange rate (REER) both in the short and medium run—what they call the BEER. The acronym BEER is often used to indicate, by extension, a whole family of models that follow similar methodologies.

**11.2.2.1 The Standard BEER Model.** The theoretical basis of the BEER model is the risk-adjusted uncovered interest parity condition in real terms. By definition, the log excess return on foreign exchange (FX) is equal to the interest rate differential plus the appreciation rate of the foreign currency,

$$z_{t+k} = i_t^* - i_t + (s_{t+k} - s_t) \tag{11.2}$$

where $s_t$ is the natural logarithm of the exchange rate (defined as the domestic price of foreign currency, so that an increase in $s_t$ denotes appreciation of the foreign currency), and $i_t$ and $i_t^*$ are the continuously compounded $k$-period domestic and foreign riskless interest rates, respectively. In terms of the log real exchange rate, defined as $q_t = s_t + p_t^* - p_t$, where $p_t^*$ and $p_t$ are the logs of the foreign and domestic price levels, respectively, Equation 11.2 can be rewritten as

$$z_{t+k} = r_{t+k}^* - r_{t+k} + q_{t+k} - q_t \tag{11.3}$$

where $r_{t+k}$ and $r_{t+k}^*$ denote domestic and foreign real interest rates, respectively. In general, the expected excess return, $E_t z_{t+k}$, will be equal to a time-varying risk premium, $\rho_t$, so that

$$q_t = E_t(q_{t+k}) + E_t(r_{t+k}^* - r_{t+k}) - \rho_t \tag{11.4}$$

That is, the equilibrium real exchange rate reflects expectations of future real exchange rates, expectations of future real interest rate differentials, and a time-varying risk premium.

To make their model empirically tractable, Clark and MacDonald make the further assumption that the unobservable expectations of the exchange rate are a function of long-run economic fundamentals, that is, $E_t(q_{t+k}) = \beta' Z_t$, where $Z_t$ denotes a vector of fundamental variables and $\beta$ is a vector of coefficients. Clark and MacDonald identify the fundamental variables as the terms of trade, the relative price of nontraded to traded goods (proxying for Harrod-Balassa-Samuelson effects), and net foreign assets (NFAs). Moreover, they proxy the time-varying risk premium $\rho_t$ with the relative supply of domestic and foreign debt, arguing that an increase in the relative supply of outstanding domestic debt relative to foreign debt will increase the domestic risk premium, thereby requiring a depreciation of the current equilibrium exchange rate (Giorgianni, 1997).

Empirically, the BEER is generally estimated using the fitted values of a cointegration relationship between the REER and a set of fundamentals such as those illustrated above. For example, Clark and MacDonald (1998) use the Johansen (1988) method that allows for the existence of multiple cointegrating vectors. Extensions of the BEER approach are among the most popular fair value models among policy institutions and in the financial industry. For example, see the IMF equilibrium real exchange rate (ERER) approach and Goldman Sachs's GSDEER model discussed later in this section.

A related approach is the so-called capital enhanced equilibrium exchange rate (CHEER), introduced by Johansen and Juselius (1992) and MacDonald and Marsh (1997), and later extended by MacDonald and Marsh (2004). The starting point is the view that nominal exchange rates may be misaligned from their PPP-implied level because of nonzero interest rate differentials (what Macdonald and Marsh (1997) call the "Casselian view" of PPP). A cointegration relation is therefore estimated between nominal exchange rates, domestic and foreign price levels, and domestic and foreign interest rates. In this approach, the estimated speed of convergence tends to be faster than the typical PPP adjustment based on univariate models, and the inferred nominal exchange rate forecasts have some degree of short-term predictive ability when compared to the random walk benchmark.

#### 11.2.2.2 The Permanent Equilibrium Exchange Rate (PEER).

The BEER model introduced in the previous section can be used to estimate what Clark and MacDonald (1998) call the current misalignment, based on current values of fundamentals. However, knowing that current values may depart substantially from sustainable or long-run levels, a number of researchers have been investigating the fair value of the real exchange rate consistent with its long-run fundamentals.

Huizinga (1987) and Cumby and Huizinga (1990) use, respectively, univariate and multivariate Beveridge–Nelson decompositions in order to decompose the real exchange rate into the sum of permanent and transitory components. The permanent component is then considered to be the permanent equilibrium exchange rate (PEER).

More recently, the PEER model of Clark and MacDonald (2004) is a direct extension of the BEER models outlined above. Clark and MacDonald use the method developed by Gonzalo and Granger (1995) in order to decompose the fundamentals in permanent and transitory components, where the former are used to identify the long-run value of the fundamentals, which are then used to calculate fair value. The fundamentals are the same as in the BEER approach, but the terms of trade and the government debts ratio are dropped in the empirical analysis.

#### 11.2.2.3 The Equilibrium Real Exchange Rate (ERER) Approach.

The IMF ERER approach obtains the fair value of a country's currency by directly estimating a reduced-form equation, which models the equilibrium exchange rate as a function of medium-term fundamentals.

The medium-term adjustment of the real exchange rate is then calculated simply as the difference between the current, projected value of the exchange rate and the corresponding estimated, equilibrium value.

In its most recent version (Lee et al., 2008; Ricci et al., 2008), the ERER approach is employed for estimating equilibrium CPI-based REERs for 48 countries. The choice of fundamentals is partly driven by theories of real exchange rate determination and partly by data availability issues. The medium-term fundamentals most notably include measures for NFA positions, relative productivity differentials between the tradable and nontradable sectors, and terms of trade. These measures have been widely employed in reduced-form estimation of equilibrium exchange rates (see for example Lane and Milesi-Ferretti, 2004).

NFAs are included because countries that are net debtors will need more depreciated real exchange rates in order to stimulate future trade surpluses to service their external liabilities. Productivity differentials are used to proxy for Harrod-Balassa-Samuelson effects. The measure of terms of trade used in the ERER reflects only the prices of imported and exported commodities. Higher commodity prices tend to imply an appreciating real exchange rate through income or wealth effects. Other fundamentals included in the analysis are government consumption, a trade restriction index, and a proxy for price controls.

The ERER approach uses panel dynamic ordinary least squares (DOLS) in order to estimate the following long-run cointegrating relationship between the log of the REER, $q$, and the set of fundamentals:

$$q_{i,t} = \alpha_i + \beta' Z_{i,t} + \sum_{j=-p}^{j=p} \gamma_j' \Delta Z_{i,t+j} + \varepsilon_{i,t} \tag{11.5}$$

where $Z$ is the vector of fundamentals, $\Delta$ denotes the first-difference operator, $\beta$ and $\gamma_j$ are coefficients vectors, $\alpha_i$ are country fixed effects, $\varepsilon_{i,t}$ denotes the residuals, and $i$ and $t$ denote the country and time, respectively. Given that REERs are index numbers, their levels are not comparable across countries, so that country fixed effects are used.

The panel DOLS specification (Eq. 11.5) is used because inference in a panel fixed effect cointegrating relationship would be flawed in the presence of correlation between the residuals and the stationary component of the unit-root processes of the regressors. Adding leads and lags of first differences of the regressors automatically removes this correlation (Stock and Watson, 1993; Mark and Sul, 2003).

The ERER approach then uses an error-correction-mechanism (ECM) specification in order to assess the speed of adjustment of the real exchange rate to its long-run equilibrium value:

$$\Delta q_{i,t} = c_i + \delta(q_{i,t-1} - \alpha_i - \beta' Z_{i,t-1}) + \lambda q_{i,t-1} + \phi' \Delta Z_{i,t} + \psi' \Delta Z_{i,t-1} + \eta_{i,t} \tag{11.6}$$

Ricci et al. (2008), in their analysis of 48 industrial countries and EMs for the period 1980–2004, estimate an adjustment coefficient $\delta$ that implies a half-life for deviations from the equilibrium level of the exchange rate of around 2.5 years.

**11.2.2.4 The Goldman Sachs Dynamic Equilibrium Exchange Rate (GSDEER).** The first version of the GSDEER model was introduced in the mid-1990s (Goldman Sachs, 1996) and was a simple, adjusted PPP model allowing for Harrod-Balassa-Samuelson effects. The coefficient on productivity was assumed to be unity. The model was not estimated but in fact calculated by applying inflation and productivity differentials to an initial reference period, at which the bilateral exchange rates were assumed to be in equilibrium. The latter was determined by judgment with strong focus on the size of current account (CA) imbalances. Calculated misalignment values were available for the currencies of advanced economies.

At the same time, Goldman Sachs developed a second fair value model for EM currencies,[2] which was essentially a BEER model with a relatively large number of model inputs reflecting external sustainability—a choice driven by the fact that EM currency crises were frequent at the time. Specifically, the following variables were used: terms of trade, the degree of openness to foreign trade, the share of long-term capital inflows as a percentage of GDP, the amount and composition of government spending, and the level of international interest rates (Goldman Sachs, 1996).

These two models were later merged into a unified BEER-style approach estimated with panel DOLS cointegration techniques with country fixed effects (O'Neill et al., 2005). More specifically, the equilibrium exchange rate was estimated as a function of terms of trade differentials, productivity differentials, and the relative NFA position between two countries. The real exchange rate was calculated using CPI indices.

Given that the GSDEER model is estimated in a panel for approximately 30 currencies, the choice of variables is partly driven by the availability of data. To allow out-of-sample projections of fair value estimates, Goldman Sachs uses its in-house forecasts for the input variables.

This generation of GSDEER model has been re-estimated about every 2 years with some modifications at each iteration. Recently, the NFA variable has been excluded as its significance dropped and given that the sign of the associated coefficient flipped and became counterintuitive, indicating that rising external liabilities were associated with an appreciating fair value (Fuentes and Meechan, 2007). As a result, the GSDEER fair value estimates now do not depend on variables of external imbalances.

Another major issue faced by the authors related to what we discuss later in Section 11.3.2: short samples for some countries or a history of managed exchange rates for others may severely bias the estimation of the intercept of reduced-form fair value models. In turn, errors in the estimation of the intercept

[2]This model was called the Goldman Sachs Dynamic Equilibrium Emerging Markets Exchange Rate (GSDEEMER) model.

will translate in a biased estimate of the fair value level of the exchange rate. In the latest version of the GSDEER model, Goldman's economists (Stolper et al., 2009) argue that most of the data problems leading to a biased estimate of the intercept will also lead to the violation of the assumption of cointegration between the exchange rates and the fundamentals. Consequently, they test the cross-sectional residuals for stationarity. Their results show that the hypothesis of a unit root in the residuals is particularly unlikely to get rejected for the following:

- currencies with a history of managed exchange rates, typically in developing Asia;
- currencies that have been subject to periods of hyperinflation, typically in Latin America;
- currencies with short samples, in particular, in Central and Eastern Europe.

For those cases in which the unit-root hypothesis cannot be rejected, Stolper et al. (2009) adjust the country fixed effects of the GSDEER model by estimating a cross-sectional model based on the Penn effect, as the one described in Section 11.2.1.

### 11.2.3 THE UNDERLYING BALANCE (UB) APPROACH

The UB approach asserts that the fair value of a currency is the level of the exchange rate that is consistent with a country's internal and external balance. Most applications of the UB approach identify internal balance as a country's economic activity being at full potential output (i.e., zero output gap). External balance can be broadly defined as a country's CA position being at equilibrium or at sustainable levels, but different interpretations of what "equilibrium" or "sustainable" exactly mean have given rise to different implementations of this approach in the literature. The UB approach has its roots in the pioneering work of Meade (1951); Metzler (1951); Nurkse (1945), and Swan (1963), in their attempts to characterize the equilibrium in an open economy. More than most other fair value models, the UB approach explicitly considers external imbalances to derive fair value estimates. We discuss further the implications of this important choice in Section 11.3.3.

The UB approach starts from the balance of payments identity, which expresses the CA in terms of either a change in NFAs ($\Delta$NFA) or the excess domestic savings ($S$) over domestic investment ($I$), that is,[3]

$$\text{CA} = \Delta\text{NFA} = S - I \tag{11.7}$$

The equilibrium exchange rate is then found as the level of the exchange rate that closes the gap between the underlying current account (UCUR) and the saving-investment/current account "norm" or "target" net capital flows. The

[3]Here, as is the case for most empirical applications of the UB approach, we abstract from possible effects of the valuation channel on the external adjustment process. Accounting for valuation effects, the change in NFAs is equal to the CA plus the net capital gain on foreign assets and liablilties.

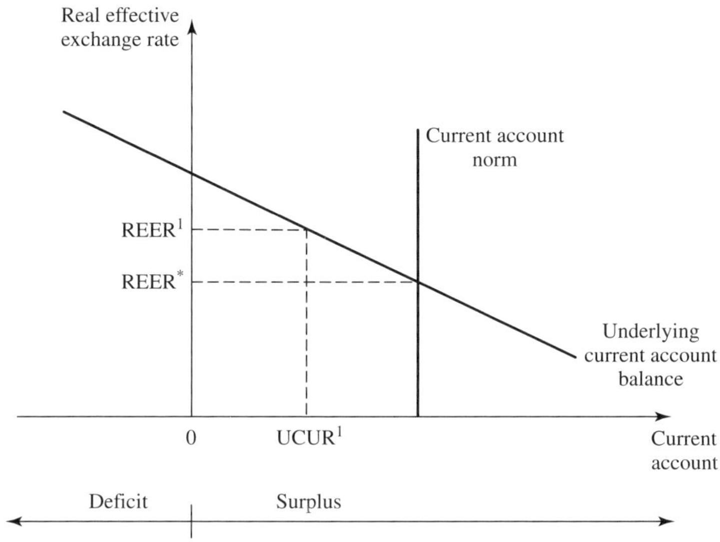


**FIGURE 11.1 Underlying balance approach. The figure illustrates the underlying balance approach described in the main text.**

UCUR is defined as the CA set to prevail in the medium run when countries are at internal balance, whereas the current account norm reflects some equilibrium or sustainable value of $(S-I)$ or $\Delta$(NFA).

Figure 11.1 provides a summary of the approach. The UCUR line is downward sloping because an appreciation of the REER (corresponding here to an increase in its level) tends to be associated with a declining CA, for a given level of output. The CA norm, instead, is generally assumed to be independent of the level of the exchange rate, so that the line is vertical. The equilibrium level of the REER, denoted as REER*, is therefore associated with the intersection of the two lines.

The estimation of the UCUR and the CA norm are distinguishing features of the empirical applications of the UB approach. We consider down here the two most prominent cases, that is, the "fundamental equilibrium exchange rate" (FEER) in Section 11.2.3.1 and the IMF macroeconomic balance (MB) approach in Section 11.2.3.2.

The different flavors of the UB really only differ in the way they estimate—or calculate—the CA norm. In a second step, all models use a virtually identical procedure to calculate the needed exchange rate ajustment for the CA to reach this target.

Countries with high ratios of exports and imports to GDP (i.e., countries that are more open to trade) will require smaller exchange rate adjustments in order to achieve CAs consistent with macroeconomic balance. This effect can be seen from Figure 11.1: an increase in trade openness, other things being equal, will tend to flatten the UCUR line, resulting in a smaller movement in the REER to move from the current level $\text{REER}^1$ to the equilibrium level REER*.

Analytically, denoting the trade-balance-to-GDP ratio as tb, we have that

$$\text{tb} = \frac{P_X X}{\text{GDP}} - \frac{P_M M}{\text{GDP}} \tag{11.8}$$

where $M$ and $X$ are import and export volumes, and $P_M$ and $P_X$ are prices of imports and exports in local currency, respectively.[4] The total differential of tb with respect to the real exchange rate $Q$ is

$$\frac{\partial \text{tb}}{\partial Q} = \frac{\partial X}{\partial Q}\frac{P_X}{\text{GDP}} + \frac{\partial P_X}{\partial Q}\frac{X}{\text{GDP}} - \frac{\partial M}{\partial Q}\frac{P_M}{\text{GDP}} - \frac{\partial P_M}{\partial Q}\frac{M}{\text{GDP}} \tag{11.9}$$

Assuming that exports are priced in local currency (so that $\frac{\partial P_X}{\partial Q} = 0$) and that imports are priced in foreign currency (so that they are unit elastic with respect to $Q$, $\frac{\partial P_M}{\partial Q} = -\frac{P_M}{Q}$), Equation (11.9) can be rewritten as

$$\frac{\partial \text{tb}}{(\partial Q)/Q} = \eta_X \frac{P_X X}{\text{GDP}} - (\eta_M - 1)\frac{P_M M}{\text{GDP}} \tag{11.10}$$

where $\eta_X = \frac{\partial X}{\partial Q}\frac{Q}{X}$ is the export elasticity and $\eta_M = \frac{\partial M}{\partial Q}\frac{Q}{M}$ is the import elasticity, with $\eta_X < 0$ and $\eta_M > 0$. This implies that, for given export and import elasticities, the impact of a change in the exchange rate will be roughly proportional to trade openness.

**11.2.3.1 The Fundamental Equilibrium Exchange Rate (FEER).** The term FEER is often used as a synonym for the exchange rate that is consistent with internal and external balance, and therefore falls into the broad category of models that follow the UB approach discussed above.

However, here we use the term FEER to indicate more narrowly the model first developed by Williamson (1983, 1994), given its major influence in the development of exchange rate fair value models. Williamson (1983) defines the FEER as the REER "generating for every country a CA surplus or deficit equal to the underlying capital flow over the cycle, given that the country is pursing internal balance as best it can and not restricting trade for balance of payments reasons" (Chapter 2, p. 14).

The main distinguishing feature of FEER with respect to other UB models (especially, the CGER MB model discussed in Section 11.2.3.2) is the definition of external balance in terms of "underlying" capital flows. The focus here is on computing the REER that equates the underlying CA to an equilibrium level of capital flows. This level is derived not through estimation procedures but mostly by judgmental considerations, and is often assumed to be a constant proportion of GDP (Williamson and Mahar, 1998). This is why Wren-Lewis (1992) defines

[4]In what follows, we assume that the trade balance is the sole source of CA adjustments, consistent with the IMF approach.

the FEER model as a "method of calculation" (as opposed to an econometric estimation) of the equilibrium exchange rate.

Highlighting the normative content of the FEER approach, Bayoumi et al. (1994) name the approach as "desired equilibrium exchange rate" (DEER). The DEER is therefore the exchange rate consistent with internal balance and a target CA explicitly set (or "desired") by policymakers. In their application, Bayoumi et al. (1994) calculate the DEER for a number of countries in 1970 in order to analyze the breakup of the Bretton Woods system. They use a 1% target CA surplus, as this was the approximate stated objective of the US government during the discussions that led to the Smithsonian Agreement in 1971 (in general, a 1% target CA surplus was also widely supported by the IMF for industrial countries in the 1960s, see also Polak, 1995, p. 749).

In a more recent example of judgmental CA targets, Cline and Williamson (2008a, 2011) discuss the appropriate set of CA targets for a number of developed and emerging economies. They start from the "presumption" that external imbalances should not exceed 3% of GDP in the medium run for any country, and then refine the CA target based on judgmental considerations for each country.

As such, the FEER model is generally considered to be a method of assessment of currency misalignment, rather than a model of exchange rate determination. However, it implicitly assumes that the actual exchange rate will exhibit a tendency to revert to its fair value, at least in the medium run.

**11.2.3.2 The Macroeconomic Balance (MB) Approach.** The MB approach is probably one of the oldest methods to estimate a currency's fair value by the IMF. Early attempts date back to at least 1967, when an IMF team led by Marcus Fleming computed the required magnitude of the devaluation of the sterling to bring the UK balance of payments in equilibrium (Polak, 1995). This approach has been subsequently developed over the years until its current form (see Artus, 1978, for a formal exposition of an early version of the model, far before the establishment of the CGER).

In this approach, the fair value of a currency is identified by calculating the exchange rate adjustment that would eliminate the difference between the CA balance projected over the medium term and the "CA norm" (also called *saving-investment norm* in earlier versions), that is, an estimated equilibrium CA balance over the same horizon.

The MB approach, in its most recent version (Lee et al., 2008), is implemented in three steps. First, the CGER estimates the equilibrium relationship between the CA, expressed as a ratio to GDP, and a set of fundamentals. These fundamentals include the fiscal balance, demographics, NFAs, oil balance, economic growth, and dummies for economic crises and financial centers (for extensive studies of the medium-term determinants of CAs, see also Debelle and Faruqee, 1996; Chinn and Prasad, 2003). The medium-term equilibrium relationship is estimated via panel data regressions, using 4-year averages of the data.

The second step is to compute CA norms by applying the estimated coefficients of the panel regression to the medium-term values of the regressors.

These medium-term values are mostly taken from the IMF's World Economic Outlook (WEO) database, and are generated by IMF's country experts.

The third step involves computing the real exchange rate adjustment that would close the gap between the CA norm (estimated in the first two steps) and the UCUR balance, as discussed above. As UCUR, the IMF typically uses WEO medium-term projection of the level of the CA.

### 11.2.4 EXTERNAL SUSTAINABILITY (ES) APPROACH

The CGER ES approach calculates the equilibrium exchange rate that would bring the CA or trade balance from its projected medium-term level to the level that would stabilize the NFA position of a country. Unlike the IMF MB and ERER approaches, the ES approach requires only few inputs (such as the prevailing growth and rates of return on external assets and liabilities) to be implemented, without the need of any direct econometric estimations of equilibrium relationships.

The concept of ES is analogous to the one of public debt sustainability, but with the object of the analysis being the whole economy instead of the public sector alone. According to the IMF, ES is reached when a country meets its intertemporal budget constraint (IMF, 2002, 2008), which implies that the net present value (NPV) of future CA or trade surpluses must be equal or greater than the NPV of that country's external liabilities. This condition is automatically met when the external debt-to-GDP ratio is either stable or declining.

Starting from a country's intertemporal budget constraint, it can be shown that the CA that stabilises NFA positions to a predetermined level $b^s$ (expressed as a ratio to nominal GDP) can be expressed as

$$\text{ca}^S = \frac{g + \pi(1+g)}{(1+g)(1+\pi)} b^S \tag{11.11}$$

where $g$ is the growth rate of real GDP, and $\pi$ is the rate of change of the GDP deflator.

Analogously, we can apply the same approach to compute the NFA-stabilizing trade balance. Denoting the gross real interest rates as $(1+r) = \frac{(1+i)}{(1+\pi)}$, we can write the NFA-stabilizing trade balance as

$$\text{tb}^S = -\frac{r-g}{1+g} b^S \tag{11.12}$$

Therefore, given the assumed values for $g$, $\pi$, and $r$, the NFA-stabilizing CAs and trade balances can be readily computed without the econometric estimation of any equilibrium relationship. Clearly, a drawback of this approach is that the choice of benchmark level of NFA, $b^S$, will be to some extent arbitrary.

We can compare the NFA-stabilizing values of the CA or trade balance, obtained using Equations (11.11) and (11.12), to their actual values and apply trade elasticities in order to calculate the required change in the REER.

Given their simplicity, Equations (11.11) and (11.12) have straightforward implications. For example, the NFA-stabilizing CA is proportional to the GDP growth rate, so that a faster-growing economy can afford to run larger CA deficits. Moreover, if the rate of return on external assets and liabilities is greater than the GDP growth rate, an increase in the former implies, ceteris paribus, a larger trade surplus for a debtor country, whereas a creditor country can afford larger trade deficits (with this relation being inversed if the rate of return is less than the growth rate).

### 11.2.5 THE NATURAL REAL EXCHANGE RATE (NATREX)

Stein (1994) defines the natural real exchange (NATREX) as "the exchange rate that would prevail if speculative and cyclical factors could be removed while unemployment is at its natural rate" (Stein, 1994, p. 135). As for the FEER model, the NATREX model is based on the UB approach.

The NATREX model explicitly recognizes different dynamics for medium- and long-run equilibrium exchange rates. Speculative and cyclical factors influence the exchange rate at the short horizon, whereas the medium term is dominated by the stock of capital, the stock of foreign debt, and a number of fundamentals. The long-term equilibrium exchange rate is determined solely by the fundamentals, as the stock of capital and foreign debt are assumed to settle at their long-run, steady state values. A number of different fundamentals have been proposed in empirical work, the most important of which are identified as domestic and foreign productivity, and domestic and private propensity to save (the so-called "social thrift") both at home and abroad.

In the empirical implementations, the NATREX is generally estimated similarly to the BEER, that is, by identifying a cointegrating relation between the real exchange rate and a number of fundamentals. Some of these fundamentals are not directly observable and thus must be proxied. For example, Stein (1994) uses real GNP growth rates in order to proxy the growth of capital stock at home and abroad. Moreover, the rate of change of foreign debt is proxied using the CA to GNP ratio, and propensity to save is proxied by private and public consumption as a ratio of GNP. The ratios are used in order to abstract from cyclical factors, the same reason for which most of the variables are taken as twelve-quarter moving averages. For a detailed exposition of the NATREX approach, see Stein (2006).

### 11.2.6 THE INDIRECT FAIR VALUE (IFV)

In this section, we discuss an indirect approach to modeling fair value, which is frequently used in financial markets. Relatively few macroeconomic assumptions are being made with regard to the drivers of the fair value. Instead, the approach depends on the assumption that speculative activity is the principal cause for misaligned exchange rates. To our knowledge, this IFV approach has not been previously formalized in the academic literature.

Market participants use this kind of model as a way to assess where the exchange rate would be had speculative activity not pushed it away from a loosely defined fair value concept. The idea that speculative activity can create these deviations is based on two assumptions. First, speculative order flow has an impact on exchange rates (Lyons, 2001). Second, one has to assume that speculative order flow is mean reverting over the medium term. The latter is a corollary of the definition of speculative activity, which is based on the assumption that speculators will at some stage reverse their position and realize either a profit or a loss.

Two measures of speculative positioning often employed in this approach are risk reversals or international money market (IMM) positioning (Mogford and Pain, 2006). The former is defined as the difference between the implied volatility between comparable out-of-the-money call and put options. When the majority of speculative investors expect appreciation, demand for call options will likely rise relative to the demand for puts. As a result the relative price, and implied volatility, will increase for the call options relative to the put options. The second measure is based on the weekly Commitments of Traders (COT) Report, which contains information about the positioning size of so-called noncommercial traders on the IMM futures exchange, part of the Chicago Mercantile Exchange (CME).[5] The report is restricted to data for the most liquid exchange rates against the US dollar.

These measures of speculative positioning tend to be stationary and highly correlated with spot exchange rates (Campa et al., 1998; Mogford and Pain, 2006). Moreover, indicators of speculative positioning also tend to be strongly autocorrelated (Dunis and Lequeux, 2001), which implies that periods of speculatively driven misalignments tend to persist for a certain time, but typically not more than a few months.

Most measures of speculative positioning have a clearly defined neutral point. For example, risk reversals are equal to zero when the implied volatilities of equivalent out-of-the-money call and put options are identical. A similar argument applies to the net positions of noncommercial traders on the IMM. In practice, however, indicators of speculative positioning tend to oscillate around a nonzero mean. Speculative investors may on average perceive that the appreciation of a currency is more likely than the depreciation, or vice versa. Moreover, these indicators can display structural breaks or trend stationarity.

In practice, these factors tend to affect the choice of sample size. On one hand, the sample has to be large enough to guarantee stationarity and the mean reverting properties of the indicators of speculative positioning. On the other hand, longer samples create the risk of having to deal with trends or structural breaks in the positioning variable. Practitioners tend to look at daily or weekly data with sample sizes between 6 months and 3 years, which emphasizes the more trading-oriented concept of fair value underlying this approach. This approach also highlights that the statistical properties of the input variables play a far bigger role than in most other concepts of fair value.

More formally, we can express the relation between the level of the exchange rate and the variables of speculative positioning in the following way:

$$e_t = \beta' Z_t + \theta' S_t + \varepsilon_t \tag{11.13}$$

[5] See www.cftc.gov/marketreports/commitmentsoftraders/index.htm for details on the COT reports.

where $e_t$ is the spot exchange rate observed in the market, $Z_t$ is a vector of broadly defined fundamentals, $S_t$ contains variables reflecting speculative activity, $\varepsilon_t$ is a residual term, and $\beta$ and $\theta$ are coefficient vectors. Given that the focus is on relatively short-term deviations from fair value, and daily or weekly data, some of the fundamental variables in $Z_t$ can potentially be approximated by linear and higher-order time trends.

The exchange rate $e_t$ is typically expressed in nominal terms and expected to display some form of long-run relationship with $Z_t$. Equation (11.13) is estimated using cointegration techniques, hence $e_t$ and $Z_t$ are expected to display unit roots, whereas $S_t$ is expected to be stationary around a constant mean, as mentioned above. When these criteria are not satisfied, the model fails to produce a fair value estimate.

Having estimated Equation (11.13), it is possible to use the parameter estimates to calculate fair value in the following way:

$$\bar{e}_t = \hat{\beta}' Z_t + \hat{\theta}' \bar{S} \tag{11.14}$$

with the overbar denoting the value of $S$ that is consistent with neutral speculative positioning. As we discussed above, neutral speculative positioning is not well defined in the presence of a nonzero mean in the $S$, though in most cases the natural choice would be to simply use the sample mean.

With most of the focus on modeling the transitory forces, users of these fair value models are typically agnostic with regards to the choice of fundamental variables in $Z_t$. Moreover, as practitioners tend to focus on very short-term deviations from fair value, there is a strong preference for financial and macro data available at daily or weekly frequency.

We illustrate the concept using the exchange rate of the Canadian dollar against the US dollar from January 2004 to January 2007. The daily spot exchange rate is regressed on the difference between US and Canadian 2-year swap rates, as well as linear, quadratic, and cubic time trends. We use 3-month 25-delta risk reversals as a measure of speculative positioning in the regression. We conducted several unit-root tests to confirm that the exchange rate and interest rate differential likely display a unit root over the sample, while risk reversals are likely stationary. Indeed, Figure 11.2 shows that risk reversals behave as a stationary time series with a sample mean, which is very close but not equal to zero.

Figure 11.3 illustrates the results. The black line represents the observed daily exchange rate between the US and Canadian dollars. The light gray line displays the fitted value of the regression using the observed values of all right-hand variables. Finally, the dark gray line represents the IFV, which describes where the exchange rate would have been without the influence of speculative activity. This fair value is computed using Equation (11.2.14), that is, as the fitted exchange rate but using the sample mean of the risk reversals instead of the observed values.

As Figure 11.3 shows, misalignment from the IFV of up to 10% occurred in the sample considered. Moreover, it seems that much of the short-term swings in the exchange rate seem to be related to speculative positioning. However,

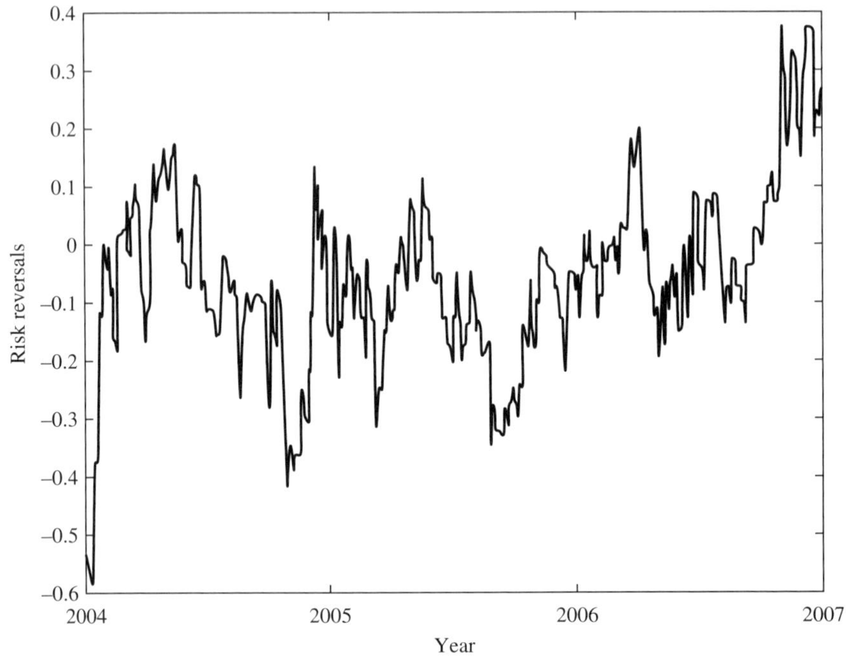


**FIGURE 11.2** USD/CAD 3-month 25-delta risk reversals. Notes: The figure shows risk reversals for 3-month 25-Delta out-of-the-money options for the Canadian dollar against the US dollar.

as discussed earlier in this section, the IFV concept does not shed light on the macroeconomic factors driving medium- and longer-term trends. Therefore, we have to rely on other fair value concepts in order to understand the determinants of the trend appreciation of the Canadian dollar's fair value estimate visible in the figure.

## 11.3 Implementation Choices and Model Characteristics

In the previous section, we introduced the main families of fair value models, including some examples of ongoing applied work by the IMF and Goldman Sachs. Interestingly, both institutions have moved toward using some combination of models. The IMF uses two related UB approaches and a BEER model, while Goldman Sachs uses a BEER model adjusted for Penn Effects. Both institutions also try to use a number of different estimation approaches, combining time series with cross-sectional techniques and, in some cases, completely avoiding econometric estimations. This trend toward combining and comparing models can be observed more broadly across the literature as well. For example, Cline

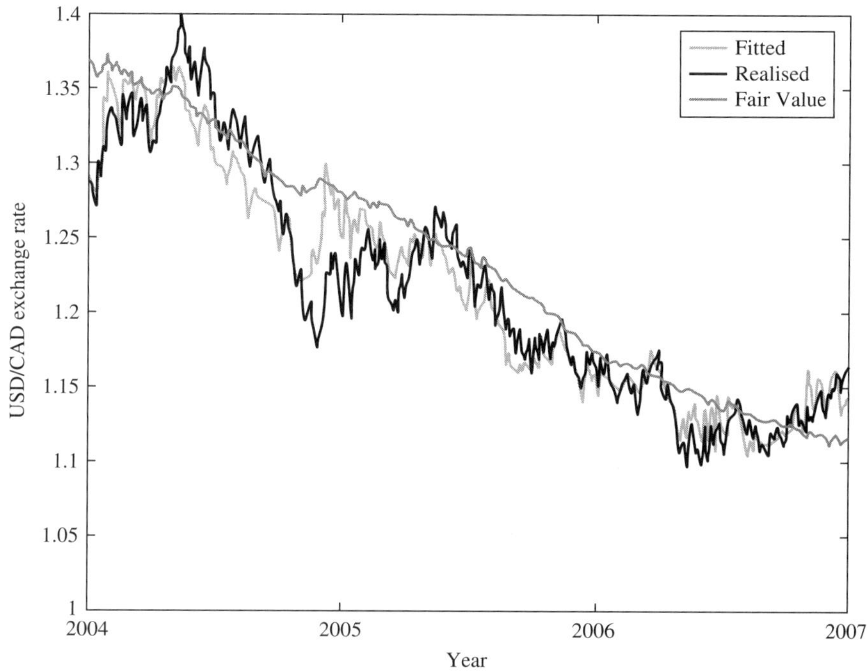


**FIGURE 11.3** Indirect fair value for USD/CAD. The figure illustrates the indirect fair value (IFV) for the daily nominal spot exchange rate of the Canadian dollar against the US dollar. The time span is between January 2004 and January 2007. The black line displays the actual observed value of the exchange rate. The light gray line displays the fitted value of a regression of the spot exchange rate on: the difference between US and Canadian 2-year swap rates; linear, quadratic, and cubic time trends; and 3-month 25-delta risk reversals. Finally, the dark gray line displays the IFV of the Canadian dollar, using the sample mean of the risk reversals as a proxy for neutral speculative positioning.

and Williamson (2008b), Dunaway et al. (2006), and Cheung et al. (2009) compare different approaches to estimate fair value for the Chinese renminbi.

The choice of the model and of the implementation technique will typically affect the estimates of fair value in a number of ways. Moreover, fair value modeling is often conducted with the specific aim of using the model systematically as a policy or investment tool, rather than as a one-off exercise. As a result, practical considerations may affect the choice of model as well. In this section, we discuss these implementation choices and model characteristics in more detail.

### 11.3.1 HORIZON/FREQUENCY

A major dimension of fair value models is the time horizon of the analysis. A number of authors have implicitly or explicitly assumed that the observed exchange rate will converge to different fair values depending on the horizon.

The speed of convergence is also one of the most important features for the applied use of fair value models.

Driver and Westaway (2004), in a framework similar to that of Clark and MacDonald (1998), start from the following reduced-form relation that relates the observed exchange rate to a number of explanatory variables:

$$e_t = \beta' Z_t + \theta' T_t + \varepsilon_t \tag{11.15}$$

where $e_t$ is the exchange rate, broadly defined,[6] $Z_t$ is a vector of medium- and long-term economic fundamentals, $T_t$ is a vector of short-term, transitory factors, $\varepsilon_t$ is a residual term, and $\beta$ and $\theta$ are coefficient vectors.

Driver and Westaway define short-run equilibrium as the exchange rate, which would pertain when its fundamentals are at their current (e.g., observed) values at time $t$, abstracting from the influence of asset market bubbles. In a notation similar to Clark and MacDonald, they define the short-term equilibrium as

$$e_t = \beta' Z_t + \theta' T_t \tag{11.16}$$

This is also similar to what Williamson (1983) and Clark and MacDonald (1998) call the *current equilibrium exchange rate*. Most BEER models use this equilibrium concept and the half-life time can typically be measured in weeks or quarters. The IFV model introduced in Section 11.2.6 typically displays even shorter half-lives that can typically be measured in days or weeks, and therefore can be considered as an attempt to identify fair value of a currency for the very short term.

The medium-run fair value[7] can be described by the following reduced-form equation,

$$\hat{e}_t = \beta' \hat{Z}_t \tag{11.17}$$

where the hat indicates that the variables abstract from cyclical components. In most empirical applications, this often translates in (i) excluding fundamentals that are typically thought to characterize only cyclical deviations from the equilibrium level[8] and in (ii) the fundamentals being set at their trend values. The PEER model in Section 11.2.2.2 can also be categorized as a medium-term fair value model.

---

[6]For illustrative purposes, we do not specify here if the exchange rate is defined in nominal or real terms, bilateral or effective.

[7]Driver and Westaway (2004) define the medium-run equilibrium as the exchange rate, which is compatible with the economy being at internal and external balance. This notion heavily influences the UB family of fair value models, see Section 11.2.3.

[8]For example, by excluding interest rate differentials from the analysis, as exchange rates tend to inherit the cyclical properties of interest rate differentials (Lustig et al., 2010).

Although consistent with a flow equilibrium, the medium-run fair value may still allow adjusting toward a long-run, stock equilibrium. For example, the NFA position may still be changing.

Using the Driver and Westaway (2004) notation again, a long-term equilibrium is defined as the point where a stock equilibrium is achieved for all agents in the economy:

$$\bar{e}_t = \beta' \bar{Z}_t \tag{11.18}$$

where the overbar denotes the long-run values of variables. Long-run fair values models are therefore mostly used when studying structural sources of misalignment. For example, a reserve currency will tend to be overvalued in the long run, as its economy will tend to run CA deficits, and therefore a depreciation will be needed for restoring the long-run equilibrium. A slightly less demanding definition of long-run equilibrium underlies the IMF ES model in Section 11.2.4, which is based on the stability of the NFA position of a country.

Fair value estimates will therefore reflect the choice in the selection of fundamentals. Particularly, models that try to directly estimate reduced-form equations such as (11.16) to (11.18) will be particularly affected: as they use the fitted value as an estimate of fair value, they tend to inherit the statistical properties of the explanatory variables used. Even relatively simple modifications, such as using a trend estimate of a fundamental variable instead of the current value, will affect the estimated magnitude and duration of exchange rate misalignments.

### 11.3.2 DIRECT ECONOMETRIC ESTIMATION VERSUS "METHODS OF CALCULATION"

One may attempt to compute currency's fair value by directly estimating a reduced-form equation relating the level of the exchange rate to a set of fundamental variables. This reduced-form equation takes generally the form of a long-run cointegrating relationship, whose short-run dynamics may be estimated using an error correction model (ECM). The BEER models discussed in Section 20.5 belong to this family.

These models are useful in order to characterize the variation of exchange rates over time. However, as these models rely on the assumption of stable long-run relations, their estimation may be plagued by the limited availability and poor quality of historical data. Especially in the case of less developed economies, the presence of small samples, systematically managed or pegged exchange rates, and data from unreliable sources may severely bias the estimated coefficients.

Another approach, for example, the one followed by the family of UB models (Section 11.2.3), is to start from a simple macroeconomic relationship between the exchange rate and an economic policy objective (such as target capital flows or CAs). Then, calculate the implied exchange rate change (from prevailing levels) that would be required in order to reach that objective. These models can be so considered as a "method of calculation" (Wren-Lewis, 1992), since they require no (or minimal) econometric estimation.

Among the advantages of this latter family of models is the fact that their simple structure makes them less reliant on data availability, and that they take policy objectives explicitly into consideration. In general, they also provide a useful reference point that can be compared to exchange rate assessments obtained using more complicated econometric models. On the other hand, the UB models often rely on relatively strong assumptions about equilibrium CA positions or trade elasticities. Even small variations in these inputs can have a substantial impact on the calculated fair value, as we discuss more in the next section.

### 11.3.3 TREATMENT OF EXTERNAL IMBALANCES

External imbalances are an implicit or explicit part of most fair value models and often are the very core of the model. However, there are a number of issues that have to be considered when using external imbalances in fair value models, for example:

- When using measures of external imbalances in time-series-based fair value models, in particular, in the BEER family of models, the estimated coefficients on the external variables often show the "wrong" (i.e., counterintuitive) signs. For example, the estimates may show that the fair value appreciates with growing CA deficits. Obviously, the idea of external sustainability would suggest the opposite, namely, that currency depreciation is needed to correct a growing CA deficits.
  One likely reasons for this empirical problem is a contamination of the estimates by cyclical effects: Most models of exchange rate determination would suggest that a small open economy facing a positive domestic demand shock will likely experience an appreciating currency at the same time as a deterioration of the CA balance. Explicitly correcting for these cyclical factors may be one solution. Alternatively, one could simply drop the external variable assuming that external imbalances will correct over the long run.
- Defining which part of an external imbalance is of cyclical or structural nature is not trivial. Policy choices can drive structural imbalances: for example, the choice of pegged or managed exchange rate regimes, the existence of sovereign wealth funds or persistent fiscal policy differentials. Structural imbalances can also be influenced by the accumulation of FX reserves or depend on the natural endowment with commodities. These factors have implications for assessing both the observed and the equilibrium levels of the CA, and therefore have to be recognized explicitly when modeling currency fair values. The UB group of fair value models is particularly sensitive to these issues, while the PPP and some BEER approaches simply assume that external imbalances will correct themselves over time.
- Many models, in particular in the UB family, use import and export demand functions to calculate the necessary exchange rate changes needed to reach an external balance target. This calculation tends to be sensitive with respect to the estimated trade elasticities—a small change in the estimated elasticities can potentially lead to large variations in the resulting

fair value (Dunaway et al., 2006), while at the same time trade elasticities tend to be extremely difficult to estimate. For example, Cheung et al. (2010) report a wide range of estimated exports and imports elasticities for China, based both on previous studies and their own calculations. Furthermore, the empirical evidence regarding the Marshall–Lerner condition is mixed. Several studies find supporting evidence for selected countries over longer horizons, but considerable doubts remain, in particular, with regard to shorter-term dynamics (Hsing, 2010; Rose, 1991).

Given the widespread use of UB models, which all rely on trade elasticities, the last point deserves further illustration. Table 11.1 presents, for different trade elasticities, the percentage change in the REER that is required to bring China's underlying CA in line with hypothetical CA targets. Panel A shows the results assuming a CA target of 0%, whereas Panel B assumes a target surplus of 3%. The table clearly shows that UB calculations are extremely sensitive with respect to the estimated trade elasticities, in particular, when they approach the region where the Marshall–Lerner condition is no longer satisfied.

Overall, the treatment of external imbalances tends to have a significant impact on fair value estimates and careful consideration of the explicit or implicit choices is important.

### 11.3.4 REAL VERSUS NOMINAL EXCHANGE RATES

In most cases, it will be reasonably easy to map the results of a nominal fair value model into real exchange rates and vice versa. But data limitations may play a role. There is a wide variety of inflation data available but not necessarily comparable across countries. Moreover, inflation data may not be available at identical frequencies across countries and hence affect the underlying horizon/frequency of the model. The vast majority of theory-driven models rely on real exchange rates. Models used by investors tend to prefer nominal exchange rates, as they are observable in the market. The Goldman Sachs GSDEER model, for example, is estimated as a real exchange rate model. The real fair value estimates are then translated into nominal fair value estimates using observed and projected inflation differentials.

### 11.3.5 BILATERAL VERSUS EFFECTIVE EXCHANGE RATE

The choice between bilateral and effective (i.e., multilateral) exchange rates is crucial when assessing exchange rate misalignments empirically.

Valuation signals from bilateral approaches are often misinterpreted when the anchor currency itself is misaligned on a multilateral basis—an issue frequently encountered in the last few years when the US dollar has been undervalued according to many fair value models. In that case, assessing multilateral misalignment may be more useful, but at the same time it may suffer more from constraints on data availability, as this approach requires collecting data from many countries.

**TABLE 11.1 Real Effective Exchange Rate Adjustment for China, Sensitivity Analysis**

| | Panel A: 0% Current Account Target | | | | | | | | | | |
|---|---|---|---|---|---|---|---|---|---|---|---|
| | | *Export Elasticities* | | | | | | | | | |
| | | −0.1 | −0.2 | −0.3 | −0.4 | −0.5 | −0.6 | −0.7 | −0.8 | −0.9 | −1.0 |
| *Import Elasticities* | 0.1 | −38.4 | −45.0 | −54.3 | −68.5 | −92.7 | −143.6 | −318.4 | 1471.7 | 222.2 | 120.2 |
| | 0.2 | −44.0 | −52.8 | −66.2 | −88.6 | −134.0 | −274.6 | 5571.4 | 250.0 | 127.9 | 85.9 |
| | 0.3 | −51.5 | −64.1 | −84.9 | −125.6 | −241.5 | −3120.0 | 285.7 | 136.6 | 89.8 | 66.8 |
| | 0.4 | −62.1 | −81.4 | −118.2 | −215.5 | −1218.8 | 333.3 | 146.6 | 94.0 | 69.1 | 54.7 |
| | 0.5 | −78.2 | −111.6 | −194.5 | −757.3 | 400.0 | 158.2 | 98.6 | 71.6 | 56.2 | 46.3 |
| | 0.6 | −105.7 | −177.3 | −549.3 | 500.0 | 171.8 | 103.7 | 74.3 | 57.9 | 47.4 | 40.1 |
| | 0.7 | −162.8 | −430.9 | 666.7 | 188.0 | 109.4 | 77.2 | 59.6 | 48.5 | 40.9 | 35.4 |
| | 0.8 | −354.5 | 1000.0 | 207.4 | 115.7 | 80.2 | 61.4 | 49.7 | 41.8 | 36.0 | 31.7 |
| | 0.9 | 2000.0 | 231.5 | 122.8 | 83.6 | 63.4 | 51.0 | 42.7 | 36.7 | 32.2 | 28.7 |
| | 1.0 | 261.7 | 130.9 | 87.2 | 65.4 | 52.3 | 43.6 | 37.4 | 32.7 | 29.1 | 26.2 |

Panel B: 3% Current Account Target

| | | *Export Elasticities* | | | | | | | | | |
|---|---|---|---|---|---|---|---|---|---|---|---|
| | | −0.1 | −0.2 | −0.3 | −0.4 | −0.5 | −0.6 | −0.7 | −0.8 | −0.9 | −1.0 |
| *Import Elasticities* | 0.1 | −23.6 | −27.7 | −33.4 | −42.1 | −57.1 | −88.4 | −195.9 | 905.7 | 136.8 | 74.0 |
| | 0.2 | −27.1 | −32.5 | −40.7 | −54.5 | −82.5 | −169.0 | 3428.6 | 153.8 | 78.7 | 52.9 |
| | 0.3 | −31.7 | −39.4 | −52.2 | −77.3 | −148.6 | −1920.0 | 175.8 | 84.1 | 55.2 | 41.1 |
| | 0.4 | −38.2 | −50.1 | −72.7 | −132.6 | −750.0 | 205.1 | 90.2 | 57.8 | 42.6 | 33.7 |
| | 0.5 | −48.1 | −68.7 | −119.7 | −466.0 | 246.2 | 97.4 | 60.7 | 44.1 | 34.6 | 28.5 |
| | 0.6 | −65.0 | −109.1 | −338.0 | 307.7 | 105.7 | 63.8 | 45.7 | 35.6 | 29.2 | 24.7 |
| | 0.7 | −100.2 | −265.2 | 410.3 | 115.7 | 67.3 | 47.5 | 36.7 | 29.9 | 25.2 | 21.8 |
| | 0.8 | −218.2 | 615.4 | 127.7 | 71.2 | 49.4 | 37.8 | 30.6 | 25.7 | 22.2 | 19.5 |
| | 0.9 | 1230.8 | 142.4 | 75.6 | 51.4 | 39.0 | 31.4 | 26.3 | 22.6 | 19.8 | 17.6 |
| | 1.0 | 161.1 | 80.5 | 53.7 | 40.3 | 32.2 | 26.8 | 23.0 | 20.1 | 17.9 | 16.1 |

The table presents, for given trade elasticities, the percentage change in the real effective exchange rate, which is required to bring China's underlying current account in line with the current account target. The required change is computed using Equation (11.10) in the main text. We use the current account projections for 2016 from the IMF WEO of April 2011 as an estimate of the underlying current account balance. We estimate the 2010 China's exports/GDP and imports/GDP ratios as 29.8% and 25.9%, respectively. Data for these ratios are from China's national statistics and the IMF. Panel A shows the results assuming a current account target of zero percent, whereas Panel B shows the results assuming a target surplus of 3% of GDP.

Effective exchange rates also depend on the weighting scheme used to calculate the basket of trading partners. Many different trade-weighted baskets are used in practice, including some alternative weighting schemes based on capital flows or even volatility. Weighting schemes with static weights suffer from lack of representativeness after a period of changing trade patterns in the global economy (Chinn, 2006).

Bilateral fair value calculations are less demanding on data availability and have the conceptual advantage of being actually observable in the markets.

In general, it is possible to transform bilateral exchange rate fair value estimates into effective exchange rate estimates, simply by applying the trade weights and calculating the geographic average. The reverse is also possible. (Alberola et al., 1999) suggest a procedure to extract bilateral misalignments from a vector of effective misalignments. See also the approach used by Cline (2008).

Finally, bilateral equilibrium exchange rates should always be globally consistent, because a world with $N$ countries can only have $N-1$ independent exchange rates (Faruqee, 1998).

### 11.3.6 TIME SERIES VERSUS CROSS SECTION OR PANEL

The choice of the estimation procedure is largely an econometric issue, which we do not discuss here, but it seems worthwhile highlighting an important trade-off when choosing between a single-equation estimate and a panel with homogeneous coefficients for all cross-sectional units.

With many countries having different economic structures, it is possible that there are different relations between macro variables and the respective currencies. Imposing the same coefficients across currencies in a panel may therefore not fully reflect the country-specific characteristics (Dunaway et al., 2006). One possible solution is to break a panel into more homogeneous subpanels and ultimately to estimate fair values for individual currencies. On the other hand, a panel allows assessing the potential influence on fair value of a factor that has not been relevant for a currency in the past. For example, the discovery of a previously unknown natural resource in a country may affect fair value, but it will be impossible to quantify the impact in a single-equation approach because of the lack of historical data. On the contrary, a panel estimate allows quantifying the impact if other currencies in the panel have been affected by a similar discovery in the past.

One possible constraint for using a panel, however, is data availability. A comparable dataset for each cross-section unit is necessary and may seriously restrict the number of possible explanatory variables and the size of the dataset.

A frequently used panel cointegration technique is the panel DOLS, see Stock and Watson (1993) and Mark and Sul (2003).

### 11.3.7 MODEL MAINTENANCE

As highlighted above, one interesting feature of fair value models is that they are often an important input for policy decisions or investments. Decision makers therefore typically demand continuously updated estimates of misalignments. This creates special demands on the timeliness of estimates, data availability, and data quality.

General model maintenance is therefore an important aspect in applied work when more than a point estimate is needed. The frequency of updates and re-estimation needs to be determined. Validation procedures may need to be implemented to assess the impact of data revisions on the fair value estimates. Fitted fair values may change when statistical agencies change the frequency, base year, or calculation of input data.

In some cases, missing time series for specific countries can be estimated with an independent model, which then has to be maintained in addition to the actual fair value model.

With additional data becoming available over time, the question of re-estimation needs to be answered. For example, Goldman Sachs re-estimates the GSDEER model every 2–3 years, while at the same time implementing potential model changes. Re-estimation also implies validation and testing of the estimates. Additional cross sections may have to be included as the needs of the user base change. Again, this would imply re-estimation. On the other hand, cross-sectional units may vanish when countries enter currency unions. All these events will likely have a more or less severe impact on misalignment estimates and hence need to be assessed carefully and quickly, before policy or investment decisions start to be influenced by issues related to model maintenance.

It is important not to underestimate this factor as complex models covering a large number of countries may rely on thousands of data series from diverse sources. A simple model that relies on a few standard input variables may prove more robust over time than a state-of-the-art model with excessively complex and time-consuming updating procedures.

What happens if the persons responsible for maintaining the fair value model leave the organisation? Without appropriate contingency planning, decision makers may suddenly no longer receive updated fair value estimates, or even worse, erroneous estimates.

## 11.4 Conclusion

A primitive notion of currency misalignment linked to the precious metal content of coins has probably been around since the antiquity. The notion that prices of tradable goods are unlikely to diverge substantially across countries can be traced back several centuries and remains a key building block of modern adjusted-PPP or BEER models. Similarly, the link between currency valuation and external imbalances has been observed in ancient times and remains an important building block of the many variants of modern UB models.

In this chapter, we have reviewed the most important families of fair value models currently in use. Most of these models have been developed over the last 20 years. Moreover, we introduce the concept of IFV, a notion of fair value frequently used by financial market participants for short-term investment decisions, but to our knowledge not previously formalized in the academic literature.

Currency fair value modeling has always been a field of interest for policymakers and investors, and fair value estimates are frequently an input for important political or financial decisions. As a result, it is important to highlight the implicit or explicit modeling and implementation choices. The two main families of fair value models used today, UB and BEER, both suffer from major problems.

The UB models are highly sensitive to assumptions of underlying cyclically adjusted external imbalances and appropriate CA targets. Moreover, even small variations in the estimation of import and export elasticities can substantially affect UB estimates of misalignment.

Some PPP and BEER models, on the other hand, are highly dependent on the availability of sufficient historical data, a particularly constraining requirement for transition economies, for example. Moreover, directly estimated BEER fair values implicitly assume that currencies have historically oscillated around fair value. This may not have been the fact in the case of managed exchange rates, in which a BEER-style fair value model may become little more than the description of the FX policy reaction function. Such a policy reaction function may still be an appropriate tool for investment decisions, though its usefulness for policy recommendations is highly questionable.

Given the variety of models, many practitioners now combine several approaches to correct or compensate for individual weaknesses. The IMF follows that path and publishes ranges of fair values rather than point estimates.

An alternative approach is to start with one preferred model and then test if the implicit or explicit assumptions are satisfied. If not, another model may help to correct biases. The latest version of Goldman Sachs' GSDEER model incorporates some basic elements of this approach.

The wide range of estimates, partly influenced by the choice of inappropriate models, often undermines the impact of policy recommendations. The ongoing debate of renminbi misalignment is probably the most obvious example. Despite the potential shortcomings the conclusion to drop fair value models altogether appears wrong, but knowing which model is relevant and in which circumstances would clearly be helpful.

Future fair value research could therefore focus on model selection strategies to help narrow the number of relevant estimates. Given that fair value modeling remains a field with many applied uses, contributions in this area would likely attract considerable interest among practitioners.

## Acknowledgments

This chapter was begun while Gino Cenedese was Summer Associate at Goldman Sachs. The authors are indebted for useful conversations and constructive comments to Ian Marsh, Lucio Sarno, and two anonymous referees. The views expressed in this chapter are those of the authors alone, and not necessarily those of the Bank of England or Goldman Sachs.

# REFERENCES


Alberola E, Cervero SG, Lopez H, Ubide A. Global equilibrium exchange rates: euro, dollar, "ins," "outs", and other major currencies in a panel cointegration framework. IMF Working Paper; 1999 Dec.

Artus JR. Methods of assessing the long-run equilibrium value of an exchange rate. J Int Econ 1978;8(2):277–299. ISSN 0022–1996.

Balassa B. The purchasing-power parity doctrine: a reappraisal. J Pol Econ 1964;72(6):584–596. ISSN 00223808.

Bayoumi T, Clark P, Symansky S, Taylor M. The robustness of equilibrium exchange rate calculations to alternative assumptions and methodologies. IMF Working Paper; 1994 Feb.

Campa JM, Kevin Chang PH, Reider RL. Implied exchange rate distributions: evidence from OTC option markets. J Int Money Finance 1998;17:117–160.

Cassel G. Abnormal deviations in international exchanges. Econ J 1918;28(112): 413–415.

Cheung Y-W, Chinn MD, Fujii E. The overvaluation of renminbi undervaluation. J Int Money Finance 2007;26:762–785.

Cheung Y-W, Chinn MD, Fujii E. Pitfalls in measuring exchange rate misalignment: the yuan and other currencies. Open Econ Rev 2009;20:183–206.

Cheung Y-W, Chinn MD, Fujii E. China's current account and exchange rate. In: Feenstra RC, Wei S-J, editors. China's growing role in world trade. Chicago: University of Chicago Press; 2010. pp. 231–271.

Chinn MD. A primer on real effective exchange rates: determinants, overvaluation, trade flows and competitive devaluation. Open Econ Rev 2006;17:115–143.

Chinn MD, Prasad ES. Medium-term determinants of current accounts in industrial and developing countries: an empirical exploration. J Int Econ 2003;59(1):47–76.

Clark PB, MacDonald R. Exchange rates and economic fundamentals: a methodological comparison of BEERs and FEERs. IMF Working Paper; 1998 May.

Clark PB, MacDonald R. Filtering the BEER: a permanent and transitory decomposition. Glob Finance J 2004;15:29–56.

Cline WR. Estimating consistent fundamental equilibrium exchange rates. Peterson Institute for International Economics Workin Paper; 2008 July.

Cline WR, Williamson J. New estimates of fundamental equilibrium exchange rates. Washington, DC: Peterson Institute for International Economics Policy Brief; 2008a.

Cline WR, Williamson J. Estimates of the equilibrium exchange rate of the renminbi: is there a consensus and if not, why not?In: Goldstein M, Lardy NR, editors. Debating China's exchange rate policy. Washington, DC: Peterson Institute; 2008b.

Cline WR, Williamson J. Estimates of fundamental equilibrium exchange rates. Washington, DC: Peterson Institute for International Economics Policy Brief; 2011.

Cumby RE, Huizinga J. The predictability of real exchange rate changes in the short run and the long run. NBER Working Paper No. 3468; 1990 Oct.

De Broeck M, Sløk T. Interpreting real exchange rate movements in transition countries. J Int Econ 2006;68:368–383.

Debelle G, Faruqee H. What determines the current account? A cross-sectional and panel approach. IMF Working Paper; 1996 June.

Deutsche Bank. Deutsche Bank guide to currency indices. 2007 Oct.

Dornbusch R, Goldfajn I, Valdés RO. Currency crises and collapses. Brook Pap Econ Act 1995;26(2):219–294.

Driver RL, Westaway PF. Concepts of equilibrium exchange rates. Bank of England Working Paper No. 248; 2004.

Du Q, Wei S-J. Sex ratios and exchange rates. NBER Working Paper No. 16788; 2011 Feb.

Dunaway S, Leigh L, Li X. How robust are estimates of equilibrium real exchange rates: The case of China. IMF Working Paper; 2006 Oct.

Dunis C, Lequeux P. The information content of risk reversals. Derivatives Use, Trading & Regul 2001;2:98–117.

Engel C. Currency misalignments and optimal monetary policy: a reexamination. Am Econ Rev 2011;101(6):2796–2822.

Faruqee H. Methodology for calculating equilibrium exchange rates and question of global consistency. In: Isard P, Faruqee H, editors. Volume 167, Exchange rate assessment: extensions of the macroeconomic balance approach, IMF Occasional Papers. Washington (DC): International Monetary Fund; 1998.

Frankel J. On the yuan: the choice between adjustment under a fixed exchange rate and adjustment under a flexible rate. CESifo Econ Stud 2006;52(2):246–275.

Fuentes M, Meechan M. The evolving GSDEER currency model. Global Viewpoint 07/03, Goldman Sachs; 2007 Jan.

Giorgianni L. Foreign exchange risk premium: Does fiscal policy matter? Evidence from Italian data. IMF Working Paper; 1997 Apr.

Goldberg LS, Kolstad CD. Foreign direct investment, exchange rate variability and demand uncertainty. Int Econ Rev 1995;36(4):855–873.

Goldman Sachs. The foreign exchange market; 1996.

Goldman Sachs. FX slices become new tradable FX currents. Global Viewpoint 09/12; 2009 Jul.

Gonzalo J, Granger CWJ. Estimation of common long-memory components in cointegrated systems. J Bus Econ Stat 1995;13:27–35.

Gourinchas P-O, Obstfeld M. Stories of the twentieth century for the twenty-first. Am Econ J Macroecon 2012;4(1):226–265.

Gupta P, Mishra D, Sahay R. Behavior of output during currency crises. J Int Econ 2007;72:428–450.

Harrod RF. International Economics. James Nisbet; 1933.

Hsing Y. Test of the Marshall-Lerner condition for eight selected Asian countries and policy implications. Glob Econ Rev 2010;38:205–214.

Huizinga J. An empirical investigation of the long run behaviour of real exchange rates. Carnegie-Rochester Conf Ser Publ Policy 1987;27:149–214.

IMF. Assessing sustainability. Technical report, Policy Development and Review Department. Washington, DC: International Monetary Fund; 2002 May.

IMF. Staff guidance note on debt sustainability analysis for market access countries. Technical report, Policy Development and Review Department. Washington, DC: International Monetary Fund; 2008 July.

IMF. World Economic Outlook. 2011April.

Johansen S. Statistical analysis of cointegration vectors. J Econ Dyn Control 1988;12:231–254.

Johansen S, Juselius K. Testing structural hypotheses in a multivariate cointegration analysis of the PPP and the UIP for UK. J Economet 1992;53(1–3):211–244.

Lane PR, Milesi-Ferretti GM. The transfer problem revisited: net foreign assets and real exchange rates. Rev Econ Stat 2004;86(4):841–857.

Lee J, Milesi-Ferretti GM, Ostry J, Prati A, Ricci LA. Exchange rate assessments: CGER methodologies. IMF Occasional Papers 261, International Monetary Fund; 2008 Apr.

Lustig H, Roussanov N, Verdelhan A. Countercyclical currency risk premia. Working Paper, MIT; 2010.

Lyons RK. The microstructure approach to exchange rates. Cambridge, London: MIT Press; 2001.

MacDonald R, Marsh IW. On fundamentals and exchange rates: A Casselian perspective. Rev Econ Stat 1997;79(4):655–664.

MacDonald R, Marsh IW. Currency spillovers and tri-polarity: a simultaneous model of the US dollar, German mark and Japanese yen. J Int Money Finance 2004;23(1):99–111.

Mark NC, Sul D. Cointegration vector estimation by panel DOLS and long-run money demand. Oxf Bull Econ Stat 2003;65(5):655–680.

Meade JE. Volume 1, The theory of international economic policy: the balance of payments. London: Oxford University Press; 1951.

Metzler LA. Wealth, saving and the rate of interest. J Pol Econ 1951;59:930–946.

Mogford C, Pain D. The information content of aggregate data on financial futures positions. Bank Engl Q Bull 2006;46:57–65.

Nurkse R. Conditions of international monetary equilibrium. Volume 4, Essays in International Finance. Princeton (NJ): Princeton University Press; 1945.

O'Neill J, Ades A, Choksy H, Nordvig J, Stolper T. Merging GSDEER and GSDEEMER: A global approach to equilibrium exchange rate modelling. Goldman Sachs Global Economic Paper No:124; 2005 May.

Polak JJ. Fifty years of exchange rate research and policy at the International Monetary Fund. IMF Staff Pap 1995;42(4):734–761.

Ricci LA. Gian Maria Milesi-Ferretti, and Jaewoo Lee. Real exchange rates and fundamentals: A cross-country perspective. IMF Working Paper; 2008 Jan.

Rodrik D. The real exchange rate and economic growth. Working Paper; 2008 Oct.

Rogoff K. The purchasing power parity puzzle. J Econ Lit 1996;34:647–668.

Rose AK. The role of exchange rates in a popular model of international trade: Does the 'Marshall-Lerner' condition hold? J Int Econ 1991;30:301–316.

Samuelson PA. Theoretical notes on trade problems. Rev Econ Stat 1964;46(2):145–154. ISSN 00346535.

Sarno L, Taylor MP. The economics of exchange rates. Cambridge: Cambridge University Press; 2003.

Stein JL. The natural real exchange rate of the US dollar and determinants of capital flows. In: Wiliamson J, editor. Estimating equilibrium exchange rates. Washington (DC): Institute for International Economics; 1994.

Stein JL. Stochastic optimal control, international finance, and debt crises. Oxford: Oxford University Press; 2006.

Stock JH, Watson MW. A simple estimator of cointegrating vectors in higher order integrated systems. Econometrica 1993;61(4):783–820.

Stolper T, Stupnitzka A, Meechan M. GSDEER—Re-estimation and test-based adjustment. Goldman Sachs: The Foreign Exchange Market 2009; 2009.

Summers R, Heston A. The Penn World Table (Mark 5): an expanded set of international comparisons, 1950–1988. Q J Econ 1991;106(2):327–68.

Swan TW. Longer-run problems of the balance of payments. In: Arndt HW, Corden WM, editors. The Australian economy: a volume of readings. Melbourne: F. W. Cheshire; 1963.

Taylor AM, Taylor MP. The purchasing power parity debate. J Econ Perspect 2004;18(4):135–158.

The Economist. 6 September 1986., 7462. p. 83.

Vaughan R. A discourse of coin and coinage. Printed by Th. Dawks, for Th. Basset, at the George, near Cliffords-Inn, in Fleet Street, London, 1675.

Williamson J. The exchange rate system. Washington (DC): Institute for International Economics; 1983.

Williamson J. Estimates of FEERs. In: Wiliamson J, editor. Estimating equilibrium exchange rates. Washington, DC: Institute for International Economics; 1994.

Williamson J, Mahar M. Current account targets. In: Wren-Lewis S, Driver R, editors. Volume 54, Real exchange rates for the Year 2000, Policy Analyses in International Economics. Washington (DC): Institute for International Economics; 1998.

Wren-Lewis S. On the analytical foundations of the fundamental equilibrium exchange rate. In: Hargreaves C, editor. Macroeconomic modelling of the long run. Aldershot: Edward Elgar; 1992.

CHAPTER TWELVE

# Technical Analysis in the Foreign Exchange Market

CHRISTOPHER J. NEELY
Federal Reserve Bank of St. Louis

PAUL A. WELLER
University of Iowa

## 12.1 Introduction

Technical analysis is the use of past price behavior and/or other market data, such as volume, to guide trading decisions in asset markets. These decisions are often generated by applying simple rules to historical price data. A technical trading rule (TTR), for example, might suggest buying a currency if its price has risen more than 1% from its value 5 days earlier. Traders in stock, commodity, and foreign exchange markets use such rules widely. Technical methods date back at least to 1700, but the "Dow Theory," proposed by *Wall Street Journal* editors Charles Dow and William Peter Hamilton, popularized them in the late nineteenth and early twentieth centuries.[1] Technical analysts—who often refer to themselves as "technicians"—argue that their approach allows them to profit

[1]Lo and Hasanhodzic (2010) survey the long history of technical analysis; they present evidence that ancient peoples tracked asset prices and might have engaged in technical analysis. Nison (1991) notes that Munehisa Homma reportedly made a fortune in eighteenth-century Japan using "candlestick" patterns to predict rice market prices. Schwager (1993, 1995) and Covel (2005) discuss how technical analysis is an important tool for many of today's most successful traders.

*Handbook of Exchange Rates*, First Edition. Edited by Jessica James, Ian W. Marsh, and Lucio Sarno.

from changes in the psychology of the market. The following statement expresses this view:

> *The technical approach to investment is essentially a reflection of the idea that prices move in trends which are determined by the changing attitudes of investors toward a variety of economic, monetary, political and psychological forces ... Since the technical approach is based on the theory that the price is a reflection of mass psychology ("the crowd") in action, it attempts to forecast future price movements on the assumption that crowd psychology moves between panic, fear, and pessimism on one hand and confidence, excessive optimism, and greed on the other.*
>
> (Pring, 1991, pp. 2–3)

Although modern technical analysis was originally developed in the context of the stock market, its advocates argue that it applies in one form or another to all asset markets. Since the era of floating exchange rates began in the early 1970s, foreign currency traders have widely adopted this approach to trading. At least some technicians clearly believe that the foreign exchange market is particularly prone to trending.

> *Currencies have the tendency to develop strong trends, stronger than stocks in my opinion because currencies reflect the performance of countries.*
>
> (Jean-Charles Gand, Société Générale Gestion, in Clements, 2010 p. 84)

> *It has been our longstanding experience that nothing trends as well or as clearly as a major currency market—not equity market indices, not commodity markets and not even long-term Treasuries.*
>
> (Walter Zimmermann, United-ICAP, in Clements, 2010 p. 197)

Academic research on the profitability of technical analysis tends to confirm the idea that foreign exchange markets trend particularly well. After reviewing the literature on technical analysis in a variety of markets, Park and Irwin (2007) conclude that technical analysis is profitable in foreign exchange and commodity futures markets but not in stock markets (also, see Silber, 1994).

This chapter briefly introduces the technical methods and then discusses how and why academic researchers have investigated these methods in the foreign exchange market. We then describe what economists have learned about technical analysis and conclude with a discussion of promising avenues of future research. Readers interested in learning more about technical methods should consult technical analysis textbooks such as Murphy (1986), Pring (1991), or Elder (1993). Readers wishing for a detailed literature review of technical analysis in currency markets should go to Menkhoff and Taylor's (2007) excellent survey.

# 12.2 The Practice of Technical Analysis

## 12.2.1 THE PHILOSOPHY OF TECHNICAL ANALYSIS

Technical analysts argue that their methods take advantage of market psychology as illustrated by the quotation from Pring (1991) above. In particular, technical textbooks such as Murphy (1986) and Pring (1991) outline three principles that guide the behavior of technical analysts.[2] The first is that market action (prices and transactions volume) "discounts" everything. In other words, an asset's price history incorporates all relevant information, so there is no need to forecast or research asset "fundamentals." Indeed, technical purists do not even look at fundamentals, except through the prism of prices, which reflect fundamentals before those variables are fully observable. Presaging recent findings by Engel and West (2005); Murphy (1986) claims that asset price changes often precede observed changes in fundamentals. The second principle is that asset prices move in trends. This is essential to the success of technical analysis because trends imply predictability and enable traders to profit by buying (selling) assets when the price is rising (falling). This is captured in the technicians' mantra "the trend is your friend." The third principle of technical analysis is that history repeats itself. Asset traders will tend to react in a similar way when confronted by similar conditions. This implies that asset price patterns will tend to repeat themselves.

Using these three principles, technical analysts attempt to identify trends and reversals of trends. These methods are explicitly extrapolative; that is, they infer future price changes from those of the recent past. Technicians argue that formal methods of detecting trends are necessary because prices move up and down around the primary (or longer-run) trend; that is, technical indicators can be constructed with data over multiple time frames from intraday to daily or multiyear horizons. Technicians may consider patterns over these multiple timeframes, placing increased emphasis on the signals from longer horizons.

Volume frequently plays a role in technical analysis. In the stock market, for example, rising volume is often said to confirm an uptrend. Some researchers on technical analysis in the stock market have evaluated rules that incorporate volume measures. Neely et al. (2010), for example, use an "on-balance-volume" rule in studying technical and fundamental predictors of the S&P 500 equity premium. But foreign exchange markets are decentralized; there are no comprehensive indicators of daily volume. Technicians in foreign exchange markets sometimes use proxies for total volume, such as volume measures from futures markets, such as the IMM Commitment of Traders, or screen-based tick counts or proprietary data from market-making banks. But foreign exchange volume remains difficult to track.

[2]Murphy (1986) and Pring (1991) provide a much more comprehensive treatment of technical analysis and these principles. Rosenberg and Shatz (1995) advocate the use of technical analysis with more economic explanation.

## 12.2.2 TYPES OF TECHNICAL ANALYSIS

There are many types of technical analysis and many ways to map current and past price and volume data into trading decisions. Broadly speaking, technicians have traditionally employed two types of analysis to distinguish trends from shorter-run fluctuations and to identify reversals: *charting* and *mechanical*(or *indicator*) methods. Charting, the older of the two methods, involves graphing the history of prices over some period—determined by the practitioner—to predict future patterns from past patterns. Charting is a very subjective system that requires the analyst to use judgment and skill in finding and interpreting patterns. Mechanical rules (i.e., indicators), on the other hand, impose consistency and discipline on the technician by requiring him to use rules based on mathematical functions of present and past exchange rates.

Charting is a complex subject, and a full discussion is well beyond the scope of this chapter. Bulkowski (2000) details the subject. Figure 12.1, however, provides a flavor of the type of patterns that technicians look for in the data and depicts what technicians describe as a "triple top"—three unsuccessful attempts to break a resistance level. The triple top shown here is in the yen/euro (JPY/EUR) market in 2009 before the price broke a support level in early 2010.[3] The triple top is a reversal pattern and generates a sell signal after a period of price increases. Figure 12.2 illustrates another type of reversal pattern, a "head-and-shoulders" pattern, for the US dollar/deutschemark (USD/DEM). The "neckline" shown in the figure joins the troughs separating the head from the two shoulders. When the exchange rate passes through the neckline, a sell signal is produced. Osler and Chang (1995) find some value in this classic pattern for some currencies.

To avoid the subjectivity involved in interpreting charts, economists have almost always studied mechanical rules. Table 12.1 shows three traditional technical rules economists have tested in the context of foreign exchange and/or equity markets: (i) filter; (ii) double moving average (MA); and (iii) channel. A filter rule produces a buy (sell) signal whenever the exchange rate rises (falls) by more than a given percentage from its most recent low (high). The choice of filter size is left to the technical analyst but typically ranges from 1/2 to 10%. An MA rule compares a short and a long MA of past prices and generates a buy (sell) signal if the short MA intersects the long MA from below (above). For example, one widely used rule, which we write as MA(5, 20), compares a 5-day and a 20-day MA. A channel rule counsels to buy (sell) the asset when its price exceeds (is less than) the maximum (minimum) over the previous $n$ days.[4] All three of these rules require technicians to choose parameters, and technical manuals provide little guidance on the appropriate values of these parameters

[3] A resistance (support) level is a set of local maxima (minima) for an asset price. These levels can be static or a function of time. George Davis of RBC Capital Markets identified this triple top example in Figure 12.1 (Clements, 2010).

[4] We define the channel rule following Taylor (1994). Sullivan et al. (1999) instead call this same channel rule a support and resistance rule. The Sullivan et al. (1999) definition of the channel rule is similar to Taylor (1994), but the rule is conditioned on a formed channel, that is, the minimum and maximum over the last $n$ days must be within $x$% of each other.

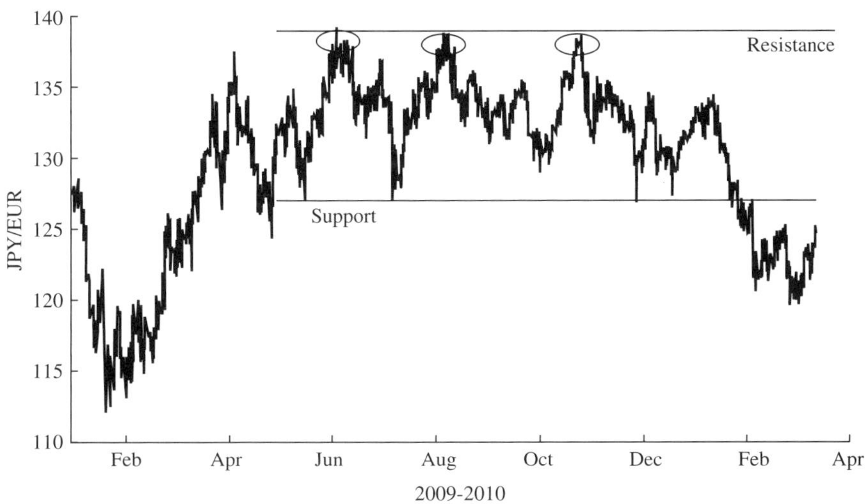


**FIGURE 12.1** A triple-top pattern in the JPY/EUR, 2009–2010. Notes: George Davis of RBC Capital Markets identifies this triple top pattern in Clements (2010).

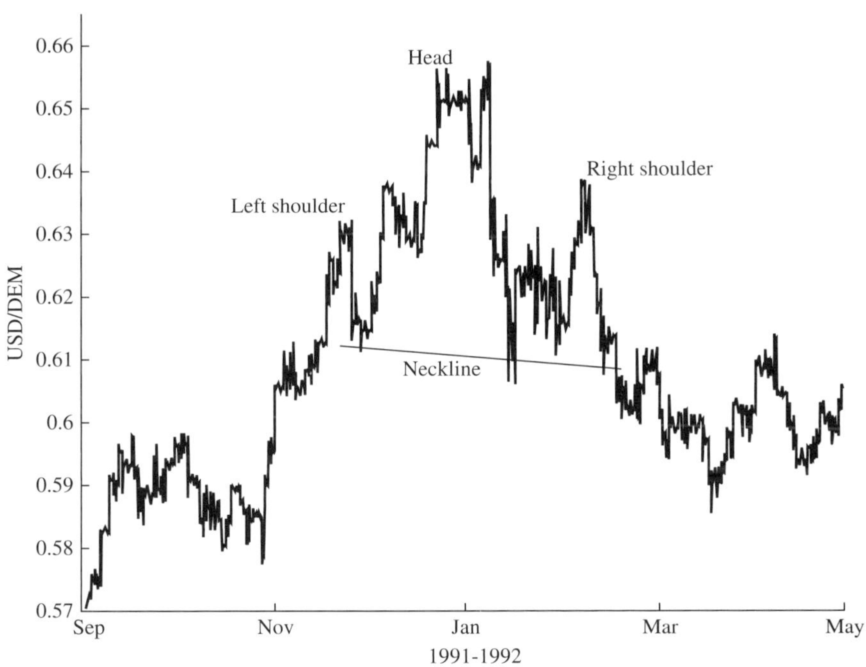


**FIGURE 12.2** A head-and-shoulders pattern in the USD/DEM, 1991–1992.

**TABLE 12.1 Traditional Technical Rules That Have Been Frequently Tested**

| Rule | Description | Mathematical expression |
|---|---|---|
| Filter | Go long (short) if the price rises (falls) y% from the local minimum (maximum). | $z_t = \begin{cases} 1 & \text{if } S_t \geq n_t(1+y) \\ -1 & \text{if } S_t \leq x_t(1-y) \\ z_{t-1} & \text{otherwise} \end{cases}$ |
| Double moving average (MA) | Go long (short) if the short moving average exceeds (declines below) the long moving average. | $z_t = \begin{cases} 1 & \text{if } \frac{1}{S}\sum_{i=0}^{S-1} S_{t-i} > \frac{1}{L}\sum_{i=0}^{L-1} S_{t-i} \\ -1 & \text{if } \frac{1}{S}\sum_{i=0}^{S-1} S_{t-i} < \frac{1}{L}\sum_{i=0}^{L-1} S_{t-i} \\ z_{t-1} & \text{otherwise} \end{cases}$ |
| Channel | Go long (short) if the price exceeds (is less than) the maximum (minimum) over the previous $n$ days plus (minus) the band of inaction. | $z_t = \begin{cases} 1 & \text{if } S_t > \max(S_{t-1}, S_{t-2}, \ldots S_{t-n})(1+y) \\ -1 & \text{if } S_t < \min(S_{t-1}, S_{t-2}, \ldots S_{t-n})(1-y) \\ z_{t-1} & \text{otherwise} \end{cases}$ |

Notes: $S_t$ is the exchange rate (dollar price of foreign currency) at time $t$, $n_t$ is the local minimum, $x_t$ is the local maximum, $y$ is the size of the band of inaction, if any, and $z_t$ is an indicator variable that equals 1 for a long position and $-1$ for a short position.

except to appeal to common practice. This introduces the possibility of data snooping and data mining biases and is a source of significant problems in any rigorous statistical test for the existence of excess returns. We consider ways of minimizing such biases in Section 12.4.

In recent practice, technicians more commonly favor several newer indicators that also use mathematical functions to determine when to buy or sell (Clements, 2010). These rules are less well known by economists and less well tested. Table 12.2 describes four of these types of rules: (i) relative strength indicator (RSI); (ii) exponentially weighted moving average (EWMA); (iii) moving average convergence divergence (MACD); and (iv) rate of change (ROC). These rules perform the same task as the traditional rules in Table 12.1—they identify trends and reversals.

In addition to charting and mechanical methods, technical analysts also use many other types of indicators. Some such indicators assign a special role to round numbers in support or resistance levels. For example, technicians interpret a crossing of a significant level, such as a yen/dollar rate of 100, as indicating

**TABLE 12.2 Technical Rules Frequently Mentioned in Technician Textbooks, Such as Elders (1993)**

| Rule name | Description | Mathematical expression |
|---|---|---|
| Relative strength indicator (RSI) | Go long if the RSI is less than 30; go short if the RSI is greater than 70. $\overline{TL}$ is the average loss over the last $n$ days, over days of loss. $\overline{TG}$ is the average gain over the last $n$ days, over days of gain. | $\mathrm{RSI}_t = 100 - \frac{100}{1+(\overline{TL}/\overline{TG})}$ $\quad z_t = \begin{cases} 1 & \text{if } \mathrm{RSI}_t \leq 30 \\ -1 & \text{if } \mathrm{RSI}_t \geq 70 \\ z_{t-1} & \text{otherwise} \end{cases}$ |
| Exponentially weighted moving average (EWMA) | Go long (short) when the short EWMA of past prices exceeds (falls short of) the long EWMA. | $z_t = \begin{cases} 1 & \text{if } \left(\frac{2}{S+1}\right) S_t + \mathrm{EMA}^S_{t-1}\left(1-\frac{2}{S+1}\right) > \left(\frac{2}{L+1}\right) S_t + \mathrm{EMA}^L_{t-1}\left(1-\frac{2}{L+1}\right) \\ -1 & \text{if } \left(\frac{2}{S+1}\right) S_t + \mathrm{EMA}^S_{t-1}\left(1-\frac{2}{S+1}\right) < \left(\frac{2}{L+1}\right) S_t + \mathrm{EMA}^L_{t-1}\left(1-\frac{2}{L+1}\right) \\ z_{t-1} & \text{otherwise} \end{cases}$ |
| Moving average convergence divergence (MACD) | Go long (short) when the difference between the short and long moving averages crosses a moving average of intermediate length from below (above). | $z_t = \begin{cases} 1 & \text{if } \mathrm{MA}^S_t - \mathrm{MA}^L_t \geq \mathrm{MA}^I_t \\ -1 & \text{if } \mathrm{MA}^S_t - \mathrm{MA}^L_t < \mathrm{MA}^I_t \\ z_{t-1} & \text{otherwise} \end{cases}$ |
| Rate of change (ROC) | Go long (short) when the rate of change crosses the predetermined oversold (overbought) level from below (above). | $\mathrm{ROC}_t = 100\left(\frac{S_t - S_{t-n}}{S_{t-n}}\right)$ $\quad z_t = \begin{cases} 1 & \text{if } \mathrm{ROC}_t \geq \mathrm{ROC}_{t-1} \text{ and } \mathrm{ROC}_t > \mathrm{OSL} \\ -1 & \text{if } \mathrm{ROC}_t \leq \mathrm{ROC}_{t-1} \text{ and } \mathrm{ROC}_t < \mathrm{OBL} \\ z_{t-1} & \text{otherwise} \end{cases}$ |

Notes: $S_t$ is the exchange rate (dollar price of foreign currency) at time $t$. $z_t$ is an indicator variable that equals 1 for a long position and $-1$ for a short position.

further movement in the same direction. For example, Creswell (1995) reported that Jorge Rodriguez, director of North American Sales at Credit Suisse, stated, "The 100 yen level for the dollar is still a very big psychological barrier, and it will take a few tests before it breaks. But once you break 100 yen, it is not going to remain there for long. You will probably see it trade between 102 and 106 for a while." Osler (2003) shows that when an exchange rate approaches a round number, such as 100 yen to the dollar, it tends to reverse its path. But when an exchange rate does cross such a level, it tends to move rapidly past it. Osler (2005) links limit orders to the very high proportion of large changes in exchange rates. Murphy (1986) discusses a number of more esoteric methods, including Elliot wave theory, Fibonacci numbers, and many other technical concepts. In addition, traders sometimes use technical analysis of one market's price history to take positions in another market, a practice called *intermarket technical analysis*.

## 12.3 Studies of Technical Analysis in the Foreign Exchange Market

### 12.3.1 WHY STUDY TECHNICAL ANALYSIS?

The widespread use of technical analysis in foreign exchange (and other) markets is puzzling because it implies that either traders are irrationally making decisions on useless information or that past prices contain useful information for trading. The latter possibility would contradict the "efficient markets hypothesis," which holds that no trading strategy should be able to generate unusual profits on publicly available information—such as past prices—except by bearing unusual risk, and the observed level of risk-adjusted profitability measures market (in)efficiency. Therefore, much research effort has been directed toward determining whether technical analysis is indeed profitable or not. One of the earliest studies, by Fama and Blume (1966), found no evidence that a particular class of TTRs could earn abnormal profits in the stock market. However, more recent research by Brock et al. (1992) and Sullivan et al. (1999) has provided contrary evidence. And many studies of the foreign exchange market have found evidence that TTRs can generate persistent profits (Dooley and Shafer, 1984; Gençay, 1999; Lee et al., 2001; Levich and Thomas, 1993; Neely et al., 1997; Poole, 1967; Sweeney, 1986; Martin, 2001).

### 12.3.2 SURVEY EVIDENCE ON THE PRACTICE OF TECHNICAL ANALYSIS

An important area of research on technical analysis has focused on documenting how and to what extent it is actually used in foreign exchange markets. This research is primarily conducted through surveys of technicians. Allen and Taylor (1990) and Taylor and Allen (1992) conduct the first such surveys on chief foreign exchange dealers in London. The responses established that almost all traders in the London foreign exchange market use technical analysis to some degree and that they tend to combine it with fundamental analysis. So, there is not an exclusive reliance on either approach to trading. In addition, the authors find that the relative weight attached to technical analysis is greater at shorter horizons. Thus, Taylor and Allen (1992) find that 90% of the respondents to their survey report using some form of technical analysis to inform their trading decisions. In addition, they find that at short horizons—less than a week—traders use technical analysis much more frequently than they do fundamental analysis, which uses economic variables such as interest rates and output growth rates to guide trading decisions.[5]

Later surveys confirmed many of these early findings. Cheung and Chinn (2001) find that 30% of US foreign exchange traders could best be characterized as technical analysts and that an increasing percentage uses technical analysis. Cheung et al. (2004) confirm previous findings that traders pay more attention to nonfundamental factors at short horizons.

More recent surveys have investigated the educational background, experience, and psychological biases of foreign exchange traders, including technical traders. Menkhoff (1997) refutes the notion that technical traders lack the experience or education of their peers who trade on fundamentals. The surveyed German technicians do not differ from nontechnicians regarding age, education, position, seniority, their firms' trading turnover, or assets under management. Menkhoff and Schmidt (2005) investigate the use of buy-and-hold, momentum and contrarian trading strategies by fund managers. Momentum traders are the least risk-averse and contrarian traders show signs of overconfidence.

Oberlechner and Osler (2012) use survey evidence from 400 North American foreign exchange traders to establish that respondents underestimate uncertainty and overestimate their own abilities. They argue that their findings help to explain the high volatility of floating exchange rates, the profitability of trend-following strategies, and the apparent irrationality of exchange rate forecasts. Finally, Clements (2010) interviews 13 prominent technicians about market efficiency, trading strategies, attitudes toward risk, and intermarket analysis.

## 12.3.3 COMPUTING SIGNALS AND RETURNS

We first review the basic procedures for evaluating TTR success before describing progress in the literature. Procedures for evaluating the profitability of trading rules vary somewhat from study to study and have evolved over the years. We briefly review reasonable and common methods for calculating such statistics. To calculate statistics for a TTR—for example, a double MA rule—researchers first compute trading signals from the daily exchange rate data.[6] The exchange rate, $S_t$, is the dollar price of foreign exchange on day $t$. The trading signals, $z_t$, properly permit both long positions (i.e., $z_t = 1$) and short positions (i.e., $z_t = -1$) in the foreign currency, since a long position in one currency is equivalent to a

[5] Menkhoff (2010) finds that the dominance of technical analysis at short horizons holds for fund managers in general.

[6] Researchers typically work with daily exchange rate data. The adjustments for higher frequency data are straightforward.

short position in the other. The following equation gives the trading signals for a double MA rule:

$$1 \quad \text{if} \quad \frac{1}{S}\sum_{i=0}^{S-1} S_{t-i} > \frac{1}{L}\sum_{i=0}^{L-1} S_{t-i} \tag{12.1}$$

$$z_t = -1 \quad \text{if} \quad \frac{1}{S}\sum_{i=0}^{S-1} S_{t-i} < \frac{1}{L}\sum_{i=0}^{L-1} S_{t-i} \tag{12.2}$$

$$z_{t-1} \quad \text{otherwise} \tag{12.3}$$

To compute excess returns, researchers typically assume that an investor holds some amount in dollars and reinvests daily at the domestic overnight interest rate. These funds can be thought of as a margin held against borrowing an equal value, either in dollars or in the foreign currency. If a trading rule signals a long (short) position in the foreign currency at date $t$, the borrowed dollars (foreign currency) are converted to foreign currency (dollars) at the closing rate for date $t$ and earn the foreign (United States) overnight rate. The domestic (foreign) overnight interest rate is $i_t$ $\left(i_t^*\right)$, and the excess return, $R_{t+1}$, to a long position in foreign currency is then given by

$$R_{t+1} = \frac{S_{t+1}}{S_t}\frac{\left(1+i_t^*\right)}{\left(1+i_t\right)}. \tag{12.4}$$

The continuously compounded (log) excess return from $t$ to $t+1$ is $z_t r_{t+1}$, where $z_t$ is the trading indicator and $r_{t+1}$ is defined as

$$r_{t+1} = \ln S_{t+1} - \ln S_t + \ln\left(1+i_t^*\right) - \ln\left(1+i_t\right). \tag{12.5}$$

Therefore, the cumulative excess return, $r$, for a trading strategy over the period from time zero to time $T$ is given by

$$r = \sum_{t=0}^{T-1} z_t r_{t+1} + n\ln\left(\frac{1-c}{1+c}\right). \tag{12.6}$$

where $n$ is the number of round-trip trades and $c$ is the one-way transaction cost.

It is generally not possible to obtain long series of interest rate and exchange rate data that are observed at the same time of day. While the lack of simultaneous data observation will introduce some error in calculated returns, there is no evidence that it introduces significant bias toward finding profitability. Further, TTRs work about as well with futures prices as with spot prices. Therefore, the lack of simultaneous timing between exchange rates and interest rates is not an important issue.

Frenkel and Levich (1975, 1977) estimate a transaction cost in the 15-basis-point range from triangular arbitrage spreads in spot markets. McCormick

(1979) reduces this estimate to about 10 basis points with more precisely timed data. Using futures data, Levich and Thomas (1993) calculate transaction costs of 2.5 basis points per futures transaction for a large institution over the period 1976–1990. They describe 4 basis points per transaction as more "conservative." Studies in the 1990s often used five basis points per change of position (Chang and Osler, 1999; Neely et al., 1997). Since 2000, spot market participants have faced spreads of two basis points or less for transactions in the range \$5–50 million.

### 12.3.4 EARLY STUDIES: SKEPTICISM BEFORE THE TIDE TURNS

Many studies of the foreign exchange market have indicated profit opportunities. Dooley and Shafer (1976, 1984); Poole (1967) and Logue and Sweeney (1977) show that filter rules were profitable over relatively short samples. Cornell and Dietrich (1978) likewise present evidence of success for both filter and MA rules. Perhaps not surprisingly, academic economists were very skeptical of these challenges to Fama's (1970) intuitively appealing efficient markets hypothesis. In a private communication, Jeffrey Shafer informed us that academics generally dismissed the findings of Dooley and Shafer (1976, 1984). The dominant view in the early 1980s was that evidence of technical trading profits must be incorrect or specific to one sample.[7]

Sweeney (1986) confirms the effectiveness of filter rules on many dollar exchange rates. By the time Sweeney (1986) was published, the tide of opinion in the profession had probably turned and economists had become aware of the profitability of filter and MA rules in foreign exchange. Sweeney (1988) and Levich and Thomas (1993) extend this understanding. Levich and Thomas (1993) examine the sample period from January 1976 to December 1990 and find average excess returns of 8.1% per annum across six filters for the JPY and numbers of similar magnitude for the DEM, British pound (GBP), and Swiss franc (CHF). Average profitability for three MA rules, MA(1, 5), MA(5, 20), and MA(1, 200), is somewhat higher. A bootstrapping exercise implies that the observed level of profit was very unlikely to be a chance occurrence. In a subsample analysis, they find some indication that profits had declined in the period 1986–1990. Later research would investigate the time variation in rule profitability more thoroughly.

### 12.3.5 PATTERN RECOGNITION, INTRADAY DATA, AND OTHER EXCHANGE RATES

Researchers have not only investigated the reasons for the apparent profitability of mechanical TTRs that use daily data but have also sought to more closely approximate the actual practice of technical analysis, which often exploits pattern analysis, high frequency transactions, and a variety of currencies.

[7]Lo (2004) describes similar resistance to the findings in Lo and MacKinlay (1988), in which they reject the random walk hypothesis for stock prices.

Although it is much more straightforward to analyze simple mechanical trading rules, researchers have made some progress in looking at more complex, pattern-based rules. In particular, Osler and Chang (1995) construct an algorithm to identify "head-and-shoulders" patterns in currency markets. They find evidence to suggest that these patterns have predictive ability in some markets. Lo et al. (2000) do further work along these lines and look at the predictive ability of several commonly used price patterns, including head-and-shoulders, in the context of equity markets. Their distinctive contribution is that they initially smooth the price series using kernel mean regression, which provides a plausible analog to the signal extraction task performed by the human brain, which filters out noise and identifies the occurrence of a price pattern. It is a step toward objective reproduction of a subjective procedure. Savin et al. (2007) extend the analysis of Lo et al. (2000) by calibrating the pattern recognition algorithm using price patterns identified by a practicing technical analyst and find evidence that the head-and-shoulders pattern has significant predictive power for stock returns for periods of up to 3 months. The kernel mean regression methodology has yet to be applied to the foreign exchange market.

Although the majority of academic studies of technical analysis have used daily data, some studies have used higher frequency data (Curcio et al., 1997; Neely and Weller, 2003; Osler, 2003; Kozhan and Salmon, 2010). Neely and Weller (2003) use half-hourly data from 1996 to examine trading rules generated by a genetic program and by a linear forecasting model. Once reasonable transaction costs are taken into account and trade is restricted to times of normal market activity, they find no evidence of positive excess returns. Kozhan and Salmon (2010) use tick-by-tick data for the pound sterling against the US dollar drawn from the Reuters D3000 trading system for separate periods in 2003 and 2008. They find that a trading rule based on a genetic algorithm can earn significant profits net of transaction costs in 2003 but that these profits disappear by 2008.

Of course, one would like to directly examine the returns to commercial trading recommendations made in real time. Gençay et al. (2003a) and (2003b) use high frequency data to compare a widely used commercial real-time trading model with technical traders and an exponentially weighted MA model, respectively. The commercial real-time model dominates its competitors in risk-adjusted return.

Other studies have extended the literature on technical analysis by studying the application of such rules to other than major dollar exchange rates. Lee and Mathur (1996) find that MA trading rules have marginal profitability for only two of six cross rates (non-USD rates). Neely and Weller (1999) show remarkable success for rules created by genetic programing in the target zones of the European Monetary System. Lee et al. (2001) discern mixed results for MA and channel rules for 13 Latin American exchange rates. Martin (2001) discovers that trading rules produce significant profits—but not after risk adjustment—for developing countries. de Zwart et al. (2009) find that both technical analysis and information from macroeconomic variables can create profitable trading strategies for emerging market exchange rates from 1997 to 2007. Likewise,

Pukthuanthong-Le et al. (2007), and Pukthuanthong-Le and Thomas (2008) find that emerging market currencies appear to provide some profit opportunities to technical rules. In summary, the evidence for technical trading profitability in cross rates is mixed but emerging markets show greater profits than recent dollar markets.

## 12.4 Explaining The Success of Technical Analysis

Research from the 1970s through the early 1990s documented a long period, perhaps 15 years, in which fairly simple technical rules—MA and filter rules—apparently produced substantial excess returns on major exchange rates. This result was puzzling because it appeared to challenge the intuitively appealing weak-form efficient markets hypothesis, which stated that past prices should not produce positive risk-adjusted returns.

Several potentially complementary hypotheses have been put forward to explain the apparent success of technical analysis. First, there are at least three ways—data snooping, publication bias, and data mining—in which the apparent returns could be spurious, an artifact of the research process. Second, the apparent returns might be consistent with a reasonably efficient market if they are compensation for bearing risk. Third, either known agents—for example, central banks—or less understood factors—for example, cognitive biases—might introduce sufficient inefficiencies to create the observed returns.

### 12.4.1 DATA SNOOPING, PUBLICATION BIAS, AND DATA MINING

Data snooping, publication bias, and data mining are three related but distinct problems that could tend to produce the false conclusion that TTRs are successful. In particular, these three issues stem from the fact that it is always possible to find ex post patterns, such as profitable trading strategies, that exist purely by chance in a specific data set and will not exist in other samples/data sets. Data snooping is the problem that researchers will choose, either consciously or unconsciously, to test rules already proved profitable on part or all of the previously tested data set.[8] Data mining is the tendency for each set of researchers to test many rules and to base the overall inference on the most successful rules: Negative test results are ignored, while positive results are taken to indicate that trading rule strategies can yield profits. Publication bias refers to the tendency of journals to more readily accept submissions with positive results (i.e., profitable trading rules) than negative results. Even if every group of researchers guards assiduously against data snooping and/or data mining, publication bias would result in the profession reading research from the studies with the most positive results.

[8]It is almost impossible to avoid some data snooping, given that data sets and plausible rules are limited.

Although practicing technicians usually use rules containing a substantial subjective element, researchers need to evaluate fixed, mechanical trading rules. Some researchers argue that one should test only those rules that are commonly used in practice to reduce the problem of drawing false conclusions from data mining. This practice exacerbates the problem of data snooping, however. Technicians routinely "backtest" rules—test them on past data—using only rules that were profitable on past data. In other words, technical analysts may have converged on a small number of rules that happen by chance to have been profitable over some historical time period. Thus, the study of those rules could be subject to data snooping bias.

Starting in the mid-1990s, studies began to consider more seriously how to confront the data snooping problem. One way to minimize this bias is to automate the rule selection procedure and minimize researcher input. Such a procedure selects rules that perform optimally during some in-sample period and then examines their performance out of sample. Neely et al. (1997) use genetic programming to identify optimal rules for six exchange rates and find evidence of significant profitability for the out-of-sample period 1981–1995. The genetic programming approach allows one to be relatively agnostic about the precise structure of any optimal rule, which reduces the chance that preconceived notions about what rules "work" may introduce data snooping bias. Gençay (1999) and others have similarly employed neural networks as "black-box" methods for generating trading rules with positive results.

Even in the absence of an automated black-box rule selection process, the practice of subdividing a sample into distinct in-sample and out-of-sample periods can also reduce the danger of data mining, as well as data snooping. The in-sample period is used to select rules that perform well during that period and the rules are then tested on the out-of-sample data. This effectively reduces a very large group of rules to a small group of selected rules that can be tested in the out-of-sample period with less concern for the number of rules or data snooping bias. Examples of in-sample/out-of-sample testing include the use of genetic programming (Neely et al., 1997) and various econometric techniques (Taylor, 1994; Dueker and Neely, 2007).

White (2000) introduces another tool—a "reality check"—to correct for the data mining bias that is inherent in testing a large group of rules in a single paper. This tool allows one to adjust significance levels as a function of the number of actual or potential rules considered. Qi and Wu (2006) apply White's reality check in the context of the foreign exchange market and find evidence that profitability survives for their 1973–1998 sample period. It is considerably weaker for their 1986–1998 subsample period. Hsu et al. (2010) test the predictive ability of trading rules on emerging market indices with the "superior predictive ability" stepwise test of Hansen (2005), which is also designed to eliminate data snooping bias. They find predictive ability but note that the emergence of exchange-traded funds appears to weaken this phenomenon.

Perhaps, the most certain solution to data snooping, data mining, and publication bias is to analyze the performance of rules in true out-of-sample tests that occur long after an important study. That is, one can test a group of rules that were examined in studies conducted sufficiently long ago that one has enough new data to carry out a true out-of-sample test. Neely et al. (2009) employ this line of attack. Of course, this technique has a substantial cost: One must wait years to employ it on past studies.

### 12.4.2 TEMPORAL VARIATION IN TRADING RULE RETURNS

Even if one is confident that one has found a profitable rule or portfolio of rules with positive returns, the significant possibility that their profitability will vary over time must be considered. It is thus necessary to test the stability of rule profitability. Several papers have taken up this challenge: Levich and Thomas (1993) note some (weak) evidence that the profitability of their rules declines in their final subsample period, 1986–1990. LeBaron (2002) finds that returns to a 150-day MA trading rule decline in the 1990s and speculates that data snooping may be responsible for earlier successes. More recently, Okunev and White (2003) and Olson (2004), using different optimizing procedures to select MA trading strategies, arrive at different conclusions on the continued profitability of trading rules. Okunev and White (2003) consider whether momentum strategies in MA rules continue to be profitable in the recent era. They find that taking simultaneous long and short positions in MA rules with the best and worst returns over the previous month produces excess returns of 45–60 basis points per month over the period 1980–2000.[9] Olson (2004) dynamically reoptimizes MA rule portfolios in successive 5-year periods from 1971 to 2000 and then tests these in successive 5-year out-of-sample periods. He finds that post-1970s returns declined to about zero by the 1990s. Schulmeister (2008) shows that the best of 1024 technical rules in the DEM/USD market were profitable out-of-sample and that rule profitability has been declining since the late 1980s. Pukthuanthong-Le et al. (2007), and Pukthuanthong-Le and Thomas (2008) extend the analysis on time variation in returns to emerging markets. They find that major currencies no longer trend reliably but markets in newly trading currencies appear to display some profit opportunities from technical rules. This finding suggests that traders in major currency markets have arbitraged away technical patterns but those patterns still exist in emerging markets.

Figure 12.3 illustrates the time variation in the returns to traditional rules. It shows the rolling mean annual return to a portfolio of the set of traditional rules used in Levich and Thomas (1993): 0.5%, 1%, 2%, 3%, 4%, and 5% filter rules, as well as MA(1, 5), MA(5, 20), and MA(1, 200) rules. This figure makes clear that the rules were profitable, on average, during the Levich and Thomas sample, 1976–1990, but tended to become much less profitable during the 1990s and 2000s. The sloping lines, which represent predicted values from a time trend model of trading rule returns, illustrate the trend decline in profitability over time. This visually confirms that traditional MA and filter rules had become unprofitable by the early 1990s.

Figure 12.3 also hints at the major difficulty in detecting time variation in the returns to TTRs in foreign exchange markets: The returns are noisy. The typical

[9] The returns were not adjusted for transaction costs.

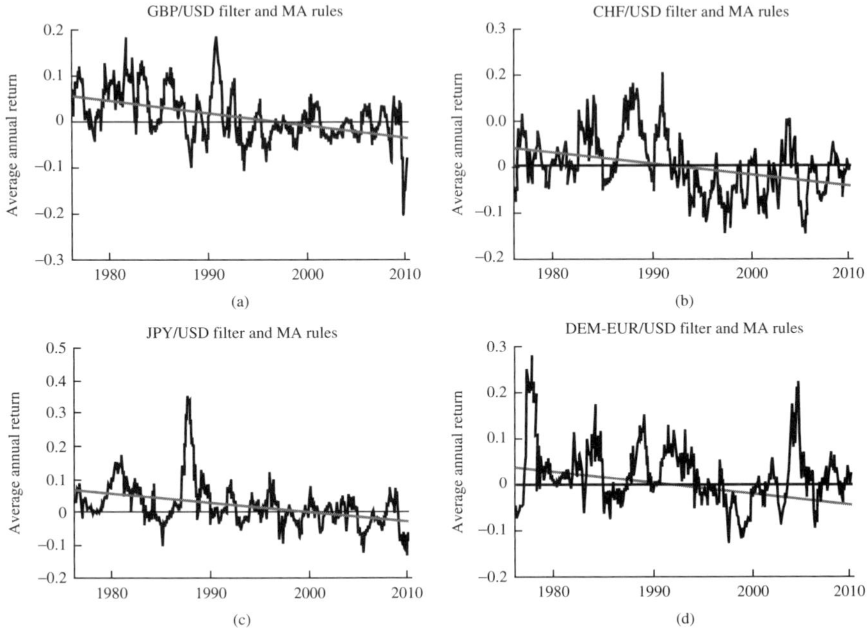


**FIGURE 12.3 (a–d) The diminishing returns to commonly tested technical trading rules, 1976–2010.**

**Notes: 1-year rolling net annual returns to portfolios made up of the commonly used filter and moving average trading rules used in Levich and Thomas (1993), as applied to the GBP/USD, CHF/USD, JPY/USD, and DEM-EUR/USD. Horizontal black lines denote zero net returns; sloping dark gray lines denote a fitted linear regression line with a constant and a time trend.**

exchange rate has an annual standard deviation around 10%. Researchers would require long samples to reliably determine that a mean trading rule return declined by 2 or 3 percentage points per annum, especially if the break date was unknown.

The temporal patterns in TTR returns can also illuminate the source of these returns. For example, if rules were profitable on some particular sample by chance, as a result of data mining, data snooping, or publication bias, then those rules would be very unlikely to remain profitable outside of the original sample. Neely et al. (2009) exploit this observation to evaluate explanations for trading rule returns by conducting true, out-of-sample tests on previously studied rules from the following papers: Levich and Thomas (1993); Neely et al. (1997); Sweeney (1986); Taylor (1994); and Dueker and Neely (2007). The rules consisted of filter, MA, and channel rules, as well as rules developed by genetic programming and econometric methods (ARIMA and Markov switching models). The logic underlying the analysis was that true, out-of-sample results permitted one to discover whether the original results reported were the result of data snooping or represented genuine profit opportunities. It was also possible to look more closely at whether profits had changed over time. The authors concluded that relatively simple technical rules were genuinely profitable on major floating exchange rates for an extended period, at least 15 years, from about 1975 to 1990. As the profitability of those simple rules became widely publicized in the academic literature, the profitability of the rules disappeared. At the same time, more complex and less well-known rules retained substantial profitability.[10]

Similarly, Kozhan and Salmon (2010), using high frequency data, find that trading rules derived from a genetic algorithm were profitable in 2003 but that this was no longer true in 2008. They attribute their finding to a dramatic rise in the volume of algorithmic trading over this period. Consistent with this explanation, Chaboud et al. (2009) report that from 2003 to 2007 the fraction of trading volume where at least one of the two counterparties was an algorithmic trader increased from almost nothing to 60% or more for the yen and euro against the dollar.

The examination of time variation in the returns to trading rules makes it clear that genuine returns existed for many years and probably still exist at lower levels for more complex rules. This raises the question as to the source of those genuine returns.

### 12.4.3 DO TECHNICAL TRADING RETURNS COMPENSATE INVESTORS FOR BEARING RISK?

Some of the early studies of technical trading in currency markets made no attempt to adjust for risk. This left open the possibility that the reported excess returns were not anomalous or an indication of market inefficiency but simply appropriate compensation for the risk incurred. Researchers have adopted a number of different risk adjustment approaches. Sweeney (1986), for example, assumes that any observed deviation from uncovered interest parity indicates the presence of a constant risk premium (or discount). A long position in foreign currency then earns a constant risk premium. Since he analyzes trading rules that do not permit short positions, he looks at the excess return earned by the trading rule (gross return less buy-and-hold return) adjusted according to the number of days the rule held a long position and thus had to earn the risk premium. He denotes the risk-adjusted return as X* and finds that observed returns remain positive after this risk adjustment (Sweeney and Lee, 1990). Although Sweeney developed the X* statistic in the context of the foreign exchange market, it would seem to be more appropriate for equities, which might exhibit an unconditional risk premium.

In a standard model of a representative agent maximizing utility over an infinite horizon, it is possible to show that the following condition should hold:

$$S_t \frac{1 + i_t}{1 + i_t^*} = E_t\left[S_{t+1}\right] + \frac{\text{cov}_t\left(M_{t+1}, S_{t+1}\right)}{E_t\left[M_{t+1}\right]}, \tag{12.7}$$

[10]In an intriguing study of a nontraditional source of technical information, Charlebois and Sapp (2007) confirm the idea that market participants can predict future asset prices. They show that information from open interest on at-the-money options produces a trading strategy that is more profitable than traditional technical trading rules.

where $M_t$ is the stochastic discount factor (marginal utility of a dollar in different states of the world). The covariance term represents the foreign currency risk premium and can be time varying. It captures the extent to which holding the foreign currency can act as a consumption hedge. If the risk premium, represented by the covariance term, is zero, we obtain the familiar uncovered interest parity condition,

$$S_t \frac{1 + i_t}{1 + i_t^*} = E_t \left[ S_{t+1} \right], \tag{12.8}$$

which predicts that the currency with the higher interest rate is expected to depreciate. The very well-documented violation of this prediction has given rise to the forward premium puzzle and is the source of the carry trade, a strategy that requires the trader to take a long position in a currency or portfolio of currencies that earns high interest rates and a short position in a currency or portfolio of currencies that earns low interest rates.

Providing a convincing model of the risk premium is the key to appropriate risk adjustment, both for TTR returns and for the carry trade. In equity markets the standard approach to risk adjustment is to use a factor model in which the stochastic discount factor is assumed to be a linear function of individual risk factors. This may be the capital asset pricing model (CAPM), in which the return on the market portfolio is the single factor or a multifactor model such as the Fama-French three-factor model. Although the CAPM has a firm theoretical foundation, there is little theoretical guidance as to choice of appropriate factors in multifactor models. The Fama-French model, which adds size and book-to-market factors to the market excess return, is widely used because of its success in explaining stock returns. It has been difficult, however, to provide a convincing link to underlying sources of risk. And there is no obvious rationale for using the model to explain currency returns. Recent work by Lustig et al. (2010) suggests that a single currency factor constructed as the return on the highest minus the return on the lowest interest rate currency portfolios may provide a parsimonious explanation of currency risk premia. They argue that the factor can explain returns to the carry trade but the model has not yet been applied to TTR returns. Brunnermeier et al. (2009) explain the returns to the carry trade through crash risk caused by the sudden unwinding of carry trades, which is associated with illiquidity. Menkhoff et al. (2012) argue that high interest currency returns are negatively related to global foreign exchange volatility, which explain the carry trade returns. In these cases, also, we do not yet know what explanatory power, if any, these factors have for TTR returns.

Risk adjustment based on the CAPM requires one to select a market portfolio. If markets are fully integrated and investors hold globally diversified portfolios, then the world market portfolio is the appropriate choice. Otherwise, it may make more sense to choose a particular country's market portfolio. Taylor (1992) looks at the beta with the S&P 500, whereas Kho (1996) uses the MSCI (world) market index. Neely et al. (1997) use both a world market index and several national indices. A general finding is that trading rule returns are unconditionally uncorrelated with sources of stock market risk. Since they are also substantially less variable, a portfolio that combines a stock index with a trading rule return will often produce a large improvement in the risk-return trade-off (Neely and Weller (1999)). However, Kho (1996) reports that allowing for time variation in the risk premium can account for much of the excess profitability of a class of MA rules.

In addition to CAPM betas, researchers have used several other risk adjustment criteria: Sharpe ratios, drawdown statistics, and measures derived specifically from utility functions, such as the $X_{eff}$ measure from Dacorogna et al. (2001). $X_{eff}$ measures the utility that the trading strategy provides to a constant absolute risk-averse individual over a weighted average of return horizons. Because it is difficult to find systematic risk exposure in foreign exchange trading rules, Sharpe ratios are among the most practically useful risk adjustment tools because they permit direct comparison of univariate risk among trading rules.

An exclusive concentration on measures of risk, to the exclusion of Knightian "uncertainty," is likely to lead to a false sense of security, among both academics and practitioners. The implicit assumption in applying any of the measures of risk mentioned above is that the environment is stationary and the past is a good guide to the future. In other words, we are dealing with a world without "black swans." Lo and Mueller (2010) have recently argued that the failure of quantitative models in finance, of which TTRs are a special case, is very often attributable to neglect of uncertainty as opposed to risk. Of course, since uncertainty is inherently unquantifiable, it is still very much an open question how best to allow it to influence the construction and application of financial models.

### 12.4.4 DOES FOREIGN EXCHANGE INTERVENTION CREATE TRADING RULE PROFITS?

One explanation for the profitability of technical trading has a long pedigree going back to Friedman (1953): Official intervention by the central bank in foreign exchange markets generates inefficiencies from which technical rules profit (Friedman, 1953; Sweeney, 1986; Kritzman, 1989). The presumed inefficiency arises from the fact that the central bank has a target for the exchange rate that may be different from its fundamental value. This may be a consequence of the imposition of short-run political objectives or a desire to limit volatility. The fact that technical rules seem to be less useful in equity and commodity markets—where there is no intervention—has buttressed the argument (Silber, 1994). LeBaron (1999) shows an intriguing correlation between days of US intervention and the profitability of MA trading rules. When one removes the returns on intervention days from the technical trading return series, the mean return to technical trading is no longer statistically significant. Szakmary and Mathur (1997) show similar results for an international data set using monthly data. But Neely (2002) uses higher frequency exchange rate data and intervention series from four monetary authorities to show that almost all the trading rule returns on intervention days occurred overnight, before intervention could plausibly have occurred. This provides convincing evidence that intervention is not a source of trading profits and that variation in the frequency of intervention does not explain changes in trading rule profitability. Intervention does not generate returns to technical trading but rather responds to strong trends from which technical traders profit.

Table 12.3 approximately reproduces LeBaron's (1999) and Neely's (2002) results for US data by applying an MA (1,150) rule to daily DEM/USD and JPY/USD data from 1979 through 1992. Using all observations, the rules make impressive and statistically significant gross annual returns on both the DEM and JPY data, at 6.97% and 8.35%, respectively. When one removes the respective intervention days, however, the gross annual returns decline to 2.07% and 3.53%, which are no longer statistically significant. The row labeled "Markov *p*-value" shows the probability that randomly removing return observations would produce as low a return as excluding intervention days. Both Markov *p*-values are low, at 8% and 5%, respectively. Here, it appears that intervention creates the returns to technical trading.

When one divides the gross returns into (i) returns before the US business day and (ii) returns during the US business day—when US intervention almost always occurred—one sees that most of the decline in returns caused by removal

**TABLE 12.3 The Effect of Removing Days of Intervention from Trading Rule Returns**

| | All DEM obs | DEM with No Intervention | All JPY obs | JPY with No Intervention |
|---|---|---|---|---|
| Obs | 3495 | 3015 | 3495 | 3287 |
| Gross AR | 6.97 | 2.07 | 8.35 | 3.53 |
| Gross AR *t*-statistic | (2.20) | (0.62) | (2.85) | (1.21) |
| Gross AR, close (*t*-1) to 9 AM (*t*) | 7.50 | 4.50 | 7.84 | 4.15 |
| Gross AR, 9 AM to close | −0.53 | −2.43 | 0.51 | −0.62 |
| Markov *p*-value | | 0.08 | | 0.05 |
| Sharpe | 0.59 | | 0.76 | |
| Trades per year | 7.08 | | 4.94 | |
| Begining date | 1/2/1979 | | 1/2/1979 | |
| Ending date | 12/31/1992 | | 12/31/1992 | |

Notes: The table reproduces the results of LeBaron (1999) and Neely (2002) on similar data and shows the results of an MA(1, 150) rule on daily foreign exchange rate data. The left-hand (right-hand) panel shows the results for DEM (JPY) data. Column 2 shows the results for all DEM observations and column 3 excludes returns on days in which US authorities intervened in the DEM market. Columns 4 and 5 show the analogous results for Japanese data. The rows show the number of observations, annual gross returns (gross AR) (no transactions costs), the *t*-statistic for the gross AR, the gross AR from the previous close to 9 AM and from 9 AM to close, the *p*-value for the test that randomly removing observations would produce as low a return as the gross return excluding intervention days, the Sharpe ratio for all observations and the number of trades per year for all observations and the sample dates.

of intervention days occurred before the US business day and almost certainly before intervention. In other words, the trading rules were especially profitable before and not after the occurrence of intervention. For example, the overnight return in the DEM market fell from 7.5% to 4.5% and that in the JPY market fell from 7.84% to 4.15%. It seems unlikely that intervention—which is sporadic and difficult to predict with any precision—would lower returns before the time of intervention. In addition, the sign of intervention is contrary to the direction of the trading signal; that is, US authorities tended to be buying (selling) dollars while technical rules were short (long) in the dollar.[11] The evidence is consistent with a story in which the US authorities typically intervene contrary to strong exchange rate trends—that is, "lean against the wind"—and TTRs tend to profit from such trends. This creates a correlation between intervention days and trading profits, but the intervention does not create those profits, it simply reacts to exchange rate trends.

The weight of empirical evidence supports the conclusion that TTRs were able to earn genuine risk-adjusted excess returns in major foreign exchange markets at least from the mid-1970s until about 1990. We can with some confidence reject explanations that rely on data mining, compensation for risk, or foreign exchange intervention. The conclusion leads one to accept that these markets were inefficient and raises this question: What was the source of the inefficiency?

### 12.4.5 DO COGNITIVE BIASES CREATE TRADING RULE PROFITS?

Evidence has steadily accumulated that suggests that financial markets are not as efficient as had once been believed. For example, stock prices display short-term momentum over periods of 6 months to a year and longer-term mean reversion (Chopra et al., 1992; De Bondt and Thaler, 1985; Jegadeesh and Titman, 1993). Such phases of momentum and reversal imply the presence of trending behavior of the kind that TTRs are designed to exploit.[12] If we combine this momentum with the evidence of strong and persistent trends in currency markets, it suggests that common factors are responsible for these patterns in different financial markets.[13] Behavioral models that depart from the standard assumption of rationality are able to account for such anomalous price patterns.

[11] Neely (1998) explains how both technical traders and central banks can make positive returns, on average, despite being on opposite sides of the market on days of intervention.

[12] Serban (2010) creates foreign exchange trading rules that combine mean reversion and momentum features, which previously have been explored in equity markets. The combination produces abnormal returns for five exchange rates. The results are grossly similar to but exceed those found in equity markets.

[13] This argument is further supported by the recent survey data presented in Menkhoff (2010) showing that fund managers in several different countries make extensive use of technical analysis and rely more heavily on it at short horizons. These results parallel the results of surveys of the foreign exchange market discussed above. Clements (2009) interviews fund managers about their views on behavioral finance.

Daniel et al. (1998) develop a model in which investors are overconfident and subject to biased self-attribution. Overconfidence manifests itself as a tendency to overestimate the precision of private information. Biased self-attribution refers to the fact that individuals are prone to thinking that favorable outcomes are due to skill and unfavorable ones to bad luck. In combination, these cognitive biases result in investors placing excessive weight on their private information. This generates a price overreaction that is only gradually reversed as new public information is revealed. In this way, price momentum and reversal are generated. With this behavioral model's emphasis on the role of private information, it might be argued that the model provides a more convincing story to explain momentum in equity markets than in the foreign exchange market, where private information plays a less prominent role. But Friesen et al. (2009) show that confirmation bias alone can generate price momentum and reversal; one need not assume that information is private. Confirmation bias is a phenomenon that has been extensively documented in experimental studies. It is characterized by the search for, or the interpretation of, evidence in ways that favor existing beliefs or expectations. It has been described as "perhaps the best known and most widely accepted notion of inferential error to come out of the literature on human reasoning" (Evans (1989) quoted in Nickerson (1998 p. 41)).

Frankel and Froot (1990) argued that the heterogeneous expectations of "chartists" and "fundamentalists" could be the source of excess volatility and bubbles in the foreign exchange market. Hong and Stein (1999) develop this idea and assume that investors are boundedly rational and unable to process all the information available. Some investors are momentum traders (the "chartists" of Frankel and Froot), and others are "newswatchers" who pay attention to fundamentals. De Grauwe and Grimaldi (2006) develop a model of heterogeneous agents in the foreign exchange market that has some similarities to the work of Hong and Stein (1999). They introduce chartists and fundamentalists—the latter are endowed with some simple learning rules—and find that the chartists trade profitably and can often dominate the market, consistent with the survey findings mentioned above.[14] Chiarella et al. (2006) create a model with boundedly rational fundamentalists and chartists who switch between fundamental and technical rules according to recent performance of the trading rules. That is, the heterogeneous traders adapt their behavior to market patterns. The authors investigate the implications for bubbles, market crashes, price resistance, and switching between price levels.[15] Hommes (2006) and LeBaron (2006) survey such heterogeneous agent models. Hommes (2011) provides experimental evidence on the importance of heterogeneity in explaining market outcomes.

[14]In a complementary approach to the theoretical models of Hong and Stein (1999) and De Grauwe and Grimaldi (2006), Schulmeister (2006) considers the empirical interaction of DEM/USD and EUR/USD trends and trading rule long-short positions.

[15]Schulmeister (2009) studies the potential interaction of trading signals and the yen–dollar exchange rate, suggesting that the response of trading signals to news might produce self-fulfilling trends.

Cognitive biases, including confirmation bias and bounded rationality, might create some departures from perfect efficiency that permit trading rules to have value. But that does not explain the time variation in the returns to trading rules or how market efficiency evolves over time.

### 12.4.6 DO MARKETS ADAPT TO ARBITRAGE AWAY TRADING RULE PROFITS?

So what might explain the long period in which researchers found that simple TTRs were profitable and the subsequent attenuation of the returns to those simple rules but the continued profitability of more complex or less studied rules? Andrew Lo (2004) put forward the adaptive markets hypothesis (AMH) that posits that financial markets gradually arbitrage away patterns as they become known. The AMH modifies the efficient markets view of the world to assert that learning, competition, and evolutionary selection pressures govern the forces that drive prices to their efficient levels. Individual agents are no longer the "hyperrational" beings of the standard paradigm, but rather boundedly rational "satisficers"—in the terminology of Herbert Simon (1955). The AMH predicts that profit opportunities will generally exist in financial markets but that learning and competition will gradually erode these opportunities as they become known. Because complexity inhibits learning, more complex strategies will persist longer than simple ones. And as some strategies decline as they become less profitable, there will be a tendency for other strategies to appear in response to the changing market environment. What is as yet unclear is the extent to which learning may mitigate or eliminate the effects of cognitive biases. Behavioral finance typically assumes that the impact of biases is persistent—rather than disappearing as the biases are recognized, as Fama (1998) suggests—but ultimately this is an empirical question.

Interestingly, the technicians interviewed in Clements (2010) often refer to forces that sound remarkably like those posited by the AMH. Not surprisingly, technicians generally believe that the EMH is badly flawed, markets contain short-lived inefficiencies, and technical analysis is well positioned to exploit them.

The AMH can be seen as an elaboration of certain ideas contained in the paradox of efficient markets put forward by Grossman and Stiglitz (1980) in the context of equity markets. As applied to the foreign exchange market, the Grossman and Stiglitz (1980) argument starts by noting that expectations about fundamentals such as national price levels, interest rates, and public debt levels determine exchange rate returns but that information about these fundamentals is costly for traders to gather and analyze. If traders cannot make some excess returns by trading on fundamentals, they will not gather and analyze fundamental information. But the traders would not be able to make excess returns on fundamental information in perfectly efficient markets. Therefore, markets cannot be perfectly efficient in that exchange rates will not always be *exactly* where fundamentals suggest they should be. One resolution to this paradox is to recognize that market analysts can recover the costs of some fundamental research by trading on marginally better information than the rest of the market. But the residual inefficiency opens up the possibility that technical traders may be able to profit from movements in exchange rates unrelated to fundamentals.

The AMH implies that profitable trading opportunities will fluctuate over time. Previously successful strategies will display deteriorating performance, and at the same time, new opportunities will appear. Most academic work has not attempted to investigate possible ways of constructing trading strategies to take advantage of this feature of the environment. A recent exception is the paper by Dempster and Leemans (2006), which uses an adaptive reinforcement learning algorithm as the basis for a fully automated system for trading in the foreign exchange market. Using data at 1-min frequency for the euro against the dollar, the authors report a gross return of 26% per annum over the period from January 2000 to January 2002.

The AMH is not yet a well-developed theory capable of generating sharp predictions. In particular, the AMH does not predict the speed of decline of risk arbitrage opportunities or the time to their extinction. Neither does it quantitatively predict how the complexity of a rule or opportunity affects its speed of decline. But the AMH provides some guidance on possible causal factors that may explain the broad findings of the literature on technical analysis.

## 12.5 The Future of Research on Technical Analysis

A major challenge for research on technical analysis is to produce a convincing theoretical underpinning for the voluminous empirical findings in the field. Some promising initial steps have already been taken in this direction. A number of competing behavioral models are able to reproduce some of the characteristics of currency markets, but it is important that these models be able to generate new predictions that can be tested. Burnside et al. (2011) is of particular interest in this regard. The authors construct a model in which overconfidence leads to overreaction to information about future inflation and provides an explanation for the forward premium puzzle and the profitability of carry trade strategies. Overconfidence can also be a source of momentum and trending in currency markets, suggesting that there may be a common underlying cause for the profitability of both TTRs and the carry trade strategy. Since their model predicts that the forward premium bias should be higher when momentum is high, we would expect to see a positive correlation between trading rule returns and carry trade profits.

An empirical challenge for technical analysis—one that has not been successfully met so far—would be to link order flow to technical trading signals and returns.[16] An example of work linking order flow with technical analysis is

[16]Although order flow is usually thought of as conveying fundamental information, we believe that it can be linked to technical analysis for the following reason: Technicians believe that technical analysis incorporates fundamental information into prices before it is fully public and the order

Gradojevic (2007), who uses order flow as one input to a trading model that combines a neural network with a fuzzy logic controller and finds that the model has significant predictive power. Although they do not explicitly link to technical trading, Rime et al. (2010) move in this direction and find that information from order flow produces a profitable trading strategy.

## 12.6 Conclusion

Technical analysis is a popular and widely used approach to trading in the foreign exchange market. Survey evidence shows that it dominates fundamental analysis at short horizons. These findings were first established for traders in the London market but have subsequently been confirmed to hold in other markets. Researchers have demonstrated that TTRs were able to generate excess returns over a long period during the 1970s and 1980s. The excess returns to relatively simple rules based on filters or MAs had disappeared by the early 1990s, but returns to more complex or sophisticated rules have persisted.

We have considered several hypotheses that the literature has advanced to explain these observations. We are able with some confidence to rule out data mining as an explanation for the early profitability of technical rules. Both out-of-sample analysis and adjustments to statistical tests indicate that the returns were genuine. Another possible explanation centers on the intervention operations of the central bank. If the central bank has a target for the exchange rate that differs from its fundamental value, then intervention may allow speculators to profit at the expense of the bank. In particular, if the central bank adopts a strategy of "leaning against the wind," then this may create predictable trends in the exchange rate that can be detected by technical analysis. However, research using high frequency data has shown that the periods of the greatest profitability precede central bank interventions. In other words, central banks have intervened to stem strong trends in the exchange rate, from which TTRs happen to profit. Therefore, intervention has been correlated with periods of high profitability for technical rules.

For the profitability of technical analysis to constitute evidence of market inefficiency, one must establish that the profits earned are not simply compensation for risk incurred. A variety of risk adjustment methods have failed to eliminate observed profits. A believer in market efficiency may argue that such tests have omitted some unknown risk factor. That argument, however, is substantially refuted by the decline in the profitability of simple rules over time, essentially to zero. It is more plausible that markets have adapted to progressively reduce profit opportunities, but at a speed that is clearly not consistent with the standard notion of market efficiency.

A proliferation of behavioral models can reproduce the trending seen in foreign exchange markets and show that technical trading can be consistently

flow literature has illustrated how order flow gradually impounds private information into prices. Therefore, order flow presumably drives the price trends that technicians exploit.

profitable in certain circumstances. The adaptive market hypothesis provides a promising framework in which such models can be further developed. Its emphasis on behavioral decision rules that depart from the standard rational paradigm, and on learning and evolutionary selection mechanisms, indicates a shift in focus in currency market research and, indeed, in financial markets in general.

## Acknowledgments

The authors thank many readers for helpful comments: Mike Dempster, Valérie Gastaldy, Ramo Gençay, Mark Hoeman, Richard Levich, Ike Mathur, participants at a Kepos Capital Management seminar and an anonymous referee. Brett Fawley provided excellent research assistance. The authors are responsible for errors. The views expressed in this paper are those of the authors and do not necessarily reflect those of the Federal Reserve Bank of St. Louis or the Federal Reserve System.

## REFERENCES

Allen H, Taylor MP. Charts, noise and fundamentals in the London foreign exchange market. Econ J 1990;100:49–59.

Brock W, Lakonishok J, LeBaron B. Simple technical trading rules and the stochastic properties of stock returns. J Finance 1992;47:1731–1764.

Brunnermeier M, Nagel S, Pedersen L. Carry trades and currency crashes. NBER Macroecon Ann 2008 2009;23:313–347.

Bulkowski TN. Encyclopedia of chart patterns. New York: John Wiley and Sons; 2000.

Burnside C, Han B, Hirshleifer D, Wang T. Investor overconfidence and the forward premium puzzle. Rev Econ Stud 2011;78:523–558.

Chaboud A, Chiquoine B, Hjalmarsson E, Vega C. Rise of the machines: algorithmic trading in the foreign exchange market, Working paper, Federal Reserve System; 2009.

Chang PHK, Osler C. Methodical madness: technical analysis and the irrationality of exchange-rate forecasts. Econ J 1999;109:636–661.

Charlebois M, Sapp S. Temporal patterns in foreign exchange returns and options. J Money Credit Bank 2007;39:443–470.

Cheung Y-W, Chinn MD. Currency traders and exchange rate dynamics: a survey of the US market. J Int Money Finance 2001;20:439–471.

Cheung Y-W, Chinn MD, Marsh IW. How do UK-based foreign exchange dealers think their market operates? Int J Finance Econ 2004;9:289–306.

Chiarella C, He X-Z, Hommes C. A dynamic analysis of moving average rules. J Econ Dyn Control 2006;30:1729–1753.

Chopra N, Lakonishok J, Ritter J. Measuring abnormal performance: do stocks overreact? J Financ Econ 1992;31:235–268.

Clements M. Technical analysis and behavioural finance in fund management. Guilford: Global Markets Media Ltd; 2009.

Clements M. Technical analysis in foreign exchange markets. Guilford: Global Markets Media Ltd; 2010.

Cornell WB, Dietrich JK. The efficiency of the market for foreign exchange under floating exchange rates. Rev Econ Stat 1978;60:111–120.

Covel MW. Trend following: how great traders make millions in up or down markets. New York: Prentice-Hall; 2005.

Creswell J. Currency market expects rate cut by Bank of Japan. Wall Street J Sept 5 1995; C16.

Curcio R, Goodhart C, Guillaume D, Payne R. Do technical trading rules generate profits? Conclusions from the intra-day foreign exchange market. Int J Finance Econ 1997;2:267–280.

Dacorogna MM, Gençay R, Müller UA, Pictet OV. Effective return, risk aversion and drawdowns. Phys A: Stat Mech Appl 2001;248:229–248.

Daniel K, Hirshleifer D, Subrahmanyam A. Investor psychology and security market under- and over-reactions. J Finance 1998;53:1839–1885.

De Bondt W, Thaler R. Does the stock market overreact? J Finance 1985;40:793–805.

De Grauwe P, Grimaldi M. Exchange rate puzzles: a tale of switching attractors. Eur Econ Rev 2006;50:1–33.

de Zwart G, Markwat T, Swinkels L, Dijk D. The economic value of fundamental and technical information in emerging currency markets. J Int Money Finance 2009;28:581–604.

Dempster MAH, Leemans V. An automated FX trading system using adaptive reinforcement learning. Expert Syst Appl 2006;30:543–552.

Dooley MP, Shafer JR. Analysis of short-run exchange rate behavior: March 1973 to September 1975. International Finance Discussion Paper No. 123, Federal Reserve Board; 1976.

Dooley MP, Shafer JR. Analysis of short-run exchange rate behavior: March 1973 to November 1981. In: Bigman D, Taya T, editors. Floating exchange rates and the state of world trade payments. Cambridge (MA): Ballinger Publishing Company; 1984.

Dueker M, Neely CJ. Can Markov switching models predict excess foreign exchange returns? J Bank Finance 2007;31:279–296.

Elder A. Trading for a living: psychology, trading tactics, money management. New York: John Wiley and Sons; 1993.

Engel C, West K. Exchange rates and fundamentals. J Pol Econ 2005;113:485–517.

Evans J. Bias in human reasoning: causes and consequences. Hillsdale (NJ): Erlbaum; 1989.

Fama EF. Efficient capital markets: a review of theory and empirical work. J Finance 1970;25:383–417.

Fama EF. Market efficiency, long-term returns, and behavioral finance. J Financ Econ 1998;49:283–306.

Fama EF, Blume M. Filter rules and stock market trading profits. J Bus 1966;39:226–241.

Frankel JA, Froot KA. Chartists, fundamentalists, and trading in the foreign exchange market. Am Econ Rev 1990;80:181–185.

Frenkel JA, Levich RM. Covered interest arbitrage: unexploited profits? J Pol Econ 1975;83:325–338.

Frenkel JA, Levich RM. Transaction costs and interest arbitrage: tranquil versus turbulent periods. J Pol Econ 1977;85:1209–1226.

Friedman M. The case for flexible exchange rates, essays in positive economics. Chicago (IL): University of Chicago Press; 1953.

Friesen GC, Weller PA, Dunham LM. Price trends and patterns in technical analysis: a theoretical and empirical examination. J Bank Finance 2009;33:1089–1100.

Gençay R. Linear, non-linear and essential foreign exchange rate prediction with simple technical trading rules. J Int Econ 1999;47:91–107.

Gençay R, Ballocchi G, Dacorogna M, Olsen R, Pictet O. Real-time trading models and the statistical properties of foreign exchange rates. Int Econ Rev 2003a;43:463–491.

Gençay R, Dacorogna M, Olsen R, Pictet O. Foreign exchange trading models and market behavior. J Econ Dyn Control 2003b;27:909–935.

Gradojevic N. Non-linear, hybrid exchange rate modeling and trading profitability in the foreign exchange market. J Econ Dyn Control 2007;31(2): 557–574.

Grossman SJ, Stiglitz JE. On the impossibility of informationally efficient markets. Am Econ Rev 1980;70:393–408.

Hansen PR. A test for superior predictive ability. J Bus Econ Stat 2005;23:365–380.

Hommes C. Heterogeneous agent models in economics and finance. In: Judd KL, Tesfatsion L, editors. Volume 2, Handbook of computational economics: agent-based computational economics. Amsterdam: North-Holland; 2006. Part 1, Chapter 9.

Hommes C. The heterogeneous expectations hypothesis: some evidence from the lab. J Econ Dyn Control 2011;35:1–24.

Hong H, Stein J. A unified theory of underreaction, momentum trading and overreaction in asset markets. J Finance 1999;54:2143–2184.

Hsu P-H, Hsu Y-C, Kuan C-M. Testing the predictive ability of technical analysis using a new stepwise test without data snooping bias. J Empir Finance 2010;17:471–484.

Jegadeesh N, Titman S. Returns to buying winners and selling losers: implications for stock market efficiency. J Finance 1993;48:65–91.

Kho B-C. Time-varying risk premia, volatility, and technical trading rule profits: evidence from foreign currency futures markets. J Financ Econ 1996;41:249–290.

Kozhan R, Salmon M. The information content of a limit order book: the case of an FX market, Working paper; 2010.

Kritzman M. Serial dependence in currency returns: investment implications. J Portf Manag 1989;16:96–102.

LeBaron B. Technical trading rule profitability and foreign exchange intervention. J Int Econ 1999;49:125–143.

LeBaron B. Technical trading profitability in foreign exchange markets in the 1990's, Working paper, Brandeis University; 2002.

LeBaron B. Agent-based computational finance. In: Judd KL, Tesfatsion L, editors. Volume 2, Handbook of computational economics: agent-based computational economics. Amsterdam: North-Holland; 2006. Part 1, Chapter 9.

Lee CI, Gleason KC, Mathur I. Trading rule profits in Latin American currency spot rates. Int Rev Financ Anal 2001;10:135–156.

Lee CI, Mathur I. Trading rule profits in European currency spot cross-rates. J Bank Finance 1996;20:949–962.

Levich RM, Thomas LR III. The significance of technical trading-rule profits in the foreign exchange market: a bootstrap approach. J Int Money Finance 1993;12:451–474.

Lo AW. The adaptive markets hypothesis: market efficiency from an evolutionary perspective. J Portf Manag 2004;30:15–29.

Lo AW, Hasanhodzic J. The evolution of technical analysis: financial prediction from Babylonian tablets to Bloomberg terminals. Hoboken (NJ): John Wiley and Sons; 2010.

Lo AW, MacKinlay AC. Stock prices do not follow random walks: evidence from a simple specification test. Rev Financ Stud 1988;1:41–66.

Lo AW, Mamaysky H, Wang J. Foundations of technical analysis: computational algorithms, statistical inference, and empirical implementation. J Finance 2000;55:1705–1770.

Lo AW, Mueller MT. WARNING: physics envy may be hazardous to your wealth. J Invest Manag 2010;8:13–63.

Logue DE, Sweeney RJ. White noise in imperfect markets: the case of the franc/dollar exchange rate. J Finance 1977;32:761–768.

Lustig H, Roussanov N, Verdelhan A. Countercyclical currency risk premia, NBER Working Paper 16427; 2010.

Martin AD. Technical trading rules in the spot foreign exchange markets of developing countries. J Multinatl Financ Manag 2001;11:59–68.

McCormick F. Covered interest arbitrage: unexploited profits: comment. J Pol Econ 1979;87:411–417.

Menkhoff L. Examining the Use of Technical Currency Analysis. Int J of Financ Econ. 1997;2(4):307–318.

Menkhoff L. The use of technical analysis by fund managers: international evidence. J Bank Finance 2010;34:2573–2586.

Menkhoff L, Sarno L, Schmeling M, Schrimpf A. Carry trades and global foreign exchange volatility. J Finance 2012;67(2):681–718.

Menkhoff L, Schmidt U. The use of trading strategies by fund managers: some first survey evidence. Appl Econ; 2005;37:1719–1730.

Menkhoff L, Taylor MP. The obstinate passion of foreign exchange professionals: technical analysis. J Econ Lit 2007;45:936–972.

Murphy JJ. Technical analysis of the futures markets. New York: New York Institute of Finance, Prentice-Hall; 1986.

Neely CJ. Technical analysis and the profitability of U.S. foreign exchange intervention. Fed Reserve Bank St Louis Rev 1998;80:3–17.

Neely CJ. The temporal pattern of trading rule returns and exchange rate intervention: intervention does not generate technical trading rule profits. J Int Econ 2002;58:211–232.

Neely CJ, Rapach DE, Tu J, Zhou G. Out-of-sample equity premium prediction: fundamental vs. technical analysis; Federal Reserve Bank of St. Louis Working Paper 2010-008B; 2010.

Neely CJ, Weller PA. Technical trading rules in the European monetary system. J Int Money Finance 1999;18:429–58.

Neely CJ, Weller PA. Intraday technical trading in the foreign exchange market. J Int Money Finance 2003;22:223–237.

Neely CJ, Weller PA, Dittmar R. Is technical analysis in the foreign exchange market profitable? A genetic programming approach. J Financ Quant Anal 1997;32:405–426.

Neely CJ, Weller PA, Ulrich JM. The adaptive markets hypothesis: evidence from the foreign exchange market. J Financ Quant Anal 2009;44:467–488.

Nickerson RS. Confirmation bias: a ubiquitous phenomenon in many guises. Rev Gen Psychol 1998;2:175–220.

Nison S. Japanese candlestick charting techniques: a contemporary guide to the ancient investment techniques of the far east. New York: Simon & Schuster; 1991.

Oberlechner T, Osler C. Survival of overconfidence in currency markets. J Financ Quant Anal 2012;47(1):91–113.

Okunev J, White DR. Do momentum-based strategies still work in foreign currency markets? J Financ Quant Anal 2003;38:425–447.

Olson D. Have trading rule profits in the currency markets declined over time? J Bank Finance 2004;28:85–105.

Osler CL. Currency orders and exchange rate dynamics: an explanation for the predictive success of technical analysis. J Finance 2003;58:1791–1820.

Osler CL. Stop-loss orders and price cascades in currency markets. J Int Money Finance 2005;24:219–241.

Osler CL, Chang KPH. Head and shoulders: Not just a flaky pattern, Federal Reserve Bank of New York Staff Report No. 4; 1995.

Park C-H, Irwin SH. What do we know about the profitability of technical analysis? J Econ Surv 2007;21:786–826.

Poole W. Speculative prices as random walks: an analysis of ten time series of flexible exchange rates. South Econ J 1967;33:468–478.

Pring MJ. Technical analysis explained. New York: McGraw-Hill; 1991.

Pukthuanthong-Le K, Levich RM, Thomas LR III. Do foreign exchange markets still trend? J Portf Manag 2007;34:114–118.

Pukthuanthong-Le K, Thomas LR III. Weak-form efficiency in currency markets. Financ Anal J 2008;64:31–52.

Qi M, Wu Y. Technical trading-rule profitability, data snooping, and reality check: evidence from the foreign exchange market. J Money Credit Bank 2006;38:2135–2158.

Rime D, Sarno L, Sojli E. Exchange rate forecasting, order flow and macroeconomic information. J Int Econ 2010;80:72–88.

Rosenberg MR, Shatz EA. The Merrill Lynch guide to understanding and using technical analysis. Merrill Lynch and Co. New York: Global Securities Research & Economics Group; 1995.

Savin G, Weller PA, Zvingelis J. The predictive power of "head-and-shoulders" price patterns in the U.S. stock market. J Financ Economet 2007;5:243–265.

Schulmeister S. The interaction between technical currency trading and exchange rate fluctuations. Finance Res Lett 2006;3:212–233.

Schulmeister S. Components of the profitability of technical currency trading. Appl Financ Econ 2008;18:917–930.

Schulmeister S. Aggregate trading behaviour of technical models and the yen/dollar exchange rate 1976–2007. Jpn World Econ 2009;21:270–279.

CHAPTER THIRTEEN

# Modeling Exchange Rates with Incomplete Information

**PHILIPPE BACCHETTA**
Department of Economics, University of Lausanne; CEPR
**ERIC VAN WINCOOP**
Department of Economics, University of Virginia; NBER

## 13.1 Introduction

Most models of exchange rate determination make a set of heroic assumptions about the information with which investors operate in the foreign exchange (FX) market. In particular, investors are assumed to (i) have identical information; (ii) perfectly know the model; and (iii) use all available information at all times. These assumptions are typical in macroeconomics and are technically convenient. However, recent research has shown that these abstractions about the information structure have crucial implications and that relaxing them can shed light on a wide range of important exchange rate puzzles. In this chapter, we review a number of models that we have developed in previous work to relax these restrictive assumptions on information. We also review some related literature.

It is not difficult to argue that the "benchmark" information structure commonly used in models of exchange rate determination bears little resemblance to reality. The assumption of common information held by all investors is inconsistent with various observations. First, there is an enormous volume of trade in the FX market (larger than in any other financial market), reflecting differences among investors. Second, investors have different expectations about

*Handbook of Exchange Rates*, First Edition. Edited by Jessica James, Ian W. Marsh, and Lucio Sarno.

future macro variables such as GDP and prices as well as future exchange rates themselves. Third, the close link between exchange rates and order flow, first documented by Evans and Lyons (2002), suggests that the exchange rate primarily aggregates private as opposed to public information.

That investors perfectly know the model is also a radical simplification of reality. There exists a considerable amount of uncertainty about the model and about structural parameters. This implies a learning process by investors, which affects their behavior. It also makes policy, especially monetary policy, more difficult. A substantial literature has documented parameter instability in macroeconomic data, while the implications of model uncertainty for monetary policy have also been investigated. There is also widespread evidence of parameter instability in financial data (see Pastor and Veronesi (2009) for a survey), including exchange rates (Rossi, 2006).

Finally, the assumption that everyone uses all available information at all times ignores the cost of continuous information processing. There are two ways in which information processing is limited. First, as we will discuss later on, most financial institutions and individual investors do not actively manage the FX exposure of external claims. They do not continuously adjust their FX holdings based on all available information as it is costly to do so. Second, even when they do change their portfolios, decisions are usually made on the basis of only a limited set of information. The best known example of this behavior is the carry trade, which may be conditioned only on interest rate differentials.

Through some simple examples, we illustrate that relaxing these restrictive assumptions about the information structure allows us to shed light on some of the biggest puzzles related to exchange rates, such as the disconnect between exchange rates and macro fundamentals and the forward discount puzzle. Our strategy is to start from a standard exchange rate model, the monetary model, and introduce various types of incomplete information. We consider only small deviations from the benchmark case, so that investors still use what they know about the model's structure to form their expectations.

The remainder of this chapter is organized as follows. In Section 13.2, we start by discussing a standard "benchmark" monetary model of exchange rate determination that makes the usual set of restrictive assumptions about the information structure. The subsequent three sections relax some of these assumptions, one at a time. In Section 13.3, we allow for information heterogeneity across investors. In Section 13.4, we introduce model uncertainty in the form of time-varying structural parameters that are unknown. Finally, in Section 13.5, we discuss what happens when investors do not continuously process all available information. Section 13.6 provides concluding remarks.

## 13.2 Basic Monetary Model

The simplest dynamic model of exchange rate determination is the monetary model. We examine the impact of incomplete information within a two-country version of this standard framework. The model is described by the following four equations:

$$m_t = p_t + \phi y_t - \alpha i_t \tag{13.1}$$

$$m_t^* = p_t^* + \phi y_t^* - \alpha i_t^* \tag{13.2}$$

$$p_t = p_t^* + s_t \tag{13.3}$$

$$E_t(s_{t+1} - s_t) = i_t - i_t^* + \psi_t \tag{13.4}$$

Equation (13.1) is a standard money market equilibrium equation, with $m_t$ being the log-money supply, $p_t$ the log-price level, $y_t$ the log-output level, and $i_t$ the interest rate. Equation (13.2) is the analogous equation for the Foreign country.[1] Equation (13.3) is a purchasing power parity equation and Equation (13.4) is an interest rate parity equation. $\psi_t$ is the deviation from uncovered interest rate parity (UIP).

Substituting Equations (13.1)–(13.3) into Equation (13.4) we obtain a first-order difference equation with a familiar solution

$$s_t = (1-\lambda)\left[f_t + E_t\sum_{j=1}^{\infty}\lambda^j f_{t+j}\right] - \lambda\left[\psi_t + E_t\sum_{j=1}^{\infty}\lambda^j \psi_{t+j}\right] \tag{13.5}$$

where $f_t = m_t - m_t^* - \phi(y_t - y_t^*)$ and $\lambda = \alpha/(1+\alpha)$.

With full information, expectations can be computed from the known process for the fundamental $f_t$ and the UIP deviation $\psi_t$. For example, when they follow an autoregressive (AR) process with AR coefficients of, respectively, $\rho_f$ and $\rho_\psi$, we have

$$s_t = \frac{1-\lambda}{1-\lambda\rho_f} f_t - \frac{\lambda}{1-\lambda\rho_\psi}\psi_t \tag{13.6}$$

In this case the exchange rate is directly linked to the observed macro fundamentals $f_t$ and $\psi_t$.

The implicit assumption behind Equation (13.6) is that investors have no information about future fundamental shocks. However, the solution is very similar when agents receive public signals about future fundamentals, such as public news variables that are featured in the literature on the impact of news shocks.[2] For example, let $v_t = f_{t+1} + \varepsilon_t$ be a piece of public information about

[1]This traditional money market equilibrium can easily be replaced by an interest rate rule, which is more typical in DSGE models. Equation 13.1 can be written as $i_t = \kappa_0 + \kappa_1(p_t - \bar{p}) + \kappa_2(y_t - \bar{y}) + \kappa_3(m_t - \bar{m})$. Often, other variables appear in interest rate rules, such as the current or expected inflation rate, but this does not fundamentally change the specification. It just involves replacing one fundamental variable in the interest rate rule, such as $m_t - \bar{m}$, with another fundamental variable, such as $\pi_t - \bar{\pi}$, where $\pi_t$ is the inflation rate.

[2]See for examples Beaudry and Portier (2006), Devereux and Engel (2006), Jaimovich and Rebelo (2008), and Lorenzoni (2010).

$f_{t+1}$, where the variance of $\varepsilon_{t+1}$ is $\sigma_v^2$. Together with the signal $f_{t+1} = \rho_f f_t + \varepsilon_{t+1}^f$, signal extraction implies $E_{t+1} f_{t+1} = a_1 f_t + a_2 v_t$, where $a_1 = \rho_f/(\sigma_f^2 d)$, $a_2 = 1/(\sigma_v^2 d)$ and $d = (1/\sigma_v^2) + (1/\sigma_f^2)$. Since $E_t f_{t+j} = \rho_f^{j-1} E_t f_{t+1}$ for $j > 1$, we then have

$$s_t = (1-\lambda)\frac{1+\lambda(a_1-\rho_f)}{1-\lambda\rho_f} f_t + (1-\lambda)\frac{\lambda a_2}{1-\lambda\rho_f} v_t - \frac{\lambda}{1-\lambda\rho_\psi}\psi_t \tag{13.7}$$

The exchange rate again depends on a set of publicly observed variables, with $v_t$ now added to the list.

This model contains all restrictive assumptions about the information structure alluded to in the introduction. All agents have the same public information. They all know the model. The parameters of the model are constant and known. Finally, all agents continuously adjust their portfolio based on all available information. This latter assumption is generally made in rational expectation dynamic portfolio choice models. In these models, the expected excess return on Foreign bonds (the UIP deviation) is then equal to a risk premium.

The model has many implications that are at odds with the data. First, it implies that the exchange rate is exclusively determined by public information. This stands in sharp contrast to the widespread evidence of a disconnect between exchange rates and observed macro variables. The best illustration of this disconnect is the well-known Meese–Rogoff puzzle. Meese and Rogoff (1983) tried to explain exchange rate movements with observed macroeconomic fundamentals and found that a fundamental-based model cannot outperform a random walk.[3] Their findings imply that the limited explanatory power of observed macro fundamentals is dominated by small sample estimation errors of reduced form parameters. This generates an even weaker fit than not using any macro fundamentals at all, as in the random walk model.

Notice that the puzzle here is not why the exchange rate is a random walk. Engel and West (2005) have shown that the benchmark model above can generate near-random-walk behavior when the discount rate $\lambda$ is close to 1 and the fundamental is an I(1) variable. The puzzle, rather, is the very limited explanatory power of observed macro fundamentals. Even when the discount rate is close to 1 and the exchange rate is close to a random walk, in standard models, changes in the exchange rate are fully determined by changes in observed macro fundamentals.

The model also implies a stable relationship between exchange rates and fundamentals. As we discuss later on, there is plenty of evidence that this relationship is highly unstable. It is for this very reason that Meese and

[3]More precisely, Meese and Rogoff (1983) estimate a linear exchange rate model based on standard fundamentals such as money supply, output, and interest rates. They use the estimated model to do a one-period-ahead forecast, but use the actual future fundamental (which implies this is not a true forecast). They do this for several periods using rolling regressions and compute the RMSE. They do the same exercise by predicting the exchange rate with a random walk. The RMSE for the random walk model is generally lower than that for the model based on fundamentals.

Rogoff (1983) conducted rolling regressions to reestimate model parameters each month.

Finally, the model suffers from the well-known forward discount puzzle for standard justifications of the UIP deviation $\psi_t$. This is most clear when we set $\psi_t$ equal to zero. Equation (13.4) then implies that high interest rate currencies tend to depreciate, while in reality, the evidence consistently shows that they tend to appreciate. The puzzle can potentially be explained when $\psi_t$ is a time-varying risk premium, as in standard models where agents continuously adjust their portfolio. But so far the quest for such a model matching the data has remained unsuccessful.[4]

We now turn to generalizations of the simple information structure above and discuss how they can generate a better fit to the data.

## 13.3 Information Heterogeneity

The first deviation from the benchmark we consider is information heterogeneity as analyzed in Bacchetta and van Wincoop (2006). There is symmetric information dispersion in the sense that agents have private signals, but no agent has superior information. There are two types of information heterogeneity. First, agents have private information about the future level of the fundamental. Second, agents have private trading needs that are only known to themselves and are unrelated to expectations about the future fundamental. Examples of this are private liquidity needs, hedging needs, or private investment opportunities. This leads to a source of demand or supply of Foreign bonds that is unrelated to expected returns and is unobservable in the aggregate.

The main implication of having private information about future fundamentals is that the exchange rate becomes a source of information. Since the exchange rate reflects demand or supply from heterogeneous agents, it aggregates information about future fundamentals. However, the exchange rate is still a noisy signal, as in the noisy rational expectation literature, because of the unrelated private trading needs.

These two types of information heterogeneity lead to three changes to the model Eqs. (13.1)–(13.4). First, the UIP deviation $\psi_t$ is equal to a risk premium. The "nonspeculative" liquidity or hedging needs are unrelated to expected returns and represent a separate source of risk. This risk premium is unobserved as it depends on the aggregate net supply of Foreign bonds associated with liquidity or hedge trade. While agents know their own liquidity or hedge trade, they cannot observe it at the aggregate.

The second change is that the expectation $E_t s_{t+1}$ now needs to be replaced by the average expectation $\bar{E}_t s_{t+1}$ across all agents. We assume that there is

[4]See surveys by Lewis (1995) and Engel (1996). Burnside et al. (2011) find that there is very little connection between excess returns on currency strategies and a wide range of possible risk factors. Verdelhan (2010) has had some success based on a model with habit formation, but his explanation relies on the close link between consumption and real exchange rates that is not observed in the data.

a continuum of agents in the interval [0,1]. Finally, agents receive a private signal about future fundamentals. For simplicity, we assume that agents receive a private signal about the fundamental next period. Agent $i$ receives the signal $v_t^i = f_{t+1} + \varepsilon_t^{v,i}$, where the signal error $\varepsilon_t^{v,i}$ has a $N(0, \sigma_v^2)$ distribution.[5]

In addition, we make the simplifying assumptions that $\psi_t$ is i.i.d. with variance $\sigma_\psi^2$ and that $f_t$ follows a random walk $f_{t+1} = f_t + \varepsilon_{t+1}^f$. The variance of $\varepsilon_{t+1}^f$ is $\sigma_f^2$. Substituting Equations (13.1)–(13.3) into Equation (13.4), we have

$$s_t = \lambda \bar{E}_t s_{t+1} + (1-\lambda) f_t - \lambda \psi_t \tag{13.8}$$

The model is solved in three steps. First, conjecture a solution

$$s_t = (1-\lambda_f) f_t + \lambda_f f_{t+1} - \lambda_\psi \psi_t \tag{13.9}$$

Second, for each investor, compute the expectation of $f_{t+1}$. This is done by solving a standard signal extraction problem using three sources of information: the random walk process $f_{t+1} = f_t + \varepsilon_{t+1}^f$, which is public information, the private signal, and the exchange rate equation. The exchange rate signal is $(s_t - (1-\lambda_f) f_t)/\lambda_f = f_{t+1} - \lambda_\psi \psi_t / \lambda_f$. This gives

$$E_t^i f_{t+1} = \frac{\beta^f f_t + \beta^v v_t^i + \beta^s (s_t - (1-\lambda_f) f_t)/\lambda_f}{D} \tag{13.10}$$

where $\beta^f = 1/\sigma_f^2$, $\beta^v = 1/\sigma_v^2$, $\beta^s = \lambda_f^2/(\lambda_\psi^2 \sigma_\psi^2)$, and $D = \beta^f + \beta^v + \beta^s$. Finally, we use this result to compute the expectation of $s_{t+1}$. Using Equation (13.9) and aggregating over agents, $\bar{E}_t s_{t+1}$ becomes a linear expression in $f_t$, $f_{t+1}$, and $s_t$. Substituting the result into Equation (13.8), we can solve for the unknown parameters $\lambda_f$ and $\lambda_\psi$.

This last step gives two equations in the unknowns $\lambda_f$ and $\lambda_\psi$, with $\lambda_f > 0$ and $\lambda_\psi > \lambda$. We can compare this solution to that of the public information model in which there is no information heterogeneity. In that case, the solution is Equation (13.6) with $\rho_f = 1$ and $\rho_\psi = 0$, so that $\lambda_f = 0$ and $\lambda_\psi = \lambda$.

Information heterogeneity therefore affects the exchange rate solution in two ways. First, the exchange rate now depends on the unobserved future fundamental $f_{t+1}$ as agents trade on the basis of their private signals about this future fundamental. Second, the impact of the unobserved fundamental $\psi_t$ is now amplified as $\lambda_\psi$, bigger than in the common knowledge model. This results from rational confusion over what is driving the exchange rate. An increase in the risk premium $\psi_t$ on Foreign bonds leads to an appreciation of the domestic

[5]When private signals provide information about fundamentals further in the future, it gives rise to higher order expectations, as shown in Bacchetta and van Wincoop (2006) (see also Bacchetta and van Wincoop, 2008).

currency. But there is a magnification effect under information heterogeneity.[6] Agents do not know whether the appreciation is the result of an increase in the risk premium or is simply due to more favorable private signals that others have about the future fundamental. As they give some weight to the second possibility, their expectation of $f_{t+1}$ drops, leading to a further appreciation.

These results imply a stronger disconnect between the exchange rate and observed fundamentals than under public information. They also imply that, depending on publicly observed information, the exchange rate contains information about future macro fundamentals. This is consistent with evidence reported by Engel and West (2005) and Froot and Ramadorai (2005). These results become even stronger when agents have private information about fundamentals further into the future. The rational confusion then becomes persistent. Even when $\psi_t$ is entirely transitory, a shock to $\psi_t$ will affect the exchange rate for $T$ periods when agents have information about fundamental $T$ periods into the future.

This model can also explain the close relationship between order flow and exchange rates. Evans and Lyons (2002), who first documented this relationship, define order flow as the "net of buyer-initiated and seller-initiated orders." The initiator of a transaction is the trader who acts on the basis of private information. The close link between order flow and exchange rates therefore suggests that most information is private. In the modern FX market, where almost all trade is electronic, private information is mostly channeled through market orders.

In Bacchetta and van Wincoop (2006) we break the demand for Foreign bonds into a component that only depends on private information and a component that depends on public information and the exchange rate. The first component of demand is submitted through market orders (order flow), while the second component is submitted through limit orders.[7] We then show that the exchange rate is driven by (i) public information and (ii) order flow. We show that the model can generate a very close link between the exchange rate and order flow as seen in the data.

## 13.4 Model Uncertainty

The second deviation from the benchmark case consists in considering the impact of model uncertainty, while going back to the assumption of common information across all agents. Model uncertainty was first introduced into exchange rate models in the late 1980s in order to explain the persistent

[6]Rational confusion can also occur without heterogeneity, as in Takagi (1991) who assumes that investors cannot distinguish between two fundamental shocks. However, there is no magnification effect in this case, as investors do not use the exchange rate as a source of information on others' signals.

[7]This simple allocation between market and limit orders does not affect the model's equilibrium. The solution would become much more complex if private information influenced limit orders.

expectational errors of market participants about future exchange rates and to explain the high exchange rate volatility. In the second half of the 1970s and 1980s, the dollar consistently depreciated more than investors expected, while in the early 1980s it appreciated more than investors expected. Contributions by Lewis (1989) and Kaminsky (1993) showed that such persistent expectational errors can, in fact, be perfectly rational when there is uncertainty about model parameters. Lewis (1989) considers the standard monetary model, but assumes the existence of a one-time change in the constant term of the money demand equation. By observing the data, agents gradually learn about the new value of the constant term. Kaminsky (1993) assumes that money growth is equal to a drift term plus a random innovation. The drift term can switch between two values based on a Markov process. In both cases, agents learn about the unknown parameters through Bayesian updating.

To illustrate the mechanism for such consistent expectational errors, assume that the fundamental $f_t$ in our simple monetary model follows the process

$$\Delta f_t = \delta + \beta \Delta f_{t-1} + v_t \tag{13.11}$$

Investors do not know $\delta$. They form Bayesian expectations by observing $\Delta f_t$, starting with a prior belief $\delta_0$. A large value of $\Delta f_t$ can be the result of either a high value of $\delta$ or a large draw of the transitory shock $v_t$.

Now assume that $\delta$ increases, leading to a large value of $\Delta f_t$. Investors will then increase their expectation of $\delta$, but not as much as the actual change in $\delta$ as they give weight to the possibility that there is only a transitory increase in $\Delta f_t$ associated with $v_t$. This means that actual future values of $\Delta f$ are larger than investors expect. The exchange rate therefore depreciates more than investors expect. This will continue as long as the expectation of $\delta$ by investors is below the true value. Since the learning process is gradual, this can indeed last a long time, leading to persistent expectational errors. Nonetheless, agents are perfectly rational.

Tabellini (1988) emphasized that such a framework can lead to increased exchange rate volatility relative to the case in which parameters are known. The logic behind this is as follows. An increase in $v_t$ leads to an exchange rate depreciation. However, when $\delta$ is unknown, agents will increase their expectation of $\delta$, which raises the expectation of future levels of $\Delta f$, which in turn leads to an even larger depreciation.

Bacchetta and van Wincoop (2011) emphasize a different implication of model uncertainty. They show that it can lead to a highly unstable reduced form relationship between the exchange rate and macro fundamentals even if the true structural parameters are constant.[8] This is driven by uncertainty about the level of parameters that generates confusion about the interpretation of the data. We now develop this point by introducing structural parameter uncertainty in the model.

[8]This instability, however, is not sufficient to explain the Meese–Rogoff result. For a discussion, see Bacchetta et al. (2010).

Let us add money demand shocks $\nu_t$ and $\nu_t^*$ to the money demand equations (Eqs. (13.1) and (13.2)) and define $b_t = \nu_t - \nu_t^*$. Assume that these aggregate money demand shocks are unobserved, so that $b_t$ is an unobserved macro fundamental. From Equations (13.1)–(13.3) of the monetary model we have

$$i_t - i_t^* = \frac{1}{\alpha}s_t - \frac{1}{\alpha}(m_t - m_t^*) - \frac{1}{\alpha}(\phi(y_t - y_t^*) + b_t) \tag{13.12}$$

Assume that agents do not know the value of the parameter $\phi$. They also do not know the value of $b_t$. However, through interest rates, money supplies, and exchange rate, they do learn the value of

$$\phi(y_t - y_t^*) + b_t \tag{13.13}$$

For illustrative purposes, we make a couple of simplifying assumptions. First, we assume that $m_t - m_t^*$ and $y_t - y_t^*$ follow random walk processes. Second, we assume that $b_t$ is i.i.d. with variance $\sigma_b^2$. Finally, we assume that starting in period 1 the parameter $\phi$ is drawn from a distribution with mean $\bar{\phi}$ and standard deviation $\sigma_\phi^2$. Agents can learn over time about the value of the parameter from the observation of $\phi(y_t - y_t^*) + b_t$.

Substituting the expression for the interest differential Eq. (13.12) into Eq. (13.4) and solving $s_t$ by integrating forward gives

$$s_t = (m_t - m_t^*) - ((1-\lambda)\phi + \lambda E_t\phi)(y_t - y_t^*) + (1-\lambda)b_t \tag{13.14}$$

This implies that the impact of the fundamental $y_t - y_t^*$ on the exchange rate is

$$\frac{\partial s_t}{\partial(y_t - y_t^*)} = -((1-\lambda)\phi + \lambda E_t\phi) \tag{13.15}$$

We can compare this to the case where $\phi$ is a known constant. From Equation (13.6), setting $\rho_f = 1$, the derivative is $-\phi$. As mentioned before, the discount rate $\lambda$ is close to 1. This implies that the impact of the fundamental $y_t - y_t^*$ on the exchange rate depends almost exclusively on the expectation of $\phi$ rather than $\phi$ itself.

The expectation of $\phi$ may bear very little relationship to the actual $\phi$. To see this, we use Kalman filter formulas to update expectations of $\phi$. Let $p_t$ be the perceived variance of $\phi$ at time $t$. We start in period 1 with $E_1\phi = \bar{\phi}$ and $p_1 = \sigma_\phi^2$. Subsequently, the expectation and variance evolve according to

$$p_t = p_{t-1}\alpha_t \tag{13.16}$$

$$\alpha_t = \frac{\sigma_b^2}{(y_t - y_t^*)^2 p_{t-1} + \sigma_b^2} \tag{13.17}$$

$$E_t\phi = \alpha_t E_{t-1}\phi + (1-\alpha_t)\phi - \frac{p_{t-1}}{(y_t - y_t^*)^2 p_{t-1} + \sigma_b^2}(y_t - y_t^*)b_t \tag{13.18}$$

$\alpha_t$ captures the speed of learning. In a more general example with multiple unknown parameters and persistence of $b_t$, Bacchetta and van Wincoop (2011) show that learning can be very slow. It may take more than a century for the variance to be reduced by half.

The key equation is Equation (13.18), which shows how the expectation of $\phi$ evolves over time. If the last term on the right-hand side is equal to zero, the expectation is a weighted average of the expectation last period (with weight $\alpha_t$ that is close to 1) and the true parameter $\phi$. But it is the last term that is key here. It depends on the product of $y_t - y_t^*$ and $b_t$. The expectation of the unknown parameter therefore depends on the product of an observed and an unobserved fundamental.

How is this possible? The reason is another type of rational confusion, which we refer to as a scapegoat effect (Bacchetta and van Wincoop, 2004). Consider an increase in the unobserved fundamental $b_t$. Using information about interest rates and the exchange rate, agents only know the aggregate of $-\phi(y_t - y_t^*) + b_t$. When $b_t$ is positive and $(y_t - y_t^*)$ is positive, agents do not know whether $-\phi(y_t - y_t^*) + b_t$ is large because $b_t$ is large or the unknown parameter $\phi$ is low. They give at least some weight to the latter possibility, therefore reducing the expectation of $\phi$, as we can see formally from Equation (13.18). Relative output becomes the scapegoat for what is really a shock to another unobserved fundamental.

The scapegoat effect implies that the relationship between the exchange rate and observed macro fundamentals can become highly unstable, and in a way that is unrelated to time variation in structural parameters themselves. In Bacchetta and van Wincoop (2011), we show that the expectation of the structural parameters can move far away from the actual unknown structural parameters, both over short and long horizons. This results in a very unstable reduced form relationship between the exchange rate and macro fundamentals.

This finding is consistent with survey evidence in the literature. Cheung and Chinn (2001) conducted a survey of US FX traders and found that the weight that traders attached to different macro indicators varies considerably over time. More recently, Fratzscher et al. (2011) use 9 years of survey data for 12 currencies to show that the weight that FX traders attach to different macro fundamentals as determinants of exchange rates varies significantly over time. They also show that these time-varying survey weights lead to time variation in the reduced form relationship between exchange rates and macro fundamentals. Finally, they provide evidence of scapegoat effects by showing that the survey weights depend on the interaction of fundamentals and noise as in Equation (13.18), using order flow data to measure the noise.[9]

[9]There is also some econometric evidence of parameter instability in reduced form exchange rate equations. See Rossi (2006) and Sarno and Valente (2009).

## 13.5 Infrequent Decision Making

As discussed in Section 13.2, in most applications, the UIP deviation in Equation (13.4) is a risk premium. Equating the expected excess return on Foreign bonds to a risk premium follows from any portfolio Euler equation that represents a trade-off between Home and Foreign bonds. It implicitly assumes that agents make new portfolio decisions each period on the basis of all available information. This assumption, although entirely standard in the literature, is nonetheless, a very strong and nonrealistic one. It implicitly assumes that all traders actively manage their FX exposure. Although there now exists an industry, developed in the late 1980s, that actively manages FX exposure (hedge funds, currency overlay managers, leveraged funds), it manages only a tiny fraction of cross-border financial holdings.[10] Banks themselves actively manage FX positions mostly intraday. Mutual funds are not allowed by law to actively reallocate between Home and Foreign assets. A Europe fund is a Europe fund and cannot suddenly start investing in US bonds. Similarly, a global bond fund cannot suddenly start shorting one country's bonds when expected returns make this attractive. Moreover, Lyons (2001) reports that financial institutions rarely devote their own proprietary capital to currency strategies. Finally, individual investors are well known to make very infrequent portfolio decisions, especially regarding pension fund allocations.

In the models that we have discussed so far, we have assumed that Equation (13.4) holds and that agents reallocate their portfolio between Home and Foreign bonds each period on the basis of all available information. We now turn to the model in Bacchetta and van Wincoop (2010) in which agents make infrequent portfolio decisions. Infrequent decisions imply that information is only gradually incorporated into the exchange rate. As initially argued by Froot and Thaler (1990) and Lyons (2001), the slow incorporation of information leads to excess return predictability and could explain the forward premium puzzle. The key aspect is not the frequency of trading, but the frequency of portfolio decision making. There is a cost to active portfolio management that makes it optimal for agents to take only infrequent portfolio decisions. To capture this feature, the model assumes overlapping investors who make a portfolio decision only in their first period. In subsequent periods, investors may trade to rebalance their portfolio, but they do not make any decisions on a new portfolio, as this is costly.

The model replaces Equations (13.1)–(13.3), which connect the interest differential to the exchange rate and some macro fundamentals, with a simple AR(1) process for the interest differential. This represents a gradually changing interest rate target. In practice, we set the Home interest rate equal to a constant $r$ and let the Foreign interest rate vary over time based on an AR process.[11]

[10] See Bacchetta and van Wincoop (2010) and Sager and Taylor (2006) for a discussion.

[11] The constant Home interest rate is the result of an exogenous constant real interest rate of $r$ and a zero-inflation monetary policy in the Home country.

The heart of the model is associated with Equation (13.4), which now changes as agents make infrequent portfolio decisions. Assume that there are overlapping generations (OLG) of agents who live $T$ periods and who make one portfolio decision for the next $T$ periods when born. The portfolio decision involves the allocation between Home and Foreign nominal bonds. Investors now care about the excess return on Foreign bonds over the next $T$ periods as they make one portfolio decision for $T$ periods. Let $q_{t+k} = s_{t+k} - s_{t+k-1} + i^*_{t+k-1} - i_{t+k-1}$ be the excess return on Foreign bonds from $t+k-1$ to $t+k$. The excess return from $t$ to $t+T$ is then $q_{t,t+T} = q_{t+1} + \cdots + q_{t+T} = s_{t+T} - s_t - fd_t - \cdots - fd_{t+T-1}$, where $fd_t = i_t - i^*_t$ is the forward discount.

Agents only consume in the last period of life. Assuming a constant rate of relative risk aversion $\gamma$, the fraction allocated to the Foreign bond is

$$b_t = \bar{b} + \frac{E_t(q_{t,t+T})}{\gamma\sigma^2} \tag{13.19}$$

where $\bar{b}$ is a constant and $\sigma^2$ depends on the risk associated with future excess returns and is constant as well in equilibrium.[12]

Agents are born with wealth of 1, which accumulates over time due to returns on their portfolio. For an investor born at time $t-k$, wealth at time $t$ is $W_{t-k,k} = \prod_{j=1}^{k} R^p_{t+k-j}$, where $R^p_{t+k-j}$ is the portfolio return from $t+k-j-1$ to $t+k-j$, which is equal to $1 + r + b_t q_{t+k-j}$. Bond market equilibrium is represented by

$$\sum_{k=1}^{T} b_{t-k+1} W_{t-k+1,t} + X_t = BS_t \tag{13.20}$$

Here $X_t$ represents exogenous purchases of Foreign bonds by noise or liquidity traders, which is calibrated to match observed exchange rate volatility and the well-known near-random-walk behavior of the exchange rate. The supply of bonds is on the right-hand side. The Foreign bond supply is fixed at $B$ in Foreign currency, which translates to $BS_t$ in the Home currency.

The model is solved by substituting the expressions for the optimal portfolios and wealth and then log-linearizing. This leads to a complicated difference equation in the exchange rate that is solved numerically. The only stochastic driver is the forward discount, which follows an AR process.

The model can account for the forward discount puzzle. The basic logic is very simple. Consider an increase in the Foreign interest rate. This leads to an increased demand for Foreign bonds, causing an appreciation of the Foreign currency. However, as agents adjust their portfolios gradually (simplified in the model through the OLG structure), there is a continued shift toward Foreign bonds that leads to a steady appreciation of the Foreign currency. This accounts for the well-established stylized fact that high interest rate currencies tend to

[12] The precise expression is $\sigma^2 = (1 - (1/\gamma))\text{var}_t(q_{t,t+T}) + (1/\gamma)\sum_{k=1}^{T} \text{var}_t(q_{t+k})$.

appreciate (the forward discount or Fama puzzle). It is also consistent with the evidence presented in Eichenbaum and Evans (1995) that after an interest rate increase, a currency continues to appreciate for 8–12 quarters before it starts to depreciate.

Four comments are worth making about this result. First, there is the question of who sells the Foreign bonds when agents continue to shift their portfolio to Foreign bonds. The answer is that the "inactive" agents at any point in time, which account for a fraction $(T - 1)/T$ of all agents, automatically take the other side through portfolio rebalancing. As the Foreign currency appreciates, these inactive agents sell Foreign bonds in order to rebalance their portfolios. Notice that this does not involve a new portfolio decision. They simply sell to keep the portfolio share allocated to Foreign bonds constant.

Second, there is the question of whether making infrequent portfolio decisions is optimal. Of course, if there is no cost to portfolio decision making, all agents would actively manage their portfolios at all times. However, the industry that actively manages FX positions charges steep fees for their services. The fees depend on the risk of the fund. At 20% risk (standard deviation of return), the typical fee is a 1% management fee plus 20% of profits, which in practice amounts to about 4%. Bacchetta and van Wincoop (2010) found that at such fees, it is indeed optimal for agents to not actively manage their portfolios. While active portfolio management leads to higher expected portfolio returns, it also involves considerable risk as future exchange rates are hard to predict. As a result, the welfare gains from active management are not sufficient to offset the fees charged.

Third, an important question is how these results change when we allow for many currencies. Diversification of the portfolio across many currencies can reduce the overall risk exposure, which can make active FX portfolio management optimal. Bacchetta and van Wincoop (2010) considered an extension calibrated to six countries (five currencies). As the risk is now diminished, it indeed becomes optimal for investors to actively manage their portfolio. However, as some agents start to actively manage their portfolio and therefore actively exploit expected excess return opportunities, in equilibrium, these expected excess returns become smaller. This in turn makes it less attractive to actively manage portfolios. There is then an equilibrium that is such that the gain from active portfolio management is exactly equal its cost and only a small fraction of agents actively manage their portfolios, as seen in the data. At the same time, the calibration shows that the excess return predictability in equilibrium corresponds closely to that seen in the data.

Finally, there might be another source of incomplete information processing in addition to infrequent decisions. When investors change their portfolio, they may do this on the basis of a limited set of information. Investors may simply observe the interest differential, as with carry trade, and invest in the high interest rate currency. Alternatively, investors may simply assume that the exchange rate follows a random walk. Bacchetta and van Wincoop (2010) introduce these assumptions in the context of infrequent trading and show that the model generates an even more negative coefficient in the Fama regression. In

Bacchetta and van Wincoop (2007), we focus on the random walk hypothesis in forming exchange rate expectations. We show that with active trading, such an assumption leads to strongly counterfactual positive Fama coefficients. However, with infrequent trading, the model can match the data.

## 13.6 Conclusion

In this chapter, we have reviewed the implications of various forms of incomplete information in an otherwise standard model of exchange rate determination. Deviations from the complete information paradigm allow us to explain various exchange rate puzzles, such as the disconnect between exchange rates and fundamentals and the forward premium puzzle.

The focus of this chapter is mainly influenced by our previous research and does not represent an exhaustive review of the existing literature. While we have examined incomplete information in versions of the standard monetary model, some papers have examined this issue in alternative models. For example, Roberts (1995) assumes imperfect information on the persistence of a shock in a dynamic Mundell–Fleming model. However, a reduced form approach is more difficult to interpret as learning is not based on optimal inference. Martinez-García (2010) introduced imperfect information in a DSGE model. He showed that consumption reacts less to shocks. This can explain that relative consumption is less volatile than exchange rates, that is, the well-known Backus–Smith puzzle.

We have also restricted our discussion to rational expectations frameworks. An entirely different direction is to consider deviations from rational expectations, where expectations are typically based on rules that ignore all or part of the information from the model. In particular, models of adaptive learning have been applied to exchange rates in many papers (Chakraborty and Evans, 2008; Lewis and Markiewicz, 2009). Often in these analyses, there is no structural model uncertainty and recursive learning schemes converge to rational expectations equilibria. In contrast, Gourinchas and Tornell (2004) consider a model where agents have incorrect beliefs about the process of the interest rate and never learn. Other models introduce more exogenous expectational rules, such as Mark and Wu (1998) and the well-known model by Frankel and Froot (1988) of chartists and fundamentalists (De Grauwe and Grimaldi, 2005). Goldberg and Frydman (1996) assume imperfect knowledge of the underlying model, so that agents use the relevant variables but ignore the model's structure and thus the precise weights of each variable. These types of models have been used to account for a wide range of exchange rate features, such as the exchange rate disconnect, high exchange rate volatility, persistent expectational errors, and the forward discount puzzle.

## Acknowledgments

We would like to thank an anonymous referee for helpful comments. Bacchetta gratefully acknowledges financial support from the National Centre of

Competence in Research "Financial Valuation and Risk Management"(NCCR FINRISK) and from the Swiss Finance Institute.

## REFERENCES


Bacchetta P, van Wincoop E. A scapegoat model of exchange rate determination. Am Econ Rev Pap Proc 2004;94:114–118.

Bacchetta P, van Wincoop E. Can information heterogeneity explain the exchange rate determination puzzle? Am Econ Rev 2006;96:552–576.

Bacchetta P, van Wincoop E. Random walk expectations and the forward discount puzzle. Am Econ Rev Pap Proc 2007;97:346–350.

Bacchetta P, van Wincoop E. Higher order expectations in asset pricing. J Money Credit Bank 2008;40:837–866.

Bacchetta P, van Wincoop E. Infrequent portfolio decisions: a solution to the forward discount puzzle. Am Econ Rev 2010;100:837–869.

Bacchetta P, van Wincoop E. On the Unstable Relationship between Exchange Rates and Macroeconomic Fundamentals mimeo; 2011.

Bacchetta P, van Wincoop E, Beutler T. Can parameter instability explain the Meese-Rogoff puzzle? NBER Semin Int Macroecon 2009 2010;61(1):125–173.

Beaudry P, Portier F. Stock prices, news and economic fluctuations. Am Econ Rev 2006;96(4): 1293–1307.

Burnside C, Eichenbaum M, Kleshchelski I, Rebelo S. Do Peso problems explain the returns to the carry trade? Rev Financ Stud 2011. Forthcoming.

Chakraborty A, Evans GW. Can perpetual learning explain the forward-premium puzzle? J Monet Econ 2008;55: 477–490.

Cheung Y-W, Chinn MD. Currency traders and exchange rate dynamics: a survey of the US market. J Int Money Finance 2001;20(4): 439–471.

De Grauwe P, Grimaldi M. The exchange rate and its fundamentals in a complex world. Rev Int Econ 2005;13(3):549–575.

Devereux MB, Engel C. Expectations and exchange rate policy. NBER working paper 12213; 2006.

Eichenbaum M, Evans CL. Some empirical evidence on the effects of shocks to monetary policy on exchange rates. Q J Econ 1995;110:975–1009.

Engel C. The forward discount anomaly and the risk premium: a survey of recent evidence. J Empir Finance 1996;3:123–192.

Engel C, West KD. Exchange rates and fundamentals. J Pol Econ 2005;113(3): 485–517.

Evans MDD, Lyons RK. Order flow and exchange rate dynamics. J Pol Econ 2002;110:170–180.

Frankel JA, Froot KA. Chartists, fundamentalists and the demand for dollars. Greek Econ Rev 1988;10(1): 49–102.

Fratzscher M, Sarno L, Zinna G. The scapegoat theory of exchange rates: the first tests mimeo.; 2011.

Froot KA, Ramadorai T. Currency returns, institutional investor flows, and exchange rate fundamentals. J Finance 2005;60(3):1535–1566.

Froot KA, Thaler RH. Anomalies: foreign exchange. J Econ Perspect 1990;4(3):179–192.

Goldberg MD, Frydman R. Imperfect knowledge and behaviour in the foreign exchange market. Econ J 1996;106:869–893.

Gourinchas P-O, Tornell A. Exchange rate puzzles and distorted beliefs. J Int Econ 2004;64(2): 303–333.

Jaimovich N, Rebelo S. Can news about the future drive the business cycle? Am Econ Rev 2008;99(4): 1097–1118.

Kaminsky G. Is There a Peso Problem? Evince from the Dollar/Pound Exchange Rate 1976–1987. Am Econ Rev 1993;83:450–472.

Lewis KK. Can learning affect exchange-rate behavior? The case of the dollar in the early 1980's. J Monet Econ 1989;23:79–100.

Lewis KK. Puzzles in international financial markets. In: Grossman GM, Rogoff K, editors. Handbook of international economics. Amsterdam: Elsevier Science; 1995. pp. 1913–1971.

Lewis V, Markiewicz A. Model misspecification, learning and the exchange rate disconnect puzzle. B.E. J Macroecon 2009;9(1) (Topics):Article 13.

Lyons RK. The microstructure approach to exchange rates. Cambridge (MA): MIT Press; 2001.

Lorenzoni G. Optimal monetary policy with uncertain fundamentals and dispersed information. Rev Econ Stud 2010;77(1): 305–338.

Mark NC, Wu Y. Rethinking deviations from uncovered interest parity: the role of covariance risk and noise. Econ J 1998;108:1686–1706.

Martínez-García E. A model of the exchange rate with informational frictions. B.E. J Macroecon 2010;10(1) (Contributions):Article 2.

Meese RA, Rogoff K. Empirical exchange rate models of the seventies: do they fit out of sample? J Int Econ 1983;14:345–373.

Pastor L, Veronesi P. Learning in financial markets. NBER WP 14646; 2009.

Roberts MA. Imperfect information: some implications for modelling the exchange rate. J Int Econ 1995;38:375–383.

Rossi B. Are exchange rates really random walks? Some evidence robust to parameter instability. Macroecon Dyn 2006;10:20–38.

Sager MJ, Taylor MP. Under the microscope: the structure of the foreign exchange market. Int J Finance Econ 2006;11:81–95.

Sarno L, Valente G. Exchange rates and fundamentals: footloose or evolving relationship? J Eur Econ Assoc 2009;7:786–830.

Tabellini G. Learning and the volatility of exchange rates. J Int Money Finance 1988;7:243–250.

Takagi S. Imperferct iinformation and the comovement of the exchange rate and the interest rate: a signal extraction approach. Int Econ Rev 1991;32:1023–1035.

Verdelhan A. A habit-based explanation of the exchange rate risk premium. J Finance 2010;65:123–145.

CHAPTER FOURTEEN

# Exchange Rates in a Stochastic Discount Factor Framework

**HANNO LUSTIG**
NBER, UCLA Anderson

**ADRIEN VERDELHAN**
NBER; Department of Finance, MIT Sloan Cambridge

## 14.1 Introduction

According to the uncovered interest rate parity (UIP) condition, expected changes in exchange rates should be equal to the interest rate differentials between foreign and domestic risk-free bonds. The UIP condition implies that a regression of exchange rate changes on interest rate differentials should produce a slope coefficient of 1. Instead, empirical work following Hansen and Hodrick (1980) and Fama (1984) consistently reveals a slope coefficient that is smaller than 1 and very often negative. The international economics literature refers to these negative UIP slope coefficients as the UIP puzzle or forward premium anomaly.

Negative slope coefficients mean that currencies with higher than average interest rates tend to appreciate and not to depreciate as UIP would predict. Investors in foreign one-period discount bonds, thus, earn the interest rate spread, which is known at the time of their investment, plus the bonus from the currency appreciation during the holding period. As a result, the forward premium anomaly implies positive predictable excess returns for investments in high interest rate currencies and negative predictable excess returns for investments in low interest

*Handbook of Exchange Rates*, First Edition. Edited by Jessica James, Ian W. Marsh, and Lucio Sarno.

rate currencies. There are two possible explanations for these predictable excess returns: time-varying risk premia and expectational errors.[1]

In this chapter, we survey empirical and theoretical risk-based approaches of exchange rates. In Section 14.2, we start by laying down the basic theoretical framework, defining stochastic discount factors (SDFs) (also known as *pricing kernels* or *intertemporal marginal rates of substitution*) and exchange rates from a financial perspective. In Section 14.3, we review the recent body of empirical evidence emerging from this financial approach of exchange rates. In Section 14.4, we review the general equilibrium models that are consistent with stylized facts on currency markets. Section 14.5 concludes.

## 14.2 Exchange Rates and Stochastic Discount Factors

The fundamental insight of asset pricing is that an asset's value is determined by both its distribution of payoffs across economic states and state prices. SDFs summarize these state prices. In this section, we first define SDFs in complete and incomplete markets. We then define exchange rates and currency risk premia in terms of domestic and foreign SDFs.

### 14.2.1 STOCHASTIC DISCOUNT FACTORS

SDFs are key components of the Euler equations that govern asset prices and returns. These Euler equations can be derived under three different assumptions: complete markets, the law of one price, or the existence of investors' preferences. We rapidly review these three assumptions here. Cochrane (2001) presents a more detailed exposition. Key references are Breeden (1979), Lucas (1978), and Harrison and Kreps (1979).

**14.2.1.1 Utility-Based Asset Pricing.** Assume that the investor derives some utility $u$ from consumption $C$ now and in the next period. This setup can be easily generalized to many periods. Let us find the price $P_t$ at time $t$ of a payoff $X_{t+1}$ at time $t+1$. Let $Q$ be the original consumption level absent at any asset purchase and let $\xi$ be the amount of the asset the investor chooses to buy. The constant subjective discount factor is $\beta$. The maximization problem of this investor is

$$\begin{aligned} &\max_{\xi}\ u(C_t) + E_t[\beta u(C_{t+1})] \\ \text{subject to: } &C_t = Q_t - P_t\xi \\ &C_{t+1} = Q_{t+1} + X_{t+1}\xi \end{aligned}$$

[1]Following Froot and Thaler (1990) and Lyons (2001), some authors depart from rational expectations in order to account for the forward premium puzzle. They assume that agents' expectations or beliefs are systematically distorted. See notably Gourinchas and Tornell (2004) and Ilut (2010). Instead, in this chapter, we focus purely on rational expectations.

Substituting the constraints into the objective and setting the derivative with respect to $\xi$ to zero yields

$$P_t u'(C_t) = E_t[\beta u'(C_{t+1})X_{t+1}]$$

where $P_t u'(C_t)$ is the loss in utility if the investor buys another unit of the asset, and $E_t[\beta u'(C_{t+1})X_{t+1}]$ is the expected and discounted increase in utility he/she obtains from the extra payoff $X_{t+1}$. The investor continues to buy or sell the asset until the marginal loss equals the marginal gain. The Euler equation is thus

$$P_t = E_t[\beta \frac{u'(C_{t+1})}{u'(C_t)} X_{t+1}] = E_t[M_{t+1}X_{t+1}].$$

where the SDF $M_{t+1}$ is defined as $M_{t+1} \equiv \beta u'(C_{t+1})/u'(C_t)$.

**14.2.1.2 Complete Markets.** Let us now abstract from utilities and assume that markets are *complete*. There are $S$ states of nature tomorrow, and $s$ denote an individual state. A contingent claim is a security that pays 1 dollar (or one unit of the consumption good) in one state $s$ only tomorrow. The price today of this contingent claim is $P_c(s)$. In complete markets, investors can buy any contingent claim (or synthesize all contingent claims). Let $\underline{X}$ be the payoff space and $X(s) \in \underline{X}$ denote an asset's payoff in state of nature $s$. Let $\pi(s)$ be the probability that state $s$ occurs. Then the price of this asset is

$$P(X) = \sum_{s=1}^{S} P_c(s)X(s) = \sum_{s=1}^{S} \pi(s)\frac{P_c(s)}{\pi(s)}X(s)$$

We define $M$ as the ratio of the contingent claim's price to the corresponding state's probability $M(s) \equiv P_c(s)/\pi(s)$ to obtain the Euler equation in complete markets

$$P(X) = \sum_{s=1}^{S} \pi(s)M(s)X(s) = E(MX)$$

**14.2.1.3 Law of One Price and Absence of Arbitrage.** Finally, assume now that markets are *incomplete* and that we simply observe a set of asset prices $P$ and their corresponding payoffs $X$. Under a minimal set of assumptions, some discount factor exists, which represents the observed prices by the same equation $P = E(MX)$. These assumptions are defined below:

**DEFINITION 14.1**

*Free portfolio formation:* $X_1, X_2 \in \underline{X} \Rightarrow aX_1 + bX_2 \in \underline{X}$ *for any real* $a$ *and* $b$.

**DEFINITION 14.2**

*Law of one price:* $P(aX_1 + bX_2) = aP(X_1) + bP(X_2)$.

Note that free portfolio formation rules out short sales constraints, bid/ask spreads, leverage limitations, etc. The law of one price says that investors cannot make instantaneous profits by repackaging portfolios. These assumptions lead to the following theorem:

**THEOREM 14.1**

*Given free portfolio formation and the law of one price, there exists a unique payoff* $X^\star \in \underline{X}$ *such that* $P(X) = E(X^\star X)$ *for all* $X \in \underline{X}$.

As a result, there exists a SDF $M$ such that $P(X) = E(MX)$. Note that the existence of a discount factor implies the law of one price: $E[M(X+Y)] = E[MX] + E[MY]$. The theorem reverses this logic. Cochrane (2001) offers a geometric and an arithmetic proof. With a stronger assumption, the absence of arbitrage, the SDF is strictly positive and thus represents some—potentially unknown—preferences. We first review the definition of the absence of arbitrage and then turn to a new theorem.

**DEFINITION 14.3**

*Absence of arbitrage: A payoff space* $\underline{X}$ *and pricing function* $P(X)$ *leave no-arbitrage opportunities if every payoff* $X$ *that is always nonnegative* ($X \geq 0$ *almost surely) and strictly positive* ($X > 0$) *with some positive probability has some strictly positive price* $P(X) > 0$.

In other words, no arbitrage says that you cannot get for free a portfolio that might pay off positively but will certainly never cost you anything. This assumption leads to the next theorem:

**THEOREM 14.2**

*No arbitrage and the law of one price imply the existence of a strictly positive discount factor* $M > 0$ *such that* $P = E(MX)$, $\forall X \in \underline{X}$.

### 14.2.2 REAL EXCHANGE RATES AND CURRENCY RISK PREMIA

We now turn to exchange rates and currency risk premia and define them in terms of SDFs. We do not need to assume that markets are complete. We simply assume free portfolio formation and the law of one price. As a result, as shown above, there exists a unique SDF in the space of traded assets.

**14.2.2.1 Real Exchange Rates.** We use a superscript $\star$ to denote a foreign variable. $M$ and $M^\star$ denote the SDFs of the domestic and foreign investors, and $Q$ is the real exchange rate in US good per foreign good. When $Q$ goes up, the US dollar depreciates in real terms. Both domestic and foreign investors have access to the return $R^\star_{t+1}$, expressed in foreign currency. The Euler conditions of both investors are

$$E_t\left[M^\star_{t+1}R^\star_{t+1}\right] = 1$$
$$E_t\left[M_{t+1}\frac{Q_{t+1}}{Q_t}R^\star_{t+1}\right] = 1$$

Since there exists a unique SDF in the space of traded assets, the change in real exchange rate is equal to

$$\frac{Q_{t+1}}{Q_t} = \frac{M^\star_{t+1}}{M_{t+1}} \tag{14.1}$$

Note that we can define the change in nominal exchange rates in a similar fashion, using the ratio of two nominal pricing kernels.

**14.2.2.2 Currency Risk Premia.** Currency risk premia correspond to *expected* currency excess returns. The most simple investment strategy on currency markets is the following: a domestic investor borrows funds at home, converts them to a foreign currency, lends at the foreign risk-free rate, and then converts back her earnings to the original currency. Thus, in logs, the currency excess return $r^e_{t+1}$ is

$$r^e_{t+1} = \Delta q_{t+1} + r^\star_t - r_t \tag{14.2}$$

where lower cases denote logs. The domestic investor gains the foreign interest rate $r^\star_t$, but has to pay the domestic interest rate $r_t$. She therefore loses if the dollar appreciates in real terms—$q$ decreases—when her assets are abroad. Note that interest rates are known at the start of the investment period. Exchange rates are thus the only source of uncertainty here. As a result, the study of these currency excess returns—also known as *carry trades*—offer key insights into exchange rates, which in turn lead to new findings on SDFs.

Bekaert (1996) and Bansal (1997) show that, if markets are complete, pricing kernels must have time-varying higher moments in order to replicate deviations from the UIP condition. Backus et al. (2001) show the implications of this necessary condition in a large class of exponentially affine asset pricing models. The argument is as follows. Log-currency risk premia are equal to the half differences in the higher conditional moments of the log-pricing kernels:

$$E_t(r^e_{t+1}) = \sum_{j=2}^{\infty} \frac{\kappa_{j,t}}{j!} - \sum_{j=2}^{\infty} \frac{\kappa^\star_{j,t}}{j!}$$

where $\kappa_j$ denotes the cumulant of order $j$ of the log-pricing kernel.[2] As UIP tests show, currency excess returns are predictable using interest rate differences. As a result, expected currency excess returns vary over time. The equation above implies that higher moments of the pricing kernels must also vary over time.

In the special case of log-normal pricing kernels and returns, the formula is even more transparent.The risk-free rates in each country are

$$r_t = -\log E_t M_{t+1} = -E_t m_{t+1} - \frac{1}{2}\text{Var}_t(m_{t+1})$$

$$\text{and } r^\star_t = -\log E_t M^\star_{t+1} = -E_t m^\star_{t+1} - \frac{1}{2}\text{Var}_t(m^\star_{t+1})$$

Using Equation 14.1, the expected change in the exchange rate is

$$E_t(\Delta q_{t+1}) = -E_t(m_{t+1}) + E_t(m^\star_{t+1}) = -r^\star_t + r_t - \frac{1}{2}\text{Var}_t(m^\star_{t+1}) + \frac{1}{2}\text{Var}_t(m_{t+1})$$

As a result, the expected log-currency excess return is equal to

$$E_t(r^e_{t+1}) = r^\star_t - r_t + E_t(\Delta q_{t+1}) = \frac{1}{2}\text{Var}_t(m_{t+1}) - \frac{1}{2}\text{Var}_t(m^\star_{t+1}) \qquad (14.3)$$

Equation 14.3 shows that in order to obtain predictable currency excess returns, log SDFs must be heteroskedastic. The same equation also highlights the link between currency excess returns and other risk premia.

**14.2.2.3 Maximal Sharpe Ratio.** To see this point, let us first define the Sharpe ratio (SR) on any return.

[2]Cumulants correspond to the coefficients in Taylor expansions of the moment generating function around the origin. As a result, the first two cumulants correspond to the mean and the variance of the log SDF.

**DEFINITION 14.4**

*The* SR *measures how much return the investor receives per unit of volatility:*

$$\mathrm{SR} = \frac{E(R^i) - R^f}{\sigma(R^i)}$$

*where* $\sigma(R^i)$ *denotes the standard deviation of the return* $R^i$.

Over the 1925–2009 period in the United States, real excess returns on the NYSE stock index have averaged 8%, with a standard deviation of 20%, and thus the SR has been about 0.4. Starting from the Euler equation and using the fact that correlations are below unity, the SR is linked to the first and second moments of SDF

$$\frac{|E(R^i) - R^f|}{\sigma(R^i)} \leq \frac{\sigma(M)}{E(M)}$$

$\sigma(M)/E(M)$ corresponds to the maximal SR attainable. When the SDF is log normal, the maximal SR is approximately equal to the standard deviation of the log SDF

$$\frac{\sigma_t(M_{t+1})}{E_t(M_{t+1})} \simeq \sigma_t(m_{t+1})$$

As a result, currency excess returns correspond to the difference in squared maximal SRs obtained on any other assets.

**14.2.2.4 High Correlation of Stochastic Discount Factors.** Exchange rates are also informative on the correlation of SDFs across countries. In order to replicate both the equity premium and the exchange rate volatility, (Brandt et al., 2006) show that pricing kernels must be highly correlated. To see this point, let us start again from Equation 14.1, which defines exchange rates. It implies that the variance of real exchange rate changes is equal to

$$\sigma^2(\Delta q) = \sigma^2(m) + \sigma^2(m^\star) - 2\rho(m, m^\star)\sigma(m)\sigma(m^\star)$$

where $\rho(m, m^\star)$ denotes the correlation among log SDFs, and $\sigma(m)$ and $\sigma(m^\star)$ denote their volatilities. In order to fit the equity premium, we know that the variance of the SDF has to be high (Hansen and Jagannathan, 1991). This condition does not depend on preferences. But if the correlation $\rho(m, m^\star)$ is small, then the variance of the exchange rate is approximately twice the variance of the SDF. Building on this observation, Brandt et al. (2006) show that the actual real exchange rate is much smoother than the theoretical one implied by asset pricing models, unless pricing kernels are highly correlated across countries.

Note that power utility would not deliver this feature. The correlation among consumption growth shocks across countries is low. Power utility thus implies a low correlation of SDFs. High risk-aversion coefficients produce high equity risk premia, but exchange rates are then too volatile (and risk-free rates are implausible). Colacito and Croce (2008) address this puzzle in Bansal and Yaron (2004)'s long-run risk model. They assume that the time-varying means of consumption growth rates are perfectly correlated across countries. Using Epstein and Zin (1989), they build a model that delivers both high equity SRs and reasonable exchange rates volatilities because SDFs are both volatile and highly correlated across countries.

## 14.3 Empirical Evidence

We have reviewed in the previous section that under fairly general conditions, changes in exchange rates and currency risk premia directly depend on the properties of SDFs. This clear link motivates empirical studies of exchange rates using financial tools and reasonings. Along this line, in this section, we first describe a key methodological innovation, that is, the use of currency portfolios, and then turn to recent findings on exchange rates based on this new method.

### 14.3.1 FROM UIP REGRESSIONS TO CURRENCY PORTFOLIOS

**14.3.1.1 UIP Regressions.** As already noted, it is well known since the work of Hansen and Hodrick (1980) and Fama (1984) that the UIP condition is flatly rejected by the data.[3] Previous work on currency risk started from UIP tests, that is, from regressions of changes in exchange rates on a constant and interest rate differentials. Since the constants are not always 0 and the slope coefficients are never 1 and very often negative, UIP tests suggest that these two coefficients are needed to determine expected currency excess returns. They imply that investors obtain excess returns when investing in higher-than-usual interest rate currencies and that interest rate elasticity is key. As a result, in order to study currency excess returns and thus currency risk, researchers had first to estimate UIP-like equations.

**14.3.1.2 Currency Portfolios.** Lustig and Verdelhan (2005) are the first to propose an alternative approach to currency risk. They show that building

[3]Dozens of papers report rejection of UIP. Bekaert and Hodrick (1993) investigate biases as an explanation of the forward premium puzzle. Hodrick (1987) and Lewis (1995) provide extensive surveys and updated regression results. Engel (2011) links deviations from UIP to exchange rates overshooting and the properties of SDFs.

portfolios of currency excess returns helps extracting currency risk premia from noisy data. Lustig and Verdelhan (2005) simply sort currencies into portfolios based on their current interest rate. This portfolio approach is more direct than the UIP regressions: it shows that investors make money by chasing high interest rates. No pre-estimation is needed. This is the exact equivalent of the Fama and French (1993) approach for equity returns. See Cochrane (2001) for a discussion of the link between standard (predictive) regressions and portfolio sorts in the equity and currency literatures. Here, investors earn large excess returns on average simply by taking long positions in baskets of currencies with currently high interest rates and taking short positions in baskets of currencies with currently low interest rates, regardless of the history of interest rate differences for individual currency pairs. The average excess returns increase from the first portfolio, with currently low interest rate currencies, to the last portfolio, with currently high interest rate currencies.

This innovation allows to focus on the aggregate component of these currency excess returns and to ignore idiosyncratic risk. It greatly simplifies the study of exchange rates. This approach to studying currencies has been adopted by several authors recently. It enabled (Ang and Chen, 2010; Christiansen et al., 2009; DeSantis and Fornari, 2008; Farhi et al., 2009; Jurek, 2008; Menkhoff et al., 2012; Kozak, 2011) to make further progress on the road to a better understanding of exchange rates. The portfolio sorting approach is quite similar to how these strategies are actually implemented in currency markets. For example, the Deutsche Bank G10 Carry Harvest Index consists of long futures contracts on the three G10 currencies associated with the highest interest rates and of short futures contracts on the three G10 Currencies associated with the lowest interest rates. The index is available online at http://www.dbfunds.db.com/Dbv/index.aspx and investors can access these returns easily through an exchange traded fund (ETF).

We now describe the basic properties of these currency portfolios. We start with annual data over a long sample. We then move to monthly data over a shorter sample for which transaction costs are available. In both cases, we report large average currency excess returns. These excess returns correspond to risk premia: they comove with consumption growth at annual frequency and with measures of global volatilities at higher frequencies.

### 14.3.2 ANNUAL CURRENCY EXCESS RETURNS AND AGGREGATE RISK

**14.3.2.1 Long Sample.** Lustig and Verdelhan (2007) show that, on average, high interest rate currencies are more exposed to aggregate consumption growth risk than low interest rate currencies in a sample with 81 currencies spanning 50 years of annual data. To uncover the link between exchange rates and consumption growth, they build eight portfolios of foreign currency excess returns on the basis of the foreign interest rates, because investors know these predict excess returns. Portfolios are rebalanced every year, so the first portfolio

**TABLE 14.1 Portfolios—Countries Sorted on Nominal Interest Rates**

| Portfolio | 1 | 2 | 3 | 4 | 5 | 6 | 7 | 8 |
|---|---|---|---|---|---|---|---|---|
| | | | 1953–2002 | | | | | |
| Mean | −2.34 | −0.87 | −0.75 | 0.33 | −0.154 | −0.21 | 2.99 | 2.03 |
| SR | −0.36 | −0.13 | −0.11 | 0.04 | −0.02 | −0.03 | 0.37 | 0.16 |
| | | | 1971–2002 | | | | | |
| Mean | −2.99 | −0.01 | −0.83 | 1.14 | −0.69 | −0.00 | 3.94 | 1.48 |
| SR | −0.38 | −0.00 | −0.10 | 0.11 | −0.07 | −0.00 | 0.39 | 0.10 |

Notes: This table reports the mean of the real excess returns (in percentage points) and the SR for a US investor. The portfolios are constructed by sorting currencies into eight groups at time $t$ based on the nominal interest rate differential at the end of period $t-1$. Portfolio 1 contains currencies with the lowest interest rates. Portfolio 8 contains currencies with the highest interest rates. The table reports annual returns for annually rebalanced portfolios.
*Source*: Lustig and Verdelhan (2007).

always contains the lowest interest rate currencies and the last portfolio always contains the highest interest rate currencies.

As one would expect from the empirical literature on UIP, US investors earn on average the negative excess returns on low interest rate currencies and large, positive excess returns on high interest rate currencies. Table 14.1, taken from Lustig and Verdelhan (2007), reports these average excess returns. The relation is almost monotonic. These returns are large even when measured per unit of risk. The SR (defined as the ratio of the average excess return to its standard deviation) on the high interest rate portfolio is close to 40%, close to the SR on US equity, while the same ratio is minus 40% for the lowest interest rate portfolio. High interest rate currencies do not depreciate as much as the interest rate difference, and as a result, US investors can generally earn positive excess returns by investing in these currencies. However, these high interest rate currencies tend to depreciate relative to low interest rate currencies in bad times for US investors.

In order to show the macroeconomic riskiness of currency excess returns in a nutshell, we now follow Lustig and Verdelhan (2008). Let us define $HML_{FX}$ (for "high minus low") as the difference in returns between the high interest rate portfolio and the low interest rate portfolio. We focus on the seventh portfolio minus the first portfolio because this produces the largest spread (5.3% per annum). Asset pricing betas measure the quantity of risk in each asset. These betas simply correspond to slope coefficients in regressions of excess returns on a constant and on risk factors. Let us consider that investors are characterized by constant relative risk aversion, the most common preferences in macroeconomics. In this case, the log SDF varies with consumption growth. By construction, the consumption $\beta$ of $HML_{FX}$ is the difference between the consumption $\beta$ of the seventh and the first portfolio ($\beta^{HML} = \beta^7 - \beta^1$). Hence, we can simply test the presence of aggregate risk by regressing $HML_{FX}$ on consumption growth. It is not the case that *all* of the consumption betas should be statistically different

TABLE 14.2 **Estimation of Consumption Betas for $\mathbf{HML_{FX}}$**

| | Panel I: Simple Regression | | | | | |
|---|---|---|---|---|---|---|
| | $\beta_c^{HML}$ | $p(\%)$ | $R^2$ | $\beta_d^{HML}$ | $p(\%)$ | $R^2$ |
| | *Panel A: Nondurables* | | | *Panel B: Durables* | | |
| 1953–2002 | 1.00 | | 4.04 | 1.06 | | 9.07 |
| | [0.44] | 2.23 | | [0.40] | 0.89 | |
| 1971–2002 | 1.54 | | 8.72 | 1.65 | | 14.02 |
| | [0.52] | 0.28 | | [0.60] | 0.63 | |

| | Panel II: Multivariate Regression | | | |
|---|---|---|---|---|
| | $\beta_c^{HML}$ | $\beta_d^{HML}$ | $\chi^2$ | $R^2$ |
| 1953–2002 | 0.07 | 1.03 | | 9.07 |
| | [0.68] | [0.62] | 9.40 | |
| 1971–2002 | 0.28 | 1.48 | | 14.90 |
| | [1.20] | [1.24] | 14.15 | |

Notes: In Panel I, each entry reports OLS estimates of $\beta_1$ in the following time-series regression of the spread on the factor: $HML_{FX,t+1} = \beta_0 + \beta_1^{HML} f_{t+1} + \varepsilon_{t+1}$, where $HML_{FX,t+1}$ is the return on the seventh portfolio minus the return on the first portfolio. The estimates are based on annual data; standard errors are reported in brackets. Following Andrews (1991), we use Newey–West heteroscedasticity-consistent standard errors with an optimal number of lags to estimate the spectral density matrix. The $p$-values (reported in %) are for a $t$-test on the slope coefficient. The factor $f_t$ is nondurable consumption growth ($\Delta c$) in the left panel and durable consumption growth ($\Delta d$) in the right panel. In Panel II, we report the multivariate regressions $HML_{FX,t+1} = \beta_0 + \beta_1^{HML} \mathbf{f}_{t+1} + \varepsilon_{t+1}$, where $\mathbf{f}_t = [\Delta c_t, \Delta d_t]$. The $\chi^2$ are for a Wald test that the slope coefficients are zero. The data are annual, and the samples cover 1953–2002 and 1971–2002.
*Source*: Lustig and Verdelhan (2008).

from zero. The interesting economic question is whether betas are different from each other and not different from zero. Since, for example, the average excess returns on the fifth and sixth currency portfolios are very close to zero, we should expect to see betas close to zero for these portfolios. This explains the focus on the "corner portfolios."

Table 14.2, taken from Lustig and Verdelhan (2008), reports consumption growth betas. The consumption growth beta of $HML_{FX}$ is 1 for nondurable and durable consumption growth in a long sample starting in 1953. It is statistically significant. As a result, the consumption capital asset pricing model (CCAPM) can account for the average return on this investment strategy of 5.3% per annum given a market price of consumption risk of around 5% per annum.

This beta is economically significant too. To see this point, let us compare currency and equity markets. As a benchmark, the consumption beta of the return on the US stock market (the return on the value-weighted CRSP index) is 0.97 for the same sample. In order to explain the average annual stock market excess return of almost 7% (over the same period) in the standard CCAPM, the price of consumption risk has to be 7.1% per annum. This market price of risk, derived from equity markets, is enough to generate large expected currency excess returns. It implies a substantial carry trade premium of $7.1 = 1.0 \times 7.1\%$ on the HML strategy, compared to 5.3% in the data. From the perspective of the CCAPM, equity and currency markets appear quite consistent.

The implied market prices of risk imply, of course, implausibly high risk-aversion coefficients if investors are characterized by power utility. This is just the equity premium puzzle of Mehra and Prescott (1985) again: average currency excess returns are as large as equity excess returns, and consumption growth is not very volatile. In order to account for the cross section of returns, power utility investors would be characterized by very high risk-aversion coefficients, thus implying counterfactual risk-free rates, as Weil (1989) noted. Currency markets are as puzzling as equity markets, but both are definitely and consistently risky. If one simply uses risk prices from stocks then the standard CCAPM already predicts a sizable carry trade risk premium. Lustig and Verdelhan (2007) show that the risk prices found for currency excess returns are similar to those obtained when estimating the same model on other test assets such as equity and bonds, even though these currency returns are not spanned by the usual factors of value and size.

**14.3.2.2 Recent Crisis.** Investments are risky if they offer low returns in bad times, when the typical investor experiences higher marginal utility growth than average. As a result, bad times are particularly informative. Yet, the evidence above pertains to samples that end in 2002, and thus miss the largest recession since WWII. We thus now rapidly review what happened during the recent Great Recession.

In the fourth quarter of 2008, the United States recorded a 4.9% (annualized) drop in real personal consumption expenditures on nondurable goods, following a 5.6% (annualized) decrease in the third quarter. These growth rates are three standard deviations below the mean US consumption growth rate in postwar data. Overall, 2008 saw large decreases in consumption growth and equity markets: −0.8% in nondurable consumption growth, −4.5% in durable expenditures growth, and −38.4% in the US stock market return.

What happened in currency markets during the same period? High interest rate currencies depreciated and low interest rate currencies appreciated. As a result, returns on currency carry trades were low exactly in bad times. No computation needed here; market data are readily available for the recent period. For example, the Deutsche Bank G10 Carry Harvest Index (and the corresponding ETF) consists of long futures contracts on the three G10 currencies associated with the highest interest rates and of short futures contracts on the three G10 Currencies associated with the lowest interest rates. The evolution of this index is clear. The recent Great Recession has erased almost all of the carry trade gains made since the end of 2002. Carry traders first enjoyed a long period of steadily high returns. From a value of 100 in 2002, the index peaked at 155 in June 2007, but by the end of 2008, it was back down to 105. Thus, a 55% cumulative gain was followed by a like decrease. During the last two quarters of 2008, we witnessed a decrease of more than 31% of the Deutsche Bank carry trade index, a negative return equivalent to three standard deviations.

In a reversal, the Deutsche Bank carry trade index recovered 16.8% during the first two quarters of 2009. Nondurable expenditures increased by 4.1%, and expenditures on durables increased by 7.4%. The US stock market recovered 4.9%. If carry trades were not risky then the opposite pattern would have been just as likely: investors would have fled from the dollar and yen directly to the Australian dollar and the Icelandic Krone during the fall of 2008, ignoring the higher-yield currencies when the crisis abated. It is, however, hard to turn the recent evidence on its head.

### 14.3.3 MONTHLY CURRENCY EXCESS RETURNS

To learn more about exchange rates, we now focus on excess returns measured at higher frequencies and after transaction costs. We follow the methodology and results of Lustig et al. (2011). Following Lustig and Verdelhan (2007), they sort countries into portfolios based on interest rates in order to study carry trade returns.

Table 14.3 illustrates violations of UIP in the cross section. We report average currency excess returns from the perspective of the US investor. These excess returns are equal to differences between foreign and US short-term interest rates and the corresponding changes in exchange rates. Currency carry trades correspond to simple investment strategies that borrow in low interest rate currencies (e.g., short the first portfolio) and that invest in high interest rate currencies (e.g., long the last portfolio). This high-minus-low strategy delivers an excess return of above 4.4% per year after transaction costs and a SR of 0.48 over the 1983–2010 sample period.

We now show that these average large excess returns on currency markets imply novel necessary conditions on domestic and foreign SDF.

### 14.3.4 IMPLICATIONS FOR STOCHASTIC DISCOUNT FACTORS

**14.3.4.1 Common Component and Heterogeneous Loadings.** Lustig et al. (2011) show that two necessary conditions for a model to replicate the empirical evidence on currency risk premia are the existence of a common component in SDFs across countries, and some heterogeneity in the loadings on this common component. These necessary conditions derive from the factor structure of the exchange rates in the currency portfolios above. The second panel of Table 14.3 reports such a principal component decomposition. The first principal component is close to the mean of these exchange rate series; it corresponds to the dollar component of all the exchange rate series (expressed in foreign currency per US dollar). The second principal component accounts for the cross section of currency excess returns: high interest rate currencies offer high excess returns on average, because they load more on this common component. To replicate this finding, pricing kernels must have a component that is common across countries and yet each country must load differently on this common component.

**TABLE 14.3 Portfolios—Countries Sorted on Nominal Interest Rates**

| Portfolio | 1 | 2 | 3 | 4 | 5 | 6 |
|---|---|---|---|---|---|---|
| | | | Panel A: Summary Statistics | | | |
| | | | *Changes in exchange rates* | | | |
| Mean | −0.87 | −1.02 | −0.96 | −2.49 | −0.81 | 2.62 |
| Std | 8.06 | 7.40 | 7.68 | 7.59 | 8.68 | 9.76 |
| | | | *Interest rate differences* | | | |
| Mean | −2.90 | −1.19 | −0.08 | 0.99 | 2.66 | 8.86 |
| Std | 0.54 | 0.48 | 0.46 | 0.51 | 0.63 | 1.87 |
| | | | *Net excess returns* | | | |
| Mean | −0.88 | −1.11 | −0.36 | 2.15 | 1.96 | 3.49 |
| Std | 8.15 | 7.46 | 7.68 | 7.64 | 8.77 | 9.77 |
| SR | −0.11 | −0.15 | −0.05 | 0.28 | 0.22 | 0.36 |
| | | | *High-minus-low net excess returns* | | | |
| Mean | | −0.23 | 0.52 | 3.03 | 2.84 | 4.38 |
| Std | | 5.44 | 5.43 | 6.23 | 6.91 | 9.03 |
| SR | | −0.04 | 0.10 | 0.49 | 0.41 | 0.48 |
| | | | Panel B: Principal Components | | | |
| 1 | 0.40 | 0.46 | 0.21 | −0.15 | 0.75 | 0.04 |
| 2 | 0.38 | 0.25 | 0.13 | −0.25 | −0.47 | 0.70 |
| 3 | 0.38 | 0.30 | 0.39 | 0.12 | −0.44 | −0.63 |
| 4 | 0.39 | 0.03 | −0.36 | 0.83 | 0.03 | 0.17 |
| 5 | 0.44 | −0.09 | −0.71 | −0.46 | −0.06 | −0.27 |
| 6 | 0.45 | −0.80 | 0.38 | −0.03 | 0.13 | 0.04 |
| %Var | 72.42 | 11.42 | 5.49 | 3.90 | 3.61 | 3.17 |
| | | | Panel C: Aggregate Volatility Betas | | | |
| $\beta$ | 0.39 | 0.24 | 0.19 | 0.10 | −0.13 | −0.79 |
| s.e | 0.12 | 0.10 | 0.10 | 0.08 | 0.13 | 0.16 |

Notes: This first panel of this table reports, for each portfolio $j$, the average change in log-spot exchange rates, the average interest rate difference (with the US as home currency), the average log-excess return, and the average return on the long short strategy. Excess returns take into account the bid–ask spreads. The next panel of this table reports, for each portfolio $j$ (row), the factor loadings on each principal component (column) of changes in exchange rates. The last line of the panel reports the percentage of the total variance explained by each principal component. The last panel reports exchange rate volatility betas $\beta^j$. These betas are obtained as the slope coefficients in regressions of portfolio exchange rates on a constant and aggregate equity volatility. Betas are reported in percentages. We report (Newey and West, 1987) standard errors computed with the optimal number of lags following (Andrews, 1991). This measure of volatility is obtained as the average across all G7 countries of equity volatility returns. The portfolios are constructed by sorting currencies into five groups at time $t$ based on short-term nominal interest rates at the end of period $t-1$. The first portfolio contains currencies with the lowest interest rates. The last portfolio contains currencies with the highest interest rates. Data are monthly, from Barclays and Reuters (Datastream). The sample period is 11/1983–12/2010.

**14.3.4.2 Exchange Rates and Global Volatility.** Finally, the currency excess returns reported in Table 14.3 imply some cross-market restrictions. They are compensations for aggregate risk, and this risk can be captured by a measure of aggregate volatility. As Lustig et al. (2011) show, changes in exchange rates differ across portfolios: high interest rate currencies tend to depreciate when aggregate equity volatility is high, while low interest rate currencies tend to depreciate. They measure monthly volatility using the standard deviation of daily equity returns. We use the average across all G7 countries of these monthly volatilities. The last panel in Table 14.3 reports exchange rate volatility betas $\beta^j$. These betas are obtained as the slope coefficients in regressions of portfolio exchange rates on a constant and aggregate equity volatility. Carry trade portfolios deliver a clear cross section of volatility betas. The corner portfolios have significantly different betas. High interest rate currencies offer high returns, because these currencies tend to depreciate in bad times. Menkhoff et al. (2012) obtain similar results with aggregate currency volatility.

An alternative explanation of our findings is that the interest rate is simply one of the characteristics that determines returns, as suggested by Bansal and Dahlquist (2000). Ranaldo and Soderlind (2008) and Habib and Stracca (2011), for example, pursue this further by arguing that some currencies are viewed simply as safe havens, and therefore earn a lower risk premium than others that are perceived as more risky. On the basis of the empirical evidence, one cannot definitively rule out a characteristics-based explanation because interest rates and slope factor betas are very highly correlated in the data. However, Lustig et al. (2011) replicate the findings described above in the data simulated from a version of their model that is calibrated to match exchange rate and interest rate moments in the actual data. In the model-generated data, they cannot rule out a characteristics-based explanation either, even though the true data generating process has no priced characteristics.

Following this rapid overview of the cross-sectional studies of exchange rates, we now turn to their time-series properties. Here, again a finance perspective offers new insights on exchange rates. Predictability of exchange rates also imply restrictions on SDFs.

### 14.3.5 PREDICTABILITY OF CURRENCY EXCESS RETURNS

Since the work by Meese and Rogoff (1983), the standard view in international economics is that individual exchange rates follow a random walk, with perhaps small departures from the random walk at very high frequencies (Evans and Lyons, 2005). This consensus emerged from the failure of a large class of models to outperform the random walk in forecasting changes in exchange rates for individual currency pairs. Forecasting has been a longstanding challenge in international economics. Twenty years ago, Froot and Thaler (1990) counted at least 75 papers on the topic. There has been no shortage since. In general, the reported $R^2$s are small and the slope coefficients borderline is significant. The existing literature, however, focuses mainly on forecasting bilateral exchange rates (see Bekaert and Hodrick (1992) and Bekaert and Hodrick (1993) for prominent examples) and not portfolios of currency excess returns. Within such settings, detecting the effect of macroeconomic variables, such as industrial production growth, on currency risk premia requires imposing tight parametric structure on the SDF (e.g., as in Dong (2006)). More recently, using portfolios of currencies and a risk-based approach, Ang and Chen (2010) show that changes in interest rates and term spreads predict currency excess returns. Adrian et al. (2010) show that the funding liquidity of financial intermediaries in the United States predicts currency excess returns on short positions in the dollar, where funding liquidity growth is interpreted as a measure of the risk appetite of these intermediaries.

We now rapidly review the results in Lustig et al. (2012). As we saw in Section 14.2, in any no-arbitrage model, the percentage change in the spot exchange rate reflects the difference between the domestic and the foreign log-pricing kernel. As a simple thought experiment, let us decompose each pricing kernel into a country-specific and a global component. Consider the average return earned by a US investor in currency markets. She borrows in US dollars and invests in all the available risk-free securities denominated in foreign currencies. With many currencies in her well-diversified portfolio, the country-specific foreign risk averages out, and the US investor is left bearing (i) the US-specific risk and (ii) the difference between the US exposure to the common risk and the average exposure of all the other countries to common risk. Let us assume that the US exposure to common risk is equal to the average exposure across all countries in the currency basket. In that case, the second source of risk exposure disappears for a US investor who is short in the dollar and long in foreign currency. She is only compensated for the U.S. risks she is exposed to and the variation in this risk premium is driven by variation in the price of US risk. The empirical evidence supports this view. The average forward discount, the average difference between foreign and US risk-free interest rates, on a broad basket of currencies is the best predictor of the average excess returns on currency markets, because, given the assumptions above, the average forward discount measures the market price of US-specific risk.

The predicted foreign currency excess returns on long position in foreign currency and short positions in the dollar are strongly countercyclical, because they inherit the cyclical properties of US-specific risk prices. Lustig et al. (2012) show that the US-specific component of macroeconomic variables such as the rate of industrial production growth actually predict future excess returns even after controlling for the average forward discount. They investigate the 1-month to 1-year ahead predictability of the excess returns on baskets of foreign currency and they obtain $R^2$s of up to 23–30% when using the average forward discount and industrial production growth as predictors. Sarno et al. (2011), using a multinational term structure model, also find that carry trade excess returns are countercyclical.

These results should not come as a surprise. Why would currency excess return predictability differ from aggregate equity and bond excess returns? A large literature documents the predictability of excess returns in equity and bond markets (see Cochrane and Piazzesi (2005) and Cochrane (2001) for a survey).

Macroeconomic and financial variables predict stock market returns, particularly at long horizons. In recent work, Duffee (2008), Joslin et al. (2010), Ludvigson and Ng (2009) report similar findings for the bond market using industrial production growth, and Swanson and Piazzesi (2008) document that payroll growth predicts excess returns on interest rate futures. Hong and Yogo (2009) show that common predictors of bond and stock returns, such as the short rate and the yield spread, also predict returns on commodity futures. Currency markets are not different.

## 14.4 Models

We turn now to three general equilibrium models that through volatile SDFs can replicate the UIP puzzle and are thus consistent with the most well-known stylized facts on exchange rates. We present these models in their chronological order of appearance. Verdelhan (2010) offers the first rational expectation model of the UIP puzzle. Bansal and Shaliastovich (2008) and Colacito (2009) explain the UIP puzzle in a Bansal and Yaron's (2004) long-run risk model, and Farhi and Gabaix (2011) in a model with disaster risk.

### 14.4.1 HABITS

We first present the general intuition for the model's mechanism, and then review a simplified version of the model that delivers key results in closed form.

**14.4.1.1 Intuition.** In this model, following Campbell and Cochrane (2001), the representative investor has external habit preferences over consumption. In bad times, when consumption is close to the habit level and investors are more risk-averse, risk-free rates are low. In this case, UIP fails just as it does in the data. What is the intuition for this result? When markets are complete, the real exchange rate, measured in units of domestic goods per foreign good, equals the ratio of foreign to domestic pricing kernels—cf. Equation 14.1. Exchange rates thus depend on foreign and consumption growth shocks. If the conditional variance of the domestic SDF is large relative to its foreign counterpart, then domestic consumption growth shocks determine variations in exchange rates. When the domestic economy receives a negative consumption growth shock, the exchange rate depreciates, lowering the return of a domestic investor long in foreign Treasury Bills. When the domestic economy receives a positive shock, the exchange rate appreciates, increasing the return of the same investor. As a result, exchange rates carry consumption growth risks, and the domestic investor expects a positive risk premium. This reasoning echoes Backus et al. (2001). When pricing kernels are conditionally log normal, as they are in this model, risk premia boil down to differences in conditional variances—cf. Equation 14.3. When the domestic pricing kernel has relatively high conditional variance, an investor who is long in foreign Treasury Bills will receive a positive risk premium.

In the habit model, the conditional variance of the pricing kernel is large in bad times, when consumption is close to the habit level and risk aversion is high. To account for the UIP puzzle in this framework, real interest rates must be procyclical, meaning low in bad times when risk aversion is high and high in good times when risk aversion is low. Under these conditions, domestic investors expect positive currency excess returns when domestic interest rates are low and foreign interest rates are high, thus resolving the forward premium anomaly. The habit model endogenously delivers such countercyclical risk aversion and procyclical real risk-free rates. Expected currency excess returns increase sharply with interest rate differentials, and this produces a negative UIP coefficient in frictionless asset markets.

**14.4.1.2 Model.** The model focuses on real risk, abstracting from money and inflation. In the model, there are two endowment economies with same initial wealth and one good. In each economy, a representative agent is characterized by external habit preferences similar to Campbell and Cochrane (2001) but with time-varying risk-free rates. The agent maximizes

$$E\sum_{t=0}^{\infty}\beta^t\frac{(C_t - H_t)^{1-\gamma} - 1}{1-\gamma}$$

where $\gamma$ denotes the risk-aversion coefficient, $H_t$ the external habit level, and $C_t$ the consumption. The external habit level corresponds to a subsistence level or social externality. It depends on consumption through the following autoregressive process of the surplus-consumption ratio, defined as the percentage gap between consumption and habit ($S_t \equiv [C_t - H_t]/C_t$):

$$s_{t+1} = (1-\phi)\bar{s} + \phi s_t + \lambda(s_t)(\Delta c_{t+1} - g)$$

Lowercase letters correspond to logs, and $g$ is the average consumption growth rate. The sensitivity function $\lambda(s_t)$ describes how habits are formed from past aggregate consumption. In both countries, idiosyncratic shocks to consumption growth are i.i.d log-normally distributed

$$\Delta c_{t+1} = g + u_{t+1}, \quad \text{where } u_{t+1} \sim \text{i.i.d. } N(0,\sigma^2)$$

"Bad times" refers to times of low surplus-consumption ratios (when the consumption level is close to the habit level), and "negative shocks" refers to negative consumption growth shocks $u$. The same features apply to the foreign representative agent. Foreign variables are denoted with a $\star$ superscript. To obtain closed-form solutions and present the main intuition, let us assume that the endowment shocks $u_{t+1}$ and $u^{\star}_{t+1}$ are independent across countries.

The model delivers time-varying risk-aversion and time-varying real risk-free rates. Since each country's habit level depends on domestic, not foreign, consumption and on aggregate, not individual, consumption, the local curvature of the utility function, or local risk-aversion coefficient, is $\gamma_t = -C_t U_{cc}(t)/U_c(t) = \gamma/S_t$.

When consumption is close to the habit level, the surplus/consumption ratio is low and the agent very risk-averse.

To obtain risk-free rates, note that the SDF is

$$M_{t+1} = \beta \frac{U_c(C_{t+1}, H_{t+1})}{U_c(C_t, H_t)} = \beta (\frac{S_{t+1}}{S_t} \frac{C_{t+1}}{C_t})^{-\gamma}$$
$$= \beta e^{-\gamma [g + (\phi - 1)(s_t - \bar{s}) + (1 + \lambda(s_t))(\Delta c_{t+1} - g)]} \tag{14.4}$$

The sensitivity function $\lambda(s_t)$ governs the dynamics of the surplus-consumption ratio:

$$\lambda(s_t) = \frac{1}{\bar{S}} \sqrt{1 - 2(s_t - \bar{s})} - 1, \text{ when } s \leq s_{\text{max}}, \text{ 0 elsewhere}$$

where $\bar{S}$ and $s_{\text{max}}$ are, respectively, the steady state and upper bound of the surplus–consumption ratio. $\bar{S}$ measures the steady-state gap (in percentage) between consumption and habit levels. Assuming that $\bar{S} = \sigma \sqrt{\frac{\gamma}{1 - \phi - B/\gamma}}$ and $s_{\text{max}} = \bar{s} + (1 - \bar{S}^2)/2$, the sensitivity function $\lambda(s_t)$ leads to linear, time-varying risk-free rates

$$r_t = \bar{r} - B(s_t - \bar{s})$$

where $\bar{r} = -\ln(\beta) + \gamma g - \frac{\gamma^2 \sigma^2}{2\bar{S}^2}$ and $B = \gamma(1 - \phi) - \frac{\gamma^2 \sigma^2}{\bar{S}^2}$. Interest rates are constant when $B = 0$. For the UIP puzzle, this is obviously not an interesting case. When $B < 0$, interest rates are low in bad times and high in good times.

**14.4.1.3 A Solution to the UIP Puzzle.** To further simplify notations, let us assume that the preferences of domestic and foreign investors are characterized by the same underlying structural parameters: the same risk-aversion coefficients ($\gamma = \gamma^*$), the same persistence and steady-state values for the surplus-consumption ratio ($\phi = \phi^\star$ and $\bar{S} = \bar{S}^\star$), and the same mean and volatility for consumption growth rates ($g = g^\star$ and $\sigma = \sigma^\star$). In this setup, we can easily derive a closed-form expression for the UIP slope coefficient.

In the model, the variance of the log SDF is equal to

$$\text{Var}_t(m_{t+1}) = \frac{\gamma^2 \sigma^2}{\bar{S}^2} [1 - 2(s_t - \bar{s})]$$

and Equation 14.3 leads to the following expected currency excess return:

$$E_t(r^e_{t+1}) = E_t(\Delta q_{t+1}) + r^\star_t - r_t = \frac{\gamma^2 \sigma^2}{\bar{S}^2} (s^\star_t - s_t)$$

The real interest rate differential is

$$r_t - r^\star_t = -B(s_t - s^\star_t).$$

As a result, the expected change in exchange rates is linear in the interest rate differential:

$$E_t(\Delta q_{t+1}) = \left[1 + \frac{1}{B}\frac{\gamma^2\sigma^2}{\bar{S}^2}\right][r_t - r_t^\star] = \gamma\left(\frac{1-\phi}{B}\right)[r_t - r_t^\star] \qquad (14.5)$$

In this framework, the UIP slope coefficient no longer needs to be equal to unity, even if consumption shocks are simply i.i.d. Since the risk premium depends on the interest rate gap, the coefficient $\alpha$ in a UIP regression can be below 1. *This means that accounting for the forward premium anomaly requires procyclical interest rates, that is,* $B < 0$.

What is the intuition behind this result? First, exchange rates covary with consumption growth shocks and command time-varying consumption risk premia. As mentioned earlier, this model implies that the local curvature of the utility function is equal to $\gamma/S_t$. A low surplus-consumption ratio (when consumption is close to the habit level), thus makes the agent more risk-averse. Using Equations 14.4 and 14.1, the change in the real exchange rate is

$$\Delta q_{t+1} = k_t + \gamma[1 + \lambda(s_t)](\Delta c_{t+1} - g) - \gamma[1 + \lambda(s_t^\star)](\Delta c_{t+1}^\star - g)$$

where $k_t$ summarizes all variables known at date $t$. In bad times, when the domestic investor is more risk averse than his foreign counterpart, the surplus-consumption ratio is lower, $s_t < s_t^\star$, and the sensitivity function is higher at home than abroad, $1 + \lambda(s_t) > 1 + \lambda(s_t^\star)$. In other words, the conditional variance of the pricing kernel is higher at home than abroad. In this case, domestic consumption shocks dominate the effect of foreign consumption shocks on the exchange rate. As a result, when the domestic economy receives a negative consumption growth shock in bad times, the exchange rate depreciates, lowering domestic returns on foreign bonds. When the domestic economy receives a positive consumption growth shock, the exchange rate appreciates, increasing domestic returns on foreign bonds. Thus, the exchange rate exposes the home investor to more domestic consumption growth risk when the domestic investor is more risk averse than his foreign counterpart. *The domestic investor therefore receives a positive currency excess return if he is more risk averse than his foreign counterpart.* When the domestic investor is less risk averse than the foreign investor, foreign consumption shocks dominate the exchange rate, and the foreign investor receives a positive excess return. Here, the risk premium is perfectly symmetric, thus taking into account the fact that positive excess returns for the domestic investor mean negative excess returns for the foreign investor. The currency risk premium is time varying because risk aversion is time varying too.

Second, *times of high risk aversion correspond to low interest rates.* In bad times, when consumption is close to the subsistence level, the surplus-consumption ratio $s_t$ is low, the domestic agent is very risk averse, and domestic interest rates are low. As we have seen, a domestic investor expects to receive a positive foreign currency excess return in times when he is more risk averse than his foreign counterpart. Thus, the domestic investor expects positive currency excess returns when domestic interest rates are low and foreign interest rates are high. This translates to a UIP coefficient less than 1. It is negative because in times of high risk aversion, a small consumption shock has a large impact on the change in marginal utility. The SDF has therefore considerable conditional variance $\text{Var}_t(m_{t+1})$, and risk premia are high. As a result, domestic currency excess returns increase sharply with risk aversion, and thus interest rate differentials.

We can reinterpret this result using Backus et al. (2001). They establish the following two necessary conditions on pricing kernels in order to reproduce the UIP puzzle: a negative correlation between the difference in conditional means and the half difference in conditional variances and a greater volatility of the latter. Let us check these two conditions. For the first one, the difference in the conditional means of the two pricing kernels is here equal to $\gamma(1-\phi)(s_t - s_t^\star)$. The currency risk premium, which is the half difference in conditional variances of the two pricing kernels, is given in Equation 14.4. The difference in conditional means and the half difference in conditional variances are clearly negatively correlated. For the second condition, the risk premium has a larger variance than the difference in conditional means if $\gamma^2\sigma^2/\bar{S}^{2}$ is above $\gamma(1-\phi)$, which is the case for procyclical interest rates ($B < 0$). This model therefore satisfies the (Backus et al. (2001) conditions.

## 14.4.2 LONG-RUN RISK

We turn now to the class of long-run risk models pioneered by Bansal and Yaron (2004). Bansal and Shaliastovich (2008), Colacito (2009), and Colacito and Croce (2008) show that this class of models also offer a potential explanation to the UIP puzzle. We first rapidly present this class of models and then show that it is possible to replicate the two (Backus et al., 2001) conditions and thus the UIP puzzle.

**14.4.2.1 Model.** The long-run risk literature works off the class of preferences due to Kreps and Porteus (1978) and Epstein and Zin (1989). Let $U_t(C_t)$ denote the utility derived from consuming $C_t$. The value function of the representative agent takes the following recursive form:

$$U_t(C_t) = \left[(1-\delta)C_t^{\frac{1-\gamma}{\theta}} + \delta\left(E_t U_{t+1}^{1-\gamma}\right)^{\frac{1}{\theta}}\right]^{\frac{\theta}{1-\gamma}}$$

The time discount factor is $\delta$, the risk-aversion parameter is $\gamma \geq 0$, and the intertemporal elasticity of substitution (IES) is $\psi \geq 0$. The parameter $\theta$ is defined by $\theta \equiv (1-\gamma)/(1-\frac{1}{\psi})$. When $\psi > 1$ and $\gamma > 1$, then $\theta < 0$ and agents prefer an early resolution of uncertainty.

On the technology side, Bansal and Shaliastovich (2008) specify the following laws of motion for consumption growth, dividend growth, and inflation. We focus below on consumption growth, which is key for the dynamics of the SDF:

$$\Delta c_{t+1} = \mu_g + x_t + \sigma_{gt}\eta_{t+1}$$
$$x_{t+1} = \rho x_t + \sigma_{xt} e_{t+1}$$
$$\sigma^2_{g,t+1} = \sigma^2_g + \nu_g\left(\sigma^2_{gt} - \sigma^2_g\right) + \sigma_{gw} w_{g,t+1}$$
$$\sigma^2_{x,t+1} = \sigma^2_x + \nu_x\left(\sigma^2_{xt} - \sigma^2_x\right) + \sigma_{xw} w_{x,t+1}$$

All shocks are i.i.d. standard normal. Real consumption growth contains a persistent long-run expected growth component $x_t$. Shocks to (short-run) consumption growth have a stochastic volatility $\sigma^2_{g,t+1}$. This volatility differs from the conditional variance of the long-run component $x_t$, which is denoted by $\sigma^2_{xt}$. These volatility processes are key: without them, expected excess returns are constant and the model cannot replicate the UIP puzzle.

A central object in the long-run risk model is the log-wealth-consumption ratio, $wc_t \equiv w_t - c_t$. It is the price-dividend ratio of a claim to aggregate consumption. It is affine in the state variables $x_t$, $\sigma^2_{gt}$, and $\sigma^2_{xt}$:

$$wc_t = \mu_{wc} + W_x x_t + W_{gs}\left(\sigma^2_{gt} - \sigma^2_g\right) + W_{xs}\left(\sigma^2_{xt} - \sigma^2_x\right)$$

The coefficients $W_x$, $W_{gs}$, and $W_{xs}$ are functions of the structural parameters. When the IES exceeds 1, an increase in expected consumption growth and a decrease in short-run or long-run consumption volatility increase the wealth-consumption ratio. The log-real SDF can now be written as a function of log-consumption growth and the change in the log-wealth-consumption ratio:

$$m_{t+1} = \left[\theta \log\delta + (\theta - 1)\kappa^c_0\right] - \gamma\Delta c_{t+1} + (\theta - 1)\left(wc_{t+1} - \kappa^c_1 wc_t\right)$$

where $\kappa^c_0$ and $\kappa^c_1$ are linearization constants, which are a function of the long-run average log-wealth-consumption ratio $\mu_{wc}$. Note that when $\theta = 1$ ($\gamma = \frac{1}{\psi}$), the above recursive preferences collapse to the standard power utility preferences, and changes in the wealth-consumption ratio are not priced; the only priced shocks are then short-run consumption growth shocks $\eta_{t+1}$. Hence, the empirical failures of the power utility model and the successes of the long-run risk model must be attributable to their respective implications for the wealth-consumption ratio. It is thus key to know the properties of this ratio. Lustig et al. (2009) estimate the wealth-consumption ratio in the data, using a preference-free no-arbitrage approach. It turns out that the Bansal and Shaliastovich (2008) model's implications are broadly consistent with the data. In particular, the long-run risk model implies that the claim to aggregate consumption is not very risky, resulting in a high mean wealth-consumption ratio and a low consumption risk premium.

**14.4.2.2 UIP Puzzle.** In this model, the time-varying consumption volatility carries a separate risk compensation and ensures that the risk premium in asset markets is time varying. In particular, periods of high macroeconomic volatility are associated with (i) an increase in nominal bond risk premium and a steeper slope of the nominal yield curve, and (ii) expected depreciation of the currency and a low domestic minus foreign interest rate differential, thus providing the economic channels for explaining the violations of expectations hypothesis and of the UIP condition.

The model delivers a closed-form expression for expected currency excess returns:

$$E_t(r^e_{t+1}) = E_t(\Delta q_{t+1}) + r^\star_t - r_t = \frac{1}{2}\gamma^2(\sigma^2_{gt} - \sigma^{\star,2}_{gt})$$

The interest rate differential across two countries is equal to

$$r_t - r^\star_t = -\frac{1}{2}(\gamma + \frac{1}{\Psi}(\gamma - 1))(\sigma^2_{gt} - \sigma^{\star,2}_{gt})$$

The expected growth components and the long-run volatilities are assumed to be perfectly correlated across the two countries. As a result, they do not drive the variation in the yield differential and foreign exchange risk premium.

The magnitude of the model-implied slope coefficients in foreign exchange projections depend on the calibration of preference and consumption growth parameters. As evident from the equations above, if the short-run consumption volatility $\sigma^2_{gt}$ is constant, the expected excess returns on foreign bonds are constant as well, so that the expectations hypothesis holds and the UIP slope coefficient should be equal to 1. On the other hand, when investors have power utility, the expected currency depreciation is constant, as the variations in foreign exchange risk premium are exactly offset by the interest rate differential between the two countries. In this case, the slope coefficient in foreign exchange regressions is 0. Bansal and Shaliastovich (2008) show that for reasonable preference and consumption growth parameters, the model produces a negative UIP slope coefficient, in line with its empirical counterpart.

We can look at the same issue through the lenses of the Backus et al. (2001) necessary conditions. As previously noted, in order to replicate the UIP puzzle models need to produce a negative correlation between the difference in conditional means and the half difference in conditional variances of log SDFs, and greater variation in the latter than in the former. The first condition is easily verified in this class of models since:

$$\begin{aligned} &\text{sign}\left\{\text{cov}\left[E_t(m^\star_{t+1}) - E_t(m_{t+1}), \frac{1}{2}\text{Var}_t(m^\star_{t+1}) - \frac{1}{2}\text{Var}_t(m_{t+1})\right]\right\} \\ &= \text{sign}\left[\frac{1-\theta}{\theta}\right] \end{aligned}$$

which is negative for $\gamma > 1$ and $\psi > 1$. The second condition is less obvious, but the usual calibrations of the long-run risk models imply that the variance of risk premium is higher than the variance of the difference in conditional means of log SDFs.

### 14.4.3 DISASTER RISK

We turn now to a third class of general equilibrium models. Farhi and Gabaix (2011) propose a theory of international time-varying risk premia in a complete markets, frictionless, and rational framework. At any point in time, a rare world disaster might occur. Disasters correspond to bad times, hence they matter for asset prices despite the fact that they occur with a low probability. Countries differ by their riskiness, that is, by how much their currency would depreciate if a world disaster were to occur. We first rapidly present their model, then turn to the UIP puzzle, and end with a short description of related work.

**14.4.3.1 Model.** The model builds on Rietz (1988) and Barro (2006). The representative agent has constant relative risk-aversion preferences. Let $\delta$ denote the constant discount factor and $\gamma$ the risk-aversion coefficient. In each period, a disaster may happen with probability $p_t$; in this case, consumption drops sharply. The consumption process is thus

$$\frac{C_{t+1}}{C_t} = \left\{ \begin{array}{ll} e^g, & \text{if there is no disaster at } t+1 \\ e^g B_{t+1}, & \text{if there is a disaster at } t+1 \end{array} \right\}$$

where $B_{t+1} > 0$. For example, if $B_{t+1} = 0.7$, then consumption falls by 30%.

The SDF is simply

$$M_{t+1} = \left\{ \begin{array}{ll} e^{-R}, & \text{if there is no disaster at } t+1 \\ e^{-R} e^{-\gamma B_{t+1}}, & \text{if there is a disaster at } t+1 \end{array} \right\}$$

where $R = \delta + \gamma g$ is the risk-free rate in an economy that would have a zero probability of disasters and $g$ the mean consumption growth rate.

In the model, a linear technology converts nontraded goods of each country into the traded good. Investing one unit of the nontraded good at time $t$ yields $exp(-\lambda s)\omega_{t+s}$ units of the traded good in all future periods $t+s$. The interpretation is that $\omega_{t+s}$ is the productivity of the export technology, and the initial investment depreciates at a rate $\lambda$. (Farhi and Gabaix, 2011) define the level of exchange rates as the present value of future export productivity.

In each country $i$, the productivity follows:

$$\frac{\omega_{i,t+1}}{\omega_{i,t}} = \left\{ \begin{array}{ll} e^{g_{\omega i}}, & \text{if there is no disaster at } t+1 \\ e^{g_{\omega i}} F_{i,t+1}, & \text{if there is a disaster at } t+1 \end{array} \right\}$$

For instance, if productivity falls by 20% during disasters, then $F_{i,t+1} = 0.8$.

As in Gabaix (2009), the intensity of disasters is stochastic. The authors define the expected "resilience" $H_{i,t}$ of each country $i$ (where $i$ denotes the home or foreign economy) as

$$H_{i,t} = p_t E_t[B_{t+1}^{-\gamma} F_{i,t+1} - 1 | \text{ disaster at } t+1] = H_i + \widehat{H}_{i,t}$$

The resilience captures how well each country's productivity is insulated from world disasters. It is a measure of the persistence in the perceived intensity of disasters.

As in (Gabaix, 2009), the authors assume that the variable component of the resilience follows a "twisted" AR(1) or linearity-generating (LG) process. The variable component of the resilience evolves as

$$\widehat{H}_{i,t+1} = \frac{1+H_{\star}}{1+H_{i,t}} e^{-\phi_H} \widehat{H}_{i,t} + \varepsilon^{H}_{i,t+1}$$

**14.4.3.2 UIP Puzzle.** In the limit of small time intervals and for small $\widehat{H}_{i,t}$, the expected change in exchange rate in a sample without disasters is

$$E_t^{ND}[\Delta q] = -\frac{\phi_H}{r_e + \phi_H}(\widehat{H}_{\star,t} - \widehat{H}_t)$$

where—to simplify notation—we assume that the two countries share the same mean productivity and consumption growth rates, preference parameters, and persistence of their resilience processes ($\phi_H = \phi_{H^\star}$). The constant $r_e$ is defined as $r_e = R + \lambda - g_\omega - \log(1+H)$.

The interest rates in the domestic and foreign economies are equal to

$$r_t = r_e - \lambda - \frac{r_e \widehat{H}_t}{r_e + \phi_H}$$

$$r_t^\star = r_e - \lambda - \frac{r_e \widehat{H}_{\star,t}}{r_e + \phi_H}$$

When a country is "risky" (low $\widehat{H}_{\star,t}$), its interest rate is high because its currency has a high risk of depreciating in bad states of the world. In addition, because $\widehat{H}_{\star,t}$ is mean reverting, risky countries are expected to be less risky in the future. As a result, the exchange rate of high interest rate countries is expected to appreciate, which is consistent with the UIP puzzle. The UIP slope coefficient in a sample without disasters is simply $-\phi_H/r_e$.

**14.4.3.3 Extensions.** Building on the work of Farhi and Gabaix (2011) and Gourio (2009), Gourio et al. (Forthcoming) extend the standard international real business cycle (RBC) model by introducing a small, stochastically time-varying risk of economic "disaster". Variations in disaster risk lead not only to changes in risk premia and asset prices but also to variations in macroeconomic quantities. An increase in the probability of disaster leads to a decline of investment and output, because higher uncertainty makes it less attractive to hold risky capital. Demand for safe assets increases, causing the yield on these assets to fall, while spreads on risky securities increase. These business cycle dynamics occur with no change in total factor productivity (TFP). In Gourio et al. (Forthcoming), the two countries have different levels of riskiness, and the recession and decline in stock prices are stronger in the country at higher risk. The exchange rate of the less risky country—the country with high interest rates—depreciates.

This model goes some way toward reconciling international RBC models with the data. In this model, (i) real exchange rates are about twice more volatile than in the basic RBC model, as they are in the data; (ii) macroeconomic aggregates are more correlated than can be accounted solely by TFP shocks; (iii) asset returns are more correlated across countries than macroeconomic aggregates, (iii) the correlation of relative consumption growth and the exchange rate is not one as in the standard model, (cf. the Backus and Smith (1993) anomaly); (iv) the UIP condition is not satisfied and a carry trade strategy delivers large annual average excess returns, compared to essentially zero in the RBC model. As in the data, high interest rate currencies depreciate and low interest rate currencies appreciate when aggregate volatility is high. The model is also consistent with basic business cycle and asset pricing facts within each country, such as the mean and volatility of equity and risk-free returns, the predictability of returns, and the correlation of asset prices and macroeconomic aggregates such as investment or output.

Building on the work of Farhi and Gabaix (2011), Farhi et al. (2009) propose a simple structural model and an estimation procedure to assess the importance of disaster risk premia. The model includes both Gaussian and disaster risk premia and can be estimated even in samples that do not contain disasters. The model points to a novel estimation procedure based on currency options with potentially different strikes. Farhi et al. (2009) implement this procedure on a large set of countries over the 1996–2008 period, forming portfolios of hedged and unhedged carry trade excess returns by sorting currencies based on their forward discounts. Farhi et al. (2009) find that disaster risk premia account for at least 25% of expected carry trade excess returns in advanced countries.

The motivation for that paper is simple. Carry trade investors can use currency options to hedge this currency risk. For example, a domestic investor who is long in the foreign currency may buy a put contract that offers a large payoff in case the foreign currency depreciates. The investor thereby protects himself against adverse movements in the exchange rate. Likewise, a domestic investor who is short in the foreign currency may buy a call contract, protecting herself against an appreciation of the foreign currency. Using different currency option contracts, investors can tailor their exposure to exchange rate risk, buying protection against adverse exchange rate movements beyond any chosen cutoff. Intuitively, different hedged investment strategies should offer returns that are commensurate with their levels of risk. For example, the difference in returns between a strategy that is immune to large adverse changes in exchange rates and one that is not immune reflects the compensation for bearing the risk of a large currency depreciation. Yet, a simple comparison across unhedged and hedged returns does not allow a correct estimation of disaster risk premia. The reason is that hedged strategies protect investors against large exchange rate changes of two types: those due to jumplike disasters and those that might occasionally happen without any jump in a world of Gaussian shocks. As a result, one needs to write down a model to disentangle these two sources of risk.

Following Backus et al. (2001), Farhi et al. (2009) start off with the law of motion of the SDF in each country. These SDFs incorporate both a traditional log-normal component, as in Lustig et al. (2011), and a disaster component, as in Farhi and Gabaix (2011). In the model, expected currency excess returns are simply the sum of Gaussian and disaster risk premia. The former arise from random shocks observed every period, while the latter are because of rare disasters.The model delivers closed-form solutions for short-dated put and call currency options, hedged currency excess returns, and risk reversals (traded option pairs that replicate a long out-of-the-money put position and a short out-of-the-money call position). These expressions lead to a simple empirical procedure to measure the compensation for disaster risk.

## 14.5 Conclusion

Hansen and Hodrick (1980) and Fama (1984) show that the UIP is rejected by the data: changes in exchange rates do not correspond to interest rate differentials, and high interest rate currencies tend to appreciate and not depreciate as the UIP condition would suggest. This finding was considered for more than 20 years as proof of market inefficiency, not any more.

This survey shows that a recent stream of the exchange rate literature, based on new empirical findings, proposes new models of exchange rates. At the core of these models are novel SDFs. These risk-based approaches offer potential solutions to the UIP puzzle in purely rational and efficient asset markets. Rejection of the UIP puzzle is not proof of market inefficiency.

Risk-based models of exchange rates solve the UIP puzzle and open new directions for research in international finance. We mention here two potential avenues for research that build on these recent findings. First, more work is needed on the link between SDFs and economic fundamentals. Properties of exchange rates translate into necessary properties of SDFs. These SDFs should be heteroskedastic and they should exhibit some common components. Moreover, countries must be heterogenous: they should differ in their loadings on these common factors. It remains to link these properties to macroeconomic variables. What is, for example, the key source of heterogeneity across countries that will affect SDFs? Second, risk-based approaches imply interesting empirical links between exchange rates and other asset markets. How do, for example, long-term bond prices and returns comove with exchange rates? What are the potential interactions between equity, bond, and currency risk premia? We leave these questions out for future research.

## REFERENCES

Adrian T, Etula E, Shin HS. Risk appetite and exchange rates. Federal Reserve Bank of New York Staff Reports 361; 2010 May.

Andrews DWK. Heteroskedasticity and autocorrelation consistent covariance matrix estimation. Econometrica 1991;59(1):817–858.

Ang A, Chen JS. Yield curve predictors of foreign exchange returns. Working Paper Columbia University; 2010.

Backus D, Foresi S, Telmer C. Affine term structure models and the forward premium anomaly. J Finance 2001;LVI(1):279–304.

Backus D, Smith G. Consumption and real exchange rates in dynamic economies with non-traded goods. J Int Econ 1993;35:297–316.

Bansal R. An Exploration of the Forward Premium Puzzle in Currency Markets. Rev Financ Stud 1997;10:369–403.

Bansal R, Dahlquist M. The forward premium puzzle: different tales from developed and emerging economies. J Int Econ 2000;51:115–144.

Bansal R, Shaliastovich I. A long-run risks explanation of predictability puzzles in bond and currency markets. Working Paper, Duke University; 2008 April.

Bansal R, Yaron A. Risks for the long run: a potential resolution of asset pricing puzzles. J Finance 2004;59(4):1481–1509.

Barro R. Rare disasters and asset markets in the twentieth century. Q J Econ 2006;121:823–866.

Bekaert G. The time variation of risk and return in foreign exchange markets: a general equilibrium perspective. Rev Financ Stud 1996;9(2):427–470.

Bekaert G, Hodrick RJ. Characterizing predictable components in excess returns on equity and foreign exchange markets. J Finance 1992;47(2):467–509. ISSN 00221082.

Bekaert G, Hodrick RJ. On biases in the measurement of foreign exchange risk premiums. J Int Money Finance 1993;12:115–138.

Brandt MW, Cochrane J, Santa-Clara P. International risk-sharing is better than you think, or exchange rates are too smooth. J Monet Econ 2006;53(4):671–698.

Breeden D. An intertemporal asset pricing model with stochastic consumption and investment opportunities. J Financ Econ 1979;7:265–296.

Campbell JY, Cochrane JH. By force of habit: a consumption-based explanation of aggregate stock market behavior. J Pol Econ 2001;107(2):205–251.

Christiansen C, Ranaldo A, Soderlind P. The time-varying systematic risk of carry trade strategies. Working Paper; 2009.

Cochrane JH. Asset pricing. Princeton (NJ): Princeton University Press; 2001.

Cochrane JH, Piazzesi M. Bond risk premia. Am Econ Rev 2005;95(1):138–160.

Colacito R. Six anomalies looking for a model. a consumption-based explanation of international finance puzzles. Working Paper; 2009.

Colacito R, Croce M. Risks for the long run and the real exchange rate. Working Paper University of North Carolina; 2008.

DeSantis RA, Fornari F. Does business cycle risk account for systematic returns from currency positioning? The international perspective. European Central Bank; 2008.

Dong S. Macro variables do drive exchange rate movements: evidence from a no-arbitrage model; 2006.

Duffee GR. Information in (and not in) the term structure. Working Paper; 2008.

Engel C. The real exchange rate, real interest rates, and the risk premium. Working Paper University of Wisconsin; 2011.

Epstein LG, Zin S. Substitution, risk aversion and the temporal behavior of consumption and asset returns: a theoretical framework. Econometrica 1989;57:937–969.

Evans MDD, Lyons RK. Meese-rogoff redux: micro-based exchange rate forecasting. Am Econ Rev 2005;95(2):405–414.

Fama EF. Forward and spot exchange rates. J Monet Econ 1984;14:319–338.

Fama EF, French KR. Common risk factors in the returns on stocks and bonds. J Financ Econ 1993;33:3–56.

Farhi E, Gabaix X. Rare disasters and exchange rates. Working Paper Harvard University; 2011.

Farhi E, Fraiberger SP, Gabaix X. Romain Ranciere, and Adrien Verdelhan. Crash risk in currency markets. Working Paper; 2009.

Froot K, Thaler R. Anomalies: foreign exchange. J Econ Perspect 1990;4:179–192.

Gabaix X. Variable rare disasters: an exactly solved framework for ten puzzles in macro-finance. Working Paper; 2009.

Gourinchas P-O, Tornell A. Exchange rate puzzle and distorted beliefs. J Int Econ 2004; 64(2):303–333.

Gourio F. Disaster risk and business cycles. Working Paper Boston University; 2009.

Habib M, Stracca L. Getting beyond carry trade: what makes a currency a safe haven. Working Paper European Central Bank; 2011.

Hansen LP, Hodrick RJ. Forward exchange rates as optimal predictors of future spot rates: an econometric analysis. J Pol Econ 1980;88(5):829–853.

Hansen LP, Jagannathan R. Implications of security markets data for models of dynamic economies. J Pol Econ 1991;99:252–262.

Harrison MJ, Kreps DM. Martingales and arbitrage in multiperiod securities markets. J Econ Theory 1979;20:381–408.

Hodrick R. The empirical evidence on the efficiency of forward and futures foreign exchange markets. Chur, Switzerland: Harwood Academic Publishers; 1987.

Hong H, Yogo M. Digging into commodities. Working Paper; 2009.

Ilut C. Ambiguity Aversion: Implications for the Uncovered Interest Rate Parity Puzzle. Working Paper Duke University; 2010.

Joslin S, Priebsch M, Singleton KJ. Risk premiums in dynamic term structure models with unspanned macro risks. Stanford University; 2010 May.

Jurek JW. Crash-neutral currency carry trades. Working Paper; 2008.

Kozak S. Bond and foreign exchange risk premia. Working Paper University of Chicago; 2011.

Kreps D, Porteus EL. Temporal resolution of uncertainty and dynamic choice theory. Econometrica 1978;46:185–200.

Lewis KK. Puzzles in international financial markets. In: Grossman G, Rogoff K, editors. Handbook of international economics. Amsterdam: Elsevier Science B.V.; 1995. pp. 1913–1971.

Lucas R. Asset prices in an exchange economy. Econometrica 1978;46(6):1429–1–54.

Ludvigson SC, Ng S. Macro factors in bond risk premia. Rev Financ Stud 2009;22(12):5027–5067.

Lustig H, Verdelhan A. The cross-section of foreign currency risk premia and consumption growth risk. Working Paper NBER 11104; 2005 May.

Lustig H, Verdelhan A. The cross-section of foreign currency risk premia and consumption growth risk. Am Econ Rev 2007;97(1):89–117.

Lustig H, Verdelhan A. Note on the cross-section of foreign currency risk premia and consumption growth risk. Working Paper NBER; 2008.

Lustig H, Roussanov N, Verdelhan A. Common risk factor in currency returns. Rev Financ Stud 2011;24(11):3731–3777.

Lustig H, Roussanov N, Verdelhan A. Countercyclical currency risk premia. Working Paper MIT; 2012.

Lustig H, Van Nieuwerburgh S, Verdelhan A. The wealth-consumption ratio. Working Paper; 2009 Aug.

Lyons RK. The microstructure approach to exchange rates. Cambridge (MA): M.I.T Press; 2001.

Meese RA, Rogoff K. Empirical exchange rate models of the seventies: Do they fit out of sample? J Int Econ 1983;14:3–24.

Mehra R, Prescott E. The equity premium: a puzzle. J Monet Econ 1985;15(2):145–161.

Menkhoff L, Sarno L, Schmeling M, Schrimpf A. Carry trades and global Fx volatility. J Finance 2012. Forthcoming.

Newey WK, West KD. A simple, positive semi-definite, heteroskedasticity and autocorrelation consistent covariance matrix. Econometrica 1987;55(3):703–708.

Ranaldo A, Soderlind P. Safe haven currencies. Working Paper; 2008 July.

Rietz TA. The equity risk premium: a solution. J Monet Econ 1988;22:117–131.

Swanson E, Piazzesi M. Futures prices as risk-adjusted forecasts of monetary policy. J Monet Econ, 2008; 55(4):677–691.

Verdelhan A. A habit-based explanation of the exchange rate risk premium. J Finance 2010;65(1):123–145.

Weil P. The equity premium puzzle and the risk-free rate puzzle. J Monet Econ 1989;24:401–424.

CHAPTER FIFTEEN

# Volatility and Correlation Timing in Active Currency Management


**PASQUALE DELLA CORTE**
Imperial College London

**LUCIO SARNO**
Cass Business School; CEPR

**ILIAS TSIAKAS**
University of Guelph


## 15.1 Introduction

The expected volatilities and correlations of asset returns are a critical input in the optimal portfolio choice of a risk-averse investor. Extensive empirical evidence indicates that both the volatility of asset returns and their correlations change over time.[1] However, forecasting the dynamics of volatility and correlation requires estimation of suitable multivariate models, which are notoriously complicated and difficult to handle. This has spurred a large body of empirical research exploring tractable multivariate models of time-varying volatility.[2] Among them,

[1]See, for example, Ang and Bekaert (2002), Longin and Solnik (1995, 2001), and Goetzmann et al. (2005).

[2]For multivariate volatility models see, e.g., Bollerslev et al. (1988), Chib et al. (2006), Diebold and Nerlove (1989), Engle and Kroner (1995), Engle et al. (2008), Gourieroux et al. (2009), Harvey et al. (1994), Ledoit et al. (2003), Philipov and Glickman (2006), and Palandri (2009).


*Handbook of Exchange Rates*, First Edition. Edited by Jessica James, Ian W. Marsh, and Lucio Sarno.

the dynamic conditional correlation (DCC) model (Engle, 2002) has emerged as a benchmark, as it provides a parsimonious and flexible framework for modeling the dynamics of asset return volatilities and correlations. Hence, it can be readily used in realistic applications of dynamic asset allocation.

This chapter addresses an essential question that lies at the core of a long line of research in empirical finance: does volatility and correlation timing matter for the optimal asset allocation of a risk-averse investor and, if so, how? We contribute to the literature on the economic value of volatility timing, which focuses primarily on the dynamics of volatilities, while, however, for the most part treats the impact of dynamic correlations as an afterthought; in some cases correlations are assumed constant (e.g., Della Corte et al. 2009), and in other cases they are modeled using rolling estimators (e.g., Fleming et al. 2001). But in no case is the effect of correlation timing separately evaluated from that of volatility timing. In this chapter we fill this gap in the literature.

Our empirical investigation begins by estimating a large set of multivariate specifications based on the DCC model. We take a Bayesian approach in estimation and asset allocation, which allows us to evaluate volatility and correlation timing in a way that accounts for parameter and model uncertainty. Our analysis also assesses the impact of other important aspects of portfolio choice, such as transaction costs, asymmetry in correlations, and richness of correlation dynamics.

The empirical analysis is based on 31 years of daily returns data on four major US dollar nominal exchange rates. As the largest financial market in the world, the foreign exchange (FX) market is geographically dispersed with a uniquely international dimension. Time-varying volatility in exchange rate returns is a stylized fact. Moreover, the FX market is a natural market to study dynamic correlations, as investors trade currencies but all prices are quoted relative to a numeraire. For example, consider the case where the US dollar is the numeraire relative to which exchange rates are quoted. Other things being equal, a shock to the US economy will likely move the US dollar in the same direction relative to all other currencies, thus generating positive correlation in all dollar exchange rates. In general, correlations between exchange rate returns will change over time because of variation in global and country-specific fundamentals as well as other factors that are specific to the FX market, such as the intervention of policy makers aimed at influencing a particular basket of exchange rates.[3]

We assess the relative economic value of volatility and correlation timing without modeling exchange rate returns as a function of state variables.[4] This is equivalent to specifying a random walk model for the spot exchange rate, which in turn is consistent with the vast majority of the empirical FX literature

[3]Note that transaction costs for professional investors in the FX market are very small (no more than 2 basis points) and currency hedge funds typically invest in a small number of currencies. Furthermore, in recent years investors can directly trade on FX volatility and correlation using volatility and correlation swaps (Della Corte et al., 2011).

[4]See Della Corte and Tsiakas (2012) in this handbook for a comprehensive statistical and economic evaluation of the predictability implied by a wide range of empirical exchange rate models for the mean.

since the seminal contribution of Meese and Rogoff (1983). Modeling the spot exchange rate as a random walk is also the basis of the widely used carry trade strategy that borrows in low interest rate currencies and invests in high interest rate currencies. The carry trade has historically delivered large economic gains by exploiting deviations from uncovered interest parity since, on average, the interest differential is not offset by a commensurate depreciation of the investment currency (Burnside et al., 2011; Menkhoff et al. 2012).

The key distinguishing feature of our analysis is the use of economic criteria. While there is an extensive literature on statistically evaluating the performance of volatility and correlation models, there is little work in formally assessing the economic value of volatility and correlation timing. A purely statistical analysis of volatility and correlation timing is not particularly informative to an investor as it falls short of measuring whether there are tangible economic gains from implementing dynamic conditional volatilities and correlations in active portfolio management. This motivates our asset allocation approach, which extends previous studies by West et al. (1993) and Fleming et al. (2001, 2003). We evaluate the dynamic allocation strategies using a constant relative risk aversion (CRRA) utility function and measure how much a risk-averse investor is willing to pay for switching from a static portfolio strategy based on the constant covariance model to one that has dynamic conditional volatility and correlation.[5]

We assess the economic value of volatility and correlation timing in a Bayesian framework, which explicitly accounts for the fact that forecasts are not known with complete precision, and the presence of estimation error will make the resulting allocation suboptimal. The Bayesian portfolio choice literature suggests that we can account for parameter uncertainty by evaluating expected utility under the investor's predictive posterior distribution, which is determined by historical data and the prior but does not depend on the parameter estimates (Barberis, 2000; Kandel and Stambaugh, 1996; and Kan and Zhou, 2007). We can thus examine the effect of parameter uncertainty on asset allocation by comparing, on the one hand, the standard (or "plug-in") method that replaces the true parameter values by their estimates with, on the other hand, the Bayesian approach that integrates estimation risk into the analysis.

In line with the Bayesian approach of Avramov (2002), Cremers (2002), and Della Corte et al. (2009), we also evaluate the impact of model uncertainty by exploring whether portfolio performance improves when combining the forecasts from the large set of models we estimate.[6] Including the benchmark static covariance model, we estimate a total of 46 model specifications, which we then combine in optimally implementing Bayesian Model Averaging (BMA).

Note that we carry out the empirical analysis both using the full sample of available data and by performing out-of-sample rolling estimation for selected models. Since out-of-sample estimation is very costly in terms of computation time, given the current state of technology, our discussion focuses primarily

[5]For related studies, see also Engle and Sheppard (2001) and Engle and Colacito (2006).

[6]We estimate the parameters of the DCC model by designing a Markov Chain Monte Carlo (MCMC) algorithm and thus contribute to the financial econometrics literature since the DCC model has yet to be estimated and evaluated using Bayesian methods.

on the full set of in-sample results. However, we find that the in-sample and out-of-sample results tend to be qualitatively identical.

To preview our key results, the performance of the dynamic allocation strategies suggests that there is high economic value in timing both the volatilities and the correlations of exchange rate returns. We find that an international investor facing FX risk will pay a performance fee of about 4% per year for volatility timing and a further 3% per year for correlation timing. This finding is robust to reasonable transaction costs as well as parameter uncertainty, model uncertainty, asymmetric correlations, and alternative specifications for volatilities and correlations. In particular, parameter uncertainty has little or no effect on the economic value of volatility and correlation timing. Furthermore, the simplest DCC specification examined here captures almost all gains from timing volatilities and correlations in the context of asset allocation across currencies. This is an important finding, which suggests that using a more sophisticated DCC specification will not necessarily enhance the performance of optimally designed portfolios relative to the simple DCC model.

The remainder of the chapter is organized as follows. In the next section, we lay out the multivariate conditional volatility and correlation models and briefly explain the Bayesian estimation methods. Section 15.3 discusses the framework for assessing the economic value of volatility and correlation timing for a risk-averse investor with a CRRA portfolio allocation strategy. The effect of parameter uncertainty on asset allocation is discussed in Section 15.4, while model uncertainty and the construction of combined forecasts are described in Section 15.5. Our empirical results are reported in Section 15.6, and Section 15.7 provides concluding remarks. We also include Appendix A with details on the volatility models employed in this chapter and Appendix B with further details on how we account for parameter uncertainty.

## 15.2 Dynamic Models for Volatility and Correlation

We model the dynamics of volatilities and correlations of exchange rate returns using a set of specifications based on the DCC model (Engle, 2002). The DCC model offers an attractive multivariate framework for the study of correlation timing because it has the following advantages: (i) it is tractable and parsimonious with a low dimension of parameters; (ii) it is flexible and can be generalized to account for asymmetric correlations while ensuring that correlations are in the $[-1, 1]$ range; (iii) it provides for a positive-definite covariance matrix; and (iv) it is straightforward to implement even when the number of assets is large.

In order to assess the economic value of volatility and correlation timing, we estimate a set of multivariate models for dynamic correlations (such as the DCC model), each under a set of univariate specifications for dynamic volatility (such as the GARCH model). In the following discussion, we describe the complete set of models we estimate.

### 15.2.1 THE SET OF MULTIVARIATE MODELS

Let $y_t = (y_{1,t}, \ldots, y_{N,t})'$ denote the $N \times 1$ vector of nominal log-exchange rate returns at time $t$:

$$y_t = \mu + \Sigma_t^{1/2} \varepsilon_t \tag{15.1}$$

where $\mu = (\mu_1, \ldots, \mu_N)'$ is the $N \times 1$ vector of unconditional means, $\Sigma_t$ is the $N \times N$ conditional covariance matrix, and $\varepsilon_t = (\varepsilon_{1,t}, \ldots, \varepsilon_{N,t})'$ is the $N \times 1$ vector of standard normal disturbances.[7]

In our analysis, the vector of means $\mu$ is constant over time. This is equivalent to specifying a random walk model for each log-exchange rate. This assumption allows us to primarily focus on the effect of dynamic volatility and correlation on asset allocation. Note that the predictability in the mean implied by a wide range of empirical exchange rate models is studied separately by Della Corte and Tsiakas (2012) in this handbook. For the conditional covariance matrix $\Sigma_t$, we use the set of specifications described below.

**15.2.1.1 The Static Benchmark.** The multivariate linear regression (*MLR*) model assumes a constant covariance matrix and represents our benchmark model. This corresponds to setting $\Sigma_t = \overline{\Sigma}$. The MLR model can be viewed as the carry trade strategy widely adopted in currency markets (e.g., Burnside et al., 2011). The alternative models presented below reflect strategies that augment the carry trade with volatility and correlation timing.

**15.2.1.2 The Constant Conditional Correlation Model.** The *constant conditional correlation* (*CCC*) model (Bollerslev, 1990) assumes constant correlations but dynamic volatilities. This model decomposes the conditional covariance matrix as follows:

$$\Sigma_t = D_t \overline{R} D_t \tag{15.2}$$

$$D_t = \text{diag}\left\{\sigma_{1,t}, \ldots, \sigma_{N,t}\right\} \tag{15.3}$$

where $D_t$ is the $N \times N$ diagonal matrix of dynamic conditional volatilities $\{\sigma_{j,t}\}$ for $j \leq N$ and $\overline{R}$ is the $N \times N$ matrix of unconditional correlations. The conditional volatilities can have any of the specifications discussed in Section 15.2.2 below. The main feature of the CCC model is that the dynamics of covariances are governed exclusively by the dynamics of volatilities since correlations are constant.

**15.2.1.3 The Dynamic Conditional Correlation Model.** The DCC model (Engle, 2002) assumes dynamic volatilities and correlations by

---

[7] See Bauwens and Laurent (2005) for a generalization of the conditional normality assumption of multivariate models.

decomposing the conditional covariance matrix as follows:

$$\Sigma_t = D_t R_t D_t \tag{15.4}$$

$$D_t = \text{diag}\left\{\sigma_{1,t}, \ldots, \sigma_{N,t}\right\} \tag{15.5}$$

$$R_t = \left(\text{diag}\left\{Q_t\right\}\right)^{-1/2} Q_t \left(\text{diag}\left\{Q_t\right\}\right)^{-1/2} \tag{15.6}$$

$$Q_t = (\overline{R} - \Gamma'\overline{R}\Gamma - \Delta'\overline{R}\Delta) + \Gamma' z_{t-1} z_{t-1}' \Gamma + \Delta' Q_{t-1} \Delta \tag{15.7}$$

where $D_t$ is the $N \times N$ diagonal matrix of dynamic conditional volatilities, $R_t$ is the $N \times N$ symmetric matrix of dynamic conditional correlations, $\overline{R}$ is the $N \times N$ matrix of unconditional correlations, $Q_t$ is an $N \times N$ symmetric positive-definite matrix, $\Gamma$ and $\Delta$ are $N \times N$ parameter matrices, and $z_t = D_t^{-1} u_t \sim N(0, R_t)$, where $u_t = y_t - \mu$.

We focus on two versions of this model. The simplest version reduces $\Gamma = \gamma$ and $\Delta = \delta$, where $\{\gamma, \delta\}$ are scalars, which are the same for all assets $i \leq N$. This is the "scalar" DCC model, which assumes that the dynamics of all correlations are driven by the same two parameters $\{\gamma, \delta\}$. A less parsimonious variant of the scalar DCC model results when the matrices $\Gamma$ and $\Delta$ are assumed to be diagonal: $\Gamma = \text{diag}\left\{\gamma_1, \cdots, \gamma_N\right\}$ and $\Delta = \text{diag}\left\{\delta_1, \cdots, \delta_N\right\}$. This is the "diagonal" DCC model, which allows for distinct dynamics in each correlation process but requires estimation of more parameters. We estimate both scalar (henceforth denoted simply as DCC) and diagonal ($\text{DCC}_{\text{diag}}$) specifications.

**15.2.1.4 The Asymmetric Dynamic Conditional Correlation Model.** The *asymmetric dynamic conditional correlation* (ADCC) model (Cappiello et al., 2006) further allows for asymmetric correlations by generalizing Equation (15.7) as follows:

$$\begin{aligned} Q_t = {} & (\overline{R} - \Gamma'\overline{R}\Gamma - \Delta'\overline{R}\Delta - \Pi'\overline{P}\Pi) \\ & + \Gamma' z_{t-1} z_{t-1}' \Gamma + \Delta' Q_{t-1} \Delta + \Pi' p_{t-1} p_{t-1}' \Pi, \end{aligned} \tag{15.8}$$

where $\Gamma$, $\Delta$, and $\Pi$ are $N \times N$ parameter matrices; $p_t = I\left[z_t < 0\right] \circ z_t$, where $I\left[\cdot\right]$ is an indicator function taking the value 1 if the argument is true and 0 otherwise and $\circ$ indicates the Hadamard product; and $\overline{P} = E\left[p_t p_t'\right]$. For example, the symmetric scalar DCC model (the simplest DCC model we consider) is obtained as a special case of the ADCC model when $\Gamma = \gamma$, $\Delta = \delta$, and $\Pi = 0$. As with the symmetric version, we estimate both scalar (ADCC) and diagonal ($\text{ADCC}_{\text{diag}}$) specifications.

The ADCC model is motivated by numerous empirical studies showing that return correlations may be asymmetric as they tend to increase in highly volatile bear markets (Ang and Chen, 2002; Longin and Solnik, 2001). This has important implications for optimal asset allocation and, for example, casts doubt on the benefits of international diversification (Ang and Bekaert, 2002). When asset returns are more volatile, investors have a stronger incentive to diversify, but it is precisely in these cases that correlations are high and diversification opportunities are low. In other words, asymmetric return correlations cause diversification opportunities to be least available when they are most needed.[8] In this context, the ADCC model allows us to determine the possible impact of asymmetric correlations on asset allocation in the FX market.

### 15.2.2 THE SET OF UNIVARIATE MODELS FOR VOLATILITY TIMING

We estimate the multivariate models under a variety of univariate specifications for the conditional variance, including some of the most popular models in the literature. The nine univariate volatility models we consider are GARCH (Bollerslev, 1986), AVGARCH (Taylor, 1986), NARCH (Higgins and Bera, 1992), EGARCH (Nelson, 1991), ZARCH (Zakoian, 1994), GJR-GARCH (Glosten et al., 1993), APGARCH (Ding et al. 1993), AGARCH (Engle, 1990), and NAGARCH (Engle and Ng, 1993). The details on the full specification of these models are available in Appendix A.

### 15.2.3 PAIRWISE MODEL COMPARISONS

In addition to the static benchmark MLR, the set of models is composed of five competing dynamic specifications CCC, DCC, $DCC_{diag}$, ADCC, and $ADCC_{diag}$ under each of the nine univariate volatility specifications listed above. In total, therefore, we estimate 46 model specifications. The principal objective of our analysis is to provide an economic evaluation of these models in the context of dynamic asset allocation. First, we assess the economic value of volatility timing simply by comparing the CCC model to the static MLR. We then measure the additional economic gains from correlation timing by comparing the DCC to the CCC model. We also assess whether there is economic value in imposing separate dynamics on correlations (diagonal DCC vs scalar DCC), whether correlation asymmetries are important (ADCC vs DCC), and finally, whether the choice of a particular volatility specification generates further economic gains.

### 15.2.4 ESTIMATION AND FORECASTING

We perform Bayesian estimation of all model parameters. The critical advantage of the Bayesian methodology is that it provides a unified framework for estimation, forecasting, and model selection, which is particularly suitable for capturing the effect of parameter and model uncertainty. Bayesian inference generally provides the posterior distribution of the parameters conditional on the data, which holds for finite samples. The posterior distribution can in turn be used as an input

[8]Recent work in empirical asset pricing shows that asymmetric correlation risk is priced in the sense that assets that payoff well when market-wide correlations are higher than expected earn negative excess returns. The negative excess return on correlation-sensitive assets can therefore be interpreted as an insurance premium (Buraschi et al., 2010; Driessen et al., 2009).

in forming Bayesian asset allocation strategies for an economically meaningful ranking of the models that accounts for parameter and model uncertainty.

In this chapter, we design an MCMC algorithm for Bayesian estimation of the DCC model. The algorithm draws insights from the Bayesian stochastic volatility algorithm of Chib et al. (2002, 2006), Kim et al. (1998), and Tsiakas (2006) and from the Bayesian univariate GARCH algorithm of Della Corte et al. (2009). The Bayesian MCMC algorithm constructs a Markov chain whose limiting distribution is the target posterior density of the parameters. The Markov chain is a Gibbs sampler in which all parameters are drawn sequentially from their full conditional posterior distribution. The Gibbs sampler is iterated 5000 times and the sampled draws, beyond a burn-in period of 1000 iterations, are treated as variates from the target posterior distribution. Our Bayesian estimation approach delivers a sample from the posterior distribution of the parameters, which is a key input to the Bayesian asset allocation.[9]

# 15.3 The Economic Value of Volatility and Correlation Timing

## 15.3.1 THE DYNAMIC STRATEGY

We design an international asset allocation strategy that involves trading the US dollar and four other currencies: the British pound, Deutsche mark/euro, Swiss franc, and Japanese yen. Consider a US investor who builds a portfolio by allocating her wealth between five bonds: one domestic (US) and four foreign bonds (UK, Germany, Switzerland, and Japan). The yield of the bonds is proxied by euro deposit rates. At the beginning of each period, the foreign bonds yield a riskless return in local currency but a risky return in US dollars. Hence the only risk the US investor is exposed to is the FX risk. Every period the investor takes two steps. First, she uses each model to forecast the one-day-ahead conditional volatilities and correlations of the exchange rate returns. Second, conditional on the forecasts of each model, she dynamically rebalances her portfolio by computing the new optimal weights that maximize utility. This setup is designed to inform us whether using one particular conditional volatility and correlation specification affects the performance of an allocation strategy in an economically meaningful way.

## 15.3.2 DYNAMIC ASSET ALLOCATION WITH CRRA UTILITY

We set up a dynamic asset allocation framework with CRRA utility for assessing the economic value of strategies that exploit predictability in volatilities and

[9] A detailed description of the MCMC algorithm is available from the authors on request. The algorithm produces estimates of the posterior means of $\theta = \{\mu, \theta_1, \theta_2\}$, where $\mu = \{\mu_i\}$ is the vector of unconditional means for assets $i \leq N$, $\theta_1$ are the parameters of each univariate GARCH-type volatility process, and $\theta_2$ are the correlation parameters. For example, for the diagonal $\text{ADCC}_{\text{diag}}$ model with GARCH volatility $\theta_1 = \{\omega_i, \alpha_i, \beta_i\}$ and $\theta_2 = \{\gamma_i, \delta_i, \pi_i\}$. Setting $N = 4$ requires 28 parameter estimates.

correlations. Consider the portfolio choice at time $t$ of an investor who maximizes the expected end-of-period utility by trading in every period $N$ risky assets and a risk-free asset. The investor problem is formally defined as follows (e.g., Brandt, 2009):

$$V_t\left(W_t, Z_t\right) = \max_{\{x_s\}_{s=t}^{T-1}} E_t\left[\frac{W_T^{1-\lambda}}{1-\lambda}\right]$$
$$s.t.\ W_{s+1} = W_s R_{p,s+1} \quad \forall s \geq t \tag{15.9}$$

where $W_T$ is the end-of-period wealth, $\lambda$ denotes the coefficient of relative risk aversion (RRA), $R_{p,s+1} = x_s'\left(R_{s+1} - R^f\right) + R^f$ is the gross portfolio return from time $s$ to $s+1$, $x_s$ is the vector of portfolio weights on the risky assets chosen at time $s$, $R_{s+1}$ is the vector of gross returns on the risky assets from time $s$ to $s+1$, $R^f$ is the gross return on the risk-free asset, and $Z_t$ is the information set available at time $t$ captured by the set of conditional volatilities and correlations.[10] In this intertemporal portfolio problem, at date $t$ the investor optimally chooses the portfolio weights $x_t$ conditional on having wealth $W_t$ and information $Z_t$, while taking into account that at every future date $s$, the portfolio weights will be optimally revised conditional on the then available wealth $W_s$ and information $Z_s$. The value function $V_t\left(W_t, Z_t\right)$ denotes the expectation, conditional on information $Z_t$, of the utility of terminal wealth $W_T$ generated by current wealth $W_t$ and the optimal portfolio weights $\left\{x_s^*\right\}_{s=t}^{T-1}$. Following Marquering and Verbeek (2004) and Han (2006), we set $\lambda = 6$, which produces portfolios with reasonable expected return and volatility.

This intertemporal allocation problem does not have a simple and tractable solution as would be the case in a mean-variance setting. We solve for the optimal portfolio choice using the method developed by Brandt et al. (2005). This is a simulation-based method that allows for nonstandard preferences, a large number of state variables, and a large number of assets with arbitrary return distributions. More importantly, the method allows us to directly use the volatility and correlation forecasts from the models in computing the dynamic weights as well as extend our analysis to a Bayesian setting where expected utility is evaluated under the posterior predictive density.

### 15.3.3 PERFORMANCE MEASURES

Following Fleming et al. (2001), we measure the economic value of volatility and correlation timing using the principle that, at any point in time, one set of estimates of the conditional volatilities and correlations is better than a second set if investment decisions based on the first set lead to higher utility. We compute the performance fee, $\Phi$, by equating the average utility of the MLR optimal portfolio with the average utility of the competing optimal portfolio

[10]Note that we allow the risk-free rate to vary over time but drop the time subscript for notational simplicity.

(say the DCC portfolio) that is subject to daily expenses $\Phi$. Since the investor is indifferent to these two strategies, we interpret $\Phi$ as the maximum performance fee she will pay to switch from the MLR to the DCC strategy. In other words, this utility-based criterion measures how much a CRRA investor is willing to pay for conditioning on dynamic volatility and correlation forecasts. To estimate the performance fee, we find the value of $\Phi$ that satisfies

$$\sum_{t=0}^{T-1} E_t\left[U\left(R^*_{p,t+1} - \Phi\right)\right] = \sum_{t=0}^{T-1} E_t\left[U\left(R_{p,t+1}\right)\right], \tag{15.10}$$

where $U(\cdot)$ is the CRRA utility function; $R^*_{p,t+1}$ is the gross portfolio return constructed using the expected return, volatility, and correlation forecasts from the *DCC* model (or another competing model); and $R_{p,t+1}$ is the gross portfolio return implied by the benchmark *MLR* model. We report $\Phi$ in annualized basis points.

### 15.3.4 TRANSACTION COSTS

The effect of transaction costs is an essential consideration in assessing the profitability of trading strategies. We account for this effect by calculating the break-even proportional transaction cost, $\tau^{\mathrm{be}}$, that renders investors indifferent to the two strategies (e.g., Han, 2006). In comparing a dynamic strategy with the benchmark MLR strategy, an investor who pays transaction costs lower than $\tau^{\mathrm{be}}$ will prefer the dynamic strategy. Since $\tau^{\mathrm{be}}$ is the proportional cost paid every time the portfolio is rebalanced, we report $\tau^{\mathrm{be}}$ in daily basis points.[11]

## 15.4 Parameter Uncertainty in Bayesian Asset Allocation

The asset allocation literature typically assumes that investors make optimal decisions with full knowledge of the true parameters of the model. In practice, model parameters have to be estimated, and if there is estimation error, the resulting allocation will be suboptimal. This gives rise to estimation risk in applications of the plug-in method, which replaces the true parameter values by their estimates. In contrast, the Bayesian approach to asset allocation integrates estimation risk into the analysis and deals with parameter uncertainty by assuming that the investor evaluates her expected utility under the predictive distribution, which is determined by historical data and the prior, but does not depend on the parameter estimates.

We consider an investor who takes into account volatility and correlation timing but is uncertain about the parameters of the model. The Bayesian

[11] In recent years, the typical transaction cost a large investor pays in the FX market is 1 pip, which is equal to 0.01 cent. For example, if the USD/GBP exchange rate is equal to 1.5000, 1 pip would raise it to 1.5001, and this would roughly correspond to 1/2 basis point proportional cost.

portfolio choice literature argues that in the presence of parameter uncertainty, the unknown objective return distribution in the expected utility maximization should be replaced with the investor's subjective posterior return distribution reflecting the information contained in the historical data and the investor's prior beliefs about the parameters. Use of predictive distributions was pioneered by Zellner and Chetty (1965) and it was used, among others, by Barberis (2000), Kandel and Stambaugh (1996), and Kan and Zhou (2007). These studies demonstrate that parameter uncertainty is an important dimension of risk, which can substantially affect the investor's optimal allocation. For example, Barberis (2000) shows that for a long-run investor, the Bayesian solution is more conservative than the plug-in approach by taking smaller positions in the risky assets. Intuitively, the Bayesian approach explicitly recognizes estimation risk as an additional source of risk, and therefore, the riskless asset becomes a more attractive investment.

In short, our plan for understanding the effect of parameter uncertainty on volatility and correlation timing is to compare, on the one hand, the allocation of an investor who uses the predictive distribution in forecasting volatilities and correlations with, on the other hand, the allocation of an investor who ignores estimation error, sampling instead from the distribution of returns conditional on fixed parameter estimates. See Appendix B for more details.

## 15.5 Model Uncertainty

Model uncertainty (or model risk) arises from the uncertainty over selecting a model specification. Consistent with our Bayesian approach, a natural criterion for resolving this uncertainty is to construct combined forecasts on the basis of posterior probability of each model. The posterior probability has three important advantages: (i) it is based on the marginal likelihood, and therefore accounts for parameter uncertainty,[12] (ii) it imposes a penalty for lack of parsimony (higher dimension), and (iii) it forms the basis of the BMA strategy discussed below. In computing the posterior probabilities, we set our prior belief to be that all models are equally likely.

We construct combined forecasts based on the BMA strategy and the Bayesian model winner (BMW) strategy (e.g., Geweke and Whiteman, 2006; and Timmermann, 2006). In assessing the economic value of combined forecasts, we treat the BMA and BMW strategies the same way as any of the individual models. For instance, we compute the performance fee and the break-even transaction cost for the BMA relative to the MLR benchmark. We apply BMA and BMW to three universes of models: (i) *VOL* is the universe of all nine univariate volatility specifications under the scalar DCC; (ii) *CORR* is the universe of the five multivariate correlation specifications

[12]Note that the marginal likelihood is an averaged (not a maximized) likelihood, and hence it integrates out parameter uncertainty. We compute the marginal likelihood as in Chib and Jeliazkov (2001).

(CCC, DCC, $DCC_{diag}$, ADCC, $ADCC_{diag}$) with GARCH volatility; and (iii) *FULL* is the complete universe of all 46 models, including the benchmark MLR.

### 15.5.1 THE BMA STRATEGY

The BMA strategy accounts directly for uncertainty in model selection, and is straightforward to implement once we have the output from the MCMC simulations (Wright, 2008). The BMA volatility and correlation forecasts are simply a weighted average of the volatility and correlation forecasts across the $K$ competing models using as weights the posterior probability of each model. Note that the BMA strategy is evaluated ex-ante as the weights are set at time $t$ and the forecasts are for time $t + 1$.

### 15.5.2 THE BMW STRATEGY

Under the BMW strategy, in each time period we select the set of one-step ahead conditional volatilities and correlations from the model that has the highest posterior probability in that period. In other words, every period the BMW strategy only uses the forecasts of the "winner" model in terms of posterior probability and hence discards the forecasts of the other models. Clearly, there is no model averaging in the BMW strategy. Similar to the BMA, the BMW strategy is evaluated ex-ante.

## 15.6 Empirical Results

### 15.6.1 DATA AND DESCRIPTIVE STATISTICS

Our analysis employs daily returns data on four major US dollar nominal spot exchange rates over the period January 1976 to December 2006 corresponding to a total of 8069 observations. The exchange rates are taken from *Datastream* and include the British pound (GBP), the Deutsche mark/euro (EUR), the Swiss franc (CHF) and the Japanese yen (JPY). After the introduction of the euro in January 1999, we use the official Deutsche mark/euro conversion rate to obtain the EUR series. The exchange rate is defined as the US dollar price of a unit of foreign currency so that an increase in the exchange rate implies a depreciation of the US dollar.

Table 15.1 reports descriptive statistics for the daily percentage exchange rate returns. For our sample period, the means are near zero, ranging from $-0.0004$ (or $-0.1\%$ per annum) for GBP to 0.0117 (or 2.9% per annum) for JPY. The daily standard deviations revolve between 0.620 for GBP (or 9.8% per annum) to 0.736 for CHF (or 11.7% per annum). Skewness is negative for two of the four FX returns, while kurtosis ranges from 6.02 for EUR to 9.78 for GBP. Finally, the average return cross-correlations are strongly positive, ranging between 0.336 and 0.819.

TABLE 15.1 **Descriptive Statistics for Daily Exchange Rate Returns**

| | GBP | EUR | CHF | JPY |
|---|---|---|---|---|
| | | *Percentage Returns* | | |
| Mean | −0.0004 | 0.0070 | 0.0095 | 0.0117 |
| Std | 0.620 | 0.653 | 0.736 | 0.664 |
| Skew | −0.356 | −0.005 | 0.083 | 0.609 |
| Kurt | 9.78 | 6.02 | 6.25 | 9.27 |
| | | *Correlation Matrix* | | |
| GBP | 1.000 | 0.557 | 0.495 | 0.336 |
| EUR | 0.557 | 1.000 | 0.819 | 0.491 |
| CHF | 0.495 | 0.819 | 1.000 | 0.543 |
| JPY | 0.336 | 0.491 | 0.543 | 1.000 |

The table summarizes the descriptive statistics for the daily percentage exchange rate returns. The data range from January 1976 to December 2006 for a sample size of 8069 daily observations.

### 15.6.2 BAYESIAN ESTIMATION

We begin by performing Bayesian estimation of the parameters of all models set out in Section 15.2. In addition to the MLR benchmark, the universe of models includes another 45 specifications: CCC, DCC, $\text{DCC}_{\text{diag}}$, ADCC, and $\text{ADCC}_{\text{diag}}$, each under nine alternative GARCH-type volatility specifications.

Table 15.2 presents the posterior mean estimates for the parameters of the asymmetric diagonal $\text{ADCC}_{\text{diag}}$ model with GARCH innovations. We only report the parameter estimates of this model because it is the most general specification that we consider in our analysis. The table shows that both volatilities and correlations are highly persistent for all four FX return series. This is a first indication that volatilities and correlations are predictable. Furthermore, the parameters $\{\pi_i\}$ indicating asymmetry in dynamic correlations are small for all exchange rates, with the exception of the British pound.

In our Bayesian framework, we assess statistical significance by reporting the highest posterior density (HPD) region for each parameter estimate. For example, the 95% *HPD* region is the shortest interval that contains 95% of the posterior distribution. We also report the numerical standard error (NSE) of each parameter, which provides a measure of convergence in the MCMC chain. Table 15.2 shows that statistical significance is much stronger for the volatility and correlation persistence parameters than for the unconditional means. However, all parameter estimates exhibit very low NSE values, thus indicating that the estimates across the MCMC iterations have converged to the posterior means.

With the parameter estimates at hand, we generate the volatility and correlation forecasts used in the asset allocation. Figure 15.1 illustrates the daily in-sample correlation forecasts from the simple DCC-GARCH model.

TABLE 15.2 **Posterior Means for the $ADCC_{diag}$–GARCH Model**

| | GBP | EUR | CHF | JPY |
|---|---|---|---|---|
| | | *Mean Parameters* | | |
| $\mu$ | 0.0036<br>(−0.0080, 0.0151)<br>[0.00009] | 0.0114<br>(−0.0010, 0.0235)<br>[0.00008] | 0.0115<br>(−0.0027, 0.0261)<br>[0.00011] | 0.0092<br>(−0.0031, 0.0216)<br>[0.00009] |
| | | *Volatility Parameters* | | |
| $\omega$ | 0.0062<br>(0.0046, 0.0081)<br>[0.00002] | 0.0040<br>(0.0027, 0.0056)<br>[0.00001] | 0.0049<br>(0.0030, 0.0073)<br>[0.00002] | 0.0046<br>(0.0030, 0.0066)<br>[0.00002] |
| $\alpha$ | 0.0682<br>(0.0579, 0.0790)<br>[0.00009] | 0.0636<br>(0.0543, 0.0732)<br>[0.00009] | 0.0545<br>(0.0460, 0.0634)<br>[0.00008] | 0.0647<br>(0.0550, 0.0752)<br>[0.00010] |
| $\beta$ | 0.9175<br>(0.9043, 0.9296)<br>[0.00012] | 0.9298<br>(0.9194, 0.9394)<br>[0.00010] | 0.9383<br>(0.9276, 0.9480)<br>[0.00010] | 0.9283<br>(0.9157, 0.9395)<br>[0.00012] |
| | | *Correlation Parameters* | | |
| $\gamma$ | 0.9809<br>(0.9782, 0.9833)<br>[0.00004] | 0.9780<br>(0.9765, 0.9797)<br>[0.00003] | 0.9793<br>(0.9775, 0.9810)<br>[0.00003] | 0.9871<br>(0.9854, 0.9886)<br>[0.00003] |
| $\delta$ | 0.1540<br>(0.1437, 0.1650)<br>[0.00020] | 0.1977<br>(0.1900, 0.2046)<br>[0.00013] | 0.1927<br>(0.1842, 0.2002)<br>[0.00014] | 0.1439<br>(0.1357, 0.1518)<br>[0.00014] |
| $\pi$ | 0.1298<br>(0.1074, 0.1522)<br>[0.00041] | 0.0460<br>(0.0241, 0.0674)<br>[0.00041] | 0.0364<br>(0.0162, 0.0566)<br>[0.00040] | 0.0334<br>(0.0114, 0.0559)<br>[0.00041] |

The table presents the Bayesian MCMC estimates of the posterior means of the $ADCC_{diag}$-GARCH model applied on daily percentage exchange rate returns from January 1976 to December 2006. The 95% highest posterior density (*HPD*) region for each parameter estimate (the shortest interval that contains 95% of the posterior distribution) is reported in parentheses, and the numerical standard error (*NSE*) in brackets.

### 15.6.3 EVALUATING VOLATILITY AND CORRELATION TIMING

We assess the economic value of FX volatility and correlation timing by analyzing the performance of dynamically rebalanced portfolios constructed using the set of forecasts from the multivariate models. Our forecasting analysis is conducted both in sample and out of sample. We first discuss the in-sample results for which we have the full range of empirical findings. The out-of-sample analysis is more focused than the in-sample analysis because it is computationally very demanding to reestimate period-by-period 46 multivariate model specifications over a 31-year sample. The out-of-sample results are reviewed at the end.

The economic evaluation focuses on the performance fee that a US investor is willing to pay for switching from the benchmark to a competing strategy. The in-sample fees are reported in Table 15.3, which shows the economic value of each volatility and correlation specification relative to the benchmark MLR

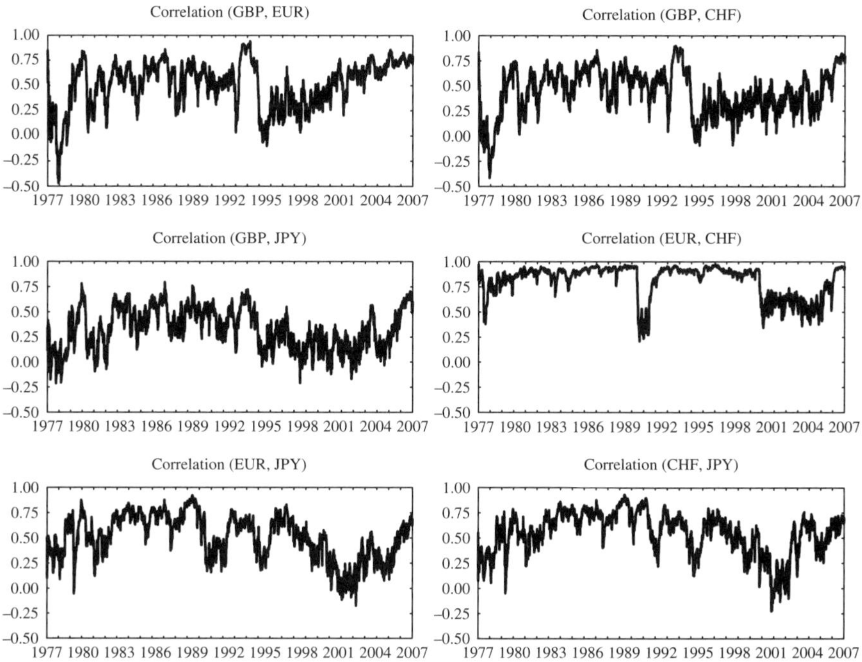


**FIGURE 15.1 Daily correlation forecasts. The figure displays the in-sample daily correlation forecasts between four US dollar exchange rate return series using the simple (scalar symmetric) DCC-GARCH model. The in-sample period uses daily observations ranging from January 1976 to December 2006.**

model. The table first reports the results for CRRA utility under the plug-in method for an extensive set of models; then, for a smaller number of selected models, we allow for parameter uncertainty only in volatilities and correlations, but not in the mean; finally, we present the results with full parameter uncertainty in the mean, volatilities, and correlations.

We first show that there is substantial economic value associated with volatility timing. Then we show that there is high economic value in timing dynamic FX correlations over and above the economic value of volatility timing. We illustrate these results by analyzing portfolio performance: switching from the static MLR to the CCC-GARCH model gives a high fee of 386 annual basis points (bps); switching from MLR to the DCC-GARCH model raises the fee to 696 bps. This is also reflected in the Sharpe ratio (SR) of the strategies: the SR rises from 1.08 for the MLR to 1.36 for CCC-GARCH and then to 1.62 for DCC-GARCH. In short, these results demonstrate that it is worth using high-dimensional multivariate models for dynamic correlations as they generate significant economic value.[13]

[13]Note that the good performance of the static MLR benchmark primarily reflects the profitability of the standard carry trade strategy and the fact that these results are in sample. As we will see

**TABLE 15.3 In-Sample Portfolio Performance**

| *Strategy* | $\mu_p$ | $\sigma_p$ | SR | $\Phi$ | $\tau^{be}$ |
|---|---|---|---|---|---|
| | | *Plug-In Method* | | | |
| MLR | 18.8 | 11.2 | 1.08 | | |
| CCC-GARCH | 22.7 | 11.8 | 1.36 | 386 | 10.5 |
| CCC-AVGARCH | 22.1 | 12.0 | 1.28 | 327 | 7.0 |
| CCC-NARCH | 22.4 | 11.9 | 1.32 | 356 | 8.4 |
| CCC-EGARCH | 22.9 | 12.1 | 1.34 | 404 | 8.5 |
| CCC-ZARCH | 22.6 | 12.1 | 1.32 | 377 | 8.1 |
| CCC-GJR-GARCH | 22.8 | 11.8 | 1.37 | 399 | 10.9 |
| CCC-APGARCH | 22.7 | 11.9 | 1.34 | 383 | 9.1 |
| CCC-AGARCH | 23.0 | 11.8 | 1.37 | 412 | 11.2 |
| CCC-NAGARCH | 23.0 | 11.8 | 1.38 | 416 | 11.3 |
| DCC-GARCH | 25.8 | 11.7 | 1.62 | 696 | 11.9 |
| $\text{DCC}_{\text{diag}} - \text{GARCH}$ | 25.7 | 11.7 | 1.62 | 691 | 11.1 |
| ADCC-GARCH | 25.7 | 11.7 | 1.62 | 691 | 11.8 |
| $\text{ADCC}_{\text{diag}} - \text{GARCH}$ | 25.8 | 11.7 | 1.62 | 694 | 11.1 |
| | | *Parameter Uncertainty in Volatilities and Correlations* | | | |
| MLR | 18.8 | 11.2 | 1.08 | | |
| CCC-GARCH | 22.7 | 11.8 | 1.36 | 386 | 10.5 |
| DCC-GARCH | 25.7 | 11.7 | 1.62 | 692 | 11.8 |
| | | *Full Parameter Uncertainty* | | | |
| MLR | 18.5 | 10.8 | 1.08 | | |
| CCC-GARCH | 22.3 | 11.4 | 1.36 | 371 | 9.9 |
| DCC-GARCH | 25.2 | 11.6 | 1.58 | 655 | 11.0 |

The table reports the in-sample economic value of selected currency strategies investing in the US dollar, British pound, Deutsche mark \ euro, Swiss franc and Japanese yen. MLR is the benchmark strategy using the MLR model, CCC is a dynamic strategy using the CCC model, and DCC is a dynamic strategy using the DCC model. The strategies build a portfolio by investing in five bonds from the US, UK, Germany, Switzerland, and Japan and using the four exchange rate forecasts to convert the portfolio return in US dollars. The annualized percentage mean, percentage volatility, and Sharpe ratio are denoted by $\mu_p$, $\sigma_p$, and SR, respectively. $\Phi$ denotes the performance fee an investor with CRRA utility and a degree of RRA equal to 6 is willing to pay for switching from MLR to one of the dynamic strategies and is reported in annual basis points. The break-even transaction cost $\tau^{be}$ is defined as the minimum daily proportional cost that cancels out the utility advantage of a given strategy and is reported in daily basis points. The *plug-in method* uses mean, volatility, and correlation forecasts without accounting for parameter uncertainty. *Parameter uncertainty in volatilities and correlations* accounts for parameter uncertainty only in volatility and correlation forecasts. *Full parameter uncertainty* accounts for parameter uncertainty in all forecasts. The sample period covers daily data from January 1976 to December 2006.

Table 15.3 reveals another important finding that justifies the choice of economic criteria in assessing alternative specifications for dynamic correlations. A purely statistical analysis may conclude that the rich correlation structure of diagonal DCC models with asymmetric correlations leads to improved performance (e.g., Cappiello et al., 2006).[14] This is not the case in evaluating correlation timing in the context of asset allocation as the choice of dynamic volatility specification (e.g., GARCH vs EGARCH) or dynamic correlation specification (e.g., DCC vs ADCC) has little effect on the results. We find that economic value is generated by making volatilities and correlations dynamic, irrespective of their exact specification. Therefore, the investor is much better off with dynamic correlations, and the simple (scalar symmetric) DCC model with GARCH volatility is as good as any other model we consider. In our framework, increasing the sophistication of the econometric specification does not enhance the economic value of the simple DCC model.

If transaction costs are sufficiently high, the period-by-period fluctuations in the dynamic weights of an optimal strategy will render the strategy too costly to implement relative to the benchmark. We evaluate the impact of transaction costs on dynamic asset allocation by computing the break-even transaction cost, $\tau^{\text{be}}$, as the minimum proportional cost that cancels out the utility advantage (and hence positive performance fee) of a given strategy. In comparing a dynamic strategy with the static MLR strategy, an investor who pays a transaction cost lower than $\tau^{\text{be}}$ will prefer the dynamic strategy. The $\tau^{\text{be}}$ values are expressed in daily basis points. Table 15.3 shows that the $\tau^{\text{be}}$ values generally revolve around 10 *bps* for constant correlation models and 11 *bps* for dynamic correlation models. Given that the cost of portfolio rebalancing for large investors in the FX market is around 1 or 2 *bps*, we conclude that the economic value of correlation timing is robust to reasonable transaction costs.[15]

#### 15.6.3.1 The Effect of Parameter Uncertainty.

The plug-in approach we have discussed so far takes the parameter estimates as true and ignores estimation error. Intuitively, however, the higher the number of parameters we estimate the more uncertain we are about the validity of our volatility and correlation forecasts. We address this concern by evaluating expected utility under the Bayesian predictive density, which reflects the posterior information contained in the returns data and the investor's prior beliefs, but does not depend on the parameter estimates. Table 15.3 shows that parameter uncertainty in second

later, the out-of-sample Sharpe ratios tend to be lower but confirm that dynamic volatilities and correlations significantly enhance the performance of dynamically rebalanced FX portfolios.

[14]We can show this by computing the log-likelihood values or posterior model probabilities. Since we focus on the economic value of the models, we do not report these statistical results, but they are available on request.

[15]We also calculate the portfolio performance of selected models using mean-variance utility since this is what is predominantly used by the literature (e.g., Della Corte et al. 2008, 2012; Fleming et al. 2001; West et al. 1993). We find that the economic value of correlation timing with mean-variance utility is still high, but with CRRA utility it tends to be a bit more pronounced, as the latter captures the effect of higher order moments. These results are available on request.

moments has little or no effect on portfolio performance. This result has a simple intuitive explanation. Volatilities and correlations are highly persistent and tend to be estimated with high precision. As a consequence, parameter uncertainty in volatilities and correlations will not play a prominent role for a one-step-ahead predictive horizon.

In contrast, parameter uncertainty turns out to be more important for the first moments, which are notoriously difficult to estimate with high precision. Our results suggest that the unconditional means in all models are hard to pinpoint with great accuracy. For example, the fee for the DCC model falls from 696 in the plug-in case to 655 in the full parameter uncertainty case, whereas the Sharpe ratio falls from 1.62 to 1.58. As discussed in Abhyankar et al. (2005), parameter uncertainty makes FX investors more cautious by taking less risk and thus expecting a lower reward-to-risk ratio. Since parameter uncertainty is an additional source of risk in asset allocation, investors will optimally choose less risky portfolios, and thus attain lower fees and lower Sharpe ratios. At any rate, despite the uncertainty over a large number of parameters, the economic gains from volatility and correlation timing remain strong.

**15.6.3.2 The Effect of Model Uncertainty.** We evaluate the effect of model uncertainty on volatility and correlation timing by exploring whether portfolio performance improves when combining the forecasts from the large set of models we estimate. We focus on the BMA and BMW strategies, which are evaluated ex-ante and are applied to three universes of models: *VOL* is the universe of all nine GARCH-type univariate volatility specifications we estimate under the simple (scalar symmetric) DCC model, *CORR* is the universe of the five multivariate correlation specifications (CCC, DCC, $\text{DCC}_{\text{diag}}$, ADCC, $\text{ADCC}_{\text{diag}}$,) with GARCH volatility; and FULL is the complete universe of all 46 models (including the benchmark MLR).

The economic value of combined forecasts is reported in Table 15.4, which assesses the impact of model uncertainty under the Bayesian predictive density. Hence we evaluate model uncertainty, while at the same time, we account for parameter uncertainty. The results in Table 15.4 indicate that there is high economic value in BMA forecast combinations and even higher value in the BMW strategy. For instance, compared to the DCC-GARCH model, which under full parameter uncertainty delivers a Sharpe ratio of 1.58, the BMA-FULL combined strategy increases the Sharpe ratio to 1.73 and the BMW-FULL raises it further to 1.81. In conclusion, accounting for model uncertainty by forming combined forecasts delivers additional economic value and makes the case for volatility and correlation timing more robust.

**15.6.3.3 Out-of-Sample Portfolio Performance.** The results reported so far are in-sample results for the period January 1976 to December 2006. In this section, we discuss out-of-sample portfolio performance. The out-of-sample period ranges from January 1986 to December 2006 and uses a rolling window of 10 years. Since this exercise is very computationally intensive, we generate daily out-of-sample forecasts using month-by-month parameter estimates for

**TABLE 15.4 In-Sample Portfolio Performance of Combined Forecasts**

| *Strategy* | $\mu_p$ | $\sigma_p$ | SR | $\Phi$ | $\tau^{\text{be}}$ |
|---|---|---|---|---|---|
| | | *Bayesian Model Averaging* | | | |
| BMA-VOL | 24.2 | 10.6 | 1.65 | 568 | 7.9 |
| BMA-CORR | 25.1 | 11.6 | 1.58 | 653 | 10.6 |
| BMA-FULL | 24.0 | 10.0 | 1.73 | 554 | 7.2 |
| | | *Bayesian Model Winner* | | | |
| BMW-VOL | 24.8 | 10.4 | 1.73 | 631 | 3.4 |
| BMW-CORR | 25.3 | 11.5 | 1.60 | 664 | 8.2 |
| BMW-FULL | 23.8 | 9.4 | 1.81 | 539 | 2.2 |

The table assesses the impact of model uncertainty on correlation timing by presenting the in-sample portfolio performance of combined forecasts. Expected utility is evaluated under the predictive density, thus accounting for parameter uncertainty. BMA denotes Bayesian model averaging and BMW Bayesian model winner, which are applied on three universes of models: *VOL* is the universe of all GARCH-type univariate volatility specifications under the scalar symmetric DCC model, *CORR* is the universe of all multivariate correlation specifications (CCC and the four DCC specifications) with GARCH volatility, and *FULL* is the complete universe of all 46 model specifications (including the benchmark *MLR*). The annualized percentage mean, percentage volatility, and Sharpe ratio are denoted by $\mu_p$, $\sigma_p$, and SR, respectively. $\Phi$ denotes the performance fee an investor with CRRA utility and a degree of RRA equal to 6 is willing to pay for switching from MLR to one of the dynamic forecast combinations and is reported in annual basis points. The break-even transaction cost $\tau^{\text{be}}$ is defined as the minimum proportional cost that cancels out the utility advantage of a given strategy and is reported in daily basis points. The sample period covers daily data from January 1976 to December 2006.

the means, volatilities, and correlations. This means, for instance, that all daily forecasts generated for January 1986 are based on parameters estimated using information up to the end of December 1985. Moreover, we focus our out-of-sample discussion on the family of DCC models with GARCH innovations since GARCH volatility performs as well as any other volatility specification.

The results are reported in Table 15.5 and show that the out-of-sample findings are qualitatively similar to the in-sample findings. The out-of-sample Sharpe ratios confirm that there is still high incremental economic value in both volatility and correlation timing: the Sharpe ratio is 0.57 for the MLR, 0.86 for the CCC, and 0.96 for the DCC. The out-of-sample Sharpe ratios are plotted in Figure 15.2. The performance fees are of the same order of magnitude as in sample: 457 bps for the CCC and 800 bps for the DCC. Again, diagonal or asymmetric DCC specifications do not add further economic value to the simple scalar symmetric DCC. Finally, the effect of full parameter uncertainty reduces the economic value of volatility and correlation timing as investors will optimally choose less risky portfolios, and thus attain lower fees and lower Sharpe ratios. With full parameter uncertainty, the Sharpe ratios are 0.56 for MLR, 0.73 for CCC, and 0.79 for DCC. Despite out-of-sample estimation and the uncertainty over a large number of parameters, there are still economic gains from volatility and correlation timing.

**TABLE 15.5 Out-of-Sample Portfolio Performance**

| *Strategy* | $\mu_p$ | $\sigma_p$ | SR | $\Phi$ | $\tau^{\text{be}}$ |
|---|---|---|---|---|---|
| | | *Plug-In Method* | | | |
| MLR | 11.2 | 10.7 | 0.57 | | |
| CCC-GARCH | 16.0 | 12.8 | 0.86 | 457 | 7.8 |
| DCC-GARCH | 19.8 | 15.4 | 0.96 | 800 | 9.7 |
| $\text{DCC}_{\text{diag}}$-GARCH | 19.1 | 14.9 | 0.94 | 732 | 8.4 |
| ADCC-GARCH | 19.6 | 15.3 | 0.95 | 774 | 9.4 |
| $\text{ADCC}_{\text{diag}}$-GARCH | 18.7 | 14.9 | 0.91 | 693 | 7.6 |
| | | *Parameter Uncertainty in Volatilities and Correlations* | | | |
| MLR | 11.2 | 10.7 | 0.57 | | |
| CCC-GARCH | 16.0 | 12.8 | 0.86 | 460 | 6.6 |
| DCC-GARCH | 19.9 | 15.4 | 0.96 | 812 | 8.4 |
| | | *Full Parameter Uncertainty* | | | |
| MLR | 11.4 | 11.2 | 0.56 | | |
| CCC-GARCH | 16.2 | 15.2 | 0.73 | 428 | 4.2 |
| DCC-GARCH | 18.3 | 16.8 | 0.79 | 613 | 4.9 |

The table shows the out-of-sample economic value of selected currency strategies investing in the US dollar, British pound, Deutsche mark \ euro, Swiss franc and Japanese yen. *MLR* is the benchmark strategy using the MLR model, CCC is a dynamic strategy using the CCC model, and DCC is a dynamic strategy using the DCC model. The strategies build a portfolio by investing in five bonds from the US, UK, Germany, Switzerland, and Japan and using the four exchange rate forecasts to convert the portfolio return in US dollars. The annualized percentage mean, percentage volatility, and Sharpe ratio are denoted by $\mu_p$, $\sigma_p$, and SR, respectively. $\Phi$ denotes the performance fee an investor with CRRA utility and a degree of RRA equal to 6 is willing to pay for switching from MLR to one of the dynamic strategies and is reported in annual basis points. The break-even transaction cost $\tau^{\text{be}}$ is defined as the minimum daily proportional cost that cancels out the utility advantage of a given strategy and is reported in daily basis points. The plug-in method uses mean, volatility, and correlation forecasts without accounting for parameter uncertainty. *Parameter uncertainty in volatilities and correlations* accounts for parameter uncertainty only in volatility and correlation forecasts. *Full parameter uncertainty*accounts for parameter uncertainty in all forecasts. The sample period covers daily data from January 1976 to December 2006. The out-of-sample period uses daily observations from January 1986 to December 2006 and sequentially updates the parameter estimates month-by-month using a 10-year rolling window.

## 15.7 Conclusion

The empirical literature in financial economics has long determined that asset return volatilities and correlations vary over time. Therefore, accurate forecasts of volatilities and correlations are critical for an investor's optimal asset allocation. This has motivated a long line of research dedicated to developing tractable multivariate volatility models. This chapter provides a

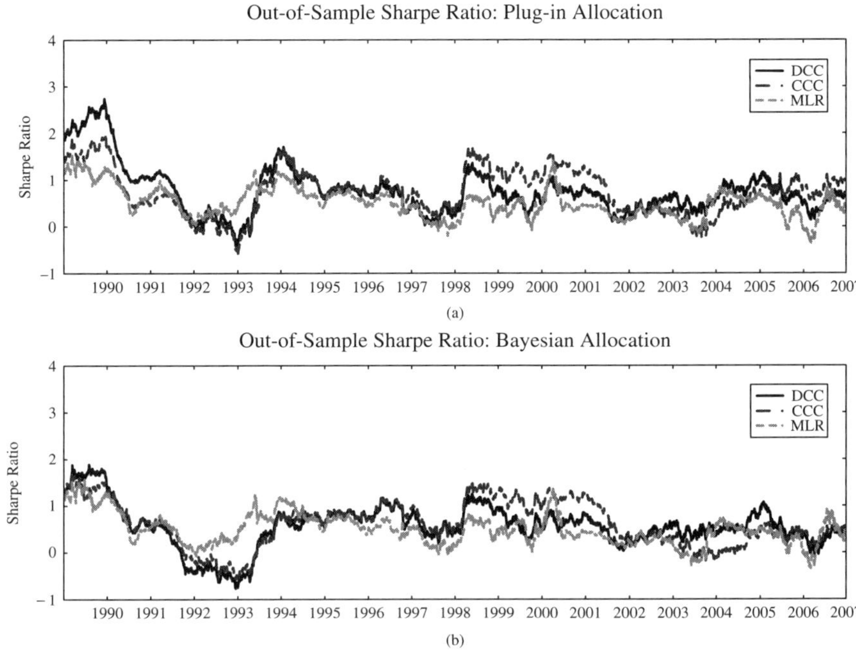


**FIGURE 15.2** **Out-of-sample Sharpe ratios. The figure displays the out-of-sample Sharpe ratios for three strategies. MLR is the benchmark strategy with static volatilities and correlations, CCC has dynamic GARCH volatilities but constant correlations, and DCC has dynamic (scalar symmetric) correlations and GARCH volatilities. (a) Plug-in allocation and (b) Bayesian allocation with full parameter uncertainty. All strategies are evaluated for a degree of RRA equal to 6. The figure displays the case of zero transaction costs. The out-of-sample period uses daily observations from January 1986 to December 2006 and sequentially updates the parameter estimates month-by-month using a 10-year rolling window. The Sharpe ratios are calculated using a 3-year rolling window and hence start in January 1989.**

comprehensive evaluation of the economic value of these models for dynamic strategies that invest in the FX market. We focus on the portfolio choice of an investor who is uncertain about the parameter estimates and the model specification.

Our analysis shows that there is high economic value in timing both FX volatilities and correlations: the performance fee for volatility timing is about 4% per year and correlation timing adds a further 3% per year. This result is robust to reasonable transaction costs, which in FX trading are generally low. It is also robust to parameter uncertainty, which has little or no effect on the economic value of volatility and correlation timing. We find that the model with the simplest structure in dynamic correlations and volatilities performs equally well as models with asymmetric correlations, richer correlation structure, or alternative volatility specifications. Despite its simplicity, therefore, the DCC model is a powerful instrument in international asset allocation. In conclusion, both volatility and correlation timing matter to an international investor, and it pays to take dynamic FX volatilities correlations into consideration in asset allocation strategies.

## APPENDIX A: UNIVARIATE MODELS FOR VOLATILITY TIMING

We estimate the multivariate correlation models under the following nine volatility specifications for each asset:

1. GARCH: Bollerslev (1986)

$$\sigma_t^2 = \omega + \alpha u_{t-1}^2 + \beta \sigma_{t-1}^2$$

2. Absolute Value GARCH (AVGARCH: Taylor, 1986)

$$\sigma_t = \omega + \alpha |u_{t-1}| + \beta \sigma_{t-1}$$

3. Nonlinear GARCH (NARCH: Higgins and Bera, 1992)

$$\sigma_t^\tau = \omega + \alpha |u_{t-1}|^\tau + \beta \sigma_{t-1}^\tau$$

4. Exponential GARCH (EGARCH: Nelson, 1991)

$$\ln\left(\sigma_t^2\right) = \omega + \alpha \varepsilon_{t-1} + \kappa\left(|\varepsilon_{t-1}| - E\left[|\varepsilon_t|\right]\right) + \beta \ln(\sigma_{t-1}^2);$$

$$\varepsilon_{t-1} = \frac{u_{t-1}}{\sigma_{t-1}}; \quad E\left[|\varepsilon_t|\right] = \sqrt{\frac{2}{\pi}}$$

5. Threshold GARCH (ZARCH: Zakoian, 1994)

$$\sigma_t = \omega + \alpha\left(|u_{t-1}| - \kappa u_{t-1}\right) + \beta \sigma_{t-1}$$

6. GJR-GARCH (Glosten et al., 1993)

$$\sigma_t^2 = \omega + \alpha\left(|u_{t-1}| - \kappa u_{t-1}\right)^2 + \beta \sigma_{t-1}^2$$

7. Asymmetric Power GARCH (APGARCH: Ding et al., 1993)

$$\sigma_t^\tau = \omega + \alpha\left(|u_{t-1}| - \kappa u_{t-1}\right)^\tau + \beta \sigma_{t-1}^\tau$$

8. Asymmetric GARCH (AGARCH: Engle, 1990)

$$\sigma_t^2 = \omega + \alpha\left(u_{t-1} + \kappa\right)^2 + \beta \sigma_{t-1}^2$$

**9.** Nonlinear Asymmetric GARCH (NAGARCH: Engle and Ng, 1993):

$$\sigma_t^2 = \omega + \alpha \left(u_{t-1} + \kappa\sigma_t\right)^2 + \beta\sigma_{t-1}^2$$

## APPENDIX B: PARAMETER UNCERTAINTY AND THE PREDICTIVE DENSITY

We account for parameter uncertainty in Bayesian asset allocation by computing the predictive density of $y_{t+1}$ as follows:

$$p\left(y_{t+1} \mid y_t\right) = \int_\theta p\left(y_{t+1}, \theta \mid y_t\right) \mathrm{d}\theta = \int_\theta p\left(y_{t+1} \mid y_t, \theta\right) \pi\left(\theta\right) \mathrm{d}\theta \qquad (15.11)$$

When the portfolio allocation problem is intertemporal, the solution should take into account the fact that the posterior distribution changes each period as the investor incorporates into her posterior beliefs information contained in new data realizations. This allows us to investigate jointly the effect of predictability and parameter uncertainty in dynamic asset allocation.[16] For instance, we can compare four different portfolio problems corresponding to four subjective data-generating processes.

- *No parameter uncertainty, no predictability*: the investor uses the point estimates of the parameters and treats means, volatilities, and correlations as constant over time. This is equivalent to using the MLR model in plug-in asset allocation.
- *No parameter uncertainty, predictability*: the investor uses the point estimates of the parameters but takes into account predictability in volatilities and correlations. This is equivalent to using the dynamic models in plug-in asset allocation.
- *Parameter uncertainty, no predictability*: the investor takes into account parameter uncertainty and treats means, volatilities, and correlations as constant over time. This is equivalent to using the MLR model in Bayesian asset allocation.
- *Parameter uncertainty, predictability*: the investor accounts for both parameter uncertainty and predictability in volatilities and correlations. This is equivalent to using the dynamic models in Bayesian asset allocation.

[16]Owing to the complexity and high dimension of the empirical models for dynamic correlation, the combination of parameter uncertainty and predictability that we examine here is slightly different from the case of full Bayesian learning considered by, for example, Brandt et al. (2005). In our Bayesian asset allocation, given the full MCMC sample of the parameters, we update the posterior second moments in every time period. However, it is not feasible to also update the parameters of the time-varying second moments. The case of full Bayesian learning would be feasible if the moments were constant over time as in the case of the MLR model.

## Acknowledgments

The authors are indebted for useful conversations or constructive comments to Torben Andersen, Federico Bandi, Luc Bauwens, Valentina Corradi, Frank Diebold, Robert Engle, Gabriele Fiorentini, Rene Garcia, John Geweke, Eric Ghysels, Xing Jin, Mico Loretan, John Maheu, Anna Pavlova, Tarun Ramadorai, Neil Shephard, Georgios Skoulakis, Jun Tu, Herman van Dijk, and Guofu Zhou as well as to participants at the 2008 Oxford-Man Conference in "Financial Econometrics and Vast Data" at Oxford, UK; the 2008 China International Conference in Finance at Dalian, China; the 2008 European Meeting of the Econometric Society at Milan, Italy; the 2008 Far Eastern and South Asian Meeting of the Econometric Society at Singapore; the 2008 Bayesian Workshop at the Rimini Center for Economic Analysis, Italy; the 2008 Small Open Economies in a Globalized World Conference at Waterloo, Canada; the 2007 Multivariate Volatility Models Conference at Faro, Portugal; and the CORE seminar at Universite Catholique de Louvain.

## REFERENCES

Abhyankar A, Sarno L, Valente G. Exchange rates and fundamentals: evidence on the economic value of predictability. J Int Econ 2005;66:325–348.

Ang A, Bekaert G. International asset allocation with regime shifts. Rev Financ Stud 2002;15:1137–1187.

Ang A, Chen J. Asymmetric correlations of equity portfolios. J Financ Econ 2002;63:443–494.

Avramov D. Stock return predictability and model uncertainty. J Financ Econ 2002;64:423–458.

Barberis N. Investing for the long run when returns are predictable. J Finance 2000;55:225–264.

Bauwens L, Laurent S. A new class of multivariate skew densities with application to generalized autoregressive conditional heteroskedasticity models. J Bus Econ Stat 2005;23:346–354.

Bollerslev T. Generalized autoregressive conditional heteroskedasticity. J Economet 1986;31:307–327.

Bollerslev T. Modeling the coherence in short-run nominal exchange rates: a multivariate generalized ARCH model. Rev Econ Stat 1990;72:498–505.

Bollerslev T, Engle RF, Wooldridge JM. A capital asset pricing model with time varying covariances. J Pol Econ 1988;96:116–131.

Brandt MW. Portfolio choice problems. In: Ait-Sahalia Y, Hansen LP, editors. Handbook of financial econometrics. New York: Elsevier; 2009.

Brandt MW, Goyal A, Santa-Clara P, Stroud JR. A simulation approach to dynamic portfolio choice with an application to learning about return predictability. Rev Financ Stud 2005;18:831–873.

Buraschi A, Porchia P, Trojani F. Correlation risk and optimal portfolio choice. J Finance 2010;65:393–420.

Burnside C, Eichenbaum M, Kleshchelski I, Rebelo S. Do peso problems explain the returns to the carry trade? Rev Financ Stud 2011;24:853–891.

Cappiello L, Engle RF, Sheppard K. Asymmetric dynamics in the correlations of global equity and bond returns. J Financ Economet 2006;4:537–572.

Chib S, Jeliazkov I. Marginal likelihood from the metropolis-hastings output. J Am Stat Assoc 2001;96:270–281.

Chib S, Nardari F, Shephard N. Markov chain Monte Carlo methods for stochastic volatility models. J Economet 2002;108:281–316.

Chib S, Nardari F, Shephard N. Analysis of high dimensional multivariate stochastic volatility models. J Economet 2006;134:341–371.

Cremers M. Stock return predictability: a bayesian model selection perspective. Rev Financ Stud 2002;15:1223–1249.

Della Corte P, Sarno L, Sestieri G. The predictive information content of external imbalances for exchange rate returns: how much is it worth? Rev Econ Stat 2012; 94: 100–115.

Della Corte P, Sarno L, Thornton DL. The expectation hypothesis of the term structure of very short-term rates: statistical tests and economic value. J Financ Econ 2008;89:158–174.

Della Corte P, Sarno L, Tsiakas I. An economic evaluation of empirical exchange rate models. Rev Financ Stud 2009;22:3491–3530.

Della Corte P, Sarno L, Tsiakas I. Spot and forward volatility in foreign exchange. J Financ Econ 2011;100:496–513.

Della Corte P, Tsiakas I. Statistical and economic methods for evaluating exchange rate predictability. In: James J, Sarno L, Marsh IW, editors. Handbook of exchange rates. London: Wiley; 2012. Forthcoming.

Diebold FX, Nerlove M. The dynamics of exchange rate volatility: a multivariate latent factor ARCH model. J Appl Economet 1989;4:1–21.

Ding Z, Engle RF, Granger C. A long-memory property of stock market returns and a new model. J Empir Finance 1993;1:83–106.

Driessen J, Maenhout P, Vilkov G. The price of correlation risk: evidence from equity options. J Finance 2009;64:1377–1406.

Engle RF. Discussion: stock market volatility and the crash of '87. Rev Financ Stud 1990;3:103–106.

Engle RF. Dynamic conditional correlation: a simple class of multivariate generalized autoregressive conditional heteroskedasticity models. J Bus Econ Stat 2002;20:339–350.

Engle RF, Colacito R. Testing and valuing dynamic correlations for asset allocation. J Bus Econ Stat 2006;24:238–253.

Engle RF, Kroner KF. Multivariate simultaneous generalized ARCH. Economet Theory 1995;11:122–150.

Engle RF, Ng VK. Measuring and testing the impact of news on volatility. J Finance 1993;48:1749–1778.

Engle RF, Sheppard K. Theoretical and empirical properties of dynamic conditional correlation multivariate GARCH. Unpublished working paper, University of California at San Diego; 2001.

Engle RF, Shephard N, Sheppard K. Fitting vast dimensional time-varying covariance models. Unpublished working paper, University of Oxford; 2008.

Fleming J, Kirby C, Ostdiek B. The economic value of volatility timing. J Finance 2001;56:329–352.

Fleming J, Kirby C, Ostdiek B. The economic value of volatility timing using 'Realized' volatility. J Financ Econ 2003;67:473–509.

Geweke J, Whiteman C. Bayesian forecasting. In: Elliott G, Granger CWJ, Timmermann A, editors. Handbook of economic forecasting. Amsterdam: Elsevier; 2006.

Glosten LR, Jagannathan R, Runkle DE. On the relationship between the expected value and the volatility of the nominal excess return on stocks. J Finance 1993;48:1779–1801.

Goetzmann WN, Li L, Rouwenhorst KG. Long term global market correlations. J Bus 2005;78:1–38.

Gourieroux C, Jasiak J, Sufana R. The wishart autoregressive process of multivariate stochastic volatility. J Economet 2009;150:167–181.

Han Y. Asset allocation with a high dimensional latent factor stochastic volatility model. Rev Financ Stud 2006;19:237–271.

Harvey AC, Ruiz E, Shephard N. Multivariate stochastic variance models. Rev Econ Stud 1994;61:247–264.

Higgins ML, Bera AK. A class of nonlinear ARCH models. Int Econ Rev 1992;33:137–158.

Kan R, Zhou G. Optimal portfolio choice with parameter uncertainty. J Financ Quant Anal 2007;42:621–656.

Kandel S, Stambaugh RF. On the predictability of stock returns: an asset-allocation perspective. J Finance 1996;51:385–424.

Kim S, Shephard N, Chib S. Stochastic volatility: likelihood inference and comparison with ARCH models. Rev Econ Stud 1998;65:361–393.

Ledoit O, Santa-Clara P, Wolf M. Flexible multivariate garch modeling with an application to international stock markets. Rev Econ Stat 2003;85:735–747.

Longin F, Solnik B. Is the correlation in international equity returns constant: 1960–1990. J Int Money Finance 1995;14:3–26.

Longin F, Solnik B. Extreme correlation of international equity markets. J Finance 2001;56:649–675.

Marquering W, Verbeek M. The economic value of predicting stock index returns and volatility. J Financ Quant Anal 2004;39:407–429.

Meese RA, Rogoff K. Empirical exchange rate models of the seventies: do they fit out of sample? J Int Econ 1983;14:3–24.

Menkhoff L, Sarno L, Schmeling M, Schrimpf A. Carry trades and global foreign exchange volatility. J Finance 2012;67:681–718.

Nelson DB. Conditional heteroskedasticity in asset returns: a new approach. Econometrica 1991;59:347–370.

Palandri A. Sequential conditional correlations: inference and evaluation. J Economet 2009;153:122–132.

Philipov A, Glickman ME. Multivariate stochastic volatility via wishart processes. J Bus Econ Stat 2006;24:313–328.

Taylor SJ. Modeling financial time series. Chichester: John Wiley and Sons, Ltd; 1986.

Timmermann A. Forecast combinations. In: Elliott G, Granger CWJ, Timmermann A, editors. Handbook of economic forecasting. Amsterdam: Elsevier; 2006.

Tsiakas I. Periodic stochastic volatility and fat tails. J Financ Economet 2006;4:90–135.

West KD, Edison HJ, Cho D. A utility-based comparison of some models of exchange rate volatility. J Int Econ 1993;35:23–45.

Wright JH. Bayesian model averaging and exchange rate forecasting. J Economet 2008;146:329–341.

Zakoian J-M. Threshold heteroskedastic models. J Econ Dyn Control 1994;18:931–955.

Zellner A, Chetty VK. Prediction and decision problems in regression models from the bayesian point of view. J Am Stat Assoc 1965;60:608–616.

# PART THREE

# FX Markets and Products

CHAPTER SIXTEEN

# Active Currency Management Part I: Is There a Premium for Currency Investing (Beta)


**GEOFFREY KENDRICK**
Nomura

**SAEED AMEN**
Nomura


## 16.1 Introduction

We use the Australian dollar (AUD) as our example. If we think of the factors which impact this currency, we can broadly split them into two categories. Firstly, we have factors specific to the AUD, which are idiosyncratic risks. For example, this can include Australian economic data and the price of commodities which Australia exports such as coal and iron. Secondly, we have factors from the broad market, which we shall term as *broad market risk*. This can include market expectations for U.S. growth and the state of global equities. The interaction between these two factors drives price action in the AUD.

The CAPM (capital asset pricing model) is a model which attempts to reconcile these two factors (French, 2003). Essentially, the model regresses an asset's returns against the broad market. The constant of this regression is known as *alpha*. Alpha basically gives an indication of the return which is specific to that asset. The gradient of this regression is known as *beta*. This gives the sensitivity


*Handbook of Exchange Rates*, First Edition. Edited by Jessica James, Ian W. Marsh, and Lucio Sarno.

of that asset to the broad market. If alpha is very low and beta is very high, we conjecture that the asset is highly correlated to the market (a beta of 1 would imply a one-to-one relationship with the market). If the beta of the asset were negative, it would imply that the asset is negatively correlated to the market. Hence, as the market rose, this asset would lose value.

In addition to simply looking at an asset's performance versus the broad market, we can also compare individual trading strategies against the broad market. The objective is to assess how much of the strategy's returns were a result of swings in the broad market or were specific to the strategy itself. If the strategy exhibits a high level of beta, but little or no alpha, it would imply that investors' returns would be similar to simply investing in the broad market (or worse if the management fee is high). In a sense, hedge funds are designed to generate alpha, strategies which are independent of the broad market direction. It is for this reason that they generally charge higher fees than funds which passively track broad markets such as S&P500.

One question we might want to ask is which asset or strategy should we pick to represent broad market returns? If we wish to compare equity based investors, using the S&P500 index as a benchmark (see Exhibit 16.1) seems to be an obvious choice. Many market participants are invested in the S&P500 and it is generally used as a barometer for equity markets by many investors. We can also use S&P500 as a proxy for the market's expectations on growth, and it is available on a much higher frequency basis than actual growth data such as gross domestic product (GDP). Similarly, for bond-based investments, there are many indices we can use to benchmark strategies, such as Bloomberg/EFFAS bond indices. For the foreign exchange markets, it is somewhat more difficult to define what broad market returns should be and what precisely we can define as beta. One reason could be that historically it has not always been seen as an investment asset class, in contrast to bonds and equities, but rather a means to transfer capital between different countries. However, we can argue that there are certain strategies which can represent broad market returns for foreign exchange investors and this is the approach that we follow in this chapter.

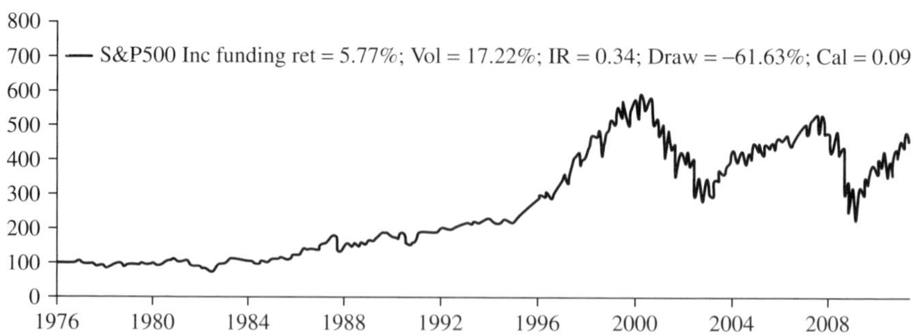


**EXHIBIT 16.1** **Total returns from S&P500 inclusive of dividend payments and after funding costs.** ***Source*****: Courtesy of Bloomberg, Nomura.**

## 16.2 Beta in the Foreign Exchange Markets

In the foreign exchange markets, it is somewhat difficult to ascertain general market returns. For one thing, at least historically, foreign exchange markets were not always thought of as an investment asset class. In addition many market participants have differing objectives. For example, central banks may trade in the market to moderate the volatility of their home currency. Companies trade FX to facilitate conducting business in foreign countries.

Hence, if we want to design a strategy which encapsulates general FX market returns, it is largely going to be confined to speculators who trade FX as if it were an investment asset class. There are several approaches we can take. We can look at indices which track the returns for currency fund managers such as the Barclay Currency Trader index. We can also construct generic systematic trading strategies, which mimic very popular strategies within FX. In this case we are thinking largely of FX carry and trend-following strategies. This is essentially our approach here in this chapter. We examine other examples such as trading the USD from a long-term directional perspective. We use the longest price histories available to conduct our analysis. We compare our generic FX carry and trend-following strategies to various benchmarks such as the S&P500 and currency fund returns.

### 16.2.1 UNDERSTANDING THE FX CARRY TRADE

The FX carry trade is probably the most popular strategy within foreign exchange markets. It is popular both within G10 and EM. However, we shall stick to looking at the carry trade from a G10 perspective given that the data history is much longer. Before we delve into the carry trade in more detail, we first need to understand how investors' returns are calculated in the FX market.

Let us take the example of an investor holding a long AUD/JPY position, which is often cited as one of the most popular carry trades within foreign exchange. We can deconstruct this trade into several parts. Essentially it involves a short position in JPY, which is used to fund a long position in AUD. As a result, the investor is paying JPY rates and receiving AUD rates. Given that AUD rates have generally been greater than JPY rates, carry returns from long AUD/JPY positions are usually positive. Over a single day, the carry is relatively small (at most several basis points). However, if the trade is held for an extended period, these small amounts of carry can accrue. So is the trade a "free lunch"? The answer is obviously no, because we are also exposed to exchange-rate fluctuations. Essentially, our total return for a spot position is made up of two components: the carry returns (i.e., AUD–JPY rates) and spot returns (i.e., AUD/JPY spot). For a carry trade to be profitable, we need our carry returns to be greater than our spot returns. We can think of accruing carry returns to be similar to collecting a risk premium.

In Exhibit 16.2, we plot the total, carry, and spot returns for a long AUD/JPY position. As we have previously noted, the carry returns make a significant contribution to the total returns. The spot returns exhibit significant volatility and are largely responsible for the drawdowns associated with this trade. The largest drawdown occurred during the Lehman crisis in 2008.

## 16.2.2 FX CARRY AS A BROADER STRATEGY

In our above example, we have cited long AUD/JPY positions as a popular implementation of the carry trade. However, in practice, if investors only hold this single position to express a carry-trade view, they will be exposed to large idiosyncratic risks with respect to Australia and Japan. However, the rationale of the trade is specifically to collect carry rather than expressing the specific view of outperformance of the Australian economy. One way to reduce this idiosyncratic risk is to create a large basket of different currency pairs to collect carry.

Typically, this involves buying several high yielding currencies funded by selling several low yielding currencies. Such a strategy needs to be relatively active in its approach given that currencies can often switch from being high yielding to low yielding (or vice versa). One example is GBP. Before the credit crunch, this was one of the highest yielding currencies within G10. However, the BoE aggressively cut rates following the collapse of Lehman Brothers. As a result GBP became one of lowest yielding currencies in G10. We construct a relatively simple example of a G10 carry model, which buys the three highest yielding currencies funded by the three lowest yielding currencies. We plot the returns of this basket in Exhibit 16.3, comparing them to the benchmark of long S&P500 positions, inclusive of USD funding costs.

Obviously, creating a carry basket does not remove the impact of broad shifts in market risk appetite. Typically, during times of strong risk appetite within the markets, a carry strategy is likely to be profitable, steadily accruing returns. When risk appetite takes a turn lower, carry trades are invariably impacted negatively, as investors seek to liquidate their holdings in risky investments (such as high yielding currencies) and seek to buy safe haven assets (such as lower yielding currencies).

In Exhibit 16.4, we have outlined the 20 months where returns from our generic carry basket were the most extreme (both positive and negative). Alongside these we have included the S&P500 returns above the risk free rate for those months. In the majority of those months in the best 20 list for carry, S&P500 returns were positive, on average around 2% each month. Conversely,

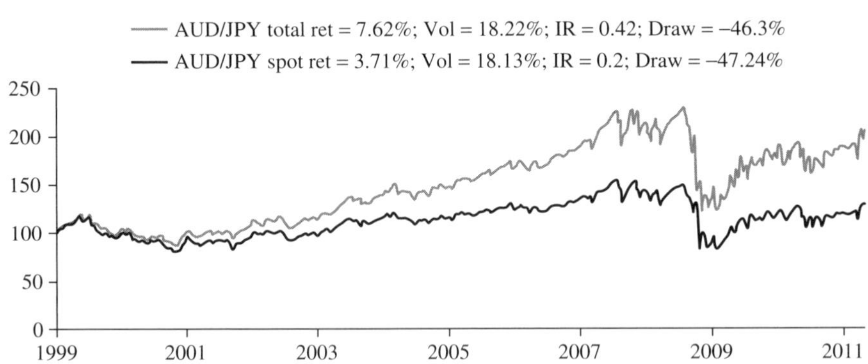


**EXHIBIT 16.2** **Long AUD/JPY total returns versus spot returns.** *Source*: **Courtesy of Bloomberg, Nomura.**

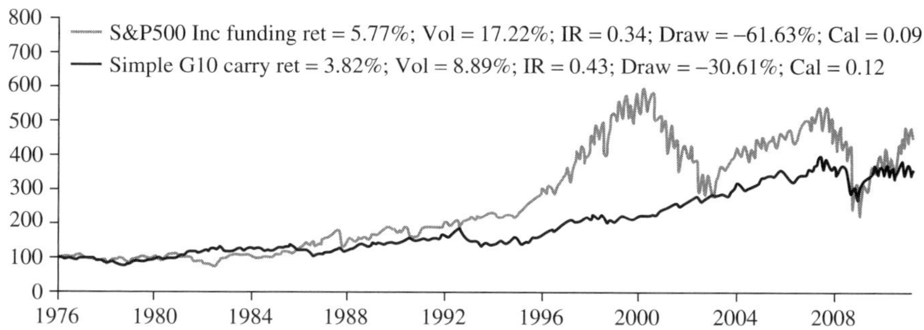


**EXHIBIT 16.3** Long G10 carry basket returns compared to returns from investing in S&P500. *Source*: Courtesy of Bloomberg, Nomura.

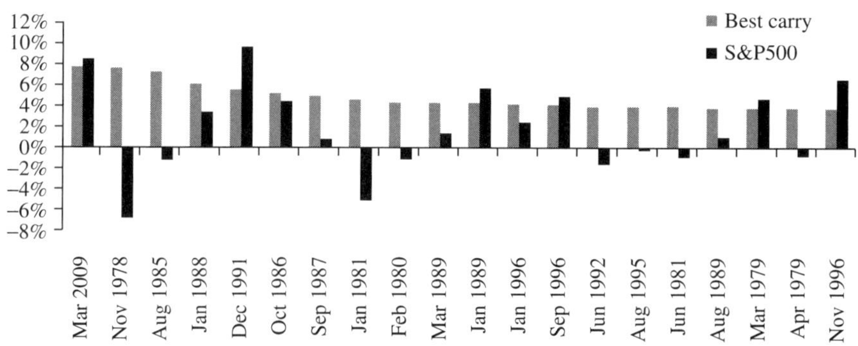


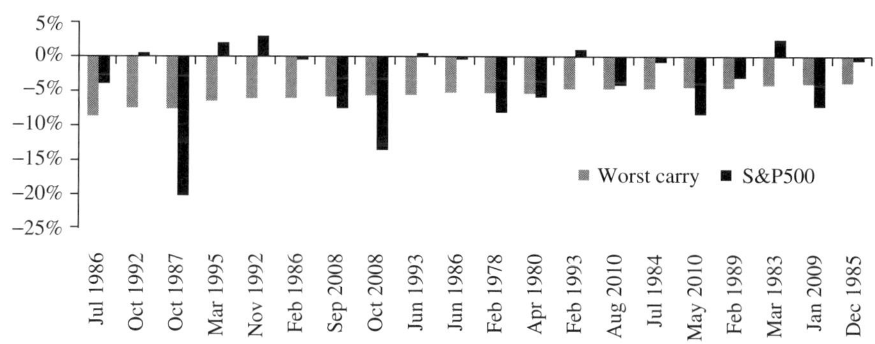


**EXHIBIT 16.4** Twenty best and worst months for G10 carry against. *Source*: Courtesy of Bloomberg, Nomura.

in the majority of those months in the worst 20 list for carry, S&P500 returns were negative with an average of about −4%. We note that most of the worst-performing months were during times of significant market stress (such as during the collapse of Lehman Brothers in 2008 and the Greek debt crisis in 2010), thus validating our earlier point that the returns from the carry trade are heavily dependent on underlying risk sentiment within the markets. In a sense, we are saying that FX carry is connected with overall market beta (as indicated by stocks).

### 16.2.3 FX TREND-BASED STRATEGIES

**16.2.3.1 Are FX Markets Always Efficient?** Another popular approach to trading within FX markets is to use a trend-following approach. Broadly speaking, trend-following strategies are seen as a subset of technical-based strategies which also include mean-reverting style strategies. The efficient market hypothesis suggests that the price of an asset reflects all publicly-available information. This seems to imply that using price information to discern trends is unlikely to be effective. However, in practice following trends in the market can be profitable, although since 2000 trends have been less easily monetized. If the market was always fully efficient then market participants would process all information at the same time. However, it is very often the case that different market participants react to news flow at differing time horizons. For example, real money fund managers would have a much longer term perspective on underlying moves in the market and hold substantial positions over extended periods. This contrasts to spot traders, who trade intraday and in many cases often close out all positions overnight. Furthermore, as discussed earlier, within the FX markets not all investors are trading purely for profit. Even traders who are speculating can, on a short-term basis, switch from an objective of seeking profit to minimizing losses. Obviously, on a longer term basis speculators do seek to profit from their trading activity, but the minimization of losses is a very important part of this.

**16.2.3.2 The Rationale for Technical-Based Strategies, Both Trend Following and Mean Reverting.** Given that we have argued that FX markets are not always efficient, it opens the door to the discussion of trend-following strategies. One of the major rationales for technical strategies is that it is essentially self fulfilling. Since a large proportion of FX traders use technicals, by implication, when a technical signal is generated (such as a moving average crossover), many market participants will likely follow the signal and therefore push up the price. Of course, many investors will trade FX based on fundamental approaches, such as relative interest rates. However, even in this case, they might use technicals to time their trade and in particular to judge where to place stops and take profits. These orders can be clustered around certain technical levels which the market participants deem as important (Exhibit 16.5). Osler[1] describes how triggering these levels can result in price cascades. Clearly, there is a fine line between having a critical mass of investors following a signal, and an excessive number. We conjecture that if an excessively large segment of the market follows a signal, it might be susceptible to front running. This would likely reduce the impact of the signal. If this was the case, then technical strategies would be more

[1] Osler (2005) — Stop Loss Orders and Price Cascades in Currency Markets — *Journal of International Money and Finance*.

**EXHIBIT 16.5 Important areas of support and resistance in EUR/USD.** ***Source*****: Courtesy of Bloomberg, Nomura.**

heavily correlated to broad-based FX fund returns. We later show that this is not the case.

**16.2.3.3 Analyzing Trend-Following Returns within FX.** Further to our discussion, we construct a trend-following model to act as a proxy for this type of trading strategy. We have tried to keep the trading rule relatively simple so that it should be more representative of how most FX market participants trade FX on a trend-following basis. We have used a similar model to that described by Lequeux and Acar.[2] Essentially, we use an equally weighted moving average model.[3] In our case we trade all the USD, EUR, and JPY crosses within G10 space.

In Exhibit 16.6, we plot our trend-following returns versus an investor's total returns for long S&P500 positions. Purely on an illustrative basis, we see

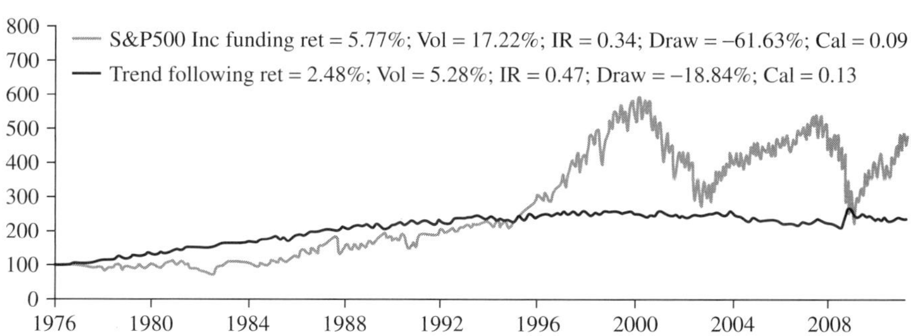


**EXHIBIT 16.6 FX-trend-following returns.** ***Source*****: Courtesy of Bloomberg, Nomura.**

[2]Lequeux and Acar (1998)—A dynamic index for managed currencies funds using CME currency contracts.

[3]We use 32D, 61D, and 117D SMA. Hence if spot is above all three moving averages, we would be invested 100%. If only two out of the three are bullish our investment would be 33% etc.

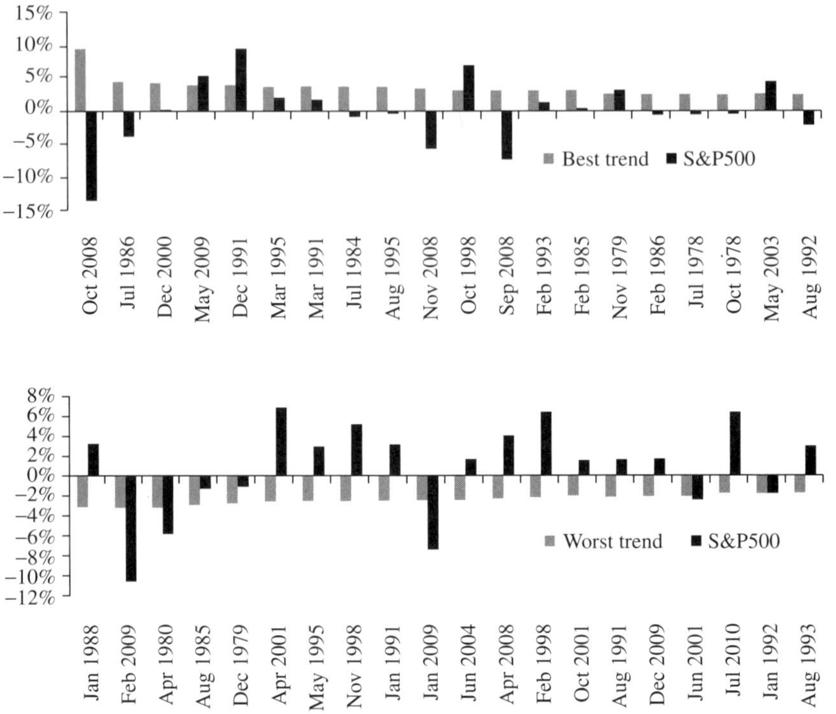


**EXHIBIT 16.7 Best and worst months for trend-following models.** ***Source*****: Courtesy of Bloomberg, Nomura.**

that the returns seem largely uncorrelated. We contrast this to FX carry returns which bore a strong relationship with S&P500. We shall expand on this point in more detail.

In Exhibit 16.7, we take a closer look at the best and worst months from our trend-following model returns. Unlike in the case of carry, it appears that the basket actually does better when S&P500 is falling heavily. Hence, the returns of a trend-following strategy can be thought of as an imperfect hedge for carry returns, which is in line with our earlier observation that trend-following returns do not appear to be correlated with S&P500.

## 16.2.4 VALUE-BASED STRATEGIES WITHIN FX

Value-based strategies can constitute another form of beta for trading FX as well as the more popular carry- and trend-based approaches. We can use purchasing power parity (PPP)[4] indices to gauge the long-term valuation of currencies. One of the most well-known PPP measures is the very simple Big Mac index published by the Economist, which takes the price of Big Macs in different currencies and

[4]Purchasing power parity.

then uses the discrepancies between them to gauge where currencies are over or undervalued.

Generally, in PPP, we try to compare the purchasing power of different currencies after removing differences in price levels, for example, using CPI. They essentially show the ratio of price for the same goods or services in different countries. In practice, most PPP measures focus on a broader array of products (rather than a single product like the Big Mac index), such as the OECD's PPP measure, which we are using here. The OECD's PPP indices are annualized time series.

Our trading rule compares the actual value of spot versus the OECD's PPP to come up with a simple over or undervaluation metric. If spot is undervalued by 20% we buy spot. Conversely, if spot is overvalued by 20%, we sell spot. We exit all trades when spot is within a range of valuation of −20/ + 20%. In Exhibit 16.8, we plot the returns for our generic FX value basket. We find that returns were fairly flat up until the mid-1990s. After that point the strategy performed a lot better.

### 16.2.5 USD DIRECTIONAL TRADE

The USD has a preeminent place within the foreign exchange market. There are several reasons for this. The USD is the world's major reserve currency. Most currencies are also primarily quoted against the USD. The vast majority of trades within the FX markets include a USD dimension. Hence, understanding the future direction of the USD is crucial to gauging the future state of foreign exchange markets. As such, we might conjecture that speculators within the foreign exchange markets are basically trading the USD, with very long-term investors positioning for a long-term decline in the USD. Hence, we could think of the USD as a beta within the foreign exchange markets. In Exhibit 16.8 we have plotted the total returns for being short USD since the 1970s, traded in equal weights against EUR, JPY, and GBP, which are the three most liquid USD crosses. We note that trading the decline in the USD has marginally been profitable over our sample although this has been characterized by large

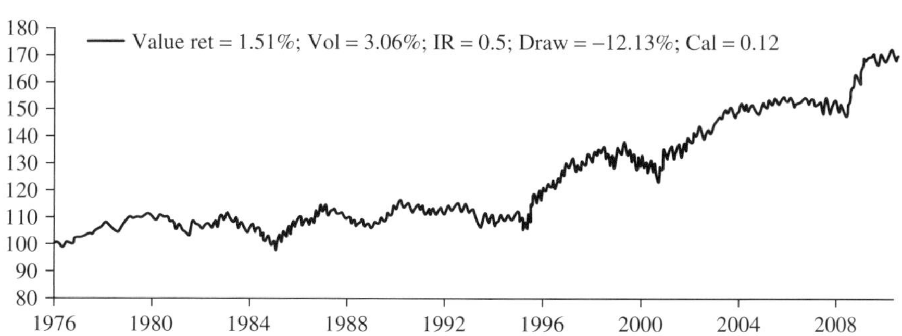


EXHIBIT 16.8 FX value returns. *Source*: Courtesy of Bloomberg, Nomura.

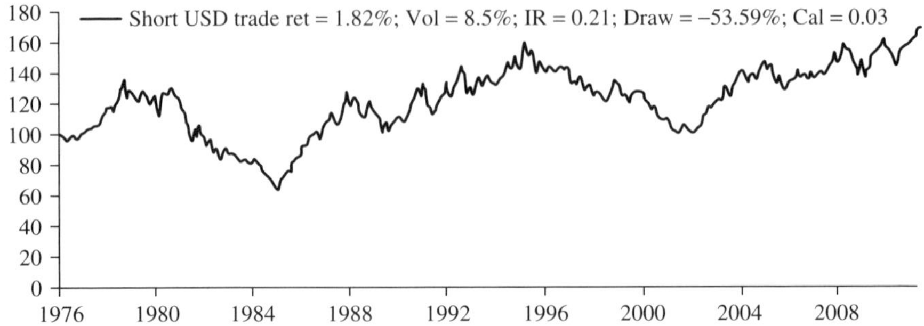


**EXHIBIT 16.9** The USD directional trade. *Source*: Courtesy of Bloomberg, Nomura.

drawdowns. In particular, there was a period of USD strength in the early 1980s. The Fed had hiked rates to stem high levels of inflation, which helped to strengthen the USD. The Plaza Accord was struck in September 1985 between the United States, Japan, France, West Germany, and the United Kingdom to devalue the USD through currency interventions. In 1987, the Louvre Accord was signed to stem any further depreciation in the USD (Exhibit 16.9).

## 16.2.6 CORRELATION BETWEEN THESE FX STRATEGIES AND OTHER FORMS OF BETA

We have discussed various strategies which could constitute a source of beta for FX market participants. In this section, we focus on FX-trend-following and carry strategies, which are the most common. Here, we investigate how correlated they are to the S&P500 which is usually considered as the most representative beta for long-only-equities investors. We have used monthly correlations, given that daily observations are subject to more noise and some of this data is only available on a monthly basis. In addition we look at the Barclay FX CTA index and the HFRX FX index. The Barclay FX CTA index of CTA's which trade currency futures and often use trend-following style strategies. The HFRX Currency index is a broader based currency fund index. It includes both discretionary and systematic currency funds and a broad range of strategies.

In Exhibit 16.10, we plot the rolling yearly correlations between FX trend and these various indices. Throughout much of our history we note that our trend-following strategy has been most heavily correlated to the Barclay FX CTA index. The rolling correlation rarely dips into negative territory. However, our trend-following basket[5] has a much more volatile correlation with S&P500, and it is often in negative territory during crises (such as 1998 and 2008). If we look at the correlations between our generic trend-following basket and the HFRX FX index, we again note that the correlations are more volatile.

[5]We use 32D, 61D, and 117D SMA. Hence if spot is above all three moving averages, we would be invested 100%. If only two out of the three are bullish our investment would be 33%, etc.

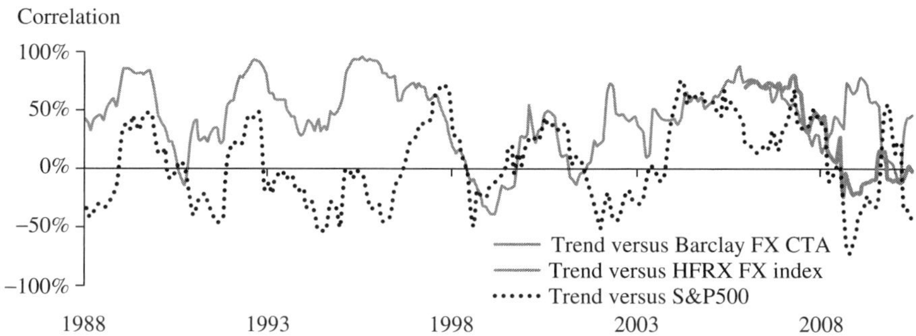


**EXHIBIT 16.10 Rolling correlation between FX trend and FX indices.** ***Source*****: Courtesy of Bloomberg, Nomura.**

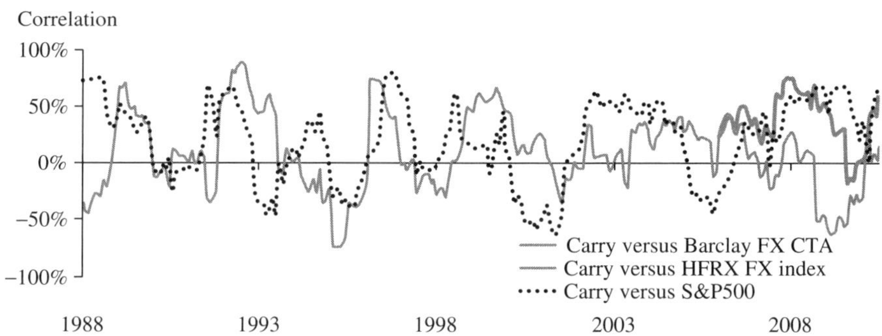


**EXHIBIT 16.11 Rolling correlation between FX carry and FX indices.** ***Source*****: Courtesy of Bloomberg, Nomura.**

In Exhibit 16.11, we repeat the same exercise. This time, however, we are comparing the rolling correlations of FX carry returns against these indices. Broadly speaking, the correlation between FX carry and S&P500 is generally positive. For the relatively small amount of history that we have for the HFRX FX index, the correlation is nearly always positive. Hence, we can surmise that for a broader base of FX funds (which area represented through HFRX FX index), FX carry might be a better descriptor of their generalized strategy. While the correlation between trend and Barclay FX CTA was largely positive, the correlation between FX carry and Barclay FX CTA is more unstable. This should not surprise us, given our earlier argument that FX-trend-following and carry strategies are not correlated and Barclay FX CTA is representative of trend-following funds within FX.

## 16.2.7 WEIGHTED PORTFOLIO OF FX STRATEGIES

In the earlier sections we have attempted to create beta for the FX markets using a single strategy, such as trend following and carry. However, this ignores the fact that more generalized FX funds (i.e., HRFX FX index) could be adopting a wide range of strategies, not purely trend following or carry. Hence, it seems like a reasonable approach to create a portfolio of trend following and carry. To weight our portfolio, we regress the returns of the carry and trend-following strategy against the monthly changes in FX funds. We use the beta coefficients from this regression to create a portfolio of carry and trend-following strategies. In Exhibit 16.12, we plot rolling correlations between this portfolio, trend-following, carry,

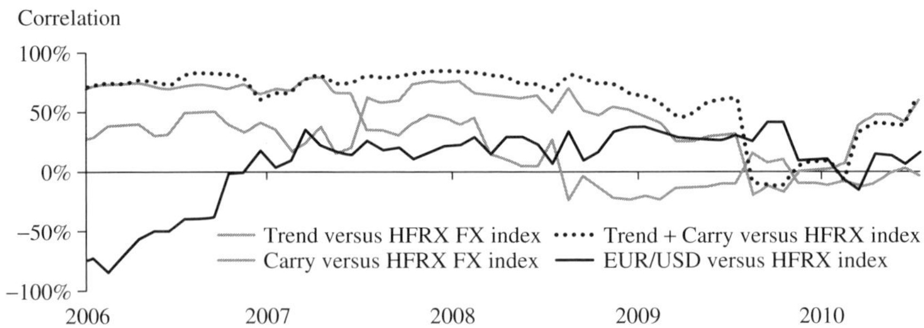


**EXHIBIT 16.12 Rolling correlation between weighted FX strategies and FX fund returns.** ***Source*: Courtesy of Bloomberg, Nomura.**

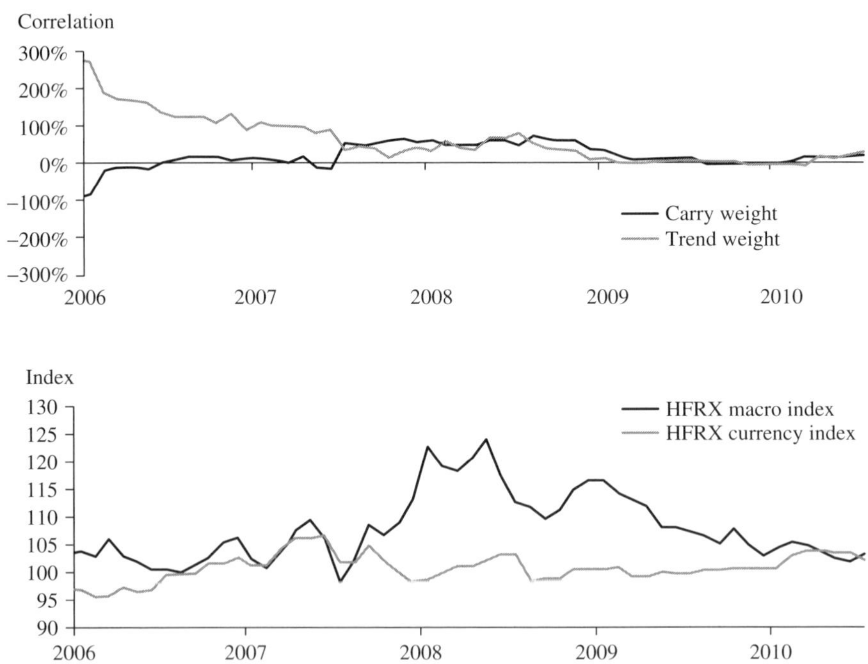


**EXHIBIT 16.13 Weights of FX carry and trend within our portfolio (top) HFRX FX and Macro fund indices (bottom).** ***Source*: Courtesy of Bloomberg, Nomura.**

and EUR/USD returns versus FX fund returns. In practice the fund data is generally lagged, so we would not be able to trade this strategy. For comparison we have also included the correlations for FX trend and carry from the previous charts. We have also plotted the correlations of EUR/USD with FX currency fund returns, in an effort to understand how much of the USD trade was driving returns.

We note that up until Sep 2009, the correlation of our mixed trend and carry portfolio was higher than the correlation of carry or trend. This suggests that a weighted portfolio is a better beta for FX currency fund returns than either strategy on its own. This suggests that the FX investors as a whole adopt a mixture of strategies rather than sticking to a single strategy such as carry or trend following. Following that period, the correlation collapsed for the three FX strategies. However, it jumped for EUR/USD, suggesting that directional USD trades were becoming more important for driving FX returns.

In Exhibit 16.13, we plot the weights of both strategies within our portfolio. Negative weights imply we are shorting the basket. We compare these weights with the underlying returns of the HFRX FX index that we plot in Exhibit 16.13. On the whole, the trend model weights are larger. This is largely because our trend-following strategy has lower volatility than carry. We note that the weights are by and large positive. However, with the beginning of the credit crunch in summer 2007 we began to see a big shift in the weights.

## 16.3 Multiple Forms of FX Beta

So far, we have mainly discussed betas from the vantage point of generic FX carry, trend, and value strategies and by looking at industry-wide indices such as the HFRX indices. Here, we investigate the various indices created by banks which can be viewed as forms of FX beta. We concentrate on various G10 FX carry indices given that a large variety of these are available from multiple banks and should be broadly comparable. Later, we do the same for trend indices.

## 16.4 Carry FX Indices from Banks

In our sample set we include a broad selection of these carry indices for discussion, DB Currency Harvest G10, Nomura G10 Carry, CitiFX Beta G10 Carry, UBS V10 FX Carry, and CS ROCI G10. The idea behind all these indices is similar to our generic carry indices, namely to buy high yielding currencies and sell low yielding currencies, so that an investor can collect carry which is in effect a risk premium. The precise methodology for selecting currency weights differs between the various indices.

Our sample is from 2002 to 2011. Our first question is to ask how similar are these various carry indices? In Exhibit 16.14, we present the long-term monthly correlations between these various strategies. The majority of these strategies have correlations of in excess of 50%, with our generic strategy. The correlations

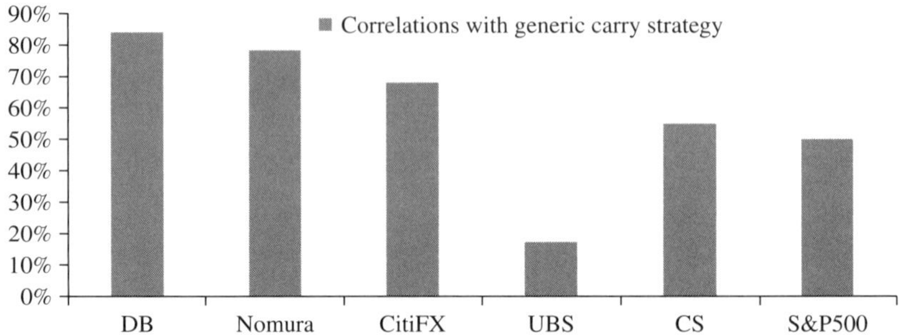


| | DB | Nomura | CitiFX | UBS | CS | S&P500 | Generic |
|---|---|---|---|---|---|---|---|
| DB | 100% | 80% | 77% | 16% | 58% | 61% | 84% |
| Nomura | 80% | 100% | 82% | 28% | 68% | 41% | 78% |
| CitiFX | 77% | 82% | 100% | 25% | 63% | 34% | 69% |
| UBS | 16% | 28% | 25% | 100% | 21% | 8% | 17% |
| CS | 58% | 68% | 63% | 21% | 100% | 28% | 55% |
| S&P500 | 61% | 41% | 34% | 8% | 28% | 100% | 51% |
| Generic | 84% | 78% | 69% | 17% | 55% | 51% | 100% |

**EXHIBIT 16.14 Monthly long-term correlations between various carry indices and generic carry strategy (top) correlations between various carry strategies (bottom).** ***Source*****: Courtesy of Bloomberg, Nomura.**

among the various strategies are also mostly above 50% (see Exhibit 16.13) and are below 90%. This suggests that although these strategies exhibit significant similarities, it would be difficult to term the strategies as identical, even though the strategies are broadly built on the same premise of collecting carry. We can obviously point to differences in methodology between the different indices as a reason why these baskets are not more closely related.

Hence, we have several different contenders for FX market beta among these carry indices. Melvin and Shand[6] note that this is in stark contrast to equity indices, where correlations can be very significant (such as between S&P500 and Dow Jones). We note that the UBS strategy exhibits the lowest correlation with the generic FX carry strategy. We also observe that its long-term correlations with other carry strategies are also comparatively low (below 30%).

In Exhibit 16.15, we plot the rolling 3M daily correlations of DB, Nomura, and UBS with our generic carry basket. We have picked these indices, given that they exhibit the highest and lowest correlations respectively of our sample. The idea is to understand how the relationship changes over time, rather than purely from a long-term perspective. We note that the DB and Nomura rolling correlations with generic carry are quite persistent throughout our sample. This is broadly consistent with their long-term correlations. With the UBS index, we see that at times the strategy has very high correlations with generic carry.

[6] Melvin and Shand (2010), Active Currency Investing and Performance Benchmarks, CESifo Working Paper No. 3052.

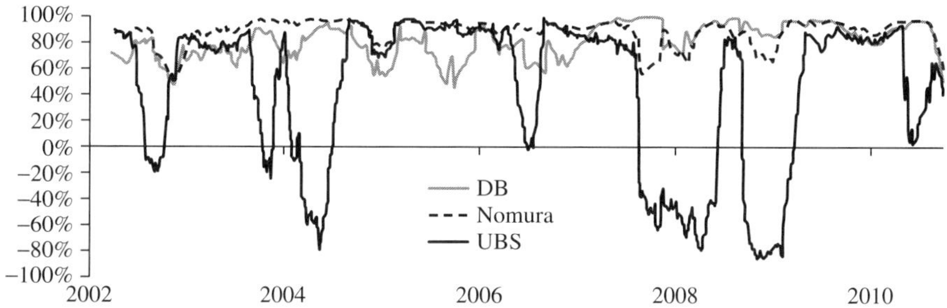


**EXHIBIT 16.15** **Rolling correlations between FX carry indices and generic FX carry strategy.** ***Source*: Courtesy of Bloomberg, Nomura.**

However, it also regularly flips into negative territory. The long-term correlation figure, we calculated earlier, masks this behavior to a certain extent. This result should not be a surprise, given that the UBS strategy also shorts carry. As a result, we cannot describe it as a long-only carry strategy.

## 16.5 Trend-Following FX Indices from Banks

In the previous section, we discussed various bank indices on FX carry. Here, we do something similar, but comparing the various trend-based indices available from various banks. As with the carry indices, the precise trading rules differ between these indices. The trend indices we shall investigate are CitiFX Beta G10 Trend, Nomura Storm FX Trend, CS FX Metrics Momentum, and Barclays Adaptive FX Trend. The general idea of these indices is to use price momentum to buy and sell currencies. We compare these against our generic trend model which we described earlier in the document.

In Exhibit 16.16, we have plotted the long-term correlations among the various trend strategies to one another and also the S&P500. We see that on a long-term basis our generic strategy is anti-correlated to S&P500. The Citi, Nomura, and CS indices have large positive correlations with our generic trend-following strategy. Interestingly, the Barclays strategy exhibits very little correlation on a long-term basis with any of the other bank indices and the generic trend strategy.

In Exhibit 16.17, we look at the 3M rolling correlations between some of the various bank trend indices versus our generic carry basket. We see that on the whole the Nomura and Citi correlations are broadly positive with our generic strategy, which fits in with long-term correlations. However, the Barclays index often displays negative correlations with our generic trend indices. This seems intuitive given that Barclays index is not a purely trend-following model. It also has a mean-reverting component.

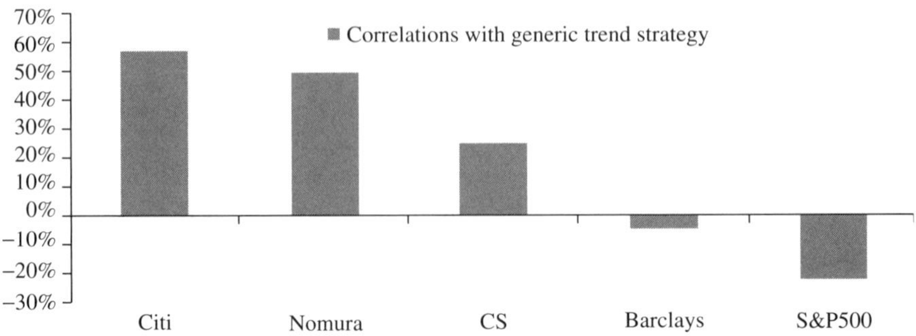


| | Citi | Nomura | CS | Barclays | S&P500 | Generic |
|---|---|---|---|---|---|---|
| Citi | 100% | 70% | 28% | 0% | −29% | 58% |
| Nomura | 70% | 100% | 33% | 4% | −19% | 50% |
| CS | 28% | 33% | 100% | 9% | −15% | 25% |
| Barclays | 0% | 4% | 9% | 100% | 3% | −5% |
| S&P500 | −29% | −19% | −15% | 3% | 100% | −22% |
| Generic | 58% | 50% | 25% | −5% | −22% | 100% |

**EXHIBIT 16.16 Monthly long-term correlations between various trend indices and generic trend strategy (top) correlations between various trend strategies (bottom).** ***Source*****: Courtesy of Bloomberg, Nomura.**

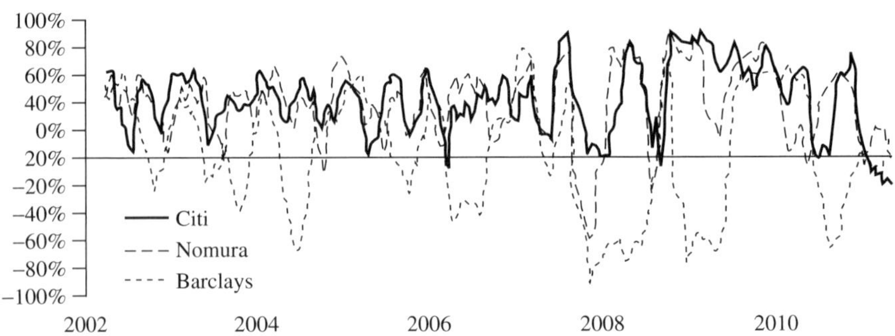


**EXHIBIT 16.17 Rolling correlations between FX trend indices and generic FX trend strategy.** ***Source*****: Courtesy of Bloomberg, Nomura.**

## 16.6 Conclusion

We have discussed that in FX there is no single index which market participants typically cite as a benchmark, unlike for example in equities where the S&P500 is an obvious candidate for market beta. However, in spite of this, we can create relatively generic FX strategies that mimic popular investment styles within the foreign exchange markets, notably carry and trend-following strategies within FX. Hence, these generic strategies can act as proxies for an FX market beta. We also examined FX value, which is often cited as a form of FX beta.

We of course need to note that this exercise for creating a proxy market beta is likely only to be suitable to capture the returns for FX market participants who are speculators, investing in FX as an asset class. Other market participants such as central banks trade within the FX market, but their trading objectives are not usually purely to maximize profit. Instead, they seek other objectives such as diversification of reserves and damping volatility in their local currency. Similarly, investors trading other asset classes trade FX to hedge or partially hedge their transactions. Here, other benchmarks might be suitable to judge their FX returns. For example, if a UK equities investor is buying S&P500, but has an active FX hedging strategy, several benchmarks they might wish to use could be comparing their returns to FX un-hedged and FX-hedged index returns.

We note that carry and trend-following strategies within FX bear little correlation with one another. When we look at FX carry compared to the S&P500, which is often considered as a form of beta for the equities markets, we note that the two strategies bear significant correlation with one another. Furthermore, carry appears to be more correlated to general FX fund returns compared to CTA currency funds. We find the reverse when comparing our trend-based strategy to CTA currency funds.

A weighted portfolio of carry and trend-following strategies can help explain a larger proportion of generalized FX fund returns than a single strategy alone. Hence, we conjecture that this weighted portfolio provides a good starting point for creating a beta which represents the benchmark for investor returns within FX markets.

We also examine the various FX carry indices created by banks that can be used as measures for FX market beta and compare them to a generic FX carry strategy. We find that although large correlations between many of these strategies suggest significant similarities between them, the strategies do still exhibit some differences. Hence, it is difficult to pick any particular strategy as being the "true" FX market beta. The same is true for FX trend indices that we compared and contrasted.

However, we can still describe them as good proxies for FX market beta.

## REFERENCES

French CW. The treynor capital asset pricing model. J Invest Manag 2003;1(2):60–72.

Lequeux P, Acar E. A dynamic index for managed currencies funds using CME currency contracts. Eur J Finance 19984(4):311–330.

Melvin M, Shand D. Active currency investing and performance benchmarks. CESifo Working Paper No. 3052; 2010 May.

Osler CL. Stop loss orders and price cascades in currency markets. J Int Money Finance 2005;24:219–41.

CHAPTER SEVENTEEN

# Active Currency Management Part II: Is There Skill or Alpha in Currency Investing?

RICHARD M. LEVICH
Stern School of Business, New York University

MOMTCHIL POJARLIEV
Hathersage Capital Management, LLC

## 17.1 Introduction

The landscape of active currency management has changed dramatically over the last 25 years. In the 1980s, while a small number of professionals engaged in speculative currency trading, an investment manager acquired currency exposure primarily as a by-product when investing in either foreign currency denominated stocks or bonds. A 1991 *Financial Times* article on the growing appeal of overseas assets for UK fund managers noted that

> *Since 1987 overseas bonds have also begun to attract interest, accounting for 2% of average assets by the end of 1989. In the view of many observers, though by no means all, they are set to become a permanent asset class in their own right in the 1990s (Dickson, 1991).*

For sure, a few boutique firms that specialized in currency viewed things differently. In 1988, an article in *Pensions and Investment Age* addressing the issue of whether foreign currency holdings ought to be hedged noted that

*Handbook of Exchange Rates*, First Edition. Edited by Jessica James, Ian W. Marsh, and Lucio Sarno.

> *Some [pension executives] also might overlay currency management onto existing international portfolios, thereby treating currency as a separate* asset class *(emphasis added; Marlene Givant, 1988).*

The realization that the currency component of an international portfolio might be actively hedged, and profitably so, led some managers to consider offering currency management as a separate product. A 1988 *Financial Times* article put it this way:

> *Fund managers can engage in more active hedging programmes on a tactical basis, but this is where the line between genuine hedging and active currency management becomes blurred. For example, many fund managers which accumulated a good in-house track record in hedging decided a few years ago to develop their experience and launch* managed currency funds, *which concentrate entirely on forecasting exchange rate movements (emphasis added; Andrew Freeman, 1989).*

A Lexis Nexis search of newspapers and periodicals for the keywords "currency" and "asset class" in the same article shows only a handful of articles each year in the years before 1990.[1] By 2007, the annual number of mentions for this pair of keywords exceeded 1100. While not all these articles referred to currency *as* an *asset class*, the notion of taking currency formally into account and separately managed by a currency professional has become part of the international investment manager's basic toolkit.

Despite all the increased attention to currencies within international portfolios, some basic questions remain. The first is whether currency exposure should be left unhedged or hedged, and if the latter, whether the hedging program should be passive (in the sense of following a set rule) or active where a manager is allowed discretion to reduce, retain, or expand currency positions.[2] A second question is whether active currency managers could offer additional return (portable alpha) to institutional investors (regardless of existing foreign currency exposure) and what is the appropriate standard for evaluating their performance. And finally, there is the empirical question of whether currency managers tend to meet, fall short of, or exceed the performance standard.

In the remainder of this chapter, we address all three questions, with our primary focus on the appropriate benchmark for performance and the empirical track record of active currency managers. We continue in the next section with a review of the types of mandates that are typically set for currency managers and the types of strategies that active currency managers might employ. The mandate plays a critical role in determining the appropriate benchmark. Section 17.3 lays out the traditional benchmark for currency fund management and then develops an alternative benchmark in which expected returns depend on certain style factors. In Sections 17.4 and 17.5, we present empirical evidence on the performance of various individual currency funds and indexes of those funds.

[1] There were no mentions of "currency" and "asset class" in the same article from 1975 until 1982. The first mention in a single article appears in 1983.

[2] See Thomas (1990) for a collection of articles that framed many of the salient issues.

The empirical evidence shows that a high proportion of the variation in returns (meaning 50%, 60%, and, in some cases, 70%, depending on the sample) can be explained by four style factors. While neither an index of funds nor an average of available funds earn alpha (relative to our alternative standard), some individual managers do. Moreover, we find some evidence of alpha persistence among individual outperforming managers.[3] Persistence is a desirable feature for plan sponsors who actively pick currency managers. These findings lead to a set of investment implications that we summarize in the final section.

## 17.2 Alternative Currency Management Mandates

While each agreement between institutional investors and their currency manager is unique, for discussion purposes, it is useful to consider first the types of mandates that are in common use and some of their key features and second, other structural and operational choices that differentiate mandates. By varying these contractual parameters, institutional investors influence their expected alpha (what we call the alpha continuum) as well as their exposure to risk.

### 17.2.1 FEATURES OF A CURRENCY MANDATE

There are two basic types of currency mandates. In an *absolute return mandate*, the investor seeks to earn a positive return, usually in excess of some benchmark, and is subject to acceptable risk levels. With a *currency overlay mandate*, on the other hand, the investor already owns a portfolio of foreign debt or equity and the objective of the mandate is either to entirely eliminate currency risk from the portfolio or only partially reduce currency risk while opportunistically going after return.[4]

In both absolute return and currency overlay mandates, the agreement will specify how much latitude the manager has to operate, identify provisions that constrain the manager, and, of course, spell out how the manager's performance will be determined and the formula for setting compensation. The main considerations stipulated in a currency mandate will include the following.

- *Passive versus Active Management*. A passive manager is constrained to simply track a predefined benchmark and does not seek to generate excess returns. Because most benchmarks are constructed from a clearly articulated

[3]Empirical evidence in Pojarliev and Levich (2010) is consistent with a significant degree of beta persistence, meaning investment style persistence, which is also advantageous for plan sponsors.

[4]Hedging within a currency overlay strategy often takes a fairly simplistic objective of establishing a predictable home currency value for assets denominated in a foreign currency. For example, consider an American plan sponsor whose financial statements and returns are prepared in USD. If the plan sponsor owns shares in Volkswagen valued at EUR 100, selling 100 EUR for USD establishes a known USD value for the foreign assets. The hedge will likely be imperfect owing to the fact that the EUR share price of Volkswagen itself will likely be sensitive to the EUR/USD exchange rate.

investment process, a passive manager often follows a systematic or rule-based approach.[5] For example, if the AFX Currency Management Index based on three moving average trading rules and seven currency pairs is used as a benchmark, then a passive manager could use these same moving average rules and currency pairs to govern his trading.[6] For an absolute return mandate, trading designed to mimic benchmarks based on carry trading, trend-following, or value trading strategies or volatility are all examples of passive strategies. For a currency overlay mandate, always fully hedging the currency position in a fixed income portfolio or always hedging 50% of the foreign currency value of the position are typical examples of passive strategies.

On the other hand, the active manager has discretion to implement a variety of trades based on different ideas. For an absolute return mandate, the active manager seeks to add value on top of the benchmark and would do so by entering into trades that deviate from the benchmark. An active currency overlay manager who felt that foreign currency had a strong chance of appreciating could hedge only 25% of the foreign currency exposure in a fixed income portfolio instead of 100% in an attempt to add extra return. Whether under an absolute return or currency overlay mandate, an active manager might adopt a systematic or rule-based investment process, a discretionally investment process, or a combination of both.

- *Allowed Currencies*. A currency mandate agreement will typically constrain the manager to operate within a set menu of currencies, perhaps restricted to the G3 or G10 countries where financial markets offer greater depth, or G20 or emerging market (EM) countries where markets are less liquid, but greater profit opportunities may be present. A wider range of allowed currencies may be more valuable in the case of an absolute return mandate, although some managers may prefer to limit themselves to only those currency pairs where they have greater expertise. In a currency overlay, the allowed currencies are often limited to those currencies in the underlying portfolio, although not always, as crosshedging can be a useful tool.

[5]Some market professionals have taken issue with this definition. Melvin and Shand (2011) note that tracking any currency trading index involves some degree of active management, as positions must be bought and sold as underlying market conditions change. While trade execution is important and can impact returns even for the manager of an S&P 500 index fund, Melvin and Shand (2011) suggest that these issues are more acute for currency where there is no natural buy and hold strategy. Melvin and Shand (2011, p. 2) conclude that "there really is no passive strategy for currency investors."

[6]The AFX Currency Management Index is based on trading in seven currency pairs weighted by their volume of turnover in the spot market, with returns for each pair based on an equally weighted portfolio of three moving average rules (32, 61, and 117 days). The seven currency pairs are EUR-USD, USD-JPY, USD-CHF, GBP-USD, EUR-JPY, EUR-GBP, and EUR-CHF.

- *Permitted Instruments*. A currency mandate agreement may also specify which instruments the manager is permitted to use. The manager may be constrained to trade spot and forwards contracts only, or he could be allowed discretion to use plain vanilla currency options or other derivative instruments such as exotic currency options (barrier or basket options, etc.). In the case of a currency overlay agreement, derivatives may offer a more efficient way of hedging particular risks in the underlying portfolio or of taking asymmetric trades that leave the underlying portfolio unharmed if the currency moves in one direction but allows the manager to benefit if the currency moves in a way that he has forecasted. In the case of an absolute return mandate, derivative instruments are often a more efficient way to obtain leverage, and so whether or not they are permitted may be linked to how much leverage is allowed by the mandate.
- *Leverage*. The degree of leverage allowed is an important consideration for absolute return mandate agreements and also for currency overlays that have some return seeking objective. A manager could be constrained to use leverage, or allowed discretion to vary leverage up to some limit, depending on market conditions. For an absolute return mandate, leverage up to a factor of 10 is typical, but greater leverage is feasible and sometimes observed in certain hedge funds or managed trading accounts. Rather than specify leverage, a currency mandate could instead specify target volatility, expected return, or worst permitted drawdown.
- *Performance Benchmark and Compensation*. Last but certainly not least, a currency mandate will specify how performance, or really outperformance, will be measured and how performance will be compensated. For an absolute return mandate, when a manager is given trading authority over a pool of funds, the benchmark for performance on those funds could be LIBID, or LIBID + $X$, or some other index denominated in the investor's base currency. Investing the assigned assets at LIBID is essentially risk free, while benchmarks greater than LIBID entail risk. When the manager receives only a line of credit against funds that are invested elsewhere, the benchmark for performance can be zero, an amount $X > 0$, or another measure of performance. A manager who never draws on the credit line, and never takes a currency position, will earn zero return and incur zero risk. Active use of the credit line in the pursuit of positive returns entails risk. Performance benchmarks for a currency overlay manager are usually designed to reflect the returns from a continuum of hedging choices from no hedging through continuous hedging of the entire underlying position. The returns from a strategy of a continuous 50% hedge are often taken as a naive benchmark for a currency overlay manager. We discuss the economic rationale for these benchmarks in Section 17.3.

Manager compensation itself often has several parameters, including in most cases an annual management fee and a performance incentive fee based on annual returns. For high net worth individuals and funds of funds that invest in currency hedge funds, the most common fee structure is a 2% per annum management fee (based on assets under management) and a 20% share of profits earned over the year.[7] Institutional clients are likely to negotiate management fees that are far lower while still being subject to the 20% performance fee. In addition, compensation is usually governed by a high watermark rule such that annual[8] performance fees are paid only to the extent that returns push the manager's cumulative returns above the previous high watermark.[9]

### 17.2.2 STRUCTURAL AND OPERATIONAL CHOICES

The agreement between an institutional investor and manager is also likely to lay out various structural or operating principles of the relationship. Perhaps the most fundamental choice is whether, or to what degree, the account is funded or unfunded. In a *funded program*, the investor designates specific funds that are placed in custody accounts where the manager is permitted to trade. For example, a pension fund sponsor might allocate \$10 million to a currency fund manager. If the mandate allows for 10 times leverage, the currency manager would have up to \$100 million AUM to invest. These funds would be placed on deposit earning LIBID unless otherwise committed to a foreign currency trading strategy. If the pension fund sponsor had begun with \$100 million in global equity holdings, carving off \$10 million for currency would change the sponsor's exposure to \$90 million in global equity, and \$10 million to \$100 million in currency, depending on the degree of leverage devoted to currency.

In an *unfunded program*, the plan sponsor retains custody of his underlying assets but earmarks some of those assets to collateralize a trading account for use by the currency manager.[10] In this case, initially, the currency manager has no assets and so faces a zero return unless trading positions are established.

In principle, an absolute return mandate could be executed through either a funded or an unfunded structure. A currency overlay mandate is more commonly implemented using an unfunded structure, as the plan sponsor may wish to retain the ability to trade the underlying foreign currency assets that require the overlay.

Other operational choices may be covered in a currency mandate such as which banks and exchanges may be used for trading. The introduction of the

---

[7]A review of the fee structure for currency funds who report through the TASS and CISDM databases shows that the 2% management fee and 20% performance fee are the modal charges. However, some managers assess fees that are higher than the "2 and 20", while others charge less.

[8]Many funds calculate performance fees based on monthly or quarterly performance, subject to lifetime or rolling high watermarks.

[9]For example, consider an absolute return mandate where initial AUM is \$100 and first year returns are 25%, pushing the AUM to \$125. The manager is paid a performance fee of 20% on the \$25 profit, so that AUM at the start of year 2 is \$120. If the manager loses 10% in year 2, AUM declines to \$108 and no performance fee is paid. If the manager gains 20% in year 3, AUM rises by \$21.6 to \$129.6. The manager is paid his performance fee only on the portion of annual profits, \$9.6 in this case, that pushes the funds AUM above the earlier high watermark of \$120.

[10]The plan sponsor may have to provide cash as collateral rather than securities. Typically, a currency overlay program for a \$100 million foreign currency portfolio could be supported by \$10 million in cash collateral.

so-called prime brokerage services by investment banks has allowed hedge fund managers to source liquidity from a variety of market makers while maintaining a credit relationship, placing collateral, and settling with a single entity—the prime broker. Thus, prime brokerage allows hedge funds, despite having a possibly limited credit history or higher risk profile, to use the prime broker's credit rating to gain access to new counterparties. Typical services offered by the prime broker are leverage, access to market liquidity, and consolidated settlement, clearing, and reporting. The availability of prime brokerage services allows more experienced currency traders and strategists to set up as currency managers who can secure sponsor mandates and operate efficiently.

### 17.2.3 THE ALPHA CONTINUUM AND IMPLICATIONS OF ACTIVE CURRENCY MANDATES

As the above discussion suggests, an agreement between an institutional plan sponsor and a currency manager has numerous features, some of which allow the manager to have greater latitude in pursuing excess returns and managing risks, while other aspects that constrain him. By agreeing on a mandate, the sponsor and currency manager target a combination of expected return and risk. At one extreme, the sponsor can design a currency overlay mandate intended to provide only currency risk reduction with no expected return; at another extreme, the sponsor can design an absolute return mandate to authorize the currency manager to hunt for the maximum alpha conditional on an acceptable level of risk.[11] Between these two extremes, we observe an alpha continuum of target alpha levels and risks.

With many possible types of mandates, each one constrained or liberated to pursue return in a unique way, it may be difficult to agree on a unique performance benchmark. Melvin and Shand (2011) highlight many of the differences in trading styles, objectives, risk management strategies, and so on that make it difficult to create a widely accepted performance benchmark in the currency asset class. We discuss alternative performance benchmarks in the next section.

## 17.3 Benchmarks for Currency Fund Management

In Section 17.2, we described two alternative currency management mandates: a currency overlay mandate and an absolute return mandate.[12] Because a currency overlay mandate is often primarily concerned with risk reduction while an absolute return mandate is more focused on generating additional returns, the methodology for benchmarking these mandates differs considerably.

[11] By definition, alpha is the difference between the absolute return earned and the return on the benchmark, so not all absolute return is included in alpha. In the next section, we propose alternative benchmarks and alpha measures.

[12] The pure alpha mandate could also be thought of as an absolute return mandate.

In the case of a currency overlay, the objective is always to hedge some portion of the preexisting currency risk in an asset portfolio. In addition, the mandate may also include the option for the overlay manager to capture some additional return via selective hedging. The currency overlay manager could be evaluated versus a benchmark of performance calculated as if 0% of the underlying exposure were hedged or as if 100% of the exposure were hedged.[13] Strange (1998) argues that ultimately the performance of managers evaluated against these benchmarks depends on whether the base currency for measuring performance appreciated or depreciated over the cycle. For this reason, Strange suggests that the 50% hedge ratio became the most popular benchmark. A currency manager is deemed to add value if he outperforms a naive strategy of hedging half the exposure, as if having no expertise to determine whether a currency was rising or falling relative to its forward premium. Strange reports that in his sample of 152 overlay programs managed by 11 firms, on average, 80% outperformed their individually specified benchmarks.[14]

In this chapter, however, our primary interest concerns the benchmarking and performance of fund managers with absolute return mandates. We identify three types of benchmarks: a traditional benchmark in widespread use among currency management professionals, an alternative benchmark based on the returns of various investment style factors, and, finally, another alternative benchmark based on the expected return for bearing foreign exchange risk.

According to the traditional benchmark, the expected rate of return associated with holding currency risk is zero. This conventional benchmark gained credence from macroeconomic models of the 1970s supplemented by financial theory according to which currency risk was diversifiable and therefore not a risk compensated by a risk premium. Another way of expressing this idea is that foreign exchange trading is a zero-sum game where every profitable position is matched by an opposite losing position.[15] According to this argument, unlike equities or real estate, currency does not generate a net profit to reward all holders of currency risk. Moreover, to the extent that currency returns were shown to exist, empirical studies showed that these returns were uncorrelated with a general market index. Currency was therefore seen as a zero-beta asset that in equilibrium was not associated with a positive expected rate of return. And finally, numerous studies argued that exchange rate changes were largely unpredictable and that the most consistent currency forecast was one based on the random walk, assuming no drift.[16] In that setting, speculators have no special ability to

[13]Strange (1998) refers to these as *polar benchmarks*.

[14]Strange also notes that in his 1998 study, the earliest mandates had been given out only 10 years earlier, or about the year the financial press first began reporting on currency as an asset class.

[15]A recent article in the *Financial Times* (December 15, 2010) Lex column also makes these points.

[16]Meese and Rogoff (1983) are responsible for this famous result. Returning to the topic years later, Rogoff (2002) writes "To make a long story short not only have a subsequent twenty years of data and research failed to overturn the Meese-Rogoff result, they have cemented it, . . . "

outforecast the market, so the expected return from currency speculation could be zero.[17]

By comparison, Arbitrage Pricing Theory (APT) offers an alternative approach for modeling the expected rate of return on financial assets.[18] APT posits that the expected return on a financial asset can be expressed as a linear function of certain macroeconomic factors or market indices. APT was developed in the context of pricing stocks.[19] More recently, Fung and Hsieh (2002) used an APT framework to model hedge fund returns. The model specification takes the form

$$R_t = \alpha + \sum_i \beta_i F_{i,t} + \varepsilon_t \tag{17.1}$$

where

- $R$, the fund's return at time $t$;
- $\alpha$, a measure of active manager skill;
- $F$, a style factor;
- $\beta$, a coefficient or factor loading that measures the sensitivity of the manager's returns to the factor; and
- $\varepsilon$, a random error term.

Fung and Hsieh (2002) note that asset-based style factors can be interpreted in the same way as traditional market indices if two conditions are satisfied. First, there must be complete transparency in how factor returns are derived. Second, the return series must be sufficiently long to produce reliable statistical results. In principle, APT could be used for modeling currency returns if suitable factors can be identified.

Finally, a variation on the above approach makes explicit allowance for currency risk factors not captured in Equation (17.1). Nucera and Valente (2010) argue that excess performance is that component of returns over and above what can be explained by the manager's exposure to a set of currency risk factors. For example, performance in excess of a carry trading index would represent excess performance only to the extent that the extra return was unrelated to other identifiable currency-related risks.

### 17.3.1 A BASIC FACTOR MODEL FOR CURRENCY RETURNS

Financial market theory tells us that the return of any portfolio can be decomposed into beta and alpha components. The beta component captures the systematic relationship between returns and the special factors driving returns. The beta component for currency might stem from exposures to risk factors or trading styles similar to how arbitrage pricing models have been used to relate equity

[17]If the random walk, no drift model is taken seriously, then the carry trade in which speculators borrow a low interest rate currency and invest in a high interest rate currency ought to earn an expected profit (subject to risk).

[18]The original formulation of the APT was by Ross (1976).

[19]For example, see Roll and Ross (1980) and Chen et al. (1986) for empirical tests relating macroeconomic variables with stock prices. See Huberman and Wang (2005) for a review article.

returns to various factors such as firm size, book value to market value ratios, market price to earnings ratios, and so on.

For currencies to qualify as an "asset class," there should be factors that correlate with or explain patterns of currency fund manager returns. Building on earlier hedge fund research, and several well-known currency trading strategies, Pojarliev and Levich (2008) propose four possible factors that could explain currency returns earned by professional managers. In generic terms, these factors are the follwing.

- *Carry*. To reflect the returns on the well-known strategy of borrowing in one or more low interest rate currencies and investing in a higher interest rate currency. A carry strategy entails risk because the low interest rate currency may depreciate, and possibly by more than the interest differential, which would result in a loss.
- *Trend Following*. To reflect the returns of investing in currencies with upside momentum financed by borrowing in currencies with downside momentum. Trend-following strategies entail many risks such as sudden reversals of trends or patterns and excessive trading costs.
- *Value*. To reflect the returns of borrowing in an overvalued currency and investing in an undervalued currency. A value strategy is exposed to the risk that currency values may become still more misaligned, that rates will be slow to revert toward the equilibrium (e.g., purchasing power parity (PPP)) value, or that the currency's long-run real exchange rate has changed consistent with a new PPP exchange rate.
- *Volatility*. To reflect the impact of currency volatility on trading returns. Different from the other three factors, this factor does not represent the return of a trading strategy,[20] but simply the change in foreign exchange volatility. Currency managers incur exposure to volatility risk not only simply by taking open currency positions but also by using options and other derivatives whose prices are sensitive to volatility.

These four factors can be proxied by well-defined trading strategies that are easily replicated and transparent within the currency domain. As Melvin and Shand (2011) stress, there are many ways to implement any of the four proposed trading styles. For example, currency managers using a value strategy could use alternative specifications of PPP and use different indicators of misalignment to trigger their buy and sell orders. Managers might also vary the menu of currencies they monitor. To be a credible and useful benchmark, the factor model should rely on trading strategies that are purposely naive and transparent. If so structured, a factor model then offers a reasonable benchmark that professionals could attain, and surpass if they have skills beyond these naive

[20]Although some currency managers trade volatility as an asset class, anecdotal evidence suggests that they represent a very small subsample of the currency management industry. We are unaware of a generic, clearly defined volatility index (investable exchange traded fund (ETF)), which is designed to capture the return of trading currency volatility as an asset class.

strategies. In the following sections, we present an overview of the empirical evidence for the four-factor model.

# 17.4 Empirical Evidence with the Barclay Currency Traders Index and Individual Fund Managers

To estimate the four-factor model, researchers require data on currency manager returns and factors that proxy for types of trading strategies and exposures that currency managers would be likely to utilize.

## 17.4.1 EMPIRICAL EVIDENCE WITH THE BARCLAY CURRENCY TRADERS INDEX

Pojarliev and Levich (2008) analyzed the returns of currency managers included in the Barclay Currency Traders Index (BCTI). The BCTI is an equal-weighted composite of managed programs that trade currency futures and forwards. The BCTI offers one representative benchmark for the performance of the currency management industry.[21] The number of funds in the BCTI varied from about 40 to 70 between 1973 and 2004 and then steadily increased to 114 in 2007. After a decline during the global financial crisis, by the end of 2010, the BCTI included 119 currency programs.

To examine the relationship between currency manager returns and style factors, Pojarliev and Levich (2008) used monthly data on the BCTI for the period from January 1990 until December 2006 (204 months). Exhibit 17.1 Panel A shows the results for Equation (17.1) for the entire sample period (row 1) and two subperiods (rows 2 and 3). The style factors for this estimation were the Citibank Beta1 G10 Carry Index[22] as a proxy for a carry factor, the

[21] Other possible sources of data on overall currency fund returns include the Currency Managers Index prepared by Parker Global Strategies, the CISDM CTA Currency Indexes prepared by The Center for International Securities and Derivatives Markets at the University of Massachusetts Amherst, and the HFRX Currency Index prepared by Hedge Fund Research Inc. To our knowledge, the BCTI reflects the longest sample of data on currency manager returns.

[22] The Beta1 G10 Carry Index reflects returns on a long high yielding and short low yielding strategy based on 10 countries and 17 currency pairs. *Source:* The Citibank Investor Risk Advisory Group.

The AFX Index reflects returns on a trend-following strategy involving three moving average rules applied to seven currency pairs, weighted by the volume of turnover in the spot market. The seven currency pairs are EUR-USD, USD-JPY, USD-CHF, GBP-USD, EUR-JPY, EUR-GBP, and EUR-CHF.

The Beta1 G10 PPP Index reflects returns on 13 pairs of currencies selected from among the 10 major currencies, taking long positions in currencies that are more than 20% undervalued against short positions in currencies that are more than 20% overvalued, using Organization for Economic Cooperation and Development (OECD) measures of PPP as a gauge for valuation. *Source:* The Citibank Investor Risk Advisory Group.

The FX Volatility factor is a simple average of the 1-month implied volatility on EUR-USD options and USD-JPY options. *Source:* Citibank.

Equations in Panel A estimated with style factors A, and equations in Panel B estimated with style factors B.

| | Sample Period | $N$ Month | Intercept | Carry | Trend | Value | Volatility | $R^2$ |
|---|---|---|---|---|---|---|---|---|
| **Panel A** | 1. January 1990 to December 2006 | 204 | −9 bps<br>(−0.74) | 0.70<br>(3.30) | 1.28<br>(17.45) | −1.02<br>(−2.26) | 0.04<br>(0.44) | 0.664 |
| | 2. January 1990 to December 2000 | 132 | −16 bps<br>(−0.88) | 0.75<br>(2.78) | 1.45<br>(14.92) | −1.38<br>(−2.45) | −0.05<br>(−0.39) | 0.680 |
| | 3. January 2001 to December 2006 | 72 | −11 bps<br>(−1.00) | 1.04<br>(3.99) | 0.78<br>(9.72) | −0.64<br>(−1.01) | 0.34<br>(3.09) | 0.767 |
| **Panel B** | 4. January 2001 to December 2006 | 72 | −7 bps<br>(−0.69) | 0.29<br>(3.96) | 0.79<br>(10.09) | −0.07<br>(−1.25) | 0.40<br>(1.93) | 0.778 |
| | 5. January 2001 to August 2010 | 116 | −2 bps<br>(−0.21) | 0.21<br>(5.38) | 0.60<br>(10.41) | −0.09<br>(−2.65) | 0.13<br>(1.39) | 0.607 |
| | 6. January 2008 to August 2010 | 44 | 4 bps<br>(0.64) | 0.04<br>(1.85) | 0.20<br>(5.29) | −0.02<br>(−0.93) | 0.03<br>(0.71) | 0.506 |

Notes: The dependent variable in each regression is the monthly excess return of the Barclay Currency Traders Index minus the risk-free rate. $t$-statistics are in parentheses below each estimated coefficient. Style factors A are those used in Pojarliev and Levich (2008):

> The Citibank Betal G10 Carry Index is the proxy for a carry factor, the AFX Currency Management index is the proxy for the trend factor, the Citibank Beta1 G10 Purchasing Power Parity index is the proxy for the value factor and the average of the 1-month implied volatility for the EUR-USD exchange rate and for the USD-JPY exchange rate is the proxy for the volatility factor. *Source*: Citibank and Liverpool John Moores University.

Style factors B are those used in Pojarliev and Levich (2010):

> The DB Currency Harvest G10 Index is the proxy for the carry index. The AFX Currency Management Index is again the proxy for the trend factor. The DB Currency Valuation Excess Return USD Index is the proxy for the returns of a value strategy. The DB FX Volatility Index is the proxy for foreign exchange volatility. *Source*: Deutsche Bank, Bloomberg and Liverpool John Moores University.

**EXHIBIT 17.1 Excess Currency Index Returns as a Function of Four Factors**

AFX Currency Management index as a proxy for the trend factor, the Citibank Beta1 G10 PPP index as a proxy for the value factor, and the average of the 1-month implied volatility for the EUR-USD exchange rate and for the USD-JPY exchange rate as a proxy for the volatility factor.

The results are quite striking. First, the $R^2$ of the regression for the entire 17-year sample period and the two subperiods are very high, indicating that these factors (carry, trend, value, and volatility) account for roughly two-thirds to three-quarters of the variability in monthly excess returns.[23] For the entire sample, both the carry and trend factors are highly significant with positive coefficients, while value has a significant negative coefficient. The negative coefficient on value indicates that managers tended to be short value and returns were negatively impacted as the value factor tended to rise over the sample period. In the first subperiod (row 2), the coefficient of value and its *t*-value are similar to the entire sample. But in the second subperiod (row 3), the carry coefficient is larger, trend is smaller, value becomes insignificant, and volatility becomes positive and significant.

Second, for the entire sample and each subperiod, the intercept term is small and not significantly different than zero. This result implies that as a group, managers included in the BCTI on average were not able to generate alpha returns. In the 2001–2006 period, for example, after accounting for our four systematic risk factors—carry, trend, value, and volatility—the first three of which reflect returns on naive currency trading strategies, alpha was −11 basis points per month or about −1.3% per year over the 72-month period. The overall excess return on the BCTI was 8 bps per month in this period, but all of that return and more (19 bps) can be attributed to the four explanatory factors.[24]

**17.4.1.1 Robustness Checks.** As a robustness check, we reestimate Equation (17.1) using different proxies for the risk factors carry, trend, value, and volatility. The proxies are the same variables as in Pojarliev and Levich (2010).

As a proxy for the return on the carry factor, we use the Deutsche Bank (DB) Currency Harvest G10 Index. This index reflects the return of being long the three high yielding currencies against being short the three low yielding currencies within the G10 currency universe (the Bloomberg code for this factor is DBHVG10U Index).

As a proxy for the trend-following factor, we use again the AFX Currency Management Index.[25]

[23]Monthly excess returns are calculated by taking the manager's total return minus the periodic risk-free rate.

[24]On the basis of our estimated model, the 19 bps comprises 22 bps attributed to carry (equal to the carry coefficient multiplied by the average carry return), 4 bps to trend, −4 bps to value, and −3 bps to volatility.

[25]We conclude that the AFX Currency Management Index is a good proxy for the trend factor in part because it is a transparent and consistent index that is calculated by an independent third party. The AFX Index was introduced in 1998 (Lequeux and Acar, 1998) and has been used for a number of years in various research papers and is therefore known to researchers in the field.

We use the DB Currency Valuation Excess Return USD Index as the proxy for the returns of a value strategy. To gauge relative value, DB prepares a ranking based on the average daily spot rate over the last 3 months divided by the PPP exchange rate as published annually by the OECD. The DB Currency Valuation Excess Return USD index reflects the return of being long the three currencies with the highest rank (undervalued currencies) against being short the three currencies with the lowest rank (overvalued currencies) within G10 currency universe (the Bloomberg code for this factor is DBPPPUSF index).

Finally, we use the DB FX Volatility Index as the proxy for foreign exchange volatility. This index is calculated as the weighted average of 3-month implied volatility for nine major currency pairs (as provided by the British Bankers Association) with weights based on trading volume in the BIS surveys (the Bloomberg code for this factor is CVIX Index).[26] We use the first difference for this factor in Equation (17.1) as it is not a trading strategy. We use logarithmic returns for the carry, trend, and value factors.

Exhibit 17.1 Panel B shows the results for Equation (17.1) for the BCTI from January 2001 until December 2006 with these alternative proxies for risk factors. The results in row 4 are almost identical to the results in row 3. The $R^2$ for the regression is nearly identical at 78%. The trend factor exhibits similar coefficient and $t$-statistic. The estimated coefficient for the carry factor is much lower, but the $t$-statistic is similar. Value is again not significant, and volatility is only significant at a 10% significance level. The intercept term is −7 basis points and not statistically significant.

These results confirm that using alternative proxies for risk factors, the results are fairly similar and confirm that between January 2001 and December 2006, currency managers as a group delivered zero[27] alpha.[28] This result is not surprising and similar to findings in other asset classes.[29]

**17.4.1.2 Extended Sample Periods.** Exhibit 17.1 row 5 extends the sample until August 2010. The results are similar to row 4 with the notable exception that value is now significant and volatility not significant. The $R^2$ is slightly lower at 61% and the alpha slightly higher at −2 basis points but again not significant.

[26] The nine currency pairs are EUR-USD, USD-JPY, USD-CHF, USD-CAD, AUD-USD, GBP-USD, EUR-JPY, EUR-GBP, and EUR-CHF.

[27] While estimating Equation (17.1) informs us about a manager's investment style, the beta coefficients are not known ex-ante and so the alpha estimates might be biased downward. Put differently, without knowledge of the betas, Equation (17.1) is not an investable strategy that managers could mimic even if desired. To address such concerns, Pojarliev and Levich (2010) estimate a single-index model where the index ($I_t$) is an equally weighted average of the available currency strategies. If a manager then outperforms this measure of beta, even by simply reweighting the styles, this would constitute alpha from style allocations. Pojarliev and Levich (2010) report that the estimates of alpha are essentially unchanged when based on the single-factor model.

[28] Melvin and Shand (2011) consider using other proxies such as trend, carry, and value indices prepared by Citibank, Credit Suisse, and DB. The authors claim that regression results and estimates of alpha are sensitive to the selection of proxies for style factors.

[29] Leibowitz (2005) argues that not everyone can be a winner as attested by the narrowness of the list of great investors and that most investors should treat the market as being highly efficient.

Exhibit 17.1 row 6 uses only the updated sample from January 2008 until August 2010 (44 monthly observations) and represents an out-of-sample experiment.[30] The results confirm that the four-factor model has explanatory power out of sample and over a short time horizon. The $R^2$ is again quite high at 51% and the intercept (alpha) is not significant. Trend is the only significant variable during this period, which could be explained by the fact that this time period spans a very turbulent period in the financial markets including the Lehman bankruptcy in September 2008, the European sovereign debt crises in early 2010, and the "flash" crash in May 2010. In addition, the carry strategy collapsed in the second half of 2008, which could explain the zero coefficient of the carry factor. Indeed, Pojarliev and Levich (2008) found that currency managers exhibit market timing skills (increasing exposures to well-performing factors and decreasing exposure to poor-performing factors). This suggests that currency managers might have trimmed exposure to carry in the second half of 2008.[31]

### 17.4.2 INDIVIDUAL CURRENCY MANAGER RETURNS

When sufficient data are available, Equation (17.1) can be estimated for individual currency managers. Drawing on Pojarliev and Levich (2008), Exhibit (17.2) Panel A shows the regression results of the four-factor model for 34 individual currency managers included in the BCTI with a track record that spans a 6-year period from January 2001 to December 2006.

Several observations stand out. First, only eight managers exhibit positive and significant alpha (intercept). Second, the four-factor model helps to differentiate between alpha hunters, who generate returns independent of simple trading strategies, and beta grazers, whose returns are heavily correlated with the performance of those trading strategies.[32] For example, manager M2 has significant exposure toward three factors: carry, trend, and volatility. The coefficients on these three factors are highly significant and the $R^2$ (0.688) is the highest of all 34 managers. This manager generated an annualized excess return of 3.70% over the 6-year sample, but these appear to be primarily beta returns. The alpha for M2 is negative (2 bps per month) and not statistically different than zero.

On the other end of the spectrum is manager M28. The $R^2$ for M28 is 0.0347, among the lowest in the sample, suggesting that he has no significant exposure toward any of the four factors. However, manager M28 has generated a significant alpha of 0.29% per month. The average annualized excess return for manager M28 is 3.02%, a little less than the excess return generated by manager

[30]We use the four-factor model presented by Pojarliev and Levich (2008) with data available after publication.

[31]This is reaffirmed in Pojarliev and Levich (2011), where the authors show that the fraction of currency managers who significantly tracked carry sharply declined in the second half of 2008.

[32]Leibowitz (2005) introduces the terms *alpha hunter* and *beta grazer*.

Regression Results for $R_{j,t} = \alpha_j \Sigma_i \beta_{i,j} F_{i,t} + \varepsilon_{j,t}$ for managers j = 1, . . . ,34.
Panel A Based on 72 monthly observations, January 2001–December 2006.

| Manager | Intercept | *t*-Stat | Beta Carry | *t*-Stat | Beta Trend | *t*-Stat | Beta Value | *t*-Stat | Beta Volatility | *t*-Stat | $R^2$ |
|---|---|---|---|---|---|---|---|---|---|---|---|
| M1 | 0.0184 | 3.3236 | −0.655 | −0.5143 | −0.0269 | −0.0687 | −1.6564 | −0.5314 | −0.1815 | −0.3414 | 0.0189 |
| M2 | −0.002 | −1.1294 | 2.2714 | 5.4067 | 0.9036 | 6.9854 | 0.3357 | 0.3265 | 0.3762 | 2.1457 | 0.6889 |
| M3 | 0.0002 | 0.2317 | −0.3562 | −1.3858 | −0.0029 | −0.037 | 0.6393 | 1.0164 | 0.0662 | 0.6172 | 0.0401 |
| M4 | 0.0024 | 1.3573 | −0.4595 | −1.1223 | −0.2625 | −2.0827 | 2.1998 | 2.1954 | 0.3418 | 2.0002 | 0.1757 |
| M5 | −0.0034 | −1.4687 | 2.6656 | 4.8841 | 0.7108 | 4.2298 | −0.2206 | −0.1651 | 0.063 | 0.2768 | 0.5157 |
| M6 | −0.0074 | −1.2462 | 6.662 | 4.8397 | 1.7715 | 4.1797 | −0.8883 | −0.2636 | 0.2216 | 0.3857 | 0.5103 |
| M7 | 0.0015 | 3.4981 | −0.1508 | −1.4402 | 0.0155 | 0.4808 | −0.161 | −0.6284 | 0.0763 | 1.746 | 0.1658 |
| M8 | 0.0051 | 3.9239 | −0.4723 | −1.5731 | 0.0579 | 0.6264 | −0.3537 | −0.4812 | 0.2144 | 1.7106 | 0.1681 |
| M9 | 0.0086 | 1.495 | 0.1918 | 0.1436 | 0.028 | 0.0681 | 1.3053 | 0.3995 | 0.1539 | 0.2761 | 0.0058 |
| M10 | 0.0025 | 0.9721 | 0.0786 | 0.1297 | 0.0439 | 0.2355 | 0.6464 | 0.4356 | 0.0295 | 0.1167 | 0.0066 |
| M11 | −0.0015 | −4.4319 | −0.081 | −1.0098 | −0.0138 | −0.5622 | 0.2719 | 1.3853 | 0.0107 | 0.3205 | 0.0479 |
| M12 | 0.0004 | 0.11 | −1.2423 | −1.2625 | 0.5025 | 1.6586 | 2.1556 | 0.8951 | 0.7023 | 1.7099 | 0.141 |
| M13 | 0.0001 | 0.0482 | 0.1051 | 0.118 | 1.4515 | 5.2885 | −1.5816 | −0.725 | 0.5213 | 1.4012 | 0.4566 |
| M14 | 0.0109 | 1.0571 | −4.0068 | −1.6923 | 2.1114 | 2.8963 | −0.3642 | −0.0628 | −1.6972 | −1.7174 | 0.1479 |
| M15 | −0.0002 | −0.0582 | 1.972 | 2.3417 | 0.933 | 3.5983 | −2.3471 | −1.1387 | 0.3023 | 0.86 | 0.3462 |
| M16 | 0.0022 | 0.9892 | −0.1483 | −0.2876 | 0.2014 | 1.2678 | 3.5933 | 2.8459 | 0.1525 | 0.7083 | 0.1461 |
| M17 | −0.0061 | −1.4582 | 3.2239 | 3.327 | 0.1397 | 0.4685 | 4.8788 | 2.0572 | 0.1974 | 0.4882 | 0.3483 |
| M18 | −0.0018 | −1.2855 | 0.3595 | 1.0952 | −0.0601 | −0.5954 | 1.3643 | 1.6981 | 0.2302 | 1.6802 | 0.1313 |
| M19 | 0.0023 | 0.7936 | 0.5512 | 0.8039 | −0.3075 | −1.4568 | −1.9338 | −1.1523 | 0.3323 | 1.1612 | 0.0474 |

**EXHIBIT 17.2** Regression Results for Individual Currency Managers

| | | | | | | | | | | | |
|---|---|---|---|---|---|---|---|---|---|---|---|
| M20 | 0.0027 | 0.2994 | −0.7516 | −0.3602 | 5.5147 | 8.5848 | −0.574 | −0.1124 | 0.616 | 0.7074 | 0.6294 |
| M21 | −0.0041 | −0.6902 | 2.5661 | 1.8694 | 3.0227 | 7.0749 | 0.4007 | 0.118 | 0.3109 | 0.5369 | 0.5618 |
| M22 | −0.0004 | −0.1536 | 1.5987 | 2.3802 | 0.3345 | 1.6175 | 2.3903 | 1.4541 | 0.2561 | 0.9135 | 0.2505 |
| M23 | 0.0064 | 1.5299 | −0.4939 | −0.512 | 0.3493 | 1.1761 | 1.4823 | 0.6278 | 0.6301 | 1.5648 | 0.0906 |
| M24 | 0.0001 | 0.1236 | −0.5023 | −1.4654 | 0.9771 | 9.2566 | 0.6966 | 0.8302 | 0.0747 | 0.5223 | 0.6429 |
| M25 | 0.0106 | 3.3421 | −0.043 | −0.059 | 0.108 | 0.4816 | 3.6282 | 2.0347 | 0.6363 | 2.0924 | 0.1244 |
| M26 | 0.0216 | 3.9814 | −1.422 | −1.1389 | 0.1577 | 0.4102 | 1.5233 | 0.4985 | 0.7424 | 1.4245 | 0.0705 |
| M27 | −0.0003 | −0.2091 | 0.2896 | 0.7629 | 0.4485 | 3.8373 | −0.1075 | −0.1157 | 0.5799 | 3.6603 | 0.4567 |
| M28 | 0.0029 | 2.0267 | −0.0783 | −0.2363 | −0.0064 | −0.0633 | −0.1904 | −0.2346 | 0.1627 | 1.1755 | 0.0347 |
| M29 | 0.0162 | 3.5206 | −1.0116 | −0.9535 | 0.0415 | 0.1271 | 4.841 | 1.8645 | 0.8304 | 1.8753 | 0.0919 |
| M30 | 0.0027 | 0.504 | 4.059 | 3.221 | 2.0985 | 5.4085 | −8.4047 | −2.7251 | 1.1319 | 2.152 | 0.5855 |
| M31 | −0.0014 | −0.459 | 1.5484 | 2.1666 | 1.7395 | 7.905 | −2.2846 | −1.3061 | 0.4585 | 1.537 | 0.6541 |
| M32 | 0.007 | 2.0515 | −0.2912 | −0.3673 | 1.5875 | 6.5019 | −0.5135 | −0.2645 | 0.7304 | 2.2068 | 0.5621 |
| M33 | 0.0106 | 1.522 | 1.0493 | 0.6563 | −0.3504 | −0.7118 | −1.9321 | −0.4938 | 1.8784 | 2.815 | 0.1196 |
| M34 | 0.0014 | 1.2557 | 0.5082 | 1.9439 | 0.2158 | 2.6814 | −0.0213 | −0.0333 | 0.1457 | 1.3351 | 0.2583 |
| Average | 0.0032 | 0.7461 | 0.5157 | 0.6091 | 0.7187 | 2.3961 | 0.2594 | 0.3014 | 0.3323 | 1.1784 | 0.2718 |
| Maximum | 0.0216 | 3.9814 | 6.662 | 5.4067 | 5.5147 | 9.2566 | 4.8788 | 2.8459 | 1.8784 | 3.6603 | 0.6889 |
| Median | 0.0019 | 0.6488 | 0.0178 | 0.0295 | 0.2086 | 1.222 | 0.1253 | 0.0424 | 0.2792 | 1.2553 | 0.167 |
| Minimum | −0.0074 | −4.4319 | −4.0068 | −1.6923 | −0.3504 | −2.0827 | −8.4047 | −2.7251 | −1.6972 | −1.7174 | 0.0058 |

**EXHIBIT 17.2** *(Continued)*

Regression Results for $R_{j,t} = \alpha_j + \Sigma_i \beta_{i,j} F_{i,t} + \varepsilon_{j,t}$ for managers j = 1,....34.
Panel B Based on 36 monthly observations, January 2001 - December 2003.

| Manager | Intercept | *t*-Stat | Beta Carry | *t*-Stat | Beta Trend | *t*-Stat | Beta Value | *t*-Stat | Beta Volatility | *t*-Stat | $R^2$ |
|---|---|---|---|---|---|---|---|---|---|---|---|
| M1 | 0.0201 | 2.05 | −0.11 | −0.05 | −0.2 | −0.3 | −3.89 | −0.82 | −0.63 | −0.8 | 0.065 |
| M2 | −0.0022 | −1.04 | 2.28 | 5.17 | 0.93 | 6.18 | 0.73 | 0.7 | 0.23 | 1.36 | 0.821 |
| M3 | 0.0039 | 2.65 | −0.45 | −1.52 | −0.18 | −1.82 | 0.08 | 0.11 | 0.17 | 1.51 | 0.139 |
| M4 | 0.0027 | 1.07 | −0.21 | −0.41 | −0.17 | −0.95 | 1.58 | 1.28 | 0.17 | 0.86 | 0.114 |
| M5 | −0.0022 | −0.69 | 1.56 | 2.34 | 0.75 | 3.31 | 1.33 | 0.84 | 0.19 | 0.74 | 0.551 |
| M6 | −0.006 | −0.744 | 4.038 | 2.43 | 1.83 | 3.24 | 3.07 | 0.78 | 0.53 | 0.82 | 0.554 |
| M7 | 0.0018 | 2.53 | −0.11 | −0.72 | 0.02 | 0.44 | −0.11 | −0.32 | 0.04 | 0.76 | 0.102 |
| M8 | 0.0059 | 2.72 | −0.31 | −0.71 | 0.05 | 0.38 | −0.44 | −0.42 | 0.14 | 0.81 | 0.111 |
| M9 | 0.0191 | 1.65 | 1.29 | 0.54 | 0.05 | 0.07 | −1.48 | −0.26 | −0.24 | −0.26 | 0.013 |
| M10 | 0.0076 | 1.53 | 0.65 | 0.63 | 0.1 | 0.3 | −0.81 | −0.33 | −0.22 | −0.55 | 0.026 |
| M11 | −0.0008 | −1.26 | −0.03 | −0.29 | −0.02 | −0.53 | 0.15 | 0.5 | 0 | −0.12 | 0.039 |
| M12 | 0.0003 | 0.06 | 0.93 | 0.81 | 0.39 | 1 | −2.75 | −1.01 | 0.46 | 1.03 | 0.212 |
| M13 | 0.0001 | 0.02 | 1.12 | 0.86 | 1.73 | 3.9 | −4.37 | −1.42 | 0.12 | 0.23 | 0.541 |
| M14 | −0.0018 | −0.11 | −8.21 | −2.34 | 3.33 | 2.79 | 6.17 | 0.75 | −2.25 | −1.65 | 0.281 |
| M15 | 0.0032 | 0.5 | 2.55 | 1.94 | 1.36 | 3.04 | −4.73 | −1.52 | −0.08 | −0.17 | 0.455 |
| M16 | 0.004 | 1.13 | 0.22 | 0.31 | 0.12 | 0.51 | 2.97 | 1.7 | 0 | 0.02 | 0.167 |
| M17 | −0.006 | −0.92 | 4.24 | 3.2 | 0.32 | 0.71 | 4.45 | 1.42 | −0.41 | −0.8 | 0.511 |
| M18 | 0.0002 | 0.11 | 0.78 | 1.49 | −0.2 | −1.15 | 0.64 | 0.52 | 0.23 | 1.16 | 0.189 |
| M19 | −0.0017 | −0.43 | 0.66 | 0.81 | 0 | 0 | −1.17 | −0.61 | 0.11 | 0.36 | 0.035 |

**EXHIBIT 17.2** *(Continued)*

| | | | | | | | | | | | |
|---|---|---|---|---|---|---|---|---|---|---|---|
| M20 | 0.01 | 0.96 | 0.58 | 0.27 | 4.53 | 6.22 | −0.64 | −0.12 | 0.78 | 0.93 | 0.715 |
| M21 | 0.0044 | 0.51 | 2.03 | 1.15 | 2.18 | 3.61 | 2.7 | 0.65 | 0.77 | 1.12 | 0.524 |
| M22 | −0.0041 | −1.02 | 0.13 | 0.16 | 0.92 | 3.23 | 4.25 | 2.15 | 0 | 0.01 | 0.396 |
| M23 | 0.0017 | 0.26 | −1.67 | −1.26 | 1.12 | 2.5 | 3.79 | 1.22 | 0.44 | 0.87 | 0.293 |
| M24 | 0.0018 | 0.71 | −0.53 | −1.02 | 1.16 | 6.49 | 0.63 | 0.51 | −0.08 | −0.43 | 0.665 |
| M25 | 0.0167 | 3.3 | 0.53 | 0.52 | 0.16 | 0.46 | 2.59 | 1.06 | 0.58 | 1.45 | 0.18 |
| M26 | 0.0335 | 3.83 | −0.93 | −0.52 | 0.18 | 0.3 | −1.26 | −0.3 | 0.82 | 1.18 | 0.115 |
| M27 | −0.0013 | −0.5 | 0.46 | 0.84 | 0.51 | 2.74 | 1.05 | 0.81 | 0.51 | 2.43 | 0.523 |
| M28 | 0.0074 | 2.81 | 0.02 | 0.04 | −0.13 | −0.72 | −0.95 | −0.75 | 0.24 | 1.16 | 0.072 |
| M29 | 0.0246 | 2.87 | −2.29 | −1.31 | −0.14 | −0.24 | 5.03 | 1.22 | 1.33 | 1.96 | 0.165 |
| M30 | 0.0072 | 1.1 | 4.76 | 3.56 | 1.86 | 4.08 | −7.5 | −2.38 | 0.77 | 1.48 | 0.702 |
| M31 | 0.0019 | 0.42 | 1.59 | 1.67 | 1.74 | 5.36 | −1.65 | −0.73 | 0.56 | 1.52 | 0.712 |
| M32 | 0.0138 | 2.63 | 0.35 | 0.32 | 1.88 | 5.12 | −2.25 | −0.89 | 0.36 | 0.87 | 0.657 |
| M33 | 0.0101 | 0.88 | 0.74 | 0.31 | 0.26 | 0.32 | −3.65 | −0.66 | 1.2 | 1.32 | 0.134 |
| M34 | 0.0028 | 1.85 | 0.58 | 1.89 | 0.24 | 2.33 | 0.22 | 0.3 | 0.06 | 0.54 | 0.394 |
| Average | 0.0053 | 0.92 | 0.51 | 0.62 | 0.78 | 1.85 | 0.11 | 0.12 | 0.2 | 0.64 | 0.329 |
| Maximum | 0.0335 | 3.83 | 4.76 | 5.17 | 4.53 | 6.49 | 6.17 | 2.15 | 1.33 | 2.43 | 0.821 |
| Median | 0.0028 | 0.8 | 0.56 | 0.42 | 0.29 | 0.86 | 0.12 | 0.21 | 0.18 | 0.84 | 0.247 |
| Minimum | −0.006 | −1.26 | −8.21 | −2.34 | −0.2 | −1.82 | −7.5 | −2.38 | −2.25 | −1.65 | 0.013 |

**EXHIBIT 17.2** *(Continued)*

Regression Results for $R_{j,t} = \alpha_j + \sum_i \beta_{i,j} F_{i,t} + \varepsilon_{j,t}$ for managers j = 1, . . . ,34.
Panel C Based on 36 monthly observations, January 2004–December 2006.

| Manager | Intercept | *t*-Stat | Beta Carry | *t*-Stat | Beta Trend | *t*-Stat | Beta Value | *t*-Stat | Beta Volatility | *t*-Stat | $R^2$ |
|---|---|---|---|---|---|---|---|---|---|---|---|
| M1 | 0.0153 | 2.78 | 1.08 | 0.69 | 0.2 | 0.53 | 6.13 | 1.46 | 2.49 | 2.83 | 0.237 |
| M2 | −0.0025 | −0.81 | 2.62 | 3 | 0.87 | 4.01 | −0.43 | −0.18 | 0.79 | 1.61 | 0.557 |
| M3 | −0.0027 | −1.77 | 0.04 | 0.09 | 0.11 | 1.01 | 1.33 | 1.13 | 0.19 | 0.79 | 0.07 |
| M4 | 0.0017 | 0.64 | −0.44 | −0.58 | −0.33 | −1.77 | 3.68 | 1.82 | 0.75 | 1.77 | 0.273 |
| M5 | −0.0055 | −1.58 | 4.2 | 4.24 | 0.6 | 2.44 | −1.92 | −0.72 | 0.12 | 0.21 | 0.56 |
| M6 | −0.0111 | −1.23 | 10.43 | 4.08 | 1.58 | 2.48 | −4.94 | −0.72 | 0.47 | 0.33 | 0.544 |
| M7 | 0.0012 | 2.17 | −0.16 | −1.01 | 0 | 0.01 | −0.54 | −1.24 | 0.11 | 1.2 | 0.325 |
| M8 | 0.0042 | 2.61 | −0.54 | −1.18 | 0.04 | 0.36 | −0.83 | −0.67 | 0.33 | 1.27 | 0.3 |
| M9 | −0.0009 | −0.33 | −0.37 | −0.44 | −0.14 | −0.7 | 2.56 | 1.13 | 0.91 | 1.91 | 0.184 |
| M10 | −0.0023 | −1.33 | −0.13 | −0.26 | −0.08 | −0.65 | 1.61 | 1.19 | 0.53 | 1.88 | 0.163 |
| M11 | −0.0022 | −7.92 | −0.06 | −0.83 | −0.01 | −0.8 | 0.23 | 1.08 | 0.06 | 1.46 | 0.175 |
| M12 | 0.0025 | 0.39 | −3.81 | −2.14 | 0.73 | 1.65 | 11.05 | 2.31 | 1.1 | 1.1 | 0.283 |
| M13 | −0.0001 | −0.02 | −0.69 | −0.53 | 1.26 | 3.87 | 4.82 | 1.37 | 1.31 | 1.78 | 0.435 |
| M14 | 0.0139 | 1.24 | 3.59 | 1.12 | 1.12 | 1.41 | 2.27 | 0.26 | 1.36 | 0.75 | 0.139 |
| M15 | −0.0042 | −1.2 | 1.54 | 1.56 | 0.51 | 2.06 | 2.25 | 0.85 | 0.83 | 1.48 | 0.261 |
| M16 | 0.0003 | 0.12 | −0.12 | −0.14 | 0.25 | 1.22 | 4.05 | 1.83 | 0.66 | 1.43 | 0.147 |
| M17 | −0.0075 | −1.38 | 2.84 | 1.84 | −0.01 | −0.03 | 3.9 | 0.94 | 1.34 | 1.54 | 0.152 |
| M18 | −0.0031 | −2.34 | −0.15 | −0.4 | 0.04 | 0.51 | 1.17 | 1.15 | 0.17 | 0.81 | 0.059 |
| M19 | 0.0053 | 1.13 | 0.15 | 0.11 | −0.53 | −1.6 | −3.06 | −0.85 | 0.27 | 0.36 | 0.099 |

**EXHIBIT 17.2** *(Continued)*

| | | | | | | | | | | | |
|---|---|---|---|---|---|---|---|---|---|---|---|
| M20 | −0.0014 | −0.09 | −2.12 | −0.5 | 6.27 | 5.9 | −8.43 | −0.74 | 0.39 | 0.16 | 0.618 |
| M21 | −0.0107 | −1.33 | 3.42 | 1.5 | 3.56 | 6.24 | −9.58 | −1.56 | −0.17 | −0.13 | 0.677 |
| M22 | −0.0002 | −0.06 | 4.12 | 4.11 | −0.17 | −0.67 | 4.2 | 1.56 | 1.24 | 2.19 | 0.459 |
| M23 | 0.0084 | 1.59 | 0.36 | 0.24 | −0.35 | −0.94 | −0.39 | −0.09 | 0.25 | 0.29 | 0.029 |
| M24 | −0.002 | −1.25 | −0.28 | −0.61 | 0.76 | 6.64 | 0.47 | 0.38 | 0.29 | 1.12 | 0.662 |
| M25 | 0.0057 | 1.52 | −1.27 | −1.19 | −0.06 | −0.24 | 1.33 | 0.46 | −0.03 | −0.05 | 0.067 |
| M26 | 0.012 | 1.79 | −2.49 | −1.31 | −0.07 | −0.14 | 2.53 | 0.49 | 0 | 0 | 0.079 |
| M27 | 0.0006 | 0.38 | −0.41 | −0.87 | 0.36 | 3.08 | −4.65 | −3.63 | 0.06 | 0.22 | 0.627 |
| M28 | −0.0006 | −0.55 | −0.19 | −0.59 | 0.03 | 0.4 | −0.25 | −0.29 | 0.01 | 0.1 | 0.046 |
| M29 | 0.0091 | 2.3 | 0.32 | 0.29 | 0.02 | 0.1 | 4.1 | 1.36 | 0.12 | 0.2 | 0.091 |
| M30 | −0.0019 | −0.22 | 4.09 | 1.67 | 2.21 | 3.62 | −14.86 | −2.27 | 1.93 | 1.4 | 0.574 |
| M31 | −0.0038 | −0.9 | 0.7 | 0.58 | 1.62 | 5.4 | −7.25 | −2.24 | −0.54 | −0.8 | 0.62 |
| M32 | 0.0003 | 0.08 | −0.83 | −0.68 | 1.2 | 3.97 | 0.07 | 0.02 | 1.02 | 1.48 | 0.494 |
| M33 | 0.0075 | 0.89 | 3.43 | 1.44 | −0.83 | −1.39 | 7.83 | 1.22 | 4.41 | 3.29 | 0.274 |
| M34 | 0 | −0.02 | 0.44 | 0.94 | 0.14 | 1.25 | −1.72 | −1.34 | 0.15 | 0.57 | 0.204 |
| Average | 0.0007 | −0.14 | 0.86 | 0.42 | 0.61 | 1.45 | 0.2 | 0.16 | 0.67 | 1.02 | 0.308 |
| Maximum | 0.0153 | 2.78 | 10.43 | 4.24 | 6.27 | 6.64 | 11.05 | 2.31 | 4.41 | 3.29 | 0.677 |
| Median | −0.0002 | −0.04 | −0.01 | −0.03 | 0.13 | 0.77 | 0.82 | 0.42 | 0.36 | 1.11 | 0.267 |
| Minimum | −0.0111 | −7.92 | −3.81 | −2.14 | −0.83 | −1.77 | −14.86 | −3.63 | −0.54 | −0.8 | 0.029 |

EXHIBIT 17.2 *(Continued)*

Barclay Currency Traders Index represents an equally-weighted average of managed programs that trade currency futures and/or cash forwards in the inter bank market. *Source*: The Barclay Group.

The Betal G10 Carry Index reflects returns on a long high-yielding and short low yielding strategy based on 10 countries and 17 currency pairs. *Source*: Citibank Investor Risk Advisory Group.

The AFX Index reflects returns on a trend-following strategy involving three moving average rules applied to seven currency pairs, weighted by the volume of turnover in the spot market.

The Betal G10 PPP Index reflects returns on 13 pairs of currencies selected from among the ten major currencies, taking long positions in currencies that are more than 20% undervalued against short positions in currencies that are more than 20% overvalued, using OECD measures of Purchasing Power Parity as a gauge for valuation. *Source*: Citibank Investor Risk Advisory Group.

The FX Volatility Index is a simple average of the 1-month implied volatility on EUR-USD options and USD-JPY options.

*Source*: Citibank. Source for Exhibit 17.2 is Pojarliev and Levich (2008).

EXHIBIT 17.2 *(Continued)*

M2 (3.70%). However, the analysis shows that M28 has generated alpha returns, while M2 is offering beta exposure.

In Exhibit 17.2 Panel A, the estimated $R^2$ exceeds 50% for 9 of the 34 managers. This seems remarkable as our model uses only factors for developed market currencies, while the currency managers in our sample are not restricted to these markets. These results are potentially very important, as they could have implications on pricing investment mandates. Clients may be willing to pay high fees for alpha, but beta exposure should be available more cheaply.

Second, for these 34 managers, the highest exposure is toward the trend-following factor. The trend factor was significant for 15 managers. The carry factor was significant for eight managers, and volatility and value were significant for only seven and five managers, respectively. This suggests that the trend style was most prevalent among currency managers; however, other factors appeared to play a significant role for some funds. Several managers (e.g., M7, M8, and M14) had negative exposure toward carry, and one manager (M4) had a negative exposure toward the trend factor. Twenty-one of the 34 managers had a significant exposure to at least one factor, 9 of those had a significant exposure to two factors, and 2 funds had a significant exposure to three factors. Manager M30 had a significant exposure to all four factors. These results imply that managers have been diversifying across different styles by having exposure toward more than one style factor.

On the other hand, 13 of the 34 managers had no significant exposure toward any style factor. For these 13 managers, none of the coefficient $t$-statistics were significant at 95% confidence level. These managers might be classified as the true alpha hunters or they simply might be offering exposure to other trading styles or risk factors than the four considered here. Note that not all the alpha hunters managed to generate alpha (only eight managers deliver significant alpha).

To test for stability of these relationships over time, we divided the sample into two subperiods, from January 2001 to December 2003 and from January 2004 to December 2006. The regression results for these two subperiods are shown in Exhibit 17.2, Panels B and C. We identify nine managers with positive and significant alpha in the first subperiod (2001–2003), and seven of those nine continue to generate positive alpha in the second subperiod (2004–2006). No manager showed significant alpha in the second half who did not produce alpha in the first half also. This offers some indication for alpha persistence and represents good news for plan sponsors. It appears those who are strong performers are likely to remain top performers when gauged over 3-year horizons.

### 17.4.3 ALTERNATIVE INFORMATION RATIO

As discussed in Section 17.3, using the traditional benchmark for performance in a funded program, all excess returns above LIBID are counted as alpha returns. By definition, in the traditional benchmark, beta returns are zero. The information ratio (IR) under the traditional performance benchmark is then simply the annualized excess return divided by the annualized standard deviation of the excess returns.

However, the empirical results in Section 17.3 offer strong support for an alternative benchmark based on Equation (17.1) in which returns can be related to a set of style factors based on common trading strategies. In this framework, returns that might have been classified as alpha under the traditional benchmark are really more akin to beta returns. Following Equation (17.1), Pojarliev and Levich (2008) define $\alpha_j$ (alpha returns for fund manager $j$) as only that portion of excess returns that are not explained by the style factors, or

$$\hat{\alpha}_j = R_{j,t} - \sum_i \hat{\beta}_{i,j} F_{i,t} + \varepsilon_{j,t} \tag{17.2}$$

This leads to an alternative IR (IR*) that reflects the alternative alpha ($\hat{\alpha}$) divided by its standard deviation or tracking error. Calculations in Exhibit 17.3 show that for the sample of 34 managers, the mean and median values of IR* are smaller than those of the traditional IR. Furthermore, there is a substantial impact on the ranking of funds. For example, several funds (M2, M5, M6, M17, M21, and M22) show a substantial decline using IR* compared with IR. These six managers switch from positive IR values to negative IR* values. On the other hand, several funds (M7, M8, and M32) show a marked increase using IR* rather than the traditional IR. This highlights that the four-factor model could have a significant impact on the ranking of managers.

For various reasons, institutional investors are rightly concerned about how much of a manager's currency return is alpha (or excess performance) and how much is beta. First, proper return attribution could lead to some repricing for "active" currency products. Investors should not expect to pay alpha fees for exposure to currency style betas that could be delivered more cheaply. Second, currency beta might be less suitable for institutional investors when the goal is to diversify global equity exposure.[33] For example, the correlation of carry beta to global equities is −20% when global equities produce returns greater than one standard deviation above their mean, but it rises to 58% when equities generate returns more than one standard deviation below their means.[34] Thus, carry beta diversifies when it is not needed, that is, in rising markets, and it provides no diversification when it is most needed, that is, in falling markets.

---

[33]Pojarliev and Levich (2011b) show that alpha hunters offer greater diversification benefits to investors with large equity exposure than beta grazers.

[34]These correlations are based on monthly return of the MSCI World Index (in local currencies) and the DB Currency Harvest G10 Index from January 1980 until September 2010. Correlations computed using different proxies for currency beta exhibits similar pattern.

| Manager | Average Annual Return,% | Excess Annual Return,% | Std. Dev.,% | IR | Annual Alpha, % | Tracking Error, % | IR* |
|---|---|---|---|---|---|---|---|
| M1 | 22.00 | 19.34 | 14.71 | 1.31 | 22.13 | 14.57 | 1.52 |
| M2 | 6.40 | 3.70 | 8.62 | 0.74 | −2.48 | 4.81 | −0.52 |
| M3 | 2.50 | −0.16 | 3.00 | −0.05 | 0.31 | 2.94 | 0.11 |
| M4 | 5.70 | 2.98 | 5.16 | 0.58 | 2.91 | 4.68 | 0.62 |
| M5 | 5.40 | 2.73 | 8.00 | 0.36 | −4.19 | 6.24 | −0.67 |
| M6 | 10.70 | 8.00 | 22.51 | 0.36 | −8.97 | 15.75 | −0.57 |
| M7 | 4.00 | 1.35 | 1.31 | 1.03 | 1.91 | 1.20 | 1.6 |
| M8 | 7.20 | 4.53 | 3.77 | 1.2 | 6.16 | 3.44 | 1.79 |
| M9 | 14.50 | 11.80 | 15.32 | 0.77 | 10.43 | 15.27 | 0.68 |
| M10 | 6.50 | 3.78 | 6.96 | 0.54 | 3.08 | 6.94 | 0.44 |
| M11 | 0.80 | −1.87 | 0.94 | −1.99 | −1.86 | 0.92 | −2.03 |
| M12 | 1.40 | −1.26 | 12.15 | −0.1 | 0.57 | 11.26 | 0.05 |
| M13 | 2.30 | −0.37 | 13.83 | −0.03 | 0.22 | 10.20 | 0.02 |
| M14 | 8.10 | 5.42 | 29.34 | 0.18 | 13.08 | 27.09 | 0.48 |
| M15 | 5.90 | 3.18 | 11.92 | 0.27 | −0.26 | 9.63 | −0.03 |
| M16 | 7.70 | 5.04 | 6.39 | 0.79 | 2.67 | 5.90 | 0.45 |
| M17 | 7.10 | 4.43 | 13.73 | 0.32 | −7.39 | 11.09 | −0.67 |
| M18 | 2.20 | −0.49 | 4.03 | −0.12 | −2.21 | 3.76 | −0.59 |
| M19 | 5.00 | 2.27 | 8.04 | 0.28 | 2.84 | 7.84 | 0.36 |
| M20 | 6.20 | 3.52 | 39.21 | 0.09 | 3.27 | 23.87 | 0.14 |
| M21 | 5.90 | 3.24 | 23.98 | 0.13 | −5.01 | 15.87 | −0.32 |
| M22 | 8.00 | 5.31 | 8.88 | 0.6 | −0.54 | 7.68 | −0.07 |
| M23 | 9.90 | 7.24 | 11.57 | 0.63 | 7.71 | 11.04 | 0.7 |
| M24 | 2.70 | −0.02 | 6.56 | 0 | 0.22 | 3.92 | 0.06 |
| M25 | 17.60 | 14.90 | 8.91 | 1.67 | 12.73 | 8.34 | 1.53 |
| M26 | 25.70 | 22.98 | 14.82 | 1.55 | 25.99 | 14.28 | 1.82 |
| M27 | 2.70 | −0.04 | 5.89 | −0.01 | −0.42 | 4.34 | −0.1 |
| M28 | 5.70 | 3.02 | 3.86 | 0.78 | 3.51 | 3.79 | 0.93 |
| M29 | 22.70 | 19.97 | 12.74 | 1.57 | 19.53 | 12.14 | 1.61 |
| M30 | 10.00 | 7.27 | 22.39 | 0.32 | 3.32 | 14.42 | 0.23 |
| M31 | 3.70 | 1.02 | 13.90 | 0.07 | −1.71 | 8.18 | −0.21 |
| M32 | 10.30 | 7.62 | 13.71 | 0.56 | 8.50 | 9.07 | 0.94 |
| M33 | 14.70 | 11.98 | 19.49 | 0.61 | 12.72 | 18.29 | 0.7 |
| M34 | 5.70 | 2.98 | 3.47 | 0.86 | 1.72 | 2.99 | 0.57 |
| Average | 8.14 | 5.45 | — | 0.47 | 3.84 | — | 0.34 |
| Maximum | 25.70 | 22.98 | — | 1.67 | 25.99 | — | 1.81 |
| Median | 6.30 | 6.30 | — | 0.45 | 2.29 | — | 0.29 |
| Minimum | 0.80 | 0.80 | — | −1.99 | −8.97 | — | −2.02 |

Notes: Based on 72 monthly observations, January 2001–December 2006.

**EXHIBIT 17.3 Performance of Individual Currency Managers**

## 17.5 Empirical Evidence: Fund Managers on the DB FX Select Platform

Evaluating hedge fund performance is challenging due to the usual biases affecting hedge fund databases.[35] In particular, backfill and survivorship bias can be severe. Malkiel and Saha (2005) report that backfill bias averages 7.3% per year and survivorship bias averages 4.4% per year for hedge funds.

To address backfill and survivorship biases, we make use of the same database as used in Pojarliev and Levich (2010), that is, daily return data for currency managers listed on the DB FXSelect trading platform. The FXSelect data is unique relative to other hedge fund databases, as it provides actual return data; this has been made possible because gains and losses are computed by DB based on real trades processed through DB prime brokerage. The return data are audited by an independent third party. In contrast, hedge fund databases simply collect return data submitted by managers and are affected by numerous biases. This makes the FXSelect dataset especially useful to study the currency management industry.

We rely on data from April 6, 2005, until March 26, 2008, as in Pojarliev and Levich (2010) and then extended through June 30, 2010, or slightly more than 5 years overall. During this sample period, 107 currency funds were active at some point on the platform. Of these, only 67 funds were active as of June 30, 2010. We label these as *live* funds. Another 40 managers joined the platform and exited before the end of the sample period. We label these as *dead* funds. These 40 names include funds which no longer exist and funds that still exist, but delisted from the platform. Pojarliev and Levich (2011b) estimated the survivorship bias to be 5.30%, that is, similar to the results reported by Malkiel and Saha (2005). The mean annual return of all 107 funds (live and dead) while listed on the platform is roughly zero at 4 basis points. The mean annual return of only the live funds is 534 basis points.

### 17.5.1 GROUPING MANAGERS INTO A FUND OF FUNDS

As another robustness check to the results reported in Section 17.4, we consider a new portfolio, a "fund of funds" (FoF) that is composed of equally weighted positions in each of the funds available on the FXSelect platform.

The return on this index can be defined as

$$R_{\mathrm{FoF},t} = \sum_{j=1}^{n_t} \frac{R_{j,t}}{n_t} \tag{17.3}$$

[35]Fung and Hsieh (2000) examine various biases that impact the estimate of average hedge fund returns. More recently, Aggarwal and Jorion (2010) investigate bias that resulted from the merger of Tremont database into the TASS database. Aiken et al. (2010) measure the self-reporting bias attributable to funds that choose to report versus those that do not.

| | Intercept | Carry | Trend (AFX) | Value (PPP) | Volatility | $R^2$ |
|---|---|---|---|---|---|---|
| | +3bps | 0.06 | 0.28 | −0.05 | 0.00 | 0.37 |
| *t*-value | 1.71 | **5.22** | **11.90** | **−3.29** | 0.05 | |

The DB G10 Harvest Index is the proxy for the returns of a Carry strategy. *Source*: DB and Bloomberg.
The AFX Index is the proxy for the returns on a Trend strategy. *Source*: Liverpool John Moores University.
The DB FX PPP Index is the proxy for the returns of a Value strategy. *Source*: DB and Bloomberg.
The Deutsche Bank Currency Volatility Index (CVIX index) is the proxy for the foreign exchange volatility. *Source*: Deutsche Bank and Bloomberg.

**EXHIBIT 17.4 Excess Currency Index Returns as a Function of Four Factors April 6 2005–June 30, 2010, 274 weekly observations**

where
$R_{j,t}$ is the weekly return for manager $j$ at time $t$ and
$n_t$ is the number of managers available on the platform at time $t$.

This portfolio is rebalanced weekly with newly listed funds added and dead funds excluded from our FoF portfolio. As a result, every one of the 107 managers who were on the platform between April 2005 and June 2010 is included in our FoF index during their active period on the platform.

We estimate Equation (17.1) using the return of the FoF portfolio as the left-hand side variable. We use the same proxies for right-hand side variables as in Pojarliev and Levich (2010) and report the results in Exhibit 17.4. Overall, the results in Exhibit 17.4 support the four-factor model of currency trading returns. The model explains roughly 37% of the variability of the FoF portfolio returns. Trend appears to be the most significant factor. The trend coefficient is 0.28, larger than for any other factor and highly significant. On average, the managers on the FXSelect platform seem to rely on trend-following. The trend factor alone explains 28% of the variability of the excess returns of the FoF portfolio (we have regressed the returns of FoF portfolio on each individual factor, but have not reported the results). The carry coefficient is also positive and significant. The value coefficient is significant but negative, indicating that on average, managers were positioned to profit from further deviations from PPP. The volatility coefficient is zero and not significant.

The point estimate for alpha in the FoF portfolio is 3 basis points and significant at the 10% level in a two-tail test. This result implies that managers included in the FXSelect platform were able to generate some alpha on average between April 2005 and June 2010. However, the alpha was not high enough to cover fees, that is, 3 basis points of weekly alpha result in 152 basis point annual return, which might only roughly cover the management fees.[36]

[36]Our return data from the FXSelect platform are before fees. A review of the fee structure for currency funds who report through the TASS and CISDM databases shows that the 2% management fee and 20% performance fee are the modal charges.

## 17.6 Conclusions and Investment Implications

Over the last decade, institutional investors have been allocating less toward traditional assets such as equities and bonds, in favor of alternative investments such as hedge funds, private equities, and commodities. The increased interest toward alternative assets has naturally put currencies on the radar of institutional investors. Should institutional investors invest in currencies as an alternative asset class? The answer to this question is probably "yes" and the reasons are two-fold. First, the FX market offers enough depth and liquidity for large institutional investors. According to the latest Central Bank Survey of Foreign Exchange and Derivatives Market Activity (BIS, 2010), the daily average foreign exchange market turnover reached $4 trillion in April 2010, 20% higher than that in 2007. This liquidity was precious during the market turmoil in 2008. Second, returns generated by such strategies are generally uncorrelated with returns from other asset classes (Burnside et al., 2007). However, one of the challenges for institutional investors after allocating assets to currency managers is to find an appropriate benchmark to gauge the performance of these managers. Without an appropriate benchmark, the investor cannot know if he should be pleased or disappointed with the results achieved by his managers, or put differently, if these managers have demonstrated true skill or not. The lack of a well-established benchmark may be one of the reasons why allocations to currency strategies remain relatively low compared to hedge funds in general.[37]

In many studies of currency trading strategies, researchers have commonly used zero as the expected return from currency speculation and interpreted all realized returns as unusual, excess returns. In the same vein, zero has often been used as a traditional benchmark to assess the performance of currency fund managers who pursue an absolute return mandate. In contrast to the traditional benchmark, Pojarliev and Levich (2008) proposed a four-factor regression model as an alternative technique to gauge the performance of currency managers. The model estimates what portion of currency trading profits is due to exposure to these specific trading style or risk factors (or beta) and what portion is due to skill, or alpha.

In empirical tests of the four-factor model, Pojarliev and Levich (2008, 2010) use different proxies for the risk factors, but the results are strikingly similar. Depending on the time period, periodicity, and model specification, four risk factors explain 50–75% in the variability of currency fund (index) returns. We have updated some of the results with more recent data, and the general conclusions remain unchanged. A significant part of currency returns comes from exposure to a small set of factors that proxy the returns from well-known and easily implemented trading styles. As a consequence, much of what might have

[37] BarclayHedge reports that in 2010Q4, macrostyle hedge funds, which include currency strategies among several others, accounted for $115.1 billion out of an estimated $2255.6 billion in hedge fund assets under management. Similarly, currency traders were estimated at $21.55 billion out of a total of $267.6 billion in assets under management at CTA accounts.

been labeled as alpha under the traditional benchmark may become beta returns under the alternative benchmark.[38]

Although we have reported results for various proxies for the style factors, as Melvin and Shand (2011) caution, using other style factors could impact the results. In addition, other factors we have omitted (such as drawdown of capital) could matter to investors. Despite these caveats, the notion of retaining the traditional performance benchmark (i.e., zero) and forsaking the use of a limited set of style factors as an alternative benchmark seem inconsistent with our results.

For several reasons, institutional investors should be concerned about how much of a currency manager's return is alpha and how much is beta. First, proper return attribution could lead to some repricing for "active" currency products. Investors should not expect to pay alpha fees for exposure to currency style betas that could be earned more cheaply. Second, currency beta might be less suitable for institutional investors when the goal is to diversify global equity exposure.

Whether there is skill or alpha in currency management can depend on not only the benchmark for comparison but also the manager. The evidence we presented using the alternative benchmark support the contention that the average manager has no skill and after transaction costs, the average alpha is negative.[39] However, Pojarliev and Levich (2008) showed that approximately one-quarter of the managers was able to generate positive and significant alpha between 2001 and 2006. The average alpha of these "stars" has been quite high at 104 bps per month or 12.48% per year, figures that are significant in both economic and statistical terms. Importantly, this 104 bps alpha is measured after taking into account the four explanatory factors, namely, carry, trend, value, and volatility. So in some respects, currencies seem not so different from other asset classes: the average manager may deliver zero alpha, but there exist some skilled managers who are able to deliver significant alpha.

In addition, there was substantial consistency between results in the first half (2001–2003) and second half (2004–2006) of the 6-year period. We identified nine managers with positive and significant alpha in the first half of the sample, and seven of those continue to make positive alpha in the second half. This is good news for plan sponsors, as it indicates that past performance data can be an indication for future performance for individual managers.

## REFERENCES

Aggarwal RK, Jorion P. Hidden survivorship in hedge fund returns, Financ Anal J, 2010; 66(2): 69–74.

[38] Nucera and Valente (2010) have proposed another more stringent performance benchmark (i.e., returns in excess of the currency risk premia associated with exposure to currency risk).

[39] Since alpha is a zero-sum game, this is true per definition.

Aiken AL, Clifford CP, Ellis J. Out of the dark: Hedge fund reporting biases and commercial databases. working paper; 2010. Available at http://ssrn.com/abstract=1519914.

Bank for International Settlements. Triennial central bank survey: report on global foreign exchange market activity in 2010. 2010 Dec.

Burnside C, Eichenbaum M, Kleschelski I, Rebelo S. The returns to currency speculation. Am Econ Rev 2007; 97(2): 333–338.

Chen N, Roll R, Ross S. Economic forces and the stock market. J Bus 1986; 59(3): 383–403.

Dickson T. The Growing Appeal of Overseas Assets. Financial Times, Survey on Pension Fund Investment. 1991 April 18; IV.

Freeman A. Now Equity Managers Cut the Risk — Currency Hedging. Financial Times, Survey on International Fund Management. 1976 October 26: VI.

Fung W, Hsieh DA. Performance characteristics of hedge funds and commodity funds: natural vs. Spurious biases. J Financ Quant Anal 2000; 35(3): 291–307.

Fung W, Hsieh DA. Asset-based style factors for hedge fund. Financ Anal J 2002; 58(5): 16–27.

Givant M. Hedged Indexes Mulled. Pensions Invest Age. 1998 June 27: 2.

Huberman G, Wang Z. Arbitrage pricing theory. Federal Reserve Bank of New York, Staff Report no. 216; 2005 August.

Leibowitz M. Alpha hunters and beta grazers. Financ Anal J 2005; 61(5): 32–39.

Lequeux P, Acar E. A dynamic benchmark for managed currencies funds. Eur J Finance 1998; 4(4): 311–330.

Malkiel B, Saha A. Hedge funds: risk and return. Financ Anal J 2005; 61(6): 80–88.

Meese R, Rogoff K. Empirical exchange rate models of the seventies: do they fit out of sample? J Int Econ 1983; 14: 3–24.

Melvin M, Shand D. Active currency investing and performance benchmarks. J Portf Manage 2011; 37(2): 46–59.

Nucera F, Valente G. The performance of currency hedge funds and foreign exchange risk premia. working paper; 2010 Oct.

Pojarliev M, Levich RM. Do professional currency managers beat the benchmark? Financ Anal J 2008; 64(5): 18–30.

Pojarliev M, Levich RM. Trades of the living dead: style differences, style persistence and performance of currency fund managers? J Int Money Finance 2010; 29(8): 1752–1775.

Pojarliev M, Levich RM. Detecting crowded trades in currency funds. Financ Anal J 2011; 67(1): 26–39.

Pojarliev M, Levich RM. Are all currency managers equal? J Portf Manage 2011b; 37(4): 42–53.

Rogoff K. The failure of empirical exchange rate models: no longer new, but still true; 2002. Available at http://www.economic-policy.org/responses.asp.

Roll R, Ross S. An empirical investigation of the arbitrage pricing theory. J Finance 1980; 35(5): 1073–1104.

Ross S. The arbitrage theory of capital asset pricing. J Econ Theory 1976; 13(3): 341–360.

Strange B. Currency overlay managers show consistency. Pensions Invest 1998; 26(12): 26–31.

Thomas LR, editor. The currency hedging debate. London: IFR Publishing Ltd.; 1990.

CHAPTER EIGHTEEN

# Currency Hedging for International Bond and Equity Investors

**KRISTJAN KASIKOV**
CitiFX Quantitative Investor Solutions,

## 18.1 Introduction

The unprecedented volatility of exchange rates during the 2007–2008 credit crisis demonstrated that the decision to hedge or not to hedge exposure to currencies can significantly impact total portfolio return and volatility. In a period when equity prices dropped sharply, foreign investors in US equities with no currency hedges on average did better than their fully hedged counterparts. Unhedged Japanese investors, however, suffered sharp currency losses at times when global equities did badly, while hedged investors experienced smoother returns.

Experience from recent years shows that currency hedging may not always have the intended consequence of reducing portfolio volatility. The negative correlation between the US dollar and equities meant that investors who hedged their US equity exposures increased their losses via currency hedges, adding volatility to their returns.

In this chapter, we investigate the historical impact of currency hedging on the volatility and returns of foreign bond and equity investments. Our focus is entirely empirical and covers a period of several different market regimes. Relative

*Handbook of Exchange Rates*, First Edition. Edited by Jessica James, Ian W. Marsh, and Lucio Sarno.

to previous studies in the area, we expand our study to include investors with all 10 major base currencies. In addition to traditional government bond and equity index holdings, we also investigate the performance of hedging the Citi US High Yield corporate bond index.

Section 18.2 of this chapter outlines previous empirical findings on currency hedging. Section 18.3 introduces the methodology and results of our tests for the historical volatility and return impact of hedging. Section 18.4 deals with the relative merits of hedging with currency forwards versus options, and Section 18.5 investigates tracking error and optimal rebalancing frequencies and triggers of currency forward hedges. Section 18.6 presents the main conclusions from the studies.

## 18.2 Overview of Empirical Hedging Studies

Empirical studies on currency hedging typically find that while arguments for the volatility benefit of hedging are compelling in government bond portfolios, evidence for other asset classes is more mixed. There is also strong evidence that conditional hedging based on the forward premium (i.e., hedging currencies with low yield and leaving currencies with high yield unhedged) has improved total returns in the past. At the same time, there appears to be no agreement on whether currency hedging has reduced the volatility of international equity portfolios.

The arguments for a high degree of currency hedging tend to be more concentrated in early studies. Eun and Resnick (1988) show that exchange rate uncertainty is a largely nondiversifiable factor, which adversely affects the performance of foreign portfolios. Using a sample of weekly data from December 1979 to 1985, they find that currency hedging significantly improved risk-adjusted returns from foreign equity holdings for a US-dollar-based investor. Similarly, Perold and Schulman (1988) argue that the risk premium in currencies will not persist over time; with the expected long-term return from currencies zero, hedging can reduce volatility without affecting returns, giving the investor a "free lunch".

Eaker and Grant (1990) find in what was probably one of the earliest carry trade papers that hedging US dollar only when there is a forward premium outperformed both fully hedged and unhedged portfolios. Glen and Jorion (1993) conduct a similar study and find that a forward-premium-based conditional hedging improved total returns from foreign bonds and equities for a US investor, and some exposure to (higher-yielding) currencies can therefore benefit the total portfolio.

Morey and Simpson (2001) support the return benefits of dynamic forward-premium-based hedging, showing that the forward-premium-based signal works best in the 1989–1998 sample if the hedging tenor is longer term and the size of the premium is large. Simpson and Dania (2006) expand the conditional hedge rules to hedging the euro and find that the forward hedge rule produces the best ex-post efficient frontier in a sample of 1999–2003 while the strategy that never hedged is the worst.

De Roon et al. (2003) highlight the benefits of forward-premium-based hedging for a US-dollar-based equity investor investing in G5 countries, while Berggrun (2005) reaches similar conclusions for Dutch investors in a sample of 1999–2004. Thorp (2004), who investigates the behavior of Australian superannuation funds, finds that the best strategy for bonds was a complete conventional hedge, whereas selective carry-based hedging at a ratio below 20% is better for stocks in a sample of 1983–2003.

Attfield et al. (2001) expand the topic of forward-premium-based hedging to the choice of optimal instrument and prove in a simulated data set that hedging with forwards if carry is positive and with bought options if carry is negative would outperform a pure forward hedge if the current level of the exchange rate is a better predictor of its future values than the forward rate.

However, evidence on the volatility benefit of conventional hedging is more mixed. Investigating the case of a US investor, Abken and Shrikhande (1997) find that while currency hedges reduced risk in equity portfolios in the 1980–1985 sample, hedging was largely a source of negative return in the post-Plaza accord period of 1986–1996, with no improvement in volatility.

Sener (1998) investigates the interdependence between the equity and currency markets in 1988–1996 and concludes that Japanese investors, whose home currency strengthened at the time when Japanese equities were weak, have more to gain from currency hedging than, for example, US investors.

Walker (2008) finds that currency hedging of foreign equity holdings typically increases total portfolio volatility for Latin American investors in a sample of 2001–2005, as *hard currencies*, such as the US dollar, act as natural hedges against negative equity returns.

Campbell et al. (2010) investigate correlations of foreign exchange (FX) rates with stock and bond returns in a sample of 1975–2005 and find that international equity investors can minimize their equity risk by taking short positions in the Australian and Canadian dollars, Japanese yen, and British pound and long positions in the US dollar, euro, and Swiss franc. This is because the former are positively correlated with world stock markets and the correlation for the latter is negative. At the same time, they find that bond investors' risk management demands small or low volatility contribution from the currency component, pointing to high optimal hedge ratios.

Schmittmann (2010) finds in a sample of 1975–2009 that no exposure to currencies is generally the variance-minimizing strategy for international bond investors in Germany, Japan, United Kingdom, and United States. Despite covering the 2007–2009 crisis, when correlations between currencies and equities were typically strong, Schmittmann (2010) surprisingly also finds that the minimum variance hedge ratios were indistinguishable from 100% hedge at the 5% confidence level in most equity portfolios.

## 18.3 Return and Volatility Impact of Currency Hedging

### 18.3.1 THEORETICAL BACKGROUND

For better understanding of currency hedging and its impact on volatility, we outline some basic formulas of hedged and unhedged returns. The value of the unhedged asset in the investor's base currency $I_t^{\mathrm{U}}$ is given by

$$I_t^{\mathrm{U}} = I_t^* \times S_t \tag{18.1}$$

where $I_t^*$ is the value of the foreign asset at time $t$ in foreign currency and $S_t$ is the exchange rate at time $t$, measured in units of investor's home currency per one unit of foreign currency.

The log return of the unhedged asset is the sum of the asset log return in local currency and the log return on holding foreign currency:

$$i_t^{\mathrm{U}} - i_{t-1}^{\mathrm{U}} = i_t^* - i_{t-1}^* + s_t - s_{t-1} \tag{18.2}$$

where $i_t^{\mathrm{U}}$ is the log of the value of the unhedged foreign asset exposure in domestic currency at time $t$, $i_t^*$ is the log of the foreign asset value in foreign currency at time $t$, and $s_t$ is the log of the exchange rate, measured in units of investor's home currency per unit of foreign currency at time $t$ (a rise in the exchange rate means that the foreign currency appreciates and the investor's home currency depreciates).

The variance of the unhedged foreign asset return in local currency $\sigma_{i\mathrm{U}}^2$ is determined by the underlying asset variance in foreign currency $\sigma_{i*}^2$, variance of the foreign currency exposure $\sigma_s^2$, and the covariance between the foreign currency and the foreign asset:

$$\sigma_{i\mathrm{U}}^2 = \sigma_{i*}^2 + \sigma_s^2 + 2 \times \mathrm{cov}(i^*, s) \tag{18.3}$$

The covariance between the foreign asset and the currency can either be positive or negative, adding or reducing, respectively, portfolio volatility. If the foreign currency appreciates and depreciates together with the value of the foreign asset, then currency exposure in effect adds leverage to the foreign asset, making the total return more volatile. This was often the case with investments into emerging market equities, where unhedged currency exposure was a source of extra return between 2003 and 2007, while adding to the pain of investors during the 2008 crisis.

On the other hand, if the foreign currency is negatively correlated with the foreign asset value, then currency risk can reduce portfolio volatility and act as a hedge against moves in the price of the asset. This is the case with investors whose base currency and foreign assets are sensitive to risk aversion. For example, Australian investors with foreign equity holdings would have benefited from currency exposure in 2008, when most foreign currencies appreciated against the Australian dollar when global equity prices fell sharply.

The total value of the 100% hedged asset $I_t^{\mathrm{H}}$, where the currency hedge is executed and rebalanced in 1-month forwards, is given at month end $t$ by the then current value of the foreign asset in investor's base currency plus the cumulative return on the foreign currency hedge from the start of the investment up to month end $t$:

$$I_t^{\mathrm{H}} = I_t^* \times S_t + \sum_{i=1}^{t} I_{i-1}^* \times (F_{i-1} - S_i) \tag{18.4}$$

where $F_{i-1}$ is the bid of the 1-month forward exchange rate at month end $i$-1, measured in units of investor's home currency per one unit of foreign currency. This formula assumes that positive returns from the currency hedge are not invested back into the asset and negative cash flows from the forward hedge are financed from the investor's cash reserves, rather than by selling assets. While indices of hedged asset performance typically assume that this is not the case, investors with cash may prefer to do so because of time and costs associated with investing hedge returns into the asset.

In the case where hedge returns are reinvested back into the asset, the total value of the 100% hedged asset $I_t^{\mathrm{H}}$ is given at month end $t$ by multiplying the total value of the investment at the previous month end by the return of the asset (in local currency) and the return on the currency hedge:

$$I_t^{\mathrm{H}} = I_{t-1}^{\mathrm{H}} \times \left( \frac{I_t^* S_t}{I_{t-1}^* S_{t-1}} + \frac{F_{t-1} - S_t}{S_{t-1}} \right) \tag{18.5}$$

This formula assumes that the return on the currency hedge is reinvested into the asset at zero cost and the notional amount on the currency hedge is the total value of the asset, including reinvestment of currency hedge returns.

Regardless of whether the hedge returns are reinvested into the asset, the log return of the hedged asset is the sum of the asset return in local currency, the return on holding foreign currency, and the return on currency hedge:

$$i_t^{\mathrm{H}} - i_{t-1}^{\mathrm{H}} = (i_t^* - i_{t-1}^*) + (s_t - s_{t-1}) + (f_{t-1} - s_t) \tag{18.6}$$

The last two terms of the formula net off to the difference between the forward rate and spot rate $(f_{t-1} - s_{t-1})$ at inception of the hedge, representing either forward point gain or loss and transaction costs of trading the forward.

The variance of the hedged foreign asset return in local currency $\sigma_{i\mathrm{H}}^2$ is determined by the underlying asset variance in foreign currency $\sigma_{i^*}^2$, variance of forward points $\sigma_{f-s}^2$, and covariance between the underlying asset and forward points:

$$\sigma_{i\mathrm{H}}^2 = \sigma_{i^*}^2 + \sigma_{f-s}^2 + 2 \times \mathrm{cov}\left(i^*, f - s\right) \tag{18.7}$$

Since forward points tend to be small and stable, their variance and covariance with the asset returns is expected to be low. This might lead one to believe that volatility of hedged returns is typically lower than that of unhedged returns. Indeed, fully hedged returns have lower volatility than unhedged if the variance of forward points and their covariance with the underlying asset is lower than the variance of the currency exposure and the covariance between the foreign asset and the foreign currency:

$$\sigma_{f-s}^2 + 2 \times \text{cov}\left(i^*, f - s\right) < \sigma_s^2 + 2 \times \text{cov}\left(i^*, s\right) \tag{18.8}$$

Since the variance of the currency exposure $\sigma_s^2$ is typically large, the question on whether Equation (18.8) is true depends on the covariance between the asset in foreign currency and the exchange rate, measured in units of domestic currency per unit of foreign currency $2 \times \text{cov}\,(i^*, s)$. If the foreign currency is negatively correlated to the local asset, then the covariance can be significantly negative enough to offset the positive variance of currency risk and can result in lower volatility of the unhedged returns relative to hedged.

An example of this might be a foreign equity investor, whose home currency is sensitive to the same risk aversion factors as equities. This results in negative correlations between foreign currencies against the investor's home currency and equity prices, giving the investor a natural hedge in foreign currency exposure. If the negative covariance is strong enough, for example, the relationship between the US dollar and equities during the 2007–2008 crisis, then hedging currency risk may increase volatility relative to unhedged returns.

### 18.3.2 METHODOLOGY

In order to investigate the volatility and return impact of currency hedging, we construct monthly unhedged and fully hedged indices of total returns, based on the MSCI Equity indices, the Citi World Government Bond Index (WGBI) family of sovereign bond indices, and the Citi US High Yield (US HY) index of corporate debt. Our sample is from January 1985 to September 2011 determined by the earliest availability of historical asset index values. Data on asset index values is sourced from Citi and Bloomberg; exchange rates and 1-month deposit rates for forward calculations are sourced from EcoWin.

We calculate hedged and unhedged return indices separately for investors with each major base currency—US dollar, euro, British pound, Swiss franc, Japanese yen, Australian dollar, Canadian dollar, New Zealand dollar, Swedish krona, and Norwegian krone—investing in the bond and equity markets of each of the other nine economies as well as the US HY index. Before the introduction of the euro in January 1999, German assets and the mark were used as proxy for Eurozone assets and the euro.

All currency hedges are implemented in 1-month forwards on the first business day of each month based on previous day's asset closing values. We assume a fixed transaction cost of 0.06% bid-offer for the forward exchange rate.

### 18.3.2.1 Findings on Hedging Foreign Government Bonds

*Volatility impact of hedging government bonds.* The volatility of exchange rates has been typically higher than that of government bond indices. Figure 18.1 shows that unhedged bonds have, in the past, been nearly three times as volatile as the original asset in local currency, suggesting that foreign unhedged bond holdings have contained more currency risk than underlying asset risk.

Figure 18.1 and Table 18.1 show that unhedged foreign investors in Australian and Japanese government bonds have,in the past, seen the biggest volatility in their portfolios. While Japanese government bonds (JGBs) have in past varied on average 3.9% per year when measured in the Japanese yen, foreign investors have seen volatility of up to 17.5% in the (improbable) case of Australian investors holding Japanese bonds. On average, the volatility of unhedged Japanese bonds has historically exceeded the volatility of JGBs in yen by 3.7 times.

Similarly, Japanese holders of Australian government bonds have experienced 16.3% annual volatility of their investments, compared to 5.2% of the asset measured in Australian dollars. The volatility of unhedged Australian bonds has historically exceeded that of the local currency asset by an average of 2.6 times across investors from other major economies. Even UK bonds, which historically have had the highest native volatility of 6.1% per year, have contributed only half of the risk to foreign unhedged holdings.

Table 18.2 shows that the volatilities of fully hedged WGBI bond exposures have been significantly lower than those of unhedged exposures. In fact, we find that the negative difference between hedged and unhedged bond returns has been significantly different from zero on a 90% confidence level for all combinations of exposures under investigation.

As volatilities of forward points and covariance between forward points and assets have been low, the volatilities of fully hedged bonds have been very close to those of local currency assets (as per formula 18.7).

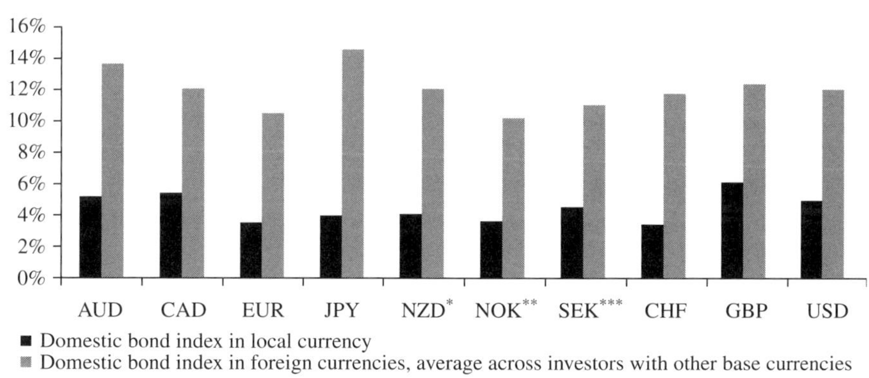


**FIGURE 18.1 Annualized volatility of WGBI bond indices in local and foreign currencies.** ***New Zealand WGBI starts October 1992. **Norwegian WGBI starts January 1995. ***Swedish WGBI starts January 1991.** ***Source:*** **Citi and EcoWin, sample: January 1985–September 2011 unless otherwise indicated.**

TABLE 18.1 **Annual Volatilities of Unhedged WGBI Bond Exposures**

| Investors' home currency | Exposure to WGBI bonds in AUD | CAD | EUR | JPY | NZD | NOK | SEK | CHF | GBP | USD |
|---|---|---|---|---|---|---|---|---|---|---|
| AUD | 5.2 | 11.4 | 13.8 | 17.5 | 8.5 | 11.0 | 11.9 | 15.4 | 15.0 | 13.6 |
| CAD | 11.4 | 5.4 | 12.2 | 15.0 | 11.4 | 10.1 | 11.8 | 13.7 | 12.8 | 8.9 |
| EUR | 13.7 | 12.0 | 3.5 | 12.8 | 11.1 | 7.1 | 7.8 | 7.1 | 9.7 | 11.4 |
| JPY | 16.3 | 14.1 | 12.0 | 3.9 | 15.0 | 14.1 | 14.3 | 11.7 | 13.4 | 11.8 |
| NZD[a] | 10.4 | 12.6 | 13.5 | 17.0 | 4.0 | 11.9 | 11.8 | 14.6 | 14.3 | 14.1 |
| NOK[b] | 13.6 | 11.7 | 7.1 | 13.8 | 11.8 | 3.6 | 8.5 | 9.2 | 10.8 | 11.8 |
| SEK[c] | 13.5 | 11.6 | 7.8 | 14.5 | 11.8 | 7.4 | 4.5 | 9.9 | 11.3 | 12.4 |
| CHF | 15.3 | 13.7 | 6.7 | 12.3 | 12.0 | 9.2 | 10.0 | 3.4 | 11.1 | 12.5 |
| GBP | 14.4 | 11.7 | 8.8 | 13.9 | 12.0 | 9.2 | 10.3 | 10.7 | 6.1 | 11.4 |
| USD | 13.3 | 9.1 | 12.0 | 13.2 | 13.4 | 11.4 | 12.7 | 13.1 | 12.5 | 4.9 |

[a]New Zealand WGBI starts October 1992.
[b]Norwegian WGBI starts January 1995.
[c]Swedish WGBI starts January 1991.
*Source:* Citi, sample: January 1985–September 2011 unless otherwise indicated.

In addition to comparing the volatilities of unhedged and fully hedged bonds, we also investigate which hedge ratios would historically have minimized the volatilities of foreign bond holdings. Table 18.3 shows the results for all major base currencies, suggesting that the higher volatility of currencies has historically dominated any potential positive correlation effects from holding foreign currencies in bond portfolios.

In most cases, the minimum volatility hedge ratios are close to 100%. Only Eurozone, Japanese, Norwegian, Swedish, Swiss, and UK holders of US Treasuries would have historically been able to reduce the volatility of returns by maintaining 5–10% exposure to the US dollar. This is because the US dollar has historically been negatively correlated with US Treasuries against the base currencies of these investors. However, this was not the case for Australian, Canadian, and New Zealand investors whose home currencies have had low correlations with US bonds.

*Return impact of hedging government bonds.* Unlike the strong volatility reduction benefit of hedging, the return impact has been more ambiguous. If uncovered interest parity held and long-term returns from currency forwards were indeed zero, then currency hedging in fixed income portfolios should be a "free lunch", with zero net long-term return, with the exception of transaction costs and a strong volatility reduction benefit.

Tables 18.4 and 18.5 show the annual returns from unhedged and fully hedged WGBI bond exposures, respectively. On the basis of a two-tailed $t$-test for difference in sample means we are unable to reject the null hypothesis that the fully hedged and unhedged returns are the same for most currency exposures on a 90% confidence level (largely due to high volatility of returns, which increases

**TABLE 18.2 Annual Volatilities of Fully Hedged WGBI Bond Exposures (in Percentage)**

| Investors' home currency | Exposure to WGBI bonds in AUD | CAD | EUR | JPY | NZD | NOK | SEK | CHF | GBP | USD |
|---|---|---|---|---|---|---|---|---|---|---|
| AUD | **5.2** | 5.5 | 3.7 | 4.0 | 4.0 | 3.6 | 4.5 | 3.5 | 6.1 | 5.1 |
| | | (−5.9) | (−10.1) | (−13.5) | (−4.5) | (−7.4) | (−7.4) | (−11.9) | (−8.9) | (−8.5) |
| CAD | 5.1 | **5.4** | 3.6 | 4.0 | 4.0 | 3.6 | 4.4 | 3.4 | 6.1 | 5.0 |
| | (−6.3) | | (−8.6) | (−11.0) | (−7.4) | (−6.5) | (−7.4) | (−10.3) | (−6.7) | (−3.9) |
| EUR | 5.1 | 5.4 | **3.5** | 3.9 | 4.0 | 3.6 | 4.4 | 3.4 | 6.1 | 4.9 |
| | (−8.6) | (−6.6) | | (−8.9) | (−7.1) | (−3.5) | (−3.4) | (−3.7) | (−3.6) | (−6.5) |
| JPY | 5.0 | 5.4 | 3.5 | **3.9** | 3.9 | 3.6 | 4.4 | 3.4 | 6.0 | 4.9 |
| | (−11.3) | (−8.7) | (−8.5) | | (−11.1) | (−10.5) | (−9.9) | (−8.3) | (−7.4) | (−6.9) |
| NZD[a] | 5.2 | 5.5 | 3.6 | 4.0 | **4.0** | 3.6 | 4.5 | 3.5 | 6.1 | 5.0 |
| | (−5.2) | (−7.1 ) | (−9.9) | (−13.0) | | (−8.3) | (−7.3) | (−11.1) | (−8.2) | (−9.1) |
| NOK[b] | 5.3 | 5.5 | 3.7 | 4.1 | 4.1 | **3.6** | 4.5 | 3.6 | 6.2 | 5.0 |
| | (−8.3) | (−6.2) | (−3.4) | (−9.7) | (−7.7) | | (−4.0) | (−5.6) | (−4.6) | (−6.8) |
| SEK[c] | 5.2 | 5.5 | 3.7 | 4.1 | 4.0 | 3.7 | **4.5** | 3.6 | 6.2 | 5.1 |
| | (−8.3) | (−6.1) | (−4.1) | (−10.4) | (−7.8) | (−3.7) | | (−6.3) | (−5.1) | (−7.3) |
| CHF | 5.0 | 5.4 | 3.5 | 3.9 | 4.0 | 3.6 | 4.4 | **3.4** | 6.1 | 4.9 |
| | (−10.3) | (−8.3) | (−3.2) | (−8.4) | (−8.0) | (−5.6) | (−5.6) | | (−5.0) | (−7.6) |
| GBP | 5.1 | 5.4 | 3.6 | 3.9 | 4.0 | 3.6 | 4.4 | 3.4 | **6.1** | 5.0 |
| | (−9.3) | (−6.3) | (−5.2) | (−10.0) | (−8.0) | (−5.6) | (−5.9) | (−7.3) | | (−6.4) |
| USD | 5.0 | 5.4 | 3.5 | 3.9 | 4.0 | 3.6 | 4.4 | 3.4 | 6.1 | **4.9** |
| | (−8.3) | (−3.7) | (−8.5) | (−9.3) | (−9.4) | (−7.8) | (−8.3) | (−9.7) | (−6.4) | |

Differences between fully hedged and unhedged volatilities are represented in parentheses.
The volatility of 100% hedged returns is lower than the volatility of unhedged returns on 90% confidence level for all exposures above.
[a]New Zealand WGBI starts October 1992.
[b]Norwegian WGBI starts January 1995.
[c]Swedish WGBI starts January 1991.
*Source:* Citi, sample: January 1985–September 2011 unless otherwise indicated.

**TABLE 18.3 Minimum Volatility Hedge Ratios for WGBI Government Bond Exposures (in Percentage)**

| Investors' home currency | Exposure to WGBI bonds in | | | | | | | | | |
|---|---|---|---|---|---|---|---|---|---|---|
| | AUD | CAD | EUR | JPY | NZD | NOK | SEK | CHF | GBP | USD |
| AUD | n/a | 100 | 103 | 103 | 101 | 97 | 95 | 102 | 102 | 101 |
| CAD | 102 | n/a | 105 | 104 | 100 | 96 | 97 | 102 | 105 | 102 |
| EUR | 99 | 96 | n/a | 100 | 95 | 96 | 93 | 105 | 99 | 92 |
| JPY | 98 | 97 | 97 | n/a | 95 | 97 | 96 | 96 | 94 | 91 |
| NZD[a] | 97 | 101 | 102 | 102 | n/a | 98 | 95 | 100 | 98 | 101 |
| NOK[b] | 102 | 98 | 107 | 101 | 98 | n/a | 103 | 104 | 105 | 96 |
| SEK[c] | 101 | 94 | 106 | 102 | 99 | 95 | n/a | 104 | 102 | 94 |
| CHF | 99 | 97 | 99 | 98 | 94 | 99 | 96 | n/a | 98 | 92 |
| GBP | 101 | 96 | 104 | 101 | 98 | 97 | 97 | 104 | n/a | 95 |
| USD | 100 | 102 | 103 | 104 | 99 | 97 | 94 | 101 | 102 | n/a |

No overhedging constraints. A hedge ratio in excess of 100 suggests that taking a theoretical net short position in the foreign currency would have further reduced volatility of returns.
[a]New Zealand WGBI starts October 1992.
[b]Norwegian WGBI starts January 1995.
[c]Swedish WGBI starts January 1991.
*Source:* Citi, sample: January 1985–September 2011 unless otherwise indicated.

the statistically significant critical thresholds). The only exceptions to this are Eurozone and Swedish investors, who have seen a significant return drag from hedging New Zealand bonds.

Despite the fact that the statistical significance of return differences has, in most cases, been low, the differences have been nonnegligible. Hedging New Zealand bond exposures into other currencies has had the biggest return impact out of all currencies, resulting in losses for all other investors. Despite the strong Japanese yen, the cost of carry in hedging has been so high that Japanese investors would have given up nearly all their gains, had they hedged their New Zealand bonds. The only exposure where Japanese investors would have made a gain from hedging since 1985 is US Treasuries, which would have returned 1.5% per more with hedges than without.

Owing to a weak US dollar over the sample period, investors with all major base currencies would have been better off with currency hedges on their US Treasury holdings. Investors whose home currencies have also traditionally offered positive carry over the US dollar, including the Australian and New Zealand dollars, British pound, and Norwegian krone, stood the most to gain from hedging.

Conversely, US investors would have lost money on currency hedging over the sample period, with the biggest losses coming from hedging exposures in the aforementioned currencies. With the exception of Australian and New Zealand fixed income investors, who benefited from strong currencies and positive carry, the return impact of hedging for all other investors has been ambiguous.

**TABLE 18.4 Annual Returns of Unhedged WGBI Bond Exposures (in Percentage)**

| | | Exposure to WGBI bonds in | | | | | | | | | |
|---|---|---|---|---|---|---|---|---|---|---|---|
| | | AUD | CAD | EUR | JPY | NZD | NOK | SEK | CHF | GBP | USD |
| Investors' home currency | AUD | 9.7 | 9.0 | 8.1 | 8.5 | 7.6 | 5.9 | 5.9 | 8.4 | 9.6 | 7.1 |
| | CAD | 9.4 | 8.7 | 7.8 | 8.2 | 8.5 | 5.5 | 6.4 | 8.2 | 9.4 | 6.8 |
| | EUR | 7.8 | 7.1 | 6.2 | 6.6 | 9.2 | 7.0 | 7.2 | 6.6 | 7.7 | 5.2 |
| | JPY | 5.5 | 4.8 | 4.0 | 4.3 | 6.7 | 5.7 | 4.1 | 4.3 | 5.4 | 3.0 |
| | NZD[a] | 8.4 | 7.8 | 6.9 | 7.3 | 7.4 | 6.3 | 5.7 | 7.2 | 8.4 | 5.9 |
| | NOK[b] | 8.6 | 7.9 | 7.0 | 7.4 | 9.0 | 6.6 | 7.1 | 7.3 | 8.5 | 6.0 |
| | SEK[c] | 9.3 | 8.6 | 7.7 | 8.1 | 10.4 | 6.9 | 8.1 | 8.0 | 9.2 | 6.7 |
| | CHF | 6.0 | 5.3 | 4.5 | 4.9 | 7.1 | 5.2 | 5.3 | 4.8 | 5.9 | 3.5 |
| | GBP | 9.1 | 8.4 | 7.5 | 7.9 | 9.4 | 7.5 | 8.2 | 7.8 | 9.0 | 6.5 |
| | USD | 10.4 | 9.7 | 8.8 | 9.2 | 9.5 | 7.3 | 6.9 | 9.1 | 10.3 | 7.8 |

[a]New Zealand WGBI starts October 1992.
[b]Norwegian WGBI starts January 1995.
[c]Swedish WGBI starts January 1991.
*Source:* Citi, sample: January 1985–September 2011 unless otherwise indicated.

Swiss and Japanese investors, who have traditionally incurred negative carry in hedging, have just about broken even on their hedges outside New Zealand and Australia. However, as is the case with all empirical results, this is dependent on the sample period and largely owes thanks to the strength of these currencies during the 2007–2008 credit crisis.

With the exception of Japanese and Swiss investors holding hedged JGBs, the return impact of hedging has been dwarfed by the benefit of the reduction in volatility, resulting in higher risk-adjusted returns for all hedged exposures. So, unless the investment into foreign government bonds is made with the strategic aim of also getting exposure to the currency, historical results show that exchange rate risk in bond portfolios should be largely hedged away.

### 18.3.2.2 Findings on Hedging US High Yield Corporate Bonds

*Volatility impact of hedging corporate bonds.* The Citigroup US HY Market Index measures the performance of below-investment-grade debt issued in US dollars by corporations in the United States and to a small extent in Canada. Owing to its lower credit quality, the High Yield Market Index has been more sensitive to risk aversion than the WGBI government bond indices. This results in different correlations between the High Yield index and currencies, affecting the results of currency hedging.

First, the annualized volatility of the High Yield Market Index has been 9.1% between January 1989 and September 2011, which compares to the 4.9% volatility of the Citi US Government Bond Index over the same period. The volatility of the High Yield index is comparable to the volatility of major exchange

**TABLE 18.5 Annual Returns of Fully Hedged WGBI Bond Exposures (in Percentage)**

| Investors' home currency | Exposure to WGBI bonds in | | | | | | | | | |
|---|---|---|---|---|---|---|---|---|---|---|
| | AUD | CAD | EUR | JPY | NZD | NOK | SEK | CHF | GBP | USD |
| AUD | **9.7** | 11.3 | 9.8 | 10.3 | 6.3 | 7.3 | 8.9 | 9.7 | 9.8 | 10.9 |
| | | (2.3) | (1.7) | (1.8) | (−1.3) | (1.4) | (3.0) | (1.3) | (0.2) | (3.8) |
| CAD | 6.4 | **8.7** | 6.9 | 7.4 | 4.0 | 4.8 | 6.7 | 6.8 | 6.9 | 8.0 |
| | (−3.0) | | (−0.9) | (−0.8) | (−4.5) | (−0.7) | (0.3) | (−1.4) | (−2.5) | (1.2) |
| EUR | 5.4 | 7.3 | **6.2** | 6.2 | 4.0 | 4.6 | 6.9 | 5.7 | 5.9 | 6.8 |
| | (−2.4) | (0.2) | | (−0.4) | (−5.2)[a] | (−2.4) | (−0.3) | (−0.9) | (−1.8) | (1.6) |
| JPY | 3.1 | 4.9 | 3.5 | **4.3** | 1.1 | 1.8 | 3.9 | 3.4 | 3.5 | 4.5 |
| | (−2.4) | (0.1) | (−0.5) | | (−5.6) | (−3.9) | (−0.2) | (−0.9) | (−1.9) | (1.5) |
| NZD[b] | 7.4 | 9.4 | 7.9 | 8.3 | **7.4** | 8.0 | 9.6 | 7.7 | 7.8 | 9.0 |
| | (−1.0) | (1.6) | (1.0) | (1.0) | | (1.7) | (3.9) | (0.5) | (−0.6) | (3.1) |
| NOK[c] | 8.0 | 9.9 | 8.4 | 8.8 | 5.6 | **6.6** | 8.6 | 8.3 | 8.5 | 9.5 |
| | (−0.6) | (2.0) | (1.4) | (1.4) | (−3.4) | | (1.5) | (1.0) | (0.0) | (3.5) |
| SEK[d] | 7.4 | 9.3 | 7.9 | 8.3 | 4.6 | 5.0 | **8.1** | 7.8 | 7.9 | 8.9 |
| | (−1.9) | (0.7) | (0.2) | (0.2) | (−5.8)[a] | (−1.9) | | (−0.2) | (−1.3) | (2.2) |
| CHF | 4.1 | 5.9 | 4.5 | 4.9 | 2.3 | 3.0 | 5.3 | **4.8** | 4.5 | 5.5 |
| | (−1.9) | (0.6) | (0.0) | (0.0) | (−4.8) | (−2.2) | (0.0) | | (−1.4) | (2.0) |
| GBP | 8.1 | 10.0 | 8.6 | 9.0 | 5.5 | 6.4 | 8.4 | 8.5 | **9.0** | 9.7 |
| | (−1.0) | (1.6) | (1.1) | (1.1) | (−3.9) | (−1.1) | (0.2) | (0.7) | | (3.2) |
| USD | 5.8 | 7.8 | 6.3 | 6.7 | 4.2 | 5.2 | 6.6 | 6.2 | 6.3 | **7.8** |
| | (−4.6) | (−1.9) | (−2.5) | (−2.5) | (−5.3) | (−2.1) | (−0.3) | (−2.9) | (−4.0) | |

Differences between fully hedged and unhedged annual returns are represented in parentheses.
[a]The difference between the unhedged and hedged return is significant on a 90% confidence level.
[b]New Zealand WGBI starts October 1992.
[c]Norwegian WGBI starts January 1995.
[d]Swedish WGBI starts January 1991.
*Source:* Citi, sample: January 1985–September 2011 unless otherwise indicated.

rates, suggesting that currency risk is not the dominant driver of return in the unhedged high yield portfolio.

Table 18.6 shows that the volatility of the unhedged US HY index has typically exceeded that of the US dollar denominated index by 3–4% per year, with the exception of Swiss and Japanese investors, who have seen bigger 5–6% volatility contributions from currency conversion. For Canadian investors, on the other hand, currency risk has added no volatility.

Currency hedging has reduced volatility relative to the unhedged asset for investors with all base currencies except the Canadian dollar. Relative to WGBI government bonds, covariances between the High Yield index and currencies have historically been stronger, resulting in less obvious benefits of a full currency hedge.

The US dollar and the US HY index have historically had negative covariances and correlations against all major currencies except the Japanese yen and the Swiss franc. These relationships have been particularly strong against currencies that have been sensitive to commodity prices and risk aversion, such as the Australian, New Zealand, and Canadian dollars, commonly known as the *commodity currencies*.

In an environment of heightened risk aversion, both low credit corporate bonds and commodity currencies have weakened, suggesting that investors with these base currencies would have benefited from foreign currency exposure. Indeed, the minimum volatility hedge ratios in Table 18.6 show that investors in Canada, Australia, and New Zealand would historically have achieved the lowest volatility in their US high yield bond portfolios with hedge ratios of 44%, 68%, and 72%, respectively. For Canadian investors, the correlation effect has been so strong that the unhedged exposure would historically have been less volatile than hedged.

For investors in Japan and Switzerland, the results have been the opposite. The yen and Swiss franc have historically reacted positively to risk aversion, leading to losses in the unhedged exposure at a time when high yield bond prices fall. For these investors, high hedge ratios would have historically produced the lowest risk.

For the remaining currencies, namely, the euro, sterling, Swedish krona, and Norwegian krone, correlations with the High Yield index have been similar to those of the commodity currencies, albeit on a weaker scale. For these base currencies, the minimum volatility of returns would have been achieved with a US dollar exposure of around 10–20%.

*Return impact of hedging corporate bonds.* Similar to hedging WGBI government bonds, we find that the return impact of hedging the US HY index into other major base currencies has historically not been statistically significant. While Table 18.7 shows that most investors would have increased returns by hedging, none of the differences between fully hedged and unhedged returns is significant on a 90% confidence level.

Table 18.7 also shows that while high hedge ratios would have lowered volatility for Japanese and Swiss investors, the negative interest rate differential

**TABLE 18.6 Annual Volatilities and Minimum Volatility Hedge Ratios of the US High Yield Index (in Percentage)**

| | Investors' home currency | | | | | | | | | |
|---|---|---|---|---|---|---|---|---|---|---|
| | AUD | CAD | EUR | JPY | NZD | NOK | SEK | CHF | GBP | USD |
| Hedged | 9.4 | 9.3 | 9.3 | 9.1 | 9.4 | 9.4 | 9.4 | 9.3 | 9.3 | n/a |
| Unhedged | 11.9 | 9 | 13.4 | 15.1 | 12.4 | 12.9 | 13.7 | 14.8 | 12.6 | 9.1 |
| Hedged-unhedged | (−2.5)[a] | (0.3) | (−4.1)[a] | (−6.0)[a] | (−3.0)[a] | (−3.5)[a] | (−4.3)[a] | (−5.5)[a] | (−3.3)[a] | n/a |
| Min vol hedge | 68 | 44 | 89 | 106 | 72 | 81 | 82 | 97 | 85 | n/a |

Differences between fully hedged and unhedged volatilities are represented in parentheses.
No overhedging constraints. A hedge ratio in excess of 100 suggests that taking a theoretical net short position in the foreign currency would have further reduced volatility of returns.
[a]The difference between the volatility of unhedged and hedged return is significant on a 90% confidence level
*Source:* Citi, sample: January 1989–September 2011.

**TABLE 18.7 Annual Returns of US High Yield Index Exposures (in Percentage)**

| | Investors' home currency | | | | | | | | | |
|---|---|---|---|---|---|---|---|---|---|---|
| | AUD | CAD | EUR | JPY | NZD | NOK | SEK | CHF | GBP | USD |
| Hedged | 10.2 | 8 | 7.8 | 5.3 | 10.6 | 9.6 | 8.9 | 6.5 | 9.9 | n/a |
| Unhedged | 8 | 7.7 | 7.5 | 5.8 | 7.3 | 7.7 | 8.7 | 5.7 | 8.9 | 8.3 |
| Hedged-unhedged | (2.2) | (0.3) | (0.3) | (−0.5) | (3.3) | (1.9) | (0.2) | (0.8) | (1.0) | n/a |

Differences between fully hedged and unhedged annual returns are given in parentheses.
None of the differences in returns is significant on a 90% confidence level.
*Source:* Citi, sample: January 1989–September 2011.

incurred in the hedge would have reduced the appeal to hedge. In case of the Japanese yen, the cost of carry has been so high that fully hedged returns would have been even lower than unhedged, taking into account the weak US dollar. Swiss investors would also have reduced their return relative to the dollar denominated index, although relative to the unhedged scenario they would have still been better off.

The benefits of hedging currency risk in exposure to the US HY index have historically been more ambiguous than hedging WGBI government bonds. The return and volatility benefits of hedging have tended to counteract each other: the high yielding and risk-sensitive base currencies, which would have benefited from some exposure to the US dollar in reducing volatility, also produced the strongest positive return impacts from the hedge. The Japanese and Swiss investors, on the other hand, who should have hedged their exposure to reduce volatility, would have benefited least in terms of total return.

However, the risk/return ratio of the hedged High Yield index would have historically been better for all investors except in Canada, suggesting that even for Japanese and Swiss investors the volatility benefit of hedging would have historically outweighed its cost. As we find that the volatility reduction benefit of hedging has historically been statistically significant while the return impact has not, hedging some currency risk on corporate bonds would be a good strategy.

Benchmark hedge ratios between 40% and 90%, with higher hedge ratios for more risk-sensitive currencies, would be a good starting point in setting up a hedge strategy for the US HY index exposure.

### 18.3.2.3 Findings on Hedging MSCI World Equities

*Volatility impact of hedging equities.* The volatility of exchange rates has historically been lower than that of equities. Figure 18.2 shows that while volatilities of unhedged equity returns in foreign currencies have been higher than those in native currencies, the differences have not been large. On average, we find that the volatility of unhedged equity exposures has been 1.14 times the volatility of equities in their home currencies across all major markets and investors' base currencies. In absolute terms, currency conversion added 2.7% points to the average equity volatility of 21.3%. This compares to a difference of 7.5% points and a ratio of 2.7 times for WGBI government bonds and 3.5% and 1.4 times for the US HY index across all other base currencies.

The relatively smaller proportion of currency risk in equities suggests that international equity investors have less potential volatility benefits from hedging than fixed income investors—the volatility of foreign equities is high both with and without currency hedges. Other factors, such as expected return from holding currencies and correlations between equities and risk-sensitive currencies, also play important roles in hedging equity holdings.

Table 18.8 shows that unhedged foreign exposures to equities in Australia, New Zealand, and Canada have been notably more volatile than the equities of these countries in their respective home currencies. This is particularly the case for Japanese and Swiss investors, who have seen the highest volatilities of their foreign holdings. This is because the commodity currencies have historically been

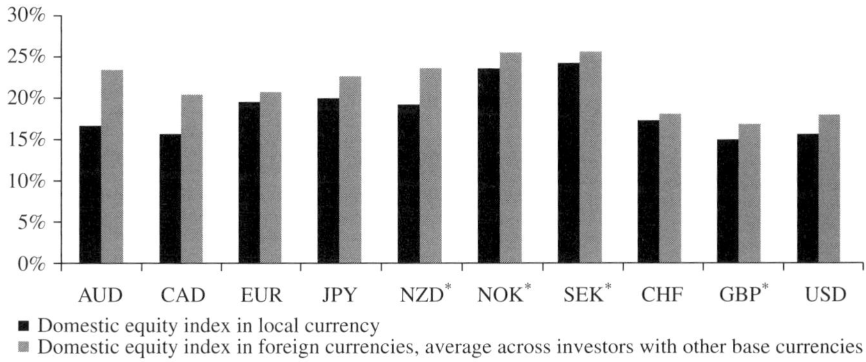


**FIGURE 18.2 Annualized volatility of MSCI equity indices in local and foreign currencies.** *New Zealand, Norwegian, Swedish, and UK MSCIs start January 1988. *Source:* Citi and EcoWin, sample: January 1985–September 2011 unless otherwise indicated.

**TABLE 18.8 Annual Volatilities of Unhedged MSCI Equity Exposures (in Percentage)**

| Investors' home currency | Exposure to MSCI equities in | | | | | | | | | |
|---|---|---|---|---|---|---|---|---|---|---|
| | AUD | CAD | EUR | JPY | NZD | NOK | SEK | CHF | GBP | USD |
| AUD | 16.7 | 17.2 | 20.0 | 22.9 | 20.0 | 23.2 | 23.7 | 18.2 | 15.4 | 16.4 |
| CAD | 21.1 | 15.7 | 19.6 | 22.1 | 21.9 | 24.3 | 24.3 | 17.4 | 15.3 | 14.2 |
| EUR | 23.8 | 21.2 | 19.6 | 22.6 | 24.0 | 25.2 | 25.4 | 16.9 | 16.2 | 18.6 |
| JPY | 25.8 | 22.8 | 23.1 | 19.9 | 25.5 | 28.3 | 28.2 | 19.5 | 19.2 | 20.1 |
| NZD[a] | 19.3 | 19.0 | 20.9 | 23.3 | 19.1 | 24.2 | 24.4 | 18.5 | 16.1 | 17.6 |
| NOK[a] | 23.2 | 20.0 | 19.4 | 22.5 | 23.2 | 23.4 | 24.8 | 16.9 | 15.7 | 17.8 |
| SEK[a] | 22.8 | 19.6 | 19.1 | 22.3 | 23.3 | 24.0 | 24.2 | 16.3 | 16.0 | 17.7 |
| CHF | 25.4 | 22.8 | 21.6 | 22.9 | 25.1 | 26.9 | 27.0 | 17.2 | 18.0 | 20.3 |
| GBP[a] | 23.6 | 20.5 | 20.3 | 22.2 | 23.8 | 25.0 | 25.3 | 17.6 | 14.8 | 18.2 |
| USD | 23.6 | 19.7 | 21.6 | 22.9 | 23.9 | 26.8 | 26.6 | 18.4 | 17.4 | 15.7 |

[a]New Zealand, Norwegian, Swedish, and UK MSCIs start January 1988.
*Source:* Citi, sample: January 1985–September 2011 unless otherwise indicated.

driven by similar factors as equities, strengthening in periods of low risk aversion and weakening when risk aversion rises.

The yen and the Swiss franc have, on the other hand, been inversely linked to risk aversion, strengthening when equity prices fall. This has resulted in positive correlations between foreign currency and equity exposures and increased unhedged equity volatility for investors in Japan and Switzerland.

Table 18.9 shows that foreign investors in Australian, Canadian, and New Zealand equities saw the biggest volatility benefits from currency hedges, with the differences in the volatility of hedged and unhedged exposures exceeding

**TABLE 18.9 Annual Volatilities of Fully Hedged MSCI Equity Exposures (in Percentage)**

| Investors' home currency | Exposure to MSCI equities in AUD | CAD | EUR | JPY | NZD | NOK | SEK | CHF | GBP | USD |
|---|---|---|---|---|---|---|---|---|---|---|
| AUD | **16.7** | 15.8 | 19.9 | 20.4 | 19.0 | 23.5 | 24.1 | 17.6 | 14.9 | 15.9 |
| | | (−1.4)[b] | (−0.1) | (−2.5)[b] | (−1.0) | (0.3) | (0.4) | (−0.6) | (−0.5) | (−0.5) |
| CAD | 16.4 | **15.7** | 19.8 | 20.3 | 19.1 | 23.4 | 24.1 | 17.5 | 14.9 | 15.8 |
| | (−4.7)[b] | | (0.2) | (−1.8)[b] | (−2.8)[b] | (−0.9) | (−0.2) | (0.1) | (−0.4) | (1.6)[b] |
| EUR | 16.1 | 15.5 | **19.6** | 20.1 | 19.2 | 23.3 | 23.9 | 17.3 | 14.8 | 15.6 |
| | (−7.7)[b] | (−5.7)[b] | | (−2.5)[b] | (−4.8)[b] | (−1.9)[b] | (−1.5) | (0.4) | (−1.4)[b] | (−3.0)[b] |
| JPY | 16.0 | 15.3 | 19.6 | **19.9** | 19.0 | 23.0 | 23.9 | 17.2 | 14.8 | 15.4 |
| | (−9.8)[b] | (−7.5)[b] | (−3.5)[b] | | (−6.5)[b] | (−5.3)[b] | (−4.3)[b] | (−2.3)[b] | (−4.4)[b] | (−4.7)[b] |
| NZD[a] | 16.6 | 15.8 | 19.9 | 20.2 | **19.1** | 23.5 | 24.0 | 17.6 | 14.9 | 15.9 |
| | (−2.7)[b] | (−3.2)[b] | (−1.0) | (−3.1)[b] | | (−0.7) | (−0.4) | (−0.9) | (−1.2)[b] | (−1.7)[b] |
| NOK[a] | 16.3 | 15.7 | 19.6 | 20.3 | 19.2 | **23.4** | 23.9 | 17.4 | 14.9 | 15.7 |
| | (−6.9)[b] | (−4.3)[b] | (0.2) | (−2.2)[b] | (−4.0)[b] | | (−0.9) | (0.5) | (−0.8) | (−2.1)[b] |
| SEK[a] | 16.2 | 15.6 | 19.7 | 20.3 | 19.3 | 23.4 | **24.2** | 17.5 | 14.9 | 15.7 |
| | (−6.6)[b] | (−4.0)[b] | (0.6) | (−2.0)[b] | (−4.0)[b] | (−0.6) | | (1.2) | (−1.1) | (−2.0)[b] |
| CHF | 16.0 | 15.4 | 19.5 | 20.0 | 19.1 | 23.2 | 23.8 | **17.2** | 14.8 | 15.5 |
| | (−9.4)[b] | (−7.4)[b] | (−2.1)[b] | (−2.9)[b] | (−6.0)[b] | (−3.7)[b] | (−3.2)[b] | | (−3.2)[b] | (−4.8)[b] |
| GBP[a] | 16.1 | 15.5 | 19.7 | 20.2 | 19.0 | 23.3 | 23.9 | 17.4 | **14.8** | 15.6 |
| | (−7.5)[b] | (−5.0)[b] | (−0.6) | (−2.0)[b] | (−4.8)[b] | (−1.7) | (−1.4) | (−0.2) | | (−2.6)[b] |
| USD | 16.4 | 15.6 | 19.8 | 20.1 | 19.0 | 23.3 | 24.0 | 17.5 | 14.8 | **15.7** |
| | (−7.2)[b] | (−4.1)[b] | (−1.8)[b] | (−2.8)[b] | (−4.9)[b] | (−3.5)[b] | (−2.6)[b] | (−0.9) | (−2.6)[b] | |

Differences between fully hedged and unhedged volatilities are given in parentheses.

[a]New Zealand, Norwegian, Swedish, and UK MSCIs start January 1988.

[b]The volatility of 100% hedged returns is different from the volatility of unhedged returns on 90% confidence level.

*Source:* Citi, sample: January 1985–September 2011 unless otherwise indicated.

the 90% confidence level for investors with all other base currencies. Japanese and Swiss investors typically saw the biggest volatility reductions in their foreign equity holdings.

The positive relationships between equities and the Australian, Canadian, and New Zealand dollars offered a natural hedge against equity prices for investors with these base currencies, reducing the volatility benefit of hedging. The differences between hedged and unhedged return volatilities are typically not statistically significant for these base currencies. In the case of Canadian investors hedging US equities, currency hedges even led to an increase in volatility.

Hedged investors with all other major base currencies have historically seen small and statistically significant reductions in the volatility of their US equity holdings. The same has also held true for US investors, with the exception of exposures in the Eurozone and Switzerland.

Table 18.10, which shows the hedge ratios that would have historically minimized the volatilities of foreign equity holdings, depicts a similar scenario. Equity investors based in Australia, Canada, and New Zealand would have in the past benefited from some foreign currency exposure, with minimum volatility hedge ratios for holdings in other countries typically between 40% and 80%. Canadian investors holding US equities are the major exception, with no hedge as the optimum strategy in the past.

In addition to the commodity currencies, the minimum volatility hedge ratios for Swedish-krona-based investors have also been on the low side of average, as this currency has also been historically sensitive to risk aversion.

Japanese and Swiss investors would, on the other hand, have benefited from high hedge ratios, exceeding 100% in most cases, to help offset the negative

**TABLE 18.10 Minimum Volatility Hedge Ratios for MSCI Equity Exposures (in Percentage)**

| | | Exposure to MSCI equities in | | | | | | | | | |
|---|---|---|---|---|---|---|---|---|---|---|---|
| | | AUD | CAD | EUR | JPY | NZD | NOK | SEK | CHF | GBP | USD |
| Investors' home currency | AUD | n/a | 72 | 50 | 70 | 79 | 44 | 44 | 55 | 55 | 54 |
| | CAD | 137 | n/a | 47 | 71 | 105 | 69 | 55 | 49 | 56 | 5 |
| | EUR | 143 | 133 | n/a | 86 | 129 | 198 | 135 | 31 | 89 | 91 |
| | JPY | 132 | 127 | 104 | n/a | 118 | 130 | 111 | 80 | 98 | 109 |
| | NZD[a] | 107 | 93 | 63 | 76 | n/a | 64 | 56 | 57 | 62 | 67 |
| | NOK[a] | 138 | 122 | 40 | 78 | 114 | n/a | 98 | 39 | 69 | 78 |
| | SEK[a] | 134 | 109 | 22 | 73 | 116 | 81 | n/a | 25 | 68 | 73 |
| | CHF | 142 | 134 | 181 | 94 | 133 | 195 | 150 | n/a | 109 | 105 |
| | GBP[a] | 133 | 127 | 70 | 74 | 117 | 109 | 88 | 55 | n/a | 87 |
| | USD | 145 | 188 | 80 | 91 | 121 | 121 | 95 | 60 | 89 | n/a |

No over- and underhedging constraints. A hedge ratio in excess of 100 suggests that taking a theoretical net short position in the foreign currency would have further reduced volatility of returns.

[a]New Zealand, Norwegian, Swedish, and UK MSCIs start January 1988.

*Source:* Citi, sample: January 1985–September 2011 unless otherwise indicated.

correlation between their home currencies and equity prices. Our long historical sample suggests that investors in the Eurozone, United Kingdom, and the United States would have been better off with relatively high hedge ratios, with the exception of exposures in Switzerland.

It is worth bearing in mind that the long sample used here downplays the impact of unusual market conditions during the 2007–2008 credit crisis, when correlations between currencies and equities were stronger than those in the past. This is particularly true for the negative correlation between the US dollar and US equities, which would have called for even lower minimum volatility hedge ratios for foreign investors and higher hedge ratios for US investors during the crisis.

*Return impact of hedging equities.* Similar to government bonds and the US HY index, we find that hedging has had a statistically insignificant impact on returns of foreign equity holdings. On the basis of a two-tailed $t$-test for difference in sample means, we are unable to reject the null hypothesis that the fully hedged and unhedged returns are the same for all combinations of major base and exposure currencies on a 90% confidence level.

Tables 18.11 and 18.12 show that the effects of hedging broadly mirror those seen in government bonds and US corporate bonds. There are only minor differences arising from different asset performance—the two equity bear markets of the last decade have impacted hedge returns relative to bonds—and in some cases, also from different sample start dates.

Foreign investors with US equity exposures would have, in the past, been better off by hedging the US dollar exposure into their home currencies, which has resulted in reduced volatility, as well as due to the weak dollar, increased returns. This is even true for investors in Japan and Switzerland, whose strong home currencies have more than made up for the cost of carry in hedging.

**TABLE 18.11 Annual Returns of Unhedged MSCI Equity Exposures (in Percentage)**

| | | Exposure to MSCI equities in | | | | | | | | | |
|---|---|---|---|---|---|---|---|---|---|---|---|
| | | AUD | CAD | EUR | JPY | NZD | NOK | SEK | CHF | GBP | USD |
| Investors' home currency | AUD | 6.8 | 6.6 | 6.3 | 3.5 | −1.1 | 6.0 | 8.0 | 10.4 | 2.6 | 6.5 |
| | CAD | 6.5 | 6.3 | 6.0 | 3.2 | −0.8 | 6.3 | 8.3 | 10.2 | 2.9 | 6.3 |
| | EUR | 4.9 | 4.7 | 4.5 | 1.7 | 0.0 | 7.2 | 9.3 | 8.5 | 3.8 | 4.7 |
| | JPY | 2.7 | 2.5 | 2.2 | −0.5 | −1.8 | 5.1 | 7.2 | 6.2 | 1.8 | 2.4 |
| | NZD[a] | 5.6 | 5.4 | 5.1 | 2.3 | −0.5 | 6.6 | 8.7 | 9.2 | 3.2 | 5.3 |
| | NOK[a] | 5.7 | 5.5 | 5.2 | 2.4 | −0.2 | 7.0 | 9.1 | 9.3 | 3.6 | 5.4 |
| | SEK[a] | 6.4 | 6.2 | 5.9 | 3.1 | 0.8 | 8.0 | 10.1 | 10.0 | 4.6 | 6.1 |
| | CHF | 3.2 | 3.0 | 2.7 | 0.0 | −1.3 | 5.8 | 7.8 | 6.7 | 2.4 | 2.9 |
| | GBP[a] | 6.2 | 6.0 | 5.7 | 2.9 | 0.9 | 8.1 | 10.2 | 9.8 | 4.7 | 5.9 |
| | USD | 7.4 | 7.3 | 7.0 | 4.1 | 0.1 | 7.2 | 9.3 | 11.1 | 3.8 | 7.2 |

[a]New Zealand, Norwegian, Swedish and UK MSCIs start January 1988.

Source: Citi, sample: January 1985–September 2011 unless otherwise indicated.

**TABLE 18.12 Annual Returns of Fully Hedged MSCI Equity Exposures (in Percentage)**

| Investors' home currency | Exposure to MSCI equities in: AUD | CAD | EUR | JPY | NZD | NOK | SEK | CHF | GBP | USD |
|---|---|---|---|---|---|---|---|---|---|---|
| AUD | **6.8** | 8.5 | 7.0 | 4.2 | −0.9 | 6.5 | 10.4 | 10.5 | 4.2 | 9.5 |
| | | (1.9) | (0.7) | (0.7) | (0.2) | (0.5) | (2.4) | (0.1) | (1.6) | (3.0) |
| CAD | 4.0 | **6.3** | 4.4 | 1.7 | −2.9 | 4.6 | 8.3 | 7.7 | 2.2 | 6.9 |
| | (−2.5) | | (−1.6) | (−1.5) | (−2.1) | (−1.7) | (0.0) | (−2.5) | (−0.7) | (0.6) |
| EUR | 3.4 | 5.4 | **4.5** | 1.1 | −3.1 | 4.7 | 8.5 | 7.4 | 2.1 | 6.3 |
| | (−1.5) | (0.7) | | (−0.6) | (−3.1) | (−2.5) | (−0.8) | (−1.1) | (−1.7) | (1.6) |
| JPY | 1.4 | 3.3 | 1.9 | **−0.5** | −5.5 | 2.4 | 5.9 | 5.1 | −0.5 | 4.3 |
| | (−1.3) | (0.8) | (−0.3) | | (−3.7) | (−2.7) | (−1.3) | (−1.1) | (−2.3) | (1.9) |
| NZD[a] | 4.6 | 6.8 | 5.4 | 2.6 | **−0.5** | 6.7 | 10.6 | 8.7 | 4.3 | 7.8 |
| | (−1.0) | (1.4) | (0.3) | (0.3) | | (0.1) | (1.9) | (−0.5) | (1.1) | (2.5) |
| NOK[a] | 5.8 | 7.7 | 6.4 | 3.3 | −1.3 | **7.0** | 10.6 | 9.8 | 4.0 | 8.6 |
| | (0.1) | (2.2) | (1.2) | (0.9) | (−1.1) | | (1.5) | (0.5) | (0.4) | (3.2) |
| SEK[a] | 5.2 | 7.1 | 5.7 | 2.7 | −2.0 | 5.7 | **10.1** | 9.1 | 3.2 | 8.0 |
| | (−1.2) | (0.9) | (−0.2) | (−0.4) | (−2.8) | (−2.3) | | (−0.9) | (−1.4) | (1.9) |
| CHF | 2.4 | 4.3 | 3.1 | 0.0 | −4.3 | 3.7 | 7.3 | **6.7** | 0.8 | 5.2 |
| | (−0.8) | (1.3) | (0.4) | (0.0) | (−3.0) | (−2.1) | (−0.5) | | (−1.6) | (2.3) |
| GBP[a] | 6.0 | 8.0 | 6.6 | 3.5 | −1.2 | 6.7 | 10.5 | 10.0 | **4.7** | 9.0 |
| | (−0.2) | (2.0) | (0.9) | (0.6) | (−2.1) | (−1.4) | (0.3) | (0.2) | | (3.1) |
| USD | 3.8 | 5.8 | 4.2 | 1.5 | −3.0 | 4.8 | 8.4 | 7.4 | 2.1 | **7.2** |
| | (−3.6) | (−1.5) | (−2.8) | (−2.6) | (−3.1) | (−2.4) | (−0.9) | (−3.7) | (−1.7) | |

Differences between fully hedged and unhedged annual returns in parentheses.
None of the differences between the unhedged and hedged return is significant on a 90% confidence level.
[a]New Zealand, Norwegian, Swedish, and UK MSCIs start January 1988.
*Source:* Citi, sample: January 1985–September 2011 unless otherwise indicated.

For example, a yen-based investor who invested in US equities in January 1985 would have earned just 2.4% per year without hedging and 4.3% with full currency hedges. Nevertheless, the cost of hedging has been high, as a domestic US-dollar-based investor would have earned 7.2% per year on the same investment.

Table 18.11 shows that low interest rates and the strong Yen have put Japanese investors in a particularly unfavorable position. Our results show that unhedged Japanese investors experienced the lowest equity returns in all major markets, including their own, where they lost 0.5% per year. Table 18.12 shows that returns to hedged Japanese investors have also been the lowest in all major markets, owing to the cost of carry.

Japanese investors with US dollar exposure have been faced with two difficult choices: hedge and lose money from the negative interest rate differential and do not hedge and lose even more money from the strong yen and face increased portfolio volatility. The results for Swiss investors have been largely similar, although their portfolios were at least helped by the good performance of their domestic equity market.

The weak US dollar, which has benefited hedged investors elsewhere, reduced returns for hedged investors in the United States. Owing to the low risk-adjusted returns of equities, the impact of the reduction in return has been proportionately larger than the reduction in volatility, so hedging has led to even lower risk-adjusted returns for hedged US investors. The opposite has been true for foreign investors with US equity exposure, who have seen currency hedges increase their risk-adjusted returns.

Unlike government and corporate bonds, the impact of currency hedges on risk-adjusted equity returns has been more mixed. Owing to the relatively modest impact on volatility, at least in proportion to the underlying asset volatility, the impact on risk-adjusted returns depends more on the uncertain return impact of hedging.

The question of hedging foreign equities is therefore as much a question of return as well as volatility, and there is more scope for active currency management in equity portfolios than fixed income portfolios. While we show that hedging has in many cases brought statistically significant volatility reductions to equity holdings, the impact on return has been higher in proportion to the often meager underlying performance of the asset, even if not strictly significant in statistical terms.

As investors typically aim for higher risk-adjusted returns, that is, an increase in return and reduction in volatility or a relatively small reduction in return relative to a big reduction in volatility, there are no unambiguous conclusions to be drawn from historical performance, which even for the relatively long period covered are dependent on the sample choice.

A combination of a passive hedge benchmark, chosen with the aim of reducing portfolio volatility, and the ability to change the hedge ratio relative to the benchmark, with the aim of adding long-term returns by going short and long foreign currencies relative to the hedge benchmark, seem to be the most appropriate choice for international equity investors. The hedge benchmark can be chosen based either on historical volatility minimizing results or simply on the basis of minimum regret, which if long-term expected returns from currencies are zero, would point to a benchmark of 50%.

### 18.3.3 SUMMARY OF FINDINGS ON THE RETURN AND VOLATILITY IMPACT OF CURRENCY HEDGING

Our investigation on the historical impact of currency hedging in government bond, corporate bond, and equity portfolios suggests that the most important topics in deciding whether and how much to hedge are the following.

1. *Risk-Adjusted Returns of the Underlying Asset*. If the investor aims to maximize the ratio of return over volatility then the optimal hedge strategy depends on the expected risk-adjusted return from the underlying asset. For assets with return/risk ratios in excess of one (e.g., total returns from holding bonds), it is important to maintain the smooth return profile of the asset and not let currency conversion risk jeopardize risk-adjusted returns, especially if the volatility of the exchange rate is higher than that of the asset. Unless there is reason to expect that holding foreign currency exposure can reduce volatility through favorable correlation effects, currency risk in the portfolio should be largely hedged away. On the other hand, assets with low return/risk ratios, such as equities, are more sensitive to the return impact of hedging. If the risk-adjusted return is low to start with, then equal reductions in return and volatility will lead to a fall in the risk-adjusted return. Maximizing returns via a dynamic hedge relative to a fixed benchmark better suits assets with low return-to-risk ratios.
2. *Relative Volatility of the Asset and the Currency Exposure*. Government bonds, which have had significantly lower volatility than currencies, have benefited most from currency hedges, with the volatility benefits of hedging clearly outweighing the impact on return. US low credit corporate bonds have had similar or slightly lower volatility than exchange rates, with most investors benefiting from some currency hedges in terms of higher risk-adjusted returns. Equities, on the other hand, have been more volatile than currencies, giving relatively modest volatility benefits of hedging and mixed impacts on risk-adjusted returns.
3. *Correlation Between the Foreign Asset and Currency*. If the foreign currency exposure is negatively correlated with the underlying asset (e.g., foreign investors holding US equities or low credit bonds), then the investor can achieve lower portfolio volatility by holding foreign currency. The minimum volatility hedge ratios depend on the relative volatility and the asset, as well as on the strength of the correlation, although correlations between assets and currencies have rarely been strong enough to justify no hedge as the least volatile option.
4. *The Cost of Hedging*. Owing to positive historical returns to the FX carry trade, we find strong historical correlations between the 1-month interest rate differentials and fully hedged returns relative to unhedged returns.

The correlations have been higher in government bonds and US corporate bonds, where we find results of 60% and 73%, respectively. For equities, the correlation across all base and exposure currencies has been 50%. This suggests that interest rate differentials have been an important driver of hedge returns, even when taking the poor performance of the carry trade during the credit crisis into account.

# 18.4 Hedge Instruments—Currency Forwards versus Options

Once the investor has decided to hedge the foreign currency exposure, the next important question is which instruments to use. In this section, we look at the relative benefits of hedging with currency forwards and options, investigating their impact on hedge cash flows, effective hedge ratios, and total return.

## 18.4.1 WHY DO HEDGE CASH FLOWS MATTER?

Managing hedge cash flows has become increasingly important for investors because of both the increased volatility of currencies during the 2007–2008 credit crisis and the increased correlations between assets and currencies. The problem is particularly sensitive in the case of hedge losses, which generate negative cash flows against mark-to-market currency gains on underlying assets.

From the point of view of hedged asset indices, the concept of cash flows seems trivial—negative cash flows from currency hedges are covered by realizing the simultaneous currency gains on underlying assets, which is achieved by selling off some of the foreign assets (at zero cost). However, in practice, there are several reasons why investors may prefer to handle hedge cash flows separately from the asset.

First, selling assets to cover hedge losses may be costly and difficult, especially the hedge losses happen in a portfolio of illiquid assets or in times of reduced market liquidity. Second, selling assets makes the performance of the asset conditional on the performance of currency hedges and reduces its future potential gains. And finally, selling assets to cover hedge losses may send a wrong signal to the investor's clients or management, questioning the necessity of currency hedges.

Anecdotal evidence, at least among long-term real money investors (such as pension funds), suggests that most hedgers tend to handle hedge cash flows from a separate cash reserve, which among other things accumulates gains from currency hedges as well as pays for their losses. The cash from hedge gains is reinvested into underlying assets only when the cash reserve grows too large relative to its strategic allocation target. On the other hand, if currency hedges produce losses larger than the cash available, then the investor needs to sell some liquid assets, which can, for example, lead to a situation, where currency losses on foreign equities or alternative investments lead to a reduced allocation to government bonds.

For these reasons, most investors tend to be averse to large cash losses from currency hedges, even if they are offset by equally large mark-to-market gains on foreign assets. Currency forwards, which offer the most effective (high delta) protection against currency risk, also produce the largest cash losses if the investor's home currency weakens.

Table 18.13 shows the average and worst historical negative cash flows from 1-month forward hedges for all major currency crosses, including the cost of carry and assuming a 100% hedge ratio. According to the table, while average hedge losses have typically been between −1% and −3% per month, the worst-case outcomes have extended well into double digits, with Australian investors losing as much as 23.3% on their Japanese yen hedges in October 2008, a month when the Japanese MSCI index dropped also by 23.6%. This added up to a lot of pain.

We find that investors in New Zealand and Australia have suffered the worst negative cash flows from 1-month forwards, followed by investors with pound sterling and Swedish krona as base currency. The euro, on the other hand, has tended to weaken less dramatically, resulting in mostly single-digit worst-case losses and an average overall loss of −2.1% per month.

Another interesting feature of Table 18.13 is the asymmetry of worst hedge losses. This is the most apparent in the Japanese yen, which has historically tended to strengthen more sharply than weaken. While foreign investors have on average lost 19.7% in their worst-case yen hedges, Japanese investors have lost an average of 12.1% in their worst hedges on foreign currencies. A similar asymmetry also applies to the Swiss franc, albeit on a weaker scale.

On the other hand, the Australian and New Zealand dollars, Swedish krona, and pound sterling have tended to weaken more sharply than gain. Nowhere is this more obvious than the euro against sterling, where UK investors have suffered the worst loss of 12.9%, while the maximum loss for Eurozone investors hedging UK assets has been only 6.7%.

Investors with risk-sensitive base currencies have historically been more vulnerable to hedge losses. This skew in risk has historically been compensated by higher domestic yields (or the higher yields have possibly led to increased sensitivity to risk aversion due to the carry trade), as we find a 95% significant correlation of −0.5 between the worst hedge losses in Table 18.13 and the average historical 1-month carry over the same period.

### 18.4.2 HISTORICAL PERFORMANCE OF HEDGING WITH OPTIONS

One way of controlling the cash flow at risk from the hedge is to implement the hedge with bought options, where the loss is limited to the premium paid. Rather than entering into a forward contract, that is, taking on an obligation to sell the foreign currency at a future date, the investor buys the right to sell the foreign currency, paying a premium to cover for the risk that the home currency weakens and the right will not be exercised. For this reason, we refer to options as *bought options* to differentiate them from other more forward-like option structures such

**TABLE 18.13 Average and Worst Historical 1-Month Forward Losses, Long Investor's Home Currency (in Percentage)**

| Investors' home currency | Exposure currency: AUD | CAD | EUR | JPY | NZD | NOK | SEK | CHF | GBP | USD |
|---|---|---|---|---|---|---|---|---|---|---|
| AUD | **n/a** | −2.3 | −3.0 | −3.8 | −2.0 | −2.9 | −2.9 | −3.4 | −3.2 | −2.7 |
| | | (−10.5) | (−12.9) | (−23.3) | (−12.8) | (−13.4) | (−12.1) | (−16.3) | (−19.3) | (−15.9) |
| CAD | −2.4 | **n/a** | −2.6 | −3.3 | −2.5 | −2.4 | −2.4 | −3.2 | −2.6 | −1.6 |
| | (−8.7) | | (−8.9) | (−18.7) | (−12.6) | (−8.4) | (−10.3) | (−10.7) | (−12.6) | (−11.6) |
| EUR | −2.9 | −2.5 | **n/a** | −3.1 | −2.7 | −1.2 | −1.3 | −1.3 | −1.6 | −2.6 |
| | (−10.6) | (−10.4) | | (−18.6) | (−9.6) | (−7.9) | (−7.4) | (−10.2) | (−6.7) | (−10.9) |
| JPY | −3.4 | −3.0 | −2.3 | **n/a** | −3.1 | −2.6 | −2.6 | −2.4 | −2.4 | −2.5 |
| | (−12.8) | (−13.1) | (−10.6) | | (−16.9) | (−8.8) | (−14.5) | (−10.1) | (−11.2) | (−11.0) |
| NZD | −2.1 | −2.5 | −2.9 | −3.9 | **n/a** | −2.9 | −2.8 | −3.2 | −3.0 | −3.0 |
| | (−17.2) | (−14.5) | (−15.9) | (−20.5) | | (−14.4) | (−16.8) | (−17.4) | (−16.9) | (−15.1) |
| NOK | −2.8 | −2.4 | −1.1 | −3.4 | −2.6 | **n/a** | −1.3 | −1.8 | −1.9 | −2.5 |
| | (−10.0) | (−10.6) | (−8.2) | (−21.2) | (−9.5) | | (−5.7) | (−9.9) | (−7.9) | (−13.9) |
| SEK | −2.7 | −2.5 | −1.3 | −3.4 | −2.9 | −1.4 | **n/a** | −2.0 | −2.0 | −3.0 |
| | (−12.3) | (−10.4) | (−13.1) | (−19.0) | (−11.4) | (−12.6) | | (−13.4) | (−15.2) | (−13.7) |
| CHF | −3.2 | −3.0 | −1.1 | −2.8 | −3.1 | −1.7 | −1.7 | **n/a** | −2.0 | −3.0 |
| | (−11.7) | (−13.2) | (−7.1) | (−17.5) | (−12.5) | (−8.1) | (−10.2) | | (−10.4) | (−15.8) |
| GBP | −2.7 | −2.3 | −1.7 | −3.4 | −2.8 | −1.9 | −1.9 | −2.2 | **n/a** | −2.3 |
| | (−14.1) | (−14.2) | (−12.9) | (−20.5) | (−14.8) | (−10.0) | (−9.9) | (−14.7) | | (−14.3) |
| USD | −2.8 | −1.5 | −2.5 | −2.9 | −2.6 | −2.6 | −2.6 | −2.8 | −2.5 | **n/a** |
| | (−11.3) | (−8.6) | (−10.9) | (−17.9) | (−15.3) | (−8.4) | (−13.0) | (−12.7) | (−14.4) | |

Worst losses are given in parentheses.
*Source:* Citi, sample: January 1985–September 2011.

as risk reversals, seagulls, and participating forwards, which also involve taking short positions in options.

The limited downside risk is one of the biggest advantages of a bought option hedge for an investor. Table 18.14 shows the average and worst-case losses on 1-month at-the-money-forward options (options where the strike is equal to the 1-month forward rate). Similar to Table 18.13, the results assume a 100% hedge ratio and trading at midmarket rates. With the exception of the shorter sample period, to account for the later development of the liquid options market in more exotic major currency crosses, the results in Tables 18.13 and 18.14 are directly comparable.

The results of Table 18.14 show that average hedge losses in bought at-the-money-forward option hedges have been around −1% to −1.2% per month, representing mostly the cost of buying the options. The average loss from the options hedge has been about 0.15% smaller than the average cost of premium across all currencies, accounting for the fact that some options expire in the money but are not enough to offset the cost of the premium.

The average loss of −1% to −1.2% in options hedges compares to an average loss of −2.1% (euro-based investors) to −2.9% (Australian-dollar-based investors) in forward hedges. In extremes, bought option hedges have rarely lost more than 2–4% per month, with the exception of Japanese yen crosses where unprecedented levels of implied volatility at the end of 2008 pushed up the prices of option premiums and resulted in up to 7% monthly losses for Australian investors hedging the yen. But relative to the −23.3% loss on the forward hedge, this is still an improvement.

Compared to hedging with currency forwards, hedging with bought options has historically significantly reduced the risk of negative cash flows from the hedge. Periods when the home currency weakens, it is clearly preferable to hedge with an option rather than a forward. However, during periods when the home currency strengthens, it is better to hedge with a forward, which fully participates in the currency gain without the cost of the premium.

The total return of options versus forward hedges is therefore very sensitive to the choice of the sample period and the strength or weakness of the investor's home currency within it. Table 18.15 shows the annualized monthly difference between at-the-money-forward option and forward hedge returns for matching sample periods between September 2002 and 2011.

The results show that investors who have benefited from hedging would have been better off with forward hedges, at least from a total return point of view. Investors with the Australian and New Zealand dollars would have been the worst off in option hedges, while Japanese, UK, and US investors would have benefited from hedging by options rather than forwards, confirming the theoretical findings of Attfield et al. (2001), who show that hedging with options under negative carry outperforms hedging with forwards if the forward rate is a poor predictor of spot.

Hedging with a bought at-the-money-forward option outperforms the forward if the investor's home currency weakens by more than the paid premium for the option. In an environment where currencies fail to move toward forward

**TABLE 18.14 Average and Worst Historical 1-Month At-the-Money-Forward Option Hedge Losses, Long Investor's Home Currency (in Percentage)**

| Investor's home currency | Exposure currency: AUD | CAD | EUR | JPY | NZD | NOK | SEK | CHF | GBP | USD |
|---|---|---|---|---|---|---|---|---|---|---|
| AUD | **n/a** | −1.0 | −1.0 | −1.5 | −0.8 | −1.0 | −1.1 | −1.1 | −1.0 | −1.3 |
| | | (−3.2) | (−3.7) | (−7.0) | (−1.4) | (−3.1) | (−3.0) | (−2.9) | (−2.4) | (−4.8) |
| CAD | −1.1 | **n/a** | −1.1 | −1.4 | −1.2 | −1.2 | −1.2 | −1.2 | −1.0 | −1.0 |
| | (−3.9) | | (−2.8) | (−4.3) | (−2.7) | (−3.3) | (−3.1) | (−2.8) | (−2.3) | (−3.0) |
| EUR | −1.0 | −1.0 | **n/a** | −1.1 | −1.2 | −0.8 | −0.7 | −0.5 | −0.8 | −1.1 |
| | (−2.7) | (−2.5) | | (−4.6) | (−2.4) | (−2.2) | (−2.2) | (−1.4) | (−2.4) | (−2.7) |
| JPY | −1.5 | −1.3 | −1.2 | **n/a** | −1.6 | −1.4 | −1.4 | −1.1 | −1.3 | −1.1 |
| | (−5.3) | (−3.4) | (−3.5) | | (−4.4) | (−3.9) | (−3.8) | (−2.8) | (−3.6) | (−2.4) |
| NZD[a] | −0.8 | −1.2 | −1.1 | −1.5 | **n/a** | −1.3 | −1.2 | −1.2 | −1.2 | −1.2 |
| | (−2.4) | (−3.3) | (−2.9) | (−5.9) | | (−3.3) | (−3.3) | (−3.7) | (−3.5) | (−4.1) |
| NOK[a] | −1.2 | −1.3 | −0.7 | −1.3 | −1.3 | **n/a** | −0.8 | −0.8 | −1.0 | −1.2 |
| | (−4.1) | (−3.5) | (−2.1) | (−5.1) | (−2.7) | | (−2.2) | (−2.4) | (−2.7) | (−3.6) |
| SEK | −1.1 | −1.3 | −0.6 | −1.4 | −1.3 | −0.8 | **n/a** | −0.8 | −0.9 | −1.2 |
| | (−3.9) | (−3.3) | (−2.0) | (−5.2) | (−3.0) | (−2.3) | | (−2.4) | (−3.0) | (−3.4) |
| CHF | −1.2 | −1.1 | −0.5 | −1.0 | −1.3 | −1.0 | −0.8 | **n/a** | −0.9 | −1.1 |
| | (−4.2) | (−3.4) | (−2.0) | (−3.8) | (−3.2) | (−3.0) | (−2.7) | | (−2.7) | (−2.7) |
| GBP | −1.1 | −1.1 | −0.8 | −1.3 | −1.2 | −1.0 | −1.0 | −0.9 | **n/a** | −1.0 |
| | (−4.0) | (−3.2) | (−2.2) | (−4.9) | (−3.3) | (−3.2) | (−2.6) | (−2.5) | | (−3.1) |
| USD | −1.3 | −1.1 | −1.0 | −1.1 | −1.4 | −1.3 | −1.2 | −1.0 | −0.9 | **n/a** |
| | (−4.5) | (−3.1) | (−3.1) | (−3.5) | (−2.8) | (−3.5) | (−3.2) | (−2.0) | (−2.3) | |

Worst losses given in parentheses.
[a]The sample starts March 2004 for AUDNOK, January 2005 for NZDNOK, and April 2004 for NZDSEK.
*Source:* Citi, sample: September 2002–September 2011 unless otherwise indicated.

**TABLE 18.15 Annualized Difference Between Monthly At-the-Money-Forward Option and Forward Returns, Trading at Midmarket Rates, Long Investor's Home Currency (in Percentage)**

| | | Exposure currency | | | | | | | | | |
|---|---|---|---|---|---|---|---|---|---|---|---|
| | | AUD | CAD | EUR | JPY | NZD | NOK | SEK | CHF | GBP | USD |
| Investors' home currency | AUD | n/a | −3.5 | −3.9 | −1.2 | 0.2 | −5.5 | −4.9 | −2.9 | −4.6 | −2.9 |
| | CAD | 1.7 | n/a | 0.1 | −0.4 | 2.7 | −1.1 | −0.8 | 1.4 | −1.7 | −2.3 |
| | EUR | 1.9 | 0.7 | n/a | 0.2 | 1.3 | −0.9 | −2.3 | 0.9 | −0.8 | −1.2 |
| | JPY | 4.4 | 0.2 | 0.1 | n/a | 3.2 | 0.7 | −0.3 | 0.3 | −0.8 | −3.7 |
| | NZD[a] | 0.6 | −2.0 | −3.9 | −2.2 | n/a | −3.3 | −4.0 | −4.5 | −4.1 | −3.1 |
| | NOK[a] | −2.8 | −1.4 | −1.6 | −0.2 | −1.0 | n/a | −2.2 | −0.9 | −2.0 | −2.7 |
| | SEK[a] | 0.8 | −0.3 | −2.2 | −0.5 | 0.5 | −1.4 | n/a | −0.7 | −1.4 | −1.2 |
| | CHF | 2.0 | 1.2 | 0.1 | −0.5 | −0.2 | −1.0 | −1.6 | n/a | −1.3 | −1.1 |
| | GBP | 3.2 | 0.9 | 1.1 | 1.2 | 3.0 | 0.6 | 0.4 | 1.5 | n/a | −1.4 |
| | USD | 6.0 | 1.4 | 1.9 | −0.7 | 5.2 | 1.1 | 2.0 | 3.0 | −0.2 | n/a |

[a]The sample starts March 2004 for AUDNOK, January 2005 for NZDNOK, and April 2004 for NZDSEK.

*Source:* Citi, sample: September 2002–September 2011 unless otherwise indicated.

rates, spending premium on the option has compared favorably to buying the home currency at a forward premium. This has helped option hedges outperform forwards in historically large negative carry hedges, such as hedging into the yen or Swiss franc. Options have also helped limit hedge losses for the weak US-dollar-based investors in this particular sample period.

Bought option hedges thus outperform forwards if hedging results in a negative cash flow—if the investor's home currency weakens, the delta on the option and the effective hedge ratio fall toward zero, leaving the investor with no hedge if the option expires out of the money. While this might be desirable from a total return point of view, the variable delta of options means that the "efficiency" of the bought option in offsetting moves in foreign currency exposure is lower than that of the forward hedge.

Figure 18.3 shows the effective hedge ratios calculated as the value or delta of the currency hedge divided by the value of the underlying asset, for a Eurozone investor, hedging US equities with currency forwards and at-the-money-forward options and targeting a 50% hedge ratio. The hedge instruments have tenor 3 months and are implemented monthly in proportions of one-third of the then current asset value.

The effective hedge ratio of the currency forward is more stable since it is only a function of the underlying asset movement—if US equities fall, the Eurozone investor becomes overhedged and if equity prices rise, underhedged. For the bought option hedge, the effective hedge ratio is a function of the delta of open options and movements in underlying equity prices.

If the euro strengthens, both the delta of the call options and the effective hedge ratio increase. On the other hand, if the euro weakens, the effective hedge

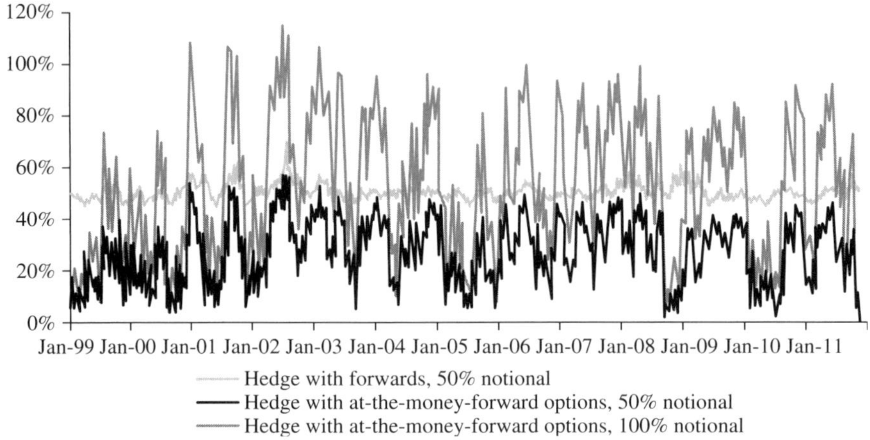


**FIGURE 18.3** **Effective hedge ratios of Eurozone investor hedging US equities with 3-month currency forwards and at-the-money-forward options, layered monthly.** ***Source:*** **Citi, sample: January 1999–September 2011.**

ratio falls, resulting in a volatile effective hedge ratio with a mean lower than that of the forward hedge ratio (if the notional amounts on the bought options are the same as on forward trades). In fact, the average effective hedge ratio of the bought option hedges with 50% notional in Figure 18.3 is 26.1%, which is close to the 50% inception delta of the at-the-money-forward options, adjusted for the 50% target hedge ratio. For equivalent notional amounts, hedging with bought options has resulted being underhedged relative to a forward hedge.

For equivalent delta amounts, Figure 18.3 shows that the investor should have bought at-the-money-forward options in twice the notional amount as the forward, resulting in a volatile effective hedge ratio between 0% and 115% and an average hedge cover of 50.2%.

Options are therefore better suited for return-oriented investors whose aim is to find the most economical hedge rather than minimize asset volatility. The delta of the bought options is specific to the tenor and entry time of the options. If the options are close to expiry and out of the money, the resulting low effective hedge ratio means that the hedge will no longer offset any weakness in the foreign currency at that point in time.

### 18.4.3 SUMMARY OF FINDINGS ON HEDGING WITH OPTIONS VERSUS FORWARDS

When deciding the optimal hedge instrument, the investor should consider the following.

1. *The Strategic Aim of the Currency Hedge*. Currency forwards are the most efficient in offsetting foreign currency risk and should be used if the aim of the hedge is to minimize volatility of the foreign asset. Investors, holding

inherently volatile underlying assets, who are looking for the most economical hedge or are sensitive to the risk of large negative cash flows from hedge instruments should consider using options. Options have historically tended to outperform forward hedges, if the hedge incurs large negative carry or the investor's home currency weakens.

2. *The Ability to Meet Negative Hedge Cash Flows*. If the investor's underlying asset is illiquid, for example, land, real estate, and other alternative investments, it may be better to hedge with long-term bought options rather than currency forwards. Maximum negative cash flows from bought option hedges have been considerably lower than those from forward hedges (for equivalent notional amounts) and are known beforehand and thus easier to plan for.
3. *Effective Hedge Ratios*. The variable delta of option hedges creates volatile hedge ratios and makes the current effective hedge dependent on the tenor and entry time of open options. If the options are out of the money and close to expiry, the investor's hedge against foreign currency weakness is low. "Layering" the options, that is, entering fixed proportions of the hedge at different times, can help smooth the effective hedge ratio.
4. *Active Hedge Management*. Options can be a good complement to forward hedges, if implemented tactically in anticipation of home currency weakness as a safer alternative to taking the hedge off. They can be used to express active views on the currency with the aim of increasing the total return of the hedge.

## 18.5 Managing Tracking Error in Forward Hedges

### 18.5.1 HOW OFTEN TO REBALANCE?

Most hedged investors target a constant ratio between the value of the hedge (in foreign currency) and the value of the foreign asset, known as *constant hedge ratio*. However, if the value of the asset moves, then the effective hedge ratio deviates from target, creating tracking error. Tracking error leaves the hedger effectively with a short foreign currency (overhedged), if the underlying asset value drops. If the foreign asset price rises, the hedger is left with a long foreign currency position relative to the benchmark (underhedged), creating a potential mark-to-market risk.

The size of the tracking error depends on the volatility of the underlying asset price and the type of hedge instrument, as discussed in the previous section. For simplicity, this section assumes the investor hedges with currency forwards, which are the preferred instruments for hedgers who care about tracking error.

Figure 18.4 shows the effective hedge ratios of a Eurozone investor, who fully hedges the Citi US Government Bond Index, Citi US HY Market Index,

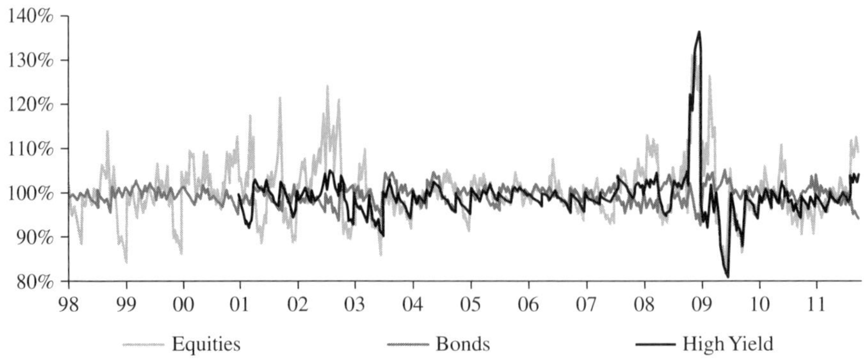


**FIGURE 18.4 Effective hedge ratios of Eurozone investor hedging US equities, government, and high yield bonds with quarterly hedge rebalancing.** *Source:* **Citi, sample: January 1998–October 2011.**

and MSCI US with quarterly forwards, adjusting the value of the hedge back to the value of the underlying asset at the end of each quarter (quarterly rebalancing). Owing to the lower volatility of the US government bond exposure, the effective hedge ratio of bonds has been closer to the 100% target than the effective hedge ratio on US equities and high yield bonds. The daily standard error between the actual and the target hedge ratio was 1.9% for the bond index, compared to 5.2% for high yield bonds and 6.8% for equities.

The tracking errors from government bonds and equities have historically tended to offset each other, with equities more likely resulting in an overhedge relative to the benchmark (because of their bigger downside volatility) and bonds resulting in an underhedge. This suggests that tracking error in multiasset portfolios is likely to be lower than that for a single asset, if correlations between assets are low or negative. Tracking error from high yield corporate bonds has been similar to that of equities, leaving investors overhedged in periods of high risk aversion and weak equity performance.

In addition to asset volatility and momentum, the size of tracking error also depends on the rebalancing frequency. If the value of the hedges is adjusted to match the value of the asset frequently, there is less scope for asset price to move significantly and create tracking error in the hedge. If hedges are rebalanced infrequently, for example, quarterly or less often, there is scope for more tracking error.

Table 18.16 shows the tracking errors (standard deviations of daily differences between effective and target hedge ratios) across all bond and equity markets as a function of regular hedge rebalancing frequencies. Because tracking error is measured in the foreign exposure currency, the results in Table 18.16 are applicable to all investors regardless of their base currency, that is, the tracking error with monthly rebalancing in US equities is the same 0.9% for Eurozone, UK, and all other investors.

The results in Table 18.16 first show that tracking error of the currency hedge has been lowest in government bond portfolios. With regular monthly

**TABLE 18.16 Daily Standard Errors Relative to a 100% Hedge Benchmark as Function of Regular Hedge Rebalancing Frequency (in Percentage)**

| | *Exposure to Citi bond indices in* | | | | | | | | | | |
|---|---|---|---|---|---|---|---|---|---|---|---|
| | AUD | CAD | EUR | JPY | NZD | NOK | SEK | CHF | GBP | USD | USD High Yield[a] |
| Weekly | 0.4 | 0.4 | 0.3 | 0.2 | 0.3 | 0.3 | 0.3 | 0.3 | 0.5 | 0.4 | 0.6 |
| Monthly | 0.9 | 0.8 | 0.7 | 0.5 | 0.7 | 0.7 | 0.8 | 0.7 | 1.1 | 1 | 2.2 |
| Quarterly | 1.6 | 1.5 | 1.4 | 0.9 | 1.3 | 1.3 | 1.6 | 1.3 | 2 | 1.9 | 5.2 |
| Six-monthly | 2.2 | 1.9 | 1.9 | 1.3 | 1.8 | 1.8 | 2.2 | 2 | 2.6 | 2.5 | 7.4 |
| | *Exposure to MSCI equity indices in* | | | | | | | | | | |
| | AUD | CAD | EUR | JPY | NZD | NOK | SEK | CHF | GBP | USD | |
| Weekly | 1.4 | 1.7 | 2 | 2 | 1.5 | 2.4 | 2.4 | 1.8 | 1.7 | 1.7 | |
| Monthly | 3.2 | 3.9 | 4.5 | 4.7 | 3.4 | 5.4 | 5.4 | 3.7 | 3.7 | 3.8 | |
| Quarterly | 5.9 | 7.2 | 8.5 | 7.7 | 5.6 | 10.1 | 9.7 | 6.7 | 6.1 | 6.8 | |
| Six-monthly | 7.9 | 11.1 | 11.4 | 11.6 | 7.4 | 18.8 | 13 | 9.1 | 8.3 | 9 | |

[a]Daily values of the Citi US High Yield Market Index start in January 2001.
*Source:* Citi, sample: January 1998–September 2011 unless otherwise stated.

rebalancing, the average daily difference between the hedge ratio and the 100% hedge benchmark has been typically less than 0.8%, with the exception of United States, United Kingdom, and Australia, which have had more volatile bond markets.

Monthly rebalancing in equities has produced daily tracking errors between 3% and 4%, more than three times the errors seen in government bonds. Investors with exposure to Norwegian and Swedish equities have seen tracking error in excess of 5% because of the higher volatility of these markets.

Tracking error in US high yield bonds has been nearly as high as in US equities. However, this result is influenced by the spike in the effective hedge ratio in 2008 when corporate bond prices plummeted. Tracking error in corporate bonds before October 2008 was roughly half the level seen in the entire sample.

The relative tracking errors from bonds and equities have been proportional to their respective underlying asset volatilities, although theoretically it is possible for volatile asset prices with weak momentum to cause less tracking error than slowly but consistently trending ones.

For investors who aim to be always hedged on target, the only solution would be to rebalance the hedge with the same frequency at which the asset value is marked to market. In our example, it would imply rebalancing daily, which is clearly not feasible in terms of both the high workload and transaction volumes and costs. So what is the optimal rebalancing frequency of bond and equity hedges?

This question can be answered by looking at the trade-off between trade volumes and tracking error. Rebalancing hedges frequently would result in low tracking error, but high trading volumes. The opposite is true for infrequent rebalancing, which has resulted in lower trading volumes, but high tracking error.

Historical results suggest that this trade-off is nonlinear, with relatively sharp initial declines in transaction volumes per each marginal increase in tracking error, as the investor moves from daily to less frequent rebalancing, followed by sharp increases in tracking error and relatively modest marginal cost savings in infrequent rebalancing.

Figure 18.5 illustrates this relationship for a Eurozone investor, hedging assets in the United States. For all three asset classes—equities, government, and high yield bonds—the investor's trade-off between tracking error and rebalancing volumes is a convex function, with the lowest optimal combinations roughly around monthly frequency.

Rebalancing more frequently than once a month has historically brought sharp marginal increases in trading volumes and costs with diminishing marginal reductions in tracking error. Rebalancing less frequently than roughly once a month has brought bigger marginal increases in tracking error with lower marginal reductions in trading volumes.

Assuming that the investor cares equally about minimizing both tracking error and transaction volumes arising from rebalancing trades, it is possible to find optimal rebalancing frequencies that minimize the combined "cost". We

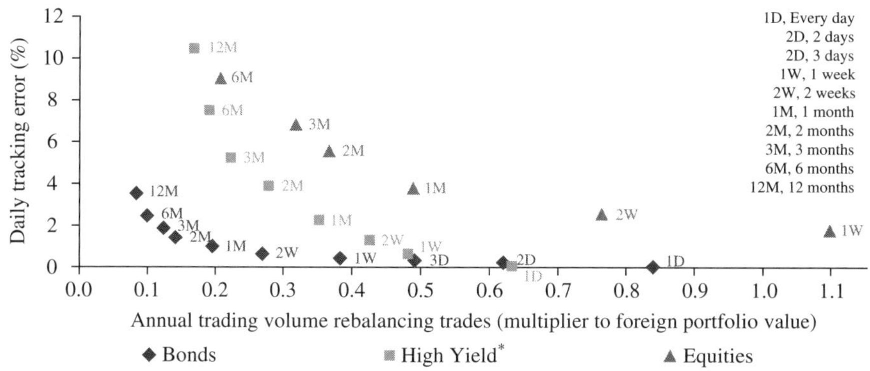


**FIGURE 18.5 Tracking error and rebalancing volumes as a function of regular rebalancing frequency for Eurozone investor hedging US equities, government, and high yield bonds.** ***Source:*** **Citi, sample: January 1998–September 2011 unless otherwise stated.**

do this by calculating historical trading volumes and tracking errors for a large number of regular rebalancing frequencies and find a combination that satisfies:

$$\min\sqrt{e^2 + c^2} \tag{18.9}$$

where $e$ is the annualized tracking error (the standard deviation of daily differences between the effective and target hedge ratio, multiplied by the square root of 260) and $c$ is the annual trading volume of rebalancing trades, as percentage of foreign asset value. This method is equal to finding the rebalancing frequency with the closest point to zero on Figure 18.5 with the exception that the tracking error scale has been annualized to make it comparable to the trading volume measure.

Table 18.17 shows the resulting optimal rebalancing frequencies, which indeed vary between 2 weeks and 2 months. For the less volatile fixed income exposures, the lowest combination of tracking error and rebalancing volume has been achieved, with rebalancing on average every 33 working days or 1.5 months. The only exception is the US HY index, which has had both high volatility and strong trends, resulting in an optimal rebalancing frequency of just 13 working days or roughly every two and a half weeks.

The more volatile equities, on the other hand, would have required slightly more frequent rebalancing, with the average optimal length at 21 working days or almost exactly one calendar month. We find a weak negative relationship between the annual volatility of underlying asset and the optimal rebalancing frequency, with the correlation of −0.1 across all MSCI equity exposures. However, this relationship has been completely absent in government bonds, suggesting that other factors, such as asset price momentum, also play an important role in determining how often to rebalance.

**TABLE 18.17 Tracking Error and Trading Volume Minimizing Rebalancing Frequencies, Working Days**

| | *Exposure to Citi bond indices in* | | | | | | | | | | |
|---|---|---|---|---|---|---|---|---|---|---|---|
| | AUD | CAD | EUR | JPY | NZD | NOK | SEK | CHF | GBP | USD | USD High Yield[a] |
| Working days | 39 | 39 | 39 | 23 | 39 | 26 | 20 | 24 | 39 | 39 | 13 |
| T/E, %[b] | 1 | 1 | 0.9 | 0.5 | 0.9 | 0.7 | 0.7 | 0.8 | 1.3 | 1.1 | 1.5 |
| Volume, %[c] | 13.5 | 13 | 13.5 | 7.9 | 13.6 | 13.7 | 17.1 | 13.2 | 16.3 | 13.5 | 39.1 |
| | *Exposure to MSCI equity indices in* | | | | | | | | | | |
| | AUD | CAD | EUR | JPY | NZD | NOK | SEK | CHF | GBP | USD | |
| Working days | 29 | 26 | 26 | 23 | 12 | 17 | 23 | 16 | 15 | 24 | |
| T/E, %[b] | 3.3 | 4 | 4.6 | 4.1 | 2.4 | 4.4 | 5.2 | 3.2 | 2.9 | 3.7 | |
| Volume, %[c] | 52.8 | 71.1 | 64.8 | 54.3 | 44.7 | 89.8 | 89.8 | 59.2 | 48.9 | 45.4 | |

[a]Daily values of the Citi US High Yield Market Index start in January 2001.
[b]Standard deviation of daily differences between effective and target hedge ratios.
[c]Annual average volume of rebalancing trades, % foreign asset value.
*Source:* Citi, sample: January 1998–September 2011 unless otherwise stated.

## 18.5.2 TRIGGER-BASED VERSUS REGULAR REBALANCING

Although rebalancing hedges at regular intervals has historically been effective in controlling tracking error, monitoring the hedge ratio only once a month leaves the investor vulnerable to sharp intramonth moves in asset prices, leading to temporary large deviations in hedge ratios. A good example of this is October 2008, when the collapse in US equities left foreign investors 131% hedged by the end of the month, which is significantly more than the 3.7% expected tracking error from monthly rebalancing.

To avoid tracking error arising from unusual market volatility, the investor may prefer to set a rebalancing trigger rather than a regular rebalancing interval. The rebalancing trigger is monitored daily or as frequently as the asset value is marked to market. If the effective hedge ratio deviates from target by more than the trigger amount, the value of the hedges is adjusted to match the value of the asset.

Although being somewhat higher maintenance than a regular rebalancing frequency (the effective hedge ratio would have to be calculated more frequently), this approach has historically tended to achieve slightly better tracking error and volume combinations than regular rebalancing frequencies, as triggers lead to rebalancing only when it is most needed.

The choice of appropriate trigger width depends on the volatility and momentum in the underlying asset as well as the target hedge ratio (the impact of asset price moves on the effective hedge ratio is proportional to the target hedge).

Table 18.18 shows the tracking error and trading volume minimizing rebalancing triggers for a 100% hedge target, where the optimal triggers are chosen according to formula (18.9) above. Optimal triggers for lower hedge target should be scaled accordingly, that is, a 7% trigger for a 100% hedge target is equivalent to a 3.5% trigger band around a 50% benchmark hedge ratio.

The results of Table 18.18 show that rebalancing on triggers only would have achieved similar or slightly lower tracking errors than regular rebalancing, but with savings in annual rebalancing volumes for most exposures. The savings are more apparent for the more volatile US HY index and MSCI equity indices.

On average, we find that rebalancing government bonds with a 1.8% trigger, that is, adjusting the value of the hedges if the effective hedge ratio deviated outside 98.2% and 101.8%, would have offered the best tracking error and trading volume in government bonds. The optimal trigger for the more volatile equities was higher, averaging 8.5% across the big developed markets.

The results of Table 18.18 are more closely linked to the volatility of the underlying asset. The optimal triggers for both government bonds and volatilities showed roughly 70% correlation with the underlying asset volatility. On average, we find that optimal rebalancing trigger amounted to 30–40% of the annual volatility of the underlying asset.

## 18.5.3 SUMMARY OF FINDINGS ON HEDGE REBALANCING

When hedging with currency forwards and aiming to maintain a constant ratio between the value of currency hedges and the value of the underlying asset, the investor should consider the following.

**TABLE 18.18 Tracking Error and Trading Volume Minimizing Rebalancing Triggers for 100% Hedge Ratio Target (in Percentage)**

| | | | | | *Exposure to Citi bond indices in* | | | | | | |
|---|---|---|---|---|---|---|---|---|---|---|---|
| | AUD | CAD | EUR | JPY | NZD | NOK | SEK | CHF | GBP | USD | USD High Yield[a] |
| Trigger, % | 2.25 | 2.00 | 1.50 | 1.00 | 1.75 | 2.25 | 1.25 | 1.75 | 2.25 | 2.00 | 3.50 |
| T/E, %[b] | 1.0 | 0.9 | 0.7 | 0.4 | 0.7 | 0.9 | 0.6 | 0.8 | 1.0 | 0.9 | 1.6 |
| | (0.0) | (−0.1) | (−0.2) | (0.0) | (−0.2) | (0.2) | (−0.1) | (0.0) | (−0.3) | (−0.2) | (0.1) |
| Volume, %[c] | 13.2 | 14.0 | 15.9 | 7.7 | 13.3 | 9.8 | 16.2 | 11.5 | 19.6 | 15.8 | 26.4 |
| | (−0.2) | (0.9) | (2.5) | (−0.2) | (−0.2) | (−3.8) | (−0.9) | (−1.7) | (3.4) | (2.2) | (−12.7) |
| | | | | | *Exposure to MSCI equity indices in* | | | | | | |
| | AUD | CAD | EUR | JPY | NZD | NOK | SEK | CHF | GBP | USD | |
| Trigger, % | 7.0 | 10.0 | 8.5 | 8.5 | 5.5 | 12.5 | 11.0 | 8.5 | 6.5 | 7.0 | |
| T/E, %[b] | 3.1 | 4.1 | 3.7 | 3.8 | 2.6 | 5.3 | 4.8 | 3.6 | 2.9 | 3.2 | |
| | (−0.2) | (0.1) | (−0.8) | (−0.3) | (0.3) | (0.9) | (−0.4) | (0.4) | (0.0) | (−0.5) | |
| Volume, %[c] | 49.0 | 53.5 | 58.2 | 41.8 | 30.6 | 57.1 | 78.6 | 37.7 | 37.7 | 43.3 | |
| | (−3.8) | (−17.7) | (−6.6) | (−12.4) | (−14.1) | (−32.7) | (−11.2) | (−21.5) | (−11.2) | (−2.1) | |

Differences between optimal trigger and optimal regular rebalancing are represented in parentheses.

[a]Daily values of the Citi US High Yield Market Index start in January 2001.

[b]Standard deviation of daily differences between effective and target hedge ratios.

[c]Annual average volume of rebalancing trades, % foreign asset value.

*Source:* Citi, sample: January 1998–September 2011 unless otherwise stated.

1. The simplest and lowest maintenance strategy would be to rebalance the hedges every 2 weeks or once a month. Less volatile government bonds can be rebalanced every 6–8 weeks. This strategy is easy to maintain since it does not require the investor to calculate or monitor the effective hedge ratio frequently. On the downside, regular rebalancing is vulnerable to unusually sharp market moves, which can leave the investor significantly over- or underhedged between the chosen rebalancing dates.
2. In order to reduce the risk of large tracking error, the investor can choose the rebalance hedges only if the effective hedge ratio deviates from target by more than a certain trigger amount. Our calculations show that for a 100% hedge target, triggers of around 1.8% and 3.5% would have worked well for government bonds and US HY bonds, respectively. The more volatile equity exposures would have achieved the best tracking error and trading volume trade-off, with an average trigger of 8.5%. The trigger width is dependent on the hedge target; for targets below 100%, the triggers should be scaled down accordingly. This is a higher maintenance strategy since it involves monitoring the effective hedge ratio more frequently, but because it produces rebalancing trades only when they are needed, it usually achieves savings in trading volume relative to rebalancing at regular intervals.
3. If the investor aims to protect a certain effective hedge ratio band, then the rebalancing trigger should be set lower than the tolerance level in order to avoid breaching the band when asset prices move sharply. Trigger-based rebalancing "triggers" once the trigger limit has already been breached.
4. The choice of optimal rebalancing trigger width depends on the volatility of the underlying asset. Our calculations suggest that the best tracking error and rebalancing volume trade-offs would have been achieved with triggers around 30–40% of the annual volatility of the underlying asset (in local currency units). The optimal trigger width should be reviewed regularly or tied to the level of asset volatility (e.g., one-third of the annualized volatility in a rolling window subject to a minimum and maximum) to avoid getting caught out by changes in market regime.
5. Trigger-based rebalancing can result in small but persistent tracking error if asset values trend slowly. In order to avoid the build-up of persistent tracking error, consider adding a less frequent trigger, for example, in addition to monitoring the breach of the 8% trigger on a daily basis, rebalance at month ends when the effective hedge ratio deviates from target by more than 4%.

## 18.6 Conclusions

In this chapter, we investigated the historical performance of currency hedges in exposures to foreign government and high yield corporate bonds and equities. From a theoretical point of view, we establish that the volatility of fully hedged returns is lower than that of unhedged if the variance of forward points and their covariance with the underlying asset is lower than the variance of the currency exposure and the covariance between the foreign asset and the foreign currency. As the variance of the currency exposure is typically large, unhedged assets can only be less volatile than hedged if the covariance between the foreign asset and the foreign currency is strongly negative. In this case, the investor can use the positive relationship between its home currency and the foreign asset to offset moves in the foreign asset.

Historical results show that currency hedging has had a statistically significant effect of reducing volatility in exposures to foreign government bonds and US HY corporate bonds, with the exception of Canadian investors. The volatility reduction benefits of hedging equities have been mostly limited to exposures to Australia, Canada, and New Zealand.

Owing to the large volatility of currency and asset returns, we find that the return impact of currency hedging is typically not statistically significant. The return impact of hedging in government bonds has been small in comparison to the large reduction in volatility, leading to higher risk-adjusted returns in hedged bonds. The same also holds true for the Citi US HY Market Index, albeit to a lesser extent.

Risk-adjusted returns on equities, which have had inherently higher volatility, have been affected more by the return impact of hedging, as the volatility reduction has been typically modest relative to the underlying asset volatility. Equity portfolios have been therefore better candidates for more active management of currency risk, which can be a source of additional return.

Selling the foreign currency via forward contracts is the most popular method of hedging among investors. However, losses on currency hedges caused significant cash flow problems during the credit crisis when currency volatility rose to unprecedented levels. We show that hedging by buying call options on the home currency has significantly reduced the negative tail of cash flows and is therefore better suited for investors with illiquid underlying portfolios and/or small cash reserves.

On the other hand, option hedges have created significantly more volatility in effective hedge ratios when compared to forward hedges and are therefore less suited for investors who target a constant hedge ratio and prioritize volatility reduction over total return and cash flows. For investors who want to manage tracking error in the hedge (i.e., minimize the difference between the effective and target hedge ratio), we find that adjusting the value of the hedge to match the value of the underlying asset roughly once or twice a month has worked well. For the less volatile government bond exposures, rebalancing hedges every other month has offered the lowest combination of tracking error and transaction volumes.

In addition, we show that rebalancing currency hedges based on triggers has worked at least as well as rebalancing at regular intervals while protecting the investor against large moves in the effective hedge ratio. The best hedge rebalancing strategy combines elements from both regular and trigger-based rebalancing.

# REFERENCES

Abken PA, Shrikhande MM. The role of currency derivatives in internationally diversified portfolios. Federal Reserve Bank of Atlanta Economic Review, Third Quarter; 1997. pp. 34–59.

Attfield C, Glod M, James J. Options and forwards compete for best hedge. Quant Finance 2001;1(1):9–11.

Berggrun L. Currency hedging for a dutch investor: the case of pension funds and insurers, *De Nederlandsche Bank Working Paper No. 054*; 2005 Oct.

Campbell JY, Serfaty-de Medeiros K, Viceira LM. Global currency hedging. J Finance 2010;LXV(1):87–121.

Eaker MR, Grant DM. Currency hedging strategies for internationally diversified equity portfolios. J Portf Manag 1990;17(1):30–32.

Eun CS, Resnick BG. Uncertainty, forward contracts, and international portfolio selection. J Finance 1988;43(1):197–215.

Glen J, Jorion P. Currency hedging for international portfolios. J Finance 1993;48(5):1865–1886.

Morey MR, Simpson MW. To hedge or not to hedge: the performance of simple strategies for hedging foreign exchange risk. J Multinatl Financ Manag 2001;11:213–223.

Perold AF, Schulman EC. The free lunch in currency hedging: implications for investment policy and performance standards. Financ Anal J 1988;44(3):45–50.

De Roon FA, Nijman TE, Werker BJM. Currency hedging for international stock portfolios: The usefulness of mean–variance analysis. J Bank Finance 2003;27:327–349.

Sener T. Objectives of hedging and optimal hedge ratios: US vs Japanese investors. J Multinatl Financ Manag 1998;8:137–153.

Schmittmann JM. Currency hedging for international portfolios, *IMF Working Paper*, WP/10/151; 2010.

Simpson MW, Dania A. Selectively hedging the Euro. J Multinatl Financ Manag 2006;16:27–42.

Thorp S. That courage is not inconsistent with caution: currency hedging for superannuation funds. University of New South Wales, unpublished working paper; 2004.

Walker E. Strategic currency hedging and global portfolio investments upside down. J Bus Res 2008;61:657–668.

CHAPTER NINETEEN

# FX Reserve Management


**MICHAEL J. PAULUS**
Managing Director, Hongkong and Shanghai Banking Corporation (HSBC)


## 19.1 FX Reserve Management

Reserve management is a dynamic process that ensures adequate official public sector foreign assets are readily available to and controlled by the authorities for meeting a defined range of objectives for a country or union. In this context, a reserve management entity (usually the central bank) is normally made responsible for the management of reserves and associated risks.

Reserve management must always be seen in the broader national policy and economic context. Its operational function and objectives do not exist in a vacuum. Increasingly it must also be seen in the context of global political and economic realities and policies (*Source*: RBS Reserve Management Trends-Forward, 2010). It is somewhat like a fish; although an independent body, its temperature cannot significantly differ from the water in which it swims.

## 19.2 FX Reserve Uses

The holding of reserves is a form of "self-insurance" against financial shocks and sudden stops in access to international capital markets. It enhances the credibility of monetary policy. Specifically, the potential uses of FX reserves can be classified in a variety of ways.

- *Intervention.* Intervention in the FX market with a view to influencing the exchange rate and/or maintaining orderly market conditions.


*Handbook of Exchange Rates*, First Edition. Edited by Jessica James, Ian W. Marsh, and Lucio Sarno.

- *Country Payments.* Execution of payments for goods and services for the country, particularly during times when obtaining external financing is difficult or impossible.
- *Emergency Liquidity.* Granting of emergency liquidity assistance to various sectors of the economy, typically the banking sector.
- *Investor Confidence.* Underpinning of investor confidence in the country's ability to meet its FX commitments, thereby also limiting the probability of financial crisis and possibly also reducing the cost of external funding (the "war chest" motive).
- *Government Payments.* Execution of payments for the government, possibly in the context of broader debt management operations.
- *Execution of Monetary Policy.* Support of domestic monetary policy liquidity management operations, for example, through FX swaps, effectively using FX claims as collateral.
- *Investment of Excess Balances.* Investment of balances in excess of foreseeable liquidity/transaction needs (*Source*: BIS Paper #38, p. 2).
- *Funding of Development/Sovereign Wealth Funds.* Excess reserves have increasingly been used to create/fund new Development and Sovereign Wealth Funds such as in China and Korea with significant market and asset price implications of their own.

## 19.3 FX Reserve Sources

At any given point in time, a country's stock of FX reserves reflects two sources of accumulation. First is an accumulation as a deliberate policy to build up the stock of reserves in order to meet potential future uses. An example is the buildup of reserves by Asian central banks following the Asian debt crisis of 1997 and to a lesser extent, following the global financial crisis of 2008/2009 (Fig. 19.1). The second is an accumulation as a by-product of the implementation of policies aimed at managing the exchange rate, which requires adjustment in that stock. In recent years, persistent FX intervention with a view to resisting upward pressure on the exchange rate has played a key role in many countries. This raises the possibility that the stock of FX reserves may be larger than desirable for foreseeable future uses. Unless there is FX debt outstanding that can be retired, it will generally not be easy to reduce it without risking "unwinding" the original effect on the exchange rate. While the desirable amount of FX reserves in light of potential future uses is difficult to determine with any precision, above a certain level, consideration of the deployment of "excess reserves" becomes more relevant. It is interesting to note that this "point" shifts in time and with experience. For example, many central banks believed that they had significant amounts of "excess reserves" before the recent global financial crisis. During the crisis, what had been thought to be "excess," proved to be "not enough" in the view of market participants. (*Source*: BIS Paper #38, p. 4)

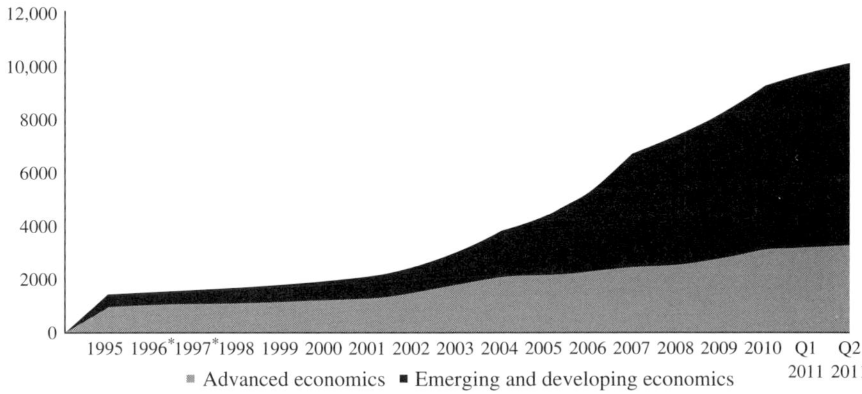


FIGURE 19.1 **Foreign currency reserve holding (US$ Bn). *Countries with sizable reserves either joined (began reporting) the sample or left (stopped reporting) the sample. *Source*: IMF Statistics Department, COFER database, and International Financial Statistics.**

## 19.4 Objectives of Reserves Management

There are three basic objectives of reserve management, which have remained constant over the years.

- *Safety.* Capital preservation is the first principal of reserve management. One does not want to lose the basic capital accumulated or invested.
- *Liquidity.* There are two distinct but closely related notions of liquidity.
  - *Market Liquidity.* An instrument is said to be liquid if transactions in it can take place rapidly and with little price impact.
  - *Funding Liquidity.* The ability to raise funds at short notice either through the sale of an asset (i.e., US Treasuries) or access to external funding (i.e., central bank swap lines) (*Source*: BIS Paper #38, p. 4)
- *Return.* This relates to the interest earned or profit made from the investments made with reserves. Historically, this has been the least important of the three objectives. However, with the rapid accumulation of reserves over the past 10 years, leading to what some might consider "excess reserves", has made the "returns" objective more of a focus.

## 19.5 Techniques of Reserve Management

Reserve management is not static and is a constant trade-off between the three objectives of safety, liquidity, and return. These can vary considerably over time, as we have seen over the past several years. The challenge for reserve managers has several dimensions. First is to map the uses of the reserves in clear trade-offs between risk and return, second is to clearly define the risk preference/tolerance level, and third is to create a portfolio structure that reflects these decisions. (*Source*: BIS Papers # 38) Consequently, it is a constantly evolving process of balancing policy, market, economic, and political objectives.

## 19.6 Historical Perspective

Gold has traditionally been the mainstay of reserves, comprising more than 50% of total reserves until the mid-1980s. Subsequently, gold holdings have continuously declined as both a percentage of reserves and also in total amount held as many central banks, particularly since 2000, have disposed of their gold holdings. This was largely due to a greater focus on returns and also falling gold prices since the peak gold price of 1980. In real terms, today's gold price of about $1800 is still roughly about 10% below the 1980 peak (Fig. 19.2).

The trends in reserve management reached a turning point at about the turn of the century. Before the year 2000, most central banks, particularly those of the major industrialized countries (the G-7 if you will), adhered to the "safety" and "liquidity" rule of reserve management. "Return" traditionally followed a far distant third. Several important factors combined in the late 1990s leading to a major shift in reserve management with a greater emphasis on "yield" and investment diversification.

- *Rapidly Growing FX Reserves.* Partially driven by the reaction to the 1997 Asian debt crisis, Asian central banks embarked on an objective of restoring,

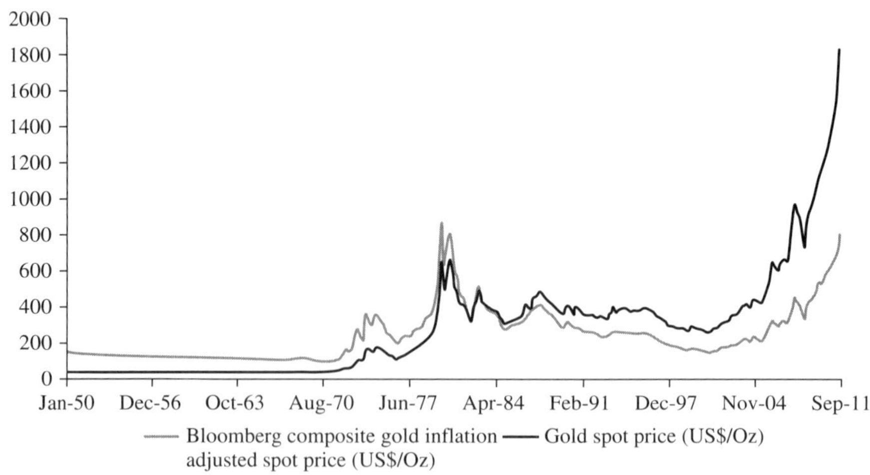


**FIGURE 19.2** **Gold price index.** ***Source*: Bloomberg.**

and increasing their holding of Foreign Exchange reserves. They have succeeded in remarkable manner.

- *US Budget Surpluses.* The US ran budget surpluses from FY 1998 through FY 2001. These surpluses were projected to grow, suggesting that US government debt, already declining, might be eliminated. (Difficult to believe in the current environment.) Although the surpluses did not last long, it was long enough for the outstanding debt of the United States to decline and to change market participant perception of possible elimination of US Treasuries.
- *Introduction of the Euro.* With the introduction of the Euro, 50% of the legacy country reserves were transferred to the ECB. The remainder, held by national central banks, could be invested with the return objective given a higher priority.
- *Legitimized "Returns" as an Objective.* Some central banks, often seen as "rogue" entities, actively managed their reserves for return for many years. This was not seen as quite legitimate among the "proper" central banks. However, the introduction of the Euro and the managing of reserves more actively by the Europeans, legitimized and even encouraged a more aggressive approach to reserve management. (*Source*: IMF Working paper WP/10/150, pp. 5–10).
- *Professionalism of Reserve Management.* Growing acceptance of the concept that a central bank needs to have at least some investments in systemically important asset classes in order to be able to fully understand their features and functioning of the market. Mortgage-backed securities would be an example. Increased use of benchmarks accelerated this trend.
- *Gold Sales.* Central bank sales of gold continued through the first decade of the century as gold was not seen as a reliable producer of returns. Also the introduction of the Euro, as cited above, and the decline in both nominal and real gold prices from the 1980 peak encouraged this development (Fig. 19.2). Interestingly, as total reserves have surged the past few years, some countries have begun accumulating gold for their reserves once again.

## 19.7 What Assets Do Central Banks Hold?

As a result of the above influences, the investments of central banks have expanded over the years and currently consist of the following investment types/categories, generally in order of least risk.

- Gold
- US Treasury bills
- Government notes & bonds
- Government notes & bonds (below AA)
- Supranational bonds
- Agency debt (Fannie & Freddie)

- RMBS/covered bonds
- Bank deposits
- Asset-backed securities
- Corporate bond (investment grade)
- Corporate bonds (below BBB)
- Index-linked bonds
- Equities
- Alternative investments (hedge funds, etc.)
- Derivatives (for alpha and hedging)
- Other investments

The choice of investable assets continues to evolve. Some central banks are currently considering investing in natural resources (i.e., oil, gas, minerals, etc.)

## 19.8 Constraints

The decision to emphasize one objective over another is subject to a number of institutional, environmental, historical, and psychological constraints.

- *Ultimate Goals of the Institution.* Reserve management operations should not interfere with, and at best should support, the goals that are typically associated with securing monetary stability and contributing to financial stability.
- *Domestic Governance Environment*
  - — Reputational concerns, paramount in central banks, tend to strongly inhibit risk tolerance
  - — Institutional statutes, which may include the restriction on the universe of investible assets
  - — Relationship with the Government, in the context in which the central bank feels that budgetary independence is important for its operational independence. Rules for distribution of profits to the government and possibly interacting with accounting provisions can induce the central bank to define comfort levels of risk in relation to its capital. (*Source*: BIS Paper #38, p. 8)
- *Implicit Rules of Acceptable Behavior by Public Interest Institutions in an International Environment.* In their FX operations, central banks are generally careful not to affect the prices of the instruments in which they operate (other than their own currency). This is not just for reasons applicable to private sector market participants (e.g., avoiding having markets move against them when they transact). It also reflects a wish not to disturb prices in those units of account for which their peers are responsible. This can narrow the range

of currencies in which they are comfortable operating and possibly the scope for active portfolio management.

- *Factors Internal to the Institution.* The human and technological resources at its disposal, such as technical know-how and the IT infrastructure.
- *Historical Experience.* "Near Death" experiences which occurred during the 1997 Asia Financial Crisis and to a lesser extent, the 2008/09 Global Financial Crisis, where central banks depleted their reserves or markets perceived they did not have enough, influences both the amount of reserves held and also emphasizes or reemphasizes the value of safety and liquidity.

## 19.9 External Managers

As central banks have broadened their investable universe over the years, they have also increasingly made use of external managers to invest a part of their reserves. In most cases, this has been relatively small but some have reportedly outsourced more than 15% of their reserves. External advisors are used primarily to develop the central bank's own in-house expertise and to gain access to asset classes for which in-house knowledge was lacking, such as mortgage-backed securities. (*Source*: BIS Paper #40, pp. 2–8). Since the financial crisis, many Central Banks are rethinking the use of external managers as they evaluate the performance of external managers during the crisis (often poor) and reconsider the range of investable assets.

## 19.10 Costs of Accumulation and Holding of Reserves

It is important to note that accumulating and holding reserves and managing them well does entail opportunity and other costs.

- *Sterilization.* Accumulating reserves presents challenges for the central banks as it results in an injection, usually not warranted or wanted, into the domestic banking system. This requires that central banks embark on sterilization actions to drain the excess liquidity by issuing short-term bills or notes. This can cause significant losses for the central banks. For example, a central bank is holding US Treasury bills that are currently paying 0.50% interest. However, the central bank issues notes of a similar maturity in their currency to drain liquidity but pays interest of 2%. All things being equal, there will be a loss of 150 bps for the amount of reserves accumulated.
- *Volatile or Declining Asset.* This is particularly true of Emerging Market economies, such as China, where the outlook for long-term economic growth would strongly suggest that their currencies will rise significantly against the dollar and Euro (USD and Euro currently comprising 90% of all reserves). Holding dollar and Euro assets then presents a particular challenge.

As their currencies rise, the value and return of reserve assets, as measured against their local currencies, is likely to decline with potential ramifications for returns and also funds flowing to the government or SWF.

- *Opportunity Cost.* The capital tied up in holding large and excess reserves raises the issue as to whether a more effective and efficient use would have been for capital infrastructure, health care, or education in those countries. There are a number of studies that suggest the cost is not insignificant, ranging roughly between 0.5% and 1.85% of GDP (*Source*: Summers, "Reflections on Global Account Imbalances and Emerging Markets Reserve Accumulation," p. 5; Rodrik, "The Social Cost of Foreign Exchange Reserves," p. 2; and Levy-Yeyati, "The Cost of Reserves"). In addition, there are potential inflationary consequences of converting reserves into local currency and these must be weighed against other factors.

## 19.11 Diversification

Surprisingly, despite all the discussion and rhetoric, there is, in fact, little evidence of currency diversification since the start of the floating rate period almost 40 years ago. In 1973, at the beginning of the floating rate period, holdings of USDs represented 76% of total reserve holdings. Subsequently, USD holdings have ranged between a high of 80% in 1977 and a low of 51% in 1990 while averaging 65.4% over the period. In the past 15 years, the percentage of reserves held in dollars has been remarkably stable, fluctuating between 62% and 71% since 1995, with the high coming in late 2001, shortly following the record low of the EUR of about 0.82 cents. USD holdings have averaged 66% during the 15-year period. The Euro has gained marginally over the time period and now represents almost 30% of reserves with the remaining 10% in sterling, yen, Swiss francs, and "others" (Fig. 19.3). There are a number of reasons the dollar continues to hold its predominant place including its role as the global "cash" currency, the basis for exchange rate arrangements, invoicing foreign transactions, and so on. (For additional detail, see below.) From a larger perspective, the US and Euro area economies combined account for close to 50% of global GDP (Fig. 19.5). (*Source*: ADB, Jong-Wha Lee, p. 25).

## 19.12 Challenges to Diversification and Size of Reserves

Although there is constant dialog and discussion about the desire and need for reserve diversification away from the dollar, recent events during the global financial crisis have, in fact, solidified the role of the dollar and US Treasuries, at least temporarily.

During the crisis, a number of currencies came under severe downward pressure, prompting significant intervention by a variety of central banks to support their local currencies. While the downward pressure on these currencies

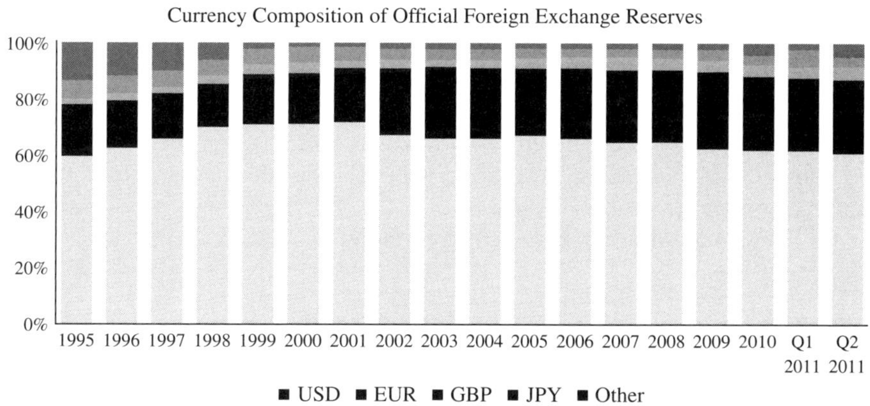


**FIGURE 19.3** Currency composition of official foreign exchange reserves. *Countries with sizable reserves either joined (began reporting) the sample or left (stopped reporting) the sample. *Source*: IMF Statistics Department COFER database and International Financial Statistics.

abated relatively quickly, there were several periods of extreme pressure. Many central banks and reserve managers observing or participating in these events took away three lessons from the crisis.

- *Never Enough.* Before the crisis, many central banks were holding record levels of reserves and believed that they had more than enough FX reserves to meet any challenge to their currencies. This proved not to be the case. Market participants challenged these assumptions and continued to pressure currencies such as the Korean won. It was only with the establishment of swap lines with the Federal Reserve that the pressure abated. Consequently, as the crisis has faded some central banks made it an objective not only to restore their reserves to previous record high levels but to push them significantly higher as a matter of policy.
- *Liquidity is King and US Treasuries are Best.* During the crisis, as markets became less liquid or closed completely, reserve managers came to a renewed appreciation of the role of US Treasuries. It was one of the few functioning markets where central banks could liquidate assets quickly and in large size, in a nondisruptive manner, to obtain the dollars they needed to defend their currencies.
- *Dollar Intervention is Most Effective.* As reserve managers have known for many years, it is most effective to intervene to support one's currency with US dollars. This lesson was highlighted once again during the crisis. Owing to market mechanisms and the role of the dollar, it was clear that intervening with dollars to support one's own currency was the most effective and efficient. In addition, as mentioned above, one could obtain liquidity rather easily by selling Treasuries and other dollar-denominated assets.

There is a large body of academic work that addresses and discusses the adequacy and size of reserves. This chapter does not address these specifically. Suffice to say that by most academic measures, many countries have an "excess" of reserves. However, reserve managers are responsible for dealing with extreme, unusual, and unexpected volatility during crises, which shape their perception and subsequent assessments of risk and actions. The case of Bank of Korea's almost complete depletion of their reserves in 1997 and the intense pressure against the won again in 2008 are recent examples.

## 19.13 Changing Role of the Dollar as the International Reserve Currency

The role of the dollar has been challenged quite frequently by many commentators over the years, most recently due to the global financial crisis and before that, the emergence of the Euro. Nevertheless, it remains the preeminent international currency. While changes in its global status are possible, factors such as the large size and dynamism of the US economy, dollar pricing of oil, and other commodities, its' use as a major form of global physical currency, lack of a significantly better alternative, and simple inertia will likely perpetuate the dollar's role for a significant amount of time.

Fundamentally, the dollar plays a central role in international trade and finance as both a store of value and a medium of exchange. Most countries have chosen the dollar to be the vehicle currency, in the conduct of monetary policy (for countries with small or limited bond markets), the invoice currency of choice in international trade, the preferred official intervention currency, and the principal official reserve asset. Its prominence is mainly due to the following factors:

- **Major Form of Cash Currency**
  - The majority of dollar banknotes are estimated to be held outside the United States (Fig. 19.4). More than 70% of hundred-dollar notes and nearly 60% of twenty- and fifty-dollar notes are held abroad, while two-thirds of all US banknotes have been in circulation outside the country since 1990.
  - Approximately $580 billion in physical US currency outstanding was circulating overseas at the end of March 2009.
- **Main Currency for Exchange Rate Arrangements**
  - The US dollar plays the role of a central currency even though alternative choices are available. Many countries have dollar-based exchange rate arrangements.
  - According to the Reinhart and Rogoff (2004) approach, seven countries currently are dollarized or have currency boards using the dollar and 89 have a pegged exchange rate against the dollar (Table 19.1). The share of countries linking their currency to the dollar in some manner has been

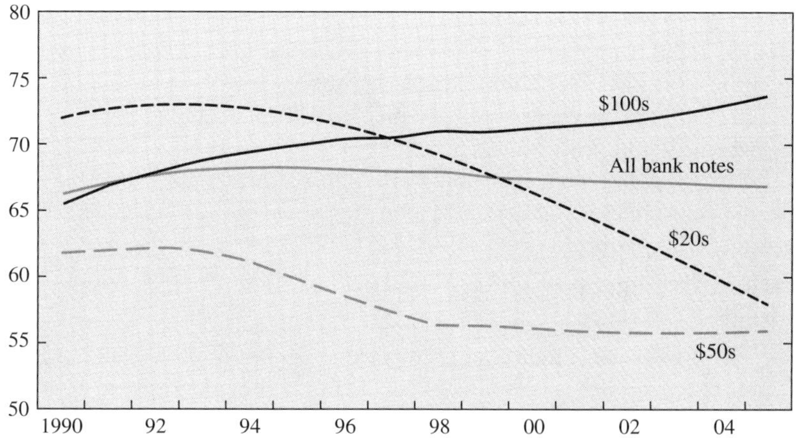


FIGURE 19.4 **Share of US banknotes held outside the United States.** ***Source*: Federal Reserve Bank of New York estimates, based on US Treasury Department (2006).**

TABLE 19.1 **Countries Reporting Dollar-Based Exchange Rate Arrangements**

| | Number of Countries | | | |
|---|---|---|---|---|
| Arrangement | 1995 | 2000 | 2005 | 2007 |
| Dollarized or formed currency board | 9 | 8 | 7 | 7 |
| Pegged exchange rate regime against dollar | 82 | 85 | 90 | 89 |
| Maintained managed floats with dollar as reference currency | 6 | 8 | 6 | 8 |
| Total reporting | 207 | 207 | 207 | 207 |
| Memo: | | | | |
| Currency linked to dollar (%) | 47 | 49 | 50 | 50 |
| Gross domestic product linked to dollar (%) | 21 | 29 | 31 | 36 |

*Source:* Reinhart and Rogoff (2004); Ilzetzki, Reinhart, and Rogoff (2008); authors calculation.

stable since 1995, and this group represents more than a third of world GDP (excluding the United States).

- **Invoicing Foreign Transactions**
  — Use of the dollar for invoicing far exceeds that which could be explained by exports to the United States alone.
- **Major Part of FX Reserves**
  — Global foreign exchange reserves total more than US$ 9 trillion of which +60% is in dollars. (*Source*: FRBNY Current Issues, January 2010)

- **Size of US Economy**
  - Much has been made of the relative decline of the US economy vis-á-vis other countries. While true, the US economy is still the dominant global economy by any measure, producing +20% of global GDP. China, which has moved into the number two spot and produces 8% of global GDP, still less than half that of the United States (Fig. 19.5). Indeed, the economies of China and Japan combined still do not equal the size of the US economy.
- **Lack of Willingness of Other Countries to Allow Their Currency to be a Reserve Currency**
  - There are benefits for a country to have their currency as the global reserve currency, including seigniorage, the ability to borrow easily in ones' own currency, and so on. However, there are significant costs involved as well. Open capital markets, loss of control of one's own money supply, the need to run trade and current account deficits in order to supply the world with liquidity, the unrequested and unlimited use of one's currency for intervention operations, the responsibility of one's central bank to be the world's "defacto" central bank with global, in addition to domestic, responsibilities, and so on. Some countries have simply refused to allow their currencies to become a reserve currency. During the late 1980s and early 1990s, Germany was encouraged by other countries to allow the Deutsche Mark (DM) to play a larger and more prominent role as a reserve currency. The Bundesbank objected largely on the grounds of losing control of the German money supply and the unrequested and unlimited use of the DM for intervention operations and refused to take on the international responsibility others expected. The moment subsequently passed as the cost of reunification mounted and the movement toward the Euro-dominated policy from the mid-1990s onward. During the same period, Japanese monetary authorities were similarly reluctant to have the yen assume that responsibility. With the difficulties the Japanese economy began to experience in the early 1990s, that moment too passed.
  - Discussions of other currencies becoming significant reserve currencies usually founder on two basic issues; first, the size of the underlying economy that the currency reflects and; second, the long-term and firm commitment to open capital markets with the resultant loss of control. The psychological factor is also important. Policymakers, thought leaders and the population at large, must generally support the extra burden and responsibility of being a reserve currency. Few countries/currency areas are willing to accept the responsibility. It means one's monetary and economic policy is watched with minute intent and is open to constant scrutiny as well as "voting" by financial markets. The recent criticism of the Fed's Quantitative Easing policy is a case in point. Few countries in the world want to assume that role or are psychologically prepared to accept their policies being open to constant debate and reaction of

global financial markets and foreign policymakers on a daily, even hourly basis. China appears to be far from assuming such a responsibility or a commitment to open markets.

- **The US Defends the Role of the Dollar**
  — The United States defends the role of the dollar both publically and privately but generally in a measured and quiet way. The mantra of a "strong dollar is in the interest of the United States" since 1995 is one way. The United States believes that the best way to ensure the dollar remains the dominant reserve currency is to publically focus on ensuring open markets in the United States and that economic fundamentals are sound. US Secretary Tim Geithner has said "I think the dollar remains the world's dominant reserve currency, I think that is likely to continue for a long period of time. And as a country, we will do what is necessary to make sure we are sustaining confidence in our financial markets and in the productive capacity of this economy and in our long-term fundamentals." (Washington Post, March 26, 2009). Privately, government officials try to discourage developments that will erode the dollar's status. Specifically, lobbying quietly to continue to have internationally traded commodities, such as oil, to be priced in dollars. In addition, the United States takes a benign view of others using the dollar for intervention and other purposes. For example, countries do not have to ask the United States if they can use the dollar to defend their currencies. This provides a level of confidence and comfort during crises that the United States will not be an obstacle to the swift and effective conduct of FX intervention or monetary policy. The United States does not object to other countries tying their currencies to the dollar, formally or informally, another form of maintaining the dollar's role. In other words, the most effective defense of the dollar as the reserve currency is to allow and encourage it to continue to be widely used for a variety of international purposes. The depth of the US Treasury and Agency debt markets also adds to the attractiveness of the dollar as countries can easily store and retrieve dollars by selling and buying US Treasuries, still the largest and most liquid asset market in the world.

## 19.14 Reserve Management if the Dollar is Replaced as the Reserve Currency

Replacing the dollar as the preeminent reserve currency is not likely to happen any time soon. However, one might speculate as to what changes would be needed in reserve management should this come to pass. Clearly, moving out of the dollar and into one or more alternative currencies would happen over time. The real issue facing reserve managers is likely to be where and what to invest in—what can reserve managers invest in that is "safe and liquid"? It is relatively easy to envisage a scenario when the USD, Euro, and the RMB will be the three

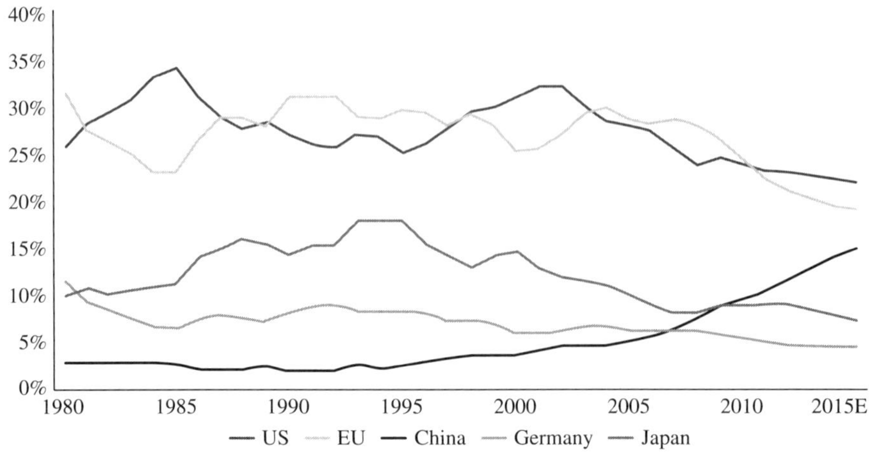


FIGURE 19.5 Percentage of world GDP (nominal). *Source*: Economic Intelligence Unit.

major reserve currencies. However, will reserve mangers quickly arrive at owning a significant portion of the outstanding sovereign debt of a country or zone? Will that hinder reserve managers in the conduct of monetary or intervention policy, that is, the liquidity of the investments? How will countries, such as China, view large-scale selling of its bonds during a crisis or a loss of confidence by other central banks? This harkens back to one of the real strengths of the dollar. US officials take a benign view on the use of the dollar for intervention purposes and the buying and selling of US Treasuries and Agencies. Will other monetary officials in other potential reserve countries take a similar approach?

It is possible to speculate that the world could end up with two or three major reserve currencies but the management of the reserves might very well vary. For example, let's speculate that in 2035, a country might want to hold three reserve currencies: USD, EUR, and RMB. Most of their reserve holdings of USD may be in Treasuries, as they provide the safest and most liquid asset. Another part would be invested in less liquid EUR assets as the EUR is not as useful in intervention. Finally, even less liquid investments might be in RMB as these investments may pay a higher return but are not nearly as useful as USDs during a crisis. A similar situation occurs now between the USD and the Euro.

There have been growing discussions and facilities established for the cross holding of local currency swap lines, particularly in Asia. The challenge for reserve managers is that holding currencies of other Asian countries, for example, are not particularly useful in a crisis where investment liquidity and ability to intervene in a meaningful way to support one's currency is required. On the trade side, these lines can be useful cushions. However, reserve mangers tend to be concerned primarily with movements in the capital markets and less with trade flows. The Chiang Mai Initiative did not live up to its hopes during the financial crisis as countries such as Korea turned to the Fed and not to their counterparts in Asia for support.

## 19.15 Conclusion

Accumulating, holding, and investing of foreign exchange reserves continues to be hot topics of study and debate both academically and by reserve managers themselves. The three basic objectives of safety, liquidity, and return ensure a certain amount of ongoing tension in the management of reserves. The importance of these objectives varies over time. During and following the recent financial crisis, the objectives of safety and liquidity, always at the top of a reserve manager's mind, gained greater importance—but for how long? Reserve management is a dynamic processes and therefore more art than science.

The role of the dollar as the world's primary reserve currency will be tested in the coming years and decades. The multifaceted roles the dollar plays in international finance, the openness of the US economy and its capital markets, and the support of US policymakers makes it difficult to see an end to the dollar's primacy. However, it is likely to be joined by other "reserve" currencies over time.

## Acknowledgments

I would like to offer my sincere thanks to Sushilkumar Jain and Jacky Mizele for their research, comments, and suggestions in preparing this chapter.

All views and opinions expressed in this book are the personal views and opinions of the author and not those of any party or organization to which the author may be affiliated (including The Hongkong and Shanghai Banking Corporation Limited and any member of the HSBC Group), and such views and opinions are not sponsored by any such party or organization.

## REFERENCES

Aizeman J. Alternatives to sizeable hoarding of international reserves: lessons from the global liquidity crisis, VOXEU.org. Centre for Economic Policy Research; 2009.

Aizeman J, Sun Y. The financial crisis and sizable international reserves depletion: from 'fear of floating' to the 'fear of losing international reserves?' Working Paper 15308. National Bureau of Economic Research; 2009.

Akdogan K. Volume 10, Foreign exchange reserve demand: an information value approach, Central Bank Review. Central Bank of the Republic of Turkey; 2010.

Aristovnik A, Cec T. Compositional analysis of foreign currency reserves in the 1999–2007 period: the Euro vs. The dollar as leading reserve currency, MPRA Paper No. 14350. Slovenia: University of Ljubljana, Faculty of Administration; 2009.

Article FEDPOINT, U.S. Foreign Exchange Intervention, Federal Reserve Bank of New York 2007.

Basu K. The mechanics of central bank intervention in foreign exchange markets, CAE Working Paper #09-02. Department of Economics, Cornell University; 2009.

Bergman M. Foreign exchange market intervention. International Monetary Economics, University of Copenhagen; 1995.

Cardon P, Coche J. Strategic asset allocation for foreign exchange reserves. Risk Management For Central Bank Foreign Reserves, European Central Bank; 2004. pp. 13–29.

Claudio B, Ebbesen J, Galati G, Health A. FX reserve management: elements of a framework, BIS Papers No 38. Monetary and Economic Department, Bank for International Settlements; 2008.

Cline WR, John W. Currency wars? Peterson Institute for International Economics; 2010.

Cooper RN. The future of the dollar. Peterson Institute for International Economics; 2009.

Dhakal GP. Volume 3, Foreign reserves: potential source of financing for development (Lessons in Good Practices from Selected Countries). Asia-Pacific Trade and Investment Review; 2007.

Downes PT. Managing foreign exchange reserves: a basic guide to the process. Finance & Development; 1989.

Eichengreen B, Flandreau M. The rise and fall of the dollar, or when did the dollar replace sterling as the leading reserve currency? 2008.

Eichengreen B, Flandreau M. The federal reserve, the Bank of England and the rise of the dollar as an international currency, 1914-39. BIS Working Papers No 328. Monetary and Economic Department, Bank for International Settlements; 2010.

Frank N, Heiko H. The effectiveness of central bank interventions during the first phase of the subprime crisis. Middle East and Central Asia Department, International Monetary Fund; 2009.

Frankel J. The euro could surpass the dollar within ten years, VOXEU.org. Centre for Economic Policy Research; 2008.

Goldberg LS. Is the international role of the dollar changing? Volume 16(1), Current issues in economics and finance. Federal Reserve Bank of New York; 2010a.

Goldberg LS. What is the status of the international roles of the dollar, VOXEU.org. Centre for Economic Policy Research; 2010b.

Goodhart CAE. The changing role of central banks, BIS Working Papers No 326. Monetary and Economic Department, Bank for International Settlements; 2010.

Greenberg MR. Quarterly Update: Foreign Exchange Reserves in Brazil, Russia, India, and China. Center for Geoeconomic Studies, Council on Foreign Relations; 2010.

Greenspan A. World Bank's conference on Recent Trends in Reserves Management; Washington (DC); 1999 29 April.

Ingves S. Guidelines for foreign exchange reserve management: accompanying documents. Prepared by the Monetary and Exchange Affairs Department, International Monetary Fund; 2003.

International Relations Committee Task Force. The Accumulation Of Foreign Reserves, Occasional Paper Series No. 43. European Central Bank; 2006.

Kenen PB. The role of the dollar as an international currency, Occasional Papers 13. New York: Group of Thirty; 1983.

Knight MD. Presentation at the Brussels Economic Forum, Bank for International Settlements; 2006.

Krugman PR. The International Role of the Dollar: Theory and Prospect, Exchange Rate Theory and Practice; University of Chicago Press; 1984. ISBN: 0-226-05096-3-261–278.

Kyereboah-Coleman A. Reserves and foreign exchange in the macroeconomic context. Accra, Ghana: WAIFEM; 2009.

Lewis NE. China's foreign exchange reserves: unintentional means to a strategic end, council on foreign relations. Huffington Post; 2010.

McCauley RN, Fund BSC. Choosing instruments in managing dollar foreign exchange reserves. BIS Q Rev 2003:39–46.

Nuges J. Foreign Exchange Reserve Management, No.19 Handbooks in Central Banking. Centre for Central Banking Studies, Bank of England.

Papaioannou E, Portes R. Costs and benefits of running an international currency. Economic Papers 348. European Commission; 2008.

Pihlman J, Han van der H. Procyclicality in Central Bank Reserve Management: Evidence from the Crisis, Monetary and Capital Markets Department, International Monetary Fund; 2010.

Posen AS. Why the Euro will not rival the dollar. Peterson Institute for International Economics; 2008.

Robert P, Nick C. RBS reserve management trends. Central Banking Publications; 2010.

Rodrik D. The social cost of foreign exchange reserves, Working Paper 11952. National Bureau of Economic Research; 2006.

Rybinski K, Sowa U. Global reserves management; 2007.

Sack BP. Managing the Federal Reserve's balance sheet. Markets Group of the Federal Reserve Bank of New York; 2010.

Staff of the International Monetary Fund. Guidelines for Foreign Exchange Reserve Management, ISBN 1-58906-260-4. International Monetary Fund; 2004.

Summers LH. Reflections on global account imbalances and emerging markets reserve accumulation. India: L.K. Jha Memorial Lecture Lawrence H. Summers Reserve Bank of India Mumbai; 2006.

The International Role Of The Euro, European Central Bank; 2008.

Trichet J-C. Ten years of the euro—successes and challenges, Speech by President of the European Central Bank; 2009.

Truman EM, Wong A. The Case for an International Reserve Diversification Standard, WP06—2. Institute for International Economics; 2006.

Williamson John. Why SDRs could rival the dollar. Peterson Institute for International; 2009.

Yeyati EL. The cost of reserves. Centro de Investigación en Finanzas, Universidad Torcuato Di Tella; 2006.

Yeyati EL. What drives reserve accumulation (and at what cost)? VOXEU.org. Centre for Economic Policy Research; 2010.

CHAPTER TWENTY

# High Frequency Finance: Using Scaling Laws to Build Trading Models

**ALEXANDRE DUPUIS and RICHARD B. OLSEN**
Olsen Ltd., University of Essex

## 20.1 Introduction

The availability of large amounts of tick-by-tick data, in excess of 50,000 data points per day (Glattfelder et al., 2010), oanda, ebs has opened up new opportunities for model building. It is now possible to follow an empirical approach and develop models bottom up by analyzing empirical data and searching for statistical properties.

The analysis of high frequency data is nontrivial: ticks (i.e., quoted prices) are irregularly spaced in time in an intricate sequence. The available literature essentially suggests two ways to handle this issue (Dacorogna et al., 2001; Engle and Russell, 2006). The first method suggests aggregating price information by interpolating prices between fixed and predetermined times. The drawback of this method is the loss of intratime information during active periods and the multiplication of price information during quiet periods, when insufficient data is available. With the second approach, one can consider a time series made of ticks and times between their occurrences (i.e., duration); this is referred to as a *point process* (Bauwens and Hautsch, 2009). Point processes are valuable because they incorporate durations and allow analytical results to be derived; however, they have the disadvantage that time is measured in terms of physical units, and therefore, point processes neither adapt to the changing market activity nor

*Handbook of Exchange Rates*, First Edition. Edited by Jessica James, Ian W. Marsh, and Lucio Sarno.

differentiate between a minute of early morning calm and a minute during a hectic news announcement.

We propose a different way to analyze high frequency data: an event-based approach in which the time series is dissected based on market events where the direction of the trend changes from up to down or vice versa. We identify alternating directional changes (DCs) as a price move of magnitude $\lambda$ from the last price extreme, be it a high or a low when a downward or upward directional change is to be observed, respectively (Guillaume et al., 1997). Physical time is substituted with the so-called intrinsic time incremented by one unit whenever a directional change occurs. This approach is well suited to deal with tick-by-tick data because it is not constrained by any fixed time grid and naturally adapts to the market activity. With this methodology, we can model the price curve as a superposition of different $\lambda$ price curves based on directional changes.

We have discovered 12 new scaling laws (Glattfelder et al., 2010) that researchers had failed to previously identify. The scaling laws are powerful tools for model building: they are a frame of reference to relate different values to each other. We use the scaling laws to compute the equivalent of a Richter scale in geology (Richter, 1958) for financial markets. The scale of market quakes (SMQ, Bisig et al., 2012) is an objective measure of the impact of political and economic events in foreign exchange and used as a support tool for decision makers and commentators in financial markets or as an input for an economic model measuring the impact of fundamental economic events.

The discovery of the 12 new scaling laws can be used as a cornerstone for model building. They provide a dynamic frame of reference, which is a kind of anchor for the rest of the model. One of the scaling laws relates the total length of the coastline of the price curve as a function of the threshold of observation. If we sum up all the price changes bigger or equal to 0.05% after subtracting potential transaction costs, then the 1-year coastline is an astounding 1600% compared to a price risk of 30%. The length of the coastline is the result of the ongoing imbalance between buyers and sellers and reflects a lack of market liquidity, when there are not enough market participants ready to take the other side of the immediate buy or sell flow.

We have developed a new class of trading models that is based on the scaling law of price overshoots. The algorithm opens countertrend positions, when there is an imbalance of buy and sell volume and a price overshoot occurs. The position is closed out as soon as the position is back in a profit. The model takes advantage of the long coastline and the recurring price rebounds and improves the price average of the position by adding and subtracting to the position during the temporary rebounds and generating incremental return that speeds up the time for the closing of the position. Besides generating return, the strategy provides liquidity to the market and reduces its overall volatility; this has economic value because it lowers uncertainty, thus increasing economic efficiency. The lack of correlation with other asset classes and investment strategies makes high frequency finance strategies an attractive new asset class with unique features: stable returns. An additional advantage is the liquidity of these strategies because investments can be closed out at any time.

The strategy can also be embedded as part of a dynamic currency overlay; in conjunction with a static hedge, the dynamic hedge generates incremental return and reduces overall risk: the dynamic hedge increases the size of its position, whenever the underlying asset appreciates too rapidly, and starts to offset the static hedge by building up long positions, whenever the asset drops too rapidly. The incremental returns of the dynamic component turn currency hedging into an attractive financial product.

The chapter is organized as follows. In Section 20.2, we define the event-based framework in some detail. The scaling laws are then presented in Section 20.3. Section 20.4 introduces the SMQ and analyzes SMQ events during the course of several years for major currency pairs. The main features of our trading model algorithm are then described in Section 20.5, where we discuss monthly statistics of executed trades. Finally, we conclude and discuss further work.

## 20.2 The Intrinsic Time Framework

The foreign exchange (FX) market is usually analyzed as a homogeneous sequence of returns $r$ defined as the price difference over a fixed period of time (Dacorogna et al., 2001). This metric is used for a discontinuous time series: over weekends, trading comes to a standstill or, inversely, at news announcements, there are spurts of market activity. Ideally, time should be a dynamic object that adapts itself to market activity. To achieve this goal, we propose an event-based approach that analyzes the time series in terms of price directional changes of a given amplitude $\lambda$ (Glattfelder et al., 2010). Within this framework, time flows unevenly: any occurrence of a directional change represents a new *intrinsic* time unit. Intrinsic time flows to the beat of events and is thus better suited to model the dynamics of the underlying processes.

The dissection algorithm identifies the occurrence of a price change $\lambda$ from the last high or low (i.e., an extrema), whether it is in an up or down mode, respectively. At each occurrence of a directional change, there is the so-called overshoot associated with the previous directional change. The overshoot is defined as the difference between the price level at which the last directional change occurred and the extrema before the next directional change is triggered. Figure 20.1 shows how the price curve is dissected into directional change and overshoot sections.

Formally, we map the time series of prices into sequences of directional changes and price overshoots as follows. Let $\Lambda = \{\lambda_0, \ldots, \lambda_{n_\lambda - 1}\}$ be the set of $n_\lambda$ price thresholds onto which time series is mapped. The initial condition of the sequence is $x_0$, the initial price; $t_0$, the initial physical time; and $m_0$, the mode that switches between up and down indicating in which direction the directional change is expected. An initial condition affects at most the first two pairs (directional change, overshoot), and let the subsequent pairs in the sequence to synchronize with any other sequence obtained with a different initialization.

A given $\lambda_i$ discretizes the time series into a set of prices $X_i(t) = \{x_0^i(t_0^i), \ldots, x_{n_i-1}^i(t_{n_i-1}^i), x(t)\}$ occurring at times $T_i(t) = \{t_0^i, \ldots, t_{n_i-1}^i, t\}$, where $x(t) =$

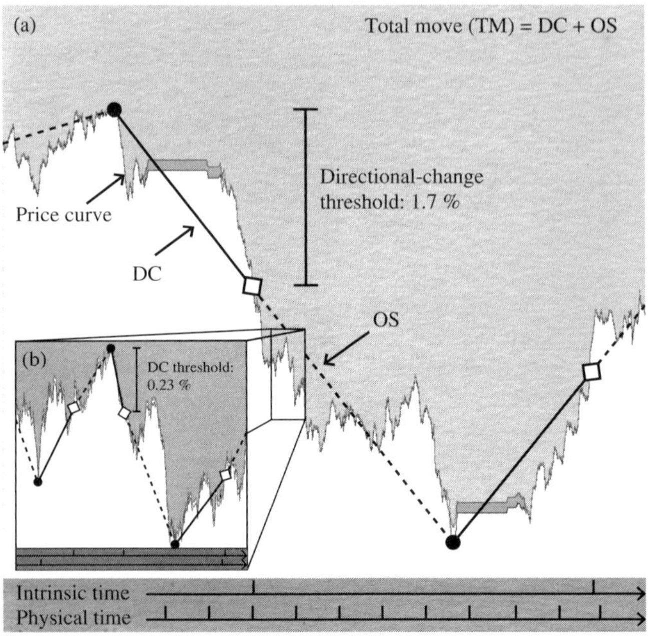


**FIGURE 20.1** Projection of a (a) 2-week, (b) zoomed-in 36-h price sample onto a reduced set of the so-called directional-change (DC) events defined by a threshold (a) $\lambda = 1.7\%$, (b) $\lambda = 0.23\%$. These DC events (diamonds) act as natural dissection points, decomposing a total-price move between two extremal price levels (bullets) into the so-called DC (solid lines) and overshoot (OS, dashed lines) sections. Timescales depict physical time ticking evenly across different price-curve activity regimes, whereas *intrinsic time* triggers only at DC events.

$(\text{bid}(t) + \text{ask}(t))/2$ is the midprice at time $t$. We highlight that the last elements of the set $(x(t), t)$ are temporary, as they do not correspond to a turning point yet but represent the state of the process at time $t$. We compute the number of turning points (i.e., the occurrence of a directional change) as $n_e^i = \lfloor n_i/2 \rfloor$. The series of amplitude of directional changes $\Delta_i$ is defined as

$$\Delta_i(t) = \left\{\delta_0^i, \ldots, \delta_{n_e^i-1}^i, \delta_{n_e^i}^i(t)\right\} = \left\{\frac{x_{2j+1}^i - x_{2j}^i}{x_{2j}^i}\right\} \tag{20.1}$$

where $0 \leq j \leq n_e^i$. The discreteness of the time series of prices prevents $|\delta_j^i| = \lambda_i$. The discrepancy is, however, small and is on average within the spread. The series of amplitudes of overshoots $\Omega_i$ is written as

$$\Omega_i(t) = \left\{\omega_0^i, \ldots, \omega_{n_e^i-1}^i, \omega_{n_e^i}^i(t)\right\} = \left\{\frac{x_{2(j+1)}^i - x_{2j+1}^i}{x_{2j+1}^i}\right\} \tag{20.2}$$

Durations of directional changes or price overshoots are similarly defined by replacing prices $x$ by physical time $t$ in Equations (20.1) and (20.2).

Algorithm 20.1 shows a pseudocode that gives further details on how to dissect the time series of prices.

**ALGORITHM 20.1 Dissect the price curve from time $t_0$ and measure overshoots with a $\lambda_i$ price threshold**

**Require:** initialise variables ($x^{\text{ext}} = x(t_0)$, *mode* is arbitrarily set to *up*, $X_i = x_0$, $T_i = t_0$)

```
update latest X_i with x(t)
update latest T_i with t
if mode is down then
    if x(t) > x^ext then
        x^ext ← x(t)
    else if (x^ext − x(t))/x^ext ≥ λ_i then
        x^ext ← x(t)
        mode ← up
        X_i ← x(t)
        T_i ← t
    end if
else if mode is up then
    if x(t) < x^ext then
        x^ext ← x(t)
    else if (x(t) − x^ext)/x^ext ≥ λ_i then
        x^ext ← x(t)
        mode ← down
        X_i ← x(t)
        T_i ← t
    end if
end if
```

Section 20.3 explores the relationships between the quantities introduced above and empirically shows that a large number of scaling laws exist. We then introduce a novel way to measure market activity by inspecting the behavior of an aggregate of $\omega^i_{n^i_e}(t)$ over $i$ on a continuous basis.

## 20.3 Scaling Laws

Scaling laws establish invariance of scale and play an important role in describing complex systems (Barabasi and Albert, 1999; Newman, 2005; West et al., 1997. In finance, there is one scaling law that has been widely reported (Ballocchi et al., 1999; Corsi et al., 2001; Dacorogna et al., 2001; Di Matteo et al., 2005; Galluccio et al., 1997; Mantegna and Stanley, 1995; Müller et al., 1990; Guillaume et al., 1997): the size of the average absolute price change (return) is scale-invariant to the time interval of its occurrence. This scaling law has been applied to risk management and volatility modeling (Di Matteo, 2007; Gabaix et al., 2003; Ghashghaie et al., 1996; Sornette, 2000), even though there has been no consensus among researchers for why the scaling law exists (Barndorff-Nielsen and Prause, 2001; Bouchaud, 2001; Farmer and Lillo, 2004; Joulin et al., 2008; Lux, 2006).

Searching for new scaling laws, we analyze the price data of the FX market, which is a complex network of interacting agents: corporations, institutional and retail traders, and brokers trading through market makers, who themselves form an intricate web of interdependence. We consider five years of tick-by-tick data for 13 exchange rates through November 2007 (see Glattfelder et al. (2010) for a description of the data set).

An exchange rate often moves by 10–20% within a year. However, since the seminal work of Mandelbrot (1963), we know about the fractal nature of price curves. The coastline, roughly being the sum of all price moves of a given threshold, at fine levels of resolution, may be far longer than one might intuitively think. But how much longer? The scaling laws described in this chapter provide a surprisingly accurate estimate and not only highlight the importance of considering tail events (Sornette, 2002) but also set these in perspective with the remarkably long coastline of price changes preceding them.

## 20.3.1 THE NEW SCALING LAWS

Interest in scaling relations in FX data was sparked in 1990 by a seminal paper relating the mean absolute change of the logarithmic midprices, sampled at time intervals $\Delta t$ over a sample of size $n\Delta t$, to the size of the time interval (Müller et al., 1990)

$$\langle|\Delta\chi|\rangle_p = \left(\frac{\Delta t}{C_\chi(p)}\right)^{E_\chi(p)} \tag{20.3}$$

where $\Delta\chi_i = \chi_i - \chi_{i-1}$ and $\chi_i = \chi(t_i) = (\ln \text{bid}_i + \ln \text{ask}_i)/2$ is the logarithmic midprice of a currency pair at time $t_i$, and $E_\chi(p)$, $C_\chi(p)$ are the scaling-law parameters. The averaging operator is $\langle x\rangle_p = \left(1/n\sum_{j=1}^{n} x_j^p\right)^{1/p}$, usually with $p \in \{1, 2\}$, and $p$ is omitted if equal to one. Note that for law (20.3), the data is sampled at fixed time intervals $t_i = i\Delta t$. This requires a time interpolation scheme (described in Glattfelder et al. (2010)), which we will also employ when necessary. Throughout the chapter, we consider a simpler definition of the price given by $x_i = (\text{bid}_i + \text{ask}_i)/2$, where price moves are defined as $\Delta x_i = (x_i - x_{i-1})/x_{i-1}$. Although the definition of $x_i$ loses the mathematical feature of $\chi_i$ of behaving antisymmetrically under price inversions (e.g., $\chi_i^{\text{EUR-USD}} = -\chi_i^{\text{USD-EUR}}$), it is more natural because, practically, percentages are more intuitive to manipulate than differences between logarithmic values. However, considering either $\chi_i$ or $x_i$ leads to very similar results even for large spread values.

Later, in 1997, a second scaling law was reported by Guillaume et al. (1997), relating the number $N(\Delta\chi_{\rm dc})$ of directional changes to the directional-change sizes $\Delta\chi_{\rm dc}$

$$N(\Delta\chi_{\rm dc}) = \left(\frac{\Delta\chi_{\rm dc}}{C_{N,\rm dc}}\right)^{E_{N,\rm dc}}. \tag{20.4}$$

In Glattfelder et al. (2010), and reviewed here, we confirm laws (20.3) and (20.4), considering $x_i$ (Fig. 20.3a–c), and report on 12 new independent scaling laws holding across 13 exchange rates and for close to three orders of magnitude. Tables of the estimated parameter values for all the laws and for the 13 exchange rates, as well as for a Gaussian random walk (GRW) model, are provided in Glattfelder et al. (2010). Table 20.1 shows the estimated scaling-law parameters for EUR-USD. We start the enumeration of the laws by a generalization of Equation (20.4) that relates the average number of ticks observed during a price move of $\Delta x$ to the size of this threshold

$$\langle N(\Delta x_{\rm tck})\rangle = \left(\frac{\Delta x}{C_{N,\rm tck}}\right)^{E_{N,\rm tck}} \tag{20.5}$$

where a tick is defined as a price move larger than (in absolute value) $\Delta x_{\rm tck} =$ 0.02%. The definition of a tick can, however, be altered without destroying

**TABLE 20.1 Estimated Scaling-Law Parameter Values Considering EUR-USD**

| Name | Equation | $E$ | $C$ |
|---|---|---|---|
| Tick count | 20.5 | 1.93 | $2.1 \times 10^{-2}$ |
| Price move count | 20.6 | −1.93 | $9.5 \times 10^{0}$ |
| Maximum price move | 20.7 ($p = 1$) | 0.52 | $1.9 \times 10^{5}$ |
| Maximum price move | 20.7 ($p = 2$) | 0.49 | $1.3 \times 10^{5}$ |
| Time of price move | 20.8 | 1.93 | $1.2 \times 10^{-3}$ |
| Time of directional change | 20.9 | 1.88 | $1.1 \times 10^{-3}$ |
| Total-price move | 20.13 | 0.98 | $4.9 \times 10^{-1}$ |
| Overshoot move | 20.13 | 1.0 | $9.9 \times 10^{-1}$ |
| Time of total move | 20.16 | 1.89 | $1.1 \times 10^{-3}$ |
| Time of directional change | 20.16 | 1.85 | $1.6 \times 10^{-3}$ |
| Time of overshoot | 20.16 | 1.91 | $1.4 \times 10^{-3}$ |
| Total-move tick count | 20.17 | 1.89 | $1.9 \times 10^{-2}$ |
| Directional-change tick count | 20.17 | 2.02 | $4.2 \times 10^{-2}$ |
| Overshoot tick count | 20.17 | 1.87 | $2.3 \times 10^{-2}$ |
| Cumulative total move | 20.18 | −0.94 | $2.0 \times 10^{2}$ |
| Cumulative total move with costs | 20.18 | −0.98 | $1.5 \times 10^{2}$ |
| Cumulative directional change | 20.18 | −0.95 | $8.8 \times 10^{1}$ |
| Cumulative overshoot | 20.18 | −0.92 | $1.1 \times 10^{2}$ |

the scaling-law relation. In essence, this law counts the average number of ticks observed during every price move $\Delta x$. Law (20.5) is plotted in Figure 20.2. The second law counts the average yearly number $N(\Delta x)$ of price moves of size $\Delta x$

$$N(\Delta x) = \left(\frac{\Delta x}{C_{N,x}}\right)^{E_{N,x}} \tag{20.6}$$

We annualize the number of observations of laws (20.4) and (20.6) by dividing them by 5, the number of years in our data sample. Law (20.6) and all the following scaling laws are given in Figure 20.3 The next scaling law relates the average maximal price range $\Delta x_{\max}$, defined as the difference between the high and low price levels, during a time interval $\Delta t$, to the size of that time interval

$$\langle \Delta x_{\max} \rangle_p = \left(\frac{\Delta t}{C_{\max}(p)}\right)^{E_{\max}(p)} \tag{20.7}$$

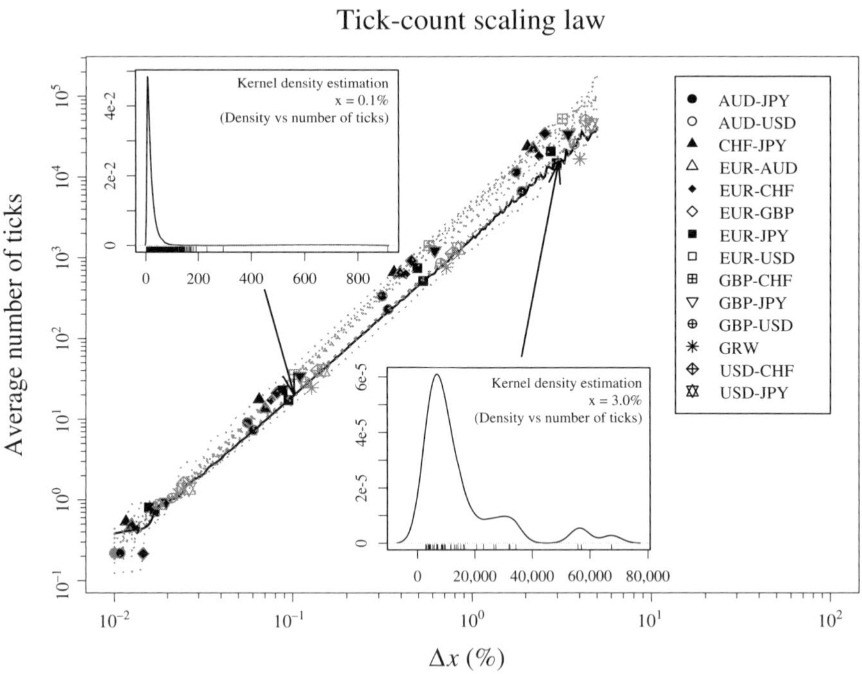


**FIGURE 20.2** Scaling law (20.5) is plotted, where the $x$-axis shows the price move thresholds of the observations and the $y$-axis, the average tick numbers. A tick is defined as a price move of 0.02%. The solid line shows the raw data for EUR-USD. For the remaining 12 currency pairs and the Gaussian random walk benchmark model, the raw data is displayed with dots. Insets show the distribution of the EUR-USD observations (drawn above their $x$-axis) for selected threshold values of 0.1% and 3.0%. See Glattfelder et al. (2010) for the values of the estimated scaling-law parameters.

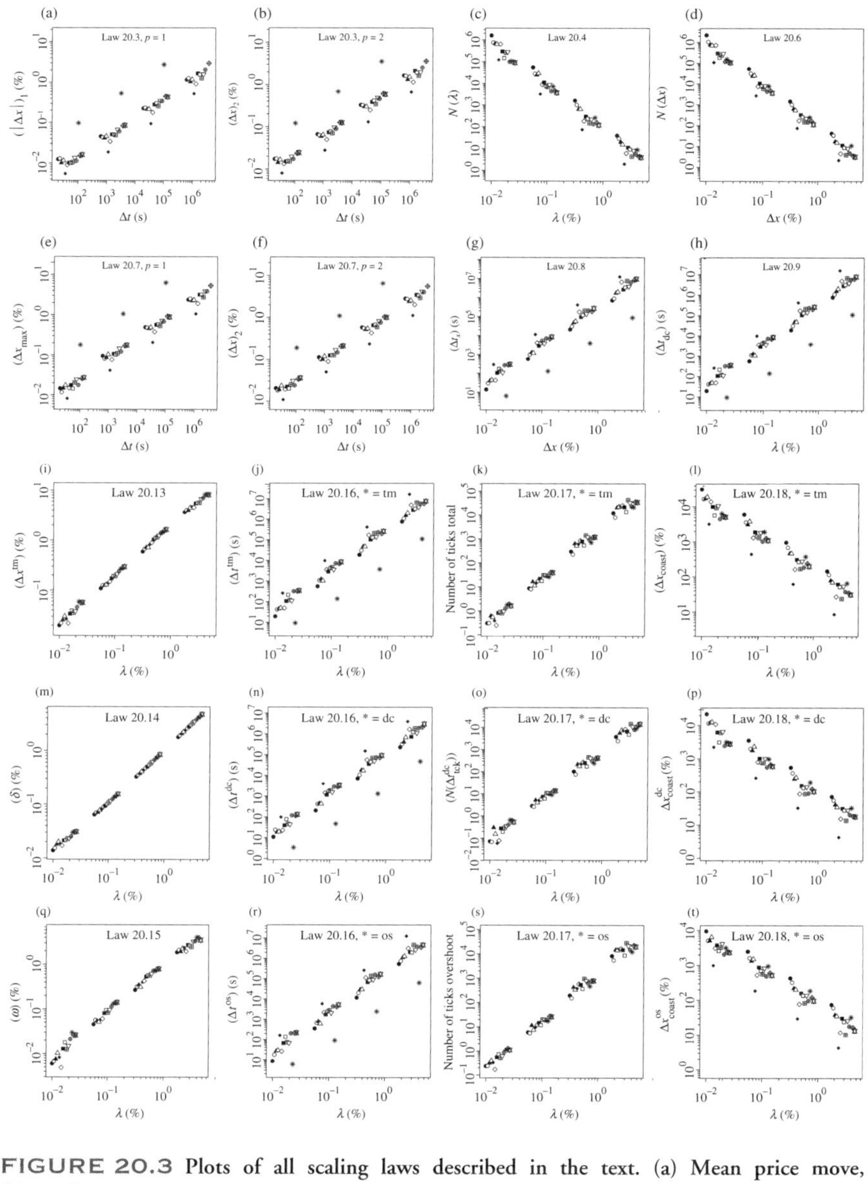

**FIGURE 20.3** Plots of all scaling laws described in the text. (a) Mean price move, (b) quadratic mean price move, (c) directional-change count, (d) price move count, (e) maximum price move, (f) quadratic mean maximum price move, (g) mean time of price move, (h) time during directional changes, (i) total-price move, (j) time of total move, (k) total-move tick count, (l) coastline (cumulative total move), (m) directional-change move, (n) time of directional change, (o) directional-change tick count, (p) cumulative directional change, (q) overshoot move, (r) time of overshoot, (s) overshoot tick count, and (t) cumulative overshoot. Symbols are as in Figure 20.2. The raw data is plotted for the 13 currency pairs with dots and for the Gaussian random walk model with dashes. See Glattfelder et al. (2010) for the values of the estimated scaling-law parameters.

where $\Delta x_{\max} = \max\{x(\tau); \tau \in [t - \Delta t; t]\} - \min\{x(\tau); \tau \in [t - \Delta t; t]\}$ and Equation (20.7) holds for $p = 1, 2$.

The statistical properties of a GRW are, as is well known, different to the observed empirical data in many respects (Mandelbrot and Hudson, 2004). Having said this, it is striking how closely this simple model can reproduce many of the average statistical properties of the real market. Notable differences are seen in law (20.7) (Figs 20.3e and f), which reveal an unintuitive result: the bell-curve distribution of price moves leads to an average maximal price move that is roughly eight times larger than that observed for the empirical data.

We have also discovered laws relating the time during which events happen to the magnitude of these events. Law (20.8) relates the average time interval $\langle \Delta t_x \rangle$ for a price change of size $\Delta x$ to occur to the size of the threshold

$$\langle \Delta t_x \rangle = \left( \frac{\Delta x}{C_{t,x}} \right)^{E_{t,x}} \tag{20.8}$$

and similarly, considering directional changes of threshold $\lambda$

$$\langle \Delta t_{\mathrm{dc}} \rangle = \left( \frac{\lambda}{C_{t,\mathrm{dc}}} \right)^{E_{t,\mathrm{dc}}} \tag{20.9}$$

Thus, laws (20.8) and (20.9) relate the average numbers of seconds that elapse between consecutive price moves and directional changes, respectively.

Next, we unveil a set of scaling laws emerging from the identification of directional-change events that make up the so-called total-move (TM) segments, which themselves decompose into directional-change (DC) and overshoot (OS) parts. The total-price move, waiting time, and number of ticks can then be written as

$$\langle |\Delta x^{\mathrm{tm}}| \rangle = \langle |\delta| \rangle + \langle |\omega| \rangle, \tag{20.10}$$

$$\langle \Delta t^{\mathrm{tm}} \rangle = \langle \Delta t^{\mathrm{dc}} \rangle + \langle \Delta t^{\mathrm{os}} \rangle, \tag{20.11}$$

$$\langle N(\Delta x^{\mathrm{tm}}_{\mathrm{tck}}) \rangle = \langle N(\Delta x^{\mathrm{dc}}_{\mathrm{tck}}) \rangle + \langle N(\Delta x^{\mathrm{os}}_{\mathrm{tck}}) \rangle. \tag{20.12}$$

This decomposition leads to nine additional scaling laws, where the average values are functions of the directional-change thresholds $\lambda$

$$\langle |\Delta x^{\mathrm{tm}}| \rangle = \left( \frac{\lambda}{C_{x,\mathrm{tm}}} \right)^{E_{x,\mathrm{tm}}} \tag{20.13}$$

$$\langle |\delta| \rangle = \left( \frac{\lambda}{C_{x,\mathrm{dc}}} \right)^{E_{x,\mathrm{dc}}} \tag{20.14}$$

$$\langle |\omega| \rangle = \left( \frac{\lambda}{C_{x,\mathrm{os}}} \right)^{E_{x,\mathrm{os}}} \tag{20.15}$$

$$\langle \Delta t^* \rangle = \left( \frac{\lambda}{C_{t,*}} \right)^{E_{t,*}} \tag{20.16}$$

$$\langle N(\Delta x^*_{\text{tck}}) \rangle = \left( \frac{\lambda}{C_{N,*}} \right)^{E_{N,*}} \tag{20.17}$$

where $*$ stands for $\{\text{tm}, \text{dc}, \text{os}\}$. Note that $\langle|\delta|\rangle = \lambda$ holds by construction. The actual deviation to $E_{x,\text{dc}} = 1$ and $C_{x,\text{dc}} = 1$, as seen in Glattfelder et al. (2010), is given by the increasing noise for small thresholds, as the impact of the effect of a tick exceeding the exact threshold systematically overestimates $\langle|\delta|\rangle$ (Fig. 20.3m). The average parameter values (across the 13 currency pairs) of law (20.13) display a peculiar feature: on average, a directional change $\lambda$ is followed by an overshoot of the same magnitude $\langle|\omega|\rangle \approx \lambda$ ($E^{\text{av}}_{x,\text{os}} \approx 1.04$ and $C^{\text{av}}_{x,\text{os}} \approx 1.06$), making the total move double the size of the directional-change threshold $\langle|\Delta x^{\text{tm}}|\rangle \approx 2\lambda$ ($E^{\text{av}}_{x,\text{to}} \approx 0.99$ and $C^{\text{av}}_{x,\text{to}} \approx 0.51$). This result is also found by computing the probable path of the price within a binomial tree as $0.5\Delta x + 0.5^2\, 2\Delta x + 0.5^3\, 3\Delta x + \cdots = \Delta x \sum_i^n i\, 0.5^i \xrightarrow{n\to\infty} 2\Delta x$. A similar feature holds for the waiting times and number of ticks: $\langle|\Delta t^{\text{os}}|\rangle \approx 2\langle|\Delta t^{\text{dc}}|\rangle$ and $\langle \text{N}(\Delta x^{\text{os}}_{\text{tck}})\rangle \approx 2\langle \text{N}(\Delta x^{\text{dc}}_{\text{tck}})\rangle$. Although in terms of size the overshoot price move is approximately as big as the direction-change threshold, it contains roughly twice as many ticks and takes twice as long to unfold.

Considering cumulative price moves instead of the averages in law (20.3) leads to another triplet of laws

$$\Delta x^*_{\text{cum}} = \sum_{i=1}^{n} |\Delta x^*_i| = \left( \frac{\lambda}{C_{\text{cum},*}} \right)^{E_{\text{cum},*}} \tag{20.18}$$

This concludes the presentation of 17 new scaling laws: we count Equation (20.7) twice for $p = 1, 2$ and omit the trivial scaling law $\langle|\delta|\rangle \propto \lambda$. In Glattfelder et al. (2010), we actually show that 12 laws are independent and hence can be understood as primary laws.

### 20.3.2 THE COASTLINE

We now have the necessary tools in hand to come back to the measurement of the length of the coastline. The total-move scaling law (20.18) allows us to estimate its size as a function of the resolution defined by the directional-change threshold. Considering thresholds of 0.01%, 0.1%, 1%, and 5%, one finds the average lengths of the annualized coastline to be 22,509%, 2046%, 186%, and 34.8%, respectively. So by decreasing the threshold of resolution 500-fold, the length of the coastline decreases by a factor of 650. Similarly, looking at the GRW, we find 14,361%, 1946%, 264%, and 65.2%, respectively. The 500-fold decrease in resolution entails a coastline decrease by a factor of only 220, highlighting the fact that GRW has fewer small moves and more middle-sized moves than the empirical price curves. Not surprisingly, taking transaction costs into account breaks the scaling law for small thresholds. However, it is still possible to evaluate the length of the coastline by employing the scaling relation for the interval [0.1%, 5%] and measuring it for 0.05%. Thus, for the thresholds 0.05%, 0.1%, 1%, and 5% the new average coastline lengths are now 1,604%, 1,463%, 161%, 34.5%. For the 0.05% threshold (which occurs on average every 15 min), we measure an average daily coastline of 6.4%. The range of these average daily coastline lengths is from 1.8% for EUR-CHF to 9.1% for AUD-JPY.

## 20.4 The Scale of Market Quakes

Scaling laws relate price moves, duration, and frequency; let us use this scaling-law methodology to measure multiscale events such as market responses due to news announcements or price jumps due to endogenous factors, such as lack of liquidity (Joulin et al., 2008). Although a considerable amount of research has been devoted to quantifying market impact of such events, see for example Bauwens et al. (2005), Bouchaud (2009), Chaboud et al. (2004), Dominguez (2003), Engle and Ng (1993) and references therein, there has been to our knowledge only one attempt at quantifying multiscale events (Zumbach, 2000) where the authors propose a scale that is a weighted average of returns over different (physical) time horizons. This approach suffers from the rigidity of physical time and does not seem to measure comparable magnitudes over different currency pairs. To alleviate these issues, and also inspired by the Richter scale Richter (1958), we propose a methodology to quantify these multiscale events along a scale, the SMQ (Bisig et al., 2012), which defines a tick-by-tick metric allowing us to quantify market quakes on a continuous basis where we monitor the excess price moves from one directional change to the next, that is, the price overshoots. In the rest of this section, we summarize the main findings from Bisig et al. (2012).

The SMQ can be used in different ways; decision makers can use the indicator as a tool to filter the significance of market events. The output of the SMQ can be used as an input to forecasting or trading models to identify regime shifts and change the input factors.

Every occurrence of a directional change triggers a new overshoot that oscillates between $-\lambda$ and any positive value until it decreases by $-\lambda$ from its recent price extreme causing the next directional change. Figure 20.4(a) shows the overshoot dynamics.

To measure the market activity over a range of price scales, we define an average overshoot $\bar{\omega}$ as

$$\bar{\omega}(t) = \frac{1}{n_\lambda} \sum_{i=1}^{n_\lambda} \omega^q(t, \lambda_i) \tag{20.19}$$

where $n_\lambda$ is the number of thresholds $\lambda_i$ and the superscript $q$ denotes the quantile taken from the historical distribution of price overshoot associated to a

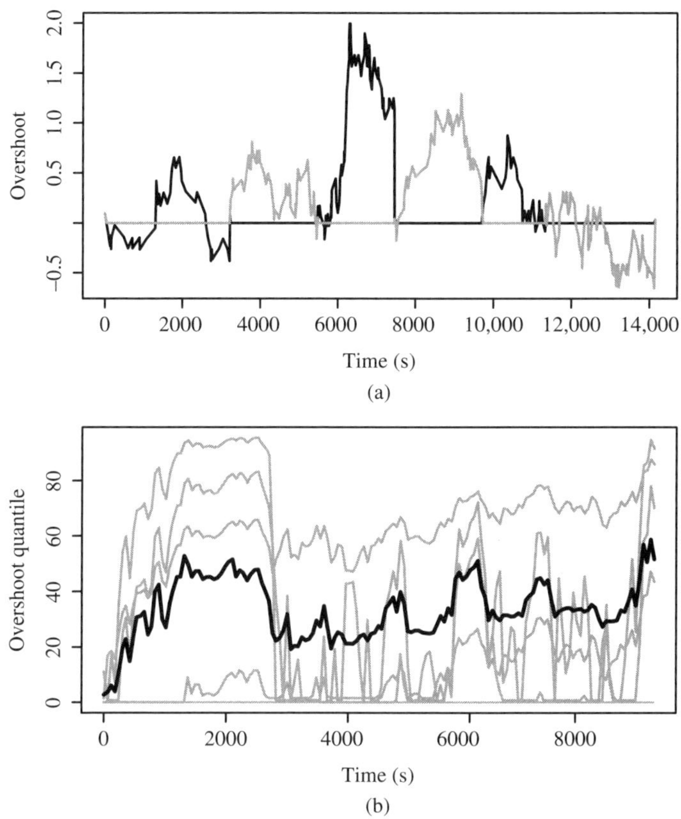


**FIGURE 20.4** **Sample evolution of (a) the price overshoot $\omega(t)$ and (b) the average price overshoot $\bar{\omega}(t)$. (a) Alternated gray and black lines show the overshoot normalized by $\lambda$. (b) A subset of the $n_\lambda$ thresholds are shown in gray and the black line shows the average overshoot $\bar{\omega}(t)$. Overshoots are measured in quantiles to ensure a normalized measurement.**

threshold $\lambda$ and computed from tick-by-tick date from December 1, 2005, up to December 31, 2008. Overshoots are expressed in quantiles to ensure a normalized measurement and to be averaged over different thresholds. We consider evenly distributed thresholds and set $\lambda_i = i\ 0.05\%$ with $i$ running from 1 to $n_\lambda = 100$. Figure 20.4(b) shows the time evolution of $\bar{\omega}$.

We now describe the way the average overshoot $\bar{\omega}(t)$ is converted into a unique number: the SMQ $\mathcal{S}(t)$. It is defined as

$$\mathcal{S}(t) = \frac{1}{n_a} \sum_{i=0}^{n_a} \mathcal{F}\left(\bar{\Omega}\left(t + \left(\frac{2i}{n_a} - 1\right)\delta t\right)\right) \tag{20.20}$$

where $\delta t$ is the time window, $n_a = \delta t/\delta t_a$ is the time discretization of the average and the set $\bar{\Omega}(t) = \{\bar{\omega}(\tau) - \langle\bar{\omega}(\tau)\rangle_{\bar{\Omega}(t)} | t - \delta t \leq \tau \leq t + \delta t\}$. The average operator $\langle\cdot\rangle_{\bar{\Omega}(t)}$ is used to prevent high or low plateaux to correspond to significantly different frequencies. The operator $\mathcal{F}(\cdot)$ is defined as

$$\mathcal{F}(\bar{\Omega}(t)) = \frac{1}{\lfloor n_f/2+1 \rfloor} \sum_{k=1}^{\lfloor n_f/2+1 \rfloor} \frac{|X_{k-1}|}{k} \tag{20.21}$$

where $n_f = \delta t / \delta t_f$ is the time discretisation of $\bar{\Omega}(t)$, $\lfloor \cdot \rfloor$ is the floor operator, and $|X_k|$ is the magnitude of the Fourier frequency computed from the discretized set $\Omega(t)$. The average is done only over half of the frequencies as the Fourier transform of a real signal is symmetric around the middle of the spectrum. The weighting ensures the robustness of the operator $\mathcal{F}(\cdot)$ to small perturbations.

Figure 20.5(a–h) shows the behavior of EUR-USD and the SMQ on the occasion of eight releases of nonfarm employment numbers Bureau of Labour Statistics. The wide variety of market responses: a steep drop (f), the same price move amplitude as in (f) but happening within a longer time period (e), little reaction from the market (c), volatile market (g and h), or a drop immediately followed by a recovery (b and g) is characterized by our methodology computing a single number within the SMQ. As expected, we observe that the steep drop (f) is associated with a higher value than (e), where the difference between the two scenarios is mainly the time for the price move to occur. Scenario (b), which could well go unnoticed as the original price level does not seem to be altered by the news announcement, is given a significant SMQ magnitude that is comparable to (e).

We also noticed in Figure 20.5a, b, and d that peaks of SMQ magnitude do not always coincide with releasing time, as the market response can take a few hours to operate.

As in the case of earthquakes, after-quakes occur, such as in (a and g), and have, in contrast to what is shown here, also been observed to be stronger than the original quake. The initial market impact can trigger margin calls that can trigger a far bigger secondary market shock.

Figure 20.5i shows the distribution of the SMQ magnitude of two sets of events versus the maximum price move that occurred within the next 12 hours following the events. The first events considered are 27 nonfarm employment change announcements between 2007 and 2009, and the second ones are 4687 SMQ magnitude peaks observed between December 2005 and March 2009, where a SMQ magnitude peak corresponds to a value $\mathcal{S}(t)$, where $\mathcal{S}(t) > \mathcal{S}(t \pm \delta t_a)$.

We observe a conelike structure where high values are not associated with any small price moves whereas large price moves can relate to small SMQ values. A high value necessarily implies that high price thresholds have been activated, but a noticeable price move can happen as a jump in the market and therefore does not necessarily correspond to a large SMQ value.

We stress here that we have opted for designing a scale that has a fixed frame of reference, implying that the average of observed SMQ magnitudes as well as their frequency can change over time, see Bisig et al. (2012) for analysis and discussion.

Here, we have restricted ourselves to EUR-USD and only considered US news. The same analysis can be done for other currency pairs and news events.

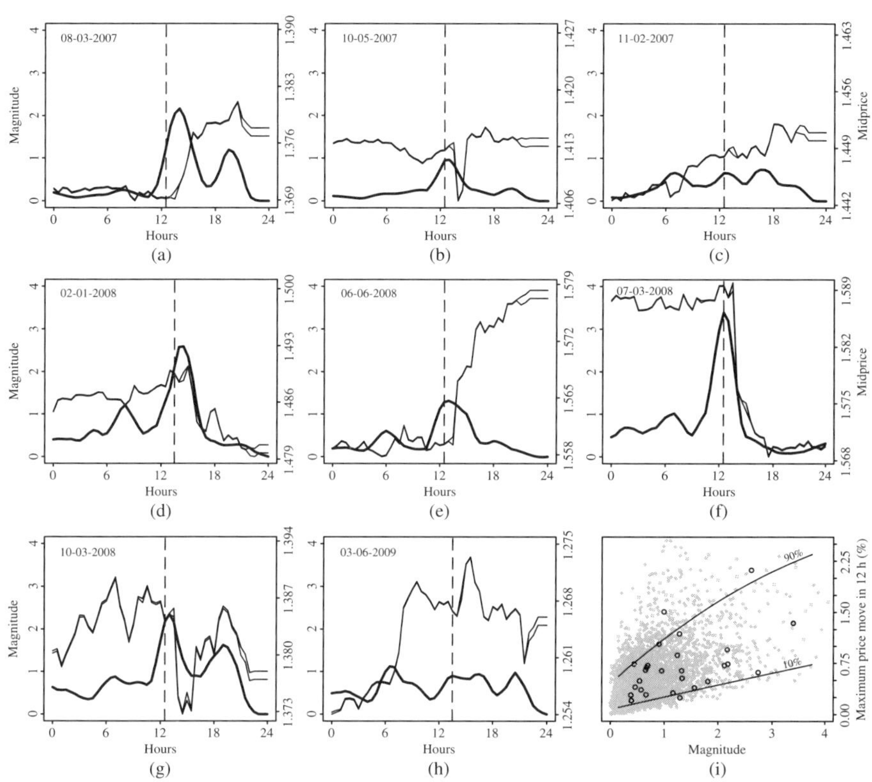

**FIGURE 20.5** (a–h) Behavior of EUR-USD (thin lines) and the SMQ (thick line). The announcement time is the dashed line, and its date appears on the top left of the figure. (i) Distribution of the SMQ magnitude of two sets of events versus the maximum price move that occurred within the next 12 h following the events. The first events (black circles) are 27 nonfarm employment change announcements between 2007 and 2009, and the second ones (gray dots) are 4687 SMQ magnitude peaks observed between December 2005 and March 2009 where a SMQ magnitude peak $\mathcal{S}(t)$ is defined as $\mathcal{S}(t) > \mathcal{S}(t \pm \delta t_a)$. The 10% and 90% quantiles of the distribution are shown.

We are, as we write, applying this methodology to eight currencies and publish SMQ values for the main international news events at the www.olsen.ch.

# 20.5 Trading Models

## 20.5.1 OVERVIEW

In this section, we describe a new class of trading models. At Olsen, we use this type of trading model in a portfolio of more than 20 currency pairs. The positions of the trading models are countertrend, meaning that a price move down triggers a buy; a price up move, a sell. These models provide liquidity to the market. Typically, prices move down when there is a lack of buyers, and they move up when there are not enough sellers. By being countertrend, we help balance demand and supply.

A trading model is made of basic agents: the so-called coastline traders that are described in some detail below. The strength of our models is the fact that these agents are identical across currency pairs. The only difference is the price scale $\lambda$ at which they operate, which adapts to the changing volatility regimes.

## 20.5.2 COASTLINE TRADER

A coastline trader is a process that exploits profit opportunities contained in the long coastline of prices. As seen above, the coastline is made of the price moves up and down at a given price scale $\lambda$. As we shall see, trading the coastline generates profits that is used to improve the price average and speed up the closure of the position. On the price scale $\lambda$, the state of the process is defined by its exposure $e_\tau$, price average $a_\tau$, and the length of overshoot $l_\tau$, where $\tau > 0$ is the age of the process expressed as the number of events. An event is the occurrence of a price move of size $\lambda$. We now describe the state variables and the way the process evolves.

A coastline trader is initialized when a price overshoot of magnitude $\omega$ is observed. A common choice is to set $\omega = 1 \cdot \lambda$ following the results shown above, stating that the average overshoot length is equal to the originating price move. Negative and positive price moves initialize long and short processes, respectively, with initial price average $a_0 = x_0$, where $x_\tau$ is the current bid or ask whether the process is short or long, respectively. The process has initially an exposure $e_0$ set to $G(l_0 = 0)$, where $G$ is a function describing position increments. The quantity $l_\tau > 0, \forall \tau$ measures the price overshoot expressed as the number of $\lambda$ price moves the process is in, from the current price to $a_0$. Note that here the price overshoot does not end when an opposite $\lambda$ price move occurs but when the process is, as we shall see, in a profit and closes itself.

The occurrence of a new $\pm\lambda$ price move respectively decreases or increases the counter $l_\tau$ and makes the process state to evolve. In case of an increase $(l_{\tau+1} = l_\tau + 1)$, a trade of size $\Delta e_\tau = G(l_{\tau+1})$ is made and the exposure becomes

$$e_{\tau+1} = e_\tau + G(l_{\tau+1}) \tag{20.22}$$

The new trade improves the price average, which reads

$$a_{\tau+1} = \frac{a_\tau e_\tau + x_\tau G(l_{\tau+1})}{e_{\tau+1}} \tag{20.23}$$

where $x_\tau$ is the ask or bid price when the process is long or short, respectively.

On the other hand, when the length of the overshoot decreases by one unit ($l_{\tau+1} = l_\tau - 1$), part of the position $\Delta e_\tau = \gamma G(l_\tau)$ is closed and the exposure becomes

$$e_{\tau+1} = e_\tau - \gamma G(l_\tau) \tag{20.24}$$

where $0 \leq \gamma \leq 1$ tunes the size of closing trades. The larger the $\gamma$, the more the coastline is traded as every up and down is fully traded. On the other hand, setting $\gamma$ close to 1 usually implies that a stronger price recovery is needed for the process to be in a profit. We usually set $\gamma = 0.5$.

Closing part of the position generates a profit $\pi_{r,\tau}$ expressed as

$$\pi_{r,\tau} = \lambda^* \gamma G(l_\tau) x_{\text{bid},\tau} \tag{20.25}$$

where the price $x_{\text{bid},\tau}$ is the bid price at time $\tau$ (the bid is taken as the profit is positive) and where $\lambda^* \approx \lambda$ is the inner price move (i.e., where the spread has been deducted) that just occurred. Giving the discreteness of the time series of prices, $\lambda^*$ is close to $\lambda$ but usually not equal.

Because a profit is taken, the price average after having taken profit worsens and becomes

$$a_{\tau+1} = \frac{(a_\tau - \bar{x}_\tau)e_\tau - \pi_{r,\tau}}{e_{\tau+1}} + \bar{x}_\tau \tag{20.26}$$

where $\bar{x}_\tau$ is the bid or the ask prices when the process is long or short, respectively.

We use the total realized profit $\pi_r = \sum \pi_{r,\tau}$ to improve the price average of the position. The coastline is thus used as a tool to manage positions. For that, we introduce an altered price average, the so-called realized average $a^r_\tau$, that takes the total realized profit $\pi^r$ into account

$$a^r_\tau = \frac{(a_\tau - \bar{x}_\tau)e_\tau + \pi_r}{e_\tau} + \bar{x}_\tau \tag{20.27}$$

A coastline trader process ends up its life when it is in a profit, that is, to say when $\pi = (\bar{x}_t - a^r_\tau)e_\tau \geq \pi_0$, where $\pi_0 = 2\delta/3$ is the profit objective and $t$ is the time expressed in physical time as a position can be in a profit in between events.

Figure 20.6 shows a possible coastline trading scenario. When an overshoot happens, a coastline trader is launched at time 1. With every $+\lambda$ price move, the position grows by an additional $G(1) + G(2)$. If at time 4, the size of the overshoot reduces by one unit, then the exposure is reduced by $G(2)$ units. Note that here, as $\gamma = 1$, the process makes full use of the coastline and minimizes exposure. On the other hand, this setting implies that a stronger price recovery is needed before the position is back in a profit. The trader continues to trade the

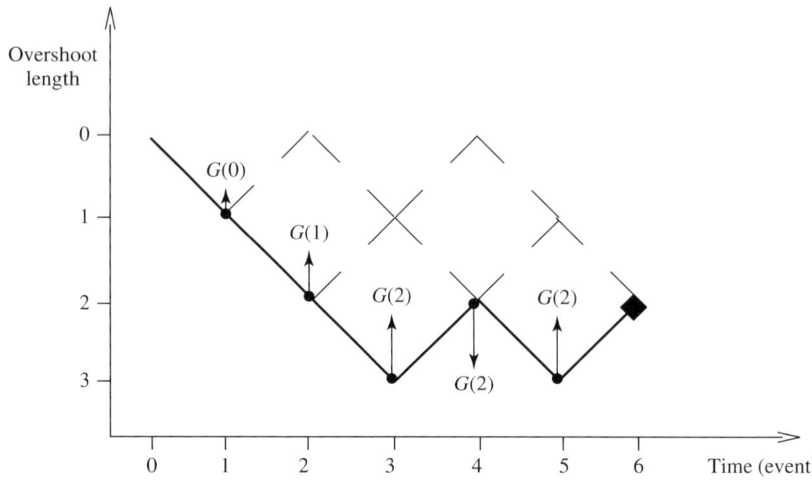


**FIGURE 20.6** Occurrence of a coastline investment strategy.

coastline until the position. Then at time 5, the overshoot increases by one unit and the exposure grows by an additional $G(2)$. The exposure is now identical to the one at time 3, but the realized average is smaller. However, in this scenario, the realized average is still not close enough to end the process. Finally, at time 6, the process is terminated and the position is closed, when the profit target has been reached.

## 20.5.3 MONTHLY STATISTICS

Figure 20.7 shows monthly statistics computed from the execution on a sample account of our investment strategy using coastline trading models, the so-called AF program ols. The trading models of Olsen are based on the above algorithm, and they also include additional risk management mechanisms to manage risk. The running period is 23 months from November 2009 to September 2011 within a portfolio of 24 currency pairs: AUD-CAD, AUD-JPY, AUD-NZD, AUD-USD, CAD-JPY, CHF-JPY, EUR-AUD, EUR-CAD, EUR-CHF, EUR-GBP, EUR-JPY, EUR-NZD, EUR-USD, GBP-AUD, GBP-CAD, GBP-CHF, GBP-JPY, GBP-USD, NZD-CAD, NZD-JPY, NZD-USD, USD-CAD, USD-CHF, and USD-JPY. In Figure 20.7(a), we observe a smoothly increasing cumulated profit that corresponds to the sum of 23 monthly profits for which 16 of them are positive. Figure 20.7(b) shows the distribution of the monthly number of trades summing up to more than $830,000$ executed trades. Even though the standard deviation of the sample is large, it is informative to compute the average number of executed trades per minute: $830,000/23/30/24/60 \approx 1$ trade per minute. We observe in Figure 20.7b and c that the trading models react to market activity and provide liquidity when needed. Indeed the lower activity in December 2009 and in the summer of 2010 is due to holidays season. In

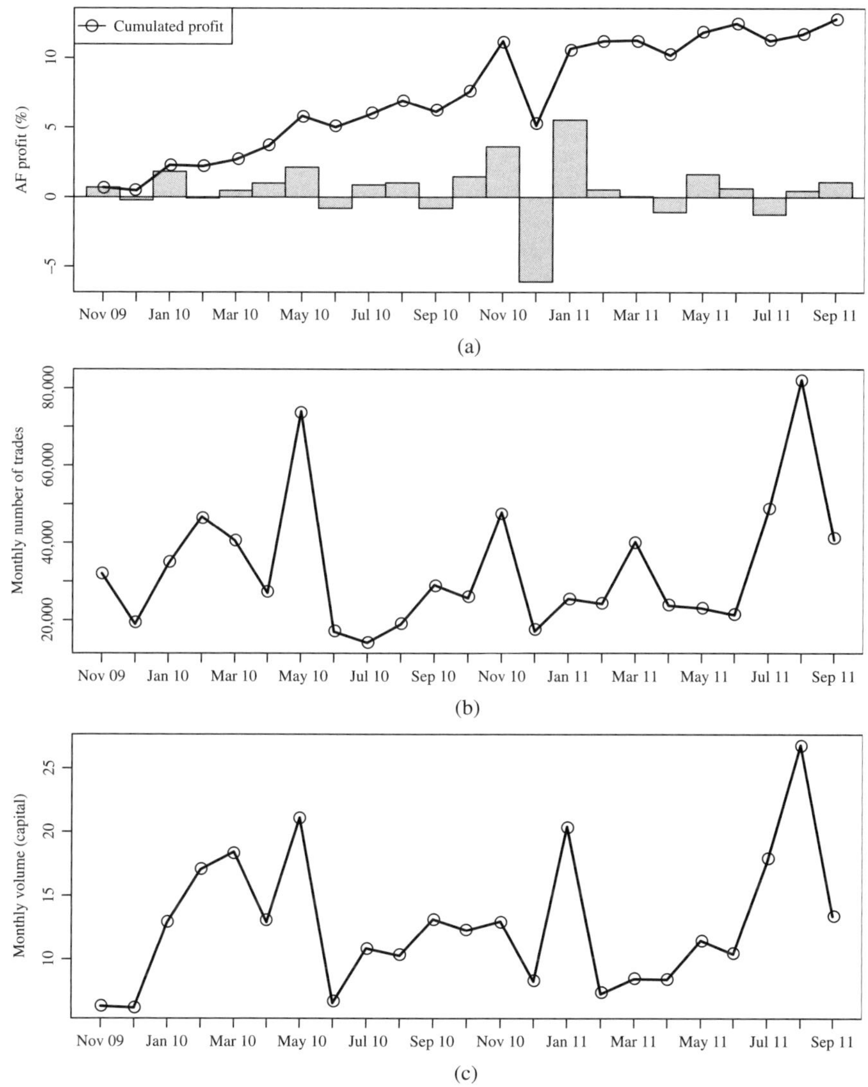


**FIGURE 20.7** Monthly statistics of the execution of our trading models on a sample account. Here we show numbers corresponding to the AF program ols. The running period is 23 months from November 2009 to September 2011 within a portfolio of 24 major currency pairs. (a) Bars and the solid line show monthly and cumulated profit, respectively. (b) Monthly number of trades. (c) Monthly volume expressed in multiple of capital. Volume is defined as the sum of the absolute value of executed trades.

contrast, the fairly high activity in May 2010 and August 2011 are, respectively, the result of the flash crash on May 6, 2010, and the CHF approaching parity against the EUR at an extraordinary pace, followed by the SNB establishing a floor in EUR-CHF.

## 20.6 Conclusion

As we have seen during the current economic crisis, financial markets are unstable. The price instability is a result of demand and supply not balancing each other out for periods of time. We have been able to show that currency markets have distinct statistical properties in the form of scaling laws that have not been discovered before because researchers did not analyze market data using intrinsic time. These properties are useful in several respects. First, it has allowed us to design a SMQ that measures the impact of political and economic events. Second, using the approach of intrinsic time we have shown that it is possible to develop a new class of trading models that balances demand and supply. We have presented an algorithm that generates incremental returns from the long coastline of price moves and inject liquidity into the market, thus contributing to overall market stability and thereby to the overall well-being.

We actually take for granted that these *unexpected* events are bounded, and even more, we assume that they will eventually revert themselves to bounce back where they were. But what if all market participants decide otherwise and all act synchronously as they recently did in the flash crash of May 6, 2010? Should we not have ways to prevent this system from slipping dangerously closer and closer to the precipice? And at the same time generate profit? We believe we should and have partially solved this challenging task by designing high frequency countertrading models providing liquidity when and where it is needed. More work remains to be done and our progress can be followed at www.olseninvest.com.

## Acknowledgments

We thank J. B. Glattfelder for discovering the scaling laws and T. Bisig and V. Impagliazzo for designing the Scale of Market Quakes.

## REFERENCES

Ballocchi G, Dacorogna MM, Hopman CM, Müller UA, Olsen RB. The intraday multivariate structure of the eurofutures markets. J Empir Finance 1999;6:479.

Barabási A-L, Albert R. Emergence of scaling in random networks. Science 1999;286:509.

Barndorff-Nielsen OE, Prause K. Apparent scaling. Finance Stoch 2001;5:103.

Bauwens L, Hautsch N. Modelling financial high frequency data using point processes. In: Anderson TG, et al., editors. Handbook of financial time series. Springer 2009.

Bisig T, Dupuis A, Impagliazzo V, Olsen RB. The scale of market quakes. Quant. Finance 2012; 12:501. Reprinted by permission of the publisher (Taylor & Francis), www.tandfonline.

Bouchaud J-P. Power laws in economics and finance: some ideas from physics. Quant Finance 2001;1:105.

Bouchaud J-P. Economics needs a scientific revolution. Nature 2009;457:147.

Bureau of Labor Statistics 2007–2009. Available at www.bls.gov.

Chaboud A, Chernenko S, Howorka E, Iyer R, Liu D, Wright J. The high-frequency effects of U.S. macroeconomic data releases on prices and trading activity in the global interdealer foreign exchange market. Board of Governors of the Federal Reserve System; Volume 823; 2004.

Corsi F, Zumbach G, Müller UA, Dacorogna MM. Consistent high-precision volatility from high-frequency data. Econ Notes Rev Bank Finance Monet Econ 2001;30:183.

Dacorogna MM, Gençay R, Müller UA, Olsen RB, Pictet OV. An introduction to high-frequency finance. San Diego (CA): Academic Press; 2001.

Di Matteo T. Multi-scaling in finance. Quant Finance 2007; 7:21.

Di Matteo T, Aste T, Dacorogna MM. Long term memories of developed and emerging markets: using the scaling analysis to characterize their stage of development. J B ank Finance 2005;29:827.

Dominguez K. The market microstructure of central bank intervention. J Int Econ 2003;59:25.

Engle RF, Ng VK. Measuring and testing the impact of news on volatility. J Finance 1993;48:1749.

Engle RF, Russell JR. Analysis of high frequency financial data. In: Ait-Sahalia Y, Hansen LP, editors. Handbook of financial econometrics. 2006. Forthcoming Elsevier.

Farmer JD, Lillo F. On the origin of power-law tails in price fluctuations. Quant Finance 2004;4:C7.

Gabaix X, Gopikrishnan P, Plerou V, Stanley HE. A theory of power-law distributions in financial market fluctuations. Nature 2003;423:267.

Galluccio S, Caldarelli G, Marsili M, Zhang Y-C. Scaling in currency exchange. Physica A 1997;245:423.

Ghashghaie S, Talkner P, Breymann W, Peinke J, Dodge Y. Turbulent cascades in foreign exchange markets. Nature 1996;381:767.

Glattfelder JB, Dupuis A, Olsen RB. Patterns in high-frequency FX data: Discovery of 12 empirical scaling laws. Quant Finance 2010;11:599. Reprinted by permission of the publisher (Taylor & Francis), www.tandfonline.

Guillaume DM, Dacorogna MM, Davé RD, Müller UA, Olsen RB, Pictet OV. From the bird's eye to the microscope: a survey of new stylized facts of the intra-daily foreign exchange markets. Finance Stoch 1997;1:95.

Joulin A, Lefevre A, Grunberg D, Bouchaud J-P. Stock price jumps: news and volume play a minor role. Wilmott Mag 2008. Sept/Oct, 46, 1 (2008).

Lux T. Financial power laws: empirical evidence, models, and mechanisms. Economics working papers; 2006.

Mandelbrot BB. The variation of certain speculative prices. J Bus 1963;36:394.

Mandelbrot BB, Hudson RL. The (mis)behavior of markets. New York: Basic Books; 2004.

Mantegna RN, Stanley HE. Scaling behavior in the dynamics of an economic index. Nature 1995;376:46.

Müller UA, Dacorogna MM, Olsen RB, Pictet OV, Schwarz M, Morgenegg C. Statistical study of foreign exchange rates, empirical evidence of a price change scaling law, and intraday analysis. J Bank Finance 1990;14:1189.

Newman MEJ. Power laws, Pareto distributions and Zipf's law. Contemp Phys 2005;46:323.

Omrane WB, Bauwens L, Giot P. News announcements, market activity and volatility in the euro/dollar foreign exchange market. J Int Money Finance 2005;24:1108.

Richter CF. Elementary seismology. San Francisco (CA): Freeman; 1958.

Sornette D. Fokker-Planck equation of distributions of financial returns and power laws. Physica A 2000;290:211.

Sornette D. Why stock markets crash: critical events in complex financial systems. Princeton (NJ): Princeton University Press; 2002.

West GB, Brown JH, Enquist BJ. A general model for the origin of allometric scaling laws in biology. Science 1997;276:122.

www.olsen.ch.

www.olseninvest.com.

www.oanda.com.

www.ebs.com.

Zumbach GO, Dacorogna MM, Olsen JL, Olsen RB. Measuring shock in financial markets. Int J Theor Appl 2000;3:347.

CHAPTER TWENTY ONE

# Algorithmic Execution in Foreign Exchange

JAMES E. DALTON
Citibank Foreign Exchange

## 21.1 Introduction

The spot foreign exchange (FX) market continues to evolve at a rapid pace. Hardly, a day goes by without an article hitting the press describing the spectacular growth of market volumes driven by quantitative trading models and the increasing globalization of trade flows. Given the trillions of dollars in volume quoted, traders familiar with the mechanics of other asset classes might assume that the seemingly bottomless liquidity circulating around the globe would negate the requirement to look to execution strategies that have been successfully deployed in the Equity Markets. (Particularly given the compression of spreads throughout the past 5 years) yet, there are significant savings to be made by adopting algorithms for the appropriate type of FX orderflow. For an increasing number of institutions, the combination of transparency, cost savings, and anonymity that an algorithmic provider can offer makes them an important option to have available complimenting traditional risk pricing when managing execution. The growth in volume has arrived alongside significant changes in market microstructure and just as in other asset classes; algorithmic tools are finding their way onto the desktops of traders across the globe.

This chapter steps through the progression we have seen in this field over recent years and some of the execution tools becoming available for traders to help them navigate a continuously transforming marketplace.

*Handbook of Exchange Rates*, First Edition. Edited by Jessica James, Ian W. Marsh, and Lucio Sarno.

Algorithmic trading can mean many different things, and it is easy to confuse the different business models that the word "algo" can infer. In the interests of clarity, refer to the following definitions in order to categorize the trading behavior that falls into the various algorithmic buckets.

*Electronic Market Making:* The electronic provision of liquidity to electronic brokers, exchanges or to clients directly.

*Systematic Proprietary Trading:* This is the business of trading signals generated from mathematical models.

*High Frequency Arbitrage:* This is the business of exploiting a range of electronic "tells" to enter very short-term positions (many of which are subsecond) while taking on as little risk as possible. Arbitrage players exploit a range of market behavioural traits, from naïve order placement strategies and the difference in dealing protocols on the various exchanges, through to the different speeds which firms are able to support via their connectivity infrastructure.

*Algorithmic Execution:* The systematic execution of client orders utilizing many of the processes and software, which have evolved out of the activities mentioned above.

### 21.1.1 DRAWING FROM THE EQUITY MARKET

The first generation of execution algorithms that were introduced to FX clients were very simple TWAP (time weighted average price) order types. These were typically setup to run against a single bank or series of bank price streams via the early providers of liquidity aggregation services. The value equation was pretty straightforward; break an order into little pieces and spread it out over time in order to minimize the bid offer spread you pay, as well as the market impact. Similar techniques were originally deployed on the program trading desks of equity brokers. While at first, this methodology helped reduce the market impact of larger institutional orders, this behavior gave rise to the first generation of systematic arbitrage players who effectively monitored and took advantage of the predictability of the approach.

The evolution of algorithmic execution in equities is well documented and has given rise to alternative exchanges, dark pools, and crossing networks (for example, please see Appendix A). The exchanges themselves continue to invest millions of dollars into the technology infrastructure required to support the exponential increase in both speed and transaction quantities the market demands to function. Any large buy-side player has dozens of brokers lined up with a list of algorithms to choose from for execution, ranging from simple participation or volume-linked strategies through to the latest iterations of liquidity seeking algorithms that dynamically respond to market conditions in real time. Many brokers can now offer customization services and in some cases the ability to link algorithms based on shifts in price or volatility. The A-Team group provide an excellent annual reference guide that details the breadth of products available from various banks and brokers (Appendix A).

### 21.1.2 WHAT IS GOING TO WORK FOR FOREIGN EXCHANGE?

At first glance, porting strategies directly from equities and deploying them in FX would appear to make sense. There are, however, significant differences between the two markets that need to be taken into account. To begin with, the bulk of FX trading is still conducted over-the-counter (OTC). This leaves many participants in the dark when it comes to the actual amount of volume dealt at any given price level, unlike equities where traded volumes are publicly available (information on which many of the popular equity algorithmic strategies are dependent).

When comparing the structures of both markets, we can see a degree of convergence taking place, as internalization capabilities gather pace in equities and are combined with the DMA (direct market access) offerings already established. That is pretty much where the similarities end, to understand why you need to consider the way FX market structure has evolved. Whichever way you look at it, roughly 50% of all FX transactions are now initiated and managed by an algorithm via an API connection to a bank or electronic broker. The most effective way to engage with this market going forward will be via algorithms. Not many buy-side firms have the resource bandwidth or budget required to develop independent strategies, it will be up to the sell side to create product in this space in order to support the growing demand.

Figures 21.1 and 21.2 illustrate the changes in market structure over the past decade.

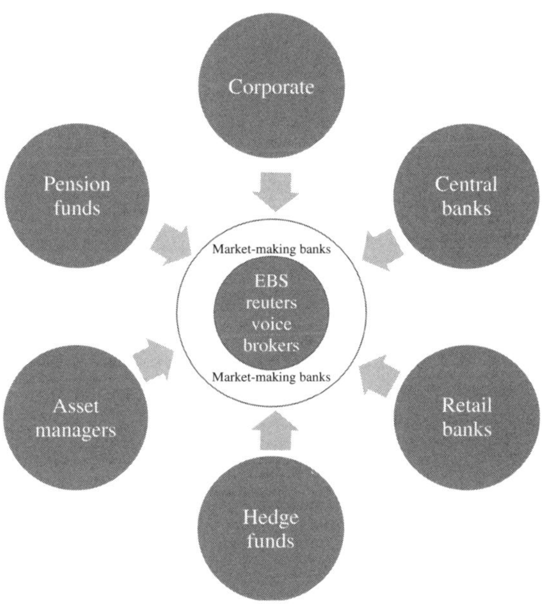


FIGURE 21.1 Market structure 10 years ago.

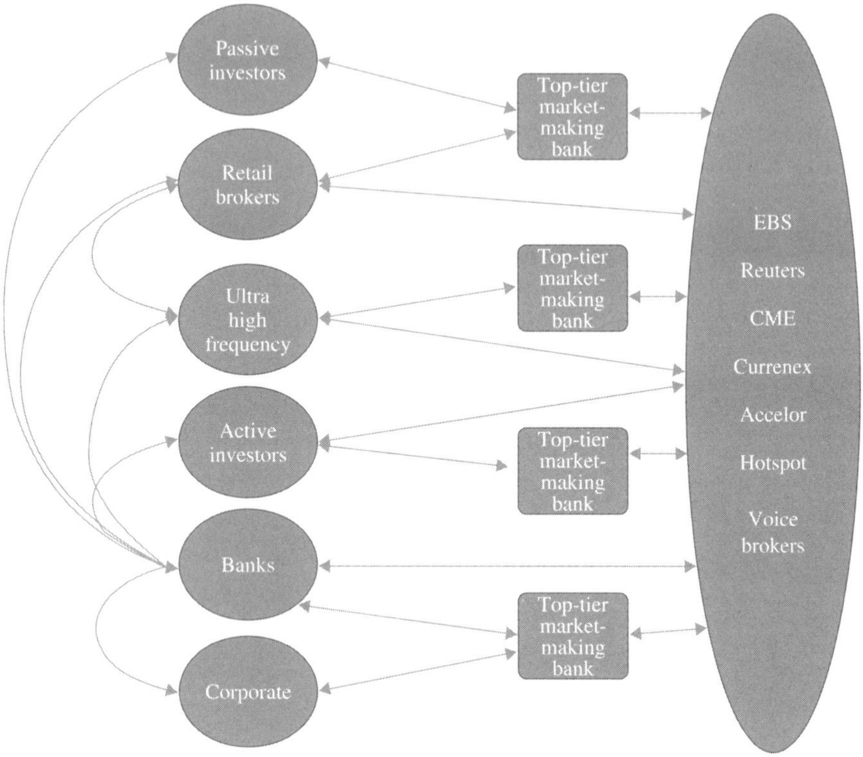


FIGURE 21.2 Current structure.

At this point, the majority of buy-side clients were dependent on one or more direct bank relationships in order to access FX liquidity.

Market-making banks called each other directly for pricing and trading through the voice and electronic broker community. Market information was concentrated amongst the major players and the bid/offer spreads quoted were significantly wider than what is available today.

Electronic trading has transformed the marketplace into one where the lines between client and competitor are increasingly blurred. To accurately represent every liquidity provision relationship type would create a chart akin to a spider's web; in the diagram above, any reference to the multi-bank trading channels that service much of the traditional buy side has been intentionally left out. You can assume that nearly all client to bank relationships are one-to-many. The main points to note are the following:

- Prime brokerage services have brought numerous participants directly onto the liquidity pools that were historically controlled by banks and brokers. Volume growth from the statistical arbitrage and non-bank market makers has been enormous in recent years.

- The direct market between banks is almost exclusively serviced by API connections and single-bank portals (while top-tier banks no longer call each other directly).
- The number of ECNs (such as LAVA, Hotspot, or Currenex) and exchanges offering anonymous trading services has grown.
- Banks and non-bank market makers are sometimes in direct competition for client business.
- The top tier of market-making banks has captured the lion's share of client volume.
- The retail market has grown to the point where it is a recognized customer group that banks compete aggressively for.
- Aggregation technology is now commonplace with multiple vendors competing for market share of bank and hedge fund trading desks. These platforms are beginning to focus on clients currently served by ECNs that have cornered a large segment of the traditional investor FX volume as an untapped market.
- Buy-side clients are increasingly taking advantage of both anonymous and direct-trading channels.

However, the most significant change is the pace at which information now rattles around the marketplace and how this impacts price.

Any aggressive activity on the CME will have an immediate effect on the prices shown in EBS; likewise significant divergence of an economic indicator from its estimated value will instantly change the size and skew of the spreads available on just about any destination available to trade.

This has given rise to a generation of quantitative analysts and programmers, who have been drawn into both the bank and non-bank market makers and who control an increasing share of market liquidity. There are thousands of electronic eyes on the market, ready to profit from one false step or latent price; failure to navigate this environment with the appropriate level of awareness and the right combination of technology is going to cost money. The adoption of algorithmic execution tools makes clear sense for any business that trades regularly or in size.

## 21.2 Key Components of an Algorithmic Execution Framework

### 21.2.1 SMART ORDER ROUTING (SOR)

A core competitive element within any algorithmic framework is the ability to receive and interpret market data from multiple destinations as quickly as possible, in order to be able to act on the intelligence gathered before opportunities pass. The same infrastructure is used to manage order placement on the range of exchanges or liquidity pools you can trade on.

While the software required to implement a market aggregation capability is easily acquired via a growing number of EMS vendors (execution management system), they will not on their own provide the "smarts" required to deliver an edge in terms of SOR (smart order routing). To get this right, you need to be constantly refining the logic that determines the best destination at a point in time to hit a price or post an order. Best price can mean more than just the absolute value of a price available (net of brokerage). An aggressive algorithm will take into account different factors to a passive algorithm when prioritizing order flow. If there are identical prices available on two electronic broker platforms, a passive strategy will generally be directed toward the price with the most volume behind it and may very well consume only a subset of the volume available in order to avoid signaling to market. On the other hand, it may avoid the more liquid destination, if the market participants on that platform are more predatory and the likelihood of order flow being gamed there is higher. An aggressive algorithm may simply go for both at once or it may prioritize one over another if the matching protocol on one exchange decreases the probability of an attempt to deal being completed successfully.

This is a very tactical portion of any algorithmic team's focus. As new order types and functionality are enabled on the APIs connecting to the dominant brokerages, every market maker and execution specialist is compelled to spend time evaluating the benefit or impact of adjusting their order placement logic.

The combinations are endless and the ongoing changes in market structure make SOR a perpetual research and development project.

### 21.2.2 INTELLIGENCE

This is where the quants really begin to add value, and where the emerging algorithmic execution service providers will seek to develop competitive advantage. Building intelligence into any algorithmic platform involves the painstaking process of sifting through terabytes of tick data and looking for statistical patterns that can help you predict liquidity, locate meaningful correlations between instruments, or determine real market volume. Every country's currency trades in a unique way, ebbs and flows of natural trade, combined with investor-related activity, creates a volume profile that can differ significantly between pairs. The volume profile of a currency at a microstructure level is crucial input toward any liquidity-linked execution solution. (See comparison between EURUSD and USDCAD in Figure 21.3. Note that CAD liquidity does not increase until the NY/London overlap, whereas EUR sees a pickup in the early hours.)

The lack of complete market data can make tracking volume difficult, any model that is built needs to be continually refined.

True intelligence can inject a layer of quality into an execution strategy that will provide an edge as more of the market steps back from trading by hand.

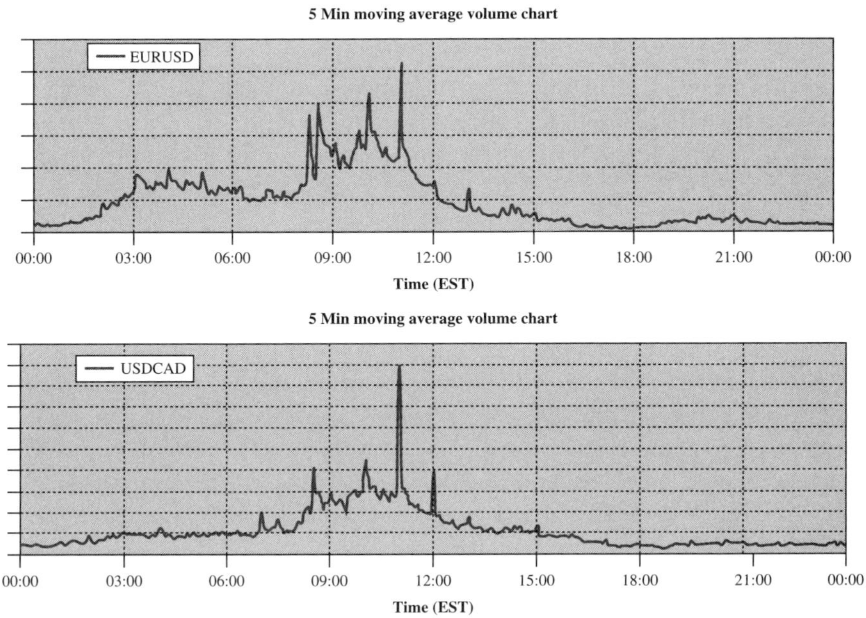


FIGURE 21.3 Liquidity curves for EURUSD and USDCAD.

Intelligence helps you optimize the timing and speed of execution; SOR takes care of the tactical implementation once a decision to execute has been made.

### 21.2.3 SPEED

Speed is vital and the game played by the ultrahigh frequency market makers or arbitrage houses has shifted from milliseconds to microseconds; this has raised the bar in terms of the investment required by banks to keep pace with the street. Many of the fastest firms on the street have created their own bespoke exoskeletal infrastructure, fine-tuned to perform in a high velocity environment. For firms without the expertise required to build something bespoke, there are multiple vendor solutions on the market that can offer ready baked functionality alongside consulting services. Colocation services, where infrastructure housing trading models are placed within close proximity to exchanges or connectivity hubs, were the domain of Futures and Equity houses up until recent times. There are now numerous firms that have invested heavily in the FX market and can provide specialist hosting and connectivity solutions for both buy-side and sell-side players. Data centers are strategically located as close as possible to matching engines and exchanges, all in the name of eliminating the latency inherent in legacy networks. While the costs associated with maintaining a competitive edge are significant, they can pale in comparison to the scale of opportunities lost in a fast moving market when running slower infrastructure.

## 21.3 Types of Algorithms

There are numerous strategies available for traders to use right now, they range in characteristics and need to be sufficiently understood before you begin applying them to your order flow. The list following contains an overview of what each style offers.

### 21.3.1 TIME SLICERS

TWAP algorithms are already used extensively and perform the basic function of minimizing spread over a predetermined time horizon.

They range from the simplest of drones executing small clips into a single or aggregated stream of prices at regular intervals through to peg and pay strategies. These will attempt to avoid paying spread by posting interest into markets while observing randomization parameters around order size and aggression timings. They work just fine for passive orders; however, their performance is generally tied to market direction, kind of like beta returns on an index portfolio. If the target interval for execution is set too aggressively, they can underperform significantly.

### 21.3.2 SWEEPER

This type of algorithm sends a series of "fill or kill" orders out to multiple markets within a predetermined limit price. They are designed to soak up maximum liquidity within the shortest time frame possible. Typically deployed when there is an immediate need to clear risk and will very likely cause short-term disruption to the market (Figure 21.4).

### 21.3.3 ICEBERG

This is really more a smart order type than an algorithm and many of the ECNs provide these as part of their generic order suite. The idea is simple, show a tip on the bid (if buying) that is a small proportion of your total amount and replace at market as each prior order is filled. They can be submitted on exchanges or hosted within an algorithmic engine. Close observation is required when running these, as you can find yourself chasing a moving target unless you have an aggression function incorporated (Figure 21.5).

### 21.3.4 OPPORTUNISTIC

A combination of the previous two categories, an opportunistic algorithm is often built with a variety of aggression settings. The level of aggression generally determines how much is completed by crossing the spread. These will often contain discretion parameters that deal faster into a tighter market and slow down if spreads gap (Figure 21.6).

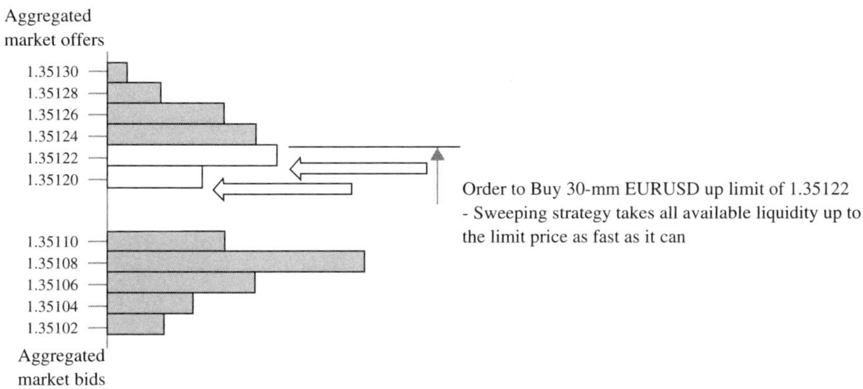


FIGURE 21.4 Sweeper.

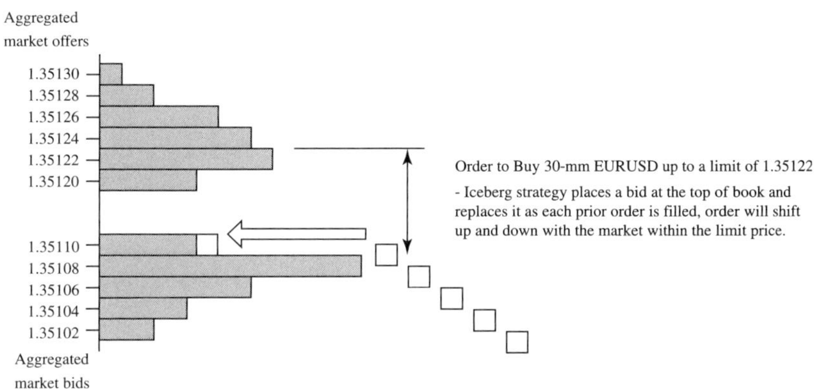


FIGURE 21.5 Iceberg.

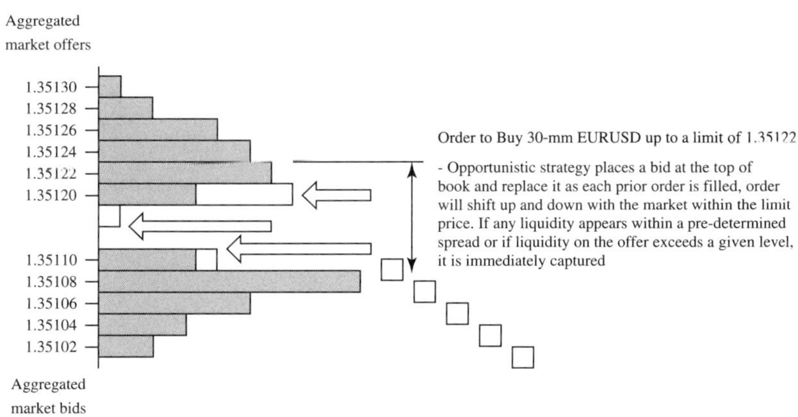


FIGURE 21.6 Opportunistic.

### 21.3.5 PARTICIPATORS

While relatively simple to build for an equity strategy, the lack of absolute volume data in FX makes targeting a percentage of market volume hard to achieve. Building a successful participation algorithm, requires the development of a proxy measure of volume that is sufficiently accurate to enable you to execute without disrupting the market. VWAP (volume weighted average price) algorithms are a derivative of the same logic (Figure 21.7).

### 21.3.6 INTERNALIZATION STRATEGIES

These are provided by the top tier of banks that handle a significant proportion of electronic client flow. There are countless methods that can be used to construct an internalization algorithm and each bank approaches it differently. The underlying principle is that the portfolio of flows from clients across multiple currencies and crosses enables orders to be run into the risk book at an optimal speed, minimizing the need to tap into the external market and protecting your order information from prying electronic eyes (Figure 21.8).

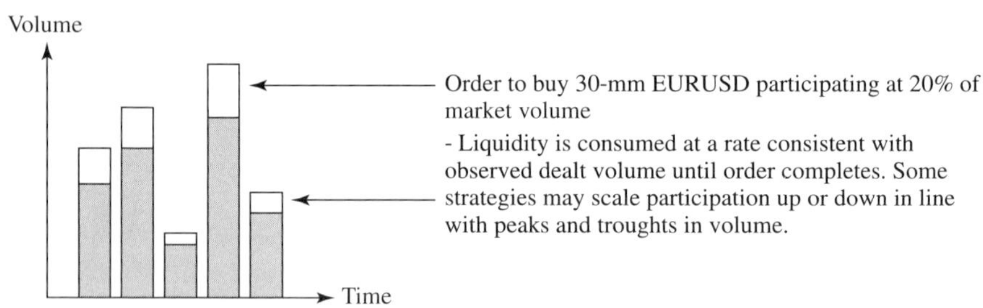


FIGURE 21.7 Participator.

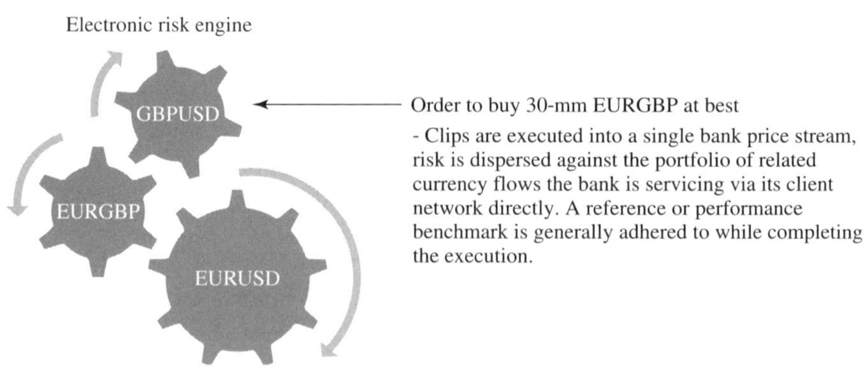


FIGURE 21.8 Internalization strategy.

### 21.3.7 DYNAMIC ALGORITHMS

Essentially a high frequency trading model tuned to optimize execution on a real-time basis. The hardest to construct and yet to hit the street; this type of algorithm will attempt to enhance performance while in action by reacting to a combination of price, volatility, and predictive signals.

## 21.4 What Execution Strategies are Most Effective?

As a general rule of thumb, if your trading goals and performance are centred on targeting specific market levels or taking advantage of short-term volatility, then risk pricing or aggressive algorithms are the only way to execute. For more strategic or passive trades, the adoption of algorithms is likely to enhance your bottom line.

Fredrik Wingren from Informed Portfolio Management (IPM) in Stockholm has extensive experience running FX algorithms for execution. "As a systematic model driven asset manager, minimising slippage is a key element in reducing transaction costs. With IPM's medium-long term investment approach, it makes little sense to execute as a block trade and pay a premium. Rather, we rather use algorithms to adapt to the size and speed of the execution in actual liquidity conditions and accept the volatility risk over the longer execution period."

Figure 21.9 details the range of drivers of execution and the optimal execution methods assigned to them.

**Short Term Trading**

Drivers of execution
- Price action
- Technical signals
- Flow information
- News
- Arbitrage

Execution requirements
- Speed
- Tight spreads
- Immediate confirmation

Execution methods
- Bank portals
- Multi-bank portals
- Liquidity aggregators
- Aggressive algorithms
- Phone

**Positioning/Hedging**

Drivers of execution
- Currency models
- Macro perspective
- Balance sheet hedging
- Portfolio hedging
- Currency overlay

Execution requirements
- Minimum market impact
- Rate transparecy
- Automation
- Cost control

Execution methods
- Bank portals
- Multi-bank portals
- Passive algorithms
- Aggressive algorithms
- Phone

**Secondary FX**

Drivers of execution
- Cash management
- Transition management
- Securities settlement
- Index rebalancing

Execution requirements
- Minimum market impact
- Rate transparency
- Automation
- Cost control

Execution methods
- Bank portals
- Multi-bank portals
- Passive algorithms
- Benchmark or WM
- Custodial services

FIGURE 21.9 Identifying your execution needs.

### 21.4.1 MEASURING PERFORMANCE

Transaction cost measurement in FX is still a subjective process in many institutions and in some cases almost ignored. Running algorithms provides traders and asset managers with a framework within which they can begin to accurately gauge the most cost-effective approach to execution. Having access to transparent, time stamped data around executions will help firms determine what solution to deploy based on their trading style, order size, market conditions, and currency pair.

Any method of execution applied to market order flow needs to be measured against more than a single benchmark in order to establish its level of effectiveness.

The appropriate benchmark depends on the nature of the algorithm deployed, how it has been configured to run, and any underlying execution goals.

If a trader sets and manages limits on an order while it runs, or if a very long duration is set for an execution, that discretionary input needs to be taken into account, as net execution performance will be very closely tied to the execution trader's market knowledge and decision-making skills. In the case of a very passive execution over a long period, the market average price or a volume weighted average become the only relevant benchmarks.

The litmus test for an algorithmic strategy is a direct comparison to available risk pricing over a portfolio of trades, if risk pricing cannot be improved on, then switching to an alternative algorithm or back to risk pricing is the next logical step. Passing this test is no small feat, as ongoing competition for client volume amongst major sell-side players has ensured that risk spreads remain extraordinarily tight.

## 21.5 Looking Forward

Ongoing investment in front office technology and the endless stream of market initiatives launched in an attempt to catch a slice of the FX pie will ensure that algorithmic execution remains in focus for the future. The ability to provide quality algorithms will be promoted by banks eager to maintain relevance with their clients. Competition can also be expected from a number of agency style service providers, introducing products in much the same way that equity market makers and proprietary trading firms have for listed instruments. Dark pools of liquidity have been introduced to the market in various guises over recent years with minimal take-up; the potential is there for them to gain momentum in the future. There is no stopping market evolution, in the current environment, any offering that provides a combination of savings, transparency, and automation is bound to continue to attract attention.

## APPENDIX A

See http://www.a-teamgroup.com/article/algorithmic-trading-directory-2011-edition/.

# REFERENCES

Trading and Exchanges: Market Microstructure for Practitioners: Larry Harris.

The Speed Traders: An Insider's Look at the New High-Frequency Trading Phenomenon That is Transforming the Investing World—Edgar Perez.

Algorithmic Trading and DMA: An introduction to direct access trading strategies—Barry Johnson.

CHAPTER TWENTY TWO

# Foreign Exchange Strategy Based Products

AYSU SECMEN
Citigroup Centre

## 22.1 Introduction

Investable foreign exchange (FX) indices and FX-strategy-based products have grown substantially over the past few years. There are a number of institutions now that offer as investments a wide range of indices tracking the performance of FX strategies such as carry or trend. None of these offerings were available 10 years ago. This growth is fueled by an ever increasing demand to gain exposure to the returns from active currency investments. A large number of investors ranging from retail to institutional are after the returns from the FX market. Whether the reason behind this interest is a desire to find alternative sources of positive returns or to achieve diversification, currencies are becoming increasingly popular and FX is starting to claim the place it deserves in investment portfolios.

A recent survey conducted by RBC Capital Markets in 2010 of 102 asset managers who manage a total of approximately $4.1 trillion of assets showed that currency tops the list of asset classes that fund managers are most likely to move into over the next 12 months, ahead of equities and commodities. This presents a clear contrast to the situation as recently as 10 years ago, when FX was seen only as a nuisance and as an undesired and often ignored side effect instead of an opportunity. So what has changed in the last decade? What is the reason that investable FX indices and strategy-based products have recently become so appealing?

*Handbook of Exchange Rates*, First Edition. Edited by Jessica James, Ian W. Marsh, and Lucio Sarno.

In this chapter, we provide an overview of investable FX indices and FX-strategy-based products. In Section 22.2, we start with a brief history of FX market since the collapse of the Bretton Woods System and then show how the market and its players have grown. In Section 22.3, we outline how investable FX indices have evolved and explain why FX has gained popularity as an asset class on its own. Finally, we show that investments in currencies are attractive both in absolute and relative terms, as well as from a portfolio diversification point of view.

## 22.2 Evolution of the Foreign Exchange Market

### 22.2.1 DISAPPOINTING EARLY YEARS

FX is a relatively young market and currencies as liquid market instruments have come rather late to the stage in the history of global markets. The Bretton Woods conference held in July 1944 aimed to redesign the world monetary system and is a key milestone in the history of modern currencies. As a result of the conference, a system of coordinated exchange rate management was set up that remained in place until the early 1970s. Under the Bretton Woods agreement, currencies were not permanently fixed but managed with occasional devaluations allowed to correct for imbalances in the balance of payments. During this time period of adjustable pegs, currencies were naturally not seen as instruments that could be traded to make profit. However, once the Bretton Woods System collapsed in the 1970s and currencies started to move freely, FX started to become interesting to investors.

After the collapse of Bretton Woods, exchange rates were initially expected to move according to monetary models. However, Meese and Rogoff's (1983) findings regarding the failure of economic models in forecasting exchange rates was a major disappointment and a source of confusion. In their pioneering work on exchange rate predictability in "Empirical Exchange Rate Models of the Seventies: Do they fit out-of-sample?" the authors compared the out-of-sample forecasting accuracy of various time series and structural models of exchange rates. They found that a random walk model could forecast as well as any of the tested models at 1- to 12-month horizons. Hence, both in academia and in the investment community, it was generally agreed that currencies at best follow a random walk and are impossible to forecast. Investors were discouraged by findings similar to Meese and Rogoff's (1983) and stayed away from currencies.

In the early years of the free floating regime, investors with international exposures or corporations with overseas businesses mostly ignored the impact currencies had on their bottom line. This had limited impact, as international exposures were still relatively low and larger investments tended to be in neighbor countries where there were strong links between currencies.

During the 1970s and into the 1980s, FX was not viewed as an asset class, as it was considered to be a zero-sum game. If currencies follow a random walk, how is it possible to forecast them and make money? Investors saw currencies as a source of volatility but not return. Another contributing factor to this view was the fact that FX is a rate of exchange and not an index ultimately linked to ownership of some underlying item of value. To buy a currency, one has to sell another currency. Hence, one investor's gain is another's loss. Unlike stocks, exchange rates do not have any positive growth expectations, and consequently there is no passive buy and hold strategy like in equities. Because of these arguments, FX market "beta" was thought to be zero and currencies were not included in traditional investment portfolios with equities and bonds.

### 22.2.2 EMERGENCE OF "PUZZLES" IN FX

In the late 1980s and early 1990s, with enough high quality data available and the help of advances in computing, academics started looking in detail into the behavior of exchange rates and research in currencies took off. A large amount of empirical research appeared and slowly consistent themes and "anomalies" or "puzzles" kept surfacing in FX. New evidence showing the profitability of simple trading rules in currencies emerged.

One of these anomalies is famously known as the *forward-rate puzzle* and is closely related to the carry trade, one of the most popular trading strategies in FX. Uncovered interest parity (UIP) asserts that expected returns on foreign and domestic deposits should be equal when converted to the same currency and hence the expected change in the spot rate should be equal to the interest rate differential. If UIP holds, forward rates must be unbiased predictors of spot rates. If the domestic interest rates are lower (higher) then the currency should appreciate (depreciate). However, evidence shows that this is not the case, and in fact, spot rates are more likely to move away from the forward rates instead of moving toward them. This implies that UIP does not hold and profits can thus be generated by doing the so-called carry trade, that is, using forward contracts to short low yielding currencies against the high yielding ones. Profits are essentially earned on the interest rate differential between the countries of the currency pair assuming that the spot does not move too far against the higher-yielding one. The early findings of Bilson (1981) and the frequently quoted paper of Fama (1984) are among the first papers documenting the existence of the forward-rate puzzle. The failure of UIP is now almost unanimously accepted by both the academia and the finance practitioners.

The other well-documented anomaly from the late 1980s and early 1990s was the profitability of momentum trading and the trending behavior of currencies. We call this an anomaly because it is a direct violation of efficient market hypothesis that asserts that one should not be able to generate profits by using the past price action as the current price should contain all relevant information. Several papers documented that currencies demonstrate statistically significant trends and show some degree of serial correlation. Levich and Thomas (1993); Sweeney (1986); Taylor and Allen (1992), and Silber (1994) are among the many who investigated the significance of momentum trading and have shown that profits can be made. A study by Park and Irwin (2004), which provides a comprehensive review of the theoretical and empirical studies on technical trading shows that there were 42 studies on the topic from 1960 to 1987 and the number more than doubled between 1988 and 2004, increasing to 92. Of course, some papers refute the value of momentum strategies and the like, but Park and Irwin (2004) show that for currencies, the number of studies showing profitability of technical trading is far higher than the number showing no profits. The explanations for the existence of the anomaly include the herding behavior of traders, central bank interventions, and risk premium, among others.

Following the strong academic evidence, momentum- and carry-based trading gained popularity in the investment community during the 1990s. It became clear that if one could correctly judge where an FX rate was headed, there was money to be made, regardless of the question of whether it is an asset or not.

During this decade, increased globalization led to an exponential growth in cross-border trading that in turn resulted in an increase in trading volume in the FX market. As their international exposures grew, corporations and investors began to realize that they could no longer ignore the impact of currencies. The FX market began to take off. Bid-offer spreads narrowed, liquidity spread to emerging market currencies, and FX developed beyond having just market makers and takers. Proprietary traders, CTAs, and hedge funds began to develop as a community and their interest in trading FX grew along with them. The highly predictable era preceding the introduction of the Euro strengthened investors' belief that currency movements could be reliably forecast, and the depth and liquidity of the new European currency tempted bigger players to the market. Currency overlay and active management became more accepted as investment strategies. Surveys published during these years by consultancies revealed with overwhelming evidence that currency trading could indeed add value. Strange (1998), who examined the performance of 152 individual overlay programs managed by 11 firms, showed that currency overlay managers have generated about 1.9% return per year on an average over a 10-year period from 1988 to 1998. Two years later, a study conducted by Baldridge et al. (2000) had similar results. All these developments helped making the case for currency trading and by the time of the new millennium, currency had become widely accepted as an asset class.

### 22.2.3 GROWTH OF FX MARKET TURNOVER AND CURRENCY MANAGERS

The growth and changing composition of the FX market can be best seen by looking at the results of the Bank of International Settlements (BIS) surveys. BIS conducts a triennial survey of FX market activity since 1989. The objective of the survey is to provide the most comprehensive and internationally consistent information on the size and structure of global FX markets. The results of the latest survey show that today with its average daily turnover above $4 trillion FX is the largest and most liquid market in the world. This turnover is about eight

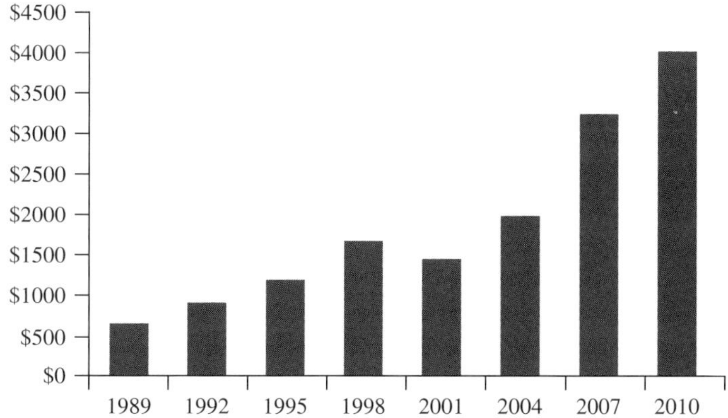


**FIGURE 22.1** Average daily global foreign exchange market turnover (in billions of US dollar). *Source*: Bank of International Settlements.

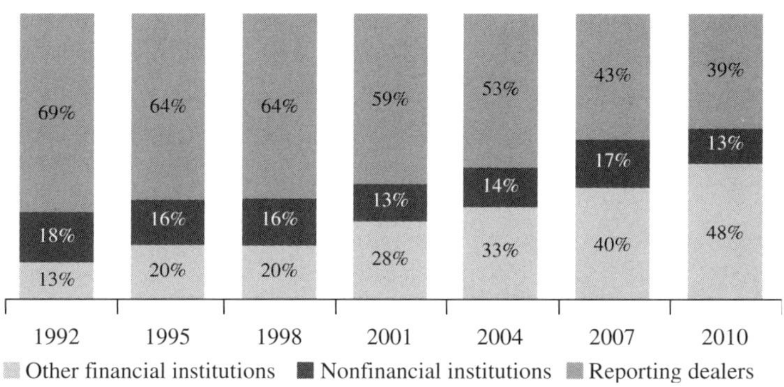


**FIGURE 22.2** Share of market turnover by counterparty. *Source*: Bank of International Settlements.

times the daily turnover of the world equities and five times to that of the US bond market. Even in the darkest moments of the recent global crisis, FX trades could still be done fairly smoothly albeit at higher bid-offer spreads.

Figure 22.1 shows how the trading in the FX market has grown since 1989. The current average daily turnover in the global FX market is about 6.4 times the turnover in 1989 and has increased by an average of 33% between consecutive surveys. Figure 22.2 shows the share of turnover by counterparty. This graph is helpful in understanding the changing composition and importance of different players in the market. Brief descriptions of the counterparty categories as defined by BIS[1] are given below:

- "Reporting dealers" are defined as financial institutions that actively participate in local and global FX and derivatives markets. These are mainly large

[1] See Triennial Central Bank Survey Report on Global Foreign Exchange Market Activity in 2010.

commercial and investment banks and securities houses that (i) participate in the interdealer market and/or (ii) have active business with large customers such as large corporate firms, governments, and other nonreporting financial institutions; in other words, reporting dealers are institutions that are actively buying and selling currency and OTC derivatives both for their own account and/or to meet customer demand. In practice, reporting dealers are often those institutions that actively or regularly deal through electronic platforms such as EBS or Reuters dealing facilities. The category of reporting dealers also includes the branches and subsidiaries of institutions operating in multiple locations that have sales desks, but not necessarily trading desks, which conduct active business with large customers.

- "Other financial institutions" are defined as those financial institutions that are not classified as reporting dealers. Thus, the term mainly covers all other financial institutions, such as smaller commercial banks, investment banks, and securities houses, and in addition mutual funds, pension funds, hedge funds, currency funds, money market funds, building societies, leasing companies, insurance companies, financial subsidiaries of corporate firms, and central banks.
- "Nonfinancial institutions" are defined as any counterparty other than those described above, that is, mainly nonfinancial end users such as corporations and governments.

We see that trading in currency markets has increased over 20% between 2007 and 2010. The survey shows that the higher global FX market turnover is mostly associated with the increased trading activity of hedge funds, pension funds, mutual funds, and insurance companies. The turnover in this category grew by 42%, increasing from $1.3 trillion to $1.9 trillion between 2007 and 2010. Just 9 years ago, the total daily turnover in this category was a mere $346 billion. The surge in trading for this segment of the market is a clear evidence that FX is now seen as a true asset.

The rising popularity of FX as a viable investment strategy can also be seen by looking at the number of programs in the Barclay Currency Traders Index shown in Figure 22.3. This index is one of the longest running indices measuring the performance of currency managers. It is an equally weighted composite of managed programs that trade currency futures and cash forwards in the interbank market. Currently, the index consists of 119 currency programs. From 1999 to 2010, the number of currency managers in Barclay Currency Traders Index has increased from 47 to 119.

Looking at the total assets under management, we get a similar picture. Figure 22.4 shows the assets under management for both the Barclay Currency Traders and Managed Futures indices. Note that the latter index covers all CTA assets under management, but currency futures and options are one of the most significant instruments in managed futures programs. In the past 11 years, the total amount of assets of currency managers almost tripled, rising from $6 billion to $17.5 billion. Similarly, the assets under management for the managed futures increased from $41 billion in 1999 to $223 billion in 2010.

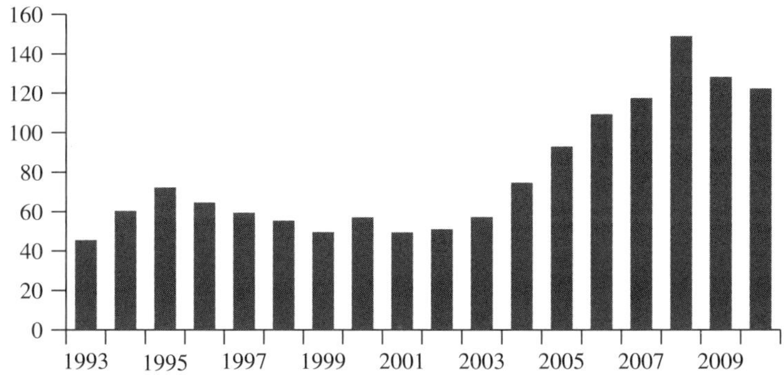


**FIGURE 22.3** **Number of programs in Barclay currency traders index.**
*Source*: BarclayHedge.

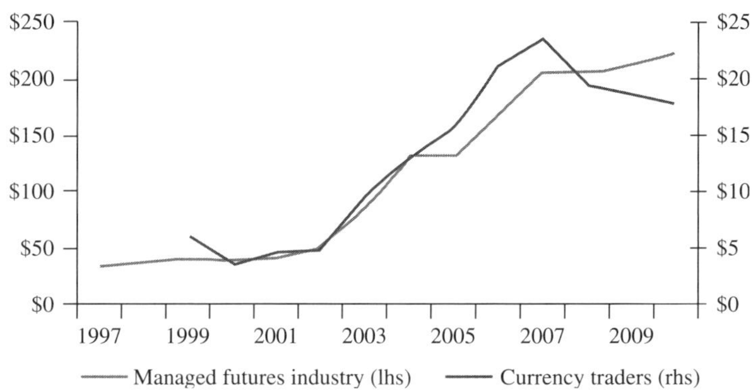


**FIGURE 22.4** **Assets under management (in billions of US dollar).** *Source*: **BarclayHedge.**

Obviously, the growth shown in Figure above is driven by the success of investors who make profits trading currencies. We have already mentioned that several surveys conducted in the 1990s and 2000s consistently showed that currency managers can generate positive returns. Table 22.1 and Figure 22.5 show the performance of currency trading programs for which we have the longest history. One of the indices used is the Barclay Currency Traders Index as mentioned earlier. The other one is the CTA Asset Weighted Currency Index that reflects the performance of currency CTAs reporting to the Center for International Securities and Derivatives Markets (CISDM) at the University of Massachusetts Amherst.

Both the Barclay and CISDM indices have information ratios around 0.7 since 1990 and show that currency programs have generated 6.7% and 8.0% per year on average, respectively. It is clear that there were ample return opportunities in the currency market in the last few decades even while the existence of a beta in FX was being questioned.

**TABLE 22.1 Performance of Currency Trading Programs**

| | Barclay Currency Traders Index | CISDM CTA Asset Weighted Currency Index |
|---|---|---|
| Annual return | 6.7% | 8.0% |
| Annualised risk | 9.8% | 10.6% |
| Information ratio | 0.68 | 0.75 |
| Max drawdown | 15.8% | 33.0% |

*Source*: BarclayHedge, CISDM.

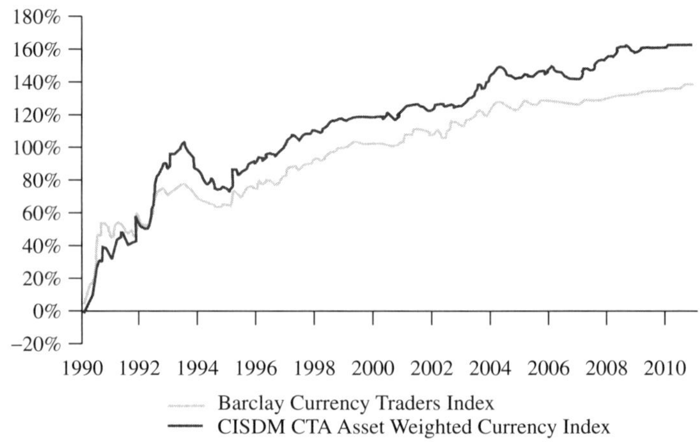


FIGURE 22.5 Performance of currency trading programs. *Source*: BarclayHedge, CISDM.

## 22.3 Foreign Exchange Investable Indices and Strategy-Based Products

### 22.3.1 WHY PROFIT OPPORTUNITIES EXIST?

We showed in Section 22.1 how much FX market has grown over the years and how big it actually is compared to the bond and equity markets. If the market is so deep with tight spreads, should we not expect the inefficiencies to be traded away? How is it possible to make money from FX?

The efficient market hypothesis assumes that investors are rational and are all profit oriented. However, in the FX market, the majority of the players are not motivated by profits from FX. The trading volumes are dominated by players whose goal is not necessarily to make money from FX. Currencies are bought or sold by central banks driven by policy; by corporations for hedging purposes, to make payments for expenses, or to repatriate earnings; by funds to rebalance international equity or bond exposures; and, finally, by tourists. According to estimates, a substantial portion of the daily trading volume is not profit oriented and is instead based on a need to simply exchange currencies. This means that the pure profit-oriented volume does not dominate the total volume traded. Hence, the FX market economically is inefficient and returns can potentially be generated.

Note that the alpha seeking portion of the currency market is included in "other financial institutions" in Figure 22.2. The share of the daily turnover for this category has increased from 13% to 48% between 1992 and 2010. However, note that the majority of this category is still nonspeculative as far as FX goes and includes passive players investing in international portfolios.

### 22.3.2 BETA AND ALPHA IN FOREIGN EXCHANGE

Assuming that the FX market is indeed inefficient and some profit opportunities exist, what are some basic FX investment styles? As mentioned earlier, even though there is no simple "buy and hold" strategy like in equities, there are transparent and simple investment strategies following systematic rules that can be used to generate consistent returns from currencies. Three of the most common strategies are carry, momentum, and valuation. They continue to be the foundations of systematic FX trading and are widely used by the investment community while also backed by substantial academic research as we mentioned in Section 22.2.2.

- *Carry*. This strategy buys higher-yielding currencies and sells lower yielding ones with the aim of earning a positive return if the spot rate fails to move toward the forward rate. There are variants of this strategy, but many investors simply rank 1- or 3-month deposit rates and buy the currencies associated with the highest ranks and sell the ones with the lowest ranks. This strategy is used to trade both developed and emerging market currencies.
- *Momentum*. This strategy is based on the idea that there is consistency in short- and medium-term currency moves. If a currency has appreciated then it is likely to continue to appreciate in the short term, and vice versa. The simplest version of this strategy ranks the currency pairs by the absolute magnitude of spot moves over the past month or quarter and takes positions in currency pairs that have experienced the largest moves in the past. This strategy is used to trade both developed and emerging market currencies.
- *Valuation*. This strategy assumes that exchange rates will converge to fair value when misvaluations are significantly large. In simplest versions of this strategy, measures such as OECD purchasing power parities are used for fair-value estimates and currencies are ranked by the absolute magnitude of the misvaluations between the spot rates and the fair-value estimates. Positions are taken in pairs which have the largest misvaluations assuming that there will be a convergence to fair value.

In early 2007, we introduced the CitiFX Beta index that combines the three currency trading styles above into a simple and transparent benchmark. The

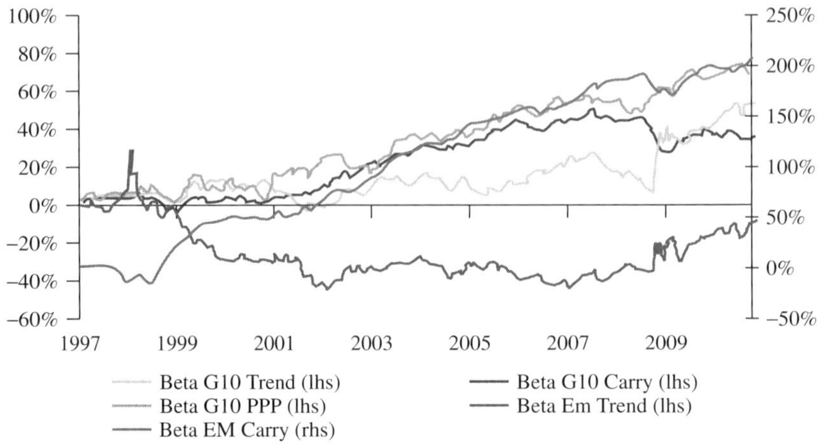


FIGURE 22.6 CitiFX Beta indices cumulative returns. *Source*: Citi.

TABLE 22.2 **Performance of CitiFX Beta Indices**

| | Beta G10 Trend, % | Beta G10 Carry, % | Beta G10 PPP, % | Beta EM Trend, % | Beta EM Carry, % |
|---|---|---|---|---|---|
| Annual return | 3.9 | 2.3 | 5.0 | −1.2 | 14.4 |
| Annualised risk | 11.0 | 6.1 | 9.3 | 11.4 | 10.7 |
| Information ratio | 0.4 | 0.4 | 0.5 | −0.1 | 1.3 |
| Max drawdown | 23 | 24 | 13 | 69 | 25 |

*Source*: Citi.

index represents the market portfolio return for currencies. In Figure 22.6 and Table 22.2, we show the performance of the CitiFX Beta indices for different styles since 1997.

Citigroup was one of the earliest FX providers to launch such indices and many others have followed suit. These types of indices are often called *beta*, *benchmark*, or *style* indices. Figure 22.7 and Table 22.3 illustrate the performance of various portfolios obtained by combining individual styles. As the names suggest, Beta Max consists of all five indices; Beta Carry trades carry concept in G10 and EM; Beta Trend trades the momentum concept in both markets; and Beta G10 and Beta EM are made up of models that trade G10 and EM currencies, respectively.

Both the individual and combined indices have historically positive performance indicating that in general trading following these major styles would have been profitable. Who would say no to an annual return of 4.9%? In addition, there are benefits from diversification that will be addressed later.

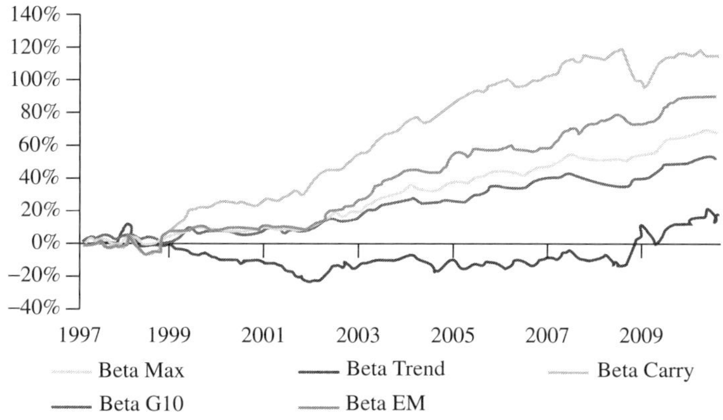


FIGURE 22.7 **CitiFX Beta portfolio cumulative returns.** ***Source*: Citi.**

TABLE 22.3 **Performance of Beta Portfolios**

| | Beta Max, % | Beta Trend, % | Beta Carry, % | Beta G10, % | Beta EM, % |
|---|---|---|---|---|---|
| Annual return | 4.9 | 1.4 | 8.3 | 3.7 | 6.6 |
| Annualised risk | 4.3 | 9.2 | 6.9 | 5.1 | 7.0 |
| Information ratio | 1.1 | 0.1 | 1.2 | 0.7 | 1.0 |
| Max drawdown | 6 | 37 | 23 | 10 | 14 |

*Source*: Citi.

Some of the FX benchmark indices including the ones offered by Citigroup are investable. Clients are able to trade them individually or in combination, and also trade "with" the style or "against" it. The ability to rapidly buy and sell these indices provides a new trading tool to express broad macro views with instant access to a portfolio of currencies that reflect those views.

Table 22.4 provides a list of FX benchmark indices provided by various institutions. The historical performance of these indices is shown in Figure 22.8 and Table 22.5. For this comparison, all indices are adjusted with a leverage factor so that they all have the same volatility as Citi's Beta Max portfolio. For institutions that provide multiple style benchmark indices as opposed to an aggregate one, the individual indices are combined with equal weights to obtain an aggregate one. Note that even though the trading rules might differ, most of the indices listed below show very high degree of correlation indicating that there is a consensus in the industry in terms of what constitutes "beta" in the FX market.

The major innovation in recent times, which has facilitated the growth of FX as an asset class has been the development of these benchmark indices.

**TABLE 22.4 Foreign Exchange Benchmark Indices**

| Institution | Index Name | Index Description |
|---|---|---|
| Citi | CitiFX | CitiFX Beta is a family of investable indices replicating the performance of most widely used trading styles in FX. The CitiFX Beta indices invest both in G10 and EM currencies and change the portfolio composition monthly by taking positions in the most attractive currencies for each style. The strategies include G10 Trend, G10 Carry, Emerging Market Trend, Emerging Market Carry, and G10 PPP. The indices that have been designed to allow clients to go both long and short provide a new and low cost tool to trade a market view. |
| Deutsche Bank | DB Currency Returns | The DBCR is an investable index that captures the long-term systematic returns available by investing in the world's currency markets. It replicates the three strategies most widely employed in the FX market and wraps them all into a single nondiscretionary index with daily liquidity. |
| Credit Suisse | FX Metrics | FX Metrics is a set of currency portfolios that replicate widely used macro-driven strategies. The strategies employed are carry, which takes advantage of the systematic bias in forward rates; momentum, which captures the trending behavior of currencies over the medium term; value, which is based on signals derived from the Credit Suisse Fair Value model; terms of trade, which invests in currencies experiencing a positive trade shock and sells currencies affected by negative shocks; growth, which tracks the relative performance of currencies with strong economic momentum against currencies with weak cyclical indicators; and emerging markets, which takes advantage of the expected appreciation of emerging markets currencies. |
| RBS | RBS FX Naïve Indices | RBS FX Naive indices are a family of indices representing the returns from volatility, carry, trend, and valuation type of strategies. |

*Source*: Company Websites, Bloomberg.

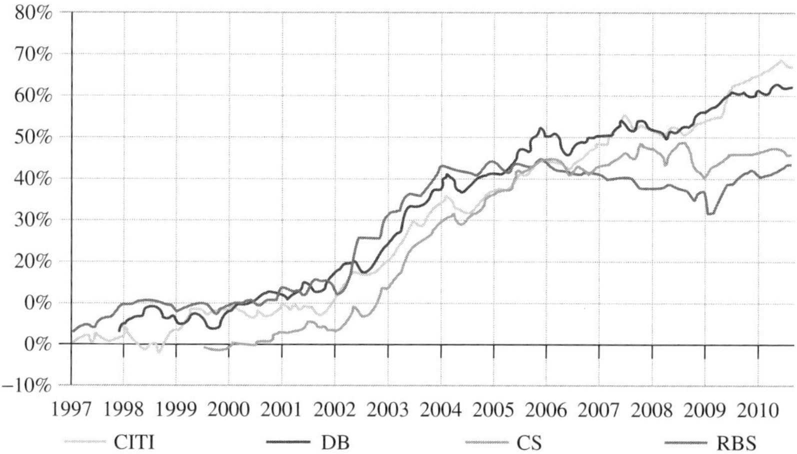


FIGURE 22.8 Foreign exchange benchmark indices. *Source:* Citi, Bloomberg.

TABLE 22.5 **Foreign Exchange Benchmark Indices**

| | CITI, % | DB, % | CS, % | RBS, % |
|---|---|---|---|---|
| Annual return | 4.9 | 4.8 | 4.1 | 3.1 |
| Annualised risk | 4.3 | 4.5 | 4.3 | 4.3 |
| Information ratio | 1.1 | 1.1 | 0.9 | 0.7 |
| Max drawdown | 6 | 7 | 10 | 13 |

*Source*: Citi, Bloomberg.

Interestingly, the motivation behind the earliest indices and index like return series was not necessarily to enable them to be traded but to create a series of "market returns" in the active FX space for benchmarking purposes.

However, just as in equities when indices became popular 25 years ago, once an index is available, many investors will want to buy and sell it directly. This simultaneously bypasses all the problems traditionally associated with currencies as an asset class and permits exposure to hedge fund like returns without paying hedge fund levels of fees. Moreover, a level of flexibility becomes available, which was previously not available. For example, an investor who feels the carry trade is under pressure can take out a short contract on the index for a month. The need for separate indices, representing different styles of trading such as carry, trend, or volatility, is also now apparent. This development once more mirrors the developments in equity and bond space where style and geographic indices are commonplace.

The next natural step after the creation of beta indices was the creation of more active "alpha"-type indices. As the name suggests, alpha indices are based on more sophisticated trading rules than their beta counterparts and try to generate excess returns beyond the ones offered by the pure style indices. Compared to the benchmark indices, the alpha indices might trade more often and usually have regime filters, which turn on or off the underlying models depending on whether the current market conditions are conducive or not. These indices enable investors who are not necessarily FX specialists to gain easy access to a market that promises attractive returns. These indices replicate investment strategies that would have been in the past only accessible via investments in hedge funds.

Figure 22.9 and Table 22.6 show the performance of a set of alpha portfolios called *CitiFX Thematic Indices* created by Citigroup. Each index represents a different multistrategy FX portfolio, where the underlying individual strategies are more sophisticated than the benchmark versions. The strategies with common themes are selected and combined into diversified portfolios. A brief description of each portfolio is given below:

*Global Carry*. For investors wanting to have a systematic carry exposure. The objective is to provide investors with a risk controlled way of exploiting the forward-rate bias in both the G10 and EM space.

*Balanced*. For investors wanting to have exposure to major investments styles. The objective is to provide investors with a well-diversified pool of strategies covering carry, fundamental, and momentum styles.

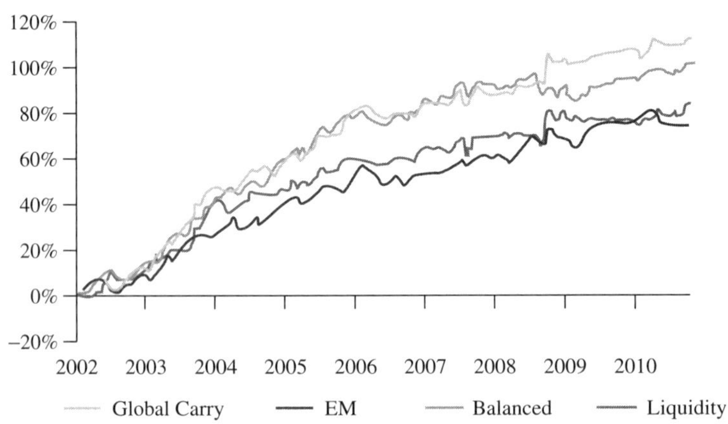


FIGURE 22.9 CitiFX Alpha thematic indices. *Source:* Citi.

TABLE 22.6 **CitiFX Alpha Thematic Indices**

| | Global Carry, % | Emerging World, % | Balanced, % | Liquidity, % |
|---|---|---|---|---|
| Annual return | 12.2 | 8.5 | 10.8 | 9.2 |
| Annualised risk | 8.1 | 8.3 | 8.1 | 7.8 |
| Information ratio | 1.5 | 1.0 | 1.3 | 1.2 |
| Max drawdown | 8 | 11 | 17 | 5 |

*Source*: Citi.

*Liquidity*. For investors only wanting exposure to G10 currencies. The objective is to provide clients with a broad spectrum of investment styles while avoiding the risks associated with EM currencies.

*Emerging World*. For investors who want exposure to emerging market currencies only. The objective of the index is to provide investors with a risk controlled way of investing in EM currencies.

The returns shown in Figure 22.9 are attractive, and it is hard to believe that investors for years resisted treating FX as an asset class. Having said that, obviously constructing the portfolios shown in the figure and trading them is no trivial task. For investors wishing to gain easy a to FX and earn returns, such as the ones shown in figure, investable indices are the easiest solution.

Table 22.7 shows the FX indices launched by various institutions. This is by no means an exhaustive list, however it covers all major institutions and is meant to give an idea about where the market perceives the opportunities to exist. The historical performance of these indices is shown in Figure 22.10 and Table 22.8.

The descriptions in Table 22.7 illustrate that even though products based on multiple strategies are available, carry is a dominant trading theme in FX and some of the products available for investors involve only carry trades. It is also worth noting that while, in general, diversified FX products did not experience similar losses to those seen in equities, there has been a drop in the performance in the last few years compared to the 2002–2007 time period.

### 22.3.3 WHY IS FX ATTRACTIVE?

According to the Tower Watson 2010 Global Pension Asset Study, at the end of 2009 pensions in the seven largest markets (Australia, Canada, Japan, Netherland, Switzerland, United Kingdom, and United States) had on an average 54.4% allocated to equities, 26.9% to bonds, and 17.4% to other assets (includes property and alternative investments). Even though the allocation to alternatives is still small compared to equity and bond allocations, historical survey results reveal that institutional investors are well aware of the dangers of lack of diversification and have been gradually increasing their exposure to alternatives in the last 10 years. Figure 22.11 shows the average composition of pension portfolios in 1999, 2004, and 2009.

While pension allocation to alternative assets was only 6% back in 1999, it increased to 14% in 2004 and is currently 17.4%. Figure 22.12 shows pension allocations to alternatives in 2009 individually for the largest markets. We see that with the exception of Japan and United Kingdom, the allocation to alternatives is above 20% in 2009. There are similar surveys showing evidence of a move away from equities toward alternatives driven by both disappointing returns from equities and a desire for diversification.

Among the so-called alternative assets, the only market that has the liquidity and the depth to make large allocations possible is FX. Liquidity is one of the key attractive aspects of currencies and implies that investors can trade in substantial

TABLE 22.7 **Additional Foreign-Exchange-Strategy-Based Indices**

| Institution | Index Name | Index description |
|---|---|---|
| Citi | CitiFX Alpha Thematic Indices | The CitiFX Alpha Thematic Indices are designed to offer investors diversification in investment styles and market exposure. Systematic FX trading models with common themes are selected and combined into four diversified indices. Each index comprises of a fixed set of trading models targeting and equal contribution of risk. The indices aim to generate returns with low volatility and also low correlation to traditional asset classes. |
| Barclays Capital | Intelligent Carry Index | The Barclays Capital Intelligent Carry Index adopts an innovative strategy to enable investors to capture returns from foreign currency markets. The index is designed to reflect the total return of an "intelligent carry strategy," which, through an objective and systematic methodology, seeks to capture the returns that are potentially available from a strategy of investing in high yielding currencies with the exposure financed by borrowings in low yielding currencies. The strategy trades only G10 currencies. |
| Deutsche Bank | DBCR Dynamic Index | The DBCR Dynamic is an investable index that captures the long-term systematic returns available by investing in the world's currency markets. It replicates the three strategies most widely employed in the FX market and wraps them all into a single nondiscretionary index with daily liquidity. The DBCR Dynamic makes a variable allocation between strategies determined by logical rules based on previous year's performance. |
| Credit Suisse | FX Factor Index | The CS FX Factor Index generates alpha by dynamically adjusting exposure to different FX strategies in response to changing market conditions. The strategies employed by FX Factor are the same six strategies that make up the family of FX Metrics indices. |
| UBS | UBS V10 Enhanced FX Carry Strategy | The UBS V10 Enhanced FX Carry Strategy is an algorithmic strategy that exploits the forward bias in the currency forward markets. The strategy uses a sophisticated filter to anticipate or react to times of market stress and reverse the positioning of the portfolio to deliver enhanced returns. |
| JP Morgan | JP Morgan Income Indices | The JP Morgan Income indices track returns from both interest rate carry and currency appreciation of an equally weighted basket of currency pairs selected for risk-adjusted returns. Income FX selects four pairs from a universe of 14 G10 currency pairs. Income EM selects five pairs from Emerging Markets. |

*Source*: Company Websites.

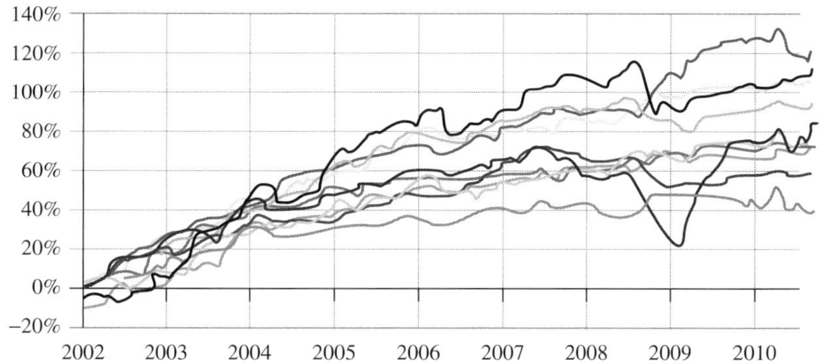


**FIGURE 22.10** **Foreign exchange alpha indices.** ***Source*****: Citi, Bloomberg.**

**TABLE 22.8 Foreign Exchange Alpha Indices**

| | Citi Global Carry, % | Citi EM, % | Citi Balanced, % | Citi Liquidity, % | DB, % | CS, % | UPS, % | BC, % | JP Income FX, % | JP Income EM, % |
|---|---|---|---|---|---|---|---|---|---|---|
| Annual return | 12.2 | 8.5 | 10.8 | 9.2 | 4.5 | 8.2 | 14.0 | 6.8 | 9.7 | 13.0 |
| Annualised risk | 8.1 | 8.3 | 8.1 | 7.8 | 7.4 | 5.3 | 9.5 | 6.4 | 13.4 | 13.0 |
| Information ratio | 1.5 | 1.0 | 1.3 | 1.2 | 0.6 | 1.5 | 1.5 | 1.1 | 0.7 | 1.0 |
| Max draw-down | 8 | 11 | 17 | 5 | 11 | 4 | 17 | 22 | 50 | 28 |

*Source*: Citi, Bloomberg.

size without causing a move in exchange rates, and they can also close positions and withdraw from the market at short notice. Even during the extremely volatile times in the middle of the recent financial crisis, investors were able to execute large size deals relatively easily even in emerging market currencies. Another related advantage of the FX market is its relatively low transaction costs.

Even though liquidity, tight spreads, and a 24-h open market are appealing features, the major attraction of investing in FX is the returns it provides. In fact, FX returns are attractive not only in absolute terms but also in relative terms. In Figure 22.13 and Table 22.9, we compare the performance of FX, equities, bonds, and commodities since 1997. Note that for this comparison, the MSCI

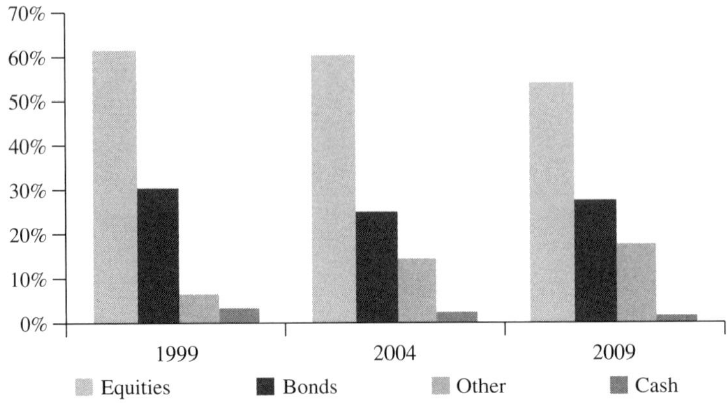


**FIGURE 22.11** Aggregate asset allocation of pensions in seven largest markets. *Source:* Tower Watson.

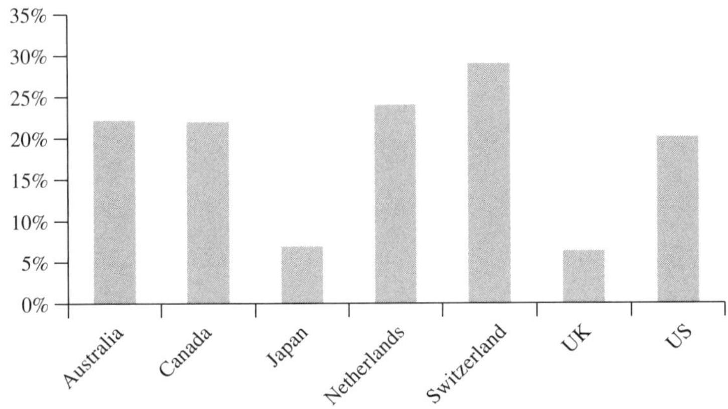


**FIGURE 22.12** Allocation to alternative assets for pensions in 2009. *Source:* Tower Watson.

World Index is used to represent equities, the S&P GS Commodity Index is used for commodities, and the 100% hedged Citi World Government Bond Index is used for bonds. For FX, we use the CitFX Liquidity Index. To have a fair comparison, the excess returns for equities, commodities, and bonds are normalized for CitiFX Liquidity risk. The normalization factors are calculated as ratio of the standard deviations of returns.

We see that for the same level of risk, FX provides the highest returns and has the second highest risk-adjusted returns following bonds. Not only FX returns are attractive but also the maximum drawdown is much less severe as well. During the recent crisis, well-diversified FX portfolios were relatively safe and did not experience the collapse seen in equities and commodities. This actually brings us to another one of the key features of FX, which is its low correlation to traditional assets.

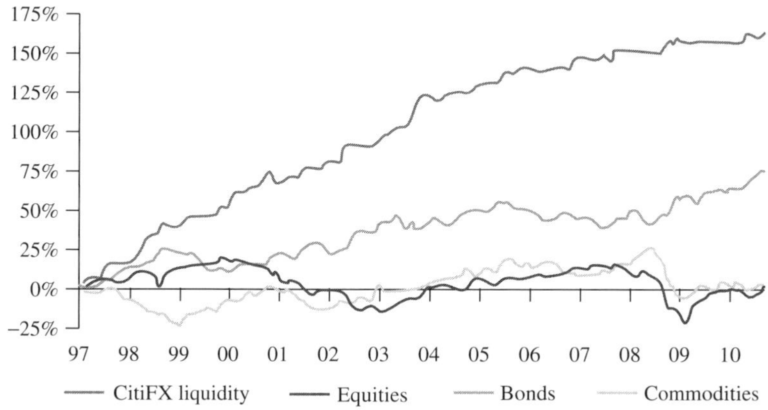


FIGURE 22.13 FX versus traditional assets. *Source:* Citi, Bloomberg.

TABLE 22.9 **FX Versus Traditional Assets**

| | CitiFX, % | Equities, % | Bonds, % | Commodities, % |
|---|---|---|---|---|
| Annual return | 11.9 | 0.2 | 5.3 | 0.2 |
| Annualised risk | 7.9 | 7.9 | 7.9 | 7.9 |
| Information ratio | 1.5 | 0.0 | 1.9 | 0.0 |
| Max drawdown | 6.0 | 30.0 | 17.1 | 22.3 |

*Source*: Citi, Bloomberg.

TABLE 22.10 **Correlations of Monthly Changes**

| | CitiFX, % | GSCI, % | Equities, % | Bonds, % | VIX, % | HF, % |
|---|---|---|---|---|---|---|
| CitiFX | **100** | | | | | |
| Commodities | **12** | 100 | | | | |
| Equities | **−6** | 16 | 100 | | | |
| Bonds | **−4** | −6 | −22 | 100 | | |
| VIX | **11** | −13 | −72 | 18 | 100 | |
| CS Tremont HF | 4 | 27 | 62 | −17 | −40 | 100 |

*Source*: Citi, Bloomberg.

FX investments are not exposed to the same risk factors as traditional assets. FX-based indices can do well in both bull and bear markets. The FX market as a whole can not crash in the same manner as equity markets do since a loss in one currency is always a gain in another. This can lead to low correlations to other assets and traditional risk factors, and has been cited as key reasons for the increased shift in allocations to FX.

Table 22.10 shows the correlations between the CitiFX Liquidity Index and other indices since 1997 based on the monthly changes rather than on the levels

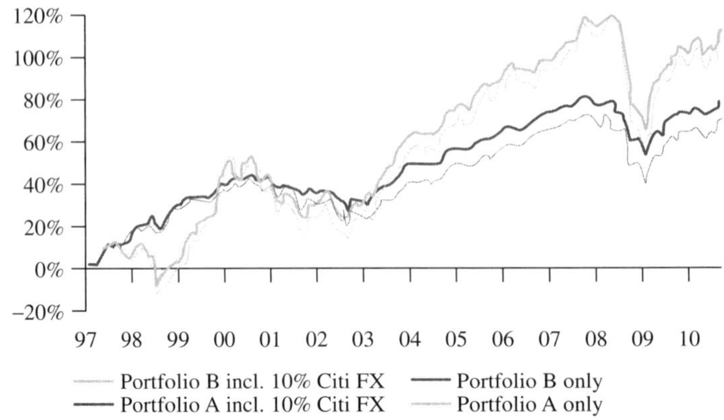


**FIGURE 22.14** **Adding FX exposure to investment portfolios.** ***Source:*** **Citi, Bloomberg.**

**TABLE 22.11** **FX Versus Traditional Asset Excess Returns**

| | PA, % | PA + CitiFX, % | PB, % | PB + CitiFX, % |
|---|---|---|---|---|
| Annual return | 5.1 | 5.8 | 7.9 | 8.3 |
| Annualised risk | 8.1 | 7.3 | 16.5 | 14.9 |
| Information ratio | 0.6 | 0.8 | 0.5 | 0.6 |
| Max drawdown | 33.2 | 29.1 | 62.8 | 55.8 |

*Source*: Citi, Bloomberg.

of the indices. Even though many of the correlations to FX rose in the midst of the crisis, FX in general has low correlations to other assets and its inclusion into multiasset portfolios can be very beneficial.

The benefit of adding FX exposure to a traditional portfolio is illustrated with an example in Figure 22.14 and Table 22.11. We start with two multiasset portfolios, one slightly more conservative than the other, and we show the impact of adding a small FX exposure. Again, we use the CitiFX Liquidity Index to represent active FX returns.

Portfolio A (PA): Conservative portfolio that consists of 50% Citi World Government Bond Index, that is hedged 100% and 50% MSCI World Equities, unhedged.

Portfolio B (PB): Aggressive portfolio that consists of 25% NASDAQ, 25% S&P GS Commodity, 25% MSCI Emerging Markets, and 25% CSTremont Global Hedge Funds; all unhedged.

In both cases, we add 10% FX exposure. Note that the weights of the existing strategies in Portfolio A and B are normalized after adding the CitiFX Liquidity Index. For example, PA with 50% equities and 50% bond becomes 10% CitiFX Liquidity, 45% equities and 45% bonds in PA + CitiFX.

Even a small allocation to FX has on an average added 68 bp per year since 1997 to Portfolio A's return and 40 bp to Portfolio B. More importantly, FX exposure has reduced the volatility and drawdown of both portfolios.

Obviously, the portfolio composition of an investor will vary, but the conclusion from the two examples above can be generalized. As shown in Table 22.10, currency returns have exhibited low correlations to traditional assets and hence their inclusion to traditional portfolios can reduce risk. This is one of the main attractive features of FX-strategy-based products and has probably contributed to the fact that currency allocations have increased in the last few years.

### 22.3.4 WHY USE STRATEGY-BASED FX PRODUCTS?

Today, investors use strategy-based products and investable currency indices for the same reason they use products and indices based on traditional assets. These indices provide easy access to multistrategy portfolios with a relatively low cost. They are a means of outsourcing expertise. Most diversified strategies demand the capacity to physically book and process multiple FX deals potentially every day. Not all the investors who would like to take advantage of currency returns have this ability. Thus, a new product type has evolved—the active FX return index—whereby investors may buy exposure to an active FX strategy, which is managed and administered by a third party via a fund, swap, or note. The interest in these products has ballooned in recent years, as more traditional investments have severely underperformed.

When the first equity indices were published daily in newspapers, their creators probably never anticipated that their simple combinations of share values would launch an industry, which now routinely values the most sophisticated derivatives based on those very indices that are now quoted tick-by-tick on exchanges throughout the world. We can expect evolution to go much faster for FX; already many of the indices may be bought and sold, and optionlike capital guarantee structures are being developed based on them.

There are a variety of OTC products available based on the strategy-based FX indices including the following:

- *OTC Options*. The investor pays an upfront premium and gets the positive/negative performance of the index
- *Total Return Swaps*. The investor receives/pays the performance of the index
- *Securitized Products*.
- *Delta-1*. The investor gets a full exposure to positive and negative performance of the index
- *Capital Protected Notes*. The investor profits from an appreciation of the index with a limited downside

These investable products are attractive because they do not have the 2–20% fee structure of hedge funds. Unlike hedge funds, where the investment rules are totally opaque, these products offer some degree of transparency. In most cases, clients can follow their positions in various strategies on a live platform. The indices have the flexibility to be funded or unfunded and the returns can be in any base currency. They are easy to get in and out and provide weekly or daily liquidity.

## 22.4 Conclusion

There is growing interest in FX as an asset class. Even though the allocation to FX still remains low compared to the allocations to more traditional assets, there is evidence that FX is increasingly in demand. Part of this demand is driven by the recent disappointing performance of equities. Currency investments are not exposed to the same risk factors as equities and bonds, and hence they do not exhibit a high correlation to traditional assets. Furthermore, there are well-documented anomalies that exist in the FX market. Since the majority of the players in the FX market are not profit focused, these inefficiencies continue to be exploited and still exist.

Strategy-based indices and products give investors easy access to FX as an asset class. These indices provide exposure to multistrategy portfolios with a relatively low cost. From retail to institutional, investors can now gain the same attractive returns enjoyed by FX specialists. While the initial beta type FX strategy indices and products were created for benchmarking purposes and only to give exposure to simple FX styles, the later alpha versions are more sophisticated. These indices replicate investment strategies that would have been in the past only accessible via investments in hedge funds. We can expect FX indices and products to evolve and expand to cater for the growing investor demand.

## REFERENCES

Baldridge J, Meath B, Myers H. Capturing alpha through active currency overlay. Russell Research Commentary; 2000.

Bilson JFO. The 'Speculative Efficiency' hypothesis. J Bus 1981;54:435–451.

Fama EF. Forward and spot exchange rates. J Monet Econ 1984;14:319–338.

Levich RM, Thomas LR. The significance of technical trading rule profits in the foreign exchange market: a bootstrap approach. J Int Money Finance 1993;12:451–474.

Meese RA, Rogoff K. Empirical exchange rate models of the seventies: do they fit out of sample. J Int Econ 1983;14:3–24.

Park C-H, Irwin SH. The profitability of technical analysis: a review. AgMAS Project Research Report; 2004.

Silber WL. Technical trading: when it works and when it doesn't. J Derivat 1994;1:39–44.

Strange B. Currency overlay managers show consistency: in the long run, count on them for adding value. Pensions and Investments; 1998.

Sweeney RJ. Beating the foreign exchange market. J Finance 1986;41:163–182.

Taylor MP, Allen H. The use of technical analysis in the foreign exchange market. J Int Money Finance 1992;11:304–314.

CHAPTER TWENTY THREE

# Foreign Exchange Futures, Forwards, and Swaps

**NAOHIKO BABA**
Goldman Sachs Japan Co. Ltd.

**YUJI SAKURAI**
UCLA Anderson School of Management

**FRANK PACKER**
Bank for International Settlements

## 23.1 Introduction

This chapter provides an overview of the markets for foreign exchange (FX) futures, forwards, and swaps. In contrast to the FX spot market where traded currencies are settled immediately (within 2 days after the transaction in practice), FX futures, forward, and swap contracts involve transactions to buy or sell currencies that are settled on a future date.

FX derivatives markets have been regarded as one of the most well-developed, liquid, and efficient markets. In its Triennial Central Bank Survey of Foreign Exchange and Derivatives Market Activity, the Bank for International Settlements (BIS) reported that as of end-April 2010, the global daily turnover of FX swaps and outright forwards amounted to \$1765 billion and \$475 billion, respectively, while that of FX spot stood at \$1490 billion. The turnover of FX swaps and outright forwards combined increased more than 2.5 times from 1998 through 2010. Such significant growth of FX derivatives markets has provided investors and bond issuers with much greater flexibility in accessing hedging, speculative

*Handbook of Exchange Rates*, First Edition. Edited by Jessica James, Ian W. Marsh, and Lucio Sarno.

and arbitrage opportunities with regard to foreign currency-denominated assets and liabilities.

How efficiently these FX derivatives markets function can be gauged by examining the so-called the covered interest parity (CIP) conditions, which correspond to no arbitrage conditions between domestic and foreign interest rates when the associated cash flow is covered by FX forwards. Empirical research on the CIP conditions used to be one of the central topics in the field of international finance at least until the mid-1980s. The early literature rigorously investigated whether the CIP condition held for major currency pairs against the US dollar, in particular, and what factors could explain deviations when the condition failed. Over time, however, thanks to technological progress on the trading and settlements front and growing liberalization of cross-border capital flows, the maintenance of CIP conditions became the norm in international finance, and this topic lost interest as a research topic for an extended period.

Since the 1990s, financial institutions have increased their global reliance on FX and cross-currency swaps as the key markets for foreign currency funding, as they accumulated foreign currency-denominated, typically US dollar, assets on their balance sheets. Following the outbreak of the global financial crisis in the summer of 2007, which peaked in the autumn of 2008 following the bankruptcy of Lehman Brothers, even such liquid and efficient markets experienced problems. Market liquidity was reduced amid heightened counterparty risk concerns, despite the conventional understanding that these swaps are effectively collateralized contracts. There was an unprecedented surge in the demand for US dollar funds, as many non-US financial institutions crowded into the markets to secure US dollar liquidity, which disrupted FX swap markets and their longer-term counterparts, the cross-currency swap markets.

Such dislocations in the FX and cross-currency swap markets manifested themselves as a significant collapse of the CIP condition. The recent substantial dislocations in the FX and cross-currency swap markets under the global financial crisis rekindled interest in this topic among researchers, giving them an opportunity to recognize how important a role these swap markets had played in financial markets.

It should be noted, however, that the FX markets traded smoothly over the crisis period, compared with equity and fixed income markets. For example, at the height of the crisis, VIX (S&P implied volatility) and US dollar swaptions implied volatility (3-month forward 3-year term) surged almost seven times and six times the level as of the beginning of 2007, respectively, while FX implied volatility (euro/dollar) rose only about 3.5 times during the same period.

The rest of the chapter is organized as follows: Section 23.2 describes the basic mechanism and market size of FX futures, outright forwards, and swaps and their relationship to CIP conditions. Section 23.3 discusses two prominent cases of dislocations in the FX and cross-currency markets: (i) the Japan premium case in the late 1990s and (ii) the global financial crisis that started in the summer of 2007.

## 23.2 Market Basics and Size

### 23.2.1 FX OUTRIGHT FORWARDS AND FUTURES

An outright FX forward contract is a contract where two parties agree to deliver, at a fixed future date, a specified amount of one currency in exchange for another. The only difference from an FX spot contract is that an FX forward is settled on any preagreed date, which is 3 or more business days after the deal, while the FX spot is settled or delivered on a date no later than 2 business days after the deal.

Suppose a US company purchases a product from a Japanese company with payment of 1 million yen due in 90 days. This importer owes yen for future delivery. The current price of the yen is assumed to be 100 yen per dollar. Over the next 90 days, however, the yen might rise against the US dollar, raising the US dollar cost of the product. This importer can avoid this FX risk by entering into a 90-day forward contract with a bank at the price of, say, 98 yen per dollar, which corresponds to the FX forward rate (see Fig. 23.1 for illustration of outright forward contract). In addition to the hedging purpose as shown in this example, FX forward contracts can also be used for speculative trades that take on FX risk by betting on a rise or fall of future FX rates.

FX forward contracts are traded over the counter (OTC), that is, a network of banks and brokers, which allows customers to enter into forward contracts at a currently agreed-upon rate of exchange. Unlike futures contracts, forward contracts are not standardized. Instead, terms and conditions of each contract are negotiated separately.

Some emerging countries' currencies cannot be traded directly in the forward market. This is because those governments put controls on the capital flows, thereby protecting their economies from speculative trading and a rapid change in global market conditions. Such currencies include the Chinese Yuan Renminbi, Korean won, Russian ruble, and Brazilian real. In some cases, a trader may get a forward contract on these currencies that does not result in delivery of the currency, but instead calls for settlement of the net amount in US dollars or other major currencies. These instruments are called *nondeliverable forwards* (NDFs). Unlike a normal forward contract, parties do not exchange principal at the maturity of an NDF. NDFs can be arranged offshore without the need to access the local currency markets, which enables traders to obtain hedging

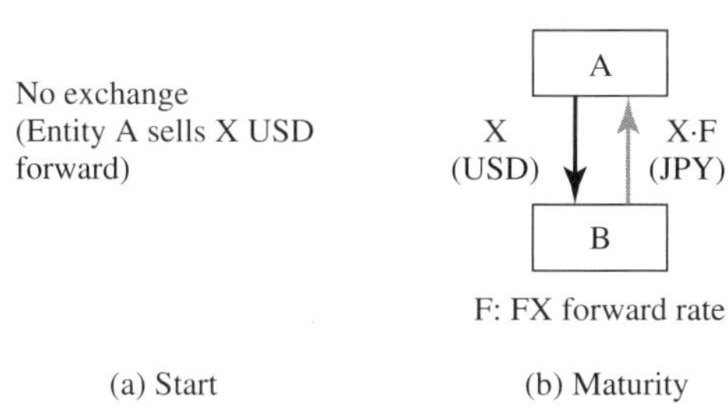


FIGURE 23.1 Outright FX forward.

opportunities against FX risk that would otherwise be considered unhedgeable. The amount of profit or loss would be determined by the FX spot rate at the time of settlement in comparison with the forward rate (see Fig. 23.2 for illustration of NDF contract). The use of NDFs has been growing, particularly in Asian currencies.

On the other hand, an FX (currency) futures contract is a standardized forward contract traded on organized exchanges rather than negotiated and traded on an OTC basis. The size of the FX futures market has been small compared with the OTC FX markets.[1] Most contracts have physical delivery. Therefore, at the end of the last trading day, actual payments are made in each currency, although traders can close out their contracts at any time before the contract's delivery date.

Futures contracts are channeled through a clearinghouse and marked to market on a daily basis, by which counterparty credit risk is reduced significantly. Also, the clearinghouse guarantees that a contract can be canceled simply by buying a second contract that reverses the first contract and netting out the position. In a forward contract, however, if a holder wants to close out or reverse a position, there has to be a second contract, and if the second contract is arranged with a different counterparty from the first, there are two contracts and two counterparties, with two separate types of counterparty credit risk (See Table 23.1 for more details on institutional differences between FX forwards and futures).

FX futures were first listed at the Chicago Mercantile Exchange (CME) in 1972, less than 1 year after the Bretton Woods system of fixed exchange rates was abandoned. Commodity traders at the CME, who did not have access to the interbank FX markets established the International Monetary Market (IMM), and launched seven FX futures against the US dollar. Today, more than

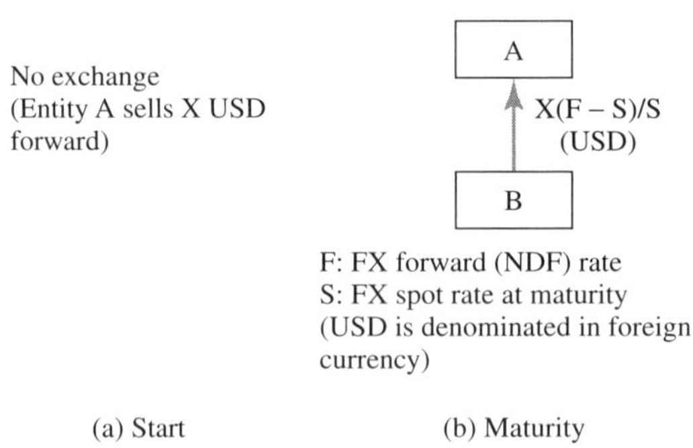


**FIGURE 23.2** **Nondeliverable forward** (NDF).

[1]According to the 2010 BIS Triennial survey, average daily turnover in exchange-traded currency products for all currencies was \$166 billion compared with \$3981 billion in OTC instruments including spot, outright forwards, and swaps.

**TABLE 23.1 Main Institutional Differences Between FX Forwards and Futures**

| | FX Forwards | FX Futures |
|---|---|---|
| Counterparty | Financial institutions | Clearing house |
| Maturity | Negotiated | Typically, IMM dates (third Wednesday in March, June, September, and December) |
| Amount | Negotiated | Standard contract size (integer multiple of) |
| Fees | Bid–ask spread | Bid–ask spread plus commissions |
| Collateral | Negotiated | Margin account |
| Settlement | At maturity | Most positions closed early |
| Margin call | Negotiated | Mark-to-market, daily |

20 currency pairs, largely against the US dollar or the euro, are traded at the CME. The CME is still the dominant exchange, but other exchanges also trade FX futures. Those include Euronext London and the New York Board of Trade, the Chicago Board of Trade (CBOT), Tokyo Financial Exchange (TFX), and Intercontinental Exchange (ICE).

Figure 23.3 shows the IMM futures positions for major currency pairs against the US dollar on a net basis (long minus short). The CME reports the future positions as of every end-Tuesday to the US Commodity Futures Trading Commission (CFTC) and the CFTC releases the data in the Commitments of Traders (COT) reports on its website every Friday. Of particular interest to market observers among the reported data are the positions held by noncommercial traders. This category of traders includes hedge funds and commodity trading advisors (CTAs) who often build their positions for speculative purposes, betting on the directions of future FX spot rates.[2] By contrast, commercial traders basically use these futures for hedging purposes. Net futures positions tend to move symmetrically between commercial and noncommercial traders, as shown in Figure 23.3. In other words, when noncommercial traders bet on the appreciation of the euro against the US dollar, for example, by holding net long euro positions, commercial traders tend to hold net short euro positions to hedge the future appreciation of the euro.

It is often argued that IMM noncommercial positions include speculative carry trade positions, where low interest yielding currencies are used as funding currencies for investments in high interest yielding currencies. During the period from 2005 through mid-2007 when carry trades were very active, the yen and the Swiss franc were often used as funding currencies and the pound sterling, the euro, and other emerging currencies, such as the Australian dollar, were used as target currencies for such trades. This tendency can be seen in Figure 23.3 where

[2]A CTA is a firm registered with the CFTC. It receives compensation for giving investors advice on options, futures, and the actual trading of managed futures accounts.

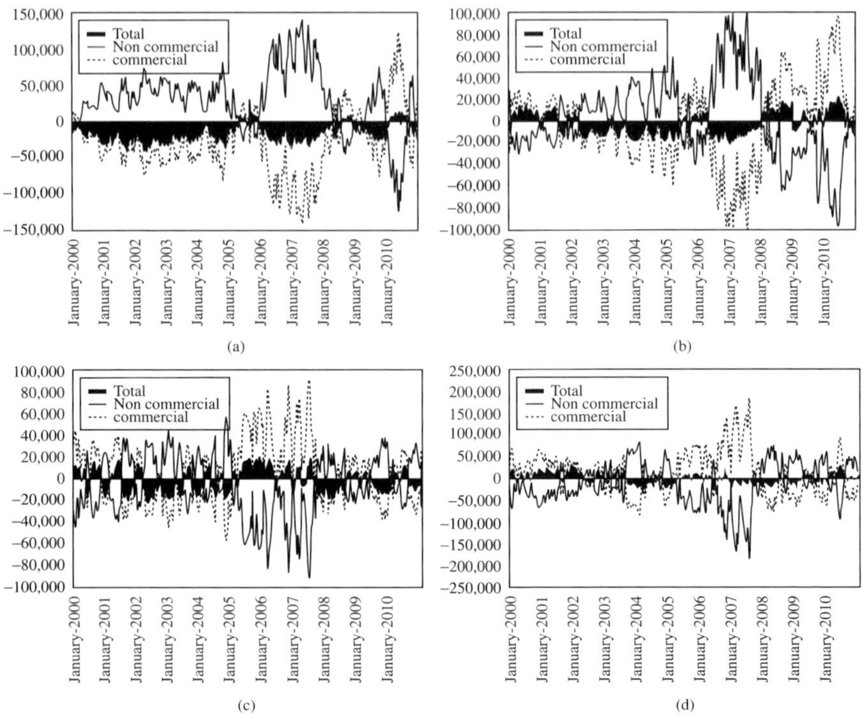


**FIGURE 23.3** **Net FX futures positions. (a) Euro, (b) pound sterling, (c) Swiss franc, and (d) Japanese yen. Note: The figures are weekly number of IMM contracts on a net basis (long minus short) as of each end-Tuesday reported by the CME to the CFTC, excluding nonreportable contracts. The units are 125,000 (euro), 62,500 (pound sterling), 125,000 (Swiss franc), and 12,500,000 (yen), respectively.** ***Source:*** **CFTC.**

the yen and the Swiss franc registered large net short positions for noncommercial traders, while the pound sterling and the euro showed large net long positions.[3]

## 23.2.2 FX SWAPS AND CROSS-CURRENCY SWAPS

### 23.2.2.1 FX Swaps

*Mechanism.* An FX swap is a short-term (mostly less than 1 year) OTC contract in which one party borrows a currency from, and lends another currency simultaneously to the same party (See Fig. 23.4 for EUR/USD swap). Put differently, an FX swap has two separate legs settling on two different dates, even though it is arranged as a single transaction. The use of FX swaps can be

[3]These carry trade positions were typically built by combining two different pair against the US dollar such as the net short yen position and the net long euro position, although the CME currently lists cross-rate pairs not including the US dollar such as the yen–euro pair so that traders can bet on FX directions directly without using the US dollar as an intermediary.

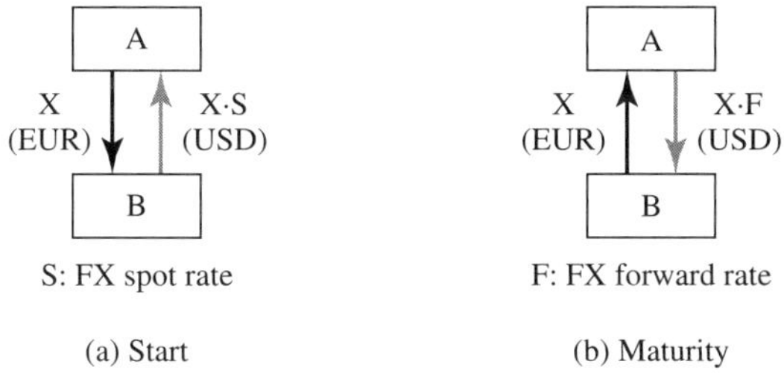


FIGURE 23.4 FX swap.

thought of the combination of actual borrowing and lending of two currencies on a collateralized basis (Melnik and Plaut (1992)).

FX swaps have generally been employed by financial institutions to fund foreign currencies for themselves and their customers including exporters and importers, as well as institutional investors who wish to hedge their positions of foreign bonds against the associated FX risk. FX swaps have also been used as a tool for speculative trading. Among these motives, the use of FX swaps for the foreign currency funding has increased significantly, particularly since the 1990s.

When non-US financial institutions need US dollars, they can borrow directly in the dollar cash market, or combine domestic currency borrowing with an FX swap. For example, an institution funding itself in euros but desiring dollars could swap the euro proceeds for dollars, in effect by selling euros for dollars at the FX spot rate and entering into a forward contract in the reverse direction at maturity (Fig. 23.4). FX swaps are conventionally priced as $F_{t,t+s} - S_t$ (forward discount rate).

*Pricing of FX swaps and short-term CIP.* The total cost of raising US dollars using euros as a funding currency through the FX swap market is often called the *FX swap-implied dollar rate* from the euro. The equality of the FX swap-implied dollar rate and dollar cash rate defines a condition of indifference as

$$\frac{F_{t,t+s}}{S_t}\left(1 + r_{t,t+s}^{\mathrm{EUR}}\right) = 1 + r_{t,t+s}^{\mathrm{USD}} \tag{23.1}$$

Here, the left-hand side of Equation (23.1) corresponds to the FX swap-implied dollar rate from the euro, where $S_t$ is the FX spot rate between the dollar and the euro at time $t$, $F_{t,t+s}$ is the FX forward rate contracted at time $t$ for exchange at time $t+s$, and $r_{t,t+s}^{\mathrm{EUR}}(r_{t,t+s}^{\mathrm{USD}})$ is the uncollateralized euro (dollar) interest rate from time $t$ to time $t+s$. $F_{t,t+s}/S_t$ essentially corresponds to the euro/dollar forward discount rate. Equation (23.1) is equivalent to the CIP condition in the international finance literature. CIP states that interest rate differentials between currencies should be perfectly reflected in the FX forward discount rates, since otherwise an arbitrager could transact in the markets to make a risk-free profit.

The early literature, using data through the 1970s, finds that the short-term CIP condition does not appear to hold invariably even for major currency pairs such as pound sterling/US dollar. Persistent deviations from CIP are attributed to such factors as transaction costs (Branson (1969); Frenkel and Levich (1975, 1977)), political risk, or capital controls (Aliber (1973); Dooley and Isard (1980)) and lags in executing arbitrage (Frenkel and Levich (1975)). Among these factors, transaction costs are thought of as the most relevant in the literature during this period. In addition, Taylor (1989) finds that deviations from short-term CIP tends to emerge during periods of uncertainty such as in 1979 when the European Monetary System was launched.

By the mid-1980s, a growing number of studies appear to support the maintenance of short-term CIP conditions for major currency pairs. This is accounted for largely by declining transaction costs, as the significant technological progress was being made on the trading and settlements front amid the growing liberalization of capital movements across borders.[4] Such empirical evidence is provided by McCormick (1979) and Clinton (1988), for example.

As the holding of CIP increasingly came to be viewed as a norm, empirical studies on this topic became quite rare until the 2000s, when more detailed transaction-based data became available to researchers. Akram et al. (2008, 2009) investigate deviations from the short-term CIP condition using tick data in 2004 and find economically significant CIP deviations, albeit short lived.

Another important development that brought back the attention of researchers to this topic was the emergence of counterparty credit risk and liquidity risk as major sources of the CIP failure, particularly when the financial system was under increased stress. As shown in Figure 23.5, which shows the 3-month CIP deviations between each of four major currencies (euro, pound sterling, Swiss franc, and yen) and the US dollar observed in the FX swap market from the late 1990s, prominent examples of the CIP failure include the late 1990s in Japan and the period of global financial crisis from 2007 through 2009 to be discussed in Section 23.3.

*Relationship between FX outright forwards and FX swaps.* It should be noted here that outright forward positions can be built by combining spot and swap positions, thus creating so-called synthetic forward positions. In fact, because of higher market liquidity of spot and swap transactions than outright forward transactions, banks often cover their forward positions resulting from their customers' orders by constructing such synthetic positions. In many cases, forward rates for customers quoted by banks are calculated by backward induction from the cost of constructing the corresponding synthetic forward positions.

[4]The United Kingdom dismantled controls on capital outflows in 1979. Japan also removed the capital controls in 1979. France and Italy abolished their capital controls in 1986, followed by Spain and Portugal to meet a 1990 deadline for liberalization set by the European Community.

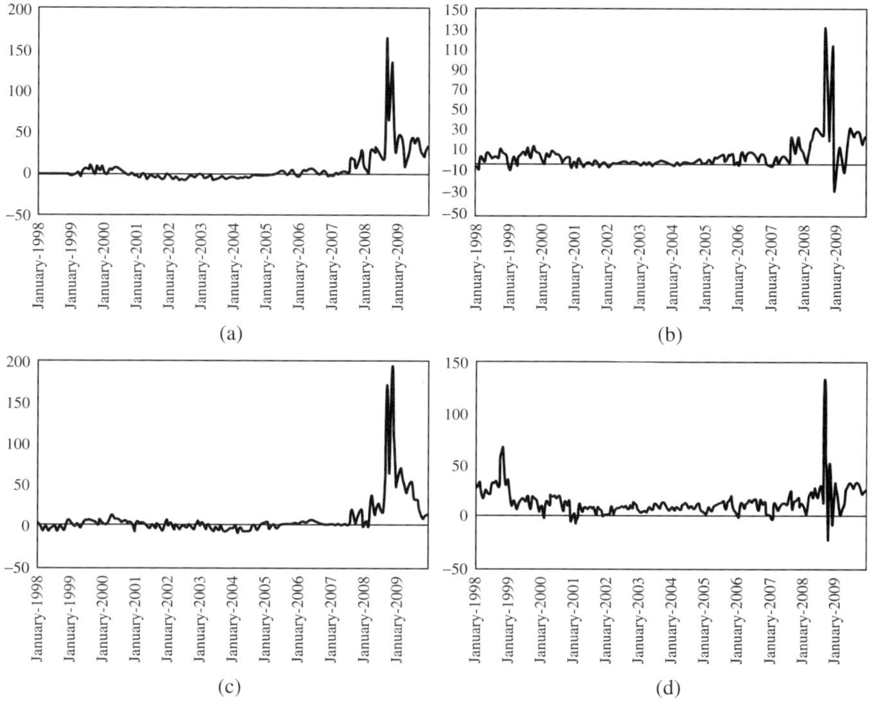


**FIGURE 23.5** **Short-term CIP deviations against the US dollar (bp). (a) Euro, (b) pound sterling, (c) Swiss franc, and (d) Japanese yen. Note: The short-term CIP deviation is defined as the 3-month FX swap-implied US dollar rate from each currency minus 3-month US dollar Libor, where 3-month Libor in each currency is used to calculate the FX swap-implied US dollar rate. The 10-day moving average is used. *Source:* Bloomberg.**

Figure 23.6 illustrates how to construct an FX forward position in practice. In this example, a Japanese exporter wishes to sell the US dollar and buy the yen with a bank 3 months from now to hedge FX risk associated with its future US dollar-denominated revenue, as shown in Figure 23.6a. The bank now has the position that is reverse to the exporter's, as shown in Figure 23.6b. The bank then attempts to cover and square this position by combining an FX swap position and a spot position, as shown in Figure 23.6c. In this way, the bank calculates the forward rate for the exporter from the FX spot rate and the forward discount rate (FX swap price).

#### 23.2.2.2 Cross-Currency Swaps

*Mechanism.* Market participants argue that FX swaps are somewhat costly at maturities greater than 2 years because of relatively low market liquidity. Thus, for such longer maturities, cross-currency swaps have been extensively

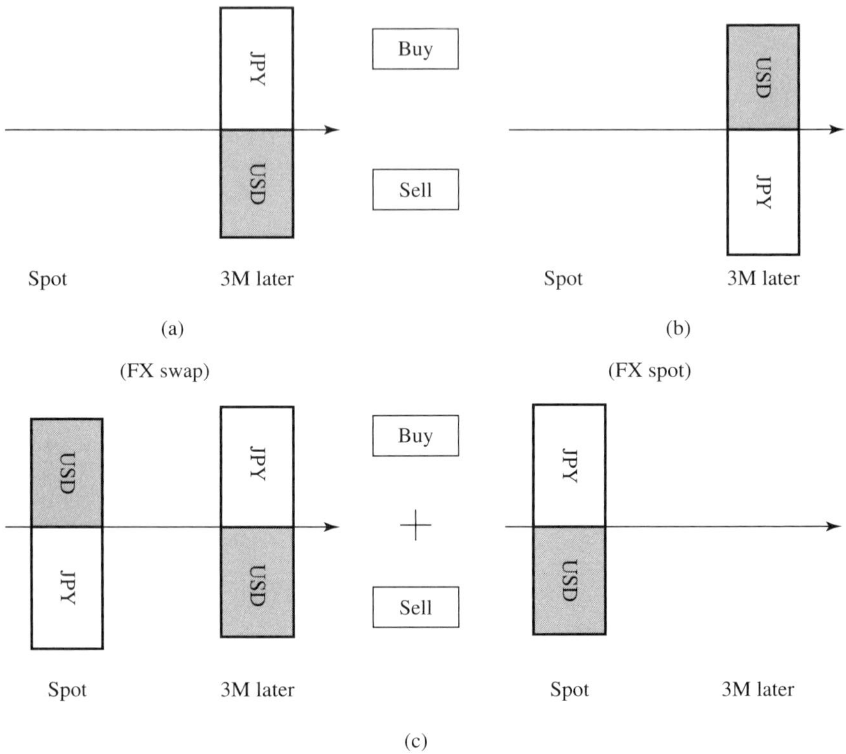


**FIGURE 23.6 Constructing an FX outright forward position using an FX swap. (a) Exporter's position, (b) bank's position, and (c) bank's hedge position.**

used instead. There are numerous types of cross-currency swap contracts, among which the most widely used in recent years is the cross-currency basis swap.

A cross-currency basis swap is a contract in which one party borrows one currency from another party and simultaneously lends the same value, at current spot rates, of a second currency to the same party. The parties involved in such swaps are financial institutions, either acting on their own or as agents for nonfinancial corporations. The main purpose of the use of cross-currency basis swaps for nonfinancial corporations is to fund their foreign direct investment in foreign currencies. Cross-currency basis swaps have been also used as a tool for converting currencies of liabilities, particularly by issuers of bonds denominated in foreign currencies. These swaps can allow issuers desiring liabilities of a certain currency to access the investor base available in another. Mirroring the tenor of the transactions they are meant to fund, most cross-currency basis swaps are long term, generally ranging between 1 and 30 years in maturity.

In such a swap contract, parties effectively borrow from each other in different currencies, exchanging principals at both the start and maturity of the swap, as well as regular interest rate payments (Fig. 23.7). Since the amount of future principal payment is fixed at the start of the contract, cross-currency basis

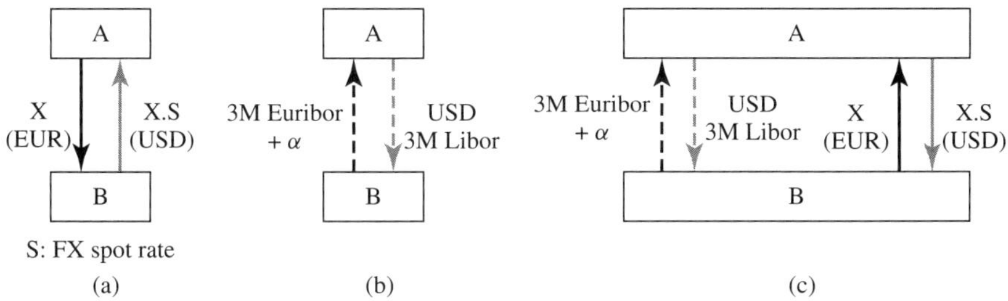


**FIGURE 23.7** **Cross-currency basis swap. (a) Start, (b) during the term, and (c) maturity.**

swaps are largely free from FX risk, but entail replacement cost, as are FX swaps. Although the structure is different from FX swaps, cross-currency swaps serve the same economic function as FX swaps.

The conventional quoting procedure for cross-currency basis swaps is as follows: A euro/US dollar 10-year basis swap, for example, is typically quoted as Euribor plus $\alpha$ basis points versus dollar Libor flat. This means that the lender/borrower of dollar/euro funds is obligated to pay Euribor plus $\alpha$ basis points generally every 3 months in exchange for receiving dollar Libor flat. In this manner, the prices for swaps $\alpha$ turn negative (positive) when there is strong demand for dollar (euro) funds relative to euro (dollar) funds.

*Pricing of cross-currency basis swaps and long-term CIP.* Because the interest rates exchanged in cross-currency basis swaps are floating rates, for the comparison with the short-term CIP condition reflected in the FX swap prices, a conversion of floating to fixed rates via interest rate swaps is necessary. As shown in Popper (1993), among others, after this conversion and abstracting from potential distortions, the long-term CIP condition for the cross-currency swap market can be written as

$$1 + r_{t,t+s}^{\mathrm{USD}} = \left(1 + r_{t,t+s}^{\mathrm{EUR}}\right) + \left[\left(1 + r_{t,t+s}^{\mathrm{USD}}\right) - \left(1 + r_{t,t+s}^{\mathrm{EUR}} + \alpha\right)\right] \tag{23.2}$$

Equation 23.2 indicates that $\alpha$ should be zero when long-term CIP holds. Therefore, $\alpha$ measures the deviation from long-term CIP. $\alpha$ can turn negative if there is strong demand for dollars. As is the case with short-term CIP, for long-term CIP to hold strictly requires negligible transaction costs, as well as the lack of political risk, counterparty credit risk and liquidity risk. Duffie and Huang (1996) show that cross-currency swaps are subject to more exposure to counterparty risk than are interest rate swaps, due to the exchange of notional amounts.

Using data of cross-currency swaps up until the early 1990s, Popper (1993) and Fletcher and Taylor (1996) find that nonnegligible deviations existed from the CIP condition at various times using cross-currency swap prices, but such deviations were diminishing over time.

Figure 23.8 shows long-term (1-, 5-, and 10-year) CIP deviations observed in the cross-currency basis swap market for the same currency pairs as in

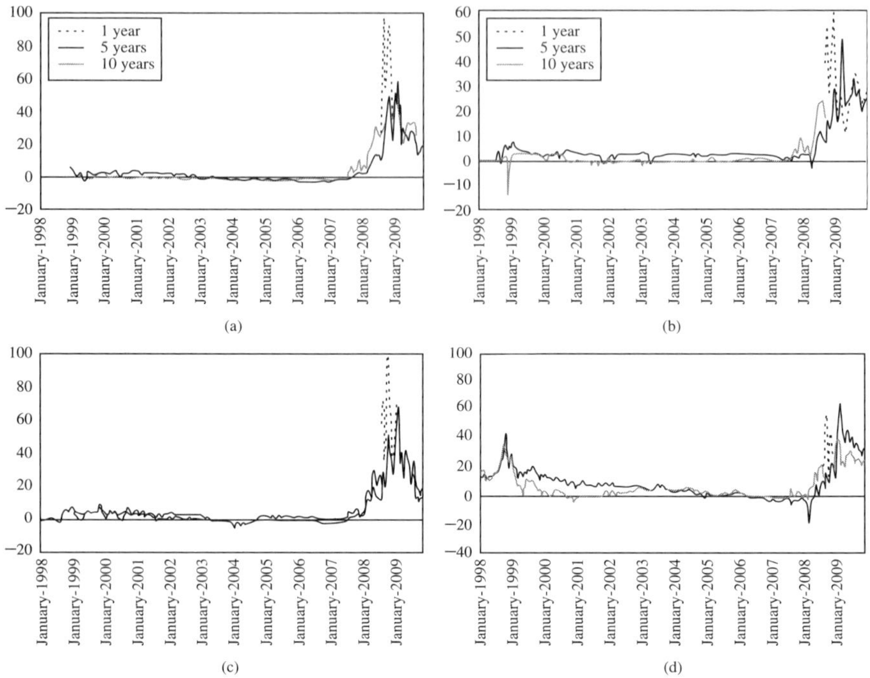


**FIGURE 23.8 Long-term CIP deviations against the US dollar (bp). (a) Euro, (b) pound sterling, (c) Swiss franc, and (d) Japanese yen. Note: The long-term CIP deviation is defined as the price of each cross-currency swap multiplied by −1. Thus, the deviation in positive territory indicates a positive US dollar premium in the cross-currency swap market over US dollar Libor. The 10-day moving average is used. *Source:* Bloomberg.**

Figure 23.5. On the whole, the market trend is very similar to the short-term CIP deviations. The CIP conditions appear have roughly held until mid-2007 except for the yen/US dollar pair. Deviations from long-term CIP soared following the Lehman failure, as was also the case with short-term CIP deviations.

*Hedging schemes using cross-currency basis swaps.* As mentioned above, cross-currency basis swaps are extensively used to hedge foreign currency-denominated assets and liabilities, thereby providing investors and bond issuers with great flexibility in terms of currency diversification. Figure 23.9 illustrates such basic hedging schemes for foreign currency-denominated bonds for portfolio investors and bond issuers, respectively. A US dollar-based portfolio investor, for example, can convert returns from euro-denominated fixed-rate bonds to dollar Libor-based (floating) returns by combining a cross-currency basis swap and an interest rate swap with a foreign currency bond investment, as shown in Figure 23.9a. Specifically, a US dollar-based investor first raises EUR

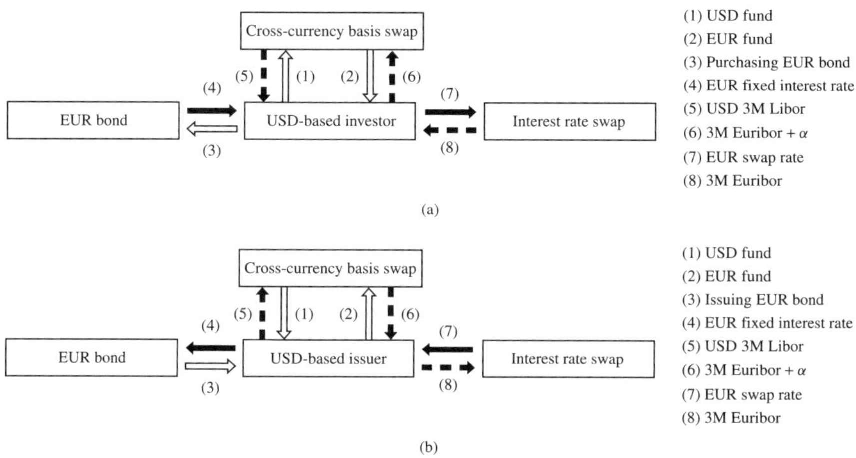


**FIGURE 23.9 Hedging schemes for foreign currency-denominated assets and liabilities using a cross-currency basis swap. (a) Hedging foreign currency-denominated assets and (b) hedging foreign currency-denominated liabilities.**

fund from USD fund via a cross-currency swap, and then uses the EUR fund to purchase a EUR bond. He/she can further utilize an interest rate swap to hedge interest rate risk.

Similarly, a US dollar-based bond issuer can diversify issuing currencies of their bonds, thereby tapping different currency investor bases, by using a cross-currency basis swap. It goes without saying that when the cross-currency swap price deviates from the CIP condition described above, investors and issuers can take advantage of the price deviations until such arbitrage activities dissipate the deviations in price, and restore the nonarbitrage CIP condition.

### 23.2.3 MARKET SIZE

**23.2.3.1 Amount Outstanding.** Figure 23.10 shows the amounts outstanding of FX futures, forwards, and swaps from the 1990s. The following points are of particular note.

*Phenomenal growth through 2008.* Market growth was phenomenal through 2008. This is largely attributable to the widespread use of FX futures and forwards, which include synthetic forwards using FX swaps, for speculative trading strategies such as carry trades. In addition, between the surfacing of subprime loan problem in the summer of 2007 and the Lehman failure in the autumn of 2008, FX and currency swaps posted further growth.[5] The

[5]See Brunnermeier (2009) and Taylor and Williams (2009) for details on the subprime loan problem and its effects on money markets.

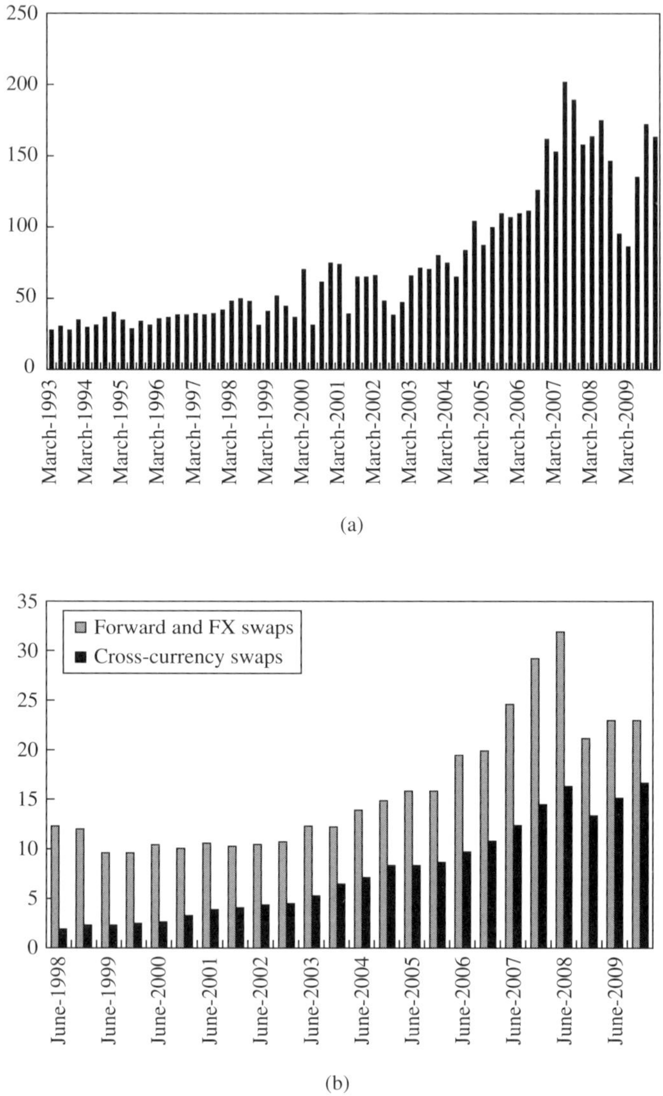


**FIGURE 23.10 Amounts outstanding of FX futures, forwards, and swaps.(a) FX futures (billion USD) and (b) FX forwards/swaps and currency swaps (trillion USD). Note: Notional principal amounts outstanding. *Source:* BIS.**

main reason for this is as follows: European financial institutions increased their reliance on FX and cross-currency swaps, amid deteriorating funding liquidity in the interbank money market and heightened concerns over their creditworthiness, to secure US dollars to support troubled US conduits to which they had committed backup liquidity facilities.

*Contraction after the Lehman failure in 2008.* In the wake of the Lehman failure, however, all instruments saw an unprecedented fall in market size. The Lehman failure further raised already heightened concerns over counterparty risk among financial institutions to such an extent that even the volume of effectively collateralized transactions of FX and cross-currency swaps decreased significantly, as market liquidity deteriorated.

Furthermore, particularly when compared with the short-term FX futures and swaps markets, the fall in longer-term currency swaps following the Lehman failure was moderate, and the recovery in market size was more prompt. This development reflects the fact that the epicenter of the global market crisis following the Lehman failure was the short-term money market so that relatively short-term markets such as FX swaps were more affected than the longer-term market of currency swaps.

*OTC versus exchange-traded FX derivatives.* The market size is much larger for OTC derivatives of FX forwards and swaps than exchange-traded derivatives of FX futures. A large share of OTC markets should primarily reflect the value of higher flexibility and usability of the OTC instruments in these markets, compared to the exchange-traded standardized products. Also, in recent years, financial institutions' higher demand for foreign currency funding in the FX swap market contributed to a further expansion, reflecting the increased need of European financial institutions to fund their accumulated US-dollar assets since the late 1990s (Baba et al., 2009).

**23.2.3.2 Turnover.** Figure 23.11 shows the global average daily turnover of FX-related OTC instruments and exchanged-traded derivatives.

Similar to the case of the amounts outstanding, turnover of each instrument experienced significant growth particularly until 2007. Even after the global financial crisis from 2007, the FX spot market maintained rapid growth, while the growth of the FX swap market slowed down significantly. Another noteworthy point is that turnover of cross-currency swaps is very low, compared even with exchange-traded derivatives, not to mention other OTC instruments. This is possibly attributable to the fact that the use of cross-currency swaps is typically associated with funding of foreign direct investment and issuance of long-term foreign currency-denominated bonds, and thus short-term speculative trading has been relatively quite limited in that market.

## 23.3 Dislocations of the FX and Cross-Currency Swap Markets under Financial Crises

### 23.3.1 JAPAN PREMIUM CASE IN THE LATE 1990s

In the autumn of 1997, concerns over the stability of the Japanese financial system heightened because of the nonperforming loan problem that had remained

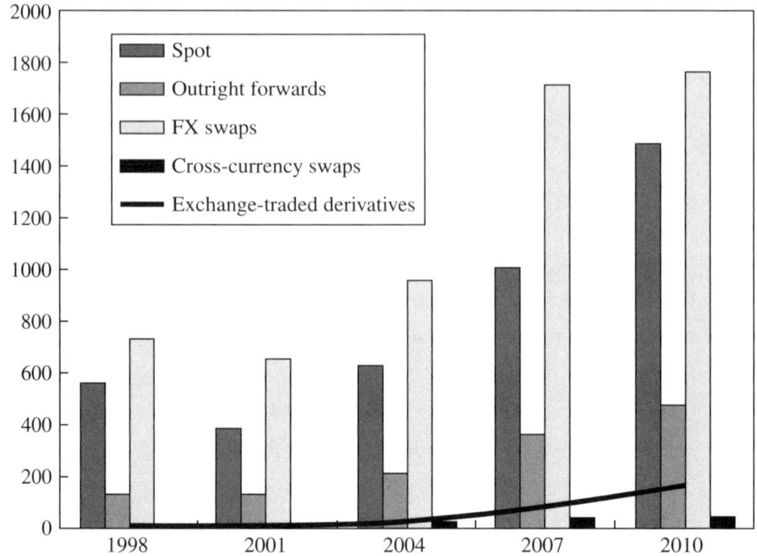


**FIGURE 23.11** **Global daily turnover (billion USD). Note: Adjusted for local and cross-border interdealer double counting. Exchange-traded derivatives include futures and options.** ***Source:*** **BIS.**

unsettled since the collapse of the asset bubbles in the early 1990s. Eventually, November of this year witnessed a series of failures of financial institutions: Sanyo Securities, Hokkaido Takushoku Bank, Yamaichi Securities, and Tokuyo City Bank.[6]

In the meantime, a premium that Japanese were required to pay over other banks in the offshore interbank US dollar funding market—so-called "Japan premium"—emerged around mid-October and then increased substantially toward the beginning of November in the wake of the failure of Sanyo Securities. This failure triggered downgrades in credit ratings of a wide range of Japanese financial institutions and the Japan premium reached a peak in the beginning of December 1997 (Covrig et al., 2004; Peek and Rosengren, 2001).

The extreme difficulty for Japanese financial institutions to raise US dollars in the offshore funding market made them turn to the FX and cross-currency swap markets. Owing to its effectively collateralized structure, the FX swap-implied dollar rate from yen was relatively stable, at least until early November.

Over time, however, one-sided order flow of US dollar funding made the FX and cross-currency swap markets dislocate as well, amid increased concerns over the counterparty risk of Japanese financial institutions (Hanajiri, 1999). After calming down in early 1998, the Japan premium and the deviations from CIP in the FX and cross-currency swap markets reemerged in the summer of 1998 and continued until the end of the year, when two large banks, Long-Term

[6]The case of Sanyo Securities was the first defaulting financial institution in postwar Japan. This was also the first default in the uncollateralized call market.

Credit Bank of Japan and Nippon Credit Bank, were nationalized (Figs. 23.5 and 23.8). The large depreciation of the US dollar against the yen in October, 1998 reflected the unwinding of carry trades, which was triggered by growing concern about a huge loss of LTCM.

## 23.3.2 THE GLOBAL FINANCIAL CRISIS FROM 2007

**23.3.2.1 Major currencies.** Dislocations in the FX and cross-currency swap markets and resultant CIP deviations after the surfacing of the subprime loan problem in the summer of 2007 are largely ascribed to the US dollar shortages of European financial institutions. The dollar shortages stemmed from a sharp growth in the US-dollar assets on their balance sheets over the past decade, which markedly outpaced the growth in their retail dollar deposits (McGuire and von Peter, 2009). This made them become heavily reliant on the FX and cross-currency swap markets for dollar funding.

Following the surfacing of the subprime problem, European financial institutions were obliged to increase dollar funding to support troubled US conduits to which they had committed backup liquidity facilities, and at the same time, interbank funding liquidity deteriorated amid heightened concerns about the creditworthiness of financial institutions on a global basis. Then, an increasing number of European institutions moved to convert their currencies into US dollars via FX swaps, resulting in impaired liquidity in the FX swap market.

Turning to the literature focusing on this early stage of the crisis, Baba et al., 2008 document that impaired market liquidity, as measured by bid–ask spreads, for example, characterizes the short-term euro/US dollar and pound sterling/US dollar swap markets, claiming that this is consistent with a predominance of orders to exchange European currencies for US dollars and counterparty risk concerns. In subsequent analysis, Baba and Packer (2009a) find that counterparty risk significantly explains the deviations in the short-term euro/dollar swap pricing. On the other hand, Coffey et al. (2009) find that borrowing constraints on financial institutions help to account for the CIP deviation.

Concerns over the stability of the global financial system then surged following the bankruptcy of Lehman Brothers on September 15, 2008. The sharp rise in counterparty risk concerns led to even more intense pressures in global funding markets. Greater demand for dollars hit both secured and unsecured term lending markets. Discontinuation of dollar flows from US money market mutual funds (MMFs) to European banks triggered by large capital outflows from US prime MMFs further exacerbated the problem (Baba et al. (2009)).

As many European financial institutions increasingly struggled to obtain dollars in the unsecured funding markets, they turned more to the FX swap market as a primary channel for securing dollars. This led to a sizable shift in FX forward prices, with the implied dollar funding rate observed in FX swaps on many major currencies rising sharply above US dollar Libor, for example. Dealers reported that bid–ask spreads on FX swaps increased to as much as 10 times the levels that had prevailed before August 2007 (Melvin and Taylor, 2009).

Using data after the Lehman failure as well, Baba and Packer (2009b) find a significant change in the role of counterparty risk before and after the Lehman failure. Before the Lehman failure, the credit standing of European financial institutions compared with that of US financial institutions was a main driver of dislocations. After the Lehman failure, however, short-term CIP deviations were positively affected by the counterparty risk of both European and US financial institutions. This result is consistent with the view that dollar shortages shifted from a localized problem among European institutions into a global phenomenon.[7]

With regard to the dislocations in the longer-term cross-currency basis swap market, the general observed tendency has been that the longer the maturity, the smaller the deviations. This reflects the fact that the epicenter of the global financial crisis, particularly following the Lehman failure, was in short-term money markets (Baba, 2009). In addition, Baba and Sakurai (2011) find that credit spreads of both European and US financial institutions have significant predictive power for regime switches between the normal regime and the crisis regime in the cross-currency swap pairs between major European currencies and the US dollar.

**23.3.2.2 Emerging countries' currencies.** Following the Lehman failure, foreign banks' lending to emerging market countries contracted sharply and many domestic banks in emerging markets faced difficulties in borrowing in the interbank market, as they faced much higher costs of obtaining dollars. Under such circumstances, there was an abrupt drop in gross international claims on many of these countries (Fig. 23.12).[8] This is particularly the case for Korea, Australia, and Brazil, where synchronized move was found between international claims and CIP deviations, while it was found, albeit less clear for Hungary.

Among these, Korea, in fact, experienced a severe retreat of global banks' lending, which led to the most significant dislocations in the Korean won/dollar swap market. In this regard, Baba and Shim (2010) find that CDS spreads of Korean banks play a significant role in explaining the short-term deviations from CIP for the Korean won/dollar pair before the Lehman failure. After that, a significant role of VIX is found to be a significant driver of deviations from CIP.[9]

Another study on the emerging market currencies is that of Fong et al. (2010), who attribute the CIP deviation for the Hong Kong dollar/US dollar pair to both counterparty risk and funding liquidity risk.

[7] Hui et al. (2010) find similar results to Baba and Packer (2009a).

[8] Gross international claims are the sum of cross-border claims in all currencies and local claims in foreign currencies of international banks.

[9] The VIX is the 30-day implied volatility of S&P 500 index options, calculated and released by the Chicago Board Options Exchange. The VIX is often regarded as a proxy for the global risk appetite.

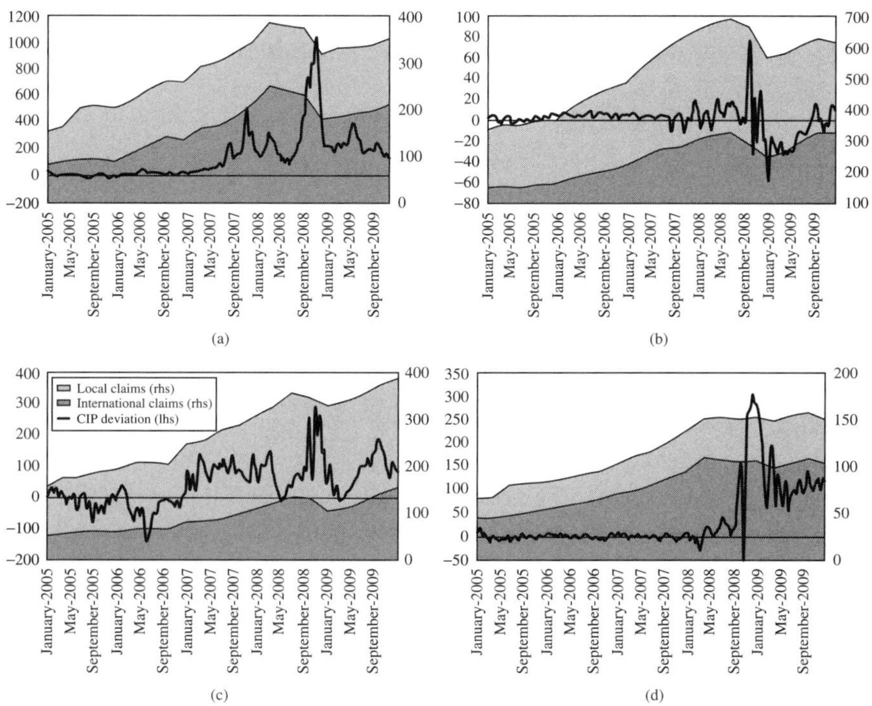


**FIGURE 23.12** Short-term CIP deviations against US dollar (bp) and foreign claims (billion USD) for selected emerging countries' currencies. (a) Korean won, (b) Australian dollar, (c) Brazilian real, and (d) Hungarian forint. Note: The short-term CIP deviation is defined as the 3-month FX swap-implied US dollar rate from each currency minus 3-month US dollar Libor, where as a funding currency interest rate, 91-day certificate of deposit rate is used for Korean won, 3-month bank bill rate for Australian dollar, and Budapest interbank rate for Hungarian forint. For Brazilian real, cupom cambial is used as the 3-month FX swap-implied US dollar rate. The 10-day moving average is used. International claims are consolidated cross-border claims in all currencies and local claims in foreign currencies. Local currency claims are local currency claims of reporting banks' foreign offices on local residents, calculated at constant end-Q4 exchange rates. *Source:* Bloomberg, Datastream, BIS.

**23.3.2.3 Policy Measures to Address the Dislocations in the FX Swap Markets.** On December 12, 2007, the US Federal Reserve announced the establishment of swap lines, or "reciprocal currency arrangements", with the European Central Bank (ECB) and the Swiss National Bank (SNB).[10,11] At that time, the ECB could swap euro for up to $20 billion and the SNB could

[10]For more details, see Baba and Packer (2009b) and Fleming and Klagge (2010).

[11]These were the first established since September 11, 2001, when the terrorist attacks disrupted financial infrastructure.

swap Swiss francs for up to $4 billion, respectively. Drawing on these funds, the ECB and the SNB were able to lend the dollar proceeds of swaps to their local counterparties with eligible collateral.

Toward March 2008, concerns about systemic risk resurfaced and stresses in the FX swap market intensified again. In response, on March 11 the Federal Reserve authorized increases in the swap lines with the ECB and the SNB to $30 billion and $6 billion, respectively. On May 2 the Federal Reserve authorized further increases in swap lines with them to $50 billion and $12 billion, respectively. On July 30, the Federal Reserve announced the addition of 84-day funds auction via the TAF. It was also announced that the ECB and SNB also would make available funds of 84-day maturity in their dollar auctions.

To further address the problems in dollar funding markets that had worsened following the Lehman failure, on September 18, the Federal Reserve authorized a more than two-fold increase in the swap lines to the ECB and SNB of $110 and $27 billion, respectively. At the same time, new dollar swap lines were opened to the Bank of Japan (BOJ), the Bank of England (BOE), and the Bank of Canada. As the financial crisis intensified, there followed a rapid-fire increase in the amount of the dollar swap lines over the next few weeks. Finally, on October 13, the swap lines with several central banks were announced to be unlimited.

In the debate over the effectiveness of central bank swaps, there is little agreement over what the appropriate target variable should be. Baba and Packer (2009a,b) and Coffey et al. (2009) measure the effectiveness of the central bank swaps in terms of their effect on the CIP deviations. By contrast, Obstfeld et al. (2009) focus on the changes in the FX spot rate, treating the swaps as means to defend the value of the domestic currency.

Analysis of the establishment of central bank swap lines on the CIP deviations suggests that they were quite effective. Baba and Packer (2009b) find that dollar-term funding auctions by the ECB, SNB, and BOE, as well as the Federal Reserve's commitment to provide unlimited dollar swap lines in October 2009, significantly ameliorated the FX swap dislocations. This result is largely supported by Hui et al. (2010). With regard to deviations from CIP for the Korean won/US dollar pair, Baba and Shim (2010) find that the Bank of Korea's use of the swap lines with the Federal Reserve was effective in alleviating dislocations in the swap market, whereas the provision of funds using its own foreign reserves was not.

By contrast, analysis of the effects of central bank swap lines on FX spot rates has suggested more mixed results. Obstfeld et al. (2009) interpret the swap lines as additions to reserve holdings available to support the FX value of the domestic currency. As such, they judge the amounts of the swap lines to have been small in the cases of Brazil, Korea, and Singapore, but possibly substantial in the cases of Hungary and Mexico.

## 23.4 Conclusion

FX derivatives markets, including futures, forwards, and swaps grew significantly from the 1980s. These markets provided investors and bond issuers with much greater flexibility in accessing hedging, speculative, and arbitrage opportunities with regard to foreign currency-denominated assets and liabilities. Reflecting these developments, CIP conditions came to hold for major currency pairs from the mid-1980s. Since the 1990s, financial institutions have increasingly relied on FX and cross-currency swaps as markets for foreign currency funding.

During the 2007–2008 financial crisis, these markets experienced a dislocation because of non-US financial institutions' high level of demand for US dollars amid heightened counterparty risk concerns until central banks established swap lines effectively. That said, over the crisis period, FX markets traded relatively smoothly. Overall FX markets were less adversely affected than equity and fixed income markets.

## Acknowledgments

The authors thank Jessica James (the editor) and anonymous referee for useful suggestions and comments. All the remaining errors are solely our responsibility. The views expressed in this chapter are those of the authors and do not necessarily reflect those of Goldman Sachs or the Bank for International Settlements.

## REFERENCES

Akram FQ, Rime D, Sarno L. Arbitrage in the foreign exchange market: Turning on the microscope. J Int Econ 2008; 76: 237–253.

Akram FQ, Rime D, Sarno L. Does the law of one price hold in international financial markets? Evidence from tick data. J Bank Finance 2009; 33: 1741–1754.

Aliber RZ. The interest rate parity theorem: a reinterpretation. J Pol Econ 1973; 81: 1451–1459.

Baba N. Dynamic spillover of money market turmoil from FX swap to cross-currency swap markets: evidence from the 2007–2008 turmoil. J Fixed Income 2009; 18: 24–38.

Baba N, McCauley RN, Ramaswamy S. US dollar money market funds and non-US banks. BIS Quarterly Review; 2009 Mar. pp. 65–81.

Baba N, Packer F. Interpreting deviations from covered interest parity during the financial market turmoil of 2007–2008. J Bank Finance 2009a; 33: 1953–1962.

Baba N, Packer F. From turmoil to crisis: dislocation in the FX swap market before and after the failure of Lehman Brothers. J Int Money Finance 2009b; 28: 1350–1374.

Baba N, Packer F, Nagano T. The spillover of money market turbulence to FX swap and cross-currency swap markets. BIS Quarterly Review; 2008 Mar. pp. 73–86.

Baba N, Sakurai Y. When and how US dollar shortages evolved into the full crisis? Evidence from the cross-currency swap market. J Bank Finance 2011; 35: 1450–1463.

Baba N, Shim I. Policy responses to dislocations in the FX swap market: the experience of Korea. BIS Quarterly Review; 2010 June. pp. 29–39.

Branson WH. The minimum covered interest differential needed for international arbitrage activity. J Pol Econ 1969; 77: 1028–1035.

Brunnermeier MK. Deciphering the liquidity and credit crunch 2007–08. J Econ Perspect 2009; 23: 77–100.

Clinton Kelvin. Transaction costs and covered interest arbitrage: theory and evidence. J Pol Econ 1988; 96: 358–370.

Coffey N, Hrung WB, Sarkar A. Capital constraints, counterparty risk, and deviations from covered interest rate parity. Federal Reserve Bank New York Staff Report. No. 393; 2009.

Covrig V, Low BS, Melvin M. A yen is not a yen: TIBOR/LIBOR and the determinants of the Japan premium. J Financ Quant Anal 2004; 39: 193–208.

Dooley MP, Isard P. Capital controls, political risk and deviations from interest rate parity. J Pol Econ 1980; 88: 370–384.

Duffie D, Huang M. Swap rates and credit quality. J Finance 1996; 51: 921–950.

Fleming MJ, Klagge NJ. The Federal Reserve's foreign exchange swap lines. Federal Reserve of New York Current Issues in Economics and Finance; 2010. p. 16.

Fletcher DJ, Taylor LW. "Swap" covered interest parity in long-date capital markets. Rev Econ Stat 1996; 78: 530–538.

Fong W-M, Valente G, Fung JKW. Covered interest arbitrage profits: the role of liquidity and credit risk. J Bank Finance 2010; 34: 1098–1107.

Frenkel JA, Levich RM. Covered interest arbitrage: unexploited profits? J Pol Econ 1975; 83: 325–338.

Frenkel JA, Levich RM. Transaction costs and interest arbitrage: tranquil versus turbulent periods. J Pol Econ 1977; 85: 1209–1226.

Hanajiri T. Three Japan premiums in autumn 1997 and autumn 1998: why did premiums differ between markets? Bank of Japan Financial Market Working Paper Series 99-E-1; 1999.

Hui C-H, Genberg H, Chung T-K. Funding liquidity risk and deviations from interest-rate parity during the financial Crisis of 2007–2009. Int J Finance Econ 2010. Forthcoming.

McCormick F. Covered interest arbitrage: unexploited profits? Comment. J Pol Econ 1979; 87: 411–417.

McGuire P, von Peter G. The US dollar shortage in global banking. BIS Quarterly Review; 2009 Mar pp. 47–63.

Melnik A, Plaut SE. Currency swaps, hedging, and the exchange of collateral. J Int Money Finance 1992; 11: 446–461.

Melvin M, Taylor MP. The crisis in the foreign exchange market. J Int Money Finance 2009; 28: 1317–1330.

Obstfeld M, Shambaugh JC, Taylor AM. Financial instability, reserves, and central bank swap lines in the panic of 2008. Am Econ Rev 2009; 99: 480–86.

Peek J, Rosengren ES. Determinants of the Japan premium: action speaks louder than words. J Int Econ 2001; 53: 283–305.

Popper H. Long-term covered interest parity: evidence from currency swaps. J Int Money Finance 1993; 12: 439–448.

Taylor JB, Williams JC. A black swan in the money market. Am Econ J Macroecon 2009; 1: 58–83.

Taylor MP. Covered interest arbitrage and market turbulence. Econ J 1989; 99: 376–391.

# CHAPTER TWENTY FOUR

# FX Options and Volatility Derivatives: An Overview from the Buy-Side Perspective

**OLEG SVIRSCHI**
Record Currency Management

## 24.1 Introduction

The next few sections provide an overview of foreign exchange (FX) options from the buy-side perspective. The content is split into four main parts: the first two parts are more theoretical and the second two are more practical.

The first part discusses a general "market for options" concept, if an option can be replicated, why the market for options exists and why one may need an option contract. It is followed by a brief outline of the Black–Scholes framework and the main assumptions this framework makes in order to derive the Black–Scholes formula. We demonstrate how these assumptions are quite far from reality and several stylized facts from the FX market show the divergence. As the assumptions are violated, we see how the FX market has adapted to incorporate "reality" into option prices. We discuss further the parallel between an option contract and portfolio insurance strategies, and we see that the cost of an option can be presented as the expected cost of a portfolio insurance strategy.

In the second part, we identify FX options-market participants and we present how they interact with each other. We build a naive volatility trading strategy using options, selling expensive volatility. We also consider a Black Swan strategy, where we buy cheap options to create a protection against potential

*Handbook of Exchange Rates*, First Edition. Edited by Jessica James, Ian W. Marsh, and Lucio Sarno.

losses in the rest of a hypothetical portfolio. We try to answer the question whether the FX volatility is an asset class by looking at the value added of the strategies discussed.

The third part is more practical and is dedicated to professionals who already have an understanding of what an option is and would like to develop their FX option intuition. The part ends with the presentation of Black Swan strategies and discussion on the volatility as an asset class in FX.

The fourth part is dedicated to expressing market views. If one has a particular view on the market, either directional in terms of spot or in terms of volatility, basic FX derivative instruments that can be used to express that view is outlined. I dedicate some space to discuss some practicalities around building a Black Swan fund and finish by presenting solutions for hedging currency exposure of illiquid assets.

## 24.2 Why Would One Bother With an Option?

### 24.2.1 HISTORY

Before early 1970s, exchange rates were in general fixed, but after the Bretton Wood agreement[1] was abandoned, currencies started to shift against each other, causing volatility. The theory is that exchange rates have to float as they are the mechanisms that tackle global trade imbalances. With fixed exchange rates, importers and exporters do not need to think about currency issues; however, such a short-term benefit can create long-term economic problems. When exchange rates are fixed, the long-term economic problem should be solved by the self-regulatory nature of the market, but the short-term financial issue of revenue fluctuation is quite troublesome for the treasurers of importing and exporting companies. Floating exchange rates create volatility and uncertainty and, therefore, there is a natural demand to eliminate this uncertainty at a certain cost. Treasurers of importing and exporting companies became the first participants in the currency forward market. A forward contract provides a mechanism by which this risk is eliminated. The problem that treasurers faced was that when a forward contract produced a negative cashflow, which should, in theory, be offset by a profit, the negative cashflow would be immediately crystallized as a negative P&L, while the profit from the underlying assets remained a projected number and would need to be crystallized in the future. However, if sales went down, the offset would not be covered completely. Treasurers were very smart and they tended to roll these negative P&L contracts without crystallizing them, but no matter how big the parachute is, it will land eventually. They came up with the idea that as soon as the contract entered negative territory they could sell it, and on recovery they could buy it back with the same maturity. Thus, the first replication of an option appeared. Neil Record, the chairman of Record PLC was one of the pioneers of this method

[1] See Filippo Cesarano "Monetary Theory and Bretton woods: The construction of an International Monetary Order" (Cesarano, 2006).

in currencies in the early 1980s. Such deals in the 1980s were very attractive because the currency market was liquid in comparison to equities and it trended. However, risk is not eliminated completely with such a method, as it does not hedge continuously and, even if it does, the cost of hedging varies.

At that time equity options already existed and they were even priced using Black–Scholes or the 0.4 rule of thumb.[2] Only in 1983 was the Black–Scholes model adapted to the FX market by Garman and Kohlhagen. Essentially this minor variation of the Black–Scholes formula needed 10 years (from 1973 to 1983) of empirical data. In these 10 years, currency options were, of course, traded, but no one was sure what the price of an FX option should be. And again the first people who traded currency options were corporate treasurers. A corporate company whose revenues were in currency X, and whose costs are in the currency Y, would sell a call on X and put on Y because if X appreciated then they could cover this option because their costs were much lower. If X depreciated, they were compensated with the option revenue. They could also buy a call option on currency Y in case currency Y appreciated against X and their costs soared.

### 24.2.2 FX OPTIONS

A currency option is a financial contract, which gives its holder the right but not the obligation to buy/sell a certain amount of currency at a certain price (strike price) at a certain time (maturity).

The Black–Scholes formula,[3] which appeared in 1973, changed the world of option pricing. The formulae states that the price of an European option (call or put) is given by the following formulae:

$$V_{\text{call}} = \mathrm{e}^{-r_d t} \left( FN\left(d_1\right) - KN\left(d_2\right) \right) \tag{24.1}$$

$$V_{\text{put}} = \mathrm{e}^{-r_d t} \left( KN\left(-d_2\right) - FN\left(-d_1\right) \right) \tag{24.2}$$

where

$$\begin{aligned} t &= \text{time to maturity} \\ F &= \text{forward price of the underlying currency, } F = S\mathrm{e}^{(r_d - r_f)t} \\ d_1 &= \frac{\ln(F/K) + 0.5\sigma^2 t}{\sigma\sqrt{t}}, \quad d_2 = \frac{\ln(F/K) - 0.5\sigma^2 t}{\sigma\sqrt{t}} \\ \sigma &= \text{implied volatility} \\ N(x) &= \text{cumulative normal distribution} \end{aligned}$$

[2] $0.4 \times \text{vol} \times \sqrt{(t)}$ is the rough calculation of the cost of ATMF (At-the-money-forward) option with maturity t as a percentage of the strike price. It can be derived from the Black–Scholes formulae when the strike is equal to the forward price and then divided by strike.

[3] See Black and Scholes (1973).

if the market dynamics evolves according to the assumptions stated below. In spite of the elegant mathematical solution, the law of one price[4] that the Black–Scholes model relies on breaks down in real life. Nevertheless, the Black–Scholes model is widely used, but more as a wrapper for underlying volatility and interest rate models. In the Black–Scholes framework, an option's payoff can be replicated using a certain amount of underlying (foreign currency forward) and a money market instrument (domestic currency deposit). This raises the question why options still exist if they can be replicated.[5] If options really were redundant, they would not be traded as a separate market.

The key is in the following assumptions the Black–Scholes framework relies on:

- continuous trading
- no transaction costs
- constant interest rates
- geometric Brownian motion.

If these assumptions hold then a delta hedging procedure proposed by Black and Scholes can replicate an option's payoff at a cost given by the Black–Scholes formulae. Let us imagine that a trader sold a call option on EUR/USD and received a premium for this option. Now, if the market moves against him and in favor of the holder of the option, that is, EUR/USD appreciates, then the trade will experience a loss. To hedge against this loss, the trader needs to buy EUR/USD in the amount that matches the sensitivity of the option. The delta is the first-order derivative of the option premium to the movements in the underlying. Therefore, delta provides the sensitivity of the hedging position, hence the name *delta hedging*. Every time underlying moves, the delta changes; therefore, the position in the underlying has to be adjusted. By how much the delta has to be adjusted? The answer can provide the second derivative of the option premium to the underlying gamma. While delta can be hedged by taking a positing in the underlying, gamma can be hedged only by taking an opposite position in options. Besides directional risk that can be hedged by taking positions in the underlying, there is a mark to market risk, and this is when the volatility at which an option was priced changes in the market. In other words, if the market is pricing an option at a different level of perceived risk then the value of the option changes. Vega of an option measures this sensitivity. We can summarize these three important Greeks and their formulae in the table below:

[4]The law-of-one-price in the context of the Black–Scholes derivation means that the price of an option derived as an expected value of payoffs and the price of the option derived as the cost of hedging the claim is the same.

[5]See Hakansson (1979).

| Greek Letter | General Formulae | Delta of a Call | Delta of a Put |
|---|---|---|---|
| Delta ($\Delta$) | $\frac{\delta V}{\delta S}$ | $e^{-r_f t} N(d_1)$ | $-e^{-r_f t} N(-d_1)$ |
| Gamma ($\Gamma$) | $\frac{\delta^2 V}{\delta S^2}$ | $e^{-r_f t} \frac{n(d_1)}{S\sigma\sqrt{t}}$ | $e^{-r_f t} \frac{n(d_1)}{S\sigma\sqrt{t}}$ |
| Vega(v)[a] | $\frac{\delta V}{\delta \sigma}$ | $S\sqrt{t} e^{-r_f t} n(d_1)$ | $S\sqrt{t} e^{-r_f t} n(d_1)$ |

[a]Strictly speaking vega is not a greek letter.

The assumptions do not hold in reality. First, delta hedging cannot be continuous, and any attempt to hedge continuously will result in unbearable trading costs. The classic example is the market crash in 1987 when portfolio managers were following portfolio insurance strategies that could theoretically give the same payoff as a put option. The problem in 1987 was a liquidity squeeze when no one on the other side was willing to buy the underlying asset prices plummeted and the insurance was ineffectual. The problem with portfolio insurance schemes and delta hedging is their vulnerability to sudden market dislocations, using the language of an options desk—they are short gamma. If someone replicates an option using the underlying and a risk-free asset, the situation the long and short gamma can be schematically presented as in Figures 24.1 and 24.2.

The holder of an option contract Figure 24.1 will always be better off than a delta hedger who replicates their payoff. For any market move, the option will

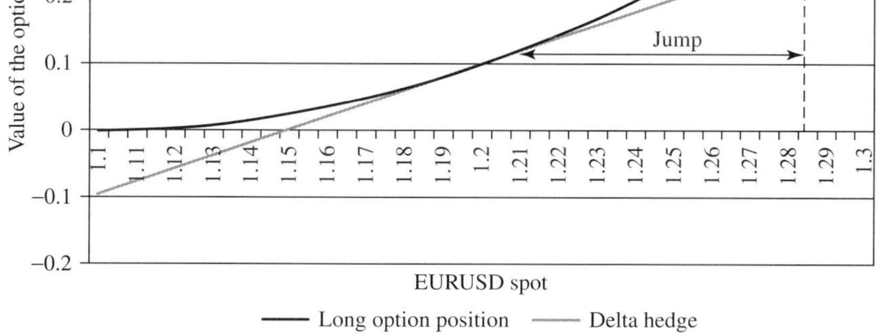


FIGURE 24.1 **Long gamma.**

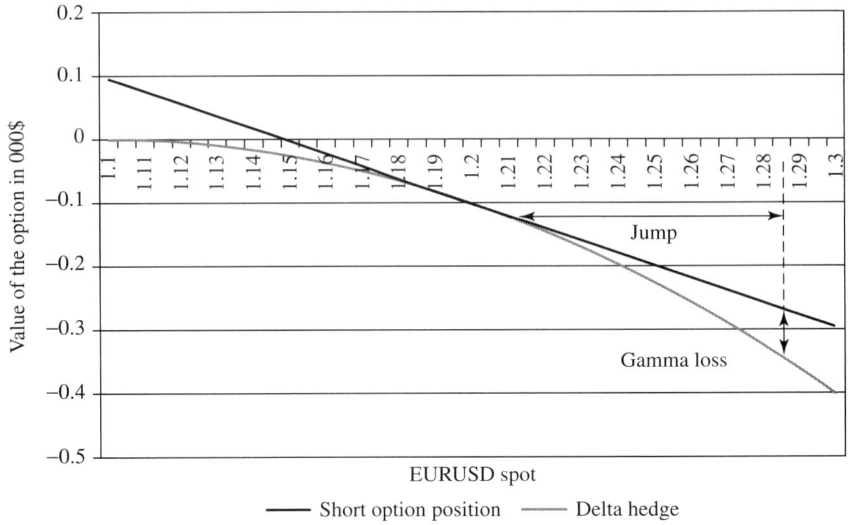


FIGURE 24.2 **Short gamma.**

gain more and lose less than the delta hedge due to the time value, or gamma, that is given by the following formula:

$$\frac{1}{2}\sigma^2 S^2 \Gamma \delta t \phi^2 \tag{24.3}$$

where $\phi$ is a number drawn from the standard normal distribution.

The expected value of the previous formula is simply given by

$$\frac{1}{2}\sigma^2 S^2 \Gamma \delta t \tag{24.4}$$

as the expected value of $\phi^2$ is just its variance.

For a long option, gamma is positive, therefore the difference between delta hedging and holding the option is positive. If gamma is negative, that is, we sold an option to a client and we are trying to replicate it using all sorts of delta hedging techniques, there will be a loss in our portfolio due to that gamma. But, as you know, there is no free lunch. For the gamma gains, we paid a premium. Similarly, we receive a premium to cover the gamma losses. This risk cannot be replicated using forward contracts of other linear instruments; therefore, the market for options that provides the risk management of the gamma exists and has flourished over time (Fig. 24.3).

For purchasers of insurance, their goal is to have a payoff that is the maximum between what they have now and what they would have if they invested in a risky asset. As this payoff is convex in nature, the expected value of this payoff is greater than the payoff of expected values. Portfolio insurance strategies[6] only

[6]Eric Bouye "Portfolio Insurance: A Short Introduction" (Bouyé, 2009).

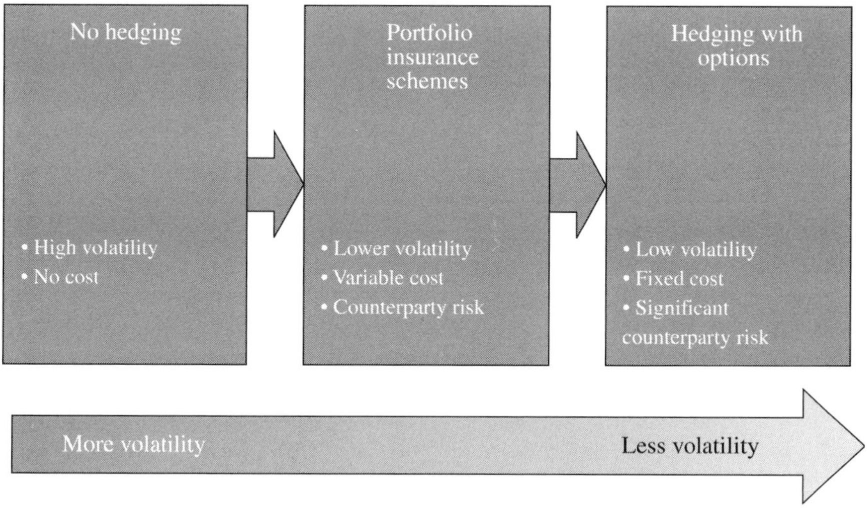


FIGURE 24.3 **Stages of hedging.**

approximate the payoff in the first order but still run a risk. So there is still a basis risk that remains between options payoff and a dynamic replication strategy. The price of the option depends on that risk.

As an example of the portfolio insurance strategy, let us consider a stop-loss strategy. The strategy buys a currency forward if the currency trades at $F$, and sells as soon as the price goes below $F$. Schematically this strategy is presented in Figures 24.4 and 24.5.

We can say that the payoff of the stop-loss strategy is given by $\text{Max}(S_T - F_0, 0)$, where $S_T$ is the end value of the currency spot at time $T$ and $F_0 = S_0 e^{(r_d - r_f)T}$ is the currency forward price at the time of initiation of the strategy.

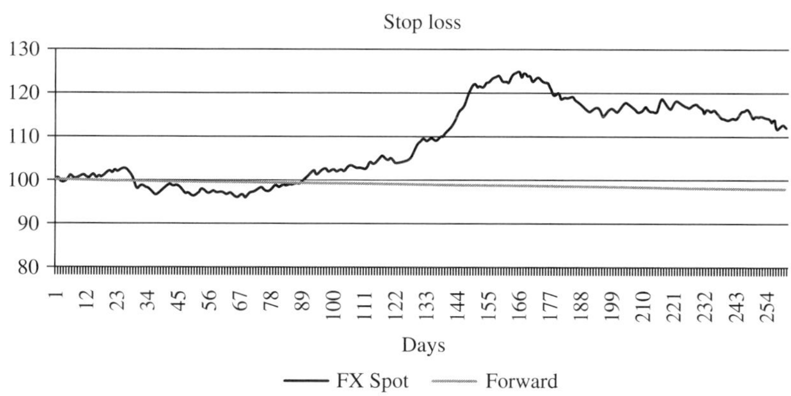


FIGURE 24.4 **Stop loss.**

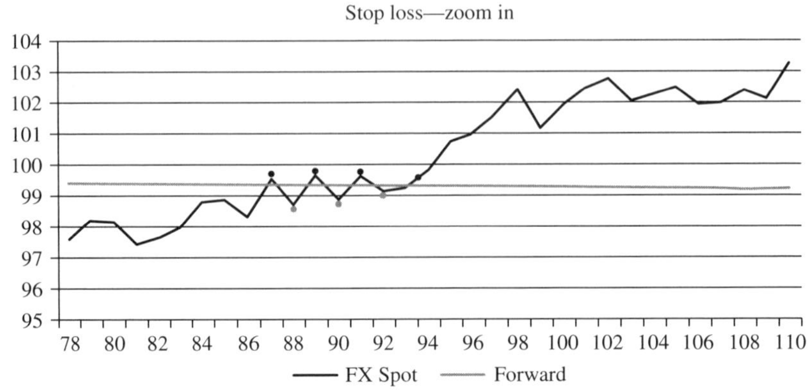


FIGURE 24.5 **Stop loss—zoom in.**

The slope of the forward line implies that the spot trades at a discount. As soon as the spot crosses the forward line and is in-the-money, we buy a forward that matures at time $T$, and as soon as the spot crosses the forward line and is out-the-money, we sell forward that matures at time $T$. In other words, we always transact at a present value. If so, then the cost of this strategy appears to be zero. Where is the catch? The catch is that we do not trade at the forward price, as we need to know where the spot is moving. Hence, the price at which we buy at the moment $t$ will be strictly greater than and the same holds for the sell. The prices at which we buy are shown in black in the diagram and the prices at which we sell are shown in gray. These small slippages constitute the cost of such a portfolio insurance. The cost will vary and is a random variable itself. This random variable is called *local time* and the expected value of local time, having the assumptions from the Black–Scholes framework is given by the Black–Scholes formula.[7] If the spot tends to trend, that is, spot changes have a positive serial correlation, then the cost of the stop-loss strategy will be lower on average than the Black–Scholes price. However, if the spot changes are negatively serially correlated then the average cost of such insurance will be greater than the Black–Scholes price. Therefore, the stop-loss strategy is a kind of trend following strategy. Generally speaking, the stop-loss strategy is equivalent to delta hedging with the assumption of zero volatility.[8] In delta hedging the error depends on how close the volatility input in the delta is to realized volatility. Therefore, assuming zero volatility makes the cost of the stop loss very uncertain, hence, risky and where there is risk, there will be another derivative trying to mitigate that risk at a certain cost.[9]

---

[7] P. Carr, R Jarrow Stop-Loss Start-Gain paradox (Carr and Jarrow, 1990).

[8] Rebonatto, Volatility and correlation (Rebonatto, 2004).

[9] See "Contract paying future variance along the strike" in "Toward a Theory of volatility trading" by Carr and Madan (1998).

## 24.3 Market for FX Options

### 24.3.1 OVERVIEW

According to the latest BIS report,[10] average daily turnover in the options market is US$207 billion. This is based on the face amount of options being transacted. This represents only 5% of the total FX daily turnover of around US$4 trillion. At the same time, spot transactions represent US$1.5 trillion. According to multiple sources in investment banks, options generate around 30% of the spot turnover due to delta hedging and gamma adjustments. Actually the turnover in the spot market generated by options can be greater, as the initial delta will be almost 0.5 on average; and then all further gamma trades will create additional flow on a daily basis (Table 24.1).

Another interesting set of numbers that give us a flavor of the market are the amounts outstanding (Table 24.2). You can see that, from 2007 to 2010, the notional amount outstanding went down, while the gross market values went up. The percentage is approximately the average cost of an option. This percentage was almost double what it had been 3 years ago. One reason for this is the volatility—the price of insurance went up following the crisis. Another reason is that the time to maturity of the outstanding options has increased, as investors are paying long-term premium to be hedged for longer, again based on their experience during 2007–2008.

**TABLE 24.1 BIS Report, Global Foreign Exchange Market Turnover**

Global foreign exchange market turnover[a]
Daily averages in April, in billions of US dollars

| Instrument/Maturity | 1998 | 2001 | 2004 | 2007 | 2010 |
|---|---|---|---|---|---|
| *Foreign exchange instruments* | 1527 | 1239 | 1934 | 3324 | 3981 |
| Spot transactions[b] | 568 | 386 | 631 | 1005 | 1490 |
| Outright forwards[b] | 128 | 130 | 209 | 362 | 475 |
| Up to 7 days | 65 | 51 | 92 | 154 | 219 |
| Over 7 days | 62 | 80 | 116 | 208 | 256 |
| Foreign exchange swaps[b] | 734 | 656 | 954 | 1714 | 1765 |
| Up to 7 days | 528 | 451 | 700 | 1329 | 1304 |
| Over 7 days | 202 | 204 | 252 | 382 | 459 |
| Currency swaps | 10 | 7 | 21 | 31 | 43 |
| Options and other products[c] | 87 | 60 | 119 | 212 | 207 |
| *Memo:* | | | | | |
| Turnover at April 2010 exchange rates[d] | 1705 | 1505 | 2040 | 3370 | 3981 |
| Estimated gaps in reporting | 49 | 30 | 116 | 152 | 144 |
| Exchange-traded derivatives[e] | 11 | 12 | 26 | 80 | 168 |

[a]Adjusted for local and cross-border inter-dealer double-counting (ie "net-net" basis).
[b]Previously classified as part of the so-called "Traditional FX market".
[c]The category "other FX products" covers highly leveraged transactions and/or trades whose notional amount is variable and where a decomposition into individual plain vanilla components was impractical or impossible.
[d]Non-US dollar legs of foreign currency transactions were converted into original currency amounts at average exchange rates for April of each survey year and then reconverted into US dollar amounts at average April 2010 exchange rates.
*Sources:* FOW TRADEdata: Futures Industry Association; various futures and options exchanges. Reported monthly data were converted into daily averages of 20.5 days in 1998, 19.5 days in 2001, 20.5 in 2004, 20 in 2007 and 20 in 2010.

[10]Triennial Central Bank Survey, Report on global FX market activity in 2010.

**TABLE 24.2 Global Positions in OTC Derivatives Markets by Type of Instrument**

Global positions in OTC derivatives markets by type of instrument[a]
Amounts outstanding, in billions of US dollars

| | Positions at end-June 2007 | | | Positions at end-June 2010 | | |
|---|---|---|---|---|---|---|
| | National amounts | Gross market values | %[b] | National amounts | Gross market values | %[b] |
| Foreign exchange contracts | 57,604 | 1612 | 2.8 | 62,933 | 3,158 | 5.0 |
| Outright forwards and FX swaps | 29,775 | 668 | 2.2 | 31,935 | 1,330 | 4.2 |
| Currency swaps | 14,130 | 666 | 4.7 | 18,890 | 1,372 | 7.3 |
| Options | 13,662 | 279 | 2.0 | 12,107 | 456 | 3.8 |
| Other | 37 | — | — | 1 | — | — |
| Memo: Exchange-traded currency contracts[c] | 326 | — | — | 386 | — | — |

[a]Adjusted for inter-dealer double-counting.
[b]Gross market values as a percentage of notional amounts.
[c]*Sources*: FOW TRADEdata; Futures Industry Association; various futures and options exchanges.

## 24.3.2 PLAYERS

FX options-market participants can be broadly classified as

- suppliers of insurance
- consumers of insurance (hedgers)
- market makers
- insurance brokers
- speculators
- central banks.

*Suppliers of insurance* are typically the balance sheet holders who would like to improve their yield by selling a covered option; for example, Japanese corporate or European corporate investors. Investment banks can also supply options by delta hedging, but predominantly investment banks try to offset a short option position by finding it somewhere cheaper and delta hedging the residuals. In major investment banks when an option is booked by traders, it is immediately booked together with a proper delta hedge transaction, so when the option arrives to the book, it is pretty much delta neutral. Then all other hedges, such as vega or gamma, if necessary, are applied to the whole book. If a bank has a good insight on the future currency movement then the hedging position will be taking advantage of that insight. So the bid/offer spread earned by the bank is reinvested and the whole desk acts as an independent player. Another important category of insurance suppliers are systematic hedge funds, as they act as insurance companies and run their proprietary actuary models.

*Consumers of insurance* are the players who have too much risk in their portfolios and need to reduce it. It could be an American corporate or international investors exposed to unrewarded currency risk, such as investors in foreign assets. They tend to strip out the volatility of their portfolios caused by currency using options or portfolio insurance, and then lever back the portfolio with an alternative type of investment. Most of the global macrohedge funds express their views by buying options, as it gives them proper leverage in case they are right and limited loss if they are wrong.

*Market makers* provide the market with liquidity, they connect buyers and sellers and most of their earnings are given by the bid/offer spread on implied volatility. We can say that most of the market makers in the FX options space are investment banks with an independent volatility model. A market maker would typically earn only bid/offer spread on vanilla options and will use its proprietary model to price an exotic instrument. As an exotic instrument often tries to reduce upfront cost, there is a premium to be earned by market makers (investment banks) who are trying to separate different risks into vanilla options and only offer to the market players those bits to which they are most sensitive. Market makers can synthesize options by delta hedging them, and they are rewarded for taking on this risk by charging more for the option. Of course, there is a balance to be aware of: the more you hedge the more expensive the option; but the more a bank charges, the more clients go to another bank who undertakes more risk. On the other hand, the more risk a bank undertakes, the greater the counterparty risk for the client.

*Insurance brokers* mainly transact for retail consumers, which are small size hedge funds, wealthy individuals, etc.

*Speculators* are relative value players in the volatility market, they tend to buy options when they are cheap and sell them when they are expensive, relative to the level of expected realized volatility given by their proprietary models.

*Central banks* transact in the FX options markets, although very rarely. Central banks are, in a way, balance sheet providers; they can sell or buy options depending on the goal of the bank. Most of the time the goal of the bank is to keep the currency exchange rate in a certain corridor. This goal can be achieved by selling options to the market assuming that the market will be hedging its position. For instance, the SNB in 2010 sold straddles in the market to support the Swiss Franc from appreciation against the Euro and did it quite successfully for a period of time.

FX derivatives instruments can be classified into three categories as follows:

- vanilla puts and calls and combination of those,
- exotic options such as barrier options, one touch digital options, and baskets, and
- volatility derivatives, such as volatility swaps and forward volatility agreements (FVAs).

As with the equity derivatives market, exotic options are typically cheaper upfront for a client to buy. But most of the time this cheapness is only relative, as exotics are more expensive on a relative basis. This happens because of the fact

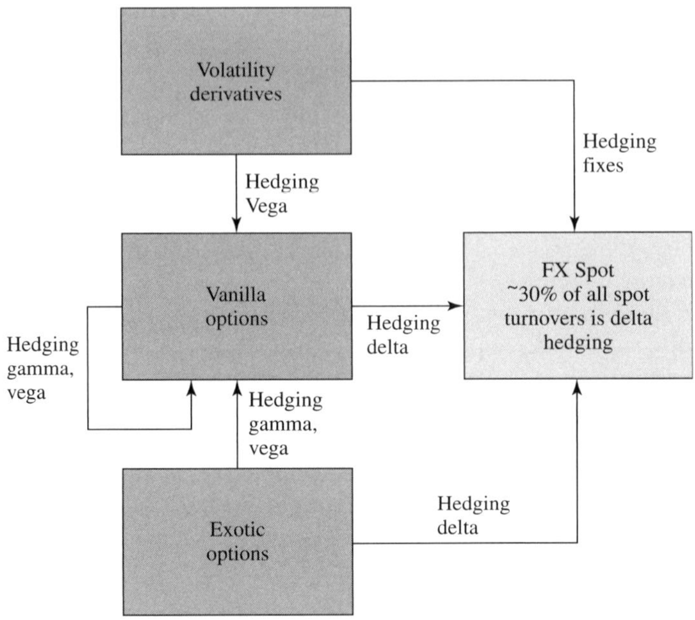


**FIGURE 24.6** **FX options hedging flows.**

that the cost of production of such an option is more expensive and, therefore, the margin is bigger, in spite of the fact that the upfront price of that option is lower.

Every option from the sell-side perspective requires hedging, and these are the flows that arise to hedge different categories of options. Vanilla options are hedged using spot and other vanilla options, exotic options are hedged with vanilla and (rarely) spot, while volatility derivatives are hedged with vanilla options and with spot depending on the type of the option (Figs. 24.6 and 24.7).[11]

### 24.3.3 SETTING THE PRICE

The price of an FX option is determined by the implied volatility, which is determined by a trader who actively makes the market. A trader works with the volatility surface[12] and sets the bid/offer implied volatility. Then, the trader will use their underlying model to know what implied moments of the distribution to expect. If their findings coincide with their view the prices remain; otherwise the trader will readjust the volatilities. To set a fair price for a contingent claim is difficult because a series of strong assumptions need to be made. The most important assumption that FX options traders usually make are

[11]The best way to hedge an option is to offset it with another option at the same terms at a better price and with a minimum counterparty risk.

[12]To define the price of vanilla call or put, it is required to know the maturity and the strike. The implied volatility as a function of maturity of an option and the strike can be represented as a surface, it is called *volatility surface*.

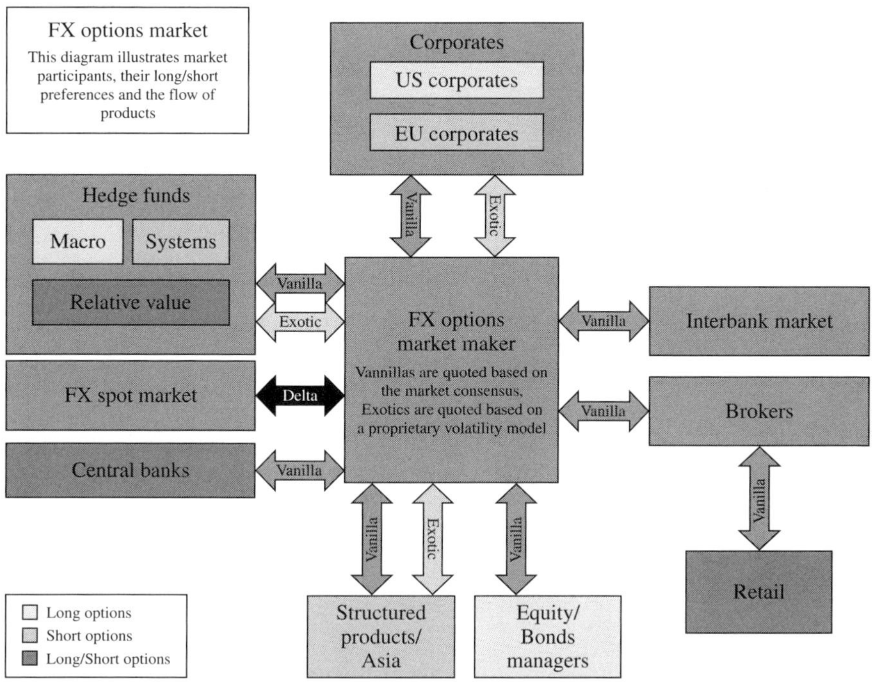


FIGURE 24.7 FX options market.

- **Expected realized volatility** The following factors are taken into account when this judgment is performed:
  - What is the market now?—analysis of supply and demand of options on the current situation in the market place.
  - What is the level of historic volatility?—analysis of the liquidity in the market.[13]
- **Expected skewness**
  - Current level of risk reversals, changes relative to the past, and analysis of demand and supply, especially if interest rates are changing as the skewness of the currency pair correlates with interest rates differential.[14]
  - Watching for a build up of a speculative position in spot, which may lead to a sharp unwind in the underlying. As the skewness may represent the crash risk premium, the trader needs to assess it properly.

[13] Important considerations regarding the volume and the volatility are made by Gatheral here: http://finmath.stanford.edu/seminars/docs/ml2004win.pdf.

[14] The correlation might exist because of the number of structured products that involve purchase of OTM (Out-the-money) options on the interest rate differential proceeds, the greater the differential, the greater the demand.

- **Expected kurtosis**
  - Current level of butterflies, changes relative to the past, analysis of demand and supply. Are any trends or sharp moves expected in either direction?
- **Expected term structure** A PCA (principal component analysis) analysis can show that the term structure of the volatility has three main principal components, which explain most of its variance:
  - parallel shift—when there is a demand/supply of a specific strike or maturity; typically the entire surface will respond, otherwise arbitrage opportunities may arise.
  - "steepener" that changes the relative price of the short- and long-term volatilities—this happens when the general level of risk aversion changes. In a risky environment, there is a greater demand for short-term options, especially in the interbank market and in benign environment the curve flattens but still with a long-term volatility premium priced in.
  - "gull" that changes the relative volatility of the medium term versus the short- and long term—this happens because of a specific event in the medium-term future, which is anticipated by the market.

Besides all of these factors that just approximate trader's intuition, there is a gut feel and the memory of the past experiences, both of which are absolutely path dependent and differ from one trader to another.

## 24.4 Volatility

### 24.4.1 OVERVIEW OF MODELS

Another assumption that the Black–Scholes framework relies on is that the volatility is constant over time (geometric Brownian motion) and that the same volatility may be used to price options at different strikes and at different maturities. This is simply not consistent with market observations, especially in FX. Of course, the volatility surface did not exist back in 1973. However, the smile[15] in volatility across different strikes consistently featured in the market in the 14 years after the market crash of 1987.[16] The volatility of the FX market changes over time. See Figure 24.8 for an illustration.

Time-varying volatility is another source for the risk in options-market making—and again another source for the creation of a derivative. For example, the FVA is quite a popular structured product offered by many banks in which the buyer has to purchase an ATMF straddle for an agreed maturity, at a starting at a point in future.

[15] Implied volatility as a function of the strike price at a fixed maturity usually represents a U-shape function, hence the name *smile*.

[16] E. Derman, Risk regimes of volatility (Derman, 1999).

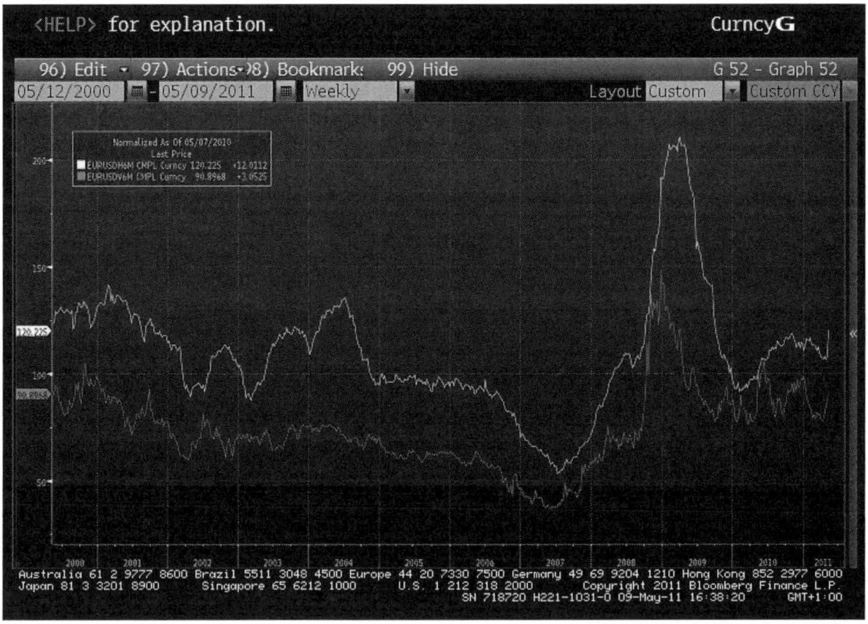


FIGURE 24.8 Implied volatility versus historic volatility EUR/USD.

People are learning machines, who always adapt to new circumstances and learn from the past. The Black–Scholes model became a reference point, a starting point for any model that learnt what went wrong in the past in terms of the initial assumptions made and adapted to new market paradigms. The introduction of the jump component, making the volatility stochastic,[17] and then combining these two approaches together, together represent a very interesting class of models that can provide a buy-side options researcher with additional information.

The behavior of the volatility of spot changes determines the behavior of option prices, as the volatility of spot determines the cost of hedging an option. We pointed out earlier that in the FX market we can have discontinuities due to various reasons as follows:

- central bank intervention
- liquidity squeeze.

They can be modeled as jumps. The presence of jumps leads to an enhancement of the geometric Brownian motion model by adding a jump component. The equation of motion is as follows:

$$dS = \mu S dt + \sigma S dZ + (e^{\alpha+\beta\varepsilon} - 1) S dq \tag{24.5}$$

[17] Stochastic volatility models assume that volatility of spot is not constant but evolves dynamically in a random manner, typically mean revering around a certain predefined parameter.

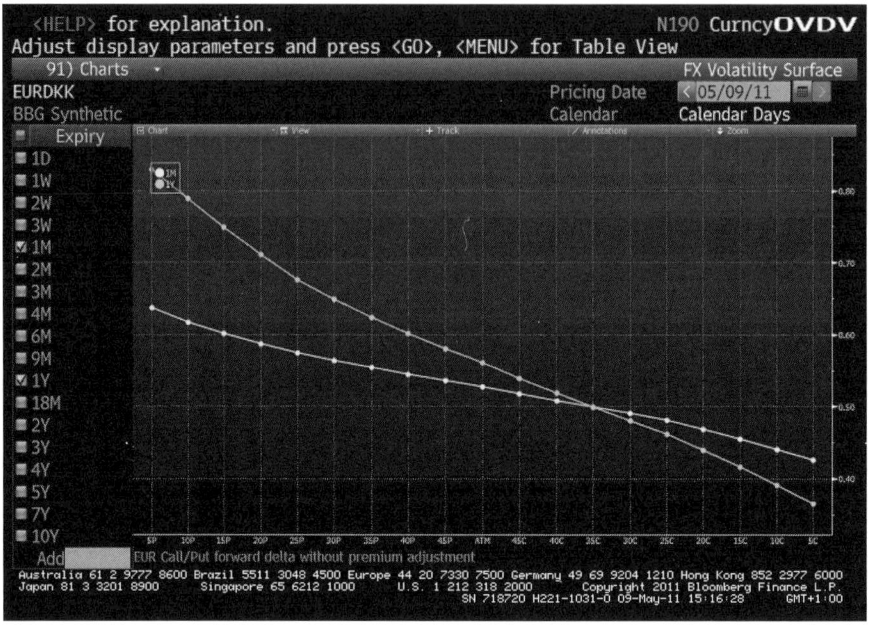


FIGURE 24.9 EUR/DKK implied volatility smiles.

We refer to the model as *BSJ*, Black–Scholes with a jump or a jump diffusion model. Such a model is more consistent with market observations and can fit a smile in FX options quite well. From the buy-side perspective, the information enclosed in the calibrated parameters of the jump component is quite valuable: if the jump in the currency is expected, for example, a central bank announcement, or possible intervention, or even break of peg, then the Poisson jump coefficients tell us the size, magnitude, and probability of the jump expected. And now if you as a manager think that this is too much or too little you can decide to take action. Let us consider an example. In Figure 24.9, there is a EUR/DKK volatility smile created from options that mature in 1 year's time:

The calibration of this model is done using the characteristic function method.[18] Briefly, the methodology contains the following several steps:

1. The price of an option is given by Black–Scholes using the volatility surface from the market.
2. The option price equation is a function of the characteristic function[19]:

$$C(S,K,T) = S - \sqrt{SK}\frac{1}{pi}\int_0^{\inf} \frac{du}{u^2+\frac{1}{4}} \mathrm{Re}\left[e^{-iuk}\phi_T\left(u-\frac{i}{2}\right)\right] \quad (24.6)$$

[18]The matlab code is available on demand.

[19]Carr, Madan 1999 "Options valuation using the fast Fourier transform" (Carr and Madan, 1999).

3. The characteristic function is found using Levy–Khintchine representation of the spot change differential equation. For the Black–Scholes model, the function is $\phi_T(u) = e^{-\frac{1}{2}u(u+i)\sigma^2 T}$. More details on different characteristic functions can be found in Gatheral 2004.[20]
4. Find such parameters of the characteristic function, which minimize the price of options along the surface.

Table 24.3 shows the result of the calibration of the 1y smile in EUR/DKK. The EUR/DKK currency pair is pegged and moves only in a very narrow band. In spite of this, the implied volatility of this currency pair is quite high, even while the historic volatility is around 0.5% annualized. Table 24.3 shows that the probability of a sudden jump is 8%. This is the level at which the market prices it. If an event happens then the jump is more likely to be down, that is, in the direction of appreciation of the Danish Krone and the size of this jump is quite uncertain. This information provides us with the following insights:

1. The spread between pure implied volatility and realized volatility could represent an opportunity, as long as the bid/offer spread allows it.
2. The jump can be associated with relevant events that are taking place around one of the currencies in the pair. For example, the current problems with the euro may cause the Danish economy to repeg the currency at a higher rate; the probability of that event in the absence of other events can be given by the probability of the jump.

Although the jump model can be consistent with the volatility skew, the time-varying volatility or stochastic volatility model is another way to model the smile in FX. For an example, we can consider the Heston model. The beauty of this model is that it has a closed form solution and, using the same calibration method of characteristic function, the parameters can be calibrated quite easily. Another enhancement that can be made is to add jumps first to the spot equation and then to the volatility equation. Such models are classed as SVJ and SVJJ.[21] A family of volatility models, which are relatively parsimonious and provide information about the FX market is presented in Figure 24.10.

The number of models that can fit the volatility surface and model the FX smile is enormous: SABR, the local volatility model, the Double–Heston model,

**TABLE 24.3 Decomposition of the Smile into Random Walk and a Jump Component**

| Currency Pair | Volatility of Spot | Probability of Jump (lambda) | Average Size of the Jump | Standard Deviation of the Jump |
|---|---|---|---|---|
| EUR/DKK | 1% | 8% | −1% | 4% |

[20] Gatheral "Volatility Surface" (Gatheral, 2004b).

[21] Gatheral "Volatility Surface" (Gatheral, 2004b).

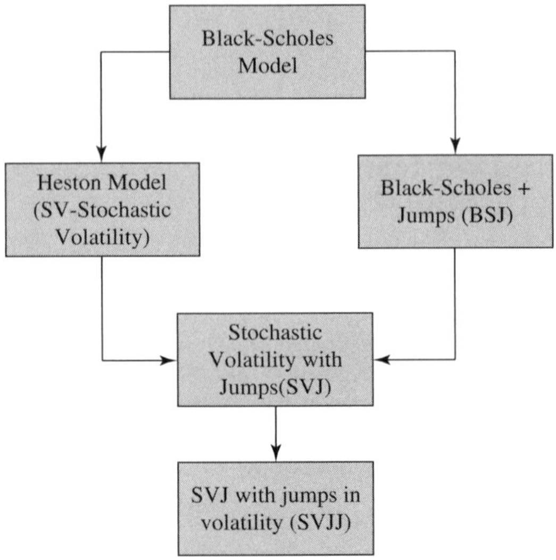


FIGURE 24.10 Parsimonious volatility models.

the stochastic correlation model, and many more. In other words, the more parameters you add, the greater fit you get. Other volatility models may work better than the two models described above for one reason: they fit the curve better. The reason we focus on the class of models described in the diagram is because the parameters can be easily interpreted; therefore, investment decisions can be made faster and with more clarity, as the reason for using options in the analysis is the extraction of information about market beliefs.

Although these models are quite parsimonious, they may not fit the volatility smile with the greatest precision. The class of models that seems to work in the FX market and is becoming a market standard is the local volatility model and mixed model. The last class of models represents just a blending of different models such as local volatility and stochastic volatility. The weights are again determined using the best fit principle.

### 24.4.2 SOME STYLIZED FACTS AND IMPLIED MOMENTS

The distribution of currency returns is not normal. It can be observed that currency returns exhibit nonzero correlation between volatility and spot returns (leverage effect,[22] skewness), and that they exhibit fat tails (extreme moves, kurtosis). All higher order moments of the distribution should be reflected in the options market and they are to a certain extent. The skewness of the realized distribution can be associated with the asymmetry of the volatility smile, while

[22]The notion leverage effect comes from the equity world, which means when the share price of the company goes down, then the leverage of the company increases and the stock becomes more volatile—negative correlation between volatility of the stock and the rate of change of price.

fat tails can be associated with the level of implied volatility for extreme strikes in comparison to ATM (at the money). For the second, third, and fourth moments, there is a mapping from realized to implied volatility.

The OTC currency market quotes volatility in terms of the delta-neutral straddle, 10-delta and 25-delta risk reversals, ("riskies") and butterfly spreads ("fly"):

$$\begin{aligned}
\mathrm{ATMV}_T &= \mathrm{IV}_T(0) \\
\mathrm{RR}_T(10) &= \mathrm{IV}_T\left(d_{10}^c\right) - \mathrm{IV}_T\left(d_{10}^p\right) \\
\mathrm{RR}_T(25) &= \mathrm{IV}_T\left(d_{25}^c\right) - \mathrm{IV}_T\left(d_{25}^p\right) \\
\mathrm{BF}_T(10) &= \left(\mathrm{IV}_T\left(d_{10}^c\right) + \mathrm{IV}_T\left(d_{10}^p\right)\right)/2 - \mathrm{ATMV}_T \\
\mathrm{BF}_T(25) &= \left(\mathrm{IV}_T\left(d_{25}^c\right) + \mathrm{IV}_T\left(d_{25}^p\right)\right)/2 - \mathrm{ATMV}_T
\end{aligned} \tag{24.7}$$

where $d_{10}^p, d_{25}^p$ are the deviation from the ATM level of put options and $d_{10}^c, d_{25}^c$ for call options, respectively.

There are the following rule-of-thumb approximations of high order moments using market quotations:

$$\begin{aligned}
\sigma_T &\approx \mathrm{ATMV}_T \\
s_T &\approx \frac{2.3409\mathrm{RR}_T(10)}{\mathrm{ATMV}_T} \\
k_T &\approx \frac{14.6130\mathrm{BF}_T(10)}{\mathrm{ATMV}_T}
\end{aligned} \tag{24.8}$$

And for 25 delta:

$$\begin{aligned}
s_T &\approx \frac{4.4478\mathrm{RR}_T(25)}{\mathrm{ATMV}_T} \\
k_T &\approx \frac{52.7546\mathrm{BF}_T(25)}{\mathrm{ATMV}_T}
\end{aligned} \tag{24.9}$$

The derivations of these relationships is based on the observation that

$$\mathrm{IV}_T(d) = \sigma_T\left(1 - \frac{1}{6}s_T d - \frac{1}{24}k_T\left(1 - d^2\right)\right) \tag{24.10}$$

And has been summarized by P. Carr and L. Wu.[23]

[23] P Carr and L. Wu "The information content of straddles, risk reversals and butterfly spreads" (Carr and Wu, 2005).

Realized moments are estimated using the following expressions:

$$\begin{aligned} \widehat{\sigma} &= \sqrt{\frac{1}{N}\sum_{i=1}^{N} r_i^2} \\ \widehat{s} &= \frac{1}{N\widehat{\sigma}^3}\sum_{i=1}^{N} r_i^3 \end{aligned} \tag{24.11}$$

$\widehat{k} = \frac{1}{N\widehat{\sigma}^4}\sum_{i=1}^{N} r_i^4 - 3$, where $r_i$ is currency daily returns, and $N$ is number of observations in the sample.

As the volatility surface is quoted in annualized volatility, then the expressions above need to be scaled appropriately. In the fourth part, we see how to use these expressions.

### 24.4.3 IS VOLATILITY AN ASSET CLASS?

An asset is a resource with economic value that an individual, corporation, or country owns or controls with the expectation that it will provide future benefit.[24] When we think about an asset we think about something tangible: in case of bonds, it is a coupon and the yield at the prevailing rate of interest; in case of equities, it is the future dividends. Volatility is a barometer of uncertainty and risk in the market. The greater the volatility, the lower is the reward/risk ratio of a currency position, and for this reason a long position in volatility may compensate a risk taker for lower risk/reward ratios.

The concept of volatility is similar to the concept of inflation. There is realized inflation, that is, by how much prices went up or down in the past, and expected inflation, which is how much the market is pricing in at a particular moment in certain yields on a treasury curve. Finally, there is future realized inflation that is not known. In this, it is the same as future realized volatility, which is similarly unknown.

When a fixed income instrument is bought, a bond for instance, there is a risk that the future realized inflation is going to deteriorate the value of the bond. Therefore, there should be a reward for this risk and demand for a premium, a discount in the value of the bond that will compensate a risk taker. This also happens with volatility: when we sell an option, the level of realized volatility during a period of holding can be higher, and therefore the option premium we paid in the beginning must compensate fully for the increasing risk of the realized volatility. In terms of risk premium drivers, we can identify the following similarities with bonds[25]:

Exposure to volatility by definition should not be correlated with other conventional risks as volatility exposure is market or delta neutral. The more uncertainty is in the market the more return the volatility strategy should yield.

---

[24] Investopedia.

[25] E Derman (Trading Volatility as an asset class) (Derman).

**TABLE 24.4 Risk Premium Drivers of Volatility and Fixed Income**

| Risk Premium Drivers | Buying a Bond | Selling an Option (Volatility) |
|---|---|---|
| Satisfying needs of the market | Provision with capital: government and corporations require capital to generate more wealth, and so will offer a premium. One can think of this as a default risk or a risk of sudden value deterioration. | Provision with insurance: markets requires insurance, and corporations will pay for it to protect themselves against a sudden jump in the spot market. For this reason, the gap risk has to be rewarded in the options. |
| Path risk | Inflation risk: while a bond is held, its value can remain high, but the purchasing power of money can deteriorate. Therefore, the locking of the capital in the bond till maturity presents a risk that inflation may be higher than expected; and one needs to be compensated for this risk. Theoretically, this inflation should be reflected in rates and can then be viewed as a market risk (see below); but this is only a theoretical assumption. | Realized volatility risk: if an option is sold, its value can remain high. However, the risk of this option to end in the money, due to high realized volatility, is also higher; and consequently this drags up the payoff to the counterparty. When an option is sold, the seller must be compensated for this risk. |
| Market | Interest rate risk: change in interest rate affects the value of the bond. Therefore, the mark to market value of the bond is at risk. This bond is still the same in the sense that the coupon payments and the principal amount are expected to be the same. | Implied volatility risk: if an investor sold an option at the rate of 10% implied annualized volatility, and if subsequently the price of volatility increases by 5%, the mark to market value of investor's liability also goes up. If he wants to buy it back from the market, he will have to pay more than he acquired at its sale. Again, he should be compensated for this risk (Table 24.4). |

And similarly the greater the quantity of movements the greater is the return of the volatility strategy. Moreover, in the presence of the negative skewness in the market, the positive returns in volatility are negatively correlated with the market and therefore exposure to volatility helps diversify the downside risk.

Like interest rates, volatility has its own term structures, two of which should be highlighted: the term structure of implied volatility, which is the expected volatility over different horizons; and the term structure of realized volatility, which is the volatility at daily, weekly, monthly, or any other frequency of observation. Bearing this in mind, there is a set of opportunities in both realized and implied markets:

- *Implied Volatility Market*. Market for options, variance swaps, volatility swaps, and correlation swaps, which offers premium for volatility sellers
  - *Volatility premium*, harvesting the differential between implied and realized volatility. Such premium prevails in short-dated options, as there could be an excess demand for cheap gamma. This strategy involves selling short-dated options and creating a book of positions and then hedging only residual risks employing delta hedging.
  - *Path premium*, harvesting path premium is based on the mean-reverting property of volatility. When volatility is high then the strategy sells options, and when volatility is low, the strategy tends to buy options. The highs and lows are determined by the nature of the mean reversion a manager believes in. A currency pair example can be EUR/CHF, when a relatively calm regime is succeeded by a turbulent regime and vice versa.
  - *Crash premium*, similar to volatility premium, but in this case a manager models the behavior of the skewness of the smile, and then sells the skew and buys volatility when volatility is too high, and vice versa. For example, one could sell an OTM put with expensive volatility and buy an ATM put with cheap volatility.
  - *Term structure*, there is a premium in the long-dated options, the term *structures* are typically upward sloping, and so the forward volatility is priced at a premium. This strategy can be built using forward volatility agreements, or rebalancing calendar spreads.
  - *Relative value*, looking at the implied volatility surface anomalies can be identified at different strikes, maturities, and currency pairs. The main principle is to see what is the cost of a greek per unit of premium spent. Some volatility hedge funds operate in exactly this niche when they source the live implied volatility quotes from several providers and compare their models.
  - *Realized volatility/correlation premium*, strategies involving buying and selling volatility using vanilla options need to be delta hedged. As will emerge later, delta hedging P&L has more sources of uncertainty, and this not only exposes a manager to the view he is pursuing but also exposes the strategy to model risk and the risk of spot path dependency. Variance swaps (volatility swaps) or correlation swaps eliminates the problem, as is discussed below.
- *Realized volatility market*, "managed futures" type of strategies: trending and market making
  - *Trending*, momentum strategies provide positive exposure to the long-dated realized volatility and negative exposure to the short-dated realized

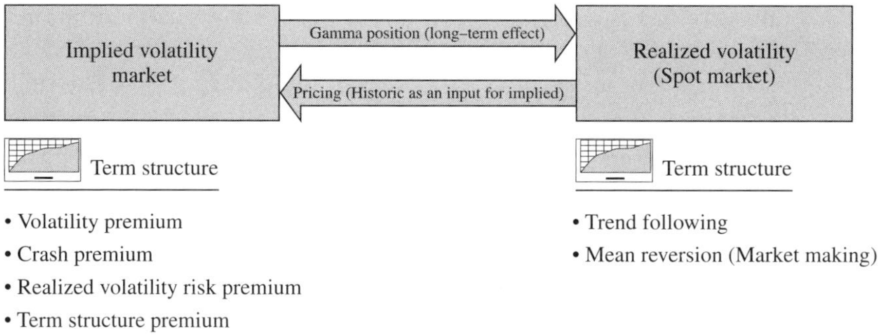


**FIGURE 24.11** Opportunities in the volatility market.

volatility. However, there are some points to be aware of in exploiting the volatility using trend following strategies. They are covered by Kremer, Krishnan and Malek[26]

- *Mean reversion (market making)*, this is the opposite of trending and provides negative exposure to the long-dated realized volatility, and positive exposure to the short-term realized volatility. One example is a reverse delta hedge of an imaginary long straddle: if the market reverts to the mean, the gamma scalping profits are kept as if the straddle has been sold (Fig. 24.11).

The equity market is the champion of financial engineering, but the currency market is catching up by implementing products that are popular in the equity world. Over the next few sections, we present the main innovative products that migrated to the currency market from the equity market. Such products as variance swaps and correlations swap allow an investor to take a precise position in variance or in correlation, bypassing any directional exposures. It is argued that in the equity market there is a variance risk premium, which a buyer of fixed variance pays.[27] In times of market stress, variance is elevated and pays off to the buyer, therefore a variance swap is a protection against turbulent periods, and especially when the variance in the portfolio hits an investor.

As variance spikes in times of distress, the correlation between assets tends to take extreme values. Generally, in times of distress, the correlation between all risky premia approaches 1. At the same time, the volatility is negatively correlated with the risk premium, and in times of distress, this correlation tends toward $-1$. Therefore, being long correlation means that when the correlation between assets in the portfolio is rising, the portfolio loses diversification and becomes increasingly risky, while this risk is offset by a long position in a correlation instrument.

[26]P., Kremer, H.P.Krishnan, M. Malek, 2004, "Trend Following as a Long Volatility Strategy" (Kremer et al., 2004).

[27]P Carr 1999 "Variance Risk Premium" (Carr, 1999).

**24.4.3.1 Broad Technicalities.** What does "being long volatility" mean? Immediately one thinks of holding a put and/or call on a currency pair. But holding a naïve position in options besides exposure in volatility creates other, perhaps undesirable, exposures such as directional exposures or delta exposures. It can be argued that these can be hedged, but hedging is not a straight forward procedure, since in order to hedge, one needs take a bet on future realized volatility. It was shown by Mougeot that a delta-hedged option position P&L can be decomposed into three parts[28]:

$$P\&L = (\sigma_i^2 - \widehat{\sigma}^2)Tg_0 + (\widehat{\sigma}^2 - \sigma_h^2)T\left[g_0 - \frac{1}{T}\int_0^T g_t \mathrm{d}t\right] + \int_0^T (\widehat{\sigma}^2 - \sigma_t^2)g_t \mathrm{d}t \tag{24.12}$$

Here $\sigma_i$ is the implied volatility at which the option was initially priced, $\sigma_h$ is the volatility at which the option was delta hedged, $\sigma_t$ is the instantaneous volatility during the lifetime of the option, $\widehat{\sigma}$ is the realized historic volatility during the lifetime of the option,[29] and finally $g_t = \frac{e^{r(T-t)}}{2\sigma_h}\frac{\delta}{\delta\sigma}V\left(S_t, T-t; \sigma_h\right)$.

It is thus made clear that the P&L arises from three sources. The first is the risk that realized volatility will be different from implied volatility; the second is the fact that hedging is done at implied rather than realized volatility; and finally, the third is the volatility path dependency risk. If the volatility does not change during the lifetime of the option, the last term will be zero.

**24.4.3.2 Variance Swap.** As has been discussed, delta hedging comes with some risks, and sometimes it is better to outsource warehousing of these risks to an investment bank or a broker. In exchange, it is possible to acquire an instrument that provides exposure to the future realized volatility. A variance swap is a contract that pays the differential between future realized variances and a predetermined variance strike (Fig. 24.12).

The market convention for realized variance is

$$\widehat{\sigma}^2 = \frac{A}{N-1}\sum_{i=1}^{N}\ln\left(\frac{S_i}{S_{i-1}}\right)^2 \tag{24.13}$$

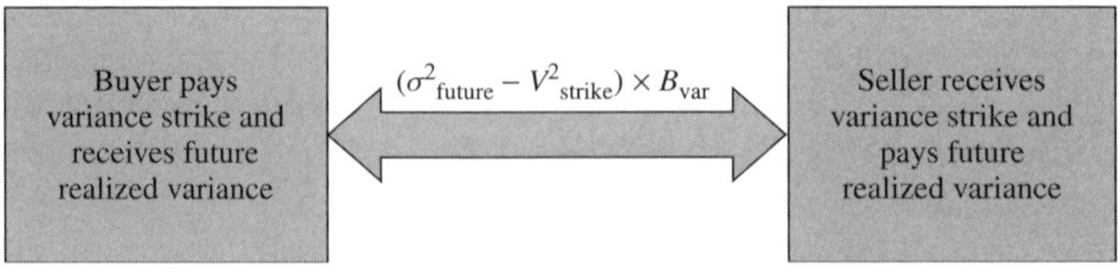


FIGURE 24.12 The payoff of a variance swap.

[28] Mougeot 2004, "Volatility Investing Handbook," BNP Paribas (Mougeot, 2004).

[29] $\widehat{\sigma}^2 = \frac{1}{T}\int_0^T \sigma_t^2 \mathrm{d}t$.

$S_i$ is fixing of spot exchange rate along the lifetime of the swap. Fixings are agreed at a certain time of the day often WM fixings are used. "A" is the day count factor, since variance has to be calculated per annum: if we have $N$ fixing points and total $M$ calendar days, then $A = N/M \times 365$. If the variance strike $V^2$ is the quote a bank or a broker provides then the payoff is simply $B_{\text{VAR}} * (\widehat{\sigma}^2 - V^2)$, where $B$ is the variance notional.

The notional expresses the sensitivity to the variance, but usually it is more convenient to express the notional as volatility notional or vega notional. Vega notional can be approximately calculated from the variance notional and strike:

$$B_{\text{vega}} = 2V \times B_{\text{VAR}} \tag{24.14}$$

How is it possible to ascertain whether the quote of $V$ is "fair"? First of all, it must be understood where a market maker takes his quote from. Mathematically, pricing of a variance swap is explained by Carr and Madan.[30] The main result of their findings is that the fair strike is given by the following formula:

$$V^2 = \frac{2e^{rT}}{T}\left[\int_0^{F_0} \frac{1}{K^2} P(K)\,\mathrm{d}K + \int_{F_0}^{\inf} \frac{1}{K^2} C(K)\,\mathrm{d}K\right] \tag{24.15}$$

Here $r$ is the domestic interest rate and $T$ is the time to maturity of the variance swap. The term in breakers is inversely weighted by the square of the strike puts and calls. $F_0$ can be taken as the forward at $T$, and the formula then segments the volatility smile into small chunks to approximate the value of these integrals, and so to obtain a reference price for the fair value of the variance swap.

**24.4.3.3 Correlation Swap.** Another currency product that first appeared in the equity market is the correlation swap. The correlation swap allows one to take a view on the correlation between two currency pairs. Like a variance swap, a correlation swap exchanges the realized correlation into strike correlation multiplied by a notional, and the payoff can be expressed as in Figure 24.13.

The realized correlation is calculated according to the following convention:

Let $n$ be the number of spot fixing rates in the correlation rate period. Let $S_{a,i}$ $(i = 1, 2, \ldots, n)$ be the spot fixing rates on fixing time of currency pair "a." Let $R_{a,i}$ $(i = 2, 3, \ldots, n)$ be the daily log returns, $R_{a,i} = \ln\left(\frac{S_{a,i}}{S_{a,i-1}}\right)$

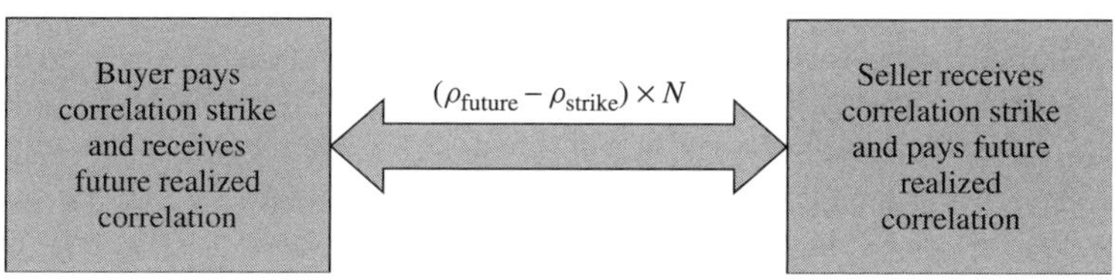


FIGURE 24.13 The payoff of a correlation swap.

[30] P. Carr and D. Madan, 2001, "Towards the theory of volatility trading" (Carr and Madan, 2001).

**TABLE 24.5 Correlation Swap Termsheet**

| | |
|---|---|
| Trade Date: | 09-Mar-10 |
| Effective Date: | 10-Mar-10 |
| Seller: | XYZ Insurance Corp. |
| Buyer: | BANK XYZ |
| Calculation Agent: | BANK XYZ |
| Notional Amount: | USD 10,000 per correlation point |
| First Currency Pair (a) | GBPUSD, number of units of USD per GBP |
| Second Currency Pair (b) | GBPNOK, number of units of NOK per GBP |
| Upfront payment | USD 40,000 paid by the Buyer to the Seller |
| Fixed correlation Rate: | 32.00% |
| First Fixing Date: | 10-Mar-10 |
| Expiration Date: | 09-Mar-11 |
| Fixing source | WMR 4pm Ldn |
| Settlement Currency: | USD |
| Settlement Date: | 11-Mar-11 |

of currency pair $a$; $\bar{R}_a$ be the average of daily returns of currency pair $a$, $\bar{R}_a = \frac{1}{n-1}\sum_{1=2}^{n} R_{a,i}$; and $\sigma_a$ be the volatility of the daily returns of currency pair $a$, $\sqrt{\frac{1}{n-2}\sum_{i=2}^{n}(R_{a,i} - \bar{R}_a)^2}$. Similarly, for currency pair $b$, the settlement correlation rate $= \frac{\frac{1}{n-2}\sum_{i=2}^{n}(R_{a,i}-\bar{R}_a)(R_{b,i}-\bar{R}_b)}{\sigma_a\sigma_b}$. The settlement formula is $100 \times$ (Fixed correlation rate $-$ Settlement correlation rate) $\times$ Notional amount. An example term sheet is given in Table 24.5.

Having the expected future variance formulated mentioned earlier is useful, as it allows one to estimate the expectation regarding the expected realized correlation. The correlation between two currency pairs can be expressed as a function of volatilities (cosine rule):

$$\rho = \frac{\sigma^2_{\text{GBPUSD}} + \sigma^2_{\text{GBPNOK}} - \sigma^2_{\text{USDNOK}}}{2\sigma_{\text{GBPUSD}}\sigma_{\text{GBPNOK}}} \tag{24.16}$$

Now, we take the expectation of this correlation. The expectation of a ratio is not a ratio of expectations, but if we assume that the convexity given by the volatility of each individual variance is not high, then we can estimate the expected realized correlation from variance swap quotes, hence obtaining an expected realized correlation.[31] Most banks price correlation swaps using Monte Carlo methods, as they allow an assessment of the expected value of correlation given the cosine rule. Thus, in FX, the valuation of a swap will depend on the underlying model for volatility, and so it can be thought of as a vega risk to a certain extent.

[31] Qing Deng 2009, "Correlation SWAPs and dynamic correlation models" (Deng, 2009).

**24.4.3.4 Opportunities in FX Volatility.** Emergence of volatility funds in equity markets made fund managers look for new opportunities that the currency market can offer. This is because, as more businesses become multinational, there emerges an increasing need for currency hedging; and hence the premium for writing options increases. After the floatation of the major currencies in the early 1970s, there have always been imbalances that the leaders of G-n countries tried to solve. Indeed, with the benefits that come with floatation, such as the abolishment of capital controls, the development of international trade, and the ability to run an independent monetary policy, there are also disadvantages. As an example of potential volatility opportunity, the 2011 events in the Swiss Franc can be considered, when the SNB pegged the currency to the Euro to counteract the appreciation of the Swiss Franc, which was becoming intolerable for the small but vibrant Swiss economy. The peg reduced volatility but not opportunity.

As the emerging market economies are becoming more competitive and the undervaluation of their currencies is no longer required to attract investment and flow, their currencies will appreciate and become more floating. This will create opportunities for volatility fund managers who can provide liquidity in derivatives in the emerged regions: although the emerging market options are widely traded, they are traded only to the extent of how free their float is.

There are several areas to focus on when assessing long-term opportunities in FX volatility:

- *Pegs*. While assessing long-term opportunities in the FX market, it is worth paying attention to currencies that are pegged. Currencies such as DKK, SAR, CHF, TWD, and CNY experience a lot of pressure, economical as well as political. The law of the impossible trinity[32] makes a fixed exchange rate economy vulnerable to capital flows and shadow monetary policy. Monitoring the level of reserves of a central bank and level of inflation can help in ascertaining pressures.
- *Volatility Mean Reversion*. Very low volatility means that the currency is coupled to another currency that cross experiences low volatility. This coupling has an economic effect. Again, like in the case of a peg, any differences in inflation expectations or rates can create some pressure. Yet, when volatility is too high, it is worth looking at the volatility of currency pairs of countries that have intense trading relationships: high volatility in USD/CAD or EUR/CZK can be a sign of opportunity.
- *Volatility Overreaction*.[33] The volatility surface is modeled using PCA. The first principal component explains parallel shifts in the surface; the second

[32] In economics, the impossible trinity describes a situation in which it is impossible for a country to maintain all three elements of monetary policy: (i) stable exchange rate; (ii) independent monetary policy; and (iii) no capital controls. According to the impossible trinity principle, at least one policy mechanism has to be sacrificed.

[33] J. Stein, "Overreactions in the options market"—although the article focuses on the equity market, the behavioral side of the analysis is suitable for the currency market also (Stein, 1989).

explains the twists in the term structure; and the third finally explains the twists in the smile. The long-term volatility overreaction comes from shocks in the short-term volatility, and the long-term volatility tends to be elevated as the first principal component governs the model. In other words, when the volatility surface moves, it usually moves in the short maturities much more actively than in the long maturities. But even the movements in the long maturities tend to be an overreaction. A similar effect can be present in the smile: after a shock, the smile may get steeper than is sustainable, creating an opportunity.

- *Historic Levels*. As was discussed before, the price for an option is set partly from historic considerations. Therefore, it makes sense to look at the past historic volatility and compare it with the prevailing level of the implied; and also to look at the historic level of the implied and to compare it to the current level of the implied. This two-dimensional volatility radar can be very helpful for spotting extreme movements on different horizons (Fig. 24.14).

### 24.4.4 ANTI-BLACK SWAN STRATEGIES

FX options are used in volatility strategies, amongst which selling short-term options are often seen as a strategy. The analysis of such a strategy can be straightforward. The strategy picks a certain predefined number of selected currency pairs and sell straddles on those currency pairs, which mature in 1 month's time (this is the typical duration of the short-volatility strategy). The same process is repeated every month. The selection is based on the systematic observation that the implied volatility is higher than the historic volatility (Fig. 24.15).

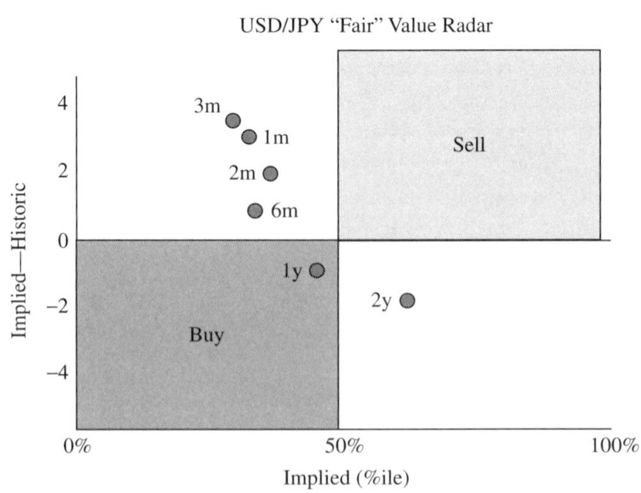


FIGURE 24.14 "Fair" value radar.

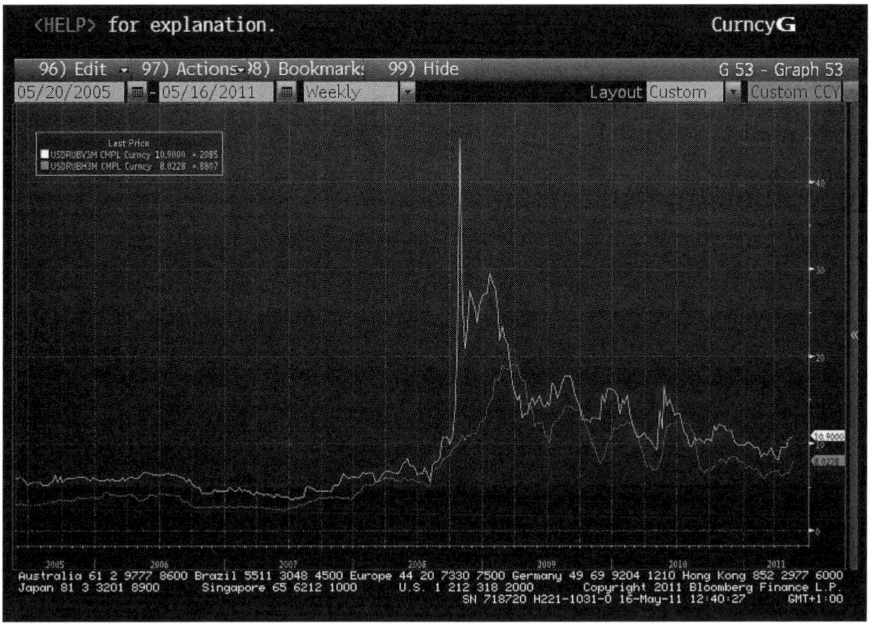


FIGURE 24.15 Implied versus historic volatility USD/RUB.

There are several possible explanations for this misalignment as follows:

1. *Expectations of Structural Changes*. Changes in interest rates announced by central banks frequently produce jumps and disconnects, therefore the expectation of these changes can drive option traders to hedge their gamma position. This can be done using short-term options, as they have the highest gamma.
2. *Overreaction*. After a hurricane, insurance prices are still high; similarly, after a jump, the implied volatility does not typically come back immediately to the level it used to be before the jump (Fig. 24.16).

Another interesting signal for trading volatility strategies is the spread between historic and implied volatility. Implied volatility is priced by investment banks, although it is driven by supply and demand. Option traders use their past experience of hedging the options sold to set the prices for implied volatility. As option traders see the demand for options, the implied volatility reflects this demand, as does the spread, as the demand for options will not create volatility in the spot market. However, these markets are very closely linked via the delta hedging procedure. As the spread between implied and historic volatility increases, the sell side builds their negative gamma position. The negative gamma position of the sell side will translate into delta hedging flows; as the gamma is negative, then any move in spot will be followed by a delta hedge amplifying trend in the market. Trends created by delta hedgers may damage the performance

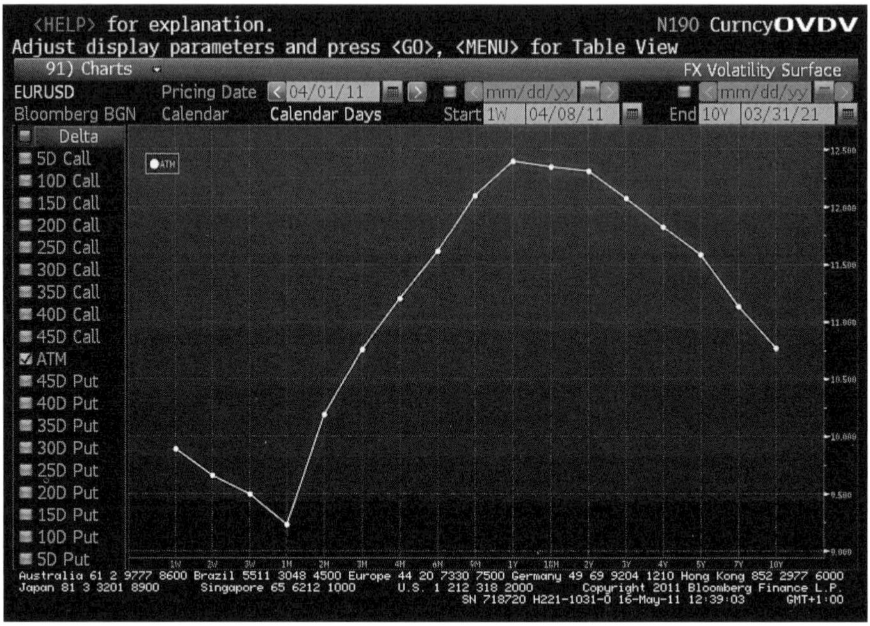


FIGURE 24.16 Implied volatility term structure, ATM, EUR/USD.

of the short-volatility strategy, therefore it may be helpful to put into place a delta hedge for protection. The reverse situation is similar, a positive gamma position means that banks, who are typically hedging, will be dampening trends; therefore, one could consider increasing the risk.

In Figure 24.17, you can see the performance of the naïve short-volatility strategy when 1m ATMF straddles of four currency pairs EUR/USD, JPY/USD, CHF/USD, and GBP/USD are sold. The strategy performed quite well from 2005 to 2008, and recovered after the crisis as the volatility was very high. Typically such strategy will perform well when there is a systematic spread between implied and historic volatility, that is, when the implied volatility is systematically more expensive.

The volatility premium is considered as an independent of other currency factors such as carry, value, momentum, and growth. However, the correlation of short volatility such strategies with carry increased during the crisis.

## 24.4.5 BLACK SWAN STRATEGIES

Black Swan strategies have gained increased popularity since the 2008 crisis and since the publication of Taleb's book.[34] According to the author, a Black Swan is a surprise event that has a major impact and can be rationalized by hindsight. When we refer to Black Swan strategies in a financial context, we mean strategies that payoff in such surprise events. In order to get a payoff, certain financial

[34]"The Black Swan" N. Taleb 2007 (Taleb, 2007).

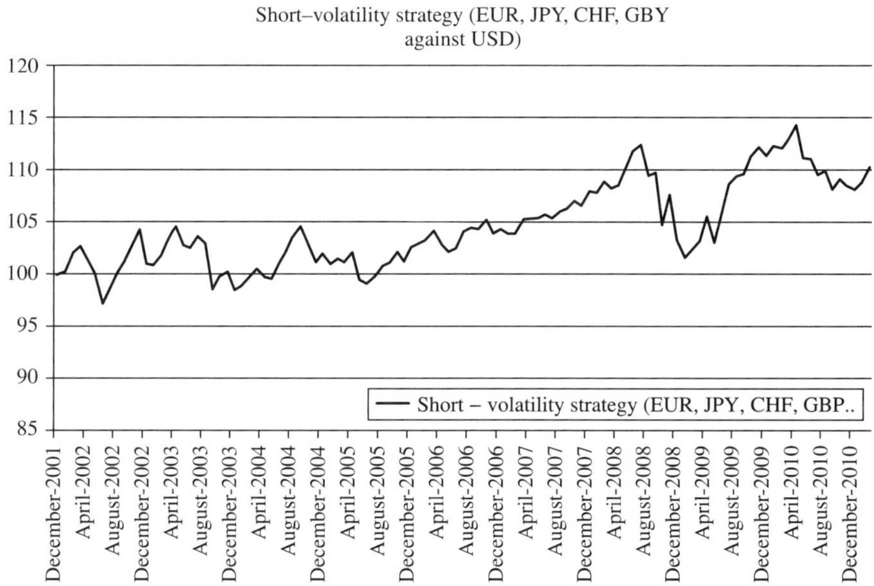


FIGURE 24.17 **Short-volatility strategy (Anti-Black Swan).**

instruments have to be purchased and, in case of a rare event, the value of the instrument will increase to produce the desired payoff. If the event is a surprise how do we know what instruments to purchase? We follow our *suspicions*. In the subprime crisis of 2007, if no one asked how much those houses were really worth then nothing might have happened. The price- or value-discovery process may take some time, and it is not only about the belief that there is a mismatch between price and value but also about the horizon of investment. One of the famous examples of a Black Swan strategy and is the story of John Paulson who made his bet against subprime CDOs. He built his strategy on a simple fact: while house prices in the US had grown very slowly between 1975 and 2000, the expansion of credit brought on by loose monetary policy had speeded up the house price inflation since 2000. His analysis suggested that the prices should revert to the long-term trend line and eventually collapse. Mr. Paulson asked many funds to finance his strategy, but a lot of doors were closed as fund managers did not want to wait for the bubble to burst and argued that spending around 10% per year on insurance (on credit default swaps, in Paulson's case) would create drawdown for investors and might not payoff.

When everyone understands and suspects that they are holding an asset that is no longer valuable, then it is quite hard to avoid a crash, as situations such as bank runs are very hard to stop. Politicians impose regulations such as banning short selling, or banning CDSs, but these measures did not prove to work in practice. Such measures stimulate the gap between fundamental value and the price in the market, while the unwind will come sooner or later. The greater the gap, the bigger the drop in price, therefore the greater is the impact for the holder of the asset who probably mark-to-markets their holding.

You can argue that a Black Swan strategy is just a value strategy, but there is one important aspect in which they are different: the Black Swan strategy expects the price to adjust to its fundamental value very fast, and not erode with time. In other words, there should be an impact, something which astonishes and surprises.

Before I describe how Black Swan strategies work, I would like to point out that the manager of a Black Swan strategy has to have a special gift to see things in an unconventional way.[35] Two Nobel Prize laureates, Kahneman and Tversky, cognitive psychologists, describe a simple experiment, in which a group of people were told to imagine that they had $300. They were then given a choice between receiving another $100 or tossing a coin, where if they won they got $200 and if they lost they got nothing. The majority of us prefer to receive another $100. In the second experiment, they told people to imagine that they had $500, and then asked them if they would rather give up a $100 or toss a coin and pay $200 if they lost and nothing at all if they won. The majority of us prefer to toss the coin in this case. In both experiments, the choices are probabilistically equivalent, but in the case of a certain gain, we do not like to risk it, while when we are confronted with a potential loss we prefer to gamble it away. It is like with the carry strategy we prefer small gains with the risk of an unwind. A Black Swan strategy is opposite, it losses small amounts every day (bleeding) but eventually receives a big gain. This is summarized in Table 24.6.

We can see that the conventional behavior, once prevailing, leads to a negatively skewed outcome distribution, as it accumulates small positive gains against large negative occasional losses. On the other hand, a Black Swan manager's outcome distribution is positively skewed, as it accumulates small negative losses, followed by occasional big gains. The first strategy represents a market beta strategy where a premium is received in exchange for providing capital to finance a business. In FX, it represents a carry strategy where a premium is received in exchange for providing capital to a deficit country. The second strategy can only be properly implemented using derivatives, as they provide

**TABLE 24.6 Kahneman and Tversky Experiment**

| | Conventional Behavior | Black Swan Manager |
|---|---|---|
| Confronted with gain | Keep a small gain (+100); either a risk premium or a carry return | Gamble to increase the gain (0, +200)—lever an option portfolio and hope to win at some point |
| Confronted with loss | Gamble in hope to get rid of the loss (0 or −200), hoping that in the case of a unwind luck will be on their side | Accept a small loss (−100)—accept the decay of an option position |

[35]The more in-depth discussion is presented by Malcolm Gladwell, publication in the New Yorker, 2002, which is available on his blog (http://www.gladwell.com/2002/2002_04_29_a_blowingup.htm).

the continuity and convexity required. Both strategies have their pluses and minuses. A conventional strategy is exposed to sudden crashes, given the current complexity of the global financial system, it is very challenging to model the left wing of the distribution to assess potential losses. On the other hand, a Black Swan strategy has an uncertainty related to how long the strategy will be bleeding for.

The most important step in building a Black Swan strategy is to be able to narrow the universe of opportunities and to concentrate on the unthinkable. To build a simple strategy, we will use Table 24.4. In order to increase our gain, a strategy needs to be levered, therefore more capital has to be spent on options. If we spend more capital on options, then the losses we are going incur will be substantial and the life of the strategy before we run out of money will be much shorter. Therefore, we need to cheapen the premium we pay. One way is to move the strike really far out of the money so that we can buy more options on the same premium. Another parameter to consider is the maturity of options. The exciting bit about this is that premium does not grow linearly. It grows slower, at the pace of the square root of time. Thus, the time decay for out-of-the-money long-dated options is very slow in comparison to ATM short-dated options.

Let us consider an exercise where we have a limited premium, and on this premium we can buy few options ATM or more options out of the money and the volatility smile is flat. In Figure 24.18, you can see that we spent the same amount on options, but in the first case we buy an ATM option, in the second case we buy 15% OTM options, and in the third case we buy 30% OTM options. The payoffs are presented in Figure 24.18. We can see that the far OTM case seems more attractive as it gives greater delta, gamma, and vega,

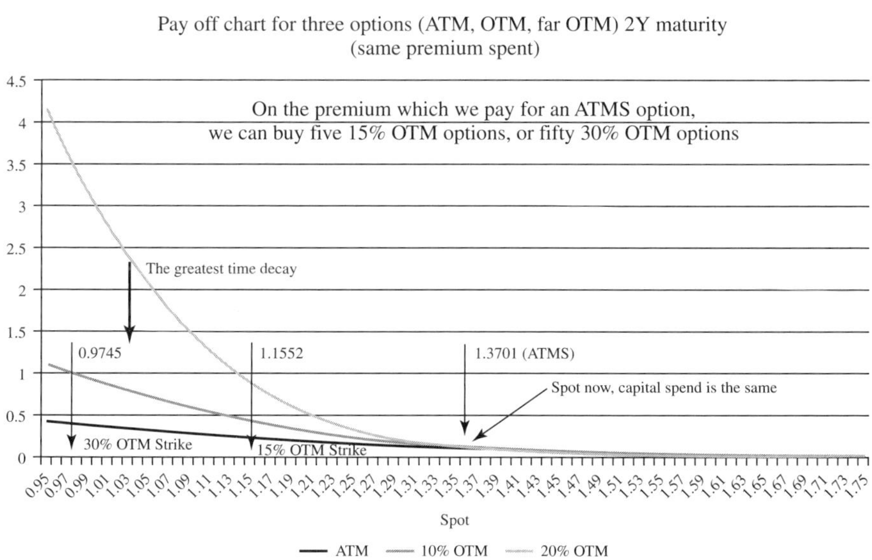


**FIGURE 24.18** **The leverage versus time decay.**

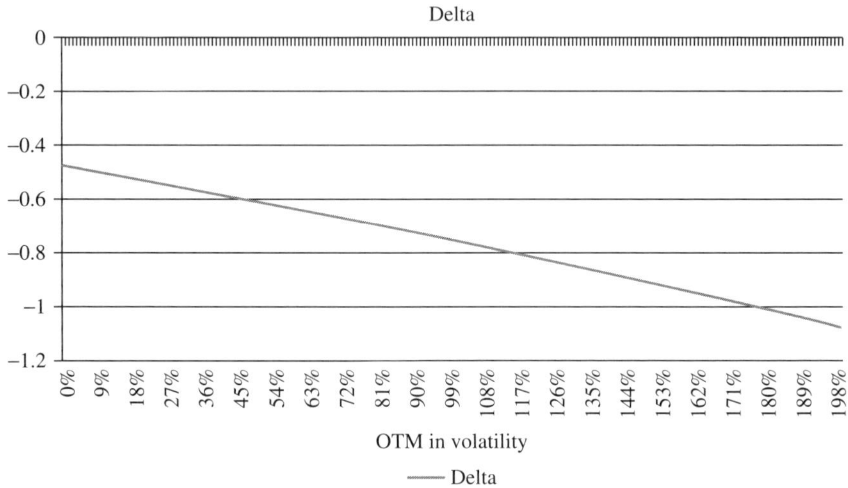


**FIGURE 24.19** **Delta of options position with the same premium spent.**

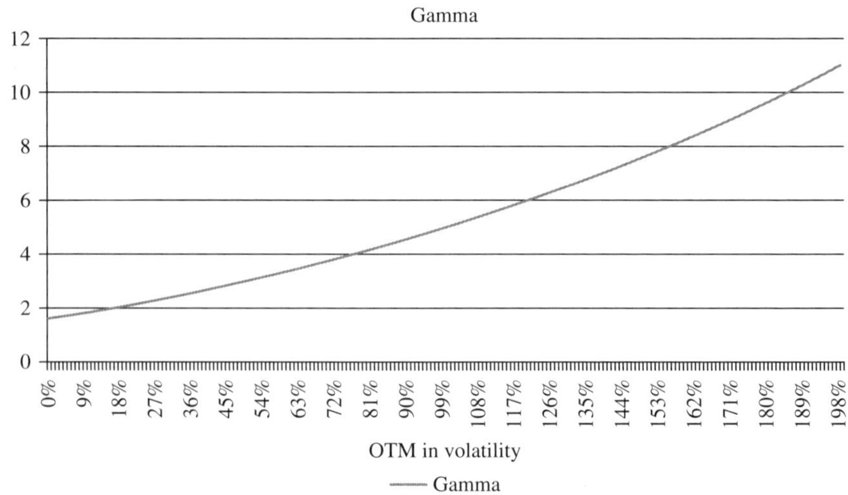


**FIGURE 24.20** **Gamma of options position with the same premium spent.**

but the catch is that the theta of this structure is very expensive, in other words, the speed at which the green line will approach the axis is much higher. In the next set of figures (Figs. 24.19–24.22), you can see how delta, gamma, theta, and the probability of being in the money (conventional Black–Scholes) change as we go OTM. As we can buy more options, the delta of the overall position has greater magnitude (on the figure we have put options, so the delta is negative); the same holds for gamma and vega, but the time decay increases. Therefore, a leveraged position in OTM options will decrease in value faster with time than an ATM position that is worth the same premium.

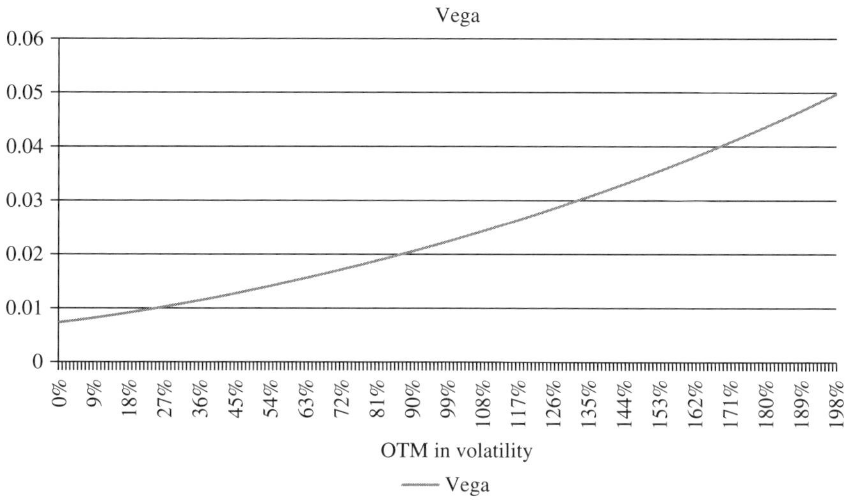


**FIGURE 24.21** **Vega of options position with the same premium spent.**

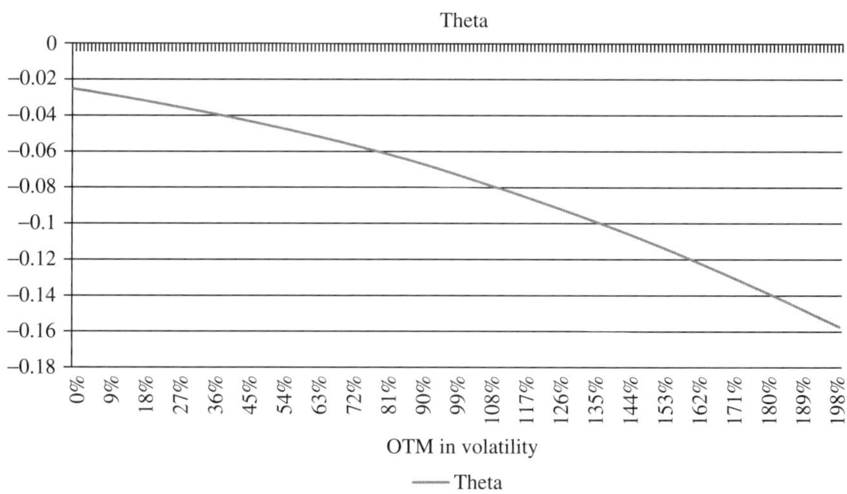


**FIGURE 24.22** **Theta of options position with the same premium spent.**

If a manager expects the Black Swan event to happen very soon, then the best way to maximize the return is to buy far OTM options as time decay is not a concern. On the other hand, if the manager is wrong about the time of arrival of the event, then the position in the far OTM options will bleed theta and the green line will be shrinking quite fast.

A naive indicator of suspicion in the market is volatility. Trends in volatility may lead to a sell off event, therefore turbulence and depreciation. A dynamic Black Swan strategy can buy options as soon as they become more and more valuable in volatility terms. The greater the volatility in the market the greater the leverage of the options should be, as soon as the volatility decreases, the leverage is reduced and the remaining premium is stored for further purchases of options. The rule is not to spend more than $x$% per year (depending on the tolerance of the investor). The drawback of this strategy is that not all trends in volatility lead to rare negative events and rare negative events may not be preceded by trend in implied volatility. Also, the spread in volatility market can cause additional costs; the greater is the volatility the greater is the bid/offer spread, therefore such a dynamic strategy may be quite expensive. Another dynamic strategy can do opposite and buy options as soon as they become cheaper and bet on the complacency of the market and suspect a problem when everyone else do not.

The number of firms that exploit Black Swans is not that great in comparison to hedge fund managers, but this number is growing. In Table 24.7, I mention just the most notorious Black Swan names, which featured in the press and on the internet, subject to survival bias.

The marketing of Black Swan funds is built around tail risk hedging, as the main focus of these strategies is not to make money but to diversify a portfolio of risky assets and create a layer of protection. However, the difference between a naive long volatility strategy and a Black Swan strategy is that a Black Swan strategy is more selective in terms of the options that make up the portfolio. A Black Swan strategy targets fat tails that are very hard to imagine, while a naive long volatility strategy buys the volatility of currency pairs, which correlate with the rest of portfolio.

**TABLE 24.7 Black Swan Funds—Who is Out There?**

| Name of the Manager | Comments |
|---|---|
| Empirica Capital | The fund of Nassim Taleb, the originator of the Black Swan idea. One of the funds, Empirica Kurtosis, was reported to have a 60% return in 2000 followed by losses in 2001 and 2002. The fund is closed now. Beside teaching and writing books, Taleb is now also advising other funds such as Universa |
| Universa | Universa is run by Mark Spitznagel, former partner of Taleb's from Empirica. The fund AUM is US$6 billion and operates on the US stock market |
| Pimco | The biggest bond manager of the world has gathered US$23 billion in the Black Swan hyperinflation fund |
| Capula IM | A bond manager, offers tail risk hedging, with around US$2 billion under management |
| 36 South Capital Advisors | Featured with the Black Swan Fund SPC, which was closed in May 2009 returning to its clients 96.3% p.a. returns |
| Cornwall Capital | "The Big Short" a book that partially describes the activity of the fund and its manager Michael Lewis is an exciting read. The philosophy of the company is that options are priced on past volatility and cannot foresee Black Swan events, therefore opportunities exist |

As Black Swan strategies are targeting fat-tail risks, the instruments with which such strategies operate are far OTM options or ATM options of pegged currency pairs. For example, a 2y ATM USD/HKD may put cost up to 1%; this is 0.5% per annum spent on a Black Swan. Or one could buy a 2y 10 delta strike EUR/SEK put, which will cost approximately the same in percentage terms.

The majority of Black Swan strategies operate with long-dated options, as they are also exposed to the volatility wind up due to high vega. Long-dated options also help lock in interest rates, and in low interest rate regimes can provide an additional carry exposure. We can use a naive long volatility strategy to create a proxy for a Black Swan strategy and to create a benchmark against which to measure the performance of a Black Swan manager.

## 24.5 FX Options from the Buy-Side Perspective

### 24.5.1 STRIKE VERSUS LEVERAGE

In FX, we are always bullish and bearish simultaneously. If we buy EUR/USD then we sell USD/EUR. An option helps express a view in a risk-managed way, and of course there is a price to pay: the premium. A very confident player will not buy an option as their belief is so strong that they do not see any use in it. That confident investor would prefer a forward or spot contract. The more risk averse the player, the more protection is necessary to make them play; hence, the market for insurance. But there is another element that makes options very attractive instruments for speculation: the leverage. Let us suppose you can spend 2% of your wealth to invest or to gamble in the FX market. With this 2%, you can either buy another currency or buy an option, either put or call, or an exotic instrument that can be even cheaper. Let us also assume that the investment horizon is 1 year and that the option you are considering is the EUR/USD put. In Table 24.8, I present different strategies that involve buying a currency forward, buying a EUR/USD put at the money forward, and buying an out-the-money put.

Now let us analyze these three strategies more closely. In all three strategies, we allocate 2% of our capital to bet on EUR/USD.

In the first strategy, we do not use leverage at all, we enter in a FX forward trade on all margin. Of course, we could borrow some more to leverage this FX forward trade, but as we know, the market is exposing us to sharp move. Hence, the broker will charge a higher spread, and we will be paying the spread on the money that we borrowed, which adds to costs. With options, however, the cost is embedded in the options spread, but during the whole year, we can sleep well at night. Let us assume that we do not run any counterparty risk at the moment. In case of a favorable outcome, the first strategy makes $400,000, which is 0.4% of the capital and in the unfavorable outcome we loss almost the same.

Let us see what options offer us in terms of return on capital. The ATMF option is quite expensive given the volatility of 13.65%. The premium of 5.46%

**TABLE 24.8 Investor Choices**

| | FX Forward | ATMF Call | OTM Call |
|---|---|---|---|
| Capital ($) | 100,000,000 | 100,000,000 | 100,000,000 |
| Strike (ATMF) | 14.164 | 14.164 | 1.05 |
| Premium in $ (1 euro notional) | 0 | 0.07733544 | 0.04455 |
| Spent $ | 0 | 2,000,000 | 2,000,000 |
| Spent as percentage of capital | 0% | 2% | 2% |
| Implied volatility | — | 13.65% | 13.65% |
| Premium in percentage-foreign | 0.00% | 5.46% | 2.97% |
| Forward delta percentage-foreign | 1 | 0.05 | 0.35 |
| Delta notional adjusted | 1,412,030 | 12,930,682 | 15,712,762 |
| Notional multiplier (leverage) | 1,412,030 | 25,861,364 | 44,893,378 |
| Premium of option (foreign) | 1,412,030 | 25,861,364 | 44,893,378 |
| Premium of option (domestic) | 2,000,000 | 36,630,037 | 67,340,067 |
| Scenario1 | 1.07 | 1.07 | 1.07 |
| Scenario2 | 1.01 | 1.01 | 1.01 |
| Breakeven | 14.164 | 14.937 | 154.455 |
| Outcome 1 (USD) | 2,400,452 | 7,334,283 | 8,978,676 |
| Outcome 2 (USD) | 1,553,234 | 0 | 0 |
| Total wealth 1 (USD) | 100,400,452 | 105,334,283 | 106,978,676 |
| Total wealth 2 (USD) | 99,553,234 | 98,000,000 | 98,000,000 |
| Return on capital 1 | 0.4% | 5.3% | 6.9% |
| Return on capital 2 | −0.4% | −2.0% | −2.0% |

can be simply approximated as 0.4× volatility; this rule of thumb worked even before the Black–Scholes.[36] The premium in dollars (domestic currency) is 7.7 cents per 1 option of 1 euro notional. How many options can we buy if we can spend $2,000,000? This is our notional multiplier: 25,861,364 options. The notional in the euro therefore will be just 25,861,364. So the payoff of this option is $25,861,364 \times \text{Max}(S - K, 0)$. Now, let us look at the delta of this option; 0.5 is quite right for an ATMF option. The delta adjusted by notional is around 13 million. It provides a great deal of sensitivity to the market in comparison to the previous strategy. In case of the favorable outcome, the money spent turns into a $7.3 million profit providing a 5% return on capital with only 2% drawdown. The strategy that involves the OTM option seems even more successful as the leverage is much higher, also the delta notional is higher as well providing with the sensitivity to the market. Schematically, these three strategies look as in Figure 24.23.

If interest rates environment pays 2% on the 1y US dollars deposit, then the rest of the capital $98,000,000 can be invested in the deposit to compensate

[36]Why we never used Black–Scholes (Taleb and Haug).

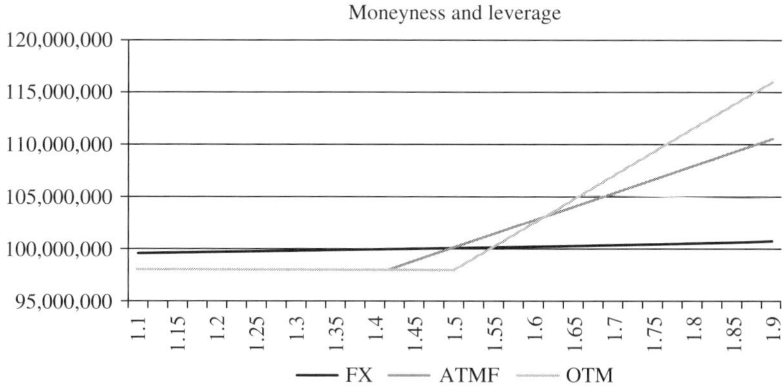


FIGURE 24.23 Strike versus leverage.

for the premium.[37] Such structured products are called *guaranteed return on investment notes* as investor receives back the capital initially invested sacrificing any interest rates that might be accrued in the period of holding.

The strategy that involves an FX forward provides you with an immediate profit if the market moves in the right direction, while the options strategies need to breakeven before they become profitable. However, as soon as they become profitable, the profitability increases much faster. The question for the directional player is: what is the optimal strike that

1. provides us with the necessary depth; and
2. is cost effective?

## 24.5.2 IMPLIED DISTRIBUTION

In order to calculate the probability of reaching breakeven, we need to assume a certain distribution of currency returns over a period of time. The reference distribution is the risk neutral distribution, which is built using the smile. The implied distribution shape depends on the interpolation method we are using to approximate the smile. Here, I use SVI method proposed by Gatheral.[38] In FX options, we observe five implied volatilities per each maturity. These points help in fitting the SVI parameterization (Fig. 24.24):

$$\sigma^2 = a + b\rho\left(\ln\left(\frac{K}{F}\right) - m\right) + \sqrt{\left(\ln\left(\frac{K}{F}\right) - m\right)^2 + \nu^2} \tag{24.17}$$

[37]Strictly speaking $100,000,000/(1+2\%) = 98,039,215$.

[38]Quasi-Explicit Calibration of Gatheral's SVI model (Zeliade Systems, 2009) (Zeliade Systems, 2009).

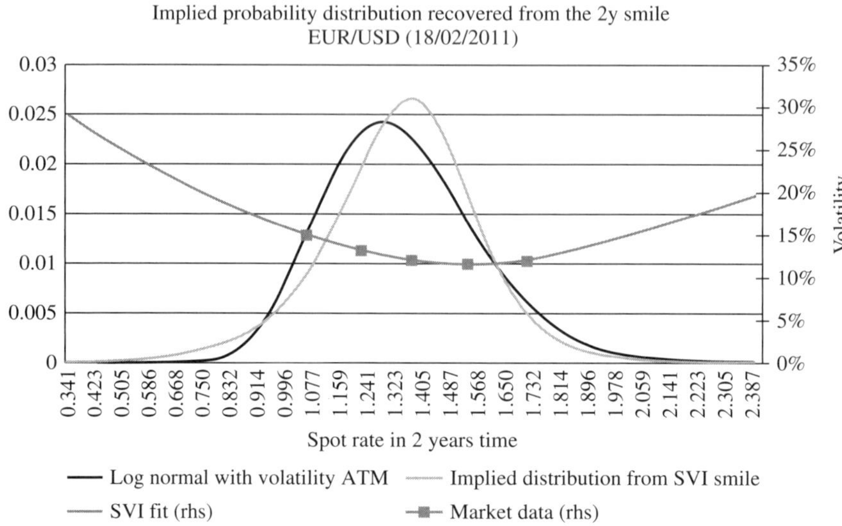


**FIGURE 24.24 Implied probability distribution.**

1. Interpolate smile using the SVI (stochastic volatility inspired) approach[39]
2. Define a step of interpolation $\delta$
3. Calculate prices of calls at each strike using interpolated volatility
4. Apply Breeden and Litzenberger (Breeden and Litzenberger, 1978) functional expression for the risk neutral density:

$$\frac{\partial^2 c}{\partial K^2} = \mathrm{e}^{-r_{\mathrm{d}}T} g\left(S_T\right) \tag{24.18}$$

where $c$ is the price of the call, $K$ is the strike, $r_{\mathrm{d}}$ is the domestic interest rate, and $g\left(S_T\right)$ is risk neutral probability density function. As our observations are discrete, we approximate the second-order derivative:

$$\frac{\partial^2 c}{\partial K^2} = \frac{c_1 + c_3 - 2c_2}{\delta^2} \tag{24.19}$$

where $c_1, c_2, c_3$ are call prices for strikes $K - \delta, K, K + \delta$, respectively.

Any systematic discrepancy between implied expectations and realized moments explained in the previous section can be exploited by creating a trading strategy. Table 24.9 gives a summary of trading strategies that exploit different misalignments:

Each investment bank involved in the FX options market has its own volatility model. The quality of the model is assessed by how well the model

[39]"A parsimonious arbitrage-free implied volatility parameterization with application to the valuation of volatility derivatives", Jim Gatheral, 2004 (Gatheral, 2004).

**TABLE 24.9 Strategies to Exploit Spreads in Implied Versus Realized Distributions**

| | Observation | Trading Strategy |
|---|---|---|
| Volatility | Realized volatility is persistently statistically lower than implied volatility $\sigma_T > \hat{\sigma}\sqrt{365}$ | Selling an ATM option and delta hedging it[a] |
| Skewness | Realized volatility is persistently statistically greater than implied volatility | Reverse delta hedging plus an option to hedge gamma as it is cheap. |
| | $\sigma_T < \hat{\sigma}\sqrt{365}$ | Similar calculations to the above |
| | Realized skewness is persistently statistically lower than implied skewness $s_T > \hat{s}/\sqrt{N}$ | Sell risk reversal and delta hedge |
| Ambiguous skewness | Realized skewness is persistently statistically greater than implied skewness $s_T < \hat{s}/\sqrt{N}$ | Buy risk reversal and reverse delta hedge |
| | $\text{RR}_T(10)\ 1.9\text{RR}_T(25)$ | Sell 10-delta risky and buy 25-delta risky, delta hedge the rest |
| Kurtosis | $\text{RR}_T(10) < 1.9\text{RR}_T(25)$ | Buy 10-delta risky and sell 25-delta risky, delta hedge the rest |
| | Realized kurtosis is persistently statistically lower than implied kurtosis $k_T > \hat{k}/N$ | Sell fly and delta hedge |
| Ambiguous kurtosis | Realized kurtosis is persistently statistically greater than implied kurtosis $k_T < \hat{k}/N$ | Buy fly and reverse delta hedge |
| | $\text{BF}_T(10)\ 3.61\text{BF}_T(25)$ | Sell 10-delta fly and buy 25-delta fly, delta hedge the rest |
| Ambiguous kurtosis | $\text{BF}_T(10) < 3.61\text{BF}_T(25)$ | Buy 10-delta fly and sell 25-delta fly, delta hedge the rest |

[a] When we sell an option we obtain $0.4\sigma_T\sqrt{T}$, but when we delta hedge we on average pay $0.4\hat{\sigma}\sqrt{365xT}$.

fits past observations. Traders rely on the model but input their own volatility, risk reversals, and butterflies for each maturity they want to trade around. These quotations are based on market experience, observations of realized volatility, memory, and momentum; in other words, what worked for a trader in the past should work for them in the future.[40] Any significant differences exceeding the bid/offer spread, between models, especially for options OTM are averaged away in the interbank market. Therefore, when a bank quotes and trades a vanilla option, it typically makes money out of the bid/offer spread by quoting the market. So the use of different models by banks does not have much impact on the prices of vanilla options. The volatility surface represents an agreement between market participants, a sort of collective consciousness. If a bank is not sure about some extreme values of the volatilities surface, it will widen the bid/offer spread for these particular options to discourage other banks from abusing it. Although the prices of vanilla options are not affected by the choice of model of one particular bank, the prices of exotic derivatives are totally model dependent.

The purpose of most exotic FX options is to offer a cheaper upfront alternative to the vanilla option, by injecting small elements of risk back into the option, elements which the buyer may be happy to accept. The amount of resources required to produce all the mathematics and the quotations, the hedging and support of these instruments is huge. Why then are investment banks so keen to push these products that are apparently cheaper? The following are a few possible reasons:

- *Leverage*. Demand creates supply, exotic instruments would have not existed if clients, such as corporate and/or hedge funds, did not ask the sell side to tweak the original vanilla option and to offer something cheap in exchange that the client will buy more and increase the leverage. An example can be a barrier knock-out (KO) option, see the definition in Table 24.8. This option seized to exists when a certain barrier is breached. Such an option costs less than equivalent vanilla option, therefore more barrier options can be bought and the potential payoff can be increased.
- *Business Margin*. It is like buying 2 l of coke in a plastic bottle versus 0.33 l in a glass bottle. The difference in price is not proportional to the quantity of liquid in these bottles.[41] The small bottle will be more expensive in relative terms than a 2 l bottle, but in absolute terms, a 2 l bottle is more expensive. Typically, the volatility of OTM options is higher than ATM—the relative price of the option is higher, although the absolute price of the option is lower.
- *Utility*. Every hedger has their own attitude to risk, therefore, their own utility profile. A variety of exotic instruments offers different utility profiles,

[40]The concept of pricing a contingent claim can be rhetoric. I raise my wallet in the air—how much would you pay for it?

[41]It will be proportional to the cost of advertising, to a less extent manufacturing, of these different products.

and there will be one that matches the profile of the decision maker and their business structure. Hedgers and corporate treasurers care about the cost of protecting their cashflows, as this is their direct responsibility. Therefore, they can forego those aspects of risk that do not directly impact those cashflows.

Some frequently used exotic instruments in the FX market are summarized in Table 24.10.[42]

### 24.5.3 LONG-DATED OPTIONS VERSUS SHORT-DATED OPTION

We discussed the cross-section of the volatility surface. The term *structure* is of interest not only in terms of the information it can provide but also in terms of the opportunities it can offer. The volatility term structure in a normal environment (low volatility benign environments) usually has an upward sloping shape where the volatility of long-term options is greater than the volatility of short-term options. The upward sloping volatility surface makes forward volatility even more expensive. The forward volatility of the T1 months option that starts in T2 time will be the following:

$$\sigma_{T1,T2} = \sqrt{\frac{(T1 + T2)\,\sigma^2_{T1+T2} - T1\sigma^2_{T1}}{T2}} \tag{24.20}$$

If the volatility term structure is steep then we have

$$\sigma^2_{T1+T2} > \sigma^2_{T1}, \sigma_{T1,T2} = \sqrt{\frac{(T1 + T2)\,\sigma^2_{T1+T2} - T1\sigma^2_{T1}}{T2}}$$
$$= \sqrt{\sigma^2_{T1+T2} + \frac{T1\left(\sigma^2_{T1+T2} - \sigma^2_{T1}\right)}{T2}} > \sigma_{T1+T2}$$

We can see that the future implied volatility in T2 will not always be as forward volatility suggests and some recent academic papers spotted that there is a bias in the forward volatility "prediction."[43] It seems to be that most of the time forward volatility overestimates implied volatility. This bias represents a long-term volatility premium and theoretically can be extracted using FVA. An FVA is an agreement to buy or sell an ATM forward straddle at a prespecified volatility on a particular date in the future. This future date is known as the *strike set date*. On the strike set date, the strike of the straddle is determined, but

[42]For a full list of exotic FX options and structured products, please see U Wystup, "FX Options and structured products" (Wystup, 2006).

[43]"The Forward Volatility Bias in Foreign exchange" P. Della Corte, et al., (Della Corte et al., 2009).

**TABLE 24.10 Basic Exotic Instruments**

| Exotic Instrument | Summary |
|---|---|
| One touch | It is a bet whether a certain level will be touched during a certain time to expiration. If the level is touched then a notional amount is paid to the buyer. No touch is just an opposite bet that is widely offered by investment banks |
| Range | The same as one touch, but now it has two levels, one is above the current spot level and the other is below the current spot level. More expensive than one touch as the probability of payout increases, but range no touch is cheaper. One touch, no touch, and range options can be used by market participants who exploit mean reversion. Such strategies systematically sell synthetic straddles by reverse delta hedging. In case a certain currency pair exits a mean-reversion corridor, a rebate is received |
| Knock Out (KO) option (put or call)—barrier is out of the money | The same as either put or call option, but as soon as a certain level (barrier) out of the money is touched, the option is canceled—knocks out. It is cheaper than a plain vanilla, but does not fully protect the buyer if the barrier is touched because the market can revert back and there will be no protection. In a way, it is a bet on the path of the spot. |
| Knock-in (KI) option (put or call) American barrier[a]—barrier is out of the money | This option starts to be an option if a certain barrier is touched. Knock in + knock out = vanilla |
| Reverse knock-out (RKO) option American barrier—barrier is in the money | Reverse knock out is a knock-out option where the barrier is in the money. This category of options is very popular, but if the market touches most of the barriers then barrier options become unpopular again until the memory remedies old wounds. The delta hedging flow that is created by RKO barrier options can be huge the spot is moving toward the barrier shortly before maturity (bad neighborhood).[b] The delta position accumulates the more the option moves in the money, but as soon as the barrier is touched, traders realize the delta hedging profit besides the option premium—the spring effect |
| Reverse knock-in (RKI) option—American barrier—barrier is in the money | Reverse knock in is a option that only become activated when a certain barrier in the money is touched. Reverse knock in + Reverse knock out = vanilla |

[a]American style barrier is the barrier that is constantly monitored, while the European barrier is considered only at expiry.
[b]Deutsche bank "Global FX Gamma Report."

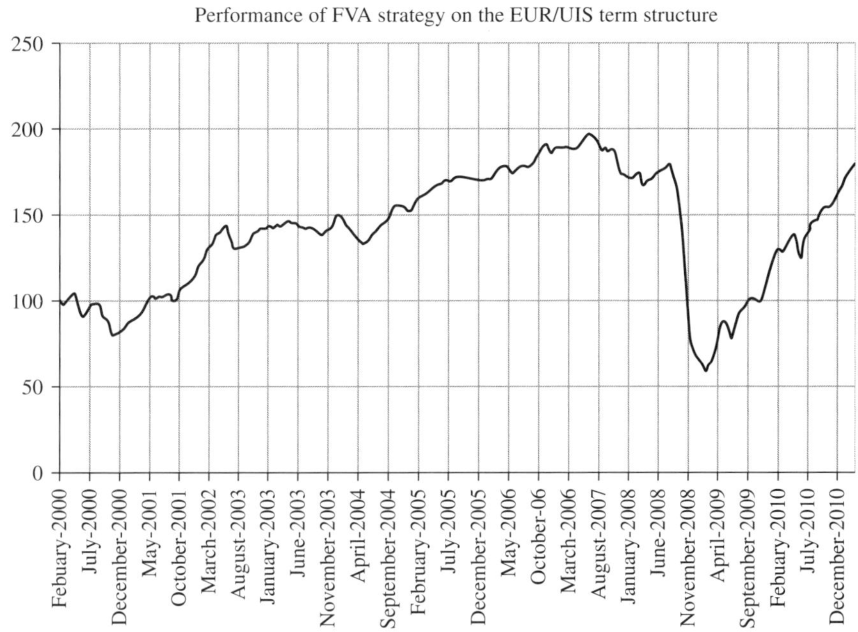


FIGURE 24.25 **Forward volatility agreement strategy.**

the premium is determined on the trade date. Consider the strategy of buying (selling) FVAs when forward implied volatility is lower (higher) than current spot implied volatility. In this example, we compare 1M spot implied volatility to the 1M forward implied volatility for EUR–USD. Note that instead of FVA contracts, straddles are used to replicate the position (Fig. 24.25).

In practice, transacting FVA agreements is more problematic, as banks are aware of the direction of the trade most of the time, therefore the quotes they provide will be with their interest in the forward volatility premium. The long-term volatility premium is paid by hedgers who buy long-dated options and do not want to rebalance their hedges too often, as it involves uncertainty when it comes to the level of volatility at which the option is going to be rebalanced. An FVA is typically hedged using a series of calendar spreads and involves delta hedging of these spreads as well.

We discussed that a view can be taken on realized volatility versus implied volatility, and you have seen the list of strategies that can exploit inefficiencies in different misalignments between probability moments. One could take a view that the implied volatility is low or high, and it will revert to a fair value given by a proprietary model. Implied volatility is mean reverting and some mean-reverting models can be helpful in fitting the past and giving market players confidence when projecting the future. If you are not model based and you foresee a turbulent time in the market, then the easier your instruments are, the more effective your bet (Table 24.11).

**TABLE 24.11 Basic Exotic Instruments**

| Strategy Matrix | | Spot View: Bearish | Spot View: Neutral | Spot View: Bullish |
|---|---|---|---|---|
| Volatility view | Bearish | Buy a put, sell two calls, buy a put with RKO[a] | Sell FVA, sell a straddle, sell a range, buy a no touch | Buy a call, sell two puts, buy a call with RKO |
| | Neutral | Buy a put/put spread, sell a call/call spread, risk reversal—buy a put and finance it with a short call | Are you sure? | Buy a call/call spread, sell a put/put spread, risk reversal—buy a call and finance it with a short put |
| | Bullish | Buy a put, buy a put with RKI (reversal kick in) | Buy FVA, buy a straddle, buy a range, sell a no touch | Buy a call, buy a call with RKI |

[a]If the volatility is low, the probability of touching the barrier is low.

### 24.5.4 BLACK SWAN FUND

There is an element of path dependency in exploiting fat tails. Fat-tail events can appear in the short term or in the long run. If a fat-tail event appears in the short run then it is typically a jump or a series of disruptions in the market, but in the long run, a rare event manifests itself as a trend that reaches levels inconceivable in the past, but now quite explainable with the benefit of hindsight. In other words, the short-run rare event is a break from short-run volatility and the long-run rare event is a break out of medium-term volatility.[44] There is a series of ready-made products offered by investment banks, which can deliver returns under these conditions, but the majority of such products they are one offs and do not give an investor exposure if circumstances suddenly change.

For example, an investor believes that there will be a "Black Swan" event involving the euro related to the debt situation in the Eurozone, and they would like to exploit this event. Let us assume that the level of the EUR/USD now is 1.45. This investor may be a victim of path dependency. Suppose they buy a put with the strike OTM 1.40. Then the EUR/USD appreciates to 1.50, and then from there drops to 1.41. The investor might perhaps gain something if they are lucky and to sell their OTM option as it moved closer to the money and the volatility in the market increased, but the bank will not be willing to buy this option back and the bid/offer spread will not be the best. So the

[44]In fact, we can refer to this as a break out of serial correlation, see Andrew Lo variance test (Lo and McKinley, 1988).

market participant has got it right in terms of the stress, but the timing was wrong. In order to get the timing right, the investor would need to pay either for research—which is uncertain—or to buy a Black Swan fund.

Such funds are new and they are all based on options (cushion) and leverage. They are responsive to short-term shocks. The objective of the fund is to make a positive return out of certain Black Swan events with a certain limit spent on options. The difference between a structured product with an embedded long option and a fund is that the fund manager has discretion in terms of spending your premium and, typically, the premium will be spent gradually if the fund is systematic, securing every level in the market and trying to find the best relative value in the FX options. A systematic Black Swan fund smoothes the timing effort by buying different options at different horizons and every month spends a certain portion of premium. A discretionary fund overrides the systematic approach by taking decisions based on views but it still needs a systematic element to smooth the timing.

There are several issues that arise in such a fund as follows:

- *The Most Cost-Effective Way of Maintaining Market Sensitivity*. If an option loses its market value there is nothing that can be done except spending more and upgrading the delta. Therefore, not all of the allocation has to be spent on premium on day 1. A systematic fund would define a delta corridor it would like to maintain and then spend money gradually by buying more into the cushion. There is a VaR approach that monitors the risk of decline in market value of the cushion and does not allow more spending if a certain level is hit.
- *New Subscriptions and Redemptions*. If a new investor comes in the fund then the cushion becomes mutual. If the cushion of new investor has different Greeks, which can be either advantageous or disadvantageous; therefore, the role of the discretionary manager is to provide fair treatment for all parties, while a systematic fund will be designed to accommodate new joiners, though the calculations are complex.

### 24.5.5 CURRENCY HEDGING OF ILLIQUID ASSETS

Funds with significant foreign currency exposure can find the performance of their underlying assets disguised, undermined, and sometimes overwhelmed by short-term currency volatility. Indeed, conventional currency hedging for property funds, venture funds, and other illiquid asset classes is proving much more difficulty now than before the credit crunch. Banks' reluctance to lend has meant that foreign currency borrowing (a natural hedge) is much less readily available, and the short horizons of forward contracts mean that unpredictable cash flows can prove very challenging to funds in the volatile conditions currently prevailing in the currency market. Funds that decide to hedge their currency exposure face difficulties due to lack of credit, lack of cash to buy insurance, correlation of FX and underlying asset, and lack of visibility. These issues are briefly discussed below, and methods of tackling them are proposed as follows:

- *Lack of Credit*. Credit is required in case of underperformance of hedges. A credit line can be granted on a collateralized basis, and while the assets are liquid, it is easy for a creditor to liquidate assets in case of failure to pay. For illiquid funds, however, when the underlying risks are hard to value, it may be difficult to get credit. In this scenario, hedging would become problematic, especially when facing large cash flow volatility. An insurance premium can be a solution, as it provides an asymmetric payoff capping the negative volatility.
- *Lack of Cash to Buy Insurance*. Insurance can be expensive as it depends on the market expectation of future movements. However, insurance costs can be reduced in several ways: (i) by considering a hedge only after a certain threshold using out-the-money instruments; and (ii) by considering longer maturities, as the premium grows with the square root of time rather than linearly. As investments in illiquid funds are long term, the options that provide hedging should also mature in the far future, 3–5 years. The advantage of options is that the price grows with the square root rather than arithmetically; therefore, if the long-term premium that was discussed earlier is excluded, a 2-year ATM option will cost only 1.4 times of what a 1-year option costs. If the volatility in 5 years is 12% then ATMF option will cost $0.4 \times 12\% \times \sqrt{5} = 10\%$. To pay 10% for insurance costs for an illiquid fund is significant. But the fund can still borrow 10% and pay installments of 2% per year. If this is still too high then moving options out-the-money can considerably cheapen the insurance. Thus, options provide a flexible mechanism for picking the right insurance at the right time.
- *Underlying Correlation*. While hedging, it is useful to consider the correlation of currency movements and the value of the underlying asset. If the correlation is positive, as it is, for example, for a commercial property in Turkey, the asset is valued in local currency, and its value moves together with the value of the currency in dollars. Therefore, the currency exposure magnifies the risk of the underlying asset. Hedging in this particular example should be carefully evaluated, as buying options on Turkish lira can be expensive because of the negative carry and the high volatility. Thus, a cheaper proxy can be considered, where (i) implied volatility is not that high, (ii) carry is not so expensive, and (iii) provides fundamental and quantitative links high correlation and similar regimes. Note, however, that some currencies such as JPY have negative correlations with assets historically.
- *The Lack of Valuation Visibility Over Long-Term Horizons*. An important question is what should be the notional of the option: in other words, how much should be hedged. In the case of a liquid asset, there is a procedure of rebalancing, and the company adjusts its hedges to match the value of the underlying exposure. If the valuation is not clear, then hedging becomes more difficult. Rebalancing of hedges could be an expensive exercise, especially as in a climate of market uncertainty, there is a significant bid-offer spread on options. If the valuation is less visible then hedging with long-dated options and committing the premium for a long horizon could be going too far. In

this case, an alternative would be to hedge just the floor, the value beyond which the asset is unlikely to fall.

There are several classes of funds—including, notably, property investment trusts/funds and private equity funds—which have currency mismatches between their investment target currency and their base or investor currency. Traditionally funds like these would use FX forward contracts to hedge currency exposures, or, in the case of property funds, they would use target-currency (foreign) debt as an implicit hedge. However, property-based borrowing is more difficult and expensive to maintain now than previously, and many funds are running at much lower, and sometimes zero, levels of borrowing.

As discussed before, the premium can be reduced by going either out of the money or selling some barriers. Five-year barrier options can be relatively cheap, as the probability of touching the barrier will be substantial; and so this strategy could be risky. An alternative is to outsource the decision on timing to a currency manager, who will be looking after the position, and who could provide recommendations. Typically, an active manager should be able to

- provide analysis, recommendations, and execution of the lowest cost/most efficient horizon, maturity structure, and out-of-the-moneyness for each of the foreign currencies to be hedged. The target should be based on the after-cost expected breakeven;
- propose a feasible hedge ratio based on knowledge of the market;
- provide market-to-market reporting.

## Acknowledgment

I would like to thank Jessica James and Stephane Knauf for this opportunity, and also John Quayle for useful discussions about FX options market at his trading desk, Bella Noyen and Diana Ples for help in shaping this document to a proper readable form.

## REFERENCES

Black F, Scholes M. The pricing of option and corporate liabilities. J Pol Econ 1973; 81:637–654.

Bouyé E. Portfolio insurance: a short introduction; 2009 May 27. Available at SSRN: http://ssrn.com/abstract=1416790

Breeden D, Litzenberger R. Prices of state contingent claims implicit in options prices. J Bus 1978;51:621–651.

Carr P. Variance risk premium; 1999.

Carr P, Jarrow R. The stop-loss start gain paradox and option valuation: a new decomposition into intrinsic and time value. Rev Financ Stud 1990;3(3):469–492.

Carr P, Madan D. Toward a theory of volatility trading. In: Jarrow R, editor. Volatility. Risk Publications; 1998. http://ebooks.cambridge.org/chapter.jsf?bid=CBO97805115 69708&cid=CBO9780511569708A023.

Carr P, Madan DB. Option valuation using the fast Fourier transform. J Comput Finance 1999;2:61–73.

Carr P, Madan D. Towards the theory of volatility trading; 2001.

Carr P, Wu L. The information content of straddles, risk reversals and butterfly spreads; 2005.

Cesarano F. Monetary theory and bretton woods: the construction of an international monetary order. New York: Cambridge University Press; 2006.

Della Corte P, Sarno L, Tsiakas I. The forward volatility bias in foreign exchange; 2009.

Deng Q. Correlation SWAPs and dynamic correlation models; 2009.

Derman E. Regimes of volatility. RISK 1999 April.

Derman E. Trading volatility as an asset class, a series of presentations. Available at http://www.ederman.com/new/docs/gaim-trading_volatility.pdf

Gatheral J. A Parsimonious Arbitrage-Free Volatility Parametrization with Application to the Valuation of Volatility Derivatives, Presentation, Global Derivatives and Risk Management Conference, May 2004.

Gatheral J. Volatility surface: a practitioner guide. Wiley; 2004b.

Hakansson N. The fantastic world of finance: progress and the free lunch. J Financ Quant Anal 1979;14:714–734.

Kremer P, Krishnan HP, Malek M. Trend following as a long volatility strategy; 2004.

Lo A, McKinley C. Stock market prices do not follow random walks: evidence from a simple specification test; 1988.

Mougeot. Volatility Investing Handbook, BNP Paribas; 2004.

Rebonatto R. Volatility and correlation. 2nd ed. New York: John Wiley and Sons; 2004.

Stein J. Overreactions in the options market. J Finance 1989;XLIV(4): 1011–1023.

Taleb N. The black swan: the impact of the highly improbable; 2007.

Taleb N, Haug EG. Why we never use Black-Scholes. 2007. http://www.maths-fi.com/article_Why_we_have_never_used_the_Black_Scholes_Merton_Option_Pri cing_Formula_Haug_Taleb_nov_2007.pdf.

Wystup U. FX Options and structured products; 2006.

Zeliade Systems. Quasi-Explicit Calibration of Gatheral's SVI model; 2009.

# PART FOUR

# FX Markets and Policy

CHAPTER TWENTY FIVE

# A Common Framework for Thinking about Currency Crises

**ROBERT FLOOD**
University of Notre Dame

**NANCY MARION**
Dartmouth College

**JUAN YEPEZ ALBORNOZ**
University of Notre Dame

## 25.1 Introduction

There are two schools of thought concerning economic crises in general and currency crises in particular. In the first, the pre-1978 orthodoxy, economic crises are attributed to arbitrary big shifts in expectations or sudden large disturbances. This view of crises is intellectually comfortable because it associates a big effect with a big shock. Moreover, since the roots of the crises are either outside the realm of economics or due to large unforecastable disturbances, there is little additional work to be done by empirical economists tracing crises back to economic fundamentals. We credit Mackay (1852, reprinted in 2008) and Kindleberger (1978, reprinted in 2000) and other secondary-sourced compilations of amusing anecdotes with developing and preserving this mindset.[1]

[1]Although not related directly to the modern crisis literature, economic historians, for example, Garber (2000) and Goldgar (2007), are now providing primary-source historical research accounts

*Handbook of Exchange Rates*, First Edition. Edited by Jessica James, Ian W. Marsh, and Lucio Sarno.

The second school, which we call the *fundamentals approach to crises*, was developed by researchers working at the Board of Governors of the Federal Reserve System (the Fed) in the late 1970s and early 1980s.[2] This approach was pioneered by Salant and Henderson (1978) (S&H), who challenged orthodoxy by developing a model of a predictable crisis in which speculators' self-interest leads to market-based dismantling of unsustainable government policies. In the S&H fundamentals approach, there is still room for big shocks to have big effects—but observing a crisis does not necessarily lead researchers to look for big precipitating shocks or arbitrary and self-serving or self-fulfilling expectations shifts. While there is room in the fundamentals approach for mathematical curiosities, such as bubbles, or ambiguous government policies to lead to arbitrary results, odd-ball model solutions and fuzzy implications are not the stars of the story.

Perhaps because the ideas originating with S&H help to confront many real-world events while providing a fascinating modeling playground, the literature on speculative attacks and currency crises has grown too large for us to survey comprehensively. Here, we focus on some of the literature's key insights and intriguing quirks and illustrate that they are all part of a common framework.[3]

Through amazing prescience or perhaps just by coincidence, the S&H paper gave economists a way to think about currency crises just as a wave of such crises broke over foreign exchange markets. In Figure 25.1, we see that the number of currency crises per year in developing countries approximately doubled from the mid-1970s to the mid-1980s, peaking at over 23 crises per year in 1990 according to Reinhart and Rogoff (2009).[4]

Salant and Henderson applied their ideas to a government fixing the price of gold in terms of goods. In their model, a steady private gold-consumption drain depletes the government gold stock, leading eventually to collapse of the gold-price-fixing policy. Paul Krugman visited the Fed while the S&H ideas were being developed. He realized that the S&H approach applied not just to the historical gold standard but to many contemporary policies as well. Krugman (1979) adapted the S&H approach to unsustainable fixed exchange rates. Presently, we will use the government policy of fixing the exchange rate as a metaphor for all sorts of government policies that speculators can bet against. *That is really the crucial issue here—can speculators bet against the policy?* If so, the analysis shows how such speculation can influence policy outcomes.

---

challenging some of the sensational stories pulled by Kindleberger (1978, 2000) from the popular press and bone-to-pick pamphleteers.

[2]We were tempted to refer to speculative attacks based on fundamentals as the "Fed View," but while the approach was developed at the Fed, it did not represent official Federal Reserve policy any more than the Mundell-Fleming-(Polak) model represented official IMF policy.

[3]Flood and Marion (1999) provided a fairly comprehensive survey over 10 years ago. As a measure of the popularity/relevance of the subject, we checked Google Scholar recently for "currency crisis" and got over 25,000 hits.

[4]Reinhart and Rogoff (2009) define a currency crash as an annual depreciation versus the US dollar (or the relevant anchor currency) of 15% or more.

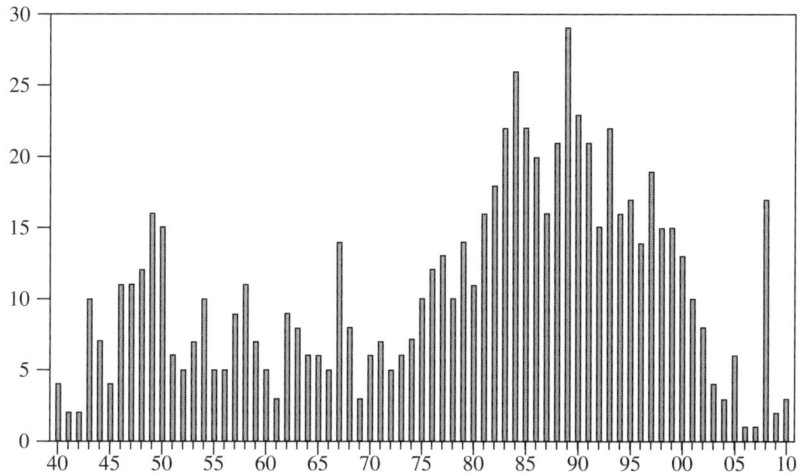


FIGURE 25.1 **Occurrence of currency crises in developing countries, 1940–2010.**

Beginning in 1980, Robert Flood was at the Fed for a few years and Peter Garber consulted there intermittently. During that period, Flood and Garber (1984a,b) (F&G) wrote two papers on speculative attacks. In 1984a, F&G linearized and clarified the model in Krugman's (1979) paper. The F&G model (1984a) is now known as the *Krugman-Flood-Garber (KFG) model*. The KFG model produces distributions of the size and timing of a speculative attack. It also produces an infinite range of arbitrary and self-fulfilling attack dates and sizes due to (possible) post-crisis exchange-rate bubbles. Flood and Garber (1984a) chose to assume away arbitrary self-fulfilling attacks produced by such math anomalies.

The rest of the chapter is organized as follows: In Section 25.2, we present the basic KFG model. In Section 25.3, we argue that the rest of the currency-crisis literature is really a set of data-driven extensions of this basic model. No attempt is made to develop fully or to do justice to the many post-KFG contributions. Our goal is to show how the basic KFG model can be adapted to incorporate the later contributions. Section 25.4 makes some observations about empirical work on the KFG model. Section 25.5 concludes.

## 25.2 The KFG Model

In the KFG model, the monetary authority fixes the exchange rate initially by offering to buy or sell international reserves at the fixed exchange rate. In the background is some set of higher-priority polices that make the fixed rate unsustainable. Since government's commitment to the exchange rate is limited and at odds with the higher-priority policies, the fixed rate will eventually be abandoned in a currency crisis. The KFG model is about determining the probability distribution for the timing of the crisis.

Fixing the exchange rate is a monetary policy, so the model is organized around the money market:

$$m(t) - p(t) = \delta - \alpha i(t) + \gamma y(t) + w(t) \tag{25.1}$$

where time is measured discretely, $m(t)$ is the log of high powered money at time $t$, $p(t)$ is the log domestic price level, $i(t)$ is the domestic interest rate, $y(t)$ is the log domestic output, $w(t)$ is a money-demand shock, and $\alpha > 0$, $\gamma > 0$, and $\delta \gtreqless 0$ are fixed parameters.

Uncovered interest parity (UIP) is imposed. Thus,

$$i(t) = i^*(t) + E_t s(t+1) - s(t) \tag{25.2}$$

where $i^*(t)$ is the foreign-currency interest rate, $s(t)$ the log-exchange rate quoted as the domestic-currency price of foreign exchange, and $E_t$ is the expectations operator conditional on full information from time $t$.

Purchasing power parity is not imposed. Instead,

$$p(t) = p^*(t) + s(t) + v(t) \tag{25.3}$$

where $p^*(t)$ is the log foreign price level and $v(t)$ is a shock.

Log-linearized high power money is made up of weighted average log domestic credit and log international reserves:

$$m(t) = \bar{m} + \phi d(t) + (1 - \phi) r(t) \tag{25.4}$$

where $d(t)$ is log domestic credit, $r(t)$ is log international reserves, and $\bar{m}$ and $\phi$ are linearization constants.

Substituting Equations (25.2)–(25.4) into Equation (25.1) and rearranging terms yields

$$(1 - \phi) r(t) + z(t) - s(t) = -\alpha[E_t s(t+1) - s(t)] \tag{25.5}$$

where

$$z(t) = \bar{m} + \phi d(t) - p^*(t) - v(t) - \delta + \alpha i^*(t) - \gamma y(t) - w(t) \tag{25.6}$$

is the *market fundamental*. Normally, the lower bound on reserves is set at $r(\min) = 0$.[5] The market fundamental is an exogenous forcing variable.

Define $\tilde{s}(t)$ to be the *shadow exchange rate*, which is the exchange rate that would prevail if reserves were at the lower bound, $r(t) = r(\min) = 0$, and the

[5]There is nothing special about setting $r(\min) = 0$ as the lower bound. Recall that $r$ is the log of reserves, so setting $r(\min) = 0$ is setting the minimum reserve level at unity. The important point is that the government's commitment to the fixed exchange rate is limited. Blanco and Garber (1986) set the reserve lower bound at an arbitrary constant and then estimate the constant.

exchange rate was allowed to float freely. Under these conditions, the general solution for the shadow exchange rate is

$$\tilde{s}(t) = \sum_{i=0}^{\infty} \frac{E_t z(t+i)}{(1+\alpha)} \left(\frac{\alpha}{1+\alpha}\right)^i + \lim_{i\to\infty} \left(\frac{\alpha}{1+\alpha}\right)^i E_t \tilde{s}(t+i) \qquad (25.7)$$

For now, specialize the solution by the following:

**1.** assuming away exchange-rate bubbles, which implies

$$\lim_{i\to\infty} \left(\frac{\alpha}{1+\alpha}\right)^i E_t \tilde{s}(t+i) = 0 \qquad (25.8)$$

**2.** assuming a constant growth-rate process for the market fundamental

$$z(t+1) = \mu + z(t) + u(t+1) \qquad (25.9)$$

where $\mu$ is a positive constant and $u(t+1)$ is a mean-zero white noise shock.[6]

With assumptions (1) and (2), the solution for $\tilde{s}(t)$ becomes

$$\tilde{s}(t) = \lambda_0 + \lambda_1 z(t) \qquad (25.10)$$

where $\lambda_0 = \alpha\mu$ and $\lambda_1 = 1$.

Figure 25.2 illustrates the conditions of the speculative attack. When the shadow rate is less than the fixed rate, speculators do not attack the fixed rate because an attack would give them capital losses; the fixed exchange rate, speculators' purchase price, is greater than $\tilde{s}(t)$, the price at which speculators could sell the reserves they buy from the government. Instead, they attack when the shadow rate equals or exceeds the fixed rate. Thus, the fixed exchange rate is abandoned when $\tilde{s}(t) \geq \bar{s}$, where $\bar{s}$ is the fixed rate.

To illustrate the model's workings in the simplest way, consider a world of certainty, so that $u(t+i) = 0$ for all $t$. The attack takes place when $\tilde{s}(t) = \alpha\mu + z(t) = \bar{s}$. In certainty, $z$ follows $z(t) = z(0) + \mu t$. Let $T$ be the attack date. Therefore, $\alpha\mu + z(0) + \mu T = \bar{s}$ characterizes the attack time, which is[7]

$$T = \frac{\bar{s} - \alpha\mu - z(0)}{\mu} \qquad (25.11)$$

The model is more relevant to data, however, when $u(t)$ comes from a stochastic distribution. When $u(t)$ is stochastic, the probability of a currency crisis next

[6]Behind the scenes may be a profligate government, financing a fiscal deficit by printing money.

[7]For simplicity, we ignore that $T$ must be an integer in discrete-time. Equation (25.11) is literally correct only in the limit when $t$ is a continuous variable.

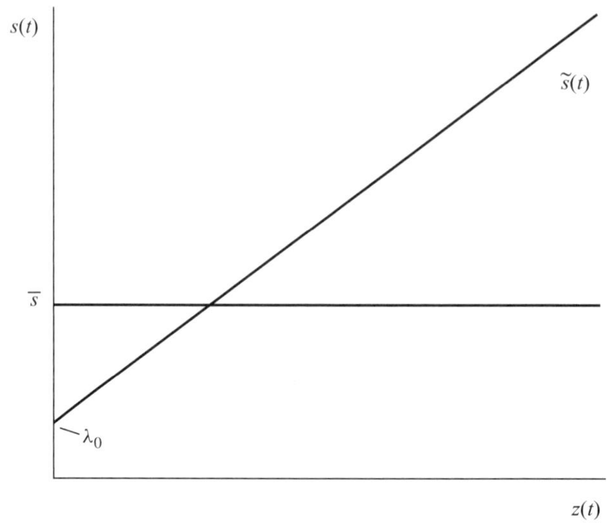


FIGURE 25.2 **Fixed rate $\bar{s}$, shadow rate $\tilde{s}$, as a function of fundamentals $z(t)$.**

period is the probability that the shadow rate next period equals or exceeds the fixed rate

$$\text{prob}\left(\tilde{s}\left(t+1\right) \geq \bar{s}\right) = \text{prob}\left(\lambda_0 + \lambda_1 z\left(t+1\right) \geq \bar{s}\right) \tag{25.12}$$

The value of $z(t)$ where the shadow rate equals the fixed rate is the critical value, $\bar{z}$. This critical value fulfills: $\lambda_0 + \lambda_1 \bar{z} = \bar{s}$, so $\bar{z} = \left(\bar{s} - \lambda_0\right)/\lambda_1$.

The probability of a crisis next period depends on the state of the world (model) this period. Given the assumed forcing process, the state is summarized by the level of the forcing variable $z(t)$. We adopt the notation

$$\text{prob}\left(z(t)\right) = \text{prob}\left(z\left(t+1\right) > \bar{z} \mid z(t)\right) \tag{25.13}$$

or

$$\begin{aligned} \text{prob}\left(z(t)\right) &= \text{prob}\left(z(t) + \mu + u(t+1) > \bar{z}\right) \\ &= \text{prob}\left(u(t+1) > \bar{z} - \mu - z(t)\right) \end{aligned} \tag{25.14}$$

where prob $(z(t))$ is the probability of a crisis at time $t+1$ based on the state at time $t$, $z(t)$.

For example, suppose $u(t)$ is drawn from the uniform distribution with upper bound $\sigma$ and lower bound $-\sigma$. The probability density function is rectangular with height $1/2\sigma$ and base $2\sigma$.[8]

Figure 25.3 illustrates the probability density of $u(t)$ and the function relating $z(t)$ to the probability of a crisis.

[8] The base width of the uniform is proportional to the standard deviation of the $u$ shock, $\sigma/\sqrt{3}$.

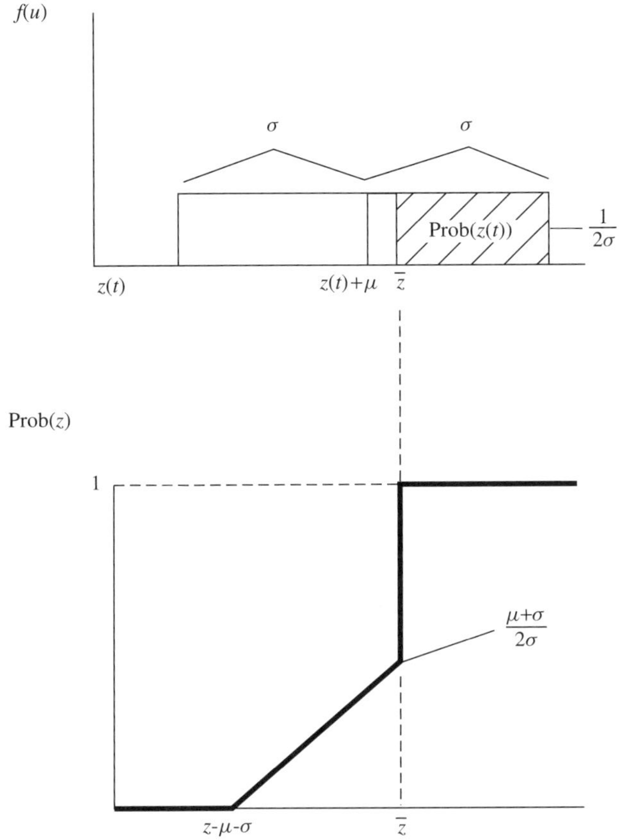


**FIGURE 25.3** Crisis probabilities with a uniformly distributed shock.

Near the origin, there is no shock from the assumed distribution big enough to push next period's $z$ above the critical value, $\bar{z}$. The probability of a crisis next period is, therefore, 0. As we move to higher values of $z$, it is possible for a shock to push next period's $z$ above the critical value. The probability of a currency crisis, therefore, is positive. The complete description of prob $(z(t))$ is

$$\text{prob}\,(z(t)) = 0, \quad z(t) < \bar{z} - \mu - \sigma \tag{25.15}$$

$$\text{prob}\,(z(t)) = \frac{z(t) + \mu + \sigma - \bar{z}}{2\sigma}, \quad \bar{z} - \mu - \sigma \leq z(t) < \bar{z} \tag{25.16}$$

$$\text{prob}\,(z(t)) = 1, \quad z(t) \geq \bar{z} \tag{25.17}$$

The function prob $(z(t))$ is flat from 0 to $z(t) = \bar{z} - \mu - \sigma$, at which point the function rises linearly with $z(t)$ at the rate $1/2\sigma$. At $z(t) = \bar{z}$, if $(\mu + \sigma)\,/\,(2\sigma) < 1$, the function *jumps* from $(\mu + \sigma)\,/\,(2\sigma)$ to unity. Notice that for big $\sigma$ or small $\mu$, the probability of a crisis at $\bar{z}$ approaches 0.5.

The probability calculated in the above example turns out to be the main object of inquiry in empirical work on crisis prediction. We call the reader's attention to a simple, but often neglected, point illustrated in Figure 25.3. The probability of crisis generally does not go smoothly to unity. The probability jumps from some fraction to unity as the shadow exchange rate reaches the fixed rate. To understand why the probability may jump, think of an object taking a random walk without drift across a table. When the object is balanced on the very edge of the table, the probability that it will fall with the next step is not necessarily unity because there remains a chance that the next step will be away from the table's edge.

## 25.3 Extensions

The KFG model stripped down both private and government behavior to bare essentials to provide sharp implications about the timing of speculative attacks. The model extensions have concentrated mainly on making government policy more realistic. We show below how such extensions can be accommodated in the KFG framework.

### 25.3.1 ATTACK-CONDITIONAL MONETARY POLICY

Flood and Garber (1984b) wrote a second paper using the Salant and Henderson framework. The second paper was about a speculative attack on a nominal gold-price-fixing scheme. The paper was motivated by discussions in Washington in the early 1980s, concerning the possible return to the gold standard.[9] The theory was essentially the same as in S&H and in KFG, but there was an added twist. At the urging of Stephen Salant, Flood and Garber (1984b) added an attack-conditional post-attack monetary policy change. In terms of the KFG model, this amounts to having different rates of domestic-credit growth before, $\mu$ (0), and after, $\mu$ (1), the speculative attack with $\mu$ (1) > $\mu$ (0).

Figure 25.4 shows how attack-conditional policy alters the model.

This example of attack-conditional policy inserts a range of indeterminacy into the KFG model. Now, there are two shadow rate lines. The higher line reflects the higher fundamentals growth rate, $\mu_1$. Along the lower line the fundamentals growth rate is $\mu_0 < \mu_1$. For this example, we take the higher fundamentals growth to be due to higher growth of domestic credit. If, following an attack, monetary policy were switched from $\mu_0$ to $\mu_1$ the intersections of the two shadow rate lines separate the fundamentals into three regions. For $z$ to the left of $z_B$, there is no profit to be made by speculators whether $\mu$ equals $\mu_1$ or $\mu_0$. Between $z_B$ and $z_A$, while $\mu = \mu_0$, if speculators attack, the attack will raise $\mu$ to $\mu_1$ and will thereby be self-fulfilling. If speculators do not attack in this

[9] Flood and Garber (1984b) grew out of a series of briefing memos written for Fed Governors Charles Partee, Emmitt Rice and Henry Wallich, who were the Fed representatives on President Reagan's Gold Commission. See http://tradingoptionslab.com/blog/gold-versus-discretion-ron-paul-debates-charles-partee/

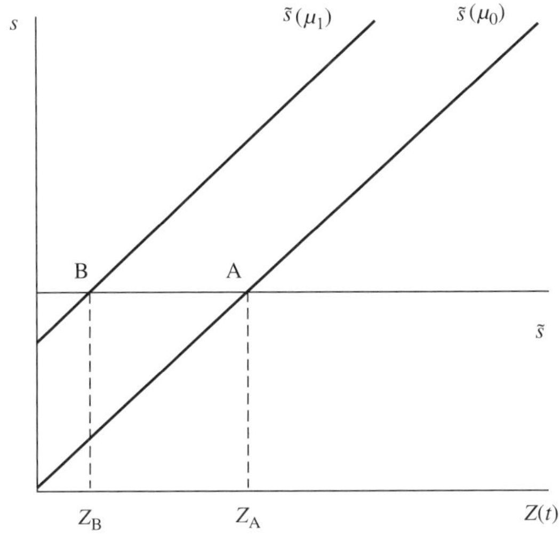


FIGURE 25.4 **Attack states with attack-conditional policy shift.**

range then the fixed rate can be sustained up to $z = z_A$. When $z \geq z_A$, the fixed rate will be attacked. The interesting aspect of the solution multiplicity explored in Flood and Garber (1984b) is that attack-conditional monetary policy can lead to indeterminate outcomes in the private market.

### 25.3.2 DEVALUATION

In the basic KFG model, it is assumed that the currency is allowed to float indefinitely in the foreign exchange market after a speculative attack. It is just as likely—perhaps more so—that with a crisis impending, the monetary authority would temporarily close the foreign exchange window and devalue the currency. Such was the policy followed by Mexico in the 1976 and 1981–1982 devaluations studied by Blanco and Garber (1986).[10]

Blanco and Garber (B&G) turned KFG into a model of devaluation under market pressure by adding the following devaluation rule:

$$\text{If } \tilde{s}(t) > \bar{s}(t) \text{ then reset } \bar{s} \text{ at } \bar{s}\,(t+1) = \bar{s}(t) + \delta u(t) \tag{25.18}$$

In Equation (25.18), $\bar{s}(t)$ is the fixed exchange rate upon entering period $t$, $\bar{s}\,(t+1)$ is the postdevaluation fixed rate, which becomes the relevant rate when the monetary authority discovers that the attack is imminent; $\delta$ is a positive parameter and $u(t)$ is the disturbance term of the fundamentals' process. In the B&G model, the shadow exchange rate is calculated as in the basic KFG model, but the unconditional expected rate of change of the exchange rate that is relevant for the opportunity cost of holding domestic money is equal to the product of the

[10]The first drafts of Blanco and Garber (1986) were written while Peter Garber visited the Fed.

probability of devaluation and the expected percentage devaluation, conditional on devaluation next period.

Although the KFG model performed well in the Mexican case and in a few others where fundamentals grew explosively, it did not perform as well in cases where fundamentals were merely highly volatile. Obstfeld's (1994) response to the hard-to-explain 1992–1993 European currency crises was to rehabilitate mathematically the pre-1978 orthodoxy that crises are (or may be) caused by arbitrary shifts in expectations. Obstfeld's work built on both the assumed-away solutions mentioned above and on the mathematically attractive solution multiplicity in the bank-runs work of Diamond and Dybvig (1983). Although the multiple-equilibria stories may seem to be just mathematical apologies for models that do not work well, we think that is too harsh a judgment. They are not entirely "throw your hands-in-the-air ... anything-can-happen" stories. Often in this work, there is range of fundamentals where the models have precise predictions and another fundamentals range where the models' implications are fuzzy, see Figure 25.4. The size and importance of such prediction difficulties can often be traced back to explicitly stated or implicitly assumed ambiguities or conditionality in government policies.[11]

Obstfeld made two points. First, governments have goals other than the fixed exchange rate and government finance, the latter modeled in KFG as an exogenous $z(t)$ process. Second, pursuit of those goals unmentioned in KFG may require devaluing the currency regardless of the value of the shadow exchange rate. The example Obstfeld used was a government targeting output or employment in addition to the fixed exchange rate. The devaluation was a discretionary policy used as an escape clause to stimulate the real sector during a business-cycle down turn.[12] Like all the models we have discussed, there are several solutions to Obstfeld's model, arising in this case because government policy reacts to private expectations of government policy.

Obstfeld's modification is to the devaluation rule. Essentially he expands the devaluation rule to be

$$\text{If: } \tilde{s}(t) > \bar{s}(t) \text{ then reset } \bar{s} \text{ at } \bar{s}\,(t+1) = \tilde{s}(t) + \delta u(t) \tag{25.19}$$

$$\text{Or if: } y(t) < \bar{y} + gs(t) \text{ then reset } \bar{s} \text{ at } \bar{s}\,(t+1) = \tilde{s}(t) + \tau \tag{25.20}$$

where $\tau$ is a fixed devaluation size and $gs(t)$ is a nonfundamental random shock. An interesting aspect of the Obstfeld model, which is surveyed less superficially in Flood and Marion (1999), is that an optimizing government may find several values of $y(t)$ where it is optimal to devalue, with each of these values a rational expectations equilibrium.[13] The lesson here and in Flood and Garber (1984b) is

[11]Obstfeld's devaluation work is sometimes called *second generation*. We find such nomenclature unhelpful and refer to Obstfeld's work using his name and describing his contribution.

[12]Kydland and Prescott (1977) made the case for monetary rules; Flood and Isard (1989) added to such rules a seldom-to-be-used escape clause.

[13]We label the nonfundamental shock in Equation (25.20) $gs\,(t)$ for fun and as acknowledgement of the widely reported role of Mr. George Soros in the 1992 European currency crises.

that when government policy is poised to react to private-sector behavior that, in turn, is responding to government policy, the resulting private behavior may surprise policy makers.

### 25.3.3 STERILIZATION AND INTEREST RATE DEFENSE

Flood et al. (1996) extended the KFG model by reminding us that policy authorities seldom allow a speculative attack to make much difference for the money supply—reserve losses are sterilized. For example, Figure 25.5, taken from Flood et al. (1996), depicts international reserves, domestic credit, and the monetary base in the period just before and just after the 1994 crisis in Mexico.

This figure illustrates that the Mexican authorities did not allow international reserve losses to have a negative impact on the monetary base during the crisis period.

Reserve-loss sterilization presents a problem for KFG because the private attack is timed such that the money-supply decrease from the reserve loss is matched by a post-attack interest rate increase, with no adjustment of the exchange rate needed at the time of the attack and no profits generated in the attack. If the money supply does not decrease in the attack, however, the KFG model cannot support a pre-attack fixed exchange rate even for a moment. The attack must come the instant the inconsistent polices are implemented. Profits from the attack on reserves are transferred immediately to speculators.

As it turns out, however, the problem is easy to fix and Flood et al. (1996) showed one way to do it.

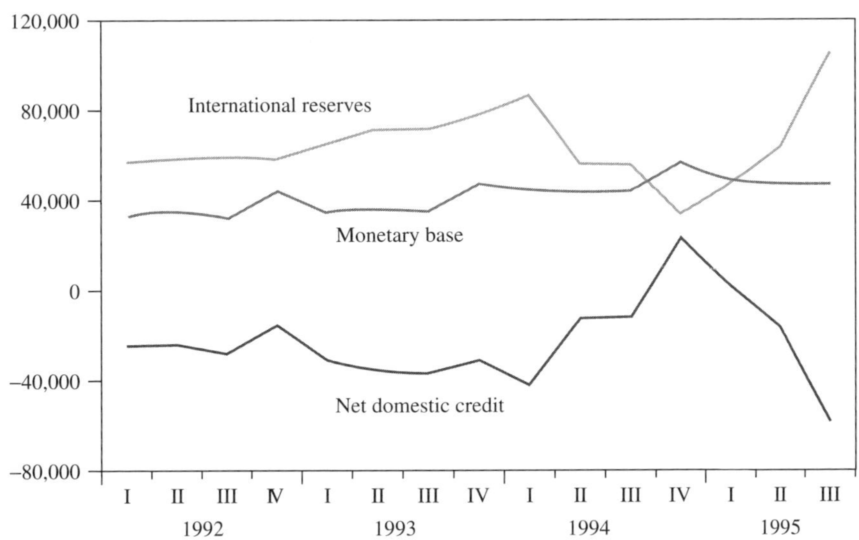


**FIGURE 25.5** Mexican base money by component (in thousands of pesos).

Instead of relying on the uncovered interest parity assumption in Equation (25.2), Flood et al. (1996) instead used

$$i(t) = i^*(t) + [E_t s(t+1) - s(t)] + \beta \left( b(t) - b^*(t) - s(t) \right) \quad (25.21)$$

The new term, $\beta\,(b(t) - b^*(t) - s(t))$, is a bond-based risk premium, with $\beta > 0$ a constant, $b(t)$ the log quantity of domestic government bonds in private hands, and $b^*(t)$ the log quantity of foreign-government bonds in private hands. By adding the bond-based risk premium to the UIP relation, Flood et al. (1996) engineered the attack to take place such that $i$ will not jump at the instant of the foreseen attack. Instead, when the expected rate of change of the exchange-rate jumps from 0 to $\mu$, the risk premium falls by exactly the same amount. The risk premium will decrease both because the domestic monetary authority must purchase domestic bonds to sterilize the reserve loss and because reserves are held as foreign-government bonds. When speculators buy the government's reserve holdings, that purchase is an increase private holding of foreign-government bonds. The attack-timing equation for this model is similar to the original KFG equation, but now it is risk-premium parameters rather than money-market parameters that govern attack timing.

Flood et al. (1996) were able to accommodate reserve-loss sterilization using a bond-based risk premium, but there is nothing special about the risk premium method. The idea taken from Salant and Henderson, which is the mechanism in KFG also, is that a foreseen speculative attack is inherently a market-caused adjustment in a quantity—reserves held privately. In the original KFG, the reserve loss caused a decrease in high power money that matched a decrease in money demand brought about by the increase in the interest rate. In Flood et al. (1996), the attack on reserves plus sterilization generated an open-market purchase of domestic credit and an increase in the world private stock of foreign-government debt to match the post-attack expected depreciation of the domestic currency. In both KFG and Flood et al. (1996), the important point is not the specific mechanism. Indeed, the point we take from Salant and Henderson is that the private sector can bring about changes in supply or in demand to accommodate the speculative attack without requiring an anticipated price change.

Flood et al. (1996) presented a risk-premium model in a setup where there was no risk, which was a bit odd. Flood and Marion (1996) showed how to derive the risk premium when the Flood et al. (1996) model incorporates risk. Flood and Marion (1996), F&M make $\beta$ (in Eq. 25.21) endogenous using a mean-variance portfolio model. F&M found $\beta(t) = \psi \mathrm{Var}_t\,(s\,(t+1))$, where $\psi$ is a positive constant and $\mathrm{Var}_t\,(s\,(t+1))$ is the step-ahead variance of the log-exchange rate (percentage variance). This turns Equation (25.21) into

$$i(t) = i^*(t) + [E_t s(t+1) - s(t)] + \psi \mathrm{Var}_t \left( s_{t+1} \right) \left( b(t) - b^*(t) - s(t) \right) \quad (25.22)$$

Where $\beta$ in Flood et al. (2005) was important in determining the response of the exchange rate to a shock, that is, the variance of the exchange rate, now the exchange-rate response and hence its variance depend on exchange-rate variance.

This modification gives rise to multiple solutions. Flood and Marion argue, however, that only one of the solutions is the fundamentals solution. The others are mathematical curiosities—such as bubbles.

It is convenient, at this point, to recognize that a government's defense of a fixed exchange rate may involve also changing the government-controlled short-term interest rate. This is known at the *interest rate defense* (IRD) of a fixed exchange rate. The IRD is not available in the basic KFG model because UIP pins down the domestic-currency interest rate. Evidently, however, policymakers do not feel constrained by UIP and try to use domestic-currency interest rates to attract foreign-currency reserves. Recall, for example, that Sweden hiked the 3-day Kroner interest rate to 500% (at an annualized rate) during the 1992 European currency crisis, evidence that the Riksbank did not feel constrained by UIP.[14]

Economists have been skeptical about the effectiveness of the IRD, but various modeling mechanisms have been proposed. Bensaid and Jeanne (1997) studied the harm an IRD might do to the real side of the economy. (In KFG, this could be modeled by making output endogenous.) Drazen (2003) approached the IRD as a signaling device about government characteristics. (In KFG, such signals may interact with private beliefs about future values of $z(t)$.) Lahiri and Vegh (2003, 2007) and Flood and Jeanne (2005) employed KFG-style models without UIP to emphasize the impact of the IRD on the government budget.[15]

### 25.3.4 LENDER OF LAST RESORT AND CURRENCY CRISES

More recent currency crises, such as the Asian crises, have been part of country-wide systemic financial crises with dramatic negative consequences for real activity.[16] These systemic crises drew attention to another government promise with priority over a fixed exchange rate. In particular, a banking system collapse may induce a government to bail out the banks at the expense of the fixed exchange rate. The papers by Chang and Velasco (2001) and Burnside et al. (2001) illustrate the point—in slightly different ways.

In these papers, currency crises and banking crises are tied together by the government's budget constraint. Banks enter the scene via their balance sheets, which can exhibit problems due to the following:

1. fundamentals-based vulnerability, for example, bad loans, currency-mismatches, which may be due to excessive risk taking (Dooley, 2000), or

[14] Of course, the 500% number is not *prima facie* evidence of departures from UIP. The New York Times reported September 17, 1992 that the market was "very thin."

[15] See Kraay (2003) for an empirical evaluation of the efficacy of the IRD.

[16] Although, here, we ignore the interaction of currency crises with the real economy, this interaction is large (Lahiri and Vegh, 2007).

2. arbitrary liquidity vulnerability in the sense of Diamond and Dybvig (1983).[17]

In the systemic-crisis models, the government has made a promise to fix the exchange rate and a promise to act as the *lender of last resort* (LOLR) to domestic banks. Both promises rely on fixed government resources. In the models, and in the data, the LOLR promise has higher priority than does the fixed-rate promise. Defending each of the two promises requires the government to dip into the same finite trough of taxpayer wealth. If the banking system requires a government bailout while the exchange rate is still fixed, the process of bailing out the banks may exhaust government reserves or require raising new taxes—including seigniorage—thereby inflating domestic credit and endangering the fixed-rate promise.

To model this process, we return to the basic KFG model but with another twist—financing the LOLR promises to the banking system. To understand the resulting currency crisis, we do not really need to model the functioning of the banking system itself, only the government's reaction to banking system distress. Assistance takes two forms in the literature. In Chang and Velasco (2000), the monetary authority opens the discount window extending domestic credit to the banks—so when the banks are in distress $d(t)$ jumps up. While the exchange rate is fixed, with no change in nominal money demand, adding to domestic credit brings on reserves losses. The currency crisis is either immediate or brought forward in time. Instead of using just the discount window, as in Burnside et al. (2001), the government gives a continuing (flow) seigniorage-based subsidy to the fragile banking system. In terms of the KFG model, we can represent this continuing subsidy as an increase in $\mu$, the time rate of change of the fundamental, $z$. We represent the post-Asian LOLR-based extensions as follows. If the banking system needs no help, the $z(t)$ process continues along its exogenous path as in basic KFG. But if the banking system needs help, the $z$ process becomes

$$z(t+1) = \mu^{+} + z\left(t^{+}\right) + u(t+1) \tag{25.23}$$

where $\mu^{+} > \mu$ and/or $z\left(t^{+}\right) > z(t)$.

The LOLR extensions invoke a policy-regime-switching trigger and a banking collapse not considered explicitly before.[18] The policy switch is the change in the domestic-credit process. Although the literature treats banking distress as a complete surprise, it would be straightforward to make the banking distress forecastable.[19]

---

[17]The forecastable collapse of banks due to insolvency was studied by Flood and Garber (1981) and Flood and Marion (2004).

[18]The banking bailout is an example of the attack-conditional policy switch suggested by Salant and depicted in Figure 25.4.

[19]This is a policy-switching problem of the type investigated by Flood and Garber (1981).

## 25.4 Empirical Work

The first empirical work on speculative attacks was done by Blanco and Garber (1986). They applied the KFG model to currency crises in Mexico in 1976 and 1981–1982. B&G applied KFG directly with the exception that in the crisis the monetary authority devalues the currency instead of allowing a run on international reserves. Preemptive devaluation is a common response to impending currency crises, as the devaluation protects reserve stocks.

We replicate two figures (Figs. 25.6 and 25.7) taken from B&G that illustrate the empirical content of their work. Figure 25.6 depicts the shadow-exchange-rate-driven series of "exchange rates conditional on devaluation" (ERCD) as given by Equation (25.18), the sequence of fixed exchange rates and the devaluation dates. In the figure, as the ERCD rises toward the sequence of fixed exchange rates the probability of one-quarter-ahead devaluation also rises.

In Figure 25.7, we have reconstructed the B&G devaluation probabilities and plotted the actual devaluation dates. Clearly, the probability of a crisis rose as a crisis approached. Notice also that in the quarter before each devaluation occurred, the probability of a crisis never approached unity. In the quarter just before the 1976 devaluation, the highest probability reached 20% and in the 1981–1982 devaluations the probability was just under 30%. This is just what the KFG model predicts (Fig. 25.3).

A number of successful empirical applications followed in B&G's footsteps.[20] The B&G empirical methodology involved a money-market-based structural study with attack probabilities based on the KFG model. Confidence in the

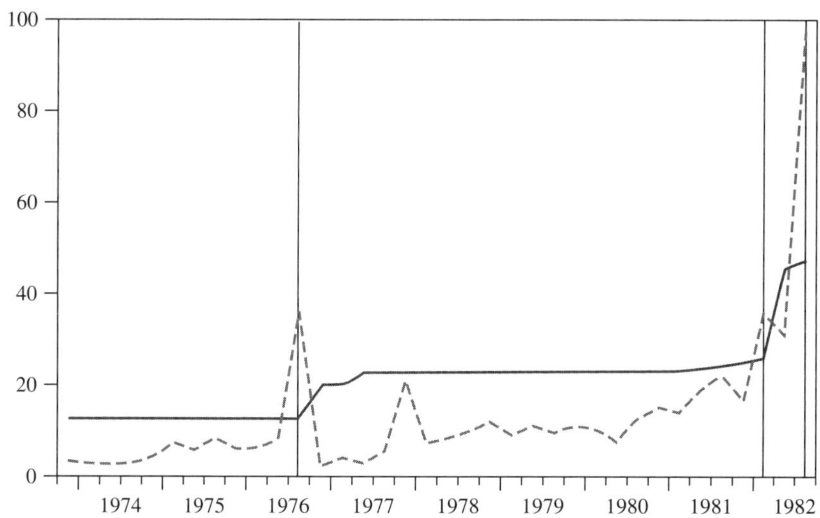


**FIGURE 25.6** Exchange rates and devaluation dates from B&G. Solid line is the fixed exchange rate. Hatched line is the exchange rate conditional on devaluation.

[20] For example, see Goldberg (1994) and Cumby and van Wijnbergen (1989).

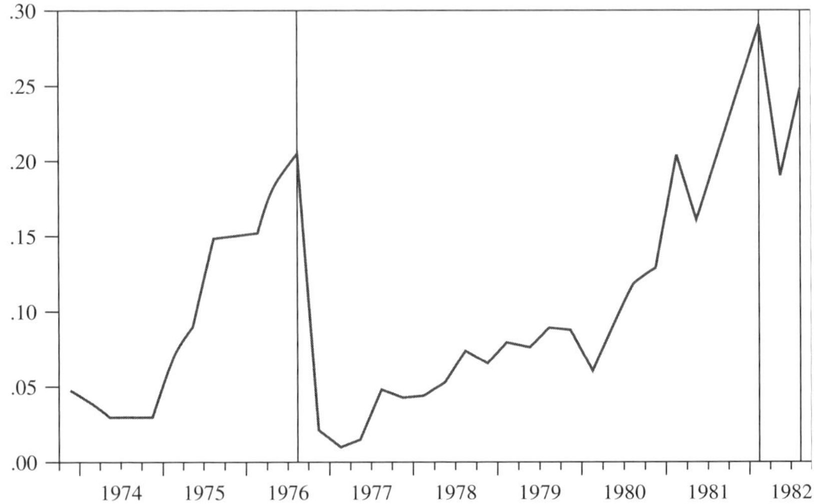


FIGURE 25.7 **Devaluation probabilities from B&G.**

structure B&G used diminished as researchers found both money-demand instability in developed and developing countries and speculative attacks absent excessively expansionary government policy. The later empirical work, for example, Eichengreen et al. (1995), Frankel and Rose (1996), and Kaminsky and Reinhart (1999), is explicitly nonstructural, using censored-dependent variable models, for example, Logit, to estimate crisis probabilities based on a wide range of lagged variables, including those suggested in KFG. The post B&G empirical results are disappointing when compared to the results in B&G.

Flood and Marion (1999) surveyed the empirical work on the KFG model and on currency crises and banking crises more broadly. They concluded that crises are hard to relate to market fundamentals—no surprise there. Since the (1999) survey was written, Kumar et al. (2003) have shown that the empirical correlation between crises and fundamentals may be stronger than previously thought. Kumar et al. (2003) used a logit model with substantial success to predict crises out of sample. They found that a logit model based on lagged values of market fundamentals suggested by theory produces crisis probabilities that match well with observed crises. More convincing still, Kumar et al. (2003) used their model's out-of-sample predictions to take simulated positions in the foreign exchange market and found that "substantial profits" could have been made using their model.

## 25.5 Conclusion

Our goal has been to show how a lot of the newly minted ideas on currency crises relate back to a common intellectual ancestor, Salant and Henderson (1978)—as seen through the lens of the KFG model. The essential idea in S&H is that speculators betting against a government policy will influence the success, failure, or at least duration of that policy in a forecastable way. Fundamentals may differ across crises, and that is to be expected, but the ways we think about those fundamentals draws on a common construct. Finally, we are skeptical about the long-lasting usefulness of odd-ball model solutions, for example, bubbles or other arbitrary indeterminacies, as explanations of crises. Economists normally refer to data unrelated to fundamentals as *unexplained residuals*.

## REFERENCES

Bensaid B, Jeanne O. The instability of fixed exchange rate systems when raising the nominal interest rate is costly. Eur Econ Rev 1997;41(8):1461–1478. Elsevier.

Blanco H, Garber P. Recurrent devaluation and speculative attacks on the Mexican Peso. J Pol Econ 1986;94(1):148–166.

Burnside C., Prospective deficits and the Asian currency crisis. J Polit Econ, 2001;109:1155–1194.

Chang R, Velasco A. Financial fragility and the exchange rate regime. J Econ Theory 2000;92:1–34.

Chang R., Velasco A. A model of financial crises in emerging markets. Quart J Econ; V116:489–517.

Cumby R, van Wijnbergen S. Financial policy and speculative runs with a crawling peg: Argentina 1979–1981. J Int Econ 1989;27:111–127.

Diamond D, Dybvig P. Bank runs, deposit insurance and liquidity. J Pol Econ 1983;91:401–419.

Dooley M. A model of crises in emerging markets. Econ J 2000;110(460):256–272.

Drazen A. Interest rate defense against speculative attack as a signal: a primer. In: Dooley MP, Frankel JA, editors. Managing currency crises in emerging markets. Chicago: University of Chicago Press; 2003.

Eichengreen B, Rose A, Wyplosz C. Exchange market mayhem: the antecedents and aftermath of speculative attacks. Econ Policy 1995;21:249–312.

Flood R, Garber P. An economic theory of monetary reform. J Pol Econ 1980;88(1):24–58.

——. A systematic banking collapse in a perfect foresight world. NBER Working Paper No. 691; 1981.

——. Flood R, Kramer C. Collapsing exchange-rate regimes: some linear examples. J Int Econ 1984a;17:1–13.

——. Gold monetization and gold discipline. J Pol Econ 1984b;92(1):90–107.

——, Flood R., Isard P., Monetary Policy Strategies. IMF Staff Papers 1989;36 (September 1989) pp. 612–32.

——, Flood R, Jeanne O. An Interest Rate Defense of a Fixed Exchange Rate? Journal of International Economics, July 2005, pp. 471–484.

Flood R, Marion N. Speculative Attacks: Fundamentals and Self-Fulfilling Prophecies, NBER WP 5789, October 1996.

____. Perspectives on the recent currency crisis literature. Int J Finance Econ 1999;4(1):1–26; Reprinted in Calvo G, Dornbusch R, Obstfeld M, editors. Money, capital mobility, and trade: essays in honor of Robert A. Mundell. Cambridge: MIT Press; 2001.

____, A model of the joint distribution of banking and currency crises, J Int Money Finan 2004;23:841–65.

Frankel J, Rose A. Currency crashes in emerging markets: an empirical treatment. J Int Econ 1996;41:351–366.

Garber P. Famous first bubbles: the fundamentals of early manias. Boston (MA): MIT Press; 2000.

Goldgar A. Tulipmania: money, honor and knowledge in the dutch golden age. Chicago: University of Chicago Press; 2007.

Goldberg L. Predicting exchange rate crises: Mexico revisited. J Int Econ 1994;36:413–430.

Kaminsky G, Reinhart C. The twin crises: the causes of banking and balance-of-payments problems. Am Econ Rev 1999;89(3):473–500.

Kindleberger C Manias, panics and crashes: a history of financial crises. Boston (MA): MIT Press; 1978, 2000.

Kraay A. Do high interest rates defend currencies during speculative attacks? J Int Econ 2003;59:297–321.

Krugman P. A model of balance of payments crises. J Money Credit Bank 1979;11:311–325.

Kumar M, Moorthy U, Perraudin W. Predicting emerging market currency crashes. J Empir Finance 2003;10:427–454.

Kydland F, Prescott E. Rules rather than discretion: the inconsistency of optimal plans. J Pol Econ 1977;85(3):473–492.

Lahiri A, Vegh C. Delaying the inevitable: interest rate defense of balance of payments crises. J Pol Econ 2003;111:404–424.

____. Output costs, currency crises and interest rate defense of a peg. Econ J 2007;117(516):216–239.

Mackay C. Extraordinary Popular Delusions and the Madness of crowds. 1852, reprinted 2008, BN Publishing.

____. Obstfeld M. The logic of currency crises. Cahiers Economiques et Monetaires, Bank of France 43; 1994. pp.189–213.

Reinhart CM, Rogoff KS. This time it's different: eight centuries of financial folly. Princeton (NJ): Princeton University Press; 2009.

Salant S, Henderson D. Market anticipations of government policies and the price of gold. J Pol Econ 1978;86:627–648.

# CHAPTER TWENTY SIX

# Official Intervention in the Foreign Exchange Market

**MARCEL FRATZSCHER**
European Central Bank

## 26.1 Introduction

On September 15, 2010, the Bank of Japan conducted a massive intervention in the foreign exchange market, buying a market-estimated USD 24 billion in order to weaken the yen. The yen depreciated by about 3%, from below YEN/USD 83 to above 85, on that day. To put the magnitude of this intervention into perspective, this USD 24 billion single-day intervention is larger than the total of all interventions conducted by the US Federal Reserve since 1990 and more than six times larger than US interventions in the entire year 1985, when United States, European, and Japanese authorities conducted concerted interventions to weaken the US dollar following the famous Plaza Accord. By mid-October 2010, about 4 weeks after the intervention by Japanese authorities, the YEN/USD exchange rate had returned to its preintervention level.[1]

Official interventions in FX markets are by no means limited to advanced economies. Quite the opposite: most advanced economies have ceased or at least drastically reduced their direct intervention activity in FX markets over the past 15 years, whereby it has been primarily emerging market economies (EMEs) that have increased substantially their FX interventions. Following the Asian financial crisis of the 1990s, global FX reserve holdings by central banks of EMEs rose

[1] Similarly, G7 authorities conducted a concerted intervention on the yen in March 2011, following the disaster due to the earthquake, tsunami, and nuclear accident.

*Handbook of Exchange Rates*, First Edition. Edited by Jessica James, Ian W. Marsh, and Lucio Sarno.

from USD 0.838 trillion in 1999 to USD 5.5 trillion in mid-2010 (Table 26.1). China is the largest reserve holder, holding USD 2.6 trillion in Q2 2010, which amounts to more than 45% of China's own GDP. Yet, China is not alone in this trend as several other EMEs hold similar even larger reserves as shares of their domestic GDP.

The specific example of the Japanese interventions on September 15, 2010 and March 2011, and the general point about the overall magnitude and speed of FX reserve accumulation at the global level both underscore that official interventions in FX markets are now more important than ever. What is the motivation behind authorities' drive to intervene in FX markets? And are authorities effective, and under what conditions, in achieving their intervention objectives? The aim of this chapter is to address these two issues about the motivation and trend as well as about the effectiveness of official FX interventions.

TABLE 26.1 **Evolution of Global FX Reserve Holdings**

| | **1999** | **2000** | **2001** | **2002** | **2003** | **2004** | **2005** | **2006** | **2007** | **2008** | **2009** | *2010* |
|---|---|---|---|---|---|---|---|---|---|---|---|---|
| *All emerging econ* | **838** | **904** | **974** | **1169** | **1508** | **1953** | **2305** | **2885** | **3897** | **4302** | **5051** | **5514** |
| *Emerging Asia* | *643* | *693* | *769* | *943* | *1207* | *1569* | *1819* | *2215* | *2907* | *3318* | *4034* | *4433* |
| China | 155 | 166 | 212 | 286 | 403 | 610 | 819 | 1066 | 1528 | 1946 | 2399 | 2648 |
| Hong Kong | 96 | 108 | 111 | 112 | 118 | 124 | 124 | 133 | 153 | 183 | 256 | 266 |
| India | 32 | 37 | 45 | 67 | 98 | 125 | 131 | 170 | 267 | 247 | 259 | 265 |
| Indonesia | 26 | 28 | 27 | 31 | 35 | 35 | 33 | 41 | 55 | 49 | 60 | 80 |
| Korea | 74 | 96 | 102 | 121 | 155 | 198 | 210 | 238 | 262 | 200 | 265 | 285 |
| Malaysia | 30 | 26 | 27 | 31 | 41 | 62 | 66 | 78 | 95 | 86 | 86 | 90 |
| Philippines | 13 | 13 | 13 | 13 | 14 | 13 | 16 | 20 | 30 | 33 | 39 | 46 |
| Singapore | 77 | 80 | 76 | 82 | 96 | 113 | 116 | 136 | 163 | 174 | 188 | 214 |
| Taiwan | 106 | 107 | 122 | 162 | 207 | 242 | 253 | 266 | 270 | 292 | 348 | 381 |
| Thailand | 34 | 32 | 32 | 38 | 41 | 48 | 51 | 65 | 85 | 108 | 134 | 157 |
| *EMEA* | *56* | *71* | *72* | *93* | *135* | *197* | *275* | *414* | *614* | *557* | *553* | *565* |
| Russia | 8 | 24 | 33 | 44 | 77 | 125 | 182 | 304 | 479 | 427 | 413 | 423 |
| Saudi Arabia | 18 | 18 | 15 | 17 | 18 | 23 | 24 | 26 | 32 | 28 | 38 | 38 |
| South Africa | 6 | 6 | 6 | 6 | 6 | 13 | 19 | 23 | 30 | 31 | 32 | 35 |
| Turkey | 23 | 22 | 19 | 27 | 34 | 36 | 51 | 61 | 73 | 71 | 70 | 69 |
| *Latin America* | *139* | *140* | *133* | *133* | *167* | *187* | *210* | *257* | *376* | *428* | *464* | *517* |
| Argentina | 34 | 34 | 20 | 10 | 14 | 20 | 28 | 32 | 46 | 46 | 48 | 51 |
| Brazil | 36 | 33 | 36 | 38 | 49 | 53 | 54 | 86 | 180 | 207 | 239 | 275 |
| Chile | 15 | 15 | 14 | 15 | 16 | 16 | 17 | 19 | 17 | 23 | 25 | 26 |
| Colombia | 8 | 9 | 10 | 11 | 11 | 14 | 15 | 15 | 21 | 24 | 25 | 27 |
| Mexico | 31 | 34 | 40 | 46 | 56 | 61 | 67 | 68 | 78 | 85 | 91 | 108 |
| Venezuela | 15 | 16 | 12 | 12 | 21 | 23 | 30 | 37 | 34 | 42 | 35 | 29 |

*Sources:* Bloomberg and Haver.

Turning to the first question about the motivation and trend of FX interventions, Section 26.2 of this chapter lays out the main elements of the debate currently ongoing among policymakers, including in the G20, about the underlying motives behind official FX interventions. Some stress the importance of a precautionary motive behind the reserve accumulation in EMEs, that is, among countries and regions that had been subject to speculative attacks and subsequently devastating financial crises in the 1990s. In this view, FX reserves provide a self-insurance mechanism against volatile capital flows and sudden stops. On the contrary, others note that the massive FX interventions by EMEs over the past decade have had primarily the motive of having weak and undervalued exchange rates, so as to improve competitiveness and exports as well as to attract foreign investment, with the ultimate aim of fostering economic growth and development. The risk of pursuing such a strategy is that it becomes incompatible if several economies pursue the same path, giving rise to what is often referred to as *competitive devaluations* or what Brazil's Minister of Finance Mantega in September 2010 coined a "currency war," that is, a vicious cycle in which official FX interventions by some trigger similar behavior by other countries in order to maintain or gain competitiveness. The following quotes illustrate today's controversy surrounding official FX interventions and policy:

> *"We are in the midst of an international currency war"*
> (Brazil's Finance Minister Mantega, 28/09/10, Source: Reuters News)

> *"The conditions for a major appreciation of the renminbi do not exist [. . .] China would suffer major social upheaval [. . .] The main cause of the US trade deficit is not the exchange rate of the Chinese currency, but the structure of investment and savings"*
> (China's Premier Wen, 23/09/10, Source: Reuters News)

> *"China has not done everything that needs to be done [. . .] What we have said [to China] is that you need to let your currency rise in accordance with the fact that your economy is rising, you are getting wealthier, and you are exporting a lot. [The renminbi is] valued lower than market conditions say it should be [which gives China] an advantage in trade."*
> (US President Obama, 21/09/10, Source: Reuters News)

> *"If there is a drastic [yen] change, such intervention is unavoidable [. . .] there is a common recognition among G20 nations that overly rapid currency movements are undesirable [. . .] the issues of China's renminbi and Japan's yen are completely different"*
> (Japan's Prime Minister Kan, 21/09/10, Source: Reuters News)

Yet, there is not only the issue of consistency and conflict among policymakers who attempt to pursue similar FX strategies via official interventions. FX interventions have various other costs and benefits, both for the domestic economy and for the global economy as a whole. Importantly, official FX interventions have a bearing on the autonomy and effectiveness of other policy tools; in particular, monetary policy which, in many instances, is severely constrained when FX interventions play a significant role in the policy mix. FX interventions may also hinder an efficient allocation of capital and impose direct financial costs for domestic policymakers. Moreover, at the global level, FX interventions have been shown to distort global financial markets by affecting substantially global market liquidity, capital flows, and the yield environment for a broad set of asset classes.

This leads to the questions: Do official interventions succeed in moving exchange rates in the desired way, and under what conditions do they do so? And through what channels do interventions function? Section 26.3 of this chapter turns to these questions about the effectiveness of official FX interventions. The section starts by presenting a simple stylized model in the spirit of microstructure models, which treat the exchange rate as an asset price that depends on several actual and expected fundamentals. Next, the section presents empirical evidence derived from the two methodological approaches that have dominated empirical studies about the effect and effectiveness of official FX interventions. It highlights that there is evidence that FX interventions may be effective in both moving the level of exchange rates as well as by affecting the underlying volatility of FX markets. Importantly, the success of official interventions is conditional on a multitude of factors; in particular, the market environment as well as how exactly the interventions are conducted.

Moreover, Section 26.3 discusses and analyzes the different channels through which official interventions may function. While studies for the 1980s indicate that FX interventions during that period may in part have functioned through a portfolio balance channel, evidence for recent intervention episodes indicate that nowadays a coordination channel, and to some extent a signaling channel, may have become more relevant as channels through which interventions work.

Importantly, Section 26.3 not only focuses on the effectiveness of actual FX interventions, that is, FX purchases and sales by monetary authorities, but also on the role and effectiveness of communication about exchange rates, or oral interventions. In fact, many advanced economies—such as the United States, the euro area, and the United Kingdom—have moved away from using actual FX interventions since the mid-1990s and have since primarily used communication as their primary policy tool to guide and influence FX markets. Hence, while in some cases, communication is an important complement to actual FX interventions, in other instances, communication has become a substitute. Section 26.3 closes by discussing the evidence about the effectiveness of this form of oral FX interventions, showing that these indeed tend to exert, in many instances, a marked effect on FX markets, primarily through a coordination channel.

The chapter is structured as follows. The next section provides a number of stylized facts about the use of official FX interventions, discusses the possible motives that drive policymakers, and outlines potential costs and benefits from such actions. Section 26.3 then provides a review of the effectiveness of official FX interventions and its underlying channels. Section 26.4 summarizes the findings and draws lessons from the experience with FX interventions.

## 26.2 Official FX Interventions and Reserve Accumulation: Stylized Facts, Motives, and Effects

The accumulation of foreign exchange reserves by the monetary authorities of emerging and developing economies is back on the international policy agenda. After the Asian financial crisis of 1997, international reserve accumulation accelerated rapidly, reaching as much as 13% of global GDP in 2009. While the increase in the stocks of FX reserves as a share of GDP of the high income countries has been relatively small (from 6% in 1999 to <8% in 2008), the rise in the ratio of reserves-to-GDP of the low and middle income countries (from 12% to 25%), in particular in East Asia (from 12% to 30%) and especially of China (from 15% to 45%), has been striking (Fig. 26.1).

Following the 2007–2009 global financial crisis, this process has experienced a new acceleration, following a short-lived episode of reserve depletion between end-2008 and the beginning of 2009. The overall level of reserves in EMEs alone reached over USD 6 trillion in mid-2010, USD 1 trillion more than at the peak before the 2007–2009 financial crisis.

How should one assess this rapid pace of official FX interventions and reserve accumulation? What are the motives behind this massive intervention activity? A first important motive for official FX interventions that policymakers in EMEs keep emphasizing is that of a precautionary motive. The severe economic and social costs of the 1997 Asian crisis convinced Asian governments that large international reserve holdings are a necessary tool to protect the economy from sudden stops of capital inflows. The precautionary demand for reserves was first explained by the buffer stock models of Hamada and Ueda (1977) and Frenkel and Jovanovic (1981), while more recent papers present representative-agent

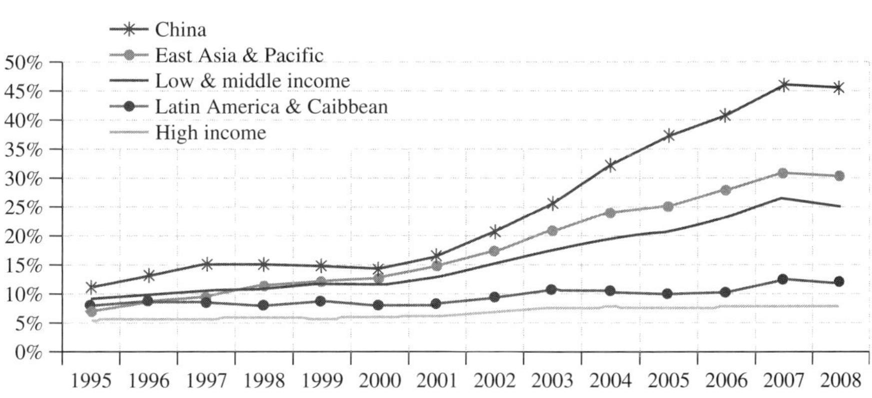


**FIGURE 26.1** International reserves as a share of GDP (%), 1995–2008. *Source*: World Development Indicators Mileva (2010).

models in which reserve accumulation reflects an insurance policy against bad states of nature (e.g., Aizenman and Lee, 2007; Caballero and Panageas, 2005, Jeanne and Rancière, 2008). Aizenman and Marion (2003) develop an insurance model, in which agents are loss averse. In this case, it can be optimal to hold large reserve balances even when there is a sizeable equity premium, such that the return on domestic capital far exceeds the return on the safe asset.

Closely related to the idea of the precautionary demand for FX reserves is the role of reserves in supporting the countercyclical use of fiscal policy. In Aizenman and Marion (2003), policymakers in a country with limited access to foreign capital use FX reserves to finance public expenditure instead of raising taxes during recessions. In this model, the optimal amount of reserve holdings allows the policymakers to smooth the tax burden and consumption over time.

One of the most controversial issues in the international policy debate currently is the question about how important this precautionary motive is for FX interventions and reserve accumulation. Many observers doubt that the sharp increase and the massive level of FX reserves of EMEs can reflect a pure insurance motive. The argument is that reserve accumulation may primarily reflect a third motive for FX interventions and reserve accumulation, namely to foster export-led growth via weak and undervalued exchange rates, which support the competitiveness and growth of the export sectors of the economy. There is indeed evidence that weaker exchange rates support growth (see e.g., Dollar, 1992; Hausmann et al., 2005) find that rapid growth accelerations sustained for a period of several years are related with real exchange rate depreciations. Rodrik (2008) shows that higher growth occurs, on average, after 10 years of undervaluation in developing countries. Levy-Yeyati and Sturzenegger (2007) explore a related channel of transmission between exchange rate undervaluation and GDP growth and find that central bank interventions indeed lead to a weak exchange rate and, in turn, to higher saving and investment. By shifting resources from consumers to financially constraint firms, real devaluation boosts savings and investment.

Other by-products are that reserve accumulation is usually associated with M2 growth via sterilization, which may potentially contribute to the deepening of domestic financial markets. Moreover, many EMEs have created and transferred excess international reserves to sovereign wealth funds, which then make strategic investments.

Despite these motives and potential benefits from FX interventions, FX reserve accumulation is associated with potentially large costs and risks (e.g., Bini Smaghi, 2010). The former consist of the opportunity cost of foregone domestic investment and consumption, which tends to be higher for developing countries as their marginal utility of consumption is higher and their infrastructure needs larger. If reserve accumulation is the consequence of having a fixed exchange rate, then additional costs include lack of monetary policy autonomy and possibly financial repression (Lardy, 2008). According to the IMF (2010), a more general measure of the cost of accumulating FX reserves should also include welfare costs associated with externalities at the national and the global levels, such as the contribution to global imbalances. Some countries' pursuit of current account surpluses may result in protectionist policies and competitive devaluations by other countries with which they compete directly in export markets. In addition, large reserve accumulation may over time undermine the quality of the reserve assets, if the debt levels of the reserve-issuing countries become unsustainable. Finally, by depressing interest rates, FX reserve accumulation may encourage excessive risk-taking and volatile capital flows.

Which of these different hypotheses is true? What is the dominant motive for official FX interventions and reserve accumulation? The gauge an answer to this question, a number of studies have developed benchmarks that capture the level of reserves needed for precautionary motives, that is, to provide adequate insurance against sudden stops and capital flights.

The oldest benchmark for reserve adequacy is based on the coverage of imports, often using as a transparent rule of thumb that reserves should cover 3–4 months of imports (e.g., Wjinholds and Kapteyn, 2001). As countries liberalized their capital accounts in the 1990s, they were increasingly exposed to large and volatile capital flows, which made the trade-related reserve adequacy yardstick inadequate. In 1999, a new rule—what today is known as the *Greenspan–Guidotti rule*—was proposed which implied the full coverage of short-term external debt at remaining maturity (Greenspan, 1999; Guidotti, 1999). The Greenspan–Guidotti rule has since been criticized for failing to account for the possibility of other forms of capital flight, for example, by domestic investors. Obstfeld et al. (2008) argue in favor of monitoring the ratio of reserves-to-M2, that is, the size of domestic financial liabilities that could potentially be converted into foreign currency. On the basis of historical evidence, Wjinholds and Kapteyn (2001) suggest a ratio of 5–10% of M2 for flexible exchange rate regimes and 20% of M2 for fixed regimes.

Looking first at the aggregate across all EMEs, the evidence indicates that the international reserve build up by EMEs over the past decade has exceeded any standard reserve adequacy measures associated with a self-insurance motive against possible shocks. In Figure 26.2, the black and dashed lines track the traditional benchmarks—the 3-months-of-imports rule and the Greenspan–Guidotti rule that requires foreign exchange reserves to cover the stock of short-term debt—and indicate that the need for global reserves would be less than one-third of the present stock of foreign exchange reserves.

Other reserve adequacy benchmarks yield very similar messages. For example, the current level of reserves would still be twice the benchmark of 6 months of imports, which was the average ratio of imports to reserves across all emerging economies when global reserves peaked before the crisis (line with triangles in Fig. 26.2). The same conclusion holds if the Greenspan–Guidotti rule was modified to require the ratio of reserves to short-term debt to be 330% in each country—which was the ration on average across all countries before the crisis—rather than 100% (line with squares). Finally, even if one regards the ratio of reserves to domestic money supply as another benchmark for assessing the adequacy of reserves, this ratio increased steadily during the past decade: while the ratio of reserves to broad money supply in emerging economies was only 15% in 2000, currently it is around 40%.

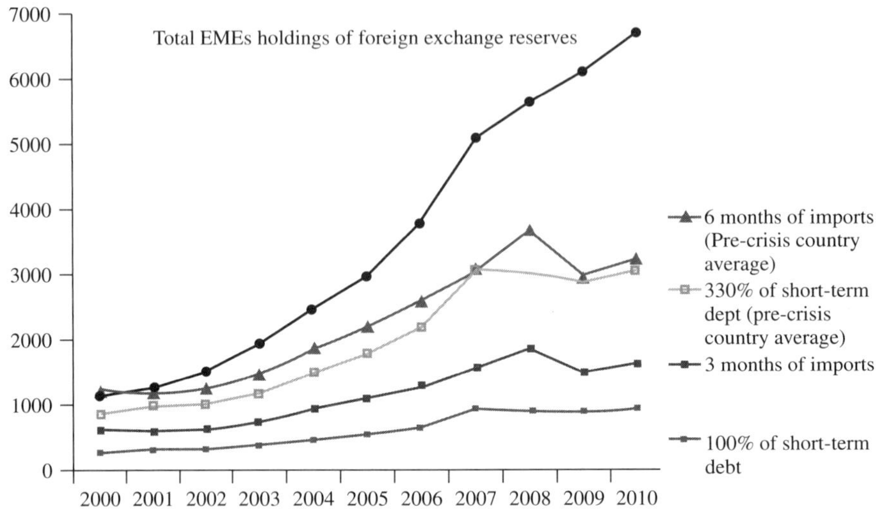


**FIGURE 26.2** **EME reserves and reserve adequacy benchmarks (USD billion).** ***Source*: Bini Smaghi (2010).**

While the benchmarks for precautionary accumulation of reserves look insufficient to explain the acceleration in global official holdings of foreign assets, it would not be appropriate to assess all reserve-accumulating countries in the same way. Interestingly, if one deducts from Figure 26.2 those economies which the IMF judges to have an undervalued currency, the difference between actual reserve accumulation and the nontraditional benchmarks narrows considerably (Fig. 26.3). Hence, what this suggests is that countries with high reserve ratios are

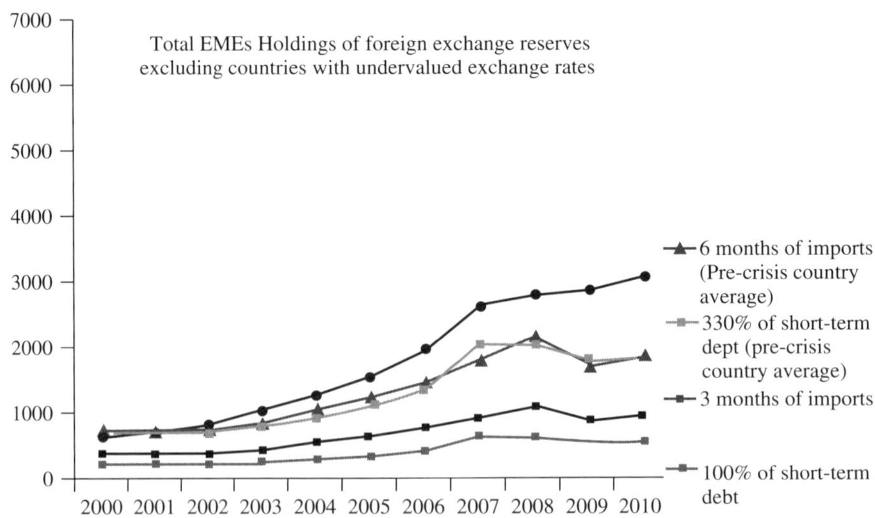


**FIGURE 26.3** **EME reserves and reserve adequacy benchmarks (USD billion)—excluding countries with undervalued exchange rates.** ***Source*: Bini Smaghi (2010).**

those that tend to have undervalued exchange rates. This is another indication that an exchange rate objective may indeed be a key driver behind official FX interventions and reserve accumulation.

In summary, the stylized facts presented in this section suggest that the acceleration of FX interventions by EMEs over the past decade has been exceeding standard benchmarks that may be consistent with a precautionary motive and that FX interventions have become particularly prevalent for countries with undervalued exchange rates. All these facts point toward the interpretation that much of the dramatic increase in official FX interventions is indeed explained by a motive to manage and guide domestic exchange rates.

## 26.3 Empirical Evidence on the Effectiveness of Official FX Interventions

Are FX interventions effective and successful in achieving their objective? While the choice and management of exchange rate regimes are treated in depth in other chapters of this handbook, much of the empirical literature has focused on the question of the effectiveness of FX interventions in floating exchange rate regimes.[2] The reason for this is twofold. The first is that in managed exchange rate regimes—where frequently also some forms of capital controls are in place—the effect of FX interventions on exchange rates is hard to determine as markets may not function freely and face various distortions. The second, more pragmatic reason has to do with the availability of data on official FX interventions. This has been one of the most severe constraints for researchers when addressing the issue of effectiveness of interventions. To date, it has been mainly the advanced economies that have published their FX intervention activity, although such data is partially becoming available also for a small set of emerging economies. Hence, the focus in this section is on the effectiveness of interventions for the three major global currencies: the US dollar, the yen, and the euro (and Deutsche mark before the creation of the euro in 1999).

This section proceeds by presenting a simple stylized model to define the concept of "effectiveness" of official interventions and to illustrate the different channels through which policymakers may succeed in managing exchange rates. The second part then discusses the evidence of effectiveness of interventions for the G3 currencies using a time-series methodology, as most commonly used in the academic literature. The third part complements this with the evidence that stems from event-study approaches which consider interventions as clusters and primarily take a longer-term time horizon to measure the effectiveness of interventions. The section draws on and links to the conceptual and empirical work provided by Fratzscher (2005, 2008, 2009).

[2] Surveys of the FX intervention literature are provided by Edison (1993); Sarno and Taylor (2001), and Neely (2005). Blinder et al. (2008) provide a broader survey on communication, including for FX.

### 26.3.1 A SIMPLE CONCEPTUAL FRAMEWORK

The exchange rate is commonly modeled in a standard asset-pricing framework, in which the log exchange rate $s_t$ reflects the discounted value of private agents' expectations about future fundamentals $f_{t+i}$:

$$s_t = (1 - \theta) \sum_{i=0}^{\infty} \theta^i E_t \left( f_{t+i} \mid \Omega_t \right) \tag{26.1}$$

with $\theta$ as the discount factor and $\Omega_t$ the public information set available to agents at time $t$. To analyze the effect of oral and actual interventions, it is useful to formulate a dynamic specification of the model. The foreign exchange risk premium $\rho$ is the return required by investors in excess of the risk-free return, which is the sum of the interest rate differentials at home ($i$) relative to abroad ($i^*$) and the expected change in the spot rate: $E[\Delta s_{t+1} - i_t + i_t^*]$. Using this definition to substitute into Equation 26.1, the dynamic model can be formulated as

$$\Delta s_{t+1} = \left( i_t - i_t^* + \rho \right) + (1 - \theta) \sum_{i=0}^{\infty} \theta^i \left[ E_{t+1} \left( f_{t+1+i} \mid \Omega_{t+1} \right) - E_t \left( f_{t+1+i} \mid \Omega_t \right) \right] \tag{26.2}$$

which implies that the change in the spot rate has an expected component—the first term on the right-hand side—and an unexpected component—the second term on the right-hand side, which is the new information about fundamentals that becomes available publicly: $\Delta s_{t+1} - E_t \left( f_{t+1} \mid \Omega_t \right)$.

How do FX interventions work and how are they used? In principle, the literature has focused on three broad channels: the portfolio balance channel, the signaling channel, and a coordination channel.

In the portfolio balance channel, actual foreign exchange interventions—both when sterilized and when nonsterilized—alter the relative supply of domestic and foreign financial assets. This induces a change in the price of these assets, thereby affecting a change in the relative value of the currencies involved. Given the imperfect substitutability, in Equation 26.1, interventions can be understood to affect the spot rate by altering the foreign exchange risk premium $\rho$. In their seminal work, Dominguez and Frankel (1993) present empirical evidence for some effectiveness of official interventions through the portfolio balance channel for the 1980s. However, the portfolio balance channel is likely to have become less relevant over time. First, this may in part to be due to the rapid integration of financial markets over the past two decades, which has made financial assets of different countries better substitutes, and second, due to the enormous increase in the size of foreign exchange market volumes.

Much of the literature has focused on the role of a second channel, the signaling channel. In this channel, interventions affect expectations of investors and asset prices by signaling either private information of the monetary authorities about relevant economic fundamentals and/or revealing the authorities' intentions about future policy. The term signaling channel was coined by the work of Mussa (1981), who argues that actual foreign exchange intervention may indeed have influenced exchange rates through this channel in the 1970s. Conceptually, in the signaling channel, interventions influence the spot rate by altering expectations about future fundamentals, that is, the second term on the right-hand side of Equation 26.2.

As to the third channel, communication policies may affect asset prices via a coordination channel. This channel implies that public statements by monetary authorities function as a coordination device that induces market views to converge and move in a particular direction over the medium term. The presence of a coordination channel in foreign exchange markets has also been suggested by Sarno and Taylor (2001). To illustrate the functioning of the coordination channel, one needs to turn to micro-based models of exchange rates (Evans and Lyons, 2002).[3] The main premise of the micro-based models is that information is not common knowledge but differs among market participants. Trading among agents is the process through which private information about fundamentals becomes public and is shared by participants. In essence, it is this heterogeneity of information and the trading process that allows for the functioning of the coordination channel of interventions. Micro-based models distinguish between different types of market participants, in particular, between market makers and traders. To illustrate the functioning of the coordination channel, consider the following modified model of Equation 26.2:

$$\Delta s_{t+1} = \left(i_t - i_t^* + \rho\right) + (1-\theta) \sum_{i=0}^{\infty} \theta^i \left[E_{t+1}^m \left(f_{t+1+i} \mid \Omega_{t+1}\right) - E_t^m \left(f_{t+1+i} \mid \Omega_t\right)\right] \tag{26.3}$$

where the market maker's expectations, $E^m$, now determine the evolution of the spot rate, in contrast to Equation 26.2. This difference, however, is important because what it indicates is that interventions may influence exchange rates not only by providing new, public information but also by inducing a revision of expectations by market makers. This revision may result not from the availability of new information but may simply reflect the coordination and incorporation of private information into market prices through the trading process. Hence, an intervention may not constitute new information per se but may coordinate trading decisions by helping to unify opinions about fundamentals and risks among traders, thereby altering the desired portfolio allocations and the exchange rate.

Following this theoretical motivation of Equations 26.2 and 26.3, a stylized and simplified version of the empirical model for the effects of interventions $IA_t$

[3]Other important contributions to this literature are Dominguez (2003); Osler (2005); Peiers (1997); Vitale (1999, 2003), among others.

that is widely used in the literature can be formulated as

$$\Delta s_t = \alpha + \sum_j \left(\beta_1^j IA_t^j\right) + \delta_1 \left(i_t^H - i_t^F\right) + \sum_d \chi_1 X_t + \varepsilon_{1,t} \quad j = H, F \qquad (26.4)$$

with $\varepsilon \sim \left(0, h_t\right)$, $\Delta s_t$ as the change in the log exchange rate of home (H) versus the foreign (F) economy; $IA_t$ as FX interventions by home or foreign authorities; and $X_t$ as a vector of controls that may capture a broad set of fundamentals, including interest rate differentials. Ideally, one would also like to proxy for the risk premium $\rho$, but it is unobservable and therefore not explicitly modeled.

While estimating (Eq. 26.4) may tell us something about the effectiveness of official interventions in terms of the level of exchange rates, it does not allow us to gauge whether interventions manage to reduce volatility and market uncertainty. The most common empirical approach in the literature has therefore been to estimate (Eq. 26.4) in an ARCH framework, so that the effect of interventions on FX volatility can be tested empirically. Choosing an EGARCH specification yields a conditional variance equation of the form

$$\log\left(h_t\right) = \tau_1 + \omega_1 \left( \left| \frac{\varepsilon_{1,t-1}}{\sqrt{h_{t-1}}} \right| - \sqrt{2/\pi} \right) + \phi_1 \log\left(h_{t-1}\right) + \kappa_1 \left( \frac{\varepsilon_{1,t-1}}{\sqrt{h_{t-1}}} \right) + \sum_j \left(\eta_1^j \left| IA_t^j \right| \right) + \sum_d \xi_1^d W_t^d, \quad j = H, F \qquad (26.5)$$

where the conditional variances of the exchange rate ($h_t$) are functions of the past variance ($h_{t-1}$) and innovations ($\varepsilon_{t-1}$), the absolute values of interventions $IA_t$ of both the home and foreign policymakers (as well as the day-of-the-week effects $W_t$).

## 26.3.2 TIME-SERIES APPROACH: EVIDENCE ON EFFECTIVENESS AND CHANNELS

This section provides empirical estimates for model (Eqs. 26.4 and 26.5), focusing on a time-series approach using the described EGARCH specification, for the case of the USD/YEN and USD/EUR and interventions by United States, Japanese, and German/euro area authorities between 1990 and 2010. As discussed above, the reason for this choice of currencies has to do with the data availability on interventions. Intervention data for these three is publicly available from the respective central banks and includes both the days when they occurred as well as the amounts and currencies against which they took place. Moreover, we extend the model of Equations 26.4 and 26.5 to include not only actual FX interventions but also FX communication—or oral interventions—by the authorities in the three economies. As discussed above, such an extension

**TABLE 26.2 Summary Statistics for Official FX Interventions by G3 Authorities, 1990–2010**

| | US Federal Reserve All Interventions | | | Bundesbank/ECB All Interventions | | | Bank of Japan All Interventions | | |
|---|---|---|---|---|---|---|---|---|---|
| | All | Buy FX | Sell FX | All | Buy FX | Sell FX | All | Buy FX | Sell FX |
| *Number of intervention days* | | | | | | | | | |
| 1990–2004 | 84 | 27 | 57 | 87 | 43 | 44 | 278 | 251 | 27 |
| 1990–1994 | 74 | 25 | 49 | 79 | 39 | 40 | 131 | 104 | 27 |
| 1995–1998 | 9 | 1 | 8 | 4 | 4 | 0 | 59 | 59 | 0 |
| 1999–2004 | 1 | 1 | 0 | 4 | 0 | 4 | 88 | 88 | 0 |
| 2005–2010 | 0 | 0 | 0 | 0 | 0 | 0 | 1 | 1 | 0 |
| *Magnitude of interventions (average, USD million)* | | | | | | | | | |
| 1990–2004 | 284 | 202 | 323 | 1591 | 2589 | 617 | 1554 | 1697 | 223 |
| 1990–1994 | 203 | 125 | 242 | 1709 | 2811 | 634 | 385 | 427 | 223 |
| 1995–1998 | 821 | 833 | 819 | 419 | 419 | — | 1706 | 1706 | — |
| 1999–2004 | 1500 | 1500 | — | n/a | — | n/a | 3192 | 3192 | — |
| 2005–2010 | — | — | — | — | — | — | 24,000 | 24,000 | — |

Note: Amounts for the actual interventions of the ECB in 2000 and the Bank of Japan in 2010 were not announced. The numbers used here are those reported by Reuters News, based on financial market reports.

*Sources:* US Federal Reserve, Bundesbank, Bank of Japan, Reuters.

may be important as authorities in all three economies are increasingly using communication as a tool to influence FX markets.[4]

Table 26.2 provides summary statistics for the number and size of FX interventions since 1990. For Japan and Germany, most actual interventions occurred against the US dollar, although there have been some instances in which Japanese authorities also intervened against the mark or the euro and Germany in support of ERM currencies in the early 1990s. What is striking is that the average daily intervention amounts over the sample period were generally quite small for today's standard, namely mostly less than USD 1 billion. Interestingly, while the intervention amounts generally increased over time, the intervention days declined substantially.

The starting point of the empirical analysis is the estimation of model (Eqs. 26.4 and 26.5) over the full sample period 1990–2009. Overall, Table 26.3 shows the first key finding that actual and oral interventions have generally been

[4]Fratzscher (2005, 2006, 2009) provides a detailed account of FX communication, about the data as well as about the underlying policy discussion. Other empirical work on the role and effectiveness of exchange rate communication policies are by Jansen and de Haan (2005) who focus on the impact of communication—primarily about monetary policy—of the Bundesbank and the ECB mainly on exchange rate volatility and find the communication in most cases had indeed a statistically significant impact. Beine et al. (2004) analyze statements of officials about actual interventions and confirm that such statements may indeed play an important role in moving markets.

**TABLE 26.3 Effectiveness of Actual Interventions and Oral Interventions—G3 Economies**

| | Conditional Mean Equation | | Conditional Variance Equation | |
|---|---|---|---|---|
| | Coefficients | Standard Error | Coefficients | Standard Error |
| **A. US dollar–euro exchange rate** | | | | |
| US oral intervention $IO^{US}$ | −0.124[a] | *0.047* | 0.016 | *0.016* |
| Ge/EA oral intervention $IO^{GE/EA}$ | 0.198[a] | *0.056* | −0.031 | *0.021* |
| US actual intervention $IA^{US}$ | −0.044 | *0.127* | 0.050 | *0.052* |
| Ge/EA actual intervention $IA^{GE/EA}$ | 1.536[a] | *0.389* | 0.556[a] | *0.134* |
| Interest rate differential[d] | −0.005 | *0.004* | −0.002 | *0.003* |
| LR test[e] | 8.356[a] | | | |
| **B. Yen–US dollar exchange rate** | | | | |
| US oral intervention $IO^{US}$ | 0.149[a] | *0.053* | −0.016 | *0.017* |
| Ja oral intervention $IO^{JA}$ | −0.155[a] | *0.051* | −0.008 | *0.017* |
| US actual intervention $IA^{US}$ | 1.287[a] | *0.267* | 0.822[a] | *0.119* |
| Ja actual intervention $IA^{JA}$ | −0.059[a] | *0.013* | −0.007[d] | *0.004* |
| Interest rate differential[d] | 0.007 | *0.006* | −0.004 | *0.004* |
| LR test[e] | 8.223[a] | — | — | — |

[a]Indicates significance at the 99% level.
[b]Indicates significance at the 95% level.
[c]Indicates significance at the 90% level.
[d]Interest rate differential for US dollar–euro exchange rate is the difference of 3-month money market rates in the United States minus the one in the euro area and correspondingly for the yen–US dollar exchange rate.
[e]LR test is a test of whether the model with intervention variables has a higher explanatory power than the model without intervention variables.
*Sources:* Fratzscher (2008).

effective in influencing the level of the US dollar–euro and yen–US dollar exchange rates. All signs are as expected.

As to actual interventions, these also have a significant effect on exchange rates. For instance, a USD 1 billion sale of foreign exchange by German/euro area in the US dollar–euro market has been associated with a 1.54% move of the exchange rate in the desired direction. By contrast, US actual interventions have no statistically significant effect on the US dollar against the DEM, in line with much of the literature on actual interventions discussed above, although they do seem to exert a significant effect on the US dollar–yen. Moreover, the effect of a USD 1 billion actual intervention by Japanese authorities on the yen–US dollar has a much smaller effect on the yen–dollar of around 0.06%. Note that these results for the yen–US dollar are similar to those found in Ito (2003) for a shorter time period.

As to oral interventions in the US dollar–euro market, German/euro area interventions in this market, on average, lead to a 0.20% change of the US dollar–mark/euro exchange rate on the day of the statement. US oral interventions have a somewhat smaller effect, moving the exchange rate by about 0.12%. The effects of US and Japanese oral interventions in the yen–dollar market are similar in magnitude at around 0.15% each. Overall, these effects may not appear to be very large individually. However, given the relatively steady frequency of communication by G3 monetary authorities, these effects are indeed relatively strong overall.

One important query is to what extent these parameter estimates are stable over time. As pointed out also, for example, by Ito (2003) for the case of Japan, variation in monetary policy reaction functions, market conditions, and size might change the effectiveness of interventions. To gauge the extent to which time variations are present for the sample of 1990–2003, splitting the sample indeed shows that the effect of actual and oral interventions have become smaller over time, yet remain statistically significant even in the 2000s (Table 26.4).

**26.3.2.1 Channels of Intervention Effectiveness.** This finding leads to the question of why and through which channels of interventions have tended to be effective. In particular, do official interventions influence exchange rates primarily through the signaling channel, that is, by signaling future monetary policy or actual interventions, or through the coordination channel, that is, by coordinating expectations across market participants?

Determining the channels of effectiveness is important from a policy perspective in order to understand what policy can do—and what it cannot do—to influence foreign exchange markets. However, it is also inherently difficult because expectations of market participants, and in particular their diversity, cannot be observed or measured accurately. This section provides a number of empirical tests that aim at getting at the underlying mechanisms of the effects of interventions. For this purpose, the model (Eqs. 26.4 and 26.5) is extended in order to be able to test for alternative hypotheses within the EGARCH framework.

Do interventions affect the exchange rate because they signal changes in future policy? Monetary authorities have two direct policy tools to exert influence over the exchange: monetary policy and actual FX purchases and sales. For instance, a statement by an official in support of the domestic currency may be perceived by market participants to raise the likelihood of future actual interventions. Alternatively, it may be understood to signal a tightening of interest rates in the future. Indeed, the literature has shown that G7 authorities in

**TABLE 26.4 Effectiveness of interventions–Changes Over Time**

| Period | Conditional Mean Equation | | | | Conditional Variance Equation | | | |
|---|---|---|---|---|---|---|---|---|
| | PRE-1999 | | POST-1999 | | PRE-1999 | | POST-1999 | |
| | Coefficients | Standard Error | Coefficients | Standard Error | Coefficients | Standard Error | Coefficients | Standard Error |
| **A. US dollar–euro exchange rate** | | | | | | | | |
| US oral intervention $IO^{US}$ | −0.145[a] | *0.065* | 0.048 | *0.073* | 0.021 | *0.036* | −0.093 | *0.144* |
| Ge/EA oral intervention $IO^{GE/EA}$ | 0.456[b] | *0.104* | 0.164[a] | *0.086* | 0.037 | *0.048* | −0.098 | *0.196* |
| US actual intervention $IA^{US}$ | −0.058 | *0.139* | — | — | 0.002 | *0.023* | — | — |
| Ge/EA actual intervention $IA^{GE/EA}$ | 1.257[b] | *0.423* | — | — | 0.083[b] | *0.020* | — | — |
| Interest rate differential[c] | −0.005 | *0.004* | −0.006 | *0.004* | −0.002 | *0.003* | −0.003 | *0.003* |
| **B. Yen–US dollar exchange rate** | | | | | | | | |
| US oral intervention $IO^{US}$ | 0.208[b] | *0.077* | 0.102 | *0.091* | −0.080 | *0.067* | 0.225[b] | *0.107* |
| Ja oral intervention $IO^{JA}$ | −0.148[a] | *0.085* | −0.170[c] | *0.086* | 0.127[b] | *0.043* | −0.068 | *0.128* |
| US actual intervention $IA^{US}$ | 1.110[b] | *0.329* | — | | 0.881[b] | *0.214* | — | |
| Ja actual intervention $IA^{JA}$ | −0.090[b] | *0.033* | −0.018[b] | *0.008* | 0.004[b] | *0.001* | 0.062[b] | *0.012* |
| Interest rate differential[c] | 0.013 | *0.005* | 0.006 | *0.005* | −0.005 | *0.005* | −0.005 | *0.003* |

[a]Indicates significance at the 90% level.
[b]indicates significance at the 99% level.
[c]indicates significance at the 95% level.
[d]The cutoff is December 31, 1998. The specification chosen is the benchmark model from Table 26.3. "—" indicates that there have been too few actual interventions by US or euro area authorities after 1998 to obtain estimates for this subsample.
[e]Interest rate differential for US dollar–euro exchange rate is the difference of 3-month money market rates in the United States minus the one in the euro area and correspondingly for the yen–US dollar exchange rate.
*Source:* Fratzscher (2008.)

the 1970s and 1980s may have sometimes used actual interventions to signal the direction of future monetary policy, and in a few instances also after a monetary policy change in order to reverse some of the undesired exchange rate effects from changes in monetary policy (Bonser-Neal et al., 1998; Kaminsky and Lewis, 1996; Lewis, 1995).

Concerning monetary policy, the hypothesis is therefore that interventions are more effective in altering the exchange rate if they are perceived to be followed by corresponding monetary policy decisions—that is, a strengthening intervention is followed by monetary tightening and a weakening intervention is backed by a subsequent easing. Similarly, following the arguments of the literature, interventions may also be more effective if they are preceded by corresponding monetary policy actions.[5]

Table 26.5 shows the results for three sets of empirical tests on the potential signaling role of monetary policy. For actual interventions, the findings indicate that these tend to be in a few cases more effective if they are consistent with the direction of monetary policy—that is, when past and future monetary policy decisions are in accordance with the actual intervention—(model 1), if they are followed by corresponding monetary policy changes in the next meeting (model 2), and if they are consistent with the changes in the last policy meeting (model 3). However, no such systematic differences exist for oral interventions. In fact, in some cases, oral interventions have a somewhat (although not statistically significant) stronger effect if they go in the opposite direction of past or future monetary policy decisions.

As an alternative channel, actual and oral interventions may affect the exchange rate through a coordination channel in which they influence the dispersion in expectations and function as a coordination device for beliefs of market participants. It is hard to measure this channel directly as market participants' expectations, and their dispersion cannot be observed directly. Nevertheless, it is worthwhile shedding light on the importance of the coordination channel by using various proxies for conditions and beliefs in FX markets.

A first hypothesis is that interventions may have a larger impact on FX markets in an environment of large uncertainty (e.g., Sarno and Taylor, 2001). Two proxies for FX market uncertainty are used: first, the historical volatility from model (Eqs. 26.4 and 26.5) above. The alternative measure of uncertainty is the implied volatility based on over-the-counter (OTC) option contracts, which is a proxy for a forward-looking measure of uncertainty in FX markets.[6]

---

[5]It should be noted that the effectiveness of actual interventions may depend not only on actual past and future monetary policy decisions but, in particular, also by expectations about future monetary policy, including its longer-term path. Although it would desirable to test for the role of changes in expectations, such data is unfortunately not available for the sample period.

[6]The trading volume of OTC options is substantially larger and thus the market deeper than that of exchange-traded options. The data used here has 1-month maturity and comes from Citibank, which is a major player in the market of OTC currency options. The quotes used are daily ones with fixed moneyness—that is, a given distance between the forward rate and the strike price of the option. For a detailed discussion of OTC currency options and actual interventions, see Galati and Melick (2002).

**TABLE 26.5 The Signaling Channel: Monetary Policy**

| | (1) Direction of Monetary Policy | | (2) If Change in Next Monetary Policy Meeting | | (3) If Change in last Monetary Policy Meeting | |
|---|---|---|---|---|---|---|
| | $H_0$: same direction<br>$H_1$: opposite direction | | $H_0$: same direction<br>$H_1$: opposite direction | | $H_0$: same direction<br>$H_1$: opposite direction | |
| Conditional Mean Equation | Coefficients | Standard Error sig. | Coefficients | Standard Error sig. | Coefficients | Standard Error sig. |
| **A. US dollar–euro exchange rate** | | | | | | |
| US oral intervention $IO^{US}$ | $H_0$:−0.048 | *0.102* | −0.174[b] | *0.071* | −0.109[b] | *0.063* |
| | $H_1$: −0.071 | *0.138* | −0.079 | *0.064* | −0.128[b] | *0.074* |
| Ge/EA oral intervention $IO^{GE/EA}$ | $H_0$: 0.165[c] | *0.074* | 0.153[b] | *0.083* | 0.270[c] | *0.092* |
| | $H_1$: 0.414[b] | *0.209* | 0.241[c] | *0.082* | 0.214[c] | *0.086* |
| US actual intervention $IA^{US}$ | $H_0$: −0.244 | *0.578* | −0.348[c] | *0.107* | −1.156[c] | *0.296*[+] |
| | $H_1$: −0.562[b] | *0.344* | −0.242 | *0.226* | −0.082 | 0.120 |
| Ge/EA actual intervention $IA^{GE/EA}$ | $H_0$: −0.446 | 0.359[+] | 1.608[c] | *0.315* | 1.719[c] | *0.306* |
| | $H_1$: 2.881[c] | *0.500* | 1.968 | *2.594* | 0.694 | *2.659* |
| **B. Yen–US dollar exchange rate** | | | | | | |
| US oral intervention $IO^{US}$ | $H_0$ 0.049 | *0.178* | 0.169[b] | *0.072* | 0.078 | 0.072[+] |
| | $H_1$: 0.218[b] | *0.094* | 0.127[b] | *0.070* | 0.270[c] | *0.094* |

| | | | | | | |
|---|---|---|---|---|---|---|
| Ja oral intervention $IO^{JA}$ | $H_0$: −0.530 | *0.566* | −0.158[b] | *0.068* | −0.343[c] | *0.107* |
| | $H_1$: 0.089 | *1.373* | −0.155[b] | *0.075* | −0.155[b] | *0.066* |
| US actual intervention $IA^{US}$ | $H_0$: 0.079 | *0.399* | 0.165 | 0.114+ | 1.042[c] | 0.163+ |
| | $H_1$: 0.496 | *0.364* | 0.615[c] | *0.219* | 0.179 | *0.165* |
| Ja actual intervention $IA^{JA}$ | $H_0$: 3.737[c] | 1.282+ | 0.056[c] | *0.013* | −0.069 | *0.066* |
| | $H_1$: 0.149 | *0.101* | 0.121[b] | *0.048* | −0.007 | *0.275* |

[a]indicates significance at the 95% level.
[b]indicates significance at the 90% level.
[c]indicates significance at the 99% level.
+ indicates whether coefficients of H0 and H1 are significantly different from each other at the 90% level.
(1) "Same direction" means that IO or IA occur in the opposite direction of the current monetary policy trend, that is, an intervention to strengthen the domestic currency during an easing cycle or an intervention to weaken it during a tightening cycle. "Opposite direction" implies the opposite case.
(2) "Same direction" means that IO or IA occur in the same direction of the change in the next monetary policy meeting, that is, an intervention to strengthen the domestic currency when the central bank will raise interest rates in the next meeting or an intervention to weaken it when the central bank will lower interest rates. "Opposite direction" implies the opposite case.
(3) "Same direction" means that IO or IA occur in the same direction of the change in the last monetary policy meeting, that is, an intervention to strengthen the domestic currency when the central bank has raised interest rates in the last meeting or an intervention to weaken it when the central bank has lowered interest rates. "Opposite direction" implies the opposite case.
*Source:* Fratzscher (2008).

Table 26.6 shows strong evidence that interventions, and in particular oral interventions, have significantly larger effects when uncertainty is high. In fact, interventions are found to have a significant effect on the level of exchange rates only in an environment of relatively large uncertainty. Overall, the effect of oral interventions on exchange rates is mostly around two to three times larger if market volatility is high as compared to when it is low. Moreover, the estimates are very similar for the two proxies for exchange rate uncertainty, yielding similar point estimates when using historical volatilities and when employing implied volatilities.

As a second hypothesis, it has been argued that new information, such as that induced by interventions, may have a stronger effect when market participants are positioned strongly in one particular direction of the exchange rate (e.g., Evans and Lyons, 2002). Two proxies for market "positioning" are employed: first, risk reversals are standardized option contracts that indicate the positioning of participants in FX markets.[7] For instance, a positive price of the USD–EUR risk reversal contract indicates that markets are long in euro and tend to expect a euro appreciation. Accordingly, a negative price of the USD–EUR risk reversal signals a positioning toward a stronger US dollar. A second and more crude proxy for market positioning is the past exchange rate trend. It has been argued in the literature (e.g., Fatum and Hutchison, 2003; Sarno and Taylor, 2001) that actual interventions tend to lean-against-the-wind, that is, go against and attempt to reverse the exchange rate trend.

Table 26.6 also shows the result for these proxies of market positioning. Both actual and oral interventions are found to be substantially more effective if they are leaning-with-the-wind, that is, if they are supportive of the predominant market sentiment and positioning. In fact, leaning-against-the-wind interventions generally have no significant effect on exchange rates. In most cases, leaning-with-the-wind interventions are substantially and statistically significantly larger than interventions of the opposite type.

**26.3.2.2 Caveats.** What do the findings of this time-series approach imply? It should be noted that the only statistically valid inference one can make is about the impact effect of interventions, or what is here called *effectiveness*. The next section focuses on the permanence of the effects of official FX interventions. Nevertheless, what matters for the success of an intervention strategy is also the frequency and, in case of actual interventions, the magnitude of interventions, that is, the cumulated impact effects. A compelling example is the small estimated coefficient for Japanese actual interventions on the yen–US dollar exchange rate of −0.059. This estimate suggests that the Japanese authorities need to purchase about USD 17 billion to weaken the yen by 1%. Given that the Bank of Japan purchased foreign exchange of roughly USD 178 billion in 2003, the estimated coefficient suggests that, ceteris paribus, Japanese interventions in 2003 moved

[7] More precisely, a risk reversal is a contract that comprises the simultaneous selling of an out-of-the-money put option and the purchase of an out-of-the-money call option on a given currency pair. As for the implied volatilities, the data source is Citibank.

**TABLE 26.6 The Coordination Channel: Market Uncertainty and Market Positioning**

| Conditional Mean Equation | Historical Exchange Rate Volatility | | Implied Exchange Rate Volatility | | Past Exchange Rate Trend | | Positioning Risk Reversals | |
|---|---|---|---|---|---|---|---|---|
| | $H_0$: High<br>$H_1$: Low | | $H_0$: High<br>$H_1$: Low | | $H_0$: Leaning-against-wind<br>$H_1$: Leaning-with-wind | | $H_0$: Leaning-against-wind<br>$H_1$: Leaning-with-wind | |
| | Coefficients | Standard Error Significance | Coefficients | Standard Error Significance | Coefficients | Standard Error Significance | Coefficients | Standard Error Significance |
| **A. US dollar–euro exchange rate** | | | | | | | | |
| US oral intervention $IO^{US}$ | $H_0$: −0.284[a] | 0.059+ | −0.184[a] | 0.046+ | 0.006 | 0.065+ | −0.046 | 0.084+ |
| | $H_1$: 0.033 | *0.079* | −0.083 | *0.088* | 0.285[a] | *0.072* | −0.355[b] | *0.156* |
| Ge/EA oral interv. $IO^{GE/EA}$ | $H_0$: 0.300[a] | 0.076+ | 0.351[c] | *0.191* | −0.009 | 0.093+ | 0.068 | 0.060+ |
| | $H_1$: 0.122 | *0.088* | 0.130 | *0.093* | 0.333[a] | *0.073* | 0.337[a] | *0.093* |
| US actual intervention $IA^{US}$ | $H_0$: −0.252[b] | *0.121* | −0.345 | *0.470* | 0.190 | 0.158+ | −0.162 | 0.489+ |
| | $H_1$: −0.584 | *0.405* | −0.356 | *0.298* | −1.257[a] | *0.201* | −0.846[a] | *0.033* |
| Ge/EA actual interv. $IA^{GE/EA}$ | $H_0$: 1.637[a] | *0.309*+ | 1.978[a] | 0.422+ | 0.017 | 0.485+ | 0.114 | 2.510+ |
| | $H_1$: 0.067 | *0.272* | 0.098 | *0.124* | 2.831[a] | *0.476* | 2.126[a] | *0.922* |

(*Continued*)

TABLE 26.6 (*Continued*)

| | | | | | | | | |
|---|---|---|---|---|---|---|---|---|
| **B. Yen–US dollar exchange rate** | | | | | | | | |
| US oral intervention $IO^{US}$ | $H_0$: 0.248[a] | 0.067+ | 0.234[b] | 0.083+ | 0.017 | 0.082+ | 0.117 | *0.119* |
| | $H_1$: 0.063 | *0.087* | 0.056 | *0.079* | 0.301[a] | *0.073* | 0.270[c] | *0.144* |
| Ja oral intervention $IO^{JA}$ | $H_0$: −0.217[a] | 0.065+ | −0.111 | *0.089* | 0.082 | 0.084+ | −0.093 | *0.317* |
| | $H_1$: −0.059 | *0.077* | −0.079 | *0.089* | −0.551[a] | *0.067* | −0.159 | *0.115* |
| US actual intervention $IA^{US}$ | $H_0$: 0.842[a] | 0.185+ | 1.881[c] | *1.108* | 0.155 | 0.193 | −0.008 | 0.444+ |
| | $H_1$: −0.030 | *0.110* | −0.067 | *0.075* | 0.471[a] | *0.121* | 1.181[a] | *0.391* |
| Ja actual intervention $IA^{JA}$ | $H_0$: −0.068 | *0.080* | −0.032 | *0.043* | −0.042 | 0.027+ | −0.032 | *0.036* |
| | $H_1$: −0.101 | *0.144* | −0.043 | *0.038* | −0.264[a] | *0.007* | −0.098[a] | *0.030* |

[a]indicates significance at the 99% level.
[b]indicates significance at the 95% level.
[c]indicates significance at the 90% levels.
+indicates whether coefficients of H0 and H1 are significantly different from each other at the 90% level.
"High" exchange rate volatility is defined as when the respective measures are above their medians.
"Leaning-against-the-wind" interventions are those that go in the opposite direction of the exchange rate trend or the market positioning.
"Leaning-with-the-wind" interventions are defined analogously.
*Source:* Fratzscher (2008).

the yen about 11% lower against the US dollar. Although the true effect of these interventions may have been different since the effectiveness of interventions varies depending on factors such as market conditions, trends, coordination, and so on, the purpose of this example is to make the important point that FX intervention policies can indeed exert a sizeable influence on overall exchange rate developments in the medium term.

Another caveat is that interventions may possibly be endogenous in that they respond to certain exchange rate developments rather than being purely exogenous. As discussed in Sarno and Taylor (2001), many interventions are leaning against the exchange rate trend, that is, they try to stem an ongoing, undesired trend. However, this implies that if endogeneity was an issue the estimates of Table 26.3 may be downward biased and the true effect may be even larger than indicated. A second potential caveat is that interventions may be anticipated by the markets. However, this case would also lead to a downward bias of the coefficients and strengthen rather than weaken the conclusions of Table 26.3.

In summary, this section establishes the first key result of the paper, namely that official interventions (both actual and oral) have indeed tended to be an effective policy tool for G3 authorities in some cases. Moreover, oral interventions also generally tend to lower uncertainty and volatility in the markets, whereas actual interventions have generally raised currency volatility. As to the channels, the evidence of the literature—an example of which has been presented here—is consistent with the argument that official FX interventions function primarily through a coordination channel rather than the signaling channel.

### 26.3.3 EVENT-STUDY APPROACH: EVIDENCE ON LONGER-TERM EFFECTIVENESS

The premise of standard macroeconomic models of exchange rates is that efficient markets should price in all relevant information instantaneously so that the contemporaneous effect of any type of news, such as interventions, should also constitute the permanent effect. However, the drawback of the time-series approaches that are most commonly used in the intervention literature, usually based on a GARCH-type framework at a daily or intradaily frequency as discussed in the previous section, is that interventions effects cannot be identified beyond one or at most a few days (e.g., Beine et al., 2002; Dominguez, 2003). However, from a policy perspective, a "successful" intervention should imply that (a) it alters the course of the exchange rate in the medium- to long term and (b) it achieves the ultimate long-run objective of the policymaker.

The rapidly evolving literature on microstructure-based exchange rate models, building on the work by Evans and Lyons (2002); Peiers (1997), and Osler (2003), suggests that there may be dynamic effects of how exchange rates incorporate new information. For instance, Evans and Lyons (2005) show that macroeconomic news have a dynamic effect that may take several days to be fully priced into foreign exchange markets. They relate this dynamic effect to the fact that news change the signed transaction volume, or order flow, for a sustained period of time, thereby affecting exchange rates for a number of days. Similarly, in their review of the literature on foreign exchange interventions, Sarno and Taylor (2001) argue that monetary authorities may affect markets over a prolonged period of time as their interventions may function as a coordination device for market participants or through what they call a coordination channel.

Following the rationale of this microstructure work, a literature on the effectiveness of official FX interventions has emerged, which uses event-study approaches to tackle the issue of long-run effectiveness or "success," of official FX interventions. The premise of this approach is that interventions should be treated and analyzed as events, that is, as clusters of interventions, rather than as individual interventions in isolation from each other.[8] In essence, this event-study approach then reduces the dimensionality of measuring the effectiveness of events into a single dimension by distinguishing whether an event was ultimately a "success" or a "failure" in achieving a particular objective. The methodology used in the present paper is related to the seminal work by Fatum and Hutchison (2003); Humpage (1999), and Fratzscher (2008) for G3 currency interventions.

#### 26.3.3.1 Measuring the "Success" of an Intervention Event.

For measuring the "success" of events, event-study approaches in essence reduce the dimensionality of the exchange rate evolution into a discrete variable of whether an intervention event moved the exchange rate in the desired way ($S = 1$) or not ($S = 0$). Four alternative criteria are used to evaluate the success of intervention events. These four criteria relate to exchange rates changes $\Delta s$ before ("pre"), after ("post") and during the event ("eve") and the event type or objective of the intervention event ($I$), with $I < 0$ indicating an attempt to weaken the domestic currency and $I > 0$ to strengthen it.

$$
\begin{aligned}
\text{“event” criterion} \quad & (\Delta s^{\text{eve}} > 0,\ I > 0) \ \text{or}\ (\Delta s^{\text{eve}} < 0,\ I < 0) \\
\text{“direction” criterion} \quad & \left(\Delta s^{\text{post}} > 0,\ I > 0\right) \ \text{or}\ \left(\Delta s^{\text{post}} < 0,\ I < 0\right) \\
\text{“reversal” criterion} \quad & \left(\Delta s^{\text{post}} > 0,\ I > 0 \text{ iff } \Delta s^{\text{pre}} < 0\right) \\
& \ \tilde{} or \left(\Delta s^{\text{post}} < 0,\ I < 0 \text{ iff } \Delta s^{\text{pre}} > 0\right) \\
\text{“smoothing” criterion} \quad & \left(\Delta s^{\text{post}} > \Delta s^{\text{pre}},\ I > 0 \text{ iff } \Delta s^{\text{pre}} < 0\right) \\
& \ \tilde{}\text{or}\ \left(\Delta s^{\text{post}} < \Delta s^{\text{pre}},\ I < 0 \text{ iff } \Delta s^{\text{pre}} > 0\right)
\end{aligned}
$$

First, the "event" criterion tests whether the direction of the exchange rate change during the event is consistent with the interventions themselves, that is, whether an intervention to, for example, strengthen the currency indeed leads to such a change during the event. Second, the "direction" criterion tests whether the exchange rate movement over the post-event window is in the desired direction. Many interventions are of the "leaning-against-the-wind" type

[8] MacKinlay (1997) provides a detailed overview of the use of this type of event-study methodology in different fields of the literature.

by trying to reverse or smooth the pre-event exchange rate movements. The third and fourth criteria are therefore defined only for these types of interventions. The third criterion is the "reversal" criterion that tests whether the intervention event succeeds in appreciating the currency after the event if it was depreciating before or in depreciating it when it was appreciating before the event. Fourth, the "smoothing" criterion is less demanding in its definition of "success" by investigating merely whether intervention events manage to reduce or smooth the strength of the pre-event exchange rate movements.

Under the condition that the exchange rate change is never exactly zero—which holds for all the different event-study windows—the sign test is used to test whether the number of "successes" ($n_+$) is larger than 50% or equivalently larger than the number of "failures" ($n_-$), with the null hypothesis as $n_+ \sim \textit{binomial}\ (n, p = 0.5)$ and with $n$ as the total number of events. A key point to stress is that each of the success criteria makes an implicit assumption about the underlying counterfactual. The first three criteria take a change of zero as counterfactual, and indeed, the unconditional probability in the data, when excluding periods of interventions, of observing a positive change in the exchange rate is 50.4% and the mean daily exchange rate change at 0.0030%. However, the issue is different for the "smoothing" criterion as the unconditional probability of observing a change in the daily exchange rate that is consistent with this criterion is 75%. Hence, the null for the "smoothing" criterion is $n_+ \sim \textit{binomial}\ (n, p = 0.75)$.

#### 26.3.3.2 Empirical Findings.

On the basis of the same G3 data described in the previous section, Table 26.7 presents the results for the different success criteria. The first columns indicate the percentage of successes in all events for each of the success criteria, the second column the corresponding $p$-values, and the third column the mean difference in the exchange rate change under the different criteria. The pre- and post-event windows in the benchmark specification are chosen to be 5 days, although below I also show the sensitivity of event "successes" to different pre- and post-window lengths.

Overall, there is overwhelming evidence that both actual and oral intervention events for the G3 economies have been successful. Turning first to oral interventions in the euro–dollar market, 75% of the events succeeded in moving the exchange rate in the desired direction during the event ("event" criterion) and still almost two-thirds of the events managed in doing so after the event ("direction" criterion). Both these success criteria are statistically significantly higher than $p = 50\%$ at the 1% significance level. The success rate of the "reversal" criterion is somewhat lower at around 63%, although it is still statistically significantly at the 5% level. The highest rate of "success" is obtained by the "smoothing" criterion where 88% of the events managed to at least reduce the exchange rate movement in the 5-day pre-event period. Finally, the results for oral interventions in the dollar–yen market are very similar, with the only exception that the success rate based on the "event" criterion fares worse.

The success of actual interventions is mostly comparable to that of oral interventions although there are also some differences. Most strikingly, and

**TABLE 26.7 Success Criteria of Event-Study Approach—G3 Economies**

| | Combined US and Euro Area | | | Combined US and Japan | | |
|---|---|---|---|---|---|---|
| Success Criteria | % Success (%) | *p*-value | % Exchange Rate Change (%) | % Success (%) | *p*-value | % Exchange Rate Change (%) |
| Event criterion | | | | | | |
| Oral interventions | 75.6 | 0.002 | 0.577 | 56.5 | 0.168 | 0.474 |
| Actual Interventions | 44.4 | 0.760 | 0.962 | 40.0 | 0.923 | 1.146 |
| Direction criterion | | | | | | |
| Oral interventions | 65.1 | 0.004 | 0.466 | 65.2 | 0.010 | 0.409 |
| Actual interventions | 66.7 | 0.119 | 0.752 | 77.5 | 0.003 | 0.993 |
| Reversal criterion | | | | | | |
| Oral interventions | 62.7 | 0.046 | 2.109 | 65.9 | 0.030 | 2.249 |
| Actual interventions | 69.2 | 0.133 | 2.897 | 81.3 | 0.003 | 2.780 |
| Smoothing criterion | | | | | | |
| Oral interventions | 88.2 | 0.001 | 2.109 | 90.9 | 0.001 | 2.249 |
| Actual interventions | 82.4 | 0.006 | 2.897 | 88.6 | 0.002 | 2.780 |

The success criteria are defined as in the text and are based on 5-day windows before and after the events. The $p$-values are obtained from a sign test of whether the number of "successes" ($n_+$) is larger than the number of "failures" ($n\_$), with the null hypothesis as $n_+ \sim binomial(n, p = 0.5)$ for the first three criteria and $n_+ \sim binomial(n, p = 0.75)$ for the smoothing criterion and with $n$ as the total number of events.
*Source:* Fratzscher (2007).

maybe surprisingly, the success rate of actual interventions during intervention events is <50%, that is, they more often fail to move the exchange rate in the desired direction during the event as compared to after the event. There are several possible explanations. One may be related to the fact that some actual interventions are conducted in secret and hence may take some days to be fully priced into the market. Moreover, this finding may underline that interventions should be analyzed as events and not individually in isolation, that is, intervention events may stop only when policymakers have achieved their objective, thus explaining why the post-event success rate is, in some cases, substantially higher than the event success rate for both exchange rates.

Finally, an important issue is how robust the results are to changing the length of the pre- and post-event time window. Figure 26.4 shows the evolution of the direction, reversal, and smoothing criteria for pre- and post-event windows ranging from 1 to 40 days and for the actual interventions in the euro–dollar market. The solid lines indicate the success rate of the different criteria, and the dotted lines indicate the corresponding $p$-values. The key finding of this analysis is that the success rate remains relatively stable and falls only moderately when extending the time window. The $p$-values reveal that intervention events are statistically successful at the 10% level for all time windows from 1 to 40 days.

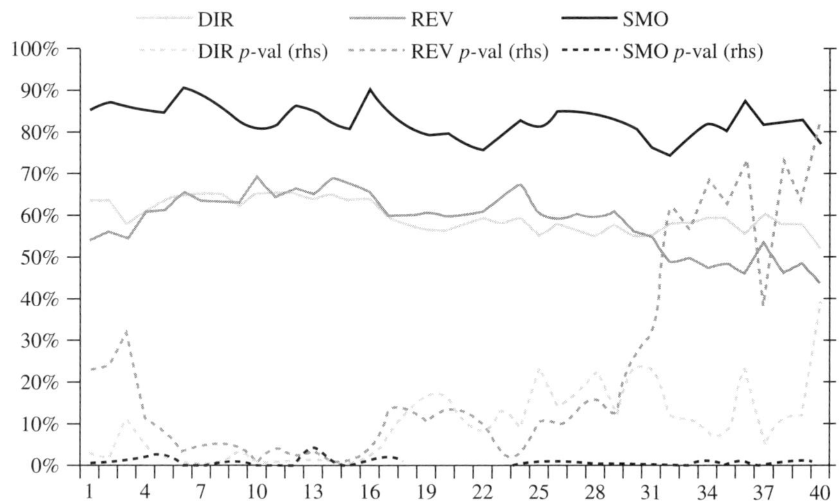


**FIGURE 26.4** **Evolution of the success criteria over post-event window, actual G3 interventions. *Source*: Fratzscher (2007). The solid lines show the percentage share of successes in total events for the direction criterion (DIR), the reversal criterion (REV), and the smoothing criterion (SMO) from 1 to 40 days after the end of the actual intervention events (combined US and Japan). The dotted lines show the corresponding *p*-values (right-hand side *y*-axis).**

In summary, the evidence suggests that both actual and oral interventions by G3 authorities have been effective in achieving their desired objectives. Oral interventions appear to be more successful during the events, while actual interventions have a somewhat higher success rate than oral interventions when they are of the "leaning-against-the-wind" type and attempt to reverse the previous exchange rate trend.

**26.3.3.3 Channels of Effectiveness.** As the final step of the analysis, the section turns to the channels through which interventions function and thus ultimately may allow authorities to conduct successful interventions. As discussed in the Introduction, actual interventions may work through a portfolio balance channel, a signaling channel, or a coordination channel. By contrast, by their very nature oral interventions can be effective only via the latter two of these channels, as they do not alter directly existing portfolio holdings, thus rendering the portfolio balance channel irrelevant.

Focusing on the coordination channel, this channel implies that interventions are more likely to be successful in an environment of large market uncertainty or when they are closely coordinated. To test these hypotheses directly, I take the findings of intervention successes in Table 26.1 and test for the determinants of success in a logit model. Table 26.8 shows the results for various explanatory factors relevant for the coordination channel and related to exchange rates and coordination for all combined interventions in the euro–dollar and the dollar–yen markets. For oral FX interventions, the estimates of the odds ratios indicate that oral intervention events are more successful if they are leaning with the trend, that is, go in the same direction as the exchange rate trend during the pre-event period (model 1, Table 26.8). The odds ratio for oral interventions is, however, statistically significant at the 5% level only for the event criterion. The odds ratio of 1.99 implies that an oral intervention event is twice as likely to be successful if it goes in the same direction as the pre-event exchange rate trend.

Oral intervention events are also more likely to be successful if exchange rates were volatile before the event and if they were strongly misaligned, that is, if deviation from PPP is above average. Here, the odds ratios are statistically significant for the event and the direction criteria and lie between 2.4 and 3.2. Both these findings are indicative that interventions tend to be more successful when market uncertainty is high or misalignments large, that is, an environment in which interventions may indeed function as a coordination device.

**TABLE 26.8 Determinants of Success of Actual and Oral FX Interventions—G3 Economies**

| | Exchange Rate | | | | | |
|---|---|---|---|---|---|---|
| Odds Ratios | (1) Trend<br>$X_1$: leaning with<br>$X_0$: leaning against | | (2) Volatility<br>$X_1$: high<br>$X_0$: low | | (3) PPP Deviation<br>$X_1$: large deviation<br>$X_0$: small deviation | |
| Success criteria: | Odds Ratio | *p*-value | Odds Ratio | *p*-value | Odds ratio | *p*-value |
| *Event criterion* | | | | | | |
| Oral interventions | 1.994[a] | 0.038 | 2.883[a] | 0.047 | 3.169[a] | 0.019 |
| Actual interventions | 2.446[b] | 0.059 | 1.299 | 0.605 | 1.897 | 0.197 |
| *Direction criterion* | | | | | | |
| Oral interventions | 1.450 | 0.389 | 2.445[b] | 0.069 | 2.922[a] | 0.022 |
| Actual interventions | 2.596[b] | 0.052 | 2.503[b] | 0.074 | 1.381 | 0.711 |
| *Reversal criterion* | | | | | | |
| Oral interventions | — | — | 1.294 | 0.530 | 1.526 | 0.449 |
| Actual interventions | — | | 3.599[a] | 0.042 | 1.309 | 0.656 |
| *Smoothing criterion* | | | | | | |
| Oral interventions | — | | 1.468 | 0.509 | 1.493 | 0.472 |
| Actual interventions | — | | 1.429 | 0.597 | 0.905 | 0.883 |
| | **Coordination** | | | | | |
| Odds Ratios | (4) Frequency<br>$X_1$: coordination<br>$X_0$: no coordination | | (5) IO–IA<br>$X_1$: coordination<br>$X_0$: no coordination | | (6) Foreign IO or IA<br>$X_1$: coordination<br>$X_0$: no coordination | |
| Success criteria | Odds Ratio | p-value | Odds Ratio | p-value | Odds ratio | p-value |
| *Event criterion* | | | | | | |
| Oral interventions | 3.219[a] | 0.001 | 2.328[b] | 0.048 | 2.002 | 0.188 |
| Actual interventions | 4.562[b] | 0.016 | 1.662 | 0.427 | 4.122[b] | 0.016 |

(*Continued*)

TABLE 26.8 (*Continued*)

| | | | | | | |
|---|---|---|---|---|---|---|
| *Direction criterion* | | | | | | |
| Oral interventions | 1.322 | 0.507 | 1.920 | 0.146 | 3.400[b] | 0.037 |
| Actual interventions | 1.125 | 0.819 | 2.572[c] | 0.074 | 2.561[b] | 0.039 |
| *Reversal criterion* | | | | | | |
| Oral interventions | 1.573 | 0.422 | 1.384 | 0.589 | 2.011 | 0.405 |
| Actual interventions | 1.371 | 0.607 | 1.719 | 0.371 | 1.600 | 0.744 |
| *Smoothing criterion* | | | | | | |
| Oral interventions | 1.141 | 0.308 | 1.451 | 0.559 | 2.769 | 0.175 |
| Actual interventions | 1.656 | 0.478 | 1.575 | 0.503 | 0.585 | 0.709 |

[a]indicates significance at the 95% level.
[b]indicates significance at the 90% level.
[c]indicates significance at the 99% level.
(1) "Leaning against" the trend means that IO or IA intends to reverse the trend of the 2-week pre-event period, whereas "leaning with" attempts to strengthen the trend. As the reversal and smoothing criteria are only defined for leaning-against-the-wind events, the respective success determinants cannot be obtained for these measures.
(2) "High" means that IO or IA event occurs in periods when exchange rate volatility is high, that is, above its median value, in the past 2 weeks, and "low" when the intervention takes place during periods of low volatility.
(3) "Large deviation" means that IO or IA events takes place when level of exchange rate deviates more than its period median from the PPP exchange rate; "small deviation" implies the opposite.
*Source:* Fratzscher (2007).
[a]indicates significance at the 99% level.
[b]indicates significance at the 95% level.
[c]indicates significance at the 90% level.
(1) "Coordination" means that intervention events comprise multiple interventions, whereas "no coordination" implies that an event only has a single oral intervention or actual intervention.
(2) "Coordination" means that, in case of an IO event, the also supporting actual interventions occur during the event, whereas "no coordination" implies that no such support takes place.
(3) "Coordination" implies that mutually supporting oral interventions take place in both countries, for example, in Japan and in United States, during the same event; "no coordination" means the no such coordination takes place.
*Source:* Fratzscher (2007).

Moreover, oral intervention events are more likely to be successful if they are coordinated, that is, if they occur in clusters, if they are supported through actual interventions during the event, and if they coincide with supportive oral interventions by foreign monetary authorities. The success criteria for which this is the case are again the event and the direction criteria.

Turning to actual interventions, the results are in some regards similar and other very different to those for exchange rate communication. The results are similar in that actual intervention events tend to be more successful if they are leaning with the pre-event exchange rate trend and occur in periods of large exchange rate volatility and uncertainty. They are also more likely to be successful if they are coordinated domestically and internationally.

In summary, the evidence presented suggests that official FX intervention events, whether through actual FX purchases and sales or orally, tend to be more successful when they go in the same direction as the pre-event exchange rate trend, and if they occur in periods of large volatility and uncertainty and when exchange rates are misaligned. They are also more successful if they are coordinated domestically and with communication or actual interventions of foreign authorities. Overall, this again provides support for the hypothesis that official interventions have primarily function through a coordination channel in influencing G3 exchange rates.

## 26.4 Conclusions

What are the motives behind official interventions? Are they successful in affecting exchange rates? And through what channels and mechanisms do interventions do so? The chapter has focused on these three questions, presenting empirical evidence and drawing on a large and continuously growing literature at the intersection of international macroeconomics and finance. As to the first of these questions, while there may be a precautionary motive behind some of the reserve accumulation in EMEs over the past decade, the chapter has presented evidence that suggests that these have primarily been driven by the motive of having weak and undervalued exchange rates, so as to improve competitiveness and exports as well as to attract foreign investment. Such a policy of EMEs has not only raised the risk of a "currency war," in which several countries pursue competitive devaluations, but it also has various costs and benefits, in particular in terms of a loss of monetary policy autonomy, the misallocation of capital, and global financial market distortions.

As to the second question, the evidence from the two methodological approaches—time-series and event-study models—indicate that FX interventions may indeed be effective in both moving the level of exchange rates and by affecting the underlying volatility of FX markets. Importantly, the success of official interventions is conditional on a multitude of factors, in particular the market environment as well as how exactly the interventions are conducted.

As to the third issue, evidence for recent intervention episodes indicate that nowadays a coordination channel, and to some extent a signaling channel, may have become the dominant channels through which interventions work. Importantly, the chapter focuses not only on the effectiveness of actual FX interventions, that is, FX purchases and sales by monetary authorities, but also on the role and effectiveness of communication about exchange rates by policymakers or oral interventions. In fact, many advanced economies—such as the United States, the euro area, and the United Kingdom—have moved away from using FX interventions since the mid-1990s and have since primarily used communication as their primary policy tool to guide and influence FX markets.

## 26.5 Acknowledgements

I would like to thank Ettore Dorrucci, Arnaud Mehl, Elitza Mileva, an anonymous referee, and the editors for input and discussions. The views expressed in this chapter are those of the author and do not necessarily reflect those of the European Central Bank.

## REFERENCES


Aizenman J, Jinjarak Y, Park D. International reserves and swap lines: substitutes or complements? NBER Working Paper No. 15804; 2010.

Aizenman J, Lee J. International reserves: precautionary versus mercantilist views, theory and evidence. Open Econ Rev 2007; 18:191 –214.

Andersen T, Bollerslev T, Diebold F, Vega C. Micro effects of macro announcements: real-time price discovery in foreign exchange. Am Econ Rev 2003; 39(1): 38–62.

Beine M, Bénassy-Quéré A, Lecourt C. Central bank intervention and foreign exchange rates: new evidence from FIGARCH estimations. J Int Money Finance 2002; 21: 115–144.

Beine M, Laurent S, Lecourt C. Central bank intervention and exchange rate volatility: evidence from a switching regime analysis. Eur Econ Rev 2003; 47(5): 891–911.

Bini Smaghi L. Reserve accumulation: the other side of the coin. Speech at the 5th High-level EMEAP-Eurosystem Seminar, Sydney; 2010. Available at http://www.ecb.europa.eu/press/key/date/2010/html/sp100210.en.html

Blinder A, Ehrmann M, Fratzscher M, Jansen DJ, De Haan J. Central bank communication and monetary policy: a survey of the evidence. J Econ Lit 2008; XLVI(4): 910–945.

Bonser-Neal C, Roley V, Sellon G. Monetary policy actions, intervention, and exchange rates: a reexamination of the empirical relationships using federal funds rate target data. J Bus 1998; 71(2):147–77.

Caballero RJ, Panageas S. A quantitative model of sudden stops and external liquidity management. NBER Working Paper 11293; 2005.

Dollar D. Outward-oriented developing economies really do grow more rapidly: evidence from 95 LDCs, 1976–1985. Econ Dev Cult Change 1992; 40/3: 523–544.

Dominguez K. The market microstructure of central bank intervention. J Int Econ 2003; 59: 25–45.

Dominguez K, Frankel J. Does foreign exchange intervention matter? The portfolio effect. Am Econ Rev 1993; 83(5): 1356–1369.

Edison H. The Effectiveness of Central-Bank Intervention: A Survey of the Literature after 1982. Special Papers in International Economics 18, Princeton University; 1993.

Evans M, Lyons R. Order flow and exchange rate dynamics. J Pol Econ 2002; 110: 170–180.

Evans M, Lyons R. Do currency markets absorb news quickly? J Int Money Finance 2005; 24(2): 197–219.

Fatum R, Hutchison M. Is intervention a signal of future monetary policy? Evidence from the federal funds futures market? J Money Credit Bank 1999; 31(1): 54–69.

Fatum R, Hutchison M. Is sterilized foreign exchange intervention effective after all? An event study approach. Econ J 2003; 113: 390–411.

Fratzscher M. Strategies of exchange rate policy in G3 economies. Econ Lett 2005; 89(1): 68–74.

Fratzscher M. On the long-term effectiveness of exchange rate communication and interventions. J Int Money Finance 2006; 25(1): 146–167.

Fratzscher M. Oral interventions versus actual interventions in FX markets—An event-study approach. Econ J 2008; 118:1–28.

Fratzscher M. How successful is the G7 in managing exchange rates? J Int Econ 2009; 79(1): 78–88.

Frenkel JA, Jovanovic B. Optimal international reserves: a stochastic framework. Econ J 1981; 91/362:507–514.

Greenspan A. Currency reserves and debt. Remarks before the World Bank Conference on Recent Trends in Reserve Management. Washington (DC); 1999 Available at http://www.federalreserve.gov/BoardDocs/Speeches/1999/19990429.htm

Guidotti P. Remarks at a G3 seminar at bonn. (unpublished transcript); 1999.

Hamada K, Ueda K. Random walks and the theory of optimal international reserves. Econ J 1977; 87/347:722–742.

Hausmann R, Pritchett L, Rodrik D. Growth accelerations. J Econ Growth 2005; 10:303–329.

Humpage O. US intervention: assessing the probability of success. J Money Credit Bank 1999; 31: 732–747.

International Monetary Fund. Reserve Accumulation and International Monetary Stability; 2010.

Ito T. Is foreign exchange intervention effective? The Japanese experience in the 1990s. In: Mizen P, editor. Monetary history, exchange rates and financial markets, essays in honour of Charles Goodhart. Cheltenham; 2003. pp. 125–153.

Jansen D, de Haan J. Talking heads: the effects of ECB statements on the Euro-Dollar exchange rate. J Int Money Finance 2005; 24(2): 343–361.

Jansen D, de Haan J. Were verbal efforts to support the euro effective? A high-frequency analysis of ECB statements. Eur J Pol Econ 2007; 23(1): 245–259.

Jeanne O, Ranciére R. The optimal level of international reserves for emerging market countries: a new formula and some applications. CEPR Discussion Paper Series No. 6723; 2008.

Kaminsky G, Lewis K. Does foreign exchange intervention signal future monetary policy? J Monet Econ 1996; 37(2):285–312.

Kearns J, Rigobon R. Identifying the efficacy of central bank interventions: evidence from Australia and Japan. J Int Econ 2004; 66(1): 31–48.

Lardy NR. Financial repression in China. Peterson Institute for International Economics Policy Brief No. PB08-8; 2008.

Levy-Yeyati E, Sturzenegger F. Fear of appreciation, Policy Research Working Paper 4387. Washington (DC): World Bank; 2007.

Lewis K. Are foreign exchange intervention and monetary policy related and does it really matter? J Bus 1995; 68(2):185–214.

MacKinlay AC. Event studies in economics and finance. J Econ Lit 1997; 35: 13–39.

Mileva E. The benefits of international reserves for developing countries. Mimeo European Central Bank; 2010.

Mussa M. The role of official intervention. New York: Group of Thirty; 1981.

Neely C. An analysis of recent studies of the effect of foreign exchange intervention. Fed Reserve Bank St. Louis Rev 2005; 87(6): 685–717.

Obstfeld M, Shambaugh JC, Taylor AM. Financial stability, the trilemma, and international reserves. NBER Working Paper 14217; 2008 Aug.

Osler C. Currency orders and exchange-rate dynamics: an explanation for the predictive success of technical analysis. J Finance 2003; 58: 1791–1819.

Osler C. Stop-loss orders and price cascades in currency markets. J Int Money Finance 2005; 24: 219–241.

Peiers B. Informed traders, intervention, and price leadership: a deeper view of the microstructure of the foreign exchange market. J Finance 1997; 52: 1589–1614.

Reitz S, Taylor M. The coordination channel of foreign exchange intervention: a nonlinear microstructural analysis. Working Paper, Deutsche Bundesbank; 2006.

Rodrik D. The real exchange rate and economic growth. Brook Pap Econ Act 2008;3(2): 365–412.

Sarno L, Taylor M. Official intervention in the foreign exchange market: is it effective, and if so, how does it work? J Econ Lit 2001; 39: 839–868.

Taylor M. Is official exchange rate intervention effective? Economica 2004; 71:1–11.

Vitale P. Sterilized central bank intervention in the foreign exchange market. J Int Econ 1999; 49(2):245–67.

Vitale P. Foreign exchange intervention: how to signal policy objectives and stabilise the economy. J Monet Econ 2003; 50: 841–870.

Wjinholds JOB, Kapteyn A. Reserve adequacy in emerging market economies. IMF Working Paper WP/01/143; 2001.

CHAPTER TWENTY SEVEN

# Exchange Rate Misalignment—The Case of the Chinese Renminbi

**YIN-WONG CHEUNG**
Department of Economics and Finance, City University of Hong Kong, University of California

## 27.1 Introduction

Exchange rates are a key macroeconomic price in international economics. And, exchange rate misalignment is perceived to be the culprit of both domestic and global economic ills, including inflationary pressures, trade imbalances, and misallocation of resources within an economy and across trading partners (Hinkle and Montiel, 1999). Since the 1970s, the debate on currency valuation and misalignment has recurred several times and has involved different currencies. The recent contentious debate on the Chinese currency valuation vividly exemplifies the complexity of assessing the extent of misalignment.

During the 2000s, the meteoric rise in China's trade surpluses has put its foreign exchange policy under close scrutiny. One common view is that China has intentionally depressed the value of its currency, the renminbi (RMB), to gain unfair advantages in the global market. As a result, China has built up huge trade surpluses in the 2000s. In addition to global imbalances, the RMB misalignment induces chronic inflationary pressure on the Chinese economy. There are repeated calls from the international community urging China to ease global imbalances by revaluing its currency.

*Handbook of Exchange Rates*, First Edition. Edited by Jessica James, Ian W. Marsh, and Lucio Sarno.

In the subsequent sections, the recent debate about the RMB valuation is used to illustrate the difficulty of determining the degree of misalignment. The theme is not to argue whether the RMB is overvalued or undervalued. Instead, the theme is to highlight a few selected factors that could make assessing the exact level of misalignment difficult.

To assess the RMB misalignment, we have to determine whether the RMB is misaligned or not and, if so, by how much. The assessment has to overcome some theoretical and empirical hurdles. First, standard results in exchange rate economics suggest that it is quite difficult to determine the right, or in economic jargon the equilibrium, exchange rate. Since misalignment is a measure of deviation from the equilibrium exchange rate, an inability to pin down the equilibrium rate implies that it is hard to exactly evaluate the related misalignment.

Even if a theoretical specification is chosen to model the equilibrium exchange rate, the ability to infer the actual level of misalignment is hindered by some practical statistical considerations. For instance, alternative ways to make the theoretical framework operational could lead to different misalignment estimates. The preciseness of the misalignment is also affected by the usual statistical caveats, including sampling uncertainty, serial correlation, and estimation robustness. Indeed, as illustrated in the subsequent sections, empirical estimates of the RMB misalignment could spread across a wide range.

The next section outlines the background of the RMB valuation debate. Section 27.3 uses the RMB case to illustrate the complexity of evaluating exchange rate misalignment. Specifically, the fundamental equilibrium exchange rate (FEER) approach and the Penn effect regression are used to illustrate the sensitivity to assumptions of the key parameters in a given model, sampling uncertainty, serial correlation adjustment, and data revision. Some concluding remarks are offered in Section 27.4.

## 27.2 Background

Over the past three decades, China has been one of the fastest growing countries in the world. A few years into the twenty-first century, the world has no doubt that China is a prominent trading country, a popular foreign direction investment destination, and a major manufacturing center in the global economy.

The RMB valuation received scant attention for most of the modern China's history. Since 1993, China has maintained a stable exchange rate against the US dollar. Its ballooning trade surplus and level of international reserves have put China's *de facto* peg policy in the limelight. Questions have recently been raised as to whether China's foreign exchange policy has led to an undervalued currency that gives Chinese exporters an unfair advantage over their competitors. The valuation of RMB has become the center of economic and political rows between China and its trading partners.

For instance, the 2010 IMF Article IV Consultation Staff Report (IMF, 2010) assesses that the RMB "remains substantially below the level that is consistent with medium-term fundamentals." However, the Chinese authorities offered alternative interpretations of evidence that the Staff used to draw the undervaluation assessment. The Staff assessment was also not agreed by several Directors of the IMF Executive Board (IMF, 2010). Further, as recent as October 2011, the US Senate passed a bill that was interpreted as a possible legislation against the "undervalued" RMB. Indeed, some US officials hold the view that, by holding down the value of the RMB, China directly or indirectly triggered the 2007–2008 global financial crisis and prevented a proper global rebalancing after the crisis.

Given its growing economic prowess, the extent of RMB misalignment and its implications are of great relevance to policy makers and financial institutions. For economists, the RMB is undervalued when it can be exchanged for a lower amount of, say, the US dollar than what economic fundamentals indicate it should be worth. Before we can define the level of misalignment, the overarching issue is how to define, in economic jargon, the equilibrium value of the RMB. A related question on the link between misalignment and the trade balance will be briefly commented in the next section.

In exchange rate economics, there is very limited consensus on which is the right exchange rate model. Further, different models might be relevant for economies with different economic structures and over different time horizons. China has undergone rapid structural changes, transitioning from central planning to greater market orientation over the last couple of decades. Even now China can be characterized as a hybrid economy, with strong elements of both "planned" and "market" systems. Although it is an integral part of a financially globalized world, China still retains a wide array of capital controls.

The well-known Dornbusch overshooting model is a useful setting to expound the role of time horizon in interpreting an exchange rate trajectory. Under the overshooting framework, the exchange rate in the short run can be different from its long-run equilibrium value and, at the same time, is consistent with market fundamentals. That is, the equilibrium path of the exchange rate can deviate from its long-run value in the short run, and observed misalignment does not necessarily imply a disequilibrium scenario. These special attributes and considerations heighten concerns regarding the appropriate model for determining RMB's equilibrium value.

In the absence of a consensual exchange rate model, we should interpret any currency misalignment estimates with great care. Undervaluation, overvaluation, or currency misalignment in general could be in the eye of the beholder. Whether there is misalignment or not depends on which economic model or what time horizon one has in mind. In addition to theoretical considerations, the complexity of valuing the RMB is compounded by the usual difficulties affecting empirical exercises. Some of these difficulties are discussed in the context of RMB valuation in the next section.

## 27.3 Undervalued or Overvalued

The inability of structural macro and time-series models to explain exchange rate movements is well documented by Meese and Rogoff (1983). Their result that these models cannot out perform a naive random walk specification has proven robust. For many years, researchers have found it difficult to reject the hypothesis that major country exchange rates follow a random walk under floating exchange rate regimes (Cheung et al., 2005; Meese and Rogoff, (1983); Rogoff, 1996). An implication of this finding is that the prospect of having a commonly agreed framework to assess exchange rate misalignment is pretty unpromising.

### 27.3.1 THE FEER MISALIGNMENT ESTIMATE

There is no shortage of RMB misalignment estimates that vary considerably from one study to the other. Table 27.1 updates the list of recent estimates of the degree of RMB misalignment in Cheung et al. (2010a). One striking observation is the dispersion of these misalignment estimates, ranging from a 44% undervaluation to an over 100% overvaluation.

The differences in the estimates come not only from different model specifications but also from models with similar theoretical underpinnings. Even if we drop the extreme overvaluation cases, the remaining estimates are still spread over a rather wide range. These vastly different estimates allow individuals to pick and select the one that is consistent with their own agenda. Most studies,

**TABLE 27.1 Some Recent RMB Misalignment Estimates**

| Estimate | As of | Source |
|---|---|---|
| +49% | July 2011 | The Economist (2011), Big Mac Index |
| +33% | March 2009 | Cline and Williamson (2010), FEER |
| +31%[a] | 2005 | Subramanian (2010), Penn Effect |
| +21%[b] | End of 2008 | Goldstein and Lardy (2009), External Balance |
| +17.5[b] | 2009 | Wang and Hu (2010), FEER, external balance |
| +10% | 2010Q1 | Tenengauzer (2010), external balance |
| +2.56% | 2009Q4 | Stupnytska et al. (2009), BEER |
| −5% | 2008 | Cheung et al. (2010a) |
| −13.4% | 2008Q4 | Hu and Chen (2010), FEER |
| −16.8% | September 2009 | Cheung et al. (2010a), relative PPP, real US exchange rate |
| −36% | December 2009 | Cheung et al. (2010a), real PPP, trade-weighted exchange rate |
| −(>)100% | — | Schnatz (2011), FEER |

Undervaluation (+), overvaluation (−).
[a]The average of estimates from adjusted data.
[b]The average of estimates.

surprisingly, did not explicitly address the notorious difficulty of determining the extent of RMB undervaluation.

These estimates were obtained from typical theoretical frameworks, including relative purchasing power parity, the Penn effect, the behavioral equilibrium exchange rate model, the FEER approach, and the macroeconomic balance effect approach. Cheung et al. (2010b), for instance, offer some discussions and comments on these approaches while Cenedese and Stolper (Forthcoming) present an extensive review of the equilibrium exchange rate models that are commonly used to assess exchange rate misalignment.

Conceivably, it is not unreasonable to expect different estimates from different theoretical settings. It is quite perplexing, however, to obtain different misalignment estimates from models that have a similar theoretical underpinning. We use the FEER approach, which is quite commonly referred to in discussions on exchange rate misalignments in emerging economies, including China to illustrate the sensitivity of misalignment estimation. It is noted that the FEER approach is quite closely related to other fundamental or fair value models including the macroeconomic balance effect approach.

Schnatz (2011) succinctly illustrates the limitations and sensitivity of the FEER framework. The FEER approach postulates that current account balance could be nonzero in the medium term. The determination of the equilibrium exchange rate involves a two-step procedure. First, the "normal" current account balance is identified. The norm could be determined on a judgmental basis that depends on researchers' priors or via an empirical approach. In the second stage, trade elasticities are used to back out the "equilibrium" exchange rate that would generate the normal current account balance. Thus, the FEER equilibrium exchange rate depends on, among other things, the values assigned to the current account norm and the trade elasticities.

What is China's current account norm? Sieving through the literature, the value could range from a low of a 2.8% of GDP deficit (Williamson and Mahar, 1998) to a high of a 8.4% surplus (Medina et al., 2010). The norm of 8.4% is a projected value for 2014 (Medina et al., 2010, Table 27.1). A large norm is usually driven by data from the post-2000 period during which China experienced substantial current account surpluses. The extent of RMB undervaluation is inversely related to the size of China's current account norm, *ceteris paribus* (Wang and Hu, 2010). It is noted that China's current balance surplus was 5.23% in 2009 and 5.19% in 2010. If the norm is assumed to be near or at the high end of 8.4%, then the RMB is likely to be *overvalued* or, at least, the case for undervaluation is very weak! Apparently, this possibility is not well articulated in, say, the media coverage.

The estimation of China's trade behavior presents a quite formidable empirical task. In general, Chinese export and import price elasticities are not very precisely and robustly estimated. These estimates tend to be quite sensitive to the inclusion of time trends and control variables in the regressions.[1] A

[1] See Ahmed (2009), Aziz and Li (2008), Kwack et al. (2007), Mann and Plück (2007), Thorbecke and Smith (2009), and Marquez and Schindler (2007). Some earlier studies are reviewed in Cheung et al. (2010c).

problematic phenomenon is that some of these estimates do not satisfy the Marshall–Lerner condition and, for these cases, an increase in trade surplus can follow a RMB appreciation. Such a possibility is illustrated by Figure 27.1, which plots China's real effective exchange rate (an increase implies appreciation) and trade balance. It is quite apparent that the RMB exchange rate moves with China's trade surplus in a "procyclical" manner—specifically, the RMB appreciation after the 2005 policy change was met with an increase in the trade surplus.

Figure 27.2, which is adopted from Schnatz (2011), depicts the dramatic change in the misalignment estimate across different China's trade elasticity estimates found in the literature. The RMB misalignment estimate could go from an undervaluation of 40% to an overvaluation of over 500%! While the extreme overvaluation estimate is implausible, the exercise vividly illustrates the fragility of the exchange rate misalignment estimation. Either the magnitude or the sign of misalignment estimate crucially depends on the assumed values of the current account norm and trade elasticities.

The variability of the FEER misalignment estimate is also documented by, say, Dunaway et al. (2009), Hu and Chen (2010), and Wang and Hu (2010). These studies demonstrate that equilibrium RMB real exchange rate estimates exhibit substantial variations in response to small perturbations in model specifications, explanatory variable definitions, and sample periods. In

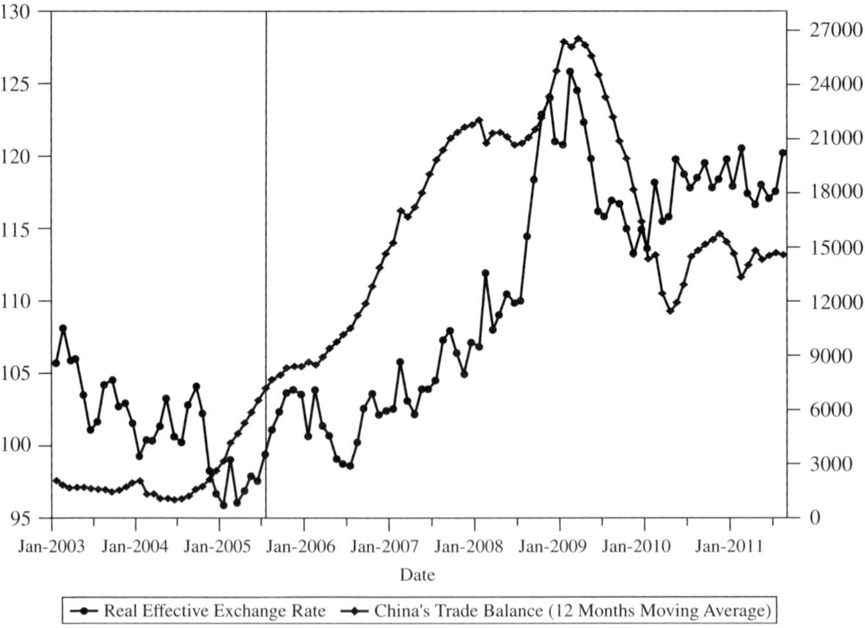


**FIGURE 27.1** China's real effective exchange rate and trade balance.

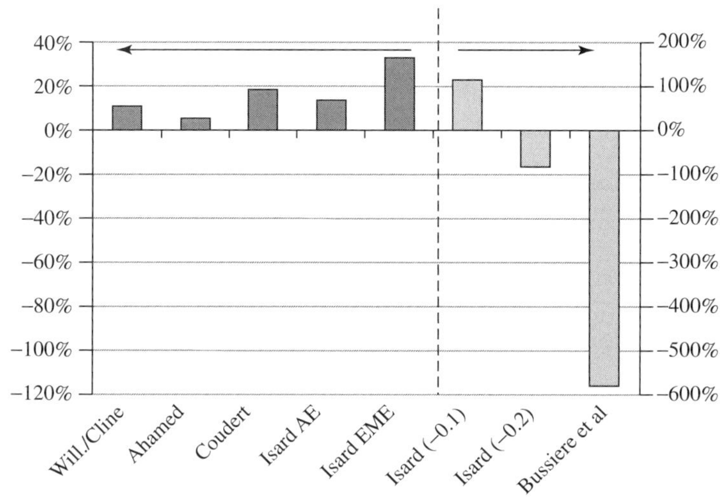


FIGURE 27.2 FEER sensitivity to changes in the trade elasticities (Schnatz, 2011). Undervaluation (+); overvaluation (−).

other words, inferences regarding currency misalignment could be very sensitive to small changes in the way the equilibrium exchange rate is estimated.

### 27.3.2 THE PENN EFFECT REGRESSION

In this section, results from the Penn effect regression are used to illustrate the implications of sampling uncertainty, serial correlation adjustment, and data revision. The basic Penn effect regression equation is given by

$$r_i = \beta_0 + \beta_1 y_i + u_i \tag{27.1}$$

where $r_i$ and $y_i$ are, respectively, country $i$'s national price level and real *per capita* income in logs and relative to the corresponding US variables. The national price level, indeed, is the reciprocal of the PPP-based real exchange rate—an increase in $r_i$ means an appreciation of the currency.[2] Henceforth, we call $r_i$ the real exchange rate for brevity.

The Penn effect is based on the acute observation that price levels vary with income levels. That is, a high income country tends to have a high real exchange rate. The empirically robust positive association between national price levels and real per capita incomes is documented by a series of Penn studies

[2]The term *national price level* is potentially confusing for those who are not familiar with the Penn effect regression using PPP-based data. In this context, the national price level is in fact a relative price with the US price level as the reference and, thus, is equivalent to the inverse of the real exchange rate.

(Kravis and Lipsey; 1983, 1987; Kravis, et al., 1978; Samuelson, 1994; Summers and Heston, 1991). In passing, we note that, after taking income levels into consideration, the so-called Big Mac Index approach will suggest the RMB was 3% overvalued in July 2011 instead of 44% undervalued as stated in Table 27.1 (The Economist, 2011).

The Penn effect framework has been adopted in the recent debate on RMB misalignment (Cheung et al., 2007; Coudert and Couharde, 2007; Frankel, 2006). The inference of currency misalignment based on Equation (27.1) hinges upon the robust positive Penn effect and the implicit assumption that real exchange rates may be overvalued or undervalued, but they are at the equilibrium level on average. Specifically, for a given currency, the empirical degree of misalignment is given by its estimated residual from Equation (27.1). To ensure data compatibility, the empirical analysis is typically conducted with PPP-based real exchange rates and GDP measures.

Using the PPP-based data from the *World Development Indicators* downloaded in 2006, Cheung et al. (2007) reported the panel regression result

$$r_i = -0.134 + 0.299y_i + \hat{u}_i \qquad (27.2)$$

the coefficient estimates are statistically significant. The pooled least squares result is based on data from 160 countries for the period 1975–2004. The estimated level of undervaluation for China in 2004 is a stunning 53.3%.

In general, the magnitudes of undervaluation estimates reported here and in the subsequent discussion are quite robust to various sensitivity tests, which include (i) grouping countries according to their stages of development, income levels, and geographical locations; (ii) splitting the sample into two subsample periods 1975–1989 and 1990–2004; and (iii) allowing for the effects of various combinations of control variables such as demographics, government policy, financial development, corruption, capital controls, and trade balances.

To what extent we could treat the estimated level as the actual level of the RBM undervaluation? Are the data informative enough for conducting a definite statistical inference? Figure 27.3 traces out the Chinese currency's time path, its equilibrium values estimated from the Penn effect regression, and the associated standard error bands. The standard error bands are the usual statistical device to capture sampling uncertainty associated with an estimator and are indicative of the possible range in which the true value of the variable of interest could be found.

According to the point estimates, the RMB started its devaluation trend in the mid-1980s. Nevertheless, the actual RMB rate is always within the two standard errors band. That is, if we apply the usual statistical inference approach, the Chinese currency's level of undervaluation is not statistically significantly different from zero. Another way to interpret the result is that the data are not sufficiently informative to tell the predicted and the actual exchange rate values apart.

In regression analysis, the presence of serial correlation could affect both the estimation and inference results. Indeed, the adjustment for serial correlation

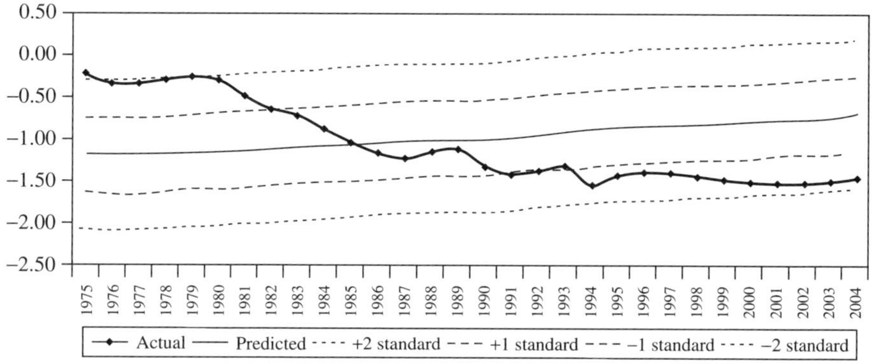


FIGURE 27.3 **Actual and predicted RMB values, the 2006 vintage data.**

in regression analysis is a common and relevant practice. It turns out that the estimated residuals in Equation (27.2) display substantial serial correlation. Using the Prais–Winsten method to control for serial correlation, the estimated regression becomes

$$r_i = -0.026 + 0.147y_i + \hat{u} \tag{27.3}$$

the two coefficient estimates are again statistically significant though the Penn effect as given by the slope coefficient is weaker. The implication of controlling for serial correlation is illustrated in Figure 27.4. The predicted RMB values and their standard errors bands are based on the Penn effect regression using the Prais–Winsten method.

The impact of serial correlation adjustment on the current misalignment analysis is nontrivial. The standard errors bands in Figure 27.4 are, as expected, noticeably narrower than those in Figure 27.3. A striking result is that, in 2004, the RMB is not undervalued but is 0.2% overvalued. Even though the misalignment estimate is again not statistically significant, the sheer shift in the magnitude and the direction of the estimate itself should make us reassess our ability to precisely estimate the degree of misalignment.

### 27.3.3 DATA REVISION

The reliability of Chinese data has been a subject of concern among academic researchers; especially applied researchers. Instead of questioning the quality of official Chinese data, we consider an instance of data revision initiated by a World Bank project. The PPP-based data used to generate results presented in the previous section were based on price information obtained from the 1993 International Comparison Program benchmark. In 2008, the World Bank, in cooperation with the Asian Development Bank, reported new estimates of output and price level data measured in PPP terms, which are based on new benchmark data on prices generated by the 2005 International Comparison

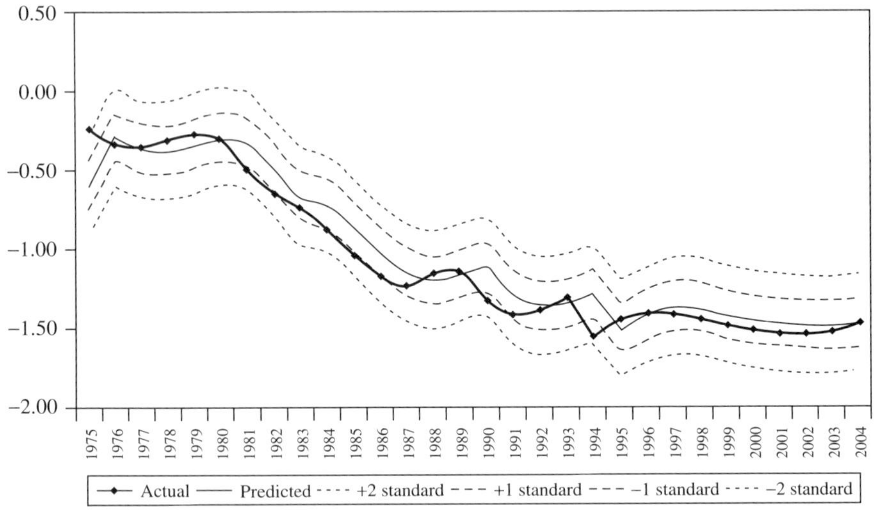


FIGURE 27.4 Actual and predicted RMB values, the 2006 vintage data (Prais–Winsten).

Project (Asian Development Bank, 2007; International Comparison Program, 2007; World Bank, 2008a,b). These data are believed to be more accurate than those previously available.

These new PPP-based data are quite different from the corresponding ones in the previous version. An often cited example is that the 2005 China's PPP-based *per capita* GDP is 39% smaller than previously estimated. Some countries, indeed, have their 2005 *per capita* GDPs revised up or down by 50% or more (World Bank, 2008c). What is the implication of these drastic data revisions for assessing currency misalignment?

The result of fitting Equation 27.1 using the updated data is given by

$$r_i = -0.295 + 0.174 y_i + \hat{u}_i \tag{27.4}$$

The updated data on 176 countries for 1980–2008 were downloaded from the World Development Indicator dataset in 2010. Using the Prais–Winsten method to account for serial correlation, the result is modified to

$$r_i = -0.018 + 0.160 y_i + \hat{u}_i \tag{27.5}$$

The coefficient estimates in Equations (27.4) and (27.5) are all statistically significant.

Apparently, the empirical Penn effect survives the data revision and, indeed, the magnitudes of the Penn effect are comparable to those derived from the previous data set. While the robustness of the Penn effect is asserted, the same cannot be said for misalignment estimates.

Figures 27.5 and 27.6 plot the time path of the Chinese currency, its estimated equilibrium values based on Equations (27.4) and (27.5), and their

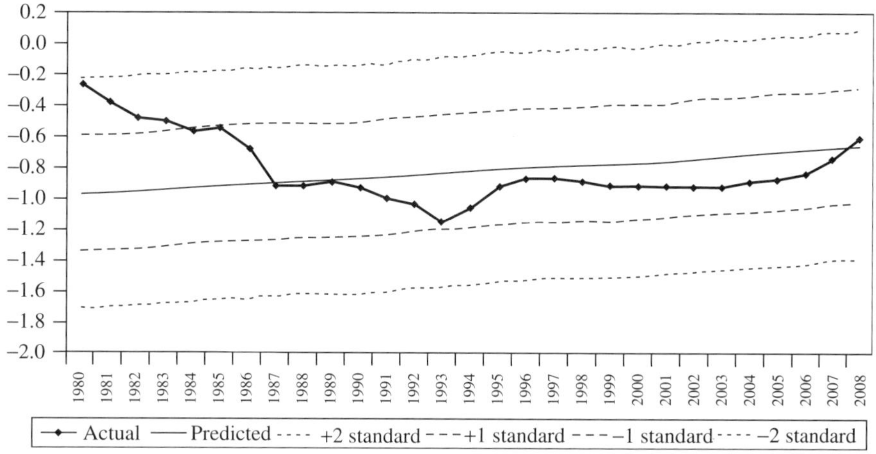


FIGURE 27.5 Actual and predicted RMB values, the 2010 vintage data.

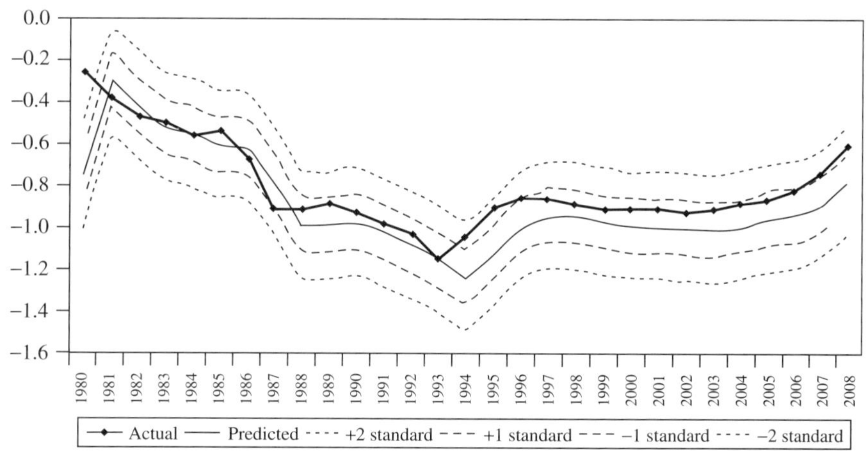


FIGURE 27.6 Actual and predicted RMB values, the 2010 vintage data (Prais–Winsten).

standard error bands. Note that in these two figures, the PPP-based real RMB exchange rate is the one from the updated dataset and is quite different from the "old" one depicted in Figures 27.3 and 27.4.

The implication of the data revision for the RMB misalignment debate is quite apparent. The sample uncertainty associated with equilibrium exchange rate estimates is similar to the one observed in previous cases. The magnitude of misalignment estimates, however, changes in a discernable manner. Before adjusting for serial correlation, the 2004 estimate is reduced to a 15.32% undervaluation from the previously estimated 53.3%. By 2008, the revised data indicate that the RMB is overvalued!

After controlling for serial correlation, the RMB is estimated to be 13.26% overvalued in 2004. Indeed, the RMB is overvalued during most of the sample period in Figure 27.6. The previous finding of substantial misalignment is not robust to the data revision following the 2005 International Comparison Project. The use of updated data alters not only the magnitude of the misalignment estimate but also the direction of misalignment.

## 27.4 Concluding Remarks

The current study draws on the seemingly unending debate on the value of the RMB to illustrate a few difficulties affecting a typical exchange rate misalignment assessment exercise. The debate on exchange rate misalignment has recurred, albeit with varying degrees of intensity, in the international community over the last few decades. To what extent could the debate be grounded in firm economic theory? Standard results in exchange rate economics do not offer a consensual model to determine the equilibrium exchange rate. Without a commonly agreed on model, it is hard to assess the extent of exchange rate misalignment. The RMB case is of no exception.

Our discussion focuses on the susceptibility of misalignment estimates to a few selected factors, including the values assigned to the key parameters in a given model, sampling uncertainty, serial correlation adjustment, and data revision. The implications of these factors are illustrated using results derived from the FEER approach and the Penn effect regression, which are commonly used in assessing exchange rate misalignment.

Comparing results from some plausible scenarios, it cannot be ignored that the empirical evidence on RMB undervaluation is weaker than the one commonly posited in the media. The RMB misalignment estimate is quite sensitive to variations in the selected factors listed in the previous paragraph. In addition to the estimates suggesting severe undervaluation that mirror the one reported in, say, the financial press, there are empirical results suggesting the RMB is quite fairly valued or is overvalued. It is important to emphasize that our theme is not to argue whether the RMB is undervalued or not—the point is that the evidence on the inability to precisely estimate exchange rate misalignment is quite pronounced, and hence we have to exercise considerable caution in interpreting any misalignment estimates.

At first glance, our discussion seems unhelpful to, say, policymakers and financial professionals, who conduct their operations here and now in the real world. The inability to pin down the precise level of misalignment, however, should be interpreted positively. The imprecision of a misalignment estimate in fact is in accordance with the well-known result that it is quite difficult to model exchange rates in general. Ignoring what we do not know does not help analyze the actual degree of misalignment. Given these considerations, it is prudent to avoid making a hasty policy decision based on a typical misalignment assessment exercise. Specifically, it is not advisable to make a particular drastic and swift exchange rate move without taking the uncertainty surrounding a misalignment estimate into consideration.

## Acknowledgments

The chapter draws on joint work conducted with Menzie Chinn and Eiji Fujii. Eiji kindly provided most of the figures.


## REFERENCES


Ahmed S. Are chinese exports sensitive to changes in the exchange rate? International Finance Discussion Paper No. 987. Washington (DC): Federal Reserve Board; 2009.

Asian Development Bank. Purchasing power parities and real expenditures. Manila, Philippines: Asian Development Bank; 2007.

Aziz J, Li X. China's changing trade elasticities. China World Econ 2008; 16(3): 1–21.

Cenedese G, Stolper T. Currency fair value models. In: James J, Marsh IW, Sarno L, editors. The handbook of exchange rates. Forthcoming. Chapter 6.

Cheung Y-W, Chinn MD, Fujii E. The overvaluation of renminbi undervaluation. J Int Money Finance 2007; 26(5): 762–785.

Cheung Y-W, Chinn MD, Fujii E. Measuring renminbi misalignment: where do we stand? Korea World Econ 2010a; 11: 263–296.

Cheung Y-W, Chinn MD, Fujii E. Measuring misalignment: latest estimates for the Chinese renminbi. In Evenett S, editor. The US-Sino currency dispute: new insights from economics, politics and law. London: Centre for Economic Policy Research. AVoxEU.org Publication; 2010b. pp. 79–90. Chapter 10.

Cheung Y-W, Chinn M, Fujii E. China's current account and exchange rate. In: Feenstra R, Wei S-J, editors. China's growing role in world trade Chicago. U.Chicago Press for NBER; 2010c. pp. 231–271. Chapter 9.

Cheung Y-W, Chinn M, Garcia Pascual A. Empirical exchange rate models of the nineties: are any fit to survive? J Int Money Finance 2005; 24: 1150–1175.

Cline WR, Williamson J. Notes on equilibrium exchange rates: January 2010, Policy Brief PB10-2. Washington (DC): Peterson Institute for International Economics; 2010.

Coudert V, Couharde C. Real equilibrium exchange rate in china: is the renminbi undervalued? J Asian Econ 2007; 18(4): 568–594.

Dunaway S, Leigh LA, Li X. How robust are estimates of equilibrium real exchange rates: the case of China. Pac Econ Rev 2009; 14(3): 361–375.

The Economist. Currency comparisons, to go; 2011. Available at http://www.economist.com/blogs/dailychart/2011/07/big-mac-index

Frankel J. On the Yuan: the choice between adjustment under a fixed exchange rate and adjustment under a flexible rate. CESifo Econ Stud 2006; 52(2): 246–275.

Goldstein, Morris and Nicholas Lardy. The Future of China's Exchange Rate Policy, Policy Analyses in International Economics 87. Washington, DC: Peterson Institute for International Economics. 2009.

Hinkle LE, Montiel PJ. Exchange rate misalignment. New York: Oxford University Press for World Bank; 1999.

Hu C, Chen Z. Renminbi already overappreciated: evidence from FEERs (1994–2008). China Econ 2010; 26: 64–78.

International Comparison Program. Preliminary Results: Frequently Asked Questions, mimeo; 2007. Available at http://siteresources.worldbank.org/ICPINT/Resources/backgrounder-FAQ.pdf.

International Monetary Fund. People's Republic of China: 2010 Article IV Consultation—Staff Report; 2010. Available at http://www.imf.org/external/pubs/ft/scr/2010/cr10238.pdf.

Kravis IB, Heston A, Summers R. International comparisons of real product and purchasing power. Baltimore (MD): The Johns Hopkins University Press; 1978.

Kravis IB, Lipsey RE. Toward an explanation of national price levels, Princeton Studies in International Finance No. 52. Princeton (NJ): International Finance Center, Princeton University; 1983.

Kravis IB, Lipsey RE. The assessment of national price levels. In: Arndt SW, Richardson JD, editors. Real financial linkages among open economies. Cambridge (MA): MIT Press; 1987. pp. 97–134.

Kwack SY, Ahn CY, Lee YS, Yang DY. Consistent estimates of world trade elasticities and an application to the effects of Chinese Yuan (RMB) appreciation. J Asian Econ 2007; 18: 314–330.

Mann C, Katerina P. The US trade deficit: a disaggregated perspective. In: Clarida R, editor. G7 current account imbalances: sustainability and adjustment. U. Chicago Press; 2007.

Marquez J, Schindler JW. Exchange-rate effects on China's trade. Rev Int Econ 2007; 15(5): 837–853.

Medina L, Prat J, Thomas A. Current Account Balance Estimates for Emerging Market Economies. IMF Working Paper 10/43; 2010.

Meese R, Rogoff K. Empirical exchange rate models of the seventies: do they fit out of sample? J Int Econ 1983; 14: 3–24.

Rogoff K. The purchasing power parity puzzle. J Econ Lit 1996; 34: 647–668.

Samuelson P. Facets of Balassa-Samuelson thirty years later. Rev Int Econ 1994; 2(3): 201–226.

Schnatz B. Global imbalances and the pretence of knowing FEERs. Pac Econ Rev 2011; 16 (5), 604–615.

Stupnytska A, Stolper T, Meechan M. GSDEER On Track: Our Improved FX Fair Value Model. Global Economics Weekly No. 09/38 (Goldman Sachs Global Economics, October 28); 2009.

Subramanian A. New PPP-based estimates of renminbi undervaluation and policy implications, Policy Brief PB10-18. Washington (DC): Peterson Institute for International Economics; 2010.

Summers R, Heston A. The penn world table (Mark5): an expanded set of international comparisons. Q J Econ 1991; 106(2): 327–368.

Tenengauzer D. RMB: the People's currency, EM FX and Debt Spotlight (21 April 2010), Bank of America-Merrill Lynch; 2010.

Wang T, Hu H. How undervalued is the RMB? Asian Economic Perspectives (13 April 2010), UBS Investment Research; 2010.

Williamson, John, and Molly Mahar. A Survey of Financial Liberalization. Princeton:Princeton Essays in International Finance. 1998; 211.

World Bank. Global purchasing power parities and real expenditures: 2005 international comparison program. Washington (DC): International Comparison Program and International Bank for Reconstruction and Development; 2008a.

World Bank. ICP 2003–2006 Handbook; 2008b. Available at http://go.worldbank.org/MW520NNFK0.

World Bank. Comparison of New 2005 PPPs with Previous Estimates: Appendix G Revised: Global Purchasing Power Parities and Real Expenditures. Washington (DC); 2008c.

CHAPTER TWENTY EIGHT

# Choosing an Exchange Rate Regime

**JEFFREY A. FRANKEL**
NBER; Kennedy School of Government, Harvard University

The single most important aspect of an exchange rate regime is the degree of flexibility. The matter is of course more complicated than a simple choice between fixed exchange rate and floating. One can array exchange rate regimes along a continuum, from most flexible to least, and grouped in three major categories:

- **I.** Floating corner
  - **1.** Free float
  - **2.** Managed float
- **II.** Intermediate regimes[1]
  - **3.** Target zone or band
  - **4.** Basket peg
  - **5.** Crawling peg
  - **6.** Adjustable peg

[1]The sequence within intermediate regimes is somewhat arbitrary. For example, if the band is as narrow as $2\frac{1}{4}\%$ as in the European Exchange Rate Mechanism or even 1% as under Bretton Woods, then it would properly belong closer to the fixed-rate end of the spectrum. Similarly, if the adjustable peg involved a devaluation or revaluation every time a moderate shock came along, it would properly belong closer to the flexible end of the spectrum.

*Handbook of Exchange Rates*, First Edition. Edited by Jessica James, Ian W. Marsh, and Lucio Sarno.

**III.** Institutionally fixed corner

- **7.** Currency board
- **8.** Dollarization
- **9.** Monetary Union.

This chapter reviews the state of research concerning how a country should choose where to locate along this continuum of exchange rate regimes.

The "corners hypothesis"—that countries are, or should be, moving away from the intermediate regimes, in favor of either the hard peg corner or the floating corner—was proposed by Eichengreen (1994) and rapidly became the new conventional wisdom with the emerging market crises of the late 1990s.[2] But it never had a good theoretical foundation. The feeling that an intermediate degree of exchange rate flexibility is inconsistent with perfect capital mobility is a misinterpretation of the principle of the impossible trinity. To take a clear example, Krugman (1991) shows theoretically that a target zone is entirely compatible with uncovered interest parity. The corners hypothesis began to lose popularity after the failure of Argentina's quasi currency board in 2001. Many countries continue to follow intermediate regimes and do not seem any the worse for it.

Attempts to address the optimal degree of exchange rate flexibility within a single theoretical model are seldom very convincing. Too many factors are involved. Better instead to enumerate the arguments for and against exchange rate flexibility and then attempt to weigh them up. This chapter considers five advantages of fixed exchange rates, followed by five advantages for exchange rate flexibility. We then turn to analysis of how to weigh the pros and cons to choose a regime. The answer depends on characteristics of the individual country in question.

## 28.1 Five Advantages of Fixed Exchange Rates

We consider here five advantages of fixing. They are (i) providing a nominal anchor to monetary policy, (ii) facilitating trade, (iii) facilitating investment, (iv) precluding competitive depreciation, and (v) avoiding speculative bubbles.

Of the five advantages of fixed exchange rates, academic economists have tended to focus most on the nominal anchor for monetary policy. The argument is that there can be an inflationary bias when monetary policy is set with full discretion.[3] A central bank that wants to fight inflation can commit more credibly by fixing the exchange rate, or even giving up its currency altogether. Workers, firm managers, and others who set wages and prices then perceive that inflation will be low in the future because the currency peg will prevent the central bank from expanding even if it wanted to. When workers and firm managers have low

[2]Fischer (2001); Summers (1999).

[3]This is the classic model of dynamically consistent monetary policy. Barro and Gordon (1983); Rogoff (1985), and Calvo and Vegh (1994).

expectations of inflation, they set their wages and prices accordingly. The result is that the country is able to attain a lower level of inflation for any given level of output. The strength of the argument for basing monetary policy on an exchange rate target will depend on what alternative nominal anchors might be available; this topic will be explored in Section 28.6.

Another leading argument in favor of fixed exchange rates, especially popular among practitioners, is the second one on the list: the effect of currencies on international trade. Exchange rate variability creates uncertainty; this risk, in turn, discourages imports and exports. Furthermore, dealing in multiple currencies incurs transactions costs. Fixing the exchange rate in terms of a large neighbor eliminates exchange rate risk, and so encourages international trade, at least with that neighbor. Going one step farther and actually adopting the neighbor's currency as one's own eliminates transaction costs as well and thus promotes trade even more.

Academic economists have often been skeptical of this claim for three reasons. First, in theory, exchange rate uncertainty is merely the symptom of variability in economic fundamentals, so that if it is suppressed in the foreign exchange market, it will show up somewhere else, for example, in the variability of the price level. Second, logically, anyone adversely affected by exchange rate variability—importers, exporters—can hedge away the risk, using forward markets or other derivative markets. Third, empirically, it used to be difficult statistically to discern an adverse effect from increased exchange rate volatility on trade.

Each of these three arguments can be rebutted, however. To begin with, much nominal exchange rate volatility in fact appears to be unrelated to changes in macroeconomic fundamentals and appears to be the cause rather than the result of real exchange rate variability. Furthermore, many smaller currencies have no derivative markets, and even where such markets exist, they may charge costs for hedging (transactions costs plus the exchange risk premium), which limit their actual use. Thin trading is especially a problem for small and developing countries, but even major currencies do not have forward markets at every horizon that an importer or exporter might need. Finally, more recent econometric studies, based on large cross sections that include many small developing countries, have found stronger evidence of an effect of exchange rate variability on trade—especially on a bilateral basis, where far more data are available. Section 28.2 elaborates on this evidence.

The third argument is that fixed exchange rates facilitate international capital flows. The argument is closely analogous to the case of international trade flows: in theory, capital importers and capital exporters should be able to hedge currency differences, but in practice, risk premiums and transaction costs intervene, as can be observed in failures of interest rate parity conditions.

A fourth advantage of fixed exchange rates is that they prevent competitive depreciation. Competitive depreciation can be viewed as an inferior Nash noncooperative equilibrium, where each country tries in vain to win a trade advantage over its neighbors. In such a model, fixing exchange rates can be an efficient institution for achieving the cooperative solution. The architects of the

Bretton Woods system thought about the problem in terms of the "beggar thy neighbor" policies of the 1930s. The language of "currency wars," in which governments complain that the exchange rate policies of others unfairly undercut their competitiveness, was revived yet again when big capital flows resumed in 2010.

The final argument for fixed exchange rates is to preclude speculative bubbles of the sort that pushed up the dollar in 1985 or the yen in 1995. Bubbles can be defined as movements in the price, in this case the exchange rate, that arise not from economic fundamentals but from self-justifying expectations. In the mathematics of rational expectations, the bubble is an extra term in the solution to a differential equation.

As we already noted, some exchange rate fluctuations appear utterly unrelated to economic fundamentals. It is not just that tests using standard observable fundamentals such as money supplies and income always find most variation in exchange rates unaccounted for. After all, residual variation can always tautologically be attributed to unobserved fundamentals (e.g., the much-storied "shifts in tastes and technology"). The most persuasive evidence is a pattern that holds reliably, either across country pairs or across history: whenever a change in exchange rate regime raises nominal exchange rate variability, it also raises real exchange rate variability.[4] This observation then allows at least the possibility that, if the fluctuations that come from floating exchange rates were eliminated, there might, in fact, not be an outburst of fundamental uncertainty somewhere else. Rather, the "bubble term" in the equation might simply disappear, delivering less variability in the real exchange rate for the same fundamentals.

## 28.2 Econometric Evidence on the Bilateral Trade Effects of Currency Regimes

Economists began to take much more seriously the possibility that fixed exchange rates encourage trade with the publication of Andrew Rose's 2000 paper, "One Money, One Market . . . ," perhaps the most influential empirical international economics paper of its decade. Applying the gravity model to a bilateral data set that was sufficiently large to encompass a number of currency unions led to an eye-opening finding: members of currency unions traded with each other an estimated three times as much as with otherwise-similar trading partners. Even if Rose had not included the currency union dummy, this paper would still have been important because he had bilateral exchange rate variability on the list of variables explaining bilateral trade, and it was highly significant statistically.[5] But the attention grabber was that the currency union dummy had a far larger, and highly significant effect, above and beyond the effect of bilateral variability per se. This chapter was of course motivated by the coming of EMU in 1999, even

[4]Bahmani-Oskooee et al. (2008); Mussa (1986); Taylor (2002).

[5]The finding that a fixed exchange rate in itself also produces a statistically significant increase in bilateral trade was confirmed by Klein and Shambaugh (2006).

though estimates were necessarily based on historical data from (much smaller) countries who had adopted currency unions in the past.

Rose's remarkable tripling estimate has been replicated in various forms many times. But no sooner had he written his paper than the brigade to "shrink the Rose effect"[6]—or to make it disappear altogether—descended en masse. These critiques sometimes read to me as "guilty until proven innocent."

It is understandable that a threefold effect was greeted with much skepticism, as this is a very large number. There are five grounds for skepticism, as I classify them. The critiques need to be assessed.

The first critique is the proposition that one cannot necessarily infer from cross-sectional evidence what would be the effect in real time of countries adopting a common currency. Most pre-1999 members of currency unions had essentially never had their own national currencies, but instead used an external currency at least since independence. In such cases as Panama or most of the CFA countries in Africa, the currency arrangement goes back more than a century. In other cases, such as the Eastern Caribbean Currency Area, the currency dates from postwar independence.

Second are allegations of missing variables. The statistical association between currency links and trade links might not be the result of causation running from currencies to trade but might arise instead because both sorts of links are caused by a third factor, such as colonial history, remaining political links, complementarity of endowments, or accidents of history. Another alleged missing variable is a country's "multilateral resistance" to trade or a more specific measure of remoteness from the rest of the world.

The third critique also concerns causality: the endogeneity of the currency decision. Countries choose as partners for currency links the neighbors with whom they trade the most, rather than the other way around. Thus, the correlation observed for currency unions among other countries may be spurious.

Fourth, the estimated effect on trade simply seems too big to be believable.

Fifth, Rose's evidence came entirely from countries that were either small (e.g., Ireland and Panama) or *very* small (e.g., Kiribati, Greenland, and Mayotte). Thus, it was not clear that the estimates could be extended to larger countries such as the members of the euro. If the currency union effect were substantially more important in small and highly trade-dependent countries, that could explain subsequent small estimates for Europe.

While each of these five arguments has some validity, to each there is a better response than one might expect.

### 28.2.1 TIME-SERIES DIMENSION

First, regarding the time dimension, a logical interpretation is that, even if the full comparative static effects were to hold in the very long run after a change in regime, they might not show up in the short run, due to very substantial lags. Even 30 years may not be enough to demonstrate long-run effects. Panama

[6]The phrase is from Baldwin (2006).

reports sending more than half its exports to the United States; perhaps one reason is that it has been on the US dollar for over a 100 years. We know that other gravity influences such as colonial ties leave an effect on bilateral trade many decades after the cause has been removed.

Subsequent research on currency unions using time-series data finds that a substantial share of the tripling that Rose had estimated from the cross-sectional data, which is presumably the long-run effect, shows up within a few decades of a change. Using a 1948–1997 sample that includes a number of countries, which left currency unions during that period, Glick and Rose (2002) find that trade among the members was twice as high in the currency union period as afterward. This suggests that roughly two-thirds of the tripling effect may be reached within three decades of a change in regime. (This reasoning assumes symmetry with respect to entry into and exit from currency unions.)

### 28.2.2 OMITTED VARIABLES

The second objection concerns the possible influence of omitted factors. Rose in fact did a thorough job of controlling for common languages, colonial history, and remaining political links. The large estimated effect of a common currency remains. It seems very possible that there remain other omitted factors (including accidents of history) that influence both currency choices and trade links. Nevertheless, Rose's various extensions of the original research—these robustness tests together with the time-series results (Glick and Rose) and the common use of fixed effects—reduce some of the force of this critique.

The omitted variable that is probably of the greatest concern to the critics comes from the influential Anderson and van Wincoop (2001) paper and is usually called the *multilateral resistance term*. This takes into account the average size of a specific determinant of trade for a region. More concretely, in a cross-sectional context, the variable may come down to "remoteness." A country's remoteness is defined as *average distance* from all trading partners, a weighted average based on the sizes of the trading partners; it is expected to have a positive effect on trade between a pair of countries, controlling for the more obvious negative effect of the distance between them bilaterally. Rose and van Wincoop (2001) find that taking multilateral resistance into account should, a priori, knock the estimated value of the euro on bilateral trade down from tripling to 58% (among the original euro members).[7] Even if one goes along with van Wincoop in imposing the constraint, the currency union term apparently remains high

[7] If I understand correctly the aspect of the Anderson and van Wincoop (2001) theory that leads to numerical estimates of the effects of borders and currencies that are sharply reduced in magnitude, it is the property that the elimination of borders or currency differences within a region theoretically entails substantial diversion of trade away from the rest of the world and thus an increase in multilateral resistance. The model's insistence on the role of trade diversion may be too doctrinaire. Such trade diversion from currency unions, whatever its basis in theory, is not observed in the data, by and large. (Frankel and Rose, 2002; Micco et al., 2003. For example, the United Kingdom does not appear to have lost trade to euroland as a result of the euro.) Thus, the argument for imposing the constraints from this particular theory may not be as strong as it otherwise would be.

(i) compared to its standard error, (ii) compared to what we all thought before 2000, and (iii) compared to what happens to the FTA (free trade area) term when it is too knocked down by imposing the van Wincoop constraint.

### 28.2.3 ENDOGENEITY OF THE CURRENCY DECISION

The endogeneity of a country's choice of exchange regime is perhaps the most intractable problem with the Rose-style estimates. After all, optimum currency area theory suggests that countries should peg if they are small and open and should peg to the partners with which they trade a lot.[8] El Salvador decided to adopt the dollar because it traded a lot with the United States, rather than the other way around. In that case, the Rose finding would be spurious. Controlling for exogenous third factors such as colonial history is a partial correction, but not a complete one, because they do not completely determine trade patterns.

Many of the critiques of the Rose results, after pointing out a problem of omitted variables or endogeneity or one of the other legitimate problems, offer a purported way to address it and then report that the currency union effect disappears. Some of these responses in effect throw out most of the data in the name of addressing the (correctly emphasized) issues of endogeneity or country size; or they do something similar: put in a great many dummy variables or fixed effects, often one for every pair of countries. But since the finding of statistical significance arose only when Rose put together a large enough data set for it to show up,[9] there is not that much information gained in reducing the data set sharply and then noticing the loss in statistical significance. Most of the statistical power lies in the cross-country variation. Throw that out, and one may be left with little.

That said, the complete bilateral data set is so large and the statistical relationship is so strong that there is some firepower to spare, and it is worth using some of it to try to get at the problems of endogeneity and missing variables. Including fixed effects for countries and/or years has become standard. The results generally hold up. Adding fixed effects for *pairs* of countries in the basic specification is a bit more problematic, although reasonable as a test for robustness. When Rose (2001) tries the matching estimator of Persson (2001) on a larger data set, he still finds a significant (although smaller) effect.

One response is a before-and-after study such as Glick and Rose. It eliminates the problem that Panama has always been on the dollar because it has always traded with the United States, much as Luxembourg has long had a currency union with Belgium, because it has always traded with Belgium. Rather these results show that when a country enters or leaves a currency link, its bilateral trade responds accordingly. But none of this is to deny that endogeneity remains a likely problem. For example, an evolution in trade patterns may come first,

[8]McKinnon (1963).

[9]Earlier gravity studies had not found major evidence of currency link effects on bilateral trade, presumably because the data sets were too small to include many examples of countries with institutionally fixed exchange rates.

with the currency decision following. In theory, Ireland may have switched its currency allegiance from Britain to the Continent in response to shifting trade patterns rather than as a cause of them. Attempting to deal with the endogeneity problem should be a priority.

One response is to look at a sort of "natural experiment" designed to be as immune as possible from this sort of endogeneity argument. The experiment is the effect on bilateral trade of African CFA members of the French franc's 1999 conversion to the euro. The long-time link of CFA currencies to the French franc has clearly always had a political motivation. So, CFA trade with France could not in the past reliably be attributed to the currency link, perhaps even after controlling for common language, and former colonial status. But with the advent of the euro, 14 CFA countries woke up in the morning and suddenly found themselves *with the same currency link to Germany, Austria, Finland, Portugal*, and so on, as they had with France. There was no economic/political motivation on the part of the African countries that led them to an arrangement whereby they were tied to these other European currencies. It turns out that CFA trade with these other European countries rose with the advent of the euro (Frankel, 2010). This suggests that the monetary union's effect on trade can be declared causal.

## 28.2.4 IMPLAUSIBLE MAGNITUDE OF THE ESTIMATE

Fourth, although those who claim that the tripling number is too large to sound plausible have a point, they tend to neglect two counterarguments. In the first place, the estimated effect of currency unions is on the same order of magnitude as the estimated effects of FTAs or, if anything, larger.[10] When one applies some of the variant estimation strategies, such as the Rose–van Wincoop reparameterization, so that the estimated effect of currency unions falls, the estimated effects of regional trading arrangements tend to fall in tandem. The point estimates, significance levels, *and necessary methodological qualifications*, are comparable across the two kinds of unions: FTAs and currency unions.

In the second place, the estimated effects of currency unions are almost as big as the famous estimated effects of borders (home bias), for example, in the Canada–US context, which is at least as big as a factor of three.[11] This home bias is surprising but is a fact of life. Something needs to explain it, and there are not very many candidates other than exchange rate variability. Thus, the Rose findings remain a challenge to the traditional views of international economists, who believed that trade barriers were far more important than either currency differences or other remaining barrier frictions.

---

[10] If critics were to apply the same tough standards to both customs unions and currency unions, they would likely find the estimated magnitude at least as large in the latter case as in the former.

[11] Important studies of the effect on trade quantities, using the gravity model, are Helliwell (1998); McCallum (1995); and Nitsch (2000). Analogous studies of the effect on price arbitrage are Engel and Rogers (1996) and Parsley and Wei (2001).

### 28.2.5 COUNTRY SIZE

The fifth critique was the claim that the result from pre-1999 currency unions is relevant only for small countries, which are highly trade dependent, and not relevant for larger countries such as those in Europe. A partial response has been possible all along: there has been no evidence of the monetary union effect varying with size, within the available sample. But if one suspects a threshold effect, above which the monetary union effect diminishes, and one posits that euro members are the first to be big enough to lie above that threshold, then this could explain the gap. The question whether the largest economies are truly different can only be answered with data from those countries. Fortunately, the euro experiment is now more than 10 years old, and so we should hope to be able to answer the question. Estimation of the euro's effect, nested within the larger sort of data set used by Rose that captures trade among all countries, confirms a much smaller boost to intraunion trade, but the effect is at least statistically above zero and explicit tests show that the discrepancy in magnitude is not explained by the larger size of euro countries.[12]

In short, the surprising finding that currency unions have a surprisingly large effect on trade among members, similar in magnitude to the effect of free trade areas, still stands.

## 28.3 Five Advantages of Floating Exchange Rates

As there are five advantages to fixed exchange rates, there are also five advantages to flexible exchange rates. They are (i) national independence for monetary policy, (ii) allowing automatic adjustment to trade shocks, (iii) retaining seigniorage, (iv) retaining lender-of-last-resort capability, and (v) avoiding speculative attacks.

The leading advantage of exchange rate flexibility is that it allows the country to pursue an independent monetary policy. The argument in favor of monetary independence, instead of constraining monetary policy by the fixed exchange rate, is the classic argument for discretion, instead of rules. When the economy is hit by a disturbance, such as a fall in demand for the goods it produces, the government would like to be able to respond so that the country does not go into recession. Under fixed exchange rates, monetary policy is always diverted, at least to some extent, to dealing with the balance of payments. This single instrument cannot be used to achieve both internal balance and external balance.

Under the combination of fixed exchange rates *and complete integration of financial markets*, which, for example, characterizes EMU, the situation is more extreme: monetary policy becomes altogether powerless to affect internal balance. Under these conditions, the domestic interest rate is tied to the foreign interest rate. An expansion in the money supply has no effect: the new money flows out

[12] Frankel (2010). The estimate that the euro has boosted intraunion trade by only about 15% confirms the findings of others, such as Micco et al. (2003).

of the country via a balance-of-payments deficit, just as quickly as it is created. In the face of an adverse disturbance, the country is unable to use monetary policy to counter its effects. After a fall in demand, the recession may last until wages and prices are bid down, or until some other automatic mechanism of adjustment takes hold, which may be a long time. By freeing up the currency to float, on the other hand, the country can respond to a recession by means of monetary expansion and depreciation of the currency. This stimulates the demand for domestic products and returns the economy to desired levels of employment and output more rapidly than would be the case under the automatic mechanisms of adjustment on which a fixed-rate country must rely.

The unfortunate reality is that few countries, especially few developing countries, have been able to make effective use of discretionary monetary policy. But even if one gives up on deliberate changes in monetary policy, there is a second advantage of floating: that it allows automatic adjustment to trade shocks. The currency responds to adverse developments in the country's export markets or other shifts in the terms of trade by depreciating, thus achieving the necessary real depreciation even in the presence of sticky prices or wages. The argument goes back to Meade (1951) and Friedman (1953).

The third and fourth advantages of a flexibly managed currency are two important advantages of an independent central bank that the government thereby retains: seigniorage and lender-of-last-resort ability. The central bank's ability to earn seignorage is partially lost if the rates of money creation and inflation are limited to those of the external currency to which it is pegged and which it must hold as foreign exchange reserves. Seigniorage is lost *entirely* under a rigid institutional commitment such as a currency board, dollarization, or—certainly—full monetary union.

The central bank's ability to act as a lender of last resort for the banking system depends, to a degree, on the knowledge that it can create as much money as necessary to bail out banks in difficulty. In the 1990s, some claimed that a country that moved to the firm-fix corner and allowed foreign banks to operate inside its borders, such as Argentina, would not need a lender of last resort because the foreign parents of local banking subsidiaries would bail them out in time of difficulty. Unfortunately, Argentina's experience in 2001 disproved this claim.

The fifth argument for a flexible exchange rate corresponds to the fifth argument in favor of fixing. Recall that the case for stabilizing the exchange rate arose from a disadvantage of free floating: occasional speculative bubbles (possibly rational, possibly not) that eventually burst. However, for a country that stops short of full dollarization, pegged exchange rates are occasionally subject to unprovoked speculative attacks (of the "second-generation" type[13]).

This disadvantage of pegging became even more evident in the 1990s than previously: a tendency toward currency mismatch, that is borrowers' effectively unhedged exposure in foreign currency (possibly rational, possibly not), ending badly in speculative attacks and multiple equilibrium. Some even argue for

[13]Obstfeld (1986).

floating on the grounds that it would be beneficial to introduce gratuitous volatility into the exchange rate in order to discourage unhedged borrowing in foreign currency.[14] Although that may sound implausible, emerging markets that introduced more exchange rate variability after the currency crises of the 1990s do seem to have reduced currency mismatch in the subsequent round of capital inflows (2002–2007), and thereby to have coped better with the shock of the 2008–2009 global financial crisis. Countries in the outer periphery of Europe, especially Eastern Europe, did not do this, and they are the ones that initially suffered the most from the global recession.

The bottom line, however, is that overvaluation, excessive volatility, and crashes are possible in either regime, peg, or float.

## 28.4 How to Weigh Up the Advantages of Fixing Versus Floating

Which dominate: the advantages of fixing or the advantages of floating? Empirical attempts to evaluate performance are hampered by the fact that de facto exchange rate regimes frequently differ from de jure: countries do not in practice follow the regime that they have officially declared. Many governments that say they float in fact do not float.[15] Many governments that say they peg do not in fact hold the peg for long.[16] Many governments that say they follow some version of a basket, in fact fiddle surreptitiously with the weights in the basket.

Some studies have attempted to classify countries according to their de facto exchange rate regime and then to test which categories have superior economic performance, judged by growth and other measures. This literature is entirely inconclusive. To oversimplify the findings of three important studies only a little: Ghosh et al. (2000) found that hard pegs work best, Levy-Yeyati and Sturzenegger (2001, 2003) concluded that floats perform best, and Reinhart and Rogoff (2004) found that limited flexibility is best!

Why such different answers? There are two major reasons, one relatively more pedestrian and the other more enlightening. First, the de facto classification schemes do not correspond to each other. A country's currency may be classified by one author as pegged and by another as floating.[17],[18] To that extent, it is no surprise that the authors get different answers as to performance. Secondly,

[14]Eichengreen and Hausmann (1999); Velasco and Chang (2006), and Arteta (2005).

[15]This is the "fear of floating" of Reinhart (2000) and Calvo and Reinhart (2002).

[16]Klein and Marion (1997); Obstfeld and Rogoff (1995).

[17]Frankel, Jeffrey, Sergio Schmukler and Luis Servén. 2000. Verifiability and the Vanishing Intermediate Exchange Rate Regime. Brookings Trade Forum 2000, edited by Susan Collins and Dani Rodrik. Washington DC: Brookings Institution.

[18]Bénassy-Quéré et al. (2004); Frankel (2003) and Frankel and Xie (2010). Tavlas et al. (2008) survey the classification studies. One reason for big differences in classification outcomes is big differences in methodology. A more fundamental problem is that many countries in fact do not typically follow any single regime for longer than a year or so without changing parameters, if not changing regimes altogether.

and more interestingly from an economic viewpoint, the question as to what exchange rate regime is best should depend on the circumstances of the country in question. No single exchange rate regime is right for all countries. This proposition may sound obvious, but there are some who tend to recommend hard pegs for all, some who tend to recommend floating for all, and some who tend to recommend intermediate regimes such as target zones for all.[19] Although some of the aforementioned studies include regressions that condition on some country variables, the list of variables is not extensive or definitive.

We need a framework for thinking about the characteristics that suit a country or other geographic area for fixing or floating or intermediate regimes, the characteristics that determine the relative weight that should be placed on the advantages and disadvantages considered above. The traditional framework was the theory of optimum currency areas, which focused on trade and stabilization of the business cycle. Thinking has evolved since then. In the 1990s, a focus on financial markets and stabilization of speculation added some additional country characteristics to the list, such as a need to import credibility from abroad. More recently, factors such as financial development and terms of trade volatility have made a comeback.

An optimum currency area is sometimes defined broadly: as a region that should have its own currency and own monetary policy. I prefer a definition with more content. First, let us note that smaller units tend to be more open and internationally integrated than larger units. Then, an OCA can be defined as *a region that is neither so small and open that it would be better off pegging its currency to a neighbor nor so large that it would be better off splitting into subregions with different currencies.* "Openness" here means international integration along many dimensions, of which trade is just the first.

## 28.5 Country Characteristics That Should Help Determine the Choice of Regime

A list of criteria that qualify a country for a relatively firm fixed exchange rate, versus a more flexible rate, should include at least the following nine characteristics:

1. Small size and openness, as reflected, for example, in the ratio of tradable goods to GDP (McKinnon, 1963). Advantages of fixing, such as facilitation of trade, tend to be larger for these countries and advantages of floating, such as discretionary monetary policy, tend to be smaller.[20]
2. The existence of a major-currency partner with whom bilateral trade, investment, and other activities are already high or are hoped to be high in the future. In theory, a country can peg to a basket of foreign currencies if

[19]Frankel (1999). An example from each of the three schools, respectively: Hanke and Schuler (1994); Larrain and Velasco (2001), and Williamson (2000).

[20]Romer (1993).

necessary to match a geographically diversified trade pattern. But, in practice, a peg to a single dominant trade partner, if one exists, is simpler and more credible.

3. *Symmetry of shocks*. This term refers to high correlation of cyclical fluctuations between the home country and the country that determines policy regarding the money to which pegging is contemplated. The condition is important because, if the domestic country is to give up the ability to follow its own monetary policy, it is better if the interest rates chosen by the larger partner are more often close to those that the domestic country would have chosen anyway.[21]
4. *Labor mobility*. When monetary response to an asymmetric shock has been precluded, it is useful if workers can move from the high unemployment region to the low unemployment region. This is the primary mechanism of adjustment across states within the monetary union that is the United States. Mundell (1961) focused on labor mobility when he originally coined the term optimum currency area.
5. *Countercyclical fiscal transfers*. Within the United States, if one region suffers an economic downturn, the federal fiscal system cushions it; one estimate is that for every dollar fall in the income of a stricken state, disposable income falls by only 70 cents. Such fiscal cushions are mostly absent at the international level. (Even where substantial transfers exist, for example, in the European Union, they are rarely very countercyclical.)
6. *Countercyclical remittances*. In any given year, inflows or outflows of migration are a relatively small fraction of the labor force. Emigrants' remittances, however, (i) constitute a large share of foreign exchange earnings in many developing countries, (ii) are variable, and (iii) appear to be countercyclical.[22] They seem to respond to the *difference* between the cyclical positions of the sending and receiving country. This makes it a bit easier for a country such as El Salvador, for example, to give up the option of setting its monetary policy differently from what the United States does. Remittances will achieve some of the smoothing.[23]
7. *Political willingness to give up some monetary sovereignty*. Some countries look on their currency with the same sense of patriotism with which they look on their flag. It is not a good idea to force subordination to the US dollar (or the euro or any other foreign currency) down the throats of an unwilling public. Otherwise, in times of economic difficulty, the public is likely to blame Washington, DC (or Frankfurt).
8. *Level of financial development*. Countries seldom float without first having developed financial markets. Aghion et al. (2005) argue that fixed rates

[21] Bayoumi and Eichengreen (1994); Mundell (1961).

[22] Frankel (2011), and other references cited therein.

[23] Sophisticated theories of intertemporal optimization say that regular capital flows should play the smoothing role too. In practice, however, private capital flows do not appear to be countercyclical. Kaminsky et al. (2005); Mendoza and Terrones (2008); and Reinhart and Reinhart (2009).

are better for countries at low levels of financial development; because financial markets are thin, the benefits of using exchange rate flexibility to accommodate real shocks are outweighed by costs of financial shocks. As markets develop, exchange flexibility becomes more attractive. They proxy financial market development by the ratio of Private Credit to GDP and estimate 40% as the threshold above which flexibility dominates. Similarly, Husain et al. (2005) find that only for richer and more financially developed countries do flexible rates work better than fixed rates, in the sense of being more durable and of delivering higher growth without inflation.

9. *Origin of shocks.* An old textbook wisdom holds that fixed rates work best if shocks are mostly internal demand shocks (especially monetary), but floating rates work best if shocks tend to be supply shocks or real shocks (especially external trade shocks). The theory is that floating rates can automatically accommodate or adjust to real shocks. Developing countries tend to be more prone to real or supply shocks than advanced economies. Natural disasters are one variety of supply shocks; Ramcharan (2007) finds empirically that floating countries weather them better. Terms of trade fluctuations are a more common variety of real shock. Again, high variability in the terms of trade makes it more likely that a floating exchange rate dominates a pegged exchange rate. Support for the effectiveness of floating rates in dealing with terms of trade shocks comes from Broda (2004); Edwards and Yeyati (2005); Edwards (2011), and Rafiq (2011).[24]

## 28.6 Alternative Nominal Anchors

A government or central bank that is impressed with the advantages of exchange rate flexibility cannot simply opt for a float and figure that it is then finished with the choice of currency regime. It must also consider, if the exchange rate is not to be the anchor for monetary policy, what is to be the nominal anchor instead (and how tightly to commit to it).

There are a variety of possible candidates for nominal anchor. Two are historical anachronisms: the price of gold under the gold standard and the money supply under monetarism. Neither of them has been a popular choice in recent decades. Two more candidates are economists' proposals to address the difficulties of the first two: a commodity standard would soften vulnerability to big fluctuations in a single commodity (the gold market) and nominal income targeting would negate the effect of big fluctuations in velocity (i.e., in the money market). Neither of those two has ever been tried, for some reason.

The leading candidate in recent years has been inflation targeting (IT). There are many variations on this approach to monetary policy: focusing on headline versus core CPI, price level versus inflation, forecasted inflation versus actual, and so forth. Some interpretations of IT are flexible enough to include output in

[24] Because small countries tend to be less diversified in their exports, criterion 9 can sometimes be at odds with criterion 1.

the target at relatively short horizons. But all orthodox interpretations focus on the CPI as the choice of price index. This choice may need rethinking in light of heightened volatility in prices of oil, minerals, and agricultural products and, therefore, in the terms of trade in many countries.

A CPI target can lead to anomalous outcomes in response to terms of trade fluctuations. If the price of imported oil or food rises on world markets, a CPI target induces the monetary authority to tighten money enough to appreciate the currency—the wrong direction for accommodating an adverse movement in the terms of trade. If the price of the export commodity rises on world markets, a CPI target *prevents* monetary tightening consistent with appreciation as called for in response to an improvement in the terms of trade. In other words, the CPI target gets it exactly backward.

One alternative is to use a price index that reflects a basket of goods produced, including those exported, in place of an index that reflects the basket of goods consumed, including those imported. It could be an index of export prices alone or a broader index of all goods produced domestically.[25] The argument is that one wants to accommodate the terms of trade, allowing the currency to appreciate when the export prices go up, not when import prices go up.

Theoretical models of IT typically miss the issue of terms of trade vulnerability, either because they are not designed for open economies or else they rely on well-functioning international capital flows for the accommodation of trade shocks. But a model that ignores the tendency for international finance to disappear in times of trouble is not very useful for choosing an exchange rate regime.

## REFERENCES

Aghion, Philippe, Philippe Bacchetta, Romaine Ranciere, and Kenneth Rogoff. "Exchange Rate Volatility and Productivity Growth: The Role of Financial Development," Journal of Monetary Economics, 2009, 56(4), 494–513.

Anderson J, van Wincoop E. Gravity with gravitas: solution to the border puzzle. Am Econ Rev 2001; 93(1): 170–192.

Arteta C. Exchange rate regimes and financial dollarization: does flexibility reduce currency mismatches. Top Macroecon 2005; 5(1): 1–28.

Bahmani-Oskooee M, Hegerty S, Kutan A. Do nominal devaluations lead to real devaluations? Evidence from 89 countries. Int Rev Econ Finance 2008; 17: 644–70.

Baldwin R. The Euro's trade effects. European Central Bank Working Paper No. 594; 2006 March.

Barro R, Gordon D. A positive theory of monetary policy in a natural rate model. J Pol Econ 1983; 91(4): 589–610.

[25]For Pegging the export price index (PEPI), see Frankel (2005). For product price targeting (PPT), see Frankel (2011).

Bayoumi T, Eichengreen B. One money or many? Analyzing the prospects for monetary unification in various parts of the world, Studies in International Finance 76. Princeton NJ: Princeton University Press; 1994.

Bénassy-Quéré A, Coeuré B, Mignon V. On the identification of de facto currency pegs. J Jpn Int Econ 2004; 20(1): 112–27.

Broda C. Terms of trade and exchange rate regimes in developing countries. J Int Econ 2004; 63(1): 31–58.

Calvo G, Reinhart C. Fear of floating. Q J Econ 2002; 117(2): 379–408.

Calvo G, Vegh C. Inflation stabilization and nominal anchors. Contemp Econ Policy 1994; 12: 35–45.

Council on Foreign Relations. Safeguarding prosperity in a global financial system: the future international financial architecture. Washington (DC): Institute for International Economics; 1999.

Edwards S. Exchange rates in emerging countries: eleven empirical regularities from Latin America and East Asia. NBER Working Paper 17074; 2011 May.

Edwards S, Yeyati EL. Flexible exchange rates as shock absorbers. Eur Econ Rev 2005; 49(8): 2079–2005.

Eichengreen B. International monetary arrangements for the 21st century. Washington (DC): Brookings Institution; 1994.

Eichengreen B, Hausmann R. Exchange rates and financial fragility. New challenges for monetary policy. Kansas City (MO): Federal Reserve Bank of Kansas City; 1999.

Engel C, Rogers J. How wide is the border? Am Econ Rev 1996; 86: 1112–1125.

Fischer S. Exchange rate regimes: is the bipolar view correct? J Econ Perspect 2001; 15(2): 3–24.

Frankel J. No single exchange rate regime is right for all countries or at all times. Essays in international finance. Princeton (NJ): Princeton University Press; 1999. p. 215.

Frankel J. Experience of and lessons from exchange rate regimes in emerging economies. Monetary and Financial Cooperation in East Asia. Hampshire, England: ADB (Macmillan); 2003.

Frankel J. Peg the export price index: a proposed monetary regime for small countries. J Policy Model 2005 Houndmills, Basingstoke, Hampshire, RG21 6XS, England; 27(4): 495–508.

Frankel J. The estimated effects of the euro on trade: why are they below historical effects of monetary unions among smaller countries? In: Alesina A, Giavazzi F, editors. Europe and the Euro: 100(2): Univ. of Chicago Press; 2010. pp. 169–218.

Frankel J. A comparison of monetary anchor options, including product price targeting, for commodity-exporters in latin America. Washington (DC): Economia, Brookings Press; 2011: 12(1). NBER WP 16362.

Frankel J, Rose A. An estimate of the effect of common currencies on trade and income. Q J Econ 2002; 117:437–466.

Frankel J, Schmukler S, Servén L. Verifiability and the vanishing intermediate exchange rate regime. In: Collins S, Rodrik D, editors. Brookings trade forum 2000. Washington (DC): Brookings Institution; 2000. pp. 59–123.

Frankel J, Xie D. Estimation of de facto flexibility parameter and basket weights in evolving exchange rate regimes. Am Econ Rev 2010;100.

Friedman M. The case for flexible exchange rates. In: Friedman M, editor. Essays in positive economics. Chicago: University of Chicago Press; 1953. pp. 157–203.

Ghosh A, Gulde A-M, Wolf H. Currency boards: more than a quick fix? Econ Policy 2000; 31: 271–335.

Glick R, Rose A. Does a currency union affect trade? The time series evidence. Eur Econ Rev 2002; 46: 1125–1–51.

Hanke SH, Schuler K. Currency boards for developing countries: a handbook. San Francisco (CA): ICS Press; 1994.

Helliwell J. How much do national borders matter? Washington (DC): Brookings Institution Press; 1998.

Husain A, Mody A, Rogoff K. Exchange rate regime durability and performance in developing Vs. Advanced economies. J Monet Econ 2005; 52: 35–64.

Kaminsky G, Reinhart C, Végh C. "When It Rains, It Pours: Procyclical Capital Flows and Macroeconomic Policies," NBER Macroeconomics Annual 2004, Volume 19, National Bureau of Economic Research, Inc.; 2005. pp. 11–82

Klein M, Marion N. Explaining the duration of exchange-rate pegs. J Dev Econ 1997; 54(2): 387–404.

Klein M, Shambaugh J. Fixed exchange rates and trade. J Int Econ 2006; 70(2): 359–383.

Krugman P. Target zones and exchange rate dynamics. Q J Econ 1991; 106: 669–682.

Larrain F, Velasco A. Exchange rate policy in emerging markets: the case for floating, Studies in international economics 224. Princeton (NJ): Princeton University Press; 2001.

Levy Yeyati E, Sturzenegger F. Exchange rate regimes and economic performance. IMF Staff Papers; 2001 Feb.

Levy Yeyati E, Sturzenegger F. To float or to trail: evidence on the impact of exchange rate regimes on growth. Am Econ Rev 2003; 93(4), Sept. 1173–1193.

Levy Yeyati E, Federico S. "Exchange Rate Regimes and Economic Performance," IMF Staff Papers; 2001, February.

Levy Yeyati E, Federico S. "To Float or to Trail: Evidence on the Impact of Exchange Rate Regimes on Growth," American Economic Review, 2003, 93(4), Sept. 1173–1193.

McCallum J. National borders matter: Canada-U.S. regional trade patterns. Am Econ Rev 1995; 85: 615–23.

McKinnon R. Optimum currency areas. Am Econ Rev 1963; 53: 717–724.

Meade J. The theory of international economic policy. London: Oxford University Press; 1951.

Mendoza E, Terrones M. An anatomy of credit booms: evidence from macro aggregates and micro data. NBER Working Paper No. 14049; 2008 May.

Micco A, Stein E, Ordoñez G. The currency union effect on trade: early evidence from EMU. Econ Policy 2003; 18: 315–43.

Mundell R. A theory of optimum currency areas. Am Econ Rev 1961; 51: 509–517.

Mussa M. Nominal exchange rate regimes and the behavior of real exchange rates: evidence and implications, Carnegie-Rochester Conference Series on Public Policy, Elsevier No. 25. 1986. pp. 117–214.

Nitsch V. National borders and international trade: evidence from the European Union. Can J Econ 2000; 33: 1091–1105.

Obstfeld M. Rational and self-fulfilling balance-of-payments crises. Am Econ Rev 1986; 76(1): 72–81.

Obstfeld M, Rogoff K. The mirage of fixed exchange rates. J Econ Perspect 1995; 9(4): 73–96.

Parsley D, Wei S-J. Explaining the border effect: the role of exchange rate variability, shipping costs, and geography. J Int Econ 2001; 55(1): 87–105.

Persson T. Currency unions and trade: how large is the treatment effect? Econ Policy 2001; 33: 435–448.

Rafiq MS. Sources of economic fluctuations in oil-exporting economies: implications for choice of exchange rate regimes. Int J Econ Finance 2011; 16(1): 70–91.

Ramcharan R. Does the exchange rate regime matter for real shocks? Evidence from windstorms and earthquakes. J Int Econ 2007; 73(1): 31–47.

Reinhart C. The mirage of floating exchange rates. Am Econ Rev 2000; 90(2): 65–70.

Reinhart C, Reinhart V. Capital flow bonanzas: an encompassing view of the past and present. In: Frankel J, Pissarides C, editors. NBER international seminar in macroeconomics 2008. Chicago: University of Chicago Press; 2009.

Reinhart C, Rogoff K. The modern history of exchange rate arrangements: a reinterpretation. Q J Econ 2004; 119(1): 1–48.

Rogoff K. The optimal degree of commitment to an intermediate monetary target. Q J Econ 1985; 100: 1169–1189.

Romer D. Openness and inflation: theory and evidence. Q J Econ 1993; 108(4): 869–903.

Rose A. One money, one market: estimating the effect of common currencies on trade. Econ Policy 2000; 15(30): 9–44.

Rose A. Currency unions and trade: the effect is large. Econ Policy 2001; 33: 449–461.

Rose A, van Wincoop E. National money as a barrier to trade: the real case for monetary union. Am Econ Rev 2001; 91-2: 386–390.

Summers L. Building an international financial architecture for the 21st century. Cato J 1999; 18(3): 321–330.

Tavlas G, Dellas H, Stockman A. The classification and performance of alternative exchange-rate systems. Eur Econ Rev 2008; 52(6): 941–963.

Taylor A. A century of purchasing power parity. Rev Econ Stat 2002; 84: 139–50.

Velasco A, Chang R. Monetary policy and the currency denomination of debt: a tale of two equilibria. J Int Econ 2006; 69: 150–175.

Williamson J. Exchange rate regimes for emerging markets: reviving the intermediate option. Washington (DC): Peterson Institute for International Economics; 2000.

# Index


Absolute returns
behavioral finance framework, volatility clustering, 118–119
currency mandate for, 471–477
Accumulation costs, foreign exchange reserves, 549–550
Active currency management
allowed currencies, 472
alpha continuum and implications, 475
alternative information ratio, 491–493
alternative mandates, 471–475
Barclay currency index, 479–483
extended sample periods, 482–483
robustness checks, 481–482
benchmarks, 475–479
basic factor model, currency returns, 477–479
currency investing premium, 451–467
current trends in, 469–471
DB FX Select Platform fund managers, 494–495
empirical results, 432–440
Bayesian estimation, 433–434
data and descriptive statistics, 432–433
volatility and correlation evaluation, 434–440
foreign exchange puzzle evolution and, 600
individual manager returns, 483–491
investment implications, 496–497
leverage, 473
parameter uncertainty
Bayesian asset allocation, 430–431
predictive density, 443
volatility and correlation evaluation, 437–438
passive *vs.* active management, 471–472
performance benchmark and compensation, 473
permitted instruments, 473
structural and operational choices, 474–475
value-based strategies, 458–459
volatility and correlation timing, 421–442
dynamic models, 424–428
multivariate models, 425–427
weighted portfolio, FX strategies, 461–463
Active hedge management, currency hedging, 531
Adaptive market hypothesis, trading rule profits and, 365–366
Adaptive reinforcement learning algorithm, technical trading and, 366
Adjustable pegs
currency trends and, 141–142
exchange rate rules, 147–148
Adjusted purchasing power parity, fair value currency models, 315–316
Agent-based models, behavioral finance framework, 113–114


*Handbook of Exchange Rates*, First Edition. Edited by Jessica James, Ian W. Marsh, and Lucio Sarno.

Agent information gaps, mainstream exchange rate models, 112
Agent interactions
  currency-trading models, 80–83
  macro/micro perspectives, 77–78
  micro-based macromodel, 96–105
Aggregate income, portfolio shifts currency trading model, 85–88
Aggregate interdealer order flow, 83–85
Aggregate risk, stochastic discount factor, currency excess returns, 399–403
Aggregation bias, law of one price and, 197–198, 199–200
Algorithmic execution
  electronic trading and, 32
  foreign exchange markets, 583–594
    dynamic algorithms, 593
    effective execution strategies, 593
    equity market derivation, 584
    future research issues, 594
    iceberg, 590–591
    intelligence, 588–589
    internalization strategies, 592
    market structure and, 585–587
    opportunistic, 590–591
    participators, 592
    performance measurement, 594
    smart order routing, 587–588
    speed, 589
    sweepers, 590–591
    time slicers, 590–591
  liquidity in market and, 12–15
  multibank trading platforms, 37–38
Allowed currencies, active currency management, 472–475
Alpha indices
  active currency management
    continuum and implications, 475
    currency investing premium, 451–467
  options in FX, Black Swan strategies and, 677–681
  strategy-based foreign exchange products and, 605–613
Alternative information ratio, active currency management, 491–493
Amounts outstanding
  derivatives in foreign exchange markets, 633–635
  options in FX, 653–654
Anchor rate
  exchange rate regime selection and, 778–779
  in fixed rate exchange regimes, 766–768
Ancient period, purchasing power parity in, 163–164
Anti-Black Swan strategies, options in FX, 672–674
Arbitrage
  in ancient period, 163–164
  fundamentalist rule, 125
  high-frequency arbitrage, algorithmic execution, 584
  law of one price and barriers to, 195–198
  macro/micro perspectives, 77–78
  no-arbitrage conditions
    derivatives foreign exchange markets, 622
    stochastic discount factor, exchange rate analysis, 393–394
  portfolio shifts model, 86
  stochastic discount factor, exchange rate analysis, absence of, 393–394
  trading rule profits and, 365–366
  unit root property, 116
Arbitrage pricing theory (APT), active currency management, 477
ASEAN countries, 140
Asia, growth of currency trading in, 5–6
Ask prices. *See also* Bid-ask spreads
  history of, 22
  interdealer trading, 16
Asset allocation
  active currency management
    dynamic asset allocation, CRRA utility, 428–429
    parameter uncertainty, Bayesian asset allocation, 430–431
  exchange rate analysis, mean variance predictions, 231–236
Asset class
  currency as, 469–470
  options in FX, volatility as, 664–672
  strategy-based foreign exchange products as, 597–618
Asset-demand function, portfolio balance exchange model, 50–51
Asset market approach, foreign exchange rate models, 45–46

Asset pricing
currency hedging volatility, 523–524
foreign exchange reserves costs, 549–550
intervention effectiveness and, 723–726
stochastic discount factor, exchange rate analysis, utility-based pricing, 391–393
Asset-pricing bubbles, depreciation decomposition, 76–77
Asymmetric dynamic conditional correlation (ADCC), active currency management, 426–427
Asymmetric information, foreign exchange market and, 19–20
Asymptotic pooled regression models, 268–272
Attack-conditional monetary policy, crisis management, 704–705
Attacks, Krugman-Flood-Garber model of crisis management, 701–704
Augmented monetary model, 52
Augmented purchasing power parity
comparative-static computation, 165
theoretical background, 162–163
Austria, floating exchange rates and paper standard in, 171–172
Autobahn trading platform, 26
Automated interface (AI), electronic trading and, 32
Autoregression vectors, nominal exchange models, out-of-sample simulations, 52–54
Available information, incomplete information, exchange rate modeling, 375–376
infrequent decision making, 385–388
monetary model, 378–379
Average absolute price change, scaling law, 565–566
AVGARCH models. *See* Univariate modeling

Backus-Smith puzzle, incomplete information, exchange rate modeling, 388
Bail outs, currency crisis management, lender of last resort model, 709–710
Balanced investments, strategy-based foreign exchange management, 610–611
Balance of payments rules, managed international monetary systems and, 148–149
Balance sheets variables, financial globalization and, 64
Balassa-Samuelson framework. *See also* Harrod-Balassa-Samuelson effect
productivity-based models, 56–58
purchasing power parity and, 56
real models of real exchange rate, 54, 56–60
Bank Restriction Period
bullionism and, 170–171
metallic standards, 172
Barclay currency index (BCTI)
active currency management, 479–483
extended sample periods, 482–483
robustness checks, 481–482
strategy-based foreign exchange products and, 602–604
BARX single-bank trading system, 26
Bayesian mechanism
active currency management, 423–424
empirical results, 433–434
estimation and forecasting, 427–428
parameter uncertainty, Bayesian asset allocation, 430–431
behavioral finance models, 114
exchange rate model uncertainty, 382–384
Bayesian model averaging (BMA), active currency management, 423–424
model uncertainty, 431–432
Beggar-thy-neighbor behavior, exchange rate regimes and, 150–153
Behavioral equilibrium exchange-rate (BEER) models, 53–54
fair value currency, 316–320
Goldman Sachs dynamic equilibrium exchange rate model, 319–320
permanent equilibrium exchange rate model, 317–319
standard model, 316–317
Behavioral finance framework
adaptive market hypothesis, technical trading, 365–366

Behavioral finance framework (*continued*)
alternative exchange rates models and, 113–114
Black Swan strategies and, 675–681
exchange rate puzzles, 114–122
foreign exchange rate prototype, 122–127
future model applications, 127–129
mainstream exchange rate models, 111–112
Benchmark strategies
active currency management
alpha factors, 475–479
basic factor model, currency returns, 477–479
currency investing premium, 452–467
performance benchmark and compensation, 473–475
algorithmic execution, foreign exchange markets, 594
strategy-based foreign exchange products, 605–611
Beta indices
active currency management
correlations with FX strategies, 460–461
currency investing premium, 451–467
foreign exchange markets, 453–463
multiple beta forms, 463
carry trades
active currency management, 453–456
time-varying risk and rare events, 308–311
carry trades and, 302–304
options in FX, Black Swan strategies and, 677–681
strategy-based foreign exchange products and, 605–613
Beveridge-Nelson decompositions, permanent equilibrium exchange rate model, fair value currency, 317
Biased self-attribution, trading rule profits and, 364–365
Bid-ask spreads
electronic trading and narrowing of, 28–29
retail aggregators and, 33–34
exchange rate analysis, transaction costs, 234–236
global custodian banks, 18
interdealer spot trading, 15–17
retail investors and, 14–15
strategy-based foreign exchange products and, 600–604
Bid price, asymmetric information, 19
Big Mac Index, value-based strategies, purchasing power parity, 458–459
Bilateral exchange rate, fair value currency models, 333, 336–337
Bilateral trade, exchange rate regime effects, 768–773
Bimetallic standard, history, 135
BIS Triennial surveys, 5–10, 27, 29
active currency management, 496–497
forwards and swaps turnover information, 621–622
options in FX, 653–654
strategy-based foreign exchange products and, 600–604
Bivariate modeling
metallic standards, 172
purchasing power parity, 162–163
Black-box selection process, technical testing, 356–357
Black-Scholes formula, options in FX
basic properties, 647–653
historical perspective, 647
volatility models, 658–681
Black Swan fund, options in FX, 690–691
Black Swan strategies
options in FX, 674–681
technical trading returns, risk analysis, 361
Bologna-Claremont Monetary Convergence, 153
Bonds
currency crisis management, sterilization and interest rate defense, 708–709
currency hedging, 501–541
foreign government bonds, 507–511
high yield corporate bonds, 511–516
nominal exchange rate, 46
portfolio balance models, 49–51
risk premium and order flow, 64–65

Bonn Summit, 140, 146
Bootstrap algorithm, exchange rate analysis, predictive ability, 230–231
Border effect, law of one price and, 194–195
Bounded rationality, trading rule profits and, 364–365
Brady bonds, 141
Break-even transaction costs, exchange rate analysis, 234–235
Bretton Woods system
  evolution of foreign exchange markets and, 598–599
  history of, 137–138
  market forces and demise of, 150–151
  options in FX following abandonment of, 646–647
  outright forwards and futures trading and abandonment of, 624–626
  post-Bretton Woods exchange rate regimes and, 133–135
    pooled regression models, 266–267
  post-collapse exchange rate models, 49–54, 111–114
  purchasing power parity and, 203–205, 211–213
BRIC countries, post-Bretton Woods exchange rate regimes and, 134–135
Brokers. *See also* Prime brokerage (PB)
  electronic brokers, 23
  evolution of market structure and, 21–22
  retail aggregators as, 18–19
  voice brokers, 22
Brownian motion, options in FX, volatility models, 659–681
Bubbles
  asset-pricing, 76–77, 144–145
  behavioral finance models, 113–114
  fixed rate exchange regimes, 768
  floating exchange rate regimes and, 774–779
  Krugman-Flood-Garber model of crisis management, 701–704
  trading rule profits and, 364–365
  unit root property, 117–118
Budget surpluses, foreign exchange reserves, 547
Bullionist periods, purchasing power parity in, 170–171
Business margins, options in FX, 686–687
Butterfly spreads, options in FX, volatility modeling, 663–664
Buy-and-hold investors, multibank platforms, 37–38
Buy-side perspective, options in FX, 645–646, 681–693
  Black Swan funds, 690–691
  currency hedging, illiquid assets, 691–693
  implied distribution, 683–687
  long-dated *vs.* short-dated options, 687–690
  strike *vs.* leverage, 681–683

Calculation methods, fair value currency model implementation, 331–332
Call options, options in FX, 647–648, 663
Capital asset pricing model (CAPM)
  active currency management, currency investing premium, 451–467
  carry trades, 283–285
    monthly return models, 293–295
  technical trading returns, risk analysis, 360–361
Capital enhanced equilibrium exchange rate (CHEER) model, fair value currency, 317
Capital mobility
  balance of payments rules and, 148–149
  portfolio balance exchange model, 50–51
Capital protected notes, strategy-based foreign exchange products, 617–618
Capital sustainability, nominal exchange rate models, 49–54
Carry trades
  active currency management, 423–425
    bank indices, 463–465
    basic factor model, 478–479
    risk appetite, 454–455
  beta factors in, 453–456
  currency returns factors, 299–308
    betas, 302–304
    cross-sectional analysis, 304–307
    currency skewness factor, 302
    currency volatility factor, 302

Carry trades (*continued*)
forward discount sorting, 300
linear factor model, 307–308
sorted portfolio factors, 300–302
defined, 285–286
forward exchange rate puzzle
emergence and, 600
incomplete information, exchange rate modeling, 376, 387–388
liquidity and, 13
monthly return models, 293–295
outright forwards and futures trading and, 625–626
quarterly return models, 295, 297–298
retail-oriented platforms, 33–34
returns measurement, 286–289
returns pricing, 290–293
risk analysis and, 283–311
stochastic discount factor, currency risk premia, 395–396
strategy-based foreign exchange products and, 605–611
Cash currency
options in FX, hedging of, 692
US Dollar as, 552–555
Cash flow, currency hedging, 524–525
Cash-in-advance constraint, two-good models, 59
Causality, purchasing power parity, 165–166
Center for International Securities and Derivatives Markets (CISDM), strategy-based foreign exchange products and, 603–604
Central banks
active currency management
carry indices, 463–465
trend indices, 465–466
cross-currency swap dislocation in global financial crisis and, 637–640
currency crisis management, lender of last resort model, 709–710
floating exchange rate regimes and, 774–779
foreign exchange reserves, 547–548
options in FX options, 655
reaction functions, 60–63
technical trading and, 367–368
Central counterparties (CCPs), electronic trading and, 35
Channels for intervention
event-study analysis of, 737–744
overview of, 718–719
time-series analysis of, 726–737
Characteristic function method, options in FX, volatility models, 660–681
Charting
technical analysis, 346–350
trading rule profits and, 364–365
Chartist rules, foreign exchange market behavioral prototype, 122–127
Chiang-Mai Initiative, 140
Chicago Board of Trade (CBOT), outright forwards and futures trading and, 625–626
Chicago Mercantile Exchange (CME), 9, 33
fair value currency models, indirect fair value, 326–328
outright forwards and futures trading and, 624–626
China
key currency competition and, 145
misalignment of exchange rates, renminbi case study, 749–760
post-Bretton Woods exchange rate regimes and, 134–135
premodern monetary system in, 163–165
CitiFX beta index, strategy-based foreign exchange products, 605–611, 615–617
CitiFX Thematic Indices, strategy-based foreign exchange management, 610–611
Clower constraint, two-good real exchange rate model, 59–60
Coastline of price curves, scaling laws and, 562–563
Coastline trading model
monthly statistics, 578–579
scaling laws and, 576–578
Cognitive limitations
mainstream exchange rate models and, 111–112
trading rule profits and cognitive bias, 363–365

Coin standards
in colonial-era United States, 169–170
in premodern economies, 163–165
Cointegration methods
bullionist periods and, 170–171
nominal exchange models, 52–54
portfolio shifts currency-trading model, order flow and FX returns, 91
purchasing power parity, 167–168
purchasing power parity and, 56
Combined forecasts, exchange rate analysis, 235–236
economic evaluation, 251–256
Commitments of Traders (COT)
fair value currency models, indirect fair value, 326–328
philosophy of technical analysis, 345
Committee of Twenty
Bretton Woods reforms and, 137–138
post-Bretton Woods exchange rate regimes and, 134–135
Commodity currencies
currency hedging, high yield corporate bonds, 513–516
current trading trends for, 7–8
Commodity prices, foreign exchanges and, 3–4
Commodity trading advisors (CTAs)
forward exchange rate puzzle emergence and, 600
liquidity needs of, 12–13
Common information assumption, incomplete information, exchange rate modeling, 375–376
uncertainty, 381–384
Comparative-static computation, purchasing power parity, 165
Competitive depreciation, fixed rate exchange regimes, 767–768
Competitive devaluations, interventions, 717–719
Complete markets, stochastic discount factor, exchange rate analysis, 392–393
Complex dynamics, behavioral finance framework, agent-based models, 113–114
Computing signals, technical analysis, 351–353
Confirmation bias, trading rule profits and, 364–365
Constant conditional correlation (CCC) model, active currency management, 425
Constant hedge ratio, hedge rebalancing, 531–536
Constant relative risk aversion (CRRA), active currency management
dynamic asset allocation, 428–429
overview, 423–424
Consumer Price Index (CPI)
exchange rate regime selection and, 778–779
purchasing power parity, 208–213
Consumption betas, stochastic discount factor, currency excess returns, 400–403
Consumption capital asset pricing model
carry trades, 283–285
quarterly return models, 295, 297–298
stochastic discount factor, currency excess returns, 401–403
Consumption growth, stochastic discount factor, currency excess returns, economic crises and, 402–403
Contingent claims, stochastic discount factor, exchange rate analysis, 393
Continuous Linked Settlement (CLS), electronic trading and, 24
Contrarian trading, technical analysis, 351
Coordination channels for interventions
effectiveness of, 724–726
overview of, 718–719
time-series analysis, 726–737
Corners hypothesis, exchange rate regimes, 766–779
Corporate bonds, currency hedging, 511–516
Corporate customers
asymmetric information in foreign exchange trading and, 20
liquidity needs of, 14
multibank trading platforms, 37–38
Correlation premium, options in FX, volatility as asset class, 666–672
Correlation swap, options in FX, volatility as asset, 669–672

Correlation timing, active currency management, 421–443
beta factors correlation, 460–461
dynamic models, 424–428
economic value, 428–430
evaluation of, 434–440
Cost, insurance and freight (CIF), law of one price and, 195–198
Countercyclical fiscal transfers, exchange rate regime selection and, 777–779
Countercyclical remittance, exchange rate regime selection and, 777–779
Counterparty credit risk
cross-currency swap dislocations and, 638–640
swap trading of foreign exchanges, 628
Country characteristics, exchange rate regimes and
selection based on, 776–779
size, 773
Country payments, foreign exchange reserves, 544
Covered interest parity (CIP)
carry trades, 286
cross-currency swaps, 631–632
global financial crisis and, 638–640
derivatives foreign exchange markets, 622
exchange rate analysis, predictive regressions, 227–228
swap trading of foreign exchanges, 627–628
Crashes
trading rule profits and, 364–365
unit root property, 117–118, 126
Crash premium, options in FX, volatility as asset class, 666–672
Credit risk
central counterparties, 35–36
retail aggregator avoidance of, 18–19
Credit support annex, 40
Crisis management in foreign exchange markets
empirical models, 711–712
Krugman-Flood-Garber model
attack-conditional monetary policy, 704–705
basic principles, 699–704
devaluation, 705–707
extensions, 704–710
lender of last resort, 709–710
sterilization and interest rate defense, 707–709
overview, 697–699
Cross-currency analysis
nominal exchange models, 53–54
stochastic discount factor, 397–398
Cross-currency basis swaps, 629–633
Cross-currency swaps, foreign exchange markets, 629–633
dislocations in, 635–640
hedging schemes, 632–633
mechanisms, 629–631
pricing and long-term CIP, 631–632
Cross-sectional analysis
currency factors, carry trades and, 304–307
fair value currency models, 337
Cumulated trade balance (CTB)
foreign exchange intervention and, 51
nominal exchange rate models, 51–54
Cumulative order flow, portfolio shifts currency-trading model, foreign exchange returns and, 88–91
Currency boards, exchange rate regimes, 141–143, 147, 155
Currency coding, 7–8
Currency crises. *See* Crisis management in foreign exchange markets
Currency fair value models. *See* Fair value currency models
Currency forwards. *See* Forwards in foreign exchange markets
Currency futures. *See* Futures market in foreign exchange
Currency hedging
cash flow impact, 524–525, 531
costs of, 523–524
currency forwards *vs.* options, 524–531
foreign government bonds, 507–511
forwards *vs.* options, 504–506
international bond and equity investors, 501–541
options in FX, illiquid assets, 691–692
strategic aim of, 530–531
Currency instruments
active currency management, 473–475
classification of, 9–10
Currency investing premium, active currency management, 451–467

Currency managers, strategy-based foreign exchange products and, 600–604
Currency mandates, active currency management, 471–475
  alpha continuum, 475
Currency misalignment
  fair value currency models, 313–314
  misalignment of exchange rates, renminbi case study, 749–760
Currency options, 9, 40
Currency overlay mandate
  active currency management, 471–475
  foreign exchange puzzle evolution and, 600
Currency portfolios, stochastic discount factor
  nominal interest rates, 403–404
  UIP regressions, 398–399
Currency regimes, history of, 135–138
Currency returns, exchange rate economics and, 11–12
Currency returns factors
  active currency management benchmarks, 477–479
    basic factor model, 477–479
    individual managers, 483–491
  carry trades, 299–308
    betas, 302–304
    cross-sectional analysis, 304–307
    currency skewness factor, 302
    currency volatility factor, 302
    forward discount sorting, 300
    linear factor model, 307–308
    sorted portfolio factors, 300–302
  price discovery, 11–12
Currency risk premia, stochastic discount factor, real exchange rates, 395
Currency swaps, 5, 9, 40
Currency-trading models, 80–105
  dominance of US dollar in, 6–8
  exchange rate regimes and, 141–143
  exchange rates, order flows, and macroeconomy, 95–96
  geography and composition, 4–6
  micro-based macromodel, 96–105
  portfolio-shifts model, 81–88
Currency unions
  country size and, 773
  time-series analysis, 770
Currency volatility indices
  active currency management, 471–475
  carry trades, risk factors, 302
  laissez-faire exchange rate performance and costs, 139
Currency wars, intervention effectiveness and, 744
Currenex multibank trading system, 25–29
Current account balance
  fair value currency models
    external sustainability approach, 324–325
    underlying current account conditions, 320–324
  portfolio balance exchange model and, 51–54
Current equilibrium exchange rate, fair value currency model implementation, horizon/frequency approach, 330–331
Custodial trades, 18, 29
Customer orders, currency-trading models, 81–95
Customer profiling, electronic trading, 31
Customer trade internalization, electronic trading and, 30–31

Data mining, technical analysis, 355–357
Data releases
  exchange rate analysis, economic fundamentals, 237–242
  Monte Carlo simulation, 272–275
  portfolio shifts currency-trading model, 81–88
    foreign exchange returns and, 91
    order flows and macrodata releases, 91–92
  purchasing power parity, real exchange rate and, 205–213
  technical analysis, 353–355
Data revision, misalignment of exchange rates, renminbi case study, 757–760
Data snooping, technical analysis, 355–357
Dealers, in foreign exchange market, 11–12
  liquidity and, 15–16
Declining assets, foreign exchange reserves costs, 549–550

Decomposition
of depreciation rates, spot-rate dynamics, 74–77
returns, micro-based macromodel, 103–105
Deficits, balance of payments rules and, 148–149
Delta-1 products, strategy-based foreign exchange products, 617–618
Delta hedging, options in FX
Black-Scholes formula, 648–653
volatility modeling, 663–664, 668–672
Demand side factors, purchasing power parity and, 56
Depreciation rates
decomposition of, spot-rate dynamics, 74–77
fixed rate exchange regimes, 767–768
macro and microeconomic perspectives, 77–80
micro-based macromodel, 99–100
portfolio shift currency trading model, order flows and returns, 88–91
Derivatives in foreign exchange markets
basic parameters, 623–626
cross-currency swaps, 629–633
financial crises dislocations, 635–637
global financial crisis of 2007, 637–640
outstanding amount, 633–635
over-the-counter trading *vs.,* 635
overview, 621–622
size parameters, 623–626, 633–635
swap trading and, 626–629
turnover, 635
Desired equilibrium exchange rate (DEER), fair value currency models, underlying balance approach, 323–324
Devaluation
currency crisis management
empirical models, 711–712
Krugman-Flood-Garber crisis management model, 705–707
interventions, competitive devaluations, 717–719
Developing countries, currency crises in, 698–699
Development fund, foreign exchange reserves, 544
Dickey-Fuller test
foreign exchange market behavioral prototype, 126–127
unit root principle, behavioral finance framework, 116–118
Difference limen, foreign exchange market behavioral prototype, 123–127
Direct econometric estimation, fair value currency model implementation, 331–332
Directional-change (DC) events
intrinsic time framework, 563–565
scaling laws and, 566–571
coastline modeling, 571–572
total-move segments, 570–571
tick data analysis, 562–563
Directional trading, active currency management, 459–460
Direct market access (DMA), foreign exchange market structure, algorithmic execution, 585–587
Disaster risk, stochastic discount factor, exchange rate models, 414–417
Disconnect puzzle
behavioral finance framework, 114–115
exchange rate analysis, 221–224
Discounted mean squared error (DMSE), exchange rate analysis, 236
Discrete choice theory, foreign exchange market behavioral prototype, 124–127
Dislocations in foreign exchange markets, cross-currency swaps and, 635–640
Dissection algorithm, intrinsic time framework, high frequency finance, scaling models, 563–565
Distributed random draws, fat-tailed distributed exchange rate returns, behavioral finance framework, 119–122
Diversification
foreign exchange reserves, 550–552
strategy-based foreign exchange products and, 597–598
Dividend shocks, portfolio shifts currency trading model, 84–88
Dodd-Frank Act, central counterparties and, 35

Dollarization, exchange rate regimes, 771–772
Dornbusch-Frankel sticky price monetary model
  long-horizon predictions, 53
  real exchange rates, 60n.22
Dornbusch overshooting model, misalignment of currency, renminbi case study, 751–760
Double-Heston model, options in FX, volatility modeling, 661–681
Double moving average rule, technical analysis, 351–353
Dow Theory, technical analysis, foreign exchange markets, 343–344
Dow theory, technical trading rules, 343–344
Drivers of FX rates, risk premium, macrodrivers, 103–105
Dynamic algorithm, algorithmic execution, foreign exchange markets, 593
Dynamic conditional correlation (DCC), active currency management
  economic value of volatility and correlation, 428–430
  models, 424–428
  multivariate analysis, 425–426
  overview, 422–424
Dynamic ordinary least squares (DOLS)
  cointegrating vectors, nominal exchange models, 54
  fair value currency models, 318–320
  productivity-based models, Balassa-Samuelson framework, 58
Dynamic structural general equilibrium (DSGE), foreign exchange rate models, 45–46
Dynamic volatility, active currency management, models, 424–428

Econometric methods
  behavioral finance framework, unit root principle, 116–118
  exchange rate dynamics, 221–260
    data releases, 237–244
    predictability, 231–236
  exchange rate regime analysis, 768–773
  fair value currency model implementation, direct econometric estimation *vs.* calculation, 331–332
Economic integration, laissez-faire exchange rate performance and, 139
Economic policy, exchange rate regimes coordination, 140
Economic value. *See* Present value model
Effective exchange rate, fair value currency models, 333, 336–337
Efficient market hypothesis
  active currency management, 456–458
  behavioral finance framework, unit root principle, 116–118
  forward exchange rate puzzle emergence and, 599–600
  strategy-based foreign exchange products and, 604–618
  technical analysis, 350, 365–366
EGARCH models. *See* Univariate modeling
Electronic Brokering Services (EBS)
  electronic trading and, 23–24
  multibank trading platforms, 37–38
  portfolio shifts currency-trading model, order flow and FX returns, 91
Electronic trading
  algorithmic execution, 584
  bid-ask spreads and, 28–29
  central counterparties, 35
  customer profiling, 31
  customer trade internalization, 30
  end-customers and, 24–29, 32–35
  evolution in foreign exchange markets of, 21–22
  foreign exchange volume increase and, 4–6
  high frequency trading and, 33
  historic evolution of, 22–23
  interdealer market, 24–29
  liquidity aggregators, 35
  major dealing bank innovations, 30–32
  market concentration and, 29
  operating efficiency of, 28–29
  prime brokerage, 31–32
  recent developments, 30–35
  retail aggregators, 33–34
  transparency enhancement and, 27
  white labeling, 30
Electrum, history of, 135

Elliot wave theory, technical analysis, 350
Emerging-market economies
  cross-currency swap dislocations and, 638–640
  currency crises in, 698–699
  exchange rate regimes, global market integration, 140–141
  floating exchange rate regimes in, 774–779
  interventions in, 715–719
    reserve accumulation and, 719–723
  market share of, 8
  post-Bretton Woods exchange rate regimes and, 134–135
  strategy-based foreign exchange management, 611
Empirical models
  active currency management, 423–424, 432–440
    Barclay currency index (BCTI), 479–483
  behavioral finance framework, unit root principle, 116–118
  carry trades, 293–308
  currency crisis management, 711–712
  exchange rate dynamics, 237–256
    data releases, 237–242
    economical evaluation, 249–256
    predictive regressions, 242–244
    statistical evaluation, 244–249
  hedging studies, 502–503
  intervention effectiveness, 723–744
  micro-based macromodel, 106–107
  microeconomic approaches, foreign exchange markets, exchange rates, order flows and macroeconomy, 100–103
  nominal exchange rate models, 51–54
  portfolio balance exchange model, 51–54
End-customers
  currency-trading models, 81–95
  electronic trading for, 24–29, 32–35
  liquidity for, 12–15
Endogeneity, exchange rate regimes, 771–772
English bullionist period, purchasing power parity in, 170–171
Equally weighted portfolios, carry trades, 284–285
Equal status countries, purchasing power parity and, 174–175
Equilibrium conditions
  micro-based macromodel, 98–100
  portfolio shifts currency-trading model, 83–88
  purchasing power parity, 165
  stochastic discount factor, exchange rate analysis, 398–407
Equilibrium exchange rate models, fair value currency, 316–317
  underlying balance approach, 320–324
Equilibrium real exchange rate (ERER) model, fair value currency, 316–319
  external sustainability approach, 324–325
Equity markets
  active currency management, 452
  algorithmic execution, 584
  currency hedging, 501–541
    MSCI world equities, 516–523
  trading volume, foreign exchange turnover and, 4–6
Error-correction-mechanism
  fair value currency model implementation, direct econometric estimation *vs.* calculation, 331–332
  fair value currency models, 318–319
Error correction term (ECT), cointegrating vectors, nominal exchange models, 52–54
Euro (EUR)
  foreign exchange reserves, 547
  key currency competition and, 145
  trading volume for, 7–8
Euronext London, 625
European Monetary System (EMS)
  exchange rate regimes and, 140
  Guidelines to Floating and, 147–148
European option, options in FX, Black-Scholes formula, 647–653
Event-study approach, intervention effectiveness analysis, 737–744
Excess balance investment, foreign exchange reserves, 544
Excess demand function, foreign exchange market behavioral prototype, 123–127

Excess returns
active currency management
Barclay currency traders index, 479–481
currency mandates, 471–475
information ratio, 491–493
manager benchmarks, 475–479
carry trades, 287–289
micro-based macromodel
current macroconditions and, 100–102
future macroconditions, 102–103
risk premium macrodrivers, 103–105
stochastic discount factor
annual returns and aggregate risk, 399–403
currency risk premia, 395–396
monthly returns, 403
predictability, currency excess returns, 405–406
technical analysis, 351–353
Excess volatility puzzle, behavioral finance framework, 114–115
Exchange rate dynamics. *See also* Disconnect puzzle
asymmetric information of corporate customers and, 20
currency trends and, 141–143
current systems, 144–145
economic policy coordination, 140
emerging market economic integration, 140–141
future prospects for, 144–153
global imbalances and financial crises of 2007–2009, 143–144
history of, 135–138
hollowing out hypothesis testing, 154–156
market discipline, 139–140
micro-based macromodel, 95–100
post-Bretton Woods developments in, 133–135
quotation conventions for, 8
statistical and economic predictions concerning, 221–260
combined forecasts, 235–236
dynamic FX strategy, 231
empirical results, 237–256
data releases, 237–242
economical evaluation, 249–256
predictive regressions, 242–244
statistical evaluation, 244–249
evaluation techniques, 228–231
mean-variance dynamic asset allocation, 231–232
performance measures, 232–234
predictive regressions, 226–228
present value model, 224–226
transaction costs, 234–235
technical analysis, 353–355
Exchange rate puzzles
behavioral finance framework, 114–122
disconnect puzzle, 114–115
excess volatility puzzle, 114–115
fat-tailed distributed exchange rate returns., 119–122
unit root property, 115–118
volatility clustering, 118–119
statistical analysis, 221–224
Exchange rate regimes
evolution of, 133–156
selection criteria for, 765–779
Exchange rate rules, managed international monetary systems, 146–148
Exchange rates, stochastic discount factor framework
common component and heterogeneous loading, 403–404
complete markets, 393
cross-country correlations, 397–398
currency excess returns
annual returns and aggregate risk, 399–403
monthly returns, 403
currency risk premia, 395–396
disaster risk models, 414–417
empirical evidence, 398–407
global volatility, 405
habit preferences, 407–411
intuition, 407–408
model for, 408–409
uncovered interest rate parity puzzle, 409–411
law of one price, 393–394
long-run risk models, 411–413
maximal Sharpe ratios, 396–397
models, 407–417
non-arbitrage conditions, 393–394
predictability, 405–407

Exchange rates, stochastic discount factor framework (*continued*)
real exchange rates, 395
uncovered interest rate parity, 391–392
regressions to currency portfolios, 398–399
utility-based asset pricing, 392–393
Execution management systems (EMS), algorithmic execution, foreign exchange markets, smart order routing, 588
Execution methods, electronic foreign exchange trading, 26–29
Execution strategies, algorithmic execution, foreign exchange markets, 593
Exotic instruments, options in FX, 686–690
Expectational errors, stochastic discount factor, exchange rate analysis, 392
Expected realized volatility, options in FX, 657–658
Expected skewness, options in FX, 657–658
Expected term structure, options in FX pricing, 658
Expected utility, foreign exchange market behavioral prototype, 122–127
Experienced utility, foreign exchange market behavioral prototype, 122–127
Exponentially weighted moving average (EWMA), technical analysis, 348–350
Export price index (XPI), purchasing power parity computations, 168–169
Extended sample periods, active currency management, Barclay currency index (BCTI) models, 481–483
External imbalances, fair value currency model implementation, 332–333
External managers, foreign exchange reserves, 549
External sustainability, fair value currency models, 319–320, 324–325
Extrapolative heuristics, foreign exchange market behavioral prototype, 122–127
Extrema, dissection algorithm and, 563–565
Factor productivity. *See* Total factor productivity
Fair game paradigm, behavioral finance framework, unit root principle, 117–118
Fair value currency models
adjusted PPP:
Harrod-Balassa-Samuelson and Penn effects, 315–316
behavioral equilibrium exchange rate models, 316–320
Goldman Sachs dynamic equilibrium exchange rate model, 319–320
permanent equilibrium exchange rate model, 317–319
standard model, 316–317
evolution of, 313–315
external sustainability approach, 324–325
implementation approaches, 328–337
bilateral *vs.* effective exchange rate, 333–336
direct econometric estimation *vs.* calculation methods, 331–332
external imbalances, 332–333
horizon/frequency, 329–331
model maintenance, 336–337
real *vs.* nominal exchange rates, 333
time series *vs.* cross section or panel, 336
indirect fair value, 325–328
natural real exchange rate, 325
taxonomy, 315–320
underlying balance approach, 320–324
fundamental equilibrium exchange rate, 322–323
macroeconomic balance approach, 323–324
Fallacy of composition, mainstream exchange rate models, 112
Fama-French three-factor model
carry trades, 283–285
monthly return models, 293–296
returns pricing, 291–293
stochastic discount factor, UIP regressions, currency portfolios, 398–399
technical trading returns, risk analysis, 360–361

Fama regression, incomplete information, exchange rate modeling, infrequent decision making, 386–388
Fat-tailed distributed exchange rate returns
behavioral finance framework, 119–122
options in FX
Black Swan strategies and, 680–681
volatility modeling, 662–681
Fibonacci numbers, technical analysis, 350
Fill or kill algorithm, algorithmic execution, foreign exchange markets, 590–591
Filter rules, technical analysis, 353–355
Financial development, exchange rate regime selection and, 777–779
Financial globalization, exchange rates and impact of, 63–64
Financial institutions
liquidity needs of, 12–13
swap trading of foreign exchanges, 626–630
Financial integration, exchange rate regimes, 138–144
Fiscal policy, interventions and, reserve accumulation, 720–723
Fisher relation, monetary exchange models, 48–49
Fixed exchange rates
in colonial-era United States, 169–170
in interwar period, 177–180
laissez-faire performance and, 138–139
options in FX and, 646–647
regimes based on, 766–779
advantages of, 766–768
Fixed income, options in FX, volatility as asset class, 664–672
Flexible exchange rates
floating exchange rate regime, 765, 773–779
laissez-faire performance and, 138–139
market discipline, 139–140
Flexible price monetary model, 46–49
long-horizon predictions, 52–54
quantitative results, 60
Floating exchange rates
in colonial-era United States, 169–170
options in FX and, 646–647
purchasing power parity and, 171–172, 173–175
regimes based on, 765, 773–779
Forecast error, depreciation decomposition, 75–77
Forecasting power
active currency management models, 427–428
exchange rate analysis, economic evaluation, 249–256
micro-based macromodel, future macroconditions, 102–105
panel data exchange rate determination, 267–268
pooled panel-data regression *vs.* time-series regression, 265–278
portfolio shifts currency trading model, order flows, 92–95
purchasing power parity testing, 165–166
Theil's U-Statistic, data illustration using, 275–278
Foreign currency unit (FCU), carry trades, 285–286
Foreign exchange markets. *See also* Forwards and Futures foreign exchange markets
algorithmic execution in, 583–594
dynamic algorithms, 593
effective execution strategies, 593
equity market derivation, 584
future research issues, 594
iceberg, 590–591
intelligence, 588–589
internalization strategies, 592
market structure and, 585–587
opportunistic, 590–591
participators, 592
performance measurement, 594
smart order routing, 587–588
speed, 589
sweepers, 590–591
time slicers, 590–591
asymmetric information and, 19–20
basics and size parameters, 623–626
behavioral model, 122–127
beta in, 453–463
crisis management in, 697–712
cross-currency swaps, 629–633

Foreign exchange markets (*continued*)
currency trading geography and composition, 4–7
derivatives, 621–622
current and future trends, 641
electronic trading revolution in, 21–22
financial crises dislocations, 635–637
financial globalization impact on, 63–64
global financial crisis of 2007, 637–640
hedging practices in, 13–14
history of, 135–138
instruments traded on, 9
interventions in, 715–745
liquidity in, 12–15
macroeconomic approaches to, 44–65
microeconomic approaches to, 73–107
multibank trading platforms for, 35–38
outstanding amounts, 633–635
players and information in, 11–13
reaction functions, 60–63
regulation of, 9–11
reserve management, 543–557
accumulation and holding costs, 549–550
central bank assets, 547–548
constraints, 548–549
diversification, 549
dollar as international reserve currency, 552–555
external managers, 549
future issues, 557
historical perspective, 546–547
objectives, 545
replacement of dollar as international reserve currency, 555–556
reserve sources, 544–545
reserve uses, 543–544
size and diversification challenges, 549–552
techniques, 545–546
size parameters, 623–626, 633–635
spot-rate dynamics, 74–80
structure of, 3–4
swap trading in, 9, 626–629
technical analysis, 343–368
trading volumes, 4–6
turnover in, 635
Foreign exchange rate
behavioral finance framework, prototype development, 122–127
misalignment of, Chinese renminbi case study, 749–760
Foreign exchange rates, future modeling trends for, 60–64
Foreign government bonds, currency hedging, 507–511
Forward discounts
carry trades, 284–285
currency sorting, 300–301
incomplete information, basic monetary model, 379
incomplete information, exchange rate modeling, infrequent decision making, 386–388
Forward premium exchange rate puzzle, 221–224
emergence of, 599–600
incomplete information, exchange rate modeling, infrequent decision making, 385–388
stochastic discount factor, 391–392
Forwards in foreign exchange markets
basic principles and size parameters, 623–626
currency hedging, 524–531
error tracking, 531–536
market size and, 633–635
options in FX and, 655–656
outright forwards, 623–626
turnover, 635
Forward volatility agreements (FVAs), options in FX
buy-side perspective, 687, 689
role of, 655
volatility models, 658–681
Fourier transform, scale of market quakes methodology, 574–575
Fractal price curves, scaling laws and, 566–571
Fractional integration, purchasing power parity, 167
France, fixed exchange rates in, 179–180
Fréchet-type distribution, fat-tailed distributed exchange rate returns, behavioral finance framework, 119–122

Free on board (FOB), law of one price and, 195–198
Front running, trade regulation and, 10
Fundamental disequilibrium
exchange rate rules and, 146–148
history of exchange rates, 137–138
Fundamental equilibrium exchange rate (FEER)
fair value currency, underlying balance approach, 320–324
misalignment of exchange rates, renminbi case study, 750–760
under and overvaluation, 752–755
Fundamentalist rule, foreign exchange market behavioral prototype, 123–127
Fundamentals approach to crisis management, 698
Fundamental shocks, incomplete information, exchange rate modeling, basic monetary model, 377–379
Fundamental trading, trading rule profits and, 364–365
Funded programs, active currency management, 474–475
Fund of funds, active currency management, manager grouping, 494–495
Future macroconditions, micro-based macromodel, order flows and, 102–105
Futures market in foreign exchange, 9n.6, 40
basic principles and size parameters, 623–633
market size and, 633–635
outright futures, 623–626
turnover, 635
FXall multibank system, 25–29
FX Connect, launching of, 24–25
FX futures, 9, 40
"FXFX" page, electronic trading and, 23–24
*FX MarketSpace,* 35
FX swap-implied dollar rate, 627–628
FX Trader System, 26

G5 countries, law of one price and purchasing power parity in, 203
G20 countries
global inflation targeting, 152–153
macroeconomic policies and, 150
Gamma of an option, options in FX
Black-Scholes formula, 648–653
Black Swan strategies and, 677–681
GARCH models. *See* Univariate modeling
Gaussian random walk (GRW) model, scaling laws, high frequency trading, 567–571
coastline modeling, 571–572
General equilibrium model, real exchange rate, 54–60
Generalized method of moments (GMM), carry trades
cross-sectional analysis, currency factors, 304–307
linear factor models, sorted currency and stock market portfolios, 307–308
monthly return models, 293–296
quarterly return models, 295–299
returns pricing, 291–293
General price index, purchasing power parity and, 55–56
General-to-specific modeling, purchasing power parity, cointegration and, 168
Genetic programming, technical analysis, temporal variations, 359
Genoa International Monetary Conference of 1922, 150–151
Geometric index, purchasing power parity in, price indices and law of one price, 192–193
Global carry trades
options in FX and, 646–647
strategy-based foreign exchange management, 610–611
Global custodian banks, foreign exchange market and, 17–18
Global distribution of currency trading, trends in, 5–6
Global financial crisis of 2007–2009
cross-currency swap dislocations and, 637–640
imbalances caused by, 143–144
Global imbalance
balance of payments rules and, 148–149
exchange rate regimes, 134–135

Global imbalance (*continued*)
financial crisis of 2007–2009, 143–144
macroeconomic policy and, 149–150
Global inflation targeting, proposals for, 151–153
Globalization
laissez-faire exchange rate performance and, 139
official interventions and, 715–719
Global liquidity, post-Bretton Woods exchange rate regimes and, 134–135
Goldman Sachs dynamic equilibrium exchange rate model (GSDEER), fair value currency, 319–320
Gold sales, foreign exchange reserves, 547
Gold standard
floating exchange rates and PPP and, 171–172
history of, 135–138
interwar fixed exchange rates and, 177–180
managed floating rate vs, 175
post-Bretton Woods exchange rate regimes and, 133–135
purchasing power parity and, 172
U. S. return to, 177
Gourinchas-Rey model, 63–64
Government payments
currency crisis management, sterilization and interest rate defense, 708–709
foreign exchange reserves, 544, 548
Granger causality
bullionist periods and, 170–171
purchasing power parity, 166
reaction functions, exchange-rate modeling, 61–63
Great Depression, exchange rate regimes and, 136
Greenback period (United States)
floating exchange rates and PPP in, 171–172
real exchange rates during, 177
Greenspan-Giudotti rule, interventions, 721–723
Gresham's law, currency regime history and, 135–138
Gross domestic product (GDP)
currency trends and, 142–143
foreign exchange turnover and, 4–6
purchasing power parity, 55–56
deflator, 168–169, 208–213
Gross national product deflator
purchasing power parity and, 168–169
return to gold standard and, 178–180
Guaranteed return on investment notes, options in FX, buy-side perspective, 683
Guatemala, purchasing power parity in, 176
Guidelines to Floating, exchange rate rules and, 147–148
Gumbel distribution, fat-tailed distributed exchange rate returns, 120–122

Habit preferences, stochastic discount factor, exchange rate models, 407–411
intuition, 407–408
model for, 408–409
uncovered interest rate parity puzzle, 409–411
Half-life estimation, law of one price and, barriers to arbitrage and nonlinearities, 196–198
Hard currencies, hedging of currency exposure, 503
Hard pegs
exchange rate regimes and, 142
fixed *vs.* floating exchange rate regimes, 775–779
Harrod-Balassa-Samuelson effect
fair value currency models, 315–316
purchasing power parity
price indices and law of one price, 193
transitory and structural disparities, 204–205
Head-and-shoulders pattern, technical analysis, 346–350, 354–355
Hedge funds
active currency management, 452
arbitrage pricing theory, 477–478
currency mandates, 473–475
DBS Select Platform managers, 494–495
liquidity needs of, 12–13
Hedge ratios
constant hedge ratio, 531–536

currency hedging
equity exposures, 519–523
forwards *vs.* options, 531
Hedging of currency exposure
active currency management, 470–471
cross-currency swaps, 632–633
empirical models, 502–503
international bond and equity markets, 501–541
options in FX
Black-Scholes formula, 649–653
illiquid assets, 691–692
return and volatility impact, 504–524
Hedging of foreign exchanges, 13–14
Herstatt risk, electronic trading and, 24
Heston models, options in FX, volatility modeling, 661–681
Heterogeneous agents
incomplete information, exchange rate modeling, 379–381
stochastic discount factor, exchange rates, common component and heterogeneous loadings, 403–404
Heuristic rules, foreign exchange market behavioral prototype, 122–127
High frequency arbitrage, algorithmic execution, 584
High frequency data, analysis of, 561–563
High frequency traders
electronic trading and, 33
liquidity in market and, 15
multibank trading platforms, 37–38
scaling laws modeling, 561–580
basic laws, 565–566
coastline trader, 571–572, 576–578
intrinsic time framework, 563–565
monthly statistics, 578–579
new laws, 566–571
scale of market quakes, 572–575
trading models, 575–578
technical analysis, temporal variations, 359
High yield corporate bonds, currency hedging, 511–516
Hill estimator, foreign exchange market behavioral prototype, 127
Historical analysis
options in FX, volatility modeling, 672–674
purchasing power parity, 161–181
Holding costs, foreign exchange reserves, 549–550
Hollowing out hypothesis
currency trading, 141–143
testing of, 154–156
Home bias, exchange rate regimes, 771–772
Homo economicus hypothesis, mainstream exchange rate models, 112
Hooper-Morton real exchange rate model, 51–52
Horizon/frequency approach, fair value currency model implementation, 329–331
Hot-potato trading
inventory half-life and, 17
in telephone era, 22
Hotspot FX, 25

Iceberg algorithm, algorithmic execution, foreign exchange markets, 590–591
Iceberg transport costs, law of one price and, 196–198
Illiquid assets, options in FX, currency hedging of, 691–692
Implied distribution, options in FX, buy-side perspective, 683–687
Implied moments, options in FX, volatility modeling, 662–664
Implied volatility market, options in FX
historic volatility *vs.,* 672–674
volatility as asset class, 666–672
Imports
corporate customers, 20
foreign exchanges and, 3–5
Impulse response functions, law of one price and purchasing power parity, 202–203
Incomplete information, exchange rate modeling and, 375–388
basic monetary model, 376–379
future research issues, 388
information heterogeneity, 379–381
infrequent decision making, 385–388
uncertainty, 381–384
Index-based products, strategy-based foreign exchange management, 611–617

Indicator methods, technical analysis, 346–350
Indirect fair value (IFV), fair value currency models, 325–328
Individual managers, active currency management, currency returns, 483–491
Inflation
  depreciation rate decomposition, 74–75
  excess returns and macroinformation, 101–102
  exchange rate analysis, present value model, 222–223
  exchange rate regime selection and, 778–779
  in fixed rate exchange regimes, 766–768
  foreign exchanges and, 3–4
  global nominal anchor proposal, 151–153
  macro/microperspectives, 77–78
  misalignment of exchange rates, renminbi case study, 749–760
  order flows and future macroconditions, 102–105
Inflationary bias, in fixed rate exchange regimes, 766–768
Inflation gaps, exchange-rate modeling, 61–62
Information
  exchange rate modeling, incomplete information, 375–388
  in foreign exchange markets, 11–12
  heterogeneity, exchange rate modeling, 379–381
Information ratio, active currency management, 491–493
Infrequent decision making, exchange rate modeling, 385–388
Initiators of trade, spot-rate dynamics, 80, 94
In-sample testing
  active currency management, volatility and correlation evaluation, 434–440
  technical testing, 356–357
Institutional investors, foreign exchange trade costs and, 18
Insurance brokers, options in FX options, 655
Insurance suppliers, options in FX options, 654–655
Integrated variables, nominal exchange models, 52–54
Intelligence, algorithmic execution, foreign exchange markets, 588–589
Interbank markets, currency-trading models, 80–95
  portfolio shifts model, 82–88
Intercontinental Exchange, 625
Interdealer spot trading
  electronic trading and, 22–29
  example of, 8n.2
  in foreign exchange market, 15–17
  portfolio shifts currency-trading model
    data releases, 83–88
    order flows and foreign exchange returns, 88–91
  in telephone era, 22
Interest differential, monetary exchange models, 48–49
Interest rates
  currency crisis management and defense of, 707–709
  development of parity, 53–54
  parity
    exchange rate analysis, 222–227
    technical trading returns, risk analysis, 360–361
  risk premium and order flow and, 64–65
  stochastic discount factor, exchange rate analysis, 395–396
Intermarket technical analysis, defined, 350
Internalization
  algorithmic execution, foreign exchange markets, 592
  electronic trading, 30–31
International bond market, currency hedging, 501–541
International capital flow, in fixed rate exchange regimes, 767–768
International Monetary Fund (IMF)
  Bretton Woods system and, 137–138
  Consultative Group on Exchange Rate issues
    fair value currency models, 317–319, 322–324
    Guidelines to Floating, 147–148

laissez-faire exchange rate performance and, 138–139
macroeconomic policies and, 149–150
post-Bretton Woods exchange rate regimes and, 133–135
exchange rate regime classification, 142–143
International Monetary Market (IMM). *See also* Commitments of Traders (COT)
fair value currency models, indirect fair value, 326–328
outright forwards and futures trading and, 624–626
International monetary systems
future prospects for, 144–153
reform forecasts for, 150–151
International reserve currency, US dollar as
changing role of, 552–555
replacement of, 555–556
Intertemporal elasticity of substitution (IES), stochastic discount factor, exchange rate models, long-run risk, 412–413
Intertemporal marginal rates of substitution. *See* Stochastic discount factor (SDF)
Interventions
balance of payments rules, 148–149
economic policy coordination, 140
effectiveness, empirical evidence on, 723–744
event-study analysis, long-term effectiveness, 737–744
exchange rate regimes and, 133
foreign exchange reserves, 543–544, 551
framework for, 724–726
Guidelines to Floating and, 147–148
official interventions and reserve accumulation, 719–723
options in FX and, 659–662
overview of, 715–719
technical trading profits, 361–363
time-series analysis, 726–737
caveats concerning, 734–737
channels of effectiveness, 729–734
Interwar period
fixed exchange rates in, 177–180
gold standard during, 172
purchasing power parity and, 173–176
In-the-money options, options in FX and, 652–653
Intraday trading
multibank platforms, 37–38
technical analysis, 353–355
Intratime information, tick analysis, 561–563
Intrinsic time framework, high frequency finance, scaling models, 563–565
Intuition, stochastic discount factor, exchange rate models, habit preferences, 407–408
Inventory half-life, interdealer trading and, 17
Inverse cubic power law, fat-tailed distributed exchange rate returns, 120–122
Investible foreign exchange indices, strategy-based foreign exchange products and, 604–618
Investor confidence, foreign exchange reserves, 544
Investor preferences, stochastic discount factor, exchange rate models, habit preferences, 409–411

Jamaica Agreement, 138
Japanese financial system, cross-currency swap dislocations and financial crisis in, 635–637
"Japan premium," cross-currency swap dislocations and, 636–637
Jumps
options in FX, volatility models, 659–681
volatility clustering, 118–119
Just noticeable difference principle, foreign exchange market behavioral prototype, 125–127

Kalman filtering, exchange rate model uncertainty, 383–384
Key currency competition, exchange rate regimes and, 144–145
Keynesian economics
global inflation targeting, 152–153
purchasing power parity and, 174–175
return to gold standard and, 178–180

Knightian uncertainty, technical trading returns, risk analysis, 361
Knock-in option, options in FX, 688
Knock-out options, options in FX, 686–688
Krugman-Flood-Garber (KFG) model, Crisis management in foreign exchange markets
  attack-conditional monetary policy, 704–705
  basic principles, 699–704
  devaluation, 705–707
  extensions, 704–710
  lender of last resort, 709–710
  sterilization and interest rate defense, 707–709
Kurtosis, options in FX pricing, 658

Labor mobility, exchange rate regime selection and, 777–779
Labor productivity, Balassa-Samuelson model, 56–58
Laissez-faire monetary system
  economic policy coordination, 140
  emerging market integration into global economy, 140–141
  exchange rate performance, 1973–2010 and, 138–139
  global imbalances and financial crises of 2007–2009, 143–144
  market discipline, 139–140
  post-Bretton Woods exchange rate regimes and, 133–135
  regional blocs and, 145
Latin Monetary Union, 136–138, 150–151
Law of one price (LOP)
  aggregation bias and micro price studies, 199–200
  barriers to arbitrage and nonlinearities, 195–198
  border effect, 194–195
  early tests of, 194
  options in FX and, 648–649
  purchasing power parity in traded goods and, 189–215
    aggregation of data from, 205–213
    empirical evidence of, 194–200
    price indices and, 190–193
    transitory and structural disparities, 203–205
  stochastic discount factor, exchange rate analysis, 393–394
Learning process, incomplete information, exchange rate modeling, monetary models, 376–379
Legitimized returns, foreign exchange reserves, 547
Lehman Brothers bankruptcy, 9
  active currency management, 453–454
  cross-currency swap dislocations and, 637–640
  foreign exchange futures, forwards, and swaps and, 633–635
Lender of last resort
  currency crisis management, 709–710
  floating exchange rate regimes and, 774–779
Leverage
  active currency management, 473–475
  options in FX
    Black Swan strategies and, 676–681
    buy-side perspective, 681–683
    exotic instruments, 686–687
    volatility modeling, 662–681
Leveraged institutional investors, liquidity needs of, 12–13
Levy-Khintchine representation, options in FX, volatility models, 661–681
Limit-order book
  electronic trading and, 25–29
  liquidity supply information, 16
Linear factor models, carry trades, 295–298
Liquidity
  aggregators, electronic trading and, 35
  algorithmic execution, foreign exchange markets, 588–589
  asymmetric information of corporate customers and, 20
  coastline of price curves and, 562–563
  currency crisis management and, 710–711
  end-customers for, 12–15
  foreign exchange reserves, 544–545, 551
  options in FX and, 655–656
  sources of, 15–18
  strategy-based foreign exchange management, 611, 613–618
  swap trading of foreign exchanges and, 628

Liquidity squeeze, options in FX, Black-Scholes formula, 649–653
Log-linearized budget constraints, financial globalization and, 63–64
Log spot exchange rate, depreciation decomposition, 74–77
Log-wealth-consumption ratio, stochastic discount factor, exchange rate models, long-run risk, 412–413
London foreign exchange market
  dominance of, 5–6
  high frequency trading, 33
  prime brokerage executions, 32
Long-dated options, options in FX
  Black-Scholes formula, 649–653
  Black Swan strategies and, 681
  buy-side perspective, 687, 689
Long-horizon prediction, nominal exchange models, 52–54
Long-run risk, stochastic discount factor, exchange rate models, 411–413
Long sample technique, stochastic discount factor, currency excess returns, 399–403
Louvre Accord, 140
Lucas two-good model, real exchange rate, 59–60

Macrodata releases
  micro-based macromodel, excess returns and, 100–105
  portfolio shifts currency-trading model
    absence of, 84–88
    order flows and, 91–92
Macroeconomic approaches
  fair value currency models, macroeconomic balance approach, 323–324
  foreign exchange determination, 44–65
  managed international monetary systems, 149–150
  micro-based macromodel, 95–100
  spot-rate dynamics, 77–80
Mainstream exchange rate models, behavioral finance framework, 111–112
Managed floating rate, 139, 142, 147–148
  purchasing power parity and, 175
Managed international monetary systems
  balance of payments rules, 148–149
  exchange rate rules, 146–148
  macroeconomic policies and, 149–150
  trend toward, 146–150
Manager selection, active currency management
  currency returns, 483–491
  DB FX Select platform, 494–495
  fund of funds grouping, 494–495
Manipulation of markets, foreign exchanges and, 10
Margin accounts, retail aggregator liquidity and, 18
Market concentration, electronic trading and, 29
Market discipline, exchange rate regimes and, 139–140
Market efficiency
  active currency management, 456–458
  technical analysis and myth of, 351, 365–369
Market fundamentals, Krugman-Flood-Garber model of crisis management, 700–704
Market liquidity, geographic and time factors in, 5–6
Market makers
  asymmetric information and exchange rate determination, 19–20
  concentration in, 4
  foreign exchange markets, 11
  interdealer trading, 16
  options in FX, volatility as asset class, 667–672
Market-making banks, foreign exchange market structure, algorithmic execution, 586–587
Market price of risk, stochastic discount factor, exchange rate analysis, 401–403
Market psychology, philosophy of technical analysis, 345
Market quakes. *See* Scale of market quakes (SMQ)
Market segmentation, carry trades, 284–285
  cross-sectional analysis, currency factors, 307

Market size, foreign exchange futures, forwards, and swaps and, 633–635
Market structure, electronic trading and, 21–22
Markov-chain model, hollowing out hypothesis testing, 154–156
Markov chain Monte Carlo (MCMC) algorithm, active currency management, estimation and forecasting, 427–428
Markov process, exchange rate model uncertainty, 382–384
Markov-switching regimes, currency trends and, 142–143
Martingale, carry trades, returns pricing, 290–291
Maximum expected return, exchange rate analysis, mean variance dynamic asset allocation, 232–236
Maximum expected utility, exchange rate analysis, mean variance dynamic asset allocation, 232–236
Mean reversion, options in FX, volatility as asset class, 667–672
Mean-reverting heuristics
  active currency management, beta factors in, 456–457
  foreign exchange market behavioral prototype, 122–127
  law of one price and purchasing power parity, 202–203
  purchasing power parity, nonstationarity and, 166–167
Mean squared error (MSE), exchange rate analysis, 223–224
  predictive ability, 229–231
Mean-square prediction errors (MSPE)
  asymptotic pooled regression models, out-of-sample prediction, 272
  Monte Carlo simulation, 272–275
Mean variance, exchange rate analysis, dynamic asset allocation, 231–236
Mechanical methods, technical analysis, 346–350
Medieval period, purchasing power parity in, 164
Medium-run fair value, fair value currency model implementation, horizon/frequency approach, 330–331
Meese-Rogoff puzzle, incomplete information, exchange rate modeling, basic monetary model, 378–379
Metallic standards, purchasing power parity and, 172
Micro-based macromodel
  equilibrium conditions, 98–100
  future macroconditions and, 102–103
  overview, 95–98
  risk premium macrodrivers, 103–105
Microeconomic approaches, foreign exchange markets, 73–107
  currency-trading models, 80–95
  exchange rates, order flows and macroeconomy, 95–105
    empirical implications, 100–103
    micro-based macromodel, 95–100
  spot-rate dynamics, 77–80
Micro price studies, law of one price and, 199–200
Microstructure research
  exchange rates, order flows and macroeconomy, 95–96
  foreign exchange markets, 11–13, 74
    algorithmic execution, 585–587
  intervention effectiveness analysis, 737–744
Minimum volatility rule, exchange rate analysis, mean variance dynamic asset allocation, 232–236
Misalignment of exchange rates
  Chinese renminbi case study, 749–760
  floating exchange rate regimes and, 774–779
Model uncertainty
  active currency management, 431–432
  exchange rate modeling, incomplete information, 381–384
Momentum trading
  forward exchange rate puzzle emergence and, 599–600
  strategy-based foreign exchange products and, 605–611
  trading rule profits and, 364–365
Monetarist model, 48
  bullionist periods and, 170–171
  purchasing power parity, 162–163
Monetary authorities, interventions by, 724–726
  time-series analysis of, 726–737
Monetary exchange rate model, 46–49

incomplete information, basic model and, 376–379
predictive regressions, 227–228
present value model, 225–226
Monetary policy
attack-conditional monetary policy, 704–705
crisis management in currency markets, 697–712
cross-currency swap dislocation, global financial crisis and, 639–640
depreciation rate decomposition, 75–76
exchange rate regime selection and, 777–779
foreign exchange reserves and execution of, 544
interventions, effectiveness assessment, 723–744
micro-based macromodel, 96–105
Money-demand parameters, monetary exchange models, 47–49
Money demand shocks, exchange rate model uncertainty, 383–384
Money supply, nominal exchange rate, 47–48
Monte Carlo simulation
law of one price and purchasing power parity, 200–203
options in FX, correlation swap, 669–672
time-series analysis, 272–275
Monthly return models
carry trade risk factors, 293–295
coastline trading model, 578–579
Moving average convergence/divergence
technical analysis, 348–350
temporal variations, trading rule returns, 357–359
MSCI World equities
currency hedging, 516–523
strategy-based foreign exchange management, 613–614
Multibank trading (MBT) systems
electronic trading and, 24–29
foreign exchange platforms, survey of, 35–38
Multilateral netting, electronic trading and, 24
Multilateral resistance term, exchange rate regime analysis, 770
Multivariate linear regression (MLR) model, active currency management, 425
Multivariate models, active currency management, 425–427
Mundell-Fleming exchange rate model, 46
monetary exchange model comparison, 47–49
Mutual assessment process (MAP), macroeconomic policies and, 150

Natural real exchange rate (NATREX), fair value currency models, 325
Neckline patterns, technical trading, 346–350
Negative hedge cash flows, currency hedging, 531
Net foreign assets (NFAs), fair value currency models, 316–320
external sustainability approach, 324–325
underlying balance approach, 320–324
Net present value, fair value currency models, external sustainability approach, 324–325
Netting. *See* Multilateral netting
New International Macroeconomics, foreign exchange rate models, 45–46
News model of FX rates, behavioral finance framework, unit root principle, 117–118
New York Board of Trade, 625
New York foreign exchange market, dominance of, 5–6, 38
Nominal exchange rates, 46–54
anchor rate in, 766–768
empirical evidence for, 51–54
fair value currency models, real exchange rates *vs.*, 333, 336–337
global nominal anchor, 151–152
monetary model, 46–49
portfolio balance models, 49–51
present value model, 224–226
Nominal interest rates, stochastic discount factor, exchange rates, 403–404
Nondeliverable forwards (NDFs), basic principles, 623–626

Nonfinancial institutions, strategy-based foreign exchange products and, 602–604
Nonlinear dynamics
behavioral finance framework
agent-based models, 113–114
volatility clustering, 118–119
law of one price and, 195–198
Nonrelease of data, portfolio shifts currency trading model, 80–84
Nonstationarity, purchasing power parity, 166–167
Nontradable goods, law of one price and, 198–199
Numeraire, exchange rate analysis, economic evaluation, 251–256

OECD purchasing power parity, data analysis from, 210–213
On-balance volume, philosophy of technical analysis, 345
One-touch option, options in FX, 688
Operational risk, reduction of, 4, 23–25
Opportunistic algorithm, algorithmic execution, foreign exchange markets, 590–591
Opportunity costs, foreign exchange reserves, 550
Optimal FX orders and quotes, 83–86
Optimal portfolio choice, active currency management, 421–422
CRRA utility, 428–429
performance measures, 429–430
Optimum currency areas, fixed *vs.* floating exchange rate regimes, 776–779
Option relocation, options in FX, Black Swan strategies and, 677–681
Options in FX, 9, 40
buy-side perspective on, 645–646
Black Swan funds, 690–691
currency hedging, illiquid assets, 691–693
implied distribution, 683–687
long-dated *vs.* short-dated options, 687–690
strike *vs.* leverage, 681–683
currency hedging, currency forwards *vs.*, 524–531
history, 646–647
market for, 653–658
properties of, 647–653
strategy-based foreign exchange products, 617–618
volatility in, 658–681
anti-Black Swan strategies, 672–674
asset class properties, 664–672
Black Swan strategies, 674–681
model overview, 658–662
stylized facts and implied moments, 662–664
Oral interventions
effectiveness of, 724–725
event-study analysis of, 737–744
time-series analysis of, 726–737
Order flow, foreign currency
asymmetric information in foreign exchange trading and, 19–20
incomplete information, exchange rate modeling, 376–379
model uncertainty, 381–384
micro-based macromodel, 95–100
current macroconditions and, 100–105
portfolio shifts currency trading model, 85–88
forecasting powers for, 92–95
foreign exchange returns and, 88–91
macrodata releases, 91–92
price impacts, 87–88
risk premiums and, 64–65
spot-rate dynamics, macro and microeconomic perspectives, 80
technical trading and, 366–367
Order of integration, purchasing power parity, 166–167
Ordinary least squares techniques
carry trades, returns pricing, 291–293
exchange rate analysis, predictive ability, 229–231
"Other financial institutions," strategy-based foreign exchange products and, 602–605
Out-of-sample simulations (OOS)
active currency management, volatility and correlation evaluation, 438–440
asymptotic pooled regression models, 271–272
exchange rate analysis, 223–224

combined forecasts, 236
economic evaluation, 233–234
predictive ability, 228–231, 244–246
nominal exchange models, 51–54
pooled panel-data regression *vs.* time-series regression, 265–278
reaction functions, exchange-rate modeling, 60–63
technical testing, 356–357
Output gaps
depreciation rate decomposition, 75–76
exchange rate analysis, present value model, 222–223
exchange-rate modeling, 61–62
macro/microperspectives, 77–78
order flows and macroconditions, 102–103
Outright forwards in foreign exchange
basic principles and size parameters, 623–626
swap trading of foreign exchanges and, 628–629
Outright futures in forward exchange, 623–626
Overshooting
coastline trading model, 576–578
empirical models, 51–52
macro approaches to foreign exchange determination, 48
misalignment of currency, renminbi case study, 751–760
scale of market quakes methodology, 572–575
scaling law of, 562–563
intrinsic time framework, 563–565
total-move segments, 570–571
Over-the-counter (OTC) markets
central counterparties and, 35
dealers in, 11–12
foreign exchange derivatives and, 635
interdealer trading and, 16
outright forwards and futures in, 623–626
in telephone era, 22
Overvaluation, misalignment of currency, renminbi case study, 752–760

Pairwise correlation, active currency management, 427
Panel methods
exchange rate determination studies, 267–268
fair value currency analysis, 337
foreign exchange models, 53–58
Paper standards
in colonial-era United States, 169–170
floating exchange rates and, 171–172, 173–175
metallic standards and, 172
in premodern economies, 163–165
in Sweden, 170–171
Pareto law, fat-tailed distributed exchange rate returns, behavioral finance framework, 119–122
Paris Conference of 1867, 150–151
Parsimonious volatility models, options in FX, 662–681
Partial equilibrium models, early research, 74
Participator algorithm, algorithmic execution, foreign exchange markets, 592
Passive currency management, 471–472
Path premium, options in FX, volatility as asset class, 666–672
Pattern recognition, technical analysis, 353–355
Pegged exchange rates
in fixed rate exchange regimes, 766–768
floating exchange rate regimes and, 774–779
global imbalances and, 143–144
global nominal anchor, 151–152
history of, 133–134, 136–139, 141–142
misalignment of currency, renminbi case study, 750–760
options in FX, 671–672
Penn effect
fair value currency models, 315–316
misalignment of exchange rates, renminbi case study, 755–757
Pension allocations, strategy-based foreign exchange management, 611, 613
Performance measurements
active currency management
currency mandates, 473–475

Performance measurements (*continued*)
volatility and correlation timing, 429–430
algorithmic execution, foreign exchange markets, 594
exchange rate analysis, 232–234
intervention effectiveness, 723–744
Period-by-period basis
depreciation decomposition, 75–77
purchasing power parity and, 56
Permanent equilibrium exchange rate (PEER) model, fair value currency, 317
Persistence of returns, active currency management, 471, 491
Peso event risk, carry trades, 310–311
Pip exchanges, currency trading and, 8n.4
Plan sponsors, active currency management, 471, 474–475
Plaza Agreement, 140
active currency management, 460
interventions and, 715
Point process, tick data analysis, 561–563
Policy-determined interest rates, depreciation decomposition, 76–77
Pooled regression models
asymptotic consequences, 268–272
out-of-sample prediction, 271–272
predictive regression, 268–270
Monte Carlo simulation, 272–275
overview of, 265–267
Theil's U-Statistic, forecasting accuracy, 275–278
Population dynamics of traders, foreign exchange market behavioral prototype, 124–127
Portable alpha, active currency management, 470
Portals, algorithmic execution, foreign exchange markets, 587, 593
Portfolio balance exchange model, 49–51
empirical evidence, 51–54
intervention channels, 724–726
Portfolio factors, carry trades, sorting of, 300–302
Portfolio shifts (PS) currency-trading model, 81–88
daily timing in, 81–82
equilibrium conditions, 83–88
order flows and returns, 88–91
Positioning in markets, intervention effectiveness and, 734–737
Power utility model
FX determination, 60–62
stochastic discount factor, exchange rate analysis, 398, 402, 412–413
Prais-Winsten method, misalignment of exchange rates, renminbi case study, 757–760
Predictive regressions
asymptotic pooled regression models, 268–270
exchange rate analysis, 226–228
economic evaluation, 231–236
empirical models, 242–246
statistical methods, 228–231
Premium return measurement, exchange rate analysis, 233–234
Premodern economies
exchange rates in, 135–138
purchasing power parity, 163–165
Present value model, exchange rate analysis, 224–226
Price discovery process
asymmetric information and, 19–20
currency returns, 11–12
Price-impact of order flow, portfolio shifts currency trading model, 87–88
Price indices
global nominal anchors and, 151–153
purchasing power parity and, 55–56, 177
law of one price, 190–193
Price latency arbitrage, 15, 33
Pricing kernels. *See* Stochastic discount factor (SDF)
Pricing variables
cross-currency swaps, 631–632
options in FX and, 656–658
philosophy of technical analysis, 345
purchasing power parity computations, 168–169
swap trading of foreign exchanges, 627–628
Prime brokerage (PB)
active currency management, 475, 494
algorithmic execution, 586–587
electronic trading, 31–32
electronic trading and, 24

Principal component analysis (PCA), options in FX, volatility modeling, 671–672
Private information, cognitive bias in technical trading and, 364–366
Productivity-based models
  Balassa-Samuelson model, 56–58
  development of, 49, 53–54
  price variables, 56
Proprietary trading
  algorithmic execution, 584
  strategy-based foreign exchange products and, 600
Prototype behavioral model, foreign exchange market, 122–127
Proxies, active currency management, 481–482, 492, 495–497
Publication bias, technical analysis, 355–357
Public information, cognitive bias in technical trading and, 364–366
Public interest institutions, foreign exchange reserves, 548–549
Purchasing power parity (PPP)
  active currency management, value-based strategies, 458–459
  in ancient period, 163–164
  in bullionist periods, 170–171
  causality, 165–166
  in colonial-era United States, 169–170
  comparative-static computation, 165
  economic history of, 161–181
  exchange rate analysis, predictive regressions, 227
  exchange rate dynamics, empirical models, 237–244
  fair value currency models, 315–316
    capital enhanced equilibrium exchange rate (CHEER) model, 317
  floating exchange rates and, 171–172, 173–175
  foreign exchange market behavioral prototype, 125–127
  in Guatemala, 176
  intervention effectiveness and, 742–744
  interwar period, 173–176
  in interwar period, 177–180
  Krugman-Flood-Garber model of crisis management, 700–704
  law of one price and, 189–215
    aggregation bias and micro price studies, 199–200
    aggregation of data from, 205–213
    price indices and, 190–193
    transitory and structural disparities, 203–205
  managed floating rate and, 175
  in medieval period, 164
  metallic standards and, 172
  misalignment of exchange rates, renminbi case study
    data revision, 757–760
    Penn effect regression, 755–757
  modern period testing of, 169–176
  monetary exchange models, 46–49, 52–54
  nonstationarity and spurious regression, 166–167
  premodern application of, 163–165
  price variable computations, 168–169
  reaction functions, exchange-rate modeling, 61–63
  real models of real exchange rate, 54–60
  regression analysis, 165
  return to gold standard and, 177–180
  Salamanca school and origins of, 165
  in Spain, 176
  testing techniques, 165–168
  Theil's U-Statistic, forecasting accuracy, 275–278
  theories of, 162–163
  in tradable goods, 189–215
  World War I period, 172–173
"Push-pull" metaphor, asymmetric information of corporate customers and, 20
Put option, options in FX and, 649
*py* variable, real exchange rates, 60n.22

Quarterly return models, carry trades, 295, 297–298
Quasi-purchasing power parity, metallic standards and, 172
Quotes, liquidity supply information, 16

Random walk models
  active currency management, 422–423, 425

Random walk models (*continued*)
behavioral finance framework, unit root principle, 116–118
evolution of foreign exchange markets and, 598–599
exchange rate analysis
performance measurements, 233–234
predictive ability, 228–231
predictive regressions, 227
incomplete information, basic monetary model, 378–379
long-horizon predictions, 52–54
Monte Carlo simulation, 273–275
options in FX, volatility modeling, 661–681
uncertainty in, 383–384
Range option, options in FX, 688
Rare events, carry trades, time-varying risk, 308–311
Rate of change (ROC), technical analysis, 348–350
Rational expectations, depreciation decomposition and revision of, 76–77
Rational expectations (RE) paradigm
behavioral finance framework, foreign exchange market prototype, 122–127
mainstream exchange rate models, 111–112
Reaction functions, exchange-rate modeling, 60–63
Real business cycle (RBC) model, stochastic discount factor, disaster risk, 417
Real effective exchange rate (REER) model, fair value currency, 318–319
underlying balance approach, 320–324
Real exchange rate
in colonial-era United States, 169–170, 177
fair value currency models, 318–319
nominal rates *vs.*, 333–335
law of one price and purchasing power parity, 200–203
metallic standards, 172
nontradable goods, 198–199
productivity-based models, Balassa-Samuelson framework, 56–58
purchasing power parity and, 54–56
law of one price and, 205–213
transitory and structural disparities, 203–205
real models of, 54–60
stochastic discount factor, 395
two-good models, 59–60
Real interest differential model, basic principles, 48–49
Reality check, technical testing, 356–357
Realized profits, foreign exchange market behavioral prototype, 124–127
Realized volatility/correlation premium, options in FX, volatility as asset class, 666–672
Real-money investors, multibank trading platforms, 37–38
Real-time prices, 4
Rebalancing, currency hedging
frequency, 530–536
summary of findings, 537–539
trigger-based *vs.* regular rebalancing, 537
Regime changes, pooled panel-data regression exchange forecasting, 266–267
Regional currencies, key currency competition and, 145
Regional monetary agreements, exchange rate regimes and, 140
Regression analysis
data illustrations, 275–278
misalignment of exchange rates, renminbi case study, Penn effect regression, 755–757
Monte Carlo study, 272–275
overview of, 265–267
panel data exchange rate determination, 267–268
pooling, asymptotic consequences, 268–272
out-of-sample prediction, 271–272
predictive regression, full sample estimation, 268–270
purchasing power parity, 165
Regulation of foreign exchange markets, 9–11

Relative price variable, purchasing power parity and, 56
Relative risk aversion (RRA)
  active currency management, volatility and correlation timing, 429
  exchange rate analysis, performance measurements, 233–234
Relative strength indicator, technical trading and, 348–350
Relative value, options in FX, volatility as asset class, 666–672
Reporting dealers, strategy-based foreign exchange products and, 601–604
Representative agent assumption, mainstream exchange rate models, 112
Request-for-quote, electronic trading and, 25–29
Reserve accumulation
  balance of payments rules and, 149
  interventions and, 719–723
Reserve adequacy measurements, interventions and, 721–723
Reserve holdings, global evolution of, 715–719
Reserve management
  currency crisis management, sterilization and interest rate defense, 707–709
  foreign exchange markets, 543–557
    accumulation and holding costs, 549–550
    central bank assets, 547–548
    constraints, 548–549
    diversification, 549
    dollar as international reserve currency, 552–555
    external managers, 549
    future issues, 557
    historical perspective, 546–547
    objectives, 545
    replacement of dollar as international reserve currency, 555–556
    reserve sources, 544–545
    reserve uses, 543–544
    size and diversification challenges, 549–552
    techniques, 545–546
Resilience, stochastic discount factor, exchange rate analysis, disaster risk, 414–415
Resistance level, technical trading and, 346–350
Resumption Act (U.S.), 177
Retail aggregators
  electronic trading and, 33–34
  as financial institutions, 12n.10
  foreign exchange market and, 18
Retail investors, liquidity needs of, 14–15
Retail-oriented platforms, multibank trading and, 37–38
Retail price index, purchasing power parity computations, 168–169
Retail trading of FX, currency-trading models, 80–95
  portfolio shifts model, 82–88
Returns on foreign exchanges
  carry trades
    measurement, 286–289
    pricing, 290–293
  currency hedging, 504–524
    equity exposures, 520–523
    foreign government bonds, 508–511
    high yield corporate bonds, 513–516
    return indices, 506–524
    summary of findings, 523–524
  portfolio shifts currency trading model, order flows and, 88–91
  technical analysis, computing signals, 351–353
Reuters D2000–1 network
  currency-trading models, 81, 91–95
  portfolio shifts currency-trading model, order flow and FX returns, 91
reversals of trends, philosophy of technical analysis and, 345
Reverse knock-out and knock-in options, options in FX, 688
Richter scale, scale of market quakes methodology, 572–575
Risk-adjusted returns
  currency hedging volatility, 523–524
  technical trading returns, 359–361
Risk analysis
  active currency management, risk appetite, 454–455

Risk analysis (*continued*)
carry trades, 283–311
returns pricing, 290–293
traditional risk factors, 293–299
Risk aversion, stochastic discount factor, exchange rate models, habit preferences, 407–411
Risk factors, carry trades, sorted portfolios, 300–302
Risk limits, central counterparties, 35
Risk premiums
carry trades, 285
currency crisis management, sterilization and interest rate defense, 708–709
depreciation decomposition and anticipated path for, 76–77
incomplete information, exchange rate modeling, 378–379
information heterogeneity, 379–381
infrequent decision making, 385–388
micro-based macromodel, 97–98
macrodrivers of, 103–105
options in FX, volatility as asset class, 664–672
order flow and, 64–65
portfolio balance exchange model, 49–51
stochastic discount factor, real exchange rates, 395–396
Risk reversal, fair value currency models, 326–328
Risk-sharing
micro-based macromodel, 97–105
portfolio shifts model, 83–87, 95
Robustness
active currency management, Barclay currency index (BCTI) models, 481–482
fair value currency models, 328–337
Rolling window betas, carry trades, time-varying risk and rare events, 309–311
Roman Empire, purchasing power parity in, 163–164
Root mean squared error (RMSE), exchange rate analysis, predictive ability, 229–231
Rose effect, bilateral trade, exchange rate regimes, 768–773
Rule of thumb, options in FX, buy-side perspective, 681–683

SABR volatility model, options in FX, 661–681
Safe havens, stochastic discount factor, exchange rate analysis, 405
Safety, foreign exchange reserves, 545
Salamanca school, purchasing power parity and, 165
Satisficers, adaptive market hypothesis, 365–366
Scale of market quakes (SMQ)
development of, 562–563
methodology of, in high frequency finance modeling, 572–575
Scaling laws, high frequency trade modeling, 561–580
basic laws, 565–566
coastline trader, 571–572, 576–578
intrinsic time framework, 563–565
monthly statistics, 578–579
new laws, 566–571
scale of market quakes, 572–575
trading applications, 575–578
Scapegoat effect, exchange rate model uncertainty, 384
Securitized products, strategy-based foreign exchange products, 617–618
Segmented markets, financial globalization and, 64
Seigniorage, floating exchange rate regimes and, 773–779
Serial correlation, misalignment of exchange rates, renminbi case study, Penn effect regression, 756–757
Settlement risk, 23–24, 31
Shadow exchange rate, Krugman-Flood-Garber model of crisis management, 700–704
Sharpe ratio
exchange rate analysis, 233–234
discounted Sharpe ratio, 236
economic evaluation, 249–256
empirical model, 246–249
stochastic discount factor, real exchange rates, 396–397
Shock-based crisis management, 697–698

Krugman-Flood-Garber model, 702–704
Shock symmetry, exchange rate regime selection and, 777–779
Short-dated options, options in FX
Black-Scholes formula, 649–653
buy-side perspective, 687, 689
Short volatility strategies, options in FX, 673–674
Signaling channels for interventions
effectiveness of, 724–726
overview of, 718–719
time-series analysis, 726–737
Silver standard, 135–136
purchasing power parity and, 172
Simple model averaging, exchange rate analysis, combined forecasts, 236
Simulated exchange rate returns, foreign exchange market behavioral prototype, 126–129
Single-bank trading (SBT) systems
electronic trading and, 24–29
white labeling in, 30
Size of foreign exchange reserves, 551–552
Skewness factor in currency returns
carry trades, 302
options in FX, expected skewness, 657–658
Slicer algorithm, algorithmic execution, foreign exchange markets, 590–591
Smart order routing (SOR), algorithmic execution, foreign exchange markets, 587–588
Smile decomposition, options in FX, volatility modeling, 661–681
Smithsonian Agreement, 137–138, 151
Smooth transition autoregressive (STAR), law of one price and purchasing power parity, 200–203
Soft pegs, 142
Sorted portfolio factors, carry trades, 300–302
Sortino ratio, exchange rate analysis, 233–234
economic evaluation, 249–256
Sovereignty issues, exchange rate regime selection and, 777–779
Sovereign wealth funds, foreign exchange reserves, 544
Spain, purchasing power parity in, 176
Special drawing right
history of, 137–138
managed international monetary system proposals and, 146–150
post-Bretton Woods exchange rate regimes and, 134–135
Speculative positioning, fair value currency models, 325–328
Speculators
crisis management in currency markets and, 698–699
options in FX options, 655
Speed, algorithmic execution, foreign exchange markets, 589
Spot exchange rates
active currency management, 422–423
derivatives foreign exchange market and, 621–625
law of one price and, 197–198
options in FX
Black-Scholes formula, 652–653
volatility models, 659–681
Spot prices, micro-based macromodel, 96–98
Spot-rate dynamics
currency-trading models, 80–95
portfolio shifts trading model, 81–88
foreign exchange markets, 74–80
depreciation rates, decomposition, 74–77
macro/microperspectives, 77–80
micro-based macromodel, 95–105
unit root principle, behavioral finance framework, 115–118
Spot trading
contract for, 9n.5
currency distribution and turnover percentage, 6–8
dominance of, 9
turnover by counterparty type, 12–13
Spurious regression, purchasing power parity, 166–167
Squared returns, behavioral finance framework, volatility clustering, 118–119
Squawk boxes, in telephone era trading, 22
Stability and Growth Pact, 140
Standard and Poor's 500 Index, active currency management, 452–453

Stationarity
floating exchange rates and, 173–175
metallic standards and, 172
purchasing power parity, 167
in colonial-era United States, 169–170
Statistical analysis, exchange rate dynamics, 221–260
predictability applications, 228–231
Sterilization
currency crisis management, 707–709
foreign exchange reserves, 549
interventions, reserve accumulation and, 720–723
Sticky price monetary model, 46–49
purchasing power parity and, 200–201
Stochastic discount factor (SDF)
carry trade pricing, 290–293
cross-sectional analysis, currency factors, 304–307
exchange rates
common component and heterogeneous loading, 403–404
complete markets, 393
cross-country correlations, 397–398
currency excess returns
annual returns and aggregate risk, 399–403
monthly returns, 403
currency risk premia, 395–396
disaster risk models, 414–417
empirical evidence, 398–407
global volatility, 405
habit preferences, 407–411
intuition, 407–408
model for, 408–409
uncovered interest rate parity puzzle, 409–411
law of one price, 393–394
long-run risk models, 411–413
maximal Sharpe ratios, 396–397
models, 407–417
non-arbitrage conditions, 393–394
predictability, 405–407
real exchange rates, 395
uncovered interest rate parity, 391–392
regressions to currency portfolios, 398–399
utility-based asset pricing, 392–393
Krugman-Flood-Garber model of crisis management, 701–704
spot-rate dynamics, 77–80
technical trading returns, risk analysis, 359–361
Stochastic shocks, foreign exchange market behavioral prototype, 126–127
Stochastic volatility inspired (SVI) model, options in FX, implied distribution, 683–687
Stochastic volatility model, options in FX, 661–681
Stock equilibrium conditions, foreign exchange rate models, 45–46
Stop-loss strategy, options in FX, Black-Scholes formula, 650–653
Straight-through processing (STP), electronic trading and, 28–29
Strategy-based foreign exchange products
alpha and beta factors, 605–611
diversification trends, 611–617
early history, 598–599
future trends, 618
investable indices, 604–605
market turnover and currency managers, 600–604
overview, 597–598
puzzle models, 599–600
strengths of, 617–618
Strike, options in FX
buy-side perspective, 681–683
strike set-date, 687
volatility as asset, 669–672
Structural disparities, purchasing power parity in traded goods and, 203–205
Stylized facts
disconnect puzzle, 114–115
incomplete information, exchange rate modeling, infrequent decision making, 386–388
interventions and, 719–723
options in FX, volatility modeling, 662–664
Subprime loan crisis, cross-currency swap dislocations and, 637–640
Super-exclusivity, purchasing power parity computations, 162–163
Superior predictive ability stepwise testing, technical analysis, 356–357
support levels, technical analysis and, 346

Surpluses, balance of payments rules and, 148–149
SVAR model, behavioral finance framework, disconnect and excess volatility puzzles, 114–115
SVJ models, options in FX, volatility modeling, 661–662
Swap trading of foreign exchanges, 9
  market size and, 633–635
  mechanisms, 626–627
  outright forwards and, 628–630
  pricing and short-term CIP, 627–628
  turnover, 635
Swedish bullionist period, purchasing power parity in, 170–171
Sweeper algorithm, algorithmic execution, foreign exchange markets, 590–591
Synthetic forward positions, swap trading of foreign exchanges and, 628–629
Systematic proprietary trading, algorithmic execution, 584

Tail decay, fat-tailed distributed exchange rate returns, 120–122
Tail risk hedging, options in FX, Black Swan strategies and, 680–681
Take-profit orders, 20
Target zones for exchange rates, proposals for, 147–148
Tariffs, purchasing power parity and, 195–196
Taylor rule fundamentals
  exchange rate analysis, 221–224, 226
    predictive regressions, 228
  reaction functions, exchange-rate modeling, 61–63
Technical analysis, foreign exchange markets, 343–368
  active currency management, beta factors in, 456–457
  categories, 346–350
  computing signals and returns, 351–353
  data snooping, publication bias, and data mining, 355–357
  early studies, 353
  future research issues, 366–368
  pattern recognition, intraday data, and exchange rate comparisons, 353–355
  philosophy, 345
  research applications, 350
  survey of practical applications, 350–351
  trading returns, risk compensation, 359–361
  trading rule profits
    cognitive biases, 363–365
    intervention and creation of, 361–363
    market adaptation to arbitrage, 365–366
    temporal variation, 357–359
Technical trading rules (TTRs)
  adaptive market hypothesis, 365–366
  cognitive bias and profits in, 363–365
  data snooping, data mining, and publication bias, 355–357
  efficient market hypothesis, 350
  foreign exchange markets, 343–344
  forward exchange rate puzzle emergence and, 600
  intervention and profit creation, 361–363
  risk-adjusted returns, 359–361
  temporal variations, rule returns, 357–359
Telephone-era trading, foreign exchange markets, 22
Temporal variation, trading rule returns, 357–359
Term structure, options in FX pricing, 658
  volatility as asset class, 666–672
Theil's U-Statistic, forecast accuracy and, 275–278
Theta of an option, options in FX, Black Swan strategies and, 679–681
*Thomson Reuters Dealing,* 22–24
*Thomson Reuters Matching,* electronic trading and, 23
Thomson Reuters services, multibank trading platforms, 37–38
Tick data
  analysis of, 561–563
  scale of market quakes methodology, 572–575
  scaling law parameters, 567–571
Time-based sampling, nominal exchange models, 53–54

Time decay, options in FX, Black Swan strategies and, 676–681
Time-series analysis
asymptotic pooled regression models
out-of-sample prediction, 271–272
predictive regression, 269–270
carry trades, quarterly return models, 295, 297–298
exchange rate regimes, 769–770
fair value currency models, 337
interventions, 726–737
caveats concerning, 734–737
channels of effectiveness, 729–734
Monte Carlo simulation, 272–275
purchasing power parity and, 174–175
scaling model of high frequency trading, intrinsic time framework, 563–565
Theil's U-Statistic, forecasting accuracy, 275–278
tick data, 561–563
Time slicer algorithm, algorithmic execution, foreign exchange markets, 590–591
Time-varying risk
carry trades, 284–285
rare events and, 308–311
options in FX, volatility models, 661–681
stochastic discount factor, exchange rate analysis, 398
habit preferences, 407–411
Time weighted average pricing (TWAP), algorithmic execution, equity markets, 584
Timing parameters
active currency management, volatility and correlation timing, 421–443
portfolio shifts currency trading model, data releases, 85–88
Tobin tax, 149
Tokyo Financial Exchange, cross-currency swap dislocations and financial crisis in, 635–637
Total factor productivity
productivity-based models, Balassa-Samuelson framework, 56–58
stochastic discount factor, disaster risk, 417
Total-move (TM) scaling law parameters, 570–571
coastline modeling, 571–572
Total return swaps, strategy-based foreign exchange products, 617–618
Tracking errors, currency hedging, 531–536
Tradable goods
aggregation bias and micro price studies, 199–200
nontradable goods *vs.*, 198–199
purchasing power parity and law of one price, 189–215
barriers to arbitrage and nonlinearities, 195–198
border effect, 194–195
early testing, 194
price indices and, 190–193
two-good real exchange rate model, 59–60
Trade surplus, misalignment of exchange rates, renminbi case study, 753–755
Trading models. *See* Currency-trading models
Trading volume, foreign exchange turnover and, 4–6
Transaction costs
active currency management, volatility and correlation timing, 430
electronic trading, 21, 27
exchange rate analysis, 234–235
foreign exchange markets, 7–8
high frequency traders, 15
law of one price and, 196–198
stochastic discount factor, exchange rate analysis, 399, 403
Transition autoregressive (TAR) model, law of one price and, barriers to arbitrage and nonlinearities, 196–198
Transitory disparities, purchasing power parity in traded goods and, 203–205
Transparency, electronic trading enhancement of, 27
Trend following
active currency management
bank foreign exchange indices, 465–466
basic factor model, 478–479
beta factors in, 456–458

forward exchange rate puzzle
emergence and, 599–600
options in FX, volatility as asset class, 666–672
philosophy of technical analysis and, 345
scaling laws and, 562–563, 575–576
Triennial Central Bank Survey of FX Market Activity, 10–11
Trigger-based rebalancing, currency hedging, 537
Triple top, technical trading, 346–350
Trivariable theory, purchasing power parity, 162–163
*t*-statistic, exchange rate analysis, predictive ability, 230–231
Turnover
currency trading and, 4–5
foreign exchange derivatives and, 635
high frequency trading and, 33–34, 37
liquidity and, 12–13
strategy-based foreign exchange products and, 600–604
trading instruments, 9
Two-good models, real exchange rates, 59–60
Two-poles hypothesis, currency trading, 141–143
Two-tier market, currency trading, 80–81

Unbiasedness hypothesis, 64–65
Uncertainty
active currency management
model uncertainty, 431–432, 438–440
parameter uncertainty, 437–438
Bayesian asset allocation, 430–431
predictive density, 443
volatility and correlation evaluation, 437–438
exchange rate modeling, incomplete information, 381–384
intervention effectiveness and, 726–737
technical trading returns, risk analysis, 361
Uncovered interest rate parity (UIP)
carry trades, 283–285
currency crisis management
interest rate defense, 708–709
Krugman-Flood-Garber model, 700–704
exchange rate analysis, 224
empirical models, 237–244
performance measures, 232–236
predictive regressions, 227
fair value currency models, 316–317
forward exchange rate puzzle
emergence and, 599–600
incomplete information, exchange rate modeling
basic monetary model, 377–379
infrequent decision making, 385–388
monetary exchange model, 47–49
portfolio balance exchange model, 50–51
stochastic discount factor
currency portfolios, 398–399
currency risk premia, 396–397
disaster risk, 415–417
habit preferences, 409–411
long-run risk model, 412–413
research background, 391–392
Underlying balance approach, fair value currency models, 320–324
fundamental equilibrium exchange rate, 322–323
macroeconomic balance approach, 323–324
Underlying current account conditions, fair value currency models, 320–324
Undershooting, empirical models, 51–52
Undervaluation, misalignment of currency, renminbi case study, 752–760
Unfunded programs, active currency management, 474–475
Unhedged world equities, currency hedging, 516–523
United Kingdom
bullionist period in, 170–171
return to gold standard in, 177–178
United States
colonial era purchasing power parity in, 169–170
economic hegemony of, 553–555
floating exchange rates in, 173–175
gold standard return in, 177

United States (*continued*)
history of Bretton Woods system and, 137–138
Unit root principle
behavioral finance framework, 115–118
purchasing power parity and, 56
Univariate modeling
active currency management, volatility timing, 427, 442–443
bullionist periods and, 170–171
purchasing power parity, 162–163
stationarity and, 167
Universal law, fat-tailed distributed exchange rate returns, 121–122
Unleveraged asset managers, liquidity needs of, 13–14
US dollar (USD)
active currency management, directional trade, 459–460
behavioral finance framework, unit root principle, 117–118
carry trades, 285–286
financial globalization and, 64
foreign exchange reserves, interventions, 551
FX swap-implied dollar rate, 627–628
as international reserve currency
changing role of, 552–555
replacement of, 555–556
key currency competition and, 144–145
post-Bretton Woods exchange rate regimes and, 133–135
trading dominance of, 6–8
Utility-based asset pricing, stochastic discount factor, exchange rate analysis, 391–393
Utility function, options in FX, 686–687

Value-based strategies
active currency management, 458–459
basic factor model, 478–479
strategy-based foreign exchange products and, 605–611
Variance swaps, options in FX, volatility as asset, 667–672
Vector error-correction model (VECM), panel data exchange rate determination, 267–268
Vega of an option, options in FX
Black-Scholes formula, 648–653
Black Swan strategies and, 679–681
volatility as asset, 669–672
Vehicle currency trading, 7–8
Voice brokers (VBs)
electronic trading and, 22–24
in telephone era trading, 22
Volatility clustering, behavioral finance framework, 118–119
Volatility derivatives, options in FX and, 655–656
Volatility of exchange rates
active currency management
basic factor model, 478–479
dynamic models, 424–428
economic value, 428–430
evaluation of, 434–440
timing parameters, 421–443
univariate modeling, 427, 442–443
carry trades, currency volatility factor, 302
cross-currency swap dislocations and, 638–640
currency hedging, 504–524
foreign government bonds, 507–511
high yield corporate bonds, 511–516
impact of, 523–524
MSCI World equities, 516–523
exchange rate rules, 147–148
floating exchange rate regimes, 774–779
foreign exchange reserves costs, 549–550
history of, 134–135
incomplete information, exchange rate modeling, 382–388
*Laissez-faire* exchange and, 138–139
mean variance dynamic asset allocation, 232–236
options in FX
Black Swan strategies and, 679–681
models, 658–681
overreaction, 671–672
pricing variables, 656–658
purchasing power parity in traded goods and, 204–205
stochastic discount factor, global volatility, 405

Volatility premium, options in FX, volatility as asset class, 666–672
Volatility surface, options in FX pricing, 656–658
Volume
  philosophy of technical analysis, 345
  strategy-based foreign exchange products and, 600
Volume weighted average pricing (VWAP), algorithmic execution, foreign exchange markets, participator algorithms, 592
Wage-rate index, purchasing power parity computations, 168–169
Weighted portfolio strategies, active currency management, 461–463
White labeling, electronic trading and, 30
Wholesale price index (WPI)
  purchasing power parity computations, 168–169
  return to gold standard and, 178–180
World War I, purchasing power parity and, 172–173

Wiley Handbooks in

# FINANCIAL ENGINEERING AND ECONOMETRICS

Advisory Editor

**Ruey S. Tsay**

*The University of Chicago Booth School of Business, USA*

---

The dynamic and interaction between financial markets around the world have changed dramatically under economic globalization. In addition, advances in communication and data collection have changed the way information is processed and used. In this new era, financial instruments have become increasingly sophisticated and their impacts are far-reaching. The recent financial (credit) crisis is a vivid example of the new challenges we face and continue to face in this information age. Analytical skills and ability to extract useful information from mass data, to comprehend the complexity of financial instruments, and to assess the financial risk involved become a necessity for economists, financial managers, and risk management professionals. To master such skills and ability, knowledge from computer science, economics, finance, mathematics and statistics is essential. As such, financial engineering is cross-disciplinary, and its theory and applications advance rapidly.

The goal of this Handbook Series is to provide a one-stop source for students, researchers, and practitioners to learn the knowledge and analytical skills they need to face today's challenges in financial markets. The Series intends to introduce systematically recent developments in different areas of financial engineering and econometrics. The coverage will be broad and thorough with balance in theory and applications. Each volume will be edited by leading researchers and practitioners in the area and covers state-of-the-art methods and theory of the selected topic.

**Published Wiley Handbooks in Financial Engineering and Econometrics**

Bauwens, Hafner, and Laurent · *Handbook of Volatility Models and Their Applications*
James, Marsh, and Sarno · *Handbook of Exchange Rates*
Viens, Mariani, and Florescu · *Handbook of Modeling High-Frequency Data in Finance*

**Forthcoming Wiley Handbooks in Financial Engineering and Econometrics**

Bali and Engle · *Handbook of Asset Pricing*
Brandimarte · *Handbook of Monte Carlo Simulation*
Chacko · *Handbook of Credit and Interest Rate Derivatives*
Chan and Wong · *Handbook of Financial Risk Management*
Cruz, Peters, and Shevchenko · *Handbook of Operational Risk*
Florescu, Mariani, Stanley, and Viens · *Handbook of High-Frequency Trading and Modeling in Finance*

Jacquier · *Handbook of Econometric Methods for Finance: Bayesian and Classical Perspecitves*

Szylar · *Handbook of Market Risk*